Flammes

1050

AMERICAN DRAMATIC LITERATURE

A MAGNIFICENT PRODUCTION

OF THAT STERLING HISTORICAL DRAMA

UNCLE TOM'S CABIN

OR LIFE AMONG THE LOWLY.

BY HARRIET BEECHER STOWE.

A HIGH-CLASS ENTERTAINMENT

THE HISTORIC SLAVE MARKET

And many other scenes that go to form a great production of this grand old historical play.

A PAIR OF FULL-BLOODED BLOODHOUNDS

Trained to take part in the Drama, are used in the thrilling scene showing

Eliza Escaping from the Slave-hunters

The illustration on the two preceding pages is of an advertising bill for *Uncle Tom's Cabin*. Although at first a failure, in its dozen subsequent versions from 1853 (none of which Mrs. Stowe herself ever wrote or permitted), *Uncle Tom's Cabin* became the most popular play in the history of the theatre. The extreme hyperbole and the emphasis upon moral values were typical of nineteenth-century theatre advertising. (*Courtesy Theatre Collection, New York Public Library.*)

AMERICAN DRAMATIC LITERATURE

TEN MODERN PLAYS
IN HISTORICAL PERSPECTIVE

Jordan Y. Miller
ASSISTANT PROFESSOR OF ENGLISH
KANSAS STATE UNIVERSITY

McGRAW-HILL BOOK COMPANY
New York   Toronto   London   1961

Passages from the following sources have been reprinted through the courtesy of the copyright owners as herein acknowledged:

"America Takes the Stage," by Richard Moody. Copyright 1955. By permission of the Indiana University Press, Bloomington, Ind.

"A Short History of the American Drama," by Margaret G. Mayorga. Copyright 1932 by Margaret G. Mayorga.

"My First Fifty Years in the Theatre," by Owen Davis. Copyright 1950. By permission of Walter H. Baker Company, Boston.

"The Theatre through Its Stage Door," by David Belasco. Copyright 1919. By permission of Harper & Brothers, New York.

Margaret Fleming, by James A. Herne. By permission of John T. Herne.

The City, by Clyde Fitch. By permission of Richard W. Fitch, Jr.

The Easiest Way, by Eugene Walter. By permission of American Play Company, Inc., New York.

Bound East for Cardiff, by Eugene O'Neill. By permission of Random House, Inc., New York.

The Dream Play, by August Strindberg, translated by Edwin Björkman. Charles Scribner's Sons, New York.

The Hairy Ape, by Eugene O'Neill. By permission of Random House, Inc., New York.

The Adding Machine, by Elmer Rice. Copyright 1922, 1929 by Elmer L. Rice. Copyright 1923 by Doubleday, Page & Company, New York. Copyright 1949, 1950, 1956 (in renewal) by Elmer L. Rice. All rights reserved. Application for the right to perform this excerpt or the entire play should be made to Samuel French, Inc., of 25 West 45th St., New York 36, N. Y., or 7623 Sunset Blvd., Hollywood 46, Calif., or if in Canada to Samuel French (Canada), Ltd., at 27 Grenville St., Toronto, Ont.

Beggar on Horseback, by George S. Kaufman and Marc Connelly. Liveright Publishing Corporation, New York, 1924.

Shenandoah, by Bronson Howard. By permission of Samuel French, Inc., New York.

Secret Service, by William Gillette. By permission of Samuel French. This play is protected by copyright in the countries of the Berne Convention outside the United States of America, and for the right to read or perform this excerpt or the entire play before an audience in any such countries application must be made to Samuel French, Inc., 25 West 45th St., New York 36, N. Y., or if in Canada to Samuel French (Canada), Ltd., 27 Grenville St., Toronto, Ont.

What Price Glory? by Maxwell Anderson and Laurence Stallings. From "Three American Plays," copyright 1926, 1953 by Maxwell Anderson and Laurence Stallings. By permission of Harcourt, Brace and Company, Inc., New York.

Metamora, by John Augustus Stone. *Davy Crockett*, by Frank Murdoch. Both from "America's Lost Plays," edited by Barrett H. Clark. By permission of Princeton University Press, Princeton, N. J.

Uncle Tom's Cabin, revised version, by A. E. Thomas. Copyright 1934, D. Appleton-Century Co., Inc. By permission of the publishers, Appleton-Century-Crofts, Inc., New York.

The Green Pastures, by Marc Connelly. Copyright 1929 by Marc Connelly. Copyright 1957, 1958 (in renewal) by Marc Connelly. By permission of Rinehart & Company, Inc., New York.

PREFACE

The drama has too long remained the poor relation in the family of American literary art, constantly deprived of its legitimate share of attention by the well-established reputation and confirmed prestige of the elder members of the household—poetry, the essay, the novel, and the short story. Colleges and universities, aware of the national heritage in American letters, offer curricula in American studies, both as major programs for undergraduates and as fields of specialization for doctoral candidates. Course work features everything from the broad historical aspects of "movements" and "schools" to the particular study of a single writer. Unfortunately, the drama has consistently been excluded from these important family gatherings. Although upon occasion admitted to the festivities when recognition of its existence has become necessary, it has thereafter been dismissed as too crude and impoverished to be allowed extended intercourse among its artistic betters.

Sixty years ago this attitude was easily supportable. A century of domestic playmaking had produced second- and third-rate imitations of routine European styles. Melodramas and farces of the crudest sort, romantic adventures untouched by reality, sentimental tales of love and honor (amply seasoned with the spice of dishonor, properly punished), and anemic attempts at "social" discourse provided opportunity for histrionic display by leading performers and lachrymose exhibitions of sentimental identification by viewers. There was, in short, no drama worthy of the name. Forty years ago, as *playmakers* began to assume the responsibilities of *playwrights* and as small but enthusiastic groups of artists began to infuse a noticeable dignity into their staged productions, there was genuine hope for the achievement of a socially acceptable status. Today that position has been gained. While the great national dramas of Europe disappeared under police state restrictions or burned themselves out, America brought its theatre in from the frontier where it had lived too long and gave it a new position as a respected art form. Since the First World War, America has developed a large amount of dramatic writing that measures up to the demands of universal and lasting appeal characteristic of enduring literature. With public and critical acclaim from abroad (including a Nobel Prize to Eugene O'Neill in 1936) and a growing consciousness at home of the importance of domestic talent, the American drama since 1918 has become a thoroughly accredited medium for the original expression of thought on a plane with all other forms of the written language. Its study as literature cannot be ignored.

The serious American dramatist can now be successfully compared to the best of American novelists and story writers. The struggles of the human individual against the impersonal destructive forces of society have become as evident in Sidney Kingsley or Arthur Miller as they ever were in Frank Norris or Theodore Dreiser. The fears, emotions, and terrifying responsibilities of men in war described by Stephen Crane carry the same forceful impact in the plays of Arthur Laurents or Herman Wouk. The isolated loneliness of man and his attempts to find meaning in life are vivid and tragic in Eugene O'Neill just as they are in Fitzgerald or Hemingway. And the destruction of a sensitive woman in a society that she cannot understand and to which she cannot adjust her principles is as fascinating in Tennessee Williams as in Henry James.

There is no anthology exclusively designed for the study of American drama as literature. In most cases, American plays are published as part of a much larger collection of international drama. Books in which only American playwriting is treated tend to include "representative" contributions from each important writer without regard to literary worth. Some modern drama anthologies are too inclusive to enable the teacher or student to make the best classroom use of them. If a collection represents the historical development of American drama, it must perforce include plays from all periods of history, thus becoming encumbered with too much nineteenth-century trivia and too little twentieth-century literature.

In this book is assembled a balanced collection of modern American plays that meet, in one way or another, the demands of good literature, together with introductory material suitable for use in teaching American drama on the college level. It is conceived as a fully developed study of the qualities of a significant part of our native literature and may be used equally well on either the undergraduate or graduate level as a complete text in a single course, as a supplement to other dramatic studies, or as a point of departure for a more detailed study of American playwriting. A speaking acquaintance with contemporary American literature and a general knowledge of the drama as a whole are necessarily assumed.

Part 1 will help the student to form a clearer understanding of the many deficiencies of eighteenth- and nineteenth-century playwriting and to gain a deeper appreciation of the significance of the achievements since 1918. Part 1 also reviews the limited but important output of a small group of American writers of the early twentieth century who appreciated the need for a literary drama and who conscientiously wrestled with its problems. The sincerity of these "might have beens" cannot be disregarded, and their potential genius must be recognized, if only briefly. Through bibliographies and suggested readings, interested students may undertake further research.

The brief history of modern American drama precludes any satisfactory chronological sequence of plays. Instead, the collection in Part 2 relies upon dramatic *type* as the most practical arrangement. But because no work of literature springs forth in full development without historical antecedɪ play is introduced by a short essay outlining the play's artistic and hɪ background and a brief critical discussion of its importance as a paɪ American dramatic literature. As a group the plays show the lack of a cleaɪ articulated American dramatic pattern. At the same time they reveal in theɪ greatly variegated stylistic treatments the typical unsettled urgency and the nervous, forceful drive that have become what is considered a distinctive American style.

High on the list of those whom I wish to thank for their assistance in helping to make this book a reality are the students in my classes in twentieth century American drama at Kansas State University over the past several years. To them I owe sincere appreciation for their interest in what I have tried to teach and for the subsequent conviction which I gained from them that undertaking this volume was indeed practicable.

I would like also to acknowledge the assistance extended me by Professors Manuel Ramirez and Robert Pyle of the Kansas State department of modern languages in preparing my notes for *Camino Real*. To Professor Walter Meserve of the University of Kansas and Professor Bruce Ingham Granger of the University of Oklahoma go many thanks for their helpful suggestions. I am especially grateful to Professor Barry Ulanov of Barnard College for his detailed criticisms of the original manuscript.

Finally, to my wife, Elaine, and to my daughter, Sherry, for their continued enthusiasm toward the entire project and their help in manuscript preparation and proofreading, go words of praise which cannot be satisfactorily expressed in writing.

Jordan Y. Miller

CONTENTS

PART ONE

THE BACKGROUNDS OF
MODERN AMERICAN DRAMA

EARLY THEATRES AND PERFORMERS
BEFORE THE REVOLUTION

1750 TO 1770

The Uncertain Evidence before 1750

If you wish to be absolutely literal about the first dramatic performances in this hemisphere, you may choose the rituals of the North and South American Indians as a form of theatre. If you decide that "civilization" is essential, you may accept the hazy records of the Spaniards in the Southwest and the French in the Northeast, both of whom entertained theatrically on festive occasions as early as 1538 in Mexico and 1606 in Canada. The records are incomplete and unimportant; it is enough to know that very little time elapsed between the explorer's arrival in the wilderness and his desire to be entertained.

Jamestown was founded in 1607 and Plymouth thirteen years later, but actors from the professional London stage did not soon follow. Surprisingly enough, the forbiddingly hostile geography of the wilderness discouraged them less than the restrictive legislation that was devised to prevent the emigration of theatrical personnel to the Colonies. The Elizabethan theatre was continually involved in a struggle with the London city fathers and the godly churchmen who wished to deny it a legal status. Frequently only the Queen's enthusiastic support allowed the theatres to function at all. Since plague, fire, or any ca tastrophe could be directly attributed to the sinful carryings-on of acting com panies, it is not surprising that the virgin American lands were to be forcibly saved from contamination. In castigating all who entered into stage plays, William Crashaw in a sermon of 1610 concluded, "Wee resolue to suffer no Idle persons in Virginea." The good Puritans of Massachusetts were utterly terrified at the thought of any display of "ungodly and prophane" behavior. Increase Mather, genuinely alarmed, wrote in 1687 that "there is much dis course of beginning Stage-Plays in New England. The last year," he added in horror, "Promiscuous Dancing was openly practised."

Local amateur productions, although frequently opposed, did succeed in getting staged. There was a piece called *Ye Bare and Ye Cubb* of August 27, 1665, the first recorded play in English presented in the Colonies. It was written by a William Darby of Accomac County, Virginia. What it was, what it said, what it looked like are completely unknown. It must have been startling, be cause it so offended the sensibilities of a certain Edward Martin that he had the actors brought into court. They were directed to appear in "those habili ments that they then acted in" and to recite some of the dialogue. To the

3

chagrin of Martin, the company was found not guilty, and he was ordered to pay court costs. It is unusual that the Cavalier atmosphere of Virginia would entertain such a suit, for there were no specific directives against theatricals at that time.

There is suggested evidence that a Harvard undergraduate named Benjamin Colman wrote the first play by an American to be acted in this country. Like the obscure bear and cub, nothing is known except a name, *Gustavus Vasa*, and a date, 1690. In Virginia the scholars of William and Mary College are reported to have offered in 1702 the recitation of a "pastoral colloquy" before the governor. Sometime between 1699 and 1702 a Richard Hunter successfully petitioned the Acting Governor of New York for a license to produce "the acting of Play's in this Citty," but nobody knows whether or not the ambitious Mr. Hunter succeeded. By 1703 New York had a population of only 4,436 persons, slave and free, a number which could not support an extended theatrical season. The climate of opinion changed soon after Hunter got his license, for on May 6, 1709, the Governor's Council in New York forbade "play acting and prize fighting" without further explanation.

Most modern historians name Anthony Aston as the first recorded professional actor. In 1703, by his own account, he arrived in Charleston, South Carolina, "full of Lice, Shame, Poverty, Nakedness and Hunger," where he "turn'd *Player* and *Poet*, and wrote one Play on the Subject of the Country." He proceeded to New York where he spent the winter "acting, writing, courting, fighting," but we have no idea what his play was about or where he acted. The earliest known published play by an American resident was *Androboros* in 1714. It was written by "Governor Hunter" (presumably Robert Hunter and no relation to the actor, Richard Hunter), as a personal satire on the citizens of New York. There is no record of its production.

Evidence of other theatrical activity during the next several years is discouragingly spotty. Documents reveal a 1716 contract in Williamsburg, Virginia, specifying that a theatre "for the enacting of comedies and tragedies" was to be built, and in November of that year three half-acre lots were purchased for the erection of a theatre and bowling green. University activity continued at William and Mary. Performances of well-known tragedies and comedies were reported in September, 1736. Charleston was the center of eighteenth-century theatrical life. Popular plays from the London stage, an opera, and a "Pantomimic Entertainment in Grotesque Characters" involving Harlequin and Scaramouch of the Italian *commedia dell' arte*, appeared in the first two months of 1735.

The population of Philadelphia, founded in 1682, had grown to about 5,000 by 1700. The Assembly of Pennsylvania in 1700 prohibited "stageplays, masks, revels" and other "rude and riotous sports." The sober lawmakers, however, found themselves continually thwarted by the more liberal attitude of the British government, and between 1705 and 1759 four restrictive acts were repealed. When, in 1723, a "Player who has Strowled hither to act as a

Comedian" set up his stage "just without the verge of the City" the Quaker mayor was deeply perturbed but could do little about it. In 1724 a newspaper announcement spoke of the New Booth on Society Hill. What went on there, aside from "Roap dancing" and the antics of a traditional clown called Pickle Herring, remains untold.

Philadelphia holds the distinction of being the first city to have kept any detailed record of a professional acting troupe. In 1749 Addison's tragedy of *Cato* was enacted, although one diarist recorded his sorrow that "any thing of the kind was encouraged." Others felt plays were likely to make "weak and inconsiderate persons" spend too much money. Our first stage historian, William Dunlap, reports these facts: "As early as 1749 it is on record that the Magistracy of the city had been disturbed by some idle young men perpetrating the murder of sundry plays in the skirts of the town," who were subsequently arrested and made to promise good behavior. Historians doubt Dunlap's assertion that they were poor and incompetent, because fairly good evidence indicates that they were mostly professionals under Walter Murray and Thomas Kean. Where they originated is a mystery, but they are part of our first definitely recorded professional theatrical history.

New York has about as scanty a record up to 1750 as any other city. Prohibitive legislation was already extant in 1709, and from then until 1732 there is nothing in evidence. In 1732, the year George Washington was born, a playhouse of some sort existed in New York, but its origin, appearance, and size cannot be specified. In 1739 a Mr. Holt, who had "danc'd a considerable Time" at Drury Lane in London, was to appear in "A New Pantomime Entertainment in Grotesque Characters call'd the Adventures of Harlequin and Scaramouch, or the Spaniard Trick'd." The resemblance of the title to that of the harlequinade performed in Charleston in 1735 might prove a traveling company, but all of this remains in that hazy limbo of supposition and inference. Performers and patrons of the 1730s did not maintain accurate records for posterity.

After 1750: The Hallams and Douglass

Historian George C. D. Odell, painstakingly turning over every pebble for evidence of dramatic fare in the colonies, marks the year 1750 as the point where conjecture permanently gives way to historical fact. By that year New York boasted 10,000 people, 1,834 houses, and 6 fire engines. Dunlap establishes 1752 as the first date of importance, but he is evidently unfamiliar with Murray and Kean's "Company of Comedians" from Philadelphia, who performed in a 300-seat theatre in Nassau Street in 1750–1751. After a successful season, they left New York and journeyed down to Williamsburg, where they opened a new playhouse in October, 1751. As the "Virginia Company of Comedians" they flourished in performances throughout the South for another twenty years, without ever returning to New York.

In 1750 Boston witnessed a production of Otway's *The Orphan* by two unidentified young Englishmen at the Coffee House in State Street. Then, properly horrified at what had occurred, the good men of Massachusetts immediately enacted a law prohibiting any repetition of such "means of disseminating licentious maxims, and tending to immorality of conduct." Punishment was severe: £20 for allowing any location to be so used, and £5 for every time anybody was caught attending. This effectively discouraged all play acting around Massachusetts Bay for a quarter of a century, until the British Army occupied the city in 1775.

The first acting group who made a prolonged effort to bring good professional theatre to the colonies was a company of twelve adults and three children led by Lewis Hallam. After their arrival from England in 1752, their history became the history of the American theatre for many years. Hallam opened in Kean's playhouse in Williamsburg with *The Merchant of Venice* on September 15, 1752, "before a numerous and polite audience, with great applause." For about a year the group performed in Virginia as a direct competitor to Kean's Virginia Company. Their subsequent arrival in New York revealed that the city had somewhat cooled toward professional acting, presenting them with a serious problem in public apathy combined with official hostility. In an open letter to the "Publick—whose Servants they are, and whose Protection they entreat" Hallam's hard-pressed band spoke up in a New York newspaper on July 2, 1753, in a plea for help, the earliest detailed record of a road company in distress. Permission was finally received, and the company opened on September 17, 1753.

For six months, in a new playhouse which Hallam had built, this troupe produced a repertory of over thirty-five of the best of Restoration and eighteenth-century plays. When they departed for Philadelphia in 1754, professional performances in New York ceased for another four years. Although in Philadelphia the Quaker opposition was intense, governmental blessings attended the 1754 opening on condition that "nothing indecent and immoral" would be offered. After a single season, the Hallam performers went to Charleston and thence to Jamaica, where Lewis Hallam died in 1755.

Another actor-manager, David Douglass, was performing in the West Indies, and the Hallam forces joined with him. The union was so close, in fact, that Douglass married Hallam's widow in 1758 and continued to employ her as the leading lady she had always been for her first husband. They returned to New York that year, but Douglass had somehow offended the authorities, probably by seeking permission to act *after* erecting a playhouse, and had considerable difficulty in gaining official sanction. In 1759 he departed for Philadelphia, where opposition from all sides—Quaker, Lutheran, Presbyterian, Baptist—restricted his activities. His company soon headed south to perform in Annapolis and Williamsburg in 1760.

The ingenuity needed to combat public resistance to the theatre was taxed to its utmost when Douglass invaded New England. Harsh laws, such as those in Massachusetts, prevented a frontal attack, but flanking movements were often employed with skill. In the autumn of 1761, a commendatory letter from the Governor of Virginia in his pocket, Douglass fired his opening round in Newport, Rhode Island. The successful diversionary tactics appear so childishly naïve that it is difficult to explain how intelligent opposition could allow such a blatant fraud to get by. The following descriptions were actually distributed on a published handbill:

KINGS ARMS TAVERN–NEWPORT, RHODE ISLAND
On Monday, July 10th, at the Public Room of the above
Inn, will be delivered a series of
MORAL DIALOGUES
in five parts,
Depicting the evil effects of jealousy and other bad passions and proving that happiness can only spring from the pursuit of virtue.

MR. DOUGLASS will represent a noble and magnanimous Moor called Othello, who loves a young lady named Desdemona, and after he has married her, harbours (as in too many cases) the dreadful passion of jealousy.
Of jealousy, our being's bane
Mark the small cause and the most dreadful pain.

MR. ALLYN will depict the character of a specious villain, in the regiment of Othello, who is so base as to hate his commander on mere suspicion, and to impose on his best friend. Of such characters, it is to be feared, there are thousands in the world, and the one in question may present to us a salutary warning.
The man that wrongs his master and his friend,
What can he come to but a shameful end?

MR. MORRIS will represent an old gentleman, the father of Desdemona, who is not cruel or covetous, but is foolish enough to dislike the noble Moor, his son-in-law, because his face is not white, forgetting that we all spring from one root. Such prejudices are very numerous and very wrong.
Father, beware what sense and love ye lack,
'Tis crime, not colour, makes the being black.

MRS. MORRIS will represent a young and virtuous wife, who being wrong-fully suspected, gets smothered (in an adjoining room), by her husband.
Reader, attend, and ere thou goest hence,
Let fall a tear to hapless innocence.

Various other dialogues, too numerous to mention here, will be delivered at night, all adapted to the improvement of the mind and manners. The whole will be repeated on Wednesday and on Saturday. Tickets, six shillings each; to be had within. Commencement at 7. Conclusion at half past 10, in order that every spectator may go home at a sober hour, and reflect upon what he has seen before he retires to rest.

Douglass led one more skirmish against Rhode Island, this time into Providence in the summer of 1762, erecting a "schoolhouse" for his "moral dialogues." To keep up the sham, the performances were announced as Concerts of Musick, between the several parts of which would be presented, gratis, a tragedy, at least honestly named, and a Pastoral Farce, equally gratis. Finally, catching on to what was being perpetrated, the Rhode Island Assembly forbade any more such nonsense by a law "to be proclaimed throughout the streets of Providence by beat of drum." Hearing the ominous tattoo, Douglass retreated permanently to New York, where he built still another playhouse, the Beekman Street Theatre, which opened on November 18, 1761.

A matter which can understandably mystify is the ease with which these managers, operating on less than shoestrings, so casually tossed up new theatres whenever needed. Made of flimsy wooden frames, unsafe and highly combustible, they were not designed as lasting structures. One theatre was even reported to have been torn down in a riot. Candles provided light, and heating, if any, was primitive. Ventilation was never considered; seats were not made for comfort. Douglass' Beekman Street structure was 90 feet long, a common dimension for the lot frontage of a modern residential suburb, and 40 feet wide. It cost only $1,625 in the currency of the time, and could have been little but a bare shelter from the weather. Also, forty-hour workweeks and craft unions were unheard of. A week, maybe two or three, and a new theatre was ready. It is not surprising that managers could quickly regain their investments. The real surprise is that the population was not decimated by being trapped in these tinderboxes. Somehow, nobody ever seems to have been hurt.

During this time the five major colleges continued their amateur performances. The College of Philadelphia (later the University of Pennsylvania) presented *The Masque of Alfred*, the first production of native writing of which we have definite knowledge. At commencement time, 1762, the students of the College of New Jersey (Princeton) rendered a thing called *The Military Glory of Great Britain*. Harvard and Yale likewise produced undergraduate theatricals, although necessarily private. The minutes of Yale's Linonian Society, kept in the hand of Nathan Hale, report that yearly plays were given. There are many indications, in fact, that amateur play acting in homes and schools was a frequent colonial diversion. George Washington, writing home from a lonely frontier outpost, expressed his preference for a good acting role in *Cato* to the drudgery of his garrison duties.

A PERMANENT THEATRE AND THE
FIRST AMERICAN PLAYS

Just before the Conflict

Douglass and his American Company left Philadelphia at the end of 1759. When they returned in 1766, they began the immediate construction of the first permanent theatre building on the American continent, just outside the Philadelphia city limits in Southwark. It was a garish and ugly invention, with the lower portion of brick, the upper story of wood, all painted bright red. Glaring oil lamps provided illumination for what view of the stage was possible around the large obstructing pillars. Crude and uncomfortable by modern standards, it was not a jerry-built affair but lasted as a playhouse from November, 1766, until early in the nineteenth century, when it was converted into a brewery. The structure was finally torn down in 1912.

Opposition to the opening of the Southwark was strong but fruitless. Letters to the press feared the dire consequences. One correspondent presumed these "lawless vagrants" were the same as the group from New York "who were drove thence with righteous Indignation by the Inhabitants." The Quakers prayed fervently against "ensnaring and irreligious entertainments."

During the season Douglass became a major figure in the history of American drama by contracting to produce two original works by native American writers. Native writers always found it extremely difficult to peddle their wares because, aside from the inferiority of their product, they had too much competition from the standard English drama, which could be produced freely without restrictions of any type. Only a distinguished native creation could survive. Douglass' step was risky, and he finally produced only one of the two plays. The first, *The Disappointment*, by Thomas Forrest, a "Farce of Credulity," was withdrawn because it contained "personal reflections unfit for the stage." On April 24, 1767, Douglass undertook to stage his second choice, "a Tragedy written by the late ingenious Thomas Godfrey," called *The Prince of Parthia*, which thus became the first original American drama by a native author to be professionally produced. The play is a romantic tragedy, laid in Parthia near the beginning of the Christian era, full of exotic trappings, and laboriously imitative of the popular verse tragedies. Its invented plot is irrelevant to historic facts.

Meanwhile New York, though a growing city of 20,000, was unimportant as a theatre town for lack of any decent theatre building. The American

9

New York's first permanent theatre, the John Street, 1767. Note the wings and painted backdrop and the large proscenium doors of conventional eighteenth-century stages. The ladies (except one whose lack of taste has permitted her to stray) are sitting in what served as boxes. The young dandies occupy the pit benches, usually left backless in theatres of this era. (*Courtesy Museum of the City of New York.*)

Company was to change all that. On December 7, 1767, they opened a brand-new permanent home, and for about thirty years the John Street Theatre was to New York what the Southwark was to Philadelphia. It, too, was painted the traditional red, constructed mainly of wood, and, says the offended Dunlap, an "unsightly" object, "no ornament to the city." The opening season of 1767–1768 was not a success, and soon performances ceased altogether when, on October 20, 1774, the Continental Congress requested that no more stage entertainments be undertaken. Douglass returned to the West Indies in early 1775, where he and Mrs. Douglass soon died.

The Revolution and the Military Theatre

Three or four years before the outbreak of Revolutionary hostilities, writers of dramatic satire, ever a popular form of entertainment, were active on both sides. The most famous contributor to the rebel cause was Mrs. Mercy Otis Warren of Massachusetts, whose works, while probably never produced, were published between 1773 and 1775. The actual conflict inspired a number of pieces such as Hugh Henry Brackenridge's untheatrical dramatic dialogue, *The Battle of Bunkers-Hill,* 1776. The British General Burgoyne, a competent playwright, is credited with a farce, *The Blockade of Boston*. Its production in Boston in January, 1776, was violently interrupted when the soldier actors rushed pell-mell off the stage at the news of a rebel attack, all of which provided fine subject matter for further ridicule by the rebel satirists.

There was plenty of amateur activity among the occupying forces in the three major Northern cities. It is ironic that Boston, the one city which consistently refused to sanction public performances, was the scene of the earliest military theatricals. From 1775 until the evacuation in 1777 the British presented plays in the patriots' "cradle of liberty," Faneuil Hall. New York was occupied in September, 1776, and soon became the center of British social activity for the remainder of the war. The John Street Theatre was rechristened the Theatre Royal and continued during the entire occupation to produce a wide variety of plays. Howe's army briefly operated the Southwark in Philadelphia. A leading participant was the scene painter, Major John André, doomed to meet Benedict Arnold. One of his backdrops was used until the theatre burned in 1821.

The admonitions of the Continental Congress notwithstanding, amateur theatricals among the American forces were not unknown, even at that unlikely spot, Valley Forge. The Continental Army reopened the Southwark, but on October 6, 1778, Congress put teeth into their resolution against "plays and other expensive Diversions and Entertainments," by stating that "any person holding an office under the United States, who shall act, promote, encourage or attend such plays, shall be deemed unworthy to hold such office, and shall be accordingly dismissed."

Early Achievements of Independence

The end of hostilities brought the professional acting companies back from their refuge in the West Indies or in the South, particularly Maryland, where the resolution of the Continental Congress had been freely ignored. Young Lewis Hallam, continuing his father's success, and John Henry, his rival, were the leading actors of the day. Henry knocked at Philadelphia's door in July, 1782, but found it firmly bolted. Hallam made his assault early in 1784 and got one foot inside with more "lectures" in the Douglass manner. Other "pantomimical finales" and "dialogues and dumb shew" were designed to hoodwink the opposition in Philadelphia as they had in Newport. By January, 1786, Hallam had joined forces with Henry, who had reopened John Street in New York. Their Old American Company presented a full season of plays while introducing to New York audiences the comic actor, Thomas Wignell, who became one of the great stage names in the early theatre.

On April 16, 1787, the company offered the first professional production of a native American play on an American subject, Royall Tyler's *The Contrast*. Even though close to Sheridan's style in *The School for Scandal*, this comedy contains the beginnings of real American stage writing in its mild

The final scene from Royall Tyler's *The Contrast*, 1787, the first play on an American theme by an American author to receive professional production. The influences of English styles in stagecraft are obvious, even in this stilted drawing by William Dunlap. (*From the original published version,* 1790.)

satire on the artificial manners of the day. In the character of Jonathan, the bumpkin, originally played by Wignell, the play becomes more significant. This ignorant rustic, who goes to see *The School for Scandal* and thinks he is witnessing private affairs through a large hole in the wall, became the prototype of generations of stage "Yankees." *The Contrast* was published by subscription in 1790, with the name of George Washington topping the list of patrons.

The final assault on the Quaker fortress in Philadelphia was completely victorious. The opposition, now a minority, begged the government in 1788 to stop the "open contravention of the Law in the exhibition of Stage Plays, under whatsoever evasive name disguised." The appeal failed, and in March, 1789, a civic group called The Dramatic Association won a hard fight to make the theatre permanently legal. All plays thereupon dropped their thin veils of "lectures" and were presented "By Authority." The Quakers had one more try at repression in 1793, when they connected a violent yellow-fever plague with the wrath of God. The Legislature was again urged to suppress these "reproachful exhibitions" as a token of obedience to "the dispenser of life, health, and happiness." This petition also failed, and Philadelphia's theatre continued.

Philadelphia, the new nation's finest city and the center of art and culture, received America's first elegant playhouse in the Chestnut Street Theatre, which offered its first drama on February 17, 1794. As described in Thomas Pollock's "The Philadelphia Theatre in the Eighteenth Century," it was not a conventional structure, but was carefully designed by a London artist for permanence and beauty. Its horseshoe tiers of boxes, resembling the modern opera house, accommodated 900 people. When boxes, pit, and gallery were full, it could hold 2,000 spectators. No obstructions of any kind blocked the view of the stage, and the facilities for the actors were gratifyingly ample. In all respects it was an excellent and spacious theatre.

The Century's Last Decade: William Dunlap

The last eleven years of the century, 1789 to 1800, were a period of considerable activity. Although a new theatre appeared in Charleston in 1792, and a French-language theatre opened there in 1794, permanent interest began to move north. The defenses of New England were finally breached. After the death of Governor Hancock of Massachusetts, the theatre's most vigorous opponent, Boston opened its Federal Street (or, more commonly, Boston) Theatre on February 3, 1794. It was a substantial edifice, designed by a professional architect, complete with card and dancing rooms, tearooms and kitchens. In 1798, fortunately vacant, it burned to the ground in the first such destruction of a permanent playhouse in this country. It was rebuilt and operating once more by 1799.

The two important events of this last decade took place in New York, a cosmopolitan city of 23,000 and the Federal Capital. These events were the appearance of America's first native-born professional man of the theatre, William Dunlap, and the opening of the Park Theatre.

William Dunlap, popularly known as "the father of American drama," was born the son of a loyalist father in Perth Amboy, New Jersey, in February, 1766. Blinded in one eye in a childhood accident, he nonetheless pursued art as a career and studied painting in England under Benjamin West. George Washington once sat for him, and he painted portraits of contemporary actors and actresses which have become a priceless record of his age. His original play, *The Father: or American Shandyism*, was accepted by the Old American Company and produced at John Street on September 7, 1789, the second native American play to be so honored. Its success was questionable, but it brought Dunlap into the theatre where he was soon to become so important. By the end of his career he had to his credit more than sixty original and adapted works. None of his plays contain much literary merit, but even his severest critic, George Seilhamer, in "The History of the American Theatre," recognizes that notwithstanding all his faults as painter, dramatist, and historian, "he was in advance of his time." "But for him," says Seilhamer, "many details of a personal nature for the first quarter of a century after the Revolution would have been obliterated from our dramatic annals."

By 1792 Hallam and Henry's Old American Company had ceased to exist in its original form. Within two years, Henry sold out his interest to Hallam; Dunlap then bought into the group in 1796. He immediately undertook extensive production of his own original Gothic melodramas and adaptations from Continental plays, mainly French. His first tragedy, *André*, was given at the new Park Theatre in March, 1798.

Because the Old American Company had suffered severe financial reverses, great hopes were attendant upon the opening of this new Park Theatre on January 29, 1798. It was an imposing three-story structure, a sizable building compared to others in this fast-growing city of 60,000; contemporary accounts praise the omission of obstructing pillars between the auditorium and the commodious stage. But serious difficulties arrived before the doors even opened. Dunlap, who had mortgaged his childhood home to raise capital, saw the cost of the building triple from the estimated $42,000 to $130,000. Moreover, all one hundred of the owners, whose subscriptions had helped to build the house, demanded free tickets for every performance. The rather disrespectful mob that rushed through the doors on opening night left encouraging cash receipts, but this glory was immediately ended as income dropped alarmingly. Morale and income the first season were temporarily boosted by the permanent hiring of Thomas Abthorpe Cooper, a promising young tragedian, who joined the Park in *Hamlet* in February, 1798.

The second season was rescued by the happy association with the plays of August von Kotzebue, the prolific German writer, whose bloodfreezing melodramas of lustful villains, ruinous castles, and wrongfully imprisoned heroines became a gold-filled treasure chest for Dunlap. After a shaky first week of the 1798–1799 season, Dunlap produced his own adaptation of Kotzebue's *Menschenhass und Reue*, known as *The Stranger*, and, in Dunlap's words, "The success of this piece alone enabled the author to keep open the theatre." For several seasons thereafter, Dunlap was to see his fortunes hinged to the public acceptance of the type of play which Kotzebue represented. American audiences found a certain identification with this interesting German writer, whose 215 plays were popular abroad as well. His portrayal of vicious aristocracy and virtuous common men suited the temper of post-Revolution America. And, of course, the dripping sentimentality of his rags-to-riches theme was always welcome. The last season of the century, Dunlap presented fourteen Kotzebue plays.

In the midst of the final season, six days after the event, the sad news of Washington's death arrived in New York on December 20, 1799. The theatre closed for ten days, and on December 30 opened again with the stage hung in mourning. Cooper, attempting to deliver a poorly rehearsed monody on the General's death, provided an inglorious close to the eighteenth-century drama in America.

OTHER IMPORTANT THEATRE PERSONNEL BEFORE 1800

FENNELL, JAMES. Outstanding tragic actor of 1790s. Joined the Park in early 1800s. Continued speculative investments shortened his stage career.

HODGKINSON, JOHN. Brilliant young English actor engaged, with his wife, by John Henry in 1792 for Old American Company. Earliest "first-rate" actor in New York; a shareholder in the company for many years.

JEFFERSON, JOSEPH. First of the famous line, grandfather of Joseph Jefferson III. One of the great comedians with Old American Company, 1794–1830.

PLACIDE, ALEXANDER. Actor, pantomimist, dancer. Managed Charleston French-language theatre, 1794.

REINAGLE, ALEXANDER. Producing partner with Thomas Wignell at the Chestnut Street, Philadelphia. Their company competed with Old American in New York, 1790s.

ROWSON, SUSANNA. Author of popular novel, "Charlotte Temple," 1791, and several plays. Successful actress, member of elite Boston family, in a day when acting meant permanent loss of reputation.

SOLEE, JOHN J. L. Proprietor of first French theatre in Charleston, 1794. Unsuccessfully competed with established companies in New York.

AMERICAN WRITERS AND AMERICAN THEMES

Dunlap Departs: Conditions in the Early Nineteenth-century Theatre

William Dunlap lacked sound business ability, and after about ten years of ineffective management of temperamental actors and other assorted trouble-makers, he ceased his duties in bankruptcy in 1805. Nevertheless, he had brought dignity to his position, and his complete integrity as a serious artist helped to carry the American theatre and its embryonic drama forward. He continued to write for many years after 1805, although little of permanent value is preserved among his sixty plays. His "History of the American Theatre" in 1832 and his biography of the actor, George Frederick Cooke, are valuable, if often inaccurate, stage documents. The entertaining and enlightening details of the published portions of his diary give us an insight into the struggles of this conscientious but inept man. He died after a long, paralyzing illness on September 28, 1839, virtually destitute. Whether or not he was the "father" of American drama, he was the first sincerely devoted professional theatre man who strove to bring artistic quality and social respectability to the theatre.

What was it like to put on a play in the professional theatre around 1800? What were the facilities? How did the audiences behave?

Stage architecture was everywhere fairly uniform. Three tiers of boxes were grouped horseshoe-fashion around the semicircular pit, topped by a steep gallery under the eaves. A large chandelier, the major source of light, hung over the long, backless pit benches. The orchestra was crowded into its own fenced-in quarters directly in front of the stage. The performers appeared quite close to the audience on the broad acting apron that extended beyond the proscenium into the auditorium. On either side and downstage of the proscenium were the standard stage-entrance doors through which characters could step directly onto the apron in front of the curtain. The Park Theatre had apparently abandoned one of the most objectionable parts of Restoration and eighteenth-century playhouses—the private boxes that opened onto the stage itself, permitting spectators to mingle with the actors as they performed. Dunlap deplored this practice and successfully prevented it in his own theatre.

We have some very amusing observations about playgoing in the first years of the nineteenth century from a young critic who signed his name "Jonathan Oldstyle." In the following excerpts you may recognize the style of Washington Irving. "There is no place of public amusement of which I am so fond as the Theatre," he said. "To enjoy this with the greater relish, I go but seldom."

16

The first Park Theatre, New York, 1798, a tremendous improvement over the primitive John Street. The large apron and the proscenium doors are still in use, but the stage boxes, so typical of other theatres of this time, have disappeared. The horseshoe shape, with tiers of galleries, was standard theatrical architecture. The pit benches are without backs, as was customary. (*Courtesy New York Historical Society, New York.*)

The behavior of the audiences no little offended him, and he revealed the considerable difficulties the actors faced:

> As I entered the house some time before the curtain rose, I had sufficient leisure to make some observations. I was much amused with the waggery and humour of the gallery, which, by the way, is kept in *excellent* order by the constables who are stationed there. The noise in this part of the house is somewhat similar to that which prevailed in Noah's ark; for we have an imitation of the whistles and yells of every kind of animal. This, in some measure, compensates for the want of music, as the gentlemen of our orchestra are very economic of their favors. Somehow or another, the anger of the gods seemed to be aroused all of a sudden, and they commenced a discharge of apples, nuts, and gingerbread, on the heads of the honest folks in the pit, who had no possibility of retreating from this new kind of thunderbolts. I can't say but I was a little irritated at being saluted aside of my head with a rotten pippin.

The boxes inhabited by the ladies were "each a little battery in itself, and they [the ladies] all seemed eager to outdo each other in the havoc they spread around," while the critics attempted to amuse themselves during the performance by a game of cards. A companion sitting with Oldstyle "loudly complained" about the candle grease dropping into the pit from the high chandelier. Oldstyle found this a "trifling inconvenience" in the pursuit of pleasure, but his friend thought the cost "pretty dear for it;—first to give six shillings at the door, and then to have my head battered with rotten apples, and my coat spoiled by candle-grease." He further noted that "by and by I shall have my other clothes dirtied by sitting down, as I perceive every body mounted on the benches."

In structure, the playhouse had a *"heavishness"* about it, appearing rather *"under groundish"* and of a certain *"dungeon-like* look," particularly in the long narrow exits from the pit. Furthermore, Oldstyle was unhappy at the producer's disregard for authentic costume. ". . . while one actor is strutting about the stage in the cuirass and helmet of Alexander," he said, "another, dressed up in a gold-laced coat and bag-wig, . . . is taking snuff in the fashion of one or two centuries back. . . ." In conclusion, Oldstyle recommended, among other things, umbrellas for the pit, less noise in the boxes, less grog in the gallery, and "to the whole house, inside and out, a total reformation."

If the audience was noisy and uncouth, it had fair reason. After all, the primitive conditions encouraged informality. Little or no heat in the winter necessitated bundles of clothing and foot warmers, or jostling around a fireplace or a crude stove in the lobby. There was practically no ventilation in the summer. One manager is known to have attempted to cool his house by having the local fire company pump water over the roof. The gay blades on their backless pit benches were unable to sit comfortably, and as Oldstyle was aware, often preferred to stand and block the view. Seats were not reserved; slaves were often sent to hold places for their masters or mistresses. A bar served the patrons at all times. Moreover, one was never quite sure if the advertised event would appear as announced. With no reserved-ticket obligations to meet, or requirements from actor and technician unions, the manager could arbitrarily cancel or postpone an announced play at any time.

The bare and clattering stage did not help the actors to overcome the hubbub in the audience. Helpful stage equipment was minimal, with little attention given to promoting any realistic effects. The illumination from smoky, dripping candles was impossible to control except by raising or lowering the chandelier, or by clumsily snuffing the lights in the middle of a scene. Oil lamps were very little improvement, and in 1800 practical gas light was nearly twenty years away. Scenery was provided by the wing and backdrop popular for over a century. This consisted of several pieces of flat painted canvas hung from the ceiling at the back of the stage, and a series of flat or angular painted canvas "wings," on either side of the stage, extending at regular intervals from these backdrops toward the proscenium. The scene was "shifted" merely by raising or lowering a backdrop and by replacing one set of wing pieces with another, generally in full view of the audience. The curtain was lowered only after the play was over, and the tradition of clearing the stage at the end of each act made realistic action nearly impossible. Every final scene involving a "dead" body had to be provided with enough supernumeraries to tote the corpse safely off in order to leave the stage empty. The "tableau curtain," that is, lowering of the curtain with actors frozen in position on stage, did not appear until Dunlap introduced it into his own productions. After his demonstration of this highly effective and dramatically emphatic device, it was here to stay indefinitely.

John Howard Payne

After Dunlap, the first important name to be associated with the writing of American drama was John Howard Payne, whose claim to immortality rests almost wholly on a single song. Yet, beginning as a teen-age genius, he wrote, adapted, or slightly altered between fifty and sixty plays. At the age of fourteen, under the name of "Eugenius," he wrote and produced on February 7, 1806, *Julia: or The Wanderer*. It was, to use some of Odell's adjectives, stilted, absurd, formless, indecent, and vile. The precocious youngster's vocabulary and knowledge of incident were far beyond his years. He was not an original writer, however, and his themes were straight from European sources, often French. His routine structure was closely patterned after the "well-made" plays of Eugène Scribe. These followed set formulas in their dramatic construction, relying heavily for their effect on arbitrarily controlled circumstances instead of on character creation. The dramatic situation was always established through well-planned expository opening scenes, then advanced toward a precisely placed climax through carefully organized and unrealistic complications, reaching a clean-cut denouement at the end, where all loose ends were tied neatly, the whole bundle well wrapped in the polished trappings of skilful mediocrity.

Payne also relied on the increasingly popular "melodrama of tears," peopled by mysterious strangers and harsh, oppressive villains, often the parents of misunderstood maidens. Last-minute revelations, suddenly discovered letters, tearful reunions of long-lost children and parents—all these were standard equipment in plays like *Thérèse: The Orphan of Geneva*, 1821, and *Adeline: The Victim of Seduction*, 1822. His *Brutus: or the Fall of Tarquin*, of 1818 is his most dignified play; but his present fame rests on *Clari: or The Maid of Milan*, first produced at Covent Garden, London, on May 8, 1823, from which comes, for better or worse, so far as our native art is concerned, "Home, Sweet Home."

Payne was also one of the most sensational actors of his day, but we must reserve a discussion of his talents in that field for a later time.

The Admirable Aborigines

In 1766, Major Richard Rogers, of the famous scouts, Rogers' Rangers, had written an apparently unproduced play called *Ponteach* (pronounced Pontiac): *or The Savages of America*, a romantic, unreal picture of the noble red man. The stage Indian first appeared in Philadelphia on April 6, 1808, in a production in James Nelson Barker's *The Indian Princess: or La Belle Sauvage*, which presented as its heroine that Indian charmer of fact and fiction, Pocahontas. The story of John Smith and Pocahontas fitted perfectly into the popular romantic concept of the Indian. The ideal native in the raw was very mild; the Indian had not yet become the wanton, bloodthirsty scalper of the Great Plains tradition. James Fenimore Cooper's "Leatherstocking Tales" exerted strong influence on his literary contemporaries. His impossibly romantic redskins, in Mark Twain's scornful words, "an extinct race which never existed," were a favorite model. Richard Moody's description in "America Takes the Stage" is a good summary of how Barker and others pleasantly fooled their audiences:

> The Indian character in American drama became the archetype of human nobility. . . . By merely obeying his spontaneous inclinations he attained a higher moral plane than the white man could achieve through the most scrupulous observance of a rigid set of moral regulations. . . . He was brave and chivalrous, kind and gentle toward his squaw and children. . . . Even in his normal day-to-day behavior he was the epitome of the virtuous man.

There were some villainous Indians, but they were pretty well understood to be "unnatural" sons of the wilderness.

The one outstanding Indian play was John Augustus Stone's *Metamora: or The Last of the Wampanoags*, produced for the first time at the Park on December 15, 1829. It concerned the affairs of King Philip, "the grandest model of a mighty man," says the play's heroine. By 1846 a plethora of such naked nobleness caused one author to say they "had of late become a perfect nuisance." The Indian worshiper had been "overestimating the red man while viewing him through the mellow moonshine of romance," said Mark Twain, and audiences no longer accepted these exaggerations.

The white man against wilderness and hostile savage contributed a share of stage romance. James K. Paulding's *The Lion of the West*, appearing at the Park in April, 1831, introduced the bumptious, swaggering Col. Nimrod Wildfire, clad in the typical buckskin clothes and coonskin hat. He represented the first of the pugnacious but noble "critters" of the West. The best examples of the romantic frontiersman, however, came after the Civil War in Augustin Daly's *Horizon*, 1871, inspired by Bret Harte's stories, and in Frank Murdoch's *Davy Crockett* of 1872, one of the most enduringly popular frontier plays.

Yankees, Drawing Rooms, and the B'Hoys

One character who appeared in play after play was the simple, humorous, and goodhearted bumpkin, patterned after Tyler's Jonathan as interpreted by Thomas Wignell in *The Contrast*. Along with the Indian, this Yankee from New England, a farmer or shrewd-bargaining trader, was a romantically conventionalized stage figure whose exaggerated rural traits made him the first American low-comedy character. ". . . he was homely, honest in his own way, uneducated, unimaginative; . . . a keen, shrewd bargainer," says Margaret Mayorga in "A Short History of the American Drama." ". . . he was usually the personification of all that was virtuous, and if he had any obvious weakness, it was that of a fickle heart."

Jonathan Ploughboy, Jonathan Doolittle, Solon Shingle, Lot Sap Sago—all were stage Yankees in the popular plays of the day, appearing either as heroes in their own right or as supporting characters. Their popularity held for almost half a century when, like the Indian, they grew tiresome and declined in importance.

Anna Cora Mowatt's *Fashion*, which also contains a fine gentleman of the soil in Adam Trueman, is more important as the most significant American comedy of manners of this period. Like *The Contrast*, it ridicules foreign affectations, this time French instead of English. Its reception at the Park on March 24, 1845, was excitingly enthusiastic because, as Arthur Hobson Quinn writes in his history, a social satire displaying actual knowledge of the life depicted onstage was rare. It is full of the routine devices of overheard conversations and mistaken identities, but its success as a sparkling social piece has been permanent. If one is willing to accept the conventions, *Fashion* can be revived even now with remarkable ease.

The "other half" of the picture—life on the city streets—achieved a remarkable popularity, especially in the "fireman" plays. As far back as Dunlap's time there had been similar plays, but it was not until near midcentury that they became popular. Benjamin A. Baker, a New York actor-manager, created *A Glance at New York* in February, 1848, centering around Mose, the fire "b'hoy," a hard-fisted, profane volunteer fireman. Since audiences fell in love with Mose in his red shirt, plug hat, and fireman's boots, Baker produced more of the same, sending Mose to Philadelphia, California, China, and elsewhere. Once again the repetition wore thin, and Mose and his friends were nearly gone within a few years.

The Blackface Stereotype

Negro minstrelsy, says Moody, was "the only genuinely indigenous form of American drama." Blackface singers, including George Washington Dixon, alleged composer of "Old Zip Coon" ("Turkey in the Straw"), were known early in the century, and there had been Negro parts in a number of plays. But the nineteenth century introduced the conventional stereotype. Thomas D. "Jim Crow" Rice is widely assumed to be one of the earliest to deliver the shuffling "Jump Jim Crow" routine in the late 1820s, a favorite Negro song-and-dance number supposedly based on the limping dance of an old slave named Crow. It was certainly Rice who became the prototype of the Negro minstrel character. Dan Emmett, possible author of "Dixie," and his band of four known as The Virginia Minstrels, were the first to attempt a full evening of blackface song and dance at New York's Bowery Theatre in February,

1843. E. P. Christy's troupe appeared in 1846, the first to use the familiar semi-circular line-up. For some eighty years, the minstrel show was one of America's most durable forms of variety entertainment, with many metropolitan theatres specializing exclusively in its production. The best of the "end men" received salaries rivaling those of the finest legitimate stage stars.

As characters in legitimate drama, Negroes were comparatively unimportant, being used mainly as servants. Here is Moody's description:

> No realistic investigation of the Negro and his problems concerned the nineteenth-century playwright. The old "darky" was a convenient stage-type . . . that could be employed to inject a bit of comedy into the play. The realistic conception of a slave, working day after day in the fields, deprived of medical attention, scorned for any sentimental devotion to his own family, was completely overshadowed by the romantic stage-type Negro: placid, full of good humor, not easily brought to anger, loyal, faithful, honest, and with a great respect for and a great desire to emulate his master.

It was politically dangerous to present dramatically sympathetic Negro characters; the explosion of *Uncle Tom's Cabin* in 1852 was therefore not surprising. Harriet Beecher Stowe's novel was published on March 20, 1852. Because of ineffectual copyright laws, Charles W. Taylor produced his happy-ending stage version of this national sensation at Purdy's National Theatre in New York, without seeking Mrs. Stowe's permission. (She regarded the stage as sinful.) Taylor's play was the first abolitionist document to reach the stage, and for the first time in American history Negroes appeared as leading characters in a drama. Adverse critical opinion condemned the play to a run of only eleven nights. Another writer, George L. Aiken, who felt his daughter could do a good Little Eva, wrote a completely new adaptation containing most of the original story, including the unhappy ending. His version ran 100 nights at Troy, New York, succeeded in a run in Albany, and lasted over 200 nights at Purdy's in New York, where it opened July 18, 1853. At the time when a week was a long run and a month almost a sensation, the 200 successive performances were phenomenal.

At one time, *Uncle Tom's Cabin* was appearing as many as eighteen times a week. Eventually other versions appeared until practically every major actor and actress had made a try at Uncle Tom, Simon Legree, Topsy, Eliza, Gumption Cute, and all the array of characters that Mrs. Stowe had placed forever in our history. It was completely worn-out in New York before long, but elsewhere, especially as a road or tent show (often known as a "Tom Show") it has continued indefinitely. It can still be seen, if one searches far enough, in some version somewhere in the United States. By the middle of the twentieth century it had gone through no less than twelve versions and some 200,000 performances. Regardless of Mrs. Stowe's disapproval of the "wicked" stage, *Uncle Tom's Cabin* was one of the most important documents in American dramatic history.

Until the end of the nineteenth century, the stage Negro continued his stereotype as part minstrel and part noble savage. And he was in nearly all cases played by white actors in blackface. A few Negro actors appeared in early twentieth-century plays, but not until Eugene O'Neill employed a Negro to play the leading role of *The Emperor Jones* in 1920 did the race achieve the status of a genuinely serious stage character.

European Borrowings and Boucicault

In 1830, Victor Hugo wrote and produced in Paris a play called *Hernani*, which succeeded in breaking the long-standing barrier of closely observed classical "unities" and sterile, rigidly constructed plays then dominant on the French stage. Letting his romantic imagination take full control, Hugo sent his characters through multiple scenes involving castles and caves, plottings and daredeviltry far from the usual classical austerity. On opening night the defenders of the older traditions were roused to violent battle against this upstart intrusion, and riots of the first order broke out. The fatal blow, however, had been struck. Then, as soon as *Hernani* appeared in Philadelphia in the season of 1831-1832, its influence could be immediately traced in American writing.

A Philadelphia physician, Robert Montgomery Bird, was America's outstanding writer of the foreign-dominated romantic play. The one for which he is most remembered, *The Gladiator*, of 1831, was a favorite of the great actor, Edwin Forrest, who awarded Bird a prize of $1,000 for it. Spartacus, the gladiator hero, expatiates heavily on matters of freedom and tyranny, but in spite of its didactic passages the play is one of the better exotically romantic pieces of the period. Bird's best is probably *The Broker of Bogota*, 1834, of limited appeal in dealing with domestic problems of eighteenth-century Spanish South America.

George Henry Boker, another Philadelphian, follows a close second behind Bird. Instead of declaiming against tyranny and oppression, he wrote "tragedies of the patrician." His masterpiece, *Francesca da Rimini*, was produced in New York on September 26, 1855. It ran for a week, a good record for so serious a play by an American author. Practically all historians assign it qualities of dramatic intensity unknown until then. However, romantic plays of this type remained alien to American democratic ideals. Strange doings within ancient families, forced marriages for political advantage, age-old customs which foment murder and suicide out of principle, never achieved the dominance in America's dramatic literature which they enjoyed abroad.

The American stage just before the Civil War was dominated not by a native-born artist, but by an Irishman, Dion Boucicault, born in Dublin somewhere between 1820 and 1822. Like Dunlap, he was a prolific adapter of foreign plays, yet free with his own ideas in the nearly 125 pieces he authored. His *The Poor of New York* (*The Streets of New York* in later versions),

1857, taken from a French drama *Les Pauvres de Paris* of 1856, and later presented in England as *The Poor of Liverpool*, was his first important effort at Wallack's Theatre in New York. Concerned with the financial panics of 1837 and 1857, it presents crass villains, scheming bankers, suffering innocence, and a house on fire which proved exceedingly popular. Boucicault's *Jessie Brown: or The Relief of Lucknow*, 1858, based on an actual historical event in 1857, had such a villainous villain that Boucicault himself was the only actor who would play it. (He was so good that one reviewer noted in high praise that the gallery "held its breath in awe and threw nothing at him.")

The noisy displays of these melodramas were modified in Boucicault's outstanding play on a distinct American theme, *The Octoroon* of December 2, 1859. Its problem of the love of a white man for a woman of one-eighth Negro blood was an eminently dangerous theme, especially since the attack upon Harpers Ferry had occurred only a few weeks earlier. It contains plenty of action, with slave-auction scenes and another fire, this time on a steamboat, to provide the necessary pyrotechnics. Boucicault also contributed an important character in the believable and sympathetic Irish heroine in *The Colleen Bawn* of 1860. Heretofore Irish stage characters had been as misrepresented as Negroes and Indians, burlesqued and ridiculed.

Boucicault is further remembered for three important facts. First, he was foremost among the writers who successfully urged the passage of the copyright law of 1856, which gave writers control over the production and publication of their own plays. Second, he developed what has been called "stage upholstery," involving elaborate scenery and vivid theatrical effects, which replaced the uninspired wing and backdrop. Most important was his establishment of the "road" as we know it today. The 1800s were the years of the great stars, whose national tours involved playing favorite roles with a resident stock company already established in every town they visited. Boucicault, in an effort to help protect his own plays and prevent piracy, introduced the "road company." This was not a traveling repertory company, but a group which presented a single play, going from town to town neither on the strength of their variety nor on the fame of their stars, but on the reputation of the play alone. The quality of the road production was consequently raised materially, although this new system started the decline and eventual decay of the familiar resident stock company.

OTHER IMPORTANT THEATRE PERSONNEL:
1800 TO THE CIVIL WAR

CALDWELL, JAMES H. Comedian in Charleston, 1816, afterwards manager of frontier theatres. Opened Camp Theatre, New Orleans, 1824.

DRAKE, SAMUEL. Managed first successful professional acting company in West at Frankfort, Ky., 1815. Ludlow and Smith acted with him. Established theatres in Ohio valley 1815–1830.

Ludlow, Noah M. Important actor and manager on the frontier along Allegheny and Mississippi Rivers after 1815. Opened first English theatre in New Orleans, 1818. Allied with Caldwell, 1821–1824. Published valuable reminiscences.

Smith, Solomon. Actor and manager throughout frontier—Ohio, Pennsylvania, Tennessee, Kentucky, St. Louis from 1817. Wrote valuable memoirs.

Wallack, James W. Successful manager of high-class Wallack's Theatre, New York, opened 1853. Father of Lester Wallack, one of New York's great managers. His New Wallack's Theatre, 1861, offered finest acting company in America.

Warren, William. Actor at Chestnut Street Theatre under Wignell in 1800. Assumed management with Wood at Wignell's death, 1803–1826.

Wood, William. See above.

THE CENTURY OF THE GREAT ACTOR

The Theatre Expands from Coast to Coast

Until about 1850, Philadelphia was still the leading theatre town in America. Its producing companies were the best this country had to offer. On November 25, 1816, the Chestnut Street Theatre, affectionately called "Old Drury of Philadelphia," introduced gas lighting in the first major installation of this wondrous new illumination. On April 2, 1820, to the horror of the management, then negotiating for the renewal of an expired insurance policy, the theatre burned to the ground, consuming gas pipes, two pianos, an organ, all the fine wardrobe, and the library. A new and elegant Chestnut arose in 1822, lasting for another thirty years until the decline of Philadelphia's importance as a center of the American theatre. On May 1, 1855, the Chestnut finally closed and was almost immediately demolished.

Northward, in Boston, the theatre continued its struggle against Puritan opposition, but was never again forced to stop because of offense to moral or religious sensibilities. The number of theatres grew steadily during the nineteenth century. The original Federal, or "Boston," Theatre closed permanently in 1852, but a citizens' group erected a handsome new one seating 3,000. It functioned as a major American theatre from 1854 until well into the twentieth century.

Theatricals in the South remained centered in Charleston. In Richmond on December 26, 1811, a catastrophe stunned all American theatres and supplied the righteous with evidence of God's avenging hand at work. The theatre burned, but this time it was occupied; seventy-two deaths resulted by fire and panic. Stringent regulations kept many theatres closed, and the stage in the South rapidly declined soon after. By 1825 it was of minimum importance; in the 1850s Charleston, with one theatre and only 23,000 white inhabitants, had little to offer.

The theatre's expansion into the frontier reached as far south as New Orleans and as far west as San Francisco. The names of Sol Smith and Noah Ludlow became familiar along the rivers and through the backwoods. Ludlow claimed the first regular English-speaking company in New Orleans in 1818, and both he and Smith were successful managers there for many years until 1852. Kentucky had professional actors as early as 1810; Cincinnati boasted a theatre building in 1801. St. Louis had amateur theatricals in 1815, Detroit the following year. San Francisco built theatres at the time of the Gold Rush, attracting some of the best acting talent from the East. Salt Lake City had plays in 1862.

Virginia City, Nevada, at its plushiest, contained five legitimate and six variety houses running simultaneously. Wherever the West expanded, there you could find the theatre. You could also find more than competent acting, because many of the Western theatres were rewarding spots for some aspiring Hamlet to begin his career, or for some old-timer, whose days in New York were numbered, to end his.

The colorful showboats plied the navigable rivers throughout the frontier territory, east and west, north and south, and brought excellent legitimate plays to otherwise inaccessible areas. From about 1830 until the last active boat, "The Majestic," was put up for sale in 1959, showboats, although deteriorating into the presentation of minstrelsy and melodrama, were one of America's most glamorous sources of theatre. Garishly painted, lavishly decorated and equipped, their screaming steam calliopes announced their coming from miles off, and they never failed to pull in enthusiastic audiences of every description wherever they touched.

New York Takes Center Stage

The original Park Theatre burned on May 24, 1820, with the loss of all equipment, but obligingly waited until the auditorium had emptied. A new and "splendid" house opened September 1, 1821, on the same site. The new Park signified the beginning of New York's prestige as the nation's theatre center, even though this poorly lit and badly paved city of 125,000 was still confined to the lower tip of Manhattan Island.

The first serious threat to the dominance of the Park came on October 23, 1826, with the opening of the largest theatre in the country, the magnificent 3,000-seat Bowery Theatre. The fate of every single important theatre of this era promptly touched the Bowery, and it burned to the ground on May 26, 1828. Insured for $50,000, the house was rebuilt in sixty-five working days, bigger and better than ever. It was gaslit, with an 84-foot-deep stage, unequaled anywhere in America.[1]

In 1841 the Park introduced Boucicault's *London Assurance*, which, for the first time in New York, employed the now conventional "box set." The three-sided room and the imaginary fourth wall of this innovation created a realistic illusion that started the wing and backdrop on their way out.

After 1850 New York theatres multiplied and became world famous: Wallack's Lyceum, 1852; The New Wallack's, 1861; The Booth, 1869. The struggles and fortunes of these houses will no longer concern us, for we must now turn to the men who occupied their stages, and who, in reality, *were* the nineteenth-century theatre.

---

[1] The Bowery was plagued by catastrophe as no other theatre. It burned again in September, 1836, reopened in January, 1837, then repeated the cycle in April, 1845, emerging anew the following August. The Park burned down in December, 1849, and was never rebuilt. The houses were always empty at the time, and there were no casualties.

The Rise of the Star Actor

The phenomenon which dominated the nineteenth-century theatre in America as well as in Europe was the dynamic figure of the actor. His personality was fervently sought on both sides of the Atlantic, and the extent to which managers would go to secure an international name was often downright foolhardy. This stage figure was idolized in a manner which can make modern infatuations with screen stars and vocalists seem insignificant passing fancies.

The great actors were giants of their art in an era when the material supplied them was everywhere inferior. After Sheridan, English playwriting declined into a craft of completely innocuous but well-constructed sentiment and melodrama. For a century, until Wilde and Shaw (and of course Ibsen in Norway) took playwriting as a serious art form, the new plays looked more and more alike. Four or five acts of uninspired contrivance continued to flow from many pens. The classics, on the other hand, were wearing thin. After all, there was only a limited number of Shakespearean plays, many of which were seldom acted. Restoration and eighteenth-century drama began to bore audiences by their endless repetition. A repertory stock company, performing three nights a week for a full season, needed a tremendous number of plays. Hamlet, Macbeth, Lear, and Lady Teazle were showing their age.

The assistance badly needed to enliven the discouragingly insipid theatrical fare came in the person of the actor. He completely dominated everything. *He* was the evening's attraction, not the play. Edwin Forrest as Metamora, Edwin Booth as Hamlet, Joseph Jefferson as Rip Van Winkle drew the crowds; the play was often beside the point. Jealousies which grew out of some "inalienable" personal rights to a specific role were notorious. Playwrights, lacking any copyright protection, could starve on their scraps of single cash payments; but actors, in permanent possession of certain plays, could and did wax opulent on box office receipts. Understandable resentments developed between resident actors and the touring star. He knew he was in demand, able to command his own price. He was hired alone and then introduced on very short notice into the group with whom he had to play. He could bully the established supporting cast with his frequent eccentricities before quickly departing with his large profits. Audiences, trained to see a name, were reluctant to attend a starless play they already knew by heart. As the star system grew, stock companies declined and eventually gave way to the professional system of hiring a complete cast, headed by star or stars, for the run of the play only.

In spite of all the devotion their personal magnetism commanded, actors were still held in social and religious disrepute. Too often they provided the opposition with valid argument against the theatre. Drunken and disorderly themselves, arrogant and selfish, proud and boastful, they became difficult to manage and unreliable in action. The accepted social niceties were frequently denied them; aristocratic churches refused them burial services.[2] Not until Queen Victoria knighted Henry Irving in 1895 did the actor achieve an official recognition of social status.

Early Stars: Cooper, Payne, and Cooke

Thomas Abthorpe Cooper and John Howard Payne began the great acting tradition in America. Cooper's Hamlet was "transcendently excellent" said one critic, and he is known to be the first Hamlet of any real stature on the American stage. He was hardly more than twenty-one at the time of his opening night in 1798, an event extensively described in Dunlap's history. Unnamed contemporary critics spoke of his voice as "of great compass, of most melodious tone, and susceptible of the greatest variety of modulation." He was capable of "wonderful expression" in his face, and "his form in anger was that of a demon; his smile in affability that of an angel." During Cooper's lifetime of thirty years on the American stage as actor and manager of the Park after Dunlap, he appeared in sixty-four different theatres in every state then in the Union and performed some 4,500 times while traveling over 20,000 miles.

John Howard Payne made his sensational debut at the Park on February 24, 1809, as Young Norval in John Home's *Douglas*. The handsome youth was not yet eighteen, looked younger, had already produced a play in New York, and, being "fatally precocious," entered this and other major roles with abandon and success. His Romeo, Hamlet, and other parts drew extravagant praise and immense crowds wherever he went in New York, Boston, or London. Dunlap found Payne's face "remarkably handsome, his countenance full of intelligence, and his manners fascinating," but was unconvinced by his enthusiastic reception. "A child playing in the same scene with men and women, is in itself an absurdity," he wrote, "and the popularity of such exhibitions is a proof of vicious taste, or rather an absence of taste. It is the same feeling which carries the crowd to see monsters of every description."

Everybody agrees that the first mature player of international importance to appear in America was George Frederick Cooke, who opened at the Park on November 21, 1810. It is said that he was promised more than $14,000 for his troubles in coming to America from England, and troubles they indeed were as his continued problem of excessive drink followed him overseas. The difficulties of keeping the man sober were soon apparent. Dunlap took the job of attempting to get him to the theatre on time, but never wholly succeeded. In December he played *Cato* drunk and without rehearsal in such a

[2] When George Holland, a popular English comedian, died in this country in 1870, a fashionable Fifth Avenue church denied him rites. The distressed family was told by the pastor that there was "a little church around the corner that does that sort of thing." This was the Church of the Transfiguration under the Rev. George Houghton, which ever since has been known as "The Little Church Around the Corner," and has become the actor's church.

pitiful exhibition that New York never forgot it. Even after a triumphant tour to Boston and Philadelphia in 1811, New Yorkers refused to support him. He died in that city, a broken man, on September 26, 1812.

Impossibly alcoholic, crude and eccentric in public behavior (he refused to play before President Madison, whom he called "king of the Yankee Doodles"), Cooke still brought a superior form of acting into the conventional roles he interpreted. One New York newspaper of 1810 saw the basis of his genius in "the boldness and originality of his manner, the significance of his gesture, the astonishing flexibility of his countenance," added to "the thorough knowledge, not only of the text, but the meaning of his author." Concerning a Philadelphia performance of Macbeth in 1811, Washington Irving wrote, "It was sublime," and continued, ". . . when he is in proper mood, there is a truth and of course a simplicity in his performances that throws all rant, stage trick & stage effect completely in the background. . . . One of his best performances may be compared to a masterpiece of ancient statuary, where you have the human figure destitute of idle ornament."

Edwin Forrest: Fabulous and Fatal

Edwin Forrest is remembered not only as the first great American-born romantic actor, but as the first performer who took a serious interest in native American plays. Born into near poverty in Philadelphia on March 9, 1806, he appeared on the Southwark stage when only eleven. He opened at the Park in New York in his own *Othello*, on November 6, 1826, for $25 a week. The following year, aged twenty-one, he was engaged for a season of eighty nights at a guarantee of $200 a performance, an exceedingly generous offer by any standard.

Secure and prosperous, Forrest began at the age of twenty-three to award a series of prizes for native plays. He would pay an author up to $1,000 in cash for permanent and exclusive rights. After 1829 he paid out a total of some $20,000, but considering the fortune he reaped from his ownership, none of which he ever shared with an author, his generosity was far from munificent. No doubt he encouraged native talent, but in supplying himself with a number of profitable roles, his niggardly treatment of his prizewinners was wholly unjust.

Forrest's trip to England in 1845 laid the groundwork for the most violent episode in American theatrical history. William C. Macready, thirteen years Forrest's senior and of no little international fame, was acting classic Shakespearean roles in England. Personal rivalry between the two men had always been intense; when Forrest was hissed in London for his performances of *Othello* and *Macbeth*, his hot temper too hastily persuaded him that Macready was back of it. At Edinburgh in 1846, while attending Macready's *Hamlet*, Forrest asserted his right to criticize by hissing back. Thereupon, the whole foolish affair deteriorated rapidly.

The Astor Place Riot, from a contemporary lithograph by N. Currier. The smouldering feud between British tragedian William Macready and America's favorite, Edwin Forrest, erupted on May 10, 1849, into the deadliest riot ever associated with the American theatre. (*Courtesy New York Historical Society, New York.*)

On Thursday, May 10, 1849, the curtain rose on Macready's *Macbeth* at the Astor Place Opera House in New York. The theatre was packed with supporters of Macready and with the "Bowery B'hoys" who were ready to shout him off the stage to show their enthusiastic support of Forrest. The mayor of New York had made a few preparations for trouble by stationing several hundred policemen inside and outside the theatre and by alerting the militia. Macready, honestly unaware of the intensity of feeling against him, was determined to appear, but his first entrance raised such a racket that the play had to proceed in dumb show. Pleas for silence got nowhere. A mob outside, increasing into the thousands, began to show its strength by attacking the building. Paving stones crashed through 1½-inch-thick boards over the windows, previously nailed up for precaution. Eventually, with most of the New York police force besieged within the building and unable to disperse the rioters, the military advanced. After some forty-five minutes of struggle, orders were given to fire. The first volley was aimed high, but at least two more were point-blank. By the time it was all over and the area cleared, the lowest count totaled thirty-one dead and hundreds, including the law and military, wounded. Most of the fatalities were among bystanders who came to watch; the rioters themselves were mainly teen-age boys and young men who had no idea what the fight was all about. Without organization, without any important ideal behind it, the riot had been one of the weirdest on record.

In spite of a tempestuous stage style, a fatal temper, and a somewhat "herculean" physique, Forrest seems to have had the ability to move gracefully onstage and to use his voice with skill. But it was not just an expressive face or physical grace that brought his tremendous success. "He was," said one comment, "a colossus, as well intellectually as physically," and to a greater extent than any other man he "united those gifts, physical and mental, and those habits and tendencies that count in an actor." His main forte was in "delineating tumultuous passion." Forrest's Lear was one of his most tremendous roles, "Jovelike" in majesty. "I may enact Spartacus, Jack Cade, Metamora," he once told an admirer, "but, by God, sir, I *am* King Lear."

Forrest continued acting until 1871 and died the following year. He left his home and much of his considerable fortune for the maintenance of a home for retired actors, which he himself had established.

The Booths from Baltimore

Junius Brutus Booth, father of America's first great theatrical family, was born in London in 1796. He was playing *Richard III* in London by 1817, and was acclaimed in the same role in Richmond, Virginia, at the age of twenty-five. Later in 1821 he opened to tremendous popular enthusiasm at the Park. His style, in some ways more madly wild than Forrest's, maintained considerable originality, although his belief in his role could terrify those on stage with him. The anecdotes about his behavior are many. On one occasion, for instance, while playing Othello, he seemed bent on actually smothering his unfortunate Desdemona until forcibly prevented by others on stage. Liable to drunkenness and nearly maniacal though he was, his fiery, energetic performances were something to remember.

Booth bought a farm near Baltimore in 1824 and settled down with his "wife," Mary Ann Holmes, to raise his expanding family in an isolated wilderness far from the theatres in which he worked.[3] In 1847, young Edwin Booth, at the age of fourteen, began to accompany his father on tour, the only one of the children able to control the parent's mad and drunken outbursts. Edwin made his own debut on September 10, 1849, at the Boston Museum. His first major role was Richard in April, 1851, when his father, either undergoing or feigning an indisposition, told the eighteen-year-old boy to go on in his stead. An older brother, Junius, Jr., who had left home and become manager of a San Francisco theatre, persuaded Edwin and their father to take the long sea journey via the Isthmus to California in 1852. A few months later the elder Booth headed for home alone. He died on a river steamboat out of New Orleans on November 30, 1852.

---

[3] The marriage was not legitimate. Booth had married in London in 1815. Not until his son came to America from England in the 1840s was he found out. After a divorce in 1851, Booth officially married Mary Ann.

After performing in Australia and in California mining towns, Edwin Booth returned to the East in 1856. There he found his younger brother, John Wilkes, grown into a handsome, dark-eyed, self-satisfied, and stage-struck youth who resolved to be the greatest Booth of them all. Edwin continued his career and was billed in New York as "the Hope of the Living Drama" in his Richard of May 3, 1857. His acting style at this time was characterized by freedom and boldness, with great power and grandeur. He had a manly presence, with "a graceful bearing, a rich, sonorous voice of unusual compass and flexibility, mobile features, and an eye positively wonderful in its power of expression."

Booth received a great personal shock in the loss of his lovely twenty-three-year-old wife, Mary Devlin, in 1863, who had played Juliet to his Romeo, but he went on to become the leading Hamlet of his age. On November 26, 1864, he opened in New York at the Winter Garden for a run of 100 consecutive nights, an all-time record, which held far into the twentieth century. The previous night, November 25, he and his two brothers, Junius and John Wilkes, appeared together in the same play for the only time in their lives. Their performance of *Julius Caesar* was a sensation; the audience, said newspaper reports, "was fairly carried by storm from the first entrance of the three brothers side by side." Junius played Brutus, Edwin played Cassius, and John Wilkes played Marc Antony. But the 100-night *Hamlet* was the year's most important event. The *New York Herald*, never a paper to praise Booth, found that the performance was "a continual elucidation of Shakespere, . . . one of the noblest pieces of dramatic art ever seen in any land or any age."

The overwhelming national disaster of April 14, 1865, will always be associated with the name of Booth. The greatness which the family brought to the American theatre must bear a certain tarnish which can never wear completely away. John Wilkes, young, hotheaded, always seeking fame, inherited more than his share of his father's erratic temper. He wanted to be a star and resented playing secondary roles to his brothers. Junius and Edwin could not control his spirit, and when, as a violent Southern sympathizer, his egotism and desire for fame became so twisted as to lead him to his final insane act, he almost took with him the entire Booth family. Their lives were in serious danger from mob violence, and the family members were either arrested or placed under surveillance for some time.

Edwin Booth retired from the stage and vowed never to return, but his public, and his family's pocketbook, refused to let him leave. Within a year he was back. On January 3, 1866, a wildly cheering throng greeted his *Hamlet*. From then on, he was the leading actor of the American stage. His million-dollar Booth Theatre opened in New York on February 3, 1869, featuring the most elaborate stage machinery and equipment, including a fan under the auditorium for cooling in summer and warming in winter. But Booth was a poor manager. Facing bankruptcy in 1873, he turned the theatre over to Junius although he continued to act until his final *Hamlet* of April 4, 1891. He died on June 8, 1893, after having given his house to the Players' Club for their perpetual use, together with a bequest of $150,000. He was still able to leave

Booth's Theatre, New York, 1869. The heights of overwhelming Victorian elegance in theatre design are abundantly apparent. The stage, pushed far behind the immense proscenium and laden with elaborately romantic settings, has lost its apron and all of its erstwhile intimate contact with the audience. The "pit" has now become the high-priced "orchestra" with individual chairs. Elaborate proscenium boxes are about all that survive from the past. (*Courtesy Museum of the City of New York.*)

behind a fortune of a half-million dollars; he was one of the richest actors in history.

Booth had brought something new to the lively theatre of the mid- and late nineteenth century—personal integrity and an intellectual approach to his roles. Eschewing fireworks and electrically charged performances, he *interpreted* his roles; he did not merely act them. He realized that he brought dramatic literature, not just entertainment alone, to his audiences. In Booth the actor was no longer a mere performer, but had become an artist.

OTHER IMPORTANT PERFORMERS OF THE NINETEENTH CENTURY

GILBERT, JOHN. Nationally famous after 1828 for comic parts and interpretations of old men.

HACKETT, JAMES H. From 1828 popular in Yankee roles and as Falstaff.

HILL, GEORGE HANDEL. "Yankee Hill," famed after 1831 for his New England Yankee roles. Popular in England.

KEAN, EDMUND. World-famous English star; debut in New York, 1820. Brilliant, temperamental, erratic. To see him perform, said Coleridge, is like "reading Shakespeare by flashes of lightning." Refusal to act before a small audience in Boston in 1821 permanently injured his reputation in America.

KEMBLE, FANNY. Distinguished English actress. At Park, 1832. Daughter of actor, Charles Kemble. The first important woman star in America.

MATHEWS, CHARLES. Tremendously popular English comedian. His intimate, quietly humorous "Evenings" and "At Homes" were enthusiastically received everywhere. American debut, 1822–1823. His memoirs contain a valuable account of early American theatre.

RACHEL (ELIZABETH RACHEL FELIX). Actress of *Théâtre Français*, Paris. First foreign-language star to make an American tour, 1855. A failure.

THE BIRTH PANGS OF REALISM

1865 TO 1900

Plays had been produced throughout the long conflict of the Civil War. Meanwhile the position of the playmaker was, fortunately, improving, as copyright laws, weak as they were, began to place the author in a better bargaining position. He was able to be more than a mere servant of the producer or the actor, although he still found it wise to have an added income. Independent dramatists, living by their royalties, did not exist. Playwriting, not yet a profession by itself, was still a long way from being a self-sustaining art.

The Dictator and the Dean: Daly and Howard

Augustin Daly, the greatest single influence on the development of modern American drama at the close of the nineteenth century, was born in Plymouth, North Carolina, July 20, 1838. He was a theatre manager in Brooklyn as early as 1856. His first original play, the sensational hit, *Under the Gaslight*, was produced in New York on August 12, 1867. Its traditional melodramatic ingredients of villainy and last-minute rescues were reinforced by marvels of mechanical ingenuity, including a full-sized locomotive roaring across the stage. In all, Daly wrote or adapted some ninety productions, mostly from French or other Continental plays.

Daly's long and important career as a stage manager began in New York's Fifth Avenue Theatre in 1869. He developed an entirely new quality in theatrical production by putting the play, from initial reading to final curtain, directly under his virtually dictatorial control. He turned his actors away from the tempestuousness of the Forrest-Booth tradition, creating a style that was ridiculed as "emasculated," or "acting with the acting left out." Under his direction histrionics gave way to natural stage interpretation, and he insisted on a new kind of company where nobody was a "star." As he won critics and public to his well-disciplined and refined productions, playgoers came to realize that going to Daly's Theatre meant going to the best drama in America.

Bronson Howard introduced a new era into American drama by demonstrating that an American playwright could make a living solely by writing plays. In 1870, when he produced his first successful play, *Saratoga*, respect for native American drama was still limited. Daly himself showed that he believed the best subject matter came from abroad when he declared that American dramatists were "entirely right" in choosing foreign material. Although Howard's plays eventually reflected the manners of contemporary Americans, his scenes of life at the aristocratic Saratoga spa were full of characters easily recognizable at any other resort; in fact, the English adaptation was called *Brighton* and scarcely altered. When Howard offered the first version of his famous *Shenandoah*, producer Lester Wallack distrusted his Civil War theme and told Howard to place it in the Crimea so it would be a "safe" play. The advice was happily ignored.

Howard's painstaking care was one of his greatest contributions to the development of American playwriting as an art. He worked and reworked on the problems that bothered him, for he regarded the drama as a living thing based on fundamental dramatic "laws" which he could not transcend. His attitude is shown by these quotations from a lecture given at Harvard in 1886:

> A play must be in one way or another, "satisfactory" to the audience. . . . In England and America, the death of a pure woman on the stage is not "satisfactory," except when the play rises to the dignity of tragedy. The death, in an ordinary play, of a woman who is not pure . . . is perfectly satisfactory, for the reason that it is inevitable. . . . The wife who has once taken the step from purity to impurity can never reinstate herself in the world of art on this side of the grave; and so an audience looks with complacent tears on the death of an erring woman. . . . There are axioms among the laws of dramatic construction, as in mathematics. One of them is this—three hearts cannot beat as one. The world is not large enough, from an artistic point of view, for three good human hearts to continue to exist, if two of them love the third. If one of the two hearts is a bad one, art assigns it to the hell on earth of disappointed love; but if it is good and tender and gentle, art is merciful to it, and puts it out of its misery by death.

The name of Bronson Howard means practically nothing to the modern active playgoer, although his position as "dean of American drama" is readily admissible. As a professional writer for the stage he brought to American playwriting the recognition it began to deserve, artistically and financially. His satire on big business, *The Henrietta*, 1887, grossed nearly $500,000 in royalties, firm proof that the combination of skill and sound copyright protection permitted a native writer to compete successfully with any other.

Howard founded the American Dramatists Club in 1891, which later became the Society of American Dramatists and Composers. He died, with great public tribute, on August 4, 1908.

Realism: Howells, Herne, and Gillette

The stage realist of nineteenth-century drama tried to steer away from the artificialities of romantic love, exotic settings, and sentimentality. The realist preferred to let his action grow naturally out of the believable situation and familiar environment in which his characters were introduced, and he eliminated easily recognizable character "types." As the abstractions of wing and backdrop gave way to the detailed design of the box set, the stage setting became a place *within* which the character lived, not *against* which the actor merely performed. Prolonged asides and soliloquies to the audience disappeared. Actors found that, within reason, they could behave onstage much as they would behave in any public place or private home.

Subject matter became important. Characters faced with problems of everyday life did not always resolve them by the end of the play. The realist had to bypass such "laws" as Howard felt immutable. He knew that all three members of a love triangle probably lived on and that far more fallen women survived than perished. Similarly, honesty, virtue, and innocence suffered onstage as they often suffered in life; earthly rewards for good heroes and heroines were not always forthcoming, and villains frequently went unpunished. Realistic writers followed the lead of Norway's Ibsen, who once replied after being asked what happened after the final curtain of *Ghosts*, "I should never dream of deciding so delicate a question. But what is your opinion?"

Stage facilities of the late nineteenth century enabled the realist to practice his art in a fashion heretofore impossible. Finely controlled gas lighting permitted many effects which were unthinkable with candle and oil lamp. The limelight allowed brilliant and intense spot focus. Stage machinery with hydraulic lifts, revolving stages, immense fly-space, enabled all kinds of marvels to take place. Then electricity, unsteady at first but soon perfected, made infinite lighting control a permanent feature.

The nineteenth-century American drama, while second-rate, was never far divorced in theme and treatment from the main currents of other literature. It is therefore understandable that the influence of William Dean Howells, realistic novelist, short story writer, editor of *The Atlantic Monthly*, should be as strongly felt in the professional theatre as elsewhere. In his own writing Howells practiced what he continually preached, "the doctrine of truth to life in art," and the impact of his novels and sound literary criticism was felt by all serious writers for over half a century. He regarded the drama on the same level as other literature, judging it with saneness and discrimination. His direct contribution to the stage was mainly in the form of highly successful one-act farces popular with amateur groups, but in these short plays and in his few longer ones he brought to the thousands who saw and played in them the manners and social values so important in the developing realistic tradition.

The most important American proponent of the realistic "problem play" in the Ibsen tradition was James A. Herne. Strong in character development, Herne guided his protagonist through a social, economic, or moral situation to the best solution as he saw it. In his portrayal of the men and women of contemporary life he became known as the "glorifier of the common man." More than any other writer of the late nineteenth century, he was an important transitional figure. Herne wanted to apply American themes to the stage in the realistic Howells manner and to avoid the stereotyped romantic formulas. In his three most important plays, *Margaret Fleming*, 1890, *Shore Acres*, and *The Reverend Griffith Davenport*, both 1899, Herne succeeded in remaining close to the common life and the simple fundamentals of everyday existence.

William Gillette spent a good part of his long career acting in his own successful plays. His dramas emphasized action, broad movement, and exciting incident more than realistic character development, although he, like Herne, never surrendered to flatly drawn stereotypes. The printed versions of his plays are full of detailed action minutely described, for Gillette preferred that his reader and, of course, his audience, should learn to know his characters by their behavior onstage as much as by what they uttered. In all of his important works there are extended periods during which nothing is said while the actors move through some very striking stage business. To the student of American dramatic literature, Gillette's *Secret Service*, 1895, and *Sherlock Holmes*, 1899, mean two of the very best cloak-and-dagger, crime-and-pursuit plays written in the nineteenth century.

A Few Moments with Melodrama

One type of play, unrelated to good literature but still a highly important part of nineteenth-century theatre, was the melodrama.[4] Good melodrama is good theatre, and there is no reason to deny its hair-raising adventures a legitimate place on the stage. At first melodrama in English seems to have come from what Montrose Moses calls the "foreign brigand literature," involving much of the Gothic tradition of Dunlap's adaptations of Kotzebue. This concerned dastardly goings-on by dark-cloaked and sinister beings, who always spoke with foreign accents and prowled in moldy, dank castles. Individual character traits of good and evil were always clear-cut. Emphasis on visual sensation by means of stage mechanics arrived with Boucicault. Instead of castles and moldering abbeys, he accentuated the violent occurrences of contemporary life through floods, slave auctions, burning steamboats, and the creation of plain, everyday, no-good villains who walked in the bright sunlight. By 1860, the rush of lurid tales of adventure called "dime novels" gave stage melodrama new impetus. When Daly's *Under the Gaslight* sent its stage locomotive roaring toward the helpless hero tied to the rails, plausibility remained far outside the theatre. The audience, seeing these exhibitions, cared nothing for the reasons *why*, nor for rationally motivated events. They waited breathlessly for each succeeding "big scene," and gripped their seats in terror as the heroine smashed her way into the sawmill to rescue her lover from the whining blade.

One of the most prolific writers of melodrama, often called "10-20-30 mellers" because of the three admission prices of ten, twenty, and thirty cents,

---

[4] Greek *melos*, song, plus drama. Originally a play with music. The *melodrame* was an early type of romantic play with accompanying background and theme music. The association of particular musical *themes* with melodrama's villain, hero, and heroine carried over into the nineteenth century and later.

Display poster for Daly's *Under the Gaslight,* 1867. These brilliantly colored lithographs advertising the latest sensational melodrama helped to pull in large and enthusiastic audiences, who gasped in wonder at the ever-increasing marvels of nineteenth-century stage mechanics. (*Courtesy Harvard Theatre Collection.*)

was Owen Davis. He describes the credo of the creators of melodrama in his little book, "My First Fifty Years in the Theatre":

> Your hero was labeled at his first entrance. Nothing was left to inference. It was almost indispensable that he knock down the villain in the first two minutes following his entrance. . . . Instead of having your heroine pursued by some abstract thing such as fate, you had her pursued by a tangible villain bent upon cutting her throat. You piled catastrophe upon catastrophe. By the time the hero threw his protecting arms around her in the last act, she must have narrowly escaped scalping by Indians, been almost drowned in a mill-race, missed death in a train wreck, and been shot at and stabbed by the villain, to say nothing of having passed unscathed through several conflagrations, an earthquake or two, a mine cave-in, or a magazine explosion. The play only ended when you had exhausted every possible calamity, but it ended happily: it *had* to end happily. And the hero remained the hero, and the villain died as black as when he first came on.

The "tearful" melodramas of the 1862 *East Lynne* variety, or its sister piece, *Way Down East,* 1898, were slightly different. They all had their bad men and their good, but their emphasis was upon actual or implied deeds of shame, rather than upon visual sensation. In the case of proved seduction, Howard's laws were invariably applicable. No soiled female could possibly redeem herself this side of the grave. Here was the tradition of dark and stormy nights, of returning prodigal daughters, and the rigid code of "Never darken my door again."

OTHER IMPORTANT THEATRE PERSONNEL BEFORE 1900

It is difficult to break the later nineteenth century into distinct chronological sections. Personnel most active after 1900 will be found listed on page 52, following the discussion of the early twentieth century.

ANDERSON, MARY. Debut in Louisville, 1875. Played Western theatres, New Orleans to San Francisco. A classic beauty who permanently retired after fifteen active years.

BARRYMORE, MAURICE. Real name, Herbert Blythe. Born in India, educated in England. American debut, 1875. Father of Barrymore acting family.

BERNHARDT, SARAH. "The Divine Sarah." Debut at *Comédie Française*, 1862. Nine American tours, 1880–1917. World-famous, mainly in French classics.

CARTER, MRS. LESLIE. Chicago society woman who made sensational debut in Belasco's *The Heart of Maryland*, 1895.

CRABTREE, CHARLOTTE (LOTTA). Debut in California mining towns, popular in San Francisco from 1860. Her winsome personality won New York in 1864.

DAVENPORT, FANNY. Daughter of tragedian, E. L. Davenport. Debut at eight years of age; engaged by Mrs. Drew, 1862. Successful in Sardou melodramas after 1874.

DREW, GEORGIANA. Sister of John, mother of Barrymore family.

DREW, MRS. JOHN. Played regular roles in melodrama from age of five. Managed Arch Street Theatre, Philadelphia, 1861, one of most brilliant stock companies in America. The greatest actress-manager in history. Grandmother of Barrymores.

IRVING, SIR HENRY. Born John Henry Brodribb. Brought great personal dignity to the stage. His *Hamlet* of 1874 set London record of 200 performances. With Ellen Terry had tremendous career in America and England. Knighted, 1895. Buried in Westminster Abbey.

JEFFERSON, JOSEPH III. Third of the famous family. Rose to fame with Laura Keene in *Our American Cousin*, 1858. His Rip Van Winkle and Bob Acres in *The Rivals* were world famous.

KEAN, CHARLES. Son of Edmund Kean. New York debut, 1846. Produced first full-scale historically accurate productions of tragedy.

KEENE, LAURA. Star of *Our American Cousin*, 1858, the play Lincoln was attending when assassinated. The first woman to attempt to form her own acting company.

LANGTRY, LILLIE. Born on Island of Jersey, known as "The Jersey Lily." Appeared in New York, 1882. A great symbol of feminine beauty, she had a town in Texas named after her.

MANSFIELD, RICHARD. German-born, appeared in New York, 1883. An overnight star, and a famous Cyrano in 1898.

MODJESKA, HELENA. Came to America from Poland, 1876. Performed in San Francisco, 1877. Debut at Daly's. Her 1883 happy-ending *A Doll's House* failed.

NEILSON, ADELAIDE. One of the great beauties of her age. Famed in England for Juliet, 1868. Toured America coast to coast after 1872.

REHAN, ADA. Irish-born, stage debut at fourteen. Apprentice with Mrs. Drew in Philadelphia. Twenty years with Daly after 1879. A famous Katharine in *The Taming of the Shrew*.

SOTHERN, E. A. Came from England, 1852. Famous as Lord Dundreary, *Our American Cousin*, from 1858 to 1880.

TERRY, ELLEN. Loveliest English actress of her time. Irving's leading lady, 1878. Famous for Portia and Lady Macbeth. Bernard Shaw adored her, wrote plays for her. A scandalous private life did not interfere with a great career.

WALLACK, LESTER. A greatly admired and much respected New York stage manager from Civil War to 1888.

THE PERIOD OF TRANSITION

The Picture at the Turn of the Century

New York, with the merger of its five boroughs in the spring of 1897, became a metropolis of 3,000,000 people in a nation of about 70,000,000. It was the undisputed entertainment center of the country. Theatre buildings multiplied rapidly. By 1894 there were thirty-nine playhouses and eight music halls headed north on Manhattan Island toward the present Times Square. An orchestra seat for the finest attraction cost about $2, a gallery seat, 50 cents. For a dime, if you didn't mind what you saw or under what conditions you saw it, you could still watch hero, heroine, and villain in the decaying halls of the Bowery. In 1909, up on Central Park West, the huge New Theatre (later known as the Century) brought hopes for a dignified art theatre before its gigantic stage and high production costs defeated its noble purpose.

The theatres were not confined merely to New York or other large cities. Throughout the country the "opera house" was a standard monument in any respectable town; resident stock companies were active everywhere. Regularly scheduled traveling shows were a part of everybody's entertainment. Outlying districts were rapidly becoming the broad and unbounded area known as "the road," while the metropolitan centers surrounding New York soon became the "try-out cities." In New Haven, Philadelphia, Boston, Washington, or Wilmington the new productions flexed their muscles, worked out the kinks, and spiced up or toned down their dialogue. Chicago, St. Louis, Detroit, or Pittsburgh became the big towns where a hit would visit after the stamp of success had already been imprinted in the narrow band of city blocks along Broadway.

The first American production of Shaw was *Arms and the Man* at the Herald Square Theatre on September 17, 1894; it had sixteen performances. In 1905, when Daly produced *Mrs. Warren's Profession*, the play was banned in New Haven, and both Daly and his star were arrested by the New York police for presenting an immoral play. (An understanding judge soon released them.) Ibsen received scattered attention in some limited productions. A happy-ending version of *A Doll's House* called *Thora* failed in 1883; the original play was staged in December, 1889. *Ghosts* shocked audiences in 1894. Oscar Wilde's *The Importance of Being Earnest* was at the Empire on April 22, 1895, and his *An Ideal Husband* had been staged the previous March at the Lyceum.

The more popular English writers whose plays appeared steadily on the New York stage were Henry Arthur Jones and Sir Arthur Wing Pinero.

Although both men are generally considered major contributors to the making of the modern English stage, their critical reputations have declined below the permanent status of Wilde and Shaw. After 1907 and *The Silver Box*, John Galsworthy's plays appeared with regularity.

Runs were getting longer and longer during these years. One or two hundred consecutive performances soon became commonplace. Stars were not yet willing to endure the multiple-year, 1,000-night runs expected today, for they wisely preferred to vary their diet with two or more plays annually. Long runs, as always, were no reflection of artistic worth. Musicals, which ran longer than legitimate plays, were no better. The toast of the town in 1900 was an extravagant song-and-dance item called *Florodora*, which ran for an astounding 505 performances. Six of the most beautiful young ladies of the show world appeared as the Florodora Sextette. Young New York was completely infatuated with them, and each girl received lavish gifts, ranging from great showers of jewels and furs to horses and houses—and money.

Unfortunately the theatre remained primarily the show place of the stars. The average ticket-buyer attended much the same type of play that had been familiar to him from the time of the Civil War: unrealistic romance and frequent adaptations of popular novels and foreign plays, especially "from the French." This was the age of the great display; the theatre was an exhibition hall, not a library. The prevailing attitude of theatre men was expressed by the powerful theatre manager, Charles Frohman, known everywhere as "C. F." This man, so influential that railroads gave his private Pullman the same precedence as that of the President of the United States, defended this theatrical way of life when he said, "We regard the workman first and the work second. Our imaginations are fired not nearly so much by great deeds as by great doers." Hence we remember the glitter of the names of those "workmen," those "doers," whom Frohman sponsored, much more than we recall the art of the writers who created for them. From the 1890s and the 1900s came dozens of actors and actresses whose personalities still suggest a time of wondrous glamor and excitement.

Probably the best representative of everything "gay" about the "Gay Nineties" was that fabulous beauty with the "rare figure and delightful voice," Lillian Russell, who first appeared on Tony Pastor's variety stage right out of Iowa in 1880 at the age of nineteen. For over twenty years in musical comedy, and later in legitimate drama, she was the national symbol of everything glamorous.

Among those who contributed dignity without need of great physical beauty was Minnie Maddern Fiske, wife of producer Harrison Grey Fiske. One of the most distinguished legitimate artists of the early century, she emphasized the intellectual approach to her roles without depending on her own personal attractiveness. She was known throughout her professional career simply as Mrs. Fiske. Her personal integrity as both serious actress and high comedienne was a major help in the continual struggle of the actor to achieve public respectability. She appeared onstage in New York and on the road from the 1880s almost up to the very day of her death in 1932.

One of the first genuine "gentlemen" of the American stage and a leading idol of the 1890s was dignified John Drew. His thin, trim-mustachioed face precisely fitted the sophistication of the model drawing-room performer. He was personally respected everywhere, and his influence was felt on and off the stage for fifty years. In 1923, at the age of seventy, he still performed as Sir Peter Teazle in *The School for Scandal* to the Lady Teazle of his distinguished niece, Ethel Barrymore. This charming beauty made her first starring appearance in 1901; she and her two brothers, John and Lionel, proceeded to become the most famous American acting family since the Booths.

Some of the men and women of the 1890s and 1900s maintained the distinction of an individual style with which they were more or less permanently identified. Into this category falls James O'Neill, who owned one of the most lucrative stage properties of any actor, *The Count of Monte Cristo*. He performed this melodrama up and down the country for decades after 1883, recreating Edmund Dantes before practically every inhabited locale in America. Joseph Jefferson did the same in his own version of *Rip Van Winkle*, which he began to play in 1865 and continued until the year before his death in 1905. Then there was the charming, captivating, girlish Maude Adams, a Frohman graduate. At twenty-five she achieved immediate success in James M. Barrie's special adaptation of *The Little Minister* in 1897. Barrie wrote several plays for her, including the phenomenal *Peter Pan*. This fantasy of 1905 was to become one of the most permanently successful plays in the American theatre. Of all the important stars in those years when public infatuation with theatrical performers was at its highest pitch, Miss Adams was perhaps the most universally loved in an outright, adoring, worshipful manner.

Another outstanding personality was the young, enthusiastic song-and-dance man, George M. Cohan. In 1901, after years with his parents and sister as "The Four Cohans" in popular vaudeville routines, he entered the legitimate stage with a play of his own. This energetic trouper, a "Yankee Doodle Dandy, born [in 1878] on the Fourth of July," as he never tired of singing, became a leading actor-playwright of the early twentieth century. His was a sense of pure theatre, and although the sentimentalities of his plays and musicals like *Broadway Jones* or *Forty-five Minutes from Broadway* were far removed from dramatic literature, he exhibited tremendous understanding of the best qualities of genuine family entertainment—clean, respectable, tuneful, and immensely popular. Even today there are those who find his songs among the best musical-comedy numbers ever written.

Monopoly Takes Over

Thriving on the star system it fostered, the theatre remained a strictly commercial enterprise. The attitude of Frohman and others enabled the businessman to gain an ironclad upper hand which seriously retarded the development of dramatic artistry for a considerable time. The most direct interference came from the formation in 1896 of a well-meaning but irresistible enterprise known as the Syndicate. It started out as a sound business arrangement, conceived in order to facilitate the movements of important road shows throughout the country. Its founders, some half-dozen important showmen, decided there would be more efficiency in sending the shows, through the agency of a central booking office, into theatres all over the country on a carefully predetermined timetable. For the performers it meant no scheduling worries, and for the individual theatre managers it meant regular topnotch shows at substantial savings. On paper the plan sounded good. In practice, under the leadership of Marc Klaw and A. L. Erlanger, who gave the Syndicate its name, it became a terrifyingly powerful monopoly. What it eventually succeeded in doing was to seize control of virtually every important theatre from coast to coast. Soon no production without a Klaw and Erlanger contract could enter certain cities under any conditions short of pitching tents in cow pastures, as the great Sarah Bernhardt was forced to do. Hopeful managers quickly found themselves the complete slaves of an impersonal New York organization. Second-rate plays, losing ground in New York, could be sent on tour and forced into any theatre, where the manager would have to show them or be run out of business. The prosperous shows would remain in New York, depriving the road of the good theatre it was supposed to be paying for. Eager new actors had to satisfy Charles Frohman, a Syndicate member, or face little chance of getting a start. Writers, of course, were almost completely at the group's mercy.

In 1906 the Syndicate controlled about 700 theatres. Before controlling legislation existed, the best way to fight such an organization was with an equally strong trust. This was supplied by Lee, J. J., and Sam S. Shubert from Syracuse. By 1905 Sam, aged twenty-nine, was managing three New York playhouses and eight out of town. After his tragic death in a train wreck that year, his brothers erected a Sam S. Shubert Memorial Theatre in every city they could enter and began to give the Syndicate a battle royal. In the end, challenged everywhere, Klaw and Erlanger gave up. The Shuberts never achieved the same absolute monopoly, although they operated a majority of the legitimate theatres in this country well into the 1950s. At that time a Federal antitrust suit compelled them to surrender a good portion of their holdings.

THOSE WHO TRIED

David Belasco, Superrealist and Showshop Genius

Dramatic historians, writing soon after the First World War, tried hard to discover literary value in early twentieth-century American drama, but later perspective shows that the accomplishments were not quite what they had once appeared to be. There were many writers who tried, however, and a few who just about succeeded.

Placing the name of David Belasco first in line of "those who tried" is misleading in so far as good literary drama is concerned. As an artist of the *theatre*, he unquestionably stood alone; as an artist of the written *drama* he was second-rate. For all that, to remove him summarily from a discussion of pre-World War I drama would prove impossible, simply because of his great personal devotion to the theatre as an institution. If there was ever an individual who regarded the entire legitimate theatre with serious intent and with the utmost integrity it was certainly David Belasco. In this sense he was an outstanding *professional*; simultaneously, he was peddling the wares of a highly *commercial* enterprise. He successfully fought the Syndicate by building his own theatres, but this did not make him any more the purveyor of dramatic art than Klaw and Erlanger themselves. Both Belasco and the Syndicate were skilled merchants selling their store of goods to a public who had been given little opportunity to choose the quality of their purchase.

In 1882, at twenty-nine years of age, after successful management in the Far West, Belasco became stage manager of the small and intimate Madison Square Theatre in New York, where experimentation was encouraged and struggling native writers welcomed. As "manager" he held the powers now associated with the terms "producer" and "director," which enabled him to apply his own artistic interpretations to each production. In his work at the Madison Square, Belasco became the first of the modern directors who visualized the entire stage picture as a product of the integrated talents of actor, scene designer, lighting technician, and director. This was a significant step forward; yet Belasco was never able to define his own safe limits. He not only closely controlled his actors, but he continually endangered the entire play when he smothered it beneath the heavy weight of highly visual but dramatically impractical stage machinery.

Belasco, the showman, had a minimum appreciation of writing; he continually sought what he himself could do for a play apart from its own dramatic qualities. In his book, "The Theatre through the Stage Door," he tells of his

constant attempts at scenic literalism. During his production of Eugene Walter's
The Easiest Way his difficulties mounted:

> We tried to build the scene in my shops, but, somehow, we could not make
> it look shabby enough. So I went to the meanest theatrical lodging-house I
> could find in the Tenderloin district and bought the entire interior of one of
> the most dilapidated rooms—patched furniture, threadbare carpet, tarnished
> and broken gas fixtures, tumble-down cupboards, dingy doors and window-
> casings, and even the faded paper on the walls.

How he removed the paper he does not say.

Belasco continued producing plays almost until his death in 1931. "I hear a
lot about 'the Belasco method,'" he wrote, "and I suppose it originates from
the importance and emphasis I place upon every minute detail which makes
for truth in my theatre." His "truth," unfortunately, involved such wholly
unnecessary detail that the real truths of which the theatre is capable were lost.

Clyde Fitch: Hack Writer and Devoted Professional

Clyde Fitch did not direct, or produce, or act. We cannot honestly call
him a dramatist, either, but we can agree that for two decades this man was
without question the most successful *playmaker* in the American theatre.

Born in 1865, dead by 1909, Fitch was one of the most prolific writers on
the modern American stage. Within twenty years he composed sixty-two plays
in all, of which thirty-six were original. This average of nearly three a year
meant that two, three, or four of his plays were running in New York at one
time. Such haste could not possibly bring the dignity of permanent literary
value, but the fact that he is not a subject of revival today does not mean that
his influence was unfelt. In subject matter and in character he opened many
doors which permitted his followers to venture into fields unthinkable a few
years earlier. Had he lived, perhaps he would have achieved the eminence
toward which he seemed so surely headed. Instead, he remains important, but
only as a figure of transition.

In 1901 Fitch broke away from his early hack writing of foreign adaptations
when he proved in *The Climbers* that the public was willing to see a play
based on American social behavior. It had been repeatedly rejected by all the
best New York producers because the sudden switch from the funeral of Act I
into comedy and social commentary was held untenable. When the play
eventually appeared, audiences overflowed in three-deep standing room as they
sought to catch a glimpse of themselves portrayed in this ironic, satiric attack
upon their own ridiculous and shallow behavior. Through his awareness of the
sounds and patterns of actual speech and his comprehension of the personalities
of the characters he created, Fitch peopled his stage with credible individuals
in the midst of a recognizable American scene, speaking the language of everyday life convincingly and accurately. The success of *The Climbers* broke

down the reluctance of producers to recognize the value of American dramatic themes, and thereafter Fitch became the acknowledged interpreter of the local New York scene so familiar to him.

Although Fitch's characters were strongly conceived, he assigned traits to his central figures which too often made them simply stage "types." In *The Girl with the Green Eyes*, 1902, his heroine is possessed of an inborn and unconquerable jealousy; in *The Truth*, 1907, she has inherited a streak of habitual petty lying. In plays purportedly "realistic," Fitch's use of "inherited" faults made some rather precarious genetic assumptions. Furthermore, he continually threw roadblocks directly into the paths of his "realistic" characters merely to create dramatic tensions. A husband, under a false sense of integrity, could sacrifice his wife's social position because "honor" forbade him to reveal a proved blackguard, or a reasonably honest young man could be quickly corrupted because life in "the city" does such things to people. Fitch continually turned his original themes into superficial hackneyed stories, manufactured for star actors. Happy endings, curtain reconciliations, sudden and unanticipated changes in the fortunes of his characters still revealed that realism was only skin-deep. Beneath was the soft body of romanticism.

None the less, in his brief and active life, Clyde Fitch was the first American writer to receive a genuine international reputation. His better plays were translated into many languages. *The Truth* was famous in England and on the Continent long before it succeeded at home. Fitch was a virtual commuter between Europe and the United States, continually planning more plays. Before his death from appendicitis while traveling in Europe, he had taken long strides toward creating a respectable literary American drama, although he never quite completed the journey. Perhaps he never would have.

William Vaughn Moody: Poet and Philosopher

The early death at forty-one of William Vaughn Moody in 1910 was a greater loss than Fitch's, for in Moody there was the promise of a philosophic and intellectual approach to dramatic literature that Fitch never achieved. Moody's training was academic, not theatrical; he was first an instructor at Harvard and later a professor of English at the University of Chicago. Even more unusual, his first ideal was to create a native *poetic* drama. Although his two produced plays were finally put into prose, he remains historically significant in his successful resistance to the artistic dictates of the Syndicate and in his defiance of the long traditions established by Daly and Belasco.

Moody's two plays achieve a literary quality surpassing anything that Fitch was able to attain because of their feeling for *idea* rather than for mere character trait or social phenomenon. Moody related these ideas to the characters themselves, avoiding stereotypes and caricatures and eliminating artificial obstructions devised only to heighten the stage effect. He was concerned about human society's difficulties and complexities, and he preferred to face them rather than to turn away without recognizing their often unpleasant impact upon the human being.

In *The Great Divide* of 1906, Moody wrote a timely play with an immediately apparent message, for it contrasted the mores of staid and Puritan New England with the freer and less rigid code of the West. Its greater importance lies in the timelessness of its distinct idea: the affirmation of the right of a person to establish and maintain his own individual character in the face of an opposing tradition. Moody's hero, the "wild" Westerner, shows his Eastern-bred wife that there may be substantial division geographically and morally between East and West, but that neither need attempt to tell the other how to behave, for neither is quite able to cope with the pattern of behavior typical of the other.

Moody proceeded further in his intellectual approach with the more dangerous theme of divine power in *The Faith Healer* of 1909. Aside from its element of hocus-pocus and romantic mystery, it does investigate the question of one's ability to believe deeply in his faith and to act upon that belief. It avoids becoming a religious tract, and, instead, becomes the portrayal of a search for what Moody called the "higher climax of character." Though a commercial failure, *The Faith Healer* was a significantly encouraging step. If Moody had survived, perhaps our native drama of ideas would have reached an earlier maturity.

Sheldon, MacKaye, and Mitchell: Art and Sophistication

The American theatre world held Edward Sheldon in the highest respect during his career of twenty-two years and sixteen plays, but today, except in histories of the drama and the memories of those who knew him, he is all but forgotten. A dramatist who "almost made it," Sheldon brought to the stage his gift of distinguishing reality from stage convention, and his ability to build good drama from what was basically an "untheatrical reality."

The distinction between his philosophy and Belasco's can be seen by contrasting Sheldon's first success, *Salvation Nell*, 1908, with almost any of Belasco's attempts at superrealism. For Sheldon, the purpose of a strikingly realistic setting was not to ask that the audience take note of the oaken planks on the bar, nor to recognize that the tables and chairs might once have rested in a legitimate saloon. His interest was in the believability of the characters whom he made to live within this atmosphere. Unlike Fitch's unpleasant men and women, who somehow always reached the final curtain morally much improved, Sheldon's characters could remain unsavory individuals even to the end, for they moved within an authentic background without the traps of conventional romanticism.

In two plays of significance, Sheldon could almost be considered a writer of "thesis" plays. In *The Nigger*, 1909, he handles race prejudice in the story of a Southern governor who is revealed as a mulatto. In *The Boss*, 1911, he advances the premise, hitherto dramatically impossible, that a thoroughly bad marriage could eventually be made into something essentially good, an accomplishment which Bronson Howard's "laws" would never have permitted.

In the 1920s Sheldon suffered a paralyzing illness which removed him from active life, although he lived as a friend and adviser to all theatre people until 1946. Once again, only speculation can assume what he might have been. His "Boss" remains too close to stereotype, and his Southern governor is destroyed through revelations of his past which smack too much of melodramatic sensation—faults which show that Sheldon had not attained the kind of permanence needed to give his plays the lasting attraction of good literature.

One writer who was confident that an artistic and literary theatre in America could exist on a grand scale and whose efforts sought to prove it was Percy MacKaye, the son of Steele MacKaye, author of a record-breaking nineteenth-century melodrama of tears, *Hazel Kirke*. The younger MacKaye was a professor of poetry and drama at Miami University, Oxford, Ohio. Like his father, he dreamed of a theatre for all people in terms of huge choruses, casts of hundreds, and the integration of every theatrical art including music, design, poetry, acting, and Belasco's switchboard. His early unsuccessful plays, such as *The Canterbury Pilgrims* of 1909 and *Jeanne d'Arc* of 1906 attempted to blend poetic dialogue and operalike massed crowds. His spectacles, like *St. Louis*, presented in that city's Forest Park in 1914, represented the broad community enterprise that he felt was so essential to the growth and prosperity of the American theatre. This kind of "civic theatre" although impractical was very close to his heart, and MacKaye was foremost in recognizing that the maintenance of an active living drama in America lay more with the average citizen in his own community than in the limited areas of New York.

Although in their individual ways both MacKaye and Belasco were failures as they attempted to reach "art," MacKaye turned the technical devices of Belasco into much more acceptable artistic material. The increasing popularity of the annual symphonic pageant-dramas such as Paul Green's *The Common Glory* and *The Lost Colony* is today's direct inheritance from the conceptions of both Steele and Percy MacKaye.

Considerably apart from our concern with poetry or scenic art stands Langdon Mitchell, whose *The New York Idea* of 1906 was the first real try at American comedy of manners. Nothing like it had ever been attempted before. The play unquestionably stands apart from others of its decade because of its daring and sophistication. It does not rely on the problems of other American "social" or "domestic" comedies in their praise of the "American way" against the decadence of European habits. Instead, Mitchell found his ancestor in the English drawing-room comedy, going straight back to Sheridan and Congreve. The action takes place in a world where intricate social ritual and sharp wit from a razor-edged tongue are automatically assumed. Its problems center upon the intricacies of marriage by whim and divorce at will, lightly tossing aside the provincial naïveté of mating for life and for love.

Langdon Mitchell was a one-shot writer, for he never again achieved anything like the widespread appeal of *The New York Idea*. A critic may easily overpraise this singular effort, or he may mistakenly underemphasize its current importance, but no one can gainsay that the impact of the play was sufficient to give it a permanent place in the historical study of American drama.

OTHER IMPORTANT THEATRE PERSONNEL BEFORE 1918

BARRYMORE, ETHEL. One of Charles Frohman's loveliest stars. Debut in 1901 in Fitch's *Captain Jinks of the Horse Marines*. Maintained great stature as stage and screen performer into the 1950s.

BARRYMORE, JOHN. "The Great Profile." Youngest of the Barrymores, he was most famous during the 1920s for his Hamlet and other serious roles.

BARRYMORE, LIONEL. Powerful dramatic actor of early 1900s. Became world famous on screen in 1930s and 1940s.

BATES, BLANCHE. One of Belasco's most famous stars after 1897, particularly in *The Girl of the Golden West*, 1905.

DUSE, ELEONORA. Italian-born, played Juliet at Verona at the age of fourteen. American debut, 1893, as Camille. Famous in Ibsen roles. Second in fame to Bernhardt.

GOODWIN, NAT. Famous for his burlesques and light comedy.

MARLOWE, JULIA. English-born. First success as Barbara Frietchie, 1899. E. H. Sothern's leading lady.

MILLER, HENRY. Arrived from England at Booth's, 1880. Popular star and manager at his own theatre in New York, 1918. Son Gilbert a leading producer in later years.

SKINNER, OTIS. Apprenticed with Booth, Modjeska, and others. Star in his own right, 1906. Popular in swaggering male roles. Father of comedienne, Cornelia Otis Skinner.

SOTHERN, E. H. Son of E. A. Sothern. Acted with his father at Park, 1879. Became famous much later for his Shakespearean roles with Julia Marlowe, and his François Villon in *If I Were King*, 1901.

THE TURNING POINT

The Free Theatres of Europe

In 1914 a book called "The New Movement in the Theatre" by Sheldon Cheney listed the shortcomings of native American dramatic writing. Striving toward the theatrical instead of the dramatic, American plays achieved strength at the expense of subtlety and depth. In trying to bring the public what it wanted, the native writer depended too much on comic relief and melodrama. Not many years after 1914 the changes which Cheney desired began to take place, and the American drama was able to throw off the shackles of Daly and Belasco commercialism.

In order fully to understand the significance of Cheney's "new movement," we must go back to the close of the century to survey the steps taken in France, Germany, and other countries to overcome a considerable amount of the same artistic deficiency too long apparent in American drama. The French stage of the nineteenth century was gripped by the tradition of the well-made play; England at the same time was doing little better with a surfeit of garish melodramas and sobbing sentimentalities of routine scripts. The theatre was actually stagnating, and there seemed little opportunity to bring it out of this condition because the entire commercial structure would be in imminent danger of collapse should it be weakened in any way by the introduction of untried procedures.

The first major break from this inanition occurred in France. André Antoine presented on March 30, 1887, a bill of one-act plays before a tiny audience on a minuscule stage in Montmartre. Antoine's style of production was revolutionary. Gone were the stereotypes of conventional characters and situations, along with all attendant unnatural stage behavior. Antoine attempted to show that thoughtful and artistic interpretation could be applied without the distracting conventions of the commercial theatre and that unpleasant subject matter need not be watered down or consciously avoided for fear of driving away a morally offended audience. By 1894 his *Théâtre Libre* had firmly established him as a successful and fearless leader, who refused to watch the theatre starve through the stubborn refusal or ignorant inability of regular producers to recognize the existence of a genuine and enthusiastic audience response for what he knew to be excellent theatre.

Other countries followed. The *Freie Bühne* of Berlin, established in 1889, devoted its efforts to much the same kind of production with even more direct influence on the German theatre as a whole than Antoine had exerted in

France. Max Reinhardt, one of the most famous producers of the twentieth century, opened the *Kleines Theater* in Berlin in 1902. In Sweden, August Strindberg founded a little theatre in Stockholm in 1907, where many of his own unconventionally expressionistic and naturalistic works were produced. In 1898 Constantin Stanislavsky had formed the Moscow Art Theatre. In 1899 William Butler Yeats and Lady Gregory had been strong forces in starting what became, by 1904, the internationally famed Abbey Theatre of Dublin.

The effect of all these theatres varied from country to country. Their main accomplishment was to offer a stage for the public appearance of many new writers whose plays could find an audience in none of the usual channels. Brieux in France, Shaw in England, Hauptmann in Germany, Strindberg, Chekhov, Ibsen, and others, regularly fed their output into these small houses, which eventually became a permanent influence in the betterment of dramatic creations everywhere at the close of the nineteenth century. To Cheney the free-theatre movement was effective because the theatre was now open to new types of drama which encouraged a natural style of acting and permitted a much more simplified stage setting than the "crassly artificial" or "consciously spectacular" backgrounds of the past.

The American Art Theatre

The development of American art theatres was late, but it came at an appropriate time. By the beginning of the First World War the center of the English-speaking *theatrical* world was shifting to New York, but not until just after the war was it apparent that the *dramatic* center was shifting as well. During the four years of the conflict the art theatres encouraged the production of native plays unsuited for the big professional stages, so that by the end of the struggle those trained in the art-theatre tradition could enter directly into competition which would force the unreceptive Broadway producers increasingly to give ground.

Two New York groups may claim nearly all our appreciation. The first was the Washington Square Players, organized in 1914. The life of this organization lasted only four years, but it drew considerable attention from New York critics and public for its avowed policy of presenting only plays of artistic merit. For 50 cents one could see Shaw, Andreyev, Ibsen, Maeterlinck, and Chekhov—all writers who had found rough going on the commercial stage.

Of more lasting importance, because of their interest in native talent as opposed to the off-beat plays from abroad, were the Provincetown Players. They were not a professional stage organization in the same sense as the Washington Square Players, for among the members were poets, novelists, and other artists of assorted talents. They were a radical set, artistically and politically, but their aims were high. Moreover, they provided for young writers a hearing nowhere else available. In 1915 the Provincetown Players presented their first plays on the front porch of a Cape Cod summer home, after which

The Guild Theatre, New York, 1925. All the distracting frills of the nineteenth century are gone, even the boxes. The seats are comfortable, sight lines clear, the auditorium uncluttered in its architectural simplicity. The 1920s saw the last great era of theatre construction; no legitimate house has been erected in New York in nearly thirty years. (*Courtesy Theatre Collection, New York Public Library.*) *Reproduced by permission from Coward-McCann, Inc., New York.*

one of their members offered an old fishing shack at the end of a pier, wherein could be set up an improvised stage and seating for about sixty people. For the first production of 1916 the Players chose a new one-acter called *Bound East for Cardiff*, by a young man nobody had ever heard of, a terribly shy, unimpressive, heavy-drinking vagabond, who had shown up with a collection of unproduced manuscripts. The success of young Eugene O'Neill's first staged play was instantaneous.

The Provincetown Players then moved into New York for a winter season and converted an unused stable into a tiny theatre. From 1916 until 1922 the original group remained intact; reorganization came in 1922, and until 1929 the Playwrights' Theatre, as it was officially named, was a respected and profoundly influential producing company. More than any other force in the early twentieth-century American theatre, the Provincetown Players demonstrated the commercial possibility of true art in the professional theatre.

One further area must be considered before we go on. This is the realm of the college and university theatre. We must step back to 1905 at Harvard University, where the most serious academic effort to bring some sort of artistic guidance to the theatre was started. In that year Prof. George Pierce Baker began his noncredit course called English 47, dramatic composition, which was a euphemism for playwriting. Interested students were free to enroll and to receive instruction in methods of dramatic technique. Professor Baker eventually was permitted to give academic credit for his popular "47 Workshop," but the administrative line was firmly drawn there, and Baker was refused all requests for facilities in which to stage his students' works. With or without official approval the class became very famous, and from Baker's guidance emerged critics, designers, and writers, including Eugene O'Neill, who became important forces in the contemporary American theatre. Baker moved to Yale in 1925 to head a new department of drama in a completely equipped, fully professional theatre. For another decade he built this graduate professional school into one of the leading academic institutions of its type. Others have since followed Baker's lead, and today the course work and full-scale productions of university schools of theatre and drama throughout the country are direct and important contributors to the vitality of continuing American dramatic art.

With the founding of the Theatre Guild in 1919, organized by many of the former members of the Washington Square Players, America received its first permanent art theatre devoted to the presentation of the best domestic and foreign drama. When the Guild became the producing agent for Eugene O'Neill in the late 1920s, America's first successful commercial art theatre and its most distinguished practicing playwright joined forces to show that no longer was there any need to apologize for or to belittle American accomplishments in dramatic literature. It was now possible to recognize native dramatic art, to produce it, and to praise it, with success throughout the world for the most noteworthy creations. The American poet, novelist, and essayist had a new companion—the American literary dramatist.

A CHRONOLOGY OF SIGNIFICANT EVENTS IN THE AMERICAN THEATRE 1598 TO 1918

The Facts before 1750

1598, Apr. 30   A *comedia* by a Spanish captain presented on the Rio Grande near today's El Paso.

1606, Nov. 14   A French masque given at Port Royal, Acadia.

1607   Jamestown, Va., settled.

1620   Plymouth, Mass., settled.

1640–1652   At least two tragedies by Corneille produced in Quebec.

1664   English take over New York from the Dutch.

1665, Aug. 27   *Ye Bare and Ye Cubb*, by William Darby, Accomac County, Va. First recorded play in English in American colonies.

1670   Charleston, S.C., founded.

1682   Philadelphia founded.

1690   Unreliable evidence suggests *Gustavus Vasa*, by Benjamin Colman, given by Harvard students.

1699–1702   Appearance of Richard Hunter, first man to secure license to present plays in New York. Nothing more is known.

1700   Assembly of Pennsylvania prohibits "stage-plays, masks, revels" and other "rude and riotous sports."

1702   A "pastoral colloquy" given by students of William and Mary College for Governor of Virginia.

1703, January   Anthony Aston appears in Charleston. Writes that he "turned *Player* and *Poet* and wrote one Play on the Subject of the Country." Play is unknown. By his own record, Aston turned up as actor in New York, probably in the following winter.

1709, May 6   Governor's Council in New York forbids play acting.

1714   Judge Samuel Sewall in Boston opposes plan to present a play in the Council Chamber. Play unknown.

————   *Androborus*, satire by "Governor Hunter" (probably Robert Hunter) of New York. First known publication of a play in America. No recorded performance.

1716, July 11   First recorded contract to build a theatre in the colonies at Williamsburg, Va.

1723   Philadelphia records its first acting company when "a Player who has Strowled hither to act as a Comedian" appears "just without the verge of the city."

1724   Appearance of acrobats and comedians at "New Booth" on Society Hill, Philadelphia's first recorded theatre.

1732, Dec. 6   Performance of *The Recruiting Officer* at "New Theatre" in New York. Location unknown.

1735, Jan. 18   First recorded production in Charleston: Otway's *The Orphan*, in a courtroom.

1736, Feb. 12   Opening of Dock Street Theatre, Charleston.

————, Sept. 10   Students of William and Mary present *Cato*, and a series of Restoration comedies on following days.

1749, August   Actors under Walter Murray and Thomas Kean present *Cato* in Plumsted's Warehouse, Philadelphia. This is Philadelphia's first recorded professional performance, and this is the first professional company of which there is any detailed record. Their origin remains unknown.

1750 *until the Revolution*

1750   The year which marks beginning of detailed records of the theatre in America.

1750   Performance of *The Orphan* in Boston Coffee House by two unidentified Englishmen.

————, February   Arrival of Murray and Kean in New York.

————, March   General Court of Massachusetts passes "An Act to Prevent Stage-Plays and other Theatrical Entertainments."

————, Mar. 5   Murray and Kean open with *Richard III* in Nassau Street playhouse (a room in a large building) in New York.

1751   Appearance of David Douglass in West Indies.

————, October   Opening of Murray and Kean playhouse in Williamsburg. Beginning of their "Virginia Company of Comedians" which flourished in South for twenty years.

1752, Sept. 15   First appearance in America of Lewis Hallam company of twelve adults and three children in *The Merchant of Venice* at Murray and Kean's Williamsburg playhouse.

1753, July 2   Hallam stranded in New York, publishes plea for help in first record of a road company in distress.

————, Sept. 17   Hallam opens in New York in rebuilt Nassau Street playhouse.

1754, Apr. 15   Hallam opens at "New Theatre" (Plumsted's warehouse) in Philadelphia.

1755   Lewis Hallam dies in Jamaica, his company subsequently disbanding.

1758–1759   Hallam's company reorganized under David Douglass. Mrs. Hallam, now Mrs. Douglass, remains leading lady; Lewis Hallam, Jr., eighteen, is leading man. Subsequently company opens at Cruger's Wharf, New York.

1759, Apr. 5   Douglass opens at Society Hill, Philadelphia, and continues for extensive season until December.

1760, Mar. 3   Douglass opens his new theatre in Annapolis.

1761, Summer   Douglass invades New England with "Moral Lectures" in Newport, Rhode Island.

————, Nov. 18   Opening of Douglass' Beekman Street Theatre, New York.

1762, August   Rhode Island Assembly passes restrictive legislation to prevent stage plays.

1766   Formal organization of American Company under Douglass and Lewis Hallam, Jr.

————   *Ponteach*, by Maj. Robert Rogers, first publication of a play by an American resident on an American subject.

————, November 12   Opening of Douglass' Southwark Theatre, Philadelphia, the first permanent playhouse in America. It stood until 1912.

1767, Apr. 24 *The Prince of Parthia,* by Thomas Godfrey. The first professional production of a play written by an American.

————, Dec. 7 Opening of Douglass' John Street Theatre, the first permanent theatre in New York.

1773 *The Adulateur,* the first of Mrs. Mercy Otis Warren's satiric attacks on New England Tories. As far as is known, none of her works were ever produced.

1774, Oct. 20 Resolution by the Continental Congress discouraging all extravagance and dissipation, including "exhibition of shews."

1774–1776 Period of Rebel and Tory satires and patriotic verse dramas. Important titles: *The Group,* 1775, by Mrs. Warren; *The Battle of Bunkers-Hill,* by Hugh Henry Brackenridge, and *The Blockade,* performed by General Burgoyne's soldiers, both 1776. Also, same year, *The Blockheads,* often attributed to Mrs. Warren, and John Leacock's *The Fall of British Tyranny.*

1775, Feb. 2 Douglass and Hallam depart for Jamaica to await end of the conflict.

1777–1782 Operation of John Street Theatre as Theatre Royal by occupying British troops.

1778, Oct. 6 Second and more drastic resolution by Congress against "plays and other expensive Diversions and Entertainment."

1779, Mar. 30 Legislature prohibits all theatrical entertainment in Pennsylvania.

From the Revolution to the Civil War

1784 Lewis Hallam, Jr., returns to mainland from Jamaica. Opens a brief, if technically illegal, season in Philadelphia at Southwark.

1785 Hallam joined by John Henry to form Old American Company.

1787, Apr. 16 *The Contrast,* by Royall Tyler. First professional production of a native American play on a native American subject in New York at John Street.

1789, Mar. 2 Repeal of Pennsylvania law against theatre.

————, Sept. 7 William Dunlap's first play to be produced: *The Father: or American Shandyism,* at John Street.

1792 "New Exhibition Room" opens in Boston. Closed same year by the sheriff.

1793 Repeal of restrictive legislation in Massachusetts and Rhode Island. Opening of theatre in Newport.

1794, Feb. 3 Opening of Federal Street (Boston) Theatre in Boston.

————, Feb. 17 Opening of Wignell and Reinagle's Chestnut Street Theatre in Philadelphia, the first elaborate and well-planned American theatre.

1796, Spring Dunlap buys into the Old American Company and becomes manager.

1798, Jan. 29 Opening of the Park Theatre in New York under Dunlap's management.

————, Feb. 2 Burning of the Federal Street Theatre in Boston, the first playhouse destroyed by fire in America.

————, Dec. 10 First production of Dunlap's adaptation of Kotzebue: *The Stranger.*

1800 Wignell and Reinagle open National Theatre in a hotel in Washington, the first theatre in the new Capital.

1805 Departure of Dunlap in bankruptcy from the Park.

1810–1812 Tour of George Frederick Cooke, first great internationally famous actor on American stage.

1811, Dec. 26   Richmond, Virginia, theatre burns with loss of seventy-one lives. First fatal fire in American theatre.

1812   Opening of Walnut Street Theatre, Philadelphia. First competition for the Chestnut.

1815, December   First successful professional theatre group in the West at Frankfort, Kentucky, under Samuel Drake.

1816, Nov. 25   Introduction of gas lighting into Chestnut Theatre.

1818   Appearance of first English-speaking company in New Orleans under Noah Ludlow.

1820, Apr. 2   Chestnut Street Theatre burns in Philadelphia.

————, May 24   Park Theatre burns in New York.

————, Nov. 27   Debut of Edwin Forrest, age 16.

1821, September   Opening of the rebuilt Park Theatre.

————   Debut of Junius Brutus Booth in Richmond.

1822   Opening of rebuilt Chestnut Theatre.

1824, Jan. 1   Opening of James Caldwell's Camp Theatre in New Orleans.

1826, Oct. 23   Opening of the 3,000-seat Bowery Theatre, New York. First real competition for the Park.

1827   Tremont Street Theatre opens in competition with Boston Theatre.

————   Caldwell opens a theatre in St. Louis.

1833   Caldwell's magnificent St. Charles Theatre opens in New Orleans.

1841, Oct.   *London Assurance*, by Dion Boucicault at Park. The first appearance of the box set, destined to replace the wing and backdrop.

1843, Feb. 6   First New York performance of the Virginia Minstrels.

1845, Mar. 24   *Fashion*, by Anna Cora Mowatt. The first genuine American comedy of manners.

1847   J. B. Rice constructs first theatre in Chicago.

1849, May 10   Astor Place Riot, New York. Thirty-one dead, hundreds injured.

————, Sept. 10   Debut of Edwin Booth in Boston.

————, Oct. 18   First professional production of a play in California, *The Bandit Chief* at Eagle Theatre, Sacramento.

1852, Mar. 20   Publication of "Uncle Tom's Cabin" in book form.

1853, July 18   Opening of *Uncle Tom's Cabin* at Purdy's, New York. Became the most popular play in the history of the theatre.

1854   Opening of the new Boston Theatre.

1855   First appearance of Dion Boucicault in this country in his own *Grimaldi* in Cincinnati.

1856, Aug. 18   First American copyright law to give author sole right to print, publish, act, perform, and present his own plays.

1861   Brigham Young erects Salt Lake Theatre.

1864, Nov. 25   For the only time in their lives, Junius Brutus, Jr., Edwin, and John Wilkes Booth appear in the same play, *Julius Caesar*.

————, Nov. 26   Opening of Edwin Booth's 100-night *Hamlet*.

From the Civil War to 1918

1865, Apr. 14   John Wilkes Booth assassinates President Lincoln, Ford's Theatre, Washington. Edwin Booth goes into "permanent" retirement.

1866, Jan. 3   Edwin Booth returns triumphantly with *Hamlet*.

1869   Daly takes over management of Fifth Avenue Theatre.

————, Feb. 3   Opening of the million-dollar Booth Theatre, New York.

1870, Dec. 21   Production of *Saratoga*, by Bronson Howard, first professional American playwright to earn his living entirely by writing plays.

1878   Gilbert and Sullivan first appear in New York with production of *H. M. S. Pinafore*.

1880, Feb. 12   Opening of Steele MacKaye's Madison Square Theatre. Featured two stages raised or lowered into place by an elevator mechanism.

————, Nov. 7   Debut of Sarah Bernhardt at the Booth in *Adrienne Lecouvreur*.

1882   Appearance of David Belasco as manager of Madison Square.

1883   First Ibsen produced in New York, Helena Modjeska's happy-ending *A Doll's House* entitled *Thora*. A failure. Sir Henry Irving first appears in New York.

1889, Sept. 9   Charles Frohman's first great success as New York manager with Howard's *Shenandoah*. One of the first plays in which author received royalties for every performance, $100,000 the first year.

1890   America's first "problem play" in Ibsen tradition, *Margaret Fleming*, by James A. Herne.

1891   First international copyright takes effect.

1893   Failure of Steele MacKaye's gigantic pageant-opera house, the Spectatorium, in Chicago.

————, Jan. 23   Eleonora Duse appears in New York as Camille.

————, Jan. 25   Opening of Charles Frohman's Empire Theatre.

1896   Klaw and Erlanger Syndicate organized.

1897   First New York production of Shaw: *Arms and the Man*.

1899, Nov. 29   Opening of *Ben-Hur*, the first supercolossal production, complete with live horses on treadmills.

1903, Dec. 30   Iroquois Theatre fire in Chicago. In eight minutes of panic, over 500 people died in rush to the few accessible exits. Fire did comparatively little damage.

1905   George Pierce Baker begins his English 47 at Harvard. Shubert Brothers begin to challenge Klaw and Erlanger.

————, Oct. 10   Shaw's *Mrs. Warren's Profession* a sensation in New York. Producer Daly and star arrested and acquitted.

1909, Nov. 6   Opening of the New Theatre, Central Park West, as an art theatre devoted to permanent repertory.

1912   Organization of the Dramatists Guild to help give legal protection to playwrights.

1915   First productions by Washington Square Players and Provincetown Players.

1916   Provincetown Players produce the first play by Eugene O'Neill, *Bound East for Cardiff*.

1918, December   Formation of the Theatre Guild.

SUGGESTED TOPICS FOR FURTHER INVESTIGATION
AND REPORT

These suggestions do not attempt to cover all the important points of theatrical history or dramatic literature. They can, however, be of help in stimulating an interest that may lead to more comprehensive study. Use the bibliographies on pages 68 to 73, together with the materials found in the anthologies which reprint many of the plays, for assistance in further investigation.

A list of topics similar to this one will also be found after each play in Part 2.

1. Using Odell's "Annals" alone or with other detailed histories such as Ireland, Seilhamer, or Hornblow, trace the struggles with official censorship and public opposition to the theatre in America up to 1789.

2. Read Tyler's *The Contrast* and Mowatt's *Fashion*. Discuss their imitative styles, and determine their originality in comparison with their earlier model, Sheridan's *The School for Scandal*.

3. A study of the development of theatre buildings makes an interesting investigation. Dunlap's "History," Odell's "Annals," Seilhamer, and Brown are all helpful. Report on one of the following periods: (*a*) From earliest times up to the opening of the Park under Dunlap in 1798; (*b*) From 1798 until the Civil War; (*c*) New York theatres from the Civil War until the opening of the Century Theatre in 1909. Take note of structural and mechanical improvements, conventions of architecture and *décor*, and take account of those historically significant.

4. Read Godfrey's *The Prince of Parthia* and an eighteenth-century tragedy, such as Addison's *Cato* or John Home's *Douglas*, two of the most popular English plays of the age. Compare and contrast their styles, and evaluate any contribution you think Godfrey made in his own effort.

5. Read some of the Revolutionary and pre-Revolutionary patriotic dramas and satires from both sides, especially Mrs. Warren's. Most of these are available on Readex Microprint. Also, read some of the patriotic poems such as Freneau's and Brackenridge's *The Rising Glory of America*. Discuss their effectiveness as propaganda.

6. Using the general histories, or any of the special books by those who participated, investigate the theatre of the frontier in a geographical area which interests you.

7. Read Graham's book, "Showboat," the history of the river showboats, and Edna Ferber's novel, "Showboat," which was made into one of the most popular musical comedies in history. Compare and contrast the historical and imaginative aspects of river theatricals.

8. Try to secure a Gothic horror play such as Dunlap's *Fontainville Abbey* or *Ribbemont*, both available in microprint. At any rate, read some later melodramas like Daly's *Under the Gaslight*, Boucicault's *The Octoroon*, or Bartley Campbell's *The White Slave*. Also, try to include at least one melodrama of tears, such as Mrs. Wood's *East Lynne*, or Lottie Parker's *Way Down East*. Compare and contrast the styles of these sensational plays.

9. Read two or three Indian plays, such as Rogers' *Ponteach*, Barker's *The Indian Princess*, Custis' *Pocahontas*, and Stone's *Metamora*. Consider these in the light of Cooper's Indians as seen in "The Deerslayer" or "The Last of the Mohicans." Discuss the plays as they represent the romantic concept of the noble savage.

10. See if you can secure some of the older Western plays, like James Kirk Paulding's *The Lion of the West*, Louisa Medina's version of Bird's *Nick of the Woods*, Daly's *Horizon*, Murdoch's *Davy Crockett*, Belasco's *The Girl of the Golden West*, or any of Augustus Thomas' Western dramas. Discuss their picture of the frontiersman.

11. Read *Uncle Tom's Cabin, The Octoroon*, Edward Sheldon's *The Nigger*, and Eugene O'Neill's *The Emperor Jones*. Discuss any aspect you wish about the use of the Negro and of racial prejudice as a subject for dramatic treatment.

12. Read Bird's *The Gladiator*, or *The Broker of Bogota*, Boker's *Francesca da Rimini*, Willis' *Tortesa the Usurer*, or any of the many exotically romantic plays of the early nineteenth century. What influences of American thought and culture do you find inserted into these plays?

13. Study Felheim's "The Theatre of Augustin Daly" and read two or three of Daly's plays. Report on his importance to our national drama and theatre.

14. Read Howard's *The Henrietta, Saratoga, Shenandoah*, and *The Banker's Daughter*. Estimate how well Howard sticks to his own "immutable laws" of dramaturgy. (Quinn's history reprints much of Howard's opinion.)

15. Read several of Howell's plays and determine why they were not extensive commercial successes.

16. After reading *Secret Service* or *Sherlock Holmes* or both, compare Gillette's melodramatic style with Daly's, Boucicault's, or any other writer's.

17. Read several of Belasco's plays. Discuss their shortcomings as good drama, as well as some of their important contributions.

18. Read several of Fitch's plays. Trace his development as a playwright from his early attempts through *The Truth, The City*, etc.

19. In histories, magazine and newspaper references, and his own books, study Percy MacKaye's ideas for civic and community theatres. Read what you can about his productions of outdoor pageants at St. Louis and elsewhere. Discuss the feasibility of his ideas, and contrast his pageant-dramas with the present-day symphonic dramas of Paul Green and others.

20. Investigate further the free theatres of Europe. Report on their development and their influences between 1890 and 1914.

21. Study the development of the art theatres in America. Report on the contributions of the Washington Square Players and the importance of the Provincetown Players.

A SELECT LIST OF AMERICAN DRAMA FROM COLONIAL TIMES TO 1918

This list will provide the student with a readily available tabulation of significant plays and playwrights before 1918. It includes only the most important plays of each author.

No attempt is made in this book to include a list of play anthologies for the simple reason that it is impossible to keep up with their publication. Many of the plays can be found in a variety of standard collections; the wise student will check his library card catalogue. Nearly all of the many editions of Quinn's anthology, "Representative American Plays," or those of Moses' "Representative American Dramas," can be found anywhere. There are two major sources of otherwise unavailable eighteenth- and nineteenth-century American plays. The first is the twenty-volume edition of "America's Lost Plays," edited by Barrett H. Clark and published in 1941 by the Princeton University Press. The few plays in the following list which are available in this collection are noted (ALP). The second source is "Three Centuries of Drama," a file of Readex Microprint cards, edited by Henry W.

Wells, published in New York in 1952. This extensive set includes a microprint reproduction of each play published in England up to 1800 and in America up to 1830. Plays available in the two American volumes of this collection are marked with an asterisk*. For a complete list of plays by author, and the facts of their publication, see the most recent printing of Quinn's dramatic histories.

Dates indicate composition or, if known, first production; otherwise, first publication. Plays and playwrights discussed in the text of Part 1 are listed without comment. Others are frequently annotated.

Anonymous.
> *The Battle of Brooklyn, 1776.
>
> *The Blockheads: or The Affrighted Officers, 1776. Often attributed to Mercy Otis Warren. These two pieces were part of the outpouring of patriotic satire and drama during the Revolution.
>
> *The Military Glory of Great Britain, 1762. A college exercise, more of a dramatic dialogue than a play, performed at Princeton commencement.

Barker, James Nelson. First important writer of plays on native American themes, but in the romantic tradition.
> *The Indian Princess: or La Belle Sauvage, 1808.
>
> *Marmion: or The Battle of Flodden Field, 1812.
>
> *Superstition, 1824. One of the earliest plays about New England witchcraft trials.

Belasco, David.
> The Darling of the Gods (with John Luther Long), 1902.
>
> The Girl of the Golden West, 1905. A favorite "Western" play in the Belasco tradition. Made into an opera by Puccini, and starred Enrico Caruso.
>
> The Heart of Maryland, 1895 (ALP). A complicated and sensational Civil War melodrama featuring the heroine swinging on a bell clapper. Much inferior to the war plays of Howard and Gillette.
>
> Hearts of Oak (with James A. Herne), 1879.
>
> Madame Butterfly (with John Luther Long), 1900.
>
> The Return of Peter Grimm, 1911. Delves into the supernatural; one of Belasco's most famous.

Bird, Robert Montgomery.
> The Broker of Bogota, 1834.
>
> The Gladiator, 1831. A Forrest prize play, and one of the actor's favorite roles.
>
> Oralloossa, Son of the Incas, 1832.

Boker, George Henry.
> Francesca da Rimini, 1855.

Boucicault, Dion.
> Arrah-na-Pogue, 1864. The best of his Irish plays.
>
> The Colleen Bawn: or The Brides of Garryowen, 1860. The first play to present a sympathetic stage picture of the Irishman, heretofore ridiculed and satirized.
>
> London Assurance, 1841.
>
> The Octoroon, 1859.
>
> The Poor of New York, 1857. One of the most famous melodramas involving the theme of rich against the poor, complete with burning buildings, etc.
>
> The Shaughraun, 1874. Considered by many to be his best. Contains his own most popular starring role.

Brackenridge, Hugh Henry.
The Battle of Bunkers-Hill, 1776. One of the Revolutionary dramas of patriotism.
Cohan, George M.
A listing of Cohan's musicals would not be worthwhile since most of them are unavailable. The few noted here are among his best-remembered straight plays.
Broadway Jones, 1912. Made into musical, *Billie*, in 1928.
Get Rich Quick Wallingford, 1910. Based on story by George R. Chester.
The Governor's Son, 1901. His first play after leaving the family vaudeville group, "The Four Cohans."
Seven Keys to Baldpate, 1913. Popular mystery melodrama of its time, adapted from Earl Derr Biggers.
The Tavern, 1920.
Conrad, Robert T.
Jack Cade, 1835. Another of Forrest's most popular roles.
Crothers, Rachel. Highly successful woman playwright of first decades of twentieth century. Her comedies of sex and sophistication were long popular. The following are her plays before 1920:
He and She, 1911. A rival to Mitchell's *The New York Idea* as an early high comedy.
A Man's World, 1909. Her first important play, concerning the double standard of love.
Custis, George Washington Parke. A writer of successful Indian plays in the tradition of the "noble savage."
The Indian Prophecy, 1827.
Pocahontas: or The Settlers of Virginia, 1830. Outstanding Indian play, portraying Pocahontas as a mature woman.
Daly, Augustin.
Horizon, 1871.
Under the Gaslight, 1867.
Dunlap, William.
André, 1798. One of the best Arnold-André plays of the Revolutionary period.
The Father: or American Shandyism, 1789. (Later, 1806, *The Father of an Only Child*.)
Fontainville Abbey, 1795. First of his Gothic horror tales, this adapted from Mrs. Radcliffe's novel.
Ribbemont: or The Feudal Baron, 1796.
The Stranger, 1798.
Fitch, Clyde.
Barbara Frietchie, 1899. Loose adaptation of Whittier's poem. Makes ninety-year-old Barbara a young teen-age maiden.
Beau Brummel, 1890. His first play and first success.
Captain Jinks of the Horse Marines, 1901. The play in which Ethel Barrymore made her successful debut.
The City, 1909. Posthumously produced. Fitch considered it his best play.
The Climbers, 1901.
The Girl with the Green Eyes, 1902.
The Truth, 1907

Freneau, Philip.
  *The Rising Glory of America, 1772. One of first patriotic verse pieces. Written
    with Hugh Henry Brackenridge.
Gillette, William.
  Held by the Enemy, 1886.
  Secret Service, 1895.
  Sherlock Holmes, 1899. Gillette created the leading roles of Captain Thorne in
    Secret Service, and Holmes, his most famous part. He was so closely identified
    with these roles that almost nobody else could play them with success.
Godfrey, Thomas.
  *The Prince of Parthia, written 1759, produced 1767, four years after Godfrey's
    death.
Herne, James A.
  Hearts of Oak, 1879 (with David Belasco). His first important play.
  Margaret Fleming, 1890. The first serious handling of the problem of adultery in
    the Ibsen technique.
  The Reverend Griffith Davenport, 1899. (ALP)
  Sag Harbor, 1899.
  Shore Acres, 1892.
Howard, Bronson.
  The Banker's Daughter, 1878. (ALP)
  The Henrietta, 1887. An early satire on big business.
  Saratoga: or Pistols for Seven, 1870.
  Shenandoah, 1888.
Howells, William Dean. None of Howells' longer plays were ever especially suc-
    cessful in the commercial theatre, but his influence on developing realistic
    techniques was large. This list is merely a sampling of his best-known plays.
  The American Claimant (with Mark Twain), 1887.
  A Counterfeit Presentment, 1877.
  The Mouse Trap, 1889 (one act).
  The Parlor Car, 1876 (one act).
  The Sleeping Car, 1883 (one act).
Hunter, Robert.
  *Androboros, 1714. First play known to be published in America.
Hoyt, Charles H. A writer of light comedy and farce, very popular in late nine-
    teenth century.
  A Texas Steer, 1890. A broad farce about a Texan in Washington.
  A Trip to Chinatown, 1891. (ALP). Famous for introducing the song "Reuben
    and Rachel."
Jefferson, Joseph, III.
  Rip Van Winkle, 1865, 1895. Technically, Jefferson was not the author. The play
    had several versions, but Boucicault's 1865 was a favorite. Finally Jefferson re-
    vised it himself in 1895, and the text is now known "as played by Joseph
    Jefferson."
Leacock, John.
  *The Fall of British Tyranny, 1776. A famous Revolutionary patriotic drama.
MacKaye, Percy.
  The Canterbury Pilgrims, 1909.

Jeanne d'Arc, 1906.

The Scarecrow, 1908. Not produced until 1910. His most famous play, a fantasy based on Hawthorne's "Feathertop."

MacKaye, Steele.

Hazel Kirke, 1880.

Mitchell, Langdon.

The New York Idea, 1906.

Moody, William Vaughn.

The Faith Healer, 1909.

The Great Divide, 1909. (Originally *The Sabine Woman*, 1906.)

Mowatt, Anna Cora.

Fashion, 1845.

Murdoch, Frank H.

Davy Crockett, 1872. (ALP) As played by Frank Mayo, widely popular frontier play.

Paulding, James Kirk.

The Lion of the West, 1831. Introduced one of the early Western heroes, Nimrod Wildfire.

Payne, John Howard.

Adeline: The Victim of Seduction, 1822.

Brutus: or The Fall of Tarquin, 1818. Readex Microprints also contains a unique prompt copy of this play.

Charles the Second: or The Merry Monarch (with Washington Irving), 1824.

Clari: or the Maid of Milan, 1823.

Julia: or The Wanderer, 1806.

Thérèse: The Orphan of Geneva, 1821.

Peabody, Josephine Preston.

The Piper, 1910. One of the few poetic dramas successful in the twentieth century. It won first prize in contest for best play to open the new Stratford-on-Avon playhouse.

Rogers, Robert.

Ponteach, 1766. The first play published in America by a native writer on a native American subject.

Sheldon, Edward.

The Boss, 1911.

The Nigger, 1910.

Romance, 1913.

Salvation Nell, 1908. One of Mrs. Fiske's great successes, noted for its realistic settings.

Stone, John Augustus.

Metamora: or The Last of the Wampanoags, 1829. (ALP). A great Forrest role. The existing version is incomplete.

Thomas, Augustus. Well known for his plays of Western local color and for his interest in the supernatural.

Alabama, 1891.

Arizona, 1899. Probably his most famous Western play.

As a Man Thinks, 1911. Further pursuit of mental processes.

The Copperhead, 1918.

In Mizzoura, 1893.

The Witching Hour, 1907. His first study of the powers of inherited tendencies and of mental telepathy.

Tyler, Royall.

*The Contrast, 1787.

Walter, Eugene.

The Easiest Way, 1908. The first American play consciously to turn away from the happy ending. Its second act setting by Belasco was very famous.

Warren, Mrs. Mercy Otis.

*The Adulateur, 1773.

*The Group, 1775. Two of the most famous Revolutionary satires.

Williams, Jesse Lynch.

Why Marry? 1917. (Originally *And So They Were Married*, 1914.) The first Pulitzer Prize Play, a popular high comedy.

Willis, Nathaniel Parker.

Tortesa the Usurer, 1839. Popular romantic drama in the European tradition.

Wood, Mrs. Henry.

East Lynne, 1863. Actually adapted by Clifton W. Tayleure from Mrs. Wood's novel. The most popular of the tearful melodramas of midcentury, it has passed into the language as a symbol of everything sickishly sentimental and pathetically maudlin.

Woodworth, Samuel.

*The Forest Rose, 1825. Famous for "The Old Oaken Bucket."

A SELECTED BIBLIOGRAPHY OF THE AMERICAN THEATRE BEFORE 1918

This limited bibliography includes most of the important books that will enable the student to pursue further study of any historical point discussed in Part 1 of this text. Detailed histories, such as those by Quinn, Mayorga, Hughes, and Hewitt, all contain extensive bibliographies of their own, which this list makes no attempt to duplicate. Once investigation is started, the student should be able to expand his readings to the limit of his school's library. Nearly all the standard histories and biographies will be available in any library of moderate size, although a number of the more specialized volumes may require further search. The brief annotations will assist in determining the value of each book in the student's specific field of interest.

General Histories

These are broad general histories of the American drama and the American theatre. They form the basis of all comprehensive studies of the American stage and have contributed heavily to the formation of Part 1 of this text. Some, of course, are considerably out-of-date, but they were all conceived as inclusive surveys of the American theatre as a whole.

Anderson, John: "The American Theatre and the Motion Picture in America," The Dial Press, Inc., New York, 1938. *The history is brief, but this large folio-type volume has a superb collection of pictures, which comprise almost half the book.*

Brown, T. Allston: "History of the American Stage," Dick and Fitzgerald, New York, 1870. *Not to be confused with Brown's larger effort devoted to New York theatres.*

Coad, Oral Sumner, and Edwin Mims, Jr.: "The American Stage," in "The Pageant of America," Yale University Press, New Haven, Conn., 1929, vol. 14. *Well illustrated, but encyclopedic in form. It is also now much out-of-date.*

Crawford, Mary Caroline: "The Romance of the American Theatre," Little, Brown & Company, Boston, 1913. *An informal history of dominant personalities and general trends. Excellent for nineteenth century. Interesting, but not a detailed scholarly study.*

Dunlap, William: "A History of the American Theatre," J. and J. Harper, New York, 1832. *There are later editions available. The first detailed history of the American stage, told by our first important playwright and manager. Frequently inaccurate and highly personal, but it is a priceless document without which most of our early histories would be sorely incomplete.*

Hewitt, Barnard: "Theatre U.S.A.: 1668–1957," McGraw-Hill Book Company, Inc., New York, 1959. *An excellent book, being a unique informal history of the theatre told through extensive passages from contemporary critical eomment and news reports. Well illustrated. Should be a part of every reference library.*

Hornblow, Arthur: "A History of the Theatre in America," J. B. Lippincott Company, Philadelphia, 1919, 2 vols. *One of the standard histories by an eminent critic and editor. Mostly about theatre, minimum of dramatic history.*

Hughes, Glenn: "A History of the American Theatre, 1700–1950," Samuel French, Inc., New York, 1951. *A fine, easy-to-read, general history of the theatre. Illustrations of early theatres. Much of the material seems reduced from details in Odell, but a handy reference.*

Ireland, Joseph N.: "Records of the New York Stage," T. H. Morrell, New York, 1866, 2 vols. *Now very rare. The first comprehensive study of our theatre, supplanted by Odell.*

Mayorga, Margaret G.: "A Short History of the American Drama," Dodd, Mead & Company, Inc., New York, 1932. *An informal history, giving broad treatment of all important writers, lacking the detailed accounts of Quinn's more inclusive volumes.*

Morris, Lloyd: "Curtain Time," Random House, Inc., New York, 1953. *A delightful informal history containing many stories and illustrations.*

Moses, Montrose J.: "The American Dramatist," Little, Brown & Company, Boston, 1925. *Separate chapters on all major writers. Fine discussions of Dunlap, Payne, Boucicault, etc. Some helpful chronological tables.*

Odell, George C. D.: "Annals of the New York Stage," Columbia University Press, New York, 1927–1949. *A fifteen-volume collection, each volume profusely illustrated, comprising the complete history of every conceivable kind of theatrical entertainment in New York from the beginning until 1894. A prodigious effort, without which no research in the American theatre is possible. Moreover, it is delightfully written in an amusing, witty style, which far removes it from the pedantry of similar works. While mainly about New York, its first volume does survey much of the colonial history elsewhere.*

Quinn, Arthur Hobson: "A History of the American Drama from the Beginning to the Civil War," Appleton-Century-Crofts, Inc., New York, 1943.

———: "A History of the American Drama from the Civil War to the Present Day," Appleton-Century-Crofts, Inc., New York, 1936. *These two volumes (the second volume is actually two books in one, separately paginated) are the standard history of drama in America, and both have been brought up-to-date into the 1940s in successive reprintings. The books review all the writers of any consequence, and include plots, outlines, and critical comment, biographical notes, etc. They are not a history of the theatre. Quinn is often much too kind to many second-rate writers in whom he wishes to find literary value. But no other volume or set compares with them.*

Seilhamer, George O.: "The History of the American Theatre," Globe Printing House, Philadelphia, 1888–1891, 3 vols. *Cut short by Seilhamer's death, this work includes only the very early theatre. An important predecessor of Odell.*

Special Histories

These books are helpful for the study of specific theatres outside of New York, or for special studies of the New York theatre itself. For personal accounts, rather than general histories, see the next section of this Bibliography, *Biographies and Personal Reminiscences.*

Blake, Charles: "An Historical Account of the Providence Stage," G. H. Whitney, Providence, R. I., 1868.

Brown, T. Allston: "A History of the New York Stage, 1732–1901," Dodd, Mead & Company, Inc., New York, 1903, 3 vols. *These three large volumes are little more than a chronological run-down of every production in every theatre in New York. It is not an easy history to read, lacking the personal touch of Odell's more complete work.*

Carson, William G. B.: "The Theatre on the Frontier," University of Chicago Press, Chicago, 1932. *Early years of the St. Louis theatre.*

Clapp, William W., Jr.: "A Record of the Boston Stage," James Munroe, Boston and Cambridge, 1853. *A small volume recording Boston's theatre history until 1850. Very fine account of early New England theatre.*

Daly, Charles P.: "First Theatre in America," Dunlap Society, New York, 1896. *A short book attempting to correct some of Dunlap's errors.*

Felheim, Marvin: "The Theatre of Augustin Daly," Harvard University Press, Cambridge, Mass., 1956. *The mid- and late-century theatre as it revolved around this famous manager.*

Ford, Paul Leicester: "Washington and the Theatre," Dunlap Society, New York, 1899. *Monograph of theatre of early republic.*

Gagey, Edmund M.: "The San Francisco Stage," Columbia University Press, New York, 1950.

Graham, Philip: "Showboat," University of Texas Press, Austin, Tex., 1951. *A complete, well-illustrated history of the river showboats.*

Hapgood, Norman: "The Stage in America, 1897–1900," The Macmillan Company, New York, 1901. *Concentrated review of end-of-century theatre. Fine discussion of the Syndicate, then in full power.*

Henderson, Myrtle E.: "History of the Theatre in Salt Lake City," Deseret Book Co., Salt Lake City, Utah, 1941.

Hoole, W. Stanley: "The Ante-bellum Charleston Theatre," University of Alabama Press, Tuscaloosa, Ala., 1946.

Kendall, John S.: "The Golden Age of the New Orleans Theatre," Louisiana State University Press, Baton Rouge, La., 1952.

MacMinn, George R.: "The Theatre of the Golden Era of California," Caxton Printers, Ltd., Caldwell, Idaho, 1941.

"Managers in Distress: The St. Louis Stage, 1840–1844," St. Louis Historical Documents, St. Louis, Mo., 1949.

Morehouse, Ward: "Matinee Tomorrow," McGraw-Hill Book Company, Inc., New York, 1949. *Informal history of American stage from 1898 to 1948. Well illustrated with anecdotes and pictures.*

Pollock, Thomas Clark: "The Philadelphia Theatre in the Eighteenth Century," University of Pennsylvania Press, Philadelphia, 1933. *The history of the original theatres up to 1799, including a complete daybook of all productions for the century. Companion to Odell's New York "Annals."*

Reed, James D.: "Old Drury of Philadelphia," University of Pennsylvania Press, Philadelphia, 1932. *History of the two Chestnut Street theatres, 1800–1835, and daily record of all productions. Supplement to Pollock.*

Tompkins, Eugene: "The History of the Boston Theatre, 1854–1901," Houghton Mifflin Company, Boston, 1908. *All productions and casts. Many pictures of performers. Supplements Clapp.*

Willard, George O.: "History of the Providence Stage, 1762–1891," R. I. News Co., Providence, R. I., 1891.

Willis, Eola: "The Charleston Stage in the XVIII Century," The State Co., Columbia, S.C., 1924.

Wilson, Arthur Herman: "A History of the Philadelphia Theatre, 1835–1855," University of Pennsylvania Press, Philadelphia, 1935. *Continuation of studies started by Pollock and Reed.*

Biographies and Personal Reminiscences

This list is highly selective and attempts to include only those books that will facilitate further pursuit of matters discussed in the text. There are many more biographies and autobiographies of famous theatre people which the bibliographies in other histories generally include. See Quinn, Mayorga, Hewitt, etc.

Barnes, Eric W.: "The Lady of Fashion: Anna Cora Mowatt," Charles Scribner's Sons, New York, 1954.

————: "The Man Who Lived Twice: The Biography of Edward Sheldon," Charles Scribner's Sons, New York, 1956.

Belasco, David: "The Theatre through Its Stage Door," Harper & Brothers, New York, 1919. *Personal account of many of Belasco's efforts.*

Binns, Archie: "Mrs. Fiske and the American Theatre," Crown Publishers, Inc., New York, 1955.

Bradley, Edward S.: "George Henry Boker," University of Pennsylvania Press, Philadelphia, 1927.

Coad, Oral Sumner: "William Dunlap: A Study of His Life and Works," Dunlap Society, New York, 1917.

Daly, Joseph F.: "Life of Augustin Daly," The Macmillan Company, New York, 1917.

Dunlap, William: "Diary of William Dunlap," in collections of the *New York Historical Society Collections,* 1930 and following years, vols. 62–64. *Three volumes of the available manuscript. Good for research, but not for casual reading.*

————: "Memoirs of George Frederick Cooke," D. Longworth, New York, 1813, 2 vols. *The lengthy biography of our first great visiting actor by the man who shepherded him around.*

Frohman, Daniel: "Memories of a Manager," Doubleday & Company, Inc., New York, 1911.

———— and Isaac F. Marcosson: "Charles Frohman, Manager and Man," Harper & Brothers, New York, 1916.

Gould, Thomas R.: "The Tragedian," Hurd & Houghton, New York, 1868. *Biography of Junius Brutus Booth.*

Harrison, Gabriel: "John Howard Payne," J. B. Lippincott Company, Philadelphia, 1885.

Jefferson, Joseph: "The Autobiography of Joseph Jefferson," Century Company, New York, 1890.

Ludlow, Noah M.: "Dramatic Life as I Found It," G. I. Jones, St. Louis, 1880.

MacKaye, Percy: "Epoch: The Life of Steele MacKaye," Liveright Publishing Corporation, New York, 1927, 2 vols.

Mathews, Anne Jackson: "Memoirs of Charles Mathews, Comedian," Richard Bentley, London, 1838. *Although this is a series of letters and notes from a famous British comedian who twice visited America, it contains some of the best accounts of the early nineteenth-century American theatre.*

Moody, Richard: "Edwin Forrest," Alfred A. Knopf, Inc., New York, 1960. *A complete and scholarly account of the life of America's first great actor.*

Moses, Montrose J.: "The Fabulous Forrest," Little, Brown & Company, Boston, 1929. *A good popular biography.*

———— and Virginia Gerson: "Clyde Fitch and His Letters," Little, Brown & Company, Boston, 1924.

Mowatt, Anna Cora: "The Autobiography of an Actress," Ticknor, Reed, and Fields, Boston, 1854.

Ruggles, Eleanor: "Prince of Players," W. W. Norton & Company, Inc., New York, 1953. *This biography of Edwin Booth reads almost like a novel.*

Smith, Solomon Franklin: "The Theatrical Apprenticeship of Sol Smith," Carey and Hart, Philadelphia, 1846.

————: "Theatrical Management in the West and South for Thirty Years," Harper & Brothers, New York, 1868. *Both of these books by the famous actor-manager of the Western frontier are fascinating and entertaining, particularly the latter, with its many anecdotes and its all too few amusing drawings.*

Walsh, Townsend: "The Career of Dion Boucicault," Dunlap Society, New York, 1915.

Wood, William B.: "Personal Recollections of the Stage," H. C. Baird, Philadelphia, 1855. *Wood was one of the managers in Philadelphia during the early and middle nineteenth century.*

Miscellaneous

A limited list of some of the more important special books.

Birdoff, Harry: "The World's Greatest Hit: Uncle Tom's Cabin," S. F. Vanni, New York, 1947.

Cheney, Sheldon: "The Art Theatre," Alfred A. Knopf, Inc., New York, 1925. *Character, ideals, and organization of art theatres with examples from America and Europe.*

————: "The New Movement in the Theatre," Mitchell Kennerley, New York, 1914. *Early account of the developing changes in late nineteenth- and early twentieth-century theatre.*

Cooke, John Esten: "The Virginia Comedians: or Old Days in the Old Dominion," D. Appleton & Company, Inc., New York, 1854. *A unique novel, based on the Hallams in Virginia. Highly fictional, but it presents many interesting points concerning colonial stages.*

Deutsch, Helen, and Stella Hanau: "The Provincetown: A Story of the Theatre," Farrar, Straus & Cudahy, Inc., New York, 1931. *The complete story of the Provincetown Players told by two who were there.*

Disher, M. Willson: "Melodrama: Plots that Thrilled," Rockliff Publishing Corporation, London, 1954. *Although this deals mainly with English productions, several American plays are included, and its interesting account of melodramatic types is highly entertaining.*

Hartman, John Geoffrey: "The Development of American Social Comedy from 1787 to 1936," University of Pennsylvania Press, Philadelphia, 1939. *A published dissertation of some interest.*

Hutton, Laurence: "Curiosities of the American Stage," Harper & Brothers, New York, 1891. *Discussion of American stage phenomena—native themes, infant prodigies, etc.*

Isaacs, Edith J. R.: "The Negro in the American Theatre," Theatre Arts Books, New York, 1947. *Fine, illustrated account of the position of the Negro in our theatre history.*

MacKaye, Percy: "The Civic Theatre," Mitchell Kennerley, New York, 1912.

————: "Community Drama," Houghton Mifflin Company, Boston, 1917. *These two volumes expound MacKaye's ideas of the popular drama through community enterprise.*

Moody, Richard: "America Takes the Stage: Romanticism in American Drama and Theatre, 1750–1900," Indiana University Press, Bloomington, Ind., 1955. *Excellent review of romanticism in nineteenth-century theatre—native themes in drama, acting, stage design, etc.*

————: "The Astor Place Riot," Indiana University Press, Bloomington, Ind., 1958. *The only complete treatment of the fatal Forrest-Macready feud, complete with illustrations.*

Moses, Montrose J.: "The American Dramatist," Little, Brown & Company, Boston, 1925. *Accounts of important writers. Convenient chronological tables.*

———— and John Mason Brown: "The American Theatre as Seen by Its Critics, 1752–1934," W. W. Norton & Company, Inc., New York, 1934. *Fine collection of critical opinion of many major productions. Unlike Hewitt's "Theatre U.S.A." in that it attempts no unified historical account.*

PART TWO

AN ANTHOLOGY OF
DRAMATIC ART SINCE 1918

Eugene O'Neill at the time of *The Iceman Cometh*, 1946. A product of the small art-theatre movement of the First World War period, O'Neill almost single-handedly turned the American trade of playmaking into the literary art of playwriting as he became our first dramatist of international stature. (*Cover portrait for Time Magazine by Boris Artzybasheff; copyright, Time, Inc., 1946.*)

THE MODERN REALISTIC DRAMA

The term *drama*, in its modern restricted sense, has come to mean a play that is fundamentally serious in its treatment of a mature theme, developed realistically toward a logical and appropriate conclusion neither tragic nor necessarily comic, but *satisfactory* in relation to the created events. The experiences which the characters meet may be the same found in any other kind of play—violent, amusing, saddening, exhilarating—but the final curtain need not necessarily find all the problems resolved, all the questions answered. There is no inevitability of a tragic catastrophe, nor is there the pleasant solution of a comedy's "happy" ending. So long as the conclusion rises satisfactorily out of the action, all is well. In other words, a *drama* is a modern "straight" or "serious" play. It has almost completely replaced *tragedy* as the opposite number of *comedy* in today's theatre vocabulary.

The Matter of the Problem Play

The advent of modern realistic techniques and the development of the serious, nontragic drama encouraged the simultaneous growth of an important dramatic form called simply the "problem" play. All serious plays contain problems, but the difference between the *problem of a play* and a *play about a problem* is considerable. In the first instance, matters of revenge, love, indecision, or hate may create problems, but their function is to help establish the pattern of dramatic conflict and character development or to further the discussion of certain moral or philosophic principles. The problem, in itself, does not become of primary importance. In the second instance, however, the play exists for the sake of presenting and analyzing a specific problem that relates directly to the existing social, political, or moral climates of opinion. The spectators see the difficulties of those on stage not as abstractions or broad generalizations, but as concrete difficulties which they can understand and readily interpret in relation to their own experiences. The dramatic presentation may vary from mere observation and awareness that the problem exists to a demand that the audience assume interest enough to initiate prompt remedial action.

The failure of most problem plays to survive after many years lies in the removal of their problems from public concern. Plays created in the heat of great political or social unrest seldom endure except as historical curiosities. Such is the case with the majority of the "social" dramas which developed in

America during the Great Depression. These plays by Odets, Lawson, Wexley and others were some of the most exciting pieces our theatre has ever seen, but their vehemence and alarm are no longer needed, for they talk of matters which time and legislative reform have altered. The writer who would attack a problem with determination must face the very likely prospect that his work, although enthusiastically received, will gain but momentary support.

Uncertain Steps in the Nineteenth Century

Steele MacKaye's *Hazel Kirke* of 1880, one of the most successful plays of the nineteenth century, took some of the first faltering steps toward modern dramatic realism. Its routine melodrama involves the standard complication of the beautiful young daughter, Hazel, driven into an apparently illegal elopement by refusal to marry the suitor chosen by her stern, unbending father. The father's curse and the realization that she may be living in sin sends Hazel plunging into her father's millpond. Arthur, the husband, appears in time to rescue his bride and reveal the legality of the marriage. Parental forgiveness arrives just before the curtain descends on a blissful family tableau.

It is difficult to take the play seriously today. It is written in an artificial, stagy language, and suspense builds upon transparently artificial contrivances. The most notable evidence of originality is the absence of any melodramatic "villain." The two men who seek the heroine's love are both sympathetic and decent, and MacKaye's treatment of them points to his awareness of character and incident closer to valid human experience.

James A. Herne's *Margaret Fleming* of 1890 can safely be called America's first realistic "problem" play. It represents a considerable advance in technique within the ten years after *Hazel Kirke*. The influences of Ibsen are obvious in the play's sincere presentation of a respectable American couple living moderately prosperous lives who are faced with a serious domestic crisis that they must in some way meet while still continuing to live.

The problem is an ancient one: adultery. Philip Fleming, a successful manufacturer happily married to a beautiful and devoted wife, has momentarily slipped into the ways of his more carefree years and fathered a child by a defenseless working girl. By putting his third party out of her misery by death Herne bows to certain of Howard's "laws," and he cannot avoid some contrived theatrical effects, such as threatening Margaret with blindness if her system, weakened in childbirth, receives further shock. The easily anticipated jolt comes in her discovery of her husband's misdeed, made even more sensational by the meeting of husband and wife at the scene of the crime.

Still, what occurs in the play's development can nearly always be justified realistically in view of what has already occurred in the past. The final handling of the "unforgivable" sin of faithlessness as worked out by Philip and Margaret Fleming is completely plausible. Herne refuses to make a martyr of his wronged wife and simultaneously refuses to kill off his evil-doing

The Penthouse Theatre, University of Washington, 1940, the first permanent theatre designed especially for arena productions. The performance becomes absolutely central, and the elaborate settings and theatre fixtures of tradition have been eliminated. (*Courtesy University of Washington, Seattle.*)

husband. Each one suffers a permanent wound, but each knows the other is in genuine need of help. The solution, even if oversentimental (it holds promise of Margaret's returned sight), is eminently satisfactory while avoiding the triteness of being merely "happy." In the closing scene, Philip asks if he will ever be forgiven:

MARGARET (*shaking her head and smiling sadly*). There is nothing to forgive. And, I want to forget.
PHILIP (*bewildered by her magnanimity, but full of hope*). Then you will let me come back to you? You will help me to be a better—a wiser man?
MARGARET (*smiling gently*). Yes, Philip.

* * *

PHILIP. Dear, not now—but in the future—some time—away in the future—perhaps, the old Margaret—
MARGARET. Ah, Philip, the old Margaret is dead. The truth killed her.
PHILIP. Then—there is no hope for me? (*There is a dignity and a growing manliness in his demeanor as the scene progresses.*)
MARGARET (*warmly*). Yes, every hope.

PHILIP. Well, what do you want me to do? Shall I go away?

MARGARET. No. Your place is here. You cannot shirk your responsibilities now.

PHILIP. I do not want to shirk my responsibilities, Margaret. I want to do whatever you think is best.

MARGARET. Very well. It is best for us both to remain here, and take up the old life together. It will be a little hard for you, but you are a man—you will soon live it down.

*   *   *

MARGARET. There is no use now lamenting what was done yesterday. That's finished. Tomorrow? What are you going to do with that?

PHILIP. There does not seem any "tomorrow" worthwhile for me. The past—

MARGARET. The past is dead. We must face the living future. Now, Philip, there are big things ahead for you, if you will only look for them. They certainly will not *come* to *you*. I will help you—we will fight this together.

At the curtain, Philip goes out into the garden to see his children, because Margaret has brought Philip's other motherless infant to raise as their own.

The play was not a commercial success, and producers long hesitated to stage it anywhere. In its original version, Margaret and Philip did not come together again. Mrs. Herne, who created the original Margaret in 1890, revised the play for its present published form. She felt that the character of Margaret and the personality of Philip would enable them to be reconciled. In the way the play is written, she is probably right.

The Twentieth-century Approach

Clyde Fitch's *The City*, posthumously produced in 1909, clearly demonstrates the confusion in dramatic and theatrical techniques which prevented plays of this type from becoming permanently valuable pieces of dramatic literature. Fitch sincerely attempted an "honest" revelation of certain human vices, particularly as urban life intensified them, and in *The City* he became increasingly daring in the subject matter he discussed and the strength of the dialogue in which he expressed it. The dramatic situation is legitimate: a family bored with petty small-town life, eager to move into the glamorous excitement of city living where one may "breathe in gasoline on Fifth Avenue" instead of smelling new-mown hay. The family naïveté and the pitfalls awaiting such innocent victims could provide a strong central theme. Fitch *thinks* he is developing a valid point, but what he actually does is much the same thing he so often did in his earlier plays. He descends from a dramatically valid theme into a discouragingly heavy reliance upon stage trickery and blatant melodramatics. Instead of revealing his ideas through careful and logical character development and realistic incident, he repeatedly takes his sound points and uses them for violent physical shocks which destroy what he is trying to say. *The City*, like most of his plays, ends on a false note of happy solution and insincere sentiment which merely "proves" that in spite of all the problems in life, things are bound to come out in the end.

Excerpts from the play show how Fitch undermined his effects. The father in *The City* has died before the family moves to New York, and the son, George, has learned that the play's blackmailing villain, Hannock, is his own illegitimate half brother. When George's sister, Cicely, reveals the horror of her secret marriage to Hannock, the following occurs:

> GEORGE (*with excitement*). She *isn't* your wife!—(HANNOCK *looks at him and sneers.* GEORGE's *rage at* HANNOCK *is only governed by the tragedy of the whole thing.*) Your marriage wasn't any marriage!
> HANNOCK (*a little frightened, and very angry now*). What do you mean?—
> GEORGE (*looks toward the door where* CICELY *has gone, and with difficulty manages to control his voice, as he lowers it*). Cicely is your *sister!*
> HANNOCK (*with a cry*). Cicely is *what?*
> GEORGE. *Your sister!*
> HANNOCK (*sees "red," and goes nearly mad*). You're a God-damn liar!

The use of this blasphemous profanity, never before uttered on the professional New York stage, is only a preface to the lurid events to come. Hannock, who has already made clear his addiction to dope by using the needle in full view of the audience, "*making guttural sounds, . . . working his hands, his mouth and his chin wet with saliva . . . his whole body wracked and trembling,*" refuses to believe the truth. Later, when Cicely has entered:

> GEORGE. Cicely! Are you strong? Are you brave? You must hear something *unbelievably terrible!*
> HANNOCK (*holding out his hand beggingly*). Come along, don't listen to him! (*She makes a movement toward* HANNOCK.)
> GEORGE. You *can't!* (*Taking hold of her.*)
> CICELY. *I will!* Leave go of me! (*Struggling desperately.*)
> GEORGE (*puts his arms about her, and holds her in his arms—her back to him*). My poor child, he's your—(HANNOCK, *without warning, pulls out a pistol from his hip pocket, and shoots her dead in* GEORGE's *arms.*)

For this final act of perverse violence the audience has been completely unprepared, and Fitch has instantly sacrificed any ideal of dramatic realism for a sensational but wildly inappropriate scene.

At the end of the play, George is ruined by his own connivances, a result of inherited traits from his father's shady character. He is determined to regain his self-respect, and in the closing scene his socially prominent sweetheart gives him courage:

> ELEANOR. The man who has done wrong, and can own it up, . . . because it is the right thing to do, and because—leaving the world out of it—*he had to be honest with himself!*—that—George—is the man I look up to ten times more than the one who was *born* good and lived good because he never was tempted to enjoy the spoils of going wrong! It's the man whom it costs

something to be good,—that's what makes real character! . . . and thank God, your real self has triumphed! *Today* you *are* the man I loved yesterday!

GEORGE (*looking away*). Now, I know what those people mean who say a man gets all the *Hell* that's coming to him *in this world*,—(*looking at her*)—and *all the Heaven*, too!

THE CURTAIN FALLS.

The same year, 1909, also saw Eugene Walter's *The Easiest Way*. The play is important for its success in proving that commercial reward was possible without the hope of a pleasant solution or a last-minute reprieve. "It was the first bold denial of the happy ending in modern American drama," said Burns Mantle in selecting it as the best representative of its season. The play also demonstrated that tolerably good writing could lift a production above the smothering detail in which Belasco, its producer, insisted on burying it.

Arbitrary plot manipulation is often at work in *The Easiest Way*, but Walter faces life "realistically" in assuming that genuine love and affection can flourish even though both Laura Murdock and John Madison are products of a considerably tarnished past. They are confident that each can be redeemed by love. Laura returns to New York to await her sweetheart, who temporarily remains in the Far West to win his fortune by his energetic honesty. As soon as the second-act curtain rises it is too patently evident that Laura will fail to keep her vow. No person of her temperament could possibly remain firm under the appalling slum conditions now visible, especially in view of the escape that Walter offers her through the repeated opportunities she has to return to her old life.

The second-act setting is the design which so challenged Belasco that he went out to buy, floor to ceiling, the shoddiest New York rooming-house hovel he could find (see page 48). The printed description continues for two full pages of double-column type and reveals the handicaps against which Belasco's actors had to struggle. Every sordid detail of the room's decaying trashy atmosphere visible to the audience is described down to the last soot smudge and cobweb. The degree to which Belasco's suffocating naturalism extended, however, is revealed in the catalogue of items beyond audience vision and of no possible dramatic use. Here are some examples:

> *On the dresser is a pincushion, a bottle of cheap perfume, purple in color and nearly empty; a common crockery match-holder, containing matches; . . . a handkerchief box, powder box and puff, rouge box and rouge paw, hand mirror, small alcohol curling iron-heater; . . . scissors, curling tongs, hair comb and brush, and a small cheap picture of John Madison; a small work-box containing a thimble and thread, and stuck in the pincushion are a couple of needles threaded. Directly to the left of the bureau is a broken-down washstand, on which is a basin half full of water, a bottle of tooth powder, toothbrushes and holder, soap and soapdish, and other cheap toilet articles, and a small drinking glass.*

The Kalita Humphreys Theatre, Dallas, Texas, 1960, the only theatre designed by the late Frank Lloyd Wright. Its huge apron and giant turntable incorporate elements of platform, arena, and proscenium stages in a completely new concept of theatre construction. The many acting areas on and around the stage encourage highly imaginative productions. (*Courtesy Dallas Theatre Center.*)

Under the mattress at the head of the bed is a heavy cardboard box about thirty inches long, seven inches wide, and four inches deep, containing about one hundred and twenty-five letters and eighty telegrams tied in about eight bundles, with dainty ribbon. One bundle must contain all practical letters of several closely written pages each, each letter having been opened. They must be written upon business paper and envelopes such as are used in newspaper offices and by business men.

Almost none of this museumlike setting, except one or two of the letters, becomes important in the action. As a valid stage effect, it is a monstrous failure.

In the best romantic tradition, Walter rewards the perseverance of young Madison by giving him a fortune in Nevada mining and sends him jubilantly into New York to surprise Laura in the life of sin she has re-entered. The discovery is a violent blow. Throughout the final scene the play builds toward its "bold denial." John twists the knife driven through Laura's heart by passing his righteous judgment upon her. "I guess you don't know what a decent sentiment is," he says. "Laura, you're not immoral, you're just unmoral, kind o' all out of shape, and I'm afraid there isn't a particle of hope. With you it is the easy way, and it always will be. . . . And you'll sink until you're down to the very bed-rock of depravity. I pity you."

When he is gone, Laura faces her fate, demanding that her maid "dress up my body and paint up my face" as she heads for Rector's "to make a hit, and to hell with the rest." As the curtain slowly descends, a hurdy-gurdy strikes up a tune *"peculiarly suggestive of the low life, the criminality and prostitution that constitute the night excitement of that section of New York City known as the Tenderloin"* and it brings to Laura's eyes *"a panorama of the inevitable depravity that awaits her."* She can only stagger off the stage *"with infinite grief, resignation, and hopelessness"* murmuring "O God—O my God."

Although Walter's hell-on-earth destruction of his fallen woman is an echo of Bronson Howard's "laws," he tried to offer more than established stage tradition to justify it.

Eugene O'Neill's *Bound East for Cardiff* of 1916 must be considered not only because of its historical significance to the Provincetown Players but also because it proved conclusively that a writer who took his artistic efforts seriously could be commercially successful.

The conditions of production were inauspicious and primitive. At one end of a fishing shack which held an audience of sixty people, a few men in a tiny space portrayed the passing of a dreary night of agony aboard a plodding tramp steamer. There was no plot, no action, and a considerable amount of talk in a variety of fairly obvious national dialects. But as the audience watched and listened, they knew that what went on in front of them was making history. Through the use of words alone, through what the men uttered and the way they uttered it, the writer was able to convey the indifference, despair, callousness, and crude but genuine devotion to one another felt by a group of ignorant, hard-drinking but sympathetic ship crewmen. Helpless amidst them, one of their number was dying of injuries from a terrible fall, grasping at the few pleasant memories left him as he realized his approaching death. The whole drama of living and dying was packed into a few short minutes of stage dialogue. Here were no musical-comedy funny men in sailor suits, but the kind of human beings with whom O'Neill had spent his derelict youth, the value of whose lives and deaths in telling a dramatic story he brilliantly recognized.

The closing moments of the play show the simplicity and genuinely deep feeling that O'Neill was able to infuse into all his early plays of the sea:

> YANK. . . . It's hard to ship on this voyage I'm goin' on—alone! (DRISCOLL *reaches out and grasps his hand. There is a pause, during which both fight to control themselves.*) My throat's like a furnace. (*He gasps for air.*) Gimme a drink of water, will yuh, Drisc? (DRISCOLL *gets him a dipper of water.*) I wish this was a pint of beer. Oooohh! (*He chokes, his face convulsed with agony, his hands tearing at his shirt front. The dipper falls from his nerveless fingers.*)
>
> DRISCOLL. For the love av God, what is ut, Yank?

YANK (*speaking with tremendous difficulty*). S'long, Drisc! (*He stares straight in front of him with eyes starting from their sockets.*) Who's that?

DRISCOLL. Who? what?

YANK (*faintly*). A pretty lady dressed in black. (*His face twitches and his body writhes in a final spasm, then straightens out rigidly.*)

DRISCOLL (*pale with horror*). Yank! Yank! Say a word to me for the love av hiven! (*He shrinks away from the bunk, making the sign of the cross. Then comes back and puts a trembling hand on YANK's chest and bends closely over the body.*)

COCKY (*from the alleyway*). Oh, Driscoll! Can you leave Yank for arf a mo' and give me a 'and?

DRISCOLL (*with a great sob*). Yank! (*He sinks down on his knees beside the bunk, his head on his hands. His lips move in some half-remembered prayer.*)

COCKY (*enters, his oilskins and sou'wester glistening with drops of water*). The fog's lifted. (*COCKY sees DRISCOLL and stands staring at him with open mouth. DRISCOLL makes the sign of the cross again.*)

COCKY (*mockingly*). Sayin' 'is prayers! (*He catches sight of the still figure in the bunk and an expression of awed understanding comes over his face. He takes off his dripping sou'wester and stands, scratching his head.*)

COCKY (*in a hushed whisper*). Gawd blimey!

THE CURTAIN FALLS.

The professional New York theatre soon welcomed the full-length treatment of realistically developed, logically concluded serious plays—the modern realistic drama. O'Neill continued for a while to keep the trail marked with *Beyond the Horizon, Anna Christie,* and some unsuccessful, though often well-produced attempts like *The Straw, Welded,* and *Diff'rent.* Sidney Howard's *The Silver Cord,* George Kelly's *Craig's Wife,* Owen Davis' Pulitzer prize-winning *Icebound* all took their important places and have become permanent American realistic "classics." The use of stage naturalism, with detailed settings closely allied with the propounded dramatic theme, was astonishingly successful in Sidney Kingsley's *Dead End* and Elmer Rice's *Street Scene.*

The realistic "problem" play found its finest exposition in the works of young Clifford Odets. The numbing grip of the Great Depression forced old and young alike to question the social system which denied millions of its members a living, or at best permitted a bare subsistence to those lucky enough to work. The 1930s therefore witnessed the growth of the "social" dramatist who praised the laboring man and condemned the wicked exploiters. In the organization of the Group Theatre this "left-wing" element found its home, and in Odets its strongest voice. Skyrocketing to fame with the violent call to the barricades in *Waiting for Lefty* of 1935, Odets produced in his *Awake and Sing, Paradise Lost,* and *Rocket to the Moon* three highly literate and dramatically sound pleas for the "proletariat," whose struggle he saw as his own and the nation's. A work of out-and-out Communist propaganda in *'Til the Day I Die* did not materially weaken his position, and after his subsequent disillusionment in the revolutionary cause and the disbanding of the Group Theatre, Odets has remained in later plays like *The Country Girl* one of our best serious, realistic dramatists.

In O'Neill, Howard, Kelly, Kingsley, Odets and all the rest, the American stage had grown up—and it could now leave to the young giant in Hollywood the ancient privilege of painting life in its happiest "ever-after" colors.

The Little Foxes

The Little Foxes is one of the finest examples of the craft of playmaking combined with the qualities of excellent realistic drama. As a "well-made play" it is superb; as a piece of realism, it is entirely convincing; as a drama, it is continuously absorbing, arriving at a denouement that is satisfactorily in keeping with the theme of the entire work without aspiring to tragedy or bowing to the improbable sentimentalities or compromises of a happy ending.

Structurally, the play is a "beautiful example of stage economy" as one opening-night critic observed. There is not a single wasted step or superfluous word. Everything that happens on stage is a direct contribution to the development of character, plot, and theme. While the sordid plans and conspiracies are carefully unwound, Miss Hellman simultaneously reveals the depth of each character who takes part in them. Those who stand on the outside of the vicious scheming are no less precisely drawn, and their comments and reactions contribute as much to the story as do those of the plotters themselves. Meanwhile, the theme of social degradation and moral decay is being propounded with skill.

The entire first act is an outstanding example of dramatic exposition. The revelation of the past weaves naturally and unobtrusively through the opening dialogue. From the moment of Birdie's breathless, overgay entrance and Oscar's sadistic smashing of her pleasure, the strains of personal antagonism become immediately clear. In front of their guest the vicious clan display their ignorance, their hypocrisy, and their greed, while Marshall, the outsider, serves as catalyst to bring out details the audience must know. The remaining acts maintain this well-built structure as each scene further intensifies what has already been adroitly established. There is not a single loose end throughout the entire play to distract or mislead at any point.

Tight construction does not necessarily mean a fine play, and although Miss Hellman has proven that the style of the well-made play is not unworthy of modern use, she has made her work far more than an exhibit of facility in maneuvering a plot. Her characters talk and move in a believably realistic fashion, without seeming to be arbitrarily led through mechanical paces for the mere creation of an effect. The concentrated evil of her central characters, whose lack of any saving grace of human compassion makes the sordidness virtually unrelieved, could be taken as evidence of the writer's direct intercession without regard to logical probability. This interference is not as direct as it might seem. These people exist in an historical period when material fortunes were based on merciless capitalizing on the opportunity at hand regardless of consequences. They live in a geographical locale where "polite" society is still torn apart by a desire to cling to old beliefs and by an inability to recognize the kind of change which must come. The characters of *The Little Foxes* are conceived and remain as a natural part of the society in which they live, unattractive and repugnant as human beings, fascinating in their horror as snarling beasts. Moreover, the Hubbards are in complete control of their destinies. Outside influences work on them with great strength, to be sure, but there is no evidence of any compulsion or raw force of nature that has placed them where they are, contrary to their own desires. Nothing around them in their physical or social world compels them to act as they do. As opportunists, vicious and without conscience, they proceed entirely on their own, make their own decisions, and have no one but themselves to whom they must render account. The drama of their ugly lives is believably real.

The individual characters in *The Little Foxes* uniformly maintain their convincing identities as dramatic creations because their baseness has emerged from plausible· reality and is explained in logical fashion. No one is asked to accept Regina as simply a scheming woman or as the vixen of the den deprived of the understandable human qualities of her sex. She is a woman in every physical sense, beautiful, a gracious and dignified hostess, and one who seeks the things a woman is expected to desire—elegance, social position, public respect. Her cold, inhuman perversity in fighting for her goals gives her considerable stature in modern drama. Oscar and Ben cause awe-stricken shudders as the ruthless infighting begins. Their barefaced encouragement of Leo's treachery and the blackmail by which they force him deeper into the trap may be nightmare contradictions of parental responsibilities, but they are evolved from realistically acceptable premises.

The sympathetic Birdie, too, proceeds through the play as a complete and well-drawn human being. Her pitiful, childish withdrawal into her past does not make her merely an object of pity without reason. The reasons are expounded, all within character, and without unnecessary and interfering exposition. Her ineffectual attempts to stem the irresistible machine of evil which threatens to make Alexandra's life a duplicate of her own, together with her one revealing outburst, make her dramatically important. She represents the reverse of the tarnished coin, but her side is exactly as counterfeit as her husband's.

If the play is to be kept from becoming a ludicrous Grand Guignol of horror, it must have some character toward whom unqualified audience sympathies can extend. Both Horace and Alexandra compete for this sympathy, not merely by virtue of their contrast to the others, but by a strength equal to the force of the opposition. Horace's appeal is limited because he must play the deadly game by the enemy's rules. Alexandra, however, can remain detached and receive the audience's complete sympathy. By the end of the play it is assumed that she *can* escape if she has the courage to pursue her resolve to do so. Because she has developed acceptable strength and integrity within the play, there is every reason to believe she will succeed.

The Little Foxes is not melodrama as described by Owen Davis or as practiced by Augustin Daly, but it frequently employs melodrama with good effect. Any intensely exciting stage action developed primarily for the sake of a thrill and strong emotional impact through terror, shock, fear, or suspense is *melodramatic*. The *melodrama*, as a dramatic type, consists of a planned succession of thrilling sequences, culminating in the destruction of the forces of evil by the forces of good through the triumph of justice. A *melodramatic play*, such as *The Little Foxes*, makes successful use of scenes of melodrama that are natural, acceptable parts of the drama itself. They arise from established character and situation and further the movement of the play without distraction. Two important scenes are vividly melodramatic. The first begins in Act II with the tense exchange between Regina and Horace, and ends in the violent upstairs argument while the other jungle beasts plan to divide the spoils. The second is, of course, the heart attack, a harrowing event of pure melodrama from the start of the argument, through the broken bottle and the collapse on the stairs. To see how skilled use of melodrama can further the effect of a realistic style, compare either of these scenes with Cicely's murder in *The City*.

The Little Foxes ends in triumph and defeat for both sides. Horace has been cheated, yet through Regina he is able to cheat Oscar and Ben. Regina now seems in full control, but her victory is no guarantee of permanent power, either over her brothers or over Alexandra. Alexandra's curtain line is powerful, and yet there is no proof that she will break away. There is no "ending" except Alexandra's question, which probably is more foreboding to Regina than she can possibly admit.

It would be foolish to say that *The Little Foxes* is a document of social reform. The play, none the less, is a problem play in the same general way that *Margaret Fleming* is a problem play. Neither makes an effort to arouse public reaction, but each presents a straightforward discussion of problems facing certain members of society. The problem of *The Little Foxes* is broader than the four walls of a home, but it is no less important, for it represents the misfortune of all human beings who have found themselves deprived of former self-respect but unable to regain the strength and confidence to oppose the evil which rushes into the vacuum. Placing the action in 1900 provides a certain aesthetic distance, and there may be a temptation to dismiss the events as part of a long-disappeared historical era. This helps, perhaps, to relieve the intense and taxing severity of the play, but it does not automatically deny the existence of the basic social problem.

The subject matter of *The Little Foxes* could not have received its present treatment before the development of the realistic drama. The nineteenth century would have demanded a full-scale melodrama, complete with punishment of the evil planners and victory for the defenders of justice. Fitch's corrupt big city contained the same evil persons, but Fitch had to saddle his worst character with blackmail, murder, and dope, and to restore all survivors to grace. Miss Hellman needs none of this. She and her audience both know that respectable society will always have Reginas, Oscars, and Bens to fight, and that there are also Horaces and Alexandras to fight them. But she does not have to reveal how it all comes out in the end, for neither she, nor her audience, really knows.

Lillian Hellman

Lillian Hellman was born in New Orleans on June 20, 1905. She was educated at New York and Columbia Universities and received her master of arts degree at Tufts College in 1940. She has nearly always been associated with literature and the theatre, having spent several years in the 1920s as a publisher's manuscript reader and as a playreader. Before 1930 she had also been a book reviewer for the New York *Herald Tribune*, and she was a theatrical press agent for a short while. She was married for a time to Arthur Kober, a playwright. During the Spanish civil war she spent some time in Spain with the Loyalists in 1937 and returned a confirmed anti-Nazi.

Miss Hellman's first dramatic attempt was a collaboration with Louis Kronenberger called *The Dear Queen*, which was never produced. Her own first play was *The Children's Hour* in 1934, a distinguished success that brought considerable praise for the author's powerful, adult treatment of the forces of evil in a neurotic, maladjusted child. After *Days to Come*, a failure of 1936, came *The Little Foxes*, still widely regarded as her best work. It also provided Tallulah Bankhead with her first important and highly praised dramatic role. *Watch on the Rhine*, 1941, concerned the difficulties of an anti-Nazi refugee family in Washington and was a successful wartime play. *The Searching Wind*, 1944, did not live up to expectations. *Another Part of the Forest* in 1946 depicted the Hubbard family twenty years before *The Little Foxes* and might have been considered her best had not the earlier "sequel" been so much better. *The Autumn Garden* appeared in 1951, and her adaptation in 1955 of Jean Anouilh's story of Joan of Arc, *L'Alouette*, called *The Lark*, in Miss Hellman's version brought considerable praise for its star, Julie Harris. A generally enthusiastic critical reception met *Toys in the Attic* in 1960. This play tells of the evils that befall a family made suddenly and unexpectedly wealthy. It was awarded the New York Drama Critics' Circle prize for the best play of the 1959–1960 season. Miss Hellman has worked on many motion pictures, including her own *The Little Foxes*, and other adaptations, such as Sidney Kingsley's *Dead End* in 1937.

THE LITTLE FOXES
by
Lillian Hellman

Take us the foxes, the little foxes, that spoil the vines;
for our vines have tender grapes.

Scene from Act II, original production of *The Little Foxes*. The details of authentic costumes, setting, and properties contribute to the reality of the scene, while unobtrusively maintaining their place as background to the believably drawn characters and logically developed action that are typical of well-written modern realistic drama. (*Theatre Arts Magazine. Photo by Vandamm.*)

The Little Foxes opened at the National Theatre in New York on February 15, 1939. It ran for 410 performances, and closed on January 20, 1940. The original cast:

ADDIE	*Abbie Mitchell*
CAL	*John Marriott*
BIRDIE HUBBARD	*Patricia Collinge*
OSCAR HUBBARD	*Carl Benton Reid*
LEO HUBBARD	*Dan Duryea*
REGINA GIDDENS	*Tallulah Bankhead*
WILLIAM MARSHALL	*Lee Baker*
BENJAMIN HUBBARD	*Charles Dingle*
ALEXANDRA GIDDENS	*Florence Williams*
HORACE GIDDENS	*Frank Conroy*

Produced and staged by Herman Shumlin
Settings designed by Howard Bay
Costumes designed by Aline Bernstein

There has been no attempt to write Southern dialect. It is to be understood that the accents are Southern.

ACT ONE

SCENE: *The living room of the Giddens home, in a small town in the deep South, the spring of 1900. Upstage is a staircase leading to the second story. Upstage, right, are double doors to the dining room. When these doors are open we see a section of the dining room and the furniture. Upstage, left, is an entrance hall with a coatrack and umbrella stand. There are large lace-curtained windows on the left wall. The room is lit by a center gas chandelier and painted china oil lamps on the tables. Against the wall is a large piano. Downstage, right, are a high couch, a large table, several chairs. Against the left back wall are a table and several chairs. Near the window there are a smaller couch and tables. The room is good-looking, the furniture expensive; but it reflects no particular taste. Everything is of the best and that is all.*

AT RISE: ADDIE, *a tall, nice-looking Negro woman of about fifty-five, is closing the windows. From behind the closed dining-room doors there is the sound of voices. After a second,* CAL, *a middle-aged Negro, comes in from the entrance hall carrying a tray with glasses and a bottle of port.* ADDIE *crosses, takes the tray from him, puts it on table, begins to arrange it.*

ADDIE (*pointing to the bottle*). You gone stark out of your head?

CAL. No, smart lady, I ain't. Miss Regina told me to get out that bottle. (*Points to bottle.*) That very bottle for the mighty honored guest. When Miss Regina changes orders like that you can bet your dime she got her reason.

ADDIE (*points to dining room*). Go on. You'll be needed.

CAL. Miss Zan she had two helpings frozen fruit cream and she tell that honored guest, she tell him that you make the best frozen fruit cream in all the South.

ADDIE (*smiles, pleased*). Did she? Well, see that Belle saves a little for her. She like it right before she go to bed. Save a few little cakes, too, she like— (*The dining-room doors are opened and quickly closed again by* BIRDIE HUBBARD. BIRDIE *is a woman of about forty, with a pretty, well-bred, faded face. Her movements are usually nervous and timid, but now, as she comes running into the room, she is gay and excited.* CAL *turns to* BIRDIE.)

BIRDIE. Oh, Cal. (*Closes door.*) I want you to get one of the kitchen boys to run home for me. He's to look in my desk drawer and— (*To* ADDIE.) My, Addie. What a good supper! Just as good as good can be.

ADDIE. You look pretty this evening, Miss Birdie, and young.

BIRDIE (*laughing*). Me, young? (*Turns back to* CAL.) Maybe you better find Simon and tell him to do it himself. He's to look in my desk, the left drawer, and bring my music album right away. Mr. Marshall is very anxious to see it because of his father and the opera in Chicago. (*To* ADDIE.) Mr. Marshall is such a polite man with his manners and very educated and cultured and I've told him all about how my mama and papa used to go to Europe for the music— (*Laughs. To* ADDIE.) Imagine going all the way to Europe just to listen to music. Wouldn't that be nice, Addie? Just to sit there and listen and— (*Turns and steps to* CAL.) Left drawer, Cal. Tell him that twice because he forgets. And tell him not to let any of the things drop out of the album and to bring it right in here when he comes back. (*The dining-room doors are opened and quickly closed by* OSCAR HUBBARD. *He is a man in his late forties.*)

CAL. Yes'm. But Simon he won't get it right. But I'll tell him.

BIRDIE. Left drawer, Cal, and tell him to bring the blue book and—

OSCAR (*sharply*). Birdie.

BIRDIE (*turning nervously*). Oh, Oscar. I was just sending Simon for my music album.

OSCAR (*to* CAL). Never mind about the album. Miss Birdie has changed her mind.

BIRDIE. But, really, Oscar. Really I promised Mr. Marshall. I— (CAL *looks at them, exits.*)

OSCAR. Why do you leave the dinner table and go running about like a child?

BIRDIE (*trying to be gay*). But, Oscar, Mr. Marshall said most specially he *wanted* to see my album. I told him about

the time Mama met Wagner, and Mrs. Wagner gave her the signed program and the big picture. Mr. Marshall wants to see that. Very, very much. We had such a nice talk and—

OSCAR (*taking a step to her*). You have been chattering to him like a magpie. You haven't let him be for a second. I can't think he came South to be bored with you.

BIRDIE (*quickly, hurt*). He wasn't bored. I don't believe he was bored. He's a very educated, cultured gentleman. (*Her voice rises.*) I just don't believe it. You always talk like that when I'm having a nice time.

OSCAR (*turning to her, sharply*). You have had too much wine. Get yourself in hand now.

BIRDIE (*drawing back, about to cry, shrilly*). What am I doing? I am not doing anything. What am I doing?

OSCAR (*taking a step to her, tensely*). I said get yourself in hand. Stop acting like a fool.

BIRDIE (*turns to him, quietly*). I don't believe he was bored. I just don't believe it. Some people like music and like to talk about it. That's all I was doing. (LEO HUBBARD *comes hurrying through the dining-room door. He is a young man of twenty, with a weak kind of good looks.*)

LEO. Mama! Papa! They are coming in now.

OSCAR (*softly*). Sit down, Birdie. Sit down now. (BIRDIE *sits down, bows her head as if to hide her face. The dining-room doors are opened by* CAL. *We see people beginning to rise from the table.* REGINA GIDDENS *comes in with* WILLIAM MARSHALL. REGINA *is a handsome woman of forty.* MARSHALL *is forty-five, pleasant-looking, self-possessed. Behind them comes* ALEXANDRA GIDDENS, *a very pretty, rather delicate-looking girl of seventeen. She is followed by* BENJAMIN HUBBARD, *fifty-five, with a large jovial face and the light graceful movements that one often finds in large men.*)

REGINA. Mr. Marshall, I think you're trying to console me. Chicago may be the noisiest, dirtiest city in the world but I should still prefer it to the sound of our horses and the smell of our azaleas. I should like crowds of people, and theaters, and lovely women— *Very* lovely women, Mr. Marshall?

MARSHALL (*crossing to sofa*). In Chicago? Oh, I suppose so. But I can tell you this: I've never dined there with *three* such lovely ladies. (ADDIE *begins to pass the port.*)

BEN. Our Southern women are well favored.

LEO (*laughs*). But one must go to Mobile for the ladies, sir. Very elegant worldly ladies, too.

BEN (*looks at him very deliberately*). Worldly, eh? *Worldly*, did you say?

OSCAR (*hastily, to* LEO). Your uncle Ben means that worldliness is not a mark of beauty in any woman.

LEO (*quickly*). Of course, Uncle Ben. I didn't mean—

MARSHALL. Your port is excellent, Mrs. Giddens.

REGINA. Thank you, Mr. Marshall. We had been saving that bottle, hoping we could open it just for you.

ALEXANDRA (*as* ADDIE *comes to her with the tray*). Oh. May I *really*, Addie?

ADDIE. Better ask Mama.

ALEXANDRA. May I, Mama?

REGINA (*nods, smiles*). In Mr. Marshall's honor.

ALEXANDRA (*smiles*). Mr. Marshall, this will be the first taste of port I've ever had. (ADDIE *serves* LEO.)

MARSHALL. No one ever had their first taste of a better port. (*He lifts his glass in a toast; she lifts hers; they both drink.*) Well, I suppose it is all true, Mrs. Giddens.

REGINA. What is true?

MARSHALL. That you Southerners occupy a unique position in America. You live better than the rest of us, you eat better, you drink better. I wonder you find time, or want to find time, to do business.

BEN. A great many Southerners don't.

MARSHALL. Do all of you live here together?

REGINA. Here with me? (*Laughs.*) Oh, no. My brother Ben lives next door. My brother Oscar and his family live in the next square.

BEN. But we are a very close family. We've always wanted it that way.

MARSHALL. That is very pleasant. Keeping your family together to share each other's lives. My family moves around too much. My children seem never to come home. Away at school in the winter; in the summer, Europe with their mother—

REGINA (*eagerly*). Oh, yes. Even down here we read about Mrs. Marshall in the society pages.

MARSHALL. I dare say. She moves about a great deal. And all of you are part of the same business? Hubbard Sons?

BEN (*motions to* OSCAR). Oscar and me. (*Motions to* REGINA.) My sister's good husband is a banker.

MARSHALL (*looks at* REGINA, *surprised*). Oh.

REGINA. I am so sorry that my husband isn't here to meet you. He's been very ill. He is at Johns Hopkins. But he will be home soon. We think he is getting better now.

LEO. I work for Uncle Horace. (RE-GINA *looks at him.*) I mean I work for Uncle Horace at his bank. I keep an eye on things while he's away.

REGINA (*smiles*). Really, Leo?

BEN (*looks at* LEO, *then to* MARSHALL). Modesty in the young is as excellent as it is rare. (*Looks at* LEO *again.*)

OSCAR (*to* LEO). Your uncle means that a young man should speak more modestly.

LEO (*hastily, taking a step to* BEN). Oh, I didn't mean, sir—

MARSHALL. Oh, Mrs. Hubbard. Where's that Wagner autograph you promised to let me see? My train will be leaving soon and—

BIRDIE. The autograph? Oh. Well. Really, Mr. Marshall, I didn't mean to chatter so about it. Really I— (*Nervously, looking at* OSCAR.) You must excuse me. I didn't get it because, well, because I had—I—I had a little headache and—

Oscar. My wife is a miserable victim of headaches.

Regina (*quickly*). Mr. Marshall said at supper that he would like you to play for him, Alexandra.

Alexandra (*who has been looking at* Birdie). It's not I who play well, sir. It's my aunt. She plays just wonderfully. She's my teacher. (*Rises. Eagerly.*) May we play a duet? May we, Mama?

Birdie (*taking* Alexandra's *hand*). Thank you, dear. But I have my headache now. I—

Oscar (*sharply*). Don't be stubborn, Birdie. Mr. Marshall wants you to play.

Marshall. Indeed I do. If your headache isn't—

Birdie (*hesitates, then gets up, pleased*). But I'd like to, sir. Very much. (*She and* Alexandra *go to the piano.*)

Marshall. It's very remarkable how you Southern aristocrats have kept together. Kept together and kept what belonged to you.

Ben. You misunderstand, sir. Southern aristocrats have *not* kept together and have *not* kept what belonged to them.

Marshall (*laughs, indicates room*). You don't call this keeping what belongs to you?

Ben. But we are not aristocrats. (*Points to* Birdie *at the piano.*) Our brother's wife is the only one of us who belongs to the Southern aristocracy. (Birdie *looks toward* Ben.)

Marshall (*smiles*). My information is that you people have been here, and solidly here, for a long time.

Oscar. And so we have. Since our great-grandfather.

Ben (*smiles*). Who was *not* an aristocrat, like Birdie's.

Marshall (*a little sharply*). You make great distinctions.

Ben. Oh, they have been made for us. And maybe they are important distinctions. (*Leans forward, intimately.*) Now you take Birdie's family. When my great-grandfather came here they were the highest-tone plantation owners in this state.

Leo (*steps to* Marshall. *Proudly*).

My mother's grandfather was *governor* of the state before the war.

Oscar. They owned the plantation, Lionnet. You may have heard of it, sir?

Marshall (*laughs*). No, I've never heard of anything but brick houses on a lake, and cotton mills.

Ben. Lionnet in its day was the best cotton land in the South. It still brings us in a fair crop. (*Sits back.*) Ah, they were great days for those people—even when I can remember. They had the best of everything. (Birdie *turns to them.*) Cloth from Paris, trips to Europe, horses you can't raise any more, niggers to lift their fingers—

Birdie (*suddenly*). We were good to our people. Everybody knew that. We were better to them than— (Marshall *look up at* Birdie.)

Regina. Why, Birdie. You aren't playing.

Ben. But when the war comes these fine gentlemen ride off and leave the cotton, *and* the women, to rot.

Birdie. My father was killed in the war. He was a fine soldier, Mr. Marshall. A fine man.

Regina. Oh, certainly, Birdie. A famous soldier.

Ben (*to* Birdie). But that isn't the tale I am telling Mr. Marshall. (*To* Marshall.) Well, sir, the war ends. (Birdie *goes back to piano.*) Lionnet is almost ruined, and the sons finish ruining it. And there were thousands like them. Why? (*Leans forward.*) Because the Southern aristocrat can adapt himself to nothing. Too high-tone to try.

Marshall. Sometimes it is difficult to learn new ways. (Birdie *and* Alexandra *begin to play.* Marshall *leans forward, listening.*)

Ben. Perhaps, perhaps. (*He sees that* Marshall *is listening to the music. Irritated, he turns to* Birdie *and* Alexandra *at the piano, then back to* Marshall.) You're right, Mr. Marshall. It is difficult to learn new ways. But maybe that's why it's profitable. *Our* grandfather and *our* father learned the new ways and learned how to make them pay. (*Smiles nastily.*) *They* were in trade. Hubbard Sons, Merchandise. Others, Birdie's family, for example, looked down on them. (*Settles back in chair.*) To make a long story short, Lionnet now belongs to *us*. (BIRDIE *stops playing.*) Twenty years ago we took over their land, their cotton, and their daughter. (BIRDIE *rises and stands stiffly by the piano.* MARSHALL, *who has been watching her, rises.*)

MARSHALL. May I bring you a glass of port, Mrs. Hubbard?

BIRDIE (*softly*). No, thank you, sir. You are most polite.

REGINA (*sharply, to* BEN). You are boring Mr. Marshall with these ancient family tales.

BEN. I hope not. I hope not. I am trying to make an important point— (*Bows to* MARSHALL.) for our future business partner.

OSCAR (*to* MARSHALL). My brother always says that it's folks like us who have struggled and fought to bring to our land some of the prosperity of your land.

BEN. Some people call that patriotism.

REGINA (*laughs gaily*). I hope you don't find my brothers too obvious, Mr. Marshall. I'm afraid they mean that this is the time for the ladies to leave the gentlemen to talk business.

MARSHALL (*hastily*). Not at all. We settled everything this afternoon. (MARSHALL *looks at his watch.*) I have only a few minutes before I must leave for the train. (*Smiles at her.*) And I insist they be spent with you.

REGINA. *And* with another glass of port.

MARSHALL. Thank you.

BEN (*to* REGINA). My sister is right. (*To* MARSHALL.) I am a plain man and I am trying to say a plain thing. A man ain't only in business for what he can get out of it. It's got to give him something here. (*Puts hand to his breast.*) That's every bit as true for the nigger picking cotton for a silver quarter, as it is for you and me. (REGINA *gives* MARSHALL *a glass of port.*) If it don't give

him something here, then he don't pick the cotton right. Money isn't all. Not by three shots.

MARSHALL. Really? Well, I always thought it was a great deal.

REGINA. And so did I, Mr. Marshall.

MARSHALL (*leans forward. Pleasantly, but with meaning*). Now you don't have to convince me that you are the right people for the deal. I wouldn't be here if you hadn't convinced me six months ago. You want the mill here, and I want it here. It isn't my business to find out why you want it.

BEN. To bring the machine to the cotton, and not the cotton to the machine.

MARSHALL (*amused*). You have a turn for neat phrases, Hubbard. Well, however grand your reasons are, mine are simple: I want to make money and I believe I'll make it on you. (*As* BEN *starts to speak, he smiles.*) Mind you, I have no objections to more high-minded reasons. They are mighty valuable in business. It's fine to have partners who so closely follow the teachings of Christ. (*Gets up.*) And now I must leave for my train.

REGINA. I'm sorry you won't stay over with us, Mr. Marshall, but you'll come again. Any time you like.

BEN (*motions to* LEO, *indicating the bottle*). Fill them up, boy, fill them up. (LEO *moves around filling the glasses as* BEN *speaks.*) Down here, sir, we have a strange custom. We drink the *last* drink for a toast. That's to prove that the Southerner is always still on his feet for the last drink. (*Picks up his glass.*) It was Henry Frick, your Mr. Henry Frick, who said, "Railroads are the Rembrandts of investments." Well, *I* say, "Southern cotton mills *will be* the Rembrandts of investment." So I give you the firm of Hubbard Sons and Marshall, Cotton Mills, and to it a long and prosperous life. (*They all pick up their glasses.* MARSHALL *looks at them, amused. Then he, too, lifts his glass, smiles.*)

OSCAR. The children will drive you to the depot. Leo! Alexandra! You will drive Mr. Marshall down.

LEO (*eagerly, looks at* BEN *who nods*). Yes, sir. (*To* MARSHALL.) Not often Uncle Ben lets *me* drive the horses. And a beautiful pair they are. (*Starts for hall.*) Come on, Zan.

ALEXANDRA. May I drive tonight, Uncle Ben, please? I'd like to and—

BEN (*shakes his head, laughs*). In your evening clothes? Oh, no, my dear.

ALEXANDRA. But Leo always— (*Stops, exits quickly.*)

REGINA. I don't like to say good-bye to you, Mr. Marshall.

MARSHALL. Then we won't say good-bye. You have promised that you would come and let me show you Chicago. Do I have to make you promise again?

REGINA (*looks at him as he presses her hand*). I promise again.

MARSHALL (*touches her hand again, then moves to* BIRDIE). Good-bye, Mrs. Hubbard.

BIRDIE (*shyly, with sweetness and dignity*). Good-bye, sir.

MARSHALL (*as he passes* REGINA). Remember.

REGINA. I will.

OSCAR. We'll see you to the carriage. (MARSHALL *exits, followed by* BEN *and* OSCAR. *For a second* REGINA *and* BIRDIE *stand looking after them. Then* REGINA *throws up her arms, laughs happily.*)

REGINA. And there, Birdie, goes the man who has opened the door to our future.

BIRDIE (*surprised at the unaccustomed friendliness*). What?

REGINA (*turning to her*). *Our future.* Yours and mine, Ben's and Oscar's, the children— (*Looks at* BIRDIE's *puzzled face, laughs.*) Our future! (*Gaily.*) You were charming at supper, Birdie. Mr. Marshall certainly thought so.

BIRDIE (*pleased*). Why, Regina! Do you think he did?

REGINA. Can't you tell when you're being admired?

BIRDIE. Oscar said I bored Mr. Marshall. (*Then quietly.*) But he admired *you.* He told me so.

REGINA. What did he say?

BIRDIE. He said to me, "I hope your sister-in-law will come to Chicago. Chicago will be at her feet." He said the ladies would bow to your manners and the gentlemen to your looks.

REGINA. Did he? He seems a lonely man. Imagine being lonely with all that money. I don't think he likes his wife.

BIRDIE. Not like his wife? What a thing to say.

REGINA. She's away a great deal. He said that several times. And once he made fun of her being so social and high-tone. But that fits in all right. (*Sits back, arms on back of sofa, stretches.*) Her being social, I mean. She can introduce me. It won't take long with an introduction from her.

BIRDIE (*bewildered*). Introduce you? In Chicago? You mean you really might go? Oh, Regina, you can't leave here. What about Horace?

REGINA. Don't look so scared about everything, Birdie. I'm going to live in Chicago. I've always wanted to. And now there'll be plenty of money to go with.

BIRDIE. But Horace won't be able to move around. You know what the doctor wrote.

REGINA. There'll be millions, Birdie, millions. You know what I've always said when people told me we were rich? I said I think you should either be a nigger or a millionaire. In between, like us, what for? (*Laughs. Looks at* BIRDIE.) But I'm not going away tomorrow, Birdie. There's plenty of time to worry about Horace when he comes home. If he ever decides to come home.

BIRDIE. Will we be going to Chicago? I mean, Oscar and Leo and me?

REGINA. You? I shouldn't think so. (*Laughs.*) Well, we must remember tonight. It's a very important night and we mustn't forget it. We shall plan all the things we'd like to have and then we'll really have them. Make a wish, Birdie, any wish. It's bound to come true now. (BEN *and* OSCAR *enter.*)

BIRDIE (*laughs*). Well. Well, I don't know. Maybe. (REGINA *turns to look at* BEN.) Well, I guess I'd know right off what I wanted. (OSCAR *stands by the upper window, waves to the departing carriage.*)

REGINA (*looks up at* BEN, *smiles. He smiles back at her*). Well, you did it.

BEN. Looks like it might be we did.

REGINA (*springs up, laughs*). Looks like it! Don't pretend. You're like a cat who's been licking the cream. (*Crosses to wine bottle.*) Now we must all have a drink to celebrate.

OSCAR. The children, Alexandra and Leo, make a very handsome couple, Regina. Marshall remarked himself what fine young folks they were. How well they looked together!

REGINA (*sharply*). Yes. You said that before, Oscar.

BEN. Yes, sir. It's beginning to look as if the deal's all set. I may not be a subtle man—but— (*Turns to them. After a second.*) Now somebody ask me how I know the deal is set.

OSCAR. What do you mean, Ben?

BEN. You remember I told him that down here we drink the *last* drink for a toast?

OSCAR (*thoughtfully*). Yes. I never heard that before.

BEN. Nobody's ever heard it before. God forgives those who invent what they need. I already had his signature. But we've all done business with men whose word over a glass is better than a bond. Anyway it don't hurt to have both.

OSCAR (*turns to* REGINA). You understand what Ben means?

REGINA (*smiles*). Yes, Oscar. I understand. I understood immediately.

BEN (*looks at her admiringly*). Did you, Regina? Well, when he lifted his glass to drink, I closed my eyes and saw the bricks going into place.

REGINA. And *I* saw a lot more than that.

BEN. Slowly, slowly. As yet we have only our hopes.

REGINA. Birdie and I have just been planning what we want. I know what I want. What will you want, Ben?

BEN. Caution. Don't count the chickens. (*Leans back, laughs.*) Well, God would allow us a little daydreaming. Good for the soul when you've worked hard enough to deserve it. (*Pauses.*) I think I'll have a stable. For a long time I've had my good eyes on Carter's in Savannah. A rich man's pleasure, the sport of kings, why not the sport of Hubbards? Why not?

REGINA (*smiles*). Why not? What will you have, Oscar?

OSCAR. I don't know. (*Thoughtfully.*) The pleasure of seeing the bricks grow will be enough for me.

BEN. Oh, of course. Our greatest pleasure will be to see the bricks grow. But we are all entitled to a little side indulgence.

OSCAR. Yes, I suppose so. Well, then, I think we might take a few trips here and there, eh, Birdie?

BIRDIE (*surprised at being consulted*). Yes, Oscar. I'd like that.

OSCAR. We might even make a regular trip to Jekyll Island. I've heard the Cornelly place is for sale. We might think about buying it. Make a nice change. Do you good, Birdie, a change of climate. Fine shooting on Jekyll, the best.

BIRDIE. I'd like—

OSCAR (*indulgently*). What would you like?

BIRDIE. Two things. Two things I'd like most.

REGINA. Two! I should like a thousand. You are modest, Birdie.

BIRDIE (*warmly, delighted with the unexpected interest*). I should like to have Lionnet back. I know you own it now, but I'd like to see it fixed up again, the way Mama and Papa had it. Every year it used to get a nice coat of paint— Papa was very particular about the paint—and the lawn was so smooth all the way down to the river, with the trims of zinnias and red-feather plush. And the figs and blue little plums and the scuppernongs— (*Smiles. Turns to* REGINA.) The organ is still there and it wouldn't cost much to fix. We could have parties for Zan, the way Mama used to have for me.

BEN. That's a pretty picture, Birdie. Might be a most pleasant way to live.

(*Dismissing* BIRDIE.) What do you want, Regina?

BIRDIE (*very happily, not noticing that they are no longer listening to her*). I could have a cutting garden. Just where Mama's used to be. Oh, I do think we could be happier there. Papa used to say that *nobody* had ever lost their temper at Lionnet, and *nobody* ever would. Papa would never let anybody be nasty-spoken or mean. No, sir. He just didn't like it.

BEN. What do you want, Regina?

REGINA. I'm going to Chicago. And when I'm settled there and know the right people and the right things to buy —because I certainly don't now—I shall go to Paris and buy them. (*Laughs.*) I'm going to leave you and Oscar to count the bricks.

BIRDIE. Oscar. Please let me have Lionnet back.

OSCAR (*to* REGINA). You are serious about moving to Chicago?

BEN. She is going to see the great world and leave us in the little one. Well, we'll come and visit you and meet all the great and be proud you are our sister.

REGINA (*gaily*). Certainly. And you won't even have to learn to be subtle, Ben. Stay as you are. You will be rich and the rich don't have to be subtle.

OSCAR. But what about Alexandra? She's seventeen. Old enough to be thinking about marrying.

BIRDIE. And, Oscar, I have one more wish. Just one more wish.

OSCAR (*turns*). What is it, Birdie? What are you saying?

BIRDIE. I want you to stop shooting. I mean, so much. I don't like to see animals and birds killed just for the killing. You only throw them away—

BEN (*to* REGINA). It'll take a great deal of money to live as you're planning, Regina.

REGINA. Certainly. But there'll be plenty of money. You have estimated the profits very high.

BEN. I have—

BIRDIE (OSCAR *is looking at her furiously*). And you never let anybody else

shoot, and the niggers need it so much to keep from starving. It's wicked to shoot food just because you like to shoot, when poor people need it so—

BEN (*laughs*). I have estimated the profits very high—for myself.

REGINA. What did you say?

BIRDIE. I've always wanted to speak about it, Oscar.

OSCAR (*slowly, carefully*). What are you chattering about?

BIRDIE (*nervously*). I was talking about Lionnet and—and about your shooting—

OSCAR. You are exciting yourself.

REGINA (*to* BEN). I didn't hear you. There was so much talking.

OSCAR (*to* BIRDIE). You have been acting very childish, very excited, all evening.

BIRDIE. Regina asked me what I'd like.

REGINA. What did you say, Ben?

BIRDIE. Now that we'll be so rich everybody was saying what they would like, so *I* said what *I* would like, too.

BEN. I said— (*He is interrupted by* OSCAR.)

OSCAR (*to* BIRDIE). Very well. We've all heard you. That's enough now.

BEN. I am waiting. (*They stop.*) I am waiting for you to finish. You and Birdie. Four conversations are three too many. (BIRDIE *slowly sits down.* BEN *smiles, to* REGINA.) I said that I had, and I do, estimate the profits very high—for myself, and Oscar, of course.

REGINA (*slowly*). And what does that mean? (BEN *shrugs, looks toward* OSCAR.)

OSCAR (*looks at* BEN, *clears throat*). Well, Regina, it's like this. For forty-nine per cent Marshall will put up four hundred thousand dollars. For fifty-one per cent— (*Smiles archly.*) a controlling interest, mind you, we will put up two hundred and twenty-five thousand dollars besides offering him certain benefits that our (*Looks at* BEN.) local position allows us to manage. Ben means that two hundred and twenty-five thousand dollars is a lot of money.

REGINA. I know the terms and I know it's a lot of money.

BEN (*nodding*). It is.

OSCAR. Ben means that we are ready with our two-thirds of the money. Your third, Horace's I mean, doesn't seem to be ready. (*Raises his hand as* REGINA *starts to speak.*) Ben has written to Horace, I have written, and you have written. He answers. But he never mentions this business. Yet we have explained it to him in great detail, and told him the urgency. Still he never mentions it. Ben has been very patient, Regina. Naturally, you are our sister and we want you to benefit from anything we do.

REGINA. And in addition to your concern for me, you do not want control to go out of the family. (*To* BEN.) That right, Ben?

BEN. That's cynical. (*Smiles.*) Cynicism is an unpleasant way of saying the truth.

OSCAR. No need to be cynical. We'd have no trouble raising the third share, the share that you want to take.

REGINA. I am sure you could get the third share, the share you were saving for me. But that would give you a strange partner. And strange partners sometimes want a great deal. (*Smiles unpleasantly.*) But perhaps it would be wise for you to find him.

OSCAR. Now, now. Nobody says we *want* to do that. We would like to have you in and you would like to come in.

REGINA. Yes. I certainly would.

BEN (*laughs, puts up his hand*). But we haven't heard from Horace.

REGINA. I've given my word that Horace will put up the money. That should be enough.

BEN. Oh, it was enough. I took your word. But I've got to have more than your word now. The contracts will be signed this week, and Marshall will want to see our money soon after. Regina, Horace has been in Baltimore for five months. I know that you've written him to come home, and that he hasn't come.

OSCAR. It's beginning to look as if he doesn't want to come home.

REGINA. Of course he wants to come home. You can't move around with heart trouble at any moment you choose. You know what doctors are like once

they get their hands on a case like this—

OSCAR. They can't very well keep him from answering letters, can they? (REGINA *turns to* BEN.) They couldn't keep him from arranging for the money if he wanted to—

REGINA. Has it occurred to you that Horace is also a good businessman?

BEN. Certainly. He is a shrewd trader. Always has been. The bank is proof of that.

REGINA. Then, possibly, he may be keeping silent because he doesn't think he is getting enough for his money. (*Looks at* OSCAR.) Seventy-five thousand he has to put up. That's a lot of money, too.

OSCAR. Nonsense. He knows a good thing when he hears it. He knows that we can make *twice* the profit on cotton goods manufactured here than can be made in the North.

BEN. That isn't what Regina means. (*Smiles.*) May I interpret you, Regina? (*To* OSCAR.) Regina is saying that Horace wants *more* than a third of our share.

OSCAR. But he's only putting up a third of the money. You put up a third and you get a third. What else could he expect?

REGINA. Well, *I* don't know. I don't know about these things. It would seem that if you put up a third you should only get a third. But then again, there's no law about it, is there? I should think that if you knew your money was very badly needed, well, you just might say, I want more, I want a bigger share. You boys have done that. I've heard you say so.

BEN (*after a pause, laughs*). So you believe he has deliberately held out? For a larger share? (*Leaning forward.*) Well, I don't believe it. But I do believe that's what *you* want. Am I right, Regina?

REGINA. Oh, I shouldn't like to be too definite. But I could say that I wouldn't like to persuade Horace unless he did get a larger share. I must look after his interests. It seems only natural—

OSCAR. And where would the larger share come from?

REGINA. I don't know. That's not my

business. (*Giggles.*) But perhaps it could come off your share, Oscar. (REGINA *and* BEN *laugh.*)

OSCAR (*rises and wheels furiously on both of them as they laugh*). What kind of talk is this?

BEN. I haven't said a thing.

OSCAR (*to* REGINA). *You* are talking very big tonight.

REGINA (*stops laughing*). Am I? Well, you should know me well enough to know that I wouldn't be asking for things I didn't think I could get.

OSCAR. Listen. I don't believe you can even get Horace to come home, much less get money from him or talk quite so big about what you want.

REGINA. Oh, I can get him home.

OSCAR. Then why haven't you?

REGINA. I thought I should fight his battles for him, before he came home. Horace is a very sick man. And even if *you* don't care how sick he is, I do.

BEN. Stop this foolish squabbling. How can you get him home?

REGINA. I will send Alexandra to Baltimore. She will ask him to come home. She will say that she wants him to come home, and that *I* want him to come home.

BIRDIE (*suddenly*). Well, of course she wants him here, but he's sick and maybe he's happy where he is.

REGINA (*ignores* BIRDIE, *to* BEN). You agree that he will come home if she asks him to, if she says that I miss him and want him—

BEN (*looks at her, smiles*). I admire you, Regina. And I agree. That's settled now and— (*Starts to rise.*)

REGINA (*quickly*). But before she brings him home, I want to know what he's going to get.

BEN. What do you want?

REGINA. Twice what you offered.

BEN. Well, you won't get it.

OSCAR (*to* REGINA). I think you've gone crazy.

REGINA. I don't want to fight, Ben—

BEN. I don't either. You won't get it. There isn't any chance of that. (*Roguishly.*) You're holding us up, and that's not pretty, Regina, not pretty. (*Holds up his hand as he sees she is about to speak.*) But we need you, and I don't want to fight. Here's what I'll do: I'll give Horace forty per cent, instead of the thirty-three and a third he really should get. I'll do that, provided he is home and his money is up within two weeks. How's that?

REGINA. All right.

OSCAR. I've asked before: where is this extra share coming from?

BEN (*pleasantly*). From you. From your share.

OSCAR (*furiously*). From me, is it? That's just fine and dandy. That's my reward. For thirty-five years I've worked my hands to the bone for you. For thirty-five years I've done all the things you didn't want to do. And this is what I—

BEN (*turns slowly to look at* OSCAR. OSCAR *breaks off*). My, my. I am being attacked tonight on all sides. First by my sister, then by my brother. And I ain't a man who likes being attacked. I can't believe that God wants the strong to parade their strength, but I don't mind doing it if it's got to be done. (*Leans back in his chair.*) You ought to take things better, Oscar. I've made you money in the past. I'm going to make you more money now. You'll be a very rich man. What's the difference to any of us if a little more goes here, a little less goes there—it's all in the family. And it will stay in the family. I'll never marry. (ADDIE *enters, begins to gather the glasses from the table.* OSCAR *turns to* BEN.) So my money will go to Alexandra and Leo. They may even marry some day and— (ADDIE *looks at* BEN.)

BIRDIE (*rising*). Marry—Zan and Leo—

OSCAR (*carefully*). That would make a great difference in my feelings. If they married.

BEN. Yes, that's what I mean. Of course it would make a difference.

OSCAR (*carefully*). Is that what *you* mean, Regina?

REGINA. Oh, it's too far away. We'll talk about it in a few years.

OSCAR. I want to talk about it now.

BEN (*nods*). Naturally.

REGINA. There's a lot of things to consider. They are first cousins, and—

OSCAR. That isn't unusual. Our grandmother and grandfather were first cousins.

REGINA (giggles). And look at us. (BEN giggles.)

OSCAR (angrily). You're both being very gay with my money.

BEN (sighs). These quarrels. I dislike them so. (Leans forward to REGINA.) A marriage might be a very wise arrangement, for several reasons. And then, Oscar has given up something for you. You should try to manage something for him.

REGINA. I haven't said I was opposed to it. But Leo is a wild boy. There were those times when he took a little money from the bank and—

OSCAR. That's all past history—

REGINA. Oh, I know. And I know all young men are wild. I'm only mentioning it to show you that there are considerations—

BEN (irritated because she does not understand that he is trying to keep OSCAR quiet). All right, so there are. But please assure Oscar that you will think about it very seriously.

REGINA (smiles, nods). Very well. I assure Oscar that I will think about it seriously.

OSCAR (sharply). That is not an answer.

REGINA (rises). My, you're in a bad humor and you shall put me in one. I have said all that I am willing to say now. After all, Horace has to give his consent, too.

OSCAR. Horace will do what you tell him to.

REGINA. Yes, I think he will.

OSCAR. And I have your word that you will try to—

REGINA (patiently). Yes, Oscar. You have my word that I will think about it. Now do leave me alone. (There is the sound of the front door being closed.)

BIRDIE. I—Alexandra is only seventeen. She—

REGINA (calling). Alexandra? Are you back?

ALEXANDRA. Yes, Mama.

LEO (comes into the room). Mr. Marshall got off safe and sound. Weren't those fine clothes he had? You can always spot clothes made in a good place. Looks like maybe they were done in England. Lots of men in the North send all the way to England for their stuff.

BEN (to LEO). Were you careful driving the horses?

LEO. Oh, yes, sir. I was. (ALEXANDRA has come in on BEN's question, hears the answer, looks angrily at LEO.)

ALEXANDRA. It's a lovely night. You should have come, Aunt Birdie.

REGINA. Were you gracious to Mr. Marshall?

ALEXANDRA. I think so, Mama. I liked him.

REGINA. Good. And now I have great news for you. You are going to Baltimore in the morning to bring your father home.

ALEXANDRA (gasps, then delighted). Me? Papa said I should come? That must mean— (Turns to ADDIE.) Addie, he must be well. Think of it, he'll be back home again. We'll bring him home.

REGINA. You are going alone, Alexandra.

ADDIE (ALEXANDRA has turned in surprise). Going alone? Going by herself? A child that age! Mr. Horace ain't going to like Zan traipsing up there by herself.

REGINA (sharply). Go upstairs and lay out Alexandra's things.

ADDIE. He'd expect me to be along—

REGINA. I'll be up in a few minutes to tell you what to pack. (ADDIE slowly begins to climb the steps. To ALEXANDRA.) I should think you'd like going alone. At your age it certainly would have delighted me. You're a strange girl, Alexandra. Addie has babied you so much.

ALEXANDRA. I only thought it would be more fun if Addie and I went together.

BIRDIE (timidly). Maybe I could go with her, Regina. I'd really like to.

REGINA. She is going alone. She is getting old enough to take some responsibilities.

OSCAR. She'd better learn now. She's almost old enough to get married. (*Jovially*, *to* LEO, *slapping him on shoulder*.) Eh, son?

LEO. Huh?

OSCAR (*annoyed with* LEO *for not understanding*). Old enough to get married, you're thinking, eh?

LEO. Oh, yes, sir. (*Feebly*.) Lots of girls get married at Zan's age. Look at Mary Prester and Johanna and—

REGINA. Well, she's not getting married tomorrow. But she is going to Baltimore tomorrow, so let's talk about that. (*To* ALEXANDRA.) You'll be glad to have Papa home again.

ALEXANDRA. I wanted to go before, Mama. You remember that. But you said *you* couldn't go, and that *I* couldn't go alone.

REGINA. I've changed my mind. (*Too casually*.) You're to tell Papa how much you missed him, and that he must come home now—for your sake. Tell him that you *need* him home.

ALEXANDRA. Need him home? I don't understand.

REGINA. There is nothing for you to understand. You are simply to say what I have told you.

BIRDIE (*rises*). He may be too sick. She couldn't do that—

ALEXANDRA. Yes. He may be too sick to travel. I couldn't make him think he had to come home for me, if he is too sick to—

REGINA (*looks at her, sharply, challengingly*). You *couldn't* do what I tell you to do, Alexandra?

ALEXANDRA (*quietly*). No. I couldn't. If I thought it would hurt him.

REGINA (*after a second's silence, smiles pleasantly*). But you are doing this for Papa's own good. (*Takes* ALEXANDRA'S *hand*.) You must let me be the judge of his condition. It's the best possible cure for him to come home and be taken care of here. He mustn't stay there any longer and listen to those alarmist doctors. You are doing this entirely for his sake. Tell your papa that I want him to come home, that I miss him very much.

ALEXANDRA (*slowly*). Yes, Mama.

REGINA (*to the others. Rises*). I must go and start getting Alexandra ready now. Why don't you all go home?

BEN (*rises*). I'll attend to the railroad ticket. One of the boys will bring it over. Good night, everybody. Have a nice trip, Alexandra. The food on the train is very good. The celery is so crisp. Have a good time and act like a little lady. (*Exits*.)

REGINA. Good night, Ben. Good night, Oscar— (*Playfully*.) Don't be so glum, Oscar. It makes you look as if you had chronic indigestion.

BIRDIE. Good night, Regina.

REGINA. Good night, Birdie. (*Exits upstairs*.)

OSCAR (*starts for hall*). Come along.

LEO (*to* ALEXANDRA). Imagine your not wanting to go! What a little fool you are. Wish it were me. What I could do in a place like Baltimore!

ALEXANDRA (*angrily, looking away from him*). Mind your business. I can guess the kind of things *you* could do.

LEO (*laughs*). Oh, no, you couldn't. (*He exits*.)

REGINA (*calling from the top of the stairs*). Come on, Alexandra.

BIRDIE (*quickly, softly*). Zan.

ALEXANDRA. I don't understand about my going, Aunt Birdie. (*Shrugs*.) But anyway, Papa will be home again. (*Pats* BIRDIE'S *arm*.) Don't worry about me. I can take care of myself. Really I can.

BIRDIE (*shakes her head, softly*). That's not what I'm worried about. Zan—

ALEXANDRA (*comes close to her*). What's the matter?

BIRDIE. It's about Leo—

ALEXANDRA (*whispering*). He beat the horses. That's why we were late getting back. We had to wait until they cooled off. He always beats the horses as if—

BIRDIE (*whispering frantically, holding* ALEXANDRA'S *hands*). He's my son. My own son. But you are more to me—more to me than my own child. I love you more than anybody else—

ALEXANDRA. Don't worry about the horses. I'm sorry I told you.

BIRDIE (*her voice rising*). *I am not worrying about the horses. I am worry-*

ing about *you*. You are *not* going to marry Leo. I am not going to let them do that to you—

ALEXANDRA. Marry? To Leo? (*Laughs.*) I wouldn't marry, Aunt Birdie. I've never even thought about it—

BIRDIE. But they have thought about it. (*Wildly.*) Zan, I couldn't stand to think about such a thing. You and— (OSCAR *has come into the doorway on* ALEXANDRA's *speech. He is standing quietly, listening.*)

ALEXANDRA (*laughs*). But I'm not going to marry. And I'm certainly not going to marry Leo.

BIRDIE. Don't you understand? They'll make you. They'll make you—

ALEXANDRA (*takes* BIRDIE's *hands, quietly, firmly*). That's foolish, Aunt Birdie. I'm grown now. Nobody can make me do anything.

BIRDIE. I just couldn't stand—

OSCAR (*sharply*). Birdie. (BIRDIE *looks up, draws quickly away from* ALEXANDRA. *She stands rigid, frightened. Quietly.*) Birdie, get your hat and coat.

ADDIE (*calls from upstairs*). Come on, baby. Your mama's waiting for you, and she ain't nobody to keep waiting.

ALEXANDRA. All right. (*Then softly, embracing* BIRDIE.) Good night, Aunt Birdie. (*As she passes* OSCAR.) Good night, Uncle Oscar. (BIRDIE *begins to move slowly toward the door as* ALEXANDRA *climbs the stairs.* ALEXANDRA *is almost out of view when* BIRDIE *reaches* OSCAR *in the doorway. As* BIRDIE *quickly attempts to pass him, he slaps her hard, across the face.* BIRDIE *cries out, puts her hand to her face. On the cry,* ALEXANDRA *turns, begins to run down the stairs.*) Aunt Birdie! What happened? What happened? I—

BIRDIE (*softly, without turning*). Nothing, darling. Nothing happened. (*Quickly, as if anxious to keep* ALEXANDRA *from coming close.*) Now go to bed. (OSCAR *exits.*) Nothing happened. I only—I only twisted my ankle. (*She goes out.* ALEXANDRA *stands on the stairs looking after her as if she were puzzled and frightened.*)

CURTAIN

ACT TWO

SCENE: *Same as Act One. A week later, morning.*

AT RISE: *The light comes from the open shutter of the right window; the other shutters are tightly closed.* ADDIE *is standing at the window, looking out. Near the dining-room doors are brooms, mops, rags, etc. After a second,* OSCAR *comes into the entrance hall, looks in the room, shivers, decides not to take his hat and coat off, comes into the room. At the sound of the door,* ADDIE *turns.*

ADDIE (*without interest*). Oh, it's you, Mr. Oscar.

OSCAR. What is this? It's not night. What's the matter here? (*Shivers.*) Fine thing at this time of the morning. Blinds all closed. (ADDIE *begins to open shutters.*) Where's Miss Regina? It's cold in here.

ADDIE. Miss Regina ain't down yet.

OSCAR. She had any word?

ADDIE (*wearily*). No, sir.

OSCAR. Wouldn't you think a girl that age could get on a train at one place and have sense enough to get off at another?

ADDIE. Something must have happened. If Zan say she was coming last night, she's coming last night. Unless something happened. Sure-fire disgrace to let a baby like that go all that way alone to bring home a sick man without—

OSCAR. You do a lot of judging around here, Addie, eh? Judging of your white folks, I mean.

ADDIE (*looks at him, sighs*). I'm tired. I been up all night watching for them.

REGINA (*speaking from the upstairs hall*). Who's downstairs, Addie? (*She appears in a dressing gown, peers down from the landing.* ADDIE *picks up broom, dustpan and brush and exits.*) Oh, it's you, Oscar. What are you doing here so early? I haven't been down yet. I'm not finished dressing.

OSCAR (*speaking up to her*). You had any word from them?

REGINA. No.

OSCAR. Then something certainly has happened. People don't just say they are arriving on Thursday night, and they haven't come by Friday morning.

REGINA. Oh, nothing has happened. Alexandra just hasn't got sense enough to send a message.

OSCAR. If nothing's happened, then why aren't they here?

REGINA. You asked me that ten times last night. My, you do fret so, Oscar. Anything might have happened. They may have missed connections in Atlanta, the train may have been delayed—oh, a hundred things could have kept them.

OSCAR. Where's Ben?

REGINA (*as she disappears upstairs*). Where should he be? At home, probably. Really, Oscar, I don't tuck him in his bed and I don't take him out of it. Have some coffee and don't worry so much.

OSCAR. Have some coffee? There isn't any coffee. (*Looks at his watch, shakes his head. After a second* CAL *enters with a large silver tray, coffee urn, small cups, newspaper.*) Oh, there you are. Is everything in this fancy house always late?

CAL (*looks at him surprised*). You ain't out shooting this morning, Mr. Oscar?

OSCAR. First day I missed since I had my head cold. First day I missed in eight years.

CAL. Yes, sir. I bet you. Simon he say you had a mighty good day yesterday morning. That's what Simon say. (*Brings* OSCAR *coffee and newspaper.*)

OSCAR. Pretty good, pretty good.

CAL (*laughs, slyly*). Bet you got enough bobwhite and squirrel to give every nigger in town a Jesus-party. Most of 'em ain't had no meat since the cotton picking was over. Bet they'd give anything for a little piece of that meat—

OSCAR (*turns his head to look at* CAL). Cal, if I catch a nigger in this town going shooting, you know what's going to happen. (LEO *enters.*)

CAL (*hastily*). Yes, sir, Mr. Oscar. I didn't say nothing about nothing. It was Simon who told me and— Morning, Mr. Leo. You gentlemen having your breakfast with us here?

LEO. The boys in the bank don't know a thing. They haven't had any message. (CAL *waits for an answer, gets none, shrugs, moves to door, exits.*)

OSCAR (*peers at* LEO). What you doing here, son?

LEO. You told me to find out if the boys at the bank had any message from Uncle Horace or Zan—

OSCAR. I told you if they had a message to bring it here. I told you that if they didn't have a message to stay at the bank and do your work.

LEO. Oh, I guess I misunderstood.

OSCAR. You didn't misunderstand. You just were looking for any excuse to take an hour off. (LEO *pours a cup of coffee.*) You got to stop that kind of thing. You got to start settling down. You going to be a married man one of these days.

LEO. Yes, sir.

OSCAR. You also got to stop with that woman in Mobile. (*As* LEO *is about to speak.*) You're young and I haven't got no objections to outside women. That is, I haven't got no objections so long as they don't interfere with serious things. Outside women are all right in their place, but *now* isn't their place. You got to realize that.

LEO (*nods*). Yes, sir. I'll tell her. She'll act all right about it.

OSCAR. Also, you got to start working harder at the bank. You got to convince your Uncle Horace you going to make a fit husband for Alexandra.

LEO. What do you think has happened to them? Supposed to be here last night— (*Laughs.*) Bet you Uncle Ben's mighty worried. Seventy-five thousand dollars worried.

OSCAR (*smiles happily*). Ought to be worried. Damn well ought to be. First he don't answer the letters, then he don't come home— (*Giggles.*)

LEO. What will happen if Uncle Horace don't come home or don't—

OSCAR. Or don't put up the money? Oh, we'll get it from outside. Easy enough.

LEO (*surprised*). But *you* don't want outsiders.

OSCAR. What do I care who gets my share? I been shaved already. Serve Ben right if he had to give away some of his.

LEO. Damn shame what they did to you.

OSCAR (*looking up the stairs*). Don't talk so loud. Don't you worry. When I die, you'll have as much as the rest. You might have yours *and* Alexandra's. I'm not so easily licked.

LEO. I wasn't thinking of myself, Papa—

OSCAR. Well, you should be, you should be. It's every man's duty to think of himself.

LEO. You think Uncle Horace don't want to go in on this?

OSCAR (*giggles*). That's my hunch. He hasn't showed any signs of loving it yet.

LEO (*laughs*). But he hasn't listened to Aunt Regina yet, either. Oh, he'll go along. It's too good a thing. Why wouldn't he want to? He's got plenty and plenty to invest with. He don't even have to sell anything. Eighty-eight thousand worth of Union Pacific bonds sitting right in his safe deposit box. All he's got to do is open the box.

OSCAR (*after a pause. Looks at his watch*). Mighty late breakfast in this fancy house. Yes, he's had those bonds for fifteen years. Bought them when they were low and just locked them up.

LEO. Yeah. Just has to open the box and take them out. That's all. Easy as easy can be. (*Laughs.*) The things in that box! There's all those bonds, looking mighty fine. (OSCAR *slowly puts down his newspaper and turns to* LEO.) Then right next to them is a baby shoe of Zan's and a cheap old cameo on a string, and, *and*—nobody'd believe this— a piece of an old violin. Not even a whole violin. Just a piece of an old thing, a piece of a violin.

OSCAR (*very softly, as if he were trying to control his voice*). A piece of a violin! What do you think of that!

LEO. Yes, sirree. A lot of other crazy things, too. A poem, I guess it is, signed with his mother's name, and two old schoolbooks with notes and— (LEO *catches* OSCAR's *look. His voice trails off. He turns his head away.*)

OSCAR (*very softly*). How do you know what's in the box, son?

LEO (*stops, draws back, frightened, realizing what he has said*). Oh, well. Well, er. Well, one of the boys, sir. It was one of the boys at the bank. He took old Manders' keys. It was Joe Horns. He just up and took Manders' keys and, and—well, took the box out. (*Quickly.*) Then they all asked me if I wanted to see, too. So I looked a little, I guess, but then I made them close up the box quick and I told them never—

OSCAR (*looks at him*). Joe Horns, you say? He opened it?

LEO. Yes, sir, yes, he did. My word of honor. (*Very nervously looking away.*) I suppose that don't excuse *me* for looking— (*Looking at* OSCAR.) but I did make him close it up and put the keys back in Manders' drawer—

OSCAR (*leans forward, very softly*). Tell me the truth, Leo. I am not going to be angry with you. Did you open the box yourself?

LEO. *No, sir, I didn't.* I told you I didn't. No, I—

OSCAR (*irritated, patient*). I am *not* going to be angry with you. (*Watching* LEO *carefully.*) Sometimes a young fellow deserves credit for looking round him to see what's going on. Sometimes that's a good sign in a fellow your age. (OSCAR *rises.*) Many great men have made their fortune with their eyes. Did you open the box?

LEO (*very puzzled*). No. I—

OSCAR (*moves to* LEO). Did you open the box? It may have been—well, it may have been a good thing if you had.

LEO (*after a long pause*). I opened it.

OSCAR (*quickly*). Is that the truth?

(LEO *nods.*) Does anybody else know that you opened it? Come, Leo, don't be afraid of speaking the truth to me.

LEO. No. Nobody knew. Nobody was in the bank when I did it. But—

OSCAR. Did your Uncle Horace ever know you opened it?

LEO (*shakes his head*). He only looks in it once every six months when he cuts the coupons, and sometimes Manders even does that for him. Uncle Horace don't even have the keys. Manders keeps them for him. Imagine not looking at all that. You can bet if I had the bonds, I'd watch 'em like—

OSCAR. If you had them. (LEO *watches him.*) *If* you had them. Then you could have a share in the mill, you and me. A fine, big share, too. (*Pauses, shrugs.*) Well, a man can't be shot for wanting to see his son get on in the world, can he, boy?

LEO (*looks up, begins to understand*). No, he can't. Natural enough. (*Laughs.*) But I haven't got the bonds and Uncle Horace has. And now he can just sit back and wait to be a millionaire.

OSCAR (*innocently*). You think your Uncle Horace likes you well enough to lend you the bonds if he decides not to use them himself?

LEO. Papa, it must be that you haven't had your breakfast! (*Laughs loudly.*) Lend me the bonds! My God—

OSCAR (*disappointed*). No, I suppose not. Just a fancy of mine. A loan for three months, maybe four, easy enough for us to pay it back then. Anyway, this is only April— (*Slowly counting the months on his fingers.*) and if he doesn't look at them until fall, he wouldn't even miss them out of the box.

LEO. That's it. He wouldn't even miss them. Ah, well—

OSCAR. No, sir. Wouldn't even miss them. How could he miss them if he never looks at them? (*Sighs as LEO stares at him.*) Well, here we are sitting around waiting for him to come home and invest his money in something he hasn't lifted his hand to get. But I can't help thinking he's acting strange. You laugh when I say he could lend you the bonds if he's not going to use them himself. But would it hurt him?

LEO (*slowly looking at* OSCAR). No. No, it wouldn't.

OSCAR. People ought to help other people. But that's not always the way it happens. (BEN *enters, hangs his coat and hat in hall. Very carefully.*) And so sometimes you got to think of yourself. (*As* LEO *stares at him,* BEN *appears in the doorway.*) Morning, Ben.

BEN (*coming in, carrying his newspaper*). Fine sunny morning. Any news from the runaways?

REGINA (*on the staircase*). There's no news or you would have heard it. Quite a convention so early in the morning, aren't you all? (*Goes to coffee urn.*)

OSCAR. You rising mighty late these days. Is that the way they do things in Chicago society?

BEN (*looking at his paper*). Old Carter died up in Senateville. Eighty-one is a good time for us all, eh? What do you think has really happened to Horace, Regina?

REGINA. Nothing.

BEN (*too casually*). You don't think maybe he never started from Baltimore and never intends to start?

REGINA (*irritated*). Of course they've started. Didn't I have a letter from Alexandra? What is so strange about people arriving late? He has that cousin in Savannah he's so fond of. He may have stopped to see him. They'll be along today some time, very flattered that you and Oscar are so worried about them.

BEN. I'm a natural worrier. Especially when I am getting ready to close a business deal and one of my partners remains silent *and* invisible.

REGINA (*laughs*). Oh, is that it? I thought you were worried about Horace's health.

OSCAR. Oh, that too. Who could help but worry? I'm worried. This is the first day I haven't shot since my head cold.

REGINA (*starts toward dining room*). Then you haven't had your breakfast. Come along. (OSCAR *and* LEO *follow her.*)

BEN. Regina. (*She turns at dining-*

room door.) That cousin of Horace's has been dead for years and, in any case, the train does not go through Savannah.

REGINA (laughs, continues into dining-room, seats herself). Did he die? You're always remembering about people dying. (BEN rises.) Now I intend to eat my breakfast in peace, and read my newspaper.

BEN (goes toward dining room as he talks). This is second breakfast for me. My first was bad. Celia ain't the cook she used to be. Too old to have taste any more. If she hadn't belonged to Mama, I'd send her off to the country. (OSCAR and LEO start to eat. BEN seats himself.)

LEO. Uncle Horace will have some tales to tell, I bet. Baltimore is a lively town.

REGINA (to CAL). The grits isn't hot enough. Take it back.

CAL. Oh, yes'm. (Calling into the kitchen as he exits.) Grits didn't hold the heat. Grits didn't hold the heat.

LEO. When I was at school three of the boys and myself took a train once and went over to Baltimore. It was so big we thought we were in Europe. I was just a kid then—

REGINA. I find it very pleasant (ADDIE enters.) to have breakfast alone. I hate chattering before I've had something hot. (CAL closes the dining-room doors.) Do be still, Leo. (ADDIE comes into the room, begins gathering up the cups, carries them to the large tray. Outside there are the sounds of voices. Quickly ADDIE runs into the hall. A few seconds later she appears again in the doorway, her arm around the shoulders of HORACE GIDDENS, supporting him. HORACE is a tall man of about forty-five. He has been good looking, but now his face is tired and ill. He walks stiffly, as if it were an enormous effort, and carefully, as if he were unsure of his balance. ADDIE takes off his overcoat and hangs it on the hall tree. She then helps him to a chair.)

HORACE. How are you, Addie? How have you been?

ADDIE. I'm all right, Mr. Horace. I've just been worried about you. (ALEX-

ANDRA enters. She is flushed and excited, her hat awry, her face dirty. Her arms are full of packages, but she comes quickly to ADDIE.)

ALEXANDRA. Don't tell me how worried you were. We couldn't help it and there was no way to send a message.

ADDIE (begins to take packages from ALEXANDRA). Yes, sir, I was mighty worried.

ALEXANDRA. We had to stop in Mobile over night. Papa— (Looks at him.) Papa didn't feel well. The trip was too much for him, and I made him stop and rest— (As ADDIE takes the last package.) No, don't take that. That's father's medicine. I'll hold it. It mustn't break. Now, about the stuff outside. Papa must have his wheel chair. I'll get that and the valises—

ADDIE (very happy, holding ALEXANDRA's arms). Since when you got to carry your own valises? Since when I ain't old enough to hold a bottle of medicine? (HORACE coughs.) You feel all right, Mr. Horace?

HORACE (nods). Glad to be sitting down.

ALEXANDRA (opening package of medicine). He doesn't feel all right. (ADDIE looks at her, then at HORACE.) He just says that. The trip was very hard on him, and now he must go right to bed.

ADDIE (looking at him carefully). Them fancy doctors, they give you help?

HORACE. They did their best.

ALEXANDRA (has become conscious of the voices in the dining room). I bet Mama was worried. I better tell her we're here now. (She starts for door.)

HORACE. Zan. (She stops.) Not for a minute, dear.

ALEXANDRA. Oh, Papa, you feel bad again. I knew you did. Do you want your medicine?

HORACE. No, I don't feel that way. I'm just tired, darling. Let me rest a little.

ALEXANDRA. Yes, but Mama will be mad if I don't tell her we're here.

ADDIE. They're all in there eating breakfast.

ALEXANDRA. Oh, are they all here?

Why do they *always* have to be here? I was hoping Papa wouldn't have to see anybody, that it would be nice for him and quiet.

ADDIE. Then let your papa rest for a minute.

HORACE. Addie, I bet your coffee's as good as ever. They don't have such good coffee up north. (*Looks at the urn.*) Is it as good, Addie? (ADDIE *starts for coffee urn.*)

ALEXANDRA. No. Dr. Reeves said not much coffee. Just now and then. I'm the nurse now, Addie.

ADDIE. You'd be a better one if you didn't look so dirty. Now go and take a bath. Change your linens, get out a fresh dress and give your hair a good brushing—go on—

ALEXANDRA. Will you be all right, Papa?

ADDIE. Go on.

ALEXANDRA (*on stairs, talks as she goes up*). The pills Papa must take once every four hours. And the bottle only when—only if he feels very bad. Now don't move until I come back and don't talk much and remember about his medicine, Addie—

ADDIE. Ring for Belle and have her help you and then I'll make you a fresh breakfast.

ALEXANDRA (*as she disappears*). How's Aunt Birdie? Is she here?

ADDIE. It ain't right for you to have coffee? It will hurt you?

HORACE (*slowly*). Nothing can make much difference now. Get me a cup, Addie. (*She looks at him, crosses to urn, pours a cup.*) Funny. They can't make coffee up north. (ADDIE *brings him a cup.*) They don't like red pepper, either. (*He takes the cup and gulps it greedily.*) God, that's good. You remember how I used to drink it? Ten, twelve cups a day. So strong it had to stain the cup. (*Then slowly.*) Addie, before I see anybody else, I want to know why Zan came to fetch me home. She's tried to tell me, but she doesn't seem to know herself.

ADDIE (*turns away*). I don't know. All I know is big things are going on. Every-body going to be high-tone rich. Big rich. You too. All because smoke's going to start out of a building that ain't even up yet.

HORACE. I've heard about it.

ADDIE. And, er— (*Hesitates—steps to him.*) And—well, Zan, she going to marry Mr. Leo in a little while.

HORACE (*looks at her, then very slowly*). What are you talking about?

ADDIE. That's right. That's the talk, God help us.

HORACE (*angrily*). *What's* the talk?

ADDIE. I'm telling you. There's going to be a wedding— (*Angrily turns away.*) Over my dead body there is.

HORACE (*after a second, quietly*). Go and tell them I'm home.

ADDIE (*hesitates*). Now you ain't to get excited. You're to be in your bed—

HORACE. Go on, Addie. Go and say I'm back. (ADDIE *opens dining-room doors. He rises with difficulty, stands stiff, as if he were in pain, facing the dining room.*)

ADDIE. Miss Regina. They're home. They got here—

REGINA. Horace! (REGINA *quickly rises, runs into the room. Warmly.*) Horace! You've finally arrived. (*As she kisses him, the others come forward, all talking together.*)

BEN (*in doorway, carrying a napkin*). Well, sir, you had us all mighty worried. (*He steps forward. They shake hands. ADDIE exits.*)

OSCAR. You're a sight for sore eyes.

HORACE. Hello, Ben. (LEO *enters, eating a biscuit.*)

OSCAR. And how you feel? Tip-top, I bet, because that's the way you're looking.

HORACE (*coldly, irritated with OSCAR's lie*). Hello, Oscar. Hello, Leo, how are you?

LEO (*shaking hands*). I'm fine, sir. But a lot better now that you're back.

REGINA. Now sit down. What did happen to you and where's Alexandra? I am so excited about seeing you that I almost forgot about her.

HORACE. I didn't feel good, a little

weak, I guess, and we stopped over night to rest. Zan's upstairs washing off the train dirt.

REGINA. Oh, I am so sorry the trip was hard on you. I didn't think that—

HORACE. Well, it's just as if I had never been away. All of you here—

BEN. Waiting to welcome you home. (BIRDIE *bursts in. She is wearing a flannel kimono and her face is flushed and excited.*)

BIRDIE (*runs to him, kisses him*). Horace!

HORACE (*warmly pressing her arm*). I was just wondering where you were, Birdie.

BIRDIE (*excited*). Oh, I would have been here. I didn't know you were back until Simon said he saw the buggy. (*She draws back to look at him. Her face sobers.*) Oh, you don't look well, Horace. No, you don't.

REGINA (*laughs*). Birdie, what a thing to say—

HORACE (*looking at* OSCAR). Oscar thinks I look very well.

OSCAR (*annoyed. Turns on* LEO). Don't stand there holding that biscuit in your hand.

LEO. Oh, well. I'll just finish my breakfast, Uncle Horace, and then I'll give you all the news about the bank— (*He exits into the dining room.*)

OSCAR. And what is that costume you have on?

BIRDIE (*looking at* HORACE). Now that you're home, you'll feel better. Plenty of good rest and we'll take such fine care of you. (*Stops.*) But where is Zan? I missed her so much.

OSCAR. I asked you what is that strange costume you're parading around in?

BIRDIE (*nervously, backing toward stairs*). Me? Oh! It's my wrapper. I was so excited about Horace I just rushed out of the house—

OSCAR. Did you come across the square dressed that way? My dear Birdie, I—

HORACE (*to* REGINA, *wearily*). Yes, it's just like old times.

REGINA (*quickly to* OSCAR). Now, no fights. This is a holiday.

BIRDIE (*runs quickly up the stairs*) Zan! Zannie!

OSCAR. Birdie! (*She stops.*)

BIRDIE. Oh. Tell Zan I'll be back in a little while. (*Whispers.*) Sorry, Oscar. (*Exits.*)

REGINA (*to* OSCAR *and* BEN). Why don't you go finish your breakfast and let Horace rest for a minute?

BEN (*crossing to dining room with* OSCAR). Never leave a meal unfinished. There are too many poor people who need the food. Mighty glad to see you home, Horace. Fine to have you back. Fine to have you back.

OSCAR (*to* LEO *as* BEN *closes dining-room doors*). Your mother has gone crazy. Running around the streets like a woman— (*The moment* REGINA *and* HORACE *are alone, they become awkward and self-conscious.*)

REGINA (*laughs awkwardly*). Well. Here we are. It's been a long time. (HORACE *smiles.*) Five months. You know, Horace, I wanted to come and be with you in the hospital, but I didn't know where my duty was. Here, or with you. But you know how much I *wanted* to come.

HORACE. That's kind of you, Regina. There was no need to come.

REGINA. Oh, but there was. Five months lying there all by yourself, no kinfolks, no friends. Don't try to tell me you didn't have a bad time of it.

HORACE. I didn't have a bad time. (*As she shakes her head, he becomes insistent.*) No, I didn't, Regina. Oh, at first when I—when I heard the news about myself—but after I got used to that, I liked it there.

REGINA. You *liked* it? (*Coldly.*) Isn't that strange. You liked it so well you didn't want to come home?

HORACE. That's not the way to put it. (*Then, kindly, as he sees her turn her head away.*) But there I was and I got kind of used to it, kind of to like lying there and thinking. (*Smiles.*) I never had much time to think before. And time's become valuable to me.

REGINA. It sounds almost like a holiday.

HORACE (*laughs*). It was, sort of. The first holiday I've had since I was a little kid.

REGINA. And here I was thinking you were in pain and—

HORACE (*quietly*). I was in pain.

REGINA. And instead you were having a holiday! A holiday of thinking. Couldn't you have done that here?

HORACE. I wanted to do it before I came here. I was thinking about us.

REGINA. About us? About you and me? Thinking about you and me after all these years. (*Unpleasantly.*) You shall tell me everything you thought—some day.

HORACE (*there is silence for a minute*). Regina. (*She turns to him.*) Why did you send Zan to Baltimore?

REGINA. Why? Because I wanted you home. You can't make anything suspicious out of that, can you?

HORACE. I didn't mean to make anything suspicious about it. (*Hesitantly, taking her hand.*) Zan said you wanted me to come home. I was so pleased at that and touched it made me feel good.

REGINA (*taking away her hand, turns*). Touched that I should want you home?

HORACE (*sighs*). I'm saying all the wrongs things as usual. Let's try to get along better. There isn't so much more time. Regina, what's all this crazy talk I've been hearing about Zan and Leo? Zan and Leo marrying?

REGINA (*turning to him, sharply*). Who gossips so much around here?

HORACE (*shocked*). Regina!

REGINA (*annoyed, anxious to quiet him*). It's some foolishness that Oscar thought up. I'll explain later. I have no intention of allowing any such arrangement. It was simply a way of keeping Oscar quiet in all this business I've been writing you about—

HORACE (*carefully*). What has Zan to do with any business of Oscar's? Whatever it is, you had better put it out of Oscar's head immediately. You know what I think of Leo.

REGINA. But there's no need to talk about it now.

HORACE. There is no need to talk about it ever. Not as long as I live. (*HORACE stops, slowly turns to look at her.*) As long as I live. I've been in a hospital for five months. Yet since I've been here you have not once asked me about—about my health. (*Then gently.*) Well, I suppose they've written you. I can't live very long.

REGINA (*coldly*). I've never understood why people have to talk about this kind of thing.

HORACE (*there is a silence. Then he looks up at her, his face cold*). You misunderstand. I don't intend to gossip about my sickness. I thought it was only fair to tell you. I was not asking for your sympathy.

REGINA (*sharply, turns to him*). What do the doctors think caused your bad heart?

HORACE. What do you mean?

REGINA. They didn't think it possible, did they, that your fancy women may have—

HORACE (*smiles unpleasantly*). Caused my heart to be bad? I don't think that's the best scientific theory. You don't catch heart trouble in bed.

REGINA (*angrily*). I didn't think you did. I only thought you might catch a bad conscience—in bed, as you say.

HORACE. I didn't tell them about my bad conscience. Or about my fancy women. Nor did I tell them that my wife has not wanted me in bed with her for— (*Sharply.*) How long is it, Regina? (*REGINA turns to him.*) Ten years? Did you bring me home for this, to make me feel guilty again? That means you want something. But you'll not make me feel guilty any more. My "thinking" has made a difference.

REGINA. I see that it has. (*She looks toward dining-room door. Then comes to him, her manner warm and friendly.*) It's foolish for us to fight this way. I didn't mean to be unpleasant. I was stupid.

HORACE (*wearily*). God knows I didn't either. I came home wanting so much not to fight, and then all of a sudden there we were. I got hurt and—

REGINA (*hastily*). It's all my fault. I

didn't ask about—about your illness because I didn't want to remind you of it. Anyway I never believe doctors when they talk about— (*Brightly.*) when they talk like that.

HORACE (*not looking at her*). Well, we'll try our best with each other. (*He rises.*)

REGINA (*quickly*). I'll try. Honestly, I will. Horace, Horace, I know you're tired but, but—couldn't you stay down here a few minutes longer? I want Ben to tell you something.

HORACE. Tomorrow.

REGINA. I'd like to now. It's very important to me. It's very important to all of us. (*Gaily, as she moves toward dining room.*) Important to your beloved daughter. She'll be a very great heiress—

HORACE. Will she? That's nice.

REGINA (*opens doors*). Ben, are you finished breakfast?

HORACE. Is this the mill business I've had so many letters about?

REGINA (*to* BEN). Horace would like to talk to you now.

HORACE. Horace would not like to talk to you now. I am very tired, Regina—

REGINA (*comes to him*). Please. You've said we'll try our best with each other. I'll try. Really, I will. Please do this for me now. You will see what I've done while you've been away. How I watched your interests. (*Laughs gaily.*) And I've done very well too. But things can't be delayed any longer. Everything must be settled this week— (HORACE *sits down.* BEN *enters.* OSCAR *has stayed in the dining room, his head turned to watch them.* LEO *is pretending to read the newspaper.*) Now you must tell Horace all about it. Only be quick because he is very tired and must go to bed. (HORACE *is looking up at her. His face hardens as she speaks.*) But I think your news will be better for him than all the medicine in the world.

BEN (*looking at* HORACE). It could wait. Horace may not feel like talking today.

REGINA. What an old faker you are! You know it can't wait. You know it

must be finished this week. You've been just as anxious for Horace to get here as I've been.

BEN (*very jovial*). I suppose I have been. And why not? Horace has done Hubbard Sons many a good turn. Why shouldn't I be anxious to help him now?

REGINA (*laughs*). Help him! Help him when you need him, that's what you mean.

BEN. What a woman you married, Horace. (*Laughs awkwardly when* HORACE *does not answer.*) Well, then I'll make it quick. You know what I've been telling you for years. How I've always said that every one of us little Southern businessmen had great things— (*Extends his arm.*)—right beyond our finger tips. It's been my dream: my dream to make those fingers grow longer. I'm a lucky man, Horace, a lucky man. To dream and to live to get what you've dreamed of. That's *my* idea of a lucky man. (*Looks at his fingers as his arm drops slowly.*) For thirty years I've cried bring the cotton mills to the cotton. (HORACE *opens medicine bottle.*) Well, finally I got up nerve to go to Marshall Company in Chicago.

HORACE. I know all this. (*He takes the medicine.* REGINA *rises, steps to him.*)

BEN. Can I get you something?

HORACE. Some water, please.

REGINA (*turns quickly*). Oh, I'm sorry. Let me. (*Brings him a glass of water. He drinks as they wait in silence.*) You feel all right now?

HORACE. Yes. You wrote me. I know all that. (OSCAR *enters from dining room.*)

REGINA (*triumphantly*). But you don't know that in the last few days Ben has agreed to give us—you, I mean—a much larger share.

HORACE. Really? That's very generous of him.

BEN (*laughs*). It wasn't so generous of me. It was smart of Regina.

REGINA (*as if she were signaling* HORACE). I explained to Ben that perhaps you hadn't answered his letters because you didn't think he was offering you enough, and that the time was getting short and you could guess how much he needed you—

HORACE (*smiles at her, nods*). And I could guess that he wants to keep control in the family.

REGINA (*to* BEN, *triumphantly*). Exactly. (*To* HORACE.) So I did a little bargaining for you and convinced my brothers they weren't the only Hubbards who had a business sense.

HORACE. Did you have to convince them of that? How little people know about each other! (*Laughs.*) But you'll know better about Regina next time, eh, Ben? (BEN, REGINA, HORACE *laugh together.* OSCAR's *face is angry.*) Now let's see. We're getting a bigger share. (*Looking at* OSCAR.) Who's getting less?

BEN. Oscar.

HORACE. Well, Oscar, you've grown very unselfish. What's happened to you? (LEO *enters from dining room.*)

BEN (*quickly, before* OSCAR *can answer*). Oscar doesn't mind. Not worth fighting about now, eh, Oscar?

OSCAR (*angrily*). I'll get mine in the end. You can be sure of that. I've got my son's future to think about.

HORACE (*sharply*). Leo? Oh, I see. (*Puts his head back, laughs.* REGINA *looks at him nervously.*) I am beginning to see. Everybody will get theirs.

BEN. I knew you'd see it. Seventy-five thousand, and that seventy-five thousand will make you a million.

REGINA (*steps to table, leaning forward*). It will, Horace, it will.

HORACE. I believe you. (*After a second.*) Now I can understand Oscar's self-sacrifice, but what did you have to promise Marshall Company besides the money you're putting up?

BEN. They wouldn't take promises. They wanted guarantees.

HORACE. Of what?

BEN (*nods*). Water power. Free and plenty of it.

HORACE. You got them that, of course.

BEN. Cheap. You'd think the governor of a great state would make his price a little higher. From pride, you know.

(HORACE *smiles.* BEN *smiles.*) Cheap wages. "What do you mean by cheap wages?" I say to Marshall. "Less than Massachusetts," he says to me, "and that averages eight a week." "Eight a week! By God," I tell him, "*I'd* work for eight a week myself." Why, there ain't a mountain white or a town nigger but wouldn't give his right arm for three silver dollars every week, eh, Horace?

HORACE. Sure. And they'll take less than that when you get around to playing them off against each other. You can save a little money that way, Ben. (*Angrily.*) And make them hate each other just a little more than they do now.

REGINA. What's all this about?

BEN (*laughs*). There'll be no trouble from anybody, white or black. Marshall said that to me. "What about strikes? That's all we've had in Massachusetts for the last three years." I say to him, "What's a strike? I never heard of one. Come South, Marshall. We got good folks and we don't stand for any fancy fooling."

HORACE. You're right. (*Slowly.*) Well, it looks like you made a good deal for yourselves, and for Marshall, too. (*To* BEN.) Your father used to say he made the thousands and you boys would make the millions. I think he was right. (*Rises.*)

REGINA (*they are all looking at* HORACE. *She laughs nervously*). Millions for *us*, too.

HORACE. Us? You and me? I don't think so. We've got enough money, Regina. We'll just sit by and watch the boys grow rich. (*They watch* HORACE *tensely as he begins to move toward the staircase. He passes* LEO, *looks at him for a second.*) How's everything at the bank, Leo?

LEO. Fine, sir. Everything is fine.

HORACE. How are all the ladies in Mobile? (HORACE *turns to* REGINA, *sharply.*) Whatever made you think I'd let Zan marry—

REGINA. Do you mean that you are turning this down? Is it possible that's what you mean?

BEN. No, that's not what he means. Turning down a fortune. Horace is tired. He'd rather talk about it tomorrow—

REGINA. We can't keep putting it off this way. Oscar must be in Chicago by the end of the week with the money and contracts.

OSCAR (*giggles, pleased*). Yes, sir. Got to be there end of the week. No sense going without the money.

REGINA (*tensely*). I've waited long enough for your answer. I'm not going to wait any longer.

HORACE (*very deliberately*). I'm very tired now, Regina.

BEN (*hastily*). Now, Horace probably has his reasons. Things he'd like explained. Tomorrow will do. I can—

REGINA (*turns to BEN, sharply*). I want to know his reasons now! (*Turns back to HORACE.*)

HORACE (*as he climbs the steps*). I don't know them all myself. Let's leave it at that.

REGINA. We shall not leave it at that! We have waited for you here like children. Waited for you to come home.

HORACE. So that you could invest my money. So that is why you wanted me home? Well, I had hoped— (*Quietly.*) If you are disappointed, Regina, I'm sorry. But I must do what I think best. We'll talk about it another day.

REGINA. We'll talk about it now. Just you and me.

HORACE (*looks down at her. His voice is tense*). Please, Regina, it's been a hard trip. I don't feel well. Please leave me alone now.

REGINA (*quietly*). I want to talk to you, Horace. I'm coming up. (*He looks at her for a minute, then moves on again out of sight. She begins to climb the stairs.*)

BEN (*softly. REGINA turns to him as he speaks*). Sometimes it is better to wait for the sun to rise again. (*She does not answer.*) And sometimes, as our mother used to tell you, (REGINA *starts up stairs.*) it's unwise for a good-looking woman to frown. (BEN *rises, moves toward stairs.*) Softness and a smile do more to the heart of men— (*She disappears.* BEN *stands looking up the stairs. There is a long silence. Then, suddenly,* OSCAR *giggles.*)

OSCAR. Let us hope she'll change his mind. Let us hope. (*After a second* BEN *crosses to table, picks up his newspaper.* OSCAR *looks at* BEN. *The silence makes* LEO *uncomfortable.*)

LEO. The paper says twenty-seven cases of yellow fever in New Orleans. Guess the flood waters caused it. (*Nobody pays attention.*) Thought they were building the levees high enough. Like the niggers always say: a man born of woman can't build nothing high enough for the Mississippi. (*Gets no answer. Gives an embarrassed laugh. Upstairs there is the sound of voices. The voices are not loud, but* BEN, OSCAR, LEO *become conscious of them.* LEO *crosses to landing, looks up, listens.*)

OSCAR (*pointing up*). Now just suppose she don't change his mind? Just suppose he keeps on refusing?

BEN (*without conviction*). He's tired. It was a mistake to talk to him today. He's a sick man, but he isn't a crazy one.

OSCAR (*giggles*). But just suppose he is crazy. What then?

BEN (*puts down his paper, peers at* OSCAR). Then we'll go outside for the money. There's plenty who would give it.

OSCAR. And plenty who will want a lot for what they give. The ones who are rich enough to give will be smart enough to want. That means we'd be working for them, don't it, Ben?

BEN. You don't have to tell me the things I told you six months ago.

OSCAR. Oh, you're right not to worry. She'll change his mind. She always has. (*There is a silence. Suddenly* REGINA'S *voice becomes louder and sharper. All of them begin to listen now. Slowly* BEN *rises, goes to listen by the staircase.* OSCAR, *watching him, smiles. As they listen* REGINA'S *voice becomes very loud.* HORACE'S *voice is no longer heard.*) Maybe. But I don't believe it. I never did believe he was going in with us.

BEN (*turning on him*). What the hell do you expect me to do?

OSCAR (*mildly*). Nothing. You done your almighty best. Nobody could blame you if the whole thing just dripped away right through our fingers. You can't do a thing. But there may be something I could do for us. (OSCAR *rises*.) Or, I might better say, Leo could do for us. (BEN *stops, turns, looks at* OSCAR. LEO *is staring at* OSCAR.) Ain't that true, son? Ain't it true you might be able to help your own kinfolks?

LEO (*nervously taking a step to him*). Papa, I—

BEN (*slowly*). How would he help us, Oscar?

OSCAR. Leo's got a friend. Leo's friend owns eighty-eight thousand dollars in Union Pacific bonds. (BEN *turns to look at* LEO.) Leo's friend don't look at the bonds much—not for five or six months at a time.

BEN (*after a pause*). Union Pacific. Uh, huh. Let me understand. Leo's friend would—would lend him these bonds and he—

OSCAR (*nods*). Would be kind enough to lend them to us.

BEN. Leo.

LEO (*excited, comes to him*). Yes, sir?

BEN. When would your friend be wanting the bonds back?

LEO (*very nervous*). I don't know. I—well, I—

OSCAR (*sharply. Steps to him*). You told me he won't look at them until fall—

LEO. Oh, that's right. But I—not till fall. Uncle Horace never—

BEN (*sharply*). Be still.

OSCAR (*smiles at* LEO). Your uncle doesn't wish to know your friend's name.

LEO (*starts to laugh*). That's a good one. Not know his name—

OSCAR. Shut up, Leo! (LEO *turns away slowly, moves to table.* BEN *turns to* OSCAR.) He won't look at them again until September. That gives us five months. Leo will return the bonds in three months. And we'll have no trouble raising the money once the mills are

going up. Will Marshall accept bonds? (BEN *stops to listen to sudden sharp voices from above. The voices are now very angry and very loud.*)

BEN (*smiling*). Why not? Why not? (*Laughs.*) Good. We are lucky. We'll take the loan from Leo's friend—I think he will make a safer partner than our sister. (*Nods toward stairs. Turns to* LEO.) How soon can you get them?

LEO. Today. Right now. They're in the safe-deposit box and—

BEN (*sharply*). I don't want to know where they are.

OSCAR (*laughs*). We will keep it secret from you. (*Pats* BEN's *arm.*)

BEN (*smiles*). Good. Draw a check for our part. You can take the night train for Chicago. Well, Oscar (*Holds out his hand.*) good luck to us.

OSCAR. Leo will be taken care of?

LEO. I'm entitled to Uncle Horace's share. I'd enjoy being a partner—

BEN (*turns to stare at him*). You would? You can go to hell, you little— (*Starts toward* LEO.)

OSCAR (*nervously*). Now, now. He didn't mean that. I only want to be sure he'll get something out of all this.

BEN. Of course. We'll take care of him. We won't have any trouble about that. I'll see you at the store.

OSCAR (*nods*). That's settled then. Come on, son. (*Starts for door.*)

LEO (*puts out his hand*). I was only going to say what a great day this was for me and— (BEN *ignores his hand.*)

BEN. Go on. (LEO *looks at him, turns, follows* OSCAR *out.* BEN *stands where he is, thinking. Again the voices upstairs can be heard.* REGINA's *voice is high and furious.* BEN *looks up, smiles, winces at the noise.*)

ALEXANDRA (*upstairs*). Mama—Mama—don't . . . (*The noise of running footsteps is heard and* ALEXANDRA *comes running down the steps, speaking as she comes.*) Uncle Ben! Uncle Ben! Please go up. Please make Mama stop. Uncle Ben, he's sick, he's so sick. How can Mama talk to him like that—please, make her stop. She'll—

BEN. Alexandra, you have a tender heart.

ALEXANDRA (*crying*). Go on up, Uncle Ben, please— (*Suddenly the voices stop. A second later there is the sound of a door being slammed.*)

BEN. Now you see. Everything is over. Don't worry. (*He starts for the door.*) Alexandra, I want you to tell your mother how sorry I am that I had to leave. And don't worry so, my dear. Married folk frequently raise their voices, unfortunately. (*He starts to put on his hat and coat as* REGINA *appears on the stairs.*)

ALEXANDRA (*furiously*). How can you treat Papa like this? He's sick. He's very sick. Don't you know that? I won't let you.

REGINA. Mind your business, Alexandra. (*To* BEN. *Her voice is cold and calm.*) How much longer can you wait for the money?

BEN (*putting on his coat*). He has refused? My, that's too bad.

REGINA. He will change his mind. I'll find a way to make him. What's the longest you can wait now?

BEN. I could wait until next week. But I can't wait until next week. (*He giggles, pleased at the joke.*) I could but I can't. Could and can't. Well, I must go now. I'm very late—

REGINA (*coming downstairs toward him*). You're not going. I want to talk to you.

BEN. I was about to give Alexandra a message for you. I wanted to tell you that Oscar is going to Chicago tonight, so we can't be here for our usual Friday supper.

REGINA (*tensely*). Oscar is going to Chi— (*Softly.*) What do you mean?

BEN. Just that. Everything is settled. He's going on to deliver to Marshall—

REGINA (*taking a step to him*). I demand to know what— You are lying. You are trying to scare me. *You haven't got the money.* How could you have it? You can't have— (BEN *laughs.*) You will wait until I— (HORACE *comes into view on the landing.*)

BEN. You are getting out of hand. Since when do I take orders from you?

REGINA. Wait, you— (BEN *stops.*) How *can* he go to Chicago? Did a ghost arrive with the money? (BEN *starts for the hall.*) I don't believe you. Come back here. (REGINA *starts after him.*) Come back here, you— (*The door slams. She stops in the doorway, staring, her fists clenched. After a pause she turns slowly.*)

HORACE (*very quietly*). It's a great day when you and Ben cross swords. I've been waiting for it for years.

ALEXANDRA. Papa, Papa, please go back! You will—

HORACE. And so they don't need you, and so you will not have your millions, after all.

REGINA (*turns slowly*). You hate to see anybody live now, don't you? You hate to think that I'm going to be alive and have what I want.

HORACE. I should have known you'd think that was the reason.

REGINA. Because you're going to die and you know you're going to die.

ALEXANDRA (*shrilly*). Mama! Don't— Don't listen, Papa. Just don't listen. Go away—

HORACE. Not to keep you from getting what you want. Not even partly that. (*Holding to the rail.*) I'm sick of you, sick of this house, sick of my life here. I'm sick of your brothers and their dirty tricks to make a dime. There must be better ways of getting rich than cheating niggers on a pound of bacon. Why should I give you the money? (*Very angrily.*) To pound the bones of this town to make dividends for you to spend? You wreck the town, you and your brothers, *you* wreck the town and live on it. Not me. Maybe it's easy for the dying to be honest. But it's not my fault I'm dying. (ADDIE *enters, stands at door quietly.*) I'll do no more harm now. I've done enough. I'll die my own way. And I'll do it without making the world any worse. I leave that to you.

REGINA (*looks up at him slowly, calmly*). I hope you die. I hope you die soon. (*Smiles.*) I'll be waiting for you to die.

ALEXANDRA (*shrieking*). Papa! Don't— Don't listen— Don't—

ADDIE. Come here, Zan. Come out of this room. (ALEXANDRA *runs quickly to* ADDIE, *who holds her.* HORACE *turns slowly and starts upstairs.*)

CURTAIN

ACT THREE

SCENE: *Same as Act One. Two weeks later. It is late afternoon and it is raining.*

AT RISE: HORACE *is sitting near the window in a wheel chair. On the table next to him is a safe-deposit box, and a small bottle of medicine.* BIRDIE *and* ALEXANDRA *are playing the piano. On a chair is a large sewing basket.*

BIRDIE (*counting for* ALEXANDRA). One and two and three and four. One and two and three and four. (*Nods—turns to* HORACE.) We once played together, Horace. Remember?

HORACE (*has been looking out of the window*). What, Birdie?

BIRDIE. We played together. You and me.

ALEXANDRA. *Papa* used to play?

BIRDIE. Indeed he did. (ADDIE *appears at the door in a large kitchen apron. She is wiping her hands on a towel.*) He played the fiddle and very well, too.

ALEXANDRA (*turns to smile at* HORACE). I never knew—

ADDIE. Where's your mama?

ALEXANDRA. Gone to Miss Safronia's to fit her dresses. (ADDIE *nods, starts to exit.*)

HORACE. Addie.

ADDIE. Yes, Mr. Horace.

HORACE (*speaks as if he had made a sudden decision*). Tell Cal to get on his things. I want him to go an errand. (ADDIE *nods, exits.* HORACE *moves nervously in his chair, looks out of the window.*)

ALEXANDRA (*who has been watching him*). It's too bad it's been raining all day, Papa. But you can go out in the yard tomorrow. Don't be restless.

HORACE. I'm not restless, darling.

BIRDIE. I remember so well the time we played together, your papa and me. It was the first time Oscar brought me here to supper. I had never seen all the Hubbards together before, and you know what a ninny I am and how shy. (*Turns to look at* HORACE.) You said you could play the fiddle and you'd be much obliged if I'd play with you. *I* was obliged to *you*, all right, all right. (*Laughs when he does not answer her.*) Horace, you haven't heard a word I've said.

HORACE. Birdie, when did Oscar get back from Chicago?

BIRDIE. Yesterday. Hasn't he been here yet?

ALEXANDRA (*stops playing*). No. Neither has Uncle Ben since—since that day.

BIRDIE. Oh, I didn't know it was *that* bad. Oscar never tells me anything—

HORACE (*smiles, nods*). The Hubbards have had their great quarrel. I knew it would come some day. (*Laughs.*) It came.

ALEXANDRA. It came. It certainly came all right.

BIRDIE (*amazed*). But Oscar was in such a good humor when he got home, I didn't—

HORACE. Yes, I can understand that. (ADDIE *enters carrying a large tray with glasses, a carafe of elderberry wine and a plate of cookies, which she puts on the table.*)

ALEXANDRA. Addie! A party! What for?

ADDIE. Nothing for. I had the fresh butter, so I made the cakes, and a little elderberry does the stomach good in the rain.

BIRDIE. Isn't this nice! A party just for us. Let's play party music, Zan. (ALEXANDRA *begins to play a gay piece.*)

ADDIE (*to* HORACE, *wheeling his chair to center*). Come over here, Mr. Horace, and don't be thinking so much. A glass of elderberry will do more good. (ALEX-ANDRA *reaches for a cake.* BIRDIE *pours herself a glass of wine.*)

ALEXANDRA. Good cakes, Addie. It's nice here. Just us. Be nice if it could always be this way.

BIRDIE (*nods happily*). Quiet and restful.

ADDIE. Well, it won't be that way long. Little while now, even sitting here, you'll hear the red bricks going into place. The next day the smoke'll be pushing out the chimneys and by church time that Sunday every human born of woman will be living on chicken. That's how Mr. Ben's been telling the story.

HORACE (*looks at her*). They believe it that way?

ADDIE. Believe it? They use to believing what Mr. Ben orders. There ain't been so much talk around here since Sherman's army didn't come near.

HORACE (*softly*). They are fools.

ADDIE (*nods, sits down with the sewing basket*). You ain't born in the South unless you're a fool.

BIRDIE (*has drunk another glass of wine*). But we didn't play together after that night. Oscar said he didn't like me to play on the piano. (*Turns to* ALEX-ANDRA.) You know what he said that night?

ALEXANDRA. Who?

BIRDIE. Oscar. He said that music made him nervous. He said he just sat and waited for the next note. (ALEXANDRA *laughs.*) He wasn't poking fun. He meant it. Ah, well— (*She finishes her glass, shakes her head.* HORACE *looks at her, smiles.*) Your papa don't like to admit it, but he's been mighty kind to me all these years. (*Running the back of her hand along his sleeve.*) Often he'd step in when somebody said something and once— (*She stops, turns away, her face still.*) Once he stopped Oscar from— (*She stops, turns. Quickly.*) I'm sorry I said that. Why, here I am so happy and yet I think about bad things. (*Laughs nervously.*) That's not right, now, is it? (*She pours a drink.* CAL *appears in the door. He has on an old coat and is carrying a torn umbrella.*)

ALEXANDRA. Have a cake, Cal.

CAL (*comes in, takes a cake*). Yes'm. You want me, Mr. Horace?

HORACE. What time is it, Cal?

CAL. 'Bout ten minutes before it's five.

HORACE. All right. Now you walk yourself down to the bank.

CAL. It'll be closed. Nobody'll be there but Mr. Manders, Mr. Joe Horns, Mr. Leo—

HORACE. Go in the back way. They'll be at the table, going over the day's business. (*Points to the deposit box.*) See that box?

CAL (*nods*). Yes, sir.

HORACE. You tell Mr. Manders that Mr. Horace says he's much obliged to him for bringing the box, it arrived all right.

CAL (*bewildered*). He know you got the box. He bring it himself Wednesday. I opened the door to him and he say, "Hello, Cal, coming on to summer weather."

HORACE. You say just what I tell you. Understand? (BIRDIE *pours another drink, stands at table.*)

CAL. No, sir. I ain't going to say I understand. I'm going down and tell a man he give you something he already know he give you, and you say "understand."

HORACE. Now, Cal.

CAL. Yes, sir. I just going to say you obliged for the box coming all right. I ain't going to understand it, but I'm going to say it.

HORACE. And tell him I want him to come over here after supper, and to bring Mr. Sol Fowler with him.

CAL (*nods*). He's to come after supper and bring Mr. Sol Fowler, your attorney-at-law, with him.

HORACE (*smiles*). That's right. Just walk right in the back room and say your piece. (*Slowly.*) In front of everybody.

CAL. Yes, sir. (*Mumbles to himself as he exits.*)

ALEXANDRA (*who has been watching* HORACE). Is anything the matter, Papa?

HORACE. Oh, no. Nothing.

ADDIE. Miss Birdie, that elderberry going to give you a headache spell.

BIRDIE (*beginning to be drunk. Gaily*).

Oh, I don't think so. I don't think it will.

ALEXANDRA (*as* HORACE *puts his hand to his throat*). Do you want your medicine, Papa?

HORACE. No, no. I'm all right, darling.

BIRDIE. Mama used to give me elderberry wine when I was a little girl. For hiccoughs. (*Laughs.*) You know, I don't think people get hiccoughs any more. Isn't that funny? (BIRDIE *laughs.* HORACE *and* ALEXANDRA *laugh.*) I used to get hiccoughs just when I shouldn't have.

ADDIE (*nods*). And nobody gets growing pains no more. That is funny. Just as if there was some style in what you get. One year an ailment's stylish and the next year it ain't.

BIRDIE (*turns*). I remember. It was my first big party, at Lionnet I mean, and I was so excited, and there I was with hiccoughs and Mama laughing. (*Softly. Looking at carafe.*) Mama always laughed. (*Picks up carafe.*) A big party, a lovely dress from Mr. Worth in Paris, France, and hiccoughs. (*Pours drink.*) My brother pounding me on the back and Mama with the elderberry bottle, laughing at me. Everybody was on their way to come, and I was such a ninny, hiccoughing away. (*Drinks.*) You know, that was the first day I ever saw Oscar Hubbard. The Ballongs were selling their horses and he was going there to buy. He passed and lifted his hat—we could see him from the window —and my brother, to tease Mama, said maybe we should have invited the Hubbards to the party. He said Mama didn't like them because they kept a store, and he said that was old-fashioned of her. (*Her face lights up.*) And then, and *then,* I saw Mama angry for the first time in my life. She said that wasn't the reason. She said she was old-fashioned, but not that way. She said she was old-fashioned enough not to like people who killed animals they couldn't use, and who made their money charging awful interest to poor, ignorant niggers and cheating them on what they bought. She was very angry, Mama was. I had never seen her face like that. And then sud-

denly she laughed and said, "Look, I've frightened Birdie out of the hiccoughs." (*Her head drops. Then softly.*) And so she had. They were all gone. (*Moves to sofa, sits.*)

ADDIE. Yeah, they got mighty well off cheating niggers. Well, there are people who eat the earth and eat all the people on it like in the Bible with the locusts. Then there are people who stand around and watch them eat it. (*Softly.*) Sometimes I think it ain't right to stand and watch them do it.

BIRDIE (*thoughtfully*). Like I say, if we could only go back to Lionnet. Everybody'd be better there. They'd be good and kind. I like people to be kind. (*Pours drink.*) Don't you, Horace; don't you like people to be kind?

HORACE. Yes, Birdie.

BIRDIE (*very drunk now*). Yes, that was the first day I ever saw Oscar. Who would have thought— (*Quickly.*) You all want to know something? Well, I don't like Leo. My very own son, and I don't like him. (*Laughs, gaily.*) My, I guess I even like Oscar more.

ALEXANDRA. Why did you marry Uncle Oscar?

ADDIE (*sharply*). That's no question for you to be asking.

HORACE (*sharply*). Why not? She's heard enough around here to ask anything.

ALEXANDRA. Aunt Birdie, why did you marry Uncle Oscar?

BIRDIE. I don't know. I thought I liked him. He was kind to me and I thought it was because he liked me too. But that wasn't the reason— (*Wheels on* ALEXANDRA.) Ask why *he* married *me.* I can tell you that: he's told it to me often enough.

ADDIE (*leaning forward*). Miss Birdie, don't—

BIRDIE (*speaking very rapidly, tensely*). My family was good and the cotton on Lionnet's fields was better. Ben Hubbard wanted the cotton and (*Rises.*) Oscar Hubbard married it for him. He was kind to me, then. He used to smile at me. He hasn't smiled at me since. Everybody knew that's what he married me for. (ADDIE *rises*.) Everybody but me. Stupid, stupid me.

ALEXANDRA (*to* HORACE, *holding his hand, softly*). I see. (*Hesitates*.) Papa, I mean—when you feel better couldn't we go away? I mean, by ourselves. Couldn't we find a way to go—

HORACE. Yes, I know what you mean. We'll try to find a way. I promise you, darling.

ADDIE (*moves to* BIRDIE). Rest a bit, Miss Birdie. You get talking like this you'll get a headache and—

BIRDIE (*sharply, turning to her*). I've never had a headache in my life. (*Begins to cry hysterically*.) You know it as well as I do. (*Turns to* ALEXANDRA.) I never had a headache, Zan. That's a lie they tell for me. I drink. All by myself, in my own room, by myself, I drink. Then, when they want to hide it, they say, "Birdie's got a headache again"—

ALEXANDRA (*comes to her quickly*). Aunt Birdie.

BIRDIE (*turning away*). Even you won't like me now. You won't like me any more.

ALEXANDRA. I love you. I'll always love you.

BIRDIE (*furiously*). Well, don't. Don't love me. Because in twenty years you'll just be like me. They'll do all the same things to you. (*Begins to laugh hysterically*.) You know what? In twenty-two years I haven't had a whole day of happiness. Oh, a little, like today with you all. But never a single, whole day. I say to myself, if only I had one more *whole* day, then— (*The laugh stops*.) And that's the way you'll be. And you'll trail after them, just like me, hoping they won't be so mean that day or say something to make you feel so bad—only you'll be worse off because you haven't got my Mama to remember— (*Turns away, her head drops. She stands quietly, swaying a little, holding to the sofa.* ALEXANDRA *leans down, puts her cheek on* BIRDIE's *arm*.)

ALEXANDRA (*to* BIRDIE). I guess we were all trying to make a happy day. You know, we sit around and try to pre-tend nothing's happened. We try to pretend we are not here. We make believe we are just by ourselves, some place else, and it doesn't seem to work. (*Kisses* BIRDIE's *hand*.) Come now, Aunt Birdie, I'll walk you home. You and me. (*She takes* BIRDIE's *arm. They move slowly out*.)

BIRDIE (*softly as they exit*). You and me.

ADDIE (*after a minute*). Well. First time I ever heard Miss Birdie say a word. (HORACE *looks at her*.) Maybe it's good for her. I'm just sorry Zan had to hear it. (HORACE *moves his head as if he were uncomfortable*.) You feel bad, don't you? (*He shrugs*.)

HORACE. So you didn't want Zan to hear? It would be nice to let her stay innocent, like Birdie at her age. Let her listen now. Let her see everything. How else is she going to know that she's got to get away? I'm trying to show her that. I'm trying, but I've only got a little time left. She can even hate me when I'm dead, if she'll only learn to hate and fear this.

ADDIE. Mr. Horace—

HORACE. Pretty soon there'll be nobody to help her but you.

ADDIE (*crossing to him*). What can I do?

HORACE. Take her away.

ADDIE. How can I do that? Do you think they'd let me just go away with her?

HORACE. I'll fix it so they can't stop you when you're ready to go. You'll go, Addie?

ADDIE (*after a second, softly*). Yes, sir. I promise. (*He touches her arm, nods*.)

HORACE (*quietly*). I'm going to have Sol Fowler make me a new will. They'll make trouble, but you make Zan stand firm and Fowler'll do the rest. Addie, I'd like to leave you something for yourself. I always wanted to.

ADDIE (*laughs*). Don't you do that, Mr. Horace. A nigger woman in a white man's will! I'd never get it nohow.

HORACE. I know. But upstairs in the armoire drawer there's seventeen hundred dollar bills. It's money left from my trip. It's in an envelope with your name. It's for you.

ADDIE. Seventeen hundred dollar bills! My God, Mr. Horace, I won't know how to count up that high. (*Shyly.*) It's mighty kind and good of you. I don't know what to say for thanks—

CAL (*appears in doorway*). I'm back. (*No answer.*) I'm back.

ADDIE. So we see.

HORACE. Well?

CAL. Nothing. I just went down and spoke my piece. Just like you told me. I say, "Mr. Horace he thank you mightily for the safe box arriving in good shape and he say you come right after supper to his house and bring Mr. Attorney-at-law Sol Fowler with you." Then I wipe my hands on my coat. Every time I ever told a lie in my whole life, I wipe my hands right after. Can't help doing it. Well, while I'm wiping my hands, Mr. Leo jump up and say to me, "What box? What you talking about?"

HORACE (*smiles*). Did he?

CAL. And Mr. Leo say he got to leave a little early cause he got something to do. And then Mr. Manders say Mr. Leo should sit right down and finish up his work and stop acting like somebody made him Mr. President. So he sit down. Now, just like I told you, Mr. Manders was mighty surprised with the message because he knows right well he brought the box— (*Points to box, sighs.*) But he took it all right. Some men take everything easy and some do not.

HORACE (*puts his head back, laughs*). Mr. Leo was telling the truth; he *has* got something to do. I hope Manders don't keep him too long. (*Outside there is the sound of voices.* CAL *exits.* ADDIE *crosses quickly to* HORACE, *puts basket on table, begins to wheel his chair toward the stairs. Sharply.*) No. Leave me where I am.

ADDIE. But that's Miss Regina coming back.

HORACE (*nods, looking at door*). Go away, Addie.

ADDIE (*hesitates*). Mr. Horace. Don't talk no more today. You don't feel well and it won't do no good—

HORACE (*as he hears footsteps in the hall*). Go on. (*She looks at him for a second, then picks up her sewing from table and exits as* REGINA *comes in from hall.* HORACE's *chair is now so placed that he is in front of the table with the medicine.* REGINA *stands in the hall, shakes umbrella, stands it in the corner, takes off her cloak and throws it over the banister. She stares at* HORACE.)

REGINA (*as she takes off her gloves*). We had agreed that you were to stay in your part of this house and I in mine. This room is *my* part of the house. Please don't come down here again.

HORACE. I won't.

REGINA (*crosses toward bell-cord*). I'll get Cal to take you upstairs.

HORACE (*smiles*). Before you do I want to tell you that after all, we have invested our money in Hubbard Sons and Marshall, Cotton Manufacturers.

REGINA (*stops, turns, stares at him*). What are you talking about? You haven't seen Ben— When did you change your mind?

HORACE. I didn't change my mind. *I* didn't invest the money. (*Smiles.*) It was invested for me.

REGINA (*angrily*). What—?

HORACE. I had eighty-eight thousand dollars' worth of Union Pacific bonds in that safe-deposit box. They are not there now. Go and look. (*As she stares at him, he points to the box.*) Go and look, Regina. (*She crosses quickly to the box, opens it.*) Those bonds are as negotiable as money.

REGINA (*turns back to him*). What kind of joke are you playing now? Is this for my benefit?

HORACE. I don't look in that box very often, but three days ago, on Wednesday it was, because I had made a decision—

REGINA. I want to know what you are talking about.

HORACE (*sharply*). Don't interrupt me again. Because I had made a decision, I sent for the box. The bonds were gone.

Eighty-eight thousand dollars gone. (*He smiles at her.*)

REGINA (*after a moment's silence, quietly*). Do you think I'm crazy enough to believe what you're saying?

HORACE (*shrugs*). Believe anything you like.

REGINA (*stares at him, slowly*). Where did they go to?

HORACE. They are in Chicago. With Mr. Marshall, I should guess.

REGINA. What did they do? Walk to Chicago? Have you really gone crazy?

HORACE. Leo took the bonds.

REGINA (*turns sharply then speaks softly, without conviction*). I don't believe it.

HORACE (*leans forward*). I wasn't there but I can guess what happened. This fine gentleman, to whom you were willing to marry your daughter, took the keys and opened the box. You remember that the day of the fight Oscar went to Chicago? Well, he went with my bonds that his son Leo had stolen for him. (*Pleasantly.*) And for Ben, of course, too.

REGINA (*slowly, nods*). When did you find out the bonds were gone?

HORACE. Wednesday night.

REGINA. I thought that's what you said. Why have you waited three days to do anything? (*Suddenly laughs.*) This *will* make a fine story.

HORACE (*nods*). Couldn't it?

REGINA (*still laughing*). A fine story to hold over their heads. How could they be such fools? (*Turns to him.*)

HORACE. But I'm not going to hold it over their heads.

REGINA (*the laugh stops*). What?

HORACE (*turns his chair to face her*). I'm going to let them keep the bonds— as a loan from you. An eighty-eight-thousand-dollar loan; they should be grateful to you. They will be, I think.

REGINA (*slowly, smiles*). I see. You are punishing me. But I won't let you punish me. If you won't do anything, I will. Now. (*She starts for door.*)

HORACE. You won't do anything. Because you can't. (REGINA *stops.*) It won't do you any good to make trouble because I shall simply say that I lent them the bonds.

REGINA (*slowly*). You would do that?

HORACE. Yes. For once in your life I am tying your hands. There is nothing for you to do. (*There is silence. Then she sits down.*)

REGINA. I see. You are going to lend them the bonds and let them keep all the profit they make on them, and there is nothing I can do about it. Is that right?

HORACE. Yes.

REGINA (*softly*). Why did you say that I was making this gift?

HORACE. I was coming to that. I am going to make a new will, Regina, leaving you eighty-eight thousand dollars in Union Pacific bonds. The rest will go to Zan. It's true that your brothers have borrowed your share for a little while. After my death I advise you to talk to Ben and Oscar. They won't admit anything and Ben, I think, will be smart enough to see that he's safe. Because I knew about the theft and said nothing. Nor will I say anything as long as I live. Is that clear to you?

REGINA (*nods, softly, without looking at him*). You will not say anything as long as you live.

HORACE. That's right. And by that time they will probably have replaced your bonds, and then they'll belong to you and nobody but us will ever know what happened. (*Stops, smiles.*) They'll be around any minute to see what I am going to do. I took good care to see that word reached Leo. They'll be mighty relieved to know I'm going to do nothing and Ben will think it all a capital joke on you. And that will be the end of that. There's nothing you can do to them, nothing you can do to me.

REGINA. You hate me very much.

HORACE. No.

REGINA. Oh, I think you do. (*Puts her head back, sighs.*) Well, we haven't been very good together. Anyway, I don't hate you either. I have only contempt for you. I've always had.

HORACE. From the very first?

REGINA. I think so.

HORACE. I was in love with *you*. But why did *you* marry *me?*

REGINA. I was lonely when I was young.

HORACE. *You* were lonely?

REGINA. Not the way people usually mean. Lonely for all the things I wasn't going to get. Everybody in this house was so busy and there was so little place for what I wanted. I wanted the world. Then, and then— (*Smiles.*) Papa died and left the money to Ben and Oscar.

HORACE. And you married me?

REGINA. Yes, I thought— But I was wrong. You were a small-town clerk then. You haven't changed.

HORACE (*nods, smiles*). And that wasn't what you wanted.

REGINA. No. No, it wasn't what I wanted. (*Pauses, leans back, pleasantly.*) It took me a little while to find out I had made a mistake. As for you—I don't know. It was almost as if I couldn't stand the kind of man you were— (*Smiles, softly.*) I used to lie there at night, praying you wouldn't come near—

HORACE. Really? It was as bad as that?

REGINA (*nods*). Remember when I went to Doctor Sloan and I told you he said there was something the matter with me and that you shouldn't touch me any more?

HORACE. I remember.

REGINA. But you believed it. I couldn't understand that. I couldn't understand that anybody could be such a soft fool. That was when I began to despise you.

HORACE (*puts his hand to his throat, looks at the bottle of medicine on table*). Why didn't you leave me?

REGINA. I told you I married you for something. It turned out it was only for this. (*Carefully.*) This wasn't what I wanted, but it was something. I never thought about it much but if I had (HORACE *puts his hand to his throat.*) I'd have known that you would die before I would. But I couldn't have known that you would get heart trouble so early and so bad. I'm lucky, Horace. I've always been lucky. (HORACE *turns slowly to the medicine.*) I'll be lucky again. (HORACE *looks at her. Then he puts his hand to his throat. Because he cannot reach the bottle he moves the chair closer. He reaches for the medicine, takes out the cork, picks up the spoon. The bottle slips and smashes on the table. He draws in his breath, gasps.*)

HORACE. Please. Tell Addie— The other bottle is upstairs. (REGINA *has not moved. She does not move now. He stares at her. Then, suddenly as if he understood, he raises his voice. It is a panic-stricken whisper, too small to be heard outside the room.*) Addie! Addie! Come— (*Stops as he hears the softness of his voice. He makes a sudden, furious spring from the chair to the stairs, taking the first few steps as if he were a desperate runner. On the fourth step he slips, gasps, grasps the rail, makes a great effort to reach the landing. When he reaches the landing, he is on his knees. His knees give way, he falls on the landing, out of view.* REGINA *has not turned during his climb up the stairs. Now she waits a second. Then she goes below the landing, speaks up.*)

REGINA. Horace. Horace. (*When there is no answer, she turns, calls.*) Addie! Cal! Come in here. (*She starts up the steps.* ADDIE *and* CAL *appear. Both run toward the stairs.*) He's had an attack. Come up here. (*They run up the steps quickly.*)

CAL. My God. Mr. Horace— (*They cannot be seen now.*)

REGINA (*her voice comes from the head of the stairs.*) Be still, Cal. Bring him in here. (*Before the footsteps and the voices have completely died away,* ALEXANDRA *appears in the hall door, in her raincloak and hood. She comes into the room, begins to unfasten the cloak, suddenly looks around, sees the empty wheel chair, stares, begins to move swiftly as if to look in the dining room. At the same moment* ADDIE *runs down the stairs.* ALEXANDRA *turns and stares up at* ADDIE.)

ALEXANDRA. Addie! What?

ADDIE (*takes* ALEXANDRA *by the shoul-*

ders). I'm going for the doctor. Go up-stairs. (ALEXANDRA *looks at her, then quickly breaks away and runs up the steps.* ADDIE *exits. The stage is empty for a minute. Then the front door bell begins to ring. When there is no answer, it rings again. A second later* LEO *appears in the hall, talking as he comes in.*)

LEO (*very nervous*). Hello. (*Irritably.*) Never saw any use ringing a bell when a door was open. If you are going to ring a bell, then somebody should answer it. (*Gets in the room, looks around, puzzled, listens, hears no sound.*) Aunt Regina. (*He moves around restlessly.*) Addie. (*Waits.*) Where the hell— (*Crosses to the bell cord, rings it impatiently, waits, gets no answer, calls.*) Cal! Cal! (CAL *appears on the stair landing.*)

CAL (*his voice is soft, shaken*). Mr. Leo. Miss Regina says you stop that screaming noise.

LEO (*angrily*). Where is everybody?

CAL. Mr. Horace he got an attack. He's bad. Miss Regina says you stop that noise.

LEO. Uncle Horace— What— What happened? (CAL *starts down the stairs, shakes his head, begins to move swiftly off.* LEO *looks around wildly.*) But when — You seen Mr. Oscar or Mr. Ben? (CAL *shakes his head. Moves on.* LEO *grabs him by the arm.*) Answer me, will you?

CAL. No, I ain't seen 'em. I ain't got time to answer you. I got to get things. (CAL *runs off.*)

LEO. But what's the matter with him? When did this happen— (*Calling after* CAL.) You'd think Papa'd be some place where you could find him. I been chasing him all afternoon. (OSCAR *and* BEN *come quickly into the room.*)

LEO. Papa, I've been looking all over town for you and Uncle Ben—

BEN. Where is he?

OSCAR. Addie just told us it was a sudden attack, and—

BEN (*to* LEO). Where is he? When did it happen?

LEO. Upstairs. Will you listen to me, please? I been looking for you for—

OSCAR (*to* BEN). You think we should go up? (BEN, *looking up the steps, shakes his head.*)

BEN. I don't know. I don't know.

OSCAR (*shakes his head*). But he was all right—

LEO (*yelling*). *Will you listen to me?*

OSCAR (*sharply*). What is the matter with you?

LEO. I been trying to tell you. I been trying to find you for an hour—

OSCAR. Tell me what?

LEO. Uncle Horace knows about the bonds. He knows about them. He's had the box since Wednesday—

BEN (*sharply*). Stop shouting! What the hell are you talking about?

LEO (*furiously*). I'm telling you he knows about the bonds. Ain't that clear enough—

OSCAR (*grabbing* LEO's *arm*). You God-damn fool! Stop screaming!

BEN. Now what happened? Talk quietly.

LEO. You heard me. Uncle Horace knows about the bonds. He's known since Wednesday.

BEN (*after a second*). How do you know that?

LEO. Because Cal comes down to Manders and says the box came O.K. and—

OSCAR (*trembling*). That might not mean a thing—

LEO (*angrily*). No? It might not, huh? Then he says Manders should come here tonight and bring Sol Fowler with him. I guess that don't mean a thing either.

OSCAR (*to* BEN). Ben— What— Do you think he's seen the—

BEN (*motions to the box*). There's the box. (*Both* OSCAR *and* LEO *turn sharply.* LEO *makes a leap to the box.*) You ass. Put it down. What are you going to do with it, eat it?

LEO. I'm going to— (*Starts.*)

BEN (*furiously*). Put it down. Don't touch it again. Now sit down and shut up for a minute.

OSCAR. Since Wednesday. (*To* LEO.) You said he had it since Wednesday. Why didn't he say something— (*To* BEN.) I don't understand—

LEO (*taking a step*). I can put it back. I can put it back before anybody knows.

BEN (*who is standing at the table, softly*). He's had it since Wednesday. Yet he hasn't said a word to us.

OSCAR. *Why? Why?*

LEO. What's the difference why? He was getting ready to say plenty. He was going to say it to Fowler tonight—

OSCAR (*angrily*). Be still. (*Turns to BEN, looks at him, waits.*)

BEN (*after a minute*). I don't believe that.

LEO (*wildly*). *You* don't believe it? What do I care what *you* believe? I do the dirty work and then—

BEN (*turning his head sharply to LEO*). I'm remembering that. I'm remembering that, Leo.

OSCAR. What do you mean?

LEO. You—

BEN (*to OSCAR*). If you don't shut that little fool up, I'll show you what I mean. For some reason he knows, but he don't say a word.

OSCAR. Maybe he didn't know that we—

BEN (*quickly*). That Leo— He's no fool. Does Manders know the bonds are missing?

LEO. How could I tell? I was half crazy. I don't think so. Because Manders seemed kind of puzzled and—

OSCAR. But we got to find out— (*He breaks off as CAL comes into the room carrying a kettle of hot water.*)

BEN. How is he, Cal?

CAL. I don't know, Mr. Ben. He was bad. (*Going toward stairs.*)

OSCAR. But when did it happen?

CAL (*shrugs*). He wasn't feeling bad early. (ADDIE *comes in quickly from the hall.*) Then there he is next thing on the landing, fallen over, his eyes tight—

ADDIE (*to CAL*). Dr. Sloan's over at the Ballongs. Hitch the buggy and go get him. (*She takes the kettle and cloths from him, pushes him, runs up the stairs.*) Go on. (*She disappears. CAL exits.*)

BEN. Never seen Sloan anywhere when you need him.

OSCAR (*softly*). Sounds bad.

LEO. He would have told *her* about it. Aunt Regina. He would have told his own wife—

BEN (*turning to LEO*). Yes, he might have told her. But they weren't on such pretty terms and maybe he didn't. Maybe he didn't. (*Goes quickly to LEO.*) Now, listen to me. If she doesn't know, it may work out all right. If she does know, you're to say he lent you the bonds.

LEO. Lent them to me! Who's going to believe that?

BEN. Nobody.

OSCAR (*to LEO*). Don't you understand? It can't do no harm to say it—

LEO. Why should I say he lent them to me? Why not to you? (*Carefully.*) Why not to Uncle Ben?

BEN (*smiles*). Just because he didn't lend them to me. Remember that.

LEO. But all he has to do is say he didn't lend them to me—

BEN (*furiously*). But for some reason, he doesn't seem to be talking, does he? (*There are footsteps above. They all stand looking at the stairs. REGINA begins to come slowly down.*)

BEN. What happened?

REGINA. He's had a bad attack.

OSCAR. Too bad. I'm sorry we weren't here when—when Horace needed us.

BEN. When *you* needed us.

REGINA (*looks at him*). Yes.

BEN. How is he? Can we—can we go up?

REGINA (*shakes her head*). He's not conscious.

OSCAR (*pacing around*). It's that—it's that bad? Wouldn't you think Sloan could be found quickly, just once, just once?

REGINA. I don't think there is much for him to do.

BEN. Oh, don't talk like that. He's come through attacks before. He will now. (REGINA *sits down. After a second she speaks softly.*)

REGINA. Well. We haven't seen each other since the day of our fight.

BEN (*tenderly*). That was nothing.

Why, you and Oscar and I used to fight when we were kids.

OSCAR (*hurriedly*). Don't you think we should go up? Is there anything we can do for Horace—

BEN. You don't feel well. Ah—

REGINA (*without looking at them*). No, I don't. (*Slight pause.*) Horace told me about the bonds this afternoon. (*There is an immediate shocked silence.*)

LEO. The bonds. What do you mean? What bonds? What—

BEN (*looks at him furiously. Then to* REGINA). The Union Pacific bonds? *Horace's* Union Pacific bonds?

REGINA. Yes.

OSCAR (*steps to her, very nervously*). Well. Well what—what about them? What—what could he say?

REGINA. He said that Leo had stolen the bonds and given them to you.

OSCAR (*aghast, very loudly*). That's ridiculous, Regina, absolutely—

LEO. I don't know what you're talking about. What would I— Why—

REGINA (*wearily to* BEN). Isn't it enough that he stole them from me? Do I have to listen to this in the bargain?

OSCAR. You are talking—

LEO. I didn't steal anything. I don't know why—

REGINA (*to* BEN). Would you ask them to stop that, please? (*There is silence for a minute.* BEN *glowers at* OSCAR *and* LEO.)

BEN. Aren't we starting at the wrong end, Regina? What did Horace tell you?

REGINA (*smiles at him*). He told me that Leo had stolen the bonds.

LEO. I didn't steal—

REGINA. Please. Let me finish. Then he told me that he was going to pretend that he had lent them to you (LEO *turns sharply to* REGINA, *then looks at* OSCAR, *then looks back at* REGINA.) as a present from me—to my brothers. He said there was nothing I could do about it. He said the rest of his money would go to Alexandra. That is all. (*There is a silence.* OSCAR *coughs*, LEO *smiles slyly*.)

LEO (*taking a step to her*). I told you he had lent them— I could have told you—

REGINA (*ignores him, smiles sadly at* BEN). So I'm very badly off, you see. (*Carefully.*) But Horace said there was nothing I could do about it as long as he was alive to say he had lent you the bonds.

BEN. You shouldn't feel that way. It can all be explained, all be adjusted. It isn't as bad—

REGINA. So you, at least, are willing to admit that the bonds were stolen?

BEN (OSCAR *laughs nervously*). I admit no such thing. It's possible that Horace made up that part of the story to tease you— (*Looks at her.*) Or perhaps to punish you. Punish you.

REGINA (*sadly*). It's not a pleasant story. I feel bad, Ben, naturally. I hadn't thought—

BEN. Now you shall have the bonds safely back. That was the understanding, wasn't it, Oscar?

OSCAR. Yes.

REGINA. I'm glad to know that. (*Smiles.*) Ah, I had greater hopes—

BEN. Don't talk that way. That's foolish. (*Looks at his watch.*) I think we ought to drive out for Sloan ourselves. If we can't find him we'll go over to Senateville for Doctor Morris. And don't think I'm dismissing this other business. I'm not. We'll have it all out on a more appropriate day.

REGINA (*looks up, quietly*). I don't think you had better go yet. I think you had better stay and sit down.

BEN. We'll be back with Sloan.

REGINA. Cal has gone for him. I don't want you to go.

BEN. Now don't worry and—

REGINA. You will come back in this room and sit down. I have something more to say.

BEN (*turns, comes toward her*). Since when do I take orders from you?

REGINA (*smiles*). You don't—yet. (*Sharply.*) Come back, Oscar. You too, Leo.

OSCAR (*sure of himself, laughs*). My dear Regina—

BEN (*softly, pats her hand*). Horace has already clipped your wings and very wittily. Do I have to clip them, too?

(*Smiles at her.*) You'd get farther with a smile, Regina. I'm a soft man for a woman's smile.

REGINA. I'm smiling, Ben. I'm smiling because you are quite safe while Horace lives. But I don't think Horace will live. And if he doesn't live I shall want seventy-five per cent in exchange for the bonds.

BEN (*steps back, whistles, laughs*). Greedy! What a greedy girl you are! You want so much of everything.

REGINA. Yes. And if I don't get what I want I am going to put all three of you in jail.

OSCAR (*furiously*). You're mighty crazy. Having just admitted—

BEN. And on what evidence would you put Oscar and Leo in jail?

REGINA (*laughs, gaily*). Oscar, listen to him. He's getting ready to swear that it was you and Leo! What do you say to that? (OSCAR *turns furiously toward* BEN.) Oh, don't be angry, Oscar. I'm going to see that he goes in with you.

BEN. Try anything you like, Regina. (*Sharply.*) And now we can stop all this and say good-bye to you. (ALEXANDRA *comes slowly down the steps.*) It's his money and he's obviously willing to let us borrow it. (*More pleasantly.*) Learn to make threats when you can carry them through. For how many years have I told you a good-looking woman gets more by being soft and appealing? Mama used to tell you that. (*Looks at his watch.*) Where the hell is Sloan? (*To* OSCAR.) Take the buggy and— (*As* BEN *turns to* OSCAR, *he sees* ALEXANDRA. *She walks stiffly. She goes slowly to the lower window, her head bent. They all turn to look at her.*)

OSCAR (*after a second, moving toward her*). What? Alexandra— (*She does not answer. After a second,* ADDIE *comes slowly down the stairs, moving as if she were very tired. At foot of steps, she looks at* ALEXANDRA, *then turns and slowly crosses to door and exits.* REGINA *rises.* BEN *looks nervously at* ALEXANDRA, *at* REGINA.)

OSCAR (*as* ADDIE *passes him, irritably

to* ALEXANDRA). Well, what is— (*Turns into room—sees* ADDIE *at foot of steps.*) —what's? (BEN *puts up a hand, shakes his head.*) My God, I didn't know—who *could* have known—I didn't know he was that sick. Well, well—I— (REGINA *stands quietly, her back to them.*)

BEN (*softly, sincerely*). Seems like yesterday when he first came here.

OSCAR (*sincerely, nervously*). Yes, that's true. (*Turns to* BEN.) The whole town loved him and respected him.

ALEXANDRA (*turns*). Did you love him, Uncle Oscar?

OSCAR. Certainly, I— What a strange thing to ask! I—

ALEXANDRA. Did you love him, Uncle Ben?

BEN (*simply*). He had—

ALEXANDRA (*suddenly starts to laugh very loudly*). And you, Mama, did you love him, too?

REGINA. I know what you feel, Alexandra, but please try to control yourself.

ALEXANDRA (*still laughing*). I'm trying, Mama. I'm trying very hard.

BEN. Grief makes some people laugh and some people cry. It's better to cry, Alexandra.

ALEXANDRA (*the laugh has stopped. Tensely moves toward* REGINA). What was Papa doing on the staircase? (BEN *turns to look at* ALEXANDRA.)

REGINA. Please go and lie down, my dear. We all need time to get over shocks like this. (ALEXANDRA *does not move.* REGINA's *voice becomes softer, more insistent.*) Please go, Alexandra.

ALEXANDRA. No, Mama. I'll wait. I've got to talk to you.

REGINA. Later. Go and rest now.

ALEXANDRA (*quietly*). I'll wait, Mama. I've plenty of time.

REGINA (*hesitates, stares, makes a half shrug, turns back to* BEN). As I was saying. Tomorrow morning I am going up to Judge Simmes. I shall tell him about Leo.

BEN (*motioning toward* ALEXANDRA). Not in front of the child, Regina. I—

REGINA (*turns to him. Sharply*). I didn't ask her to stay. Tomorrow morning I go to Judge Simmes—

Oscar. And what proof? What proof of all this—

Regina (*turns sharply*). None. I won't need any. The bonds are missing and they are with Marshall. That will be enough. If it isn't, I'll add what's necessary.

Ben. I'm sure of that.

Regina (*turns to* Ben). You can be quite sure.

Oscar. We'll deny—

Regina. Deny your heads off. You couldn't find a jury that wouldn't weep for a woman whose brothers steal from her. And you couldn't find twelve men in this state you haven't cheated and who hate you for it.

Oscar. What kind of talk is this? You couldn't do anything like that! We're your own brothers. (*Points upstairs.*) How can you talk that way when upstairs not five minutes ago—

Regina (*slowly*). There are people who can't go back, who must finish what they start. I am one of those people, Oscar. (*After a slight pause.*) Where was I? (*Smiles at* Ben.) Well, they'll convict you. But I won't care much if they don't. (*Leans forward, pleasantly.*) Because by that time you'll be ruined. I shall also tell my story to Mr. Marshall, who likes me, I think, and who will not want to be involved in your scandal. A respectable firm like Marshall and Company. The deal would be off in an hour. (*Turns to them angrily.*) And you know it. Now I don't want to hear any more from any of you. *You'll do no more bargaining in this house.* I'll take my seventy-five per cent and we'll forget the story forever. That's one way of doing it, and the way I prefer. You know me well enough to know that I don't mind taking the other way.

Ben (*after a second, slowly*). None of us has ever known you well enough, Regina.

Regina. You're getting old, Ben. Your tricks aren't as smart as they used to be. (*There is no answer. She waits, then smiles.*) All right. I take it that's settled and I get what I asked for.

Oscar (*furiously to* Ben.) Are you going to let her do this—

Ben (*turns to look at him, slowly*). You have a suggestion?

Regina (*puts her arms above her head, stretches, laughs*). No, he hasn't. All right. Now, Leo, I have forgotten that you ever saw the bonds. (*Archly, to* Ben *and* Oscar.) And as long as you boys both behave yourselves, I've forgotten that we ever talked about them. You can draw up the necessary papers tomorrow. (Ben *laughs.* Leo *stares at him, starts for door. Exits.* Oscar *moves toward door angrily.* Regina *looks at* Ben, *nods, laughs with him. For a second,* Oscar *stands in the door, looking back at them. Then he exits.*)

Regina. You're a good loser, Ben. I like that.

Ben (*he picks up his coat, then turns to her*). Well, I say to myself, what's the good? You and I aren't like Oscar. We're not sour people. I think that comes from a good digestion. Then, too, one loses today and wins tomorrow. I say to myself, years of planning and I get what I want. Then I don't get it. But I'm not discouraged. The century's turning, the world is open. Open for people like you and me. Ready for us, waiting for us. After all this is just the beginning. There are hundreds of Hubbards sitting in rooms like this throughout the country. All their names aren't Hubbard, but they are all Hubbards and they will own this country some day. We'll get along.

Regina (*smiles*). I think so.

Ben. Then, too, I say to myself, things may change. (*Looks at* Alexandra.) I agree with Alexandra. What is a man in a wheel chair doing on a staircase? I ask myself that.

Regina (*looks up at him*). And what do you answer?

Ben. I have no answer. But maybe some day I will. Maybe never, but maybe some day. (*Smiles. Pats her arm.*) When I do, I'll let you know. (*Goes toward hall.*)

Regina. When you do, write me. I

will be in Chicago. (*Gaily.*) Ah, Ben, if Papa had only left me his money.

BEN. I'll see you tomorrow.

REGINA. Oh, yes. Certainly. You'll be sort of working for me now.

BEN (*as he passes* ALEXANDRA, *smiles*). Alexandra, you're turning out to be a right interesting girl. (*Looks at* REGINA.) Well, good night all. (*He exits.*)

REGINA (*Sits quietly for a second, stretches, turns to look at* ALEXANDRA). What do you want to talk to me about, Alexandra?

ALEXANDRA (*slowly*). I've changed my mind. I don't want to talk. There's nothing to talk about now.

REGINA. You're acting very strange. Not like yourself. You've had a bad shock today. I know that. And you loved Papa, but you must have expected this to come some day. You knew how sick he was.

ALEXANDRA. I knew. We all knew.

REGINA. It will be good for you to get away from here. Good for me, too. Time heals most wounds, Alexandra. You're young, you shall have all the things I wanted. I'll make the world for you the way I wanted it to be for me. (*Uncomfortably.*) Don't sit there staring. You've been around Birdie so much you're getting just like her.

ALEXANDRA (*nods*). Funny. That's what Aunt Birdie said today.

REGINA (*nods*). Be good for you to get away from all this. (ADDIE *enters.*)

ADDIE. Cal is back, Miss Regina. He says Dr. Sloan will be coming in a few minutes.

REGINA. We'll go in a few weeks. A few weeks! That means two or three Saturdays, two or three Sundays. (*Sighs.*) Well, I'm very tired. I shall go to bed. I don't want any supper. Put the lights out and lock up. (ADDIE *moves to the piano lamp, turns it out.*) You go to your room, Alexandra. Addie will bring you something hot. You look very tired. (*Rises. To* ADDIE.) Call me when Dr. Sloan gets here. I don't want to see anybody else. I don't want any condolence calls tonight. The whole town will be over.

ALEXANDRA. Mama, I'm not coming with you. I'm not going to Chicago.

REGINA (*turns to her*). You're very upset, Alexandra.

ALEXANDRA (*quietly*). I mean what I say. With all my heart.

REGINA. We'll talk about it tomorrow. The morning will make a difference.

ALEXANDRA. It won't make any difference. And there isn't anything to talk about. I am going away from you. Because I want to. Because I know Papa would want me to.

REGINA (*puzzled, careful, polite*). You *know* your papa wanted you to go away from me?

ALEXANDRA. Yes.

REGINA (*softly*). And if I say no?

ALEXANDRA (*looks at her*). Say it Mama, say it. And see what happens.

REGINA (*softly, after a pause*). And if I make you stay?

ALEXANDRA. That would be foolish. It wouldn't work in the end.

REGINA. You're very serious about it, aren't you? (*Crosses to stairs.*) Well, you'll change your mind in a few days.

ALEXANDRA. You only change your mind when you want to. And I won't want to.

REGINA (*going up the steps*). Alexandra, I've come to the end of my rope. Somewhere there has to be what I want, too. Life goes too fast. Do what you want; think what you want; go where you want. I'd like to keep you with me, but I won't make you stay. Too many people used to make me do too many things. No, I won't make you stay.

ALEXANDRA. You couldn't, Mama, because I want to leave here. As I've never wanted anything in my life before. Because now I understand what Papa was trying to tell me. (*Pause.*) All in one day: Addie said there were people who ate the earth and other people who stood around and watched them do it. And just now Uncle Ben said the same thing. Really, he said the same thing. (*Tensely.*) Well, tell him for me, Mama, I'm not going to stand around and watch you do it. Tell him I'll be fighting as hard as he'll be fighting (*Rises.*) some place where people don't just stand around and watch.

REGINA. Well, you have spirit, after all. I used to think you were all sugar water. We don't have to be bad friends. I don't want us to be bad friends, Alexandra. (*Starts, stops, turns to* ALEXANDRA.) Would you like to come and talk to me, Alexandra? Would you—would you like to sleep in my room tonight?

ALEXANDRA (*takes a step toward her*). Are you afraid, Mama? (REGINA *does not answer. She moves slowly out of sight.* ADDIE *comes to* ALEXANDRA, *presses her arm.*)

THE CURTAIN FALLS.

SUGGESTED TOPICS FOR FURTHER INVESTIGATION AND REPORT

1. Read any of the better known Belasco plays: *Madame Butterfly*, *The Girl of the Golden West*, *The Return of Peter Grimm*, and read one of Fitch's more famous efforts: *The Climbers*, *The Girl With the Green Eyes*, *The Truth*, *The City*. Compare and contrast the degrees of "realism" apparent in these plays. Also note the essential romanticism they each contain.

2. Read Walter's *The Easiest Way* and one or more of the following: Sidney Kingsley's *Dead End*, *Men in White*, or *Detective Story*, or Elmer Rice's *Street Scene*. Note carefully the various stage settings and minute directions and character descriptions, especially those attempts at "illusionism"—the creation of the illusion of reality. Try to locate some pictures of these settings, most of which can be found in familiar theatre and drama histories, the Burns Mantle collections, and certain anthologies. Which play or plays seem the most successful in bringing the atmosphere of the real thing into the theatre? Do these plays fit the category of "problem play"?

3. Read Lillian Hellman's *Another Part of the Forest*, the "sequel" to *The Little Foxes* which tells the Hubbard story twenty years earlier. Compare the two plays in style, structure, character, and theme. Which one is the better representative of the modern realistic drama?

4. Study some of the social plays of the 1930s: Odets' *Waiting for Lefty*, Wexley's *They Shall Not Die*, Blitzstein's *The Cradle Will Rock*, and the Federal Theatre plays like *One-third of a Nation* or *Power*. Discuss the effectiveness of these plays in presenting specific social ills. How much do they rely on overt "propaganda" for their effect? How much is legitimate drama?

5. Clifford Odets has been called the "American Chekhov," meaning that his plays approach the special kind of realism for which Anton Chekhov's Russian plays are so famous. Compare a play like *The Cherry Orchard*, *Uncle Vanya*, or *The Seagull*, with Odets' *Awake and Sing*, *Rocket to the Moon*, or *The Country Girl*. Attack or justify the comparison.

6. Read all of Herne's *Margaret Fleming*. Also read Strindberg's *The Father* and Ibsen's *A Doll's House*. Present an analysis of the treatments of marriage found in each of these plays.

7. Two plays about a very delicate problem—the "different" individual in society —are Lillian Hellman's *The Children's Hour* and Robert Anderson's *Tea and Sympathy*. Discuss their effectiveness in handling the problems they present.

8. Although the Hubbards in *The Little Foxes* are an evil group who seem to have no capacity for human compassion, they are presented as pretty much their own masters. However, playwrights have often discussed the "inheritance" of certain personal behavior patterns: Fitch in *The Truth* (congenital lying), *The Girl With the Green Eyes* (jealousy), or *The City* (personal corruption); Augustus Thomas in *The Witching Hour* (fear); and Maxwell Anderson's recent adaptation, *Bad Seed* (homicidal tendencies). Read at least two of these plays and determine the validity of the theme and the degree of conviction which the writer conveys.

9. The nineteenth-century playwrights, Henry Arthur Jones and Arthur Wing Pinero, were considered the first "realists" of the English stage. Read Pinero's *The*

Second Mrs. Tanqueray or *Mid-channel*, and Jones' *Saints and Sinners* or *Michael and His Lost Angel*. Compare them with the plays of a nineteenth-century American realist like Herne, or with some of the plays of Bronson Howard.

10. Read Sidney Howard's *The Silver Cord*, George Kelly's *Craig's Wife*, and Eugene O'Neill's *Anna Christie*. Discuss their values and shortcomings as representatives of modern realistic drama.

THE DEPARTURE FROM REALISM

The Two Paths of Modern Drama

The serious realistic drama like *The Little Foxes* represents only a part of what has developed stylistically in twentieth-century plays. The departures have been almost as varied as the number of writers, because the realistic style of Ibsen was immediately challenged by the imaginative minds who would not be governed by restrictions of any type.

There were two excellent reasons for the nearly simultaneous development of modern realism and its antithesis, which will, for the moment, bear the name "antirealism." First was the new-found freedom of thought which permitted the display of many previously forbidden topics. The realist, freed of the false delicacies of romanticism, took the initiative in his portrayal of the actual world of men. Unfortunately, the more the realist probed into mankind's ills, the more he became artistically removed from his subject. As he revealed man as a product of society, he increasingly approached the clinical case histories of the literary naturalist, carrying no more dramatic impact than a doctor's report to a medical journal. To the confirmed realist, this unemotional objectivity signified an arrival at honest *truth* through art. Those who denied that such "art" was truly *art* set about to use the realist's freedom while steering away from the realist's narrow world. The antirealist was sure that no permanent truths could possibly be achieved on a stage devoted so completely to literal reality.

The second reason for the separate roads taken by modern drama was the development of stage mechanics to a degree unimagined in the nineteenth century. The coming of electricity thoroughly revolutionized theatre practice, and the first to make the best use of it was the realist. Mobility and limitless control of electric lighting enabled the creation of more natural effects, while costume, makeup, and *décor* were subtly highlighted to suggest the actuality of character and scene. Impersonal objectivity, the negation of artistic interpretation, was the final achievement, witnessed in Belasco's literal and unartistic stage illusionism. The antirealist, seeking to maintain art in the theatre, saw far beyond these limits. Electricity, with its instant response, was a challenge to the fertile imagination; the facilities of the stage could be released to move as far from realism as the boundaries of the mind would go.

Expressionism, the most commonly used word to describe dramatic antirealism, is a companion to impressionism, surrealism, constructivism, and all the various refinements of the antirealistic departures. Expressionism is a species of no well-defined characteristics, and it recognizes no confining physical limits. Through exaggeration or distortion of scenery, costume, sound, and particularly lighting, the expressionistic play may express every nuance of its creator's subjective identification with his idea. Time has no meaning; logical sequence of events is not considered. Characters may be anything from allegorical symbols or comic-strip caricatures to massed crowds speaking and moving as an operatic unit. Dialogue bears no resemblance to human speech, and may be delivered in any manner from machine-gun staccato bursts to prolonged monotones of stream of consciousness. Subject matter is unlimited, but its theme nearly always considers man's loss of individuality and integrity in the midst of an increasingly mechanized and all-conforming society. The central figure of expressionism is a lost soul, for in many ways this is a literature of despair. It sees man headed toward a terrible destruction which he can avoid only by his acute awareness of its imminence.

The Important European Experimenters

The nature of expressionism is continually experimental, for it depends closely upon the novelty of effect and a constant search for unusual devices of strong impact. Successful full-scale experimentation began with August Strindberg's nightmare picture of life, *The Dream Play*, in 1902, wherein the writer expounded his opinion that to be a man is indeed a pitiful and painful thing. Strindberg is concerned with the human animal's inability to find himself in a maze of conventional philosophy, where he suffocates from dead ideas and a lack of the appreciation of beauty. There is no plot; scenes blend rapidly into other scenes in the manner of a dreaming human mind. It is a place, in Strindberg's words, "where anything may happen; everything is possible and probable. Time and space do not exist."

The following stage directions show how completely Strindberg depends upon the ingenuity of the stage carpenters and electricians:

> *The background is raised and a new one revealed, showing an old, dilapidated party-wall. In the centre of it is a gate closing a passageway. This opens upon a green, sunlit space, where is seen a tremendous blue monk's hood (aconite). . . . Further to the right is a door that has an air-hole shaped like a four-leaved clover. To the left of the gate stands a small linden tree with coal-black trunk and a few pale-green leaves. Near it is a small air-hole leading into a cellar.*

* * *

> *Without lowering of the curtain, the stage changes to a lawyer's office, and in this manner. The gate remains, but as a wicket in the railing running clear across the stage. The gate-keeper's lodge turns into the private enclosure of the Lawyer, and it is now entirely open to the front. The linden, leafless, becomes a hat tree. The billboard is covered with legal notices and court decisions. The door with the four-leaved clover hole forms part of a document chest.*

The stage is darkened and the following changes are made. The railing stays, but it encloses now the chancel of a church. The billboard displays hymn numbers. The linden hat tree becomes a candelabrum. The Lawyer's desk is turned into the desk of the presiding functionary, and the door with the clover leaf leads to the vestry.

Before it spread to America to flourish briefly in the years following the First World War, expressionism gained its strongest hold in central Europe. It was most popular in Germany, although Czech, Hungarian, and even Italian playwrights adopted many of its elements in some exceedingly fine plays. Foremost among the leading German writers were Georg Kaiser and Ernst Toller.

Kaiser's most important contribution was his "Gas" trilogy, composed of three separate plays, *The Coral*, 1917, *Gas I*, 1918, and *Gas II*, 1920. Whereas Strindberg in *The Dream Play* is concerned with suffering in all phases of life, these plays deal directly with mankind's disappearance into a mechanistic society from which he is unable to save himself. In *The Coral* the central figure is the Billionaire, rejected by both his son and daughter for his inhumane exploitation of the workers from whose ranks he himself has risen. In *Gas I*, the Billionaire's Son manufactures industrial gas. After a gigantic explosion demolishes the factory, he refuses to rebuild, for he knows the workers will become slaves to the machine. His good intentions are overcome by the massed attack of business and labor, and he surrenders. In *Gas II* the rebuilt factory functions only for war. The victorious enemy makes each worker a literal slave. The only way out is "the gas that kills" which the Billionaire Worker, son of the Billionaire's Son, throws into the midst of the factory. Every worker is immediately consumed and nothing is left but a pile of bleaching skeletons. The enemy, unable to survive, turns its machine guns upon itself. Complete extermination is society's future.

Toller was more interested in analyzing current social problems in an attitude similar to the writers of the "proletarian" or left-wing drama in America during the Depression. His most famous play, *Masse Mensch* (Man and the Masses), predicts an ultimate destruction not by machinery but by the uncontrolled mass of men tearing itself apart.

The American Attempt

Eugene O'Neill, an admirer of Strindberg's expressionistic and naturalistic plays, was the first to apply the techniques of expressionism to the American drama. His fame as a writer of powerfully realistic short plays had just been established when he gave the Provincetown Players the first important expressionistic play in this country, *The Emperor Jones* of 1920. Its theme of man's relationship to his own soul and his God is well suited to expressionistic writing, and O'Neill makes exceptional use of the stage facilities of light and sound to emphasize the deterioration of a human mind in the body of a hunted man. *The Emperor Jones*, with its monotonously beating drums and its picture of the fugitive emperor's uncontrolled terror, was a sensational critical and popular success, although there were reservations about this unusual new style as a permanent contribution to the theatre.

The Hairy Ape of 1922 made greater use of expressionism. Once more O'Neill's protagonist is a man without a place in the world, frantically seeking somewhere to belong. Yank, the apelike stoker, prowls the streets of New York in search of revenge against the society he feels has ruined him until he is at last welcomed into the crushing arms of a giant gorilla with whom he can identify himself. O'Neill employs highly stylized dialogue and numbers of massed actors in choral patterns far more than in *The Emperor Jones*. The best expressionistic portion of the play is the scene depicting the violent clash of Yank's brutish world with that of rich, haughty Fifth Avenue:

(*The crowd from church enter from the right, sauntering slowly and affectedly, their heads held stiffly up, looking neither to right nor left, talking in toneless, simpering voices. The women are rouged, calcimined, dyed, over-dressed to the nth degree. The men are in Prince Alberts, high hats, spats, canes, etc. A procession of gaudy marionettes, yet with something of the relent-less horror of Frankensteins in their detached, mechanical unawareness.*)

* * *

(*A fat, high-hatted, spatted gentleman runs out from the side street. He calls out plaintively.*) Bus! Bus! Stop there! (*and runs full tilt into . . .* YANK, *who is bowled off his balance.*)

YANK (*seeing a fight—with a roar of joy as he springs to his feet*). At last! Bus, huh? I'll bust yuh! (*He lets drive a terrific swing, his fist landing full on the fat gentleman's face. But the gentleman stands as if nothing had happened.*)

GENTLEMAN. I beg your pardon. (*Then irritably.*) You have made me lose my bus. (*He claps his hands and begins to scream.*) Officer! Officer! (*Many police whistles shrill out on the instant and a whole platoon of policemen rush in on* YANK *from all sides. He tries to fight but is clubbed to the pavement and fallen upon. The crowd at the* [store] *window have not moved or noticed this disturbance. The clanging gong of the patrol wagon approaches with a clamoring din.*)

Three other American writers, Elmer Rice, George S. Kaufman, and Marc Connelly, made excellent use of expressionism to present their pictures of the human predicament. Rice's *The Adding Machine* of 1923 contains a protagonist who is no Yank from the midst of a burning Hades of coal and soot, but a little nonentity called Mr. Zero, lost in the labyrinth of big business.

When Zero is dismissed from his position after twenty-five years of work in order to be replaced by an adding machine, this curtain scene explodes with terrific force:

Boss. I say I'm sorry to lose an employee who's been with me for so many years— (*Soft music is heard—the sound of the mechanical player of a distant merry-go-round. The part of the floor upon which the desk and stools are standing begins to revolve very slowly.*) But, of course, in an organization like this, efficiency must be the first consideration— (*The music becomes gradually louder and the revolutions more rapid.*) You will draw your salary for a full month. And I'll direct my secretary to give you a letter of recommendation—

ZERO. Wait a minute, boss. Let me get this right. You mean I'm canned?

Boss (*barely making himself heard above the increasing volume of sound*). I'm sorry—no other alternative—greatly regret—old employee—efficiency—econ-omy—business—*business*—BUSINESS— (*His voice is drowned by the music. The platform is revolving rapidly now. ZERO and the Boss face each other. They are entirely motionless save for the Boss's jaws, which open and close incessantly. But the words are inaudible. The music swells and swells. To it is added every off-stage effect of the theatre: the wind, the waves, the gal-loping horses, the locomotive whistle, the sleigh bells, the automobile siren, the glass-crash. New Year's Eve, Election Night, Armistice Day, and the Mardi-Gras. The noise is deafening, maddening, unendurable. Suddenly it culminates in a terrific peal of thunder. For an instant there is a flash of red and then everything is plunged into blackness.*)

Zero's enraged murder of the Boss results in his trial and execution, but the fate of Mr. Zero, and all the Zeroes in the world, is a never-ending cycle of increased slavery. In the afterlife to which he is sent, Zero learns how he is destined to return to operate an even greater machine, a "super-hyper-adding machine" which will be controlled only by the force of the big toe on his right foot.

Kaufman and Connelly's *Beggar on Horseback*, 1924, is a "dream play" that turns into a hilarious satire on the tremendously efficient inefficiency of modern big business. The hero, young Neil, dreams he has married the mil-lionaire's daughter instead of the girl next door, and is employed in his father-in-law's office. He seeks to begin work but is frustrated for lack of a pencil. He speaks to a stenographer:

MISS HEY. Of course you've filled out a requisition.

NEIL. No, I haven't. A piece of paper, isn't it? (*She hands him a tremendous sheet of paper. It is about twenty by thirty inches. He studies it.*) What I want is a pencil. There's a place for that to be put in, I suppose?

MISS HEY (*wearily*). Yes—where it says: "The undersigned wishes a pencil to do some work with." How old are you?

NEIL. Thirty-two.

MISS HEY (*taking the paper away*). That's the wrong form. (*She gives him another—a blue one this time.*) Parents living?

NEIL. No.

MISS HEY. What did you do with your last pencil?

NEIL. I didn't have any.

MISS HEY. Did you have any before that?

NEIL. I don't think I ever had any. (*He indicates the form.*) Is that all right?

MISS HEY. It isn't as regular as we like, but I guess it'll do.

NEIL. What do I do now? Go to someone else, don't I?

MISS HEY. Oh, yes. Sometimes you travel for days.

NEIL. Are we all crazy?

MISS HEY. Yes.

O'Neill continued to use expressionism in his search for meaning in life, specifically in the complex system of masks in both *The Great God Brown* in 1926 and *Lazarus Laughed* in 1928. Because of the ability with which expressionism could illuminate despair and fear, it was a favorite of those who wrote the "proletarian" drama of social protest and those who sought a way to peace in plays against war. John Howard Lawson's *Processional*, 1925, Clifford Odets' *Waiting for Lefty*, 1935, Irwin Shaw's *Bury the Dead* and Paul Green's *Johnny Johnson*, both of 1936, as well as the Federal Theatre Project's *Living Newspapers*, were all users of expressionism in one way or another.

Thornton Wilder's two distinguished plays, *Our Town* of 1938 and *The Skin of Our Teeth*, 1942, far apart in subject matter and dramatic appeal, will probably endure among the few highly stylized plays to survive as good American literature. Certainly *Our Town* has found its unassailable place as the favorite acting piece for young people and amateurs throughout the nation in its universally appealing compassion and sentimentality, and its highly praised Off Broadway revival in 1959 proved that it can succeed indefinitely as a professional piece as well. To call it flatly "expressionistic" is not exactly correct, because it has none of the distorted images of the expressionist. Its scenes of life in New England, except for the unorthodox presentation and the absence of properties, are completely realistic in concept. The last-act interpretation of life after death is not quite fantasy, nor is it expressionism either, yet the entire play is firmly antirealistic. There is no question concerning *The Skin of Our Teeth*. Its stylized picture of mankind's endless cycle of earthly life from savagery through "civilization" and back again has some of the most brilliant—and hilarious—episodes of expressionistic technique in modern drama. It demands close study for its attitudes in comparison with the world view of Tennessee Williams' *Camino Real*.

Expressionism had mostly burned itself out by the end of the 1930s, leaving realism as the predominant style. The experiments of the imaginative stage artist, nevertheless, left behind some permanent legacies which no realist is entirely able to ignore. Because of this gift, modern realism has a fluidity and a plasticity which add constant excitement to the business of attending the modern theatre and which prevent any attempt to create a rigid classification establishing the precise nature of "modern" drama.

Camino Real

Tennessee Williams is one of the few important playwrights since the 1930s, and practically the only one since the Second World War who has attempted to stage a full-scale expressionistic play in a large commercial theatre. So unusual was the appearance of *Camino Real* in the midst of the more orthodox productions of the 1950s that the play seemed almost like an anachronism. Williams and many other writers for two decades or more had made free use of the techniques of expressionism in their otherwise conventional plays, asking audiences to look through hazy gauze screens into dimly lit sets, or to watch characters enter through transparent walls or nonexistent doors. None, however, had formed a play in a style so completely and unreservedly expressionistic as *Camino Real*. *Expressionism* as a recognized theatrical term was so passé that not a single opening-night critic used the word anywhere in describing what he had just witnessed. The comments all mentioned the "symbolism," the "fantasy," or the "surrealism" of the play, noting its "episodic" and "exotic" qualities, on occasion linked with "poetry." But *expressionism* was as completely ignored as if it had never existed.

How much of the inability of *Camino Real* to survive beyond a very few performances on Broadway was due to audience resistance to its dramatic form, and how much to its failure to communicate as a play may not easily be determined. Certainly a large part of Williams' failure was a result of the extent of his demands on the audience. Perhaps he expected too much from modern audiences, spoon-fed on the explicitness of cinematic and electronic entertainment.

The easiest step to take when watching this play is to dismiss the entire thing as a garishly mad shambles full of more than its share of sound and fury and signifying absolutely nothing. For those who search diligently for meaning, there is an equal danger of destroying the play's value in the valiant attempt to work out a full explanation of each symbol and episode. Treating the composition as an intriguing jigsaw puzzle has serious drawbacks. There is a strong possibility that the meaning of the picture may have been missed in the enthusiasm of fitting each piece into place; or the expert puzzler who neatly solves it may discover he still has a large handful of pieces with absolutely no place to put them.

The middle ground in the case of *Camino Real* is, then, a meeting place part way, depending upon the play's intelligibility to the individual member of the audience. There can be *comprehension* without complete *understanding*. The aim of the writer is an expression of strong personal feelings and emotions. If one is offended by a particularly raw episode, or by the uninhibited language, he has every right to criticize its use. He does not, however, have the right to condemn the entire play for any momentary lapse in taste. The world Williams sees in *Camino Real* is a dismal one; it is also a repugnant and hideous one, full of vileness and degradation. It may not be *your* view, but you cannot deny Williams' right to see it so. Therefore, do not read this play, or others like it, with any thought of "solving" it or of arriving at a literal "translation." Met at least halfway, *Camino Real* is far from the dismaying jumble it would seem at first to be.

Camino Real is all expressionism. The complete auditorium from balcony and orchestra aisles to boxes and pit combine with the stage to become the acting area. Time and space are without meaning. Individual characters appear and disappear with no relation to probability—some as native inhabitants of this desolate place, others as creatures of legend, myth, and history. Upon occasion, they become symbols in the most obvious manner, and at other times they remain in disturbing obscurity. Plausibility is no concern. Scene blends into scene without pause; broad and bawdy farce intrudes upon horror, meaningless nonsense upon moments of serious thought. An over-all atmosphere of hysteria, which from time to time erupts without warning in almost uncontrolled frenzy, permeates the whole. Every possibility of electronic control in light and sound is employed to its maximum. *Décor* and costume, make-up and stage movement are grotesque, exaggerated, and distorted. In the theme itself, Williams is well within the tradition of expressionism, for he is intensely concerned with the fate of mankind in the corrupt society he has created for himself.

The *Camino Real* is the "Royal Way," the "way of life," and what happens there is the activity of life. The division between the world of privilege and the world of deprivation is explicit; between them is the common property of the public square, used by both sides, but also the haunt of the streetcleaners, as ready to receive the diamond-studded body of Lord Mulligan as that of the most defenseless nonentity. It is a no man's land, a deadly battlefield, the site of madly wild revels and open seduction. It is barren and unattractive; its fountain is dry. On either side are the extremes of life, neither of them any more attractive than the common ground between them. The Siete Mares Hotel contains elegance, but it is an elegance stained with greed, lust, and gluttony. The opposite side of the square is the ultimate depth of complete human degradation and spiritual collapse, although life at the "Ritz Men Only" is in reality no more decayed than at Gutman's house of brilliant darkness. Williams not only finds life to have no safe, attractive compromise, but he denies the existence of human dignity or self-respect at either end of the scale. One lolls in the lush, indolent over-erotic world of the Siete Mares, or he barely exists in the steamy sleeping quarters of the "Ritz Men Only," whose perverts and predators are not much different from the inhabitants across the way.

In the midst of this forbidding scene, centered within a fearful expanse of nothingness, all kinds of men and women exist. How they arrived here remains the permanent unknown, just as each person's entrance into life must always be the unsolved mystery. Williams chooses to present his permanent guests at the Siete Mares in terms of their last agonies, at that time of life when full payment for every uninhibited dissipation must be made. Casanova, the symbol of the eternal rake; Marguerite Gautier, "Camille," the image of all the enticements of the life of love; Byron, the poet, aesthete, and immoralist; all find the truth about themselves, and in themselves reflect all who would live as they have, faced with the final decision of what to make of their nearly spent lives. One may not run out on life, no matter how great his wealth or other personal resources. If he does, he also dies in the plunge of the Fugitivo.

The one man who tries to make some sense of what occurs but who is unable to succeed on his own terms any more than the others is Kilroy, the man who is always here, there, and everywhere, the personification of the innocent naïve "John Public." Kilroy has strength, proven by his golden gloves, but strength alone will not maintain existence. Kilroy's manly ability has failed him in his overexpanded, but solidly golden heart. When the symbol of his once-great strength is surrendered, it can purchase only a few items of an easily penetrated disguise in an abortive attempt to hide his true self and to flee. Kilroy, the good and the generous, is forever the fall guy, the Patsy, at the mercy of the Gutmans of the world, who can command his capture and humiliation at will. His agility and his intelligence, his innate goodness and strength, are useless, and he can only blink his electrically lighted nose on command. On the positive side, however, Kilroy represents a fine quality of humanity that even the wanton Gypsy's daughter, for all her easily accessible professional love, can recognize. To the dismay of her brassy parent, she wilfully chooses the penniless, unsuccessful Patsy. Her charms Kilroy cannot resist; even the image of his One True Woman cannot overcome his human urgencies. His symbolic, yet explicit seduction of the perennially renewed virgin becomes a hilarious counterpart to the falsely elegant courtship between Casanova and Marguerite at the other side of the square. Then Kilroy dies, but at the same time he lives. He finds his golden heart cannot purchase him a single one of the Gypsy's daughter's charms. Her own hunger satisfied, she has no further interest in his manliness, and she returns to the innocence of childhood in her infant's nightdress. Thus dead and reborn, Kilroy is able to escape, and as he prepares to cross the terror of the desert outside, the fountain flows and life seems on the verge of renewal on the Camino Real. There is, then, hope, but there is no hope without a fight or, for that matter, no hope without death.

Beyond these points, *Camino Real* can mean what the viewer wishes it to mean. In whatever way he takes it, no spectator can remain unmoved. He may attack violently, or defend with vigor, but he will be unable to deny that he has experienced a memorable evening of tremendous theatre.

Tennessee Williams

Thomas Lanier Williams was born in 1914 in Columbus, Mississippi, the son of a shoe salesman and the grandson of an Episcopalian clergyman. His ancestry included a number of Tennessee Indian fighters, from whom he chose his better-known name. He grew up in a Southern atmosphere, mainly in St. Louis. Much of his interest in literature stems from his father, who called him "Miss Nancy" and could not understand the boy's dislike for sports and outdoor activities.

Williams' interest in the pathetic women so often portrayed in his plays comes from visits with his grandfather on parish calls into the homes of the decaying gentility around St. Louis. At the age of fourteen he found that writing helped him to withdraw from an unpleasant world, and in 1928 he sold a story to a pulp magazine, *Weird Tales*, for $35.

Since the elder Williams wished his son to start earning money as soon as possible, young Tennessee dropped out of the University of Missouri in 1933 during his sophomore year. Two years of work in a shoe factory and extensive writing late at night resulted in a nervous collapse. Upon recovery he entered Washington University in St. Louis in 1936 and later the University of Iowa, where he received his B.A. in 1938.

Williams continued writing after moving to New York. At one time he was employed to recite poetry at a Greenwich Village night club. In 1939 he won a prize from the Group Theatre for four one-act plays entitled *American Blues*, and joined Theresa Helburn's and John Gassner's playwriting seminar at the New School for Social Research. In 1940 the Theatre Guild purchased *Battle of Angels*, a disastrous failure. Assistance from friends, Rockefeller Foundation grants, and the American Academy and National Institute of Arts and Letters sustained him until he was able to produce his first success, *The Glass Menagerie*, in 1945. After indifferent luck in collaborating with Donald Windham on the dramatization of a D. H. Lawrence story, *You Touched Me*, in 1946, Williams reached permanent fame, a Pulitzer Prize, and a Drama Critics' Circle Award with *A Streetcar Named Desire*. Since that time he has remained one of the dominant figures in American drama. *Summer and Smoke* in 1948 was not a Broadway success, but thrived in an Off Broadway revival at the Circle in the Square during 1952-1953. *Cat on a Hot Tin Roof* won a duplicate pair of prizes in 1954. *Orpheus Descending* was a failure in 1957, but a pair of short plays Off Broadway called *Garden District* did well in 1958. *Sweet Bird of Youth* opened in 1959 to further critical praise. A revised and somewhat shortened version of *Camino Real* received mixed reviews in an Off Broadway production in 1960.

Williams has also written a number of short stories and poems. In 1946 he published "27 Wagonsful of Cotton"; in 1950 a novel, "The Roman Spring of Mrs. Stone," and in 1954 "One Arm and Other Stories." "In the Winter of Cities," 1956, is a collection of fifty-four poems. He has also published *Baby Doll*, his first original screen play, which appeared with considerable national sensation in 1956. Other films, *Suddenly Last Summer*, and *The Fugitive Kind*, based on *Orpheus Descending*, were released in 1959 and 1960.

CAMINO REAL

by

Tennessee Williams

In the middle of the journey of our life I came to myself in a dark **wood**
where the straight way was lost.

Canto I, Dante's *Inferno*

This broad caricature of the mad fiesta from *Camino Real* successfully catches the spirit
of Williams' play. Among those present in this wild mélange are Lord Byron, Casanova,
the Gypsy's Daughter, Kilroy, the Gypsy, Marguerite Gauthier, and Gutman. (*The New
York Times. Courtesy Al Hirschfeld.*)

ORIGINAL EDITOR'S NOTE

The version of *Camino Real** here published is considerably revised over the one presented on Broadway. Following the opening there, Mr. Williams went to his home at Key West and continued to work on this play. When he left six weeks later to direct Donald Windham's *Starless Night* in Houston, Texas, he took the playing version with him and reworked it whenever time allowed. It was with him when he drove in leisurely fashion back to New York. As delivered to the publisher, the manuscript of *Camino Real* was typed on three different typewriters and on stationery of hotels across the country.

Three characters, a prologue and several scenes that were not in the Broadway production have been added, or reinstated from earlier, preproduction versions, while other scenes have been deleted.

Camino Real is divided into a Prologue and Sixteen "Blocks," scenes with no perceptible time lapse between them for the most part. There are intermissions indicated after Block Six and Block Eleven.

The action takes place in an unspecified Latin-American country.

Camino Real was first written in 1948 as a one-act play called *Ten Blocks on the Camino Real*. In its present form it had its Broadway premiere on March 19, 1953 at the Martin Beck Theatre. It ran for 60 performances. The following cast appeared in the original production:

GUTMAN	*Frank Silvera*
SURVIVOR	*Guy Thomajan*
ROSITA	*Aza Bard*
FIRST OFFICER	*Henry Silva*
JACQUES CASANOVA	*Joseph Anthony*
LA MADRECITA DE LOS PERDIDOS	*Vivian Nathan*
HER SON	*Rolando Valdez*
KILROY	*Eli Wallach*
FIRST STREET CLEANER	*Nehemiah Persoff*
SECOND STREET CLEANER	*Fred Sadoff*
ABDULLAH	*Ernesto Gonzalez*
A BUM IN A WINDOW	*Martin Balsam*
A. RATT	*Mike Gazzo*
THE LOAN SHARK	*Salem Ludwig*
BARON DE CHARLUS	*David J. Stewart*
LOBO	*Ronne Aul*
SECOND OFFICER	*William Lennard*
A GROTESQUE MUMMER	*Gluck Sandor*
MARGUERITE GAUTIER	*Jo Van Fleet*
LADY MULLIGAN	*Lucille Patton*
WAITER	*Page Johnson*
LORD BYRON	*Hurd Hatfield*

* The original production employed an Anglicized pronunciation of the title: *Cá*-mino *Ré*al.

NAVIGATOR OF THE FUGITIVO	*Antony Vorno*
PILOT OF THE FUGITIVO	*Martin Balsam*
MARKET WOMAN	*Charlotte Jones*
SECOND MARKET WOMAN	*Joanna Vischer*
STREET VENDOR	*Ruth Volner*
LORD MULLIGAN	*Parker Wilson*
THE GYPSY	*Jennie Goldstein*
HER DAUGHTER, ESMERALDA	*Barbara Baxley*
NURSIE	*Salem Ludwig*
EVA	*Mary Grey*
THE INSTRUCTOR	*David J. Stewart*
ASSISTANT INSTRUCTOR	*Parker Wilson*
MEDICAL STUDENT	*Page Johnson*
DON QUIXOTE	*Hurd Hatfield*
SANCHO PANZA	*(Not in production)*
PRUDENCE DUVERNOY	*(Not in production)*
OLYMPE	*(Not in production)*

Produced by Cheryl Crawford and Ethel Reiner, in association with
Walter P. Chrysler, Jr.
Directed by Elia Kazan, assisted by Anna Sokolow
Settings and costumes by Lemual Ayers
Incidental music by Bernardo Ségall
Production associate, Anderson Lawler

NOTES CONCERNING SOME OF THE CHARACTERS

JACQUES CASANOVA. Williams assigns a French name to the Italian adventurer
Giovanni Jacopo Casanova de Seingalt. He lived from 1725 to 1798. His published
"Memoirs" are famous for their record of his many love affairs. Although a rogue,
he was not as debauched and brutal as the traditional, and mostly fictional, Don
Juan, or Don Giovanni. The name "Casanova" has become synonymous with "great
lover."

LA MADRECITA DE LOS PERDIDOS means "Little Mother of the Lost Ones."

KILROY. During the Second World War a tradition grew up around a mysterious
character who, though never seen, always managed to reach every objective before
anyone else. He invariably left for those who followed him the same message
scrawled on any convenient object: "Kilroy was here." The ability of Kilroy to
get anywhere, no matter how remote or inaccessible, became a widespread joke.
He evolved as a kind of extension of the enterprising American GI who could
accomplish anything long before the high brass ever got around to it, always
leaving his curt message behind. Williams uses Kilroy as the symbol of youthful
innocence and strength, and of the good-in-heart who can do what almost nobody
else in the play can—escape.

BARON DE CHARLUS is a leading character in Marcel Proust's "Remembrance of
Things Past," portrayed as a masochistic homosexual approaching insanity in his
older age.

MARGUERITE GAUTIER is better known to Americans as "Camille." She is the heroine of the novel "La Dame aux Camélias" by Alexandre Dumas, *fils*, written in 1848,

and the play of the same name, also by Dumas, written in 1852. English translations of both the novel and the play are entitled "Camille." She represents Casanova's counterpart as the wanton female lover, selling her affections. She is also representative of the languishing, consumptive courtesan whose lost soul is redeemed by pure love before her agonizing death.

LORD BYRON. George Noel Gordon, Lord Byron, lived his short life from 1788 to 1824. He was the most famous English romantic writer. In *Camino Real* he enacts the part of the hero he so often created in his poetry, sad and melancholy, melodramatic, brooding upon mysterious and evil things. Byron had a reputation for wild debauchery, which he did nothing to discourage. The reference to Shelley's death is based on fact. Percy Bysshe Shelley (1792–1822) was also a famous English romantic poet, irresponsible and amoral, involved in many tempestuous love affairs. He was drowned in the Adriatic Sea, and his body was cremated.

ESMERALDA is the gypsy heroine of Victor Hugo's "Notre Dame de Paris" (better known in America as "The Hunchback of Notre Dame") of 1831. She was probably suggested to Hugo by Preciosa, in Cervantes' novelette, "La Gitanilla," 1613.

DON QUIXOTE is the hero of "Don Quixote de la Mancha," the great Spanish satirical novel by Cervantes, published in 1605 and 1615, which made fun of the prevalent exaggerated attitudes toward chivalry. Don Quixote has come to signify the individual who is inherently good, but whose ideas are impractical, and whose dreams of great accomplishments in life are preposterous and continually shifting from one impossible deed to another.

SANCHO PANZA is Don Quixote's faithful and practical-minded squire, who accompanies him on all of his escapades.

PRUDENCE DUVERNOY. A milliner friend of Marguerite Gautier.

OLYMPE. Another friend of Marguerite.

PROLOGUE

As the curtain rises, on an almost lightless stage, there is a loud singing of wind, accompanied by distant, measured reverberations like pounding surf or distant shellfire. Above the ancient wall that backs the set and the perimeter of mountains visible above the wall, are flickers of a white radiance as though daybreak were a white bird caught in a net and struggling to rise. The plaza is seen fitfully by this light. It belongs to a tropical seaport that bears a confusing, but somehow harmonious, resemblance to such widely scattered ports as Tangiers, Havana, Vera Cruz, Casablanca, Shanghai, New Orleans. On stage left is the luxury side of the street, containing the façade of the Siete Mares[1] hotel and its low terrace on which are a number of glass-topped white iron tables and chairs. In the downstairs there is a great bay window in which are seen a pair of elegant "dummies," one seated, one standing behind, looking out into the plaza with painted smiles. Upstairs is a small balcony and behind it a large window exposing a wall on which is hung a phoenix painted on silk: this should be softly lighted now and then in the play, since resurrections are so much a part of its meaning. Opposite the hotel is Skid Row which contains the GYPSY's gaudy stall, the LOAN SHARK's establishment with a window containing a variety of pawned articles, and the "Ritz Men Only" which is a flea-bag hotel or flophouse and which has a practical window above its downstairs entrance, in which a bum will appear from time to time to deliver appropriate or contra-

[1] Seven Seas.

puntal song titles. Upstage is a great flight of stairs that mount the ancient wall to a sort of archway that leads out into "Terra Incognita,"[2] as it is called in the play, a wasteland between the walled town and the distant perimeter of snow-topped mountains. Downstage right and left are a pair of arches which give entrance to dead-end streets.

Immediately after the curtain rises a shaft of blue light is thrown down a central aisle of the theatre, and in this light, advancing from the back of the house, appears DON QUIXOTE DE LA MANCHA, *dressed like an old "desert rat." As he enters the aisle he shouts, "Hola!", in a cracked old voice which is still full of energy and is answered by another voice which is impatient and tired, that of his squire,* SANCHO PANZA. *Stumbling with a fatigue which is only physical, the old knight comes down the aisle, and* SANCHO *follows a couple of yards behind him, loaded down with equipment that ranges from a medieval shield to a military canteen or Thermos bottle. Shouts are exchanged between them.*

QUIXOTE (*ranting above the wind in a voice which is nearly as old*). Blue is the color of distance!

SANCHO (*wearily behind him*). Yes, distance is blue.

QUIXOTE. Blue is also the color of nobility.

SANCHO. Yes, nobility's blue.

QUIXOTE. Blue is the color of distance and nobility, and that's why an old knight should always have somewhere about him a bit of blue ribbon . . . (*He jostles the elbow of an aisle-sitter as he staggers with fatigue; he mumbles an apology.*)

SANCHO. Yes, a bit of blue ribbon.

QUIXOTE. A bit of faded blue ribbon, tucked away in whatever remains of his armor, or borne on the tip of his lance,

his—unconquerable lance! It serves to remind an old knight of distance that he has gone and distance he has yet to go . . . (SANCHO *mutters the Spanish word for excrement as several pieces of rusty armor fall into the aisle.* QUIXOTE *has now arrived at the foot of the steps onto the forestage. He pauses there as if wandering out of or into a dream.* SANCHO *draws up clanking behind him.* MR. GUTMAN, *a lordly fat man wearing a linen suit and a pith helmet, appears dimly on the balcony of the Siete Mares, a white cockatoo on his wrist. The bird cries out harshly.*)

GUTMAN. Hush, Aurora.

QUIXOTE. It also reminds an old knight of that green country he lived in which was the youth of his heart, before such singing words as *Truth!*

SANCHO (*panting*).—Truth.

QUIXOTE. *Valor!*[3]

SANCHO.—Valor.

QUIXOTE (*elevating his lance*). *Devoir!*[4]

SANCHO.—Devoir . . .

QUIXOTE.—turned into the meaningless mumble of some old monk hunched over cold mutton at supper! (GUTMAN *alerts a pair of* GUARDS *in the plaza, who cross with red lanterns to either side of the proscenium where they lower black and white striped barrier gates as if the proscenium marked a frontier. One of them, with a hand on his holster, advances toward the pair on the steps.*)

GUARD. Vien aquí.[5] (SANCHO *hangs back but* QUIXOTE *stalks up to the barrier gate. The* GUARD *turns a flashlight on his long and exceedingly grave red face, "frisks" him casually for concealed weapons, examines a rusty old knife and tosses it contemptuously away.*) Sus papeles! Sus documentos![6] (QUIXOTE *fumblingly produces some tattered old papers from the lining of his hat.*)

GUTMAN (*impatiently*). Who is it?

[2] Unknown Land.
[3] "Courage!"
[4] "Duty!"
[5] Good Spanish would be *ven aquí.* The language on the Camino Real is apparently a kind of hybrid of Williams' own invention, based on Spanish, but there are smatterings of French and Italian thrown in.
[6] "Your papers! Your identification!"

GUARD. An old desert rat named Quixote.

GUTMAN. Oh!—Expected!—Let him in. (*The* GUARDS *raise the barrier gate and one sits down to smoke on the terrace.* SANCHO *hangs back still. A dispute takes place on the forestage and steps into the aisle.*)

QUIXOTE. Forward!

SANCHO. Aw, naw. I know this place. (*He produces a crumpled parchment.*) Here it is on the chart. Look, it says here, "Continue until you come to the square of a walled town which is the end of the Camino Real and the beginning of the Camino Real. Halt there," it says, "and turn back, Traveler, for the spring of humanity has gone dry in this place and—"

QUIXOTE (*He snatches the chart from him and reads the rest of the inscription*). "—there are no birds in the country except wild birds that are tamed and kept in—" (*He holds the chart close to his nose.*)—Cages!

SANCHO (*urgently*). Let's go back to La Mancha!

QUIXOTE. Forward!

SANCHO. The time has come for retreat!

QUIXOTE. The time for retreat never comes!

SANCHO. *I'm* going back to *La Mancha!* (*He dumps the knightly equipment into the orchestra pit.*)

QUIXOTE. *Without me?*

SANCHO (*bustling up the aisle*). With you or without you, old tireless and tiresome master!

QUIXOTE (*imploringly*). Saaaaaan-cho-ooooooooo!

SANCHO (*near the top of the aisle*). I'm going back to La Maaaaaaaan-chaaaaaaa. (*He disappears as the blue light in the aisle dims out. The* GUARD *puts out his cigarette and wanders out of the plaza. The wind moans and* GUTMAN *laughs softly as the ancient knight enters the plaza with such a desolate air.*)

QUIXOTE (*looking about the plaza*).— Lonely . . . (*To his surprise the word is echoed softly by almost unseen figures huddled below the stairs and against the* wall of the town. QUIXOTE *leans upon his lance and observes with a wry smile*—)—When so many are lonely as seem to be lonely, it would be inexcusably selfish to be lonely alone. (*He shakes out a dusty blanket. Shadowy arms extend toward him and voices murmur.*)

VOICE. Sleep. Sleep. Sleep.

QUIXOTE (*arranging his blanket*). Yes, I'll sleep for a while, I'll sleep and dream for a while against the wall of this town . . . (*A mandolin or guitar plays "The Nightingale of France."*)—And my dream will be a pageant, a masque in which old meanings will be remembered and possibly new ones discovered, and when I wake from this sleep and this disturbing pageant of a dream, I'll choose one among its shadows to take along with me in the place of Sancho . . . (*He blows his nose between his fingers and wipes them on his shirttail.*)—For new companions are not as familiar as old ones but all the same—they're old ones with only slight differences of face and figure, which may or may not be improvements, and it would be selfish of me to be lonely alone . . . (*He stumbles down the incline into the Pit below the stairs where most of the* STREET PEOPLE *huddle beneath awnings of open stalls. The white cockatoo squawks.*)

GUTMAN. Hush, Aurora.

QUIXOTE. And tomorrow at this same hour, which we call madrugada, the loveliest of all words, except the word alba, and that word also means daybreak— Yes, at daybreak tomorrow I will go on from here with a new companion and this old bit of blue ribbon to keep me in mind of distance that I have gone and distance I have yet to go, and also to keep me in mind of— (*The cockatoo cries wildly.* QUIXOTE *nods as if in agreement with the outcry and folds himself into his blanket below the great stairs.*)

GUTMAN (*stroking the cockatoo's crest*). Be still, Aurora. I know it's morning, Aurora. (*Daylight turns the plaza silver and slowly gold. Vendors rise beneath white awnings of stalls. The* GYPSY's *stall opens. A tall, courtly figure, in his late middle years* (JACQUES CASANOVA) *crosses from the* LOAN SHARK'S, *removing a silver snuff box from his pocket as* GUTMAN *speaks. His costume, like that of all the legendary characters in the play (except perhaps* QUIXOTE) *is generally "modern" but with vestigial touches of the period to which he was actually related. The cane and the snuff box and perhaps a brocaded vest may be sufficient to give this historical suggestion in* CASANOVA'S *case. He bears his hawklike head with a sort of anxious pride on most occasions, a pride maintained under a steadily mounting pressure.*)—It's morning and after morning. It's afternoon, ha ha! And now I must go downstairs to announce the beginning of that old wanderer's dream . . . (*He withdraws from the balcony as old* PRUDENCE DUVERNOY *stumbles out of the hotel, as if not yet quite awake from an afternoon siesta. Chattering with beads and bracelets, she wanders vaguely down into the plaza, raising a faded green silk parasol, damp henna-streaked hair slipping under a monstrous hat of faded silk roses; she is searching for a lost poodle.*)

PRUDENCE. Trique? Trique? (JACQUES *comes out of the* LOAN SHARK'S *replacing his case angrily in his pocket.*)

JACQUES. Why, I'd rather give it to a street beggar! This case is a Boucheron, I won it at faro at the summer palace, at Tsarskoe Selo in the winter of— (*The* LOAN SHARK *slams the door.* JACQUES *glares, then shrugs and starts across the plaza. Old* PRUDENCE *is crouched over the filthy gray bundle of a dying mongrel by the fountain.*)

PRUDENCE. Trique, oh, Trique! (*The* GYPSY'S *son,* ABDULLAH, *watches, giggling.*)

JACQUES (*reproving*). It is a terrible thing for an old woman to outlive her dogs. (*He crosses to* PRUDENCE *and gently disengages the animal from her grasp.*) Madam, that is not Trique.

PRUDENCE.—When I woke up she wasn't in her basket . . .

JACQUES. Sometimes we sleep too long in the afternoon and when we wake we find things changed, Signora.

PRUDENCE. Oh, you're Italian!

JACQUES. I am from Venice, Signora.

PRUDENCE. Ah, Venice, city of pearls! I saw you last night on the terrace dining with—Oh, I'm so worried about her! I'm an old friend of hers, perhaps she's mentioned me to you. Prudence Duvernoy? I was her best friend in the old days in Paris, but now she's forgotten so much . . . I hope you have influence with her! (*A waltz of Camille's time in Paris is heard.*) I want you to give her a message from a certain wealthy old gentleman that she met at one of those watering places she used to go to for her health. She resembled his daughter who died of consumption and so he adored Camille, lavished everything on her! What did she do? Took a young lover who hadn't a couple of pennies to rub together, disinherited by his father because of *her!* Oh, you can't do that, not now, not any more, you've got to be realistic on the Camino Real! (GUTMAN *has come out on the terrace: he announces quietly—*)

GUTMAN. Block One on the Camino Real.

BLOCK ONE

PRUDENCE (*continuing*). Yes, you've got to be practical on it! Well, give her this message, please, Sir. He wants her back on any terms whatsoever! (*Her speech gathers furious momentum.*) Her evenings will be free. He wants only her mornings, mornings are hard on old men because their hearts beat slowly, and he wants only her mornings! Well, that's how it should be! A sensible arrangement! Elderly gentlemen have to content themselves with a lady's spare time before supper! Isn't that so? Of course so! And so I told him! I told him, Camille isn't well! She requires delicate care! Has many debts, creditors storm her door! "How much does she owe?" he asked me, and, oh, did I do some lightning mathematics! Jewels in pawn, I told him, pearls, rings, necklaces, bracelets, diamond ear-drops are in pawn! Horses put up for sale at a public auction!

JACQUES (*appalled by this torrent*). Signora, Signora, all of these things are—

PRUDENCE.—What?

JACQUES. *Dreams!* (GUTMAN *laughs. A woman sings at a distance.*)

PRUDENCE (*continuing with less assurance*).—You're not so young as I thought when I saw you last night on the terrace by candlelight on the—Oh, but—Ho ho!—I bet there is *one* old fountain in this plaza that hasn't gone dry! (*She pokes him obscenely. He recoils.* GUTMAN *laughs.* JACQUES *starts away but she seizes his arm again, and the torrent of speech continues.*) Wait, wait, listen! Her candle is burning low. But how can you tell? She might have a lingering end, and charity hospitals? Why, you might as well take a flying leap into the Streetcleaners' barrel. Oh, I've told her and told her not to live in a dream! A dream is nothing to live in, why, it's gone like a—Don't let her elegance fool you! That girl has done the Camino in carriages but she has also done it on foot! She knows every stone the Camino is paved with! So tell her

this. You tell her, she won't listen to me!—Times and conditions have undergone certain changes since we were friends in Paris, and now we dismiss young lovers with skins of silk and eyes like a child's first prayer, we put them away as lightly as we put away white gloves meant only for summer, and pick up a pair of black ones, suitable for winter . . . (*The singing voice rises: then subsides.*)

JACQUES. Excuse me, Madam. (*He tears himself from her grasp and rushes into the Siete Mares.*)

PRUDENCE (*dazed, to* GUTMAN).—What block is this?

GUTMAN. Block One.

PRUDENCE. I didn't hear the announcement . . .

GUTMAN (*coldly*). Well, now you do. (OLYMPE *comes out of the lobby with a pale orange silk parasol like a floating moon.*)

OLYMPE. Oh, there you are, I've looked for you high and low!—mostly low . . . (*They float vaguely out into the dazzling plaza as though a capricious wind took them, finally drifting through the Moorish arch downstage right. The song dies out.*)

GUTMAN (*lighting a thin cigar*). Block Two on the Camino Real.

BLOCK TWO

After GUTMAN'S *announcement, a hoarse cry is heard. A figure in rags, skin blackened by the sun, tumbles crazily down the steep alley to the plaza. He turns about blindly, murmuring: "A donde la fuente?"*[7] *He stumbles against the hideous old prostitute* ROSITA *who grins horribly and whispers something to him, hitching up her ragged, filthy skirt. Then she gives him a jocular push toward the fountain. He falls upon his belly and thrusts his hands into the dried-up basin. Then he staggers to his feet with a despairing cry.*

THE SURVIVOR. La fuente está seca![8]

(ROSITA *laughs madly but the other* STREET PEOPLE *moan. A dry gourd rattles.*)

ROSITA. The fountain is dry, but there's plenty to drink in the Siete Mares! (*She shoves him toward the hotel. The proprietor,* GUTMAN, *steps out, smoking a thin cigar, fanning himself with a palm leaf. As the* SURVIVOR *advances,* GUTMAN *whistles. A man in military dress comes out upon the low terrace.*)

OFFICER. Go back! (*The* SURVIVOR *stumbles forward. The* OFFICER *fires at him. He lowers his hands to his stomach, turns slowly about with a lost expres-*

---

[7] More correctly, "*Dónde está la fuente?*" meaning "Where's the fountain?"
[8] "The fountain is dry!"

sion, looking up at the sky, and stumbles toward the fountain. During the scene that follows, until the entrance of LA MADRECITA and her SON, the SURVIVOR drags himself slowly about the concrete rim of the fountain, almost entirely ignored, as a dying pariah dog in a starving country. JACQUES CASANOVA comes out upon the terrace of the Siete Mares. Now he passes the hotel proprietor's impassive figure, descending a step beneath and a little in advance of him, and without looking at him.)

JACQUES (with infinite weariness and disgust). What has happened?

GUTMAN (serenely). We have entered the second in a progress of sixteen blocks on the Camino Real. It's five o'clock. That angry old lion, the Sun, looked back once and growled and then went switching his tail toward the cool shade of the Sierras. Our guests have taken their afternoon siestas . . . (The SURVIVOR has come out upon the forestage, now, not like a dying man but like a shy speaker who has forgotten the opening line of his speech. He is only a little crouched over with a hand obscuring the red stain over his belly. Two or three STREET PEOPLE wander about calling their wares: "Tacos, tacos, fritos . . ."–"Lotería, lotería"⁹–ROSITA shuffles around, calling "Love? Love?"–pulling down the filthy décolletage of her blouse to show more of her sagging bosom. The SURVIVOR arrives at the top of the stairs descending into the orchestra of the theatre, and hangs onto it, looking out reflectively as a man over the rail of a boat coming into a somewhat disturbingly strange harbor.)

GUTMAN (continuing).–They suffer from extreme fatigue, our guests at the Siete Mares, all of them have a degree or two of fever. Questions are passed amongst them like something illicit and shameful, like counterfeit money or drugs or indecent postcards– (He leans forward and whispers:)–"What is this place? Where are we? What is the meaning of–Shhhh!"–Ha ha. . . .

THE SURVIVOR (very softly to the audience). I once had a pony named Peeto. He caught in his nostrils the scent of thunderstorms coming even before the clouds had crossed the Sierra . . .

VENDOR. Tacos, tacos, fritos . . .

ROSITA. Love? Love?

LADY MULLIGAN (to waiter on terrace). Are you sure no one called me? I was expecting a call . . .

GUTMAN (smiling). My guests are confused and exhausted but at this hour they pull themselves together, and drift downstairs on the wings of gin and the lift, they drift into the public rooms and exchange notes again on fashionable couturiers and custom tailors, restaurants, vintages of wine, hair-dressers, plastic surgeons, girls and young men susceptible to offers . . . (There is a hum of light conversation and laughter within.)–Hear them? They're exchanging notes . . .

JACQUES (striking the terrace with his cane). I asked you what has happened in the plaza!

GUTMAN. Oh, in the plaza, ha ha!–Happenings in the plaza don't concern us . . .

JACQUES. I heard shots fired.

GUTMAN. Shots were fired to remind you of your good fortune in staying here. The public fountains have gone dry, you know, but the Siete Mares was erected over the only perpetual never-dried-up spring in Tierra Caliente,¹⁰ and of course that advantage has to be–protected–sometimes by–martial law . . . (The guitar resumes.)

THE SURVIVOR. When Peeto, my pony, was born–he stood on his four legs at once, and accepted the world!–He was wiser than I . . .

VENDOR. Fritos, fritos, tacos!

ROSITA. Love!

THE SURVIVOR.–When Peeto was one

---

⁹ Tacos are a kind of corn pancake called tortillas wrapped around meat. Fritos are fritters. Lotería means lottery tickets.
¹⁰ Hot Country.

year old he was wiser than God! (*A wind sings across the plaza; a dry gourd rattles.*) "Peeto, Peeto!" the Indian boys call after him, trying to stop him—trying to stop the wind! (*The* SURVIVOR's *head sags forward. He sits down as slowly as an old man on a park bench.* JACQUES *strikes the terrace again with his cane and starts toward the* SURVIVOR. *The* GUARD *seizes his elbow.*)

JACQUES. Don't put your hand on *me!*

GUARD. Stay here.

GUTMAN. Remain on the terrace, please, Signor Casanova.

JACQUES (*fiercely*).—Cognac! (*The* WAITER *whispers to* GUTMAN. GUTMAN *chuckles.*)

GUTMAN. The Maître 'D' tells me that your credit has been discontinued in the restaurant and bar, he says that he has enough of your tabs to pave the terrace with!

JACQUES. What a piece of impertinence! I told the man that the letter that I'm expecting has been delayed in the mail. The postal service in this country is fantastically disorganized, and you know it! You also know that Mlle. Gautier will guarantee my tabs!

GUTMAN. Then let her pick them up at dinner tonight if you're hungry!

JACQUES. I'm not accustomed to this kind of treatment on the Camino Real!

GUTMAN. Oh, you'll be, you'll be, after a single night at the "Ritz Men Only." That's where you'll have to transfer your patronage if the letter containing the remittance check doesn't arrive tonight.

JACQUES. I assure you that I shall do nothing of the sort!—Tonight or ever!

GUTMAN. Watch out, old hawk, the wind is ruffling your feathers! (JACQUES *sinks trembling into a chair.*)—Give him a thimble of brandy before he collapses . . . Fury is a luxury of the young, their veins are resilient, but his are brittle . . .

JACQUES. Here I sit, submitting to insult for a thimble of brandy—while directly in front of me— (*The singer,* LA MADRECITA, *enters the plaza. She is a blind woman led by a ragged* YOUNG MAN. *The* WAITER *brings* JACQUES *a brandy.*)—a man in the plaza dies like a pariah dog!—I take the brandy! I sip it!—My heart is too tired to break, my heart is too tired to—break . . . (LA MADRECITA *chants softly. She slowly raises her arm to point at the* SURVIVOR *crouched on the steps from the plaza.*)

GUTMAN (*suddenly*). Give me the phone! Connect me with the Palace. Get me the Generalissimo, quick, quick, quick! (*The* SURVIVOR *rises feebly and shuffles very slowly toward the extended arms of "The Little Blind One."*) Generalissimo? Gutman speaking! Hello, sweetheart. There has been a little incident in the plaza. You know that party of young explorers that attempted to cross the desert on foot? Well, one of them's come back. He was very thirsty. He found the fountain dry. He started toward the hotel. He was politely advised to advance no further. But he disregarded this advice. Action had to be taken. And now, and now—that old blind woman they call "La Madrecita"?—She's come into the plaza with the man called "The Dreamer" . . .

SURVIVOR. Donde?

THE DREAMER. Aquí![11]

GUTMAN (*continuing*). You remember those two! I once mentioned them to you. You said "They're harmless dreamers and they're loved by the people."—"What," I asked you, "is harmless about a dreamer, and what," I asked you, "is harmless about the love of the people?—Revolution only needs good dreamers who remember their dreams, and the love of the people belongs safely only to you—their Generalissimo!"—Yes, now the blind woman has recovered her sight and is extending her arms to the wounded Survivor, and the man with the guitar is leading him to her . . . (*The described action is being enacted.*) *Wait one moment!* There's a possibility that the forbidden word may be spoken! Yes! The forbidden word is about to be

---

[11] "Where? Here!"

spoken! (*The* DREAMER *places an arm about the blinded* SURVIVOR, *and cries out:*)

THE DREAMER. *Hermano!*[12] (*The cry is repeated like springing fire and a loud murmur sweeps the crowd. They push forward with cupped hands extended and the gasping cries of starving people at the sight of bread. Two* MILITARY GUARDS *herd them back under the colonnades with clubs and drawn revolvers.* LA MADRECITA *chants softly with her blind eyes lifted. A* GUARD *starts toward her. The* PEOPLE *shout "NO!"*)

LA MADRECITA (*chanting*). "Rojo está el sol! Rojo está el sol de sangre! Blanca está la luna! Blanca está la luna de miedo!"[13] (*The crowd makes a turning motion.*)

GUTMAN (*to the waiter*). Put up the ropes! (*Velvet ropes are strung very quickly about the terrace of the Siete Mares. They are like the ropes on decks of steamers in rough waters.* GUTMAN *shouts into the phone again:*) The word was spoken. The crowd is agitated. Hang on! (*He lays down instrument.*)

JACQUES (*hoarsely, shaken*). He said "Hermano." That's the word for brother.

GUTMAN (*calmly*). Yes, the most dangerous word in any human tongue is the word for brother. It's inflammatory.—I don't suppose it can be struck out of the language altogether but it must be reserved for strictly private usage in back of soundproof walls. Otherwise it disturbs the population . . .

JACQUES. The people need the word. They're thirsty for it!

GUTMAN. What are these creatures? Mendicants. Prostitutes. Thieves and petty vendors in a bazaar where the human heart is a part of the bargain.

JACQUES. Because they need the word and the word is forbidden!

GUTMAN. The word is said in pulpits and at tables of council where its volatile essence can be contained. But on the lips of these creatures, what is it? A wanton incitement to riot, without understanding. For what is a brother to them but someone to get ahead of, to cheat, to lie to, to undersell in the market. Brother, you say to a man whose wife you sleep with!—But now, you see, the word has disturbed the people and made it necessary to invoke martial law! (*Meanwhile the* DREAMER *has brought the* SURVIVOR *to* LA MADRECITA, *who is seated on the cement rim of the fountain. She has cradled the dying man in her arms in the attitude of a Pietà.*[14] *The* DREAMER *is crouched beside them, softly playing a guitar. Now he springs up with a harsh cry:*)

THE DREAMER. *Muerto!*[15] (*The* STREET-CLEANERS' *piping commences at a distance.* GUTMAN *seizes the phone again.*)

GUTMAN (*into phone*). Generalissimo, the Survivor is no longer surviving. I think we'd better have some public diversion right away. Put the Gypsy on! Have her announce the Fiesta!

LOUDSPEAKER (*responding instantly*). Damas y Caballeros![16] The next voice you hear will be the voice of—the Gypsy!

GYPSY (*over loudspeaker*). Hoy! Noche de Fiesta![17] Tonight the moon will restore the virginity of my daughter!

GUTMAN. Bring on the Gypsy's daughter, Esmeralda. Show the virgin-to-be! (ESMERALDA *is led from the* GYPSY's *stall by a severe duenna, "NURSIE," out upon the forestage. She is manacled by the wrist to the duenna. Her costume is vaguely Levantine.*[18] GUARDS *are herding the crowd back again.*) Ha ha! Ho ho

---

[12] "Brother!"

[13] "Red is the sun! Red is the sun of blood! White is the moon! White is the moon of fear!"

[14] A Pietà is the figure of the Virgin mourning over the dead body of Christ.

[15] "Dead!"

[16] "Ladies and Gentlemen!"

[17] "Night of Festivity!"

[18] The area at the eastern end of the Mediterranean.

ho! Music! (*There is gay music.* ROSITA *dances.*) Abdullah! You're on! (ABDULLAH *skips into the plaza, shouting histrionically.*)

ABDULLAH. Tonight the moon will restore the virginity of my sister, Esmeralda!

GUTMAN. *Dance, boy!* (ESMERALDA *is led back into the stall. Throwing off his burnoose,*[19] ABDULLAH *dances with* ROSITA. *Behind their dance, armed* GUARDS *force* LA MADRECITA *and the* DREAMER *to retreat from the fountain, leaving the lifeless body of the* SURVIVOR. *All at once there is a discordant blast of brass instruments.* KILROY *comes into the plaza. He is a young American vagrant, about*

twenty-seven. *He wears dungarees and a skivvy shirt, the pants faded nearly white from long wear and much washing, fitting him as closely as the clothes of sculpture. He has a pair of golden boxing gloves slung about his neck and he carries a small duffle bag. His belt is ruby-and-emerald-studded with the word* CHAMP *in bold letters. He stops before a chalked inscription on a wall downstage which says: "Kilroy Is Coming!" He scratches out "Coming" and over it prints "Here!"*)

GUTMAN. Ho ho!—a clown! The Eternal Punchinella![20] That's exactly what's needed in a time of crisis! Block Three on the Camino Real.

BLOCK THREE

KILROY (*genially, to all present*). Ha ha! (*Then he walks up to the* OFFICER *by the terrace of the Siete Mares.*) Buenas dias, señor. (*He gets no response—barely even a glance.*) Habla Inglesia? Usted?[21]

OFFICER. What is it you want?

KILROY. Where is Western Union or Wells-Fargo? I got to send a wire to some friends in the States.

OFFICER. No hay Western Union, no hay Wells-Fargo.

KILROY. That is very peculiar. I never struck a town yet that didn't have one or the other. I just got off a boat. Lousiest frigging tub I ever shipped on, one continual hell it was, all the way up from Rio. And me sick, too. I picked up one of those tropical fevers. No sick-bay on that tub, no doctor, no medicine or nothing, not even one quinine pill, and I was burning up with Christ knows how much fever. I couldn't make them understand I was sick. I got a bad heart,

too. I had to retire from the prize ring because of my heart. I was the light heavyweight champion of the West Coast, won these gloves!—before my ticker went bad.—Feel my chest! Go on, feel it! Feel it. I've got a heart in my chest as big as the head of a baby. Ha ha! They stood me in front of a screen that makes you transparent and that's what they seen inside me, a heart in my chest as big as the head of a baby! With something like that you don't need the Gypsy to tell you, "Time is short, Baby—get ready to hitch on wings!" The medics wouldn't okay me for no more fights. They said to give up liquor and smoking and sex!—To give up sex!—I used to believe a man couldn't live without sex—but he can—if he wants to! My real true woman, my wife, she would of stuck with me, but it was all spoiled with her being scared and me, too, that a real hard kiss would kill me!—So one night while she was sleeping I wrote her good-

[19] An Arab cloak and hood.

[20] Or "Pulcinella," a stock character from the Italian *commedia dell' arte* of the sixteenth and seventeenth centuries. He was generally typified by pugnaciousness, a humped back, hooked nose, and a coxcomb. His most direct descendant in modern times is Punch of Punch and Judy puppetry.

[21] Kilroy's Spanish is far from perfect. He should be saying *"Buenos días, señor. Habla inglés?"* He is probably getting his message across, however, saying "Good day, sir. Do you speak English?" The *"Usted"* is a "You" added for emphasis.

bye . . . (*He notices a lack of attention in the* OFFICER: *he grins.*) No comprendo the lingo?

OFFICER. What is it you want?

KILROY. Excuse my ignorance, but what place is this? What is this country and what is the name of this town? I know it seems funny of me to ask such a question. Loco! But I was so glad to get off that rotten tub that I didn't ask nothing of no one except my pay—and I got short-changed on that. I have trouble counting these pesos or Whatzit-you-call-'em. (*He jerks out his wallet.*) All-a-this-here. In the States that pile of lettuce would make you a plutocrat!—But I bet you this stuff don't add up to fifty dollars American coin. Ha ha!

OFFICER. Ha ha.

KILROY. Ha ha!

OFFICER (*making it sound like a death-rattle*). Ha-ha-ha-ha-ha. (*He turns and starts into the cantina.*[22] KILROY *grabs his arm.*)

KILROY. Hey!

OFFICER. What is it you want?

KILROY. What is the name of this country and this town? (*The* OFFICER *thrusts his elbow in* KILROY'S *stomach and twists his arm loose with a Spanish curse. He kicks the swinging doors open and enters the cantina.*) Brass hats are the same everywhere. (*As soon as the* OFFICER *goes, the* STREET PEOPLE *come forward and crowd about* KILROY *with their wheedling cries.*)

STREET PEOPLE. Dulces, dulces! Lotería! Lotería! Pasteles, café con leche!

KILROY. No caree, no caree![23] (*The* PROSTITUTE *creeps up to him and grins.*)

ROSITA. Love? Love?

KILROY. What did you say?

ROSITA. *Love?*

KILROY. Sorry—I don't feature that. (*To audience.*) I have ideals. (*The* GYPSY *appears on the roof of her establishment with* ESMERALDA *whom she*

secures by handcuffs to the iron railing.*)

GYPSY. Stay there while I give the pitch! (*She then advances with a portable microphone.*) Testing! One, two, three, four!

NURSIE (*from offstage*). You're on the air!

GYPSY'S LOUDSPEAKER. Are you perplexed by something? Are you tired out and confused? Do you have a fever? (KILROY *looks around for the source of the voice.*) Do you feel yourself to be spiritually unprepared for the age of exploding atoms? Do you distrust the newspapers? Are you suspicious of governments? Have you arrived at a point on the Camino Real where the walls converge not in the distance but right in front of your nose? Does further progress appear impossible to you? Are you afraid of anything at all? Afraid of your heartbeat? Or the eyes of strangers! Afraid of breathing? Afraid of not breathing? Do you wish that things could be straight and simple again as they were in your childhood? Would you like to go back to Kindy Garten? (ROSITA *has crept up to* KILROY *while he listens. She reaches out to him. At the same time a* PICKPOCKET *lifts his wallet.*)

KILROY (*catching the whore's wrist*). Keep y'r hands off me, y' dirty ole bag! No caree putas! No loteria, no dulces, nada—so get away! Vamoose! All of you! Quit picking at me![24] (*He reaches in his pocket and jerks out a handful of small copper and silver coins which he flings disgustedly down the street. The grotesque people scramble after it with their inhuman cries.* KILROY *goes on a few steps—then stops short—feeling the back pocket of his dungarees. Then he lets out a startled cry.*) Robbed! My God, I've been robbed! (*The* STREET PEOPLE *scatter to the walls.*) Which of you got my wallet? *Which* of you dirty—? Shh—Uh!

---

[22] *Café*, or canteen.

[23] The vendors are selling candy, lottery tickets, pastries, and coffee with milk, or the "*café au lait*" of the French. Kilroy's reply is probably "*No quiero*" meaning "I don't want any."

[24] *Putas*: prostitutes. *Nada*: nothing. Vamoose actually comes from Spanish *vamos*: let's go.

(*They mumble with gestures of incomprehension. He marches back to the entrance to the hotel.*) Hey! Officer! Official!—General! (*The* OFFICER *finally lounges out of the hotel entrance and glances at* KILROY.) Tiende?[25] One of them's got my wallet! Picked it out of my pocket while that old whore there was groping me! Don't you comprendo?

OFFICER. Nobody rob you. You don't have no pesos.

KILROY. Huh?

OFFICER. You just dreaming that you have money. You don't ever have money. Nunca! Nada![26] (*He spits between his teeth.*) Loco . . . (*The* OFFICER *crosses to the fountain.* KILROY *stares at him, then bawls out:*)

KILROY (*to the* STREET PEOPLE). We'll see what the American Embassy has to say about this! I'll go to the American Consul. Whichever of you rotten spivs lifted my wallet is going to jail—calaboose! I hope I have made myself plain. If not, I will make myself plainer! (*There are scattered laughs among the crowd. He crosses to the fountain. He notices the body of the no longer* SURVIVOR, *kneels beside it, shakes it, turns it over, springs up and shouts:*) Hey! This guy is dead! (*There is the sound of the* STREETCLEANERS' *piping. They trundle their white barrel into the plaza from one of the downstage arches. The appearance of these men undergoes a progressive alteration through the play. When they first appear they are almost like any such public servants in a tropical country; their white jackets are dirtier than the musicians' and some of the stains are red. They have on white caps with black visors. They are continually exchanging sly jokes and giggling unpleasantly together.* LORD MULLIGAN *has come out upon the terrace and as they pass him, they pause for a moment, point at him, snicker. He is extremely discomfited by this impertinence, touches his chest as if he felt a* palpitation and turns back inside. KILROY *yells to the advancing* STREETCLEANERS.) There's a dead man layin' here! (*They giggle again. Briskly they lift the body and stuff it into the barrel; then trundle it off, looking back at* KILROY, *giggling, whispering. They return under the downstage arch through which they entered.* KILROY, *in a low, shocked voice:*) What *is* this place? What kind of a hassle have I got myself into?

LOUDSPEAKER. If anyone on the Camino is bewildered, come to the Gypsy. A poco dinero[27] will tickle the Gypsy's palm and give her visions!

ABDULLAH (*giving* KILROY *a card*). If you got a question, ask my mama, the Gypsy!

KILROY. Man, whenever you see those three brass balls on a street, you don't have to look a long ways for a Gypsy. Now le' me think. I am faced with three problems. One: I'm hungry. Two: I'm lonely. Three: I'm in a place where I don't know what it is or how I got there! First action that's indicated is to —cash in on something—Well . . . let's see . . . (*Honky-tonk music fades in at this point and the Skid Row façade begins to light up for the evening. There is the* GYPSY's *stall with its cabalistic devices, its sectional cranium and palm, three luminous brass balls overhanging the entrance to the* LOAN SHARK *and his window filled with a vast assortment of hocked articles for sale: trumpets, banjos, fur coats, tuxedos, a gown of scarlet sequins, loops of pearls and rhinestones. Dimly behind this display is a neon sign in three pastel colors, pink, green, and blue. It fades softly in and out and it says: "Magic Tricks Jokes." There is also the advertisement of a flea-bag hotel or flophouse called "Ritz Men Only." This sign is also pale neon or luminous paint, and only the entrance is on the street floor, the rooms are above the* LOAN SHARK *and* GYPSY's *stall. One of the windows of this upper story is prac-*

---

[25] Probably *entiende*, meaning "do you understand?"
[26] *Nunca:* never. *Nada:* nothing.
[27] A little money.

tical. *Figures appear in it sometimes, leaning out as if suffocating or to hawk and spit into the street below. This side of the street should have all the color and animation that are permitted by the resources of the production. There may be moments of dancelike action—a fight, a seduction, sale of narcotics, arrest, etc.*)

KILROY (*to the audience from the apron*). What've I got to cash in on? My golden gloves? Never! I'll say that once more, never! The silver-framed photo of my One True Woman? Never! Repeat that! Never! What else have I got of a detachable and a negotiable nature? Oh! My ruby-and-emerald-studded belt with the word CHAMP on it. (*He whips it off his pants.*) This is not necessary to hold on my pants, but this is a precious reminder of the sweet used-to-be. Oh, well. Sometimes a man has got to hock his sweet used-to-be in order to finance his present situation . . . (*He enters the* LOAN SHARK'S. *A* DRUNKEN BUM *leans out the practical window of the "Ritz Men Only" and shouts:*)

BUM. O Jack o' Diamonds, you robbed my pockets, you robbed my pockets of silver and gold! (*He jerks the window shade down.*)

GUTMAN (*on the terrace*). Block Four on the Camino Real!

BLOCK FOUR

There is a phrase of light music as the BARON DE CHARLUS, *an elderly foppish sybarite in a light silk suit, a carnation in his lapel, crosses from the Siete Mares to the honky-tonk side of the street. On his trail is a wild-looking young man of startling beauty called* LOBO. CHARLUS *is aware of the follower and, during his conversation with* A. RATT, *he takes out a pocket mirror to inspect him while pretending to comb his hair and point his moustache. As* CHARLUS *approaches, the* MANAGER *of the flea-bag puts up a vacancy sign and calls out:*

A. RATT. Vacancy here! A bed at the "Ritz Men Only"! A little white ship to sail the dangerous night in . . .

THE BARON. Ah, bon soir, Mr. Ratt.

A. RATT. Cruising?

THE BARON. No, just—walking!

A. RATT. That's all you need to do.

THE BARON. I sometimes find it suffices. You have a vacancy, do you?

A. RATT. For you?

THE BARON. And a possible guest. You know the requirements. An iron bed with no mattress and a considerable length of stout knotted rope. No! Chains this evening, metal chains. I've been very bad, I have a lot to atone for . . .

A. RATT. Why don't you take these joy-rides at the Siete Mares?

THE BARON (*with the mirror focused on* LOBO). They don't have Ingreso Libero[28] at the Siete Mares. Oh, I don't like places in the haute saison, the alta staggione,[29] and yet if you go between the fashionable seasons, it's too hot or too damp or appallingly overrun by all the wrong sort of people who rap on the wall if canaries sing in your bedsprings after midnight. I don't know why such people don't stay at home. Surely a Kodak, a Brownie, or even a Leica works just as well in Milwaukee or Sioux City as it does in these places they do on their whirlwind summer tours, and don't look now, but I think I am being followed!

A. RATT. Yep, you've made a pickup!

THE BARON. Attractive?

A. RATT. That depends on who's driving the bicycle, Dad.

THE BARON. Ciao, Caro![30] Expect me at ten. (*He crosses elegantly to the fountain.*)

A. RATT. Vacancy here! A little white ship to sail the dangerous night in! (*The music changes.* KILROY *backs out of the* LOAN SHARK'S, *belt unsold, engaged in a*

---

[28] Free entry.
[29] Both phrases mean "The height of the season"; the first is French, the second is Italian.
[30] "So long, dear."

violent dispute. The LOAN SHARK *is haggling for his golden gloves.* CHARLUS *lingers, intrigued by the scene.*)

LOAN SHARK. I don't want no belt! I want the gloves! Eight-fifty!

KILROY. No dice.

LOAN SHARK. Nine, nine-fifty!

KILROY. Nah, nah, nah!

LOAN SHARK. Yah, yah, yah.

KILROY. I say nah.

LOAN SHARK. I say yah.

KILROY. The nahs have it.

LOAN SHARK. Don't be a fool. What can you do with a pair of golden gloves?

KILROY. I can remember the battles I fought to win them! I can remember that I used to be—CHAMP! (*Fade in Band Music: "March of the Gladiators" —ghostly cheers, etc.*)

LOAN SHARK. You can remember that you *used to be*—Champ?

KILROY. Yes! I used to be—CHAMP!

THE BARON. Used to be is the past tense, meaning useless.

KILROY. Not to me, Mister. These are my gloves, these gloves are gold, and I fought a lot of hard fights to win 'em! I broke clean from the clinches. I never hit a low blow, the referee never told me to mix it up! And the fixers never got to me!

LOAN SHARK. In other words, a sucker!

KILROY. Yep, I'm a sucker that won the golden gloves!

LOAN SHARK. Congratulations. My final offer is a piece of green paper with Alexander Hamilton's picture on it. Take it or leave it.

KILROY. I leave it for you to *stuff* it! I'd hustle my heart on this street, I'd peddle my heart's true blood before I'd leave my golden gloves hung up in a loan shark's window between a rusted trombone and some poor lush's long ago mildewed tuxedo!

LOAN SHARK. So you say but I will see you later.

THE BARON. The name of the Camino is not unreal! (*The* BUM *sticks his head out the window and shouts:*)

BUM. Pa dam, Pa dam, Pa dam!

THE BARON (*continuing the* BUM'S *song*). Echoes the beat of my heart! Pa dam, Pa dam—*hello!* (*He has crossed to* KILROY *as he sings and extends his hand to him.*)

KILROY (*uncertainly*). Hey, mate. It's wonderful to see you.

THE BARON. Thanks, but why?

KILROY. A normal American. In a clean white suit.

THE BARON. My suit is pale yellow. My nationality is French, and my normality has been often subject to question.

KILROY. I still say your suit is clean.

THE BARON. Thanks. That's more than I can say for your apparel.

KILROY. Don't judge a book by the covers. I'd take a shower if I could locate the "Y."

THE BARON. What's the "Y"?

KILROY. Sort of a Protestant church with a swimmin' pool in it. Sometimes it also has an employment bureau. It does good in the community.

THE BARON. Nothing in this community does much good.

KILROY. I'm getting the same impression. This place is confusing to me. I think it must be the aftereffects of fever. Nothing seems real. Could you give me the scoop?

THE BARON. Serious questions are referred to the Gypsy. Once upon a time. Oh, once upon a time. I used to wonder. Now I simply wander. I stroll about the fountain and hope to be followed. Some people call it corruption. I call it—simplification . . .

BUM (*very softly at the window*). I wonder what's become of Sally, that old gal of mine? (*He lowers the blind.*)

KILROY. Well, anyhow . . .

THE BARON. Well, anyhow?

KILROY. How about the hot-spots in this town?

THE BARON. Oh, the hot-spots, ho ho! There's the Pink Flamingo, the Yellow Pelican, the Blue Heron, and the Prothonotary Warbler! They call it the Bird Circuit. But I don't care for such places. They stand three-deep at the bar and look at themselves in the mirror and what they see is depressing. One sailor comes in—they faint! My own choice of resorts is the Bucket of Blood downstairs from the "Ritz Men Only."—How about a match?

KILROY. Where's your cigarette?

THE BARON (*gently and sweetly*). Oh, I don't smoke. I just wanted to see your eyes more clearly . . .

KILROY. Why?

THE BARON. The eyes are the windows of the soul, and yours are too gentle for someone who has as much as I have to atone for. (*He starts off.*) Au revoir . . .

KILROY.—A very unusual type character . . . (CASANOVA *is on the steps leading to the arch, looking out at the desert beyond. Now he turns and descends a few steps, laughing with a note of tired incredulity.* KILROY *crosses to him.*) Gee, it's wonderful to see you, a normal American in a— (*There is a strangulated outcry from the arch under which the* BARON *has disappeared.*) Excuse me a minute! (*He rushes toward the source of the outcry.* JACQUES *crosses to the bench before the fountain. Rhubarb is heard through the arch.* JACQUES *shrugs wearily as if it were just a noisy radio.*

KILROY *comes plummeting out backwards, all the way to* JACQUES.) I tried to interfere, but what's th' use?!

JACQUES. No use at all! (*The* STREETCLEANERS *come through the arch with the* BARON *doubled up in their barrel. They pause and exchange sibilant whispers, pointing and snickering at* KILROY.)

KILROY. Who are they pointing at? At me, Kilroy? (*The* BUM *laughs from the window. A.* RATT *laughs from his shadowy doorway. The* LOAN SHARK *laughs from his.*) Kilroy is here and he's not about to be there!—If he can help it . . . (*He snatches up a rock and throws it at the* STREETCLEANERS. *Everybody laughs louder and the laughter seems to reverberate from the mountains. The light changes, dims a little in the plaza.*) Sons a whatever you're sons of! Don't look at me, I'm not about to take no ride in the barrel! (*The* BARON, *his elegant white shoes protruding from the barrel, is wheeled up the Alleyway Out. Figures in the square resume their dazed attitudes and one or two Guests return to the terrace of the Siete Mares as—*)

GUTMAN. Block Five on the Camino Real! (*He strolls off.*)

BLOCK FIVE

KILROY (*to* JACQUES). Gee, the blocks go fast on this street!

JACQUES. Yes. The blocks go fast.

KILROY. My name's Kilroy. I'm here.

JACQUES. Mine is Casanova. I'm here, too.

KILROY. But you been here longer than me and maybe could brief me on it. For instance, what do they do with a stiff picked up in this town? (*The* GUARD *stares at them suspiciously from the terrace.* JACQUES *whistles "La Golondrina" and crosses downstage.* KILROY *follows.*) Did I say something untactful?

JACQUES (*smiling into a sunset glow*). The exchange of serious questions and ideas, especially between persons from opposite sides of the plaza, is regarded unfavorably here. You'll notice I'm talking as if I had acute laryngitis. I'm

gazing into the sunset. If I should start to whistle "La Golondrina" it means we're being overheard by the Guards on the terrace. Now you want to know what is done to a body from which the soul has departed on the Camino Real!— Its disposition depends on what the Streetcleaners happen to find in its pockets. If its pockets are empty as the unfortunate Baron's turned out to be, and as mine are at this moment—the "stiff" is wheeled straight off to the Laboratory. And there the individual becomes an undistinguished member of a collectivist state. His chemical components are separated and poured into vats containing the corresponding elements of countless others. If any of his vital organs or parts are at all unique in size or structure, they're placed on exhibition in bottles containing a very foul-smelling solution called formaldehyde. There is a charge of admission to this museum. The proceeds go to the maintenance of the military police. (*He whistles "La Golondrina" till the* GUARD *turns his back again. He moves toward the front of the stage.*)

KILROY (*following*).—I guess that's—sensible . . .

JACQUES. Yes, but not romantic. And romance is important. Don't you think?

KILROY. Nobody thinks romance is more important than me!

JACQUES. Except possibly me!

KILROY. Maybe that's why fate has brung us together! We're buddies under the skin!

JACQUES. Travelers born?

KILROY. Always looking for something!

JACQUES. Satisfied by nothing!

KILROY. Hopeful?

JACQUES. Always!

OFFICER. Keep moving! (*They move apart till the* OFFICER *exits.*)

KILROY. And when a joker on the Camino gets fed up with one continual hassle—how does he get *off* it?

JACQUES. You see the narrow and very steep stairway that passes under what is described in the travel brochures as a "Magnificent Arch of Triumph"?—Well, that's the Way Out!

KILROY. That's the way out? (KILROY *without hesitation plunges right up to almost the top step; then pauses with a sound of squealing brakes. There is a sudden loud wind.*)

JACQUES (*shouting with hand cupped to mouth*). Well, how does the prospect please you, Traveler born?

KILROY (*shouting back in a tone of awe*). It's too unknown for my blood. Man, I seen nothing like it except through a telescope once on the pier on Coney Island. "Ten cents to see the craters and plains of the moon!"—And here's the same view in three dimensions for nothing! (*The desert wind sings loudly:* KILROY *mocks it.*)

JACQUES. Are you—ready to cross it?

KILROY. Maybe sometime with someone but not right now and alone! How about you?

JACQUES. I'm not alone.

KILROY. You're with a party?

JACQUES. No, but I'm sweetly encumbered with a—lady . . .

KILROY. It wouldn't do with a lady. I don't see nothing but nothing—and then more nothing. And then I see some mountains. But the mountains are covered with snow.

JACQUES. Snowshoes would be useful! (*He observes* GUTMAN *approaching through the passage at upper left. He whistles "La Golondrina" for* KILROY'S *attention and points with his cane as he exits.*)

KILROY (*descending steps disconsolately*). Mush, mush. (*The* BUM *comes to his window. A.* RATT *enters his doorway.* GUTMAN *enters below* KILROY.)

BUM. It's sleepy time down South!

GUTMAN (*warningly as* KILROY *passes him*). Block Six in a progress of sixteen blocks on the Camino Real.

BLOCK SIX

KILROY (*from the stairs*). Man, I could use a bed now.—I'd like to make me a cool pad on this camino now and lie down and sleep and dream of being with someone—friendly . . . (*He crosses to the "Ritz Men Only."*)

A. RATT (*softly and sleepily*). Vacancy here! I got a single bed at the "Ritz Men Only," a little white ship to sail the dangerous night in. (KILROY *crosses down to his doorway.*)

KILROY.—You got a vacancy here?

A. RATT. I got a vacancy here if you got the one-fifty there.

KILROY. Ha ha! I been in countries where money was not legal tender. I mean it was legal but it wasn't tender. (*There is a loud groan from offstage above.*)—Somebody dying on you or just drunk?

A. RATT. Who knows or cares in this pad, Dad?

KILROY. I heard once that a man can't die while he's drunk. Is that a fact or a fiction?

A. RATT. Strictly a fiction.

VOICE ABOVE. *Stiff in number seven! Call the Streetcleaners!*

A. RATT (*with absolutely no change in face or voice*). Number seven is vacant. (STREETCLEANERS' *piping is heard. The* BUM *leaves the window.*)

KILROY. Thanks, but tonight I'm going to sleep under the stars. (A. RATT *gestures* "Have it your way" *and exits.* KILROY, *left alone, starts downstage. He notices that* LA MADRECITA *is crouched near the fountain, holding something up, inconspicuously, in her hand. Coming to her he sees that it's a piece of food. He takes it, puts it in his mouth, tries to thank her but her head is down, muffled in her rebozo*[31] *and there is no way for him to acknowledge the gift. He starts to cross.* STREET PEOPLE *raise up their heads in their Pit and motion him invitingly to come in with them. They call softly,* "Sleep, sleep . . .")

GUTMAN (*from his chair on the terrace*). Hey, Joe. (*The* STREET PEOPLE *duck immediately.*)

KILROY. Who? Me?

GUTMAN. Yes, you, Candy Man. Are you disocupado?

KILROY.—That means—unemployed, don't it? (*He sees* OFFICERS *converging from right.*)

GUTMAN. Jobless. On the bum. Carrying the banner!

KILROY.—Aw, no, aw, no, don't try to hang no vagrancy rap on me! I was robbed on this square and I got plenty of witnesses to prove it.

GUTMAN (*with ironic courtesy*). Oh? (*He makes a gesture asking* "Where?")

KILROY (*coming down to apron left and crossing to the right*). Witnesses! Witnesses! Witnesses! (*He comes to* LA MADRECITA.) You were a witness! (*A gesture indicates that he realizes her blindness. Opposite the* GYPSY'S *balcony he pauses for a second.*) Hey, Gypsy's daughter! (*The balcony is dark. He continues up to the Pit. The* STREET PEOPLE *duck as he calls down:*) You were witnesses! (*An* OFFICER *enters with a Patsy outfit. He hands it to* GUTMAN.)

GUTMAN. Here, Boy! Take these. (GUTMAN *displays and then tosses on the ground at* KILROY'S *feet the Patsy outfit—the red fright wig, the big crimson nose that lights up and has horn-rimmed glasses attached, a pair of clown pants that have a huge footprint on the seat.*)

KILROY. What is this outfit?

GUTMAN. The uniform of a Patsy.

KILROY. I know what a Patsy is—he's a clown in the circus who takes pratfalls but *I'm no Patsy!*

GUTMAN. Pick it up.

KILROY. Don't give me orders. Kilroy is a free agent—

GUTMAN (*smoothly*). But a Patsy isn't. Pick it up and put it on, Candy Man. You are now the Patsy.

KILROY. So you say but you are completely mistaken. (*Four* OFFICERS *press in on him.*) And don't crowd me with your torpedoes! I'm a stranger here but I got a clean record in all the places I been, I'm not in the books for nothin' but vagrancy and once when I was hungry I walked by a truck-load of pineapples without picking one, because I was brought up good— (*Then, with a pathetic attempt at making friends with the* OFFICER *to his right.*) and there was a cop on the corner!

OFFICER. Ponga selo![32]

KILROY. What'd you say? (*Desperately to audience he asks:*) What did he say?

OFFICER. Ponga selo!

KILROY. What'd you say? (*The* OFFICER *shoves him down roughly to the Patsy outfit.* KILROY *picks up the pants,*

---

[31] Shawl.

[32] "Put it on!" It should be spelled as one word, "*póngaselo.*"

shakes them out carefully as if about to step into them and says very politely:) Why, surely. I'd be delighted. My fondest dreams have come true. (*Suddenly he tosses the Patsy dress into* GUTMAN'S *face and leaps into the aisle of the theatre.*)

GUTMAN. Stop him! Arrest that vagrant! Don't let him get away!

LOUDSPEAKER. Be on the lookout for a fugitive Patsy. The Patsy has escaped. Stop him, stop that Patsy! (*A wild chase commences. The two* GUARDS *rush madly down either side to intercept him at the back of the house.* KILROY *wheels about at the top of the center aisle, and runs back down it, panting, gasping out questions and entreaties to various persons occupying aisle seats, such as:*)

KILROY. How do I git out? Which way do I go, which way do I get out? Where's the Greyhound depot? Hey, do you know where the Greyhound bus depot is? What's the best way out, if there is any way out? I got to find one. I had enough of this place. I had too much of this place. I'm free. I'm a free man with equal rights in this world! You better believe it because that's news for you and you had better believe it! Kilroy's a free man with equal rights in this world! All right, now, help me, somebody, help me find a way out, I got to find one, I don't like this place! It's not for me and I am not buying any! Oh! Over there! I see a sign that says EXIT. That's a sweet word to me, man, that's a lovely word, EXIT! That's the entrance to paradise for Kilroy! Exit, I'm coming, Exit, I'm coming! (*The* STREET PEOPLE *have gathered along the forestage to watch the chase.* ESMERALDA, *barefooted, wearing only a slip, bursts out of the* GYPSY'S *establishment like an animal broken out of a cage, darts among the* STREET PEOPLE *to the front of the Crowd which is shouting like the spectators at the climax of a corrida.*[33] *Behind her,* NURSIE *appears, a male actor, wigged and dressed austerely as a duenna, crying out in both languages.*)

NURSIE. Esmeralda! Esmeralda!

GYPSY. Police!

NURSIE. Come back here, Esmeralda!

GYPSY. Catch her, idiot!

NURSIE. Where is my lady bird, where is my precious treasure?

GYPSY. Idiot! I told you to keep her door locked!

NURSIE. She jimmied the lock, Esmeralda! (*These shouts are mostly lost in the general rhubarb of the chase and the shouting* STREET PEOPLE. ESMERALDA *crouches on the forestage, screaming encouragement in Spanish to the fugitive.* ABDULLAH *catches sight of her, seizes her wrist, shouting:*)

ABDULLAH. Here she is! I got her! (ESMERALDA *fights savagely. She nearly breaks loose, but* NURSIE *and the* GYPSY *close upon her, too, and she is overwhelmed and dragged back, fighting all the way, toward the door from which she escaped. Meanwhile—timed with the above action—shots are fired in the air by* KILROY'S *Pursuers. He dashes, panting, into the boxes of the theatre, darting from one box to another, shouting incoherently, now, sobbing for breath, crying out:*)

KILROY. *Mary, help a Christian! Help a Christian, Mary!*

ESMERALDA. *Yankee! Yankee, jump!* (*The* OFFICERS *close upon him in the box nearest the stage. A dazzling spot of light is thrown on him. He lifts a little gilded chair to defend himself. The chair is torn from his grasp. He leaps upon the ledge of the box.*) Jump! Jump, Yankee! (*The* GYPSY *is dragging the girl back by her hair.*)

KILROY. *Watch out down there! Geronimo!* (*He leaps onto the stage and crumples up with a twisted ankle.* ESMERALDA *screams demoniacally , breaks from her mother's grasp and rushes to him, fighting off his pursuers who have leapt after him from the box.* ABDULLAH, NURSIE, *and the* GYPSY *seize her again, just as* KILROY *is seized by his pursuers. The* OFFICERS *beat him to his knees. Each time he is struck,* ESMERALDA

---

[33] Bullfight.

screams as if she received the blow her-self. As his cries subside into sobbing, so do hers, and at the end, when he is quite helpless, she is also overcome by her captors and as they drag her back to the GYPSY'S *she cries to him:)*

ESMERALDA. *They've got you! They've got me! (Her mother slaps her fiercely.)* Caught! Caught! We're caught! (*She is dragged inside. The door is slammed shut on her continuing outcries. For a moment nothing is heard but* KILROY'S *hoarse panting and sobbing.* GUTMAN *takes command of the situation, thrusting his way through the crowd to face* KILROY *who is pinioned by two* GUARDS.)

GUTMAN (*smiling serenely*). Well, well, how do you do! I understand that you're seeking employment here. We need a Patsy and the job is yours for the asking!

KILROY. I don't. Accept. This job. I been. Shanghaied! (KILROY *dons Patsy outfit.*)

GUTMAN. Hush! The Patsy doesn't talk. He lights his nose, that's all!

GUARD. Press the little button at the end of the cord.

GUTMAN. That's right. Just press the little button at the end of the cord! (KILROY *lights his nose. Everybody laughs.*) Again, ha ha! Again, ha ha! Again! (*The nose goes off and on like a firefly as the stage dims out.*)

THE CURTAIN FALLS.

THERE IS A SHORT INTERMISSION.

BLOCK SEVEN

The DREAMER *is singing with mando-lin, "Noche de Ronde." The* GUESTS *murmur, "cool—cool . . ."* GUTMAN *stands on the podiumlike elevation down-stage right, smoking a long thin cigar, signing an occasional tab from the bar or café. He is standing in an amber spot. The rest of the stage is filled with blue dusk. At the signal the song fades to a whisper and* GUTMAN *speaks.*

GUTMAN. Block Seven on the Camino Real—I like this hour. (*He gives the audience a tender gold-toothed smile.*) The fire's gone out of the day but the light of it lingers . . . In Rome the continual fountains are bathing stone heroes with silver, in Copenhagen the Tivoli gardens are lighted, they're selling the lottery on San Juan de Latrene . . . (*The* DREAMER *advances a little, playing the mandolin softly.*)

LA MADRECITA (*holding up glass beads and shell necklaces*). Recuerdos, recuer-dos?[34]

GUTMAN. And these are the moments when we look into ourselves and ask with a wonder which never is lost alto-gether: "Can this be all? Is there noth-ing more? Is this what the glittering wheels of the heavens turn for?" (*He leans forward as if conveying a secret.*) —Ask the Gypsy! Un poco dinero will tickle the Gypsy's palm and give her visions! (ABDULLAH *emerges with a silver tray, calling:*)

ABDULLAH. Letter for Signor Casanova, Letter for Signor Casanova! (JACQUES *springs up but stands rigid.*)

GUTMAN. Casanova, you have received a letter. Perhaps it's the letter with the remittance check in it!

JACQUES (*in a hoarse, exalted voice*). Yes! It is! The letter! With the remit-tance check in it!

GUTMAN. Then why don't you take it so you can maintain your residence at the Siete Mares and so avoid the more somber attractions of the "Ritz Men Only"?

JACQUES. My hand is—

GUTMAN. Your hand is paralyzed? . . . By what? *Anxiety? Apprehension?* . . . Put the letter in Signor Casanova's pocket so he can open it when he recovers the use of his digital extremities. Then give him a shot of brandy on the house be-fore he falls on his face! (JACQUES *has stepped down into the plaza. He looks*

[34] Souvenirs.

down at KILROY *crouched to the right of him and wildly blinking his nose.*)

JACQUES. Yes. I know the Morse code. (KILROY'S *nose again blinks on and off.*) Thank you, brother. (*This is said as if acknowledging a message.*) I knew without asking the Gypsy that something of this sort would happen to you. You have a spark of anarchy in your spirit and that's not to be tolerated. Nothing wild or honest is tolerated here! It has to be extinguished or used only to light up your nose for Mr. Gutman's amusement . . . (JACQUES *saunters around* KILROY *whistling "La Golondrina." Then satisfied that no one is suspicious of this encounter . . .*) Before the final block we'll find some way out of here! Meanwhile, patience and courage, little brother! (JACQUES *feeling he's been there too long starts away giving* KILROY *a reassuring pat on the shoulder and saying:*) Patience! . . . Courage!

LADY MULLIGAN (*from the* MULLIGANS' *table*). Mr. Gutman!

GUTMAN. Lady Mulligan! And how are you this evening, Lord Mulligan?

LADY MULLIGAN (*interrupting* LORD MULLIGAN'S *rumblings*). He's not at all well. This . . . climate is so enervating!

LORD MULLIGAN. I was so weak this morning . . . I couldn't screw the lid on my tooth paste!

LADY MULLIGAN. Raymond, tell Mr. Gutman about those two impertinent workmen in the square! . . . These two idiots pushing a white barrel! Pop up every time we step outside the hotel!

LORD MULLIGAN.—point and giggle at me!

LADY MULLIGAN. Can't they be discharged?

GUTMAN. They can't be discharged, disciplined nor bribed! All you can do is pretend to ignore them.

LADY MULLIGAN. I can't eat! . . . Raymond, stop stuffing!

LORD MULLIGAN. *Shut up!*

GUTMAN (*to the audience*). When the big wheels crack on this street it's like the fall of a capital city, the destruction of Carthage, the sack of Rome by the white-eyed giants from the North! I've seen them fall! I've seen the destruction of them! Adventurers suddenly frightened of a dark room! Gamblers unable to choose between odd and even! Con men and pitchmen and plume-hatted cavaliers turned baby-soft at one note of the Streetcleaners' pipes! When I observe this change, I say to myself: "Could it happen to ME?"—The answer is "YES!" And that's what curdles my blood like milk on the doorstep of someone gone for the summer! (A HUNCHBACK MUMMER *somersaults through his hoop of silver bells, springs up and shakes it excitedly toward a downstage arch which begins to flicker with a diamond-blue radiance; this marks the advent of each legendary character in the play. The music follows: a waltz from the time of Camille in Paris.*) Ah, there's the music of another legend, one that everyone knows, the legend of the sentimental whore, the courtesan who made the mistake of love. But now you see her coming into this plaza not as she was when she burned with a fever that cast a thin light over Paris, but changed, yes, faded as lanterns and legends fade when they burn into day! (*He turns and shouts:*) Rosita, sell her a flower! (MARGUERITE *has entered the plaza. A beautiful woman of indefinite age. The* STREET PEOPLE *cluster about her with wheedling cries, holding up glass beads, shell necklaces and so forth. She seems confused, lost, half-awake.* JACQUES *has sprung up at her entrance but has difficulty making his way through the cluster of vendors.* ROSITA *has snatched up a tray of flowers and cries out:*)

ROSITA. Camellias, camellias! Pink or white, whichever a lady finds suitable to the moon!

GUTMAN. That's the ticket!

MARGUERITE. Yes, I would like a camellia.

ROSITA (*in a bad French accent*). Rouge ou blanc ce soir?[35]

MARGUERITE. It's always a white one,

---

[35] "Red or white this evening?"

now . . . but there used to be five evenings out of the month when a pink
camellia, instead of the usual white one,
let my admirers know that the moon
those nights was unfavorable to pleasure,
and so they called me–Camille . . .

JACQUES. Mia cara![36] (*Imperiously, very
proud to be with her, he pushes the*
STREET PEOPLE *aside with his cane.*) Out
of the way, make way, let us through,
please!

MARGUERITE. Don't push them with
your cane.

JACQUES. If they get close enough
they'll snatch your purse. (MARGUERITE
utters a low, shocked cry.) What is it?

MARGUERITE. *My purse is gone! It's
lost! My papers were in it!*

JACQUES. Your passport was in it?

MARGUERITE. My passport and my per-
miso de residencia![37] (*She leans faint
against the arch during the following
scene.* ABDULLAH *turns to run.* JACQUES
catches him.)

JACQUES (*seizing* ABDULLAH's *wrist*).
Where did you take her?

ABDULLAH. Oww!–P'tit Zoco.

JACQUES. The Souks?

ABDULLAH. The Souks!

JACQUES. Which cafés did she go to?

ABDULLAH. Ahmed's, she went to—

JACQUES. Did she smoke at Ahmed's?

ABDULLAH. Two kif pipes![38]

JACQUES. Who was it took her purse?
Was it *you*? We'll see! (*He strips off
the boy's burnoose. He crouches whimpering, shivering in a ragged slip.*)

MARGUERITE. Jacques, let the boy go,
he didn't take it!

JACQUES. He doesn't have it on him
but knows who does!

ABDULLAH. No, no, I don't know!

JACQUES. You little son of a Gypsy!
Senta![39] . . . You know who I am? I am
Jacques Casanova! I belong to the Secret
Order of the Rose-colored Cross! . . .
Run back to Ahmed's. Contact the spiv

that took the lady's purse. Tell him to
keep it but give her back her papers!
There'll be a large reward. (*He thumps
his cane on the ground to release* AB-
DULLAH *from the spell. The boy dashes
off.* JACQUES *laughs and turns triumphantly to* MARGUERITE.)

LADY MULLIGAN. Waiter! That adventurer and his mistress must not be seated
next to Lord Mulligan's table!

JACQUES (*loudly enough for* LADY
MULLIGAN *to hear*). This hotel has become a mecca for black marketeers and
their expensively kept women!

LADY MULLIGAN. Mr. Gutman!

MARGUERITE. Let's have dinner upstairs!

WAITER (*directing them to terrace
table*). This way, M'sieur.

JACQUES. We'll take our usual table.
(*He indicates one.*)

MARGUERITE. Please!

WAITER (*overlapping* MARGUERITE's
"*please!*"). This table is reserved for
Lord Byron!

JACQUES (*masterfully*). This table is always our table.

MARGUERITE. I'm not hungry.

JACQUES. Hold out the lady's chair,
cretino![40]

GUTMAN (*darting over to* MAR-
GUERITE's *chair*). Permit me! (JACQUES
bows with mock gallantry to LADY MUL-
LIGAN *as he turns to his chair during
seating of* MARGUERITE.)

LADY MULLIGAN. We'll move to *that*
table!

JACQUES.—You must learn how to carry
the banner of Bohemia into the enemy
camp. (*A screen is put up around them.*)

MARGUERITE. Bohemia has no banner.
It survives by discretion.

JACQUES. I'm glad that you value discretion. *Wine list!* Was it discretion that
led you through the bazaars this afternoon wearing your cabochon sapphire
and diamond ear-drops? You were for-

---

[36] "My dear!"

[37] Permit to remain in residence.

[38] Kif, or keef, is a narcotic from Indian hemp, smoked to produce a languorous, dreamy
tranquility.

[39] "Sit down!" Actually, "*Sentad!*"

[40] Idiot; stupid.

tunate that you lost only your purse and papers!

MARGUERITE. Take the wine list.

JACQUES. Still or sparkling?

MARGUERITE. Sparkling.

GUTMAN. May I make a suggestion, Signor Casanova?

JACQUES. Please do.

GUTMAN. It's a very cold and dry wine from only ten metres below the snowline in the mountains. The name of the wine is Quando!—meaning when! Such as "When are remittances going to be received?" "When are accounts to be settled?" Ha ha ha! Bring Signor Casanova a bottle of Quando with the compliments of the house!

JACQUES. I'm sorry this had to happen in—your presence . . .

MARGUERITE. That doesn't matter, my dear. But why don't you *tell* me when you are short of money?

JACQUES. I thought the fact was apparent. It is to everyone else.

MARGUERITE. The letter you were expecting, it still hasn't come?

JACQUES (*removing it from his pocket*). It came this afternoon—Here it is!

MARGUERITE. You haven't opened the letter!

JACQUES. I haven't had the nerve to! I've had so many unpleasant surprises that I've lost faith in my luck.

MARGUERITE. Give the letter to me. Let me open it for you.

JACQUES. Later, a little bit later, after the—wine . . .

MARGUERITE. Old hawk, anxious old hawk! (*She clasps his hand on the table: he leans toward her: she kisses her fingertips and places them on his lips.*)

JACQUES. Do you call that a kiss?

MARGUERITE. I call it the ghost of a kiss. It will have to do for now. (*She leans back, her blue-tinted eyelids closed.*)

JACQUES. Are you tired? Are you tired, Marguerite? You know you should have rested this afternoon.

MARGUERITE. I looked at silver and rested.

JACQUES. You looked at silver at Ahmed's?

MARGUERITE. No, I rested at Ahmed's, and had mint-tea. (*The* DREAMER *accompanies their speech with his guitar. The duologue should have the style of an antiphonal poem, the cues picked up so that there is scarcely a separation between the speeches, and the tempo quick and the voices edged.*)

JACQUES. You had mint-tea downstairs?

MARGUERITE. No, upstairs.

JACQUES. Upstairs where they burn the poppy?[41]

MARGUERITE. Upstairs where it's cool and there's music and the haggling of the bazaar is soft as the murmur of pigeons.

JACQUES. That sounds restful. Reclining among silk pillows on a divan, in a curtained and perfumed alcove above the bazaar?

MARGUERITE. Forgetting for a while where I am, or that I don't know where I am . . .

JACQUES. Forgetting alone or forgetting with some young companion who plays the lute or the flute or who had silver to show you? Yes. That sounds very restful. And yet you do seem tired.

MARGUERITE. If I seem tired, it's your insulting solicitude that I'm tired of!

JACQUES. Is it insulting to feel concern for your safety in this place?

MARGUERITE. Yes, it is. The implication is.

JACQUES. What is the implication?

MARGUERITE. You know what it is: that I am one of those *aging—voluptuaries*—who used to be paid for pleasure but now have to pay!—Jacques, I won't be followed, I've gone too far to be followed!—*What is it?* (*The* WAITER *has presented an envelope on a salver.*)

WAITER. A letter for the lady.

MARGUERITE. How strange to receive a letter in a place where nobody knows I'm staying! Will you open it for me? (*The* WAITER *withdraws.* JACQUES *takes the letter and opens it.*) Well! What is it?

JACQUES. Nothing important. An illus-

---

[41] In other words, smoke opium.

trated brochure from some resort in the mountains.

MARGUERITE. What is it called?

JACQUES. Bide-a-While. (*A chafing dish bursts into startling blue flame at the* MULLIGANS' *table.* LADY MULLIGAN *clasps her hands and exclaims with affected delight, the* WAITER *and* MR. GUTMAN *laugh agreeably.* MARGUERITE *springs up and moves out upon the forestage.* JACQUES *goes to her.*) Do you know this resort in the mountains?

MARGUERITE. Yes. I stayed there once. It's one of those places with open sleeping verandahs, surrounded by snowy pine woods. It has rows and rows of narrow white iron beds as regular as tombstones. The invalids smile at each other when axes flash across valleys, ring, flash, ring again! Young voices shout across valleys Hola! And mail is delivered. The friend that used to write you ten-page letters contents himself now with a postcard bluebird that tells you to "Get well Quick!" (JACQUES *throws the brochure away.*)—And when the last bleeding comes, not much later nor earlier than expected, you're wheeled discreetly into a little tent of white gauze, and the last thing you know of this world, of which you've known so little and yet so much, is the smell of an empty ice box. (*The blue flame expires in the chafing dish.* GUTMAN *picks up the brochure and hands it to the* WAITER, *whispering something.*)

JACQUES. You won't go back to that place. (*The* WAITER *places the brochure on the salver again and approaches behind them.*)

MARGUERITE. I wasn't released. I left without permission. They sent me this to remind me.

WAITER (*presenting the salver*). You dropped this.

JACQUES. We threw it away!

WAITER. Excuse me.

JACQUES. Now, from now on, Marguerite, you must take better care of yourself. Do you hear me?

MARGUERITE. I hear you. No more distractions for me? No more entertainers in curtained and perfumed alcoves above the bazaar, no more young men that a pinch of white powder or a puff of gray smoke can almost turn to someone devoutly remembered?

JACQUES. No, from now on—

MARGUERITE. What "from now on," old hawk?

JACQUES. Rest. Peace.

MARGUERITE. Rest in peace is that final bit of advice they carve on gravestones, and I'm not ready for it! Are you? Are *you* ready for it? (*She returns to the table. He follows her.*) Oh, Jacques, when are we going to leave here, how are we going to leave here, you've got to tell me!

JACQUES. I've told you all I know.

MARGUERITE. Nothing, you've given up hope!

JACQUES. I haven't, that's not true. (GUTMAN *has brought out the white cockatoo which he shows to* LADY MULLIGAN *at her table.*)

GUTMAN (*his voice rising above the murmurs*). Her name is Aurora.

LADY MULLIGAN. Why do you call her Aurora?

GUTMAN. She cries at daybreak.

LADY MULLIGAN. Only at daybreak?

GUTMAN. Yes, at daybreak only. (*Their voices and laughter fade under.*)

MARGUERITE. How long is it since you've been to the travel agencies?

JACQUES. This morning I made the usual round of Cook's, American Express, Wagon-lits Universal, and it was the same story. There are no flights out of here till further orders from someone higher up.

MARGUERITE. Nothing, nothing at all?

JACQUES. Oh, there's a rumor of something called the Fugitivo, but—

MARGUERITE. The What!!!?

JACQUES. The Fugitivo. It's one of those non-scheduled things that—

MARGUERITE. When, when, when?

JACQUES. I told you it was non-scheduled. Non-scheduled means it comes and goes at no predictable—

MARGUERITE. Don't give me the dictionary! I want to know how does one get on it? Did you bribe them? Did you offer them money? No. Of course you didn't! And I know why! You really don't want to leave here. You *think* you don't want to go because you're brave as an old hawk. But the truth of the matter—the real not the royal truth—is that you're terrified of the Terra Incognita outside that wall.

JACQUES. You've hit upon the truth. I'm terrified of the unknown country inside or outside this wall or any place on earth without you with me! The only country, known or unknown that I can breathe in, or care to, is the country in which we breathe together, as we are now at this table. And later, a little while later, even closer than this, the sole inhabitants of a tiny world whose limits are those of the light from a rose-colored lamp—beside the sweetly, completely known country of your cool bed!

MARGUERITE. The little comfort of love?

JACQUES. Is that comfort so little?

MARGUERITE. Caged birds accept each other but flight is what they long for.

JACQUES. I want to stay here with you and love you and guard you until the time or way comes that we both can leave with honor.

MARGUERITE. "Leave with honor"? Your vocabulary is almost as out-of-date as your cape and your cane. How could anyone quit this field with honor, this place where there's nothing but the gradual wasting away of everything decent in us . . . the sort of desperation that comes after even desperation has been worn out through long wear! . . . Why have they put these screens around the table? (*She springs up and knocks one of them over.*)

LADY MULLIGAN. There! You see? I don't understand why you let such people stay here.

GUTMAN. They pay the price of admission the same as you.

LADY MULLIGAN. What price is that?

GUTMAN. Desperation!—With cash here! (*He indicates the Siete Mares.*) Without cash there! (*He indicates Skid Row.*) Block Eight on the Camino Real!

BLOCK EIGHT

There is the sound of loud desert wind and a flamenco cry followed by a dramatic phrase of music. A flickering diamond blue radiance floods the hotel entrance. The crouching, grimacing HUNCHBACK *shakes his hoop of bells which is the convention for the appearance of each legendary figure.* LORD BYRON *appears in the doorway readied for departure.* GUTMAN *raises his hand for silence.*

GUTMAN. You're leaving us, Lord Byron?

BYRON. Yes, I'm leaving you, Mr. Gutman.

GUTMAN. What a pity! But this is a port of entry and departure. There are no permanent guests. Possibly you are getting a little restless?

BYRON. The luxuries of this place have made me soft. The metal point's gone from my pen, there's nothing left but the feather.

GUTMAN. That may be true. But what can you do about it?

BYRON. Make a departure!

GUTMAN. From yourself?

BYRON. From my present self to myself as I used to be!

GUTMAN. *That's* the *furthest* departure a man could make! I guess you're sailing to Athens? There's another war there and like all wars since the beginning of time it can be interpreted as a —struggle for *what?*

BYRON.—For *freedom!* You may laugh at it, but it still means something to *me!*

GUTMAN. Of course it does! I'm not laughing a bit, I'm beaming with admiration.

BYRON. I've allowed myself many distractions.

GUTMAN. Yes, indeed!

BYRON. But I've never altogether forgotten my old devotion to the—

GUTMAN.—To the *what*, Lord Byron? (BYRON *passes nervous fingers through his hair.*) You can't remember the object of your one-time devotion? (*There is a pause.* BYRON *limps away from the terrace and goes toward the fountain.*)

BYRON. When Shelley's corpse was recovered from the sea . . . (GUTMAN *beckons the* DREAMER *who approaches and accompanies* BYRON's *speech.*)—It was burned on the beach at Viareggio.—I watched the spectacle from my carriage because the stench was revolting . . . Then it—fascinated me! I got out of my carriage. Went nearer, holding a handkerchief to my nostrils!—I saw that the front of the skull had broken away in the flames, and there— (*He advances out upon the stage apron, followed by* ABDULLAH *with the pine torch or lantern.*) And there was the brain of Shelley, indistinguishable from a cooking stew!—*boiling, bubbling, hissing!*—in the *blackening—cracked—pot—*of his skull! (MARGUERITE *rises abruptly.* JACQUES *supports her.*)—Trelawny, his friend, Trelawny, threw salt and oil and frankincense in the flames and finally the almost intolerable stench— (ABDULLAH *giggles.* GUTMAN *slaps him.*)—was *gone* and the burning was *pure!*—as a man's burning should be . . . A man's burning *ought* to be pure!—*not* like mine—(a crêpe suzette—burned in brandy . . .) *Shelley's* burning was finally very *pure!* But the body, the corpse, split open like a grilled pig! (ABDULLAH *giggles irrepressibly again.* GUTMAN *grips the back of his neck and he stands up stiff and assumes an expression of exaggerated solemnity.*)—And then Trelawny[42]—as the ribs of the corpse unlocked—reached into them as a baker reaches quickly into an oven! (ABDULLAH *almost goes into another convulsion.*)—And snatched out—as a baker would a biscuit!—the *heart* of Shelley! Snatched the heart of Shelley out of the

blistering corpse!—Out of the purifying —blue-flame . . . (MARGUERITE *resumes her seat,* JACQUES *his.*)—And it was *over!* —I thought— (*He turns slightly from the audience and crosses upstage from the apron. He faces* JACQUES *and* MARGUERITE.)—I thought it was a disgusting thing to do, to snatch a man's heart from his body! What can one man do with another man's heart? (JACQUES *rises and strikes the stage with his cane.*)

JACQUES (*passionately*). He can do this with it! (*He seizes a loaf of bread on his table, and descends from the terrace.*) *He can twist it like this!* (*He twists the loaf.*) *He can tear it like this!* (*He tears the loaf in two.*) *He can crush it under his foot!* (*He drops the bread and stamps on it.*)—*And kick it away—like this!* (*He kicks the bread off the terrace.* LORD BYRON *turns away from him and limps again out upon the stage apron and speaks to the audience.*)

BYRON. That's very true, Señor. But a poet's vocation, which used to be my vocation, is to influence the heart in a gentler fashion than you have made your mark on that loaf of bread. He ought to purify it and lift it above its ordinary level. For what is the heart but a sort of— (*He makes a high, groping gesture in the air.*)—A sort of—*instrument!*—that translates *noise* into *music*, chaos into— *order* . . . (ABDULLAH *ducks almost to the earth in an effort to stifle his mirth.* GUTMAN *coughs to cover his own amusement.*)—*a mysterious order!* (*He raises his voice till it fills the plaza.*)—That was my vocation once upon a time, before it was obscured by vulgar plaudits!—Little by little it was lost among gondolas and palazzos![43]—masked balls, glittering salons, huge shadowy courts and torch-lit entrances!—Baroque façades, canopies and carpets, candelabra and gold plate among snowy damask, ladies with throats as slender as flower stems, bending and

---

[42] Edward John Trelawny was friend and companion to both Byron and Shelley. In his "Recollections" he claims to have taken Shelley's heart as Byron here describes it, although absolute proof is lacking.

[43] Palaces.

breathing toward me their fragrant breath—Exposing their breasts to me! Whispering, half-smiling!—And everywhere marble, the visible grandeur of marble, pink and gray marble, veined and tinted as flayed corrupting flesh,—all these provided agreeable distractions from the rather frightening solitude of a poet. Oh, I wrote many cantos in Venice and Constantinople and in Ravenna and Rome, on all of those Latin and Levantine excursions that my twisted foot led me into—but I wonder about them a little. They seem to improve as the wine in the bottle—dwindles . . . *There is a passion for declivity in this world!* And lately I've found myself listening to hired musicians behind a row of artificial palm trees—instead of the single—pure-stringed instrument of my heart . . . Well, then, it's time to leave here! (*He turns back to the stage.*) —There is a time for departure even when there's no certain place to go! I'm going to look for one, now. I'm sailing to Athens. At least I can look up at the Acropolis, I can stand at the foot of it and look up at broken columns on the crest of a hill—if not purity, at least its recollection . . . I can sit quietly looking for a long, long time in absolute silence, and possibly, yes, *still* possibly—The old pure music will come to me again. Of course on the other hand I may hear only the little noise of insects in the grass . . . But I am sailing to Athens! *Make voyages!—Attempt them!*—there's nothing else . . .

MARGUERITE (*excitedly*). *Watch where he goes!* (LORD BYRON *limps across the* plaza *with his head bowed, making slight, apologetic gestures to the wheedling* BEGGARS *who shuffle about him. There is music. He crosses toward the steep* Alleyway Out. *The following is played with a quiet intensity so it will be in a lower key than the later Fugitivo Scene.*) Watch him, watch him, see which way he goes. Maybe he knows of a way that we haven't found out.

JACQUES. Yes, I'm watching him, Cara. (LORD *and* LADY MULLIGAN *half rise, staring anxiously through monocle and lorgnon.*)

MARGUERITE. Oh, my God, I believe he's going up that alley.

JACQUES. Yes, he is. He has.

LORD *and* LADY MULLIGAN. Oh, the fool, the idiot, he's going under the arch!

MARGUERITE. Jacques, run after him, warn him, tell him about the desert he has to cross.

JACQUES. I think he knows what he's doing.

MARGUERITE. I can't look! (*She turns to the audience, throwing back her head and closing her eyes. The desert wind sings loudly as* BYRON *climbs to the top of the steps.*)

BYRON (*to several porters carrying luggage—which is mainly caged birds*). THIS WAY! (*He exits.* KILROY *starts to follow. He stops at the steps, cringing and looking at* GUTMAN. GUTMAN *motions him to go ahead.* KILROY *rushes up the stairs. He looks out, loses his nerve and sits—blinking his nose.* GUTMAN *laughs as he announces*—)

GUTMAN. Block Nine on the Camino Real! (*He goes into the hotel.*)

BLOCK NINE

ABDULLAH *runs back to the hotel with the billowing flambeau. A faint and far away humming sound becomes audible* . . . MARGUERITE *opens her eyes with a startled look. She searches the sky for something. A very low percussion begins with the humming sound, as if excited hearts are beating.*

MARGUERITE. Jacques! I hear something in the sky!

JACQUES. I think what you hear is—

MARGUERITE (*with rising excitement*).— No, it's a plane, a great one, I see the lights of it, now!

JACQUES. Some kind of fireworks, Cara.

MARGUERITE. Hush! LISTEN! (*She*

blows out the candle to see better above it. She rises, peering into the sky.) I see it! I see it! There! It's circling over us!

LADY MULLIGAN. Raymond, Raymond, sit down, your face is flushed!

HOTEL GUESTS (*overlapping*).—What is it?—The FUGITIVO!—THE FUGITIVO! THE FUGITIVO!—Quick, get my jewelry from the hotel safe!—Cash a check!—Throw some things in a bag! I'll wait here!—Never mind luggage, we have our money and papers!—Where is it now?—There, there!—It's turning to land!—To go like this?—Yes, go anyhow, just go anyhow, just go!—Raymond! Please!—Oh, it's rising again!—Oh, it's— SHH! MR. GUTMAN! (GUTMAN *appears in the doorway. He raises a hand in a commanding gesture.*)

GUTMAN. Signs in the sky should not be mistaken for wonders! (*The Voices modulate quickly.*) Ladies, gentlemen, please resume your seats! (*Places are resumed at tables, and silver is shakily lifted. Glasses are raised to lips, but the noise of concerted panting of excitement fills the stage and a low percussion echoes frantic heart beats.* GUTMAN *descends to the plaza, shouting furiously to the* OFFICER.) Why wasn't I told the Fugitivo was coming? (*Everyone, almost as a man, rushes into the hotel and reappears almost at once with hastily collected possessions. Marguerite rises but appears stunned. There is a great whistling and screeching sound as the aerial transport halts somewhere close by, accompanied by rainbow splashes of light and cries like children's on a roller-coaster. Some incoming* PASSENGERS *approach the stage down an aisle of the theatre, preceded by* REDCAPS *with luggage.*)

PASSENGERS.—What a heavenly trip!— The scenery was thrilling!—It's so quick! —The only way to travel! Etc., etc. (*A uniformed man, the* PILOT, *enters the plaza with a megaphone.*)

PILOT (*through the megaphone*). Fugitivo now loading for departure! Fugitivo loading immediately for departure! Northwest corner of the plaza!

MARGUERITE. Jacques, it's the Fugitivo, it's the non-scheduled thing you heard of this afternoon!

PILOT. All out-going passengers on the Fugitivo are requested to present their tickets and papers immediately at this station.

MARGUERITE. He said "outgoing passengers"!

PILOT. Outgoing passengers on the Fugitivo report immediately at this station for customs inspection.

MARGUERITE (*with a forced smile*). Why are you just standing there?

JACQUES (*with an Italian gesture*). Che cosa possa fare?[44]

MARGUERITE. Move, move, do something!

JACQUES. *What!*

MARGUERITE. Go to them, ask, find out!

JACQUES. I have no idea what the damned thing is!

MARGUERITE. I do, I'll tell you! It's a way to escape from this abominable place!

JACQUES. Forse, forse, non so![45]

MARGUERITE. It's a way *out* and *I'm* not going to miss it!

PILOT. Ici la Douane![46] Customs inspection here!

MARGUERITE. Customs. That means luggage. Run to my room! Here! Key! Throw a few things in a bag, my jewels, my furs, but hurry! Vite, vite, vite! I don't believe there's much time! No, everybody is— (*Outgoing* PASSENGERS *storm the desk and table.*)—Clamoring for tickets! There must be limited space! Why don't you do what I tell you? (*She rushes to a man with a rubber stamp and a roll of tickets.*) Monsieur! Señor! Pardonnez-moi![47] I'm going, I'm going out! I want my ticket!

[44] "What can I do?"

[45] "Perhaps, I don't know!"

[46] The pilot announces customs in French as well as English.

[47] Marguerite is unsure which language to use, tries French and Spanish for "Sir!" then "Pardon me" in French. "Vite!" is French for "Hurry!"

PILOT (*coldly*). Name, please.

MARGUERITE. Mademoiselle — Gautier — but I—

PILOT. Gautier? Gautier? We have no Gautier listed.

MARGUERITE. I'm—*not* listed! I mean I'm—traveling under another name.

TRAVEL AGENT. What name are you traveling under? (PRUDENCE *and* OLYMPE *rush out of the hotel half-dressed, dragging their furs. Meanwhile* KILROY *is trying to make a fast buck or two as a* REDCAP. *The scene gathers wild momentum, is punctuated by crashes of percussion. Grotesque mummers act as demon custom inspectors and immigration authorities, etc. Baggage is tossed about, ripped open, smuggled goods seized, arrests made, all amid the wildest importunities, protests, threats, bribes, entreaties; it is a scene for improvisation.*)

PRUDENCE. Thank God I woke up!

OLYMPE. Thank God I wasn't asleep!

PRUDENCE. I knew it was non-scheduled but I *did* think they'd give you time to get in your girdle.

OLYMPE. Look who's trying to crash it! I know damned well *she* don't have a reservation!

PILOT (*to* MARGUERITE). What name did you say, Mademoiselle? Please! People are waiting, you're holding up the line!

MARGUERITE. I'm so confused! Jacques! What name did you make my reservation under?

OLYMPE. She has no reservation!

PRUDENCE. *I have, I got mine!*

OLYMPE. *I got mine!*

PRUDENCE. *I'm* next!

OLYMPE. Don't push *me*, you old bag!

MARGUERITE. I was here first! I was here before anybody! Jacques, quick! Get my money from the hotel safe! (JACQUES *exits.*)

AGENT. *Stay in line!* (*There is a loud warning whistle.*)

PILOT. Five minutes. The Fugitivo leaves in five minutes. Five, five minutes

only! (*At this announcement the scene becomes riotous.*)

TRAVEL AGENT. *Four minutes! The Fugitivo leaves in four minutes!* (PRUDENCE *and* OLYMPE *are shrieking at him in French. The warning whistle blasts again.*) *Three minutes, the Fugitivo leaves in three minutes!*

MARGUERITE (*topping the turmoil*). Monsieur! Please! I was here first, I was here before anybody! Look! (JACQUES *returns with her money.*) I have thousands of francs! Take whatever you want! Take all of it, it's yours!

PILOT. Payment is only accepted in pounds sterling or dollars. Next, please.

MARGUERITE. You don't accept francs? They do at the hotel! They accept my francs at the Siete Mares!

PILOT. Lady, don't argue with me, I don't make the rules!

MARGUERITE (*beating her forehead with her fist*). Oh, God, Jacques! Take these back to the cashier! (*She thrusts the bills at him.*) Get them changed to dollars or —Hurry! Tout de suite![48] I'm—going to faint . . .

JACQUES. But Marguerite—

MARGUERITE. Go! Go! Please!

PILOT. Closing, we're closing now! The Fugitivo leaves in two minutes! (LORD *and* LADY MULLIGAN *rush forward.*)

LADY MULLIGAN. Let Lord Mulligan through.

PILOT (*to* MARGUERITE). You're standing in the way. (OLYMPE *screams as the* CUSTOMS INSPECTOR *dumps her jewels on the ground. She and* PRUDENCE *butt heads as they dive for the gems; the fight is renewed.*)

MARGUERITE (*detaining the* PILOT). Oh, look, Monsieur! Regardez ça![49] My diamond, a solitaire—two carats! Take that as security!

PILOT. Let me go. The Loan Shark's across the plaza! (*There is another warning blast.* PRUDENCE *and* OLYMPE *seize hat boxes and rush toward the whistle.*)

MARGUERITE (*clinging desperately to

[48] "Immediately!"
[49] "Look at that!"

the PILOT). You don't understand! Señor Casanova has gone to change money! He'll be here in a second. And I'll pay five, ten, twenty times the price of— *JACQUES! JACQUES! WHERE ARE YOU?*

VOICE (*back of auditorium*). We're closing the gate!

MARGUERITE. You can't close the gate!

PILOT. Move, Madame!

MARGUERITE. I won't move!

LADY MULLIGAN. I tell you, Lord Mulligan is the Iron & Steel man from Cobh! Raymond! They're closing the gate!

LORD MULLIGAN. I can't seem to get through!

GUTMAN. Hold the gate for Lord Mulligan!

PILOT (*to* MARGUERITE). Madame, stand back or I will have to use force!

MARGUERITE. Jacques! Jacques!

LADY MULLIGAN. Let us through! We're clear!

PILOT. Madame! Stand back and let these passengers through!

MARGUERITE. No, No! I'm first! I'm next!

LORD MULLIGAN. Get her out of our way! That woman's a whore!

LADY MULLIGAN. How dare you stand in our way?

PILOT. Officer, take this woman!

LADY MULLIGAN. Come on, Raymond!

MARGUERITE (*as the* OFFICER *pulls her away*). Jacques! Jacques! Jacques! (JACQUES *returns with changed money.*) Here! Here is the money!

PILOT. All right, give me your papers.

MARGUERITE.—My papers? Did you say my papers?

PILOT. Hurry, hurry, your passport!

MARGUERITE.—Jacques! He wants my papers! Give him my papers, Jacques!

JACQUES.—The lady's papers are lost!

MARGUERITE (*wildly*). No, no, no, THAT IS NOT TRUE! HE WANTS TO KEEP ME HERE! HE'S LYING ABOUT IT!

JACQUES. Have you forgotten that your papers were stolen?

MARGUERITE. I gave you my papers, I gave you my papers to keep, you've got my papers. (*Screaming,* LADY MULLIGAN *breaks past her and descends the stairs.*)

LADY MULLIGAN. Raymond! Hurry!

LORD MULLIGAN (*staggering on the top step*). I'm sick! I'm sick! (*The* STREET-CLEANERS *disguised as expensive morticians in swallowtail coats come rapidly up the aisle of the theatre and wait at the foot of the stairway for the tottering tycoon.*)

LADY MULLIGAN. You cannot be sick till we get on the Fugitivo!

LORD MULLIGAN. Forward all cables to Guaranty Trust in Paris.

LADY MULLIGAN. Place de la Concorde.

LORD MULLIGAN. Thank you! All purchases C.O.D. to Mulligan Iron & Steel Works in Cobh—Thank you!

LADY MULLIGAN. Raymond! Raymond! Who are these men?

LORD MULLIGAN. I know these men! I recognize their faces!

LADY MULLIGAN. Raymond! They're the Streetcleaners! (*She screams and runs up the aisle screaming repeatedly, stopping half-way to look back. The Two* STREETCLEANERS *seize Lord Mulligan by either arm as he crumples.*) Pack Lord Mulligan's body in dry ice! Ship Air Express to Cobh care of Mulligan Iron & Steel Works, in Cobh! (*She runs sobbing out of the back of the auditorium as the whistle blows repeatedly and a Voice shouts.*) I'm coming! I'm coming!

MARGUERITE. Jacques! Jacques! Oh, God!

PILOT. The Fugitivo is leaving, all aboard! (*He starts toward the steps.* MARGUERITE *clutches his arm.*) Let go of me!

MARGUERITE. You can't go without me!

PILOT. Officer, hold this woman!

JACQUES. Marguerite, let him go! (*She releases the* PILOT's *arm and turns savagely on* JACQUES. *She tears his coat open, seizes a large envelope of papers and rushes after the* PILOT *who has started down the steps over the orchestra pit and into a center aisle of the house. Timpani build up as she starts down the steps, screaming—*)

MARGUERITE. Here! I have them here! Wait! I have my papers now, I have my papers! (*The* PILOT *runs cursing up the center aisle as the Fugitivo whistle gives repeated short, shrill blasts; timpani and dissonant brass are heard. Outgoing PAS-SENGERS burst into hysterical song, laughter, shouts of farewell. These can come over a loudspeaker at the back of the house.*)

VOICE (*in distance*). Going! Going! Going!

MARGUERITE (*attempting as if half-paralyzed to descend the steps*). NOT WITHOUT ME, NO, NO, NOT WITHOUT ME! (*Her figure is caught in the dazzling glacial light of the follow-spot. It blinds her. She makes violent, crazed gestures, clinging to the railing of the steps; her breath is loud and hoarse as a dying person's, she holds a blood-stained handkerchief to her lips. There is a prolonged, gradually fading, rocketlike roar as the Fugitivo takes off. Shrill cries of joy from departing passengers; something radiant passes above the stage and streams of confetti and tinsel fall into the plaza. Then there is a great calm, the ship's receding roar diminished to the hum of an insect.*)

GUTMAN (*somewhat compassionately*). Block Ten on the Camino Real.

BLOCK TEN

There is something about the desolation of the plaza that suggests a city devastated by bombardment. Reddish lights flicker here and there as if ruins were smoldering and wisps of smoke rise from them.

LA MADRECITA (*almost inaudibly*). Donde?

THE DREAMER. Aquí. Aquí, Madrecita.

MARGUERITE. Lost! Lost! Lost! Lost! (*She is still clinging brokenly to the railing of the steps.* JACQUES *descends to her and helps her back up the steps.*)

JACQUES. Lean against me, Cara. Breathe quietly, now.

MARGUERITE. Lost!

JACQUES. Breathe quietly, quietly, and look up at the sky.

MARGUERITE. Lost . . .

JACQUES. These tropical nights are so clear. There's the Southern Cross. Do you see the Southern Cross, Marguerite? (*He points through the proscenium. They are now on the bench before the fountain; she is resting in his arms.*) And there, over there, is Orion, like a fat, golden fish swimming North in the deep clear water, and we are together, breathing quietly together, leaning together, quietly, quietly together, completely, sweetly together, not frightened, now, not alone, but completely quietly together . . . (LA MADRECITA, *led into the center of the plaza by her son, has begun to sing very softly; the reddish flares dim out and the smoke disappears.*) All of us have a desperate bird in our hearts, a memory of—some distant mother with—wings . . .

MARGUERITE. I would have—left—without you . . .

JACQUES. I know, I know!

MARGUERITE. Then how can you—still—?

JACQUES. Hold you? (MARGUERITE *nods slightly.*) Because you've taught me that part of love which is tender. I never knew it before. Oh, I had—mistresses that circled me like moons! I scrambled from one bed-chamber to another bed-chamber with shirttails always aflame, from girl to girl, like buckets of coal-oil poured on a conflagration! But never loved until now with the part of love that's tender . . .

MARGUERITE.—We're used to each other. That's what you think is love . . . You'd better leave me now, you'd better go and let me go because there's a cold wind blowing out of the mountains and over the desert and into my heart, and if you stay with me now, I'll say cruel things, I'll wound your vanity, I'll taunt you with the decline of your male vigor!

JACQUES. Why does disappointment make people unkind to each other?

MARGUERITE. Each of us is very much alone.

JACQUES. Only if we distrust each other.

MARGUERITE. We have to distrust each other. It is our only defense against betrayal.

JACQUES. I think our defense is love.

MARGUERITE. Oh, Jacques, we're used to each other, we're a pair of captive hawks caught in the same cage, and so we've grown used to each other. That's what passes for love at this dim, shadowy end of the Camino Real . . . What are we sure of? Not even of our existence, dear comforting friend! And whom can we ask the questions that torment us? "What is this place?" "Where are we?" —a fat old man who gives sly hints that only bewilder us more, a fake of a Gypsy squinting at cards and tea-leaves. What else are we offered? The never-broken procession of little events that assure us that we and strangers about us are still going on! Where? Why? and the perch that we hold is unstable! We're threatened with eviction, for this is a port of entry and departure, there are no permanent guests! And where else have we to go when we leave here? Bide-a-While? "Ritz Men Only"? Or under that ominous arch into Terra Incognita? We're lonely. We're frightened. We hear the Streetcleaners' piping not far away. So now and then, although we've wounded each other time and again—we stretch out hands to each other in the dark that we can't escape from—we huddle together for some dim-communal comfort—and that's what passes for love on this terminal stretch of the road that used to be royal. What is it, this feeling between us? When you feel my exhausted weight against your shoulder—when I clasp your anxious old hawk's head to my breast, what is it we feel in whatever is left of our hearts? Something, yes, something—delicate, unreal, bloodless! The sort of violets that could grow on the moon, or in the crevices of those far away mountains, fertilized by the droppings of carrion birds. Those birds are familiar to us. Their shadows inhabit the plaza. I've heard them flapping their wings like old charwomen beating worn-out carpets with gray brooms . . . But tenderness, the violets in the mountains—can't break the rocks!

JACQUES. The violets in the mountains can break the rocks if you believe in them and allow them to grow! (*The plaza has resumed its usual aspect.* AB-DULLAH *enters through one of the downstage arches.*)

ABDULLAH. Get your carnival hats and noisemakers here! Tonight the moon will restore the virginity of my sister!

MARGUERITE (*almost tenderly touching his face*). Don't you know that tonight I am going to betray you?

JACQUES.—Why would you do that?

MARGUERITE. Because I've out-lived the tenderness of my heart. Abdullah, come here! I have an errand for you! Go to Ahmed's and deliver a message!

ABDULLAH. I'm working for Mama, making the Yankee dollar! Get your carnival hats and—

MARGUERITE. *Here, boy!* (*She snatches a ring off her finger and offers it to him.*)

JACQUES.—Your cabochon sapphire?[50]

MARGUERITE. Yes, my cabochon sapphire!

JACQUES. Are you mad?

MARGUERITE. Yes, I'm mad, or nearly! The specter of lunacy's at my heels tonight! (JACQUES *drives* ABDULLAH *back with his cane.*) Catch, boy! The other side of the fountain! Quick! (*The guitar is heard molto vivace. She tosses the ring across the fountain.* JACQUES *attempts to hold the boy back with his cane.* AB-DULLAH *dodges in and out like a little terrier, laughing.* MARGUERITE *shouts encouragement in French. When the boy is driven back from the ring, she snatches it up and tosses it to him again, shouting:*) Catch, boy! Run to Ahmed's! Tell the charming young man that the French lady's bored with her company tonight!

[50] A jewel that is cut in a convex shape. It is polished but it has no facets.

Say that the French lady missed the Fugitivo and wants to forget she missed it! Oh, and reserve a room with a balcony so I can watch your sister appear on the roof when the moonrise makes her a virgin! (ABDULLAH *skips shouting out of the plaza.* JACQUES *strikes the stage with his cane. She says, without looking at him:*) Time betrays us and we betray each other.

JACQUES. Wait, Marguerite.

MARGUERITE. No! I can't! The wind from the desert is sweeping me away! (*A loud singing wind sweeps her toward the terrace, away from him. She looks back once or twice as if for some gesture of leave-taking but he only stares at her fiercely, striking the stage at inter-* vals with his cane, like a death-march. GUTMAN *watches, smiling, from the terrace, bows to* MARGUERITE *as she passes into the hotel. The drum of* JACQUES' *cane is taken up by other percussive instruments, and almost unnoticeably at first, weird-looking celebrants or carnival mummers creep into the plaza, silently as spiders descending a wall. A sheet of scarlet and yellow rice paper bearing some cryptic device is lowered from the center of the plaza. The percussive effects become gradually louder.* JACQUES *is oblivious to the scene behind him, standing in front of the plaza, his eyes closed.*)

GUTMAN. Block Eleven on the Camino Real.

BLOCK ELEVEN

GUTMAN. The Fiesta has started. The first event is the coronation of the King of Cuckolds.[51] (*Blinding shafts of light are suddenly cast upon* CASANOVA *on the forestage. He shields his face, startled, as the crowd closes about him. The blinding shafts of light seem to strike him like savage blows and he falls to his knees as—the* HUNCHBACK *scuttles out of the* GYPSY's *stall with a crown of gilded antlers on a velvet pillow. He places it on* JACQUES' *head. The celebrants form a circle about him chanting.*)

JACQUES. What is this?—a crown—

GUTMAN. A crown of horns!

CROWD. Cornudo! Cornudo! Cornudo! Cornudo! Cornudo![52]

GUTMAN. Hail, all hail, the King of Cuckolds on the Camino Real! (JACQUES *springs up, first striking out at them with his cane. Then all at once he abandons* self-defense, throws off his cape, casts away his cane, and fills the plaza with a roar of defiance and self-derision.*)

JACQUES. Si, si, sono cornudo![53] Cornudo! Cornudo! Casanova is the King of Cuckolds on the Camino Real! Show me crowned to the world! Announce the honor! Tell the world of the honor bestowed on Casanova, Chevalier de Seingalt! Knight of the Golden Spur by the Grace of His Holiness the Pope . . . Famous adventurer! Con man Extraordinary! Gambler! Pitch-man par excellence! Shill! Pimp! Spiv! *And—great— lover . . .*[54] (*The Crowd howls with applause and laughter but his voice rises above them with sobbing intensity*). Yes, I said GREAT LOVER! The greatest lover wears the longest horns on the Camino! GREAT! LOVER!

GUTMAN. Attention! Silence! The

[51] A husband or wife whose spouse has been unfaithful is termed a cuckold, identified by the horns which are supposed to grow from the head. The tradition of the cuckold is centuries old, and a favorite literary reference.

[52] "Cuckold!"

[53] "Yes, yes, I am a cuckold!"

[54] Casanova is calling himself as many derogatory names as he can think of. A "con man" (confidence man) is a swindler who takes advantage of his victim's confidence; a pitch-man is a glib salesman of worthless products, generally associated with carnivals; a shill is a pitch-man's confederate who places fake bets or makes fake purchases to encourage the crowd to do the same; a pimp is a prostitute's agent; and a spiv is the modern equivalent of the ancient social parasite, one who lives by his wits and does no regular work.

moon is rising! The restoration is about to occur! (*A white radiance is appearing over the ancient wall of the town. The mountains become luminous. There is music. Everyone, with breathless attention, faces the light.* KILROY *crosses to* JACQUES *and beckons him out behind the crowd. There he snatches off the antlers and returns him his fedora.* JACQUES *reciprocates by removing* KILROY's *fright wig and electric nose. They embrace as brothers. In a Chaplinesque dumb-play,* KILROY *points to the wildly flickering three brass balls of the* LOAN SHARK *and to his golden gloves; then with a terrible grimace he removes the gloves from about his neck, smiles at* JACQUES *and indicates that the two of them together will take flight over the wall.* JACQUES *shakes his head sadly, pointing to his heart and then to the Siete Mares.* KILROY *nods with regretful understanding of a human and manly folly. A* GUARD *has been silently approaching them in a soft-shoe dance.* JACQUES *whistles "La Golondrina."* KILROY *assumes a very nonchalant pose. The* GUARD *picks up curiously the discarded fright wig and electric nose. Then glancing suspiciously at the pair, he advances.* KILROY *makes a run for it. He does a baseball slide into the* LOAN SHARK's *welcoming doorway. The door slams. The* COP *is about to crash it when a gong sounds and* GUTMAN *shouts.*)

GUTMAN. SILENCE! ATTENTION! THE GYPSY!

GYPSY (*appearing on the roof with a gong*). The moon has restored the virginity of my daughter Esmeralda! (*The gong sounds.*)

STREET PEOPLE. Ahh!

GYPSY. The moon in its plenitude has made her a virgin! (*The gong sounds.*)

STREET PEOPLE. Ahh!

GYPSY. Praise her, celebrate her, give her suitable homage! (*The gong sounds.*)

STREET PEOPLE. Ahh!

GYPSY. Summon her to the roof! (*She shouts:*) ESMERALDA! (*Dancers shout the name in rhythm.*) RISE WITH THE MOON, MY DAUGHTER! CHOOSE THE HERO! (ESMERALDA *appears on the roof in dazzling light. She seems to be dressed in jewels. She raises her jeweled arms with a harsh flamenco cry.*)

ESMERALDA. OLE!

DANCERS. OLE![55] (*The details of the Carnival are a problem for director and choreographer but it has already been indicated in the script that the Fiesta is a sort of serio-comic, grotesque-lyric "Rites of Fertility" with roots in various pagan cultures. It should not be over-elaborated or allowed to occupy much time. It should not be more than three minutes from the appearance of* ESMERALDA *on the* GYPSY's *roof till the return of* KILROY *from the* LOAN SHARK's. KILROY *emerges from the Pawn Shop in grotesque disguise, a turban, dark glasses, a burnoose and an umbrella or sunshade.*)

KILROY (*to* JACQUES). So long, pal, I wish you could come with me. (JACQUES *clasps his cross in* KILROY's *hands.*)

ESMERALDA. Yankee!

KILROY (*to the audience*). So long, everybody. Good luck to you all on the Camino! I hocked my golden gloves to finance this expedition. I'm going. Hasta luega.[56] I'm going. I'm gone!

ESMERALDA. Yankee! (*He has no sooner entered the plaza than the riotous women strip off everything but the dungarees and skivvy which he first appeared in.*)

KILROY (*to the women*). Let me go. Let go of me! Watch out for my equipment!

ESMERALDA. Yankee! Yankee! (*He breaks away from them and plunges up the stairs of the ancient wall. He is halfway up them when* GUTMAN *shouts out:*)

GUTMAN. Follow-spot on that gringo, light the stairs! (*The light catches* KILROY. *At the same instant* ESMERALDA *cries out to him:*)

ESMERALDA. *Yankee! Yankee!*

GYPSY. What's goin' on down there? (*She rushes into the plaza.*)

---

[55] The cry of the spectators at a bullfight.
[56] Actually "*hasta luego*"—"see you later."

KILROY. Oh, no, I'm on my way out!

ESMERALDA. Espere un momento![57] (*The* GYPSY *calls the police, but is ignored in the crowd.*)

KILROY. Don't tempt me, baby! I hocked my golden gloves to finance this expedition!

ESMERALDA. Querido!

KILROY. Querido means sweetheart, a word which is hard to resist but I must resist it.

ESMERALDA. Champ!

KILROY. I used to be Champ but why remind me of it?

ESMERALDA. Be Champ again! Contend in the contest! Compete in the competition!

GYPSY (*shouting*). *Naw, naw, not eligible!*

ESMERALDA. *Pl-eeeeeeze!*

GYPSY. Slap her, Nursie, she's flippin'. (ESMERALDA *slaps* NURSIE *instead.*)

ESMERALDA. Hero! Champ!

KILROY. I'm not in condition!

ESMERALDA. You're still the Champ, the undefeated Champ of the golden gloves!

KILROY. Nobody's called me that in a long, long time!

ESMERALDA. Champ!

KILROY. My resistance is crumbling!

ESMERALDA. Champ!

KILROY. It's crumbled!

ESMERALDA. Hero!

KILROY. GERONIMO![58] (*He takes a flying leap from the stairs into the center of the plaza. He turns toward* ESMERALDA *and cries:*) DOLL!! (KILROY *surrounded by cheering* STREET PEOPLE *goes into a triumphant eccentric dance which reviews his history as fighter, traveler and lover. At finish of the dance, the music is cut off, as* KILROY *lunges, arm uplifted towards* ESMERALDA, *and cries: Kilroy the Champ!*

ESMERALDA. *KILROY the Champ!* (*She snatches a bunch of red roses from the stunned* NURSIE *and tosses them to* KILROY.)

CROWD (*sharply*). OLE! (*The* GYPSY, *at the same instant, hurls her gong down, creating a resounding noise.* KILROY *turns and comes down towards the audience, saying to them:*)

KILROY. Y'see? (*Cheering* STREET PEOPLE *surge towards him and lift him in the air. The lights fade as the curtain descends.*)

CROWD (*in a sustained yell*). OLE!

THE CURTAIN FALLS.

THERE IS A SHORT INTERMISSION.

BLOCK TWELVE

The stage is in darkness except for a spotlight which picks out ESMERALDA *on the* GYPSY'S *roof.*

ESMERALDA. Mama, what happened?—Mama, the lights went out!—Mama, where are you? It's so dark I'm scared!—MAMA! (*The lights are turned on displaying a deserted plaza. The* GYPSY *is seated at a small table before her stall.*)

GYPSY. Come on downstairs, Doll. The mischief is done. You've chosen your hero!

GUTMAN (*from the balcony of the Siete Mares*). Block Twelve on the Camino Real.

NURSIE (*at the fountain*). Gypsy, the fountain is still dry!

GYPSY. What d'yuh expect? There's nobody left to uphold the old traditions! You raise a girl. She watches television. Plays be-bop. Reads *Screen Secrets*. Comes the Big Fiesta. The moonrise makes her a virgin—which is the neatest trick of the week! And what does she do? Chooses a Fugitive Patsy for the Chosen Hero! Well, show him in! Admit the joker and get the virgin ready!

NURSIE. You're going through with it?

GYPSY. Look, Nursie! I'm operating a legitimate joint! This joker'll get the same treatment he'd get if he breezed down the Camino in a blizzard of G-notes! Trot, girl! Lubricate your means of locomotion! (NURSIE *goes into the*

[57] "Wait a moment!"
[58] The cry of paratroopers as they leap from the plane.

GYPSY's *stall. The* GYPSY *rubs her hands together and blows on the crystal ball, spits on it and gives it the old one-two with a "shammy" rag . . . She mutters "Crystal ball, tell me all . . . crystal ball tell me all" . . . as* KILROY *bounds into the plaza from her stall . . . a rose between his teeth.*)

GYPSY. Siente se, por favor.[59]

KILROY. No comprendo the lingo.

GYPSY. Put it down!

NURSIE (*offstage*). Hey, Gypsy!

GYPSY. Address me as Madam!

NURSIE (*entering*). *Madam!* Winchell has scooped you!

GYPSY. In a pig's eye!

NURSIE. The Fugitivo has "*fftt . . .*"!

GYPSY. In Elizabeth, New Jersey . . . ten fifty-seven P.M. . . . Eastern Standard Time—while you were putting them kiss-me-quicks in your hair-do! Furthermore, my second exclusive is that the solar system is drifting towards the constellation of Hercules: *Skiddoo!* (NURSIE *exits. Stamping is heard offstage.*) *Quiet, back there! God damn it!*

NURSIE (*offstage*). She's out of control!

GYPSY. Give her a double-bromide! (*To* KILROY:) Well, how does it feel to be the Chosen Hero?

KILROY. I better explain something to you.

GYPSY. Save your breath. You'll need it.

KILROY. I want to level with you. Can I level with you?

GYPSY (*rapidly stamping some papers*). How could you help but level with the Gypsy?

KILROY. I don't know what the hero is chosen for. (ESMERALDA *and* NURSIE *shriek offstage.*)

GYPSY. Time will brief you . . . Aw, I hate paper work! . . . NURSEHH! (NURSIE *comes out and stands by the table.*) This filing system is screwed up six ways from Next Sunday . . . File this crap under crap!—(*To* KILROY:) The smoking lamp is lit. Have a stick on me! (*She offers him a cigarette.*)

KILROY. No thanks.

GYPSY. Come on, indulge yourself. You got nothing to lose that won't be lost.

KILROY. If that's a professional opinion, I don't respect it.

GYPSY. Resume your seat and give me your full name.

KILROY. Kilroy.

GYPSY (*writing all this down*). Date of birth and place of that disaster?

KILROY. Both unknown.

GYPSY. Address?

KILROY. Traveler.

GYPSY. Parents?

KILROY. Anonymous.

GYPSY. Who brought you up?

KILROY. I was brought up and down by an eccentric old aunt in Dallas.

GYPSY. Raise both hands simultaneously and swear that you have not come here for the purpose of committing an immoral act.

ESMERALDA (*from offstage*). Hey, Chico!

GYPSY. *QUIET!* Childhood diseases?

KILROY. Whooping cough, measles and mumps.

GYPSY. Likes and dislikes?

KILROY. I like situations I can get out of. I don't like cops and—

GYPSY. Immaterial! Here! Signature on this! (*She hands him a blank.*)

KILROY. What is it?

GYPSY. You always sign something, don't you?

KILROY. Not till I know what it is.

GYPSY. It's just a little formality to give a tone to the establishment and make an impression on our out-of-town trade. Roll up your sleeve.

KILROY. What for?

GYPSY. A shot of some kind.

KILROY. What kind?

GYPSY. Any kind. Don't they always give you some kind of a shot?

KILROY. "They"?

GYPSY. Brass-hats, Americanos! (*She injects a hypo.*)

KILROY. I am no guinea pig!

GYPSY. Don't kid yourself. We're all

[59] "Sit down, please." Should be spelled "*siéntese.*"

of us guinea pigs in the laboratory of God. Humanity is just a work in progress.

KILROY. I don't make it out.

GYPSY. Who does? The Camino Real is a funny paper read backwards! (*There is weird piping outside.* KILROY *shifts on his seat. The* GYPSY *grins.*) Tired? The altitude makes you sleepy?

KILROY. It makes me nervous.

GYPSY. I'll show you how to take a slug of tequila![60] It dilates the capillaries. First you sprinkle salt on the back of your hand. Then lick it off with your tongue. Now then you toss the shot down! (*She demonstrates.*)—And then you bite into the lemon. That way it goes down easy, but what a bang!— You're next.

KILROY. No, thanks, I'm on the wagon.

GYPSY. There's an old Chinese proverb that says, "When your goose is cooked you might as well have it cooked with plenty of gravy." (*She laughs.*) Get up, baby. Let's have a look at yuh!—You're not a bad-looking boy. Sometimes working for the Yankee dollar isn't a painful profession. Have you ever been attracted by older women?

KILROY. Frankly, no, ma'am.

GYPSY. Well, there's a first time for everything.

KILROY. That is a subject I cannot agree with you on.

GYPSY. You think I'm an old bag? (KILROY *laughs awkwardly. The* GYPSY *slaps his face.*) Will you take the cards or the crystal?

KILROY. It's immaterial.

GYPSY. All right, we'll begin with the cards. (*She shuffles and deals.*) Ask me a question.

KILROY. Has my luck run out?

GYPSY. Baby, your luck ran out the day you were born. Another question.

KILROY. Ought I to leave this town?

GYPSY. It don't look to me like you've got much choice in the matter . . . Take a card. (KILROY *takes one.*) Ace?

KILROY. Yes, ma'am.

GYPSY. What color?

KILROY. Black.

GYPSY. Oh, oh—That does it. How big is your heart?

KILROY. As big as the head of a baby.

GYPSY. It's going to break.

KILROY. That's what I was afraid of.

GYPSY. The Streetcleaners are waiting for you outside the door.

KILROY. Which door, the front one? I'll slip out the back!

GYPSY. Leave us face it frankly, your number is up! You must've known a long time that the name of Kilroy was on the Streetcleaners' list.

KILROY. Sure. But not on top of it!

GYPSY. It's always a bit of a shock. Wait a minute! Here's good news. The Queen of Hearts has turned up in proper position.

KILROY. What's that mean?

GYPSY. Love, Baby!

KILROY. Love?

GYPSY. The Booby Prize!—Esmeralda! (*She rises and hits a gong. A divan is carried out. The* GYPSY'S DAUGHTER *is seated in a reclining position, like an odalisque, on this low divan. A spangled veil covers her face. From this veil to the girdle below her navel, that supports her diaphanous bifurcated skirt, she is nude except for a pair of glittering emerald snakes coiled over her breasts.* KILROY'S *head moves in a dizzy circle and a canary warbles inside it.*)

KILROY. WHAT'S—WHAT'S *HER* SPECIALTY?—Tea-leaves? (*The* GYPSY *wags a finger.*)

GYPSY. You know what curiosity did to the tom cat!—Nursie, give me my glamour wig and my forty-five. I'm hitting the street! I gotta go down to Walgreen's for change.

KILROY. What change?

GYPSY. The change from that ten-spot you're about to give me.

NURSIE. Don't argue with her. She has a will of iron.

KILROY. I'm not arguing! (*He reluctantly produces the money.*) But let's be *fair* about this! I hocked my golden gloves for this saw-buck!

NURSIE. All of them Yankee bastids want something for nothing!

---

[60] Highly distilled liquor of the maguey plant.

KILROY. I want a receipt for this bill.

NURSIE. No one is gypped at the Gypsy's!

KILROY. That's wonderful! How do I know it?

GYPSY. It's in the cards, it's in the crystal ball, it's in the tea-leaves! Absolutely no one is gypped at the Gypsy's! (*She snatches the bill. The wind howls.*) Such changeable weather! I'll slip on my summer furs! Nursie, break out my summer furs!

NURSIE (*leering grotesquely*). Mink or sable?

GYPSY. *Ha ha, that's a doll!* Here! Clock him! (NURSIE *tosses her a greasy blanket, and the* GYPSY *tosses* NURSIE *an alarm clock. The* GYPSY *rushes through the beaded string curtains.*) *Adios!* Ha ha!! (*She is hardly offstage when two shots ring out.* KILROY *starts.*)

ESMERALDA (*plaintively*). Mother has such an awful time on the street.

KILROY. You mean that she is insulted on the street?

ESMERALDA. By strangers.

KILROY (*to the audience*). I shouldn't think acquaintances would do it. (*She curls up on the low divan.* KILROY *licks his lips.*)—You seem very different from —this afternoon . . .

ESMERALDA. This afternoon?

KILROY. Yes, in the plaza when I was being roughed up by them gorillas and you was being dragged in the house by your Mama! (ESMERALDA *stares at him blankly.*) You don't remember?

ESMERALDA. I never remember what happened before the moonrise makes me a virgin.

KILROY.—That—comes as a shock to you, huh?

ESMERALDA. Yes. It comes as a shock.

KILROY (*smiling*). You have a little temporary amnesia they call it!

ESMERALDA. Yankee . . .

KILROY. Huh?

ESMERALDA. I'm glad I chose you. I'm glad that you were chosen. (*Her voice trails off.*) I'm glad. I'm very glad . . .

NURSIE. Doll!

ESMERALDA.—What is it, Nursie?

NURSIE. How are things progressing?

ESMERALDA. Slowly, Nursie— (NURSIE *comes lumbering in.*)

NURSIE. I want some light reading matter.

ESMERALDA. He's sitting on *Screen Secrets.*

KILROY (*jumping up*). Aw. Here. (*He hands her the fan magazine. She lumbers back out, coyly.*)—I—I feel—self-conscious. (*He suddenly jerks out a silver-framed photo.*)—D'you—like pictures?

ESMERALDA. Moving pictures?

KILROY. No, a—motionless—snapshot!

ESMERALDA. Of you?

KILROY. Of my—real—true woman . . . She was a platinum blonde the same as Jean Harlow. Do you remember Jean Harlow? No, you wouldn't remember Jean Harlow. It shows you are getting old when you remember Jean Harlow. (*He puts the snapshot away.*) . . . They say that Jean Harlow's ashes are kept in a little private cathedral in Forest Lawn[61] . . . Wouldn't it be wonderful if you could sprinkle them ashes over the ground like seeds, and out of each one would spring another Jean Harlow? And when spring comes you could just walk out and pick them off the bush! . . . You don't talk much.

ESMERALDA. You want me to *talk?*

KILROY. Well, that's the way we do things in the States. A little vino, some records on the victrola, some quiet conversation—and then if both parties are in a mood for romance . . . Romance—

ESMERALDA. Music! (*She rises and pours some wine from a slender crystal decanter as music is heard.*) They say that the monetary system has got to be stabilized all over the world.

KILROY (*taking the glass*). Repeat that, please. My radar was not wide open.

ESMERALDA. I said that *they* said that —uh, skip it! But we couldn't care less as long as we keep on getting the Yankee dollar . . . plus federal tax!

KILROY. That's for surely!

ESMERALDA. How do you feel about

[61] Jean Harlow was a motion picture star of the 1930s, famous for her platinum-blonde hair. Forest Lawn is the well-known Hollywood cemetery.

the class struggle? Do you take sides in that?

KILROY. Not that I—

ESMERALDA. Neither do we because of the dialectics.

KILROY. Who! Which?

ESMERALDA. Languages with accents, I suppose. But Mama don't care as long as they don't bring the Pope over here and put him in the White House.

KILROY. Who would do that?

ESMERALDA. Oh, the Bolsheviskies, those nasty old things with whiskers! *Whiskers scratch!* But little moustaches tickle . . . (*She giggles.*)

KILROY. I always got a smooth shave . . .

ESMERALDA. And how do you feel about the Mumbo Jumbo? Do you think they've got the Old Man in the bag yet?

KILROY. The Old Man?

ESMERALDA. God. We don't think so. We think there has been so much of the Mumbo Jumbo it's put Him to sleep! (KILROY *jumps up impatiently.*)

KILROY. This is not what I mean by a quiet conversation. I mean this is no where! *No where!*

ESMERALDA. What sort of talk do you want?

KILROY. Something more—intimate sort of! You know, like—

ESMERALDA.—Where did you get those eyes?

KILROY. *PERSONAL! Yeah* . . .

ESMERALDA. Well,—where did you get those eyes?

KILROY. Out of a dead cod-fish!

NURSIE (*shouting offstage*). DOLL! (KILROY *springs up, pounding his left palm with his right fist.*)

ESMERALDA. What?

NURSIE. Fifteen minutes!

KILROY. I'm no hot-rod mechanic. (*To the audience:*) I bet she's out there holding a stop watch to see that I don't overstay my time in this place!

ESMERALDA (*calling through the string curtains*). *Nursie, go to bed, Nursie!*

KILROY (*in a fierce whisper*). That's right, go to bed, Nursie!! (*There is a loud crash offstage.*)

ESMERALDA.—Nursie has gone to bed . . .

(*She drops the string curtains and returns to the alcove.*)

KILROY (*with vast relief*).—Ahhhhhhhhhh . . .

ESMERALDA. What've you got your eyes on?

KILROY. Those green snakes on you— what do you wear them for?

ESMERALDA. Supposedly for protection, but really for fun. (*He crosses to the divan.*) What are you going to do?

KILROY. I'm about to establish a beachhead on that sofa. (*He sits down.*) How about—lifting your veil?

ESMERALDA. I can't lift it.

KILROY. Why not?

ESMERALDA. I promised Mother I wouldn't.

KILROY. I thought your mother was the broadminded type.

ESMERALDA. Oh, she is, but you know how mothers are. You can lift it for me, if you say pretty please.

KILROY. Aww——

ESMERALDA. Go on, say it! Say pretty please!

KILROY. No!!

ESMERALDA. Why not?

KILROY. It's silly.

ESMERALDA. Then you can't lift my veil!

KILROY. Oh, all right. Pretty please.

ESMERALDA. Say it again!

KILROY. Pretty please.

ESMERALDA. Now say it once more like you meant it. (*He jumps up. She grabs his hand.*) Don't go away.

KILROY. You're making a fool out of me.

ESMERALDA. I was just teasing a little. Because you're so cute. Sit down again, please—*pretty* please! (*He falls on the couch.*)

KILROY. What is that wonderful perfume you've got on?

ESMERALDA. Guess!

KILROY. Chanel Number Five?

ESMERALDA. No.

KILROY. Tabu?

ESMERALDA. No.

KILROY. I give up.

ESMERALDA. It's *Noche en Acapulco!* I'm just dying to go to Acapulco. I wish that you would take me to Acapulco. (*He sits up.*) What's the matter?

KILROY. You gypsies' daughters are invariably reminded of something without which you cannot do—just when it looks like everything has been fixed.

ESMERALDA. That isn't nice at all. I'm not the gold-digger type. Some girls see themselves in silver foxes. I only see myself in Acapulco.

KILROY. At Todd's Place?

ESMERALDA. Oh, no, at the Mirador! Watching those pretty boys dive off the Quebrada!

KILROY. Look again, Baby. Maybe you'll see yourself in Paramount Pictures or having a Singapore Sling at a Statler bar!

ESMERALDA. You're being sarcastic?

KILROY. Nope. Just realistic. All of you gypsies' daughters have hearts of stone, and I'm not whistling "Dixie"! But just the same, the night before a man dies, he says, "Pretty please—will you let me lift your veil?"—while the Streetcleaners wait for him right outside the door!—Because to be warm for a little longer is life. And love?—that's a four-letter word which is sometimes no better than one you see printed on fences by kids playing hooky from school!—Oh, well—what's the use of complaining? You gypsies' daughters have ears that only catch sounds like the snap of a gold cigarette case! Or, pretty please, Baby,—we're going to Acapulco!

ESMERALDA. *Are* we?

KILROY. See what I mean? (*To the audience:*) Didn't I tell you?! (*To Esmeralda:*) Yes! In the morning!

ESMERALDA. Ohhhh! I'm dizzy with joy! My little heart is going pitty-pat!

KILROY. My big heart is going boom-boom! Can I lift your veil now?

ESMERALDA. If you will be gentle.

KILROY. I would not hurt a fly unless it had on leather mittens. (*He touches a corner of her spangled veil.*)

ESMERALDA. Ohhh . . .

KILROY. What?

ESMERALDA. Ohhhhhh!!

KILROY. Why! What's the matter?

ESMERALDA. You are not being gentle!

KILROY. I *am* being gentle.

ESMERALDA. You are *not* being gentle.

KILROY. What was I being, then?

ESMERALDA. Rough!

KILROY. I am *not* being rough.

ESMERALDA. Yes, you *are* being rough. You have to be gentle with me because you're the first.

KILROY. Are you kidding?

ESMERALDA. No.

KILROY. How about all of those other fiestas you've been to?

ESMERALDA. Each one's the first one. That is the wonderful thing about gypsies' daughters!

KILROY. You can say that again!

ESMERALDA. I don't like you when you're like that.

KILROY. Like what?

ESMERALDA. Cynical and sarcastic.

KILROY. I am sincere.

ESMERALDA. Lots of boys aren't sincere.

KILROY. Maybe they aren't but I am.

ESMERALDA. Everyone says he's sincere, but everyone isn't sincere. If everyone was sincere who says he's sincere there wouldn't be half so many insincere ones in the world and there would be lots, lots, lots more really sincere ones!

KILROY. I think you have got something there. But how about gypsies' daughters?

ESMERALDA. Huh?

KILROY. Are they one hundred percent in the really sincere category?

ESMERALDA. Well, yes, and no, and mostly no! But some of them are for a while if their sweethearts are gentle.

KILROY. Would you believe I am sincere and gentle?

ESMERALDA. I would believe that you believe that you are . . . For a while . . .

KILROY. Everything's for a while. For a while is the stuff that dreams are made of, Baby! Now?—Now?

ESMERALDA. Yes, now, but be gentle!—gentle . . . (*He delicately lifts a corner of her veil. She utters a soft cry. He lifts it further. She cries out again. A bit further . . . He turns the spangled veil all the way up from her face.*)

KILROY. I am sincere.

ESMERALDA. I am sincere.

KILROY. I am sincere.

ESMERALDA. I am sincere.

KILROY. I am sincere.

ESMERALDA. I am sincere.

KILROY. I am sincere.

ESMERALDA. I am sincere. (KILROY *leans back, removing his hand from her veil. She opens her eyes.*) Is that all?

KILROY. I am tired.

ESMERALDA.—Already? (*He rises and goes down the steps from the alcove.*)

KILROY. I am tired, and full of regret . . .

ESMERALDA. Oh!

KILROY. It wasn't much to give my golden gloves for.

ESMERALDA. You pity yourself?

KILROY. That's right, I pity myself and everybody that goes to the Gypsy's daughter. I pity the world and I pity the God who made it. (*He sits down.*)

ESMERALDA. It's always like that as soon as the veil is lifted. They're all so ashamed of having degraded themselves, and their hearts have more regret than a heart can hold!

KILROY. Even a heart that's as big as the head of a baby!

ESMERALDA. You don't even notice how pretty my face is, do you?

KILROY. You look like all gypsies' daughters, no better, no worse. But as long as you get to go to Acapulco, your cup runneth over with ordinary contentment.

ESMERALDA.—I've never been so insulted in all my life!

KILROY. Oh, yes, you have, Baby. And you'll be insulted worse if you stay in this racket. You'll be insulted so much that it will get to be like water off *a duck's back!* (*The door slams. Curtains are drawn apart on the* GYPSY. ESMERALDA *lowers her veil hastily.* KILROY *pretends not to notice the* GYPSY's *entrance. She picks up a little bell and rings it over his head.*) Okay, Mamacita! I am aware of your presence!

GYPSY. Ha-ha! I was followed three blocks by some awful man!

KILROY. Then you caught him.

GYPSY. Naw, he ducked into a subway! I waited fifteen minutes outside the men's room and he never came out!

KILROY. Then you went in?

GYPSY. No! I got myself a sailor!—The streets are brilliant! . . . Have you all been good children? (ESMERALDA *makes a whimpering sound.*) The pussy will play while the old mother cat is away?

KILROY. Your sense of humor is wonderful, but how about my change, Mamacita?

GYPSY. What change are you talking about?

KILROY. Are you boxed out of your mind? The change from that ten-spot you trotted over to Walgreen's?

GYPSY. Ohhhhh—

KILROY. *Oh, what?*

GYPSY (*counting on her fingers*). Five for the works, one dollar luxury tax, two for the house percentage and two more pour la service!—makes ten! Didn't I tell you?

KILROY.—What kind of a deal is this?

GYPSY (*whipping out a revolver*). A rugged one, Baby!

ESMERALDA. Mama, don't be unkind!

GYPSY. Honey, the gentleman's friends are waiting outside the door and it wouldn't be nice to detain him! Come on—Get going—Vamoose!

KILROY. Okay, Mamacita! Me voy![62] (*He crosses to the beaded string curtains; turns to look back at the* GYPSY *and her daughter. The piping of the* STREETCLEANERS *is heard outside.*) Sincere?—Sure! That's the wonderful thing about gypsies' daughters! (*He goes out.* ESMERALDA *raises a wondering fingertip to one eye. Then she cries out:*)

ESMERALDA. Look, Mama! Look, Mama! A tear!

GYPSY. You have been watching television too much . . . (*She gathers the cards and turns off the crystal ball as light fades out on the phony paradise of the* GYPSY's.)

GUTMAN. Block Thirteen on the Camino Real. (*He exits.*)

---

[62] Kilroy calls the Gypsy "little mamma." *Me voy:* I'm going.

BLOCK THIRTEEN

In the blackout the STREETCLEANERS
*place a barrel in the center and then hide
in the Pit.* KILROY, *who enters from the
right, is followed by a spotlight. He sees
the barrel and the menacing* STREET-
CLEANERS *and then runs to the closed
door of the Siete Mares and rings the
bell. No one answers. He backs up so he
can see the balcony and calls:*

KILROY. Mr. Gutman! Just gimme a
cot in the lobby. I'll do odd jobs in the
morning. I'll be the Patsy again. I'll light
my nose sixty times a minute. I'll take
prat-falls and assume the position for
anybody that drops a dime on the street
. . . Have a heart! Have just a LITTLE
heart. Please! (*There is no response
from* GUTMAN'S *balcony.* JACQUES *enters.
He pounds his cane once on the pavement.*)

JACQUES. Gutman! Open the door!—
GUTMAN! GUTMAN! (EVA, *a beautiful woman, apparently nude, appears
on the balcony.*)

GUTMAN (*from inside*). Eva darling,
you're exposing yourself! (*He appears
on the balcony with a portmanteau.*)

JACQUES. What are you doing with my
portmanteau?

GUTMAN. Haven't you come for your
luggage?

JACQUES. Certainly not! I haven't
checked out of here!

GUTMAN. Very few do . . . but resi-
dences are frequently terminated.

JACQUES. Open the door!

GUTMAN. Open the letter with the remittance check in it!

JACQUES. In the morning!

GUTMAN. Tonight!

JACQUES. Upstairs in my room!

GUTMAN. Downstairs at the entrance!

JACQUES. I won't be intimidated!

GUTMAN (*raising the portmanteau
over his head*). What?!

JACQUES. Wait!— (*He takes the letter
out of his pocket.*) Give me some light.
(KILROY *strikes a match and holds it over*
JACQUES' *shoulder.*) Thank you. What
does it say?

GUTMAN.—Remittances?

KILROY (*reading the letter over*
JACQUES' *shoulder*).—discontinued . . .
(GUTMAN *raises the portmanteau again.*)

JACQUES. Careful, I have— (*The portmanteau lands with a crash. The* BUM
comes to the window at the crash. A.
RATT *comes out to his doorway at the
same time.*)—fragile—mementoes . . . (*He
crosses slowly down to the portmanteau
and kneels as* GUTMAN *laughs and slams
the balcony door.* JACQUES *turns to* KIL-
ROY. *He smiles at the young adventurer.*)
—"And so at last it has come, the distinguished thing!" (A. RATT *speaks as*
JACQUES *touches the portmanteau.*)

A. RATT. Hey, Dad—Vacancy here! A
bed at the "Ritz Men Only." A little
white ship to sail the dangerous night in.

JACQUES. Single or double?

A. RATT. There's only singles in this
pad.

JACQUES (*to* KILROY). Match you for
it.

KILROY. What the hell, we're buddies,
we can sleep spoons! If we can't sleep,
we'll push the wash stand against the
door and sing old popular songs till the
crack of dawn! . . . "Heart of my heart,
I love that melody!" . . . You bet your
life I do. (JACQUES *takes out a pocket
handkerchief and starts to grasp the portmanteau handle.*)—It looks to me like you
could use a Redcap and my rates are
non-union! (*He picks up the portmanteau and starts to cross towards the
"Ritz Men Only." He stops at right
center.*) Sorry, buddy. Can't make it!
The altitude on this block has affected
my ticker! And in the distance which is
nearer than further, I hear—the Streetcleaners'—piping! (*Piping is heard.*)

JACQUES. COME ALONG! (*He lifts
the portmanteau and starts on.*)

KILROY. NO. Tonight! I prefer! To
sleep! Out! Under! The stars!

JACQUES (*gently*). I understand,
Brother!

KILROY (*to* JACQUES *as he continues
toward the "Ritz Men Only"*). Bon

Voyage! I hope that you sail the dangerous night to the sweet golden port of morning!

JACQUES (*exiting*). Thanks, Brother!

KILROY. Excuse the *corn!* I'm sincere!

BUM. Show me the way to go home! . . .

GUTMAN (*appearing on the balcony with white parakeet*). Block Fourteen on the Camino Real.

BLOCK FOURTEEN

At opening, the BUM *is still at the window. The* STREETCLEANERS' *piping continues a little louder.* KILROY *climbs, breathing heavily, to the top of the stairs and stands looking out at Terra Incognita as* MARGUERITE *enters the plaza through alleyway at right. She is accompanied by a silent* YOUNG MAN *who wears a domino.*[63]

MARGUERITE. Don't come any further with me. I'll have to wake the night porter. Thank you for giving me safe conduct through the Medina. (*She has offered her hand. He grips it with a tightness that makes her wince.*) Ohhhh . . . I'm not sure which is more provocative in you, your ominous silence or your glittering smile or— (*He's looking at her purse.*) What do you want? . . . Oh! (*She starts to open the purse. He snatches it. She gasps as he suddenly strips her cloak off her. Then he snatches off her pearl necklace. With each successive despoilment, she gasps and retreats but makes no resistance. Her eyes are closed. He continues to smile. Finally, he rips her dress and runs his hands over her body as if to see if she had anything else of value concealed on her.*)—What else do I have that you want?

THE YOUNG MAN (*contemptuously*). Nothing. (*The* YOUNG MAN *exits through the cantina, examining his loot. The* BUM *leans out his window, draws a deep breath and says:*)

BUM. Lonely.

MARGUERITE (*to herself*). Lonely . . .

KILROY (*on the steps*). Lonely . . . (*The* STREETCLEANERS' *piping is heard.*

MARGUERITE *runs to the Siete Mares and rings the bell. Nobody answers. She crosses to the terrace.* KILROY, *meanwhile, has descended the stairs.*)

MARGUERITE. Jacques! (*Piping is heard.*)

KILROY. Lady?

MARGUERITE. What?

KILROY.—*I'm—safe* . . .

MARGUERITE. I wasn't expecting that music tonight, were you? (*Piping.*)

KILROY. It's them Streetcleaners.

MARGUERITE. I know. (*Piping.*)

KILROY. You better go on in, lady.

MARGUERITE. No.

KILROY. GO ON IN!

MARGUERITE. NO! I want to stay out here and I do what I want to do! (*KILROY looks at her for the first time.*) Sit down with me please.

KILROY. They're coming for me. The Gypsy told me I'm on top of their list. Thanks for. Taking my. Hand. (*Piping is heard.*)

MARGUERITE. Thanks for taking mine. (*Piping.*)

KILROY. Do me one more favor. Take out of my pocket a picture. My fingers are. Stiff.

MARGUERITE. This one?

KILROY. My one. True. Woman.

MARGUERITE. A silver-framed photo! Was she really so fair?

KILROY. She was so fair and much fairer than they could tint that picture!

MARGUERITE. Then you have been on the street when the street was royal.

KILROY. Yeah . . . when the street was royal! (*Piping is heard.* KILROY *rises.*)

[63] A masquerade costume. Domino can mean the hood and mask, or just the black half-mask alone.

MARGUERITE. Don't get up, don't leave me!

KILROY. I want to be on my feet when the Streetcleaners come for me!

MARGUERITE. Sit back down again and tell me about your girl. (*He sits.*)

KILROY. Y'know what it is you miss most? When you're separated. From someone. You lived. With. And loved? It's waking up in the night! With that—warmness beside you!

MARGUERITE. Yes, that *warmness* beside you!

KILROY. Once you get used to that. *Warmness!* It's a hell of a lonely feeling to wake up without it! Specially in some dollar-a-night hotel room on Skid! A hot-water bottle won't do. And a stranger. Won't do. It has to be some one you're used to. And that you. *KNOW LOVES* you! (*Piping is heard.*) Can you see them?

MARGUERITE. I see no one but you.

KILROY. I looked at my wife one night when she was sleeping and that was the night that the medics wouldn't okay me for no more fights . . . Well . . . My wife was sleeping with a smile like a child's. I kissed her. She didn't wake up. I took a pencil and paper. I wrote her. Good-bye!

MARGUERITE. That was the night, she would have loved you the most!

KILROY. Yeah, *that* night, but what about *after* that night? Oh, Lady . . . Why should a beautiful girl tie up with a broken-down champ?—The earth still turning and her obliged to turn with it, not out—of dark into light but out of light into dark? Naw, naw, naw, naw!—Washed up!—Finished! (*Piping.*) . . . that ain't a word that a man can't look at . . . There ain't no words in the language a man can't look at . . . and know just what they mean, and be. And act. And *go!* (*He turns to the waiting* STREETCLEANERS.) Come on! . . . Come on! . . . COME ON, YOU SONS OF BITCHES! KILROY IS HERE! HE'S READY! (*A gong sounds.* KILROY *swings at the* STREETCLEANERS. *They circle about him out of reach, turning him by each of their movements. The swings grow wilder like a boxer. He falls to his knees still swinging and finally collapses flat on his face. The* STREETCLEANERS *pounce but* LA MADRECITA *throws herself protectingly over the body and covers it with her shawl. Blackout.*)

MARGUERITE. Jacques!

GUTMAN (*on balcony*). Block Fifteen on the Camino Real.

BLOCK FIFTEEN

LA MADRECITA *is seated; across her knees is the body of* KILROY. *Up center, a low table on wheels bears a sheeted figure. Beside the table stands a* MEDICAL INSTRUCTOR *addressing* STUDENTS *and* NURSES, *all in white surgical outfits.*

INSTRUCTOR. This is the body of an unidentified vagrant.

LA MADRECITA. This was thy son, America—and now mine.

INSTRUCTOR. He was found in an alley along the Camino Real.

LA MADRECITA. Think of him, now, as he was before his luck failed him. Remember his time of greatness, when he was not faded, not frightened.

INSTRUCTOR. More light, please!

LA MADRECITA. More light!

INSTRUCTOR. Can everyone see clearly!

LA MADRECITA. Everyone must see clearly!

INSTRUCTOR. There is no external evidence of disease.

LA MADRECITA. He had clear eyes and the body of a champion boxer.

INSTRUCTOR. There are no marks of violence on the body.

LA MADRECITA. He had the soft voice of the South and a pair of golden gloves.

INSTRUCTOR. His death was apparently due to natural causes. (*The* STUDENTS *make notes. There are keening voices.*)

LA MADRECITA. Yes, blow wind where night thins! He had many admirers!

INSTRUCTOR. There are no legal claimants.

LA MADRECITA. He stood as a planet among the moons of their longing, haughty with youth, a champion of the prize-ring!

INSTRUCTOR. No friends or relatives having identified him—

LA MADRECITA. You should have seen the lovely monogrammed robe in which he strode the aisles of the Colosseums!

INSTRUCTOR. After the elapse of a certain number of days, his body becomes the property of the State—

LA MADRECITA. Yes, blow wind where night thins—for laurel is not everlasting . . .

INSTRUCTOR. And now is transferred to our hands for the nominal sum of five dollars.

LA MADRECITA. This was thy son—and now mine . . .

INSTRUCTOR. We will now proceed with the dissection. Knife, please!

LA MADRECITA. Blow wind! (*Keening is heard offstage.*) Yes, blow wind where night thins! You are his passing bell and his lamentation. (*More keening is heard.*) Keen for him, all maimed creatures, deformed and mutilated—his homeless ghost is your own!

INSTRUCTOR. First we will open up the chest cavity and examine the heart for evidence of coronary occlusion.

LA MADRECITA. His heart was pure gold and as big as the head of a baby.

INSTRUCTOR. We will make an incision along the vertical line.

LA MADRECITA. Rise, ghost! Go! Go bird! "Humankind cannot bear very much reality."[64] (*At the touch of her flowers, KILROY stirs and pushes himself up slowly from her lap. On his feet again, he rubs his eyes and looks around him.*)

VOICES (*crying offstage*). Olé! Olé! Olé!

KILROY. Hey! Hey, somebody! Where am I? (*He notices the dissection room and approaches.*)

INSTRUCTOR (*removing a glittering sphere from a dummy corpse*). Look at this heart. It's as big as the head of a baby.

KILROY. My heart!

INSTRUCTOR. Wash it off so we can look for the pathological lesions.

KILROY. Yes, siree, that's my heart!

GUTMAN. Block Sixteen! (*KILROY pauses just outside the dissection area as a STUDENT takes the heart and dips it into a basin on the stand beside the table. The STUDENT suddenly cries out and holds aloft a glittering gold sphere.*)

INSTRUCTOR. Look! This heart's solid gold!

BLOCK SIXTEEN

KILROY (*rushing forward*). That's mine, you bastards! (*He snatches the golden sphere from the MEDICAL INSTRUCTOR. The autopsy proceeds as if nothing had happened as the spot of light on the table fades out, but for KILROY a ghostly chase commences, a dreamlike re-enactment of the chase that occurred at the end of Block Six. GUTMAN shouts from his balcony:*)

GUTMAN. Stop, thief, stop, corpse! That gold heart is the property of the State! Catch him, catch the golden-heart robber! (*KILROY dashes offstage into an*

aisle of the theatre. There is the wail of a siren; the air is filled with calls and whistles, roar of motors, screeching brakes, pistol-shots, thundering footsteps. The dimness of the auditorium is transected by searching rays of light—but there are no visible pursuers.*)

KILROY (*as he runs panting up the aisle*). This is my heart! It don't belong to no State, not even the U.S.A. Which way is out? Where's the Greyhound depot? Nobody's going to put my heart in a bottle in a museum and charge admission to support the rotten police!

[64] Quoted from T. S. Eliot, "Four Quartets," Harcourt, Brace and Company, Inc., New York, 1943. Copyright 1936 by Harcourt, Brace and Company, Inc., and reprinted with their permission.

Where are they? Which way are they going? Or coming? Hey, somebody, help me get out of here! Which way do I—which way—which way do I—*go! go! go! go! go!* (*He has now arrived in the balcony.*) *Gee, I'm lost! I don't know where I am!* I'm all turned around, I'm *confused*, I don't understand—what's—happened, it's like a—*dream*, it's—just like a—dream . . . *Mary! Oh, Mary! Mary!* (*He has entered the box from which he leapt in Block Six. A clear shaft of light falls on him. He looks up into it, crying:*) *Mary, help a Christian!! Help a Christian, Mary!*—It's like a dream . . . (*Es-*MERALDA *appears in a childish nightgown beside her gauze-tented bed on the* GYPSY's *roof. Her* MOTHER *appears with a cup of some sedative drink, cooing . . .*)

GYPSY. Beddy-bye, beddy-bye, darling. It's sleepy-time down South and up North, too, and also East and West!

KILROY (*softly*). Yes, it's—like a—dream . . . (*He leans panting over the ledge of the box, holding his heart like a football, watching* ESMERALDA.)

GYPSY. Drink your Ovaltine, Ducks, and the sandman will come on tip-toe with a bag full of dreams . . .

ESMERALDA. I want to dream of the Chosen Hero, Mummy.

GYPSY. Which one, the one that's coming or the one that is gone?

ESMERALDA. The *only* one, *Kilroy!* He was *sincere!*

KILROY. That's *right! I was*, for a while!

GYPSY. How do you know that Kilroy was sincere?

ESMERALDA. He said so.

KILROY. That's the truth, I *was!*

GYPSY. When did he say that?

ESMERALDA. When he lifted my veil.

GYPSY. Baby, they're always sincere when they lift your veil; it's one of those natural reflexes that don't mean a thing.

KILROY (*aside*). What a cynical old bitch that Gypsy mama is!

GYPSY. And there's going to be lots of other fiestas for you, baby doll, and lots of other chosen heroes to lift your little veil when Mamacita and Nursie are out of the room.

ESMERALDA. No, Mummy, never, I mean it!

KILROY. I *believe* she means it!

GYPSY. Finish your Ovaltine and say your Now-I-Lay-Me. (ESMERALDA *sips the drink and hands her the cup.*)

KILROY (*with a catch in his voice*). I had one true woman, which I can't go back to, but now I've found another. (*He leaps onto the stage from the box.*)

ESMERALDA (*dropping to her knees*). Now I lay me down to sleep, I pray the Lord my soul to keep. If I should die before I wake, I pray the Lord my soul to take.

GYPSY. God bless Mummy!

ESMERALDA. And the crystal ball and the tea-leaves.

KILROY. *Pssst!*

ESMERALDA. What's that?

GYPSY. A tom-cat in the plaza.

ESMERALDA. God bless all cats without pads in the plaza tonight.

KILROY. Amen! (*He falls to his knees in the empty plaza.*)

ESMERALDA. God bless all con men and hustlers and pitch-men who hawk their hearts on the street, all two-time losers who're likely to lose once more, the courtesan who made the mistake of love, the greatest of lovers crowned with the longest horns, the poet who wandered far from his heart's green country and possibly will and possibly won't be able to find his way back, look down with a smile tonight on the last cavaliers, the ones with the rusty armor and soiled white plumes, and visit with understanding and something that's almost tender those fading legends that come and go in this plaza like songs not clearly remembered, oh, sometime and somewhere, let there be something to mean the word *honor* again!

QUIXOTE (*hoarsely and loudly, stirring slightly among his verminous rags*). Amen!

KILROY. Amen . . .

GYPSY (*disturbed*).—That will do, now.

ESMERALDA. *And, oh, God, let me dream tonight of the Chosen Hero!*

GYPSY. Now, sleep. Fly away on the magic carpet of dreams! (ESMERALDA

crawls into the gauze-tented cot. The
Gypsy *descends from the roof.*)

Kilroy. *Esmeralda! My little Gypsy
sweetheart!*

Esmeralda (*sleepily*). Go away, cat.
(*The light behind the gauze is gradually
dimming.*)

Kilroy. This is no cat. This is the
chosen hero of the big fiesta, Kilroy, the
champion of the golden gloves with his
gold heart cut from his chest and in his
hands to give you!

Esmeralda. Go away. Let me dream
of the Chosen Hero.

Kilroy. What a hassle! Mistook for a
cat! What can I do to convince this doll
I'm real? (*Three brass balls wink brilliantly.*)—Another transaction seems to
be indicated! (*He rushes to the* Loan
Shark's. *The entrance immediately lights
up.*) My heart is gold! What will you
give me for it? (*Jewels, furs, sequined
gowns, etc., are tossed to his feet. He
throws his heart like a basketball to the*
Loan Shark, *snatches up the loot, and
rushes back to the* Gypsy's) *Doll! Behold this loot! I gave my golden heart
for it!*

Esmeralda. Go away, cat . . . (*She
falls asleep.* Kilroy *bangs his forehead
with his fist, then rushes to the* Gypsy's
*door, pounds it with both fists. The door
is thrown open and the sordid contents
of a large jar are thrown at him. He falls
back gasping, spluttering, retching. He
retreats and finally assumes an exaggerated attitude of despair.*)

Kilroy. Had for a button! Stewed,
screwed, and tattooed on the Camino
Real! Baptized, finally, with the contents
of a slop-jar!—Did anybody say the deal
was rugged?! (Quixote *stirs against the
wall of Skid Row. He hawks and spits
and staggers to his feet.*)

Gutman. Why, the old knight's
awake, his dream is over!

Quixote (*to* Kilroy). Hello! Is that
a fountain?

Kilroy.—Yeah, but—

Quixote. I've got a mouthful of old

chicken feathers . . . (*He approaches
the fountain. It begins to flow.* Kilroy
*falls back in amazement as the Old
Knight rinses his mouth and drinks and
removes his jacket to bathe, handing the
tattered garment to* Kilroy. *As he
bathes:*) Qué pasa, mi amigo?[65]

Kilroy. The deal is rugged. D'you
know what I mean?

Quixote. Who knows better than I
what a rugged deal is! (*He produces a
tooth brush and brushes his teeth.*)—Will
you take some advice?

Kilroy. Brother, at this point on the
Camino I will take anything which is
offered!

Quixote. *Don't! Pity! Your! Self!* (*He
takes out a pocket mirror and grooms
his beard and moustache.*) The wounds
of the vanity, the many offenses our egos
have to endure, being housed in bodies
that age and hearts that grow tired, are
better accepted with a tolerant smile—
like *this!*—You see? (*He cracks his face
in two with an enormous grin.*)

Gutman. Follow-spot on the face of
the ancient knight!

Quixote. Otherwise what you become
is a bag full of curdled cream—*leche
mala*, we call it!—attractive to nobody,
least of all to yourself! (*He passes the
comb and pocket mirror to* Kilroy.)
Have you got any plans?

Kilroy (*a bit uncertainly, wistfully*).
Well, I was thinking of—going on t.cm
—here!

Quixote. Good! Come with me.

Kilroy (*to the audience*). Crazy old
bastard. (*Then to the Knight.*) Donde?

Quixote (*starting for the stairs*).
Quien sabe![66] (*The fountain is now
flowing loudly and sweetly. The* Street
People *are moving toward it with murmurs of wonder.* Marguerite *comes out
upon the terrace.*)

Kilroy. Hey, there's—!

Quixote. Shhh! Listen! (*They pause
on the stairs.*)

Marguerite. Abdullah! (Gutman *has
descended to the terrace.*)

[65] "What is it, my friend?"
[66] "Where? Who knows!"

GUTMAN. Mademoiselle, allow me to deliver the message for you. It would be in bad form if I didn't take some final part in the pageant. (*He crosses the plaza to the opposite façade and shouts "Casanova!" under the window of the "Ritz Men Only." Meanwhile* KILROY *scratches out the verb "is" and prints the correction "was" in the inscription on the ancient wall.*) Casanova! Great lover and King of Cuckolds on the Camino Real! The last of your ladies has guaranteed your tabs and is expecting you for breakfast on the terrace! (CASANOVA *looks first out of the practical window of the flophouse, then emerges from its scabrous doorway, haggard, unshaven, crumpled in dress but bearing himself as erectly as ever. He blinks and glares fiercely into the brilliant morning light.* MARGUERITE *cannot return his look; she averts her face with a look for which anguish would not be too strong a term, but at the same time she extends a pleading hand toward him. After some hesi-* *tation, he begins to move toward her, striking the pavement in measured cadence with his cane, glancing once, as he crosses, out at the audience with a wry smile that makes admissions that would be embarrassing to a vainer man than* CASANOVA *now is. When he reaches* MARGUERITE *she gropes for his hand, seizes it with a low cry and presses it spasmodically to her lips while he draws her into his arms and looks above her sobbing, dyed-golden head with the serene, clouded gaze of someone mortally ill as the mercy of a narcotic laps over his pain.* QUIXOTE *raises his lance in a formal gesture and cries out hoarsely, powerfully from the stairs:*)

QUIXOTE. *The violets in the mountains have broken the rocks!* (QUIXOTE *goes through the arch with* KILROY.)

GUTMAN (*to the audience*). The Curtain Line has been spoken! (*To the wings.*) Bring it down! (*He bows with a fat man's grace as—*)

THE CURTAIN FALLS.

SUGGESTED TOPICS FOR FURTHER INVESTIGATION AND REPORT

1. Study some of Williams' more conventional plays, specifically the more "pessimistic" ones such as *A Streetcar Named Desire*, *Cat on a Hot Tin Roof*, *Sweet Bird of Youth*. How much of the world outlook of *Camino Real* is present in these plays? Are any of them more optimistic?

2. Read Strindberg's *The Dream Play*. Compare its use of the expressionistic method with that found in *Camino Real*. What are the views of human society and the fate of mankind in general found in Strindberg's play as compared with Williams'?

3. T. S. Eliot's concept of modern society in "The Waste Land" is a very famous picture of decay. Read the entire poem and discuss its attitudes in comparison with those of *Camino Real*.

4. Read the entire trilogy, *The Coral*, *Gas I*, and *Gas II*. (All three are available in Tucker and Downer's "Twenty-five Modern Plays," Harper & Brothers, 1953.) Determine how much of Kaiser's view is unduly pessimistic, how much is vindicated by events of the last thirty years. Outline his expressionistic techniques.

5. Make a study of the various stylized stage techniques such as impressionism, expressionism, surrealism, constructivism, symbolism, and the epic style. Distinguish among them, show where they often overlap, and discuss their importance on the modern stage.

6. Read Maeterlinck's *Pelléas et Mélisande*, generally regarded as a fine example of *impressionism*. Discuss its thematic and stylistic differences in contrast to any expressionistic play.

7. Read an epic play like Bertolt Brecht's *Mother Courage*. Then read one of the Federal Theatre plays from America, such as *Power*, or *One-third of a Nation*. Compare and contrast the styles and the effectiveness of the German and the American attempts. The epic style is supposed to be as purely *objective* as possible. Which succeeds better, the American or the German?

8. Discuss the American attitudes toward modern business and the position of the individual in a materialistic society as portrayed in Elmer Rice's *The Adding Machine*, Kaufman and Connelly's *Beggar on Horseback*, and Eugene O'Neill's *The Great God Brown*.

9. Expressionism was a favorite device of those who wrote the strongest antiwar plays in America during the 1920s and 1930s. Read Irwin Shaw's *Bury the Dead* and Paul Green's *Johnny Johnson*. Discuss the qualities of expressionism and their value as direct propaganda.

10. Williams and many other modern writers make use of expressionistic and other nonrealistic techniques in the midst of otherwise realistic plays. Read *The Glass Menagerie*, Williams' first success, and others, such as Arthur Miller's *Death of a Salesman*, Philip Barry's *Hotel Universe*, Elmer Rice's *Dream Girl*. Discuss the value of the stylistic mixture.

11. Expressionism—or definite "stylization"—is found in plays essentially comic as well as serious. Thorton Wilder's *The Skin of Our Teeth* and William Saroyan's two interesting attempts, *My Heart's in the Highlands* (or the one-act version, *The Man with His Heart in the Highlands*) and *The Time of Your Life* are outstanding examples. Determine what the dramatic or theatrical style of each of these plays is, and analyze the human outlook of each writer. What is the over-all attitude of each compared with Williams?

THE MATURE WAR PLAY

Traditional Limitations of Warfare on the Stage

It is impossibly difficult to reproduce onstage with any fidelity the actual physical aspects of war. Restricted in the scope of his play by the size and the facilities of the stage, the playwright has generally relegated the actual conflict to the background and has recorded the struggle through the specific actions of his central characters. Stage wars traditionally have been fought between "gentlemen." Beginning with the chronicle dramas of the Renaissance, the problems of the nobles and landed aristocrats became the main problems of war. The ordinary citizen who might suffer in the wake of their maneuvering aroused little concern. If the "enlisted man" received a part, he was probably a comic figure. The stage attitude reflected reality, since warfare and its participants were still fairly feudal, and combat was a very personal thing. Opposing forces fought limited engagements in close encounter, hand to hand, engagements that often involved the noble leaders themselves.

As time passed, the officers, another privileged class, replaced the coroneted heads. Armies were no longer made up of nobles and their knights, but they still existed on the basis of a distinct class separation between officers (gentlemen) and soldiers (rabble). Serving in the military as an officer was a prerogative reserved for and frequently an obligation of gentlemen and aristocracy. No "citizen" could easily achieve this status. The men who did the fighting were a lower level of humanity, foreign mercenaries hired to fight for countries other than their own, illiterate volunteers, and impressed men, literally kidnapped into forced service, especially in the navies.

Since, by definition, officers were gentlemen, they conducted war by fairly strict rules of gallantry. There was still an element of personal conflict between commanders, who offered extravagantly generous treatment to each other's deputations, and extended a certain gentlemanly hospitality to prisoners (so long, of course, as they were officers). Surrenders were formal affairs, including the knee-bending delivery of the sword to the conqueror. Women were inviolate and to be defended and respected by both sides.

If all of this did not universally apply to actual wartime conduct, the stage none the less reserved its right to show a heightened and generously romanticized version of it. Success was fairly certain, because, until the present century, most audiences were aesthetically removed from contact with war. The absence of aerial bombardment allowed life to proceed in nearly normal paths outside the battle zone. It was not difficult for the stage to present an unreal picture of war. The hero's romantic behavior was based on how he *ought* to perform, whether or not it was the manner in which he actually would. Heroism, honor, courage (or, in the case of the enemy, treachery, skulduggery, and cowardice) all came forth at their theatrical best.

The Early Nineteenth-century American War Play

The writer of nineteenth-century war plays in America inherited all the romantic traditions of the past, including a stilted and highly flowing blank verse. He displayed little or no actual violence, and his smartly attired officers performed their gentlemanly duties as efficiently as ever. The early American playwright could have dramatized some exciting adventures from the lately completed Revolution, for this unique conflict had witnessed farmer and shop-keeper taking up arms in defense of their own principles rather than those deemed important by a powerful few. Instead, one of the most famous plays from the period, actually written within a few years of the Revolution's end, shows all the conventional, unimaginative traits of its ancestors.

André, by William Dunlap, was written in 1798. Using the Benedict Arnold treason, Dunlap has peopled *André* with a noble collection of unbelievably honorable commissioned gentlemen. By the time the play is over, it is apparent that, aside from the platitudes liberally sprinkled throughout concerning the wretched British who oppose the magnificent American cause, the Revolution itself is quite beside the point. The central concern of the play is spying—a deed that no real officer and gentleman should ever consider even remotely his business.

Bland, "a youthful but military figure . . . Captain of horse," says Dunlap, is informed that a spy has been captured. When told, "André's his name," Bland replies in dismay, "O, it cannot be!" but O, it is, and Bland must face the fact of war that an officer as well as a rascal from the ranks can be a spy. What makes the situation even more difficult is the fact that André once saved Bland's life on the field of battle. Not wishing to die hanging, "like the base ruffian, or the midnight thief," André seeks Bland's aid in securing him a firing squad so that he can "die a soldier's death." Instead, Bland rushes straight to The General (presumably Washington) in an attempt to free his friend. The General knows the merits of Bland as an officer, and offers him promotion:

> BLAND (*with contemptuous irony*). Pardon me, Sir, I never shall deserve it.
>   (*With increasing heat.*)
>   The country that forgets to reverence virtue;
>   That makes no difference 'twixt the sordid wretch
>   Who, for reward, risks treason's penalty,
>   And him unfortunate, whose duteous service
>   Is, by mere accident, so chang'd in form
>   As to assume guilt's semblance, I serve not:
>   Scorn to serve. I have a soldier's honor,
>   But 'tis in union with a freeman's judgment,

And when I act, both prompt. Thus from my helm
I tear, what once I proudly thought, the badge
Of virtuous fellowship. (*Tears the cockade from his helmet.*) My sword I
  keep. (*Puts on his helmet.*)
Would, André, thou hadst never put thine off.
Then hadst thou through opposers' hearts made way
To liberty, or bravely pierc'd thine own! (*Exit.*)

This act of near mutiny is fortunately overlooked by the magnanimous and understanding General.

The final scene combines André's cool heroism with Bland's wild hysteria (he "*throws himself on the earth*"), and the firm moralizing of a fellow American officer, to send the 1798 audience home convinced that they have seen a great play.

After the American Civil War

The American Civil War, said Winston Churchill, was "the noblest war" and the last war between gentlemen. In many ways, this is certainly true. Its leaders, especially from the South, were the social elite; the generosity of Grant toward the defeated Lee was in the finest gentlemanly tradition.

The war was also the first truly modern war. Its tremendous slaughter produced the highest ratio of casualties to the number of combatants and the total populations involved that has ever been known. It was a fight between conscripted citizen armies of great size. It was in every sense full-scale and total war, in which none were guaranteed immunity from its destruction, and it was desperately fought over a vast land area between equal civilized nations to its complete and annihilating conclusion.

Two outstanding examples of the American Civil War play, written when the conflict was a lively memory and the thousands of veterans from either side spun their tales of horror and heroism, are Bronson Howard's *Shenandoah* of 1888, and William Gillette's *Secret Service* of 1895. They remain about as unoriginal in their attitude and as conventionally romantic in their concept as anything which preceded them. The plays bring the shooting a little closer than before, but the gentlemanly antagonists, whose personal reputation and individual honor are still of utmost importance, dominate the action.

The less effective of the two is *Shenandoah*, a drama of charging steeds and flying banners, lovely women and generous commanders. Its plot outline is simple—the familiar story of close friends who must divide their allegiances once the war erupts. They part as enemies, meet upon the battlefield, and after the war rejoin each other in Washington on friendlier terms than ever. Heartache and distress have been transitory, the war a bad dream. Nobody has suffered. There have been a few deaths, for of course *somebody* has to die, but only those who could not have lived happily ever after are dispatched, namely, a profligate son who has redeemed himself in a hero's death and a rascally spy. War comes; it roars past; it departs. All, we are glad to know, is still impossibly well.

In one scene, Jenny Buckthorn, a true-blue daughter of the regiment, whose father is a Federal general, sits on a stone post and looks out toward the maneuvering warriors just before a battle in the Shenandoah valley. Her picture of life at the front conveys the completely unrealistic view of war which was so conventional in this type of play:

> (*She imitates a trumpet signal on her closed fists.*)
> JENNY. What a magnificent line! Guideposts! Every man and every horse is eager for the next command. There comes the flag! (*As the scene progresses trumpet signals are heard without and she follows their various meanings in her speech.*) To the standard! The regiment is going to the front. Oh! I do wish I could go with it. I always do, the moment I hear the trumpets. Boots and Saddles! Mount! I wish I was in command of the regiment. It was born in me. Fours right! There they go! Look at those horses' ears! Forward. (*A military band is heard without, playing "The Battle Cry of Freedom." *JENNY* takes the attitude of holding a bridle and trotting.*) Rappity—plap—plap—plap—etc. (*She imitates the motions of a soldier on horseback, stepping down to the rock at side of post; thence to the ground and about the stage, with the various curvettings of a spirited horse. A chorus of soldiers is heard without, with the band. The music becomes more and more distant.* JENNY *gradually stops as the music is dying away, and stands, listening. As it dies entirely away, she suddenly starts to an enthusiastic attitude.*) Ah! If I were only a man! The enemy! On Third Battalion, left, front, into line, march! Draw sabres! Charge! (*Imitates a trumpet signal. As she finishes, she rises to her full height, with both arms raised, and trembling with enthusiasm.*) Ah! (*She suddenly drops her arms and changes to an attitude and expression of disappointment—pouting.*) And the first time Old Margery took me to Father, in her arms, she had to tell him I was a girl. Father was as much disgusted as I was. But he'd never admit it; he says I'm as good a soldier as any of 'em—just as I am.

Secret Service succumbs to much that we have already witnessed, but its denouement leaves room for reasonable doubt and its background of besieged Richmond is much more realistic and believable. We are again dealing with spies, and the protagonist, a Northern officer, Dumont, known locally as Captain Thorne, C.S.A., realizes what a dastardly and personally unrewarding kind of enterprise he has undertaken. He is in love with the Confederate General Varney's daughter, Edith, whose faith in him is without bounds, even upon discovering that he is the long sought Northern cloak-and-dagger man. Every element of melodrama that means positive audience attention is employed throughout this play, including secret messages, hand-to-hand fights, a spy who shoots himself to avoid detection, a fugitive hiding behind the window curtains, unexpected knocks at the door, and last-minute rescues. The love triangle is pushed for all it is worth, with the Confederate secret agent, Arrelsford, who suspects "Thorne" all along, completing the third side.

In imminent danger of his life, Thorne apologizes to Edith for what he must do. His attitude toward his work should be compared to the viewpoint on spying in *André* and to Jenny's picture of life at the front in *Shenandoah*:

> THORNE. Ha!—They're on the scent at last! (*Muttering it to himself.*) They'll get me now—and then won't take long to finish me off! (*Turns toward* EDITH.) And as that'll be the last of me—(*Moves toward her.*) As that'll be the last of me Miss Varney—(*Comes down* L.C. *near her.*) maybe you'll listen to one thing! We can't all die a soldier's death—in the roar of battle— our friends around us—under the flag we love!—No—not all! Some of us have orders for another kind of work—desperate—dare-devil work—the hazardous schemes of the Secret Service. We fight our battles alone—no comrades to cheer us on—ten thousand to one against us—death at every turn! If we win we escape with our lives—if we lose—dragged out and butchered like dogs—no soldier's grave—not even a trench with the rest of the boys—alone— despised—forgotten! These were my orders Miss Varney—this is the death I die tonight—and I don't want you to think for one minute that I'm ashamed of it.

Even though it could mean disaster for his own army, Thorne can take none but the path of personal honor. For instance, when his capture is thwarted by loyal, loving Edith and he is free to send the false messages to the Confederate army, he refuses because it would take advantage of the heroic girl who rescued him. When he is finally trapped and sentenced to die, Edith tells him that the musket balls have been removed from the firing squad's guns. In a last tremendous gesture of noble honor, he turns to the sergeant in charge "as if making an ordinary military report" and says, "You'd better take a look at your muskets—they've been tampered with." In the end, Thorne is merely imprisoned; Gillette could not permit his hero's talents and very blue blood to be wasted by the simple and logical expedient of shooting a spy.

The Attitude of a World War

Any student who has taken his basic course in American literature knows that Stephen Crane's Henry Fleming had to change his attitude toward the glories of war. Inspired by typical heroic visions, this young man seeks his "Red Badge of Courage," but learns that the soldier's life is one of boredom, death, horror, stench, starvation, and excruciating pain. War is brought down to the level of the man who gets out and shoots the gun, who must follow the orders of those honorable men on horseback (who suddenly seem most ordinarily human), and who wants to turn and run frantically until he is as far from the carnage as possible. Through this short book, in 1896, the personal experience of war and the dirty thing it is became revealed as it had never been before. The senseless brutality could hardly ever again be disguised as the romantic chivalry that writers themselves had known did not exist, but which they refused to admit on paper.

Whatever "noble" aspects still remained in the American mind were shattered in the disaster of World War I. Democracy was to be saved and Lafayette repaid, but the disillusion of what went on in the infested filth of the trenches and in the shambles of the postwar world permanently eliminated any ideas of glory. The price was questioned in the roaring, cursing explosion of Maxwell Anderson and Laurence Stalling's *What Price Glory* of 1924, which blew all previous theatrical interpretations of war completely off the stage. Here was enacted the life of the man at the front, waiting for the shell with his number on it, and the officer who, leaving his horse at home, his plumes in his trunk, and his gallantry on the shelf, enters the fray with his men and suffers their hideously grimy existence with them. He fights them for possession of their sluttish women, obscenely curses them for their ineptness, and rails against the "top brass" who wouldn't know a war if they saw one. The public reaction was, of course, one of shocked astonishment.

Two significant passages from *What Price Glory* should be compared with Bland's audience with his General in *André*, or with the companion-in-arms, glory-of-death speeches found in *Shenandoah* or *Secret Service*. The first is by Lieutenant Moore, upon discovering that Lieutenant Aldrich, the second in command, has been shot:

> MOORE. Oh, God, Dave, but they got you. God, but they got you a beauty, the dirty swine. God DAMN them for keeping us up in this hellish town. Why can't they send in some of the million men they've got back there and give us a chance? Men in my platoons are so hysterical every time I get a message from Flagg, they want to know if they're being relieved. What can I tell them? They look at me like whipped dogs—as if I had just beaten them—and I've had enough of them this time. I've got to get them out, I tell you. They've had enough. Every night the same way. (*He turns to* FLAGG.) And since six o'clock there's been a wounded sniper in the tree by that orchard angel crying "*Kamerad! Kamerad!*" Just like a big crippled whippoorwill. What price glory now? Why in God's name can't we all go home? Who gives a damn for this lousy, stinking little town but the poor French bastards who live here? God damn it! You talk about courage, and all night long you hear a man who's bleeding to death on a tree calling you "*Kamerad*" and asking you to save him. God damn every son of a bitch in the world, who isn't here! I won't stand for it. I won't stand for it! I won't have the platoon asking me every minute of the livelong night when they are going to be relieved. . . . Flagg, I tell you you can shoot me, but I won't stand for it. . . . I'll take 'em out tonight and kill you if you get in my way.

The second speech is Captain Flagg's address in "a thundering staccato" to two new lieutenants who have come up from the replacement depot:

> FLAGG. My name is Flagg, gentlemen, and I'm the sinkhole and cesspool of this regiment, frowned on in the YMCA huts and sneered at by the divisional Beau Brummells. I am a lousy, good-for-nothing company commander. I corrupt youth and lead little boys astray into the black shadows between

the lines of hell, killing more men than any other company commander in the regiment, and drawing all the dirty jobs in the world. I take chocolate soldiers and make dead heroes out of them. I did not send for you, Mister . . . (*He leans forward, and the first officer salutes and speaks: "Cunningham, sir"*) nor for you . . . (*"Lundstrom, sir," also salutes*); and I confess I am in a quandary. Four days ago I should have been more hospitable, for I had four gunnery sergeants then. Now I have two, and can't spare them to teach little boys how to adjust their diapers. I've no doubt that one of you was an all-American halfback, and the other the editor of the college paper, but we neither follow the ball nor the news here. We are all dirt, and we propose to die in order that corps headquarters may be decorated.

The New Approach of World War II

By the time it was over, the global struggle of World War II had reached into every home in the nation. No longer could the conflict be restricted to a limited area, for the threat of immediate and complete involvement hung over the home front as well as the battlefield. A successful play based on its history would have to wear a new color. The jungles and beachheads which made the trenches of *What Price Glory* seem like cozy living rooms and the frightfulness visible in the dust of Hiroshima obliterated any possibility of attempting to re-create war's violence. All of this notwithstanding, the war play as a type did survive, and in its best examples became just as dramatically effective as its predecessors.

What evolved can accurately be termed the *mature war play*. Aware that war is indeed the most horrible of the senselessly masochistic treatments man can devise for himself, the mature war play assumes that there is no need to bellow obscenities against it or piously sermonize about the hideous nature of the slaughter. The mature play accepts its war as an accomplished fact, needing no further comment or elaboration. It turns from stagy make-believe to the primary source of genuine dramatic material: the individual human being, whether foot soldier or strategic commander, whose prolonged physical and mental agonies under the inhuman tensions and literally killing strains of these wildly unnatural conditions become more terrifying than enemy shrapnel or bullets.

An indication of the path the new war play would take appeared in 1942, in Maxwell Anderson's sentimental but compassionate portrayal of the American soldier in *The Eve of St. Mark*. In many respects the play is purely conventional with its assortment of familiar character types, and it continues Anderson's attempt at authentic barracks-room language so startlingly effective in *What Price Glory*. Furthermore, the back-home scenes and the dream sequences border on the maudlin. But Anderson senses something in this play which is nowhere present in *Glory*, and he presents it with an understanding that points the way ahead. This is a sympathetic comprehension of the underlying emotions of these inexperienced young men, ejected so suddenly from their comfortable society trained for peace into a violent world trained only for war. Anderson's philosophical, poetry-quoting intellectual, Francis Marion, in no way a soldier and incapable of thinking and acting as one, would never have had an important place in *Glory*. He and all the others facing certain destruction on their isolated Pacific island are in the midst of something they cannot possibly control and but dimly understand. They did not ask to fight, and they seek only to escape alive and return home. Without ranting blasphemy and without descent into platitudinous nonsense, they do their best to survive and in the end emerge more "heroic" and far more believably human.

When Arthur Laurents presented *Home of the Brave* in 1946, the professional critics welcomed his psychological study of human relations during combat. Race prejudices, social antagonisms, and the simple but misunderstood inward delight and relief of every soldier when he sees his companion fall instead of himself, combine in a distinguished play. Laurents, like Anderson, preferred to believe that his audience was aware of the meaning of war, and chose his scenes of violence only to further the understanding of the characters' reactions to their experiences. The psychological and physical shock reveals itself in confused human reactions to very normal behavior under the stress of combat, and although the war never unnecessarily intrudes, it remains a permanent and unforgettable part of everybody's life.

The farthest removed from the actual fighting of any of the artistically successful war plays is Herman Wouk's *The Caine Mutiny Court-Martial* of 1954. It fits well into the pattern of maturity, because once more the war and all that it means are accepted without comment. The war has been directly responsible for the deeds of the men on stage. The drama is involved with bravery and cowardice under conditions of the utmost conceivable violence, but through its austere courtroom setting and its terse question-and-answer routine, it probes the underlying reasons behind the behavior of the individuals concerned while evoking the finest dramatic suspense and the best theatrical appeal. The analysis of a sick mind and the effect of that mind on those compelled to obey its twisted whims give the audience a fascinating picture of the behavior pattern of very believable human beings in a very believable wartime situation.

Command Decision

Command Decision returns to the problems of the war hero of previous generations, the Army officer. The entire play concerns the affairs of the Armed Forces' most elite personnel, not only in the high echelons, but in the service branch as well. Here are the colonels and many-starred generals of the Air Force, the "glamor boys" in the eyes of the foot-slogging GI. They fight only in the best of weather, and are quartered in comfortable shelter far from danger. Their food and drink—especially the latter—are ample and palatable, their women plentiful and accessible. The shooting war is hundreds of miles away. But Haines makes it clear from the start that his officers are very much involved in the deadly business for which they are paid, and even as officers remain decidedly human.

It is interesting to observe how Haines brings his officer personnel down to an acceptably realistic level. In order to prove that the front-line officer is likely to be no model of gentlemanly behavior, Maxwell Anderson gives Captain Flagg of *What Price Glory* the same animal behavior as his men and keeps him throughout the play in a prolonged orgy of violence. Haines is able to suggest the same thing in a few opening lines. His commanding general has no sooner entered than he is confronted with three potentially serious disciplinary cases, every one involving an officer. There is a matter of rape, another of wilful destruction of cultural treasures, and a third of desertion in the face of the enemy. The first two are quickly disposed of by the expediencies of a couple of gallons of ice cream and a private "chewing out." There is no attempt to explain away or to excuse these undignified episodes. Haines knows that such things exist, and that arm stripes or shoulder bars make no difference. He also presumes that his audience is mature enough to understand why they exist without forcing his general to set off verbal fireworks about the shame of it all. The third case, involving the recalcitrant Jenks, remains a simmering, sputtering danger, although never allowed to explode with full force.

This attitude of the opening scene sets the tone for the rest of the play. The fine drama relies on none of the melodramatics or crude brutalities so fondly exhibited in a good part of modern war literature. Although the sadistic sergeant or the psychopathic captain may provide harrowing military adventure, Haines' welcome assumption is that operational headquarters are not uniformly inhabited by sexual perverts, mental incompetents, and cowards. In *The Caine Mutiny Court-Martial* Greenwald's casual approach to the destruction of Queeg is excellent writing, and the captain's disintegration is theatre at its finest. The running battle with an obstinate and pitifully vain skipper in *Mister Roberts* is hilarious fun. The feud between *What Price Glory's* Sergeant Quirt and Captain Flagg, who have apparently spent most of their military careers fighting each other for the sluts of Hong Kong or

Manila, keeps the atmosphere charged. But the shipboard shenanigans of *Mister Roberts* or the exposure of Queeg's unbalanced mind continue to propagate the too common viewpoint that those in command are seldom little more than fools. Haines' officers have acquired a quality unknown to Quirt or Flagg; they are thoroughly respectable men, educated, intelligent, and intellectual. They are decent and restrained, but not above the use of genuine profanity which avoids artificial and ill-disguised stage euphemisms. Most of these officers are none the less efficient fighters and we need not fear for the nation's safety in their hands any less than we would in those of thick-skinned Quirt with his instinct for survival in a trench.

Because the characters of *Command Decision* are not playing at war but are seriously engaged in the ugly business of killing, Haines refuses to allow the intrusion of women for their usual stage purposes. Neither telescopic viewing of disrobed nurses nor lusting after the physical attractions of a Charmaine have any conceivable purpose here. There is an abundance of fleshly love available offstage, and its easy accessibility is quickly acknowledged—whereupon the matter ends.

After the removal of practically every convention of the modern war story, *Command Decision* proceeds on the assumption that the mature audience will be thoroughly aware that war is not a matter of tomfoolery and cannot be won either by blasphemous brute force or by ignorant bumbling. The play then becomes a serious study of the tremendous pressures and frightful loneliness forced upon the capable and conscientious general officer at command level, whose duties compel him to go beyond all human decency in order to pursue his savage business to its only conceivable conclusion. Haines reduces the meaning of war to the responsibilities of one single man, to whom must be extended the complete trust which his military position and firmly disciplined Armed Service background unquestionably demand.

The accumulated impact of the authentic but mildly emotional opening scenes of *Command Decision* provides a more devastating indictment of war than all the screaming protests ever could. Behind all the day-to-day functions of a command post with its impressive wall charts and routine reports from the last mission, certain feelings of uneasiness steadily develop. Brockhurst's fencing with the adroit and experienced Evans suggests that all is not well. By the time the first act is over, the spectator realizes that the figures so casually discussed represent the lives of hundreds of highly trained young men and their fabulously costly equipment. The true cost of military success is given a new perspective. The audience is granted the privilege of seeing how it looks through the eyes of the men who must give the orders. The almost brutal coolness with which they discuss the details of Operation Stitch adds to the surprise of discovering the truth: every major, colonel, and general involved in the entire Operation performs his job without question even though he may experience a personal revulsion of such intensity that it can become, upon occasion, fatal.

Haines develops the excellent dramatic irony of Dennis' position through his frustrating encounters with the very men whom he is doing his best to satisfy. The display of indifference, crass political expediency, and just plain ignorance by the junketing dignitaries becomes a deadly serious matter. Malcolm's poisonous sententiousness, Kane's vacillation, Brockhurst's unwarranted sneering, compound to smother the helpless Dennis in the midst of a campaign which could, were it to fail, be the destruction of every one of these self-justifying visiting firemen. Their myopic view of war from an armchair labels Dennis as a bloody butcher, while it demands his removal from the job he cannot abandon at any cost and which his critics cannot realize he so thoroughly abominates. The hypocritical award of the Legion of Merit is a depressingly vacuous gesture.

The final scene is a complete vindication of Dennis, both as an officer and as a man, yet it avoids simply making everything "come out all right." Given the intelligence which Haines has assigned to his responsible commanders, there is only one thing that the affable, ambitious Garnett can do, and he does it in the full knowledge that it may mean the quick end to his own promising career. Garnett arrives at a true concept of command somewhat late, but with the realization he can understand Dennis and take over without change, letting the discipline from their cocktail-party-bound superiors descend when it may. And in a final and deeply cutting irony, the weary Dennis is thrown back into the fray with an even more important command and without a moment's recuperation. The big wheels at the top of the whole clumsy administrative machine at last prove that they know one of their most important cogs when they see it.

A large amount of *Command Decision's* final success comes from character creation. Read any routine war play, or reflect upon the average motion picture treatment of war. Before long you will be able to foretell the dramatis personae with ease, for there is bound to be a brutal neurotic noncom, a comic sad sack from Brooklyn, a mamma's boy, a tall Texan, and a book-learned college man. The chain of events through which they pass can easily be anticipated. Haines does not fall into this wearisome pattern, and his characters develop distinct and plausible personalities. Though Sergeant Evans is *almost* the gag-quoting enlisted man, his personality as a seasoned combat veteran with a healthy disrespect for inflated rank rings true. He also helps to bring the whole affair down to an earthy level; as the only enlisted man in the play he represents, chorus fashion, the detached outside view, while speaking from intelligent experience. Malcolm, who is close to the popular ridiculous figure of the Southern Congressman, never crosses the line into caricature. He is no fool, but he is ignorantly foolish, thereby becoming a far more dangerous threat to the security of the nation he represents and purports to defend. General Kane is Haines' nearest approach to the familiar fumbling officer, although he is no more a "type" than are Malcolm and the rest.

As for Dennis, Haines could have created him in several images. Instead, he combines in his central character the qualities which make a thoroughly believable commander without in any way weakening him into a "good-Joe" out of *Mister Roberts* or finishing him off as a martyr to a lost cause. He is something of both, but he maintains his distance, commands respect, and acts with the human emotions we hope are typical of the great majority of our responsible general officers.

By recognizing that its audience will be fully aware of the broader aspects of war, its filth, carnage, destruction, and horror, *Command Decision* says more about the realities of war than any literal transcription of trench or beachhead carnage. It surrenders to no romantic make-believe nor to violence and harangue, but through its straightforward approach produces a total effect of human dignity in the midst of the worst of human depravity.

William Wister Haines

William Wister Haines was born in Des Moines, Iowa, in 1908. His mother, Ella Wister Haines, was a writer of short fiction and novels. He attended Culver Military Academy and received his bachelor of science degree from the University of Pennsylvania in 1931.

Haines' first novel was "Slim," in 1934, based on his own experiences as an electric-company lineman during the summers he attended college. "High Tension," in 1938, continued in the same vein. In 1942 he entered the Air Force and rose from first lieutenant to lieutenant colonel in the nearly 3½ years he served. The material he treats in *Command Decision* was familiar to him because of his work in such units as the 8th Composite Command, 8th Fighter Command, Headquarters Eighth Air Force and the Strategic Air Force in Europe. While with this last group he served in the office of the Assistant Chief of the Air Staff, Royal Air Force. He was in a fine position to study the responsibilities and the tremendous personal trials endured by the high-ranking officers on both sides.

Command Decision was written soon after his release from the service. It was first submitted as a play to the editors of *The Atlantic Monthly*, but was changed into a novel which the magazine serialized and then published as a book. Haines has continued to write short stories for the *Atlantic* and *The Saturday Evening Post,* and published another novel, "The Honorable Rodney Slade," in 1957.

COMMAND DECISION

by

William Wister Haines

This play is a purely imaginary work of fiction. Use of the name of any person living or dead, excepting named public figures, is unintentional coincidence.

W. W. H.

Scene from the original New York production of *Command Decision*. Haines makes excellent use of an authentic background setting to assist him in conveying to his audience the terrible strains manifest in those who must take the full responsibilities of high-level command in total war. (*Photo by Eileen Darby. Courtesy Graphic House.*)

Command Decision was first presented at the Fulton Theatre in New York on October 1, 1947. It ran for a total of 408 performances, and was later made into a successful motion picture starring James Stewart. The following cast appeared in the original production:

WAR CORRESPONDENT ELMER BROCKHURST	*Edmon Ryan*
TECH. SERGEANT HAROLD EVANS	*James Whitmore*
BRIGADIER GENERAL K. C. DENNIS	*Paul Kelly*
COLONEL ERNEST HALEY	*Edward Binns*
ENLISTED ARMED GUARD	*West Hooker*
CAPTAIN LUCIUS JENKS	*Arthur Franz*
MAJOR GENERAL ROLAND GOODLOW KANE	*Jay Fassett*
BRIGADIER GENERAL CLIFTON C. GARNETT	*Paul McGrath*
MAJOR HOMER PRESCOTT	*William Layton*
COLONEL EDWARD MARTIN	*Stephen Elliott*
LT. JAKE GOLDBERG	*John Randolph*
MAJOR DESMOND LANSING	*Lewis Martin*
MAJOR BELDING DAVIS	*Robert Pike*
MAJOR RUFUS DAYHUFF	*Walter Black*
MR. ARTHUR MALCOLM	*Paul Ford*
MR. OLIVER STONE	*Frank McNellis*
CAPTAIN G. W. C. LEE	*James Holden*
N. C. O. PHOTOGRAPHER	*Leonard Patrick*

Produced by Kermit Bloomgarden
Directed by John O'Shaughnessy
Setting and lighting by Jo Mielziner
Costumes supervised by Julia Sze

The entire action of the play takes place in the office of BRIGADIER GENERAL K. C. DENNIS at the Headquarters of the Fifth American Bombardment Division, Heavy, in England.

This office is the round-roofed end of a large Nissen hut.[1] It is a conventional rectangle with a small alcove running back a few feet upstage R. Along the R. wall, ranged from downstage upward, are a wastebasket labelled "Burn,"[2] a low sturdy chest labelled "Division Flag Locker." On wall pegs above "Division Flag Locker" hang GENERAL DENNIS's helmet, gas mask and service .45 in holster. American, British and Division flags droop from standards on floor. On R. wall of alcove are three filing cabinets, one strap-locked and labelled "Top Secret." On back wall of alcove is a pot-bellied coal stove for heating coffee. In L. wall of alcove a door gives on Operations Room; through it as action indicates the teleprinter may be heard clicking.

The back wall is covered by a curtain over the Status Board and a curtain over the map, both being opened as action indicates. Status Board is a blackboard indicating minute-by-minute operational status of planes and crews in the Division's

[1] The British equivalent of the Quonset hut, a long, narrow steel building with semicircular roof arching down to the ground to form the structure's sides.

[2] All classified documents, unfiled or otherwise unstored, and all papers associated with them, including carbon copies and the carbon paper itself, were consigned to the "Burn" basket in all military installations for destruction each day.

group. The map is a G. S. G.S. 1 x 250,000,[3] showing part of England, the Channel and North Sea, and that part of Europe roughly bounded by the 48th Parallel, North, and the 15th Meridian, East. (Note: The scale of this map is approximately one inch to four miles.)

Over the Status Board is hung a large, ripped-off section of a German fighter plane, its marking cross clearly visible to audience. At L. of map, by door in back wall, are four light-switches, two for long strip light that illuminates map and one each for lights above GENERAL DENNIS's desk and the map table. An unmounted souvenir Browning .50 machine gun stands on floor under light switches, erect, barrel wired to wall.

The door, back wall L., leads to ante-room of the GENERAL's office. Legend, "Commanding General," may be seen in reverse lettering on its opaque glass. L. of door in corner are three Tommy-guns in a rack. Along L. wall, running down, are a fire-extinguisher and A. R. P.[4] sand and water buckets and a cot. L. wall itself is a large window giving on the perimeter track and landing strips of the Operating Group based on Div. Hq. Airfield. Window is blacked out by curtains in night scenes.

R. of C. is GENERAL DENNIS's big flat-topped desk, facing L., his nameplate on lower end of it plainly discernible to audience. Armchair behind it (R.) and one for visitors just before it. L. of C. is a large (3' x 6') map table. There are a chair at its R., a draughtsman's stool behind it. A rack under it holds rolls of maps and the "Speed At Altitude, Performance Chart" of the German fighter plane, exhibited as action indicates. A long pointer, for use at map, is kept in this rack. At rise of first act curtain a 1'-½" step-up is under map table.

The First Act begins about four o'clock on a Saturday afternoon. The Second is divided; Scene One begins about ten o'clock that Saturday night. Scene Two begins about noon on Sunday, the following day. The Third Act begins about eight o'clock that same Sunday evening.

ACT ONE

Curtain rises on empty room. Coffee bubbles on stove. TECH. SGT. HAROLD EVANS *enters.* EVANS *is a tough, independent graduate gunner of twenty-five who has finished his missions and taken a job as the* GENERAL'S *man to improve his food, drink, and amusement. He pours himself coffee, goes to desk, selects and lights one of the* GENERAL'S *cigars and returns with it to coffee at table. Settles comfortably to cigar and coffee, then scowls as door opens and* WAR CORRESPONDENT ELMER BROCKHURST *enters.* BROCKHURST, *middle-aged, reflects the cocky, contemptuous power of the big magazine he represents.*

BROCKHURST. Is General Dennis in, Sergeant?

EVANS. Does it look like it?

BROCKHURST. Seriously, Joe . . .

EVANS. My name isn't Joe. Who let you in here? (BROCKHURST *goes to mask over wall map, scrutinizes it eagerly.*) Who let you in here?

BROCKHURST. I can't hear you. (EVANS *steps to tommy-gun rack, grabs a gun, ejects shell onto floor, covers* BROCKHURST.) Look out! That thing might go off!

EVANS. *Might,* hell! Who let you in here?

BROCKHURST. I've got a pass.

EVANS. I seen General Dennis tear it up.

BROCKHURST. I've got a new pass, from General Dennis's boss.

EVANS. Walk it over here, slow! (*Scared,* BROCKHURST *does.* EVANS *reads.*)

---

[3] Geographic Survey, General Staff. One inch to 250,000 feet.
[4] Air Raid Precaution.

"Elmer Brockhurst, accredited corre-spondent of *Coverage* . . ." that maga-zine with all the hatchet murders and naked dames?

BROCKHURST. Yeah.

EVANS. ". . . has my authorization to visit any Army Air Forces installation in my command . . . signed . . ." Who?

BROCKHURST. Major General R. G. Kane . . . that's who.

EVANS. A Goddamned old Major Gen-eral and can't sign his name clear enough to read . . . No . . . this *is* old Percent himself. (*He racks tommy-gun, returns pass, sits down to coffee. Relieved,* BROCKHURST *turns chummy.*)

BROCKHURST. Percent?

EVANS. Kane . . . cause of that public-ity about what percent of Germany his gallant forces destroy every afternoon, weather permitting.

BROCKHURST. He tops your boss, any-way.

EVANS. Keep away from that map. When Dennis sees you, he'll spit a snake. (BROCKHURST *flinches, pours coffee.*)

BROCKHURST. Where is that Fascist megalomaniac?

EVANS. Who?

BROCKHURST. Dennis, that's what he is, a Fascist megalomaniac.

EVANS. What's that?

BROCKHURST. A man so drunk with power he thinks he can cover anything he does with other people's blood.

EVANS. How long you been around the army?

BROCKHURST. Long enough to know that's what Dennis is.

EVANS. That's what all generals are.

BROCKHURST. Where is he, Sarge? Sleeping till the mission comes in?

EVANS. You must love that guard-house, pumping me about missions.

BROCKHURST. Having Dennis lock me in that guardhouse taught me a lot of angles. What became of that German pilot he had there?

EVANS. That isn't a lot of angles . . . that's one.

BROCKHURST. What about that German

fighter plane Dennis has under close guard in Hangar Four? . . . the one he's been flying himself lately . . . why did he take the worst losses of the war yes-terday and then send his bombers even deeper into Germany today?

EVANS. I thought you knew the angles.

BROCKHURST. I know he's got one of his own squadron Commanders under close arrest in the guardhouse right now. (EVANS *starts.* BROCKHURST *presses his advantage.*) Why?

EVANS. He's a bad boy . . . won't brush his teeth.

BROCKHURST. Don't you guys realize that a free press is your protection?

EVANS. Why don't you write your Congressman?

BROCKHURST. I think he already knows it. Cliff Garnett arrived in England last night by special plane.

EVANS. Who's he?

BROCKHURST. Brigadier General Clifton C. Garnett is Secretary to the United Chiefs of Staff in Washington.

EVANS. Oh, God! Now we'll never get the war over.

BROCKHURST. I'll bet you Dennis's war is over this week.

EVANS. You think they'd fire Dennis for one of them Pentagon bellhops?

BROCKHURST. Sarge, ever since General Lucas got killed and Dennis took over here the country's been shuddering at his losses . . . people are whispering . . . calling Dennis the Butcher of Bombard-ment . . .

EVANS. Oh, my aching back . . .

BROCKHURST. Wait and see! Cliff Gar-nett should have had this job in the first place . . . he's a smart operator and the United Chiefs trust him.

EVANS. They never fired no general yet till they'd give him the Legion of Merit . . . and Dennis ain't got one.

BROCKHURST. They can give 'em mighty quick. Going to miss your hero?

EVANS. He's no hero to me. I've just taken this job—after my twenty-eight missions[5]—to chisel my way to what I really want.

[5] After a prescribed number of combat missions, normally twenty-five, an officer or en-listed man was entitled to ground duty.

BROCKHURST. Sarge, I know R. G. Kane pretty well . . . what would you like?

EVANS. Bartender . . . in a rest camp . . . for battle-weary WACS.[6]

BROCKHURST. Listen, Sarge, Dennis is a ruptured duck. But a couple of angles on this deal would be worth some whiskey to me. What became of that German pilot Dennis had in the guardhouse?

EVANS. Whiskey or Scotch?

BROCKHURST. Bonded bourbon.

EVANS. How much?

BROCKHURST. Four bottles.

EVANS. You gave Peterson in the guard-house two cases . . . just for making the phone call that got you out of there.

BROCKHURST. I did like hell! I gave Peterson one case . . . (Stops, realizing he's tricked.) Okay. Call it a case . . . for the whole story, though.

EVANS (secretively). Dennis had him locked in there till last night . . .

BROCKHURST (eagerly). Yeah?

EVANS. . . . but yesterday the quartermaster run out of Spam.[7] Dennis said by God he'd promised the men meat for breakfast and if they wasn't no other meat we'd just have to use that Kraut pilot . . .

BROCKHURST. Okay . . . you got your joke . . . I've still got my whiskey. (BROCKHURST exits. EVANS jumps to phone and speaks into it.)

EVANS. Guardhouse . . . Corporal Peterson, this is Tech Sergeant Evans in the General's office. Bring six of them twelve marbles you just won . . . you know, them tall glass marbles with labels on 'em, to me personally in the General's ante-room . . . You heard me . . . well, Jesus Christ, I'm giving you half of 'em, ain't I? Okay . . . they better be. (Hangs up, listens, puts cigar in ashtray on desk and jumps to attention as

BRIGADIER GENERAL K. C. DENNIS enters. DENNIS is about forty, prepossessing, forceful, usually so preoccupied as to appear slightly absent-minded. Does not notice cigar but heard phone click.)

DENNIS. Was that for me?

EVANS. No, sir.

DENNIS. Any word since the strike message from the mission?

EVANS. No, sir.

DENNIS (picks up cigar and begins smoking it, his mind on business). Ask Colonel Haley to step in and have the guard bring Captain Jenks. (EVANS exits. DENNIS walks to window and studies sky. COLONEL ERNEST HALEY enters. He is Regular Army, literal, carries papers.) Anything more from the mission?

HALEY. Just Colonel Martin's radio I woke you for, sir . . . (Reads it from paper.) "Primary target plastered. Warm here. Martin."

DENNIS. "Warm . . ."

HALEY. Intelligence said they'd fight today, sir.

DENNIS. What about the weather for tomorrow?

HALEY. No change since last reading, sir.

DENNIS. Good. How many planes can I count on having? (HALEY strips curtain mask, revealing Division Status, a welter of chalk columns on a blackboard showing minute-by-minute status of Groups' planes and crews. EVANS enters quietly and stands at ease through this.)

HALEY. Thirteen Minor Repairs promised by fifteen hundred,[8] eighteen from Major Repair by twenty-three hundred, twenty-two Maidenheads from Modification arriving stations now and thirty of those weatherbound new ones took off from Iceland at eleven hundred this morning, sir.

DENNIS. Are the newcomers from

[6] Members of the Women's Army Corps.

[7] The trade name of a pork luncheon meat of Swift and Company, but assigned indiscriminately by the average soldier to all similar meats frequently served at overseas bases.

[8] Military time is kept by the twenty-four-hour clock. "Fifteen hundred" is 3 P.M. All hours before 10 A.M. are designated by a zero before the hour: 0500 is 5 A.M., or "Oh-five hundred" as it would be spoken. Minutes follow the hour number: 1730 is "seventeen thirty hours" or 5:30 P.M. This method of time indication eliminates all possible A.M. or P.M. confusion.

Iceland flying Ferry crews or replacements?

HALEY. Mostly Ferry, sir. But we've got twelve crews back from Flak houses, eighteen from Leave and Sick and twenty-eight new ones from Combat Crew Replacement Center today, sir.

DENNIS. And twelve crews finish their missions today?

HALEY. If they get back, sir.

DENNIS. We lose 'em anyway. How many would graduate tomorrow?

HALEY. Depends on who gets back today, sir.

DENNIS. Well, on averages . . . few enough to hold 'em over for an easy last mission?

HALEY. Fourteen . . . maybe. But they're your lead crews, sir.

DENNIS. How do the boys feel, Haley?

HALEY. They're too tired to feel, sir.

DENNIS. What else?

HALEY (fingering papers unhappily). Another rape case, I'm afraid, sir.

DENNIS. Combat crew or base personnel?

HALEY. A navigator, sir.

DENNIS. Nuts. When's a navigator had time to get raped?

HALEY. Complaint was he did the raping, sir. Last night.

DENNIS. Between yesterday's mission, and today's . . . ? Who's complaining, the girl or her mother?

HALEY. Her mother, sir. Mrs. Daphne Magruder, Tranquillity Cottage, The High Street, Undershot-Overhill.

EVANS. I know them people, sir.

DENNIS. No doubt. Did our boy go there alone, Haley?

HALEY. I'm afraid he did, sir.

DENNIS. Haley! I've told you before: when these boys tomcat, they're to go in pairs. How can you expect one man, flying missions, to keep the whole family happy? Have you told the Judge Advocate?

HALEY. Not yet, sir. We're badly bottlenecked for navigators and this man has ten missions more to go on his twenty-five.

EVANS. Would the General like to square . . . that is, to have this matter attended to by negotiation, sir?

DENNIS. Yes.

EVANS. If I could have two gallons of ice cream from mess supply . . .

DENNIS. Get it and get going.

EVANS. With the General's permission, sir, these matters are better negotiated after dark.

DENNIS. All right. What else, Haley?

HALEY (reading paper unhappily). Sir, the Society for the Preservation of Cultural and Artistic Treasures against Vandalism says it was our Division that bombed that cathedral. You remember, sir, the man said he was shot up.

DENNIS. I remember . . . he was shot up . . .

HALEY. Yes, sir. But next time out that man got hit himself. He's in the hospital now and says he wants to tell the truth. He says the war's turned him into an Atheist . . . and when he saw he couldn't reach the target with his bombs he threw 'em into that cathedral, just to show God what he thought of His lower echelons.

DENNIS. Could he have got back to base with his bombs?

HALEY (hedging). He was deep in France . . . with one motor shot out, sir.

DENNIS. Go to the hospital and chew his ass out. Tell him for me we don't haul bombs through the submarine belt to waste on Atheism or any other religion . . . and it better not happen again. Then write the Society it was an emergency necessary to save life. What else?

HALEY. Nothing official, sir, but . . .

DENNIS. But what? (HALEY looks sharply at EVANS, who reluctantly exits.)

HALEY. Grapevine says General Kane's in a huddle with the Hemisphere Commander, sir.

DENNIS. What's that got to do with us?

HALEY. Grapevine says there's a big meeting in Washington next week . . . and neither of them is invited.

DENNIS. That's their worry. (Then, anxiously.) What day next week?

HALEY. No one knows, sir.

DENNIS. Well, tomorrow's only Sunday . . . you're sure the weather hasn't changed?

HALEY. No, sir . . . last forecast is still fine.

DENNIS. Well, then, we'll finish *before* the meeting.

HALEY. I hope so, sir.

DENNIS. *We* haven't had any squawk from Washington yet . . . ?

HALEY. Not yet, sir.

DENNIS. Send Captain Jenks in here.

HALEY. Want me with you, sir?

DENNIS. No. I'll try him alone again. (*Checks* HALEY *at door.*) Has that cable come for Ted Martin yet?

HALEY. Not yet, sir. I've been checking. Mrs. Martin must be late with that baby.

DENNIS (*absently*). She's ten years late . . . (*Then, noticing* HALEY'S *surprise.*) Keep checking; I'd like to meet Ted with good news when he lands. (HALEY *exits.* DENNIS *takes a troubled look at the sky, seats himself with a dossier of papers at desk. A knock is heard at door.*) Come in! (CAPTAIN LUCIUS JENKS *enters, followed by an* ARMED GUARD. JENKS *is an ordinary-looking kid in flying coveralls, momentarily sullen.* GUARD *follows him to position facing desk and salutes.*)

GUARD. Guard reporting with prisoner as ordered, sir.

DENNIS. Wait outside. (GUARD *exits.*) Jenks, have you thought this over?

JENKS (*stonily*). I thought it over this morning.

DENNIS. You've had more time.

JENKS. I don't need more time.

DENNIS. Damn it, boy, don't you realize this is serious?

JENKS. I'm not getting killed to make you a record. I'll tell the court so, too, and the whole damned world.

DENNIS. What else will you tell them?

JENKS. That you lost forty bombers, four hundred men, by deliberately sending us beyond fighter cover yesterday. This morning, when we're entitled to a milk run[9] you order us even further into Germany.

DENNIS. Who told you you were entitled to a milk run?

JENKS. You big boys think flak-fodder like us can't even read a calendar, don't you? Where do the Air Forces get those statistical records for sorties and tonnages that General Kane announces regularly? They get 'em on milk runs, over the Channel Ports, the last three days of every month.

DENNIS. Twelve crews took today's target for their last mission.

JENKS. They didn't have the guts to say what they thought of it. If you big shots are entitled to a record racket, so am I.

DENNIS. You were informed, at briefing, of the purpose of this mission.

JENKS. "A very significant target that can kill a lot of our people unless we knock it out." Nuts to that pep talk! Everything in Germany's made to kill people. Why can't we have targets under fighter cover, like General Kane promised?

DENNIS. He didn't promise that.

JENKS. Anyone who knows the Army knows what Kane . . .

DENNIS. *General* Kane's . . .

JENKS. . . . General Kane's press interview meant. That day we lost nineteen over Bremfurt and the Air Corps turned itself inside out explaining. How do you think the public will take forty yesterday . . . and worse today?

DENNIS. The public isn't my business.

JENKS. How do you think it will like hearing you ordered both these attacks when Kane . . . General Kane, was absent . . .

DENNIS. And that isn't your business. You were ordered to go. After learning the target you refused.

JENKS. I've been to plenty tough targets.

DENNIS (*fingering dossier*). You aborted from the two toughest prior to yesterday.

JENKS. For mechanical malfunctions in my plane . . .

DENNIS. One engineer's examination said: "Possibly justifiable." The other said: "Defect not discernible."

JENKS. It was plenty discernible to me

---

[9] A bombing mission comparatively safe, over easy targets, lightly defended—supposedly no more dangerous than delivering the milk.

and my co-pilot will tell you the same thing, unless he's prejudiced . . .

DENNIS. He should be; he's flying your seat today, and you're a Squadron Commander . . . The Army had trusted you with Command. (*This bites,* JENKS *has begun to look scared.* DENNIS *resumes patiently.*) Now, if you've got any legitimate reason at all . . .

EVANS (*enters, announces with a note of warning*). Major General R. G. Kane and party, sir. (DENNIS *jumps to attention as* KANE *and party enter.* JENKS *steps into background.* KANE, *a shrewd man of fifty odd, tough but capable of a calculated amiability, which is currently on display, leads. Next comes* BRIGADIER GENERAL CLIFTON C. GARNETT, *a virile man in late thirties, meticulously dressed.* KANE's *aide,* MAJOR HOMER PRESCOTT, *a genteel stooge, follows.* JENKS *remains in background as* DENNIS *minds his military manners, saluting.* EVANS *exits.*)

DENNIS. I'm very sorry, sir. If I'd known you were visiting my command I should have been at the gate.

KANE. Don't speak of it, my boy! You remember Cliff Garnett, of course?

DENNIS (*offering* GARNETT *hand*). Sir, I was best man when Ted Martin married Cliff's sister.

GARNETT. Casey, how are you?

DENNIS. Fine.

GARNETT. I want you to know we all felt terribly when Joe Lucas was killed. (DENNIS *glances at* KANE, *who shakes his head slightly.*)

DENNIS. So did we.

GARNETT. But I don't mind telling you some of us in Washington were mighty glad you were here to take over his job.

KANE (*manifestly changing subject*). Cliff here wanted to see a real operational headquarters, so I brought him straight down without waiting on protocol.

DENNIS. How's the Pentagon, Cliff?

GARNETT (*nettled*). A little worried about you, Casey.

DENNIS. Well, that gives them something to do.

GARNETT. I hope it won't be something we wouldn't like.

DENNIS. Are you over for long?

GARNETT. You never know. My orders just said, "Tour of Observation . . ."

KANE (*cutting this off*). And my new aide, Major Prescott, General Dennis.

PRESCOTT. How *do* you do, sir? I'm very happy to meet the commander of our famous Fifth Division.

BROCKHURST (*enters*). I had a hunch you'd come down here today, R. G.

DENNIS. General Kane, I've forbidden this man the station.

KANE. Now, Casey, that's one of the things I came down about.

DENNIS. He was snooping in a restricted hangar and trying to worm information out of my people. I had him in the guardhouse until your counterorder.

BROCKHURST. Kane, the American people are going to be very interested in Dennis's guardhouse.

KANE (*sees* JENKS, *hastens to change subject*). Why, Captain Jenks! Delighted to see you again, my boy.

JENKS. Thank you, sir.

KANE (*throws a paternal arm around* JENKS, *and leads him to* GARNETT). Cliff, this is one of our real heroes!

GARNETT. Is this the Captain Jenks who named his Fortress the Urgent Virgin?

KANE. The best publicity we've had in this war! Three pages and ten pictures in Brockie's magazine. What brings you to headquarters today, my boy? Helping General Dennis?

DENNIS. A disciplinary matter, sir. We'll attend to it later . . . Jenks! (DENNIS *indicates door, but* KANE *stops* JENKS.)

KANE. No, no! This is what you wanted to see, Cliff; real field problems. Now, Casey, you and Captain Jenks carry on just as if we weren't here. If there's one thing I pride myself on it's not interfering with the vital work of my Divisions.

DENNIS. This isn't a matter for the press, sir.

KANE (*sharply*). Brockie is my friend,

General! (*Then, to* JENKS.) What's the disciplinary trouble, my boy? Some of those high-spirited young pilots of yours getting out of hand?

JENKS. Perhaps General Dennis will explain, sir.

DENNIS. Captain Jenks refused to fly today's mission as ordered, sir. (BROCKHURST *whistles. Others react, shocked.*)

KANE. I can't believe it.

JENKS. Do you know what today's target was, General Kane?

DENNIS (*sharply*). Captain, you're still under Security Regulations. There will be no mention of today's target before the press!

BROCKHURST. Security covers a lot, doesn't it, Dennis?

DENNIS. The life of every man we send across the Channel.

BROCKHURST. What about the life of this boy, under you?

KANE (*to* BROCKHURST). Brockie, there *is* a question of Security, if you don't mind.

BROCKHURST. O. K., R. G. I *was* trying to help you. (BROCKHURST *exits.*)

DENNIS. The target was Schweinhafen, sir.

KANE. Schweinhafen! You've begun Operation Stitch?

DENNIS. Began yesterday, sir, with Posenleben.

KANE. *Posenleben* ... yesterday? What happened?

DENNIS. Excellent results, sir. Over three-quarters total destruction.

KANE. I mean ... what were your losses?

DENNIS. Forty planes, sir.

KANE. *Forty!* Good God! Does the press know it?

DENNIS. I put a security blackout on the whole operation as we agreed.

GARNETT (*sharply*). Would someone mind telling a visitor the details of this Operation Stitch?

DENNIS. Kind of a three-horse parlay, Cliff: Posenleben, Schweinhafen ... (*Eyes* PRESCOTT *and* JENKS.) And one other.

GARNETT. Well, I thought I'd written your directive myself!

DENNIS. Some things aren't in official directives, Cliff.

GARNETT. Evidently. But the United Chiefs are still running the war, Casey. Have you taken it on yourself to change their orders?

KANE. I was going to send them a provisional plan for Operation Stitch, but ... (*Lamely.*) I didn't know General Dennis intended implementing it so soon. It takes a very rare weather condition.

PRESCOTT. The whole idea was General Dennis's, sir!

DENNIS. And I'll explain it myself, Major! Do you wish to detain Captain Jenks any further, General Kane?

KANE (*wishes he were dead, but he has to deal with this*). Did you go on the Posenleben mission yesterday, Captain?

JENKS. I did, sir. It was a bloody massacre. Today will be worse.

KANE. Any news from today's mission yet, General?

DENNIS. Colonel Martin radioed: "Primary target plastered," sir.

KANE. I mean news about losses?

DENNIS. Ted indicated fighting, sir, but no details. (GARNETT *reacts perceptibly to mention of* TED.) I see no further need of Captain Jenks at this conference, sir.

KANE. General, as you know, I pride myself on never interfering with the functioning of my subordinate echelons. But in a case that touches one of our combat personnel, I know you will forgive an older commander's concern. With your permission, I should like to speak to Captain Jenks alone.

DENNIS (*to others, stonily*). If you gentlemen will come with me ...

KANE. No, no. You and Cliff stay right here. We'll step outside. (KANE, JENKS *and* PRESCOTT *go out.* GARNETT *faces* DENNIS *accusingly.*)

GARNETT. So ... Ted Martin *is* flying missions!

DENNIS. He led the Division today ... yesterday, too.

GARNETT. Casey, do you think this is fair to my sister?

DENNIS. Cliff, when Helen married Ted, she married the service.

GARNETT. They've waited ten years for this baby. It's due this week. Ted shouldn't be flying missions at all at his age, let alone just now.

DENNIS. He gets paid to.

GARNETT (*starts, checks himself, smiles*). I went to see your family just before leaving, Casey. I've got some letters for you.

DENNIS. Thanks. How are they?

GARNETT. Fine! And terribly proud of you. That pretty daughter of yours says to tell you she's learned to spell three words.

DENNIS (*pleased, covering*). I hope one of them is "No."

GARNETT. She's a charmer, Casey. And young William Mitchell Dennis sent you special orders. You're to destroy all of Germany except one little piece he wants saved for his first bomb. He asked if I thought you could do it.

DENNIS. What did you tell him?

GARNETT. I told him, with war, you never know.

DENNIS. Let's see . . . he was ten this month. Eight more years would be pretty slow . . . even for the United Chiefs.

GARNETT (*nettled*). Casey, you're too old for this brass-baiting. The United Chiefs have their headaches, too. (*Then, with concern.*) Helen is very worried about Ted.

DENNIS. Is she?

GARNETT. You know that always was the trouble between them.

DENNIS. Was it?

GARNETT. In the old days, when you and he were testing those experimental jobs she got so she couldn't even answer the phone. That's why she wouldn't have kids then: she had no security.

DENNIS. Neither did the other girls, Cliff.

GARNETT (*defensively*). I know she left him. But think of her side of it. Five years in boarding houses on Second Lieutenant's pay. Then the morning he made First he had to call his commanding officer a goddamned fool . . .

DENNIS. That's what he was . . .

GARNETT. . . . maybe. But Ted was a Second Lieutenant again by lunch. That afternoon he turned down twelve thousand a year from the best airline in America. What would you have thought?

DENNIS. That he was a rare guy.

GARNETT. She's realized that, Casey. She did go back to him.

DENNIS. What's all this leading to?

GARNETT. Does Ted think she came back to him and is having that kid just because he *is* pretty secure now?

DENNIS. Ask Ted what he thinks.

GARNETT. He and I were never very close. You know what he thinks of you.

DENNIS. Maybe that's because I don't try to run his life.

GARNETT. You don't have to waste it. Ted is too valuable to be flying missions.

DENNIS. What's more important?

GARNETT (*hesitates, evades*). Casey, the service needs Ted . . . for bigger jobs. And he and Helen deserve a little security now. You don't have to send him at his age.

DENNIS. I don't have to send any of 'em. We could all be secure, under Hitler. (KANE, JENKS *and* PRESCOTT *enter.* KANE *is grave but more assured.*)

KANE. General Dennis, Captain Jenks is obviously the victim of a shock condition induced by the strain of his nineteen missions. It's a medical problem. All he needs is rest.

DENNIS. Sir, Captain Jenks finished ten days in a rest house on Thursday and has been medically certified fit for the completion of his twenty-five missions. (KANE *looks apoplectic.* PRESCOTT *scrambles for a new excuse.*)

PRESCOTT. Captain Jenks, did you know of any defect in your plane . . . ?

DENNIS. His co-pilot took the plane. It has not aborted.

KANE (*catching the straw*). We won't know until the plane comes back. We'll continue the investigation later, General.

DENNIS. Guard! (GUARD *enters, takes place behind* JENKS.) Return the prisoner to the guardhouse. (GUARD *and* JENKS *go out.*)

KANE. General, this is very serious.

DENNIS. Every detail will be checked, sir. It happened at five-twenty this morning. I've got the rest of the twenty-four hours to charge him.

KANE. What charge are you considering?

DENNIS. Unless something new comes up the only possible charge is "Desertion in the face of the enemy."

KANE. Good God, boy! We can't shoot a national hero!

DENNIS. Do you think you'll ever have another tough mission if you don't? At group briefing this morning when the target was uncovered I saw five men cross themselves. One fainted. But they went . . . and they know that Jenks didn't. (KANE *understands but won't face the implication.* PRESCOTT *tries again.*)

PRESCOTT. Couldn't a quiet transfer be arranged . . . to transport or training?

DENNIS. So he could go yellow there and kill passengers or students?

PRESCOTT. Precautions could be taken. There's such a thing as the end justifying the means, sir. This case would put the honor of the Army Air Forces at stake.

DENNIS. It already has. Every man in the Division knows it.

PRESCOTT. I was thinking of the larger picture.

DENNIS. You can afford to.

KANE. Homer, go talk this over with Elmer Brockhurst . . . everything.

DENNIS. Sir! . . .

KANE. Brockie has a remarkable feel for public reaction, Casey. We've got to consider every angle on this. (PRESCOTT *exits.* DENNIS *extends* JENKS' *201 file to* KANE.)[10]

DENNIS. Look at the Engineers' reports on his two previous abortions.

KANE (*ignoring file*). Have you talked to his group commander?

DENNIS. Didn't you get yesterday's report, sir?

KANE. No. I've been with the Hemisphere Commander.

DENNIS. Colonel Ledgrave went down yesterday, sir.

KANE. My God! Leddy . . . any parachutes seen?

DENNIS. Two, from the waist. But Leddy was riding with the bombardier and she exploded just as the waist gunners got out. (KANE *is visibly affected,* GARNETT *shocked.*)

GARNETT. That's Roger Ledgrave, class of '29?

DENNIS. Yeah.

GARNETT. Casey, is it necessary . . . for our own people . . . to go so often?

DENNIS. Yes.

KANE. Casey, had Leddy never mentioned Captain Jenks to you?

DENNIS. Never, sir.

KANE. That's my oversight. I had told him, in confidence, that since that publicity in *Coverage* we've been advised to be very careful of Captain Jenks.

DENNIS. I wish I had been told that, sir. (*Awkward pause,* GARNETT *breaks it.*)

GARNETT. How soon will today's mission be landing, Casey?

DENNIS. In six or seven minutes.

GARNETT. General Kane, I must insist on being briefed about this Operation Stitch. The United Chiefs will have to know.

DENNIS (*shocked*). Haven't you told him anything about it, sir?

KANE. I thought it would be fairer to let you.

DENNIS (*reacts, settles to work*). Six weeks ago a German fighter plane landed on that Number One strip, right outside the window there.

GARNETT. Shot up?

DENNIS. Not a scratch. The pilot was a Czechoslovakian engineer. He'd been forced to work for them, but when they sent him up to the Baltic to test this job he flew it here to us.

GARNETT. Accommodating of him.

DENNIS. That cross was the plane marking. I hung it there as a reminder.

GARNETT. What kind of fighter was it?

---

[10] Army file number for personnel file.

DENNIS. Focke-Schmidt 1.

GARNETT. Focke-Schmidt 1 . . . ?

DENNIS. Remember that spy's report out of Lisbon . . . on a new jet-propelled fighter . . . Messerschmidt wing, the new Serrenbach propulsion unit . . . forty-eight thousand ceiling and six hundred at thirty thousand?

GARNETT. Our people said that was impossible.

DENNIS. I know. These are the tests of it. (DENNIS *strips a curtain mask, revealing performance curves inked on graph paper. Red, blue, green and yellow curves are closely grouped, almost parallel. Above, obviously in a class by itself, is the heavy black curve of the Focke-Schmidt 1.* DENNIS *indicates colors as he talks.*) Lightning, Thunderbolt, Mustang, Spit Twelve[11] and . . . Focke-Schmidt 1!

GARNETT. Jesus Christ! . . . Oh, the German job's in kilometers.

DENNIS. No, it isn't. That's miles . . . same as the others.

GARNETT. Who made these tests?

DENNIS. Ted Martin and I.

GARNETT. Yourselves?

DENNIS. Three turns apiece.

GARNETT (*awed, tracing black curve*). You did that . . . after what the doctors told you?

DENNIS. I wanted to be sure. It gave me a week in the hospital to think things over.

GARNETT (*examines curves, impressed, rueful*). Of course our new Mustangs will be a great improvement.

DENNIS. This isn't an improvement, Cliff. This is a revolution.

GARNETT. Even so, when you get enough of our new Mustangs . . .

DENNIS. Can you arrange an armistice until we get 'em?

GARNETT. Casey, I've battled the United Chiefs for every bomber you've got. I've stuck my neck out to get you Mustangs to protect them. I've fought for this Air Corps just as hard as you have. Now, when will the Germans get these jets?

DENNIS. They have three factories entering line production now . . . or rather, they did have, yesterday morning.

GARNETT. New factories?

DENNIS. No. They've converted old bomber plants. The Czech engineer thinks they've got one operating group on conversion training already.

GARNETT. Have you lost any planes to it?

DENNIS. Lost planes don't report. But last week we wrote off three reconnaissance planes for the first time in months. They were stripped to the ribs and flying at forty thousand, but something got them.

KANE. Of course, we don't *know* it was this new jet.

DENNIS. It wasn't mice. (*Moves to map and opens it.*) I've flown this plane and we've photographed the three factories.

GARNETT. Weren't they camouflaged?

DENNIS. Perfectly. We put an infrared camera on a night fighter and caught 'em after dark with Focke-Schmidts on every apron. (*Indicates three marked spots on map.*) Posenleben, Schweinhafen and Fendelhorst. That's Operation Stitch, for Stitch in Time . . .

GARNETT. They're deep enough in, aren't they?

DENNIS. Goering is thinking better of us these days.

GARNETT. How far beyond friendly fighter cover is that? (DENNIS *swings the conventional arc, it is woefully short of the marks.*) Casey, it's murder to send bombers that far beyond friendly fighter cover.

KANE. And I don't think it's necessary. This jet fighter may have a superior capability on paper, or even when it's flown by men like Casey and Ted Martin. But when I consider American courage and airmanship . . .

DENNIS (*indicating graphed performance curves*). Courage and airmanship don't fill gaps like this, sir.

---

[11] Lightning, Thunderbolt, and Mustang are names of famous American fighter planes. The British Spit, or Spitfire, and the Hurricane won the Battle of Britain in 1940.

GARNETT. Why hasn't this technical data been reported?

DENNIS. It has. Through channels. You'll hear from it next year.

GARNETT. What's your honest opinion of this, Casey?

DENNIS. This can run us out of Europe in sixty days.

KANE (*protestingly*). That's giving them absolute perfection in production, in testing, in crew conversion, in tactics . . .

DENNIS. That's giving them thirty days to get two groups operating and thirty more to catch one of our missions for just half an hour. I put that in my report.

GARNETT (*sharply*). Why didn't you send this report to us? (DENNIS *is silent.* KANE *has to answer.*)

KANE. I did report to the United Chiefs that we could not exclude the possibility of encountering an unsuspected enemy capability which might compel retrospective alteration of our present estimate of the situation.

GARNETT. Did you approve this Operation Stitch, sir? (KANE *glares. But* GARNETT *is secretary to the United Chiefs.*)

KANE. I told General Dennis this constitutes a tactical emergency within the scope of a *Division* Commander's discretion.

DENNIS. It's my rap, Cliff. I consider the operation necessary.

GARNETT. Your losses are the United Chiefs' rap, Casey. Remember, half of them are Admirals. A very substantial body of opinion doesn't believe we can succeed with daylight precision bombardment over Germany.

DENNIS. A very substantial body of opinion didn't believe the Wright brothers could fly.

GARNETT. Casey, you'll have to know it. The United Chiefs are having a global re-allocation meeting next Tuesday.

DENNIS (*shocked*). Global *re*-allocation, next Tuesday?

GARNETT. To review the whole record.

DENNIS. Are they getting cold feet on precision bombardment?

GARNETT. It's making a terrible drain on our best industrial capacity and the very cream of our manpower.

KANE. They were upset about our losses, even before this week.

DENNIS. Cliff, were you sent here to slow us up?

GARNETT. Not specifically; but our people felt I should warn you, because you might even scare the United Chiefs into abandoning our whole B-29 strategy in the Pacific.[12]

KANE. I don't think we're justified in making a third attack tomorrow.

DENNIS. Sir! Concentration is the crux of this! You agreed to that.

GARNETT. Why?

DENNIS. Weather. It may be a month before we can get back to Fendelhorst. That's too long. (*Overscene comes the faint rising roar of the returning bombers. All hurry to window.*)

GARNETT. There they come now . . .

DENNIS. Four . . . five . . . eight . . . nine . . . (*Sound rises and then begins to recede, these planes are passing at a distant tangent.*)

GARNETT. Aren't they going to land here?

DENNIS. Not this group; they're based about ten miles north . . . (*Peers intently as sound of two more planes passes.*) . . . ten . . . eleven . . . I made it eleven.

GARNETT. So did I. What's squadron strength here? (*Sound fades completely.*)

DENNIS. Twelve . . . if it was a squadron.

KANE. My God! That isn't the remains of a group, is it?

DENNIS. Can't tell yet, sir.

KANE (*scared, nervous*). Find out! (DENNIS *reacts, checks himself, exits.*) Cliff, what will Washington think? (*Teletype up and off.*)

GARNETT. Sir, they'll think you're running a military bucket shop.

---

[12] The main heavy daylight bombers of the European theatre were the B-17 "Flying Fortresses" and the B-24s. The B-29 "Superfortresses" were assigned to the Pacific.

KANE. I was *going* to tell them but I didn't think Casey would be so impetuous. At least we are two-thirds done . . . (BROCKHURST *and* PRESCOTT *enter.*)

PRESCOTT. Sir, Brockie has some ideas I think you should hear. (*Muffled ring of phone in Ops room.*)

KANE. What's your reaction, Brockie? Tell us frankly.

BROCKHURST. You want it smooth or rough, R. G.?

KANE. Well, your honest reaction, Elmer.

BROCKHURST. Your neck's out a foot.

KANE. *My* neck . . . ?

BROCKHURST. Unless you can pass the buck to the Hemisphere Commander. You've got a hero to court martial . . . after record losses yesterday and probably again today. You've let security keep this so dark it stinks like Pearl Harbor . . . (*Faint sound of a single bomber high overhead.*) After all, the public makes these bombers and sends you these kids. It's got a right to know. (*Teletype up as* DENNIS *enters.*)

KANE. Go on, Elmer. I want General Dennis to hear your reaction. (*Teletype fades.*)

BROCKHURST. He knows it. I've warned him that the press and public . . .

DENNIS. Press and public be goddamned! Your magazine would crucify us for one headline.

BROCKHURST. When did we *ever* . . . ?

DENNIS. After Bremfurt. We needed a second attack to finish there. But by the time you got done with our losses and Washington got done with your insinuations, we were told it was politically impossible to attack there again. *Politically impossible!* Today boys were killed with cannon made at Bremfurt, since that attack.

BROCKHURST. Dennis, the Air Corps spent twenty years begging us to cry wolf at the public to get you planes. Now you've got 'em all you give us is phony official statements and alibis about security. We were asked to help Washington "prepare the country" for the news about Bremfurt. I'm sorry the plan backfired but it wasn't entirely our fault.

DENNIS. However it happened, the boys are dead.

KANE. Was that a group or a squadron, General?

DENNIS. Next to last group, sir. Some stragglers still coming. (*Overscene comes sound of more approaching bombers. All hurry to window.*) This must be Ted's group now. (*Sound builds to heavy volume through which closer sounds of individual planes with erratic, missing engines are audible.*) Eighteen . . . twenty-two . . . twenty-three . . . twenty-six . . . (*Group sound fades a little. Individual sound of one plane, engines missing wildly, rises in direct approach to building.*)

KANE. My God! They look ragged today . . .

PRESCOTT (*to* GARNETT). They look *much* better in tight formation, sir.

GARNETT. Here's one coming right at us!

PRESCOTT. Look, sir! He's got two feathered props![13]

BROCKHURST. And half his tail's shot off. . . . *Look out!* (*Sound of bomber rises.* BROCKHURST, PRESCOTT *and* GARNETT *throw themselves on floor as plane zooms over with terrific crescendo.* KANE *and* DENNIS *remain erect.* EVANS *enters.*)

EVANS. Colonel Martin's group returning, sir. (*Sound recedes. The three men on floor pick themselves up.*)

PRESCOTT (*to* GARNETT). Sorry, sir. They're not *supposed* to buzz the bases.

KANE. I'll have that pilot tried!

DENNIS. He isn't buzzing, sir. He's in trouble. (*All hurry back to window as sound rises again in circling approach.*) Good boy, he's lining up to land it!

GARNETT. Why don't they bail out . . . she's only salvage anyway!

DENNIS (*furiously*). Can't you see those red flares? He's got wounded aboard! (*Sound rises again as plane con-*

---

[13] A propeller that has been stopped because of engine trouble.

tinues circling approach, toward build-ing now.)

GARNETT. Urgent Virgin! Why, that's Captain Jenks's plane!

PRESCOTT (*to* KANE, *suggestively*). You see, sir . . . Captain Jenks's plane *is* in bad condition.

DENNIS. It's come from Germany in that condition. (*Peers tensely. Sound rises as plane roars past window, motors still missing wildly.*) *Jesus!* Look at that wheel . . . (*Shouts desperately through window.*) Pick her up, boy! *Pick her up!!!* (*Sound of plane abates, then comes the grinding, crashing sound of a nose-in. Silence. Then the whole building shakes to a thunderous concussion fol-lowed immediately by the sound of siren on meat wagons.* HALEY *enters from Ops room. Teletype up as siren fades.*)

HALEY. Left main gas tank. Total loss, sir.

DENNIS. Can you get the others down here?

HALEY. I've sent them to the other fields, sir. There's plenty of room on most of them now.

DENNIS. What was your count on this gang?

HALEY. Twenty-eight, sir. There may be stragglers.

DENNIS. Did you see Ted's plane?

HALEY. No, sir. It may be landing somewhere else, sir.

DENNIS. Aggregate tomorrow's ser-viceability as fast as possible. (HALEY *exits. Teletype off as door closes.*)

KANE (*horrified*). Tomorrow! This is worse than yesterday.

DENNIS. They got their target, sir.

EVANS (*blandly*). The photographers are waiting outside, General Kane. (KANE *looks nonplussed.*)

PRESCOTT (*takes over, severely*). What photographers?

EVANS. From Public Relations, sir.

PRESCOTT. Who ordered them and on what authority?

EVANS. I did, sir. All generals have their pictures taken everywhere they go. They say it helps the boys' morale.

KANE. Well, of course, if it helps

morale . . . We'll go along, General . . . probably drop in on some of your Group Interrogations.

DENNIS (*reaching for cap*). Very well, sir.

KANE. No, no. I wouldn't think of taking you away from here now.

GARNETT. Casey, I'll have more to say to you about this later.

KANE. Casey, you will not order to-morrow's mission until I get back. (DEN-NIS *salutes.* EVANS *holds door and then follows as* KANE, PRESCOTT *and* GARNETT *go out.* DENNIS *speaks off to Ops room, voice wracked with fear and nervous-ness.*)

DENNIS. Haley, haven't you *anything* on Ted yet?

HALEY'S VOICE (*off*). Nothing yet, sir.

DENNIS (*walks distractedly about room, gathers himself as* EVANS *enters*). You're going to wisecrack yourself right into the infantry.

EVANS. Sir, we never would have got rid of 'em without photographers.

DENNIS. They're coming back. Alert the cook.

EVANS. Sir, maybe if I was to speak to the cook . . .

DENNIS. None of that! We'll have to give 'em a good dinner. (EVANS *exits.* DENNIS *circles room distractedly again, then slumps wearily against desk as* COLONEL TED MARTIN *enters.* MARTIN *is vigorous, skeptical, in mid-thirties. Looks exhausted but exudes great vitality. Face is smoke-stained and clothes are con-spicuously drenched with dried blood.* DENNIS *can hardly speak to him at first.*) Ted . . . you all right?

MARTIN. Not a scratch.

DENNIS. What's that blood?

MARTIN. My radio man.

DENNIS. Bad?

MARTIN. Dead.

DENNIS. Oh. Anyone else?

MARTIN. Not in our plane. Got a drink?

DENNIS. Sure. Aren't they serving combat ration to the crews?

MARTIN. Yeah, but I wanted to see you quick. (DENNIS *extends bottle from desk.* MARTIN *drinks deep, continues drinking through scene.*) Ummm . . . that's better.

DENNIS. What happened?

MARTIN. Twenty-millimeter shell, right on the radio panel. Ummmm, I'm getting old. They should have had this war ten years ago.

DENNIS. How do you think I feel?

MARTIN (*contrite, covering*). Sorry, Grandpa.

DENNIS. Tell me about it. Was it rough all the way?

MARTIN. No. It was a milk run for thirty-four minutes after our fighters had to turn back. Then the whole damned Luftwaffe jumped us . . . (*Grins, drinks.*) Those boys must have a new directive, too. From then back to our fighters we shot our guns hot.

DENNIS. When did you get yours?

MARTIN. Just after I radioed you the strike signal. What about the rest?

DENNIS. Looks like forty-two with two down in the channel, so far.

MARTIN. I was afraid of that, from what I saw.

DENNIS. Did you catch fire?

MARTIN. Yes. We were having it hot and heavy so I stayed on the nose gun and Goldberg went back and put it out. He should get something for that, Casey. One of our waist gunners took one look at that fire and went right out through the bomb bay.

DENNIS. Goldberg can have whatever you recommend.

MARTIN. I'll think it over. Then after things quieted down we tried a tourniquet on the kid, but it was too late. (*Shakes head, drinks.*) Didn't I just see Old Percent and Cliff Garnett in a car?

DENNIS. Yeah. The joint's full of big wheels today.

MARTIN. Did Cliff bring any news from Helen?

DENNIS. Letters. There's no cable. I've been checking.

MARTIN. Casey, did they send Cliff over to stop Operation Stitch?

DENNIS. No. Kane hasn't even told Washington about it.

MARTIN. Then what's Cliff doing here?

DENNIS. Warning us that Washington is nervous.

MARTIN. They didn't have to send him for that.

DENNIS. The big wheels are having a Global Re-allocation meeting Tuesday.

MARTIN. Has Cliff re-allocated himself your job?

DENNIS. I think Cliff's got his eye on one of those B-29 commands in the Pacific. They start with two stars.

EVANS (*enters*). Glad to see you back, Colonel Martin. Sir, where do you want General Garnett's footlocker and bedroll?

MARTIN. General Garnett's footlocker and bedroll . . . so, he is moving in?

EVANS. They just arrived, sir.

DENNIS. Number One guest hut, Sergeant. (EVANS *exits.* MARTIN *rises, massages* DENNIS's *shoulder blades with palm.*)

MARTIN. Well, the handle doesn't stick out anyway, Casey.

DENNIS. Ted, I don't envy you Cliff for a brother-in-law, but he's an able staff officer.

MARTIN. Clifton has flown some of the hottest desks in Washington.

DENNIS. We needed those guys . . . to get planes for hoodlums like you and me.

MARTIN. Casey, no record after this war will be worth a damn without Command in it. Cliff knows this is still the best command in the Air Forces. Any brigadier alive would give his next star for your job.

DENNIS. When I finish Operation Stitch they can have it for Corporal's stripes. Thank God we're two-thirds done.

MARTIN. Casey, that's the hell of it: we aren't.

DENNIS. Ted! Are you sure you're all right?

MARTIN. Yeah. *I'm* all right.

DENNIS. You're tired. You did Posenleben yesterday and Schweinhafen today . . .

MARTIN (*forcing the words*). We didn't touch Schweinhafen today.

DENNIS (*strickenly*). What? You signalled me.

MARTIN. Mistake. Before I could correct it the radio man was dead. We plastered some goddamned place that looked exactly like it, forty miles from Schweinhafen.

DENNIS. Are you sure?

MARTIN. Positive.

DENNIS. How did it happen?

MARTIN. Sighting mistake. It was my fault, Casey. When we came on our bombing run there set a little town that looked more like Schweinhafen than Schweinhafen does; same confluence of rivers, railroad and highways, same cathedral a mile to the left, same phony road on the roof camouflage . . . you'll see it yourself in the strike pictures. I was still on the nose gun but I switched with Goldberg long enough for a look through the bombsight myself. We were both sure of it and Goldberg threw the whole load right down the chimney. The others salvoed into our smoke.

DENNIS. How do you know it wasn't Schweinhafen? Sure you weren't turned around?

MARTIN. I swung east to make sure. There was Schweinhafen with its maidenhead still showing. Did you tell Kane we'd hit it?

DENNIS. Yes. What do you think you did hit?

MARTIN. I don't know. Goldberg's checking maps and photos and target folders now. Whatever it was came apart like a powder mill. Did you get any sleep, Casey?

DENNIS (evasively). Of course. Tell me . . .

MARTIN. How much?

DENNIS. About . . . about three hours.

MARTIN. You promised me you'd get five.

DENNIS. I had work to do.

MARTIN. Casey, if you don't take better care of yourself someone else will be doing this work anyway.

DENNIS. Maybe this will give us both a rest.

MARTIN. Forty-four bombers for the wrong target. Why don't you castrate me?

DENNIS. Quit hurting. You've had this coming, Ted. It's averages.

MARTIN. What will this do to Operation Stitch?

DENNIS. Set us back one day. We'll do Schweinhafen again tomorrow and Fendelhorst Monday. I'm pretty sure the weather will hold.

MARTIN. Will Kane . . . with Global Re-allocation coming up Tuesday?

DENNIS. He'll have to.

MARTIN. Casey, he had cold feet before we started.

DENNIS. He's our Chief, Ted.

MARTIN. And a good soldier is loyal to his Chief; it says so in the book. But what kind of loyalty is that . . . to fallible men above him, half the time dopes and cowards? What about loyalty to common sense . . . and to the guys who have to do things that aren't in the book . . . like Stitch?

DENNIS. At least he didn't forbid it, Ted.

MARTIN. Did he authorize it? Did he endorse your report and go on record like a man? Not Kane. You're the goat on this one.

DENNIS. Other guys have been killed. If I get canned . . .

MARTIN. If you get canned, it's the end of honest bombardment here.

DENNIS. We've got to tell him, Ted.

MARTIN (with passion). You can't tell him, Casey! What about the guys we've already lost? If Kane quits now, they're wasted. We either finish now or we might as well take precision bombardment back to Arizona. It's us, or the Germans, this week, boy; and you're the only Commander in this hemispere with guts enough to see it through.

DENNIS. Which of us is going to tell Kane that?

MARTIN. I'll guarantee Kane won't be able to tell today's strike photos from Schweinhafen. Tomorrow we'll knock off Fendelhorst. Monday, when he orders his usual month-end milk run to the French Channel ports, we'll go back and clean up Schweinhafen.

HALEY (enters). Fifty-third Wing reports both of today's reconnaissance planes now two hours overdue, sir. (DENNIS nods. HALEY exits.)

MARTIN. Today it's reconnaissance planes! Six weeks from now it'll be whole divisions of bombers, unless we finish the job.

DENNIS. We'll finish, Ted. We'll make him finish!

MARTIN (*aghast*). Casey, you and I know what Operation Stitch means. How can you tell Kane?

DENNIS. He's our Chief, Ted. He's in command.

CURTAIN

ACT TWO

SCENE 1: *About twenty-two hundred that night. Stage is as before at rise. EVANS is discovered in a posture of slovenly relaxation in DENNIS's chair. HALEY enters to make a change on status board.*

HALEY. Where have you been for five hours?

EVANS. Sir, there were two of them women, both unhappy.

HALEY. Only two? That wouldn't have bothered me at your age.

EVANS. Well, sir, I hope it doesn't bother me, at your age. (HALEY *gapes, then both jump to attention as* DENNIS *enters.*)

DENNIS. Where's the twenty-two hundred weather map for tomorrow?

HALEY. They asked us to hold it, pending further developments, sir.

DENNIS. Bad developments?

HALEY. They didn't say so, sir; they promised them soon.

DENNIS. Bring it as fast as you get it. What about Status?

HALEY. I think I can promise four full groups for tomorrow, sir.

DENNIS. That's including last mission crews?

HALEY. Yes, sir. We're scraping bottom at that.

DENNIS (*nods, reluctantly. Sees* EVANS, *covers a grin*). How did you make out, Sergeant?

EVANS. Mission accomplished, sir.

HALEY (*with relish*). Not quite, sir. Mrs. Magruder telephoned again. Now she wants Sergeant Evans billeted in her house . . . for protection.

EVANS (*horrified*). What? . . . Look here, sir . . .

DENNIS (*amused, dead pan*). Sergeant, we've got to get ten more missions out of this navigator.

EVANS. Sir, my oath was to preserve, protect and defend the Constitution of the United States . . .

DENNIS. The United States needs navigators, Sergeant.

EVANS. Sir, I wouldn't do this to an Admiral.

DENNIS. We haven't got an Admiral handy.

HALEY (*reluctantly*). Sir, there's one more point . . . that navigator was killed on the mission today.

DENNIS (*wearily, heavily*). Oh. Have his effects examined, before they're sent home.

HALEY. It's being done, sir.

EVANS. Sir, in the circumstances, may I return to military duty?

DENNIS. Yes.

EVANS (*starts out, turns back, solicitously*). Excuse me, General, but . . . have you had your chow yet?

DENNIS. I'm still expecting General Kane for dinner.

EVANS. He'd be pretty stringy, sir. I'll get you something. (*Exits.*)

HALEY. General, the group commanders are sweating for tomorrow's order.

DENNIS. I can't send it till I find General Kane.

HALEY. They need all the time we can give 'em, sir. Most of our ground crews haven't had their clothes off for three days.

DENNIS. Neither has anyone else . . . except Sergeant Evans. (*Thinks, eyes watch.*) Cut a Field Order Tape using the data for Operation Stitch, Phase Two.

HALEY. Phase *Two* . . . sir?

DENNIS. That's what I said.

HALEY. Yes, sir. (*Starts for door, smouldering.*)

DENNIS (*checks him*). Ernie—! I'm sorry . . . I'm tired.

HALEY. Roger, sir. You ought to get some sleep, Casey. (*Exits.* DENNIS *slumps on desk, exhausted, face down. Almost sleeps. Then stirs quickly as* MARTIN *enters carrying pictures.*)

MARTIN. Sorry, Casey. Why don't you hit that sack for an hour?

DENNIS (*stirring*). You aren't pretty enough for a nurse.

MARTIN. Have you found Percent yet?

DENNIS. Not a trace . . . I've phoned everywhere.

MARTIN. He must be looking for another photographer.

DENNIS. Are these today's strikes?

MARTIN. All we got. There won't be any reconnaissance, thank God. (*They eye each other, then scrutinize pictures together.*)

DENNIS. This is the one from your plane?

MARTIN. Yeah. Just as we bombed. And this was from our last plane. Look what Goldberg did to it.

DENNIS. God! It's uncanny; these pictures would fool an expert.

MARTIN (*deliberately*). They'd better.

DENNIS. Why?

MARTIN. If you report this mistake to Kane before that Tuesday meeting, you're just giving your job to Cliff.

DENNIS. I'd like to think so.

MARTIN (*indicating cross*). And you're giving Goering those. Do you like to think that?

DENNIS. No.

MARTIN. These pictures will keep Kane happy for twenty-four hours. He doesn't know a strike photo from a gonorrhoea smear. Why do you have to tell him tonight?

DENNIS. Why did you tell me?

MARTIN. I could trust you.

DENNIS (*simply*). He trusts us. (*They're deadlocked as* KANE, GARNETT, PRESCOTT *and* BROCKHURST *enter.* MARTIN *conceals pictures.*)

KANE. Forgive us, Casey. We've had dinner.

GARNETT. Ted, old man! I want a good talk with you! How are you?

MARTIN. Still kicking.

KANE. Ted, I'm sorry you had such a rough day today, but when you're leading the Division, I never worry about the target.

DENNIS. Sir, my group commanders have got to have tomorrow's field order.

KANE. That's something we have to discuss, Casey. Cliff, will you explain?

GARNETT. Casey, you may think I've ratted on you but I felt our people had to know what's going on. I persuaded General Kane to let me telephone the Air Board in Washington.

DENNIS. What did they say?

GARNETT. Unfortunately, most of 'em are in Florida . . . at the proving grounds.

DENNIS. Testing a new typewriter?

KANE. Casey, I cannot tolerate this attitude. Our Public Relations Policy has put us where we are today.

DENNIS. It sure has.

BROCKHURST. Dennis, a free democracy cannot ignore public opinion.

DENNIS. Let's take that up when it's free again.

BROCKHURST. What?

DENNIS. The problem now is survival, Mr. Brockhurst. (EVANS *enters with sandwiches.*) They've eaten, Sergeant.

EVANS. Do they know you haven't, sir?

KANE. I'm sorry, Casey. Put them down, Sergeant. We're going soon.

EVANS. That's fine, sir. (*Unloads tray, dead pan.*)

GARNETT. But I did have a very constructive talk with Lester Blackmer. Lester was shocked, but I think I sold him on persuading the Board to let you finish Operation Stitch . . . after Tuesday.

DENNIS (*furiously—to* KANE). Sir! Did you let that little two-star stooge forbid us . . .

KANE. Certainly not! The Chief prides himself on never letting his personal staff interfere with his field commanders!

GARNETT. Casey, if you'll play ball now, everything will be fine, after Tuesday.

DENNIS. Including the weather . . . in Washington?

GARNETT. You'll get weather again.

DENNIS. When . . . after they've got

jets? I've waited five weeks for this weather. Twice we had one good day. This takes three in succession. If we ever got 'em again the big wheels would be after us for headline bombing. Submarine pens! Or covering some State Department fourflush in the Balkans.

GARNETT. Nobody can take the politics out of war. But I made Lester agree that since you *are* two thirds done . . . (LT. JAKE GOLDBERG *enters with strike photographs.* GOLDBERG *is tough of speech, gentle of manner. Like many good bombardiers he is essentially scholarly. Momentarily he is too preoccupied to notice the visitors.*)

GOLDBERG. I've found the damned thing . . . Oh . . . excuse me, sir. You said when I found it . . .

DENNIS. That's right, come in. General Kane, today's lead bombardier, Lieutenant Goldberg.

KANE. Lieutenant, a member of the big chief's advisory council in Washington just told me on the phone that the chief will be very proud of your mission today. (GOLDBERG *looks bored, but* MARTIN *is sweating bullets, tries to pull him out.*)

MARTIN. Sorry, sir. (*But* KANE *has grabbed pictures.*)

KANE. Look, Cliff! Look! Here's the highway coming in, here's the river . . . here's the factory . . .

GOLDBERG. You've got them upside down, sir.

DENNIS. General Kane, I'd like a minute alone with you, sir.

KANE. Of course, Casey. My God! Look at that destruction, Cliff! These will have to go to Washington by special plane.

PRESCOTT. Sir! I'd like to frame these, dramatically, on good white board, with a title . . . The Doom of Schweinhafen!

KANE. Yes! The very thing, Homer!

GOLDBERG. It isn't Schweinhafen, sir.

KANE. Not Schweinhafen? What are they?

GOLDBERG. The Nautilus Torpedo factory at Gritzenheim, sir.

GARNETT. Torpedo factory! General! This is very opportune! Half the United Chiefs are admirals! If we get these to that meeting . . .

KANE. I'll send my own plane! (*Claps* GOLDBERG *on the shoulder.*) You don't know what you've done for us, boy! Showing them that in the midst of the greatest air campaign in history, we still think enough of the larger picture to knock out a torpedo factory, too . . .

DENNIS. I'm sorry, sir. It wasn't *too.* It was *instead.*

KANE. Instead! You let me tell Washington you'd destroyed Schweinhafen!

DENNIS. It was a mistake. We hit this Nautilus place.

KANE. Whose mistake?

DENNIS. Mine, sir. The briefing . . .

MARTIN. The briefing was perfect. I led the division and I loused it up.

GOLDBERG. These gentlemen are covering for me, sir. I was well briefed and I was on the bombsight. I got mixed up in the fighting.

KANE (*is confused, but his chagrin has found a focal point*). Why did you *get* mixed up . . . were you scared?

GOLDBERG. Yes, sir. I'm always scared. But today . . .

KANE. Casey, what are you thinking of —entrusting a mission of this importance to a man who admits he's . . .

DENNIS (*furiously*). Sir, I should like to explain to you . . .

GOLDBERG (*to* DENNIS). It's all right, sir. General Kane doesn't understand.

KANE. Do *you* understand what I'd be justified in doing?

GOLDBERG. You ought to shoot me for wasting four hundred and forty guys this afternoon. I'd be grateful if you did. (*Turns and exits without saluting.*)

DENNIS. Sir! Lieutenant Goldberg is on the fourth mission of a *voluntary second tour of duty over German targets only.*

BROCKHURST. I think I'd take it easy on that one, R. G. (*Too late,* KANE *is stricken with contrition.*)

MARTIN (*pours it on him with repressed fury*). Sir, that boy isn't our Division Bombardier by accident. He knows there's a German order waiting for him by name and serial number. He knew it when he volunteered for a second tour. Today he hit what we both thought was the target . . . perfectly . . . I've just written him up for a cluster on his Silver Star.

KANE. Send the citation to me personally.

MARTIN (*sincerely*). Thank you, sir.

KANE. Ted, how many men in the Division know this mistake?

MARTIN. Most of 'em were too busy fighting to care where we were.

KANE. In any case you might have had a recall or change of target signal en route . . . *mightn't you?*

MARTIN. I might have.

KANE. Cliff, do you think it's fair, to the Service, to report this mistake immediately?

GARNETT. I'd have to think about that, sir.

KANE. We reported the strike in good faith. Now, with two more days on naval targets, under fighter cover, we can average down losses, set sortie and tonnage records, and put the Navy under obligation to us just before that meeting.

DENNIS. And that would be the end of Operation Stitch.

KANE. Casey, let's you and I take these pictures to your light table. (*They start out.* PRESCOTT *stops them.*)

PRESCOTT. Sir, would you ask Brockie here to help me with the wording of the picture captions? They must be right.

BROCKHURST. I'm not as interested in wordings as I was, R. G.

KANE. We need help, Brockie . . . just as you sometimes need help . . . with the censors. (BROCKHURST *starts, hesitates, then follows the beaming* PRESCOTT *out through ante-room door.* KANE *and* DENNIS *go out into Ops room.* EVANS *exits.*)

MARTIN. Well, Clifton, do you find travel broadening?

GARNETT. Ted, how long has Casey been like this?

MARTIN. Like what?

GARNETT. So strung up . . . so tense . . . ?

MARTIN. Were you sent here to replace him?

GARNETT. I don't think so.

MARTIN. What does Kane think?

GARNETT. He asked me, confidentially, if I'd been sent to replace him.

MARTIN. Jesus! You haven't done anything bad enough to be a *Major* General, have you?

GARNETT. Same old rebel, aren't you, Ted? Listen, old man, Helen is worried about your flying missions.

MARTIN. My insurance is paid up.

GARNETT. Good God, man! I don't mean that. But you know how she is.

MARTIN. I should. Look, Cliff; neither of us is going to change much. Let's drop it.

GARNETT. But you've got the kid to think of now.

MARTIN. That's the point. This isn't like the old barnstorming and testing. Nobody gets a kick out of this.

GARNETT. Exactly.

MARTIN. But if Goldberg can fly missions for my kid, so can I.

GARNETT. But, Ted, you can do so much more, with your experience.

MARTIN. What?

GARNETT. I've been fighting for bombardment in my own way. Now I think the United Chiefs are going to give me a B-29 command in the Pacific to make me prove what I've been saying.

MARTIN. Aren't those B-29s still a long way off?

GARNETT. No. They're coming faster than anyone realizes. Those jobs will be assigned very soon.

MARTIN. So . . . with a B-29 command you will get two stars?

GARNETT. And a lot of headaches.

MARTIN. Cliff, this is not conference fighting. Can you run an operational command?

GARNETT. Joe Lucas did—until he got killed. Casey's doing it. And I'm going to have something they never had.

MARTIN. What?

GARNETT. Brigadier General Ted Martin—for my Chief of Staff.

MARTIN. Me, a Chief of Staff . . . with all those papers?

GARNETT. Adjutants do that. But I need . . . the Air Corps needs . . . your operating experience out there. Incidentally, I'll be able to make you a brigadier immediately. (MARTIN *ponders deeply while* GARNETT *eyes him tensely.*)

MARTIN. Cliff, did Casey cook this up with you . . . to ground me gently . . . *after today?*

GARNETT. Good Lord, no! He doesn't even know this.

MARTIN. Then he isn't trying to get rid of me?

GARNETT. He'd rather cut his arm off. But he'll understand that the service needs you there . . . and it's your chance to make brigadier. Casey isn't selfish.

MARTIN. If you put it to him that way, he'd make me go.

GARNETT. We'll be a perfect team. I'll fight the Navy and you can fight the Japs . . .

MARTIN. And Helen makes Brigadier's wife. It's very neat, Cliff.

GARNETT. Damn it, Ted, that war's just as much for your kid as this one. Why should you throw yourself away here when by waiting . . . ?

MARTIN. The Germans aren't waiting.

GARNETT. Look, if you'd rather we both ask Casey . . .

MARTIN. No you don't. If you say a word to Casey before I think this over, the deal's off.

GARNETT. All right, but think with your head. Those B-29s can save an invasion against Japan. They can save bloody beach-heads and five years of guerrilla warfare. They've got to have the best we've got, Ted.

MARTIN. What else does Helen want?

GARNETT. She wants you to suggest a godfather for the kid. Naturally we've talked about it, but she wants your views.

MARTIN. Who does she want me to view?

GARNETT. Well, R. G. Kane is going to be a big name . . . (KANE *and* DENNIS *enter.*)

KANE. No man alive could tell these pictures from Schweinhafen . . . (*Pauses —eyes* GARNETT.) Cliff—do the United Chiefs actually study strike photos?

GARNETT (*shocked—evasive*). Well, sir, of course they're not trained photo interpreters themselves, but . . . (PRESCOTT *and* BROCKHURST *enter.* BROCKHURST *is now troubled by what he's seen and heard, but* PRESCOTT *wears the happy flush of creative endeavor.*)

PRESCOTT. Sir. I got some draughtsmen to make three-by-five mountings for the panels . . . before and after pictures . . . on good white board with glossy black lettering . . . the first title will be: "Doom of an Axis Torpedo Factory."

DENNIS. Jesus H. Christ!

KANE. General!

BROCKHURST (*respectfully*). General, I want to get this straight. Isn't a torpedo factory a worthwhile target?

DENNIS. The last one would be. The Germans wouldn't miss the first ten.

BROCKHURST. But you have to make a start, on anything worthwhile.

DENNIS. Fighting submarines by heavy bombardment is not worthwhile.

BROCKHURST. The Navy thinks it is. And most people agree.

DENNIS. Most people always think you can get something for nothing, Mr. Brockhurst. We're the only force available to strike the Germans in Germnay. To wipe out submarines by bombing would cost us every good weather day for a year.

BROCKHURST. Then why don't the United Chiefs straighten this mess out?

GARNETT. The United Chiefs are half admirals. We have to make some concessions to inter-service cooperation.

DENNIS. Did you get my memorandum to the Anointed Chiefs on that?

KANE. I didn't send it up, Casey. It was too provocative.

DENNIS. I offered the Navy a fair trade. I wrote them I'd bomb any naval target in Germany . . . the day after they took those battleships in and shelled the fighter plane factory at Brennen.

BROCKHURST. Can I use that?

KANE. God, no! Half the United Chiefs are admirals, Brockie.

BROCKHURST. Where did I get the idea this war was against the Axis?

DENNIS. General Kane, *may* I send tomorrow's field order?

KANE. Casey, I can't lose another forty planes over Schweinhafen the day after I've told them I've destroyed it.

DENNIS. Sir, you can release the Division to my discretion.

KANE. Whichever of us got hung, we'd still be sabotaging the Chief.

DENNIS. Would you rather sabotage bombardment, sir?

KANE. Casey, I've spent twenty years working for bombardment. The Chief's spent twenty-five. You kids don't know how we've fought.

MARTIN. No?

KANE. *No!* You're giving your youth. We've already given ours. I was twelve years a *Captain,* the Chief was fourteen. We took Billy Mitchell's side when it meant Siberia.[14] They sent us to a cavalry school. I was the second-best pilot in America . . . and they assigned me to keeping records of manure disposal. But we never gave up; we never quit trying. We wrote anything we could get printed, we got down on our knees to Hollywood charlatans for pictures, we did those publicity stunts . . . to educate the public and we kept our own fund for the widows. We tested without parachutes, we flew the mail through solid glue in obsolete training planes. The year Hermann Goering dominated the Munich conference our appropriation wasn't as big as the New York City Public Safety Budget . . . and we bought a lot of congressmen liquor, out of our own pockets, to get it.

BROCKHURST. General, why didn't you tell this story?

KANE. And spell it all out for the Germans? Not that they didn't know and count on it . . . but you don't tell stories in uniform. We were promised fifty thousand planes . . . and our boys were never going to fight in foreign wars . . . so the country went back to sleep and we were called back from stables and rifle ranges to make a modern air force . . . out of promises . . . and what was left over after they gave our planes and instructors to every God-damned ambassador in Washington . . .

BROCKHURST. We were told that was to get experience . . .

KANE. There wasn't any experience of daylight precision bombardment. Both the Germans and British had tried it and said it couldn't be done. The Chief said it could . . . But we'd just begun to get the tools to get started when we were in it ourselves . . . with a double war . . . and a fifty-thousand plane paper air force that didn't add up to fifty serviceable bombers . . . (*Turns to* DENNIS *defensively.*) Casey, if we'd had in Nineteen Forty-one the planes you've lost this week we would have had a Munich with the Japs that would have made Hitler's Munich look like International Rotary!

DENNIS. Sir, we've all fought, all our lives, to get an air force. Now we've got to protect our beginnings.

KANE. From what?

DENNIS (*indicating cross*). Those.

KANE. Those things? They're just our acknowledged enemies. They fight us in the open. Do you remember the fight to get our first experimental Fortress? Do you realize how much the Navy wants our planes for sub-patrol . . . and to protect the repairing of those battleships that air power couldn't hurt? Do you know how much the Army wants our pilots for company commanders? Don't you know the British want us to switch to night area bombardment? Do you know there's a plan to fly infantry supplies into China . . . *with bombers?* Do you know what it means that the United Chiefs are half admirals and the Con-

---

[14] General William Mitchell (1879–1936) was long a vigorous proponent of air power, but failed to convince the authorities, even after successfully sinking a battleship from the air. He was court-martialed and convicted in 1925 of attacking his superiors for their failure to agree with him. He was completely vindicated in later years, and posthumously awarded the Congressional Medal of Honor in 1946. The verdict, however, was never changed.

solidated Chiefs half British? Don't you realize the fight it's taken for Cliff and the others to get us any planes at all?

GARNETT. He's right, Casey. Washington's at the crossroads on us.

KANE. On Tuesday every one of those factions will be at that meeting with its own pet plan for winning the war by naval blockade, or attrition by defensive, or a good sound saber charge. And you want us to send the Chief in there with three days of prohibitive losses hanging over our theory . . .

DENNIS. Damn it, sir! It's not a theory. Ted demolished Posenleben . . .

KANE. And with time and planes and support we can do the same to every factory in Europe. But the decision is at stake now. It isn't just a few losses this week, or even a lot in six months. The Germans are going to kill more of our people, of course. But they won't be any deader than all the ones who've been killed through the last thirty years to get us air power. You can worry about Germany . . . and you should. But I'm fighting the ground forces and the Navy and the Congress and the White House and the people and the press and our allies. You think I don't know the boys call me Old Percent? You think I've enjoyed spreading this mug of mine around the press like a pregnant heiress? You think I don't know what they could do to me for the statistics I've juggled, the strike photos I've doctored, the reports I've gilded, or suppressed. I know . . . and I'd do it all again! I've spent twenty years watching my friends killed and broken and disgraced and discarded for one single idea . . . to get our God-damned country air power! (Breaks off, muses, resumes heavily.) Ted, how did the Germans fight today?

MARTIN. Rough, sir.

KANE. No sign the second day in succession hurts them too?

MARTIN. None we could see, sir.

KANE. What do you think they'll be able to do tomorrow?

MARTIN. They'll fight, sir. They don't stand short on guts over there.

DENNIS. Today's Intelligence Summary's done, sir.

KANE. Is your intelligence officer any good?

DENNIS. He's what we have. He's honest and has sense.

KANE. What is he, a synthetic?

DENNIS. Retread, sir. Artilleryman last time, insurance broker since.

KANE. Probably a good husband and father, too. Well, get him.

DENNIS (into phone). Ask Major Lansing to step in at once. (Goes to door, greets him. MAJOR DESMOND LANSING enters. He is gray-haired, self-possessed, wears good last War ribbons.)

LANSING. Major Lansing reporting as ordered, sir.

DENNIS. General Kane, my Assistant Chief of Staff for Intelligence, Major Lansing.

KANE. What will the Germans do tomorrow, Major?

LANSING. That depends upon where we go, sir.

KANE. If we go back to Schweinhafen?

LANSING. They'll order maximum effort as soon as we cross the tenth Meridian East, sir. (Indicates tenth Meridian East on map.)

KANE. How many will they have serviceable?

LANSING. Enough for a hard fight, sir.

KANE. But we've claimed over a hundred and eighty in the last two days.

LANSING. I'm aware of that, sir.

KANE. You don't believe our claims?

LANSING. No, sir.

KANE. Then why do you report them?

LANSING. Orders from your headquarters, sir.

KANE. Oh. Well, you understand that's necessary for the boys' morale. What do you think of Operation Stitch?

LANSING. It's imperative, sir. We're losing forty-odd bombers to conventional fighters for every worth-while mission now. If they get a hundred jets we'll lose a hundred and forty at a time.

KANE. Do you think the Germans know what we're up to?

LANSING. There's no information on that, sir.

KANE. What would you guess?

LANSING. That they don't, sir.

KANE. Why?

LANSING. The Germans don't like to give their superiors bad news, sir.

BROCKHURST. You shock me, Major.

KANE. How can they help reporting what's happened?

LANSING. Their information has to go up through channels, too, sir.

GARNETT. Is that a sarcasm, Major?

LANSING. It's a fact, sir. *Deutschlandsender* just announced they'd destroyed a hundred and sixty of our bombers today, sir.

BROCKHURST. Doubtless for the German boys' morale.

KANE. Major, do you mean to say that if the Germans guessed the truth about Operation Stitch they wouldn't face it among themselves?

LANSING. That would depend on who did the guessing and who did the facing, sir.

KANE. You evidently don't think much of *their* High Command.

LANSING. That's a personal opinion, sir.

GARNETT. I'd like to know how you form it, Major.

LANSING. My observation, sir, is that most soldiers and particularly air men are afflicted with Narcissism. They don't think about their enemies, they think about themselves because their mechanical problems take up all their time. The consequence is that when they've procured their planes and trained their people and learned their tactics, they have to ask amateurs, like me, what to do with them. When the results are bad they fire the amateurs and make the Commanders Field Marshals.

GARNETT (*indignantly*). We don't have Field Marshals!

LANSING (*evenly*). I happened to be thinking of Goering, sir. The battles of Britain and Malta could have been decisive. But Goering lost his nerve over the early losses and diffused his effort. By the time the truth came out the German Air Force had lost not only its offensive power but its freedom of operation. They will be judging us by their own experience.

KANE. What do you mean by that?

LANSING. The Germans never settled on one decisive target system and paid the price for it. They know that every time we've had bad losses we've switched to easy targets for a while.

KANE. If we hit Schweinhafen tomorrow, will the Germans tumble?

LANSING. You're still asking me to guess, sir. I should guess that after two jet factories in quick succession they would face the truth.

KANE. And concentrate every fighter they have in defense of Fendelhorst on Monday?

LANSING. We'd have to expect it, sir.

KANE. And even so, you think it's worth doing?

LANSING. If you wish to continue precision bombardment, sir.

KANE. Thank you, Major. (LANSING *salutes and exits.*)

GARNETT. That's a very independent Major you keep, Casey.

KANE. Of course, he's really only a civilian.

HALEY (*enters. Addresses* DENNIS). There's a weather report you should hear at once, sir. (MAJOR BELDING DAVIS, *Division Weather Officer, enters.* HALEY *exits.*)

DENNIS. Come in, Major. General Kane, my Division Weather Officer, Major Davis. Go right ahead, Davis. What is it?

DAVIS. Special Flash from Iceland, sir. Just preliminary, but a very interesting cold mass is forming eccentrically . . .

DENNIS. Never mind the genealogy; what will it do?

DAVIS. Blanket the Continent, if it matures as we expect, sir.

DENNIS. When?

DAVIS. On present indications, late Monday afternoon, sir.

DENNIS. When will it close my bases here?

DAVIS. Best estimate now is about fifteen hundred Monday, sir.

DENNIS. I always said God must love Willi Messerschmidt!

DAVIS. We'll have more for the midnight weather map, sir.

DENNIS. Bring it as you get it. (DAVIS *exits.* DENNIS *turns to* KANE.) There goes our season's weather, sir. We'll make it these next two days or bite our nails off to the elbow.

GARNETT. Casey, we can't afford two more days of heavy losses now . . . just for a theory.

DENNIS. It's not a theory! Doesn't Washington understand our losses? Do you think the Germans would fight like this if they weren't scared of our bombardment?

KANE. Homer, make a note of that for Washington. (PRESCOTT *whips out notebook, writes.*)

DENNIS. Cliff, we're doing what no one in this war has been able to do yet. We're making the German Air Force fight, on our *initiative* . . . over Germany, where it doesn't dare to refuse combat in order to rest and rebuild. And we're tearing it up . . . *over Germany!* The German Air Force has been the balance of power in this world, ever since Munich. It took the German army everywhere they've been. It beat the Polish Air Force in three days and the Norwegian in three hours . . . it forced the Maginot Line and beat the French in three weeks . . .

KANE. Homer, get this.

DENNIS. The Royal Air Force did win a brilliant battle from it, over England. It was a defensive battle, the kind we're making *Germany* fight now. Even after that the German Air Force was good enough to knock off Yugoslavia and Greece for practice, to capture Crete and dominate the Mediterranean, to chase the Russians back to Moscow and Stalingrad, to blockade the North Cape and very nearly cut the Atlantic lifeline to England. They would have done it if their High Command had backed them up with a few more planes. Now we've made them switch from bomber production to manufacturing jet fighters. We've made them pull whole Groups off the Russians and away from Rommel and put them over *there* across the Channel, *facing us.* Our own people in the Mediterranean are advancing under aerial supremacy . . .

KANE. Homer, get every word of this . . .

DENNIS. Well, get this too, Homer! The Germans know this better than we do. But they're retreating from their costliest conquests and they've broken the balance of their whole air force for just one thing. They know that Fighters, Hurricanes, and Spits saved England from either decisive bombardment or invasion. They're developing these jets to make Europe as impregnable as the British made England. And they're going to do it, just as surely as we sit here with our fingers in our asses and let them!

PRESCOTT. Do you want that in, too, sir?

KANE. Not exactly that. Don't take any more. Casey, I agree with you entirely, but we've got to wait.

DENNIS. Sirs, wars are lost by waiting. The Allies waited at Munich. The French and British waited, behind the Maginot Line. The Germans waited, to invade England. The Russians waited, until they had to fight without an Allied Army in the field. We waited, for a little more strength, to coerce Japan. Now we're forcing the fighting . . . But if we wait for the cycle to swing again, we'll be waiting for the Germans to put a roof on the continent, to neutralize the Russians and then to confront our armies on D-Day at the Channel with an air force that's already whipped us. I'm not trying to tell you that Operation Stitch will win the war. But no battle, anywhere in this war, has been won without aerial supremacy. Operation Stitch is the price of that.

KANE. Will you gentlemen wait in the ante-room? (*Others go out.* GARNETT *hesitates.*)

GARNETT. Did you mean me, too, sir?

KANE. I should like to be alone with General Dennis. (GARNETT *exits, stiffly.*) Casey, you must think me incapable of decision.

DENNIS. Sir, are there factors—on your level—that I don't know?

KANE. Nothing military.

DENNIS. Well, then, sir . . .

KANE. But if Washington screams for blood—I'd have to throw you to the wolves.

DENNIS. I understand that, sir.

KANE. If I have to jettison you, we lose our best Brigadier.

DENNIS. Thank you, sir. But we're all expendable.

KANE. If they have to jettison me, we probably lose bombardment.

DENNIS. Sir, don't you think—at the top—they expect us to fight?

KANE. I hope so, Casey, because . . . I'm releasing the Division to your discretion, with immediate effect.

DENNIS. Thank you, sir.

KANE. You're fully aware of—what may happen?

DENNIS. Perfectly, sir.

KANE. Well, I hope it doesn't. Good luck, my boy. (*Turns to door.*)

EVANS (*enters with paper*). Top Secret relay from Washington for General Kane, sir.

KANE (*takes it, reads it, crumbles visibly. Hands it to* DENNIS). My God! Read it.

DENNIS (*reading*). "Impossible contact Air Board yet. Urgently implore low losses during critical three days next. Representatives Malcolm and Stone of House Military Affairs Committee arriving England this night. Imperative their impressions our situation favorable at any price." (*Stops reading, eyes* KANE, *pretends to be thinking aloud.*) This is an opportune time to be courtmartialling a hero, isn't it, sir?

KANE. My God! Jenks is from Malcolm's State!

DENNIS. So he is.

KANE. We'll have to fix this at once . . . medically. (*Indicates phone.*)

DENNIS (*speaks into it*). Have Major Dayhuff report here immediately. (*Then to* KANE.) Sir, Jenks is bright. He'll understand his nuisance value.

KANE. We'll make it worth his while to play ball with us.

DENNIS. Are you sure we can, sir?

KANE. Bombardment's at stake. If necessary we can have Jenks declared insane from combat fatigue.

DENNIS. That's pretty strong, General.

KANE. In any case I'll have to take back that discretion I've just given you. Tomorrow you will bomb the safest naval target you can find . . . to keep these Congressmen happy.

DENNIS. Sir! This is impossible!

KANE. Nothing's impossible . . . for the service, Casey. (MAJOR RUFUS DAYHUFF, *a poised graying medical reserve officer, enters saluting smartly.*)

DAYHUFF. Major Dayhuff reporting as ordered, sir.

DENNIS. General Kane, my Division Medical Officer, Major Dayhuff.

KANE. Good evening, Major. We have a very serious problem.

DENNIS. Doctor, please tell General Kane exactly what you told me about Captain Jenks.

DAYHUFF. I've been through the case myself, sir. I've talked to the Flight Surgeon in Captain Jenks' group and I've talked to Captain Jenks himself.

KANE. What is your opinion, Doctor?

DAYHUFF. There is no medical excuse for Captain Jenks' conduct, sir. He acknowledges this and expects no medical exoneration.

KANE. Mightn't this defiance, in itself, indicate a neurosis or a psychiatric condition . . . ?

DAYHUFF. Doctors can be wrong, sir. In my opinion Jenks is normal.

KANE. Have you entered this in his record?

DAYHUFF. Not yet, sir. But I shall.

KANE. Do you think this is simple cowardice, Major?

DAYHUFF. No, sir. Cowards welcome medical excuses.

KANE. Have you no idea what's wrong with him?

DAYHUFF. A personal opinion, sir. But it's not a medical matter.

KANE. Tell me your opinion.

DAYHUFF. This boy has been corrupted by our press and publicity policy, sir. Jenks has not done anything exceptional enough for all that attention he got. He knew it and he knew that you knew it. He knew the Air Corps was not rewarding him; it was exploiting him. Most men would have laughed it off; many have. But this boy got the idea that he was too valuable to continue combat; too valuable to himself and too valuable to you.

KANE. And your medical opinion is that he's sane and responsible?

DAYHUFF. Yes, sir.

KANE. Thank you, Major (DAYHUFF *exits.*) Ummm . . . we've got to think of something, Casey.

DENNIS (*thoughtfully*). Sir, any simple lie will clear Jenks. But we need something that won't look too raw to the other crews; we don't want a mutiny.

KANE. My God, no!

DENNIS. Now, sir, Jenks is from Malcolm's State. Suppose he'd had secret orders from his Commanding General—that is, me—to hold himself in readiness for special escort duty to these distinguished visitors . . . *then* he would have been justified . . .

KANE. Why, Casey . . . *Casey!* That's perfect . . . *perfect,* my boy. When I picked you for this job a lot of people thought you were just another overage test pilot! (*Starts for door.*) I'll never forget this, my boy . . . never!

DENNIS. I'll fix it, sir . . . *as soon as I've ordered Schweinhafen for tomorrow.*

KANE (*turns, faces him, aghast*). This is blackmail.

DENNIS. Bombardment's at stake, General.

KANE. Ingenious, Casey . . . but I order you to release Captain Jenks to me.

DENNIS. Very well, sir. But I shall file formal charges against him unless you agree to let me finish Operation Stitch immediately.

KANE. Casey, this is preposterous . . . if you'll just consider . . .

DENNIS. I have considered, sir.

KANE. You realize that I might not be able to . . . protect you?

DENNIS. I do, sir.

KANE. Well, I was going to release the Division to your discretion anyway . . . if you insist on taking the personal risk . . .

DENNIS. Thank you, sir. (*Speaks into phone.*) Guardhouse . . . Dennis speaking, Lieutenant. You will release Captain Jenks to the personal custody of General Kane.

KANE. In the circumstances, Casey, I'll have to send Washington a correction on today's strike.

DENNIS. I understand that, sir.

KANE. Well, don't bother to come to the gate. (*Exits.*)

DENNIS (*slumps from strain, grabs phone, speaks into it*). Major Davis . . . what about that Iceland weather . . . nothing further, eh? Ask Colonel Haley to step in. (*Stares at map until* HALEY *enters.*) Haley, put Operation Stitch, Phase Two, Schweinhafen, on the printer at once for all Groups for tomorrow. Bomb and fuel loading as before. Routes and timings to follow as soon as we work 'em out.

HALEY. Phase *Two*, sir? You're certain, sir?

DENNIS. Get it clicking. I'll sign the order in a minute. (HALEY *exits.* MARTIN *enters, worried.*)

MARTIN. What the hell have you done now? Percent went out of here burning like a fuse.

DENNIS. Malcolm of Home Military Affairs arrives here tomorrow. Jenks is from Malcolm's State. So I agreed not to courtmartial Jenks for Kane's promise to let us finish Stitch.

MARTIN. Casey, you know Kane will never keep a tough promise.

DENNIS. I can still remember when Kane had guts.

MARTIN. You know you're cutting your own throat, don't you?

DENNIS. Maybe. We figured Stitch would cost some casualties, Ted.

MARTIN. Yeah . . . we did. I'll bet Kane signals me a recall in the air tomorrow.

DENNIS. Not you; I've alerted Claude Minter to lead them tomorrow.

MARTIN. Why?

DENNIS. He's fresh, he's rested, he's coming along fine. Claude's good . . . he's damned good.

MARTIN. I know he's good. He ought to do Fendelhorst Monday.

DENNIS. You've done two of these. I'm tired of sweating you out.

MARTIN. Are you sure that's the only reason, Casey?

DENNIS. Yes.

MARTIN. You're sure the boys wouldn't have a better chance with someone else up front?

DENNIS. Ted, it's a break for the boys every time you lead them . . . but it's no fun to sit here and think about it.

MARTIN. Well, you get paid the first of every month . . . and so do I.

DENNIS. Now listen, Ted . . .

MARTIN. Schweinhafen's *mine*, Casey.

DENNIS (*hesitates, picks up phone, speaks into it, heavily*). Haley, notify Claude Minter he's on immediate leave, for twenty-four hours. (*Hangs up, eyes* MARTIN.) Now you go get some sleep.

MARTIN. Keep your temper with those Congressmen tomorrow, will you? I don't want to come back here and find you with a Legion of Merit and a ticket home.

DENNIS. Don't worry. I can still do the office chores around here.

MARTIN. (*starts for ante-room door, stops*). Casey, Helen wants me to pick a godfather for the kid. Will you take it?

DENNIS. What are you trying to do . . . queer him for life?

MARTIN. I'm serious.

DENNIS. Well, sure.

MARTIN. And I want you to promise me something.

DENNIS. What?

MARTIN. If he ever wants to join the army, you'll take a club and beat his brains right out through his tail.

CURTAIN

SCENE 2: *About twelve hundred the next day. Curtain rises on the end of a formal presentation for the visiting Con-* gressmen. DENNIS's *office has been made into a miniature theater, with* CONGRESSMEN MALCOLM *and* STONE, PRESCOTT, BROCKHURST, *and* GARNETT *for audience. They face* KANE, *who has just finished lecturing them from graph and symbol exhibits which* EVANS *has changed for him. Among these, "Doom Of An Axis Torpedo Factory" is conspicuous.* KANE *is smiling warmly,* DENNIS *staring stonily at* MALCOLM, *who has claimed the floor.*

MALCOLM. Gennel Kane, it's mighty inspirin' foh representatives of the American people, like me an' Misteh Stone, heah, to come oveh onto foreign soil an' fin' the American Flag flyin' an' undeh it a Fiel' Commandeh who is woythy of ouah great nation an' the boys he comman's. When we get back to ouah own post of duty in the Congress in Washin'ton, I promise you that ouah great leadehs theah, mos' of whom I am fohtunate enough to count among mah closes' frien's, are goin' to hear fum mah own lips how fohtunate this country is in some of its commandehs.

KANE (*straightfaced*). Mr. Malcolm, and Mr. Stone, you must make the country understand that the credit for what we do here belongs to the boys. Command is merely a trusteeship of our sacred blood. Often at night I think on the parable of the talents. It must have been a terrible ordeal for those men who were trying to serve their master as best they could, with what they were given. But I think the greater lesson is in the humility we learn about the wisdom of the Master who knew what he was doing when he tested his subordinates. Sometimes I have to pray that our shortages here are only a test through which a Greater Wisdom is measuring our worthiness for a greater service to our people.

STONE (*has borne this bravely, as befits a veteran of the House, but he understands it*). You mean you want more planes, General?

KANE (*with force*). Mr. Stone, if the nation wants aerial supremacy we must have them.

STONE (*honestly troubled*). The nation wants aerial supremacy everywhere, General. They all tell us the same thing . . . you people over here, the people in the Pacific, the Navy . . . you're getting most of our available replacements now. And, frankly, we're appalled at the way you're eating up our boys and bombers here. What did you tell us your loss rate is?

KANE (*indicating a discarded chart*). Overall rate of four point eight nine since the beginning of our operations here, sir.

MALCOLM. What are losses this week, Gennel?

KANE. I'll have to tell you that to-morrow, Mr. Malcolm, when I've heard from the other Divisions . . . (*Trying to break it off.*) And now, gentlemen, if you'd like to inspect the station . . .

MALCOLM. Gennel Kane, the country is pretty upset about the way youah Command oveh heah is losin' planes an' crews. I and Misteh Stone have come oveh on puhpose to look into it. Now, suh, what were losses in this Division foh this week?

KANE. Have you the figures at hand, General?

DENNIS (*rising*). Ninety-six, sir.

MALCOLM. Ninety-six . . . out of what ove'all stren'th in youah Division?

DENNIS. It varies with the replacement flow; in average it runs between one-eighty and two hundred.

MALCOLM. So . . . you've lost half youah stren'th in a week?

DENNIS. Eighty-four were lost on two particularly difficult missions.

MALCOLM (*silkily*). Well . . . ! That means neah about twenty-five percent per mission in this Division as against Gennel Kane's overall average of less than five?

KANE. When these are figured into the general average, Mr. Malcolm . . .

MALCOLM. I undehstan' the gennel average, suh! Perhaps Gennel Dennis will explain the discrepancy between his Division an' that.

DENNIS. My Division has the only ex-

tension tanks for specially distant targets. Both of these operations were beyond the gasoline range of friendly fighter cover.

MALCOLM. An' the boys lost were deliberately sent beyon' that range?

DENNIS. Yes.

MALCOLM. May I ask who ohdehed these operations?

DENNIS. I did.

MALCOLM. On youah own authority?

DENNIS. Yes.

KANE. General Dennis was within his technical authority.

MALCOLM (*is no longer the cheerful clown. He talks and acts the experienced prosecutor closing for the kill*). I undehstan' the technicalities, Gennel Kane. No one expec's a man of youah responsibilities to ohdeh every attack foh every Division every night. But the fac's appeah to be that the minute youah back was toined, Gennel Dennis took it on his own self to ohdeh these disastrous attacks.

DENNIS. They were not disastrous. Posenleben was the best bombing of the war to date. You saw the pictures. As for yesterday . . .

KANE (*hastily*). The Navy has been begging us to destroy the Nautilus Torpedo Plant, gentlemen. You saw yourselves Major Prescott's presentation on "The Doom Of An Axis Torpedo Factory." That attack was a great piece of inter-service cooperation and a very bright spot in General Dennis's record.

MALCOLM. Gennel, I honoh youah loyalty to youah subohdinate, but it seems to me that ouah boys are payin' a pretty bloody price foh Gennel Dennis's recohd.

DENNIS. They're paying a bloody price for the country's record.

MALCOLM. Oh . . . ! So the *country's* responsible foh youah sendin' 'em beyon' frien'ly fighteh coveh?

DENNIS. Yes.

MALCOLM. May I ask how?

DENNIS. How did you vote on the fortification of Guam?

MALCOLM. What?

DENNIS. How did you vote on the fortification of Guam?

STONE (*chuckling*). By God! He's got you, Arthur.

MALCOLM. We'll see who's got who! Gennel Dennis, I want to know why you, puhsonally, are the only single one oveh heah that sen's his Division beyon' fighte' coveh, every time Gennel Kane got his back turned! Every otheh Division consis'en'ly increases sohties an' tonnages of bombs dropped every month. The only solitary thing you increase is losses!

DENNIS. Sorties and tonnages are meaningless except on the right targets, Mr. Malcolm. If you want statistics, the training commands in America fly more sorties than we do . . . except the ones in your State.

MALCOLM. What you sayin' about mah State?

DENNIS. That every airfield in it is under a foot of water half the year and twelve thousand feet of fog for nine months. But when we asked permission to move to where we could operate efficiently the recommendation was blocked by your committee.

STONE. General Kane, what are you attacking today?

KANE. General Dennis . . . (DENNIS *strips map curtain, revealing three tapes leading to Cherbourg, Emden and Schweinhafen. Others throng to map.*)

DENNIS. It's a three-pronged operation, gentlemen. One of our Divisions attacks the Cherbourg sub-pens. Another attacks a sub repair yard at Emden. My Division, here in the center, is attacking the Focke-Schmidt aircraft factory at Schweinhafen.

MALCOLM. Didn't I hear this Division attacked Schweinhafen yestehday?

KANE. The target was cloud-covered, Mr. Malcolm, so Colonel Martin very wisely decided to bomb the torpedo factory, which he could plainly see, instead . . .

PRESCOTT. It was a wonderful piece of air generalship. Colonel Martin is leading the Division again today.

MALCOLM. Is youah Division undeh fighteh coveh today, Gennel?

DENNIS (*at map*). To here. Another relay will pick them up here, coming out.

MALCOLM. But they'll be on theah own fum heah to heah an' back?

DENNIS. Yes.

MALCOLM. An' you sent them again on youah own authority?

DENNIS. Yes.

BROCKHURST. Gentlemen, I'm fed up. I can tell you a hatful about the problems of command!

KANE (*quickly*). Brockie, we all appreciate your interest, but . . .

GARNETT. Mr. Malcolm and Mr. Stone could be severely criticized in Washington for accepting anything but official military information. (MALCOLM *and* STONE *nod, hooked.* BROCKHURST *subsides, helpless.*)

KANE. General Dennis has worked out a very ingenious plan of attack, gentlemen. You see, these other Divisions will draw some of the German fighter groups out to the wings and so reduce concentration against Colonel Martin here in the center.

STONE. Then these other two attacks are timed to prevent concentration against Colonel Martin?

KANE. Yes.

STONE. Do you expect them to succeed, General Dennis?

DENNIS. Not entirely. They may help Colonel Martin a little.

STONE. When do these diversionary attacks bomb their targets?

DENNIS (*eyeing watch*). Very soon now.

STONE. And when does Colonel Martin bomb Schweinhafen?

DENNIS. In about fourteen minutes.

STONE. Then unless these diversions *do* succeed, he's probably fighting right now.

DENNIS. Probably. (*Awed silence.* MALCOLM *cannot stand the tension.*)

MALCOLM. Gennel Kane, I'm wahnin' you; if we eveh have anotheh of these muhderous attacks . . .

DENNIS. Our operations are determined by military directive.

HALEY (*enters*). Plotting room reports the other Divisions are just about to bomb their targets, General.

KANE. Does the radar screen show any reaction from German fighters, Colonel?

HALEY. None sighted yet, sir. (HALEY *exits.*)

MALCOLM. Then Cunnel Mahtin's got to run the gauntlet of the whole German fighter force!

KANE. If you'll come with me, gentlemen . . .

PRESCOTT. This way, gentlemen . . .

KANE. We'll have a look at that screen ourselves, down in the radar and signals room. (*Others start out.* KANE *continues pointedly.*) General Dennis will wish to remain in his office. (*As others go out,* KANE *turns frantically back to* DENNIS.) Casey, for Christ's sake be careful! Malcolm's powerful!

DENNIS. Sir, are you going to let Malcolm break our bargain?

KANE. I'll keep it if I can.

DENNIS. What we're going to do with that Jenks boy would strain a pretty tough stomach.

KANE. It's necessary, Casey, for the service.

DENNIS. I only agreed in exchange for your promise to let me finish Operation Stitch tomorrow, in spite of Malcolm.

KANE. By tomorrow Malcolm could have us both in the Quartermaster Corps in Greenland! Is everything arranged as we agreed?

DENNIS. Everything, sir.

KANE. And a good lunch?

DENNIS. Yes, sir.

KANE. And plenty to drink?

DENNIS. Why . . . I hadn't thought of that.

KANE. With *Congressmen* here . . . ? Start thinking in double triples! (KANE *exits.*)

DENNIS (*bursts out, oblivious of* EVANS). Booze! It's a wonder he doesn't want opium and slave girls.

EVANS. Put 'em on field conditions, sir . . . benzedrine and WACS.

DENNIS. Sergeant, is there plenty in the officers' bar?

EVANS. Not a drop, sir. End of the month. Quota's gone.

DENNIS. How about the medical officer?

EVANS. He's been dry ever since those Cabinet members were here, sir.

DENNIS. God damn democracy!

EVANS. Sir, there are the combat crews' ration stocks.

DENNIS. They're running low.

EVANS. There's enough for about six missions left, sir.

DENNIS. What's the dope on replacements?

EVANS. Quartermaster's doubtful, sir. Congress says we're depraving our boys with drink . . . and the stuff's getting short in Washington.

DENNIS. These statesmen can go dry for one day. Maybe it will kill them.

EVANS. Sir, General Kane ordered you . . .

DENNIS. I can't sweat whiskey, can I?

EVANS. Sir, just a few bottles from combat ration stocks . . .

DENNIS. Not a drop! Now get the hell out of here . . .

EVANS. I knew there was a catch to this job.

DENNIS. Sergeant, I told you . . . (DENNIS *watches, speechless, while* EVANS *unlocks Division flag locker and produces two bottles of excellent bourbon.*) Where did you get that?

EVANS. Present from an admirer, sir . . . (*Extends a bottle symbolically.*) It still is, sir.

DENNIS (*touched, pulling out wallet*). Nonsense! You could get a fortune for this.

EVANS. No, sir! I'd like just one thing, sir . . . to shake your hand . . . (*Extends hand hesitantly.* DENNIS *shakes warmly but with embarrassment.*)

DENNIS. What's this for?

EVANS. Telling that servant of the people what a son of a bitch he is. I didn't think you had it in you, sir.

DENNIS. Oh . . . well . . . you'd better get some glasses and water . . .

(*Then, checking* EVANS *at door.*) Sergeant . . . I appreciate this.

EVANS. Well, sir. I'd hate breaking in a new General. (EVANS *exits.*)

DENNIS (*calls off*). Haley! (HALEY *enters.*) Are they getting any fighting on those diversions?

HALEY. Not a blip, sir. General Kane is pretty scared.

DENNIS. Well, he isn't getting shot at. Get Davis with the weather. (GARNETT *hurries in, excited.* HALEY *exits.*)

GARNETT. Casey, the old man says for God's sake be more discreet. He's scared.

DENNIS (*regretfully, pityingly*). A man who's broken altitude records . . . scared of congressmen!

GARNETT. Confidentially, he knows he's pretty close to that third star.

DENNIS. I wonder if that's where it sets in. Let me know, will you?

GARNETT. You'll be likelier to let me know.

DENNIS. Don't kid me. Haven't you got one of those B-29 commands sewed up for yourself?

GARNETT. Casey, the Air Corps hasn't got B-29 commands sewed up yet, until the United Chiefs decide whether you've proved precision bombardment over here.

DENNIS. When will it be decided?

GARNETT. Ostensibly on Tuesday. But those deals are always fixed before the meetings. They may be deciding this minute.

DENNIS (*drily*). No wonder you've been jittering, Cliff.

GARNETT. Frankly, I'm not as keen for it as I was, since I've seen what command is like.

DENNIS. Don't worry; the boys do the work.

GARNETT. Casey, it takes more than boys. I hate to ask this, but I need Ted Martin for my Chief of Staff out there in the Pacific. (DENNIS *considers this slowly, while* GARNETT *watches tensely.*)

DENNIS. What can you do for him?

GARNETT. Make him a Brigadier immediately. That Command will carry two stars at the top.

DENNIS. So . . . it *will be* Major General Garnett. Congratulations.

GARNETT. It isn't final yet. But if it *does* come out that way I will need your help with Ted . . . for the good of the service.

DENNIS. How about the good of Ted?

GARNETT. Well, I pointed out to him that he makes Brigadier . . . (*Stops, confused.*) A word from you will cinch it, Casey.

DENNIS. So, he knew about this last night?

GARNETT. Casey, it isn't proselytizing when a guy's your own brother-in-law.

DENNIS (*looks at his watch and at map*). Cliff! Can't you ever do anything straight?

GARNETT. Casey, if I'd thought for a minute that you would object . . .

DENNIS. Object! Do you think I'd have let him go today if I had known this? . . . I had Claude Minter alerted to lead this attack. And I let Ted talk me into holding Claude over for Fendelhorst tomorrow. Of course the bastard didn't tell me about this.

GARNETT. I'm very sorry, Casey, but you know yourself you have to handle Ted with kid gloves . . .

DENNIS (*heavily*). Don't try to handle him, Cliff; he does that fine.

GARNETT. You mean . . . I can have him . . . ?

DENNIS. For that job . . . of course.

GARNETT. And you'll persuade him?

DENNIS. Yes.

GARNETT. Casey, I don't know how to thank you . . .

DENNIS. Save it; I'm not doing it for you.

GARNETT. I mean for Ted . . . and the service . . .

DENNIS. Those B-29s will need Ted. (HALEY *and* DAVIS *enter with weather map.*) Well, what have you got?

DAVIS. The mass is denser, but that's slowing it up. It's about eighty miles behind expected drift now, sir.

DENNIS. How much longer will that give us?

DAVIS. The Continent will be open for

bombing all day tomorrow, but this will start closing in our bases by fifteen hundred, sir.

DENNIS. How does that fit, Haley?

HALEY. Lacks twenty-two minutes, sir. We'd have to take off before first light.

GARNETT. With that gas and bombload? You'd be inviting formation collisions.

HALEY. That's been the experience, sir. (EVANS *enters with glasses. Begins setting up an improvised bar.*)

DENNIS. But even by fifteen hundred tomorrow our returning planes could still see the island from, say, fifteen thousand feet?

DAVIS. They could see where it is, sir. This stuff will stack up over England like froth on a beer until it cools enough to move on.

DENNIS. But it will be right down on the deck?

DAVIS. I'm afraid it will be a crash landing condition, sir.

DENNIS. Bring anything new as fast as you get it. (DAVIS *exits.* DENNIS *detains* HALEY.) Have every spare parachute in the Division re-packed this afternoon. Tonight, re-pack enough from the planes so you can fill out with fresh packs for tomorrow.

HALEY (*reacts, controls himself*). Very well, sir. (*Exits.*)

GARNETT (*horrified*). Casey, what the hell are you thinking of?

DENNIS. Paratroops do it. Our crews will land on a friendly island.

GARNETT. But the planes?

DENNIS. They're expendable. The boys can leave them on automatic pilot so they'll fly out to sea and not crash in the villages.

GARNETT. You'd throw away a whole Division of planes for one target?

DENNIS. If we don't finish Fendelhorst tomorrow we've thrown away precision bombardment. That's all these planes are made for.

GARNETT. Have you thought what they'll say in Washington?

DENNIS. I'm thinking what they'll say in Berlin.

BROCKHURST (*enters, chastened*). Dennis, I owe you an apology. I thought you were a butcher. Compared to Kane you're a starry-eyed Boy Scout.

DENNIS. Take your troubles with General Kane to him.

BROCKHURST. I'd take 'em to the whole country if it weren't for your censors. Kane has just sent Colonel Martin a recall signal.

DENNIS. WHAT? (*Starts for door, checks himself, looks at watch and map, half smiles.*)

GARNETT (*horrified*). He couldn't. What, exactly, did he signal?

BROCKHURST. *Discretion,* to abandon primary target for a target of opportunity under fighter cover.

GARNETT. Kane let Malcolm make him do that?

BROCKHURST. He'll tell you. He asked me to send you down there. (GARNETT *exits.* BROCKHURST *eyes* DENNIS, *who is now studying map.*) That re-call signal only establishes Kane's personal alibi. He *knows* Martin's already beyond fighter cover. Recalling him now means taking the losses without getting the result—just from fear.

DENNIS. American Commanders have to fear losses, Mr. Brockhurst.

BROCKHURST. Because of those goddamned congressmen?

DENNIS. Them and you.

BROCKHURST. By me you mean a free press?

DENNIS. And free speech. There are only two choices. Either the state controls the army or the army controls the state.

BROCKHURST. So these cross purposes and confusions and compromises are the price of democracy?

DENNIS. Payable in boys. Our freedom is not as free as it looks, but it still beats the alternative.

BROCKHURST. The boys don't pay all of it. Kane's got you framed like a picture.

DENNIS. General Kane is doing what he thinks best. You don't understand the army.

BROCKHURST. It's only people. I understand people.

DENNIS. No, it's not. It's a receivership for the failures of people. They give us these boys to wipe the slate clean. It's the last resource. The army *has* to win.

BROCKHURST. Even at the sacrifice of all humanity, honor and reason?

DENNIS. That's what war is, Mr. Brockhurst. If we win, those things may get another chance.

BROCKHURST. Dennis, is there nothing I can do to help?

DENNIS. When these boys get your freedom back for you, you might try taking better care of it. Until then the problem is killing. (KANE, GARNETT, PRESCOTT, MALCOLM, *and* STONE *enter*.)

KANE (*at door*). . . . and I don't mind telling you it's a terrible responsibility.

MALCOLM. It was a very courageous order, General . . .

STONE. But I don't understand this.

KANE (*to* DENNIS). General, as you know, I pride myself on never interfering with normal operations. But today's diversions were so obviously unsuccessful that I felt it my duty to recall Colonel Martin.

MALCOLM. It was a brilliant command decision, General. It was woyth ouah whole trip oveh heah to fin' we got some Commandehs with humanity enough not to deman' the impossible . . . foh recohds.

DENNIS. Did you get a reply from Colonel Martin, General Kane?

KANE. No. He'll probably preserve radio silence back to our fighters.

STONE (*persevering*). Then Colonel Martin already *had* gone beyond fighter cover?

KANE. Of course we're not *certain* he'd gone that far . . .

MALCOLM (*sees whiskey, extricates* KANE). Well, looky here! Drinkin' whiskey fum Gawd's own country! Wheah in the worl' did you get this oveh heah, Sahgent?

EVANS. Present to General Dennis from an admirer, sir. (*All throng to bar.*)

BROCKHURST (*recognizes whiskey,*

smiles). Yes, Sergeant, it was. (*All except* DENNIS *begin to drink. Overscene sound of teleprinter begins to clatter.* DENNIS *reacts, but* STONE *detains him, persisting with question.*)

STONE. Well—it seems to me that if Colonel Martin had already gone *beyond* fighter cover . . .

MALCOLM. You mean Cunnel Mahtin had *been sent* beyon' fighteh coveh by Gennel Dennis when he knew his own self them diversions most likely wouldn't work . . . am I right, Gennel?

DENNIS. You are.

HALEY (*enters with a message*). Liaison message from a Royal Air Force Reconnaissance plane, sir.

DENNIS. Read it.

HALEY (*reading*). "Twelve thirty-nine sighted large formation USAAF. Fortresses approx ten-forty-six East, fifty-forty North . . . Altitude twenty-two thousand, heading ninety-eight . . ."

KANE. NINETY-EIGHT . . . he's still going *into* Germany!

HALEY (*continuing reading*). "Unescorted by friendly fighters, under heavy attack, formations good over." (HALEY *exits*.)

MALCOLM (*drinks deeply*). "'Unescohted an' undeh heavy attack . . . !'" Gennel Kane, I'm wahnin' you, if we eveh have anotheh attack like this . . .

STONE. Arthur! It's not our place to criticize. If they think it's necessary.

MALCOLM. Necessary! To slaughteh American youth foh one pig-headed Brigadieh to make hisself a puhsonal recohd . . .

HALEY (*enters, hesitantly*). Message you should see, General Dennis . . .

KANE (*nervously*). Read the message, Colonel!

HALEY (*reading*). "Relay on personal cable from message center London in clear for Colonel Edward Martin: new co-pilot made first landing four-fourteen this morning everything fine, Helen."

DENNIS. Jesus! Ted's got a son! Congratulations, Uncle! (DENNIS *and* GARNETT *shake*.)

KANE (*exploits the distraction*). Gentlemen! Colonel Martin's son! (*Others throng to drink.*)

DENNIS. Haley, prepare a copy to relay to Ted, but hold it till we hear. (HALEY *exits.*)

MALCOLM. Till you heah what?

DENNIS (*eyeing watch*). His strike signal. It will be very soon now.

MALCOLM. You tellin' me this Cunnel out theah leadin' the attack been bohn a daddy an' you ain't even goin' to radio him?

DENNIS. He's busy now.

KANE (*intervening*). Fortunately, gentlemen, war also has its pleasant duties. We'll have just time for one of them, General Dennis. (DENNIS *looks rebellious, checks himself, speaks off to Ops room.*)

EVANS (*speaks off to ante-room*). Let's go. (G. I. PHOTOGRAPHER *with camera enters and takes position.*)

MALCOLM. Gennel Kane, you fixin' to have this decoration ceremony you was tellin' me about?

KANE. Right now, Mr. Malcolm. (HALEY *enters with citation and medal box.* JENKS, *in best uniform, enters after him.* MALCOLM *jumps to exploit the hero.*) Mr. Malcolm . . . Mr. Stone . . . Captain Jenks.

MALCOLM. Son, I'm proud to meet you, mighty proud! Now if you'll just stan' oveh heah with me . . . (*Grabs* JENKS, *beckons* PHOTOGRAPHER. STONE *jumps briskly to join them.*) Boy! I want a pictuah that will make all America proud of . . . the Captain, heah. (PHOTOGRAPHER *maneuvers.* MALCOLM *and* STONE *almost crowd* JENKS *out of picture.*) All right, son! *Weah* ready!

EVANS. Excuse me, sir . . .

KANE (*outraged*). WHAT . . . ?

EVANS. Would the gentlemen from Congress like to put their glasses over here before the photographing starts . . . ? (*He steps to them, takes glasses from their hands as he speaks.*)

STONE. Oh, yes . . . thank you, Sergeant.

MALCOLM. You goin' a long way in life, son! (PHOTOGRAPHER *snaps them, mugging and beaming.*)

KANE. Now, gentlemen, I think we'd better go ahead.

MALCOLM. Are you gettin' this, Elmeh boy?

BROCKHURST. I'm beginning to get it. (*All re-group rapidly.* JENKS *facing* KANE, HALEY *beside them.* MALCOLM *and* STONE *maneuver into good camera range.*)

HALEY (*reads from citation*). "Captain Lucius Jenks for outstanding heroic and meritorious conduct in aerial warfare . . ." (*Overscene sound of teleprinter clattering is heard.* EVANS *hurries to Ops room.* DENNIS *watches him anxiously.*) HALEY *continues reading.*) "Captain Jenks, first as pilot and later as Commander of the 1993rd Bombardment Squadron, Heavy . . ." (HALEY *breaks off as* EVANS *enters and hands* DENNIS *strip of paper.*)

DENNIS (*reading*). "No mistake this time. Scratch Schweinhafen for me, Ted." Jesus, Haley! He got it . . . HE GOT IT . . . *HE GOT IT!!!* Signal him about his kid! (HALEY *exits.*)

GARNETT (*raises glass*). Gentlemen! The greatest combat leader in the Army Air Forces!

KANE (*to* BROCKHURST). Brockie, I want a feature story on Colonel Martin for this! (*All throng to drink, leaving* MALCOLM *piqued, beside the forgotten* JENKS.)

MALCOLM. Gennel Kane! Ain't we goin' to be photographed with you decoratin' this hero fum mah home State?

PRESCOTT. Sir! Colonel Martin's message asks you to scratch Schweinhafen for him. Now, while the photographer is still here . . . (*Proffers crayon.* KANE *takes it to map. Congressmen stampede to get into photo.*)

KANE (*to* PHOTOGRAPHER). Are we all right, son?

PHOTOGRAPHER. Pull your blouse down over your hips, General. (PHOTOGRAPHER *trains on them, then stops as* HALEY *enters quietly, hands* DENNIS *a message.* DENNIS *reads it, puts it down quietly, steps away from it. Others watch uneasily.* GARNETT *picks it up.*)

GARNETT (*reading*). "Good luck, Casey, we're on fire and going . . ."

MALCOLM. Goin' . . . ? Finish the message, cain't you?

GARNETT. That's all there is.

MALCOLM. All . . . all . . . ? (*Steps over to* DENNIS.) Listen heah! I want to know . . .

DENNIS. Shut up!

MALCOLM (*getting it*). You mean to tell me he's . . .

DENNIS. SHUT UP!

MALCOLM. You telling me to shut up afteh you've done kilt the bes' . . . (DENNIS *grabs him by lapels, shakes him savagely.*)

KANE. Casey! (DENNIS *flings* MALCOLM *into a chair.*)

STONE. General Kane, nobody could blame General Dennis.

BROCKHURST. Let's both remember that, Mr. Stone.

GARNETT. Casey, do you realize what . . . we've done to Ted?

DENNIS. Yes.

GARNETT. But we'll have to . . . one of us will have to tell Helen.

DENNIS. I'll tell Helen . . . and then I'll tell Claude Minter's wife.

GARNETT. Claude Minter's wife? (*Eyeing him nervously.*)

DENNIS. Yes. I'll tell her I sent Claude to Fendelhorst tomorrow.

GARNETT. Fendelhorst! Tomorrow!

KANE. Casey, you leave me no choice. I am relieving you of your command with immediate effect. General Garnett, pending confirmation from Washington you will assume command of the Fifth Division. (*Then, sincerely, to* DENNIS.) I'm sorry, my boy. I'm going to recommend you for the Legion of Merit.

CURTAIN

ACT THREE

About twenty hundred that night. Curtain rises to discover room bare and serviceable as in Act One. EVANS *enters, puts name plate with* GARNETT's *name on desk, tosses* DENNIS's *nameplate into trash box. From offstage singing and mild carousal noises are audible.* EVANS *shakes head disapprovingly, puts coffee to boil and gets out cigar box.* MAJOR DAYHUFF *enters, catching* EVANS *red-handed with cigar box.*

DAYHUFF (*amused, covering it*). Good evening, Evans. Aren't you expecting the General?

EVANS. Any minute now. And I knew he'd want you to have a cigar.

DAYHUFF. Thanks.

EVANS (*extends box. It is empty*). Congressmen! Sorry, sir. I'll have this attended to.

DAYHUFF. All right. How did that wound in your arm heal, Sergeant?

EVANS (*with gesture*). Fine, Doctor. I can lift any girl in England off her feet.

DAYHUFF. So I hear. (*Mild carousal noises heard off.*) Aren't you missing a good evening for . . . recreation?

EVANS. I'll be off duty as soon as we send the order for tomorrow.

DAYHUFF. Sergeant, I had it on good authority there wouldn't be a mission tomorrow.

EVANS. Well, mine is straight from the horse's . . . that is, General Kane. When he left here he told Garnett he'd communicate his instructions as soon as he'd made an appreciation of the situation.

DAYHUFF. Can you put that into English?

EVANS. Yes, sir. Order, counter order, disorder . . . and then five feet of tele-printed hot air meaning a milk run to the nearest Channel port.

DAYHUFF. Oh. I take it you don't approve of the change?

EVANS. I expected it.

DAYHUFF. Because of the way Dennis . . . disagreed with those Congressmen?

EVANS. Hell no! They've all buried worse bodies than that. Kane and Washington have been laying for Dennis a long time.

DAYHUFF. What makes you think that?

EVANS. Dennis was trying to get the war over.

DAYHUFF. That's a harsh judgment, Sergeant.

EVANS. We got the signal from Washington confirming Garnett in two hours, didn't we?

DAYHUFF. While we're violating security, what did it say about Dennis?

EVANS. ". . . return to Washington by special plane, for reassignment."

DAYHUFF. Well, for his sake I hope it's an easier assignment.

EVANS. They'll probably make him Air Force Liaison to the Admiral commanding the Washington Aquarium.

DAYHUFF. I'm not so sure Washington will waste a man like that.

EVANS. Maybe they'll let him burn Top Secret waste paper.

DAYHUFF. When you get older it may occur to you that Command is just as tough in Washington as anywhere else. Could you figure out the difference between Kane and Dennis from official reports?

EVANS. Very fast.

DAYHUFF. How?

EVANS. Dennis always had his neck out a foot. But you have to look close for those two stars to tell Kane from a turtle. This Garnett's another.

DAYHUFF. So you'll guarantee nothing worse than a milk run tomorrow?

EVANS. After what happened to Dennis . . . listen to the boys. Disgusting, isn't it, sir?

GARNETT (enters). Good evening, Evans. Anything from General Kane?

EVANS. No, sir.

VOICE (offstage). Where's my bottle?

GARNETT. What's that racket outside?

EVANS. Just some of the boys, sir. (Bottle crash offstage.)

GARNETT. Well, call the guardhouse.

EVANS. Excuse me, sir. May I attend to this for you, sir?

GARNETT. Yes.

EVANS (goes to window, calls off). Hey, you, out there . . . shut up!

VOICE (off, evidently drunk). Who's telling me to shut up!

EVANS. I am.

VOICE. Do you know who I am?

EVANS. I don't want to know who you are.

VOICE. I am Captain George Washington Culpepper Lee!

EVANS. Well, I am Tech Sergeant Harold Evans . . .

LEE. Oh . . . a Technical Sergeant, eh . . . ?

EVANS. Speaking for Brigadier General Clifton C. Garnett! (Noise of swiftly receding feet and then silence.) Thank you, sir.

GARNETT. Thank you, Sergeant. See if there are any messages.

DAYHUFF (grins). I'm afraid I'm the real culprit, General Garnett.

GARNETT. How?

DAYHUFF. I authorized a small allotment of whiskey from combat crew ration into the messes tonight.

GARNETT. Is this usual?

DAYHUFF. No, sir. The last three days were not usual either, sir.

GARNETT. Is the whole base in this condition?

DAYHUFF. No, sir! It wouldn't run one percent. Most of them are asleep.

GARNETT. I see.

DAYHUFF. This is a very special night, sir. And they're veterans. They know they can fly a milk run tomorrow sound asleep.

GARNETT. Does the Division just assume that I'm going to order a milk run?

DAYHUFF. I'm not assuming, sir. That's what I came in to ask.

GARNETT. There are a great many factors in this decision, Major.

DAYHUFF. I represent one of them, sir.

GARNETT. What is your medical estimate, Major?

DAYHUFF. When General Dennis planned Operation Stitch he requested a medical appreciation. I estimated the men could stand three successive days.

GARNETT. Three?

DAYHUFF. We agreed that anything beyond that would have to be decided by military consideration.

GARNETT. In short, the men could do it, if General Kane ordered it?

DAYHUFF. Men can do what they have to, sir.

GARNETT. At a price, eh?

DAYHUFF. Well, sir; two-thirds of these men will be killed in a normal tour of duty anyway . . .

GARNETT. Thank you, Major. (DAY-HUFF *exits.* GARNETT *cogitates, calls off.*) Evans! (EVANS *enters.*) Any word from General Kane?

EVANS. No, sir. Coffee's ready, sir.

GARNETT. I didn't order coffee.

EVANS. You will, sir.

GARNETT (*sniffs it, likes it*). Oh, thank you, Sergeant. What else will I need?

EVANS. Cigars and whiskey, sir.

GARNETT. I almost never use them.

EVANS. Your visitors will, sir.

GARNETT. Oh. I guess you and I will be together some time, Evans. Can you suggest anything else I need?

EVANS. You need a new sergeant, sir.

GARNETT. What . . . ? Oh, you're going home to work for General Dennis?

EVANS (*bitterly*). No, sir; he wouldn't take me. I guess they use Colonels for errand boys in Washington. I've decided to go to Nevada to teach gunnery.

GARNETT. *You've* decided . . . ? What do you think this Army is?

EVANS. I'd rather not answer that, sir. But War Department Circular six-nine-five-eight-seven-dash-three says applications from graduate gunners to teach aerial gunnery will be accepted.

GARNETT. Well, if the circular authorizes it . . . ask Colonel Haley to step in. (EVANS *makes for door.* GARNETT *checks him.*) Evans, you *are* a graduate gunner?

EVANS. Yes, sir. Twenty-eight missions.

GARNETT. Would it be too much to ask these boys for a tough one tomorrow?

EVANS. I don't know, sir.

GARNETT. You must know . . . from your own experience.

EVANS. Never had this experience, sir. Nobody in the Army ever asked me anything. They just told me.

GARNETT. Ask Colonel Haley to step in. (EVANS *exits.* GARNETT *visibly sweats.* HALEY *enters.*) Good evening, Haley. Any messages?

HALEY. Other Division Commanders have sent compliments and will await your decision before planning tomorrow's mission, sir.

GARNETT. Anything from General Kane?

HALEY. No, sir.

GARNETT. Wasn't his weather conference tonight at eighteen hundred?

HALEY. Yes, sir.

GARNETT. I suppose on a tricky reading he might wait for twenty hundred developments?

HALEY. He might, sir.

GARNETT. And we haven't had *our* twenty hundred weather yet.

HALEY. Davis is marking the map now, sir. If you want it at once . . .

GARNETT. No, no. Have you final figures from today yet?

HALEY (*handing him paper*). Right here, sir.

GARNETT. Thirty-nine lost . . . four in the Channel . . . What's this?

HALEY. Both reconnaissance planes unreported again today, sir.

GARNETT. Haley, what about morale?

HALEY. Very good now, sir. What you've heard tonight is just the normal let-down between tough missions and easy ones.

GARNETT. Haley, what do these boys really think about?

HALEY. Their twenty-fifth mission, sir.

GARNETT. Of course. But what else?

HALEY. The normal things, sir. And promotion and decoration, too.

GARNETT. By the normal things, you mean . . . ?

HALEY. Yes, sir. Fortunately the villages around here are full of it.

GARNETT. I should think it would lead to trouble.

HALEY. It does, sir.

GARNETT. What kind?

HALEY. Just the normal kind, sir. These women have been at war a long time. They know the men have to be up and dressed in time for missions.

GARNETT. Is this immorality very widespread?

HALEY. Very, sir. I believe it's as bad as America.

GARNETT. So that kind of morale really takes care of itself?

HALEY. Yes, sir. Keeps down perversion, too. (*Then, briskly.*) If you're ready to go through status, sir . . .

GARNETT (*still stalling*). Haley, you really think the change of Command has helped morale?

HALEY. They're pretty cheerful tonight, sir.

GARNETT. Well, that's something. You always wonder if they'll be hostile to a new . . . face.

HALEY. All generals look alike to them, sir. (*Pause.*) They figure a new General's always good for a couple of soft missions.

GARNETT. Haley, are those last pictures developed?

HALEY. I'll find out, sir. (HALEY *exits.* GARNETT *stews, then looks up, startled, as* CAPTAIN GEORGE WASHINGTON CULPEPPER LEE *enters.* LEE *is an attractive youngster, somewhat drunk. He salutes with exaggerated formality.*)

LEE. Captain Lee reports his presence, sir.

GARNETT. Who?

LEE. Captain George Washington Culpepper Lee, sir.

GARNETT. Lee, you're drunk.

LEE. Yes, sir. I've come in to report myself for that and to apologize for singing under your window and then running away.

GARNETT. Get out of here and go to bed.

LEE. I'm sorry, sir. This hasn't happened before and won't again. (*Salutes, turns to go;* GARNETT *checks him.*)

GARNETT. Lee, did you go to Schweinhafen today?

LEE (*thoughtfully, rather fuddled*). Yes, sir. I went to Schweinhafen today and I went to Schweinhafen yesterday and I went to Posenleben Friday . . . and I've been to Hamburg . . . and Bremen . . . and Kiel . . . and Schweinfurt and Regensburg . . . (*Stops, horrified at himself.*) Excuse me, sir. I only meant to say I'd been to twenty-four of them without taking a drink and I'm ashamed of myself for singing under your window on Easter Sunday.

GARNETT. You go to bed, Lee. It's all right . . . even if it isn't Easter Sunday.

LEE. Beg your pardon, sir. It's my Easter Sunday.

GARNETT. Yours?

LEE. Yes, sir. Resurrection, sir. Today was my twenty-fourth. All I've got to do now is knock off one more little milk run and then go home and live the rest of my life.

GARNETT. Oh. Well, don't behave like this at home.

LEE. I wouldn't think of it, sir. I'm going to get married.

GARNETT. Well, congratulations!

LEE. Yes, sir. We almost did before I came over, but I thought . . . I thought she'd worry more that way.

GARNETT. I see. Now get to bed; the best of luck.

LEE. Thank you, sir. And Happy Easter to you, sir. (LEE *exits, leaving* GARNETT *to think that one over.*)

HALEY (*enters*). The pictures will be up in a minute and there's a message, sir.

GARNETT. From General Kane?

HALEY. No, sir. The last Group reports all crews provided with freshly packed parachutes for tomorrow in compliance with today's order.

GARNETT. What order?

HALEY. General Dennis's last order this morning, sir. If you remember it was not rescinded.

GARNETT. But that was for a special weather condition. Where *is* that weather man?

HALEY. Coming, sir. It's a tricky reading.

GARNETT (*hopefully*). You mean, it looks worse?

HALEY. He'll have to tell you that, sir.

GARNETT. And you're sure there's nothing from General Kane?

HALEY. Messages are brought as received, sir.

GARNETT. We'll go through Status, Haley. Just give me totals. (*They move to Status Board.*)

HALEY. I think I can promise a hundred and thirty planes by bomb loading, sir.

GARNETT. One-thirty . . . that's not really four full groups, is it?

HALEY. Today was our third successive day of intensive operations, sir. I'll bet the Germans would be glad to trade serviceability with me . . . and they only have to repair single engine fighters and find one man to a crew.

GARNETT. I wasn't criticizing . . . but we just haven't the strength that General Dennis had, have we?

HALEY. One-thirty's enough for any target in the book, if they hit it.

GARNETT. Planes, perhaps; how about crews?

HALEY. I've been able to piece out one thirty-two, sir.

GARNETT. How many would be on their last mission?

HALEY. Eighteen, sir.

GARNETT. A hundred and eighty boys . . .

HALEY. It's a break for them, sir, to finish on an easy one, if it is an easy one.

GARNETT. Of course that depends entirely on General Kane's orders.

HALEY. Yes, sir. If he sends orders. Shall I see about your weather, sir?

GARNETT (*picks up Directive Folder*). Haley, when General Dennis handed over to me this afternoon there was so much to take in I missed some of the details. It says here: "In the absence of explicit target designation or other order from higher headquarters, division commanders will exercise their own discretion . . ." When should this designation come down?

HALEY. From General Kane's eighteen hundred weather conference tonight, sir.

GARNETT. And if we hear nothing this just applies automatically?

HALEY. Automatically, sir.

MAJOR LANSING (*enters, shirt sleeves rolled up, wet hands filled with wet pictures*). Last pictures from the camera ships in the last Group on today's mission, sir.

GARNETT. There are no pictures from reconnaissance?

LANSING. No, sir. Both reconnaissance planes are unreported again today. These are all we'll have.

GARNETT. How are they?

LANSING (*spreading them for scrutiny*). Wonderful, sir. The next to last Group *did* get the casting furnaces, you see . . . here. And here where the main spar milling shop was there's nothing left but a compound crater.

GARNETT. Then it's complete?

LANSING. Schweinhafen's complete, sir.

GARNETT. I see. Nothing more on Colonel Martin . . . ? No parachutes showing in any of these strike photos?

LANSING. It was very windy over Schweinhafen today, sir. The last Group photos didn't catch any of the parachutes going down. We have one more sighting from Crew Interrogation that agrees exactly with the others. As the fire worked toward his gas tanks, Colonel Martin's plane swung away from the formation, of course, and then exploded. Four parachutes were seen to open afterwards, but there were no individual identifications.

GARNETT (*eyeing pictures*). I wish we could know what he did.

LANSING. Yes, but I'm glad he doesn't know we're not finishing the job.

GARNETT. That's not in our hands, Major.

LANSING. I understand that, sir.

GARNETT. I want you to brief me now on what targets would be best to give these boys a break tomorrow. (*They move to map. HALEY exits.*)

LANSING. The Germans won't fight for anything in France tomorrow, sir. They need a rest as badly as we do.

GARNETT. You keep records of losses and loss expectancy over the different targets, of course?

LANSING. Of course, sir.

GARNETT. Well, what would loss expectancy be . . . along the coastal fringe here, on some of these naval objectives?

LANSING. I wouldn't trust my memory for the figures, sir. But I can have a list prepared for you very quickly.

GARNETT. What would the targets be, the naval targets . . . along here?

LANSING. Minesweeper and E-boat bases along through there, sir.

GARNETT. We have attacked such objectives before, of course?

LANSING. Yes, sir. For the blooding of new Groups. Would you like a loss expectancy list prepared, sir?

GARNETT. Yes. (LANSING *makes for door.* GARNETT *checks him.*) Major, I'd like to ask you a question.

LANSING. Yes, sir.

GARNETT. If you had to decide tomorrow's mission . . . for General Kane . . . would you attack Fendelhorst?

LANSING. Fendelhorst, sir! I'm thankful I don't have to decide that.

GARNETT. But if you did?

LANSING. Sir, I'm afraid my decision would be influenced by a personal reason.

GARNETT. May I ask what that is?

LANSING. General, I regret intruding this upon your considerations. Since you ask me, I have a son, training now in a combat infantry Division, Assault . . . (*Points to cross.*) When those jets have stopped our bombardment they'll make the deadliest strafing planes ever used against ground troops. I'm sorry, sir, but I'm afraid I couldn't help thinking of my boy going up a beach against them.

GARNETT. Yes . . . but what if your boy were flying a bomber tomorrow?

LANSING. I hope I would send him to Fendelhorst, sir.

GARNETT. Thank you, Major. (LANSING *exits, leaving* GARNETT *to think that over.* HALEY *and* DAVIS *enter.*)

HALEY. Weather's ready, sir.

GARNETT. Is this the same report that General Kane is getting?

DAVIS. No, sir. This is my reading. General Kane's weather people refuse either concurrence or disagreement.

GARNETT. Isn't that unusual?

DAVIS. Very unscientific, sir.

HALEY. Often happens, sir. In such cases we operate on our own weather reading, subject to other instructions. Directive covers it, sir.

GARNETT. Well, what is it?

DAVIS (*spreading map on table*). That cold mass is still slowing down. The entire Continent will be open for bombing all day and you'll have until seventeen hundred over the bases here for landing, sir.

GARNETT. Seventeen hundred . . . five o'clock in the afternoon . . . why, that's enough for . . . anything . . . isn't it?

HALEY. Yes, sir.

GARNETT. Even without parachutes.

HALEY. Yes, sir.

GARNETT. You're sure of this, Davis?

DAVIS. Never sure with weather, sir. If anything, though, this will improve for us during the night.

GARNETT. Thank you, Major.

DAVIS. All right. (DAVIS *exits.* GARNETT *stews.* HALEY *gets down to business.*)

HALEY. General Garnett, the Group commanders need gas and bomb-loading orders. Their ground crews are so exhausted it will take them twice as long as normal tonight.

GARNETT. Haley, to be perfectly frank, I understood I was going to receive instructions from General Kane . . .

HALEY. But we haven't, sir. And our Directive says: "In the absence of explicit target designation or other orders . . ."

EVANS (*enters with message*). Message for General Garnett from General Kane, sir.

GARNETT (*faintly*). Read it. (EVANS *looks perplexed, hands message to* HALEY, *who reads.*)

HALEY (*reading*). "General Kane compelled proceed Hemisphere Commander's dinner for Congressmen London, consequently unable to attend weather conference here. Operating procedure will apply as per directive. General Kane desires express especial confidence General Garnett's discretion based on weather. Signed Saybold for Kane." (*Deadly silence.* DENNIS *enters in trench-coat, carrying cap.* GARNETT *gathers himself.*)

GARNETT. Come in, old man; I'll speak

to you in a minute, Haley. (HALEY *and* EVANS *go out.*) Sit down, Casey.

DENNIS. They've just reported my plane's landed and is taking gas. The boys are loading my stuff.

GARNETT. Damn it, man! You don't have to rush off like this.

DENNIS. The order said: "With immediate effect" . . . Cliff. I'm taking Ted's personal stuff to Helen.

GARNETT. Good. You'll go to see her at once?

DENNIS. Of course. No more news, I suppose?

GARNETT. One more crew sighting, exactly like the others, four parachutes.

DENNIS. Yeah.

GARNETT. What will you tell her?

DENNIS. The truth. She won't talk.

GARNETT. How long do we keep it quiet?

DENNIS. For Ted, I'd like eight weeks. They'd dig out every cave in Germany if they thought he was hiding in one of them.

GARNETT. Do you think he is?

DENNIS. No. Not with an explosion where he was riding.

GARNETT. Casey, if he did get down alive . . . and they caught him . . . what then?

DENNIS. If the army gets him it's probably all right. But no one can be responsible for what civilians who've been bombed will do.

GARNETT. But if the army gets him first . . . it's all right?

DENNIS. Probably.

GARNETT. I've been thinking all day about those six boys the Japanese captured . . . alive . . .

DENNIS. I won't go into that side of it with Helen.

GARNETT. She'll be thinking of it. She must have seen those pictures the Japanese released after they got through with them.

DENNIS. Cliff! Will you stop talking about it?

GARNETT. I've been thinking about it all afternoon. I was the guy who *wanted* a B-29 command. God! When I think of ordering boys out over the Japanese . . .

DENNIS. You don't have to think about it. You've got a good job here. Good luck, Cliff . . .

GARNETT. Good, is it? Read that? (*Hands* DENNIS *the message.*)

DENNIS (*reads it, speaks casually*). Hemisphere Commander's, eh? Well, they'll get real Martinis. That old son of a bitch has the best mess in London.

GARNETT. *Real Martinis* . . . while *I* have to decide about tomorrow.

DENNIS. You don't have to decide anything. You're socked in with bad weather at fifteen hundred tomorrow afternoon.

GARNETT. The weather's changed, Casey; it's good for anything.

DENNIS. The hell you say! Isn't that just like the weather for you?

GARNETT. And Kane is passing the buck to me.

DENNIS. Well, somebody's probably got a heel on his neck, too. Good luck, Cliff . . .

GARNETT. Casey! You can't run out on me like this. What am I going to do?

DENNIS. You're going to command, Clifton . . . and you will be paid the first of every month. (*Fumbles with coat as if preparing to go.*)

GARNETT. Casey, there's one more thing . . .

DENNIS (*eyeing watch*). Well . . . ?

GARNETT. I had a boy in here tonight . . . a pilot . . .

DENNIS. Bitching and screaming like a wounded eagle, I suppose?

GARNETT (*indignantly*). Hell no! He was a nice attractive kid with a lot of guts.

DENNIS. They're all nice attractive kids with a lot of guts.

GARNETT. I know, but this one was a little drunk.

DENNIS (*shocked*). Drunk in *here* . . . (*Then, reflectively.*) Oh. I suppose his co-pilot was killed on the mission today . . . I've had those . . .

GARNETT. No, no . . . that wasn't it . . .

DENNIS. Oh, just nerves? Well, the best thing with those, Cliff, is just to have the M. P.'s throw 'em into bed . . .

GARNETT. Oh, he wasn't that drunk . . .

DENNIS. They need it sometimes. Their crews will sober them up with oxygen in five minutes in the morning and then hop them up with enough benzedrine to get them through the mission. This isn't Washington, Cliff; you can't be too strict with them.

GARNETT. That's not it, Casey. This boy gave me a personal slant . . .

DENNIS. The War Department has provided you with a chaplain for that, Cliff. Tell them to do their crying to him.

GARNETT. Casey, he wasn't crying, he was happy. He told me he's going to get married.

DENNIS. And the only thing you can tell him is that you hope you won't have to kill him before he does . . . It's your baby, Cliff, but I learned long ago to let the chaplain handle those. He's our liaison with the headquarters that decides that . . . if there is one.

GARNETT. Casey! What's happened to you?

DENNIS. Just what's going to happen to you . . . and the sooner I get out of here, the sooner you can get to work. (Starts for door.)

GARNETT (checks him). Casey! If you'll help me just this once . . .

DENNIS. It isn't just this once. It's from now on.

GARNETT. When you first came over here you had Ted and Joe Lucas to talk to . . .

DENNIS. Joe never talked. He was commanding this Division then, and I was running a Group for him. That's worse. You see them at meals every day and you know a lot of them personally.

GARNETT. But at least you had Joe for a boss until he got killed in that air raid in London.

DENNIS. Did you believe that story?

GARNETT. Why . . . of course . . .

DENNIS. Well, you're old enough to know better. Joe didn't get killed in any air raid in London. It was the night after we first sent them to Mangelburg. Joe didn't want to send them. He knew they weren't ready. Kane knew it, too. But they were crowding Joe and Kane from

higher up. Joe counted them in at landing that night and then he went down to London and took a hotel room and shot himself. Then I got the job. Now it's yours. Good luck, Cliff.

GARNETT. Joe Lucas . . . did that . . . how could he?

DENNIS. You'll see how he could. Wait till you've counted in a really bad one that you've ordered yourself. Wait till you start noticing the faces of those kids on the trucks from the replacement centers . . . the new ones coming in. Wait till you start waking up in the afternoon . . . and wondering what it is that makes those faces look so much like the faces of the ones you're already killing, that same afternoon. Then go out and puke up your powdered eggs and then take veronal to get back to sleep . . . and then have them wake you up and give you benzedrine to keep you awake while you count in your stragglers and plan your next mission . . . then you'll see how Joe Lucas could have done it . . .

GARNETT. Joe Lucas! Of all the men in the service . . .

DENNIS. Yes . . . and I've wanted to do the same thing, five or six times when I've signed those field orders . . . and so will you! But that was one thing Joe did for me. He made me think that through. That only helps one guy.

GARNETT. But even after that . . . you had Ted . . .

DENNIS. Yes. I had Ted. That's one thing I've done for you, Cliff. I've killed Ted. You won't have to do that.

GARNETT. Casey, you've hated this, every minute of it, haven't you?

DENNIS. I got paid for it.

GARNETT. What will you do now, Casey?

DENNIS. Oh, I guess I still rate a Training Command. I'm going to get one out West somewhere, where I can have Cathy and the kids with me and get a day off now and then to take the boy fishing.

HALEY (enters with list). Here's the list Major Lansing prepared for you, sir.

GARNETT (dazedly). List?

HALEY. Yes, sir. You ordered it, sir.

GARNETT. Read it.

HALEY (*reading*). "Expectancy of losses from flak against French Channel port targets based on previous experience . . . Brest, 4.9 . . . Cherbourg, 3.4 . . . Calais, 2.2 . . . Dunkirk, 1.6 . . . Dieppe, 1.4 . . ."

GARNETT. That's enough . . . (HALEY *puts list on desk, starts out.*)

DENNIS (*checks him*). Ernie . . . how did *my* good-bye presents to the boys finally average out?

HALEY. Twenty-four percent Friday, twenty-six percent yesterday and twenty-nine percent today, sir.

DENNIS. Some difference between those and the Channel ports.

HALEY. Many differences, sir.

GARNETT (*low-voiced*). Haley, notify the other Divisions and all our Groups that tomorrow the Fifth Division will attack Fendelhorst.

HALEY. Yes, sir. (*Exits.*)

DENNIS (*half-laughs, awkwardly*). Well . . . Cliff! Good luck . . . *General.*

GARNETT. Save me a job in that training command, will you? (DENNIS *starts out.* EVANS *enters.*)

EVANS. Change of orders for General Dennis . . . sir . . .

DENNIS. No, you don't . . .

EVANS. From Washington, sir.

DENNIS. I've got my orders. I've gone . . . home.

EVANS. We're instructed to relay the message to your plane, sir. (*Hesitates.*)

GARNETT (*takes message, reads aloud slowly*). "With immediate effect, General Dennis will proceed via Gibraltar, Cairo, Karachi, Calcutta and Chungking to . . ." (*Stops, horrified.*) My God, Casey . . . this means a B-29 command . . .

DENNIS. No, by God! They can't! . . . I *WON'T!* (*Then, slowly.*) Cliff, does that say: "With immediate effect"?

GARNETT. I'm afraid it does, Casey.

DENNIS. Yeah . . . Evans! Get your things.

CURTAIN

SUGGESTED TOPICS FOR FURTHER INVESTIGATION AND REPORT

1. One of the best examples of the superhero is Almanzor in John Dryden's *The Conquest of Granada*, written in 1670, in the popular "heroic" style of the Restoration. A more believable young warrior, but still highly romanticized, is John Home's *Douglas*, in the play of the same name, 1756. Read these two plays and compare the heroes with characters who represent the modern attitude.

2. Look in Allardyce Nicoll's "The Development of the Theatre" or in any good illustrated history of the theatre. Study the pictures of some of the stage effects depicting violence and death as employed on the stage during the Renaissance or some other early period. Compare and contrast these scenes with those demanded by the stage directions of *What Price Glory*.

3. Read *The Trojan Women* and *Lysistrata*, ancient Greek plays by Euripides and Aristophanes. Also read Irwin Shaw's *Bury the Dead* and Paul Green's *Johnny Johnson*. These plays present the serious and the comic approaches to the ridiculous aspects of war. Discuss their similarities of approach.

4. Read Shakespeare's *Henry V*. Note carefully the portrayals of Bardolph, Pistol, and Nym, and of the national types represented by Gower, Fluellen, Macmorris, and Jamy. These are the "enlisted" men of their day, and the beginnings of citizen-officers. Compare their treatment with enlisted and junior-officer personnel in *What Price Glory*, *Command Decision*, or *Mister Roberts*. Also, notice King Henry's views as expressed in his conversation with Williams and Bates before the battle.

5. The tyrannical superior officer is a standard dramatic character. Show how the treatment of two captains, those of *Mister Roberts* by Heggen and Logan and of *The Caine Mutiny Court-martial* by Herman Wouk, result in the opposite styles of comedy and serious drama.

6. The terrible psychological stresses of combat are emphasized in *Home of the Brave* and *The Caine Mutiny Court-martial*. Discuss the various ways each author makes use of the unnatural effect these stresses have on leading characters.

7. The British counterpart to *What Price Glory* is *Journey's End* by Robert C. Sherriff. Discuss the similarities and the differences you find in these plays.

8. Make a further study of *Shenandoah* and *Secret Service*. Read also David Belasco's *The Heart of Maryland*, another well-known Civil War play. Discuss their techniques, and see if you can determine which one would be most easily revived today.

THE CREATION OF A FOLK DRAMA

What Is a Folk Tradition?

A native "folk" are those people who, through years or even generations of comparative isolation, have developed and preserved their own peculiar culture and social environment, from which comes a unified form of expression colored by a common emotion and attitude. *Folklore* is the collection of knowledge, beliefs, and customs which remain typical of an originating folk society. Pure folklore has spontaneous origins, springing from the active imagination of naïve minds, seeking to explain, to entertain, or to express emotional feelings, nearly always preserved by oral tradition. Part of folklore may be *myth*, which attempts to explain the mysteries of natural phenomena by giving the forces of nature physical shape in the persons of gods and demons. Another part may be *legend*, wherein great native heroes and heroines live almost supernatural lives. From folklore also emerges a whole pattern of *superstition*, including magic and conjuration, mystic symbols and primitive medicine. Also out of folk tradition comes *art*, visible in primitive painting and handicraft, dance, and, to a lesser extent, drama.

Folklore develops from "pockets" of culture which can never be considered typical of a nation as a whole. Large urban groups in constant communication with one another break down the barriers of isolation and destroy or assimilate old traditions. Hence, folklore becomes essentially rural, its sources remaining where direct contact among groups is difficult. Modern mass communication has diluted and corrupted many of the genuine folk cultures. Superstition, myth, and traditional distrust of those outside the group lose strength in the face of constantly expanding educational facilities. Conversely, and to its credit, this advance in communication has made possible the better preservation and dissemination of these same traditions. The origins and significance of folk cultures become meaningful as a part of an entire nation's inheritance. The most serious danger to the perpetuation of valid traditions lies in the widespread inability to recognize the difference between a genuine folk piece and a mere imitation. The word "folk" becomes too easily applied. The product of a Tin Pan Alley composer who has never seen a Tennessee mountain, and the output of a screen writer who knows nothing of the true psychology of the Southern Negro or the Great Plains sodbuster, are fabricated, sterile products whose sale makes more difficult the task of the genuine article to take its legitimate place.

American Folk Material

Most folk traditions are lost in an antiquity that America's national youth clearly lacks. American civilization was hand-carved out of a wilderness by men who brought with them the culture of another continent. None the less, there is a great quantity of indigenous folk material from the two areas within the United States which gave the new nation its purest folk heritage—the plantation South and the expanding West.

From the South came the tradition of the Negro. While it is preponderantly racial rather than regional, it is also a composite of black and white cultures, a hybrid of great strength and individuality. Its language and song, especially the primitive beauties of the spiritual, are based upon what the white man had taught his captive blacks, but they are adapted from the temperament, emotion, and manners of the Negro past. The once widespread appeal of blackface minstrelsy and the pseudo-plantation song in Stephen Foster style have often made it difficult to determine where the true Negro folk tradition in song and dance leaves off and where its imitation begins, but there is no doubt that the characteristics of the Negro slave and of the antebellum plantation South developed a completely American folk tradition.

The opening of the seemingly endless expanses of the Great Plains and the push into the western mountains produced the tradition of life in the sod shanty and covered wagon. Its folk heroes were the buffalo hunter, the homesteader, and the cowboy, representing all of the best and worst on both sides of the law. In the brief years in which the West was opened and won, there developed, in the lonely song of the night-riding cowhand to his cattle or in the raucously bawdy saloon ballad, an American folk tradition of the purest sort.

Other "pockets" of American folk culture have been important contributors to native tradition. The mountains of the upper South in Tennessee, Kentucky, and the Carolinas have probably been the most popular source of folk images next to the West, and there are many legends and tales from New England and the Hudson River. These areas lack the singularity of Western and Deep Southern patterns; the influences from England and the Continent are often easy to trace. The Indian, on the other hand, has contributed surprisingly little to the development of an American folk tradition. Native Indian lore, familiar and attractive though it is, has nevertheless made little impression upon our own. Books, plays, and poems have been written about the Indian, but he has not become assimilated as a vital element in our national heritage.

The Possibility of Folk Drama

If one sets out to write a folk song or story, he may imitate and he may suggest, but he must admit that he is writing peripherally or "in the manner of," rather than foolishly try to convince his audience that his creation is legitimately "folk." In writing drama he must acknowledge the same limitations. There are genuine folk dramas, pageants, dramatized incidents, even religious rituals, which have been a part of folklore in many parts of the world. The highly complex symbolic drama from the Far East has descended from a remote past, almost unchanged. Holiday celebrations in England, with mummers and their George-and-Dragon plays, are fully native.

Since in America it is difficult to find extensive native theatre apart from Indian rain dances and similar rituals, the writer of a folk play may not be able to point to native prototypes of his work. He must nevertheless realize that he is writing an essentially *derived* piece of work, just as is the novelist or the poet. He must meet several requirments even then, if his derivation is to be convincing. He must know his subject, both the people he is representing and the history of their culture. He must be completely, not superficially, acquainted with the mores, the ideas, and the inner drives of his characters, and he must above all be faithful in the creation of their expressed thoughts both to the intent they convey and to the dialect in which they speak. He must have a twofold, almost self-contradictory view. First he must be subjective about his topic, for he must show that he knows and understands, that he conveys compassion and sympathy for all who appear upon his stage. He cannot, on the other hand, avoid an imperative objectivity. He must stand aside, refuse to comment upon, to caricature, or to demand emotional reaction based on calculated effect at the expense of authenticity. If the writer has been honest with himself, his subject, and his audience, what appears on stage may be believed as honestly representative of what it assumes to imitate. As long as he does all this, we can accept his product as a *folk drama*, remembering at the same time that it is *in* the tradition, and does not spring forth as a part *of* the tradition.

The Romantic Distortion

Three of the favorite folk subjects in the American theatre of the nineteenth century were the Indian, the frontiersman, and the Negro, but their gross misinterpretation precluded the possibility of an authentically derived folk drama. Take for instance John Augustus Stone's *Metamora* of 1829, probably the best example of the many highly popular Indian plays of the period. Relating the plot of this story of white man's intrigue and treachery during King Philip's War would be useless; it is full of wicked rascals, ruined gentlemen, and innocent virtue. The picture of Metamora (King Philip) provides the greater interest. When all of the attacks, plots, and killings have reached their climax and Metamora is cornered by the deceiving white man, he magnificently faces death. His wife and young child are already dead:

> METAMORA. Though numbers overpower me and treachery surround me, though friends desert me, I defy you still! Come to me—come singly to me! And this true knife that has tasted the foul blood of your nation and now

is red with the purest of mine, will feel a grasp as strong as when it flashed in the blaze of your burning dwellings, or was lifted terribly over the fallen in battle.

* * *

(*They fire.* METAMORA *falls. . . .*)

METAMORA. My curses on you, white men! May the Great Spirit curse you when he speaks in his war voice from the clouds! Murderers! The last of the Wampanoags' curse be on you! May your graves and the graves of your children be in the path the red man shall trace! And may the wolf and panther howl o'er your fleshless bones, fit banquet for the destroyers! Spirits of the grave, I come! But the curse of Metamora stays with the white man! I die! My wife! My queen! My Nahmeokee! (*Falls and dies; a tableau is formed. Drums and trumpet sound a retreat till curtain. Slow curtain.*)

Equally as noble as the redskin was the hardy woodsman. Nimrod Wildfire, Bloody Nathan, and others inhabited the plays of the day, but the last and best, and in many ways the most preposterous, was Frank Murdoch's 1872 *Davy Crockett*, subtitled *Be Sure You're Right Then Go Ahead*. This good, tenderhearted, verbose young man, wise in the ways of the forest, encounters his childhood companion, Eleanor, journeying through the wilderness in the company of the villain, Crampton, and his weak nephew, Neil, betrothed to Eleanor. The girl is obviously a captive and Davy, of course, saves her from the horror of marriage against her will by abducting her as his own wife. Before he does, he must save both Eleanor and Neil, whom he has sheltered in his wayside shack in the midst of a snowstorm. Neil has been seriously injured by a mishap on the way:

ELEANOR. What is it?

DAVY. That's wolves.

ELEANOR. Wolves—! (*Screams.*)

DAVY. Don't be skeered.

ELEANOR. But—is there no danger?

DAVY. Ain't I here?

ELEANOR. Yes, but they are so dreadfully near.

DAVY. Yes, they tracked you in the snow, and smell blood.

ELEANOR. Blood!

DAVY. Take it easy, girl. This door is built of oak, I built it—and—blazes, the bar's gone!

ELEANOR. Gone! (*Wolves howl all around cabin.*)

DAVY. Yes, I split it up to warm you and your friend. Rouse him up. The pesky devils is all around the house.

ELEANOR (*goes to Neil*). Neil—help! (*Wolves throw themselves against door. Bark.*)

DAVY. Quick, there, I can't hold the door again 'em—

NEIL. I tell you, Uncle, if the girl says no, there's an end of it—

ELEANOR. My God—he is delirious!

DAVY. What!

ELEANOR. 'Tis true, nothing can save us!

DAVY. Yes, it can!

ELEANOR. What?

DAVY. The strong arm of a backwoodsman. (*Davy bars door with his arm. The wolves attack the house. Heads seen through opening in the hut and under the door.*)

TABLEAU

Harriet Beecher Stowe was the "little woman who started this war" as Lincoln is supposed to have said, with her novel "Uncle Tom's Cabin." Though her book is all but forgotten, the play, which is not hers, seems to live forever. The drama is an out-and-out polemic, the most obvious kind of propaganda, but its picture of the Negro personality was burned into the memories of generations of playgoers. The distorted image of the incorrigible Topsy ("Ise so wicked!") and the old and wise and illiterate Uncle Tom have become part of our national inheritance, it is true, but these misconceptions established a pattern for the stage Negro to follow for three-quarters of a century. Compare the portrait of Uncle Tom in this brief dialogue with Moody's description on page 22:

TOM. Is anything mo' I kin do fo' you, Massa St. Clair?

ST. CLAIR. Nothing. Oh, Tom, my boy, the whole world is as empty as an eggshell!

TOM. Yes, Massa, I knows dat, but if you-all could look up to where Miss Eva is . . .

ST. CLAIR. I do look up, Tom. I look up and I see *nothing*. I wish to God I could! It seems to be given to poor, honest fellows like you, to see what we cannot!

TOM. I reckon you kin, Marse St. Clair, if you pray to de Lawd! "Lawd, I believe, help Thou my unbelief!"

ST. CLAIR. No, Tom, I want to believe, but I cannot. I see nothing but doubt. Who knows anything about anything? Was all that beautiful love and faith but a shifting phase of feeling passing with a breath? And there is no more Eva—nothing!

TOM. Oh, yes, Massa St. Clair, there is. I knows it!

ST. CLAIR. How do you know there is? You never *saw* the Lord!

TOM. Well, Massa, you can't see pain, kin you? But you kin feel it—jes' so Ah feel de Lawd, in my soul, Massa St. Clair. When I was sold away from mah ole woman an' mah children I was jus' mos' broke up. I says they ain't nothin' left—nothin' at all. Then the Lawd He stood by me and He say: "You cheer up, Tom, they ain't nothin' to be 'fraid of!" An' wot He done do fo' me, He do for Massa St. Clair!

ST. CLAIR. Tom, I believe you're fond of me!

TOM. Ah's willin' to lay down mah life fo' you, Massa St. Clair!

A Genuine Folk Drama

By the beginning of the new century, it was apparent that accurate portrayal of folk characteristics would make good theatre material, although it was some time before the well-entrenched unrealities could be eliminated.

Until 1918 the New York stage made small use of regional subject matter outside the West.

Two men who demonstrated the great power of a sincere stage interpretation of native American types were Eugene O'Neill, a professional playwright, and Frederick Koch, a North Dakota college professor. They were instrumental in proving that a realistic approach and a demonstration of compassionate understanding of our racial and social minorities could make as fine a drama as any other subject.

In 1910 Koch founded the Dakota Playmakers at the University of North Dakota, where students were encouraged to write and present plays which used regional material. He became professor of dramatic literature at North Carolina in 1918 and subsequently organized the Carolina Playmakers, one of the most influential groups devoted to the furtherance of native drama. At first his students concentrated on the lore of their own state, but eventually expanded their interests to include all races and all regions of the South. Through tours and published collections, this university troupe brought to American playgoers (and readers) an awareness of the tragedy, comedy, and melodrama inherent in an honest presentation of the simple folk of the backwoods and hills.

O'Neill was more sensational because he wrote for the commercial Broadway stage. *The Emperor Jones* of 1920, expressionistic in style and not in the accepted sense a folk play, made a great contribution to the further success of folk subjects by establishing the professional dramatic validity of the racial theme. In addition, O'Neill proved the ability of the Negro to perform with the most skilled dramatic talents. For the first time in the history of the New York stage he employed a Negro actor in a full-length dramatic role. In 1924, O'Neill's taut story of miscegenation in *All God's Chillun Got Wings* once more proved the great power of his subject matter.

Paul Green, a product of the Carolina Playmakers, won the 1926 Pulitzer Prize with *In Abraham's Bosom*, a painfully intense, often cruelly violent story of a Negro of mixed blood and his white father and half brother, all faithfully transcribed from the people of the Carolina woods. Lula Vollmer's *Sun-Up* of 1923 turned to the poor whites in its moving story of the widow unable to understand why her son must go to fight a war of no concern to either of them. Another Pulitzer Prize in the 1923–1924 season went to Hatcher Hughes' *Hell-Bent fer Heaven*, involving the hypocrisy of superstitious evangelism. Lynn Riggs' modestly successful *Green Grow the Lilacs*, 1931, became the fantastically triumphant *Oklahoma!*, which demonstrated, in its admixture of folksy atmosphere, song, and colorful ballet, the wide appeal of folk material.

Marc Connelly's Pulitzer Prize-winning *The Green Pastures*, 1930, stands as something entirely apart from the more conventionally derived folk drama. Its beautiful portrayal of the Southern Negro's religious beliefs puts it very close to pure folk drama. In subject matter and in the utterly inoffensive charm with which it is handled, the play is a faithful guidepost to the achievements that are possible with the great store of available folk material. Richard B. Harrison's interpretation of "De Lawd," God in the frock coat of a kindly Negro preacher, was one of the memorable stage roles of the age. Compare this typical passage with the Negro in *Uncle Tom's Cabin* and in *Porgy*. God has just created Adam, a powerfully built man dressed like a Negro field hand, and has gone down to visit him:

GOD. Good mo'nin', Son.
ADAM (*with a little awe*). Good mo'nin', Lawd.
GOD. What's yo' name, Son?
ADAM. Adam.
GOD. Adam which?
ADAM (*frankly, after a moment's puzzled groping*). Jest Adam, Lawd.
GOD. Well, Adam, how dey treatin' you? How things goin'?
ADAM. Well, Lawd, you know it's kind of a new line of wukk.
GOD. You'll soon get de hang of it. You know yo' kind of a new style with me. . . .

De Lawd creates Eve, and then speaks to both of them.

GOD. . . . Now I'll tell you what I'm gonter do. I'm gonter put you in charge here. I'm gonter give you de run of dis whole garden. Eve, you take care of dis man an' Adam you take care of dis woman. You belong to each other. I don't want you to try to do too much caize yo' both kind of experiment wid me an' I ain't sho' whether you could make it. You two jest enjoy yo'self. Drink de water from de little brooks an' de wine from de grapes an' de berries, an' eat de food dat's hangin' for you in de trees. (*He pauses, startled by a painful thought.*) Dat is, in all but one tree. (*He pauses. Then, not looking at them.*) You know what I mean, my children?
ADAM and EVE. Yes Lawd. (*They slowly turn their heads left, toward the branches of an offstage tree. Then they look back at GOD.*)
ADAM. Thank you, Lawd.
EVE. Thank you, Lawd.
GOD. I gotter be gittin' along now. I got a hund'ed thousan' things to do 'fo' you take you' nex' breath. Enjoy yo'selves—

Porgy

Porgy, a derived folk drama, is in nearly every instance the best play of its kind from the period of revived folk interest in the 1920s. Dorothy and DuBose Heyward have been absolutely honest in their approach, and they remain true to the spirit of the folk society they portray. The moral outlook and the emotional responses of the characters are products of a closely knit society living by its own private code. The onlooker has no right to demand that the inhabitants of Catfish Row be anything else; in their sight, the onlooker may be far more degraded than they.

The most immediate evidence of authenticity is the dialect. It is not the "Lawd-bless-deah-ol'-Massa" routine of *Uncle Tom's Cabin,* nor the more familiar speech pattern of *The Green Pastures. Porgy* attempts to transcribe the heavy, almost unintelligible dialect of the Charleston Negro, giving it the quality of the "Gullah" which he actually speaks. After Jake, Mingo, and Sporting Life talk to "dem bones" in the opening crap game, it is not long before something different emerges. Jake's early line, "I ain't likes dat luck" is not quite what Uncle Tom would say. Whenever conventional stage dialect seems to have intruded, the sound of "Him dress she up in he own eye, till she stan' like de Queen of Sheba to he" reassures us that it has not. The demands on an actor reading these lines are far more severe than one hired to play Uncle Tom or De Lawd.

Soon after the opening curtain, Catfish Row takes on the atmosphere of the human hive that it is. As the activity of the evening progresses toward its violent climax, the audience quickly senses that this is no romanticized glossing, nor is it a picture of happy-go-lucky indolence in the childlike, naïve, comic Negro figures who pleasantly divert with their capers. These men and women are in deadly earnest about their lives, and they are going to be treated as credible human beings. Probably the most impressive effect which the Heywards gain in the entire play is their successful outlining of the wide separation of this world from "civilization" outside. The white man is the intruder, as would be expected, but he also represents a system that has no connection with and very little meaning to the life within Catfish Row. No matter how vicious the crime within the circle, the white policeman is the enemy. Not even the widowed Serena will inform against the fugitive murderer of her husband; the detective can only threaten uselessly and take a whimpering, half-imbecilic old man as hostage. "It sho' pay nigger to go blin' in dis world," sagely observes Maria. The undertaker, though unsatisfied with his pay, cannot surrender one of his kind to the hands of the white medical students and will take whatever he can get. When justice is done and Crown dies, the silence and the professed ignorance are impenetrable. Again the white man is frustrated in his attempt to force the defenses; the combat ends in a draw. It will continue indefinitely in this manner; the enemy will always find his blustering noise and his legal racial supremacy of little effect. Leader-less, without organization, all react without prompting when the outer gates are breached; the inner defenses invariably hold.

It is a different matter when one of the same society sees the opportunity to cash in on his own people's appalling ignorance. Frazier, the unscrupulous lawyer, knows that his own people will never force him into jail. In the first place, he knows they do not comprehend the white man's interpretation of the law, nor the white man's morals. They see far more meaning in surrender-ing a dollar or two of hard-begged money for a fancy piece of worthless "divorce" paper than in living by an outside code. Argument is pointless, and Archdale, the outsider, knows he can get nowhere with logic. Porgy and Bess are satisfied; they agree with Archdale's conclusion that "respectability at one-fifty" is a bargain.

Folk tradition among the Deep South Negroes is handled in detail and with integrity in *Porgy*. There is intimate knowledge and understanding, and there is also respect. Racial idiosyncrasy is never permitted to intrude beyond its natural place as a function of the whole. Audience laughter or pity cannot be derived by seeing the Negro society in contrast to the "better" quality of the white man's universe, but can only be a response to the quality of this special group itself. The singing, the "shoutin'," and the emotional releases in the wake are beautiful in their primitive passion, and the unleashed ecstasy of vivid folk color at the close of Act I is a deeply moving scene. The determina-tion to end Bess's delirium by the invocations of the "conjur' 'oman" is earnestly serious. At the height of the hurricane, when uncontrollable terror mounts to the point of almost complete mass hysteria and beats upon the audience in accumulated crescendo, the emotional climax retains the same honesty found everywhere in the play.

The Heywards have not forgotten the importance of character and plot. By avoiding usually expected stereotypes, they have eliminated simply cut, flat-dimensioned figures in a melodramatic story. They have given full life to Porgy, Bess, Crown, Sporting Life—in fact to everyone who enters or leaves the sagging gates. Porgy, a cripple, has great capacity for love and he feels the natural desire to be a whole man. He succeeds in his dispatch of Crown and shouts to Bess, "Yo' gots a *man* now!" Bess, a lost soul, unable to take care of herself, desperately needs the loving help which Porgy will murder to provide for her. Bess is a wicked woman, even by the standards of Catfish Row, but she arouses pity toward herself and a hope that she can win her struggle. She fights what is for her a successful battle, until faced with the evil so well designed in the "high-yellar" Sporting Life.

Although every important incident in these pitiful lives provides almost continual melodramatics, there is a constant feeling throughout the play that violence is something these people have learned to expect and to endure. The plot never departs beyond probability. With the Negro's easy access to drink and narcotics and with his need for release from the killing drudgery of enforced social caste, there is an always smoldering fuse that can touch off a devastating explosion with minimum effort. The frantic search for an emotional way out is brilliantly detailed in this play, so that plot and character combine with absolute conviction. Furthermore, the violence has no relationship to the Negro's plight vis-à-vis the white man's attitude. The play never descends into a social document, nowhere preaches or extols. Instead, it becomes the drama of a vibrant people's collected lives, and we can meet it on no other terms.

A Few Words about the Opera

Porgy was a moderately successful play, well received by the critics and public, and was an important part of the Theatre Guild's 1927–1928 season. As a mature treatment of the American Negro, enacted by a large colored cast, *Porgy* was a remarkable and memorable play. Today, however, both the play and the original novel on which it is based are almost completely forgotten in the brilliance of the phenomenally successful operatic version, *Porgy and Bess.*

George Gershwin, the young writer of popular musical comedies and symphonic jazz during the 1930s, had been interested in the possibilities of setting the Heywards' play to music ever since it first opened. For about two years he worked on a score which he hoped would convey the genuine native atmosphere present in the spoken play. With the help of his brother, Ira, who often teamed with him in writing the lyrics for his musical shows, and of Mr. Heyward as librettist, Gershwin fashioned what has since turned into America's nearest approach to genuine folk opera.

Porgy and Bess opened at the Alvin Theatre in New York on October 10, 1935. In both its original semioperatic form and in the subsequent longer, fully developed opera of its revival, *Porgy and Bess* has become an American classic. As one critic has stated, Gershwin need not have written any other music to have guaranteed him a preeminent position as an American composer. The opera, although changing the name slightly, remains the same story, but the music has brought an entirely new atmosphere, genuinely modern, yet soundly based upon authentic Negro song and rhythm.

Each time the opera has been revived, it has become more firmly established and more enthusiastically welcomed. After the original production, Cheryl Crawford revived it in New York in 1942. In 1952, produced by Blevin Davis and Robert Breen, it was sent on a short tour of Europe, returned to Broadway in 1953, and in 1954 started another series of European engagements.

When the first European tour was proposed in late 1952, the wisdom of the venture was seriously doubted in some quarters. Fears that it might be regarded as "cheap" and poor propaganda were completely unfounded. The opera was welcomed throughout Europe with cheers and almost endless applause. The weeklong appearance at La Scala in Milan was the longest single engagement in the history of the famous house. From Moscow to Paris to London to Belgrade the *Porgy and Bess* company, collectively and individually, became a tremendous propaganda weapon for America, bringing a personal commendation from President Eisenhower.

Dorothy and DuBose Heyward

DuBose Heyward was a native of Charleston, South Carolina, where he was born in 1885. When a young boy, he worked as a cotton checker on the wharves of that city and had firsthand contacts with the people he was later to picture in Catfish Row. He was at first a successful insurance man and then entered into a literary career in the early 1920s. He established a poetry society in Charleston, published some poems, "Carolina Chansons" in 1922, and two more, "Skylines and Horizons" in 1924 and "Jasbo Brown" in 1931. The novel, "Porgy," appeared in 1925, but has since been almost totally obscured by the much more famous and successful play and opera. Before his death in 1940, Heyward wrote the novels "Peter Ashley," 1932, "Star-spangled Virgin," 1939, about the Virgin Islanders and the Roosevelt New Deal, and the folk novel, "Mamba's Daughters," 1929. This last book was made into the successful stage production by Mrs. Heyward, and starred Ethel Waters in a distinguished performance in 1939.

Dorothy Hartzell Kuhns was born in Worcester, Ohio, in 1890. She attended Radcliffe College and studied playwriting at Harvard under Professor George Pierce Baker in his 47 Workshop, and at Columbia University. In 1923 she married DuBose Heyward. She won a playwriting prize for her first play, *Nancy Ann*, in 1924. She and her husband collaborated in the dramatization of *Porgy* which the Theatre Guild produced in 1927. After her husband's death, the Guild produced another of her plays, *Set My People Free*, concerning a slave rebellion, in 1948.

PORGY

by
Dorothy and DuBose Heyward

Original setting of Catfish Row for *Porgy*. All subsequent stagings of opera and motion picture versions have elaborated upon this design, but none have departed materially from the first version. The tightly knit, hivelike existence of the inhabitants is precisely conveyed through this near-classic in stage design. (*"Stages of the World," Theatre Arts Books. Photo by Vandamm.*)

Porgy was first produced by the Theatre Guild on October 10, 1927 at the Guild Theatre in New York. Its initial run was 217 performances, followed by a further revival run of 137 performances. The following cast appeared in the opening production:

MARIA, keeper of the cookshop	*Georgette Harvey*
JAKE, captain of the fishing fleet	*Wesley Hill*
LILY	*Dorothy Paul*
MINGO	*Richard Huey*
ANNIE	*Ella Madison*
SPORTING LIFE	*Percy Verwayne*
SERENA, ROBBINS' wife	*Rose MacClendon*
ROBBINS, a young stevedore	*Lloyd Gray*
JIM, a stevedore	*Peter Clark*
CLARA, JAKE'S wife	*Marie Young*
PETER, the honeyman	*Hayes Pryor*
PORGY, a crippled beggar	*Frank Wilson*
CROWN, a stevedore	*Jack Carter*
CROWN'S BESS	*Evelyn Ellis*
A DETECTIVE	*Stanley de Wolfe*
TWO POLICEMEN	*Hugh Rennie*
	Maurice McRae
UNDERTAKER	*Leigh Whipper*
SCIPIO	*Melville Greene*
SIMON FRAZIER, a lawyer	*A. B. Comathiere*
NELSON, a fisherman	*G. Edward Brown*
ALAN ARCHDALE	*Edward Fielding*
THE CRAB MAN	*Leigh Whipper*
THE CORONER	*Garrett Minturn*

Directed by Rouben Mamoulian
Settings by Cleon Throckmorton

The action of the play takes place in Charleston, South Carolina, in the early 1900s.

ACT ONE

SCENE 1: *Before the rise of each curtain, the bells of St. Michael's, adjacent to the Negro quarter of old Charleston, chime the hour. The chimes are heard occasionally throughout the play. Before the rise of first curtain, St. Michael's chimes the quarters and strikes eight.*
The curtain rises on the court of Catfish Row, now a Negro tenement in a fallen quarter of Charleston, but in Colonial days one of the finest buildings of the aristocracy. *The walls rise around a court, except a part of the rear wall of the old house, which breaks to leave a section of lower wall pierced at its center by a massive wrought-iron gate of great beauty which hangs unsteadily between brick pillars surmounted by pineapples carved of Italian marble.*
By day, the walls of the entire structure present a mottled color effect of varying pastel shades, caused by the at-

mospheric action of many layers of color wash. A brilliant note is added by rows of blooming flame-colored geraniums in old vegetable tins on narrow shelves attached to each window sill. All of the windows are equipped with dilapidated slat shutters, some of which are open, others closed, but with the slats turned so that any one inside could look out without being seen. The floor of the spacious court is paved with large flagstones, and these gleam in faintly varying colors under their accumulated grime.

Beyond the gate and above the wall, one sees a littered cobbled street, an old gas street lamp, and, beyond that again, the blue expanse of the bay, with Fort Sumter showing on the horizon. Over the wall can be seen masts and spars of fishing boats lying on the beach.

By night, the court depends for its illumination upon the wheezing gas lamp, and the kerosene lamps and lanterns that come and go in the hands of the occupants of the Row.

At left front is PORGY's room (door and window), and beyond it, an arch letting on an inside yard. The pump stands against the wall right back; then, on around right wall, SERENA's doorway, with her window above it, two more doors, then the door to MARIA's cookshop. Center right is seen SERENA's wash bench, and near right wall, well down front, is a table on which MARIA serves her meals during the warm weather.

As the curtain rises, revealing Catfish Row on a summer evening, the court reëchoes with African laughter and friendly banter in "Gullah," the language of the Charleston Negro, which still retains many African words. The audience understands none of it. Like the laughter and movement, the twanging of a guitar from an upper window, the dancing of an urchin with a loose, shuffling step, it is a part of the picture of Catfish Row as it really is—an alien scene, a people as little known to most Americans as the people of the Congo. Gradually, it seems to the audience that they are beginning to understand this foreign language. In reality, the "Gullah" is being

tempered to their ears, spoken more distinctly with the African words omitted.

It is Saturday night, and most of the residents of Catfish Row are out in the court, sitting watching the crap shooters or moving to and fro to visit with one neighbor, then another. Among those present are:

MARIA, matriarch of the court, massive in proportions and decisive in action.

ANNIE, middle-aged, quiet, and sedate.

LILY, loud, good-natured, the court hoyden.

CLARA, who has her baby in her arms. She is scarcely more than a girl and has a sweet wistful face.

JAKE, CLARA's husband. A successful captain of the fishing fleet; good-looking, good-natured.

"SPORTING LIFE," bootlegger to Catfish Row; a slender, overdressed, high-yellow Negro.

MINGO, young and lazy.

JIM and NELSON, fishermen.

SCIPIO, a boy of twelve, one of the numerous offspring of ROBBINS and SERENA.

ROBBINS and SERENA are still in their room on the second floor. SERENA is seen occasionally as she moves back and forth past her lighted window. She is a self-respecting "white folks" Negress, of about thirty.

The men are gathering for their Saturday-night crap game. They are grouped between gate and PORGY's room. JAKE is squatting right, MINGO center rear, and SPORTING LIFE is left, forming triangle. A smoking kerosene lamp is in center of group, and the men are tossing and retrieving their dice in the circle of light.

JAKE (rolling). Seems like dese bones don't gib me nuttin' but box cars tonight. It was de same two weeks ago, an' de game broke me. I ain't likes dat luck. (SPORTING LIFE produces his own dice, and throws with a loud grunt and snap of his fingers. MINGO snatches the dice and balances them in his hand.)

SPORTING LIFE. Damn yu', gib me dem bones. (MINGO holds him off with one hand while he hands the dice to JAKE.)

MINGO. Whut yo' say to dese, Jake?

JAKE (*examining them*). Dem's de same cockeye bones whut clean de gang out las' week. Ef dey rolls in dis game, I rolls out. (*Hands the dice back to* SPORT-ING LIFE.) Eberybody rolls de same bones in dis game, Sportin' Life—take 'em or leabe 'em. (ROBBINS *comes from door, rear right. He is a well-set-up Negro of about thirty. The window above him opens, and* SERENA *leans from sill.*)

SERENA (*pleadingly*). Honey-boy!

ROBBINS. Now, fuh Gawd's sake, don't start dat again. I goin' play—git dat.

SERENA. Ef yo' didn't hab licker in yo' right now, yo' wouldn't talk like dat. Yo' know whut yo' done promise' me las' week.

ROBBINS. All right, den, I wouldn't shoot no more dan fifty cents. (*Joins the group.* CLARA *paces up and down the court, singing softly to her baby.*) Dat ole lady ob mine hell on joinin' de buryin' lodge. I says, spen' um while yo' is still alibe an' kickin'. (*Picks up dice. Throws them with a loud grunt.*) I ain't see no buzzard 'round here yit. (JIM, *a big, strong-looking fellow, saunters over to the group of crap players. A cotton hook swings from his belt.*)

JIM. Lor', I is tire' dis night. I'm t'inkin' ob gettin' out ob de cotton business. Mebby it all right fo' a fella like Crown dat Gawd start to make into a bull, den change He min'. But it ain't no work fo' a man.

JAKE. Better come 'long on de *Sea Gull*. I gots place fo' nudder fishermans.

JIM. Dat suit me. Dis cotton hook hab swung he las' bale ob cotton. Here, Scipio, yo' wants a cotton hook? (*Throws the hook to* SCIPIO, *who takes it eagerly, fastens it at his waist, and goes about court playing he is a stevedore, lifting objects with the hook and pretending that they are of tremendous weight.* CLARA *passes the group, crooning softly.*)

CLARA. "Hush, li'l baby, don' yo' cry. Fadder an' mudder born to die."

JAKE (*standing up*). Whut! dat chile ain't sleep yit. Gib um to me. I'll fix um fo' yo'. (*Takes baby from* CLARA, *rocks it in his arms, sings.*)

"My mammy tells me, long time ago,
Son, don' yo' marry no gal yo' know.
Spen' all yo' money—eat all yo' bread,
Gone to Savannah, lef' yo' fo' dead."

(*Several of the men join in on the last line.* JAKE *rocks the baby more violently and begins to shuffle.* CLARA *watches anxiously.*)

"Spen' all yo' money. Steal all yo' clothes. Whut will become of yo', Gawd only knows."

(*The light leaves* SERENA's *window.* JAKE *swings the baby back to* CLARA.) Dere now! Whut I tells yo'. He 'sleep already. (*The baby wails. The men laugh.* CLARA *carries baby to her room. Closes door.* SERENA *comes from her door with a lamp which she sets on her wash bench. She sits beside it and looks anxiously toward crap players.*)

MARIA (*to* SERENA). Whut worryin' yo', Serena? Yo' gots one ob de bes' mens in Catfish Row. Why yo' ain't let um play widout pickin' on um?

SERENA. He gots licker in um tonight, an' Robbins ain't de same man wid licker. (MINGO *is rolling and retrieving the dice. While he does so, he looks and laughs at* ROBBINS, *then sings at him.*)

MINGO (*singing*). "My mammy tell me, long time ago,
Son don't yo' marry no gal yo' know."
(*Speaking to* ROBBINS.) Ought to be single like Porgy an' me. Den yo' kin shoot bones widout git pick on.

ROBBINS. Oh, my lady all right; only 'cept' she don' like craps. She people belong to Gob'nor Rutledge. Ain't yo' see Miss Rutledge come to see she when she sick?

MARIA (*overhearing, to* SERENA). Oh, dat Miss Rutledge come to see yuh?

SERENA. Sho! yo' ain' know dat?

MARIA. She eber sell any ob she ole clothes?

SERENA. Not she. But sometime she gib 'em away.

MARIA (*sighing*). I wish I could git a dress off she. She de firs' pusson I eber see whut hipped an' busted 'zac'ly like me.

ROBBINS (*boasting*). Yes, suh! my lady —Yo' bes' sabe yo' talk fo' dem dice. Bones ain't got no patience wid' 'omen.

MINGO. Dat's de trut'. Course dey can't git along together. Dey is all two atter de same money.

JAKE. Annie dere likes de single life, ain't it, Annie? Whut become ob dat ole fisherman used to come fo' see yo'?

ANNIE. He ain't fisherman.

JAKE. Whut he do?

ANNIE. Him ain't do nuttin' mos' all de time. Odder time, him is a shoe carpenter. (*The voice of* PETER, *the old "honey man," is heard in the street, drawing nearer and nearer.*)

PETER. Here comes de honey man. Yo' gots honey?—Yes, ma'am, I gots honey. —Yo' gots honey in de comb?—Yes, ma'am, I gots honey in de comb.—Yo' gots honey cheap?—Yes, ma'am, my honey cheap. (PETER *enters gate and closes it behind him. He is a gentle, kindly Negro, verging on senility. A large wooden tray covered with a white cloth is balanced on his head.*)

LILY (*going to meet him*). Well, here come my ole man. (*Takes tray from his head and shouts in his ear.*) Now gimme de money. (*He hands her some coins. She points to bench.*) Now go sit an' res'. (*He does as he is told. She places tray in her room and returns to circle.*)

MARIA. Yo', Scipio! Here comes Porgy! Open de gate fo' uh! (PORGY *drives up to the gate in his soapbox chariot. He is a crippled beggar of the Charleston streets, who has done much to overcome his handicap of almost powerless legs by supplying himself with a patriarchal and very dirty goat, which draws a cart made of an upturned soap box, on two lopsided wheels, which bears the inscription,* "WILD ROSE SOAP, PURE AND FRAGRANT." PORGY *is no longer young, and yet not old. There is a suggestion of the mystic in his thoughtful, sensitive face. He is black, with the almost purple blackness of unadulterated Congo blood.* SCIPIO *reluctantly interrupts his performance on a mouth organ, shuffles across court, and opens one side of the ponderous gate.* PORGY *drives through and pulls up beside the crap ring.*)

JAKE. Here de ole crap shark.

PORGY. All right, Mingo! Jake! Gib' me a han' out dis wagon. I gots a pocket full ob de buckra money, an' he goin' to any man whut gots de guts fo' shoot 'em off me! (MINGO *and* JAKE *help* PORGY *from wagon to a seat on ground at left front of circle.* SCIPIO *leads goat away through arch at rear left.* JIM *saunters to gate and looks out.*)

ROBBINS. All right, mens! Roll 'em! We done wait long 'nough.

JIM (*returning to group*). Yo' bes' wait for Crown. I seen um comin', takin' de whole sidewalk, an' he look like he ain't goin' stan' no foolin'.

PORGY. Is Bess wid um?

JAKE. Listen to Porgy! I t'ink he sof' on Crown's Bess! (*All the men laugh.*)

PORGY. Gawd make cripple to be lonely. T'ain't no use for um to be sof' on a 'oman.

MARIA. Porgy gots too good sense to look twice at dat licker-guzzlin' slut.

LILY. Licker-guzzlin'! It takes more'n licker fo' sati'fy Crown's Bess.

SERENA. Happy dus'! Dat's what it take! Dat gal Bess ain't fit for Gawd-fearin' ladies to 'sociate wid!

SPORTING LIFE. Sistuhs! You needn't worry! Gawd-fearin' ladies is de las' t'ing on eart' Bess is a-wantin' for 'sociate wid.

PORGY. Can't yo' keep yo' mout' off Bess! Between de Gawd-fearin' ladies an' de Gawd-damnin' men, dat gal ain't gots no chance.

JAKE. Ain't I tells yo' Porgy sof' on um? (*More laughter.*)

PORGY. I ain't neber swap one word wid she. (CROWN *and* BESS *appear at gate.* CROWN *is lurching slightly and* BESS *is piloting him through the entrance.* CROWN *is a huge Negro of magnificent physique, a stevedore on the cotton wharfs. He is wearing blue denim pants and tan shirt with a bright bandanna about his neck. From his belt hangs a long gleaming cotton hook.* BESS *is slender, but sinewy; very black, wide nostrils, and large, but well-formed mouth. She flaunts a typical, but debased, Negro beauty. From the occupants of Catfish Row there are cries of,* "Here comes Big Boy!" " 'Low, Crown!" " 'Low Bess," etc.)

CROWN (*to* SPORTING LIFE). All right, high stepper. Gib us a pint, and make it damn' quick. (SPORTING LIFE *pulls a flask from his hip pocket and hands it to* CROWN. CROWN *jerks out cork and takes a long pull. To* BESS.) Pay um, Bess! (BESS *settles for the bottle, then takes her seat by* CROWN, *ignoring the women of the court.* CROWN *hands her the flask, from which she takes a long pull. She meets* SERENA's *eyes, laughs at her hostility, and at once extends the bottle to* ROBBINS.)

BESS. Hab one to de Gawd-fearin' ladies. Dere's nuttin' else like 'em—t'ank Gawd! (ROBBINS *tries to resist, but the fumes of raw liquor are too much for him. He takes a deep drink.* CROWN *snatches the bottle from him, gulps the entire remaining contents, and shatters it on the flags behind him. The crap circle is now complete. The positions are as follows:*

Rear

X BESS   X CROWN

X DADDY
PETER

X MINGO   X SPORTING LIFE
X JAKE
X ROBBINS   X PORGY

Footlights

CROWN *throws coin down before him.*)

CROWN. I'm talkin' to yo' mans. Anybody answerin' me? (*They all throw down money.*)

ROBBINS (*to* JAKE). An' dem fine chillen ob mine!

CROWN. Shet yo' damn mout' an' t'row.

ROBBINS (*taken aback and rolling hastily*). Box cars again! (*They all roar with laughter.*)

MINGO. Cover 'em, brudder, cover 'em.

ROBBINS. Cover hell! I goin' pass 'em along an' see ef I kin break my luck.

MINGO. He lady ain't 'low um but fifty cent, an' he can't take no chance wid bad luck. (*All laugh at* ROBBINS.)

BESS (*with a provocative look at* SERENA). Dat all right, Honey-boy, I'll stake yo' when yo' four bits done gone.

SERENA (*to* ROBBINS). Go ahead an'

play, yo' ain't need no charity off no she-devils.

BESS (*to* ROBBINS). See whut I git fuh yo'. De she-gawds is easy when yo' knows de way. (CROWN *claps his hand over* BESS's *mouth.*)

CROWN. Shet yo' damn mout'. Yo' don' gib Mingo no chance to talk to de bones. (JAKE *has cast and lost, and the dice are now with* MINGO, *who is swinging them back and forth in his hand. Sings.*)

MINGO. "Ole snake-eye, go off an' die. Ole man seben, come down from Heaben." (*Grunts, throws, and snaps fingers.*) Seben! (*Scoops up dice.*)

CROWN. I ain't see dat seben yit. (*Snatches* MINGO's *hand and opens fingers. Looks at dice.*) Yo' done tu'n um ober.

MINGO (*to Circle*). Whut I t'row? (*Cries of* "Seben," "Jus' as he say," *etc.* MINGO *pulls in pot.*)

CROWN. Well, dere's more'n one man done meet he Gawd fuh pullin' 'em in 'fore I reads 'em. See? An' I'm a-sayin' it ober tonight. (*All ante again.*)

MINGO. Come home again to yo' pappy (*Shoots.*) Four to make! Come four! (*Shoots. Cries of* "Seben," "Crapped out," *etc.* MINGO *passes dice to* CROWN.)

CROWN. Come clean, yo' little black-eyed bitches! (*Shoots. Cries of* "Six," "Six to make," *etc.* CROWN *takes up bones and produces rabbit foot from pocket. He touches dice with it.*) Kiss rabbit foot. (*Shoots.*)

SPORTING LIFE (*reaching for dice*). Crapped out! Come to your pappy. (CROWN *extends a huge arm and brushes him back. He tries to focus his eyes on dice.*)

ROBBINS. Crown too cock-eyed drunk to read um. What he is say, Bess?

BESS. Seben.

CROWN (*scowls at* ROBBINS, *then turns to* SPORTING LIFE). I ain't drunk 'nough to read 'em, dat's de trouble. Licker ain't strong 'nough. Gimme a pinch ob happy dus', Sportin' Life. (SPORTING LIFE *takes from his pocket a small folded paper.*)

BESS. Don' gib' um dat stuff, Sportin' Life. He's ugly drunk already.

CROWN. Yo' is a good one to talk! Pay um and shut up. (*Takes the paper from*

Sporting Life, *unfolds it, and inhales the powder. Bess pays Sporting Life. Daddy Peter takes his pipe from his mouth and crowds in between Crown and Sporting Life, putting a hand on the arm of each.*)

Peter. Frien' an' dice an' happy dus' ain't meant to 'sociate. Yo' mens bes' go slow. (Crown *draws back his fist. Cries of "Leabe Uncle Peter be!" "He ain't mean no harm!" etc. Crown relaxes. Sporting Life picks up the dice.*)

Sporting Life. Huh, seben! Huh, seben! Huh, seben! (*Shoots.*) 'Leben! Come home, Fido! (*Whistles, snaps fingers, and pulls in pot. All ante.*)

Crown. Gawd damn it. I ain't read um yet. (*All laugh at him. Cries of "Crown cockeye drunk." "Can't tell dice from watermillion," etc. Crown, growling.*) All right. I'm tellin' yo'.

Sporting Life (*shooting*). Six to make! Get um again! (*Shoots.*) (*Cries of "Seben," "Crapped out," etc. Porgy takes up dice and commences to sway, with his eyes half closed. He apostrophizes dice in a sort of sing-song chant.*)

Porgy. Oh, little stars, roll me some light. (*Shoots.*) 'Leben little stars, come home. (*Pulls in pot. All ante.*) Roll dis poor beggar a sun an' moon! (*Shoots.*)

Mingo. Snake eyes!

Porgy. Dem ain't no snake eyes. Dey is a fleck ob mornin' an' ebenin' star. An' jus' yo' watch um rise fo' dis po' beggar. (*Shoots. Cries of "made um," "Dat's he point," etc. Porgy pulls in pot.*)

Crown. Roll up dat fella sleeve. (Porgy *rolls up his sleeves.*) Well, yo' gots dem damn dice conjer den. (*All ante. Porgy rolls. Cries of "Snake eyes," "Crapped out!" All ante. Robbins takes up bones, whistles, shoots, snaps them back very rapidly.*)

Robbins. Nine to make! (*Whistles, shoots, snaps fingers.*) Read um! (*Sweeps them up, and reaches for money. Crown seizes his wrist.*)

Crown. Tech dat money an' meet yo' Gawd.

Robbins. Take yo' han' off me, yo' lousy houn'! (*Turns to* Jake.) Han' me dat brick behin' yo'. (Jake *reaches*

brickbat and puts it in his free hand. Crown jerks his cotton hook out of his belt and lunges forward, bowling Robbins over, and knocking brick from his hand. Crown then steps back and kicks over lamp, extinguishing it. The stage is now dark except for the small lamp at Serena's wash bench. This lights up the woman's terrified face as she strains her gaze into the darkness. Maria, Clara and the others of her group stand behind her. From the crap ring come cries and curses. Suddenly, shutters are thrown open in right and left walls of building, and forms strain from the sills. As the shutters are banged open, shafts light from them flash across the court, latticing it with a cross play of light.*

Crown *and* Robbins *are revealed facing each other:* Crown *crouched for a spring with gleaming cotton hook extended;* Robbins *defenseless, his back to the wall. Then* Robbins *lunges under the hook and they clinch. The fight proceeds with no distinguishable words from the combatants, but with bestial growls and breath that sobs and catches in their throats. In and out of the cross-play of light they sway—now revealed, now in darkness. The watchers move back and stand around the wall. They commence a weird, high-keyed moaning that rises as the figures take the light, and subsides almost to silence when they are obscured.*

Suddenly, out of the dark, Crown *swings* Robbins *into a shaft of light.* Crown *is facing the audience and is holding* Robbins *by the throat at arms' length. With a triumphant snarl, he swings the hook downward.* Robbins *drops back toward audience into darkness, and* Crown *stands in high light. There is dead silence now. In it* Crown *looks down at his hands, opening and closing them. Then he draws his arm across his eyes. The silence is shattered by a piercing scream, and* Serena *runs across the court and throws herself on the body.* Bess *appears in the light beside* Crown. *She shakes him violently by the arm.*)

Bess. Wake up an' hit it out. Yo' ain't got no time to lose.

CROWN (*looking stupidly into the gloom at* SERENA *and the body of her man*). Whut de matter?

BESS (*hysterically*). Yo' done kill Robbins, an' de police'll be comin'. (*She starts to pull him toward the gate.*)

CROWN. Whar yo' goin' hide? Dey knows you an' me pulls togedder. (*In the half light, it can now be seen that the court has been deserted, except for* SERENA, *who sits beside the body with her head bowed, and sways from side to side with a low, steady moaning. A match is scratched and held in* PORGY'S *hand. He is crouched on his doorstep. He looks toward* ROBBINS' *body, and his face shows horror and fear. He gives a whimpering moan, and as the match burns out, he drags himself over his threshold and closes the door.*)

BESS. Dey wouldn't look fuh me here. I'll stay here an' hide. Somebody always willin' to take care ob Bess.

CROWN (*now at gate*). Well, git dis: he's temporary. I'se comin' back when de hell dies down.

BESS. All right. Only git out now. Here, take dis. (*Thrusts the money into his hand. She pushes him out of gate. He disappears into the shadows. She turns around and faces the court. It is silent and empty except for the body and* SERENA. SPORTING LIFE *steps out of the shadows under* SERENA'S *steps, startling her.*) Dat yo', Sportin' Life? Fo' Gawd's sake, gib me a little touch happy dus'. I shakin' so I can hardly stan'. (*Suddenly remembering.*) Oh, I done gib' all de money to Crown. I can't pay fo' um. But, for Gawd's sake, gib me jus' a touch!

SPORTING LIFE. Yo' ain't needs to pay fo' um, Bess. (*Pours powder into her hand.*) Sportin' Life ain't go back on a frien' in trouble like dese odder low-life critters. (BESS *quickly inhales the powder. Sighs with relief.*) Listen! I'll be goin' back up to Noo Yo'k soon. All yo' gots to do is to come wid me now. I'll hide yo' out an' take yo' on wid me when I go. Why, yo' an' me'll be a swell team! Wid yo' looks an' all de frien's I gots dere, it'll be ebery night an' all night—

licker, dus', bright lights, an' de sky de limit! (*He looks apprehensively toward gate. Takes her arm.*) Come 'long! We gots to beat it while de beatin's good. (BESS *draws away sharply from his grasp.*) Nobody 'round here's goin' to take in Crown's Bess. Yo' bes' go wid yo' only frien'.

BESS. I ain't come to dat yet.

SPORTING LIFE. Well, de cops ain't goin' find me here fo' *no* 'oman! (*Slinks out gate.* BESS *looks desperately about for shelter. She advances timidly and takes up lamp from the wash bench. She starts at rear left, and tries all of the doors as she goes. They are either locked, or slammed in her face as she reaches out to them. She comes to* MARIA'S *shop door, and as she reaches it, it is jerked open and* MARIA *confronts her.*)

MARIA (*in a tense voice*). Yo' done bring trouble 'nough. Git out 'fore de police comes.

BESS. Yo' wouldn't hab' a heart, an' let me in?

MARIA. Not till hell freeze! (*A light is lit in* PORGY'S *room, showing at window and crack in door.*)

BESS (*indicating* PORGY'S *room*). Who lib ober dere?

MARIA. He ain't no use to yo' kin'. Dat's Porgy. He a cripple an' a beggar. (BESS *seems to agree with* MARIA *that* PORGY *is of no use to her. Crosses to gate, hesitates. Then she turns slowly toward* PORGY'S *room and crosses, shuddering away from* SERENA *and the body, which she must pass on the way. She reaches the door, puts her hand on the knob, hesitates, then slowly she opens it, enters, and closes it behind her.*)

CURTAIN

SCENE 2: *St. Michael's chimes the quarters and strikes seven.*

The curtain rises on SERENA'S *room, a second story room in Catfish Row, which still bears traces of its ancient beauty in its high panelled walls and tall, slender mantel with Grecian frieze and intricate scroll work. The door is in left wall at back. Near the center of back wall a window looks toward the sea. The fireplace is in right wall. Over the mantel is a gaudy lithograph of Lincoln striking chains from the slaves. The room is vaguely lighted by several kerosene lamps, and is scantily furnished: a bed against the back wall at left, and a few chairs.*

ROBBINS' *body lies upon the bed, completely covered by a white sheet. On its chest is a large blue saucer. Standing about the bed or seated on the floor are Negroes, all singing and swaying and patting with their large feet.* SERENA *sits at the foot of the bed swaying dismally to the rhythm. They have been singing for hours. The monotony of the dirge and the steady beat of the patting has lulled several into a state of coma.*

"Deat', ain't yuh gots no shame, shame?
 Deat', ain't yuh gots no shame, shame?
 Deat', ain't yuh gots no shame, shame?
 Deat', ain't yuh gots no shame?

"Teck dis man an' gone, gone,
 Teck dis man an' gone, gone,
 Teck dis man an' gone, gone,
 Deat', ain't yuh gots no shame?

"Leabe dis 'oman lone, lone,
 Leabe dis 'oman lone, lone,
 Leabe dis 'oman lone, lone,
 Deat,' ain't yuh gots no shame?"

(The door opens and PETER *comes in. Doffs his old hat, crosses, and puts coins in saucer. The singing and swaying continue. He finds a seat at right front and begins to sway and pat with the others.* SERENA *reaches over, gets saucer, and counts coins. Replaces saucer with a hopeless expression.)*

JAKE. How de saucer stan', Sistuh? *(The singing dies gradually as, one by one, the Negroes stop to listen, but the rhythm continues.)*

SERENA *(dully).* Fourteen dolluh and thirty-six cent.

MARIA *(encouragingly).* Dat's a-comin' on Sistuh. Yo' can bury him soon.

SERENA. De Boa'd ob Healt' say he gots to git buried tomorruh.

CLARA. It cost thirty-four dolluh for

bury my grandmudder, but she gots de three carriage'.

SERENA. What I goin' to do ef I ain't gots de money?

PETER *(understanding that they refer to saucer).* Gawd gots plenty coin' fo' de saucer.

SERENA. Bless de Lo'd.

PETER. An' He goin' soften dese people heart' fo' fill de saucer till he spill ober.

SERENA. Amen, my Jedus!

PETER. De Lord will provide a grabe fo' He chillun.

CLARA. Bless de Lo'd! *(The swaying gradually changes to the rhythm of* PETER's *prayer.)*

PETER. An' he gots comfort fo' de widder.

SERENA. Oh, my Jedus!

PETER. An' food fo' de fadderless.

SERENA. Yes, Lo'd!

PETER. An' he goin' raise dis poor sinner out de grabe.

JAKE. Allelujah!

PETER. An' set him in de seat of de righteous, Amen.

SERENA. Amen, my brudder. *(They all sway in silence.)*

ANNIE *(looking toward door).* What dat?

CLARA. I hear somebody comin' up de steps now bringing much penny fo' de saucer. *(*MARIA *opens the door and looks out.)*

SERENA. Who dat?

MARIA. It's Porgy comin' up de steps.

JAKE *(starting to rise).* Somebody bes' go help um.

MARIA. He gots help. Crown's Bess is a-helpin' um.

SERENA *(springs to her feet).* What's she a-comin' here fo'? *(They are all silent, looking toward door.* PORGY *and* BESS *enter.* PORGY *looks about; makes a movement toward corpse.* BESS *starts to lead him across room.* SERENA *stands defiant, silent, till they have gone half the way.)* What yo' bring dat 'oman here fo'?

PORGY. She want to come help sing. She's a good shouter. *(*BESS, *self-possessed, leads* PORGY *on toward saucer. He* *deposits his coins. Then* BESS *stretches her hand toward saucer.*)

SERENA. I don' need yo' money fo' bury my man. (BESS *hesitates.*) I ain' takin' money off he murderer.

PORGY. Dat ain't Crown's money. I gib um to Bess fo' put in de saucer.

SERENA. All right. Yo' can put um in. (BESS *drops the money in saucer and leads* PORGY *to a place at left front. They sit side by side on the floor.* SERENA *stands glaring after them.*)

PETER (*trying to make peace*). Sing, Sistuh, sing! Time is passin', an de saucer ain't full.

SERENA (*to* PORGY). She can sit ober dere in de corner, if she want to. But she can't sing! (BESS *sits with quiet dignity; seeming scarcely to notice* SERENA'S *tone and words.*)

PORGY. Dat all right. Bess don' want fo' sing, anyway. (*The spiritual begins again.*)

"Leabe dese chillun starve, starve,
Leabe dese chillun starve, starve,
Leabe dese chillun starve, starve,
Deat', ain't yuh gots no shame?"

MINGO (*looking upward*). Dat rain on de roof?

JAKE. Yes, rainin' hard out.

PORGY. Dat's all right now fo' Robbins. Gawd done send He rain already fo' wash he feetsteps offen dis eart'.

LILY. Oh, yes, Brudder!

SERENA. Amen, my Jedus! (*The spiritual continues. The swaying and patting begin gradually and grow. Slowly* BESS *begins to sway with the others, but she makes no sound. The door is burst suddenly open and the* DETECTIVE *enters. Two* POLICEMEN *wait in the doorway. The spiritual ceases abruptly. All the Negroes' eyes are riveted on the white man and filled with fear. He strides over to the corpse, looks down at it.*)

DETECTIVE. Um! A saucer-buried setup, I see! (*To* SERENA.) You're his widow?

SERENA. Yes, suh.

DETECTIVE. He didn't leave any burial insurance?

SERENA. No, boss. He didn't leabe nuttin'.

DETECTIVE. Well, see to it that he's buried tomorrow. (*Turns away from her. Slowly circles room, looking fixedly at each Negro in turn. Each quails under his gaze. He pauses abruptly before* PETER. *Suddenly shouts at him.*) You killed Robbins, and I'm going to hang you for it! (PETER *is almost paralyzed by terror, his panic heightened by the fact that he cannot hear what the* DETECTIVE *says. His mouth opens and he cannot find his voice.*)

LILY (*to* DETECTIVE). He ain't done um.

PETER (*helplessly*). What he say?

LILY (*shouting in* PETER'S *ear*). He say yo' kill Robbins.

DETECTIVE (*laying his hand on* PETER'S *shoulder*). Come along now!

PETER. 'Fore Gawd, boss, I ain't neber done um! (*The* DETECTIVE *whips out his revolver and points it between* PETER'S *eyes.*)

DETECTIVE. Who did it, then? (*Shouting.*) You heard me! Who did it?

PETER (*wildly*). Crown done um, boss. I done see him do um.

DETECTIVE (*shouting*). You're sure you saw him?

PETER. I swear to Gawd, boss. I was right dere, close beside um.

DETECTIVE (*with satisfied grunt*). Umph! I thought as much. (*Swings suddenly on* PORGY *and points the pistol in his face.*) You saw it, too! (PORGY *trembles but does not speak. He lowers his eyes.*) Come! Out with it! I don't want to have to put the law on you! (PORGY *sits silent. The* DETECTIVE *shouts with fury.*) Look at me, you damned nigger! (PORGY *slowly raises his eyes to the* DETECTIVE'S *face.*)

PORGY. I ain't know nuttin' 'bout um, boss.

DETECTIVE (*angrily*). That's your room in the corner, isn't it? (*Points downward toward left.*)

PORGY. Yes, boss. Dat's my room.

DETECTIVE. The door opens on the court, don't it?

PORGY. Yes, boss, my door open on de cou't.

DETECTIVE. And yet you didn't see or hear anything?

PORGY. I ain't know nuttin' 'bout um. I been inside asleep on my bed wid de door closed.

DETECTIVE (*exasperated*). You're a damned liar. (*Turns away disgusted. Saunters toward door. To* POLICEMEN, *indicating* PETER.) He saw the killing. Take him along and lock him up as a material witness. (FIRST POLICEMAN *crosses to* PETER.)

FIRST POLICEMAN (*helping* PETER *to his feet*). Come along, Uncle.

PETER (*shaking with terror*). I ain't neber done um, boss.

POLICEMAN. Nobody says you did it. We're just taking you along as a witness. (*But* PETER *does not understand.*)

SERENA. What yo' goin' to do wid um?

POLICEMAN. Lock him up. Come along. It ain't going to be so bad for you as for Crown, anyway.

SECOND POLICEMAN (*to* DETECTIVE). How about the cripple?

DETECTIVE (*sourly*). He couldn't have helped seeing it, but I can't make him come through. But it don't matter. One's enough to hang Crown (*with a short laugh*)—if we ever get him.

MARIA (*to* FIRST POLICEMAN). How long yo' goin' lock um up fo'?

FIRST POLICEMAN. Till we catch Crown.

PORGY (*sadly*). I reckon Crown done loose now in de palmetto thickets, an' de rope ain't neber made fo' hang um.

DETECTIVE. Then the old man's out of luck. (*To* SERENA.) Remember! You've got to bury that body tomorrow or the Board of Health will take him and turn him over to the medical students.

PETER. I ain't neber done um, boss.

DETECTIVE (*to* FIRST POLICEMAN). Come on! Get the old man in the wagon. (PETER, *shaking in every limb, is led out. The* DETECTIVE *and* SECOND POLICEMAN *follow. A moment of desolated silence.*)

MARIA. It sho' pay black folks to go blin' in dis world.

JAKE. Porgy ain't got much leg, but he sho' got sense in dealin' wid de w'ite folks.

PORGY (*slowly, as though half to himself*). I can't puzzle dis t'ing out. Peter war a good man. An' dat Crown war a killer an' fo'eber gettin' into trouble. But dere go Peter fo' be lock up like t'ief, an' here lie Robbins wid he wife an' fadderless chillun. An' Crown gone he was fo' do de same t'ing ober again somewheres else. (*The Negroes begin to sway and moan.*)

CLARA. Gone fo' true! Yes, Jedus! (*A voice raises the spiritual, "What de Matter, Chillun?" It swells slowly. One voice joins in after another. The swaying and patting begin and grow slowly in tempo and emphasis. As before,* BESS *sways in silence.*)

"What' de mattuh, chillun?
What' de mattuh, chillun?
What' de mattuh, chillun?
Yuh can't stan' still.
Pain gots de body.
Pain gots de body.
Pain gots de body.
An' I can't stan' still.

"What de mattuh, Sistuh?
What de mattuh, Sistuh?
What de mattuh, Sistuh?
What de mattuh, Sistuh?
Yuh can't stan' still.
Jedus gots our brudder,
Jedus gots our brudder,
Jedus gots our brudder,
An' I can't stan' still."

(*The door opens and the* UNDERTAKER *bustles into the room with an air of great importance. He is a short, yellow Negro with a low, oily voice. He is dressed entirely in black. He crosses to* SERENA. *The song dies away, but the swaying continues to its rhythm.*)

UNDERTAKER. How de saucer stan' now, my sistuh? (*Glances appraisingly at saucer.*)

SERENA (*in a flat, despairing voice*). Dere ain't but fifteen dollah.

UNDERTAKER. Umph! Can't bury um fo' fifteen dollah.

JAKE. He gots to git buried tomorruh

or de Boa'd ob Healt' 'll take um an' gib um to de students.

SERENA (*wildly*). Oh, fo' Gawd's sake bury um in de grabeyahd. (*She rises to her knees and seizes the* UNDERTAKER's *hand in both hers. Imploringly.*) Don't let de students hab um. I goin' to work Monday, an' I swear to Gawd I goin' to pay yo' ebery cent. (*Even the swaying ceases now. The Negroes all wait tensely, their eyes riveted on the* UNDERTAKER's *face, pleading silently. After a moment's hesitation, the* UNDERTAKER's *professional manner slips from him.*)

UNDERTAKER (*simply*). All right, Sistuh. Wid de box an' one carriage, it's cost me more'n twenty-five. But I'll see yo' t'rough. (*An expression of vast relief sweeps into every face.* SERENA *silently relaxes across the foot of the bed, her head between her outstretched arms.*) Yo' can all be ready at eight tomorruh. It's a long trip to de cemetery. (*The* UNDERTAKER *goes out door. The Negroes gaze silently after him with eyes filled with gratitude. There is a moment of silence after his departure. Then, carrried out of herself by sympathy and gratitude,* BESS, *forgetful of the ban laid upon her, lifts her strong, beautiful voice triumphantly.*)

BESS. "Oh, I gots a little brudder in de new grabeyahd
What outshine de sun,
Outshine de sun,"

(PORGY's *voice joins hers.*)
"Outshine de sun."

(*By the fourth line, many of the Negro voices have joined in, and the song grows steadily in volume and fervor.*)
"Oh, I gots a little brudder in de new grabeyahd

What outshine de sun,
An' I'll meet um in de Primus Lan'.'"

(BESS' *voice is heard again for one brief moment alone as it rises high and clear on the first line of the chorus.*)
"I will meet um in de Primus Lan'!"

(*Then a full chorus, with deep basses predominating, crashes in on the second line of the refrain.* SERENA, *last of all, joins enthusiastically in the chorus.*)
"Oh, I'll meet um in de Primus Lan'!
I will meet um, meet um, meet um,
I will meet um, meet um, meet um,
I will meet um in de Primus Lan'!

"Oh, I gots a mansion up on high
What ain't make wid han',
Ain't make wid han',
Ain't make wid han',
Oh, I gots a mansion up on high
What ain't make wid hand',
An' I'll meet um in de Primus Lan'!"

(*The beautiful old spiritual beats triumphantly through the narrow room, steadily gaining in speed.* SERENA *is the first to leap to her feet and begin to "shout."*[1] *One by one, as the spirit moves them, the Negroes follow her example till they are all on their feet, swaying, shuffling, clapping their hands.* BESS *leads the "shouting" as she has the singing, throwing her whole soul into an intricate shuffle and complete turn. Each Negro "shouts" in his own individual way, some dancing in place, others merely swaying and patting their hands. "Allelujahs" and cries of "Yes, Lord" are interjected into the singing. And the rhythm swells till the old walls seem to rock and surge with the sweep of it.*)

CURTAIN

ACT TWO

SCENE 1: *St. Michael's chimes the quarters and strikes one. Morning. The court is full of movement, the Negroes going about their tasks. At right front, a group of fishermen are rigging their lines. They are working leisurely with much noisy laughter and banter. Occasionally, a snatch of song is heard.* PORGY *is sitting at his window. The soapbox car stands by his door, the goat is*

---

[1] "Shouting" is the term given by the Carolina Negroes to the body rhythms and steps with which they accompany their emotional songs.

inside the room. Occasionally looks out door.

JAKE. Fish runnin' well outside de bar dese days.

MINGO (*an onlooker*). Hear tell de Bufort mens bring in such a catch yesterday dat de boat look like he gots floor ob silver.

JIM. I hears dey gots to t'row away half de catch so as not glut de market.

JAKE. Yes, suh! Fish runnin' well, an' we mens bes' make de mores ob it.

JIM. Dats de trut'. Dem Septembuh storm due soon, an' fish don' like eas' win' an' muddy watuh.

ANNIE (*calling across court*). Mus' be you mens forget 'bout picnic. Ain't yo' know de parade start up de block at ten o'clock?

MINGO. Dat's de trut', Sistuh. (*The men begin to gather up their fishing gear.*)

PORGY (*at window. Solicitously*). Bess, ain't you wants to go to de picnic after all? Yo' know I is membuh in good standin' ob "De Sons and Daughters ob Repent Ye Saith de Lord."

BESS (*unseen within room*). I radder stay home wid yo'.

PORGY. Yo' gots jus' as much right to go as any 'oman in Catfish Row.

BESS (*in unconvincing voice*). I ain't care much 'bout picnic. (PORGY *is troubled. Sits in silence.*)

SPORTING LIFE (*who has sauntered over to group of fishermen*). All yo' mens goin' to de picnic?

JAKE. Goin' fo' sho'. How come yo' t'ink we ain't goin'?

SPORTING LIFE. I jus' ask. Don' hab no picnic in Noo Yo'k. Yo' folks still hab yo' picnic on Kittiwah Islan'?

JIM. Listen to Sportin' Life. He been six mont' in Noo Yo'k, an' he want to know ef we still hab we picnic on Kittiwah! (*They laugh.* SPORTING LIFE *moves off. Sits at* MARIA'S *table.* LILY *joins the group of men.*)

JAKE. All right, mens. I'm all fuh ridin' luck fur as he will tote me. Turn out at four tomorruh mornin', an' we'll push de *Sea Gull* clean to de Blackfish Banks 'fore we wets de anchor. I gots a feelin'

we goin' be gunnels under wid de pure fish when we comes in at night.

LILY. Yuh goin' fuh take de *Sea Gull* out beyond bah? (*She laughs. Calls out to* NELSON, *who is on far side of court.*) Heah dis, Nelson. Dese mens aimin' for take de *Sea Gull* to de Blackfish Banks! (NELSON *joins the group.* CLARA, *overhearing, slowly approaches, her baby in her arms.* LILY *turns to the others.*) Yo' mens bes' keep yo' ol° washtub close to home. Wait till yo' gets a good boat like de *Mosquito* 'fore yo' trabble. (*All the men and* LILY *laugh delightedly.*)

JAKE. Mosquito born in de water, but he can drown jus' de same. (*All laugh,* LILY *slapping* NELSON'S *shoulder in her appreciation.* CLARA *has stood silently beside them with anxious eyes.*)

CLARA. Jake! Yo' ain't plannin' to take de *Sea Gull* to de Blackfish Bank? It's time fuh de Septembuh storms.

JAKE (*laughing reassuringly*). Ain't yo' know we had one stiff gale las' yeah, an' he nebber come two yeah han' runnin'.

CLARA. Jake, I don' want yo' fuh go outside de bah!

JAKE. How yo' t'ink we goin' gib dat man child college edication? (*They all laugh, except* CLARA.)

CLARA. Deys odder way fuh make money sides fish.

JAKE. Hear de 'oman! Mebbe yo' like me to be a cotton picker! Huh? (*The men laugh.* SCIPIO *is playing about the court with a broad red sash pinned across his breast from shoulder to waist. It bears the legend, "Repent Ye Saith the Lord." From the boy's breast flutters a yellow ribbon with the word "Marshal." He struts about court leading an imaginary parade.* JAKE, *looking about for change of subject, sees* SCIPIO *and starts to his feet.*) Heah, Scipio! Who sash dat yo' gots? (SCIPIO *backs away.* JAKE *pursues.*) Come heah, yo'! Jus' as I t'ought. Dat's my sash! (*Not watching where he is going,* SCIPIO, *in his flight from* JAKE, *runs straight into* MARIA, *who delivers him to* JAKE.)

MARIA. Heah yo' is, Jake.

JAKE. T'ank yo' kindly, Sistuh. (*To*

Scipio, *while he rescues his sash and badge.*) How yo' t'ink I goin' lead dis picnic parade atter yo' been ruin my sash? (*Pins ribbons on his breast. Sits on washing bench. Lights pipe. The crowd begins to break up with noisy laughter and joking.* SERENA *comes in at gate, wearing a neat white apron and a hat. Crosses to* PORGY's *door, greeting her friends as she passes them.*)

SERENA (*to the men*). Fine day fuh de picnic.

JIM. Fine fuh true, Sistuh. (SERENA *knocks at* PORGY's *door.* BESS *opens it.* SERENA *pays no attention to her.*)

SERENA (*looking through* BESS). Porgy! (*Sees him at window. Crosses to him.*) Oh, dere yo' is. I gots news. I done been to see my white folks 'bout Peter.

PORGY. What dey say?

SERENA. Dey say dey gots a white gentleman frien', name ob Mistah Archdale, who is lawyer an' he can get um out. I tells um yo' is de pusson fo' um to talk to 'cause yo' gots so much sense when yo' talks to w'ite folks. An' dey say he'll come fo' see yo' 'cause he pass right by here ebery day, an' yo' is cripple. (*Turns away, ignoring* BESS. *Crosses, sits beside* JAKE, *takes out and lights her pipe.* MARIA *is serving a late breakfast to* SPORTING LIFE. JIM *and* MINGO *have joined him at table. St. Michael's chimes the quarter hour.* MARIA *crosses to pump to fill kettle. After a few puffs,* SERENA *whispers loudly to* JAKE.) It's a shame when good Christian 'omans got to lib under de same roof wid a murderin' she-debil like dat Crown's Bess.

JAKE. She don' seem to harm nobody, an' Porgy seem to like to hab she 'roun'.

MARIA. Porgy change since dat 'oman go to lib' wid he.

SERENA. How he change?

MARIA. I tell yo' dat man happy now.

SERENA. Go 'long wid yo'. Dat 'oman ain't de kin' fo' make cripple happy. It take a killer like Crown to hol' she down.

MARIA. Dat may be so, but Porgy don't know dat yet. An', 'sides, ef a man is de kin' what need a 'oman, he goin' be happy regahdless.

JAKE. Dat's de trut', Sistuh. Him dress she up in he own eye, till she stan' like de Queen ob Sheba to he.

MARIA. Porgy t'ink right now dat he gots a she-gawd in he room.

SERENA. Well, dere is gawds and gawds, an' Porgy sho' got de kin' what goin' gib um hell. Much as I likes Porgy, I wouldn't swap a word wid she.

MARIA. Dat all so, Sistuh. But yo' keep yo' eye on Porgy. He use to hate all dese chillen, but now he nebber come home widout candy ball fuh de crowd.

JAKE. I tells yo' dat 'oman— (BESS *crosses to pump with bucket.*)

SERENA. Sh! (*The three are silent watching* BESS. *She is neatly dressed, walks with queenly dignity, passes them as though they did not exist, fills her bucket, swings it easily to her head, turns from them with an air of cool scorn, and recrosses to her own door. The three look after her with varying expressions:* MARIA *interested,* SERENA *indignant,* JAKE *admiring.*)

JAKE. Dat's de t'ing. She sho ain't askin' no visit ofen none ob she neighbors.

SERENA. Yo' poor sof'-headed fool! Ain't yo' shame to set dere 'fore me an' talk sweet-mout' about dat murderin' Crown's Bess? (*Making eyes at him.*) Now, ef I was a man, I'd sabe my sof' wo'd fuh de God-fearin' 'omans.

JAKE. Ef yo' was a man— (*Pauses, looking thoughtfully at her, then shakes his head.*) No, it ain't no use. Yo' wouldn't understan'. Dat's somethin' shemale sense ain't goin' to help yo' none wid. (*Knocks ashes from his pipe.* MARIA *has turned toward her table. She suddenly puts down her kettle, strides to the table, seizes* SPORTING LIFE's *hand, opens the fingers before he has time to resist, and blows a white powder from his palm.*)

SPORTING LIFE (*furiously*). What yo' t'ink yo' doin'! Dat stuff cos' money. (MARIA *stands back, arms akimbo, staring down at him for a moment in silence.* SPORTING LIFE *shifts uneasily in his chair.*)

MARIA (*in stentorian tones*). I jus' tryin' to figger out wedder I better kill yuñ decent now, wid yo' frien' about yo'— or leabe yo' fuh de white folks to hang atter a while. I ain't say nuttin' no matter how drunk yo' gets dese boys on you'h rot-gut whisky. But nobody ain't goin' peddle happy dus' roun' my shop. Yo' heah what I say?

SPORTING LIFE. Come now, ole lady, don't talk like dese ole-fashioned, lamp-oil folks. Why, up in Noo Yo'k, where I been waitin' in a—hotel—

MARIA. Hotel, eh? I suppose dese gal' yo' tryin' to get to go back to Noo Yo'k wid yo' is goin' to be bordahs! (*Shouting.*) Don' yo' try any ob yo' Noo Yo'kin' roun' dis town. Ef I had my way, I'd go down to dat Noo Yo'k boat an' take ebery Gawd's mans what come up de gangplank wid a Joseph coat on he back an' a glass headlight on he buzzum an' drap um to de catfish 'fore he foot hit decent groun'. Yes! my belly fair ache wid dis Noo Yo'k talk. (*Bangs table so violently with her fist that* SPORTING LIFE *leaps from his chair and extends a propitiating hand toward her.*)

SPORTING LIFE. Dat's all right, Auntie. Le's you an' me be frien'.

MARIA. Frien' wid yo'! One ob dese day I might lie down wid rattlesnake, an' when dat time come, yo' kin come right 'long an' git in de bed. But till den, keep yo' shiny carcass in Noo Yo'k til de debble ready to take cha'ge ob um. (SIMON FRAZIER, *an elderly Negro dressed in black frock coat, comes in at the gate, looks about, crosses to* MARIA's *table.* MARIA *is still glaring at* SPORTING LIFE *so ferociously that* FRAZIER *hesitates,* MARIA *looks up and sees him. She is suddenly all smiles.*)

MARIA. Mornin', lawyer. Lookin' fuh somebody?

FRAZIER. Porgy live here, don't he?

MARIA. Sho' he do. Right ober dere he room.

FRAZIER. T'ank yo', Sistuh. (*Crosses toward* PORGY's *door.*)

LILY (*who is near* PORGY's *door*). Porgy! Lawyer Frazier to see yo'. (MARIA *gives* SPORTING LIFE *final glare and enters shop.* BESS *helps* PORGY *on to doorstep and returns to room.*)

FRAZIER. Mornin', Porgy.

PORGY. Mornin', lawyer.

FRAZIER. I come to see yo' on business fo' one ob my w'ite client'.

PORGY. Huh?

FRAZIER. I been in to see Mistah Alan Archdale yesterday an' he gib' me message fo' yo'.

PORGY. Who he?

FRAZIER (*in disgust*). Who he? Yo' ain't know who is Mistah Alan Archdale? He lawyer, same as me.

PORGY (*uneasily*). Whut he wants wid me?

FRAZIER. I been in to see um on private business like we lawyers always has togedder. An' he say to me, "Mistah Frazier, do yo' know dat black scoundrel dat hitchen his goat outside my window ebery mornin'?" I sez: "Yes, Mistah Archdale, I knows um." An' he say: "Well, when yo' goes out, tell um to mobe on." When I comes out, yo' is gone, so I come heah fo' tell yo'. *Mobe on.*

PORGY. Why he don't tell me heself?

FRAZIER. Yo' t'ink Mistah Alan Archdale gots time fo' tell beggar to mobe on? No, suh! He put he case in my han', an' I is authorize fo' tell yo' yo' gots to fin' nudder hitchin' place.

PORGY (*unhappily*). I been hitch on dat corner mos' a mont' now. Why he don't want me 'roun'?

FRAZIER (*scratching his head*). I ain't quite make dat out. He say sompen 'bout de goat an' de commodity advertise on de chariot. (*Pointing to cart*). "Pure an' fragrant." Dat's soap, ain't it? I gather dat he t'ink yo' goat need soap.

PORGY (*astonished*). Whut a goat want wid soap?

FRAZIER (*also puzzled*). I ain't know ezac'ly. (BESS *comes to doorway and stands behind* PORGY. FRAZIER *resumes his authoritative tone.*) All I knows is yuh gots to *mobe on!* (FRAZIER *looks up and sees* BESS.) How yo' do? (*Looks at her, scrutinizing.*) Ain't yo' Crown's Bess?

PORGY. No, suh, she ain't. She's Porgy's Bess.

FRAZIER (*sensing business*). Oh! I guess den yo' goin' be wantin' divorce.

PORGY. Huh?

FRAZIER. Ef de 'oman goin' stay wid' yo', she gots to hab divorce from Crown or else it ain't legal. (*Takes legal-looking document from pocket. Shows it to* PORGY. PORGY *looks at it, much impressed. Passes it to* BESS.)

PORGY. How much it cos'?

FRAZIER. One dollah, ef dere ain't no complications. (PORGY *looks dubious.* FRAZIER *quickly takes huge seal from his coat-tail pocket. Shows it to* PORGY.)

FRAZIER. When yo' gits divorce, I puts dis seal on de paper to show yo' has paid cash.

PORGY. Bess, yo' likes to hab divorce?

BESS (*with longing*). Whut yo' t'ink, Porgy? (*The other Negroes are gradually edging nearer to listen.*)

PORGY. I goin' buy yo' divorce. Bring me my pocketbook. (BESS *goes into room and returns immediately with a number of small coins tied up in a rag, hands it to* PORGY. *He laboriously counts out a dollar in nickels and pennies. In the meantime,* FRAZIER *is filling in document with fountain pen. Group of Negroes now listening frankly.* FRAZIER *takes coins from* PORGY. *Counts them.* BESS *holds out her hand for document.*)

FRAZIER (*pocketing coins*). Wait a minute. 'Tain't legal yet. (*Holding paper in hands, lowers glasses on his nose. Begins in solemn tones.*) Yo' name?

BESS. Bess. (FRAZIER *makes note.*)

FRAZIER. Yo' age?

BESS. Twenty-six yeah.

FRAZIER. Yo' desire to be divorce from dis man Crown?

BESS. Yas, boss.

FRAZIER. Address de co't as Yo' Honor.

BESS. Yas, Yo' Honor.

FRAZIER. When was yo' an Crown marry? (BESS *hesitates.*)

BESS. I don't rightly 'member, boss— Yo' Honor.

FRAZIER. One yeah? Ten yeah?

BESS. Ain't I done tell yo' I don' remember?

LILY. She ain't neber been marry.

FRAZIER (*to* BESS). Dat de trut'?

BESS. Yas, Yo' Honor.

FRAZIER (*triumphantly*). Ah, dat's a complication.

BESS. I ain't know dat mattered.

PORGY. Yo' can't gib she divorce? Gib me back my dollah.

FRAZIER. Who say I can't gib she divorce? But, under circumstances, dis divorce cos' two dollah. It take expert fuh divorce 'oman whut ain't marry.

BESS. Don't pay um no two dollah, Porgy. It ain't wuth it.

FRAZIER. Berry well, den, ef yo' wants to go on libbin' in sin. (*Takes coins from pocket and begins to count. Seeing that they do not weaken, he pauses abruptly in his counting.*) Seein' dat we is ole frien', I goin' make dis divo'ce dollah an' er half. (*Again takes out impressive seal.* PORGY *eyes seal, greatly impressed. Begins counting out more pennies.* FRAZIER *affixes seal. Hands it to* PORGY. *Pockets extra money.*)

FRAZIER. Dat ain't much money considerin' whut yo' gets. One dollah an er half to change from a 'oman to a lady.

BESS (*happily*). T'ank yo' kindly, Yo' Honor.

FRAZIER. Glad to serbe yo'. When yo' ready to buy license, come to me.

PORGY. Whut she want wid license? She gots divorce, ain't she?

FRAZIER. Well, yo' ought to be stylish like de white folks, an' follow up divorce wid marriage license. (PORGY *and* BESS *look quite depressed at prospect of further complications.*) Well, goodmornin', Missus Porgy. (*Turns to go. To* MARIA.) Yo' gots de cup coffee fo' sweeten my mout'?

MARIA. Sho' I is. Step right ober. (*She and* FRAZIER *enter cookshop. The court is alive with noisy laughter and action. A fish vendor is calling his wares. St. Michael's is chiming the half hour.* MARIA *is bustling back and forth serving the men at her table.* SERENA *is pumping water and calling to her friends.* ANNIE *is holding* CLARA's *baby, rocking and tossing it.* CLARA *is rearranging sash with motto "Repent Ye Saith the Lord" across* JAKE's *breast, and consulting the others as to the proper angle. The sash adjusted,* JAKE *bursts into song. "Brer Rabbit, whut yo' da do dey!"* LILY *answers with second line of song. The duet continues.* SCIPIO *runs in at gate. Runs to* SERENA.)

SCIPIO. Dey's a buckra comin'. I heah um axin' outside ef dis Catfish Row. (*The Negroes suddenly break off in their tasks.* JAKE *ceases to sing.*)

NELSON (*calling to* SERENA). Whut he say?

SERENA (*in guarded voice, but addressing the court in general*). W'ite gen'man. (*There is a sudden deep silence, contrasting strangely with noise and movement that preceded it.* ANNIE *gives* CLARA *her baby, goes quickly inside her own door.* JAKE *removes sash, puts it in pocket.* SERENA *retreats behind her tubs. The men at table give absorbed attention to their food.* MARIA *serves them in silence without looking up.* SCIPIO *becomes engrossed in tinkering with an old barrel hoop.* BESS *goes inside.* PORGY *feigns sleep.* ALAN ARCHDALE, *a tall kindly man in early middle age, whose bearing at once stamps him the aristocrat, enters the court, looks about at the Negroes, all ostensibly oblivious of his presence.*)

ARCHDALE (*calling to* SCIPIO). Boy! (SCIPIO *approaches, reluctant, shuffling.*) I'm looking for a man by the name of Porgy. Which is his room? (SCIPIO *shuffles and is silent.*) Don't you know Porgy?

SCIPIO (*his eyes on the ground*). No, suh.

ARCHDALE. He lives here, doesn't he?

SCIPIO. I ain't know, boss. (CLARA *is nearest.* ARCHDALE *crosses to her. She listens submissively, her eyes lowered.*)

ARCHDALE. I'm looking for a man named Porgy. Can you direct me to his room?

CLARA (*polite, but utterly negative*). Porgy? (*Repeats the name slowly as though trying to remember.*) No, boss, I ain't nebber heah ob nobody 'roun' dese parts name Porgy.

ARCHDALE. Come, you must know him. I am sure he lives in Catfish Row.

CLARA (*raising her voice*). Anybody heah know a man by de name Porgy? (*Several of the Negroes repeat the name to one another, with shakes of their heads.*)

ARCHDALE (*laughing reassuringly*). I'm a friend of his, Mr. Alan Archdale, and I want to help him. (SERENA *approaches. Looks keenly at* ARCHDALE.)

SERENA. Go 'long an' wake Porgy. Can't yo' tell folks when yo' see um? (*A light of understanding breaks over* CLARA's *face.*)

CLARA. Oh, yo' means Porgy! I ain't understan' whut name yo' say, boss. (VOICES *all about the court:* "Oh, de gen'man mean Porgy. How come we ain't onderstan'!" CLARA *crosses to* PORGY's *door, all smiles.*) A gen'man come fuh see Porgy. (PORGY *appears to awake.* ARCHDALE *crosses to him.*)

PORGY. How yo' does, boss?

ARCHDALE. You're Porgy? Oh, you're the fellow who rides in the goat cart. (*Sits on step.*)

PORGY. Yes, boss, I gots goat.

ARCHDALE. Tell me about your friend who got locked up on account of the Robbins murder.

PORGY (*his face inscrutable*). How come yo' to care, boss?

ARCHDALE. Why, I'm the Rutledges' lawyer, and I look after their colored folks for them. Serena Robbins is the daughter of their old coachman, and she asked them to help out her friend.

PORGY (*a shade of suspicion still in his voice*). Peter ain't gots no money, yo' know, boss; an' I jus' begs from do' to do'!

ARCHDALE (*reassuringly*). It will not take any money. At least, not much. And I am sure that Mrs. Rutledge will take care of that. So you can go right ahead and tell me all about it. (PORGY's *suspicions vanish.*)

PORGY. It like dis, boss. Crown kill Robbins, an' Peter see um do it. Now Crown gone he ways, an' dey done gots ole Peter lock up.

ARCHDALE. I see, as a witness.

PORGY. Till dey catch Crown, dey say, but ef dey keep um lock up till den, dat ole man gots er life sentence.

ARCHDALE (*under his breath*). The dirty hounds! (*He is silent for a moment, his face set and stern.* PORGY *waits.* ARCHDALE *turns wearily to him.*) Of course, we can go to law about this, but it will take no end of time. There is an easier way. (*Across the sunlit walls of Catfish Row falls the shadow of a great bird flying low, evidently just out range of vision of audience. There is a sudden great commotion in the court. Cries of "Drive um away," "Don't let um light," "T'row dis brick." Brooms are waved at the bird overhead. Bricks thrown. PORGY looks up in anxiety. BESS comes to door with broom. ARCHDALE rises in perplexity.*)

PORGY. Dribe um off, Bess! Don't let um light.

ARCHDALE. What is it? What's the matter? (*The shadow rises high. The commotion dies down.*)

PORGY. Dat's a buzzard. Yo' don' know dat bird like fo' eat dead folks?

ARCHDALE. But there's no one dead here, is there?

PORGY. Boss, dat bird mean trouble. Once de buzzard fold he wing an' light ober yo' do', yo' know all yo' happiness done dead. (*With relief, the Negroes stand watching the bird disappear in the distance. ARCHDALE also looks after it.*)

SERENA (*leaning from her window and surveying court*). It sho' make me 'shamed to see all dese superstitious colo'd folks makin' spectacle ob demself befo' de w'ite gentlemans. Ain't we all see dat buzzard sit smack on Maria's table day fo' yesterday? An' whut happen? Nuttin'! No bad luck 'tall.

MARIA (*indignantly*). Bad luck! Whut dat 'oman call bad luck? Ain't I had more drunk customer' yesterday dan any day dis mont'? Dey fair bus' up my shop. (*Goes into shop muttering indignantly.*)

ARCHDALE (*turning back to PORGY*). Now, listen. Peter must have someone to go his bond. Do you know a man by the name of Huysenberg who keeps a corner shop over by the East End Wharf?

PORGY (*his face darkening*). Yes, boss, I knows um. He rob eberybody he git he han' on.

ARCHDALE. I see you know him. Well, take him this ten dollars and tell him that you want him to go Peter's bond.

He hasn't any money of his own, and his shop is in his wife's name, but he has an arrangement with the magistrate that makes him entirely satisfactory. (*Hands PORGY a ten-dollar bill.*) Do you understand?

PORGY. Yes, boss. T'ank yo', boss. (*ARCHDALE, about to go, hesitates, looks at goat-cart.*)

ARCHDALE. Porgy, there's another little matter I want to speak to you about. The last few weeks you've been begging right under my office window. I wish you'd find another place. (*Noticing PORGY's troubled expression.*) There are lots of other street corners.

PORGY (*sadly*). I done try all de oder corner, boss. Ebery time I stop fo' beg, somebody tell' me to keep mobin'. But I been beggin' under yo' window fo' t'ree week' now, an' I beginnin' to say to myself, "Porgy, yo' is fix fo' life. Mus' be yo' is found a gentlemans whut got place in de heart fo' de poor cripple."

ARCHDALE. I have a place in my heart for the cripple but not for the goat.

PORGY. Dis bery nice goat, boss. Lawyer Frazier say yo' t'ink he need soap. But I don't see how dat can be, boss. Two week han' runnin' now dat goat eat up Serena's washin' soap.

ARCHDALE. He doesn't need it inside.

PORGY (*mystified*). Whut goat want wid soap outside? (*Suddenly enlightened.*) Oh, yo' don' like to smell um? (*FRAZIER comes from shop. Sees ARCHDALE. Approaches. Stands waiting, hat in hand. PORGY is now all smiles.*) Dat all right, boss. By tomorroh I goin' hab' dis goat wash till yo' can't tell um from one ob dose rose bush in de park.

ARCHDALE. I'm sorry, Porgy. But you must find another place.

FRAZIER. Good-morning, Mistah Archdale. I done gib dis beggar yo' message. (*Sternly to PORGY.*) 'Membuh what I tell yo'—Mobe on!

ARCHDALE. All right, Frazier. (*To PORGY.*) If Peter isn't out in a week, let me know. (*Turning to take leave.*) I suppose you're all going to the picnic today. (*The Negroes nod and smile. PORGY looks wistfully at BESS, who stands behind him in the doorway.* ARCHDALE *is crossing toward gate.*)

JAKE. Yas, boss. We goin'.

PORGY. Bess, ain't yo' change yo' mind 'bout picnic now yo' gots divo'ce? (ARCHDALE *catches word "divorce," turns.*)

ARCHDALE. Divorce?

PORGY (*proudly*). Yas, boss, Misteh Frazier jus' sell my 'oman a divo'ce. She an honest 'oman now.

ARCHDALE (*sternly, to* FRAZIER, *who is looking guilty*). Didn't the judge tell you that if you sold any more divorces he'd put you in jail? I've a good mind to report you.

FRAZIER. Mus' be dat judge fergit dat I votes de Democratic ticket.

ARCHDALE. That won't help you now. The gentleman from the North, who has come down to better moral conditions among the Negroes, says you are a menace to morals. He's going to have you indicted if you don't quit.

PORGY (*suspiciously; handing paper to* ARCHDALE). Ain't dis no good as he stan', boss? 'Cause I ain't goin' pay um fo' no more complications. (*As* ARCHDALE *glances over the paper,* PORGY *glares vindictively at* FRAZIER.) Dat lawyer come 'round heah in he By-God coat, an' fo' yo' can crack yo' teet', he gone wid yo' las' cent.

ARCHDALE (*reading*). "I, Simon Frazier, hereby divorce Bess and Crown for a charge of one dollar and fifty cents cash. Signed, SIMON FRAZIER." Well, that's simple enough. (*Examines seal.*) "Sealed —Charleston Steamboat Company." Don't you know that there is no such thing as divorce in this state?

FRAZIER. I heah tell dere ain't no such er t'ing fuh de w'ite folks; but de colo'd folks need um so bad, I ain't see no reason why I can't make one up whut sattify 'em. (*His voice breaks.*) Dem divo'ce is keepin' me alibe, boss, an' whut mo', he is keepin' de colo'd folks straight.

ARCHDALE. How's that?

FRAZIER. Dat jedge say he gots to lib togedder anyhow till dey done dead. Dat's de law, he say. But black folks ain't make dat way. I done get my black folks all properly moralize, an' now he say he goin' jail me. Ef I stops now de folks leabe each odder anyway. Ef it don't cos' de man nuttin' to leabe he wife, he ain't goin' keep she er mont'. But when he gots fuh pay dolluh to get way, he goin' t'ink twice 'fore he trabble. (ARCHDALE *keeps from laughing with difficulty.*)

BESS. Ain't mah divo'ce no good, boss? Porgy done pay one dolluh an' er half fuh it.

ARCHDALE (*looking at paper*). I could hardly say that it is legal.

BESS. Legal! Dat wo'd mean good?

ARCHDALE. Well, sometimes.

PORGY. Plenty of our frien' is divo'ce', boss.

ARCHDALE (*with accusing look at* FRAZIER, *who cringes*). So I hear. (*Again consults paper.*) You've left this man, Crown, and intend to stay with Porgy?

BESS. Yes, suh.

ARCHDALE. I suppose this makes a respectable woman of you. Um—on the whole—I'd keep it. I imagine that respectability at one-fifty would be a bargain anywhere. (*Hands papers to* BESS. *Turns back to* FRAZIER.) But remember, Frazier: *No more divorces!* Or to jail you go. I won't report you this time. (*The goat sticks its head out door.* PORGY *throws his arm around its neck.* ARCHDALE *turns to go.*) Good morning. (*Crosses toward gate.*)

FRAZIER (*close by* PORGY'S *door. Recovering from his emotion enough to speak*). Gawd bless yo', boss. Good mornin', boss.

PORGY (*imitating* FRAZIER'S *professional manner*). Mobe on, please. Mobe on! I gots er bery polite goat heah whut object to de smell ob de jail bird. (ARCHDALE, *overhearing, laughs suddenly. Goes out gate, his shoulders shaking with laughter.* FRAZIER *moves off, talks to Negroes in background, and soon leaves the court.* BESS *sits by* PORGY *on step.*) Ain't yo' hear de boss laugh?

BESS. Fo' sho' I heh um laugh.

PORGY (*hugging goat*). No, no, bruddah, we ain't goin' mobe on. When we makes de buckra laugh, we done win. We goin' spend we life under Mistah Archdale's window. Yo' watch! (*Draws himself up by door frame, goes inside. Bess remains on step. St. Michael's chimes the three-quarter hour. Preparations for the picnic are now at their height. One by one the women, when not on stage, have changed to their most gorgeously colored dresses. Men and women are now wearing sashes all bearing the legend: "Repent Ye Saith the Lord." The leaders have also badges denoting their various ranks: "Marshal," etc. Baskets are being assembled in the court. The court is full of bustle and confusion. Sporting Life saunters over to Bess, who is sitting on step wistfully watching the picnic preparations.*)

Sporting Life. 'Lo, Bess! Goin' to picnic?

Bess. No, guess I'll stay home.

Sporting Life. Picnics all right fo' dese small-town people, but we is used to de high life. Yo' an' me onderstan' each odder. I can't see fo' de life ob me what yo' hangin' 'roun dis place for! Wid yo' looks, Bess, an' yo' way wid de boys, dere's big money fo' yo' an' me in Noo' Yo'k.

Bess (*quietly*). I can't remembuh eber meet a nothin' I likes less dan I does yo'.

Sporting Life (*laughingly*). Oh, come on, now! How 'bout a little touch happy dus' fo' de ole time' sake?

Bess. I t'rough wid dat stuff.

Sporting Life. Come on! Gib me yo' hand. (*Reaches out and takes her hand, draws it toward him, and with other hand unfolds paper ready to pour powder.*)

Bess (*wavering*). I tells yo' I t'rough!

Sporting Life. Jus' a pinch. Not 'nough to hurt a flea. (*Bess snatches her hand away.*)

Bess. I done gib' up happy dus'.

Sporting Life. Tell dat to somebody else! Nobody eber gib' up happy dus'. (*Again he takes her hand and she does not resist. Gazes fascinated at the powder. Porgy's hand reaches suddenly into the open space of the door; seizes Sporting Life's wrist in an iron grip. Sporting*

Life *looks at the hand in astonishment mixed with a sort of horror.*) Leggo, yo' damn cripple! (*The hand twists Sporting Life's wrist till he relinquishes Bess' hand and grunts with pain. Then Porgy's hand is silently withdrawn.*) Gawd, what a grip fo' a piece ob a man!

Bess (*rising*). Go 'long now.

Sporting Life (*regaining his swagger*). All right! Yo' men friend' come an' dey go. But 'membuh, ole Sportin' Life an' de happy dus' here all along. (*Saunters along—goes out gate. From the distance is heard the blare of a discordant band. It is playing "My Soul's so Happy dat I Can't Sit Down," though the tune is scarcely recognizable to the audience. The Negroes, however, are untroubled by the discords. One or another sings a line or two of the song. A jumble of voices rises above the music: "Here come de orphans!" "Dere de orphan band down de block!" "Le's we go!" etc. A man passes outside the gate, stopping long enough to call in to the occupants of Catfish Row: "Eberybody gettin' in line up de block. You folks bes' hurry." Porgy comes out on doorstep to watch. Sits. Bess stands beside him absorbed in the gay scene. Porgy looks at her keenly, troubled.*)

Jake (*in the midst of his preparations*). Come 'long to de picnic, Bess! (*Does not wait for reply.*)

Porgy (*triumphantly*). Dere! Don' yo' hear Jake ask yo' fo' go? Go 'long!

Bess. Plenty ob de mens ask me. Yo' ain't hear none ob de ladies sayin' nuttin'.

Porgy. Bess, yo' can put on my lodge sash an' be just as good as any 'oman in dat crowd.

Bess (*with a little laugh*). Yo' an' me know it take more'n sash. (*The confusion grows. Picnickers once started on their way come scurrying back for forgotten bundles. Scipio runs in at gate in high excitement.*)

Scipio (*breathless; to Serena*). Ma, I gots good news fo' yo'.

Serena. What dat?

Scipio. De bandmaster say I can be a orphan. (*The song breaks out in greater volume.*)

"Sit down! I can't sit down!
Sit down! I can't sit down!
Sit down! I can't sit down!
My soul's so happy dat I can't sit down!
Cause yo' can't git yo' rights when yo' do.

I was sleepin' on a pile ob lumbah
Jus' as happy as a man could be
When a w'ite man woke me from my slumbah
An' he says, 'Yo' gots fo' work now cause yo' free.' "

(*Other voices are calling back and forth: "How dem little fella can play!" "Ain't yo' ready! Time fo' go!" "We off fo' Kittiwah!" The band plays with more abandon.* BESS *wears the expression of a dreamer who sees herself in the midst of the merrymakers. Her feet begin to shuffle in time to the music.* PORGY *does not look up, but his eyes watch the shuffling feet.*)

PORGY (*mournfully*). Yo' can't tell me yo' ain't wants to go. (*The Negroes troop across the court all carrying their baskets. In twos and threes they go out at the gate. Among the last to go,* MARIA *comes hurrying from her shop carrying a gigantic basket. Turns to follow the others. Sees* PORGY *and* BESS. *Hesitates. As though afraid of being left behind, turns again toward gate. Then resolutely sets down her basket.*)

MARIA. What de mattuh wid yo', Sistuh? Ain't yo' know yo' late fo' de picnic? (*A sudden wave of happiness breaks over* BESS's *face. She is too surprised to answer.*)

PORGY. Bess says she ain't figgerin' to go.

MARIA (*crosses rapidly to them*). Sho' she goin! Eberybody goin'. She gots to help me wid my basket. I gots 'nough fo' six. Where yo' hat? (*Reaches hat just inside door and puts it on* BESS's *head.*)

PORGY (*taking sash from pocket and holding it out to* BESS). Here my sash, Bess. (MARIA *unties* BESS's *apron. Throws it through door. Takes sash from* PORGY, *pins it across* BESS's *breast, jerking her*

peremptorily about to save time. Then starts for her basket.)

MARIA. Come 'long now!

BESS (*hesitating*). I hate fo' leabe yo', Porgy.

PORGY (*happily*). I too happy fo' hab yo' go.

MARIA. Ain't yo' goin' help me wid dis basket? (BESS *hurries to her and takes one handle of basket.*) See yo' some mo', Porgy! (MARIA *crosses rapidly to gate. To keep her hold on the basket,* BESS *is forced to hurry. Looking back.*) Goodbye—Porgy! (MARIA, *apparently seeing the others far ahead and anxious not to be left behind, breaks into a lumbering run, dragging* BESS *after her.* BESS *is waving to* PORGY *as she goes. The voices of the Negroes grow fainter. Then the last distant crashes of the band are heard, and the court is quiet.* PORGY *sits on his doorstep dreaming, gazing happily into space, rocking a little. Takes pipe from his pocket, knocks out ashes; lights it. Across the sunlit walls falls the shadow of the buzzard flying lazily over the court.* PORGY *remains in happy abstraction, oblivious of the bird. Puffs leisurely at his pipe. The shadow hovers over his door; then falls across his face. He looks up suddenly and sees the bird. Swift terror sweeps into his face.*)

PORGY (*frantically*). Get out ob here! Don' yo' light! Lef' it! Yo' hear me! Lef' it! (*He waves futile arms at it. The bird continues to hover above him.*) Get out! Somebody bring broom! Don' yo' light on my door, yo' debil! Help! Somebody help me! Oh, Gawd! (*He struggles down the steps and at last reaches the brick. The shadow wings of the bird close as it comes to rest directly over* PORGY's *door. Grasping the brick, he again looks up to take aim. His fingers slowly relax, and the brick falls to the ground.*) 'Tain't no use now. 'Tain't no use. He done lit. (PORGY *regains his seat on step and sits looking up at the bird with an expression of hopelessness as the curtain falls.*)

CURTAIN

SCENE 2: *Kittiwah Island. Moonlight revealing a narrow strip of sand backed by a tangled palmetto thicket. In the distance (right) the band is playing "My Soul's so Happy dat I Can't Sit Down." JAKE, MINGO, and several others troop across stage from left to right, swinging apparently empty baskets.*

MINGO. Dis been some picnic, but, Lor', I tired!

JAKE (*swinging his basket in a circle*). Dis basket some lighter fo' carry dan when we come out. (*Breaks into song: "My Soul's so Happy," etc. The others join in. They go off right, their song growing fainter in distance. SERENA and LILY enter, followed a moment later by BESS and MARIA. MARIA is puffing, out of breath.*)

MARIA. I ain't no han' fo' walk so fas' on a full stomach. (*Stops abruptly. Looks about her on ground.*)

SERENA. Yo' goin' miss de boat ef yo' ain't hurry, Sistuh.

MARIA. It was jus' about heah I los' my pipe. I 'membuh dere was palmetto sort ob twisted like dat.

LILY. How come yo' lose yo' pipe?

MARIA (*searching ground. The others help her*). I was sittin' under de tree a-smokin', an' I see a Plat-eye ha'nt a-lookin' at me t'rough de palmetto leaf. An', 'fo yo' can crack yo' teet', I is gone from heah, but my pipe ain't gone wid me.

LILY. Plat-eye ha'nt! What was he like?

MARIA. Two big eye' like fireball a-watchin' me.

SERENA (*scornfully*). Plat-eye ha'nt! Yo' ain't read nuttin' in de Bible 'bout Plat-eye is yo'?

MARIA. I ain't needs to read 'bout 'em. I sees 'em lookin' at me t'rough de palmetto leaf.

SERENA. Jus' like yo' hab buzzard set on yo' table two days ago, an' yo' hab' mighty ha'd time a'thinkin' up some bad luck to lay on um.

MARIA. Bad luck! Ain't I lose my pipe dat I smoke dese twenty yeah', an' my mudder smoke um befo' me?

LILY. I ain't partial to sleepin' out wid de rattlesnake'. Le's we go or de boat go widout us.

MARIA. Ef dat boat go widout me, dey's goin' to be some sick people in Catfish Row when I gets back. (*Steamboat whistles off right. MARIA answers it.*) Hold yo' halt! I ain't goin' til I gets my pipe.

BESS. Yo' bes' go along, Maria, and le's we whut is de fas' walker' look fo' um a bit.

MARIA (*pointing left*). It might hab' been a little farder back dat way I lose um. (*BESS begins to search at left and wanders off left, her eyes combing the ground.*) An' it might hab' been a little farder dese way. (*Goes off right searching. LILY follows. SERENA continues her search on stage.*)

LILY (*off right*). I ain't see um nowheres. Le's we go.

MARIA (*farther in distance*). I goin' fin' um. (*From the blackness of the thicket two eyes can be seen watching SERENA. As she turns in her quest, she sees them. For a moment, she is motionless; then her breath catches in a shuddering gasp of horror, and she flees swiftly off right. A snatch of the song rises suddenly in distance and quickly dies down again. BESS comes on from left, her head bent, still searching. A great black hand creeps slowly out among the palmetto branches and draws them aside. BESS hears the sound. Straightens, stands rigid, listening.*)

BESS (*in a low, breathless voice*). Crown?

CROWN. Yo' know bery well dis Crown. (*She turns and looks at him. He partly emerges from the thicket, naked to the waist, his cotton trousers frayed away to the knees.*) I seen yo' land, an' I been waitin' all day fo' yo'. I mos' dead on dis damn islan'!

BESS (*looks at him slowly*). Yo' ain't look mos' dead. Yo' bigger'n eber.

CROWN. Oh, plenty bird' egg, oyster, an' t'ing. But I mos' dead ob lonesome wid not a Gawd's person fo' swap a word wid. Lor' I'se glad yo' come!

BESS. I can't stay, Crown, or de boat go widout me.

CROWN. Got any happy dus' wid yo'?

BESS. No.

CROWN. Come on! Ain't yo' gots jus' a little?

BESS. No, I ain't. I done gib up dope. (CROWN *laughs loudly.*)

CROWN. It sho' do a lonesome man good to hab' he 'oman come an' swap a couple joke wid um.

BESS. Dat's de Gawd's trut'. An' sides —I gots sompen fo' tell yo'.

CROWN. Yo' bes' listen to whut I gots fo' tell yo'. I waitin' here til de cotton begin comin' in. Den libin' 'll be easy. Davy'll hide yo' an' me on de ribber boat fur as Savannah. Who yo' libin' wid now?

BESS. I libin' wid de cripple Porgy.

CROWN (*laughing*). Yo' gots de funny tas' in men. But dots yo' business. I ain't care who yo' takes up wid while I'm away. But 'membuh whut I tol' yo'! He's temporary! I guess it be jus' couple week' now 'fo' I comes fo' yo'!

BESS (*with an effort*). Crown, I got sompen fo' tell yo'.

CROWN. What dat?

BESS. I—I sort ob change' my way'.

CROWN. How you' change'?

BESS. I—I libin' wid Porgy now—an' I libin' decent.

CROWN. Yo' heah whut I tol' yo'? I say in couple week I comin' fo' yo', an' yo' goin' tote fair 'less yo' wants to meet yo' Gawd. Yo' gits dat?

BESS. Crown, I tells yo' I change'. I stayin' wid Porgy fo' good. (*He seizes her by the arm and draws her savagely toward him. The steamboat whistles.*) Take yo' han' off me. I goin' miss dat boat!

CROWN. Dere's anudder boat day after tomorruh.

BESS. I tells yo' I means what I says. Porgy my man now.

CROWN (*jeering at her*). I ain't had a laugh in weeks.

BESS. Take yo' hot han' off me. I tells yo' I stayin' wid Porgy for keeps.

CROWN. Yo' is tellin' me yo' radder hab dat crawlin' cripple dan Crown?

BESS (*taking a propitiatory tone*). It like dis, Crown—I de only 'oman Porgy eber hab'. An' I thinkin' how it goin' be if all dese odder folks goes back to Cat-fish Row tonight, an' I ain't come home to um. He be like a little chil' dat los' its ma. (CROWN, *still holding her, throws back his head and laughs.* BESS *begins to be frightened.*) Yo' can laugh, but I tells yo' I change'!

CROWN. Yo' change' all right. Yo' ain't neber been so funny. (*The boat whistles. She tries to pull away. He stops laughing and holds her tighter with lowering look. Draws her nearer.*)

BESS. Lemme go, Crown! Yo' can get plenty odder women.

CROWN. What I wants wid odder women? I gots a 'oman. An' dats yo'. See?

BESS (*trying flattery*). Yo' know how it always been wid yo', Crown—yo' ain't neber want for a 'oman. Look at dis chest, an' look at dese arm' yo' got! Dere's plenty better-lookin' gal dan me. Yo' know how it always been wid yo'. Dese five year' now I been yo' 'oman— yo' could kick me in de street, an' den, when yo' ready fo' me back, yo' could whistle fo' me an' dere I was again a-lickin' yo' han'. What yo' wants wid Bess? She gettin' ole now. (*She sees that her flattery has failed and is terrified.*) Dat boat goin' widout me! Lemme go! Crown, I'll come back fo' see yo'. I swear to Gawd I'll come on de Friday boat. Jus' lemme go *now*! I can't stop out here all night. I 'fraid! Dere's t'ings movin' in de t'icket—rattlesnake, an' such! Lemme go, I tells yo'. Take yo' han' off me!

CROWN (*holding her and looking steadily at her*). No man ever take my 'oman from me. It goin' to be good joke on Crown ef he lose um to one wid no leg' an' no gizzard. (*Draws her closer.*) So yo' is change, is yo'? (*Grips her more tightly. Looks straight into her eyes.*) Whut yo' say now?

BESS (*summoning the last of her resolution*). I stayin' wid Porgy fo' good. (*His jaw shoots forward, and his huge shoulder muscles bulge and set. Slowly his giant hands close round her throat. He brings his eyes still closer to hers. The boat whistles long and loud, but neither gives sign of hearing it. After a moment, CROWN laughs with satisfaction at what he sees in BESS's eyes. His hands leave her throat and clasp her savagely by the shoulders. BESS throws back her head with a wild hysterical laugh.)*

CROWN. I knows yo' ain't change'!

Wid yo' an' me, it always goin' be de same. See? (He swings her about and hurls her face forward through an opening in the thicket. Then, with a low laugh, he follows her. She regains her balance and goes on ahead of him. The band is still playing, but growing faint in the distance.)

CURTAIN

ACT THREE

SCENE 1: *St. Michael's chimes the half hour. Curtain. The court before dawn. Lights in a few windows: MARIA's JAKE's, PORGY's. The fishermen are preparing for an early departure.*

JAKE *(coming from his door).* Dat all de breakfas' I time fo'. *(Calls to men in MARIA's shop.)* Come on yo' mens! It almost light. *(CLARA comes from their room, the baby in her arms. Her eyes are anxious and reproachful, but she says nothing.)*

JIM *(coming from MARIA's shop, wiping his mouth).* Yo' ready Jake? We bes' be off.

JAKE. Le's we go! *(MARIA appears in her doorway, wiping hands on her apron.)*

MARIA. Good-bye, boys! Hope yo' has de same good luck today! *(JAKE quickly takes baby from CLARA's arms, kisses it hurriedly, and returns it to CLARA.)*

JAKE. 'Bye big boy! *(BESS's voice is heard from her room, droning in delirium. All the Negroes stop suddenly to listen.)*

BESS. Eighteen mile to Kittiwah—eighteen mile—palmetto bush by de sho' —rattlesnake an' such. *(JAKE crosses to PORGY's window.)*

JAKE. How Bess dis mornin'? *(PORGY appears at window.)*

PORGY. She no better.

JAKE. She still out she head? *(PORGY nods.)*

BESS. Bess goin' fin' um fo' yo'. Dat all right, Maria, Bess goin' fin' um . . . *(JAKE shakes his head sadly. Hurriedly recrosses to the other men. They go toward gate together, CLARA following.)*

JIM. I bet dat catch we made yesterday de bigges' catch eber make 'round dese parts.

NELSON. We bes' make de mores ob today. Look to me like de las' good day we goin' hab'. Gots a wet tas' to um.

JAKE. Don' yo' know dat ain't de kin' ob talk to talk 'fore my 'oman? Ain't yo' hears de raggin' I gits ebery day? *(Laughs.)* But, see! I gots 'er trained now. She ain't sayin' a word. So long, Clara! *(JAKE gives CLARA a hurried, affectionate pat and follows the other men as they troop out the gate, talking and laughing. The gate clangs shut behind them. CLARA goes silently into her room, closes door.)*

BESS. Mus' be right heah on de groun'. Bess goin' fin' um . . . *(BESS's voice drones on. MARIA, in her doorway, listens a moment. Then crosses to PORGY's door: hesitates, awed by the mystery of delirium. SERENA silently crosses the court and joins MARIA. They listen a moment longer.)*

SERENA *(in a low voice).* She still out she head? *(MARIA nods. They stand silent.)*

BESS *(from the room).* Eighteen mile to Kittiwah—palmetto bush by de sho'. Eighteen mile to Kittiwah . . . *(PETER appears outside the gate. He seems older and feebler, but his face is joyful. Pushes gate open, comes into court, looking eagerly about. Sees the two women and crosses toward them.)*

PETER. How eberybody? *(They turn and see him.)*

MARIA *(joyfully).* Ef it ain't ole Peter!

SERENA. Heah Daddy Peter home

again. Hey, yo' Lily! Heah yo' ole man. Lordy, we is glad fo' see yo'! (LILY *comes running from her door. Hurries to* PETER *and greets him joyfully.*)

LILY. Ef it ain't my ole gran'daddy!

PETER. I begin fo' t'ink mebby I ain't eber see Catfish Row— (BESS's *voice rises in a sudden wail. The women turn awestricken faces toward* PORGY's *door.* PETER, *who has not heard, is mystified by their expressions. His words die away. He looks questioningly from one to another.* BESS *again takes up her monotonous refrain.*)

BESS. Palmetto bush sort ob twisted like rattlesnake an' t'ing . . .

PETER. Whut de mattuh?

MARIA (*shouting into his ear*). Porgy's 'oman bery sick.

LILY (*shouting*). She out she head.

PETER. How long she been like dat?

MARIA. More'n a week now. Eber since we hab de picnic on Kittiwah.

SERENA. She wander off by sheself an' git lost in de palmetto t'icket. She ain't come home fo' two day.

BESS. Dat's right, Maria, I goin' fin' um —eighteen mile to Kittiwah—eighteen mile . . .

PORGY (*within room, soothingly*). Das all right, Bess. Yo' here wid Porgy now.

BESS (*monotonously*). Palmetto bush by de sho' . . . (MARIA, SERENA, *and* PETER *stand wide-eyed, looking in at the door. They do not go too near.*)

PORGY. Yo' right here wid Porgy an' nuttin' can't hurt yo'. Soon de cool wedder comin' an' chill dese febers.

PETER (*shaking his head*). Dat 'oman bery sick. (*The women nod.*)

PORGY. Ain't yo' remembuh how de cool win' come to town wid de smell ob pine tree an' how de stars is all polishin' up like w'ite folks silber? Den eberybody git well. Ain't yo' know? Yo' jus' keep still an' watch what Porgy say. (*Silence in the room.* CLARA *comes from her door carrying her baby, crosses to the gate and stands looking out toward the sea. After a moment,* PORGY *comes from his door, softly closes it behind him.*) I t'ink mebby she goin' sleep now. (*Sinks wearily on to step. Dully.*) Dat

yo' Peter? A whole week gone, now, an' she ain't no better! What I goin' do? (*A moment of silence.*)

PETER. Ef yo' wants to listen to me, I advise yo' to send she to de w'ite folks' hospital. (*Blank consternation.* MARIA *is first to find her voice.*)

MARIA (*speaking into his ears*). Fo' Gawd's sake, Peter! Ain't yo' know dey lets colo'd folks die dere so dey can gib um to de student'? I say dey gib um to de student'.

PETER. De student' ain't gits um till he done dead. Ain't dat so? Den he can't hurt um none. Ain't dat so too? An' I gots dis to say. One ob my w'ite folks is a nurse to de hospital. An' dat lady is a pure angel wid de sick colo'd folks. Ef I sick to-morruh I goin' to she, an' what she say is good wid me. I wants dis carcass took care ob while he is alibe. When he done dead, I ain't keer.

LILY (*shouting*). Yo' ain't keer wedder yo' is cut up an scatter, 'stead ob bein' bury in Gawd's own grabeyahd!

PETER. Well, mebby I ain't say I jus' as lief. But I t'ink Gawd onderstan' de succumstance an' make allowance.

PORGY (*moaning*). Oh, Gawd! Don't let um take Bess to de hospital!

SERENA (*in injured tone*). Mus' be yo' is all fegit how I pray Clara's baby out ob de convulsion. Dey ain't nebber been a sick pusson or corpse in Catfish Row dat I has refuse' my prayers. Dey is fo' de righteous an' fo' de sinner all two.

PORGY. Dat's right, Sistuh. Yo' pray ober um. Dat can't hurt um none. (SERENA *closes her eyes and begins to sway.*)

SERENA. Oh, Jedus who done trouble de watuh in de Sea of Gallerie—

PORGY. Amen!

SERENA. —an' likewise who done cas' de debil out ob de afflicted time an' time again—

PETER. Oh, Jedus! (*Begins to sway.*)

SERENA. —what make yo' ain't lay yo' han' on dis sistuh' head—

LILY. Oh, my Fadder!

SERENA. —an' sen' de debil out ob she, down a steep place into de sea, like yo' used to do, time an' time again.

PORGY. Time an' time again.

SERENA. Lif' dis poor cripple up out ob de dus'—

PETER. Allelujah!

SERENA. —an' lif' up he 'oman an' make she well, time an' time again. (*They sway a moment in silence. Then* SERENA *silently rises and departs. After a moment,* PETER *and* LILY *follow her.*)

MARIA (*in a low voice*). Listen to me. Yo' wants dat 'oman cure up, ain't yo'?

PORGY. Yo' knows I does.

MARIA. Bery well, den. Why ain't yo' sen' to Lody?

PORGY. Fo' make conjur'?

MARIA. Yo' gots two dollah? (PORGY *nods.*) Den yo' bes' waste no time. Yo' go quick to Lody an' gib she de two dollah an' tell she to make conjur' fo' cas' de debil out ob Bess. (MINGO *has sauntered in and taken a seat at the table by* MARIA's *door.*)

PORGY. How I goin' leabe Bess?

MINGO. Hey, Maria! How 'bout a little serbice?

MARIA. Here, yo' Mingo, come here! (*He crosses to them.*) Yo' do little job fo' Porgy an' I gib yo' de free breakfas' when yo' gits back. Yo' know Lody, de conjur' 'oman?

MINGO. Who don't know Lody!

MARIA. Yo' go to Lody an' tell she fo' make conjur' fo' cas' de debil out ob Porgy's Bess. He goin' gib yo' two dollah fo' she. (PORGY *has taken out his money bag and is counting out pennies.*)

MINGO. Dat long way to Lody's 'fore breakfus'.

MARIA. Listen to um! Ef yo' wa'n't dead on yo' feet, yo' could get dere an' back in ten minute'.

MINGO. Whut yo' gots fo' breakfus'?

MARIA. I gots de butts meat fo' grease yo' mout', an' de corn bread an' 'lasses fo' sweet yo' mout'.

MINGO. How 'bout er little shark steak?

MARIA. Listen to me, boy! I ain't serbe no free breakfus' alley cat.

MINGO (*belligerently*). Who you callin' alley cat?

MARIA (*despairingly*). Dis fella ain't know nuttin'! Get dis! I decides fo' my

customer' whut dey goin' hab', but ain't yo' neber been in one ob dem stylish rest'rant where de name ob all de victual' is writ up on de wall, an' you can pick an' choose 'mong um? Dat's alley cat.

PORGY. I goin' gib' yo' quarter fo' goin'.

MINGO. Ah! He ain't so far now!

PORGY (*handing him money*). Here de two dollah fo' Lody an' de quarter fo' yo'self. (MINGO *starts for gate.*)

MARIA. Dat breakfas' I promise yo' goin' be on de table in ten minute'. Ef yo' ain't hurry, he'll be cold.

MINGO. I be back fo' yo' can crack yo' teet'. (*Goes out gate and off to left. St. Michael's chimes the three-quarter hour.*)

MARIA. Quarter till five. Eben dat lazy critter can't spend more'n ten minute' *gittin'* to Lody's. By fib o'clock sure, she goin' hab she conjur' make.

PORGY (*eagerly*). Yo' t'ink dat cure she?

MARIA. I ain't t'ink. I know. Yo' watch what I say, my brudder. Bess good as cure right now. Yo' gots jus' a quartuh hour to wait. Come fib o'clock, dat 'oman well. (*Crosses to her shop. Goes about her work.* SERENA *has gone to work at her tubs. She now calls to* CLARA, *who still stands gazing out through gate.*)

SERENA. What yo' stan' dere fo', Clara? Boats must be out ob sight by now.

CLARA. Dey been out ob sight fo' long time now.

MARIA (*working at her table*). Yo' ain't gots no call fo' worry 'bout yo' man. Dis goin' be a fine day.

CLARA. I neber see de watuh look so black.

MARIA. Well, has yo' eber see it look so still?

CLARA. No. He too still. An' somet'ing in my head keep a-listenin' fo' dat hurricane bell. (*Crosses to* SERENA. *Sits on bench.*) Let me sit here wid yo', an' yo' talk a lot.

MARIA (*who has crossed to pump with kettle*). I gots a feelin'—

SERENA. What yo' gots a feelin' 'bout?

MARIA. I gots a feelin' when dat 'oman of Porgy's got lost on Kittiwah Islan' she done been wid Crown.

SERENA (*her face darkening*). Yo t'ink Crown on Kittiwah?

MARIA. I always figger he been dere in dem deep palmettuhs, an' when I hear de t'ings dat 'oman keep sayin' in she sickness, I sure ob two t'ing—one, dat he is dere, and two, dat she's been wid um.

CLARA. Yo' beliebe she still run wid Crown!

MARIA. Dem sort ob mens ain't need to worry 'bout habin' women.

SERENA. Bess goin' stay wid Porgy ef she know what good fo' she!

MARIA. She know all right, an' she lobe Porgy. But, ef dat buck come after she, dey ain't goin' be nobody 'round here but Porgy an' de goat. (*As* MARIA *speaks,* PORGY *comes from his door. The other women sign to* MARIA *to be careful. Seeing* PORGY, *she drops the subject and returns to her shop.*)

SERENA (*piling clothes in basket*). Come on, Clara, lend me a han' wid dese clothes. (CLARA, *holding baby on one arm, takes one handle of basket.* SERENA *lifts the other. They carry it through* SERENA'S *door.* PORGY *sits on his doorstep, his face tense, waiting.* DADDY PETER *comes from his door followed by* LILY, *who carries the honey tray. She places it on his head and returns to room, closing the door.* PETER *crosses toward gate, beginning instantly to chant.*)

PETER. I gots honey.—Has yo' gots honey?—Yes, ma'am, I gots honey.—You gots honey cheap? . . . (*A woman leans from an upper window and calls.*)

THE WOMAN. Oh, honey man! Honey man!

PETER (*going on*). Yes, ma'am, my honey cheap.

THE WOMAN. Hey, dere! I wants some honey! (PETER *goes out gate and off to the right.*)

PETER. You gots honey in de comb?—Yes, ma'am, I gots honey in de comb.—Heah comes de honey man!—I gots honey. (PORGY *sits waiting. St. Michael's begins to chime the hour.* PORGY *grows suddenly rigid. As the chimes continue,* MARIA *comes to her doorway and stands motionless, also listening. She and*

PORGY *gaze at each other across court with tense, expectant faces. The chimes cease.*)

PORGY (*in a low, vibrant voice*). Now de time! Oh, Gawd! (*St. Michael's strikes five. As* PORGY *and* MARIA *still wait motionless,* BESS'S *voice is heard, weakly.*)

BESS. Porgy! (PORGY *and* MARIA *are both electrified by the sound. They gaze at each other with joyful faces, but for a second neither moves.*) Porgy! Dat yo' dere, ain't it? Why yo' ain't talk to me?

PORGY (*with a half-laugh that breaks in a sob*). T'ank Gawd! T'ank Gawd! (BESS *appears in the doorway in her white nightgown. She is very weak.*)

BESS. I lonesome here all by myself. (MARIA *crosses to her quickly. Gently assists her as she lowers herself to seat beside* PORGY.)

BESS. It hot in dere. Let me sit here a while in de cool.

MARIA. I'll get yo' blanket.

PORGY. Maria, ain't she ought to go back to bed?

MARIA (*going past them into room*). Let she be. What I done tell yo'? Ain't dat conjur' cured she?

BESS. I been sick, ain't it?

PORGY. Oh, Bess! Bess!

BESS. What de mattuh?

PORGY (*almost sobbing with relief*). Yo' been bery sick! T'ank Gawd de conjur' cure yo'! (MARIA *reappears with blanket, which she wraps about* BESS.)

MARIA. I ain't goin' let yo' set here bery long. (*Returns to her shop.*)

PORGY. I got yo' back, Bess!

BESS. How long I been sick, Porgy?

PORGY. Jus' a week. Yo' come back from Kittiwah wid yo' eye like fireball, an' Maria git yo' in de bed. An' yo' ain't know me! (BESS *suddenly catches her breath in a stifled sob.*) What de mattuh, Bess?

BESS. I guess I ain't know nuttin' wid de feber—or I ain't come back at all!

PORGY. Yo' ain't come back to Porgy? (*She begins to moan hysterically.*)

BESS. No, I ain't ought to come back!

PORGY (*soothingly*). Dat all right. Don' yo' worry none, Bess. I knows yo' been wid Crown. (BESS *draws in her breath sharply, then speaks in a whisper.*)

BESS. How yo' know?

PORGY. Yo' been talk 'bout um while yo' out ob yo' head.

BESS. What I say?

PORGY. Yo' ain't say nuttin' 'cept crazy stuff, but Gawd gib cripple to know many t'ing he ain't gib strong men.

BESS. Yo' ain't want me go away?

PORGY. No, I ain't want yo' go, Bess. (*Looks at her keenly. A moment of silence.*) Yo' neber lie to me, Bess.

BESS. No, I neber lie to yo'. Yo' gots to gib me dat. (*Another silence.*)

PORGY. How t'ings stan' 'tween yo' an' Crown?

BESS (*after a pause*). He comin' fo' me when de cotton come to town.

PORGY. Yo' goin'?

BESS. I tell um—yes. (PORGY *turns his head from her and sits looking straight before him. After a moment,* BESS *reaches out timidly and lays her hand on his arm. Then she tries to encircle it with her fingers.*) Porgy! Gawd! Yo' gots de arm like stebedore! Why yo' muscle pull up like dat? (*He looks at her, his face set and stern. She cowers, her hand still on his arm.*) It make' me 'fraid! (*A pause.*)

PORGY. Yo' ain't gots nuttin' fo' be 'fraid of. I ain't try to keep no 'oman what don' want to stay. Ef yo' wants to go wid Crown, dat fo' yo' to say.

BESS. I ain't wants to go, Porgy. (PORGY *looks at her with hope.*) But I ain't yo' kin'. When Crown put he hand on me dat day, I run to he like watuh. Some day again he goin' put he han' on my t'roat. It goin' be like dyin', den. But I gots to talk de trut' to you'. When dem time come, I goin' to go. (*Silence.*)

PORGY (*in a whisper*). Ef dey wa'n't no Crown, Bess! Ef dey was only jus' yo' an Porgy, what den? (*She looks into his face with an expression of yearning. Then, suddenly, the weakness of her illness sweeps down upon her and she breaks out hysterically, trembling with fear.*)

BESS. Oh, fo' Gawd's sake, Porgy! Don't let dat man come an' handle me!

Ef yo' is willin' to keep me, den lemme stay! (*Her voice rises hysterically, broken by sobs.*) Ef he jus' don' put dem hot han' on me, I can be good! I can 'membuh! I can be happy! (*The sobs overcome her.*)

PORGY. Dere, dere, Bess. (*Pats her arm soothingly, waiting for the storm to spend itself. She grows suddenly quiet, except for occasional silent, rending sighs.*) Yo' ain't need to be afraid. Ain't yo' gots yo' man? Ain't yo' gots Porgy fo' take care ob yo'? What kin' ob mans yo' tinks yo' gots anyway, fo' let anudder mans carry he 'oman? No, sur! Yo' gots yo' man now! Yo' gots Porgy! (BESS *has become quiet. A pause.*) Dere, now. Yo' been set up too long. Let Porgy help yo' back to bed. (*He draws himself up by the door frame.* BESS *rises unsteadily and, with a hand on his arm, they make their way into the room.* PORGY *closes the door behind them.* MINGO *appears outside the gate, steadies himself against it, then staggers through and crosses to* MARIA's *table. Slumps into chair. Pounds on table, then buries head in his hands.* MARIA *comes to doorway.*)

MARIA. Oh, dat yo', Mingo! Gawd A'mighty, how yo' gits drunk so fas'! (*Goes into shop and immediately returns with breakfast things on a tray. Begins putting them before him.*) I bet yo' drink dat rot-gut stuff straight! Ain't yo' know nuff to pollute yo' whisky wid watuh?

MINGO (*pushing dishes away*). Don' want dat stuff. Wants de shark steak.

MARIA (*hands on hips*). So yo' don' want dat stuff! Bery well! Yo' wants de shark steak! Yo' t'inks I gibin' shark steak wid de free breakfas'?

MINGO. I tells yo' I wants de shark steak. (*With uncertain movements, draws a handful of change from pocket.*)

MARIA (*mollified*). Ob course, ef yo' goin' pay fo' um! (MINGO *spills the money in a pile on table. It is all pennies.* MARIA *stares at it, then at him. Her eyes are suddenly filled with suspicion.*) Where yo' gits dat money? (MINGO *looks up at her stupidly. She speaks in a ferocious whisper.*) Where yo' gits dat money? (MINGO *seems to try to recollect*.) He all pennies—jus' like Porgy gits fo' beggin'! (*She suddenly seizes him, jerks him to his feet.*) Dats Porgy's money, I tells yo', what he gibe yo' fo' Lody! (MINGO *open his mouth to protest, searching wildly for words.*) Don' yo' lie to me.

MINGO. I jus' take 'nough fo' li'l' drink. (MARIA *gives him a savage shake which seems to spill out further words.*) I t'ink Lody must have move'. I can't find she. (*With weak bravado.*) Leggo me, ole lady! (*Tries to shake off her grip.* MARIA *holds him tighter and brings her face close to his. His eyes suddenly meet hers, and he sees a look of such cold ferocity that he quails and sobs with terror.*) Oh, Jedus.

MARIA. Yo' low, crawlin' houn'! Yo' drink up de conjur' money ob a poor dyin' 'oman, an' ain't leabe she nuttin' but de Christian prayers! You listen to me! (*Slowly and impressively.*) Fo' yo' own good, I goin' lock yo' up in my closet till yo' sober nuff to keep yo' mout' shut. Den mebby I lets yo' loose. But I goin' to be where I can git my han' on yo' again! Ef yo' eber tell Porgy —or any libin' pusson—dat yo' ain't deliber dat message to Lody, I goin' hab yo' blood on my soul when I stan' at de Jedgment. Now, yo', gots dat straight in yo' head? (MINGO, *unable to speak, nods. She swings him suddenly about, hurls him into her room, and closes the door on him. Wipes her face on apron, looks with mystified expression toward* PORGY's *closed door. Baffled.*) Mus' hab' been Jedus done cure Bess after all. (*Considers a moment. Takes a few steps toward* PORGY's *door. Then stops, with decision.*) No, I be damn ef He did. He ain't gots it in um. (*Goes into her room. Bangs door behind her. For a moment, the court is empty and silent. Suddenly, the silence is broken by the deep, ominous clang of a bell, very different from the silver tone of St. Michael's. Instantly, every resident of Catfish Row, excepting* MINGO *and* BESS, *is in the court or leaning from his window. Having come, they now stand motionless, scarcely*

breathing, listening to the bell. CLARA, *with her baby, has come from* SERENA's *door, her eyes bright with terror.*) Mus' be de bell fo' a hot wave. Yo' see! He ain't goin' ring more'n twelbe.

LILY (*who has been counting half audibly*).—ten—eleben—twelbe— (*For a moment no one breathes. Then the bell rings on. Every face is suddenly rigid with horror.*)

CLARA (*wildly*). Twenty! (*She runs to the gate and looks off left.*)

SERENA (*following and seeking to comfort her*). Dat bell mus' be mistake! Ain't yo' membuh de las' hurricane? How he take two day' fo' blow up?

ANNIE. Now eberyt'ing quiet. Not a breaf ob air. (*All the Negroes have gone to the gate and are gazing off to left.*)

PORGY (*from his window*). How de Custom House flag?

SERENA. He right dere on de pole, jus' like always.

MARIA (*seeing it too, relieved*). Don' yo' see dat flag dere, Clara?

SERENA (*reassuringly to* CLARA). Dat ain't no hurricane signal, is it?

MARIA. Ain't yo' know long as de American flag wabin' ober de Custom House dat mean eberyt'ing all right, jus' like— (*They are all gazing off left at the distant flag. Suddenly, a new wave of horror sweeps simultaneously over every face.* MARIA's *speech breaks off with her lips still parted.*)

LILY (*in a low, awed voice*). Gawd! Dey take um down! (*They continue to gaze, fascinated, but* CLARA *turns away, back into the court. Her terror has given way to dull hopelessness.*)

CLARA. Dey don' hab' to run up no hurricane signal to tell me nuttin'. My head stop listenin' fo' um now.

PORGY. De mens goin' see de signal an' come home quick.

CLARA. Dey can't see dat signal from de Blackfish Banks, an' dey dere by dis time.

ANNIE (*hysterically*). How dey goin' come back wid no win' fo' de sail?

MARIA (*sternly silencing her*). Dey can row in 'fo' dis storm come. He ain't here yet, is he?

PORGY. No, he ain't here yet.

LILY. I ain't fo' worryin' 'bout t'ing dat mightn't happen 'tall. (*There is a general babble of voices: "Time 'nough fo' worry when de storm come!" "Mebby by to-morruh we habe li'l' storm!" etc. While they reassure themselves, the sea is darkening. The shutters of Catfish Row begin to flap back and forth in a sudden wind.* CLARA *stands watching the swinging shutters.*)

CURTAIN

SCENE 2: *Before the rise of the curtain the sound of the wind and water begins and swiftly swells and rises. Through the wind the chimes and bells of St. Michael's are heard, sometimes rising clear and strong as the wind lulls, then lost completely in a sudden gust.*

The curtain rises on SERENA's *room, dim and shadowy in the light of guttering kerosene lamps. The Negroes are huddled together in groups. A few have found seats on the chairs and bed. Others sit on the floor. A small group at right, including* SERENA *and* PETER, *are on their knees, swaying and singing the monotonous chant of "The Judgment Day Spiritual."* PORGY *and* BESS *sit together on the floor at left front.* CLARA *stands motionless at window, her baby in her arms. Every face is filled with fear. They shudder and draw closer together as the wind rises.*

THE SINGERS. "We will all sing togedduh, on dat day,
We will all sing togedduh on dat day,
An' I'll fall upon my knees an' face de risin' sun,
Oh, Lord, hab mercy on me!"

MARIA (*speaking above the monotonous chant*). What yo' stan' dere all de time a-lookin' out fo', Clara? Yo' can't see nuttin' in de dark.

CLARA (*gazing out between slats of closed shutters; in a flat, dull voice*). I t'ink I see a little light now 'round de edge ob dis storm. He mus' be mos' daytime. (*In a sudden silence of the wind, a faint, distant sound is heard.*)

ANNIE. What dat? Sound like a whinny.

CLARA. Somebody's poor horse in de watuh.

PORGY (*moaning*). My poor li'l' goat. He goin' to dead. Dat goat's my leg', I can't neber walk again!

MARIA. Dat's right sma't goat, Porgy. He goin' to climb on yo' bed an' keep he head out ob de watuh. Yo' watch whut I say!

PETER. Yo' bes' come sing wid we, Clara. Dat make yo' feel better.

CLARA (*suddenly hysterical*). I mos' lose my min' wid yo' singin'. Yo' been singin' de same speritual since daylight yesterday!

SERENA (*severely*). Ain't we want to be ready when de grabe gib up de dead an' Gabriel sound he trumpet?

SPORTING LIFE. I ain't so sure dis de Jedgment Day. We hab bad storm 'fore.

SERENA. Not like dis.

MINGO. I 'membuh my ma tell me, when dey hab de eart'quake here, all de colo'd people sing dat Jedgment Day speritual, waiting fo' de sound ob de trumpet. But he ain't de Jedgment Day den, an' mebby he ain't now.

SERENA. Dat may be so, but dis ain't no time fo' takin' chances. (*Bursts again into song. Her group joins her. The shutters suddenly fly apart and flap violently in the wind, drowning out the singing. The Negroes cower and draw closer together. Some of the men struggle to capture the flying shutters.* BESS *sits calm, gazing straight ahead of her.* PORGY *is watching her thoughtfully.*)

PORGY (*in a brief moment of quiet*). Yo' ain't 'fraid, Bess? (BESS *shakes her head. A pause.*) What make yo' ain't say nuttin'?

BESS. I jus' t'inkin'. (*The men finally lash the shutters together with rope.*) Yo' know whut I t'inkin' 'bout, Porgy.

PORGY. Yo' t'inkin' what storm like dis mus' be like out on de sea islands. (BESS *nods.*)

BESS. Wabe' like dese mus' wash clean across Kittiwah. (*After a moment, she lays her hand on his arm.* PORGY *looks keenly into her eyes.*)

PORGY. Yo' sorry?

BESS. I sorry fo' any man lef' out in storm like dis. But I can stop a-listenin' now fo' his step a-comin'. (*Puts her hand in his.*) I guess yo' gots me fo' keeps, Porgy.

PORGY. Ain't I tells yo' dat all 'long. (*A distant roar is heard, coming steadily nearer.*)

LILY (*terror-stricken*). Here he come now!

SERENA. Oh, Masteh! I is ready! (*The crash and roar sweep by.*)

MARIA. Yo' can se um, Clara?

CLARA. He somebody's roof goin' by.

ANNIE. Gawd A'mighty!

PETER. Oh, Jedus, hab a little pity!

SERENA. Le's we sing! (SERENA's *group begins to sing, but before they have completed a single line* CLARA *cries out loudly.*)

CLARA. Fo' Gawd's sake, sing somet'ing else! (*The singers are startled into silence. A blank pause. Then* BESS *begins to sing, "Somebody's Knockin' at de Door," and one by one the others join her till the whole room is singing.*)

ALL. "Dere's somebody knockin' at de do'.
Dere's somebody knockin' at de do'.
Oh, Mary, oh, Mart'a,
Somebody knockin' at de do'.

"It's a moaner, Lord,
Somebody knockin' at de do'.
It's a moaner, Lord,
Somebody knockin' at de do'.
Oh, Mary, oh, Mart'a,
Somebody knockin' at de do'.

"It's a sinnuh, Lord," etc.
"It's my preachuh, Lord," etc.
"It's my Jedus, Lord," etc.

(*The spiritual swells and gains in tempo; the rhythm of the patting and swaying grows. A few begin to shout.*)

PETER. I hear deat' knockin' at de door. (*Looks fearfully at door. His haunted expression draws the attention of the others. One by one, they stop singing.*)

ANNIE. What yo' say, Daddy Peter? (*The singing stops, but the rhythm continues.*)

PETER. I hear deat' knockin' at de do'. (*A horrified silence. All eyes turn to door*).

LILY (*in an awed whisper*). It mus' be deat', or Peter can't hear um.

MINGO. He ain't hear nuttin'. Nobody knock.

LILY. Yes, dey is! Somebody dere!

PETER. Deat' is knockin' at de do'.

MARIA. Open de do' an' show um nobody ain't dere.

MINGO. Open um yo'self. (MARIA *rises and starts toward door.*)

LILY (*wildly*). I tells yo' dere is somebody dere! An' Peter can't hear no libbon' person! (MARIA *hesitates. A loud knock is heard. The Negroes immediately burst into a pandemonium of terror. There are cries of "Oh, Gawd, hab' me'cy!" "Don't let um come in!" The knock is repeated, louder. Some begin to pray, but the more energetic begin piling furniture in front of door. "Bring dat dresser!" "Wedge um under de knob," etc. The door is shaken violently.*)

BESS. Dat ain't no use. Ef he death, he come' in, anyway.

MARIA (*now the most terrified of all*). Oh, Gawd! Gawd! Don't let um in! (*With a sucking sound of the wind, the door slowly opens, pushing away the flimsy furniture. Shrieks of terror and prayers fill the room.* CROWN, *bent double against the wind, enters. As one by one they gain courage to look toward the door, the prayers die away. For a moment, the Negroes stare at him in silence. Then there are cries of "Crown!" "Gawd, it's Crown!"* BESS *sits silent, rigid.* PORGY *gazes at her searchingly.*)

CROWN. Yo' is a nice pa'cel ob folks! Shut a frien' out in a storm like dis!

SERENA. Who' frien' is yo'?

CROWN. I yo' frien', Sistuh. Glad fo' see yo'! Still mopin' or has yo' got anudder man?

SERENA. I prayin' Gawd to hold back my han'.

CROWN (*laughing*). Well, he'll hold it, all right. Better try de police.

MARIA. Yo' know bery well Serena too

decent to gib' one of she own people away to de w'ite folks.

CROWN (to SERENA). Well, between yo' Gawd an' yo' manners, yo' sho' makes t'ings soft fo' a hard fella! (Sees BESS.) Oh, dere's who I'm lookin' fo'! Why ain't yo' come say hello to yo' man?

BESS. Yo' ain't my man.

CROWN. It's sho' time I was comin' back! Dere jus' ain't no 'oman a man can leabe! (Looking at PORGY.) Yo' ain't done much fo' yo'self while I been gone. Ain't dere no whole ones left?

BESS (rising and facing him). Keep yo' mout' off Porgy!

CROWN. Well, fo' Gawd's sake! Dem hymn-whiners got yo' too?

BESS. I tol' yo' I ain't goin' wid yo' no mo'. I stayin' wid Porgy fo' good.

CROWN. 'Oman! Do yo' want to meet yo' Gawd? Come here!

BESS (holding her ground). Porgy my man now.

CROWN (laughing). Yo' call dat a man! Don' yo' min'. I gots de forgivin' nature, an' I goin' take yo' back. (Reaches for her. BESS violently repulses him.)

BESS. Keep yo' han' off me!

SERENA (to CROWN). Ef yo' stick 'round here, yo' sure to get killed sooner or later. Den de w'ite folks goin' figger I done um. Dey gots it in de writin' now dat I been Robbins' wife. An' dey goin' lock me up fo' um anyway. So I might as well do um. (BESS returns to her seat by PORGY.)

CROWN (laughing). What makes yo' t'ink I goin' get killed? Ef Gawd want to kill me, he got plenty ob chance 'tween here an' Kittiwah Islan'. Me an' Him been habin' it out all de way from Kittiwah; first Him on top, den me. Dere ain't nuttin' He likes better'n a scrap wid a man! Gawd an' me frien'! (A terrific roar of wind.)

SERENA (terror-stricken). Yo' fool! Ain't yo' gots more sense dan talk 'bout Gawd like dat in a storm like dis! (Another sudden gust.)

CROWN. Gawd's laughin' at yo'!

PETER. It bery dangerous fo' we all to hab' dat blasphemin' man 'mong us. Le's we sing unto de Lord! (A woman's voice leads the spiritual, "Got to Meet de Jedgment.")

THE WOMEN. "All I know—

SEVERAL MEN. I got to meet de Jedgment.

THE WOMEN. "All I know—

THE MEN. Got to meet de Jedgment.

THE WOMEN. "All I know—

THE MEN. Got to meet de Jedgment.

TOGETHER. All I know, All I know, All I know—

THE WOMEN. "All I know—

THE MEN. I got to meet de Jedgment . . ."

(As the wind subsides, the spiritual rises strong and clear. The Negroes sing and sway for a moment uninterrupted.)

CROWN (his voice rising above the singing). Yo' folks mus' t'ink de Lord bery easy pleased ef yo' t'ink He like to listen to dat. (They sing on.) Ef it affec' Him de way it do me, yo' is gibin' um de lonesome blues. (They continue to sing. CROWN shouts above singing.) Here, here! Cut dat! I didn't come all de way from Kittiwah to sit up wid no corpses! Dem as is in such a hurry fo' de Jedgment, all dey gots fo' do is to kiss demselves good-bye an' step out dat door. Yo', Uncle Peter, here's yo' chance. The Jim Crow's leabin' an' yo' don't need no ticket! (Turning to SERENA.) How 'bout yo', Sistuh? All abo'd! What, dey ain't no trabbelers? (A roar of wind.) Dere go de train! An' yo' miss yo' chance! (The wind rises above the singing. CROWN shouts up at ceiling.) Dat's right, drown um out! Don' yo' listen to um sing! Dey don' gib yo' credit fo' no taste in music. How 'bout dis one, Big Frien'? (Sings.)

"Rock in de mountain,
Fish in de sea,
Dere neber was a fella
Take an 'oman from me."

LILY. Jedus! He goin' call down Gawd' wrath on we all! (The wind rises to its highest pitch. The Negroes huddle together in terror. They begin to sway and moan. CROWN stands in middle of room, his arms thrown wide. His voice rises above the wind.)

CROWN. Don' yo' hear Gawd A'mighty

—laughing up dere? Dat's right, Ole Frien'! Gawd laugh, an' Crown laugh back! (*Throws back his head and laughs. The wind shrieks above his laugh.*) Dat's right! Yo' like um, Gawd? I'll gib yo' anudder verse! (*Sings.*)
"I ain't no doctor,
No doctor' son,
But I can cool yo' feber
Till de doctor come."

(*While he is singing, the wind suddenly ceases. The Negroes look at one another, appalled by the suddenness of the change.*)

BESS. Mus' be de storm ober.

PORGY. He jus' takin' a res'. When de wind lull like dis, he come back soon, worse'n eber.

CROWN. Ain't I tell yo' Gawd like um? He quiet now fo' listen. (*He bursts again into song.*)
"I laugh in de country,
 I laugh in de town,
 'Cause a cripple t'ink he goin'
 Take an 'oman from Crown."
(*Then begins to shuffle.*) Come on, Bess! Yo' ain't one ob dese spiritual-whimperin' critters. What, ain't yo' gots no guts! Come 'long! Yo' used to be de bes' dancer in Charleston. Ef yo' don' want to dance wid Crown, mebby yo' new man'll dance wid yo'! (*Roars with laughter. BESS is silent. He dances a few more steps.*) Come 'long, Maria! Yo' can't tell me dese Gawd-f'arin' whiners has got yo'! (*MARIA hesitates, CROWN dances on. Laughs.*) Dis ole lady too fat fo' dance!

MARIA (*indignantly*). Who say I'm too fat! (*Gets lumberingly to her feet and begins to shuffle. MINGO begins to clap for them.*)

CROWN (*dancing*). How 'bout ole Sportin' Life? (*SPORTING LIFE joins in the dancing. PETER begins to clap.*)

LILY. Stop dat, yo' ole fool!

CROWN (*dancing near PETER and shouting in his ear*). Dis gran'daddy too ole fo' dance!

PETER (*indignant, puffing out his chest*). Who say I too ole! (*Gets laboriously to his feet and begins a feeble shuffle. A group are now forgetting their*

terror in song and dance in the middle of the room. Another group, including SERENA, are looking on disapprovingly and with fear in their faces. CLARA pays no attention to it all, gazes steadily from window. PORGY and BESS sit together, absorbed in each other. Every now and then CROWN cuts a pigeon wing before BESS. She ignores him. He laughs and dances away. A wild crescendo shriek cuts across the sound of merriment. The dancers stop in their places. Everyone turns to CLARA, who is pointing from the window, her eyes wild and horror-stricken. They all rush to the window. SERENA and ANNIE are already trying to comfort CLARA.*)

ANNIE. Course it's a boat upside down, but 'tain't de *Sea Gull.*

CLARA. It got red gunnels same as *Sea Gull.*

SERENA. Don' yo' know *Sea Gull* gots bird wid spread wing on he bow.

MINGO (*pointing*). He goin' come up ober dere now.

SERENA. You'll see! He gots no bird! Dere! Watch um! See he— (*She breaks off suddenly with widening eyes. CLARA cries out.*)

MINGO. Gawd! It de *Sea Gull* fo' true!

CLARA (*shaking off SERENA's arm*). Lemme go!

PETER. What yo' goin' do?

SERENA (*holding her*). Yo' wait now, Clara!

CLARA. Lemme go! (*Breaks from SERENA's hold. Runs frantically to the door. Then turns back suddenly to BESS.*) Bess, yo' keep my baby till I come back. (*Thrusts the baby into BESS's arms. Wrests the door open while the Negroes call protests after her.*)

BESS. Clara! Don' go! (*CLARA rushes out. The door bangs shut behind her. A startled moment of silence. They all stand looking at closed door.*)

MINGO. Dat 'oman t'ink she goin' find Jake alibe!

BESS. Clara oughtn't to be out dere by sheself.

SPORTING LIFE. Eberyt'ing quiet now.

PORGY. Dat storm comin' back any minute.

BESS. Somebody go fo' Clara. Don' leabe she out dere alone! (*No one moves.*)

SPORTING LIFE. What de fool 'oman go fo'!

MARIA. Dey ain't nobody in here got de guts ob a chicken.

MINGO. Go 'long yo'self, Auntie. Dere ain't no wabe big nough fo' drown yo'.

PETER (*starting for door*). Who goin' wid me?

BESS (*holding him back*). Yo' ain't goin', Daddy Peter! Yo' too ole. (*Looking scornfully over the room.*) Ain't dere no *man* 'round here?

CROWN. Yes! Where all dem folks been wantin' to meet de Jedgment? Go 'long! Yo' been askin' fo' somet'ing, an' yo' ain't got the gizzards to go an' get um. Now's yo' chance. (*Laughs. Goes and stands before* BESS, *looking sideways to see effect on her.*) Porgy, what yo' sittin' dere fo'? Ain't yo' hear yo' 'oman calling fo' a *man?* Yes, looks to me like only *one man* 'round here! (*Again glances toward* BESS; *then runs to door, throwing up his arms and calling. Calls the men by name: "Go 'long, Sam!" etc.*) All right, Ole Frien' up dere! We's on fo' anudder bout! (*Jerks door open and runs out. A moment of silence. The stage has grown perceptibly lighter. All the Negroes crowd to the window, looking over each other's shoulders through slats of the closed shutters.*)

PETER. Dere Clara almost to de wharf already.

BESS. De watuh deep?

SERENA. Almost to she waist.

SPORTING LIFE. Gawd! How Crown splash t'rough dat watuh! (*They watch a moment in silence. A roar of wind and water. The stage darkens suddenly. With a swift, sucking sound, the shutters fly apart. Confused cries of "Oh, Jedus! Hab' a little me'cy!" "Gawd A'mighty! De storm come back!" "Ain't I tell yo' he comin' worser'n eber."*)

SERENA (*kneeling center*). Gawd answering Crown! (*Others kneel with her, shrinking close together, moaning with terror.*)

MINGO (*at window, his voice rising*

high in horror). De wharf goin'! Gawd A'mighty!

BESS (*screaming futilely against the wind*). Clara! Clara! (*Wild shrieks of horror from all the Negroes at window. Then a terrific roar, accompanied by the splintering of timber. Then a sudden awed silence in the room.* PETER *turns the women from the window, blocking further view. They huddle together in the center of the room around* SERENA'S *group.* BESS *crosses to* PORGY. *Sits beside him, the baby in her arms. All the others fall upon their knees as with one accord they begin to sing the "Jedgment Day Spiritual."* BESS *does not sing, but sits holding the baby close, with a rapt look in her eyes.*)

"We will all pray togedduh on dat day,
We will all pray togedduh on dat day,
An' I'll fall upon my knees an' face de risin' sun.
Oh, Lord, hab mercy on me!

"We will drink wine togedduh on dat day.
We will drink wine togedduh on dat day," etc.

"We will eat bread togedduh on dat day,
We will eat bread togedduh on dat day,
An' I'll fall upon my knees an' face de risin' sun.
Oh, Lord, hab mercy on me!"

PETER (*in the midst of the singing*). Allelujah! Gawd hab mercy on de souls ob Clara an' Crown! (BESS *turns and looks directly at* PORGY. *With an expression of awe in his face, he reaches out a timid hand and touches the baby's cheek. The roar increases. The shutters fly back and forth. With fear-stricken eyes, the Negroes sway and pat and sing, their voices sometimes rising above the roar of the wind and sometimes drowned by it.* BESS *continues silent, looking straight ahead of her, tenderness, yearning, and awe in her face.* PORGY *sits watching her. The shutters crash more violently. The roar of wind and water increases. The Negroes huddle closer and sing on.*)

CURTAIN

ACT FOUR

SCENE 1: *Chimes. St. Michael's strikes one. Curtain. The court, dark except for lights around the closed shutters of a second story room at back left and the glow from* MARIA's *open door.* PORGY *is at his window but is only vaguely seen in the darkness. He holds the shutters partly closed so as to screen himself, while he is able to look out. From the second-story room comes the sound of a spiritual muffled by the closed shutters. Door to stairway at back left opens and* SERENA *comes out. Through the open door the spiritual is heard more plainly. It is sung by women's voices—a slow, mournful dirge.*

"Nelson, Nelson, don' let yo' brudder condemn yo'.

Nelson, Nelson, don' let yo' brudder condemn yo'.

Nelson, Nelson, don' let yo' brudder condemn yo'.

Way down in dat lonesome grabeyahd."

(SERENA *closes door, muffling the chant. She crosses toward her room: sees the light from* MARIA's *door and pauses.*)

SERENA. Yo' still up, Maria? How come yo' ain't sing wid we women fo' de dead in de storm?

MARIA (*coming to her doorway*). Some ob dose 'omans liable to sing all night, I too tired clearin' t'ing' up. My stove been wash' clean 'cross de street. An' 'sides, it break my heart to hear dese 'omans mournin' fo' de mens dat provide um wid bread and what was dey lover' too. All dem fine, strong mens, dead in de storm! (*In lower voice.*) It gib me de creeps, Serena, to t'ink how many ghost' mus' be listenin' 'round dis cou't to-night.

SERENA (*nervously*). I ain't no patience wid yo' talk 'bout ghost'. (PORGY *softly moves his shutter.* SERENA *starts.*) What' dat?

MARIA. Jus' Porgy watchin' at he window. (*Draws* SERENA *farther from* PORGY's *window and lowers her voice ominously.*) What' he watchin' fo'?

SERENA (*impatiently*). How I know?

MARIA. He been dere all day. He ain't gone out on de street to beg like he alway' do. An' he ain't gone up wid Bess to sing fo' de dead in de storm.

SERENA. What ob dat?

MARIA. Crown dead, ain't he? (*Lowers voice still further.*) Mus' be he t'ink Crown' ghost is a-comin' fo' trouble Bess. (SERENA *gives scornful grunt.*) Bery well, Sistuh. But I knows dis— Gawd gib dat cripple to see many t'ing yo' an' me can't see—an' if he is watch fo' sompen, den dere is sompen fo' watch fo'. (BESS, *the baby in her arms, opens door at left back. The spiritual is again heard clearly.* BESS *does not close door, but stands listening, holding baby close.* MARIA *and* SERENA *move over to listen.*)

WOMEN'S VOICES. "Jake, Jake, don' let yo' brudder condemn yo'

Jake, Jake, don' let yo' brudder condemn yo' . . ."

BESS. Dey singin' for Jake an' Clara now. I couldn't stay. (*The three women listen a moment in silence.*)

VOICES. "Clara, Clara, don't let yo' sistuh condemn yo'

Way down in dat lonesome grabeyahd . . ."

(BESS *softly closes door, muffling the singing. Turns toward her own door.*)

SERENA. What we all goin' to do wid dat poor mudderless baby?

BESS (*stopping short. Turns slowly back*). Mus' be Clara has come back already.

SERENA (*looks fearfully about her*). What yo' means?

BESS. Mus' be Clara has come back an' say somepen to yo' I ain't hear. I ain't hear her say nuttin' 'bout "we." She say, "Bess, yo' keep dis baby for me till I comes for um."

SERENA. Somebody oughts to make sure de poor chile gets a proper Christian raisin'.

BESS. Clara ain't say nuttin' to me 'bout dat, an' until she do, I goin' stan' on she las' libbin' word an' keep she baby for she till she do come back. (*Again starts toward her door. Again turns back impulsively.*) Oh, let me be, Serena. Can't yo' see I ain't de same 'oman what used to run wid Crown? Gawd wouldn't ha' let Clara gib me dis baby if He hadn't seen I was different inside. He wouldn't ha' gib me Porgy if He didn't want to gib me my chance. (*Looking down at baby.*) See! He t'ink already dat I he ma. I gots de big brightness all inside me to-day. I can't stan' not to hab eberybody kind to me to-day! (*Holds baby out to* SERENA.) Look at um now, Serena—hold um a minute. Tell um he gots a good ma what goin' stan' by um! (SERENA *takes the baby reluctantly, but responds when it touches her bosom. She rocks it in her arms.*)

SERENA. Yes—I reckon yo' gots a good ma now. She gots Gawd in she heart at las'. Yo' ain't gots no cause for fret. (*Hands baby back to* BESS, *who draws it close.*)

BESS. Ain't you see, Serena, how he scroogin' down? Dis baby know already dat he done git back home. (*Turns to go.*)

SERENA. Good-night, Sistuh. (BESS *pauses slightly, as though taken by surprise.*)

BESS. Good-night—Sistuh. (*Goes into her room. A dim light appears in the room. The shutters are closed from within.* SERENA *goes to her room.* MARIA *begins to shut up her shop for the night. Several women carrying lanterns come from the funeral room, leaving the door open. They go out of the gate. The spiritual is again heard.*)

THE SINGERS. "Ummmmm, Ummmmm, yeddy ole Egypt duh yowlin'
Way down in dat lonesome grabeyahd.

"Crown, Crown don' let yo' brudder condemn yo',
Crown, Crown, don' let yo' brudder condemn yo',

(*There is a sudden raucous laugh in the darkness.* MARIA *starts: then turns and peers into the shadows under* SERENA's *stairs.*)

MARIA. Yo' low-live skunk! What yo' hidin' round here fo'?

SPORTING LIFE (*sauntering into the light from* MARIA's *window*). Jus' listenin' to de singin'. Nice happy little tune dat. Now dey's stowin' my ole frien' Crown. (*Laughs again.* MARIA *crosses quickly: closes the door, muffling the singing.*)

MARIA (*returning to* SPORTING LIFE). Yo' ain't gots no shame—laughin' at dem poor 'omans singin' fo' dere dead mens!

SPORTING LIFE. I ain't see no sense makin' such a fuss ober a man when he dead. When a gal's man done gone, dere's plenty mens still libin' what likes good-lookin' gals.

MARIA. I know it ain't dem gals yo' is atter. Ain't yo' see Bess gots no use for yo'? Ain't yo' see she gots a man?

SPORTING LIFE. I see more'n dat, Auntie. (*Laughs as though at a joke all his own.*)

MARIA. What yo' means?

SPORTING LIFE. I see she gots two mens —an' when a 'oman gots two mens— pretty soon she ain't got one at all!

MARIA (*threateningly*). What yo' means by dat—Bess gots two mens?

SPORTING LIFE. What make yo' all so sure Crown dead?

MARIA. Ain't we see de wharf wash away under um?

SPORTING LIFE. Ain't he tell yo' Gawd an' he frien'?

MARIA (*alarmed*). Yo' is tellin' me Crown ain't dead?

SPORTING LIFE (*nonchalantly*). I ain't tellin' yo' nuttin', Auntie.

MARIA (*advancing on him threateningly*). Yas, yo' is. Yo' tellin' me ebery-t'ing yo' knows, an' damn quick! (*Corners him.*)

SPORTING LIFE. Ob course he dead! Ain't we hear um singin' he funeral song?

MARIA (*grabbing his arm and bringing her face close to his*). Yo' has seen um?

SPORTING LIFE. How can I see um if

he dead? Mus' be he ghos' I seen hangin' 'round here.

MARIA (*meditatively*). So yo' has seen um. (*Menacingly.*) Well, if Bess gots two mens, dat sho' count' yo' out. (SPORTING LIFE *laughs at her. While they talk,* PORGY's *shutters open inch by inch.*)

SPORTING LIFE. Dat jus' where I comes in. When a 'oman gots jus' one man, mebby she gots um for keep. But when she gots two mens—dere's mighty apt to be carvin'!—An' de cops takes de leabin's.

MARIA (*warningly*). Dere ain't nobody in dis court would gib' a colo'd man 'way to de cops.

SPORTING LIFE. *Oh, no,* Auntie! But dem cops is bery smart, an' dey gots it in fo' Crown, rememmbuh! An', when dat time comes, yo' can tell Bess for me dat little ole Sportin' Life is still on de premises.

MARIA (*starting for him*). Well, he ain't goin' stay bery long on my premises!

SPORTING LIFE (*hurriedly withdrawing, but not forgetting his swagger*). Dat's all right, ole lady! I was jus' leabin'. (*Saunters toward gate.* MARIA *turns back to the closing of her shop.* SPORTING LIFE *glances at her over his shoulder. Sees her engaged in barring her windows. Steps swiftly into the darkness under* SERENA's *stairs.* MARIA *finishes her work. Looks about court. Sees it's apparently empty. Goes into her shop. Locks door. A child's whimper is heard from* BESS's *room, then* BESS's *voice singing in the darkness.*)

"Hush, little baby, don' yo' cry,
 Hush, little baby, don' yo' cry,
 Hush, little baby, don' yo' cry,
 Mother an' fadder born to die.

"Heard a thunder in de sky,
 Heard a thunder in de sky,
 Heard a thunder in de sky,
 Mus' be Jedus passin' by.

"Heard a rumblin' in de groun',
 Heard a rumblin' in de groun',
 Heard a rumblin' in de groun',
 Mus' be Satan turnin' 'round'.

"Hush, little baby, don' yo' cry,
 Mother an' fadder born to die."

(*Her voice trails off sleepily and is silent. During her lullaby, the last singers have come from the funeral room and crossed to their own rooms or gone out at gate. The light in the funeral room goes out.* MARIA's *light goes out. A moment of complete darkness and silence in Catfish Row; then the sudden flash of a match in the darkness reveals* SPORTING LIFE *about to light a cigarette. He hears something at gate and hurriedly extinguishes match, with cigarette unlit.*

Against the gray background beyond the gate a gigantic figure can be seen. The gate opens very slowly and noiselessly. CROWN *comes stealthily into court; very gently closes gate behind him. Picks his way slowly and silently across court. Stops to listen. Silence. Goes on to* PORGY's *door. Again listens. Puts his hand on knob and softly tries door. Opens it very cautiously, inch by inch. When it is wide enough, he stealthily slips through. Inch by inch, the door closes. A full minute of absolute silence.* MARIA *is in her wrapper; opens her door and stands listening. Satisfied, she is turning back. A muffled thud sounds from* PORGY's *room.* MARIA *stops short. Stands motionless. Suddenly* PORGY's *laugh is heard, deep, swelling, lustful. The baby cries out.*)

BESS. (*within room. Horror in her voice*). Fo' Gawd' sake, Porgy! What yo' laughin' 'bout?

PORGY (*triumphantly*). Dat all right, honey. Don' yo' be worryin'. Yo' gots Porgy now, an' he look atter he 'oman. Ain't I don' tell you'? Yo' gots a *man* now. (MARIA *crosses the court swiftly. Opens* PORGY's *door, goes in, and closes it behind her. Again the flash of a match in the shadows.* SPORTING LIFE *lights his cigarette and continues his vigil.*)

CURTAIN

SCENE 2: *St. Michael's chimes and strikes six. The curtain rises on the court, silent and apparently deserted. After a moment, three white men appear out-side the gate. One is the* DETECTIVE *who arrested* PETER. *The second is the* CORO-NER, *a fat, easy-going, florid man. The third is a* POLICEMAN.

DETECTIVE (*to* POLICEMAN, *pointing off right.*) Bring the wagon 'round to the corner, Al, and wait for us there. (*The* POLICEMAN *goes off right. The* DETECTIVE *and* CORONER *come in at gate.*) This is the joint. I'd like to get some-thing on it this time that would justify closing it up as a public nuisance and turning the lot of 'em into the street. It's alive with crooked blacks.

CORONER (*looking around him*). Looks pretty dead to me.

DETECTIVE. Dead, hell! If you was on the force, 'stead of sitting down in the coroner's office, you'd know we don't make a move that isn't watched by a hundred pair of eyes. (*The* CORONER *looks exceedingly uncomfortable. Glanc-es apprehensively about him.*) There! Did you catch that? (*Points at a win-dow.* CORONER *starts.*) They're gone now.

CORONER. Don't know as I have much business, after all. Just to get a witness to identify the body at the inquest. Maybe you'll bring one along for me when you come.

DETECTIVE. Like hell I will! You stay and get your own witness, and I'll learn you something about handling these peo-ple, too. Now, let's see—got several leads here! The widow of Robbins, the fel-low Crown killed. That's her room there. And then there's the corpse's woman. She's living with the cripple in there now.

CORONER. What makes you think the buck was killed here?

DETECTIVE (*pointing toward sea*). Found right out there.

CORONER. Found at flood tide. Might have been washed in from miles out.

DETECTIVE. A hell of a lot you know about these people. Come on! I'll show you. (CORONER *nods and follows* DETEC-TIVE. *They stop at door leading to* SERENA'S *room.* DETECTIVE *kicks it open, and shouts up the stairs.*)

DETECTIVE. Come on down, Serena Robbins, and make it damn quick! (*There is silence for a moment, then the shutters of* SERENA'S *window are slowly opened, and* ANNIE *looks out.*)

ANNIE. Serena been sick in she bed three day, an' I been here wid she all dat time.

DETECTIVE. The hell she has! Tell her, if she don't come down, I'll get the wagon and run her in.

ANNIE. She bery sick, boss. She can't leabe she bed.

DETECTIVE. She'll leave it damn quick if she knows what's good for her. (ANNIE *disappears. A loud moaning is heard. Then* ANNIE *reappears accompanied by another woman. Between them they support* SERENA. *She wears a voluminous white nightgown, and her face and head are bound in a towel. She collapses across the window sill with a loud groan.*) Drop that racket. (SERENA *is silent.*) Where were you last night?

SERENA (*slowly and as though in great pain*). I been sick in dis bed now three day an' night.

ANNIE. We been sittin' wid she an' nursin' she all dat time.

THE OTHER WOMAN. Dat's de Gawd's trut'.

CORONER. Would you swear to that?

SERENA, ANNIE, *and* OTHER WOMAN (*in unison, as though answer had been learned by rote*). Yes, boss, we swear to dat.

CORONER (*to* DETECTIVE). There you are—an air-tight alibi. (DETECTIVE *regards* CORONER *with scorn.*)

DETECTIVE (*to* SERENA). You know damn well you were out yesterday. I've got a good mind to send for the wagon and carry you in. (*The women are si-lent.* DETECTIVE *waits, then shouts ab-ruptly.*) Well?

THE THREE WOMEN (*again in unison*). We swear to Gawd we been in dis room three day'.

DETECTIVE (*bluffing*). Ah-hh, that's what I wanted! So you swear you were in last night, eh? (*The women are frightened and silent.*) And just two months ago—right here—Crown killed your husband, didn't he? (*No answer.*) Answer me! (DETECTIVE *runs halfway upstairs.*) You'll either talk here or in jail. Get that! Did Crown kill Robbins? Yes or no! (SERENA *nods her head.*) Exactly. And last night Crown got his right here—didn't he? (*Women are silent except* SERENA, *who groans as though in pain.* DETECTIVE *pretends to construe groan as assent—triumphantly.*) Yes, and how do you know he was killed if you didn't see it?

WOMEN (*in unison*). We ain't see nuttin', boss. We been in here t'ree day an' night, an' de window been closed.

DETECTIVE (*shouting*). Look at me, Robbins! Do you mean to tell me that the man who killed your husband was bumped off right here, under your window, and you didn't know?

WOMEN (*in unison*). We ain't see nuttin', boss. We been in here—

DETECTIVE (*interrupting*). —three days and nights with the window closed. You needn't do that one again. (*Turning away disgustedly.*) Oh, hell! You might as well argue with a parrot cage, but you'll never break them without your own witnesses, and you'll never get 'em. (*The three women leave the window, closing shutters.*) Well, come along. Let's see what's here. (*Goes to* LILY *and* PETER'S *door. Throws it open.*) Come on out here, you! (LILY *comes to door.*) What's your name?

LILY (*seeing* CORONER). Do, Lord! Ef it ain't Mr. Jennings!

CORONER. Well, Lily! So you live here? (*To* DETECTIVE.) I'll answer for this woman. She worked for us for years.

DETECTIVE. That don't prove she don't know anything about this murder, does it? (*To* LILY.) What's your name?

LILY (*stubbornly*). I don' know nuttin' 'bout um.

DETECTIVE (*shouting at her*). I didn't ask you whether—

CORONER. Let me question her. (*Kindly to* LILY.) What's your name?

LILY. Do, Mr. Jennings! You ain't membuh my name is Lily Holmes?

CORONER. I know your name was Lily Holmes, but you left us to get married. What's your name now?

LILY. Lord, Mr. Jennings! I de same Lily Holmes. You ain't t'ink I goin' be responsible for dat man's name? No, suh! An' I ain't gib' um my name, nedder!

DETECTIVE (*looking through door*). That your husband? (*Calling into room.*) Come on out here, you!

LILY. I'll fetch um. (*Goes into room. Returns with* PETER.)

CORONER. Why it's the old honey man! (PETER *is terror-stricken at sight of* DETECTIVE.)

DETECTIVE (*recognizing him*). Oh, so it's you, is it? Well, Uncle, do you want to go back to jail or are you going to come clean?

LILY (*appealing to* CORONER). Ain't no use to ask him nuttin'. He deaf, an' 'sides, he ain't got good sense nohow.

CORONER. But, Lily, you didn't marry the old honey man?

LILY (*surveying* PETER). Whut wrong wid um?

CORONER. He's not a suitable age.

LILY (*puzzled*). Whut he ain't?

CORONER. Do you think he's the right age?

LILY. Sho' he de right age. He eighty-two.

CORONER. An old man like that's apt to linger on your hands. (DADDY PETER, *hearing nothing of conversation, but feeling that he is its subject, is nodding and smiling with self-appreciation.*)

LILY. No, boss. Ef I is marry to young man an' he took sick, mebbe *he* linger on my hand. But (*Points to* PETER, *who smiles more amiably.*) He ain't linger on my han'. He took sick—he gone.

CORONER. What did you marry him for?

LILY. Why, yo' see, boss, he like dis. Ain't yo' 'membuh how I used to hab' dem crazy fits ob misery in my stomach? I wake up in de night wid 'em. De doctor say to me, "Lily Holmes, one ob dese nights yo' goin' dead in yo' bed all by yo'self." So I t'ink I bes' marry dat man so as I won't go dead all by myself. But since I marry um, I gets well ob my misery, an' I ain't got no furder use for um.

DETECTIVE (*to* CORONER). Say, are you investigating a murder or just paying social calls? (*To* LILY *and* PETER.) That'll do for you two. Get inside. (LILY *and* PETER *hurriedly return to their room.*)

CORONER. Well, seems to me I get as much out of them as you do.

DETECTIVE. Come on, let's put the cripple and his woman through. I have a hunch that's where we'll find our bacon. (*Crosses toward* PORGY'S *door.* CORONER *follows.*)

CORONER. All right. Go ahead. I'm watching you handle them.

DETECTIVE. You won't find the cripple much of a witness. I tried to break him in the Robbins case but he wouldn't come through. (*Kicks the door open with a bang.*) Come on out, both of you. Step lively now! (BESS *helps* PORGY *to seat on doorstep. Then she stands by him, the baby in her arms.* DETECTIVE *enters room.*)

CORONER (*to* PORGY). What is your name? (PORGY *looks at him keenly, then reassured, smiles.*)

PORGY. Jus' Porgy. You knows me, boss. Yo' done gib' me plenty ob pennies on Meetin' Street.

CORONER. Of course! You're the goat man. I didn't know you without your wagon. Now, this Negro Crown—you knew him by sight, didn't you?

PORGY (*as though remembering with difficulty*). Yes, boss—I 'membuh um when he used to come here, long ago.

CORONER. You could identify him, I suppose. (PORGY *looks blank.*) You'd know him if you saw him again, I mean.

PORGY (*slowly*). Yes, boss, I'd know um. (*With dawning apprehension.*) But I ain't care none 'bout see um. (CORONER *laughs. Makes note in notebook. Puts it in pocket. Calls to* DETECTIVE.)

CORONER. Well, I'm through. Let's pull freight.

DETECTIVE (*appears in doorway: looks knowingly at* PORGY *and* BESS). Mighty clean floor in there. Funny it got its first scrubbing in twenty years this morning.

BESS. I scrubs my floor ebery week. You can ask dese people here 'bout um.

DETECTIVE (*sneering*). Oh, yes! More witnesses! (*Then triumphantly.*) But you missed the blood under the bed this time. (*Jerks out his gun, covers* PORGY, *shouts.*) Come, out with it! You killed Crown, didn't you? Speak up, or I'll hang you sure as hell! (PORGY *and* BESS *sit silent, with eyes lowered.*) Well?

BESS. I ain't understan', boss. Dere ain't no blood dere, an' nobody ain't kill Crown in our room.

CORONER (*drawing* DETECTIVE *aside*). For God's sake, Duggan, let's call it a day. The cripple couldn't kill a two-hundred-pound buck and tote him a hundred yards. (*Turning toward gate.*) Anyway, *I'm* through, and I've got to get along. It's 'most time for my inquest. (BESS *and* PORGY *go swiftly inside. Close door.*)

DETECTIVE (*following* CORONER *reluctantly*). Got your witness?

CORONER. Yeh. (*They go out gate and off to left. Again the court is deserted and silent. For a moment, there is no sound or movement. Then, in one of the rooms, a voice is raised singing.*)

VOICE. "Sit down! I can't sit down! Sit down! I can't sit down! My soul's so happy dat I can't sit down!"

(*Another voice joins, then another. In a moment, the empty court is ringing with the song, sung mockingly, triumphantly. Another moment, and doors and shutters begin to fly open. The Negroes come from their doors or lean from their windows, and the court is quickly filled with life and movement. They are all singing.* SERENA's *door flies open, and she comes out singing. She is fully dressed and carries a great basket of clothes, which she begins to hang on line while she sings.* BESS *helps* PORGY *on to the doorstep and sits beside him, the baby in her arms. Both are singing.* LILY *comes out carrying the honey tray.* PETER *follows. She balances it on his head.* SCIPIO *drives* PORGY's *goat cart in through archway. A Negro near the gate looks out, suddenly gives a loud hiss and waves his arms—in a warning ges-*

ture. The song ceases abruptly. SERENA *grabs her wash from the line. The Negroes return swiftly and silently to their rooms. Doors and shutters close stealthily.* BESS *attempts to help* PORGY *to his feet, but, seeing that they have no time, he sinks down again on his doorstep and pretends to doze.* BESS *goes inside, closes door.* SCIPIO *drives the goat back through archway. The court is again silent, and deserted by all but* PORGY. *A* POLICEMAN *enters from left. Comes in at gate. Looks about court. Sees* PORGY, *who is apparently oblivious of him. Crosses to* PORGY.)

POLICEMAN. Hey, you! (PORGY *opens his eyes.*) You're Porgy, aren't you? I've got something for you. (*Holds out paper.* PORGY *looks at it in alarm.* POLICEMAN *speaks kindly.*) You needn't be afraid to take it. It's just a summons as a witness at the coroner's inquest. All you've got to do is view the body and tell the coroner who it is. (PORGY *is suddenly terror-stricken. His voice shakes.*)

PORGY. I gots to go an' look on Crown's face?

POLICEMAN. Yes, that's all.

PORGY. Wid all dem w'ite folks lookin' at me?

POLICEMAN. Oh, cheer up! I reckon you've seen a dead man before. It'll be all over in a few minutes. (BESS *appears in doorway, listening, her eyes wide with horror.*)

PORGY. Dere ain't goin' be no black man in dat room 'cept me?

POLICEMAN. Just you and Crown—if you still call him one. (*Turns away.*)

PORGY (*scarcely able to speak for terror*). Boss—I couldn't jus' bring a 'oman wid me? I couldn't eben carry my—my 'oman?

POLICEMAN (*slightly impatient*). No, you can't bring anyone. Say, you're the cripple, aren't you? I'll get the wagon and carry you down. And as soon as you've seen Crown, you can come home. (*Starts for gate.*)

PORGY (*desperately*). Boss—

POLICEMAN. Now, listen, I've summoned you, and you've got to go, or it's contempt of court. I'll call the wagon for you. (*Goes out gate and off to left.*

As soon as he has gone, doors open stealthily. The Negroes come out and gather about PORGY, *speaking in low, frightened tones.*)

PORGY. Oh, Gawd! Whut I goin' to do?

BESS. Yo' got to go, Porgy. Mebby yo' can jus' make like to look at um an' keep yo' eye' shut.

MARIA. Yo' goin' be all right, Porgy. Yo' jus' goin' to be a witness.

SPORTING LIFE. I ain't so sure ob dat. (*They all look at him in alarm.*) I don' know who done de killin'. All I knows is, when de man what done um goes in dat room, Crown' wounds begin to bleed.

PORGY (*terror-stricken*). Oh, Jedus!

SPORTING LIFE. Dat's one way de cops got ob tellin' who done um.

PORGY (*in a panic, moaning*). I can't look on he face! Oh, Gawd! Whut I goin' to do!

SPORTING LIFE (*taking command of the situation*). Listen to me! Yo' do jus' as I say an' yo' won't hab' to look on he face.

PORGY. What I do, Sportin' Life?

SPORTING LIFE. Get busy, yo' people. We gots to get Porgy out ob here! Get de goat, Scipio. Here, Mingo! Yo' stan' by to gib' me a han' wid Porgy.

BESS. Don' yo' go, Porgy! He can't get away!

SPORTING LIFE. He gots to get away or dey'll hang um sure.

PORGY. Oh, Gawd! (SCIPIO *has brought the goat cart.* SPORTING LIFE *and* MINGO *are lifting* PORGY *in while he moans with terror and mutters unintelligibly.*)

SPORTING LIFE. Now, listen! Make straight for Bedens Alley. When yo' gets dere, turn in an' lie low.

MINGO. Bedens Alley too far. He'll neber make it.

SPORTING LIFE. Shut up, Mingo. I'm runnin' dis. All right, Porgy, light out!

MARIA. Quick! Start um!

BESS. Make um run! (*The clang of the patrol wagon bell is heard approaching rapidly. The Negroes stand as though paralyzed with terror.*)

MINGO. Here dey is!

Bess. Oh, Gawd! It's too late now!

Sporting Life. No, it ain't. Here, eberybody, get um in dere! (*Directs them to the archway. They drive the goat through, then mass in front of archway, hiding* Porgy *from view.* Sporting Life *saunters across the court as though he had nothing to do with the affair, and awaits developments. The patrol bell rings more slowly as the wagon slows down, then comes to a stop at left of gate just out of view. The* Policeman *again comes in at gate. Looks toward* Porgy's *door. Crosses to it abruptly. Throws it open.*)

Policeman. Hey, you there! (*Runs to gate. Calls.*) Jim! The fool's trying to make a get-away! Come on! (*Turns to the Negroes.*) Where did he go? (*They look at him with blank faces.*) All right! (*Starts for* Porgy's *door. The* Second Policeman *enters from left.*) You take that side, Jim. I'll take this. (*Goes into* Porgy's *room.* Second Policeman *goes through* Serena's *door. As soon as both* Policemen *are out of sight, the Negroes beckon to* Porgy, *who drives from archway and quickly toward gate. The shutters of an upper window are thrown open, and the* First Policeman *looks out.*)

Policeman. Hey, you! What d'you think you're doing? (Porgy *leans forward and wrings the goat's tail. The astonished animal leaps forward and goes out gate at a run.*) Jim! (*The* Second Policeman *throws open shutters of room opposite and leans from window.*) Look there! (*Points to* Porgy *as he disappears off left. Both* Policemen *burst into peals of laughter. The Negroes follow to gate, pushing it shut, looking out through bars.*)

Second Policeman. He must want to have a race. (*The two* Policemen *leave the windows and a minute later come running from doors.*)

First Policeman. Racing the wagon! That's good! (*They start toward gate.*)

Second Policeman (*laying a hand on the other's arm*). Say, let him get a start. (*They double up with laughter.*) This is going to be good!

First Policeman. Here, you all! Get away from the gate. (*The Negroes stand back. He opens gate.*) Come on now! We're off! (*They run out gate, still shouting with laughter. They run off right. The Negroes press close about gate to watch. The clang of the patrol wagon bell is heard as the vehicle sets off at top speed.*)

Annie. Oh, Gawd! Dey'll get um!

Maria. Ef he can jus' git 'round de corner!—

Lily. —Mebby dey won't fin' um.

Bess (*turning hopelessly away*). 'Tain't no use. (*The tension in the crowd of watchers suddenly relaxes, and their faces assume hopeless expressions.*) Dey got um?

Lily. Yeh. Dey got um.

Serena. Dey putting him an' de goat all two in de wagon. (Bess *sits hopelessly on her doorstep. The other Negroes return to their various rooms and tasks.* Sporting Life *saunters across court and sits down on step by* Bess. *The stage is darkening. A light appears in a window.*)

Bess. Oh, Gawd! Dey goin' carry um to look on Crown' face!

Sporting Life (*laughing*). Don' yo' worry none 'bout dat, Sistuh. Porgy ain't a witness now. Dey goin' lock um up in de jail.

Mingo (*at gate*). Dat's de trut'. Dey done turn de wagon 'round toward de jail.

Bess. Well, dat better'n makin' um look on Crown. (*Fearfully.*) Not fo' long, Sportin' Life?

Sporting Life (*sympathetically*). No, not fo' long. Jus' a yeah, mebby.

Bess. A yeah.

Sporting Life. Contempt ob court— dat's a serious offence. (Bess *drops her face into her hands.*) Jus' like I tol' yo'. Nobody home now but Bess an' ole Sportin' Life.

Bess. I ain't gots no time fo' yo'.

Sporting Life (*laughing*). Fo' sho' yo' has. Yo' jus' gots nice little vacation now fo' play 'round wid yo' ole frien'. Contempt ob court—dat serious offence. Dat man ain't be back heah fo' a yeah.

BESS (*alarmed*). Sportin' Life, yo' ain't t'ink dey puts Porgy up fo' a yeah?

SPORTING LIFE. A yeah fo' sho'. Cheer up, Sistuh ! Gib me yo' han'. (*He takes her hand. She is too preoccupied to resist.*) Ole Sportin' Life got de stuff fo' scare away de lonesome blues. (*Pours powder into her hand. BESS looks down at it.*)

BESS. Happy dus'! (*Gazes at the powder with fascinated horror.*) I ain't want none ob dat stuff, I tells yo'.

SPORTING LIFE. Ain't nuff ter hurt er flea.

BESS. Take dat stuff away! (*But she continues to hold it in her hand.*)

SPORTING LIFE. Jus' a little touch fo' ole time' sake. (*BESS suddenly claps her hand over her face. When she takes it away, it is empty. SPORTING LIFE smiles with satisfaction.*) Dat de t'ing, ain't it? An' 'membuh, dere's plenty more where dat come from. Dere's a boat to Noo Yo'k to-morruh an' I'm goin'. (*Pauses significantly. BESS says nothing.*) Why yo' such a fool, Bess? What yo' goin' to do a whole yeah heah by yo'self? Now's yo' chance. (*BESS leaps to her feet, her eyes blazing. She glares at SPORTING LIFE with contempt and hatred.*)

BESS. Yo' low, crawlin' houn'! Git 'way from my door, I tell yo'! Lef' it, yo'! Rattlesnake! Dat's whut yo' is! Rattlesnake! (*While she berates him, SPORTING LIFE lights a cigarette, continues to sit on step.*)

SPORTING LIFE. Rave on, Sistuh! But I'll be right here when yo' is wantin' dat second shot. (*BESS runs suddenly past him into her room. Slams door behind her. SPORTING LIFE sits smiling to himself and leisurely blowing smoke rings. MARIA comes to her doorway. Sees him. Crosses to him.*)

MARIA (*contemptuously*). What yo' waitin' 'round here for?

SPORTING LIFE. Jus' waitin'. (*Smokes contentedly.*)

MARIA. What yo' t'ink yo' goin' to get?

SPORTING LIFE (*with shrug of shoulders*). Uummmmmm—jus' waitin'.

MARIA (*turning scornfully away*). Yo'

don' know Bess. (*Recrosses to her shop. SPORTING LIFE watches her till she has reached her doorstep.*)

SPORTING LIFE (*in a low voice, not intended for MARIA to hear*). You don' know happy dus'. (*MARIA does not hear. Goes into shop: closes door. SPORTING LIFE continues to wait. St. Michael's chimes the half hour.*)

CURTAIN

SCENE 3: *Chimes. Two o'clock. The court is as usual, except that PORGY's door and shutters are closed. Negroes are coming and going about their tasks. PETER, LILY, and MINGO sit at MARIA's table. She is busy serving them. SCIPIO is playing near the gate. SERENA sits near her door rocking a baby in her arms and singing, "Hush little baby, don't you cry." MARIA goes into her shop. PORGY drives up outside the gate and calls softly to SCIPIO. His air is one of mystery.*

PORGY. Here, Scipio! Here Porgy back from jail. Open de gate an' don't make no noise. (*SCIPIO goes reluctantly to gate, opens it, and leads the goat inside. SERENA looks up, sees PORGY, stops singing in the middle of a bar, and hunches over the baby as though to hide it. Various Negroes about the court look up, see him, and go silently into their rooms. PORGY is too preoccupied with his secret to notice anything. He drives over and stops beside MARIA's table. LILY, PETER, and MINGO half rise, then see that it is too late to escape, and resume their seats.*)

PORGY (*in a joyous but guarded voice*). Shhh, don't nobody let on yet dat I is home again. I gots a surprise fo' Bess, an' I ain't want she to know till I gots eberyt'ing ready. (*He does not notice that the others are silent and embarrassed, and, reaching into the wagon, commences to remove packages, talking volubly all the time. He unwraps a harmonica and hands it to SCIPIO.*) Here, boy. T'row away dat ole mout' organ you gots an' start in on dis one. See, he gots picture ob brass band on um. Work on dat, an' fus' t'ing dat yo' know, yo'll be playin' wid de orphans. (*He turns to

LILY.) Here, gal, hol' up yo' head. Dat's right. I nebber did like dem ole funeral bonnet Peter buy fo' yo'. (*Unwraps a gorgeous, feather-trimmed hat and hands it to her.*) Now get underneat' dat, an' make all de red bird and de blue jay jealous. (LILY *takes hat, but is unable to speak her thanks. PORGY is hurrying on, and does not notice this. He opens a package and shakes out a gay dress, then lays it on the table.*) Now, dat's de style for Bess. She is one gal what always look good in red. (*He opens a hat and places it beside the dress.*) I reckon I is de fus' pusson anybody roun' here ebber see what go to jail po', an' leabe dere rich. But Porgy' luck ridin' high now. Ain't nuttin' can stop um. When de buckra search me in de jail, I all de time gots my lucky bones in my mout'—see! an' time I get settle' in my new boardin' house, I start to go right t'rough dem odder crap shooters like Glory Hallelujah. (*He takes a package from the cart, opens it, and holds up a baby dress.*) Now, ain't dis de t'ing! Course, de baby ain't really big 'nough for wear dress yet, but he goin' grow fas'. You watch, he goin' be in dat dress by de fus' frost. (*Continues his story.*) Yas, suh! dere warn't no stoppin' dem bones. Dey jus' gone whoopin' right t'rough dat jail, a-pullin' me after 'em. An den, on de las' day, de big buckra guard hear 'bout it, an' he come an' say I gots to gib up de bones. But I been seein' um rol wid de jailer in de watch house, an' I know he weakness. I ask dat buckra if he ain't likes me to teach um how to sing lucky to de bones 'fore I gib' dem up, an' 'fore he git 'way I done gone t'rough um fo' t'ree dollar an' seben cent an' dis shirt. (*He proudly exhibits shirt that he is wearing. His purchases are now all spread out on the table, and he looks from them to the faces of the Negroes.*) Now it time to call Bess. Oh, Bess. Here Porgy come home. (*There is a moment of absolute silence. LILY gets to her feet, buries her face in her hands, and runs to her room. PETER starts to follow. MINGO rises and goes toward MARIA's door.*) Here, Lily, Peter, Mingo,

where you all goin'? What de hell kin' ob a welcome dis fo' a man what been in jail fo' a week, an' fo' de contemp' ob court at dat. Oh, now I see. Well, yo' ain't gots to min' Bess an' me! All de time we wants to hab we frien' wid us. Eben now, we ain't wants to be jus' by weself. (*They continue to withdraw. He looks about him in growing surprise, and discovers SERENA haunched up silently over the baby.*) Why, hello! Dere's Serena. Yo' sho' work fas' Sistuh. I ain't been gone a week, an' yo' done gots a new baby. (SERENA *rises hurriedly, exposing baby for first time.*) Here, hold on. Let me see dat chile. Dat's Bess' baby, ain't it? Where yo' get um? Where Bess, anyhow? She ain't answer me.

SERENA (*calling*). Maria, come out dat cookshop. Here Porgy come home. *You* gots to talk wid um. (PORGY *drives to his own door.*)

PORGY. Bess! Ain't yo' dere, Bess? (MARIA *comes to her doorway. PORGY turns to her, his eyes wide with alarm.*) Where' Bess? (MARIA *sits on her doorstep. PORGY turns his goat and drives over to her.*) Tell me quick. Where' Bess? (MARIA *does not answer.*) Where? Where?

MARIA (*trying to put on a bold face*). Ain't we tell yo' all along, Porgy, dat 'oman ain't fit fo' yo'?

PORGY (*frantically*). I ain't ask yo' opinion. Where' Bess? (*They all shrink from telling him. Each evades, trying to leave it to the others.*)

MARIA. Dat dirty dog Sportin' Life make us all t'ink yo' is lock up fo' a yeah.

PORGY. Won't somebody tell me, where Bess?

SERENA. Bess very low in she min' 'cause she t'ink yo' is gone fo' a yeah. (*Pauses, unable to come to the point.*)

PORGY. But I home *now*. I want to tell she I is here.

SERENA. She gone back to de happy dus' an' de red eye. She been very drunk two day'.

PORGY. But where she now? I ain't care if she was drunk. I want she now.

LILY. Dat houn' Sportin' Life was for-eber hangin' 'round and gettin' she to take more dope.

PORGY (*driving again to his own door. Calls*). Bess! Bess! Won't nobody tell me—

MARIA (*following him*). Ain't we tellin' yo'? Dat houn' Sportin' Life—

PORGY (*desperately*). I ain't ask 'bout Sportin' Life. Where Bess?

SERENA. She gone, Porgy. An' I done take dis chile to gib um a Christian raisin'—

PORGY. *Where* she gone?

SERENA. Dat gal ain't neber had Gawd in she heart, an' de debil get um at last.

MARIA. 'Tain't de debil. De happy dus' done for um.

PORGY (*wildly*). Yo'—Bess?—Yo' ain't means Bess dead?

SERENA. She worse dan dead.

LILY. Sportin' Life carry she away on de Noo Yo'k boat. (*They are all silent, gazing at* PORGY. *He, too, is silent for a moment.*)

PORGY. Where dat dey take she?

MINGO. Noo Yo'k.

MARIA. Dat's way up Nort'.

PORGY (*pointing*). It dat way?

MARIA. It take two days by de boat. Yo' can't find um.

PORGY. I ain't say I can find um. I say, where it is?

MARIA. Yo' can't go after she. Ain't yo' hear we say yo' can't find um.

ANNIE. Ain't yo' know Noo Yo'k mos' a t'ousand mile' from here?

PORGY. Which way dat?

LILY (*pointing*). Up Nort'—past de Custom House. (PORGY *turns his goat and drives slowly with bowed head toward the gate.*)

MARIA. Porgy, I tells yo' it ain't no use!

LILY. Dat great big city. Yo' can't find um dere!

SERENA. Ain't we tells yo'— (*But* PORGY *is going on toward gate as if he did not hear, and they cease to protest and stand motionless watching him. As* PORGY *reaches the gate,* SCIPIO *silently opens it.* PORGY *drives through and turns to left, as* LILY *pointed.*

St. Michael's chimes the quarter hour. The gate clangs shut.)

CURTAIN

SUGGESTED TOPICS FOR FURTHER INVESTIGATION AND REPORT

1. Read the novel "Porgy." Note the alterations necessary for stage adaptation. What improvements have been made? What important portions, if any, have been omitted or changed?

2. Study the origins and development of Negro minstrelsy. Does it have any justification in being associated with a folk tradition of any sort?

3. The only other play to compare with *Porgy* as a Negro folk play is *The Green Pastures*. Compare the two plays. Which one is more justifiably "folk"? Why does not *The Green Pastures* become offensive either from racial or religious viewpoints? You might find it interesting to read the source of *The Green Pastures*, Roark Bradford's collection of stories called "Ol' Man Adam and His Chillun."

4. The explosive matter of Negro-white relations has been the subject of several important plays, not always on the folk basis. They make an interesting study, however. Read plays like Boucicault's *The Octoroon, Uncle Tom's Cabin*, O'Neill's *All God's Chillun Got Wings*, John Wexley's *They Shall Not Die*, or Gow and d'Usseau's *Deep Are the Roots*. What methods of approach to the racial problem are used at different periods? Which ones are propaganda, which serious dramatic studies? How valuable are any of them as social documents?

5. Try to secure a recording of *Porgy and Bess*. Can you determine why the opera was such an electrifying success in Europe? Evaluate Gershwin's music in relation to the text of the play. What has been gained or lost by substituting his music for spirituals?

6. The nineteenth-century Indian and frontier plays are often hard to secure. The "America's Lost Plays" series contains a few (Volume IV has *Davy Crockett*; Volume XIV has *Metamora*), and the Microprint cards of "Three Centuries of Drama" have practically everything before 1830. Other early anthologies have an assortment. Read as many as you can find and discuss their treatment of the Indian and/or the frontiersman.

7. Read a number of the one-act folk plays such as *Trifles, The Clod, Moonshine, Fixins*, and others, which can easily be found in a variety of one-act collections such as the "Best One-Act Plays" series, the "Provincetown Plays" volumes, and the collections of the Carolina Playmakers. Your library probably has many others. Discuss their effectiveness and authenticity as folk drama.

8. Study the longer plays, Vollmer's *Sun-Up*, Green's *In Abraham's Bosom, The Field God*, Hughes' *Hell-Bent fer Heaven*, Riggs' *Green Grow the Lilacs*, and others of the 1920s and 1930s. Evaluate them, individually or collectively, or in contrast with *Porgy* or *The Green Pastures*.

9. Try to find some of the later nineteenth- and early twentieth-century "Western" plays. You may have to rely on the "Burns Mantle Best Plays" series for abridged versions. Read Fitch's *The Cowboy and the Lady*, Moody's *The Great Divide*, Thomas' *Arizona*, Royle's *The Squaw Man*, or Belasco's *The Girl of the Golden West* or *The Rose of the Rancho*. How authentic do you find them? An interesting project would be to read Owen Wister's novel "The Virginian" and note how many of our present ideas of the Western hero have been influenced by that book.

10. Read some of the Irish folk plays, short ones by Lady Gregory or Lord

Dunsany, or others like Synge's *Riders to the Sea* or *The Playboy of the Western World*. Compare them with some of the Western, mountain, or Negro folk plays from America.

11. *Oklahoma!* the Rodgers and Hammerstein musical based on *Green Grow the Lilacs*, is often referred to as a folk musical. What is your opinion? How does it compare with *Porgy and Bess?*

FOUR TYPES OF COMEDY

The Fundamentals of the Comic

Comedy is strictly a *human* matter and a *social* phenomenon. Man is the only animal capable of making the contrasts and comparisons necessary to evoke laughter. When a person finds something to be comic, he automatically relates it to some aspect of humanity. Throughout his life society has established for him certain norms in shape, size, and degree, the direct products of human concepts of propriety. When they are violated or distorted in any unexpected way, and the violation is not displeasing or painful, then the human mind may judge the event as comic. Thus the comic is not a private thing; it must be shared. All causes of laughter are based on experiences held in common with other human beings.

Stage comedy in all its forms is fundamentally a process of reduction, of placing a human being lower than he would normally expect to be, thus making him an inferior, often ridiculous figure, and consequently a comic one. Whether the comedy be derived from the "lowest" elements—obscenity, physical deformity, or accidental mishap—or from the "highest"—intelligent and thought-provoking laughter based on the foibles and pretensions of highly educated, civilized individuals—it will establish one thing very clearly: that the human being is much less significant than he would like to be considered.

Objective detachment is absolutely necessary in surveying all comic situations. Carried to its logical conclusion, the comic situation is very near disaster; once any kind of emotional reaction is permitted, the comic thereupon becomes sentimental, pathetic, or unpleasantly painful. Consequently the comic writer must know the difference between the painfully distorted and the comically exaggerated. He must know not only his society's level of comic intelligence but also its extent of possible emotional identification.

There are two broad categories of comedy, *humor* and *wit*. Humorous comedy derives from what is done, witty comedy from what is said. The humorous play relies upon the mechanics of personal appearance and behavior and upon situation. The witty play depends upon the writer's ability to compose amusing dialogue, frequently independent of the elements of humor. The witty character consciously seeks to be entertaining. He asks for laughter at the expense of the audience itself, or of a third party on or off stage. The humorous character is funny in himself. He asks for laughter at his own expense. Wit is fragile, brittle, lacking depth in genuine character or satisfying incident. It demands the instant comprehension of its audience and cannot stand analysis, for it is all air. Humor, stemming from the groundwork of the play itself—the appearance and actions of those on stage—has a firm and well-established base. Each has its place, and both can operate equally well within the same comedy.

A stage comedy does not automatically assume continual laughter. Good comedy may contain suffering and death, and it need not end "happily ever after" in the usual sense. The difference between this type of comedy and serious drama is in the degree of emphasis. So long as the play presents its characters as human beings brought down to the common level of all mankind, subject to the shortcomings and ills of everyone, and capable of meeting their problems with only the weapons we all possess in normal mind and body, and so long as the ending promises at least a satisfactory future into which dramatically unpleasant situations will not intrude, the play will probably remain comic. The smile can be inward, the laugh unheard, but the play can still be comedy.

THE RARE QUALITIES OF HIGH COMEDY

What Is "High" Comedy?

Comedy at its highest level becomes essentially a matter of *idea* rather than action, making its appeal to the intellect through skilled character portrayal and polished, often highly artificial, language. Good high comedy is a rarity in the theatre because it demands a writer sufficiently gifted in talents of objective detachment and intelligent insight to be able to compose this difficult but always delightful comic form. High comedy also demands an audience willing to find its amusement in the nuances of sophisticated character behavior and clever, witty dialogue.

To gain its best effect, high comedy needs a few important ingredients. First of all, serious emphasis is placed upon the unimportant trivialities of life, while normally important matters are regarded with complete frivolity. Next, being nonromantic and nonsentimental, high comedy involves a lighthearted emphasis upon sex. Love, still the never-ending war between men and women, becomes an elaborate game, seriously played by its own set of closely followed ground rules. The result is a sexual *amorality* which cannot be judged by the conventions of any "proper" or "acceptable" morality. The best high-comedy characters may seem to live without conscience in their pursuit of sexual pleasures, but they are performing within the accepted code, not in any fashion *immoral*, but simply *unmoral*—a considerably different thing.

In order to carry conviction in what they say and do, high-comedy characters are usually fully developed human beings with independent thoughts of their own. The limits of their artificial world impose certain restrictions, of course, but the impression is of well-rounded personality. By the end of the last act, however, the typical high-comedy character will leave the stage precisely as he entered it. He will have achieved very little and developed almost not at all. When the play is all over, and all the witty dialogue has been spoken, it is apparent that everybody in a high comedy is pretty much a second-rate human being at best. The characters, for the most part, realize this fact and make no serious effort to alter the situation.

Early American Social Comedy

Although genuine high comedy has nothing to do with the "height" of the society with which it deals, its most popular form is the "social" comedy, or "comedy of manners," designed to reflect the social conventions, eccentricities, and follies of a sophisticated urban society. The English comedy of manners of the Restoration and the eighteenth century was the comedy of America as well, and Sheridan's *The School for Scandal* of 1777, the finest high comedy of the late century, contained character and incident familiar to both sides of the Atlantic. It is not surprising that our first social comedy was a close imitation of English prototypes.

Royall Tyler's *The Contrast*, 1787, was the first play by an American on an American subject to be professionally produced in this country. Its appeal derives from its ridicule of slavish imitations of English manners, in contrast to the genuinely sincere simplicity of the vigorous young world of newly free America. Even in protest, however, Tyler was unable to bring originality into his own style, as this opening discussion between Letitia and Charlotte will attest. Their dialogue could be found in almost any of a hundred similar English plays:

> LETITIA. And so, Charlotte, you really think the pocket-hoop unbecoming.
> CHARLOTTE. No, I don't say so. It may be very becoming to saunter round the house of a rainy day; to visit my grand-mamma, or to go to Quakers' meeting: but to swim in a minuet, with the eyes of fifty well-dressed beaux upon me, to trip it in the Mall, or walk on the battery, give me the luxurious, jaunty, flowing, bell-hoop. It would have delighted you to have seen me the last evening, my charming girl! I was dangling o'er the battery with Billy Dimple; a knot of young fellows were upon the platform; as I passed them I faultered with one of the most bewitching false steps you ever saw, and then recovered myself with such a pretty confusion, flirting my hoop to discover a jet black shoe and brilliant buckle. Gad! how my little heart thrilled to hear the confused raptures of—"*Demme, Jack, what a delicate foot!*" "*Ha! General, what a well-turn'd—*"
> LETITIA. Fie! fie! Charlotte! (*Stopping her mouth.*) I protest you are quite a libertine.

Not until 1845 did America receive what can fairly be called a social drama of its own in Anna Cora Mowatt's *Fashion*. Its attack on the foolishness of aspiring to French mannerisms suggests high comedy, but in many ways it is hardly more than an old-fashioned melodrama, heavily laden with scheming villains and pursued young maidens, plus a noble stage Yankee called Adam Trueman. Nevertheless, in Mrs. Tiffany the play makes amusing use of the fashionable eccentricities of the time as shown in this opening dialogue with the French maid:

> MRS. TIFFANY. Is everything in order, Millinette? Ah! very elegant, very elegant, indeed! There is a *jenny-says-quoi* look about this furniture,—an air of fashion and gentility perfectly bewitching. Is there not, Millinette?
>
> MILLINETTE. Oh, *oui*, Madame!
>
> MRS. TIFFANY. But where is Miss Seraphina? It is twelve o'clock; our visitors will be pouring in, and she has not made her appearance. But I hear that nothing is more fashionable than to keep people waiting.—None but vulgar persons pay any attention to punctuality. Is it not so, Millinette?
>
> MILLINETTE. Quite *comme il faut.*—Great *personnes* always do make little *personnes* wait, Madame.
>
> MRS. TIFFANY. This mode of receiving visitors only upon one specified day of the week is a most convenient custom! It saves the trouble of keeping the house continually in order and of being always dressed. I flatter myself that *I* was the first to introduce it amongst the New York *ee-light*. You are quite sure that it is strictly a Parisian mode, Millinette?
>
> MILLINETTE. Oh, *oui*, Madame; entirely *mode de Paris.*
>
> MRS. TIFFANY. This girl is worth her weight in gold. (*Aside.*) Millinette, how do you say *arm-chair* in French?
>
> MILLINETTE. *Fauteuil*, Madame.
>
> MRS. TIFFANY. Fo-tool! That has a foreign—an out-of-the-wayish sound that is perfectly charming—and so genteel! There is something about our American words decidedly vulgar. *Fowtool!* how refined. *Fowtool! Arm-chair!* what a difference!

The differences between plays in the *Fashion* or *Contrast* tradition and the first attempt at genuine high comedy are shown in Langdon Mitchell's successful *The New York Idea* of 1906. Mitchell's collection of socially prominent Americans perform the rituals of high comedy better than any before them ever had.

The "idea" of the play is the increasingly sophisticated attitude toward divorce. Mitchell's characters overstress this new-found freedom and try much too hard to convince one another and the audience that they are making the most of a new game. They also tend to become caricatures. A stage Englishman, complete with stereotyped English behavior, walks among a suffocatingly boring lawyer, a hypocritical clergyman, a harebrained divorcée, and a horse-mad ex-husband and wife. None of them achieve the flair and polish of the best in high comedy.

In spite of its weaknesses, *The New York Idea* is a milestone. The following scene, appearing when the proprieties of the late Victorian age were still powerful, is sophisticated to a degree undreamed of only a few years earlier.

Matthew, the minister, is discussing yesterday's sermon with the play's heroine:

MATTHEW. No, really, it was a wonderful sermon, my dear. My text was from Paul—"It is better to marry than to burn." It was a strictly logical sermon. I argued—that, as the grass withereth, and the flower fadeth, there is nothing final in nature; not even death! And, as there is nothing final in nature, not even death—so then if death is not final—why should marriage be final? (*Gently.*) And so the necessity of—eh—divorce! You see? It was an exquisite sermon! All New York was there! And all New York went away happy! Even the sinners—if there were any! I don't often meet sinners— do you?

CYNTHIA (*indulgently, in spite of his folly, because he is kind*). You're such a dear, delightful pagan! Here's your tea!

MATTHEW (*sipping his tea*). Why, my dear—you have a very sad expression!

CYNTHIA (*a little bitterly*). Why not?

MATTHEW (*with sentimental sweetness*). I feel as if I were of no use in the world when I see sadness on a young face. Only sinners should feel sad. You have committed no sin!

CYNTHIA (*impulsively*). Yes, I have!

MATTHEW. Eh?

CYNTHIA. I committed the unpardonable sin—whe—when I married for love.

MATTHEW. One must not marry for anything else, my dear!

CYNTHIA. Why am I marrying your brother?

MATTHEW. I often wonder why. I wonder why you didn't choose to remain a free woman.

CYNTHIA (*going over the ground she has often argued with herself*). I meant to; but a divorcée has no place in society. I felt horridly lonely! I wanted a friend. Philip was ideal as a friend—for months. Isn't it nice to bind a friend to you?

MATTHEW. Yes—yes! (*He sets down the teacup.*)

CYNTHIA (*growing more and more excited and moved as she speaks*). To marry a friend—to marry on prudent, sensible grounds—a man—like Philip? That's what I should have done first, instead of rushing into marriage— because I had a wild, mad, sensitive, sympathetic—passion and pain and fury—of I don't know what—that almost strangled me with happiness!

MATTHEW (*amiable and reminiscent*). Ah—ah—in my youth—I—I too!

CYNTHIA (*coming back to her manner of every day*). And besides—the day Philip asked me I was in the dumps! And now—how about marrying only for love?

MATTHEW. Ah, my dear, love is not the only thing in the world!

Improvements upon high comedy came in later plays by other writers, specifically in Jesse Lynch Williams' *Why Marry?* in 1917, the first Pulitzer Prize winner, and *Why Not?* in 1922, and in Rachel Crothers' *He and She*, 1911, and *Nice People*, 1920.

It is interesting that from 1929 to 1939, the decade of depression, proletarian drama of social protest, and the start of a new World War, American high comedy achieved its best expression. Two playwrights, S. N. Behrman, represented in this volume, and Philip Barry were by all odds the most accomplished in its creation; the choice between them as the best American high-comedy writer is difficult indeed. Barry's first success, *Paris Bound* in 1927, was a well-written comedy of manners which made a good case for the preservation rather than the severance of the marriage ties, but his *Holiday* in 1929 was a high comedy of the finest tradition. The Seton family, rich, complacent, narrow, and jealous of its social position, is shocked by the behavior of the young daughter, Linda, who would break away from the stuffy if proper household and elope with her sister's unconventional but wholly sympathetic fiancé. Through a distinctive and distinguished style, complete with the gay badinage and sincere insincerity of high comedy, Barry composed an amusing and satiric picture of the pre-Depression socially elite. A decade later, with *The Philadelphia Story*, he displayed a high-comedy touch as skilled as ever, although his comments upon the emptiness of high-society living, couched in his usual sprightly style, were somewhat more acid than before. *Hotel Universe* in 1930 was a venture into fantasy; it sent its high-comedy characters back into their past, where they were able to overcome many of the deadening illusions of their sterile adult lives.

Aside from Barry and Behrman, no other American playwrights have been as successful with the high-comedy tradition. British-born John Van Druten won acclaim with *The Voice of the Turtle* in 1943, and Samuel Taylor's *Sabrina Fair* was a notable success of 1953.

Biography

Biography comes as close to meeting the requisites of excellent high comedy as any play in American drama. Its atmosphere, character, and dialogue achieve a lustrous polished quality, an appropriate concomitant to the purely comic spirit that high comedy must unflaggingly maintain.

As soon as the opening scene is under way and the impetuous young Kurt demands to know why he is being so disrespectfully treated, the audience is aware that well-ordered routine and "proper" behavior will find no place here. The atmosphere of Marion Froude's cluttered apartment is pleasantly relaxed, totally independent of arbitrary convention, inhabited by one whose own life is not to be influenced by the preachments of hollow conformists. More than this, Behrman furthers the high-comedy spirit by adhering to the important requirement which he himself acknowledges: the lighthearted treatment of matters serious and the earnest concern for matters most trivial. His upstart radical finds his greatest worries in the fact that Marion's tardiness has taken thirty minutes from his life, or that he may be in danger of becoming "tolerant." Nolan, the would-be servant of his country, frets more about a youthful indiscretion so insignificant that his companion in sin cannot even remember him, than he does about the serious matter of making himself a worthy legislator. The attitudes of Marion and Feydak toward their own transgressions—her free love and his blatant appropriation of a dead brother's fame—completely prevent any serious concern.

Behrman consistently maintains high comedy in the second-rate nature of his leading characters. The more they talk of their own importance, the more they reveal their very ordinary human qualities. Painting himself as another William Pitt, Nolan would also play the gallant knight and share Marion's shame with her, unmindful that he is less a convincing Southern gentleman and statesman than he is a conventional moralist afraid of what others will say about him. Kurt is out to remake society in his own image, and to hurt those who block his path because he himself has been hurt. He does not see the pitifully ridiculous creature he really is, into whom Marion can peer and recognize his hopeless delusion. Marion's perception has long since labeled the mediocre Wilson as "Tympi," after the drum with the large size and hollow sound. Feydak, at least, is aware of his own limits, even while perjuring his soul.

Marion knows what everybody is, and she knows herself besides. She has no pretenses, and she can easily make fools of both Kurt and Nolan, while simultaneously offering them her sincere affection. Honest with herself and with them, she refuses to belong to either. She knows her own artistic limits, and she unhesitatingly admits them. She can never permit the serious trivialities of those around her to alter her own sane and sensible outlook— the essentially comic outlook—and her adroit handling of all their attempts to break through her defenses is constantly amusing. Being a real person, Marion can of course suffer, and we catch a brief glimpse of emotion near the final curtain when she must dismiss Kurt with genuine pain. It will soon be forgotten, however, and we must accept her attitude toward life as correct, and the ways of the others as considerably inferior.

Behrman has not neglected to make Marion and his trio of important men into solid three-dimensional characters. Marion is far from shallow, and her worldly experiences have made her into a basically thoughtful and tolerant person. Her treatment of Kurt and Nolan is neither flippant nor callous. She is not a cynical or a cruel woman. She can be seriously earnest when the occasion arises, but she wisely recognizes that the occasion is infrequent and that her own emotional stability comes from frank recognition that most things are not worth the trouble of anxious concern.

Kurt and Nolan are not as fully developed as Marion, but they retain a solid amount of good character. Kurt plays the part of the "angry young man" of his day, but Behrman is careful to let us see beneath his arrogant veneer. Nolan, full of conventional mediocrity and noble aspirations, is recognizable and understandable, though fair game for Marion's free and easy wit. In fact, he comes close to representing what most of us consider right and proper. When we are amused by Marion's handling of him and by her own exhibition of her personal liberty, we are admitting the practical and sensible aspect of her way of life while recognizing the stuffiness of our own standards. The third-act introduction of the Kinnecotts is not objectionable. Neither Kinnecott nor Slade is a vital character, and neither develops much beyond first impressions. Kinnecott approaches a caricature of the health-food addict and old-school politician who has never heard of the word "progress," but he never gets out of hand. Slade is hardly more than an interested spectator at an enjoyable show.

Although it may be hard to find the polished epigram of an Oscar Wilde or the smooth verbal sparring of a Noel Coward in the dialogue of *Biography*, still Behrman provides the glittering banter so typical of the best of high comedy. The repartee that bounces back and forth from one character to another is, of course, completely unrealistic, but it is delightful to hear and gives the illusion of complete spontaneity. Nobody is capable of indefinitely maintaining the elevated, neatly phrased conversation of high comedy, but those who hear it are pleasantly fooled into believing it possible. It provides the smooth, frictionless lubrication of the entertaining, if sometimes obvious, mechanics of a play which attempts to express the comic spirit.

High comedy, conceived and executed in the spirit of the purely comic, is a rare thing. Only a few privileged writers can handle it, and only the most adept actors can perform it without danger of becoming self-conscious or treading heavily upon the fragile lines. The actor who plays comedy well, says Behrman, is the best actor there is, because he has the sense of *awareness* of life, its comedy and its tragedy, and he realizes, with the great comic writer, that the comic intuition "gets to the heart of a human situation with a precision and a velocity unattainable in any other way." It is not surprising that a stage comedy which realizes all of this is a thing of rare perfection.

S. N. Behrman

Samuel Nathaniel Behrman, always known professionally as S. N. Behrman, is surely the finest living exponent of the polished high comedy of manners in America. He has been rivaled in this country only by Philip Barry, and although his fame has been less international than Somerset Maugham's or Noel Coward's, he has at times equaled these English writers in his work.

Behrman was born in Worcester, Massachusetts, in 1893, into a family which, surprisingly enough, did not belong to the upper-class society he has so skilfully created in his plays. He arrived at an interest in the theatre not in New York but through a local stock company; while still a high school student he wrote a one-act play which appeared in Worcester and on the Poli vaudeville circuit with Behrman often in the cast. He might have continued on the stage indefinitely had not his parents persuaded him to complete his advanced education. He attended Worcester's Clark University for two years, and then transferred to Harvard, where he took his B.A. in 1916. While there he attended George Pierce Baker's famous class in playwriting. He completed his formal education with an M.A. at Columbia University in 1918.

Behrman's first work in New York was as assistant editor and book reviewer for *The New York Times Book Review*, and he did similar work for *The New Republic*. He contributed articles and short stories to *The Smart Set*, *The Masses*, *The Freeman*, and *The New Yorker*. Playwriting was his chief interest, however, and he collaborated in unsuccessful plays with Kenyon Nicholson and Owen Davis before hitting his own stride in *The Second Man* in 1927, the play by which the Theatre Guild discovered him. It remains among his best, often regarded as a finer play than *Biography*. Soon after came the successful *Serena Blandish* in 1929, a failure called *Meteor* in the same year, and a further successful comedy, *Brief Moment*, in 1931.

Biography of 1932 is a kind of turning point in Behrman's early career, for it was the last of his more frivolous plays for some time. He became more and more concerned with the social and political issues of his day, especially as the Depression darkened and the world headed for another war. *Rain from Heaven*, 1934, *End of Summer*, 1936, and *Wine of Choice*, 1938, all attempted a combination of high comedy—and its sophisticated treatment of sex—with political discussion, but to no particular advantage. His own disturbed outlook concerning the position of the comic writer in a world on the edge of chaos was discussed at length in *No Time for Comedy* in 1939.

Behrman has not completely abandoned the high-comedy style; he demonstrated in his own adaptation of Maugham's short story, *Jane*, produced in New York in 1952, that his ability to deal joyously with the patently frivolous had not deserted him. He also composed *The Talley Method*, 1941, and *Dunnigan's Daughter*, 1945. Adaptations of note have been the very successful *Amphitryon 38*, 1937, from Giraudoux's comedy, and *Jacobowsky and the Colonel* in 1944, from Franz Werfel's original. In 1959 appeared an auto-biographical play set in Worcester of 1908 called *The Cold Wind and the Warm*.

BIOGRAPHY
by
S. N. Behrman

Ina Claire as Marion in the original production of *Biography*. The vivacious charm of Behrman's delightfully independent artist was portrayed beautifully by this talented and attractive young actress. (*Theatre Arts Magazine. Photo by Vandamm.*)

Biography was first produced by the Theatre Guild at the Guild Theatre, New York, on December 12, 1932. It closed on July 29, 1933, after a run of 267 performances. It has been the most popular of Behrman's comedies. Ina Claire created the part of Marion in one of her outstanding Broadway roles. The following cast appeared in the first production:

RICHARD KURT	*Earle Larimore*
MINNIE, MARION FROUDE's maid	*Helen Salinger*
MELCHIOR FEYDAK, a Viennese composer	*Arnold Korff*
MARION FROUDE	*Ina Claire*
LEANDER NOLAN	*Jay Fassett*
WARWICK WILSON	*Alexander Clark*
ORRIN KINNICOTT	*Charles Richman*
SLADE KINNICOTT, his daughter	*Mary Arbenz*

Directed by Philip Moeller
Settings designed by Jo Mielziner

ACT ONE

SCENE: *The studio apartment of* MARION FROUDE *in an old-fashioned studio building in West 57th St., New York. A great, cavernous room expressing in its polyglot furnishings the artistic patois of the various landlords who have sublet this apartment to wandering tenants like* MARION FROUDE. *The styles range from medieval Florence to contemporary Grand Rapids; on a movable raised platform in the center is a papal throne chair in red velvet and gold fringes. Not far from it is an ordinary American kitchen chair. The hanging lamp which sheds a mellow light over a French Empire sofa is filigreed copper Byzantine. Another and longer sofa across the room against the grand piano is in soft green velvet and has the gentility of a polite Park Avenue drawing room. Under the stairs, rear, which go up to* MARION's *bedroom, are stacks of her canvases. There is a quite fine wood carving of a Madonna which seems to be centuries old and in the wall spaces looking at audience are great, dim canvases—copies by some former tenant left probably in lieu of rent—of Sargent's Lord Ribblesdale and Mme. X.*

Whether it is due to the amenable spirit of the present incumbent or because they are relaxed in the democracy of art, these oddments of the creative spirit do not suggest disharmony. The room is warm, musty, with restful shadows and limpid lights. The enormous leaded window on the right, though some of its members are patched and cracked, gleams in the descending twilight with an opalescent light; even the copper cylinder of the fire extinguisher and its attendant axe, visible in the hall, seem to be not so much implements against calamity, as amusing museum-bits cherished from an earlier time. Every school is represented here except the modern. The studio has the mellowness of anachronism.

There is a door upstage left leading to the kitchen and MINNIE's *bedroom; a door, center, under the stairs leads into hallway. A door on the stair landing, center, leads to* MARION's *bedroom.*

TIME: *About five o'clock of an afternoon in November.*

AT RISE: RICHARD KURT *is finishing a nervous cigarette. He has the essential audacity which comes from having seen the worst happen, from having endured the keenest pain. He has the hardness of one who knows that he can be devastated by pity, the bitterness which comes from having seen, in early youth, justice thwarted and tears unavailing, the self-reliance which comes from having seen everything go in a disordered world save one stubborn, unyielding core of belief—at everything else he laughs, in this alone he trusts. He has the intensity of the fanatic and the carelessness of the vagabond. He goes to the door from the hall and calls.*

KURT. Say, you, hello there—what's your name? (MINNIE, MARION FROUDE'S *inseparable maid, a German woman of about fifty, comes in. She is indignant at being thus summarily summoned, and by a stranger.*)

MINNIE (*with dignity*). My name iss Minnie, if you please.

KURT. What time did Miss Froude go out?

MINNIE. About two o'clock.

KURT. It's nearly five now. She should be home, shouldn't she?

MINNIE. She said she vas coming home to tea and that iss all I know.

KURT (*grimly*). I know. She invited me to tea. . . . Where did she go to lunch?

MINNIE (*acidly*). That I do not know.

KURT. Did someone call for her or did she go out alone? I have a reason for asking.

MINNIE. She went out alone. Any more questions?

KURT. No. I see there's no point in asking you questions.

MINNIE. Den vy do you ask dem? (*The doorbell rings. MINNIE throws up her hands in despair. She goes out muttering: "Ach Gott." KURT is rather amused at her. He lights another cigarette. Sounds of vociferous greeting outside. "Ach mein lieber Herr Feydak[1] . . ." MELCHIOR FEYDAK, the Austrian composer, comes in. He is forty-five, tall, hook-nosed, thin-faced, a humorist with a rather sad face.*)

FEYDAK. Nun, Minnie, und so ist die schlechte. . . . ?[2] (MINNIE *makes a sign to him not to disclose their free-masonry in the presence of strangers. She is cautious. . . .*) Not home yet, eh, Minnie? Where is she? Well—well. How do they say—gallivanting—I love that word—gallivanting as usual. Well, I'll wait. It's humiliating—but I'll wait. Chilly! Brr! I don't mind so much being cold in London or Vienna. I expect it. But I can't stand it in New York. (*He warms himself before fire.*) And who is this young man?

MINNIE (*shortly*). Ich weiss nicht! . . . Er hat alle fünf minuten gefragt wo sie ist—[3] (*She goes out.*)

FEYDAK. You've offended Minnie, I can see that.

KURT. That's just too bad!

FEYDAK. We all tremble before Minnie. . . . Been waiting long?

KURT. Over half an hour!

FEYDAK. Extraordinary thing—ever since I've known Marion there's always been someone waiting for her. There are two kinds of people in one's life—people whom one keeps waiting—and the people for whom one waits. . . .

KURT. Is that an epigram?

FEYDAK. Do you object to epigrams?

KURT (*with some pride*). I despise epigrams.

FEYDAK (*tolerantly sizing* KURT *up*). Hm! Friend of Miss Froude's?

KURT. Not at all.

FEYDAK. That at least is no cause for pride.

KURT. I just don't happen to be, that's all.

FEYDAK. I commiserate you.

KURT. I despise gallantry also.

FEYDAK (*lightly*). And I thought Americans were so sentimental. . . .

KURT. And, together with other forms of glibness, I loathe generalization. . . .

FEYDAK (*drily*). Young man, we have a great deal in common.

KURT. Also, there is a faint flavor of

[1] The German *Ach Gott*, literally "Oh, God," is not much stronger than the English "Oh for goodness' sake." Minnie's offstage greeting: "Oh my dear Herr Feydak."
[2] "And now, Minnie, where's the bad girl?"
[3] "I don't know. Every five minutes he's been asking where she is."

condescension in the way you say "young man" for which I don't really care. . . .

FEYDAK (*delighted and encouraging him to go on*). What about me do you like? There must be something.

KURT. If I were that kind your question would embarrass me.

FEYDAK (*very pleased*). Good for Marion!

KURT. Why do you say that?

FEYDAK. She always had a knack for picking up originals!

KURT. You are under a misapprehension. Miss Froude did not pick me up. I picked her up. (FEYDAK *stares at him. This does shock him.*) I wrote Miss Froude a letter—a business-letter. She answered and gave me an appointment for four-thirty. It is now after five. She has taken a half-hour out of my life. . . .

FEYDAK. I gather that fragment of time has great value. . . .

KURT. She has shortened my life by thirty minutes. God, how I hate Bohemians!

FEYDAK (*innocently*). Are you by any chance—an Evangelist?

KURT. I am—for the moment—a businessman. I'm not here to hold hands or drink tea. I'm here on business. My presence here is a favor to Miss Froude and likely to bring her a handsome profit. . . .

FEYDAK. Profit! Ah! That accounts for her being late. . . .

KURT (*sceptically*). You despise profit, I suppose! Are you—by any chance—old-world?

FEYDAK. Young man, your technique is entirely wasted on me. . . .

KURT. Technique! What are you talking about?

FEYDAK. When I was a young man—before I achieved any sort of success—I was rude on principle. Deliberately rude and extravagantly bitter in order to make impression. When it is no longer necessary for you to wait around for people in order to do them favors you'll mellow down, I assure you.

KURT (*fiercely, he has been touched*). You think so, do you! That's where

you're mistaken! I'm rude now. When I'm successful I'll be murderous!

FEYDAK (*genially*). More power to you! But I've never seen it happen yet. Success is the great muffler! Not an epigram, I hope. If it is—forgive me. (*A moment's pause.* KURT *studies him while* FEYDAK *crosses to stove and warms his hands.*)

KURT. I know you from somewhere. It's very tantalizing.

FEYDAK. I don't think so. I have only just arrived in this country. . . .

KURT. Still I know you—I'm sure—I've seen you somewhere. . . .

FEYDAK (*understanding the familiarity*). Maybe you know Miss Froude's portrait of me. . . .

KURT (*doubtfully*). Yes—maybe that's it . . . may I ask. . . . ?

FEYDAK. Certainly. My name is Feydak.

KURT. The composer?

FEYDAK (*drily*). Yes. . . .

KURT. I thought he was dead. . . .

FEYDAK. That is true. But I hope you won't tell anyone—for I am his ghost. . . .

KURT (*putting this down for Continental humor and genuinely contrite*). Forgive me. . . .

FEYDAK. But why?

KURT. If you really are Feydak the composer—I have the most enormous admiration for you. I worship music above everything.

FEYDAK (*slightly bored*). Go on. . . .

KURT. I read in the paper—you're on your way to Hollywood. . . .

FEYDAK. Yes. I am on my way to Hollywood. . . .

KURT. In the new state men like you won't have to prostitute themselves in Hollywood. . . .

FEYDAK. Ah! A Utopian!

KURT. Yes. You use the word as a term of contempt. Why? Every artist is a Utopian. You must be very tired or you wouldn't be so contemptuous of Utopians.

FEYDAK (*with a charming smile*). I am rather tired. Old-world, you would call it.

KURT. You can be anything you like. . . .

FEYDAK (*satirically*). Thank you. . . .

KURT. You've written lovely music—I have a friend who plays every note of it. I didn't see your operetta when it was done here. . . . I didn't have the price . . . it was very badly done though, I heard. . . .

FEYDAK. I must explain to you—you are under a misapprehension. . . .

KURT. It was done here, wasn't it?

FEYDAK. Not about the operetta. You are under a misapprehension—about me. I am a composer—but I didn't write "Danubia." That was my brother, Victor Feydak. You are right. He is dead. You are the first person I have met in New York who even suspected it.

KURT. I'm sorry.

FEYDAK. Not at all. I am flattered. At home our identities were never confused. Is this the well-known American hospitality? It is, in some sort, compensation for his death. . . . (KURT *is embarrassed and uncomfortable. It is part of his essential insecurity; he is only really at home in protest. He wants to get out.*)

KURT. I'm sorry—I. . . .

FEYDAK (*easily*). But why?

KURT. I think I'll leave a note for Miss Froude—get that girl in here, will you?

FEYDAK. Let's have some tea—she's sure to be in any minute. . . .

KURT. No, thanks. And you might tell her for me that if she wants to see me about the matter I wrote her about she can come to my office. . . . (MARION FROUDE *comes in. She is one of those women the sight of whom on Fifth Ave., where she has just been walking, causes foreigners to exclaim enthusiastically that American women are the most radiant in the world. She is tall, lithe, indomitably alive. Unlike* KURT, *the tears in things have warmed without scalding her; she floats life like a dancer's scarf in perpetual enjoyment of its colors and contours.*)

MARION (*to* KURT). I'm *so* sorry!

FEYDAK (*coming toward her*). I don't believe a word of it! (*She is overjoyed at seeing* FEYDAK. *She can't believe for a second that it is he. Then she flies into his arms.*)

MARION. Feydie! Oh, Feydie, I've been trying everywhere to reach you—I can't believe it. . . . Feydie darling!

FEYDAK (*severely*). Is this how you keep a business appointment, Miss Froude?

MARION. How long have you waited? If I'd only known. . . . (*Suddenly conscious that* KURT *had waited too.*) Oh, I'm sorry, Mr.— Mr.— . . . ?

KURT. Kurt. Richard Kurt.

MARION. Oh, of course, Mr. Kurt. I say—could you possibly—would it be too much trouble—could you come back?

FEYDAK (*same tone*). This young man is here on business. It is more important. I can wait. I'll come back.

MARION. No, no, Feydie—no, no. I can't wait for that. I'm sure Mr. Kurt will understand. Mr. Feydak is an old friend whom I haven't seen in ever so long. It isn't as if Mr. Kurt were a regular businessman.

FEYDAK (*amused*). How do you know he isn't?

MARION (*breathless with excitement*). I can tell. He's not a bit like his letter. When I got your letter I was sure you were jowley and, you know— (*She makes a gesture.*) convex. I'm sure, Feydie—whatever the business is— (*To* KURT.) you did say you had some, didn't you?—I'm sure it can wait. A half-hour anyway. Can't it wait a half-hour? You see, Feydie and I haven't seen each other since. . . .

KURT. Vienna!

MARION (*astonished*). Yes. How did you know?

KURT. It's always since Vienna that Bohemians haven't seen each other, isn't it? I'll be back in thirty minutes. (*He goes.*)

MARION. What a singular young man!

FEYDAK. I've been having a very amusing talk with him. Professional rebel, I think. Well, my dear—you look marvelous! (*They take each other in.*)

MARION. Isn't it wonderful. . . .

FEYDAK. It is nice! (*They sit on sofa,* MARION *left of* FEYDAK.)

MARION. How long is it?

FEYDAK. Well, it's since. . . .

MARION (*firmly*). Since Vicki died.

FEYDAK. That's right. I haven't seen you since.

MARION. Since that day—we walked behind him.

FEYDAK. Yes.

MARION. I felt I couldn't bear to stay on. I left for London that night.

FEYDAK. Yes.

MARION. It's six years, isn't it?

FEYDAK. Yes. Six years last June. (*A pause.*)

MARION. What's happened since then? Nothing. . . .

FEYDAK. How long have you been here?

MARION. Two weeks.

FEYDAK. Busy?

MARION. Not professionally, I'm afraid. People are charming—they ask me to lunch and dinner and they're—"oh, so interested"—but no commissions so far. And God, how I need it. . . .

FEYDAK. I'm surprised. I gathered you'd been very successful.

MARION. It's always sounded like it, hasn't it? The impression, I believe, is due to the extreme notoriety of some of my sitters. Oh, I've managed well enough up to now—if I'd been more provident I dare say I could have put a tidy bit by —but at the moment people don't seem in a mood to have their portraits done. Are they less vain than they used to be? Or just poorer?

FEYDAK. Both, I think. . . .

MARION. Last time I came here I was awfully busy. Had great réclame because I'd been in Russia doing leading Communists. Obeying some subtle paradox the big financiers flocked to me. Pittsburgh manufacturers wanted to be done by the same brush that had tackled Lenin. Now they seem less eager. Must be some reason, Feydie. But what about you? Let me hear about you. How's Kathie?

FEYDAK. Well. She's here with me.

MARION. And Sadye?

FEYDAK. Splendid.

MARION. She must be a big girl now.

FEYDAK. As tall as you are.

MARION. Kathie used to hate me, didn't she? Frightened to death of me. Was afraid I was after Vicki's money. . . .

FEYDAK. Yes. She was afraid you'd marry him and that we should have less from him. When we knew he was dying she was in a panic.

MARION. Poor dear—I could have spared her all that worry if she'd been halfway civil to me.

FEYDAK. Kathie is practical. And she is a good mother. Those are attributes which make women avaricious.

MARION. Did Vicki leave you very much?

FEYDAK. Not very much. Half to you.

MARION. Really? How sweet of him! How dear of him!

FEYDAK. We've spent it. . . .

MARION. Of course you should.

FEYDAK. But I'll soon be in position to repay you your share. I'm on my way to Hollywood.

MARION. Are you really? How wonderful for you, Feydie! I'm so glad.

FEYDAK. You've been there, haven't you?

MARION. Yes. Last time I was in America.

FEYDAK. Did you like it?

MARION. Well, it's the new Eldorado— art on the gold-rush.

FEYDAK (*with a kind of ironic bitterness*). Vicki left me an inheritance subject, it appears, to perpetual renewal.

MARION. How do you mean?

FEYDAK. Things have been going from bad to worse in Vienna—you haven't been there since '25 so you don't know. the theatre's pretty well dead—even the first-rate fellows have had a hard time making their way. I managed to get several scores to do—but they were not— except that they were failures—up to my usual standard. . . .

MARION (*laughing, reproachful*). Oh, Feydie . . . !

FEYDAK. If it weren't for the money Vicki left me—and you!—I don't know how we should have got through at all these six years. About a month ago we reached the end of our rope—we were hopelessly in debt—no means of getting out—when the miracle happened. . . . (MARION *is excited, touches his knee with her hand.*)

MARION (*murmuring*). I can't bear it. . . .

FEYDAK. It was my dramatic agent on the phone. A great American film magnate was in town and wanted to see me. Ausgerechnet me and no other. Even my agent couldn't keep the surprise out of his voice. Why me? I asked. God knows, says the agent. Well, we went around to the Bristol to see the magnate. And, as we talked to him, it gradually became apparent. He thought I was Vicki. He didn't know Vicki was dead! He thought I had written "Danubia."

MARION. Did he say so?

FEYDAK. No—not at all. But as we shook hands at the end he said to me: "Any man that can write a tune like this is the kind of man we want." And he whistled, so out of tune that I could hardly recognize it myself, the waltz from Danubia. Do you remember it? (*He starts to hum the waltz and* MARION *joins him. They hum together, then* FEYDAK *continues to talk as* MARION *continues to hum a few more measures.*) He was so innocent, so affable that I had an impulse to say to him: "Look here, old fellow, you don't want me, you want my brother and, in order to get him, you'll have to resurrect him!" But noble impulses are luxury impulses. You have to be well off to gratify them. I kept quiet. We shook hands and here I am. Tonight they're giving me a dinner at the Waldorf Astoria for the press to meet my brother! Irony if you like, eh, Marion? (*There is a pause.*)

MARION. Feydie . . . (*A moment. He does not answer.*) Feydie—do you mind if I say something to you—very frankly?

FEYDAK. I doubt whether you can say anything to me more penetrating than the remarks I habitually address to myself.

MARION. You know Vicki was very fond of you. He used to say you put too high a valuation on genius.

FEYDAK. Because he had it he could afford to deprecate it.

MARION. Over and over again he used to say to me: "You know, Marion," he would say, "as a human being Feydie's far superior to me, more amiable, more witty, more talented, more patient. . . ."

FEYDAK (*shakes his head*). Not true. I simply give the impression of these things. . . .

MARION. You underrate yourself, Feydie. . . . How this would have amused him—this incident with the Hollywood man!

FEYDAK (*smiling bitterly*). It would rather. . . .

MARION. Why do you grudge giving him a laugh somewhere? I never had a chance to tell you in Vienna—things were so—so close and terrible—at the end—but he had the greatest tenderness for you. He used to speak of you—I can't tell you how much. "Because of this sixth sense for making tunes which I have and he hasn't," he said to me one day—not a week before he died—"he thinks himself less than me." He used to tell me that everything he had he owed to you— to the sacrifices you made to send him to the Conservatory when he was a boy. . . . The extent to which he had outstripped you hurt him—hurt him. I felt he would have given anything to dip into the golden bowl of his genius and pour it over you. And do you know what was the terror of his life, the obsessing terror of his life?—his fear of your resenting him. . . .

FEYDAK (*moved, deeply ashamed*). Marion. . . .

MARION. Don't resent him now, Feydie. . . . Why, it's such fun—don't you see? It's such a curious, marginal survival for him—that a badly-remembered waltz-tune, five years after his death, should be the means of helping you at a moment when you need it so badly. . . . It's delicious, Feydie. It's such fun! The only awful thing is the possibility that he is unaware of it. It would have pleased him so, Feydie. Must you grudge him it?

FEYDAK. You make me horribly ashamed. . . .

MARION (*brightly*). Nonsense. . . .

FEYDAK. Because I did grudge him it —yes—I won't, though—I see now that it never occurred to me how . . . (*Bursts out laughing suddenly.*) God, it is funny, isn't it. . . .

MARION (*joining in his laughter*). Of course—it's delightful. . . . (*They both laugh heartily and long.*)

MARION. And the funny thing is—you'll be much better for them out there than he would have been.

FEYDAK. Surely! They'll be able to whistle *my* tunes!

MARION. Don't you see!

FEYDAK. Oh, Lieber Schatzel,[4] come out there with me.

MARION. Can't.

FEYDAK. I wish, Marion, you would come. I never feel life so warm and good as when you are in the neighborhood.

MARION. Dear Feydie, you're very comforting.

FEYDAK. Is there someone that keeps you here?

MARION. No, there's no one. I'm quite alone.

FEYDAK. Well then . . . !

MARION. No, this isn't the moment for me, Feydie. Besides, I can't afford the journey. I'm frightfully hard up at the moment.

FEYDAK. Well, look here, I . . .

MARION. No, that's sweet of you but I couldn't.

FEYDAK. I don't see why—it's too silly. . . .

MARION. Vanity. A kind of vanity.

FEYDAK. But I owe it to you!

MARION. I suppose it is foolish in a way—but I've a kind of pride in maneuvering on my own. I always have done it—in that way at least I've been genuinely independent. I'm a little proud of my ingenuity. And do you know, Feydie, no matter how hard up I've been at different times something's always turned up for me. I have a kind of curiosity to know what it will be this time. It would spoil the fun for me to take money from my friends. Nothing so much as that would make me doubtful of my own— shall we say—marketability?

FEYDAK. Paradoxical, isn't it?

MARION. Why not? Anyway, it's a pet idée of mine, so be a darling and let me indulge it, will you, Feydie, and don't offer me money. Anyway, I've a business proposition on. . . .

FEYDAK. Have you?

MARION. That young man who was just here. Do you suppose he'll come back? Now I think of it we were a bit short with him, weren't we? I was so glad to see you I couldn't be bothered with him! (*Sound of doorbell.*) Ah! You see! (*Calls outside.*) Show him in, Minnie! (MINNIE *comes in and exits hall door to admit the visitor.*)

FEYDAK. What are you doing for dinner?

MARION. There's a young man who attached himself to me on the boat.

FEYDAK. Oh, Marion!

MARION. I seem to attract youth, Feydie. What shall I do about it?

FEYDAK. Where are you dining?

MARION. I don't know. . . . Which speakeasy? Tell me which one and I'll . . . (MINNIE *ushers in* MR. LEANDER NOLAN. *He is middle-aged, ample, handsome. Looks like the late Warren Gamaliel Harding.[5] Soberly dressed and wears a waistcoat with white piping on it. The façade is impeccable but in* NOLAN'S *eye you may discern, at odd moments, an uncertainty, an almost boyish anxiety to please, to be right, that is rather engaging.* MARION, *who expected the young man, is rather startled.* MR. NOLAN *regards her with satisfaction.*)

NOLAN. Hello, Marion.

MARION (*doubtfully, feels she should remember him*). How do you do? Er—

---

4 Darling.

5 The twenty-ninth President was distinguished by his phenomenally good looks, if by nothing else.

will you excuse me—just a second. . . . ?

NOLAN (*genially*). Certainly. (*He moves right.* MARION *walks* FEYDIE *to the hall door.*)

FEYDAK (*under his breath to her*). Looks like a commission. (*She makes a gesture of silent prayer.*)

MARION (*out loud*). Telephone me in an hour, will you, Feydie, and let me know which speakeasy. . . .

FEYDAK (*once he has her in the hallway out of* NOLAN's *hearing*). Also, du kommst ganz sicher?[6]

MARION. Vielleicht spater.[7] Bye, Feydie dear. (FEYDIE *goes out.* MARION *turns to face* NOLAN *who is standing with his arms behind his back rather enjoying the surprise he is about to give her.*)

NOLAN. How are you, Marion?

MARION (*delicately*). Er—do I know you?

NOLAN. Yes. You know me.

MARION. Oh, yes—of course!

NOLAN. About time!

MARION (*brightly insecure*). Lady Winchester's garden-party at Ascot—two summers ago. . . .

NOLAN. Guess again!

MARION. No—I know you perfectly well—it's just that—no, don't tell me. . . . (*She covers her eyes with her hand, trying to conjure him out of the past.*)

NOLAN. This is astonishing. If someone had said to me that I could walk into a room in front of Marion Froude and she not know me I'd have told 'em they were crazy . . .

MARION (*desperate*). I do know you. I know you perfectly well—it's just that . . .

NOLAN. You'll be awful sore at yourself—I warn you . . .

MARION. I can't forgive myself now—I know!

NOLAN. I don't believe it!

MARION. The American Embassy dinner in Rome on the Fourth of July—last year—you sat on my right.

NOLAN. I did not!

MARION (*miserably*). Well, you sat somewhere. Where did you sit?

NOLAN. I wasn't there.

MARION. Well, I think it's very unkind of you to keep me in suspense like this. I can't bear it another second!

NOLAN. I wouldn't have believed it!

MARION. Well, give me some hint, will you?

NOLAN. Think of home—think of Tennessee!

MARION. Oh . . . !

NOLAN. Little Mary Froude. . . .

MARION (*a light breaking in on her*). No! Oh, no!

NOLAN. Well, it's about time. . . .

MARION. But . . . ! You were . . .

NOLAN. Well, so were you!

MARION. But—Bunny—you aren't Bunny Nolan, are you? You're his brother!

NOLAN. I have no brother.

MARION. But Bunny—Bunny dear—how important you've become!

NOLAN. I haven't done badly—no.

MARION. Here, give me your coat and hat— (MARION, *taking his coat and hat, crosses upstage to piano, and leaves them there. Laughing, a little hysterical.*) You should have warned me. It's not fair of you. Bunny! Of all people—I can scarcely believe it. . . . (*A moment's pause. He doesn't quite like her calling him Bunny but he doesn't know how to stop it. She sits on model stand looking up at him as she says:*) You look wonderful. You look like a—like a—Senator or something monumental like that.

NOLAN (*sits on sofa below piano*). That's a good omen. I'll have to tell Orrin.

MARION. What's a good omen? And who is Orrin?

NOLAN. Your saying I look like a Senator. Because—I don't want to be premature—but in a few months I may be one.

MARION. A Senator!

NOLAN (*smiling*). Senator. Washington. Not Nashville.

[6] "Now you'll come, for sure?"
[7] "Maybe later."

MARION. Do you want to be a Senator or can't you help it?

NOLAN (*to whom this point of view is incomprehensible*). What do you mean?

MARION. I'll paint you, Bunny. Toga. Ferrule. Tribune of the people.

NOLAN. Not a bad idea. Not a bad idea at all. I remember now—you were always sketching me. Sketching everything. Say, you've done pretty well yourself, haven't you?

MARION. Not as well as you have, Bunny. Imagine. Bunny Nolan—a Senator at Washington. Well, well! And tell me—how do I seem to you? You knew me at once, didn't you?

NOLAN. Sure I did. You haven't changed so much—a little, perhaps.

MARION (*delicately*). Ampler?

NOLAN (*inspecting her*). No . . . not that I can notice. . . .

MARION (*with a sigh of relief*). That's wonderful. . . .

NOLAN. You look just the same. You are just the same.

MARION. Oh, you don't know, Bunny. I'm artful. How long is it since we've seen each other? Twelve years anyway. More than that—fifteen . . .

NOLAN. Just about—hadn't even begun to practice law yet. . . .

MARION. We were just kids . . . children. . . . And now look at you! I can see how successful you are, Bunny.

NOLAN. How?

MARION. White piping on your vest. That suggests directorates to me. Multiple control. Vertical corporations. Are you vertical or horizontal, Bunny?

NOLAN. I'm both.

MARION. Good for you! Married?

NOLAN. Not yet . . .

MARION. How did you escape? You're going to be, though.

NOLAN. I'm engaged.

MARION. Who's the lucky girl?

NOLAN. Slade Kinnicott. Daughter of Orrin Kinnicott.

MARION. Orrin Kinnicott. The newspaper publisher?

NOLAN. Yes. He's backing me for the Senate.

MARION. Well, if he's backing you you ought to get in. All that circulation—not very good circulation, is it? Still, one vote's as good as another, I suppose. . . .

NOLAN (*hurt*). In my own State the Kinnicott papers are as good as any . . .

MARION. Well, I wish you luck. I'm sure you'll have it. My! Senator Nolan!

NOLAN. If I get in I'll be the youngest Senator . . .

MARION. And the best-looking too, Bunny . . .

NOLAN (*embarrassed*). Well . . .

MARION. You're fussed! How charming of you! (*She sits beside him.*) Oh, Bunny, I'm very proud of you, really.

NOLAN. You see, Marion, I've been pretty successful in the law. Tremendously successful, I may say. I've organized some of the biggest mergers of recent years. I've made a fortune—a sizeable fortune. Well, one day I woke up and I said to myself: Look here, Nolan, you've got to take stock. You've got to ask yourself where you're heading. I'd been so busy I'd never had a chance to ask myself these fundamental questions before. And I decided to call a halt. You've got enough, more than enough for life, I said to myself. It's time you quit piling up money for yourself and began thinking about your fellow-man. I've always been ambitious, Marion. You know that. You shared all my early dreams . . .

MARION. Of course I did. . . .

NOLAN. Remember I always told you I didn't want money and power for their own sakes—I always wanted to be a big man in a real sense—to do something for my country and my time . . .

MARION. Yes. Sometimes you sounded like Daniel Webster, darling. I'm not a bit surprised you're going in the Senate.

NOLAN. I never thought—even in my wildest dreams. . . .

MARION. Well, you see you underestimated yourself. You may go even higher—the White House—why not?

NOLAN. I never let myself think of that.

MARION. Why not? It's no more wonderful that what's happened already, is it?

NOLAN (*Napoleon at Saint Helena*). Destiny!

MARION. Exactly. Destiny!

NOLAN (*kind, richly human, patronizing*). And you, my dear . . . ?

MARION. As you see. Obscure. Uncertain. Alone. Nowhere at all. Not the remotest chance of my getting into the Senate—unless I marry into it. Oh, Bunny, after you get to Washington will you introduce me to some Senators?

NOLAN. Well, that's premature . . . Naturally if the people should favor me I'd do what I could. I never forget a friend. Whatever faults I may have, disloyalty, I hope, is not one of them.

MARION. Of course it isn't. You're a dear. You always were. (*A moment's pause.*)

NOLAN. Who was that fellow I found you with when I came in?

MARION. An old friend of mine from Vienna—a composer.

NOLAN. You've been a lot with foreigners, haven't you?

MARION. A good deal . . .

NOLAN. Funny, I don't understand that.

MARION. Foreigners are people, you know, Bunny. Some of 'em are rather nice.

NOLAN. When I'm abroad a few weeks home begins to look pretty good to me.

MARION. I love New York but I can't say I feel an acute nostalgia for Tennessee. (*Another pause. He stares at her suddenly—still incredulous that he should be seeing her at all, and that, after all these years and quite without him, she should be radiant still.*)

NOLAN. Little Marion Froude! I can't believe it somehow. . . .

MARION. Oh, Bunny! You're sweet! You're so—ingenuous. That's what I always liked about you.

NOLAN. What do you mean?

MARION. The way you look at me, the incredulity, the surprise. What did you expect to see? A hulk, a remnant, a whitened sepulchre . . . what?

NOLAN (*uncomfortable at being caught*). Not—not at all. . . .

MARION. Tell me, Bunny, what . . . ? I won't be hurt . . .

NOLAN (*miserably, stumbling*). Well, naturally, after what I'd heard . . .

MARION. What have you heard? Oh, do tell me, Bunny.

NOLAN. Well, I mean—about your life. . . .

MARION. Racy, Bunny? Racy?

NOLAN. No use going into that. You chose your own way. Everybody has a right to live their own life, I guess.

MARION (*pats his arm*). That's very handsome of you Bunny. I hope you take that liberal point of view when you reach the Senate.

NOLAN. I came here, Marion, in a perfectly sincere mood, to say something to you, something that's been on my mind ever since we parted, but if you're going to be flippant I suppose there's no use my saying anything—I might as well go, in fact. (*But he makes no attempt to do so.*)

MARION (*seriously*). Do forgive me, Bunny. One gets into an idiom that passes for banter but really I'm not so changed. I'm not flippant. I'm awfully glad to see you, Bunny. (*An undertone of sadness creeps into her voice.*) After all, one makes very few real friends in life—and you are part of my youth—we are part of each other's youth . . .

NOLAN. You didn't even know me!

MARION. Complete surprise! After all I've been in New York many times during these years and never once—never once have you come near me. You've dropped me all these years. (*With a sigh.*) I'm afraid, Bunny, your career has been too much with you.

NOLAN (*grimly*). So has yours!

MARION. I detect an overtone—faint but unmistakable—of moral censure.

NOLAN (*same tone*). Well, I suppose it's impossible to live one's life in art without being sexually promiscuous! (*He looks at her accusingly.*)

MARION. Oh, dear me, Bunny! What shall I do? Shall I blush? Shall I hang my head in shame? What shall I do? How does one react in the face of an appalling accusation of this sort? I didn't know the news had got around so widely . . .

NOLAN. Well, so many of your lovers have been famous men. . . .

MARION. Well, you were obscure . . . But you're famous now, aren't you? I seem to be stimulating if nothing else . . .

NOLAN. If I had then some of the fame I have now you probably wouldn't have walked out on me at the last minute the way you did . . .

MARION. Dear, dear Bunny, that's not quite—

NOLAN (*irritated beyond control*). I wish you wouldn't call me Bunny. . . .

MARION. Well, I always did. What is your real name?

NOLAN. You know perfectly well . . .

MARION. I swear I don't. . . .

NOLAN. My name is Leander. . . .

MARION. Bunny, really. . . .

NOLAN. That is my name.

MARION. Really I'd forgotten that. Leander! Who was he—he did something in the Hellespont, didn't he? What did he do in the Hellespont?[8]

NOLAN (*sharply*). Beside the point.

MARION. Sorry! You say you wanted to tell me something—

NOLAN (*grimly*). Yes!

MARION. I love to be told things.

NOLAN. That night you left me—

MARION. We'd quarrelled about something, hadn't we?

NOLAN. I realized after you left me how much I'd grown to depend on you—

MARION. Dear Bunny!

NOLAN. I plunged into work. I worked fiercely to forget you. I did forget you— (*He looks away from her.*) And yet—

MARION. And yet—?

NOLAN. The way we'd separated and I never heard from you—it left something bitter in my mind—something— (*He hesitates for a word.*)

MARION (*supplying it*). Unresolved!

NOLAN (*quickly—relieved that she understands so exactly*). Yes. All these years I've wanted to see you, to get it off my mind—

MARION. Did you want the last word, Bunny dear?

NOLAN (*fiercely*). I wanted to see you, to stand before you, to tell myself— "Here she is and—and what of it!"

MARION. Well, can you?

NOLAN (*heatedly, with transparent overemphasis*). Yes! Yes!

MARION. Good for you, Bunny. I know just how you feel—like having a tooth out, isn't it? (*Sincerely.*) In justice to myself—I must tell you this—that the reason I walked out on you in the summary way I did was not, as you've just suggested, because I doubted your future— it was obvious to me, even then, that you were destined for mighty things— but the reason was that I felt a disparity in our characters not conducive to matrimonial contentment. You see how right I was. I suspected in myself a—a tendency to explore, a spiritual and physical wanderlust—that I knew would horrify you once you found it out. It horrifies you now when we are no longer anything to each other. Imagine, Leander dear, if we were married how much more difficult it would be— If there is any one thing you have to be grateful to me for it is that instant's clear vision I had which made me see, which made me look ahead, which made me tear myself away from you. Why, everything you have now—your future, your prospects—even your fiancée, Leander dear —you owe to me—no, I won't say to me—to that instinct—to that premonition. . . .

NOLAN (*nostalgic*). We might have done it together. . . .

MARION. I wouldn't have stood for a fiancée, Bunny dear—not even I am as promiscuous as that. . . .

NOLAN. Don't use that word!

MARION. But, Leander! It's your own!

---

[8] According to the old Greek myth he swam the straits of Hellespont (Dardanelles) to be with his sweetheart, Hero.

NOLAN. Do you think it hasn't been on my conscience ever since, do you think it hasn't tortured me . . . !

MARION. What, dear?

NOLAN. That thought!

MARION. Which thought?

NOLAN. Every time I heard about you —all the notoriety that's attended you in the American papers . . . painting pictures of Communist statesmen, running around California with movie comedians!

MARION. I have to practice my profession, Bunny. One must live, you know. Besides, I've done Capitalist statesmen too. And at Geneva. . . .

NOLAN (darkly). You know what I mean . . . !

MARION. You mean . . . (She whispers through her cupped hand) you mean promiscuous? Has that gotten around, Bunny? Is it whispered in the sewing-circles of Nashville? Will I be burned for a witch if I go back home? Will they have a trial over me? Will you defend me?

NOLAN (quite literally, with sincere and disarming simplicity). I should be forced, as an honest man, to stand before the multitude and say: In condemning this woman you are condemning me who am asking your suffrages to represent you. For it was I with whom this woman first sinned before God. As an honorable man that is what I should have to do.

MARION. And has this worried you— actually . . . !

NOLAN. It's tortured me . . . !

MARION. You're the holy man and I'm Thaïs! That gives me an idea for the portrait which I hope you will commission me to do. I'll do you in a hair-shirt. Savonarola. He was a Senator too, wasn't he? Or was he?[9]

NOLAN (gloomily contemplating her). I can't forget that it was I who . . .

MARION. Did you think you were the first, Bunny? Was I so unscrupulously coquettish as to lead you to believe that I—oh, I couldn't have been. It's not like me. (She crosses to right of model stand.)

NOLAN (fiercely). Don't lie to me!

MARION (sitting on stand). Bunny, you frighten me!

NOLAN (stands over her almost threateningly). You're lying to me to salve my conscience but I won't have it! I know my guilt and I'm going to bear it!

MARION. Well, I don't want to deprive you of your little pleasures but . . .

NOLAN. You're evil, Marion. You haven't the face of evil but you're evil— evil!

MARION. Oh, Bunny darling, now you can't mean that surely. What's come over you? You never were like that—or were you? You know perfectly well I'm not evil. Casual—maybe—but not evil. Good Heavens, Bunny, I might as well say you're evil because you're intolerant. These are differences in temperament, that's all—charming differences in temperament.

NOLAN (shakes his head, unconvinced). Sophistry!

MARION. All right, Dean Inge.[10] Sophistry. By the way I've met the Gloomy Dean and he's not gloomy at all—he's very jolly. (Gets up from stand.) Let's have a cup of tea, shall we? Will your constituents care if you have a cup of tea with a promiscuous woman? Will they have to know?

NOLAN. I'm afraid I can't, Marion. I have to be getting on. . . .

MARION. Oh, stay and have some tea— (Makes him sit down.) what do you have to do that can't wait for a cup of tea? . . . (Calls off.) Minnie—Minnie. . . .

MINNNIE (appears in doorway). Ja, Fraulein. . . .

MARION. Bitte—Thee. . . .[11]

MINNIE. Ja, Fraulein. . . . (She goes

---

[9] Marion's allusions are literary and historical. The heroine of Anatole France's "Thaïs" (1890) was a courtesan in Alexandria, converted to Christianity by the monk, Paphnutius, who fell in love with her. The novel was the basis for Massenet's 1894 opera. Savonarola was a fifteenth-century Florentine religious reformer.

[10] Anglican Dean of St. Paul's Cathedral, London.

[11] "Yes, miss . . ." "Tea, please."

out. MARION *smiles at* NOLAN *and sits beside him. He is quite uncomfortable.*)

NOLAN (*slightly embarrassed*). About the painting, Marion. . . .

MARION. Oh, I was only joking . . . don't let yourself be bullied into it . . .

NOLAN. I've never been painted in oils. It might do for campaign purposes. And, if I should be elected, it would be very helpful to you in Washington.

MARION. You're awfully kind, Bunny. I must tell you frankly though that the dignified Senatorial style isn't exactly my forte. However, I might try. Yes—I'll try . . . (*She gives him a long look.*) I'll go the limit on you, Bunny—when I get through with you you'll be a symbol of Dignity. Solid man. No nonsense. Safe and sane. Holds the middle course—a slogan in a frock-coat. I'll make you look like Warren G. Harding—even handsomer— Get you the women's votes.

NOLAN. Well, that'll be very nice of you. . . . (MARION *suddenly kisses him.*)

MARION. Thank you, darling! (*He is very uncomfortable, embarrassed and thrilled.*)

NOLAN. Marion . . . !

MARION. Just a rush of feeling, dear!

NOLAN. You understand that this—this commission . . .

MARION. Of course. Strictly business. Don't worry. I shan't kiss you again till it's finished.

NOLAN. I don't know whether I told you—I'm going to be married in a month.

MARION. I'll have the portrait ready for your wedding-day.

NOLAN. And I am devoted to Slade with every fibre of my being. . . .

MARION. Every fibre—how thorough!

NOLAN. I'm not a Bohemian, you know, Marion.

MARION. Don't tell me! You're a gypsy! (*She continues to study him,*

poses him, poses his hand. MINNIE *enters from left with tea tray containing teapot, cups and saucers, spoons, sugar and cream, and a plate of cakes. She puts tray on model stand and exits left.*) Oh, Bunny, what fun it'll be to do you. Thank you, Minnie. Tell me—how do you see yourself?

NOLAN. What do you mean?

MARION. In your heart of hearts—how do you see yourself? Napoleon, Scipio, Mussolini . . . ? [12]

NOLAN. Nonsense! Do you think I'm an actor?

MARION. Of course. Everybody is. Everybody has some secret vision of himself. Do you know what mine is? Do you know how I see myself? (*The doorbell rings.*)

NOLAN (*ironically*). More visitors!

MARION (*calls to* MINNIE). See who it is, will you, Minnie? . . . Probably the young man I met on the boat coming to take me to dinner.

NOLAN. What's his name?

MARION. I've forgotten. He's just a boy I met on the boat.

NOLAN. How can anybody live the way you live?

MARION. It's a special talent, dear. (*Doorbell rings again.*) Minnie, go to the door. (MINNIE *comes in and exits hallway.*) This is my lucky day, Bunny.

NOLAN. Would you mind, in front of strangers, not calling me Bunny?

MARION. Oh, of course, what is it?

NOLAN (*irritated*). Leander.

MARION (*mnemonic*). Leander—Hellespont—Leander. . . . (MINNIE *comes downstage a few feet from the door.*)

MINNIE (*just inside the room*). It's the Junge who was here before—er sagt er ist ausgeschifft da—[13]

MARION. Oh, show him in, Minnie, and bring a cup for him too.

---

[12] Although Marion is being facetious, not all the names in this list are particularly flattering. Napoleon needs no explanation; Scipio was the Roman general who defeated Hannibal in 202 B.C. Mussolini was the modern dictator of Italy, who would have restored the ancient Roman power, but his dreams collapsed in the defeat of the Rome-Berlin Axis in the Second World War. In fairness to Marion, however, she is speaking of him as an outstanding strong man of Europe, already ten years in power and at the time of the play, not yet the hated enemy he was to become.

[13] *Junge* is youngster, or young boy. Minnie's German continues: "He says he has landed there."

MINNIE (*as she goes*). Ja.

NOLAN. And don't use these extravagant terms of endearment—anybody who didn't know you would misunderstand it. . . .

MARION (*very happy*). All right darling. (MINNIE *ushers in* RICHARD KURT, *goes out, comes back again with more tea.* MARION *comes forward to greet him.*) I'm so glad to see you again, Mr. ——. . . .

KURT. Kurt.

MARION. Oh. . . .

KURT. With a K.

MARION (*reassured*). Oh—I'll try to remember. This is Senator Nolan—Mr. Kurt. . . .

NOLAN (*glowering*). I am not Senator Nolan.

MARION. But you will be. (*She offers him a cup of tea, he takes it.*) Can't I just call you that—between ourselves? It gives me such a sense of quiet power. And maybe it'll impress my visitor. Do have a cup of tea, Mr. Kurt. (*She gives him one.*)

KURT (*puts his hat on sofa left*). I am not impressed by politicians. And I didn't come to drink tea. I am here on business. (*Nevertheless he takes a hearty sip.*)

MARION. Well, you can do both. They do in England. American businessmen are so tense.

KURT. I'm not a businessman.

NOLAN. Well, whatever you are, you are very ill-mannered.

KURT (*pleased*). That's true!

MARION (*delighted*). Isn't it nice you agree? For a moment I thought you weren't going to hit it off. . . .

NOLAN. In my day if a boy came in and behaved like this before a lady he'd be horsewhipped.

KURT. Well, when you get into the Senate you can introduce a horsewhipping bill. Probably bring you great kudos.

NOLAN. You talk like a Bolshevik.

KURT. Thank you! You talk like a Senator! (MARION *wants to laugh but thinks better of it. She looks at* KURT *with a new eye.*)

MARION (*quickly offering him more tea*). Another cup, Mr. Kurt. . . .

KURT (*taking it*). Thank you.

MARION. And one of these cakes—they're very nice . . . Minnie made them —almost as good as lebkuchen. Minnie spoils me.

KURT (*taking it*). Thank you. (*Eats cake.*) Having said, from our respective points of view, the worst thing we could say about each other, having uttered the ultimate insult, there's no reason we can't be friends, Senator. Damn good cake. No lunch as a matter of fact.

MARION. That's what's the matter with him—he was hungry—hungry boy. . . .

NOLAN (*puts teacup on piano*). He probably wants to sell you some insurance. . . .

KURT. Not at all. I'm not here to sell. I'm here to buy.

MARION. A picture!

KURT. Do I look like a picture-buyer?

MARION. As a matter of fact you don't . . . but I haven't anything to sell except pictures.

KURT (*confidently*). I think you have!

MARION (*to* NOLAN). This young man is very tantalizing.

NOLAN. Well, why don't you ask him to state his proposition and have done with it?

MARION (*turns to* KURT *and repeats mechanically*). State your proposition and have done with it.

KURT (*puts his cup down on table rear of sofa left*). What a nuisance women are!

NOLAN (*starting toward him*). Why, you insolent young whelp—I've half a mind to . . .

KURT (*pleasantly*). That's an impulse you'd better control. I wrote this lady a business letter asking for an appointment. She granted it to me at four o'clock. It is now six. In that interval I've climbed these five flights of stairs three times. I've lost over an hour of my life going away and coming back. An hour in which I might have read a first-class book or made love to a girl or had an idea—an irreparable hour. That's rudeness if you like. It's unbusinesslike. It's sloppy. (*To* MARION.) Now will you see me alone or will you keep me here fencing with this inadequate antagonist?

MARION. You are unquestionably the most impossible young man I've ever met. Go away!

KURT. Right! (*He turns to go and means it and she knows that he means it. And she is consumed with curiosity. As he goes.*) So long, Senator! Yours for the Revolution!

MARION (*as he reaches the door, goes after him—pleads pitifully*). Young man! Mr. Nolan is an old friend of mine. I should consult him in any case about whatever business you may suggest. Can't you speak in front of him? (*At the same time she shakes her head to him not to go away.*)

KURT. I cannot!

MARION. Please wait a minute. . . .

KURT. All right—one. (*He picks up a magazine and leafs through it negligently.*)

MARION (*to* LEANDER). After all, Leander, I can't afford—it may be something. . . . (*She takes his arm and starts walking him to the door, whispering.*) I'm just curious to hear what he's got to say for himself. . . .

NOLAN. I'm not sure it's safe to leave you alone with a character like that. . . .

MARION. Minnie's in her room . . . with a bow and arrow!

NOLAN (*going up to hall door*). I have to go in any case—I'm late now.

MARION. When will I see you, Bunny? (*She is at door with him.*)

NOLAN (*taking up his hat and coat*). I don't know. I'm very busy. I'll telephone you.

MARION. Do. Telephone me tonight. I'll tell you what he said. It'll probably be funny.

NOLAN (*out loud at* KURT). It pains me, Marion, that you are so unprotected that any hooligan— (KURT *turns page of magazine.*) can write you and come to see you in your apartment. However, that is the way you have chosen. Good night.

MARION. Good night, dear. Are you in the book? I'll telephone you . . .

NOLAN (*hastily*). No—no—you'd better not. I shall communicate with you. Good-bye.

KURT. Good-bye, Sir Galahad. (NOLAN *starts to retort, changes his mind and, in a very choleric mood, he goes out. There is a pause.*)

MARION. Well, I'm afraid you didn't make a very good impression on him!

KURT (*putting magazine away*). That's just too bad!

MARION. That's no way for a young man to get on in the world—he's a very important person.

KURT. That's what passes for importance. You're not taken in by him, are you? Stuffed shirt—flatulent and pompous—perfect legislator!

MARION. As a matter of fact he's a very nice man—simple and kindly. (*Gets cigarettes and offers one to* KURT *who takes it and lights it. She takes one too but he forgets to light hers.*)

KURT. I bet he isn't simple and he isn't kindly. I bet he's greedy and vicious. Anyway he's a hypocrite. When a man starts worrying out loud about unprotected women you may know he's a hypocritical sensualist.

MARION. You're a violent young man, aren't you? (*Not getting light from* KURT *she lights her own. Throwing match to floor.*)

KURT. Yes. The world is full of things and people that make me see red. . . . Why do you keep calling me youth and young man? I'm twenty-five.

MARION. Well, you seem to have the lurid and uncorrected imagination of the adolescent.

KURT. Imagination! That's where you're wrong. I may tell you, Miss Froude, that I'm as realistic as anybody you've ever met.

MARION (*sitting on upstage arm of sofa, right*). Anybody who'd be so unreasonable over a nice fellow like Bunny Nolan . . . if you only knew—if only you'd been present at the interview I had with him just before you came. You'd have seen how wrong you are about him. Why, he was—he was awfully funny—but he was also touching.

KURT. You're one of those tolerant people, aren't you—see the best in people?

MARION. You say that as if tolerance were a crime.

KURT. Your kind is. It's criminal because it encourages dishonesty, incompetence, weakness and all kinds of knavery. What you call tolerance I call sloppy laziness. You're like those book-reviewers who find something to praise in every mediocre book.

MARION. You are a fanatical young man.

KURT. Having said that you think you dispose of me. Well, so be it. I'm disposed of. Now, let's get down to business. (*His manner plainly says: "Well, why should I bother to convince you? What importance can it possibly have what you think of me?" It is not wasted on* MARION.)

MARION. You are also a little patronizing . . .

KURT (*pleased*). Am I?

MARION. However, I don't mind being patronized. That's where my tolerance comes in. It even amuses me a little bit. (*Crossing to piano seat.*) But as I have to change for dinner perhaps you'd better . . .

KURT. Exactly.

MARION. Please sit down . . . (*A moment . . . She sits on piano bench facing him.*)

KURT (*goes to piano and talks to her across it*). I am the editor of a magazine called Every Week. Do you know it?

MARION. It seems to me I've seen it on newsstands. . . .

KURT. You've never read it?

MARION. I'm afraid I haven't.

KURT. That is a tribute to your discrimination. We have an immense circulation. Three millions, I believe. With a circulation of that size you may imagine that the average of our readers' intelligence cannot be very high. Yet occasionally we flatter them by printing the highbrows—in discreet doses we give them, at intervals, Shaw and Wells and Chesterton.[14] So you'll be in good company anyway. . . .

MARION (*amazed*). *I* will?

KURT. Yes. I want you to write your biography to run serially in Every Week. Later of course you can bring it out as a book.

MARION. My biography!

KURT. Yes. The story of your life.

MARION (*with dignity*). I know the meaning of the word.

KURT. The money is pretty good. I am prepared to give you an advance of two thousand dollars.

MARION. Good Heavens, am I as old as that—that people want my biography?

KURT. We proceed on the theory that nothing exciting happens to people after they are forty. . . .

MARION. What a cruel idea!

KURT. Why wait till you're eighty? Your impressions will be dimmed by time. Most autobiographies are written by corpses. Why not do yours while you are still young, vital, in the thick of life?

MARION. But I'm not a writer. I shouldn't know how to begin.

KURT. You were born, weren't you? Begin with that.

MARION. I write pleasant letters, my friends tell me. . . . But look here, why should you want this story from me—why should anybody be interested?—I'm not a first-rate artist you know—not by far—I'm just clever. . . .

KURT (*bluntly*). It's not you—it's the celebrity of your subjects. . . .

MARION (*amused*). You're a brutal young man—I rather like you . . .

KURT. Well, you've been courageous. You've been forthright. For an American woman you've had a rather extraordinary career—you've done pretty well what you wanted. . . .

MARION. The - Woman - Who - Dared sort of thing. . . . Isn't that passé?

KURT. I think your life will make good copy. You might have stayed here and settled down and done Pictorial Review covers of mothers hovering fondly over babies. Instead you went to Europe and

---

[14] Marion would indeed be in elite company. George Bernard Shaw (1856–1950) was the greatest modern English dramatist, essayist, and critic; H. G. Wells (1866–1946) was an internationally famous English novelist, journalist, and social thinker; and G. K. Chesterton (1874–1936) was a noted English biographer, historian, and essayist. All three men were still active at the time of this play.

managed to get the most inaccessible people to sit for you. How did you do it?

MARION. You'd be surprised how accessible some of these inaccessible people are!

KURT. Well, that's just what I want to get from your story. Just that. Tell what happened to you, that's all. The impulse that made you leave home, that made you go, for instance, to Russia, before the popular emigration set in, that's made you wander ever since, that's kept you from settling down in any of the places where you had a chance to get established.

MARION (*quite seriously*). But supposing I don't know that. . . .

KURT. Well, that's interesting. That enigma is interesting. Maybe, while writing, you can solve it. It's a form of clarification. The more I talk to you the more I feel there's a great story in you and that you'll have great fun telling it.

MARION. Young man, you make me feel like an institution!

KURT. Should do you a lot of good in your professional career too—we'll reprint the portraits you've made of Lenin, Mussolini, Shaw—anything you like. . . . (*She begins to laugh, quietly at first, then heartily.*)

MARION. Forgive me. . . .

KURT (*unperturbed*). What's the matter?

MARION. Something I remembered— the funniest thing—isn't it funny how the oddest things pop into your mind?

KURT. What was it?

MARION. Something that happened years ago. . . .

KURT. What?

MARION. Oh, I couldn't possibly tell you. It wouldn't be fair!

KURT. In that case it'll probably be great for the magazine. Save it!

MARION (*frightened*). You won't do anything lurid, will you?

KURT. Just print the story—just as you write it—practically as you write it.

MARION. I'm scared! (*She puts out her cigarette in ash tray on the piano.*)

KURT. Nonsense. Here's your first check. Two thousand dollars. (*He puts the check down on the table in front of her.*)

MARION (*wretched suddenly, picks up check, rises, looks at check*). I can't tell you how old this makes me feel!

KURT. Suppose I asked you to write a novel! That wouldn't make you feel old, would it? Well, I'm simply asking you to write a novel of your life. The only lively reading these days is biography. People are bored with fiction. It's too tame. The fiction-writers haven't the audacity to put down what actually happens to people.

MARION. You may be disappointed, you know. You probably see headlines in your mind. The Woman of a Hundred Affairs, The Last of the Great Adventuresses, The Magda[15] Who Wouldn't Go Home. I promise you—it won't be a bit like that.

KURT. We'll announce it next month— first installment the following month. O.K.?

MARION (*puts down check, paces down right*). Oh dear! I can't promise a thing like that—I really can't. . . .

KURT. Why not?

MARION. It'll worry me too much.

KURT. Well, don't promise. Just get to work.

MARION (*faces him*). But what'll I do first?

KURT (*getting up*). Well, if I were you I'd sit down. (*She does so helplessly on piano bench.* KURT *then gives her paper, one of his own pencils.*) There now! You're all set!

MARION (*wailing*). How can I go out to dinner—how can I ever do anything— with a chapter to write?

KURT. After all you don't have to make up anything. Just tell what happened to you. (*He lights a fresh cigarette.*)

MARION. Can I use names?

---

[15] Magda, in Sudermann's *Die Heimat* (1893), returned to home and her father's wrath as the mother of an illegitimate child.

KURT. When they're prominent, yes. The obscure ones you can fake if you want to. Nobody'll know 'em anyway.

MARION (*looks at him*). Oh . . . What's your name?

KURT (*looks at her*). I told you—my name's Kurt.

MARION. I know—with a K—I can't call you Kurt! What's your *name?*

KURT (*sulkily*). Richard.

MARION. That's better. I tell you, Dickie, when I think—when I think—of the funny men I've known . . . they're pretty nearly all brothers under the skin you know, Dickie.

KURT. Well, that, as they say in the office, is an angle. (*Suddenly her fear vanishes and she is overcome with the marvelous possibilities.*)

MARION (*jumps up and leans toward him as if to kiss him, but quickly thinks better of it*). Dickie, I think it'll be marvelous! It'll be a knockout. And imagine— (*Picking up check.*) I'm going to be paid for it! Dickie, you're an angel!

KURT (*sardonically*). That's me. Angel Kurt! Well, so long. I'll be seeing you. (*Starts upstage toward hall door.*)

MARION (*suddenly panicky*). Oh, don't go!

KURT. You don't think I'm going to sit here and hold your hand while you're remembering your conquests, do you?

MARION. Well, you can't go away and leave me like this—alone with my life. . . .

KURT. Perhaps it's time you got a good, straight, clear-eyed look at it—alone by yourself, without anybody around to hold your hand. . . .

MARION (*suddenly*). No. I don't want to. (*Shrugs her shoulders as if she were cold.*) I think it would worry me. Besides, I feel superstitious about it.

KURT (*following her downstage*). Superstitious!

MARION. Yes. A kind of—ultimate act. After you've written your biography, what else could there possibly be left for you to do?

KURT. Collect material for another!

MARION. What could you do over again—that wouldn't be repetitious? (*Sits on right arm of sofa right.*)

KURT. It's repetitious to eat or to make love, isn't it? You keep on doing it.

MARION. You're cynical!

KURT (*almost spits it out*). You're sentimental.

MARION. I am—Sentimental Journey[16] —no, that's been used, hasn't it?

KURT. Don't worry about a title—I'll get that from the story after you've finished it.

MARION. There's something about it—I don't know—

KURT. What?

MARION. Vulgar. *Everybody* spouting memoirs. Who cares?

KURT. Well, wrong hunch! Sorry to have taken your valuable time. Goodbye.

MARION (*the finality frightens her*). What do you mean?

KURT (*he is withering—crosses to her*). I'm prepared to admit I was mistaken—that's all. In your desire to escape vulgarity you would probably be—thin. You might even achieve refinement. I'm not interested. Padded episodes hovering on the edge of amour—

MARION (*turns on him*). Young man, you're insufferable!

KURT. And you're a false alarm!

MARION (*after a moment*). I congratulate you! You've brought me to the verge of losing my temper! But I tell you this—you're quite mistaken about the character of my life—and about my relations with my friends. My story won't be thin and episodic because my life hasn't been thin and episodic. And I won't have to pad—the problem will be to select. I'm going to write the damn thing just to show you. Come in tomorrow afternoon for a cocktail.

KURT. Whose memoirs are these going to be, yours or mine?

MARION. Well, you're an editor, aren't you? (*She smiles at him.*) Come in and edit.

KURT. All right, I'll come. But if you

[16] Volume of autobiographical sketches by Laurence Sterne, 1768.

aren't here I'll go away. I won't wait a minute. (*He goes out quickly.* MARION *stands looking after him, inclined to laugh, and yet affected. This is a new type even for her.*)

MARION (*she speaks to herself*). What an extraordinary young man! (*In a moment* KURT *comes back in.* MARION *is very glad to see him, greets him as if there had been a long separtaion.*) Oh, hello!

KURT (*embarrassed*). I forgot my hat! (*He can't see it at once.*)

MARION (*without moving nor looking away from him, she indicates the hat on the sofa left*). There it is! Right next to mine.

KURT (*crosses for it*). Oh yes. (*Picks up the hat.*) Thanks. (*For a moment he stands uncertainly, hat in hand, looking at* MARION *who has not taken her eyes off him. He is embarrassed.*) Well, so long!

MARION. So long. (KURT *leaves again. She stands as before looking after him. She turns toward the piano—sees the check—picks it up and reads it to make sure it's true. The whole thing has a slightly fantastic quality to her. She is very happy and excited. She waves the check in her hand like a pennant and humming she crosses to the piano seat and sits and plays the waltz from "Danubia." She sees the pad and pencil on the piano and stops playing and, picking up the pencil and the pad, she crosses to the small armchair in the upstage end of the window and sits with her feet on the window seat. She repeats the first words of the first chapter aloud to herself as she writes them down.*) I am born . . . (MINNIE *enters from door left to get the tea things she had left on the model stand.* MARION *taps the pencil on the pad as she repeats the words.*) I am born . . . (*The time seems remote to her.*) I am born—I meet Richard Kurt —Well, Minnie, here's the outline—I am born . . . I meet Richard Kurt—now all I have to do is to fill in. . . . (MINNIE, *used to having irrelevancies addressed to her, takes this program rather stolidly.*)

MINNIE. Was, Marion?[17]

MARION (*trying to get rid of her*). Fix something light, will you, Minnie . . . I'm not going out.

MINNIE. Aber der Junge kommt![18]

MARION. What Junge?

MINNIE. Der Junge dem Sie . . .[19]

MARION. Oh, yes! The Junge I met on the boat. You'll have to send him away. I can't go out tonight. From now on, Minnie, no more frivolous engagements!

MINNIE (*astonished*). Sie bleiben ganzen abend zu Hause?[20]

MARION. Yes, Minnie. I'm spending the evening alone with my life . . . (*She remembers* KURT'S *words and repeats them as if, after all, they have made a profound impression on her.*) . . . get a good, straight, clear-eyed look at it . . .

MINNIE (*picks up the tea tray and, bustling toward the kitchen, promising delights*). Ein fleisch brühe und pfannkuchen![21] (MINNIE *exits door left.*)

MARION (*already brooding over her past*). I am born. . . .

SLOWLY THE CURTAIN FALLS.

ACT TWO

SCENE: *The same. About three weeks later. Afternoon.*

AT RISE: MARION *is putting some touches on the full-length portrait of* LEANDER NOLAN *which stands away from the audience. She is wearing her working costume, baggy red corduroy trousers, a sash and a worn blue smock over a kind of sweater-jacket. She is very happy. . . . On the piano nearby are*

[17] "What, Marion?"
[18] "But the young man is coming!"
[19] "The young man whom you . . ."
[20] "You're going to stay home all evening?"
[21] "Beef broth and pancakes."

her writing things. While touching up
LEANDER *she is struck by an idea for her
book. Puts down her brush and palette
and goes to the piano to jot down some
notes. The idea pleases her. She giggles
to herself. Then she returns to her easel.*
MINNIE *comes in and stands watching
her a moment before* MARION *sees her.*

MARION (*sees* MINNIE *at last*). Oh yes,
Minnie—do you want anything?

MINNIE. You asked me to come right
away, Marion.

MARION. Did I?

MINNIE. Ja. (*Sitting on sofa right.*)
Zo! You have left a note on the kitchen
I should come in right away I am back
from the market.

MARION (*studying the portrait*). Of
course I did. That's right, Minnie.

MINNIE. Well, what did you want,
Marion?

MARION (*washing paint brush in tur-
pentine jar*). Did I tell you there'd be
two for dinner?

MINNIE. Ja. Gewiss! Das ist vy I vent
to the market.[22]

MARION. Well, I've changed my plans.
I'm dining out with Feydie after all.

MINNIE (*rising and looking at picture*).
Ach, Gott! (*She studies the portrait.*)

MARION (*looks humorously at* MINNIE
and puts her arm about MINNIE'S *shoulders*). Gut?

MINNIE. Ziemlich gut—[23]

MARION. Do you know who it is?

MINNIE. Oh, das sieht man ja gleich.
Das ist Herr Nolan![24]

MARION (*shaking her hand in gratitude*). Thank you, Minnie. (*Doorbell rings.*) See who that is, will you,
Minnie?

MINNIE. Fraulein ist zu hause?

MARION. Ich erwarte Herr Feydak.
Für ihn bin ich immer zu hause.[25]

MINNIE. (*agreeing heartily as she
crosses to the door*). Ja, Ja, der Herr
Feydak. . . . (MINNIE *goes out.* MARION
jots down a note on the pad which is on

the piano. FEYDAK *enters.* MINNIE *closes
the door and exits left.*)

MARION (*at piano*). Hello, Feydie!
Sit down!

FEYDAK. Well, my dear, which career
do I interrupt?

MARION (*laughing*). I don't know!

FEYDAK. One comes to see you with
diffidence nowadays. (FEYDAK *removes
coat and hat and places them on the upstage end of the sofa right, and sits on
the left side of the sofa.*)

MARION. While I'm painting I think
of funny things to say, funny phrases.
It won't be a serious biography, thank
God. I'm dedicating it to Vicki: "To
Vicki—the gayest person I have ever
known!" By the way, have you got any
little snapshots of Vicki—all I've got are
formal photographs with his orders. I'd
like to get something a little more intimate.

FEYDAK. I'll hunt some up for you.

MARION. Have you heard from the
Powers yet, when you are to leave?

FEYDAK. Tomorrow.

MARION (*stricken—sits right of him*).
Feydie!

FEYDAK (*fatalistically*). Tomorrow.
(*They sit.*) I shall leave you with sorrow, Marion.

MARION. I'll have no one to laugh
with.

FEYDAK. For me it's an exile.

MARION. You'll have a wonderful time.
I shall miss you terribly.

FEYDAK. Perhaps you'll come out.

MARION. Perhaps I will. I've always
wanted to go to China. If I have enough
money left from all my labors I'll stop
in on you—en route to China.

FEYDAK. That would be marvelous.

MARION. You know writing one's life
has a sobering effect on one—you get
it together and you think: "Well! look
at the damn thing . . ."

FEYDAK. Do you want to be impressive?

---

[22] "Yes. Certainly! That is why," etc. Minnie is never quite certain which language to use.
[23] "Pretty good—"
[24] "Oh, you can see that immediately. That's Herr Nolan!"
[25] "Are you at home?"
"I'm expecting Herr Feydak. I'm always at home for him."

MARION. Well, I don't want to be trivial . . .

FEYDAK. I think *you* escape that.

MARION. My friendships haven't been trivial. . . . (*She gives his hand a squeeze.*)

FEYDAK. Have you seen that bombastic young man?

MARION. Oh, yes. He comes in every once in a while to see how I'm getting on. He's quite insulting. Underneath his arrogance I suspect he's very uncertain.

FEYDAK. Oh, now, don't tell me he has an inferiority complex!

MARION. Well, I think he has!

FEYDAK. The new psychology is very confusing. In my simple day you said: "That young man is bumptious and insufferable" and you dismissed him. Now you say: "He has an inferiority complex" and you encourage him to be more bumptious and more insufferable. It's very confusing.

MARION. There's a kind of honesty about him that I like.

FEYDAK (*instantly putting two and two together*). Oh!

MARION. Nothing like that, Feydie! As a matter of fact—I don't mind telling you . . . I like him very much—

FEYDAK. I think he is destined . . .

MARION. He's not interested. He's some kind of fanatic. Social, I think: I've met that kind in Russia—quite unassailable. But I'm optimistic. . . . (*They laugh.*) Well, one must never despair, must one. Life is so much more resourceful and resilient than one is oneself. Three weeks ago when you came to see me I felt quite at the end of my rope. I didn't tell you quite but I actually didn't know which way to turn. I felt tired too—which troubled me. Well, now I find myself, quite suddenly, (*She indicates portrait.*) doing Leander and—(*She indicates manuscript on piano.*) doing myself. New Vista. Very exciting.

FEYDAK. All this enthusiasm for art alone?

MARION (*laughing*). Of course!—Feydie, what did you think?

FEYDAK. I don't believe it.

MARION. Come here and have a look at Leander!

FEYDAK (*he rises—walks to the canvas on the easel*). Hm! Formal!

MARION. It's to hang in the White House. (*She winks at him, he laughs, puts his arm around her shoulder.*)

FEYDAK. Marion, you're adorable! (*They walk downstage together, their arms around each other's shoulders, very affectionately.*)

MARION. Oh, Feydie, I'm having a wonderful time. Quiet too. Writing *enforces* silence and solitude on one. I've always lived in such a rush—a kind of interminable scherzo. . . .

FEYDAK. Good title! . . .

MARION. Think so? I'll put it down. . . . (*Writes on pad on piano. FEYDAK sits on right arm of sofa left, facing her.*) Interminable scherzo. . . . How do you spell it? A little affected. Might do for a chapter heading maybe. . . . (*Returns to him—sitting on model stand—facing him.*) But I realize now I haven't in years had time to stop and think. I sit here for hours, Feydie, and nothing comes to me. Then, suddenly, the past will come in on me with such a rush— odd, remote, semi-forgotten things of the past. Are they true? How much is true? One can never be sure, can one? I remember certain griefs and fears. I remember their existence without recalling at all their intensity—their special anguish. Why? What was the matter with me? What made them so acute? It is like recalling a landscape without color, a kind of color-blindness of the memory. (*Doorbell rings. She calls out to her factotum.*) Minnie! (*MINNIE enters left and crosses rapidly to hall door. MARION arranges the model stand on which stands the papal armchair in red and gold.*) This is probably the Hon. Nolan. He's due for a sitting. He pretends he doesn't like to have his picture painted, but I know he does. (*MINNIE enters from hallway. She is flustered and giggly.*)

MINNIE (*very high-pitched voice*). Herr Varvick Vilson!

MARION. Tympi Wilson!

MINNIE (*to* FEYDAK). Der *film star!*

FEYDAK. So?

MINNIE (*radiant*). Ja! Ja!

MARION. Oh, Feydie, you'll adore this. Ask him in, Minnie.

MINNIE (*as she goes out to admit* WILSON). Gott, ist er schön![26]

MARION. Warwick's public.

FEYDAK. And mine!

MARION (*in a quick whisper*). Whatever you do—outstay him! (MINNIE *has opened the door and* WARWICK WILSON *enters. He is very handsome, explosively emotional, and given to cosmic generalization. He is in evening clothes, a red carnation in his buttonhole.*)

WILSON (*crossing to* MARION *and kissing her hand*). Marion!

MARION. Warwick!

WILSON. Darling! How are you?

MARION. I'm splendid. Been up all night?

WILSON. No, no! This is business. (MINNIE *has crossed to kitchen door upper left, never taking her eyes from* WILSON.)

MARION. This is Mr. Feydak. Mr. Warwick Wilson, the famous film star.

WILSON (*crosses to sofa and shakes hands with* FEYDAK—*dramatically*). Feydak! *The* Mr. Feydak?

FEYDAK (*again mistaken for his brother*). Ja.

WILSON. I've heard of you indeed!

FEYDAK. Have you? Thanks.

MARION. Mr. Feydak is on his way to Hollywood. He is to write the music for . . .

WILSON (*sits on the model stand—facing front*). Of course! I am honored, Mr. Feydak—deeply honored. That unforgettable waltz—how does it go? . . . (*He starts to hum with a swaying gesture the waltz from the "Merry Widow."*) Music's my one passion!

MARION. Once you said it was me.

WILSON. A lot of good it did me!

MARION (*to* WILSON). Well, tell me . . . (*She sees* MINNIE, *who is still star-*

ing at WILSON.) Look at Minnie. The mere sight of you has upset her so that she's speechless.

MINNIE. Aber, Fraulein![27] (WILSON *rises graciously and gives* MINNIE *a friendly wave of the hand. He's no snob.* MINNIE, *speechless with delight, exits left.* WILSON *returns to his position on the model stand.*)

MARION. All right, Minnie! Warwick, Warwick! You musn't do things like that to Minnie, at her age!

WILSON (*tragically*). There you are! This face! This cursed face! I should go masked really. One has no private life!

MARION (*sits in throne chair on model stand*). What would you do with it if you had it, eh, Tympi?

WILSON (*delighted*). That nickname!

MARION. It just rolled off my tongue. Did I call you that?

WILSON. You did! You invented it. No one's called me that since you left Hollywood. And you promised to explain the significance to me, but you never did.

MARION. Did it have a significance?

FEYDAK. Marion has a knack for nicknames.

MARION. I love 'em. I'd like to do a chapter on nicknames.

WILSON (*highly pleased*). Tympi! Tympi! (*Very patronizing to* FEYDAK.) You are an intuitive person, Mr. Feydak. I can see that. (FEYDAK *ad libs: "Danke schön."*[28]) Can you imagine what she meant?

FEYDAK. Her vagaries are beyond me, Mr. Wilson.

WILSON (*leaning back toward* MARION). Speak, Oracle! No! Don't tell me now. Put it into that book you're writing.

MARION (MARION *and* FEYDAK *exchange glances*). How things get around.

WILSON. It's been in the back of my mind for years, Marion . . . to have you paint me. Now that we're both in town together . . .

---

[26] "God, is he good looking!"

[27] "But Miss!"

[28] "Thanks a lot."

MARION. Well, I'd *love* to . . .

WILSON. In the costume of the Dane. (MARION *and* FEYDAK *exchange a look. Strikes a pose.*) I'd like to be done in *his* costume. I hope, Mr. Feydak, that they won't break your spirit in Hollywood as they've almost broken mine!

FEYDAK (*with a smile*). My spirit is indestructible!

WILSON (*rises and crosses to rear of sofa and pats* FEYDAK *on the back*). I'm glad to hear it. (*Returns to left of model stand and stands with his right foot on it.*) You know, for years I've been begging them to do Shakespeare. (*Gesticulates.*)

MARION (*interrupting him*). Sit down and be comfortable.

WILSON. They simply won't listen. But I'm going to give up acting and produce!

MARION. Oh, good God! Don't do that!

WILSON. Why not?

MARION. What would Minnie do with her night off?

WILSON (*smiles*). My public, eh?

MARION. Yes!

WILSON. Quite so! (*Patronizingly.*) You artists who work in media like painting or literature— (*To* FEYDAK.) or music, that too is a beautiful art, Mr. Feydak—transcends speech—transcends everything; by saying nothing it says all.

FEYDAK. Ja! (*The doorbell rings.*)

WILSON. You are certainly lucky compared to us poor actors. We— (MINNIE *enters and crosses to hall door upper center.*) Wouldn't it be ironic if all that remained of me after I am gone were your painting of me? That is why I want it, perhaps—my poor grasp on immortality.

FEYDAK. You see, Marion, you confer immortality!

MARION. I think immortality is an over-rated commodity. But tell me, Tympi, what are you doing away from Hollywood?

MINNIE (*comes in announcing*). Der Herr Nolan! (MINNIE *then looks at* WILSON. WILSON *stands—looks at* MINNIE.)

MARION. Show him in. Show him in. (*With a lingering look at* WILSON, MINNIE *goes back. To others, after watching* MINNIE *exit.*) You see!

FEYDAK. The effect is instantaneous—like music. . . . (NOLAN *enters.* MINNIE *follows* NOLAN *in and exits into kitchen, murmuring ecstatically, "Gott! Ist er schön!", looking at* WILSON.)

MARION. Hello, Bunny. (*Introducing* NOLAN.) You know Mr. Feydak. Mr. Nolan, this is Warwick Wilson, you've heard of him. (FEYDAK *bows to* NOLAN, *who returns the bow.*)

WILSON. It's a pleasure, Mr. Nolan. I've heard of you indeed! (*They shake hands.*)

MARION. You're late for your sitting, Bunny. Will the presence of these gentlemen embarrass you? I don't mind if you don't.

NOLAN (*has entered rather worried and angry. He has a magazine rolled in his hand. He now speaks very irritatedly*). As a matter of fact, Marion . . .

MARION (*putting him in throne chair on model stand*). Oh, sit down, like a good fellow. The light is getting bad. (NOLAN *sits.* WILSON *sits on the right arm of the sofa left on which* FEYDAK *is sitting.* MARION *gets to work on* BUNNY.) How did you find me, Tympi?

WILSON. I read in a magazine that you were barging into literature . . .

NOLAN (*half rising, showing magazine*). This is true then!

MARION. Don't get up, Bunny . . . (*Nevertheless she takes the magazine and looks at it.*) Well, Dickie has gone and spread himself, hasn't he? (*She sits on sofa left between* WILSON *and* FEYDAK.) Look here, Feydie! (*Shows him the full-page announcement of her book in magazine.*)

FEYDAK (*looking*). Do you think you can live up to this?

MARION. Why will they write this sort of thing? (*Rises and goes back.*) Makes me out a kind of female Casanova. (*She drops the magazine on the stand at* NOLAN's *feet.*) Well, they'll be disappointed.

NOLAN (*bitterly*). Will they?

MARION. Bunny! (*But she thinks nothing of it—merely pushes him into a better light.*)

FEYDAK (*tactfully—he senses danger*). May I ask, Mr. Wilson—are you making a picture at the moment?

WILSON. No, I'm in New York making some personal appearances.

MARION. Personal appearances. I love that phrase. Has such an air of magnanimity about it. (*Crosses to painting.*)

WILSON. Pretty boring, I can tell you! I've got writer's cramp signing autograph books. It's a perfect martyrdom I assure you. It's no fun at all. (WILSON *crosses to stand—puts his right foot on it, leans on his knee with his right arm and studies* NOLAN, *his face not six inches away from* NOLAN'S. NOLAN *fidgets.*)

MARION. I can imagine! What's the matter, Bunny? You seem under a strain today . . . not relaxed.

NOLAN (*bursting out and glaring at all of them*). It's like being watched while you're taking a bath!

MARION. Oh, I'm so sorry, Bunny!

FEYDAK (*rising*). I quite sympathize with Mr. Nolan.

WILSON (*moves away*). Supposing I were so shy, eh, Mr. Nolan?

FEYDAK (*crosses to* MARION *who is above her easel, right*). I'm off, Marion. (*Kisses her hand.*) Auf wiedersehen![29]

MARION (*meaningfully*). You'll have to go— (WILSON *sits again on arm of sofa left.*) both of you . . .

WILSON (*rises*). I was just going myself. My next appearance is at 6:45. (*Speaks to others.*)

FEYDAK (*to help her*). Perhaps I can drop you, Mr. Wilson.

WILSON (*faces* FEYDAK). No, I'll drop you . . . (*Turns to* MARION.) I say, Marion . . . (FEYDAK, *helpless, goes upstage putting on coat.*)

MARION. Yes, Tympi?

WILSON. If you started my portrait right away and it turns out—I am sure it will turn out—you might put it in your book, mightn't you? I'm frankly sick of just appearing in fan magazines.

MARION. We'll see. Why not?

WILSON. Splendid! *Don't fail to come tonight.* Good-bye, dearest Marion. Good-bye again, Mr. Nolan. (*He starts to shake* NOLAN'S *hand but is interrupted by* MARION, *almost screaming.*)

MARION. No, no, no! Don't do *that*—don't touch him.

WILSON. Most happy! See you later. . . . (*He waves himself off at last—* MARION *returns to her easel.*)

MARION (*to* FEYDAK). Don't forget—I'm dining with you.

FEYDAK (*like the player in "Hamlet" who burlesques Polonius*). Most happy—see you later. (FEYDAK *leaves.*)

MARION (*with relief*). Now then . . .

NOLAN (*muttering to himself*). Silly ass!

MARION (*working on painting*). That young man is one of the most famous people in the world, do you realize that, Bunny? His profile follows you all over Europe—*and* Asia. Ubiquitous profile. Have you ever seen him?

NOLAN (*unswerved*). He's a silly ass!

MARION. I admit he's somewhat on that side—but that other one—that Feydie—he's the darling of the world!

NOLAN (*very short—bitterly*). Evidently!

MARION (*surprised*). Bunny!

NOLAN (*savage now*). Who isn't a darling? Everyone's a darling as far as I can see! The world's full of darlings. Your world at any rate.

MARION. But, darling . . . (*She suddenly stops—sits at right end of sofa right.*) Oh, Bunny, I remember now!

NOLAN. You remember what?

MARION. Tympi! Why I nicknamed him Tympi. Don't you see?

NOLAN. No, I don't see . . .

MARION. For tympanum—a large instrument in the orchestra producing a hollow sound. (*She beats an imaginary drum with her paint brush.*) Boom! (*Suddenly* NOLAN *quits the pose.*) What is it?

NOLAN. I can't sit today. I'm not in the mood.

[29] "Good-bye."

MARION. I could tell there was something worrying you.

NOLAN. There is something worrying me!

MARION. Well, what is it?

NOLAN. This confounded story! Are you really writing it?

MARION. Well, yes—I am.

NOLAN. What do you intend to tell?

MARION. Well, that's a rather difficult question to answer—it's like asking me what I've been doing all my life.

NOLAN. When does this biography start?

MARION (beginning to wonder about this questioning). With my birth—coincidence, isn't it?

NOLAN. All the time back home—when you were a girl in Knoxille?

MARION. Yes, of course. I've had a wonderful time going back over it all.

NOLAN. Everything?

MARION. Everything I can remember.

NOLAN. Do I come into it?

MARION (smiling to herself). You do! You certainly do!

NOLAN. You must leave me out of that story!

MARION. But Bunny, how can I possibly leave you out?

NOLAN. You must, that's all!

MARION. But how can I? You were too important—think of the rôle you played in my life. By your own confession, Bunny darling, you—you started me. That's a good idea for a chapter heading, isn't it? "Bunny Starts Me." I must put that down.

NOLAN. This is no joke, Marion. (With menace.) I warn you . . .

MARION. Warn me! Let me understand you. Are you seriously asking me to give up an opportunity like this just because . . .

NOLAN (rises and gets down from the model stand. Speaks with brutal command). Opportunity! Cheap exhibitionism! A chance to flaunt your affairs in a rag like this. (Indicating magazine on piano.) I won't be drawn into it. I can tell you that! (He is in a towering rage.)

MARION (after a pause). I know that by your standards, Bunny, I'm a loose character. But there are other standards, there just are.

NOLAN (crosses to center—drops magazine on model stand). Not in Tennessee!

MARION (rises). I'm afraid you're provincial, Bunny.

NOLAN. I'm sorry.

MARION (takes off her smock, crosses to small table down right, gets her notes, then crosses to desk upper right). I don't care what the advertisements say about my story—I know what I'm writing . . .

NOLAN. I'm sorry.

MARION. That's all right. (But this has gone pretty deep.)

NOLAN (after a pause). If you're doing this for money— (She turns and watches him.) I know you've been pretty hard up—I promise you I'll get you commissions enough to more than make up for this story. I was talking about you only the other day to my prospective father-in-law. He's a big man, you know. I am sure I can get him to sit for you . . .

MARION. The tip isn't big enough.

NOLAN (scared now that he sees the extent to which he has hurt her). Marion! . . .

MARION. It amuses me to write my life. I am pleasure-loving—you know that—I will therefore pass up the opportunity of painting your big father-in-law. I will even give up the pleasure of painting you. And we can part friends, then, can't we? (She reaches out her hand to him.) Good-bye, Bunny.

NOLAN (devastated). Marion—you can't do this to me—you can't send me away like this . . .

MARION. I don't think I've ever in my life had a vulgar quarrel with anyone. This is the nearest I've come to it. I'm a little annoyed with you for that. I think it's better we part now while we can still do so with some—dignity. Shall we?

NOLAN. You don't realize what's involved—or you wouldn't' talk like that. . . .

MARION. What is involved?

NOLAN. My entire career. That's what's involved.

MARION. Oh!

NOLAN. This is the most critical moment of my life. My fiancée's father is the most powerful leader of opinion in my state. Frankly, I depend on him for support. To have this kind of thing bandied about now might cause a permanent rift between him and me—might seriously interfere, not only with my candidacy for the Senate, but with my marriage.

MARION. They are interlocking—I quite understand.

NOLAN. A revelation of this kind—coming at this moment—might be fatal . . .

MARION. Revelation! You make me feel like—I can't tell you what you make me feel like . . . (*She laughs—semihysterically.*)

NOLAN (*sepulchral*). You must give this up, Marion.

MARION. I've met distinguished men abroad—politicians, statesmen—a Prime Minister even—and this kind of "revelation"—as you so luridly call it—is no more to them than a theme for after-dinner banter. They take it in their stride. My God, Bunny, you take it so big!

NOLAN. These people I'm depending on to elect me aren't sophisticated like you or me. (MARION *looks at* NOLAN *with some surprise.*) What I mean is—they're country people essentially—my future father-in-law is sympathetic to their point of view.

MARION. Tell me—your father-in-law, is he the man with the chest expansion?

NOLAN. He's a fine sturdy man—as you perhaps know, he makes a fetish of exercise.

MARION (*bubbling again*). You see his pictures in shorts in health magazines.

NOLAN. There's no disgrace in that.

MARION (*sits on right arm of sofa left.*) It doesn't shock me, Bunny. I was just identifying him, that's all.

NOLAN. I owe everything to Kinnicott —I wouldn't be running for the Senate right now if not for him. I can't risk offending him.

MARION. What the devil's happened to you anyway? You used to be quite a nice boy—even fun occasionally . . .

NOLAN (*wistful—turns away*). Maybe —if you had stuck to me . . .

MARION. Ts! Ts! Ts! Poor Bunny. I'm sorry for you. Really I am. (*She strokes his arm.*)

NOLAN (*suddenly passionate—faces her*). Don't touch me!

MARION (*amazed*). Bunny!

NOLAN. Do you think I'm not human!

MARION. Well, if you aren't the most contradictory . . .

NOLAN. I realized the moment I came in here the other day—the moment I saw you . . .

MARION (*interrupting*). But Bunny! you're engaged and you're going to be a Senator.

NOLAN (*walks away from her*). Forget it! Forget I ever said it. . . .

MARION. You bewilder me . . .

NOLAN (*bitterly*). I'm not surprised I bewilder you. You've spent your life among a lot of foreign counts. It's well known that foreigners are more immoral than we are.

MARION. I'm very touched. I am really. (*She kisses him in a friendly way.*)

NOLAN. Don't do that! I forbid you!

MARION. All right. I'll never attack you again, I promise.

NOLAN. I wish I had never come back into your life—it was a terrible mistake—you'd forgotten me.

MARION (*seriously*). Oh, you're wrong. First love—one doesn't forget that.

NOLAN (*passionately*). But you did! You forgot me! And if you got the chance again, you'd humiliate me again.

MARION. Humiliate! What queer notions you have— Is it a question of pride or vanity between us? We're old friends —friends.

NOLAN (*moves a step right*). Please forget this—I don't know what came over me—I . . .

MARION. Of course. There's nothing to forget. (*Moves a step toward him.*) It's quite all right, dear . . . (*She pats him on his hand.*) . . . Oh, excuse me . . .

NOLAN. I warn you, Marion—I solemnly warn you—if you persist in this—

MARION. Never in my life have I seen a man vacillate so between passion and threat . . .

NOLAN. I shall find ways to stop you. Mr. Kinnicott, my future father-in-law, is a powerful man.

MARION. I know. Extraordinary biceps.

NOLAN. I warn you, Marion. This matter is beyond flippancy.

MARION (sits). There'll be some very distinguished people in my biography. You needn't be ashamed.

NOLAN. That movie-actor!

MARION. Tympi in Hamlet costume— you in a toga. I'll print your portraits on opposite pages—my two men!

NOLAN. You are malicious!

MARION. I must admit, Bunny, that you provoke in me all my malicious impulses. You come here suddenly and you convey to me what I've missed in not marrying you. (The back-door bell rings. MINNIE crosses to answer it during MARION's speech.) You dangle before me the inventory of your felicities —a career, a fortune, a fabulous bride— and then, because I get a chance to chronicle my own adventures—you object—you tell me I mustn't! I have a nice nature, Bunny, or I should be angry—I should be indignant. (KURT enters.)

NOLAN (sharply and with threat). Now, Marion, I've warned you . . . You'll regret this.

MARION. Hello, Dickie, do talk to Bunny for a minute, will you? (Crosses to the stairs and starts up them to her bedroom.) I've simply got to change. (MINNIE enters up center and exits left.) Feydie's coming to take me out to dinner.

NOLAN. But, Marion . . .

MARION. I couldn't do anything about this in any case, Bunny dear, because I've promised Dickie. In fact, I signed something, didn't I, Dickie? Don't go away, either of you. . . . (MARION blows them a kiss and exits into her bedroom. A pause between the two men. KURT crosses downstage to above the model stand. Suddenly, NOLAN goes to KURT and reaches out his hand to him.)

NOLAN. How do you do, young man?

KURT (very much surprised). How do you do? (He looks at him narrowly, his head a little on one side, a terrier appraising a mastiff.)

NOLAN. I am very glad to see you.

KURT. Isn't that nice . . . ?

NOLAN. You may be surprised to learn that on the one occasion when we met you made quite an impression on me.

KURT. Did I?

NOLAN (sits on sofa right). You did. Sit down. In fact—I hope you don't mind—if you will allow me as a prerogative of seniority—to ask you a few questions. I have a purpose in mind and not—I trust—an idle purpose.

KURT. Shoot! (Sits.) Anything to enlighten the professor! (He knows he is going to be pumped and has decided to be casual, naive and even respectful.)

NOLAN (clearing his throat). Now then—your present position on the magazine you represent—have you been on it long?

KURT. About two years.

NOLAN. And before that?

KURT. Newspaper work.

NOLAN. And before that?

KURT. Tramping around the world. Odd jobs. Quite a variety.

NOLAN. College?

KURT. Believe it or not—Yale—two years . . . worked my way through— washed dishes.

NOLAN. Very interesting preparation . . . very interesting . . . Tell me now —your present work—do you find it interesting? Is the remuneration satisfactory?

KURT. Two hundred smackers a week. That's twice what I've ever earned in my life before.

NOLAN. Now then—to come to the point—no doubt you've heard of my prospective father-in-law, Mr. Orrin Kinnicott?

KURT. Heard of him! We pay him the compliment of imitation. He is our model, our criterion, our guiding star!

NOLAN. As you know, Mr. Kinnicott's interests are varied. He owns some powerful newspapers in my state. The other day I heard him say that he wanted a new man in Washington.

KURT (*playing naively excited*). Now that's something to give one's eye-teeth for!

NOLAN (*pleased at the result*). I think it might be possible to swing it—very possible.

KURT. God, what a break!

NOLAN. As it happens, Mr. Kinnicott is at present in town. I shall arrange an appointment for you in the next few days. Naturally, I expect you to keep the matter entirely confidential.

KURT. Naturally! You needn't worry on that score, Senator, I assure you.

NOLAN. Thank you, Mr. Kurt. That is all I ask. (*A pause.*)

KURT. Mr. Nolan—do you mind if I ask *you* something?

NOLAN. Certainly not . . .

KURT. You won't consider me impertinent?

NOLAN (*with a smile*). I don't object to impertinence, Mr. Kurt. I was often considered impertinent myself when I was your age.

KURT. Why are you making me this offer?

NOLAN. I am not making you an offer. I shall merely attempt to expedite . . .

KURT. Why? The first time we met we didn't exactly hit it off, now, did we? Why then are you going to all this trouble?

NOLAN. I have discussed you with Miss Froude, who is an old friend of mine and whose opinion I greatly respect. She thinks very highly of you, Mr. Kurt. My own impression . . .

KURT (*inexorably*). Why? What, as they say, is the pay-off?

NOLAN. I'll tell you. I'll tell you quite frankly. I don't want Miss Froude's autobiography, which you have persuaded her to write, to appear in your magazine. I want it killed!

KURT. Oh! You want it killed?

NOLAN. Exactly.

KURT. Why?

NOLAN. Marion knows why. We needn't go into that.

KURT (*wounded by a sudden and devastating jealousy*). Good God! You! You too! (MARION *enters from balcony. She is wearing a dove-colored evening dress—the gamine transformed into lady-of-the-world.*)

MARION. Well! How have you two boys been getting on? What do you think?

KURT (*seething. Crosses to foot of stairs*). I'll tell you what I think. . . .

MARION. About the dress, I mean . . . (*She does a turn for them.*)

NOLAN (*without looking up at her or the dress. He is watching KURT*). It's charming.

MARION. Thank you, Bunny. With all his faults Bunny is much more satisfactory than you are, Dickie.

KURT (*at boiling point*). He's chivalrous, he is! His chivalry is so exquisite that he has just been attempting to bribe me to keep your story from being published. His gallantry is so delicate that he's terrified about being mentioned in it.

MARION (*comes downstairs during* KURT's *speech*). Don't be so worked up about it, Dickie. You're another one who takes it big. It's catching!

KURT (*flaring at her*). You're not very sensitive. . . .

MARION. Why should I be? You misapprehend Bunny. If he doesn't want to be in the same story with me that's his business. And it's nothing to do with chivalry or gallantry or nonsense like that.

NOLAN. Marion,—this young man . . .

KURT (*taunting him*). What about Washington, Mr. Nolan? Mr. Nolan, a prospective Senator, offers to bribe me with a post in Washington controlled by his prospective father-in-law. . . .

MARION. If it's a good job take it, Dickie, by all means. . . .

KURT. I am afraid, Marion, that your code is more relaxed than mine . . .

MARION. Code, nonsense! I gave up codes long ago. I'm a big laissez-faire girl!

NOLAN. If this young man is an example of the distinguished company you've come to associate with, Marion . . .

MARION. Don't quarrel, children—please. It distresses me.

NOLAN. He's extremely objectionable.

KURT. What about Washington, now, *Senator?* Are you still willing to expedite . . . (KURT *and* NOLAN *stand glaring at each other.* MARION *tries to calm the troubled waters. Crosses to* NOLAN.)

MARION. Really, Dickie, you're very naughty. Don't mind him, Bunny. He's very young.

KURT. And incorruptible!

NOLAN. Marion, I claim the privilege of a friendship that antedates Mr. Kurt's by some years, to beg you, very solemnly, not to prostitute your talents to his contemptible, sensation-mongering rag.

KURT (*faces them*). There's a Senatorial sentence!

MARION. Hush, Dickie, hush! Bunny darling, it's true that Dickie's magazine isn't the Edinburgh Review. On the other hand, your assumption that my story will be vulgar and sensational is a little gratuitous, isn't it?

NOLAN. You *refuse* then?

MARION (*gently but with a serious overtone*). Yes. This—censorship before publication seems to me, shall we say, unfair. It is—even in an old friend—dictatorial.

NOLAN (*with an air of finality*). You leave me then no alternative. I am very sorry.

KURT. Don't let him frighten you, Marion, he can't do anything.

NOLAN. I can forgive you anything, Marion, but the fact that you value my wishes below those of this insolent young man.

MARION. But this insolent young man hasn't anything to do with it! Can't you see, Bunny—it's my own wish that is involved.

NOLAN. I have explained to you the special circumstances. If you would consent to delay publication till after election. . . . (*She turns to* KURT *to ask him to make this concession but can't get a word in. She is wedged between both of them.*)

KURT. She has nothing to do with the publication date. That's my province. Gosh, what a chance for the circulation manager in Tennessee! (*He rubs his palms together in mock anticipation of profits.*)

NOLAN (*losing his temper at last*). You are tampering with more than you bargain for Mr.— Mr.— . . .

KURT. Kurt.

MARION. With a "K."

NOLAN. There are ways of dealing with a young man like this and you'll soon find out what they are!

KURT. Them's harsh words, Senator!

NOLAN. You wait and see.

MARION. Bunny!

NOLAN. Don't speak to me! I never want to see you again! (*He goes out.*)

MARION (*really distressed*). This is awful!

KURT (*highly elated*). It's wonderful!

MARION. But I'm very fond of Bunny. Oh dear! I'll telephone him tonight . . .

KURT (*grimly*). Over my dead body!

MARION. Can it be, Dickie, that I control the election of Senators from Tennessee? (*Sits at right end of sofa left.*)

KURT (*after a moment*). How could you ever have loved a stuffed shirt like that?

MARION. He wasn't a stuffed shirt. That's the funny part. He was charming. He was a charming boy. Rather thin. Rather reticent. He was much nicer than you, as a matter of fact. . . .

KURT. I'm sure he was!

MARION. He was much less violent!

KURT (*sits*). Hypocritical old buccaneer!

MARION. He used to work hard all day and at night he studied law. We used to walk the country lanes and dream about the future. He was scared—he was wistful. How did he emerge into this successful, ambitious, overcautious—mediocrity? How do we all emerge into what we are? How did I emerge into what I am? I've dug up some of my old diaries. I was a tremulous young girl. I was eager. I believe I was naive. Look at me now! Time, Dickie . . . What will you be at forty? A bondholder and a commuter . . . Oh, Dickie!

KURT (*tensely*). I'll never be forty!

MARION (*laughing*). How will you avoid it?

KURT (*same tone*). I'll use myself up before I'm forty.

MARION. Do you think so? I don't think so. (*Rises.*) I sometimes wake up on certain mornings feeling absolutely—immortal! Indestructible! One is perpetually reborn, I think, Dickie. Everyone should write one's life, I think—but not for publication. For oneself. A kind of spiritual Spring-cleaning!

KURT. The Ego preening . . . !

MARION (*sitting on right arm of sofa left*). Well, why not? After all, one's ego is all one really has.

KURT. Reminiscence is easy. So is anticipation. It's the *present* that's difficult and most people are too lazy or too indifferent to cope with it.

MARION. It's natural for you to say that—at your age one has no past and no future either, because the intimation of the future comes only with the sense of the past . . .

KURT (*with sudden bitterness*). I see the past as an *evil thing*—to be extirpated.

MARION. How awful! (*Pause.*) Why?

KURT. That's not important.

MARION (*rises*). You freeze up so whenever I try to find out anything about you. I'm not used to that. Usually people open up to me—I'm a born confidante. But not you. . . . I'm interested too, because in an odd way I've become very fond of you.

KURT. My life's very dull, I assure you. *My* past lacks completely what you would call *glamour.*

MARION. No, Dickie. I don't believe that. I don't believe that's true of anybody's life.

KURT. Well, it's true. Moreover it's true of most people's lives. It's easy for anyone who's lived as you have to make romantic generalizations. It's very pleasant for you to believe them. Well, I shan't disillusion you. (*Turns away from her.*) Why should I? It's not important. (*She is sitting down, smoking a cigarette in a holder, watching him. He becomes conscious that she is studying him.*)

MARION. I had no idea you felt this way about me—you despise me, don't you? (*He doesn't answer.*) Don't you?

KURT. Yes.

MARION. Why?

KURT (*rises. Walks away*). Why did we start this?

MARION. You're annoyed at having even momentarily revealed yourself, aren't you? I'll have your secret, Dickie—I'll pluck out the heart of your mystery.

KURT. Secret! Mystery! More romantic nonsense. I have no secret. Nobody has a secret. There are different kinds of greed, different kinds of ambition—that's all!

MARION. Oh, you simplify too much—really I'm afraid you do. Tell me—why do you disapprove of me? Is it—as Bunny does—on moral grounds?

KURT (*right end of sofa left—angrily*). You're superficial and casual and irresponsible. You take life, which is a tragic thing, as though it were a trivial bedroom farce. You're a second-rate artist who's acquired a reputation through vamping celebrities to sit for you.

MARION (*quietly, she continues smoking*). Go on . . .

KURT. As an unglamorous upstart who has been forced to make my way I resent parasitism, that's all!

MARION. Isn't there in biology something about benevolent parasites, Dickie? Many great men, I believe, owe a debt of gratitude to their parasites, as many plants do . . . there are varieties. Again, Dickie, you simplify unduly. It is a defect of the radical and the young.

KURT. To return to the Honorable Nolan . . .

MARION. I return to him with relief . . .

KURT. He may exert pressure on us, you know . . .

MARION. How? I'm very interested. . . .

KURT. Well, for one thing, his future father-in-law might get me fired.

MARION. Could he do that?

KURT. He might. He might easily. (MARION *sits upright and looks at him.*) Some form of bribery. He might go to my chief and offer him a bigger job—anything.

MARION. All on account of my poor

little biography— It seems incredible that anyone would take all this trouble. . . .

KURT. I'd just like to see them try— I'd just like to, that's all . . .

MARION. What would you do?

KURT. Do?! I'd make the Honorable Nolan the laughing stock of the country, and his athletic father-in-law too. I'd just plaster them, that's what I'd do.

MARION. You sound vindictive.

KURT. Baby, I am vindictive!

MARION. Funny, I'm just amused. . . .

KURT. Well, everything's a spectacle to you! (*Turns away from her.*) God, how I hate detachment!

MARION. Your desire to break up Bunny is quite impersonal then.

KURT. Surgical. Just as impersonal as that.

MARION. You're a funny boy, Dickie.

KURT (*turns away from her*). I'm not funny and I'm not a boy. You've been around with dilettantes so long you don't recognize seriousness when you see it.

MARION. But it's the serious people who are funny, Dickie! Look at Bunny.

KURT (*faces her*). Yes, look at him! An epitome of the brainless muddle of contemporary life, of all the self-seeking second-raters who rise to power and wield power. That's why I'm going to do him in. (*The phone rings—for a moment they pay no attention to it.*) It's the most beautiful chance anybody ever had and I'd just like to see them try and stop me. (*Phone keeps ringing. MARION answers it.*)

MARION. Yes . . . yes . . . certainly. (*To KURT—a bit surprised.*) It's for you . . . (*She hands him hand-receiver.*)

KURT (*takes phone and talks from rear of sofa*). Yes. Hello . . . sure. Well, what about it? . . . Oh, you want to talk to me about it, do you? . . . I thought you would . . . I'll be around . . . sure . . . so long. (*He hangs up.*) They've begun! (*He is almost gay with the heady scent of battle.*)

MARION. What do you mean?

KURT. That was my chief. He wants to talk to me about your story. Kinnicott's begun to put the screws on him. He's going to ask me to kill it. All right —I'll kill it!

MARION (*faintly*). I can't believe it. . . .

KURT. Neff's had a call from the father-in-law . . .

MARION. Did he say so?

KURT. No, but you can bet he has!

MARION. I must say this puts my back up . . .

KURT. I'll make a fight for it to keep my job. But if he's stubborn I'll tell him to go to hell—and go to a publisher with your manuscript. And if I don't get quick action that way I'll publish it myself—I'll put every penny I've saved into it . . .

MARION. But why should you? Why does it mean so much to you?

KURT. Do you think I'd miss a chance like this?— It'll test the calibre of our magazines, of our press, our Senators, our morality . . .

MARION. All on account of my poor little story—how Vicki would have laughed!

KURT (*a spasm of jealousy again*). Who's Vicki?

MARION (*aware of it*). An old friend to whom I'm dedicating the biography.

KURT. Yeah! (*Sits beside her then speaks.*) Where is he now?

MARION. He's dead. (*A pause. She gets up and crosses to center.*) I've always rather despised these contemporary women who publicize their emotions. (*Another moment. She walks upstage. She is thinking aloud.*) And here I am doing it myself. Too much self-revelation these days. Loud speakers in the confessional. Why should I add to the noise? I think, as far as this story is concerned, I'll call it a day, Dickie.

KURT. What!

MARION. Let's forget all about it, shall we?

KURT. If you let me down now, I'll hate you.

MARION. Will you? Why won't you take me into your confidence then? Why won't you tell me about yourself? What are you after?

KURT (*after a moment of inhibition decides to reveal his secret dream*). My ambition is to be critic-at-large of things-as-they-are. I want to find out everything there is to know about the intimate structure of things. I want to reduce the whole system to absurdity. I want to laugh the powers-that-be out of existence in a great winnowing gale of laughter.

MARION. That's an interesting research. Of course it strikes me it's vitiated by one thing—you have a preconceived idea of what you will find. In a research biased like that from the start you are apt to overlook much that is noble and generous and gentle.

KURT (*challenging and bitter*). Have you found generosity and gentleness and nobility?

MARION. A good deal—yes.

KURT. Well, I haven't!

MARION. I'm sorry for you.

KURT. You needn't be. Reserve your pity for weaklings. I don't need it!

MARION. Are you so strong? (*A pause.* KURT *doesn't answer.*) How old are you, Dickie?

KURT (*turns away*). What difference does that make?

MARION. Who do you live with?

KURT. I live alone.

MARION. Are you in love with anybody?

KURT. No.

MARION. Where are your parents?

KURT. They're dead.

MARION. Long?

KURT. My mother is. I hardly remember her. Just barely remember her.

MARION. Your father? (*He doesn't answer.*) Do you remember your father?

KURT (*in a strange voice*). Yes. I remember him all right.

MARION. What did your father do?

KURT. He was a coal miner.

MARION. Oh! Won't you tell me about him? I'd like to know.

KURT. I was a kid of fourteen. There

was a strike. One day my father took me out for a walk. Sunny spring morning. We stopped to listen to an organizer. My father was a mild little man with kind of faded, tired blue eyes. We stood on the outskirts of the crowd. My father was holding me by the hand. Suddenly somebody shouted: "The militia!" There was a shot. Everybody scattered. My father was bewildered—he didn't know which way to turn. A second later he crumpled down beside me. He was bleeding. He was still holding my hand. He died like that. . . . (*A moment. He concludes harshly — coldly — like steel.*) Are there any other glamorous facts of my existence you would like to know?

MARION (*stirred to her heart*). You poor boy . . . I knew there was something . . . I knew. . . . !

KURT (*hard and ironic*). It's trivial really. People exaggerate the importance of human life. One has to die. (*Turns to her.*) The point is to have fun while you're alive, isn't it? Well, you've managed. I congratulate you!

MARION (*her heart full*). Dickie darling—why are you so bitter against me? Why against me . . . ?

KURT. Do you want to know that too? Well, it's because . . . (*His voice rises. She suddenly doesn't want him to speak.*)

MARION. Hush, dearest—hush—don't say any more—I understand—not any more . . . (*His defenses vanish suddenly. He sinks to his knees beside her, his arms around her.*)

KURT. Marion, my angel!

MARION (*infinitely compassionate, stroking his hair*). Dickie—Dickie—Dickie . . . Why have you been afraid to love me?

CURTAIN

ACT THREE

SCENE: *The same.* TIME: *Late afternoon. Two weeks later.*

The telephone is ringing as the curtain rises. There is a moment and MINNIE *enters and crosses to rear of the table, rear of the sofa left. She picks up the receiver.*

MINNIE (*speaking into the phone*). Hello.—No, Mr. Kurt, she's not yet back. Vot? You're not coming home to dinner?—But I've made the pfannkuchen you like— Vot?— You're tired of my damn pfannkuchen— (*She shouts angrily.*) Every night I make dinner and

you and Marion go out!—I'm *not* yelling
—Vot? Vot shall I tell Marion?— Vot?—
(*Doorbell rings.*) Vait—vait a minute.—
Someone's ringing. (*She puts the receiver
on the table and goes to the door.* MIN-
NIE *shows in* LEANDER NOLAN, *who is
followed by* ORRIN KINNICOTT, *who is a
big, well-developed Southerner, about
fifty-five, with a high-pitched voice. He
is a superbly-built man with a magnificent chest development. He is aware that
he is a fine figure of a man, impeccably
dressed in formal afternoon clothes.*)

NOLAN (*to* MINNIE, *who has preceded
him into the room*). Did Miss Froude
say she was expecting us for tea, Minnie?

MINNIE. No, Mr. Nolan. She didn't
say nothing to me.

NOLAN. Not even when she'd be back?

MINNIE (*hangs up coats*). No. She just
went out.

NOLAN. All right, Minnie. We'll wait.

MINNIE. Yes, Mr. Nolan. (*She is about
to go out into kitchen when she remembers that* KURT *is on the telephone. She
picks up the receiver and says.*) Hello—
Mr. Kurt—you dere?— Good-bye! (*She
then hangs up the receiver and exits left.*)

KINNICOTT (*querulously. Sits on sofa
right*). Did you tell her four o'clock?

NOLAN. Yes. I told her. (NOLAN's *manner with his father-in-law-to-be in this
scene conveys the beginnings of a secret
irritation, an inner rebellion.*)

KINNICOTT. Does she know I'm a busy
man?

NOLAN (*gloomily*). She's not impressed
much by busy men.

KINNICOTT. I know these fly-by-night
characters. I've dealt with 'em before
. . . Bad— (*He sniffs the air of the
room*) bad air. (*Rises—tries to open window, fails, sits on window seat.*) Bet she's
underexercised.

NOLAN. On the contrary—she's radi-
antly healthy!

KINNICOTT. Cosmetics, I bet! These fly-
by-night characters. . . .

NOLAN (*very irritated*). Why do you
keep calling her a fly-by-night character?
She's nothing of the sort!

KINNICOTT (*crosses to* NOLAN). Look
here, Leander. . . .

NOLAN. Well?

KINNICOTT. Have you been entirely
frank with me, in this matter?

NOLAN. Of course I have. . . .

KINNICOTT (*cryptic*). About the past
—yes. But I refer to the present.

NOLAN. I don't know what you mean.

KINNICOTT. I think you do know what
I mean. Sometimes the way you talk I
suspect—I suspect, Leander—that you are
still in love with this woman.

NOLAN. Nonsense! I simply tell you
that she's not a fly-by-night character.
That doesn't mean I'm in love with her!

KINNICOTT. My daughter feels the same
thing.

NOLAN. Slade! You've discussed this
with Slade!

KINNICOTT. She's discussed it with me.
She's no fool, that girl. She's noticed
things lately.

NOLAN. What things?

KINNICOTT. She says she talks to you
and that you're off somewhere else—
dreaming. I tried to put her on another
scent—but she was positive. She said:
"Come on now, dad—don't stall me—
come clean!" So I told her!

NOLAN. You did¹

KINNICOTT. Yes.

NOLAN. When?

KINNICOTT. Yesterday. Told her it happened fifteen years ago, that you were
a naive young feller, didn't know anything about women, were just naturally
taken in . . .

NOLAN. That's not true though. I was
not taken in.

KINNICOTT. There you go again—de-
fending the woman that's endangering
your entire career and using up my
energies and yours when you ought to
be home right now getting together with
folks and thinking how to cinch this here
election. Not going to be a walk-over,
you know. (*Again trying the window.*)
How do you open this thing to get some
air? (*Sits on window seat.*)

NOLAN. I don't know. What did Slade
say when you told her?

KINNICOTT. Nothin'. You know Slade's
not the talkin' kind.

NOLAN. Funny she didn't mention it to
me last night.

KINNICOTT. Didn't want to worry yer

probably . . . all wool and a yard wide that girl is. I warn you, Leander, don't tamper with the most precious and rare thing. . . .

NOLAN (*impatient of oratory*). I know —I know. The point is—what are we going to do?

KINNICOTT. 'Course I can get that young fellow—what's his name?

NOLAN. Kurt.

KINNICOTT. I can get him fired all right. From what you've told me, Leander, he's got something else up his sleeve. . . .

NOLAN. I'm afraid so.

KINNICOTT. That's what I want to find out from your lady friend. And I've got a pretty sure idea right now what it is.

NOLAN. What do you mean?

KINNICOTT. Money!

NOLAN (*still not understanding*). Money. . . . ?

KINNICOTT. Blackmail!

NOLAN. You're crazy!

KINNICOTT. You don't know much about women, Leander; when you know the sex as well as I do you'll know that every woman has blackmail up her sleeve.

NOLAN. Look here, Orrin. . . . !

KINNICOTT (*rises, confronts* NOLAN). Now, you listen to me for a moment, son. . . . This situation's gone about far enough right now. You'd better make up your mind whether you want this blackmailing female or whether you want my daughter . . . and you'd better make it up right quick.

NOLAN (*flaring up*). I resent your tone, Orrin, and I won't be ordered around as if I were a high-grade servant!

KINNICOTT. Now son, when you get control of your temper, and cool down a little bit, you'll see that my ordering hasn't been so bad for you. I'll acknowledge you were mighty successful as a lawyer, but in politics, you're nothing but a novice.

NOLAN (*resentful*). Am I? (*Doorbell.*)

KINNICOTT. Just look back a bit, that's all—I've had to push and bolster you to get you where you are.

NOLAN (*desperately*). I know—I have every reason to be grateful to you—that's the worst of it. (MINNIE *enters and crosses to hall door. Both men turn and watch to see who it is that is calling.*)

MINNIE (*speaking to someone at the door*). Ja, Fraulein?

SLADE (*off stage*). Is Miss Froude in?

MINNIE. Nein, Fraulein.

SLADE (*entering*). Well, I'll just wait. (SLADE KINNICOTT *is a good-looking, dark, high-spirited girl, a rather inspiring and healthy example of the generation growing up on D. H. Lawrence.[30] To her father and* NOLAN *as she crosses downstage between them.*) Hello.

NOLAN. Slade!

KINNICOTT (*severely*). Daughter! What are you doing here?

SLADE. Came to have my picture painted. What are you?

KINNICOTT. Your coming here at this time is most inopportune, daughter. We are here on business.

SLADE (*mischievously*). I can imagine!

NOLAN. I'm very glad you came, Slade. I want you to meet the woman whom your father has just been accusing of the most reprehensible crimes!

SLADE. I'm pretty anxious to get a load of her myself. (*Looks about the room taking it in and then sits on the left end of the sofa below the piano.*) Nice layout. Gee, I wish I were artistic. What a lucky gal she is! A paint-brush and an easel and she can set up shop anywhere in the world. That's independence for you! Gosh! (*She looks about, admiring and envious.*)

KINNICOTT. Why must you come here to get your picture painted? We have tolerable good artists in Knoxville.

SLADE. Well, if you *must* know I'm very keen to have a heart-to-heart talk with my fiancé's old girl. Natural, isn't it?

[30] Lawrence (1885–1930) was an English poet, short-story writer, and novelist much concerned with the problem of sexual relations. His most famous novel, "Lady Chatterley's Lover," long banned from this country in its original version, was finally published here in unexpurgated form in 1959. It is famous for its literally described love scenes.

KINNICOTT. No, it isn't natural!

NOLAN (*crosses angrily to window and back toward* KINNICOTT *and sits down on stool right near sofa on which* SLADE *and her father are sitting*). This is what you get for telling her, Orrin.

SLADE. If you think I didn't suspect something was up ever since Froude arrived here, you don't know your little bride. Maybe I haven't been watching the clouds gather on that classic brow! Where is my rival? Don't tell me she's holding up two big shots like you two boys.

KINNICOTT. Slade, this is no time . . . please leave us before she comes.

SLADE. Not I! Just my luck; when a story is going to come out which has something in it *I* want to read, you two killjoys are going to suppress it!

NOLAN. This isn't exactly a joke, you know, Slade. . . .

SLADE. I mean it. . . .

KINNICOTT (*sadly*). I've spoiled you, Slade—I've been too easy with you. . . .

SLADE. At least I hope you'll buy the *manuscript*. My God, father, I'm curious. Can't you understand that? I want to find out what Leander was like before he became ambitious. I've a right to know! This story might hurt you with the voters in Tennessee, Leander, but it's given me a kick out of you I didn't know was there! How did she make you, Leander—that's what I'd like to know. You've been pretty unapproachable to me but I sort of took it for granted National Figures were like that. Also I'd gotten to the point when I was going to suggest that we break our engagement, but this little incident revives my interest.

NOLAN (*furious*). Indeed!

SLADE. Yes indeed. Where is this woman? What is that secret? How to Make National Figures . . . there's a title for you!

KINNICOTT. Slade, you're talking too much! Shut up!

NOLAN (*rises and moves stool toward them a bit*). No, she isn't at all. . . . (*To* SLADE.) If your interest in me re-

quires the artificial stimulus of an episode that happened twenty years ago . . .

SLADE (*leaning toward him*). It requires something. . . .

NOLAN (*leaning closer toward her. The three heads are now close together,* KINNICOTT's *in the center*). Does it?

SLADE. It does. We were getting so that conversation, when we were alone, was rather difficult. (NOLAN *starts to argue.*)

KINNICOTT (*pushes them apart*). Children! Children!

NOLAN. We're not children! (*To* SLADE.) If our relationship is so—

SLADE. Tenuous . . . ?

NOLAN. . . . That it requires artificial . . .

SLADE. Respiration . . . ?

NOLAN. If it's as bad as that then I think perhaps we'd both better . . .

SLADE. Call it a day? . . . You'll need me in the Senate, Leander, to fill in the gaps when you get hung up in a speech. Consider carefully what you are discarding. . . .

NOLAN. If that is the case I tell you solemnly we'd better separate now.

SLADE (*mock tragedy*). Father, Leander is giving your daughter the air. Do something!

KINNICOTT. I don't blame him for being irritated. You should not be here. Please go home.

SLADE (*lights cigarette*). Don't worry, dad. I'll get him back.

KINNICOTT. This is a bad mess, Leander. And I must tell you frankly that I don't altogether approve of your attitude . . .

NOLAN. And I must tell you frankly that I don't approve of *yours*. . . .

KINNICOTT. Is that so!

NOLAN. I don't like your tone in speaking of a woman with whom at one time I had a relation of the tenderest emotion —for whom I still have a high regard. . . .

KINNICOTT. That's evident anyway!

NOLAN. When you apply to such a woman the terms you used before Slade came in, when you impute to her motives so base, you cast an equal reflection on my judgment and my character. . . .

SLADE: And that, pop, is lèse-majesté.[31]

NOLAN. And it may be perfectly true, Slade, that knowing Miss Froude has spoiled me for the flippant modernisms with which you study. . . .

SLADE. I'm dying to ask her one thing: when you made love to her in the old days did it always sound like a prepared speech on tariff schedules?

KINNICOTT. This is getting us nowhere. . . .

SLADE. Well, dad, what do you expect? Leander and I have broken our engagement since I came into this room. That's progress, isn't it?

KINNICOTT. Your coming here at this time was most unfortunate.

SLADE. Leander doesn't think so. (*Ironically.*) He's free now to pursue the lady for whom he still has a high regard. (*Rises.*) Are we no longer engaged, Leander?

NOLAN. That's not for me to say.

SLADE (*rises and shakes hands with* NOLAN). Gentleman to the last! And at the very moment—

KINNICOTT (*in despair—speaks as* SLADE *starts to speak*). Slade, if you would only go home!

SLADE (*crosses left*). Just at the very moment when I was saying to myself: Well, if a brilliant and beautiful woman who has played footie with royalty in the capitals of the world loved him, maybe there's a secret charm in him that I've overlooked—just when I was saying that and preparing to probe and discover, (*Lightly.*) he gives me the air. (*Sits on sofa left.*) By God, Orrin, there's life for you. (*Bell rings.*) Ah, that must be my rival! (NOLAN *gets up and fixes his tie, expecting* MARION. *But it is* KURT *who comes in. He faces them. He is in a white heat of anger.*)

KURT. Well, gentlemen, I'm not surprised to find you here! (*Drops hat on model stand and comes downstage left.*)

NOLAN (*about to introduce* KINNICOTT). How do you do, Mr. Kurt . . . this is. . . .

KURT. I can guess who it is. I can guess why you're here. Having failed to intimidate *me* you are here to intimidate Miss Froude. (SLADE *rises, excited by this tempest.*) Well, I can advise you that you will fail with her too.

NOLAN. This is his usual style, Orrin. Don't mind him.

KURT. I have just come from my office where I have been informed by Mr. Neff—(SLADE *stands below* KURT—*just behind him—watching him.*) whom *you* doubtless know, Mr. Kinnicott—that I could decide between publishing Miss Froude's story or giving up my job. I invited him to go to hell. That invitation I now cordially extend to you two gentlemen.

SLADE. Why doesn't somebody introduce me to this interesting young man? (*She comes toward him.* KURT *is embarrassed, but covers it in a gruff manner. He has actually not been aware of her in the room.*)

KURT. I'm sorry—I—I didn't know.

SLADE. Why are you sorry? I'm Slade Kinnicott. (*She gives him her hand. He takes it, limply.*)

KURT. Alright—alright. (*He is disarmed and feels, suddenly, rather foolish.*)

SLADE. Leander, why have you kept me apart from this young man?

KURT. I'm sorry—I . . .

SLADE. Nonsense. What's your name?

KURT. Richard Kurt.

SLADE. Go to it—(*Turns him toward others.*)

KINNICOTT (*impressively—interposing between them*). You're being very foolish, young man.

KURT (*crosses toward them—to right of model stand*). Possibly.

NOLAN. You can't argue with him. I've tried it. He's a fanatic.

KURT. But if you ask me I think *you're* being very foolish.

KINNICOTT (*who wants to find out what's in* KURT's *mind*). Are we? How do you figure that, young man?

SLADE (*parroting—crosses and sits on*

---

[31] Crime against the crown; treason.

model stand. She is having a wonderful time). Yes, how!

KINNICOTT. Oh, hush your mouth.

KURT. Because I'm going to publish Miss Froude's book myself. And I promise you that it'll be the best-advertised first book that's come out in a long time.

SLADE. Thank God! Will you send me the advance sheets? I'll make it worth your while, Mr. Kurt.

KINNICOTT. I can see you are an extremely impulsive young man. Have you ever inquired, may I ask . . . ?

SLADE (*edges a bit closer to* KURT). This is going to be dangerous! Look out, Richard. . . . (NOLAN *sits on stool, disgusted with* SLADE.)

KINNICOTT (*smoothly*). Have you inquired into the penalties for libel, Mr. Kurt?

KURT. Libel! You're going to sue me for libel, are you?

KINNICOTT (*same voice*). Yes. You and Miss Froude both . . . yes. . . .

KURT. Well, you just go ahead and try it, that's all I can tell you. Go ahead and sue. (*Crosses to above* NOLAN.) It'll put Mr. Nolan in a charming position before those *moral* constituents of his, won't it? (*Includes both* NOLAN *and* KINNICOTT.) Go ahead and sue, both of you—sue your heads off . . . ! I promise the two of you I'll give you the fight of your lives!

SLADE (*delighted*). Good for you, Richard! (MARION *comes in. She wears a long red velvet coat, and a little red cap stuck on the side of her golden head— she looks a little like Portia.[32] She is at the top of her form.*)

MARION (*beaming with hospitality*). Well! How nice! Minnie!

KURT (*goes upstage to right of* MARION). This chivalrous gentleman has just been proposing to sue you for libel— he considers . . .

SLADE (*who rises and stands just below the model stand*). I'm Slade Kinnicott.

MARION (*crosses downstage to her and they shake hands over the model stand*). How very nice of you to come! (*Turns and faces* KINNICOTT.) Is this Mr. Kinnicott? (*He bows.*) I'm so glad to see you. (*They shake hands.*) I'm so sorry to be late. (*Waves hello to* NOLAN.) Hello, Bunny.

SLADE (*this is too much for her*). Oh, my God—BUNNY! (*She sits, overcome.*)

MARION (*to* NOLAN). I'm so sorry . . .

NOLAN (*glaring at* SLADE). It's all right, Marion!

MARION. Has Minnie given you tea? I'll just . . . Minnie! (MINNIE *enters.*) Tea, Minnie, please. . . . (*To the men.*) Or cocktails—highballs . . . ?

KINNICOTT. I never drink alcoholic mixtures.

NOLAN (*asserting his independence*). I'll have a highball!

KINNICOTT. I must tell you, Leander, that I do not approve—

NOLAN. I'll have *two* whiskies straight!

MARION. Good! Highball for you, Miss Kinnicott?

SLADE. Thanks.

MARION. I'll fix them myself, Minnie. Just bring us some tea, Minnie.

KINNICOTT. Nor do I wish any tea.

KURT (*crosses down left*). Nor do I.

MARION. Do you mind if I have a cup? Do sit down, Miss Kinnicott. A tiring day. . . . (SLADE *sits on model stand.* MARION *goes up to rear of piano.*) Minnie, please bring me a cup of tea—

MINNIE. Ja, Fraulein. (*Remembering.*) A telegram for you, Fraulein.

MARION. Oh, thank you, Minnie. Just put it there on the table. (MINNIE *leaves the telegram on the table rear of the sofa left and then exits left.* MARION *removes her coat and hat and crosses to rear of piano and starts to mix the highballs.*) Now then! What is all this nice cheerful talk about a libel suit? That's what they're always having in England, isn't it, on the least provocation. It's

---

[32] Heroine of Shakespeare's *Merchant of Venice*. Marion's costume suggests the lawyer's attire in which actresses playing Portia are generally portrayed.

when you've circulated a lie about someone—defamed someone—maliciously —isn't it? Bunny! (*She gives* NOLAN *his two drinks. He takes them and returns to his position.* MARION *picks up the other glass and crosses with it to* SLADE.) Now then—whom have I defamed?

KURT. You've defamed the Honorable Mr. Nolan!

MARION (*hands drink to* SLADE). Have I? Oh, I am tired. . . . (*She sits on sofa.*) Sit by me, won't you, Miss Kinnicott?

SLADE (*sauntering over*). Thanks. (*She sits by* MARION *on the sofa.*)

MARION. You're very pretty. . . .

SLADE (*more warmly*). Thanks!

MARION. Bunny, I congratulate you. I've heard so much about you, Miss Kinnicott. And I think it's very gracious of you to come and see me. If Bunny lets me I'd like to paint you—(MINNIE *enters.*) and give you the portrait for a wedding-present. (*She rises and crosses to above model stand to get cup of tea from* MINNIE. MINNIE *exits left.*) Thank you, Minnie.

SLADE. You're very lovely.

MARION. Thank you, my dear.

SLADE. I can't tell you how curious I've been about you—I—

KINNICOTT. This is all very well—but I'm a busy man . . .

MARION (*looks at* KINNICOTT *as she crosses and sits right of* SLADE. *A moment, then* MARION *speaks*). It seems so strange to see you with all your clothes on. It seems a pity—as an artist I must say it seems a pity—to conceal that wonderful chest development that I've admired so often in The Body Beautiful.

KINNICOTT. That's neither here nor there.

MARION (*this is almost an aside to* SLADE). It seems to me that it's decidedly there. (MARION *and* SLADE *laugh quietly together.*)

KINNICOTT. Slade, you've upset everything by coming here. . . . (KURT *comes forward. He has been eaten up with irritation that the superb indignation he felt should have been so dissipated by* this cascade of small talk. He can stand it no longer.)

KURT (*crosses to right of model stand*). If you understood better what these gentlemen mean to do. . . . !

NOLAN (*protests*). It wasn't my idea!

KURT. You wouldn't be quite so friendly, Marion. . . .

MARION. I couldn't possibly be unfriendly to anyone so frank—and—and gladiatorial—as Mr. Kinnicott.

KURT (*furious at her for not letting him launch into it*). A libel suit . . . !

MARION. Oh, yes! A libel suit! It sounds so cozy. Sit down, won't you? (KINNICOTT *sits on stool.*) A libel suit. Now then—what shall it be about?

KURT. The Honorable Nolan is going to sue you for libel. . . .

NOLAN. I'll punch your head if you say that again. . . .

KURT. On the assumption that when you say in your story that you and he were lovers you are lying and defaming his character!

MARION. Dear Bunny, you must want to be a Senator very very badly!

NOLAN (*in despair*). I never said it, I tell you!

MARION. As a matter of fact, how could I prove it? Come to think of it, are there any letters? Did you ever write to me, Bunny?

NOLAN. I don't remember.

MARION. I don't think you ever did. You see—we were always—during that dim brief period of your youth—we were always so close—letters were hardly necessary, were they? Did I ever send you any letters, Bunny?

NOLAN. I don't remember, I tell you.

MARION. Neither do I. You might look around in old trunks and places and see if you can find some old letters of an affectionate nature—I'd love to read them —they'd probably make wonderful reading now. Why is it that the things one writes when one's young always sound so foolish afterwards? Has that ever occurred to you, Mr. Kinnicott?

KINNICOTT. I don't admit the fact.

MARION. No.

KINNICOTT. No. I was looking over some old editorials of mine written in the depression of 1907 and they're just as apropos today. I haven't changed my ideas in twenty-five years.

MARION. Haven't you really? How very steadfast. Now if the world were equally changeless, how consistent that would make you. (*To* KURT.) Well, there isn't any documentary evidence.

KURT. It doesn't matter. . . .

KINNICOTT. As I said before, this is getting us nowhere. Don't you think, Miss Froude, that the only way we can settle this is by ourselves? (*She smiles at him.*) I can see you're a sensible woman.

MARION. I am very sensible.

KINNICOTT. And you and I can settle this matter in short order.

KURT. You don't have to talk to him at all if you don't want to.

MARION (*smiling at* KINNICOTT). But I'd love to. I've always wanted to meet Mr. Kinnicott. There are some questions I want very much to ask him. (*To the others.*) You can all wait in my bedroom. It's fairly tidy, I think.

SLADE (*to* KURT—*rises, crosses to him*). Why don't you take me for a walk, Richard?

MARION (*as* KURT *hesitates*). Do that, Dickie. A walk'll do you good.

NOLAN. What'll I do?

MARION (*as if it were another dilemma*). You wait in my bedroom. (*Aware suddenly of the proprieties.*) No—in Minnie's bedroom. It's just next to the kitchen.

NOLAN (*defiantly*). I will! (*He exits into bedroom.*)

KURT (*sulky—he doesn't quite like the turn affairs have taken*). We'll be back in ten minutes.

SLADE (*as they go out*). You can't tell, Richard. (SLADE *and* KURT *exit*. MARION *draws a deep breath. She assumes at once with* KINNICOTT *the air of two equals, mature people talking freely to each other after they've gotten rid of the children.*)

MARION (*they cross to sofa left*). Now we can talk! It's funny—I feel we've put the children to bed and can have a quiet talk after a lot of chatter.

KINNICOTT. Same here!

MARION. Please sit down. (*They do.*)

KINNICOTT. I feel sure you and I can come to an understanding.

MARION. I'm sure we can.

KINNICOTT. Now then, about this little matter of the story— You won't mind if I speak very frankly to you. . . . ?

MARION. Not at all.

KINNICOTT. You see, Miss Froude . . .

MARION. Oh, call me Marion. Everybody does.

KINNICOTT. Thanks. Call me Orrin.

MARION. Alright, I'll try. Not a very usual name. Orrin. Fits you. Strong. Rugged strength.

KINNICOTT. Thank you.

MARION. You're welcome. What were you going to say when I interrupted you? You were going to say something. . . .

KINNICOTT. I was going to say—you're not at all what I expected to meet.

MARION. No? What did you think I'd be like? Tell me—I'd love to know.

KINNICOTT. Well, you're kind of homey—you know—folksy . . .

MARION. Folksy. (*Smiles.*) After all, there's no reason I shouldn't be, is there? I'm just a small-town girl from Tennessee. I sometimes wonder at myself—how I ever got so far away. . . .

KINNICOTT (*positively*). Metabolism!

MARION. I beg your pardon. . . .

KINNICOTT. I always say—take most of the bad men and most of the loose women and correct their metabolism and you'll correct them.

MARION. Really?

KINNICOTT (*seriously*). Absolutely. Trouble with our penology experts—so-called—is that they're psychologists—so-called—when they should be physiologists.

MARION. That is very interesting indeed. Have you ever written anything about that?

KINNICOTT. Off and on.

MARION. Any definitive work I mean?

KINNICOTT. I'm considering doing that right now.

MARION. Oh, I do wish you would!

It's extraordinary how little one knows about one's own body, isn't it? I get so impatient of myself sometimes—of my physical limitations. My mind is seething with ideas but I haven't the physical energy to go on working. I tire so quickly—and often for no apparent reason. Why is that, Mr. Kinnicott?

KINNICOTT. Defective—(*She says at same time with him.*)

MARION–KINNICOTT. Metabolism!

KINNICOTT. Tell me—

MARION. What?

KINNICOTT. Do you eat enough roughage?

MARION. I don't know, offhand.

KINNICOTT (*firmly*). Well, you should know!

MARION. As I say, Orrin—one is so ignorant of these fundamental things.

KINNICOTT (*definitely aware now of* MARION *as a personal possibility*). I can see this, Marion—if you'd met me—instead of Leander—when you were a young girl—you'd have been a different woman.

MARION. I'm sure I would. Imagine—with one's metabolism disciplined early in life—how far one could go.

KINNICOTT (*confidentially offering her hope*). It's not too late!

MARION. Isn't it?

KINNICOTT. Er. . . . (*He drops his voice still lower.*) What are you doing tomorrow evenin'?

MARION. I—I'm free.

KINNICOTT (*same voice*). Will you have dinner with me?

MARION. I'd be delighted.

KINNICOTT. Fine! Then we can go over this little matter of the story and Leander quietly. Leander isn't strong on tact. . . .

MARION. You know, some men aren't.

KINNICOTT. You and I can make a friendly adjustment.

MARION. What fun! (*They chuckle.*)

KINNICOTT. What time shall we meet? Say seven-thirty?

MARION. Let's say eight . . . do you mind?

KINNICOTT. My apartment?

MARION. If you like.

KINNICOTT. Here's my card with the address. It's a roof apartment. I'm a widower.

MARION. Irresistible combination!

KINNICOTT. By the way—

MARION. What?

KINNICOTT. Don't mention our little date for tomorrow evenin' to Leander.

MARION (*rising*). No, I agree with you. I don't think that would be wise.

KINNICOTT (*nodding trustingly—rises*). Fine! At seven-thirty?

MARION. No—no. Eight.

KINNICOTT. Oh yes . . . eight. (*A moment's pause. He visibly preens before her, buttoning his beautifully-fitting frock coat across his heroic chest.*)

MARION (*approving*). Wonderful! Wonderful!

KINNICOTT (*going toward bedroom. To her*). Do you mind if I . . . Leander . . .

MARION. Not at all.

KINNICOTT. I'll take the load off his mind. (*He goes out. She can't believe it. The whole situation is so fantastic. She flings off her little red cap and shaking with laughter collapses on the couch.* MINNIE *comes in to clear up the tea-things.*)

MARION (*as* MINNIE *enters*). It's too good to be true, Minnie. . . .

MINNIE. Vat is too good to be true?

MARION. I must write some of it down before I forget it . . . (*The bell again.* MARION *gets up to make notes on her script.*)—A widower's penthouse—(*With an irritated sigh* MINNIE *goes out to answer bell.* MARION *sits at desk jotting notes very fast.* SLADE *and* KURT *come in.* KURT *is morose.* MARION *gets up to greet them.*) Well, children?

SLADE. That walk was a total loss.

MARION (*laughing*). What did you expect?

SLADE. Well, a little encouragement—just a soupçon[33] . . .

MARION. Dickie's very serious.

[33] A very small amount.

SLADE. How did you come out with dad?

MARION. Wonderful! I'm crazy about him!

SLADE. But he got you to renege on the story . . .

MARION. Well, he thinks so. However, we're going to discuss it tomorrow evenin'.

SLADE. Thought he'd date you up—could tell by the way he eyed you. . . .

MARION. He's going to teach me how to live in a state of virtuous metabolism.

SLADE. Oh! Don't you believe it! Dad's an awful old chaser.

MARION (rather shocked). Slade!

SLADE (amused). Are you shocked?

MARION. You make me feel a little old-fashioned. (KURT is intensely irritated by this conversation.)

KURT. Where are they?

MARION. They're in there sitting on Minnie's bed. Orrin is probably telling Bunny that everything'll be all right.

SLADE (sits left of MARION). Marion. . . .

MARION. Yes. . . .

SLADE. What is there about Bunny you can't help liking? (Utterly disgusted, KURT goes to sofa down left and sits staring moodily into a gloomily-tinted future.)

MARION. He's a dear—there's something very touching about Bunny—sweet . . .

SLADE. Were you in love with him once?

MARION. Yes.

SLADE. Are you in love with him now?

MARION. No.

SLADE (in a whisper). Are you in love with—someone else?

MARION (a moment's pause). Yes.

SLADE. I thought you were. He's mad about you.—I envy you, Marion.

MARION. Do you? Why?

SLADE. You're independent. You're—yourself. You can do anything you like.

MARION. Yes, I know. But it's possible one can pay too much for independence.

I'm adrift. Sometimes—you know what seems to me the most heavenly thing—the only thing—for a woman? Marriage, children—the dear boundaries of routine . . .

SLADE. If you had married Bunny he would've given 'em to you. He's still in love with you, but he doesn't quite know it. Shall I tell him?

MARION (parrying). What are you talking about?

SLADE. I wish we could change places, Marion. You can with me but I can't with you. (KINNICOTT and NOLAN come in from the bedroom. KINNICOTT is at his most oleaginous.)

KINNICOTT (to KURT). Well, young man! Over your little temper?

KURT. No. I'm not over it! What makes you think I'm over it?

KINNICOTT. Well, well, well! As far as I'm concerned there are no hard feelings. I'm going to call up your employer myself when I get home and tell him, that as far as you are concerned, to let bygones be bygones. Can't do more than that, can I?

KURT. To what do I owe this generosity?

KINNICOTT. To the fact that in Miss Froude you have a most gracious friend and intercepter. (He gives MARION a gallant, old-South bow.) Miss Froude—this has been a very great pleasure.

MARION (rises—with an answering bow). Thank you! (SLADE also rises.)

KINNICOTT (giving her his hand). Auf wiedersehen.

MARION. Auf wiedersehen. Ich kann es kaum erwarten![34]

KINNICOTT (pretending to understand). Yes, oh, yes, yes, of course! (To SLADE.) Come, Slade. (He goes to hall door.)

SLADE. All right, dad. (To NOLAN.) Coming—Bunny?

NOLAN. Well, yes—I'm coming.

SLADE (to NOLAN). You want to stay. Why don't you?

KINNICOTT (quickly marshaling his lit-

---

[34] "Good bye. I can hardly wait!"

tle following with a military precision).
I think Leander had better come with
us—

SLADE (*to* MARION). Good-bye, Marion.

MARION (*to* SLADE). Good-bye, Slade.
(*They shake hands.*) Come to see me.

SLADE. Thanks, I will.

KINNICOTT (*smiles at* MARION). Miss
Froude! (*Bows to* MARION *who returns
his bow.*) Come, daughter. Come, Leander. (*To* KURT.) Good-bye, young
man. No hard feelings. (KURT *glares at
him.* KINNICOTT *again bows to* MARION.)
Miss Froude! (MARION *is startled into
still a third bow. He calls without looking back.*) Come, Slade! Leander!!

SLADE (*as she exits*). Bunny!

NOLAN (*lingers an instant then crosses
to* MARION). I'll be back.

MARION. When?

NOLAN. In a few minutes. All right?

MARION. I'll be in. (*He goes out quickly.* MARION *is in wonderful spirits. She
runs to* KURT *and throws her arms
around him.*) Oh, Dickie. That Orrin!
That Orrin!

KURT. What did you say to him that
put him in such good spirits?

MARION. Everything I said put him in
good spirits. I can't wait for tomorrow
evenin'. I can't wait for that dinner. It'll
probably consist entirely of roughage—
just imagine! He's the quaintest man I
ever met in my life. He's too good to be
true. (*Sits right of* KURT.)

KURT. Well, he may be quaint to you
but to me he's a putrescent old hypocrite and I don't see how you can bear
to have him come near you, say less go
to dinner with him!

MARION (*sobered by his intensity*).
You're so merciless in your judgments,
Dickie. You quite frighten me sometimes
—you do really.

KURT. And so do you me.

MARION. I do? That's absurd!

KURT. You do. It's like thinking a person fastidious and exacting and finding
her suddenly . . .

MARION. Gross—indiscriminating?

KURT (*bluntly*). Yes!

MARION. You know, Dickie, I adore
you and I'm touched by you and I love
you but I'd hate to live in a country
where you were Dictator. It would be
all right while you loved me but when
you stopped. . . .

KURT. It wouldn't make any difference
if I stopped—I shouldn't be that kind of
a Dictator . . .

MARION (*glances at him. Almost sadly*). I see you've thought of it. . . .

KURT (*inexorably*). What did you say
to Kinnicott?

MARION. Your manner is so—inquisi-
torial. I haven't been able to get used
to it.

KURT (*angry and jealous*). I heard you
tell Nolan to come back too . . . How
do you think I feel?

MARION. Dickie!

KURT. When Nolan sat there and told
me he had been your lover, I felt like
socking him. Even when we're alone
together, I can't forget that . . . yet you
encourage him, and Kinnicott— My God,
Marion, you seem to like these people!

MARION. I certainly like Slade.

KURT. Well I don't. She's conceited
and overbearing. Thinks she can have
anything she likes because she's Orrin
Kinnicott's daughter.

MARION. That's where you're wrong.
She's a nice girl—and she's unhappy.

KURT (*bitterly*). Maladjusted, I suppose!

MARION. Dickie, Dickie, Dickie! Studying you, I can see why so many movements against injustice become such absolute—tyrannies.

KURT. That beautiful detachment
again. . . . (*He is white with fury. He
hates her at this moment.*)

MARION (*with a little laugh*). You hate
me, don't you . . . ?

KURT. Yes! Temporizing with these
. . . ! Yes . . . ! I hate you. (*She says
nothing, sits there looking at him.*)
These people flout you, they insult you
in the most flagrant way. God knows
I'm not a gentleman, but it horrifies me
to think of the insufferable arrogance
of their attitude toward you . . . as if

the final insult to their pride and their honor could only come from the discovery that this stuffed shirt Nolan had once been your lover! The blot on the immaculate Tennessee scutcheon! Why, it's the God-damndest insolence I ever heard of. And yet you flirt and curry favor and bandy with them. And you're amused—always amused!

MARION. Yes. I am amused.

KURT. I can't understand such . . . !

MARION. Of course you can't. That's the difference—one of the differences—between 25 and 35!

KURT. If the time ever comes when I'm amused by what I should hate, I hope somebody shoots me. What did you tell Kinnicott?

MARION. Nothing. Simply nothing. I saw no point in having a scene with him so I inquired into his favorite subject. He gave me health hints. He thinks tomorrow night he will cajole me—through the exercise of his great personal charm—into giving up my plan to publish.

KURT. Well, why didn't you tell him right out that you wouldn't?

MARION. Because I wanted to avoid a scene.

KURT. You can't always avoid scenes. That's the trouble with you—you expect to go through life as if it were a beautifully-lit drawing room with modulated voices making polite chatter. Life isn't a drawing room . . . !

MARION. I have—once or twice—suspected it.

KURT (rises). What the devil are you afraid of, anyway? I had a scene today in the office and I was prepared for one here—until you let me down—

MARION (lightly). Prepared? I think you were eager. . . .

KURT. What if I was! It's in your behalf, isn't it?

MARION. Is it? But you forget, Dickie. You're a born martyr. I'm not. I think the most uncomfortable thing about martyrs is that they look down on people who aren't. (Thinks—looks at him.) As a matter of fact, Dickie, I don't really

understand. Why do you insist so on this story? Why is it so important—now wouldn't it be better to give it up?

KURT. Give it up!

MARION. Yes.

KURT. You'd give it up!

MARION. Why not?

KURT (obeying a sudden manic impulse). After all this—after all I've—! Oh, yes, of course! Then you could marry Nolan and live happily forever after. And be amused. Good-bye! (He rushes up center, grabs his hat from the stand as he passes it, and continues on out the door.)

MARION (rises and runs after him). Dickie!

KURT (going out the door). Good-bye!

MARION. Dickie! Dickie! (The door slams. MARION walks back into the room. A pause. She stands still for a moment; she shakes her head. . . . She is very distressed and saddened and a deep unhappiness is gnawing in her heart, an awareness of the vast, uncrossable deserts between the souls of human beings. She makes a little helpless gesture with her hands, murmuring to herself.) Poor Dickie! Poor boy! (In its Italian folder the manuscript of her book is lying on the piano before her. She picks it up—she gives the effect of weighing the script in her hand. Slowly, as if in a trance, she walks with the script to the Franklin stove downstage left and sits before it on a little stool. She opens the manuscript and then the isinglass door of the stove. The light from behind it glows on her face. She looks again down on her manuscript, at this morsel of her recorded past. She tears out a page or two and puts them into the fire. A moment and she has put the entire script into the stove and she sits there watching its cremation. The doorbell rings. As MINNIE comes in to answer it, she shuts the door of the stove quickly.)

MARION. It's probably Mr. Nolan. (MINNIE goes out. MARION makes a visible effort to shake herself out of her mood. NOLAN comes in followed by

MINNIE *who crosses stage and goes in the bedroom left.* NOLAN *is excited and distrait.*)

NOLAN. Hello, Marion. . . .

MARION. Hello, Bunny dear.

NOLAN (*sparring for time*). Excuse me for rushing in on you like this . . . I . . .

MARION. I've been expecting you.

NOLAN. That's right! I told you I was coming back, didn't I? . . .

MARION. You did—yes.

NOLAN. I must have known—I must have felt it—what would happen. . . . Marion . . .

MARION. Bunny dear, you're all worked up. Won't you have a highball?

NOLAN. No, thanks. Marion. . . .

MARION. Yes, Bunny . . .

NOLAN. I've done it!

MARION. You've done what?

NOLAN. I've broken with Slade. I've broken with Kinnicott. I've broken with all of them.

MARION. You haven't!

NOLAN. Yes! I have!

MARION. Oh—oh, Bunny!

NOLAN (*sits*). When Orrin told me what you'd done—that you were going to give up the story. . . .

MARION. But I—

NOLAN. He said he was sure he could get you to do it. It all came over me —your generosity—your wonderful generosity.

MARION (*beyond words*). Oh, Bunny! (*Sits. She is in a sort of laughing despair. He hardly notices her attitude. He rushes on.*)

NOLAN. I realized in that moment that in all this time—since I'd been seeing you —I'd been hoping you wouldn't give up the story, that you would go through with it, that my career would go to smash. . . .

MARION (*faintly*). Bunny. . . .

NOLAN. I saw then that all this—which I'd been telling myself I wanted—Slade, a career, Washington, public life—all of it—that I didn't want it, that I was sick at the prospect of it—that I wasn't up to it, that I was scared to death of it. I saw all that—and I told her—I told Slade. . . .

MARION. You did!

NOLAN. Yes.

MARION. What did she say?

NOLAN. She said she knew it. She's clever, that girl. She's cleverer than I am. She's cleverer than you are. I'm afraid of her cleverness. I'm uncomfortable with it. Marion, I know I seem stupid and ridiculous to you—just a Babbitt—clumsy—but I love you, Marion.[35] I always have—never anyone else. Let me go with you wherever you go—(*Lest she think it a "proposition."*) I mean—I want to marry you.

MARION. I'm terribly touched by this, Bunny darling, but I can't marry you.

NOLAN. Why not?

MARION. If I married you it would be for the wrong reasons. And it wouldn't be in character really—neither for me— nor for you. Besides that, I think you're wrong about Slade. She's very nice, you know. I like her very much.

NOLAN. I don't understand her. I never will.

MARION. If you did you'd like her. You better have another try. Really, Bunny, I wish you would.

NOLAN. Letting me down easy, aren't you?

MARION. It's Slade's manner that shocks you—her modern—gestures. If you really understood me—as you think you do—I'd really shock you very much, Bunny.

NOLAN. I'll risk it. Marion, my dearest Marion, won't you give me some hope? . . .

MARION (*sees she must tell him*). Besides,—I'm in love.

NOLAN (*stunned*). Really! With whom?

MARION. Dickie . . . You see, Bunny . . . (*He can't get over this. There is a*

---

[35] Hero of Sinclair Lewis' novel, "Babbitt," of 1922. The name is synonymous with conventional middle-class morality and platitudinous outlook toward politics, religion, love, etc.

considerable pause.) You see, Bunny . . .

NOLAN (*slowly*). Do you mean that you and he—you don't mean that . . . ?

MARION. Yes, Bunny.

NOLAN (*dazed*). Are you going to marry him?

MARION. No.

NOLAN (*he passes his hand over his forehead*). This is a shock to me, Marion.

MARION (*gently*). I thought it only fair to tell you.

NOLAN (*in a sudden passion*). You—you. . . . (*He feels like striking her, controls himself with difficulty.*) Anybody else but him. . . . !

MARION. You see, Bunny.

NOLAN (*after a moment—rises*). Sorry! Funny, isn't it? Joke, isn't it?

MARION. I'm terribly fond of you, Bunny. (*Takes his hand.*) I always will be. That kind of tenderness outlasts many things.

NOLAN (*blindly*). I'll go on, I suppose.

MARION. Of course you will! (NOLAN *crosses to model stand and gets his hat.* KURT *comes in. There is a silence.* NO-LAN *forces himself to look at him.* KURT *does not meet his glance.* KURT *is white and shaken—not in the least truculent.*) Good-bye, Bunny dear. Bunny!

NOLAN. Yes, Marion.

MARION. Will you do me a favor?

NOLAN. Yes.

MARION. Will you please tell Mr. Kinnicott for me—that as I've been called out of town suddenly—I can't dine with him tomorrow night. You *will* see him, won't you, and you'll tell him?

NOLAN. Yes. (NOLAN *leaves. A silence again. . . . Suddenly* KURT *goes to her, embraces her with a kind of hopeless intensity.*)

KURT (*in a whisper, like a child*). Please forgive me. . . .

MARION. Yes.

KURT. These moods come over me—I can't control myself—afterwards I hate myself—it's because I love you so much—I can't bear to. . . .

MARION. I know, dear—I know. . . .

KURT. I'm torn up all the time—torn to bits.

MARION. I know, dear . . .

KURT. When this is all blown over—could we—do you think . . .

MARION. What, dear?

KURT. If we could only go away together, the two of us—somewhere away from people, by ourselves?

MARION. Why not, Dickie? We can go now, if you want to. . . .

KURT. Now? But you're crazy. How can we possibly leave now—with the book. . . .

MARION. Dickie—I must tell you. . . .

KURT. You must tell me what?

MARION. You must be patient—you must hear me out for once—you must try to understand my point of view. (*She leads him to sofa left and sits beside him.*)

KURT. What do you mean?

MARION. You know, Dickie, I've been very troubled about you. I've been sad. I've been sad.

KURT. I was angry . . . I didn't mean . . . It was just that . . .

MARION. No, you don't understand—it wasn't your anger that troubled me. It was ourselves—the difference between us—not the years alone but the immutable difference in temperament. Your hates frighten me, Dickie. These people—poor Bunny, that ridiculous fellow Kinnicott—to you these rather ineffectual, blundering people symbolize the forces that have hurt you and you hate them. But I don't hate them. I can't hate them. Without feeling it, I can understand your hate but I can't bring myself to foster it. To you, this book has become a crusade. It couldn't be to me. Do you know, Dickie dear—and this has made me laugh so to myself—that there was nothing in the book about Bunny that would ever have been recognized by anybody. It was an idyllic chapter of first love—that's all—and there was nothing in it that could remotely have been connected with the Bunny that is now. . . .

KURT. So much the better—! Think of the spectacle they'll make of themselves—destroyed by laughter. . . .

MARION. I don't believe in destructive

campaigns, Dickie . . . outside of the shocking vulgarity of it all—I couldn't do it—for the distress it would cause. . . .

KURT. You've decided not to publish then. . . .

MARION. I've destroyed the book, Dickie.

KURT. You've destroyed it!

MARION. Yes. I'm sorry.

KURT. You traitor!

MARION. It seemed the simple thing to do—the inevitable thing.

KURT. What about *me?* You might have consulted me—after what I've . . .

MARION. I'm terribly sorry—but I couldn't possibly have published that book.

KURT (*in a queer voice*). I see now why everything is this way. . . .

MARION. I couldn't . . . !

KURT. Why the injustice and the cruelty go on—year after year—century after century—without change—because —as they grow older—people become— *tolerant!* Things amuse them. I hate you and I hate your tolerance. I always did.

MARION. I know you do. You hate my essential quality—the thing that is me. That's what I was thinking just now and that's what made me sad.

KURT. Nothing to be said, is there? (*Rises.*) Good-bye.

MARION (*rises*). All right! (KURT *starts to go. She calls after him, pitifully.*) Won't you kiss me good-bye?

KURT. All right. (MARION *goes up after him. They kiss each other passionately.*)

MARION (*whispering to him*). I would try to change you. I know I would. And if I changed you I should destroy what makes me love you. Good-bye, my darling. Good-bye, my dearest. Go quickly. (KURT *goes up stage and exits without a word. He is blinded by pain.*) Dickie. . . . ! (MARION *is left alone. She is trembling a little. She feels cold. She goes to the stove and sits in front of it, her back to it, trying to get warm. She becomes aware that her eyes are full of tears. As*

MINNIE *comes in, she brushes them away.*)

MINNIE. Are you worried from anything, Marion?

MARION. No, Minnie. I'm alright.

MINNIE. I tink maybe dot telegram bring you bad news.

MARION. Telegram? What telegram?

MINNIE. Dot telegram I bring you.

MARION. Of course—I haven't even— where is it?

MINNIE (*gets telegram from table rear of sofa left and hands it to* MARION). There it is!

MARION. Thank you, Minnie. (*Opens telegram and reads it.*) This is from heaven! Minnie, I want you to pack right away. We're leaving! (*She springs up.*)

MINNIE. Leaving? Ven?

MARION. Right away. Tonight! This is from Feydie! Listen! (*Reads telegram aloud to* MINNIE.) "Can get you commission to paint prize winners Motion Picture Academy—wire answer at once. Feydie." (*Hysterically grateful for the mercy of having something to do at once, of being busy, of not having time to think.*) Something always turns up for me! Pack everything, Minnie. I want to get out right away. (*She rushes upstage right, picks up her hat and coat and then runs to the stairs left.*)

MINNIE. Don't you tink you better vait till tomorrow?

MARION. No, Minnie. Once the temptation to a journey comes into my head I can't bear it till I'm on my way! This time, Minnie, we'll have a real trip. From Hollywood we'll go to Honolulu and from Honolulu to China. How would you like that, Minnie? (*She starts up the stairs.*)

MINNIE (*for her, enthusiastic*). Fine, Marion! (*Calls after her as she runs upstairs.*) Dot crazy Kurt he goes vit us?

MARION (*as she disappears into her bedroom*). No, Minnie—no one—we travel alone!

QUICK CURTAIN

SUGGESTED TOPICS FOR FURTHER STUDY AND DISCUSSION

1. The attitudes and behavior patterns of high comedy are not strictly "modern." They have been present in wide variation throughout dramatic history. Read Shakespeare's *Much Ado about Nothing*, Congreve's *The Way of the World*, and Molière's *The Misanthrope*. Discuss the elements of high comedy in each, and note the similarities and differences found in the three pairs of lovers, Beatrice and Benedick, Millamant and Mirabell, and Célimène and Alceste.

2. Sheridan's *The School for Scandal* remains one of the finest high comedies of all time. Present an analysis of the play to show why it has been so highly regarded and how well it meets the requirements of good high comedy.

3. Tyler's *The Contrast* is based on Sheridan's *School*, as well as upon the whole tradition of eighteenth-century comedy. *Fashion* still has many overtones of the same tradition. Read the two American plays and discuss them in relation to Sheridan.

4. Oscar Wilde was one of the greatest creators of epigrammatic dialogue in English. His characters speak in some of the most delightfully sparkling language ever written for the stage. Read *Lady Windermere's Fan*, *A Woman of No Importance*, *An Ideal Husband*, and most certainly *The Importance of Being Earnest*. Are they "high" comedy? The last-named is widely considered to be a farce, but the "highest" farce in the language. Does it belong with the others?

5. Read more of Behrman's plays, particularly *The Second Man*, *Brief Moment*, and *No Time for Comedy*. Compare them with *Biography*. Evaluate them individually or collectively as high comedies.

6. Make a comparison of Somerset Maugham and Behrman as seen in Maugham's *The Circle* and Behrman's *Biography* or *The Second Man*.

7. Noel Coward writes a highly sophisticated comedy which is not always favorably compared with Maugham or with Behrman. Read his two most famous, *Private Lives* and *Design for Living*. What is your opinion?

8. Study some of the earlier American high comedies. Read all of Langdon Mitchell's *The New York Idea*, Rachel Crothers' *He and She* or *Nice People*, Jesse Lynch Williams' *Why Marry?* Evaluate them as high comedy. Do you find that Behrman is an improvement, or merely a refinement, on their styles?

9. Philip Barry's comedies are Behrman's nearest competition. Read *Holiday*, *Paris Bound*, and *The Philadelphia Story* and determine Barry's position in relation to Behrman. In what ways is he superior? How and when is he less successful?

Satire and the Comic

Satire, said George S. Kaufman, is what closes Saturday night. There is only one trouble with this gentleman's outlook (and Kaufman of all comic writers should know it well): it is not actually true. Dramatic satire has been an important ingredient of the theatre since Aristophanes first showed the Athenian tyrants how ridiculous they looked and made them laugh at his ribald comments.

The definition of satire is simple; it is merely a work of literature, in poetry or prose, which holds human follies and vices up to ridicule. No one denies that there are plenty of these faults to be exposed. The danger which threatens the satirist with a threat of Saturday-night closing lurks in the act of exposure, because any person who would comment upon the follies of men, being himself human like the rest, is immediately announcing himself a judge of right and wrong. It is the unusual person who willingly permits himself and his pet beliefs to stand accused.

The genuine satirist, contrary to popular belief, is not particularly interested in creating laughter. His point is to cast derision, and although he may achieve laughter through acid language or humorous character, the *object* of the satire is not, *ipso facto*, a funny thing. Often the laughter that arises is uneasy; the smile or chuckle falls short of complete amusement. If the hilarity of the moment overshadows the point of the satire and laughter drowns it out, then the satirist has blunted his weapon.

Because satire does not seek laughter, it should not be confused with burlesque, lampoon, or parody, which do. These forms thrive on laughter arising directly from their exaggeration or imitation of certain well-known features of their victim. Instead of wishing to correct a human failing, they employ the chosen fault as a source of comic amusement. Burlesque and lampoon can pass beyond mere fun and become vicious personal attacks for political, social, or even artistic reasons, but their initial concept remains different from satire. In satire the folly itself is not amusing; the laughter must come from elsewhere.

Most satire in the theatre, as described by Allardyce Nicoll, is "enclosed" in comedy, because of the ease with which a point may be emphasized by laughter. For purposes of discussion, we shall use the term "comedy with a purpose"; that is, a play which bases its appeal upon the recognizable comic qualities of humankind, but which simultaneously exposes and ridicules. Therefore we shall find that no comedy with a purpose is purely satiric, because it consciously relies upon the comic for ultimate success. On the other hand, there are elements within this kind of play which stand apart from the comic in order to call the human being to task with pointed comment and serious observation.

The comedy of manners has often been associated with satire. There is no doubt that early "social" plays, as far back as *The Contrast* and *Fashion*, were satirizing the pretentious affectations of certain social groups. A fault of early twentieth-century American high comedy, like *The New York Idea*, was its unnecessary stress on some of the shortcomings of the gaily abandoned life. In the modern tradition of Behrman, Maugham, and Coward, high-comedy characters must be accepted for just what they are. Behrman in *Biography* uses Marion to deflate the overextended ego of each man, and she is a fine foil to the ridiculous Kinnicott. But nowhere is Behrman using his central characters as objects of serious satire, for he has no desire to change or correct them. They are comic characters because they are human. They are not subjects for the darts of a satirist.

Dramatic Satire in America

"Comedy with a purpose" came early in American history with the political satires written by both rebel and Tory before the Revolution. The most famous are those of Mrs. Mercy Otis Warren, whose short pieces were widely circulated in the Colonies. They are aimed at scornful laughter through broad burlesque and grotesque caricature of actual people. The value of these satires, which were probably never produced, is almost wholly lost today because the names and the events are too topical.

Appeals to the intellect were not a part of nineteenth-century American drama. The "social" comedies and the burlesques, particularly those which made fun of the overworked clichés in the Indian and frontier dramas, were popular, but until comparatively modern times very few new plays could be regarded as satiric.

Early in the twentieth century, Clyde Fitch came fairly close to social satire, particularly in parts of *The Climbers* of 1901. Its story involves melodramatic complications and love entanglements connected with a group of society women who attempt to climb back into the midst of things after having been left destitute by the death of the husband and father. The satiric opening scene takes place immediately after the funeral. For a long time producers who believed the public would be offended by its irreverent atmosphere refused to buy the play. The speakers in the following condensed passage are the widow and her daughters. They have returned home after the funeral, and do not know the poverty that awaits them. They have just ordered tea:

> MRS. HUNTER. Girls, everybody in town was there! I'm sure even your father himself couldn't have complained.
> BLANCHE. Mother!
>
> * * *
>
> JESSICA. Here's the tea—
> MRS. HUNTER. I'm afraid I can't touch it. (*Taking her place behind tea table and biting eagerly into a sandwich.*)
> JESSICA (*dryly*). Try. . . .

MRS. HUNTER (*eating*). One thing I was furious about,—did you see the Witherspoons *here* at the house?

CLARA. *I* did.

MRS. HUNTER. The idea! When I've never called on them. They are the worst social pushers I've ever known. (*She takes another sandwich.*)

CLARA. Trying to make people think they are on our visiting list! Using even a funeral to get in!

MRS. HUNTER. But I *was* glad the Worthings were here. . . . (*She takes a third sandwich.*)

BLANCHE. A great many people loved father. . . .

JESSICA. Shall we have to economize now, mother?

MRS. HUNTER. Of course not; how dare you suggest such an injustice to your *father*, and *before* the flowers are withered on his grave! (*Again becoming tearful.*) Has the new writing paper come?

BLANCHE. Yes.

MRS. HUNTER. Is the black border broad enough? They said it was the thing.

CLARA. If you had it any broader, you'd have to get white ink to write with!

MRS. HUNTER (*sweetly*). Don't be impertinent, darling!

An interesting satire of the 1920s was Eugene O'Neill's *Marco Millions*, written in 1923 but staged in 1927. It is not one of O'Neill's best, but his attack on American materialism is at least different. The protagonist is Marco Polo of historical fame, but he is a Marco Polo of rather alarming American traveling-salesman characteristics. From a young man full of innocence and virtue, who sets off with his elders on a great venture, he develops into the highly successful businessman who can sell anything and organize anybody if given half a chance. He proves his ability when the great Kublai Khan gives him the opportunity, but in so doing he loses the soul that could be his salvation. O'Neill's style, never light in any play, treads heavily, but the sharp bite of satire is well composed in scenes like the following. Marco informs the Khan how he has managed things as governor of Yang-Chau, where he has repealed the taxes on excess profits ("Imagine a profit being excess!") and on luxuries ("The great majority . . . couldn't afford luxuries"). They have been replaced by a tax on every necessity of life which "hits every man's pocket equally."

KUBLAI (*with a chilling air*). I have received a petition from the inhabitants of Yang-Chau enumerating over three thousand cases of your gross abuse of power!

MARCO (*abashed only for a moment*). Oh, so they've sent that vile slander to you, have they? That's the work of a mere handful of radicals—

KUBLAI (*dryly*). Five hundred thousand names are signed to it. (*Still more dryly.*) Half a million citizens accuse you of endeavoring to stamp out their ancient culture!

MARCO. What! Why, I even had a law passed that anyone caught interfering with culture would be subject to a fine! It was Section One of a blanket statute that every citizen must be happy or go to jail.

But, to tell the truth, I want to resign anyhow. I've done all I could. I've appointed five hundred committees to carry on my work and I retire confident that with the system I've instituted everything will go on automatically and brains are no longer needed. (*He adds as a bitter afterthought.*) And it's lucky they're not or Yang-Chau would soon be a ruin!

The Khan accepts his resignation "with deep regret" and then asks if Marco still possesses his immortal soul. Flustered, Marco replies that he hopes so, presuming that the Khan assumes that Yang-Chau would have been a good place to lose one. "Well, you wouldn't know the old town now," he concludes. "Sin is practically unseen."

The national hypocrisies and the meaningless slaughter of war provide Robert E. Sherwood's 1936 Pulitzer Prize-winning comedy, *Idiot's Delight*, with some excellent satiric targets. The play's basis is high comedy, involving a stranded entertainment troupe in Europe, and centers around the attempt by Harry, the manager, to determine if the stunning blonde "Russian" Irene is really the babe he spent a memorable night with in an Omaha hotel. As interpreted by Alfred Lunt and Lynn Fontanne, America's most polished high comedians, the play was a brilliant success. Sherwood's realization of the pointlessness of international strife and its distressing imminence at the time of the play permitted him to include some strongly ironic comments on man's mutual mayhem. The contrast between the wild brutality of the erupting conflict and the "serious" business of high-comedy frivolities was notably effective. In the following passage, Irene, the heroine, talks with her paramour, Achille Weber, a French munitions manufacturer, shortly after the Italian air force has bombed Paris. She has just expressed her great "happiness" for him because he has promoted "all this great, wonderful death and destruction."

WEBER. Yes, my dear. . . . But don't forget to do honor to Him—up there—who put fear into man. I am but the humble instrument of His divine will.
IRENE (*looking upward, sympathetically*). Yes—that's quite true. We don't do half enough justice to Him. Poor, lonely old soul. Sitting up in heaven, with nothing to do but play solitaire. Poor, dear God. Playing Idiot's Delight. The game that never means anything, and never ends.
WEBER. You have an engaging fancy, my dear.

* * *

IRENE. . . . When I am worrying about you, and your career, I have to run away from the terror of my own thoughts. So I amuse myself by studying the faces of the people I see. Just ordinary, casual, dull people. (*She is speaking in a tone that is sweetly sadistic.*) That young English couple, for instance. I was watching them during dinner, sitting there, close together, holding hands, and rubbing their knees together under the table. And I saw him in his nice, smart, British uniform, shooting a little pistol at a huge tank. And the tank rolls over him. And his fine strong body, that was so full of the capacity for ecstasy, is a mass of mashed flesh and bones—a smear of purple blood—like a stepped-on snail. But before the moment of death, he consoles himself by thinking, "Thank God *she* is safe! She is bearing the child I gave her, and he will live to see a better world." (*She walks behind* WEBER *and leans over his shoulder.*) But I know where she is. She is lying in a cellar that has been wrecked by an air raid, and her firm young breasts are all mixed up with the bowels of a dismembered policeman, and the embryo from her womb is splattered against the face of a dead bishop. That is the kind of thought with which I amuse myself, Achille. And it makes me so proud to think that I am so close to you—who make all this possible.

WEBER. Do you talk in this whimsical vein to many people?

Politics, business affairs, high society, the military—all have been exposed to the satiric pen in some of the American theatre's most popular plays. Among the writers appears the name of none other than George S. Kaufman. The well-drawn cartoon of presidential election madness in *Of Thee I Sing*, which he and Morrie Ryskind composed in 1931, took a Pulitzer Prize. *Beggar on Horseback* is top-quality Kaufman, and so are the satiric farces like *Merton of the Movies*, *The Butter and Egg Man*, and *The Man Who Came to Dinner*, written with collaborators Marc Connelly and Moss Hart. On the distaff side, Clare Boothe's unabashed attack on the "weaker" sex in *The Women* neatly impaled a whole raft of predatory females in 1936. The picture of the Pentagon in Okinawa was one of the biggest successes of the postwar period in *The Teahouse of the August Moon* in 1953, John Patrick's interpretation of military shenanigans.

Good satire—for the most part, properly seasoned with good comedy—can succeed, and as long as human beings are what they are, there is no doubt that it will continue to play through many Saturday nights for a long time.

The Male Animal

James Thurber and Elliot Nugent's dissection of a great American institution, the Homecoming football weekend, is a combination of admirably pointed satire and uproariously funny comedy. It has become a classic of its type. Whoever in the future attempts to ridicule this seasonal insanity, or tries to scorn the narrow reasoning of stadium-conscious college alumni, will have to stand comparison with the writers of *The Male Animal*.

The play has fundamental qualities of high comedy in the conflict of wits that has never ended and never will, the War between Men and Women. James Thurber is the past master at sketching the campaigns and tactics of this ageless battle. His stories and cartoons are peopled with little men lost in the frightening world of incomprehensible women. They fight back valiantly and with intelligence, at times meeting hopeless defeat, at others emerging victorious. Sometimes, as in *The Male Animal*, there are other men who must be countered, mainly ape men or bull men, giant creatures who rumble and roar and play football while sweeping the women off their feet. Then the little man must fight the intruder for the privilege of getting back into the original battle, and he must use his brains for weapons. Tommy Turner is Thurber's little man, quiet, absent-minded, inoffensive. He is ill equipped to fight for his mate, but when the occasion arises, he does his best.

This intrusion of physical combat into Tommy's life turns the play away from its high-comedy base into the farther lands of pure and simple farce. Good farce demands a fundamentally illogical or improbable situation logically developed and convincingly pursued. It is visual, full of action, independent of completely drawn characters, reliant upon sight gag and broad verbal gymnastics. The object of farce is to arouse a laugh; it cannot survive when its audience is asked to stop and think. The whole circus of loosened beasts which descend upon Tommy Turner is within the realm of farce. While Tommy attempts to make some sense of what goes on around him, he sees only a world of lunatics, who sing silly songs and search for missing cream pitchers with no indication of rational behavior.

But *The Male Animal* is not just farce, and it is not, of course, high comedy. It is a play with a deliberate message, made forcefully and tellingly in the midst of enormous fun. This fun, however, vividly accentuates the point that Thurber and Nugent are making. While the audience is laughing at Tommy's gay try as a cordial host, it also realizes that the whole ridiculous charade is a painful experience, made endurable only by an excess of cocktails, which are beyond Tommy's small capacity. The laughter is caught up short in Tommy's sudden need to defend himself under conditions most unfavorable.

Thurber and Nugent display astute awareness of the workings of the collegiate mind. So long as homage is paid to the brawn of the Wallys and Joe Fergusons, and so long as trustees and administrators cater to the alumni's demand for bigger and better stadiums, the Tommy Turners will have to remain objects of suspicion and prejudice. There is hope, though, as long as men like Turner refuse to be cowed and make themselves heard on principle. Tommy will not conform; conformity is death to original thinking and hence to the spirit of a university. Ed Keller, practicing his "Americanism," takes pride in conformity and will oppose every low-paid professor and dean along the way. After the reading of the letter and the arrival of the petition, Tommy's victory is complete and devastating, but Keller cannot understand how approval of Tommy's views can come from heroes like Stalenkiwiecz and Wierasocka. Keller's refusal to strike his flag after the direct hit that sinks him brings the final laughter of derision and scorn.

The Male Animal makes its plea for academic tolerance and independence of thought through characters who are entertaining and plausible at the same time. This comedy relies extensively on quickly recognizable individuals who act as they are expected to act; still, nobody becomes a mere parody, because Thurber and Nugent give each of them a background and an individuality which renders him understandable. The whole domestic picture of life at the Turners' is revealed in the portraits of Ellen and Tommy. It is a nice life, comfortable, quiet, moderately secure (a maid such as Cleota in an English professor's house is an unrealistic luxury), but it borders on dullness for Ellen, once the most popular girl on the dance floor. Tommy's recollection of his own shy awkwardness, Ellen's beauty in her large floppy hat, and all such incidents out of the past, are important in establishing character depth. Joe Ferguson has reasons for being what he is. The Whirling Joe of college days has never grown up; his privileged life as campus hero has carried over into private life, and he remains the loud, bone-crushing ball carrier he always was. Ed Keller, the perennial undergraduate, is closest to caricature, but he is not outside the realm of believability. The temptation to make Dr. Damon nothing but an umbrella-carrying, Ovaltine-sipping, lovable old "prof" is avoided even in his brief moments on stage. Favoring caution and rear-guard action, he is still admirable in his ability to fight back when pressed too far. Michael, Wally, Patricia—the Tommy, Joe, and Ellen of a new generation—need less delineation, for they are young, open, not yet aware of the struggles ahead of them, but they, too, maintain levels happily above the transparencies they might be in a play which could become trite.

The Male Animal is never trite. It is a charming, amusing comedy, at times wittily intelligent, at others uproariously farcical. But it is honest and it tells the truth. It also earnestly pleads for tolerance and understanding in an atmosphere designed for tolerance but contaminated by the intrusion of the unthinking mentality that can judge quality only by immediate and sensational success on the football field. It is wrong to count *The Male Animal* as predominantly satiric. The play appeals both to the intellect and to the emotions. The follies of the Ed Kellers and the Joe Fergusons are ridiculed as universal faults, visible today as well as twenty-five years ago, but the emotional needs of all the Tommy Turners who desire sympathetic understanding within their own homes are also made clear, and they are not the elements of satire.

The Male Animal is excellent comedy in nearly every respect. Its world is fundamentally comic, but its overtones are serious. It asks for laughter on nearly every occasion. And yet, when the human animal must take the form of the enraged tiger springing from his den, particularly a glasses-wearing English-teaching tiger, the play becomes more than fun. It has a purpose, beautifully sugar-coated, but strong and bitter underneath. It is easy to swallow, but once down, it has its desired effect.

Since the significance of Vanzetti's letter in *The Male Animal* may not reach the present generation, it is important to know why Tommy's innocent gesture became such a red flag to that defender of "Americanism," Ed Keller.

On December 24, 1919, two payroll messengers in Bridgewater, Massachusetts, were held up and shot. The event occurred during a time of national and international tensions caused by repeated terrorism widely attributed to "Reds" and "anarchists." The payroll robbery-murder became involved in this hysteria when two known anarchists and draft-dodgers, Niccola Sacco and Bartolomeo Vanzetti, were arrested for the crime.

The trial and subsequent appeals became an international sensation. The testimony for the defense and that for the prosecution were in many instances 100 per cent contradictory, but on July 14, 1921, Sacco and Vanzetti were found guilty. For six years, until April 9, 1927, when the men were at last sentenced to death, fruitless appeals went through every Massachusetts court. Further appeals went to the Governor of Massachusetts and to the United States Supreme Court. All failed, and the men died on August 23, 1927.

The public emotional identification with the case grew as people of liberal thought, convinced that the men had been executed for their political beliefs, clashed violently with those who were convinced that the men were deadly bomb-throwing murderers. During his imprisonment Vanzetti wrote many documents in a fine but broken style, which to men like Tommy Turner were worthy pieces of literary composition. To men like Ed Keller they were fiery propaganda from a hate-filled anarchist. As late as 1940 feelings about the case ran high, and the clash between Tommy and Ed does not represent something wholly imaginary.

In 1959 futile attempts were made in the General Court (Legislature) of Massachusetts to exonerate Sacco and Vanzetti. It may be another generation before the case is finally considered closed.

James Thurber and Elliott Nugent

To the readers of *The New Yorker*, the name of James Thurber needs no introduction. As a cartoonist, nonsense essayist, and short-story writer he has established himself as the greatest living humorist in American letters. He may well be remembered in the future as one of the finest of all time. His melancholy hounds, his little men, and the predatory, shapeless women who make life miserable have become the trademarks, in cartoon and story alike, of an excellent satirist.

Thurber was born in Columbus, Ohio, on December 8, 1894. He says that his father was "an honest politician" by trade, and the stories of life in the Thurber household suggest a continual side show inhabited by a collection of eccentrics seldom found outside a madhouse. An unfortunate childhood accident blinded young Thurber in one eye, and from then on clear vision has been a serious problem, until today he is almost totally blind. However, this affliction never interfered with the insight into human behavior which his work has constantly revealed.

From 1913 to 1917 he attended Ohio State University, where he knew Nugent and worked with him for a time on the literary magazine. Conflicting reports exist about whether or not he took his degree eventually, but it is certain that he worked for the State Department in Washington and Paris from 1918 to 1920, having been rejected by the Army because of his eyesight. Soon afterwards he began work for the Columbus *Dispatch* and the Paris edition of the Chicago *Tribune*. In 1926, one year after the magazine was founded, he joined the staff of *The New Yorker*, and although he did not long remain an editor, he has been a steady contributor ever since. By 1929 he had published his first important work, "Is Sex Necessary?" with E. B. White, also of *The New Yorker*, a parody of the current fad of sex-education books. Thurber's famous line drawings illustrated the text.

Since his first published success, Thurber has seen book after book through the press, nearly always composed of *New Yorker* items in collection, although in later years he has written for direct publication. "My Life and Hard Times," his "autobiography," appeared in 1933. Other familiar titles are: "The Owl in the Attic," 1931; "The Middle-aged Man on the Flying Trapeze," 1935; "Fables for Our Time," 1939; "The Thurber Carnival," 1945; "The Thirteen Clocks," 1950 (also made into a successful opera in 1954); "Thurber Country," 1953; and "The Wonderful O," 1957. Three of his short stories were made into plays and presented at New York's Theatre de Lys as *Three by Thurber* in 1955.

Another series of stage adaptations written by Thurber himself appeared in a successful revue called *A Thurber Carnival* in 1960.

Thurber's style lacks any definite formula, and yet his stories and cartoons are unmistakable. He has had no imitators, for he is one of those who cannot be copied. The disturbing sting, the "shiver under the laugh" that Thurber invariably conveys, will always remain a distinctive quality.

Thurber was extremely fortunate to work with his college acquaintance, Elliott Nugent, in the writing of *The Male Animal*. Nugent's background was 100 per cent theatrical, coming as he did from a long line of theatre people. He made his own debut on the professional stage at four. He attended Ohio

State University and received his B.A. in 1919; soon thereafter he began appearing on the New York stage and writing for it.

His first important role was in George S. Kaufman's *Dulcy*, in 1921. For the next three or four years he and his father, J. C. Nugent, collaborated on a series of successful plays, among them *The Poor Nut* in 1925, the prototype of *The Male Animal*. For ten years, until 1940, he worked in Hollywood as actor, writer, and director, and returned to Broadway to help produce and star in the role of Tommy Turner in *The Male Animal*. In John Van Druten's *The Voice of the Turtle* in 1943 he won the Drama Critics' Circle award for the best acting of the 1943–1944 season. Nugent also directed the movie version of *The Male Animal* starring Henry Fonda, and has continued as producer and actor on Broadway into the 1950s.

THE MALE ANIMAL

by

James Thurber and Elliott Nugent

A composite view of the general confusion in *The Male Animal*, sketched by its coauthor. While including characters who never appear—namely, the Thurber trademark apprehensively crouching center stage and the disgruntled producer with his hat on at stage left—Thurber does display the leading characters in typical poses. (*The New York Times. Courtesy James Thurber.*)

The Male Animal was first produced at the Cort Theatre, New York, on January 9, 1940. It was greeted as the finest comedy of the new season, and ran successfully for 243 performances. The following cast appeared in the first production:

CLEOTA	*Amanda Randolph*
ELLEN TURNER	*Ruth Matteson*
TOMMY TURNER	*Elliott Nugent*
PATRICIA STANLEY	*Gene Tierney*
WALLY MYERS	*Don De Fore*
DEAN FREDERICK DAMON	*Ivan Simpson*
MICHAEL BARNES	*Robert Scott*
JOE FERGUSON	*Leon Ames*
MRS. BLANCHE DAMON	*Minna Phillips*
ED KELLER	*Matt Briggs*
MYRTLE KELLER	*Regina Wallace*
"NUTSY" MILLER	*Richard Beckhard*
NEWSPAPER REPORTER	*John Boruff*

Produced by Herman Shumlin
Directed by Mr. Shumlin
Setting by Aline Bernstein
Costumes supervised by Emeline Clark Roche

ACT ONE

SCENE: *The living room of a pleasant, inexpensive little house. There is no distinction of architectural design, but someone with natural good taste has managed to make it look attractive and liveable on a very modest budget. There are some good prints on the walls. The hangings are cheerful, and the furniture, picked up through various bargains and inheritances, goes together to make a pleasing, informal atmosphere.*

The front door opens onto a porch. The wall of the room is lined with bookshelves which continue around the corner to the fireplace. Below this fireplace is a stand with a radio-phonograph. In the center of the rear wall, a bay window with window seat. This corner is used by the Turner family as a casual depository for visitors' hats and coats, although they have also a coat-rail just inside the front door. In front of the bay window, a long table backs a comfort-able couch. To the right of the bay window are more bookshelves, a small landing, and a stairway running up and off stage. In the corner below the stair near the dining-room door, a table has been prepared today to serve as a temporary bar, with a tray, cocktail shaker, and two or three bottles and glasses. On the right are two doors, one leading to the dining room, the other to another porch and back yard. Two small sofas, an arm-chair, a couple of small end or coffee tables, and one or two straight chairs complete the furnishings of the room. There are two or three vases of flowers, and the books and magazines which frequently litter this room have been put tidily away.

At the rise of the curtain, the phone on table, behind sofa is ringing. CLEOTA, *a colored maid, enters from the dining room and answers it.*

CLEOTA. Professah   Turner's   res-i-dence— Who?— You got de wrong numbah— Who?— What you say?— Oh, Mistah *Turner!* No, he ain't heah. He jus' went out to buy some likkah— Who is dis callin'? Yessuh. Yessuh. Ah doan' get dat, but Ah'll tell him Doctah Damon. Ah say Ah'll tell him. (*She hangs up phone; starts for dining room.*)

ELLEN's VOICE (*upstairs*). Who was it, Cleota?

CLEOTA. It was Doctah Damon. He say he comin' ovah to see Mistah Turner or Mistah Turner come over to see him, or sumpin'. (*She turns on lights from wall switch.*)

ELLEN (*coming downstairs*). What was that again, Cleota? (*She is an extremely pretty young woman about twenty-nine or thirty. Quick of speech and movement, she has a ready smile and a sweetness of personality that warms the room. She is completely feminine and acts always from an emotional, not an intellectual, stimulus.*)

CLEOTA. Doctah Damon doan talk up. He kinda muffles. (ELLEN *begins to put finishing touches to the room with quick efficiency, putting away magazines and books.*)

ELLEN. I'm afraid it's you that kind of muffles.

CLEOTA. Yessum. Miz Turner, Ah'm fixin' dem hor doves for de pahty. Did you say put dem black seed ones in de oven?

ELLEN. Black seed ones? Oh, heavens, Cleota, you're not heating the caviar?

CLEOTA. No'm, Ah ain't heatin' it, but taste lak' sumpin' oughtta be done to it.

ELLEN. It's to be served cold. Here, you pick up the rest of the magazines. I'll take a look at the canapés. (*Hurries off into dining room.*)

CLEOTA. Yessum. Ah ain't no hand at 'em. People where Ah worked last jus' drank without eatin' anything. (*There is the sound of whistling outside, and* TOMMY TURNER *enters. He is a young associate professor, thirty-three years old. He wears glasses, is rather more charming than handsome. His clothes are a little baggy. He has a way of disarranging his hair with his hands,* so that he looks like a puzzled spaniel at times. He is carrying chrysanthemums and two bottles of liquor, wrapped in paper and tied with string.*) Oh, hello, Mr. Turner!

TOMMY. Hello, Cleota!

CLEOTA. You bettah not mess up dis room, 'cause dey is guess comin'.

TOMMY. All right, Cleota. I'll be good. (CLEOTA *gives him a doubting look and dawdles off to dining room. We see what she means when* TOMMY *unwraps his packages. In a moment, paper and string drop about him like falling leaves. Manfully, he sticks flowers in the vase among the other flowers. A book with a gay jacket catches his eye. He looks at it disapprovingly, throws it in wastebasket.* ELLEN *enters from dining room.*)

ELLEN. Hello, dear!

TOMMY. Hello, Ellen! Those are for you. (*Indicates his flowers.*)

ELLEN. Oh, thank you, Tommy. They're lovely. (*Surveys the flowers.*)

TOMMY. The ones in the middle.

ELLEN. Yes—

TOMMY. I got the liquor, too.

ELLEN (*taking flowers out of vase*). Did you get the right kind?

TOMMY. I got both kinds. (ELLEN *picks up the litter he has made.*)

ELLEN. Tommy, you're a housewrecker, but you're nice. (*Kisses him.*)

TOMMY. Did I do something right?

ELLEN. Cleota—Cleota, will you fill this vase with water, please? (*Hands vase to* CLEOTA *in doorway.* CLEOTA *goes out.*) What became of the book that was on this table?

TOMMY. That? Oh, I threw it in the waste basket. It's trash.

ELLEN (*rescuing book*). But you can't throw it away. Wally gave it to Patricia.

TOMMY. Oh, he did?

ELLEN. Besides, it's just the right color for this room. (*Young voices are raised outside and* PATRICIA STANLEY, ELLEN's *sister, opens the door and backs into the room. She is a pretty, lively girl of nineteen or twenty. She is followed by* WALLY MYERS, *who is six-feet-one, and weighs 190 pounds, mostly muscle.*)

PAT's VOICE. Oh, Wally, quit arguing!

I'm going to dinner with Mike, and then to the rally with you. You can't feed me at the training table.

WALLY. Aw, that guy Barnes! I don't see why you have to— Oh, how do you do, Mrs. Turner—Professor Turner?

TOMMY. Hello, Butch!

ELLEN. That's Wally Myers.

WALLY (to PATRICIA). Oh, has Butch been coming here, too?

PATRICIA. Go on, get out of here, half-back. I have to get dressed. (*As she sits down and inspects a run in her stocking.*) Hey, Ellen, excited about seeing the great Ferguson, again? He just drove up to the Beta House in a Duesenberg![1] (CLEOTA *reenters with the vase; gives it to* ELLEN *and leaves.*)

ELLEN (*arranging* TOMMY'S *flowers*). Did you see him?

PATRICIA. No, the kids were telling me. Has he still got his hair?

ELLEN. I haven't seen him in ten years. We'll soon find out.

WALLY. Say, is he coming here?

ELLEN. Yes. Why don't you come back and meet him, Wally? You can tell him all about the game tomorrow.

WALLY. Gee, thanks! But nobody could tell Joe Ferguson anything about a football game. He's all-time All-American, you know. Well, thanks, Mrs. Turner. I'll be back. See you later, Pat. (WALLY *goes out.*)

TOMMY. Does he mean that now Joe belongs to the ages, like Lincoln?

ELLEN. Um-hum, in a way.

TOMMY (*crossing to bookcase*). Well, I suppose he has passed into legend. I used to admire him myself—almost.

ELLEN. Pat, why don't you and Michael stay here for dinner? Supper, rather. It's just a bite. We're all going out to eat after the rally.

PATRICIA. No, thanks. You know Michael hates Mr. Keller. He'd spit in his eye.

TOMMY. Why do we have to have Ed Keller to this party? (*Carrying three copies of* Harper's, *he sits on settee.*)

ELLEN. Oh, Joe has to have someone to talk football with. Besides, Ed's his closest friend here. He practically paid Joe's way through college. You can stand the Kellers one night.

TOMMY. Just barely. I don't know how to entertain trustees.

PATRICIA. Well, you'd better be entertaining tonight with the great Ferguson coming. (*Rises.*) Weren't you engaged to him once, Ellen?

ELLEN. Not officially. Just for fun.

PATRICIA (*going upstairs*). Baby, that can be dangerous, too!

ELLEN. Oh, Dean Damon phoned, Tommy.

TOMMY. What'd he want?

ELLEN. I don't know. Cleota answered the phone.

TOMMY. Oh—I see— Oh, I'll bet I know what it was. I saw him this morning. What do you think?

ELLEN. Oh, I don't know— Oh, Tommy, you don't mean—?

TOMMY. Yes, I do.

ELLEN. Oh Tommy, that's wonderful! It's three hundred and fifty more a year, isn't it?

TOMMY. Five hundred! I'm no piker.

ELLEN. Well, you certainly deserve it. (*Gives him a little kiss.*)

TOMMY. Now I can get you that fur coat next February. People must think I let you freeze in the winter.

ELLEN (*crossing to table*). No, they don't. And, don't worry about me— You need some new things, yourself.—I love the flowers, Tommy. And this promotion couldn't have come on a better day for me. Do you know what day it is?

TOMMY. Friday, isn't it? Why?

ELLEN. Oh, nothing—never mind. (*Glances around room.*) What became of all the match boxes? I had one in each ash tray. (*She returns and digs in his coat pocket.*)

TOMMY. I haven't seen any match boxes. What's going on here? Say, you look very pretty tonight. That's a new dress, isn't it?

---

[1] The Duesenberg was an expensive German-made car. In the 1940s a foreign car was very rare. The equivalent today would be the more expensive Jaguar or a car of similar make.

ELLEN. No— It's my hair that's bothering you. It's done a new way—

TOMMY. Doesn't bother me. I like it.

ELLEN (*who has found two match boxes*). One more.

TOMMY. Oh, you exaggerate this match-box thing. Oh! (*Hands her one.*) I ought to take you out to dinner more and show you off.

ELLEN (*redistributing match boxes*). Well, we're going out tonight after the rally.

TOMMY. I mean just the two of us. Tonight will be just like old times. Remember how Joe was always horning in on our dinner dates? I don't believe we ever had one that he didn't come over and diagram the Washington Monument play or something on the tablecloth with a pencil.

ELLEN. Statue of Liberty play, darling.

TOMMY. He was always coming. I never saw him going.

ELLEN. There's still one missing.

TOMMY. I haven't got it— (*He finds it.*) I'll bet Joe does something to get his wife down. Probably cleans his guns with doilies. Clumsy guy. Always knocking knives and forks on the floor.

ELLEN. He wasn't clumsy. He was very graceful. He was a swell dancer. (*She puts away some books.*)

TOMMY. I remember he got the first and the last dance with you, the last time we all went to a dance together.

ELLEN. Phi Psi Christmas dance, wasn't it?

TOMMY. No, the May Dance. Out at the Trowbridge Farm. Remember how it rained?

ELLEN. I remember I had the last dance with Joe because you disappeared somewhere.

TOMMY. No, I was watching—from behind some ferns.

ELLEN. They played "Three O'Clock in the Morning" and "Who?" It was a lovely night, wasn't it?

TOMMY. No, it poured down. You and Joe were dancing out on the terrace when it started. You both got soaked, but you kept right on dancing. (*Having found what he wanted,* TOMMY *returns two magazines to shelves.*)

ELLEN. Oh, yes, I remember. My dress was ruined.

TOMMY. You were shining wet—like Venus and Triton.

ELLEN. Why didn't you cut in? (*Takes magazine* TOMMY *left on coffee table to bookcase.*)

TOMMY. I had a cold. Besides, my feet hurt. (*He starts toward stairs.*) I'll dress. (*Doorbell rings.*) Lord, I hope he isn't here already. (ELLEN *admits* DAMON *and* MICHAEL. DAMON, *the head of the English Department, is a tall, thin, distinguished-looking man of some sixty-five years. He has gray hair, eyes capable of twinkling through glasses whose rims he has a habit of peering over. He talks slowly, selecting his words, in a voice at once compelling and humorous. He often hesitates, peers over his glasses before saying the last word of a phrase or a sentence.* MICHAEL BARNES *is a Senior in the Arts College, an intensely serious young man and a fine literary student. The older people who surround him find his youthful grimness about life's problems sometimes amusing, but more frequently alarming.*)

ELLEN. Oh, come in, Doctor Damon. Hello, Michael.

MICHAEL. How do you do?

TOMMY. How do you do, sir?

DAMON. Hello, Thomas!

ELLEN. Where's Mrs. Damon?

DAMON. I shall pick her up and bring her along shortly for the festivities. This is in the nature of an unofficial call.

TOMMY. Hello, Michael! You both look a little grim. Has anything happened?

DAMON. Michael has written another of his fiery editorials.

PATRICIA (*runs down the stairs*). Ellen, did you see my—oh! How do you do, Doctor Damon? Hi, Michael!

MICHAEL. H'lo!

DAMON. Sit down, my dear. I have here an editorial written by Michael for *The Lit*, which comes out tomorrow. Perhaps, to save time, one of us should read it aloud— "When this so-called

University forces such men out of its faculty as Professor Kennedy, Professor Sykes, and Professor Chapman, because they have been ignorantly called Reds, it surrenders its right to be called a seat of learning. It admits that it is nothing more nor less than a training school" (you will recognize the voice of our good friend, Hutchins, of Chicago[2]) "a training school for bond salesmen, farmers, real-estate dealers, and ambulance chasers. It announces to the world that its faculty is subservient—" (DAMON *peers over glasses at* MICHAEL.)

MICHAEL. Oh, I didn't mean you, of course, Doctor Damon.

DAMON. "—that its faculty is subservient to its trustees, and that its trustees represent a political viewpoint which must finally emerge under its proper name, which is—Fascism."

PATRICIA. Oh, Michael! There you go again!

DAMON. Wait till you hear where he has actually gone.

PATRICIA. Isn't that all?

DAMON. Unhappily, there is more.

PATRICIA. Oh, Lord! (TOMMY *sits down.*)

DAMON (*continuing*). "These professors were not Reds. They were distinguished liberals. Let us thank God that we still have one man left who is going ahead teaching what he believes should be taught."

TOMMY. Who's that?

DAMON. Sh! "He is not afraid to bring up even the Sacco-Vanzetti case. He has read to his classes on the same day Vanzetti's last statement and Lincoln's letter to Mrs. Bixby." I hope we are not alienating the many friends of Abraham Lincoln. (TOMMY *rises and glances at* MICHAEL *questioningly.*) "The hounds of bigotry and reaction will, of course, be set upon the trail of this courageous teacher, but, if they think they are merely on the spoor of a lamb they are destined to the same disappointment as

the hunters who in chasing the wild boar, came accidentally upon a tigress and her cubs. Our hats are off to Professor Thomas Turner of the English Department." That's all.

ELLEN. Tommy?

TOMMY. Michael, I think you might have consulted me about this.

PATRICIA. Michael, you fool! They'll kick you out of school for this—and Tommy too!

ELLEN. You never told me you had brought up the Sacco-Vanzetti case in your classes, Tommy.

DAMON. Yes, just what is this Vanzetti letter you have read?

TOMMY. I haven't read it yet.

MICHAEL. When you told me the other day you were going to read it, I thought you meant that day.

TOMMY. No, Michael. I just meant some day. But I was talking to you as a friend, I was not giving an interview to an editor.

ELLEN. But why were you going to read this letter, Tommy?

TOMMY. Because it's a fine piece of English composition, and I'm teaching a class in English composition. An obscure little class. I don't want any publicity, Michael. I just want to be left alone.

ELLEN. But nobody thinks of Vanzetti as a writer, Tommy.

TOMMY. It happens that he developed into an extraordinary writer. I don't think you could help being interested in the letter yourself, Doctor Damon.

DAMON. You would be surprised at my strength of will in these matters, Thomas. What I am interested in is preserving some air of academic calm here at Midwestern—and also in retaining my chair in the English department.

PATRICIA. You don't want to get Tommy kicked out of school, do you, Michael?

MICHAEL. No. I didn't think of that. I thought Mr. Turner was about the only man we had left who would read

---

[2] Robert Maynard Hutchins, then Chancellor of the University of Chicago. His youth (forty-one at the time of this play) caused him to be regarded as the "boy wonder" of United States education.

whatever he wanted to to his classes. I thought he was the one man who would stand up to these stadium builders.

TOMMY. I'm not standing up to anyone, Michael. I'm not challenging anyone. This is just an innocent little piece I wanted to read. (MICHAEL *turns away*.)

ELLEN (*rises*). I know it must be all right, Tommy, but you can't read it now. Keller and the other trustees kicked Don Chapman out last month for doing things just as harmless as this. (*Turning to* MICHAEL.) You'll have to change that editorial, Michael.

MICHAEL. I can't. The magazines were run off the presses last night. They've already been delivered to the news stands.

DAMON. They go on sale in the morning. (*To* ELLEN.) I think that our—er—tigress here may have to issue a denial tomorrow. After all, he hasn't read it yet.

ELLEN (*to* TOMMY). Yes, and you mustn't read it now.

PATRICIA. Will Michael be kicked out of school, Doctor Damon?

DAMON. Sufficient unto the day is the evil thereof, my dear. (*He gets his hat.*)

PATRICIA (*to* MICHAEL). There! You see—

DAMON (*coming to* TOMMY, *who has seated himself at the other side of the room*). I quite understand how you meant to present it, Thomas; but our good friend Mr. Keller would not. Do not underestimate Mr. Edward K. Keller. He rolls like the juggernaut over the careers of young professors.

TOMMY. I know.

DAMON (*starting to door*). Since he must be with us tonight let us confine our conversation to the—woeful inadequacies of the Illinois team.

TOMMY (*rising*). It isn't Illinois we're playing—it's Michigan.

DAMON. Oh, I must remember that. (*Goes out.*)

PATRICIA (*to* MICHAEL). There, you see! You will be kicked out.

MICHAEL. He didn't say that.

PATRICIA. Yes, he did. You needn't bother to come back for me, Michael.

I'm staying here for supper. (*Runs upstairs.*)

MICHAEL. I see. I'm sorry, Mr. Turner. I guess I got—well—carried away.

TOMMY. I know, Michael. Sometimes, when I see that light in your eye I wish I could be carried away too.

MICHAEL. Yes sir. (*He goes out grimly. There is a slight pause.*)

TOMMY. Well—

ELLEN. I'm sorry, Tommy.

TOMMY. Oh it's all right. Maybe I can read this thing later on, after all the fuss quiets down—say next spring.

ELLEN. It would still be dangerous.

TOMMY. Yes, I guess it would. I know I'm not a tiger, but I don't like to be thought of as a pussy cat either.

ELLEN (*with an understanding smile*). It's getting late. You'd better go and put on that gray suit I laid out for you.

TOMMY. Yeh, sure. (*Crosses to stairs.*)

ELLEN. And be sure your socks are right side out, and Tommy—don't try to be a tiger in front of Ed Keller.

TOMMY (*at stair landing*). I won't. I'm scared of those Neanderthal men. I'll talk about football.

ELLEN. Thank you, darling. That's swell. You know how Joe is—always cheerful. And we do want it to be a good party.

TOMMY (*starting upstairs*). I'll be cheerful. I'll be merry and bright. I'll be the most cheerful son-of-a-gun in this part of the country. (*He sings as he exits up the stairs. He disappears. We hear him singing a snatch of "Who's Afraid of the Big Bad Wolf?" The doorbell rings.*)

ELLEN (*calling upstairs*). Hurry, Tommy! They're here! (*Crosses to the door and admits* JOE FERGUSON, *followed by* WALLY MYERS.) Hello, Joe!

JOE. Ellen! How are you, baby? God, you look great! Why, you're younger and prettier than ever! If I were a braver man, I'd kiss you. Doggone it, I *will* kiss you! (*Kisses her on cheek, hugs her, lifts her off the floor—whirls her around.* WALLY *closes door.* JOE *is all that we have been led to expect: big, dynamic, well-dressed, prosperous. He is*

*full of good nature and a boundless en-
thusiasm for everything.*)

ELLEN (*catching something of his ebul-
lience*). It's terribly nice to see you
again, Joe. If I were a younger woman,
I'd say it's been all of ten years.

JOE (*whipping off his coat, he puts
down a small box on sofa*). Gosh, this is
swell! Where's the great Thomas?

ELLEN. Tommy will be right down. I
see Wally found you—so you've met?
(WALLY *hangs up* JOE's *coat*.)

JOE. Yeh. We joined forces outside.

ELLEN (*at settee*). Come on over here
and sit down.

JOE. I forgot to ask you Wally, who's
going in at the other half tomorrow?
Stalenkiwiecz?

WALLY. No, sir. Wierasocka.

JOE. Oh, is he?

WALLY. Yeh. He's a Beta. From Oregon.

JOE. Oh, yeh—yeh, I know him.

WALLY. Stalenkiwiecz is laid up. They
think he's got whooping cough. (*He sits
in center of settee beside* ELLEN.)

JOE. That's bad! I've got a thousand
fish on that game. (*Sits on settee. It is
very crowded.*)

WALLY. I think it's safe, all right, Mr.
Ferguson, but I wish we had you. Sta-
lenkiwiecz, Wierasocka, Myers, and
Whirling Joe Ferguson.

ELLEN. Do they still call you Whirling
Joe?

JOE. Oh, sure, remember how—

WALLY. Say, he was the greatest open-
field runner there ever was.

ELLEN. Yes, Joe. How does it happen
you've never even—

WALLY. Why, you made Red Grange
look like a cripple.

JOE. Aw, they say you're not so bad
yourself. Say Ellen, how's—

WALLY. Aw, I'm just fair, that's all.
(*Produces a clipping.*) This is what
Grantland Rice said about me. (*Hands
it to* JOE.)

JOE (*beginning to wish* WALLY *would
go*). Yeh.—Too bad this is Wally's last
year. We're going to miss him—eh, Ellen?

ELLEN (*pointedly*). Have you got anything to do, Wally?

WALLY. Well—the Coach wants me to
help him with the back-field next season.
Not much money in it, of course.

JOE (*hands clipping back to* WALLY).
Well, if you want my advice, don't go
in for coaching. I had a sweet offer from
Cincinnati in 'Twenty-nine. Remember
that, Ellen?

ELLEN. I remember very well. Do you
remember when—

WALLY. Nineteen twenty-nine!—I was
only twelve years old then—

TOMMY (*comes downstairs*). Hello,
Joe! It's nice to see you again!

JOE (*rises and shakes hands*). Tommy,
old man, how are you? Ten years!
Teaching must be good for you. And
Ellen, here, looks like a million bucks!
That reminds me—I came laden with
gifts. (*Turns and almost runs into*
WALLY. *He recovers and gets the small
box.*) These are a few flowering weeds—

ELLEN (*opening the box of orchids*).
Thank you, Joe. They're lovely. Tommy, will you call Cleota?

TOMMY. Sure! (*Goes into dining
room, calls.*) Cleota!

ELLEN. It's fun to get flowers. Very
festive.

JOE. Oh, it's nothing much, but I
wanted you to know I remembered the
great day. Think I'd forget it was your
birthday?

ELLEN. You never used to. (TOMMY
has rejoined them.) Tommy gave me
some flowering weeds, too—for my birthday.

TOMMY. Yes, I got her some—for
your—oh—yes— Not such nice ones, I'm
afraid. (*To* ELLEN.) I'm a lucky man.
(CLEOTA *enters.*)

ELLEN. Will you find something to
put these in, Cleota?

CLEOTA. Ah'll hafta put 'em in de sink
wit dat ice. (*Goes out with flowers.*)

JOE. Boy, it's sure great to be here!

TOMMY. It's nice to have you.—Staying long?

JOE. Got to be in Washington next
week. Well, Tommy, I see you've still
got a lot of books.

TOMMY. Oh, yes.

JOE. You know I never get a chance

to read books. (*He sits on settee again.*)

WALLY. Say, you must have a swell job! (*He sits on bench before fireplace.*)

JOE. By the time I get through at night, I'm lucky if I can keep up with what's going on in the world. Way things are changing, you gotta do that. I take fifteen magazines. That keeps me busy.

ELLEN (*linking her arm through* TOMMY'S). Tommy's had several articles in *Harper's* and the *Atlantic.*

JOE. No! Say, that's fine! But you'll have to boil them down to the *Reader's Digest* to reach me, Tommy. You know, that's a great little magazine.

TOMMY. Do you like bouillon cubes?

ELLEN (*hastily*). Tommy, you'd better make a drink.

TOMMY. Yes. We have a lot of celebrating to do. (*He goes out to dining room calling* "Cleota.")

ELLEN. How've you been, Joe? (*Sits next to* JOE.)

JOE. Fine, except for a little sinus trouble.

WALLY. You know, Mrs. Turner, I recognized him right away from that big picture in the gym. (TOMMY *reenters with bowl of ice. Mixes drinks at table.*)

ELLEN. That's fine. How's Brenda? I meant to ask before.

JOE. Fine! Great! Little heavier, maybe. We're being divorced, you know.

ELLEN. But I didn't know. Oh, Joe, I'm sorry.

JOE. Nothing to be sorry about. It's just one of those things.

TOMMY. What's the matter?

ELLEN. Joe and his wife are breaking up.

TOMMY. Oh, that's too bad.

JOE. No, it's all fine. We're both taking it in our stride. Took her out to dinner last week—along with her new boy friend.

TOMMY. Wasn't that rather complicated?

ELLEN. Oh, you're not up to date, Tommy. That's the modern way of doing things.

JOE. Sure! Take it in your stride. Gosh, Ellen, I can't take my eyes off you. (*At* WALLY'S *chuckle,* JOE *rises and changes*

the subject.) Nice little place you got here. Need any help, Tommy? I'm a demon on Manhattans. (*He is starting toward* TOMMY *when the doorbell rings.*)

TOMMY. I'm all right, thanks.

JOE. I hope that's Ed, the old scoundrel.

ELLEN (*admits the* DAMONS). I'm so glad— Hello, Mrs. Damon!

BLANCHE. Hello, Ellen dear! How do you do, Mr. Turner?

ELLEN. You must know Joe Ferguson.

BLANCHE. Oh, of course! How do you do? (JOE *bows, smiling.*)

ELLEN. This is Mrs. Damon, Joe. You remember Dean Damon?

JOE. Yes indeed! Nice to see you again, sir.

DAMON (*crossing to him and shaking hands*). Back for the slaughter of the— uh—Michigan innocents, eh?

JOE. That's right. (ELLEN *and* BLANCHE *have turned to* WALLY.)

ELLEN. Mrs. Damon, may I present Mr. Myers? (BLANCHE *shakes hands with him.*)

WALLY. How do you do?

BLANCHE. Oh, yes, of course we all know about our great fullback. (TOMMY *gives* JOE *a cocktail.*)

ELLEN. Let me help you with your coat.

BLANCHE. Thank you, dear. (*To* WALLY.) Tell me, are you nervous about the game?

WALLY. No, ma'am.

BLANCHE. Not the least little bit?

WALLY. No, ma'am.

BLANCHE. That's nice. (*Smiling at his surprise, she sits on settee.*)

DAMON (*to* JOE). I remember you not only from the gridiron but from my Shakespeare class. You slept very quietly.

JOE. I never did finish reading *Hamlet.* I always wondered how that came out. (*He laughs heartily.* DAMON *laughs politely.*)

TOMMY. Does anybody mind a Manhattan?

BLANCHE. Oh, Ellen! Could we have sherry?

ELLEN. Certainly. Tommy— (TOMMY,

who is bringing two cocktails to the DAMONS, *pauses uncertainly.*)

TOMMY. Sherry coming right up. Here, Wally. (*Gives him cocktail.*)

WALLY. No, thanks. I'm in training.

TOMMY. Well, just hold it. Sherry for you too, Doctor Damon?

DAMON (*disappointed*). When Mrs. Damon says we, she means me. Sherry, thanks. (TOMMY *drinks the left-over cocktail.*)

BLANCHE. A little sherry is such fun. (WALLY *offers her cigarette from box on coffee table.*) No thanks, I'll smoke my "Spuds"! (WALLY *lights* BLANCHE'S *cigarette.*)

PATRICIA (*coming downstairs*). Hello, everybody!

ELLEN (*presenting* PAT *to* JOE). This is my sister Patricia.

PATRICIA. How do you do?

JOE (*admiring her*). How do you *do?* My goodness! Why, you're as big and pretty as your sister. How about a drink?

PATRICIA. No, thanks. (*To* ELLEN *as she crosses to* WALLY.) Still has his hair. Hello, Wally! (TOMMY *serves sherry to* DAMONS.)

WALLY. Hi, Pat! Look, can I pick you up at Hennick's a little earlier?

PATRICIA. I'm not going to Hennick's. I'm eating here. That date's off.

WALLY. With Barnes? Say, that's swell. I got to run along, Mrs. Turner. Nice party. (*Crosses to* JOE.) Glad I met you, Joe—I mean, Mr. Ferguson. (*They shake hands.*) I'll be seeing you. Goodbye, everybody! I'll go out the back way. (*He goes out the door which leads into the garden.*)

JOE. Take it easy, old man. Don't break a leg on me. Remember, I've got a thousand fish on that game. (*Follows* WALLY *out.*)

BLANCHE. He's a handsome boy, Patricia. (*Doorbell rings.*) And seems very healthy.

PATRICIA. I have to keep in training for him. (PATRICIA *and* DAMON *sit down on the bench before the fireplace.*)

TOMMY (*going to door*). I'll get it. (ELLEN *joins* TOMMY *and greets the*

KELLERS *as they come in.* ED KELLER *is a big, loud, slightly bald man of about thirty-eight, heavy around the middle. He is a prosperous real-estate man, owns the Keller Building, is a trustee and as such, the biggest voice and strongest hand on the Board.* MYRTLE KELLER, *also in her late thirties, dresses well and is not bad-looking, was once pretty, but is now a slightly faded blonde.*)

ED. Hello, Ellen! Hi, Turner! Where is he? (*Passes* TOMMY *fast, without handshake, looking for* JOE *who reappears. The two men run to meet each other. This is a typical meeting between two old friends of the hale-and-hearty, back-slapping persuasion who haven't met for years.*) Hiya, you old rascal! Hahya, boy?

JOE (*as they clinch in the middle of the room, hugging, slapping backs, etc.*). Hello, you old son-of-a-gun! How are you, Ed? (*Crosses to* MYRTLE.) Hello, Myrtle! Gosh, I'm glad to see you! (*Hugs her, lifting her off her feet.*)

MYRTLE (*screams*). I'm glad to see you, too! Ellen—

JOE (*back to* ED). Gee, you're looking swell, Ed, old boy, old boy!

ED. Judas Priest, this is swell! How are you anyway, Joe? (*The* MEN'S *voices predominate.*)

JOE. Fine! Swell! Never better. You've put on a little weight, eh, Eddie? And what's happened to the crowning glory?

ED. Worry: real-estate, Roosevelt. Wonder I got any left.

MYRTLE. How do you do, Doctor Damon? How do you do, Mrs. Damon? Haven't seen you in a long, long time. Hello, Patricia— Oh, quiet down! Ed! (*Sits down.*) Are we late, Ellen?

ELLEN. Not at all. Just in time for the canapés.

JOE. How long's it been, Ed? Seven, eight years, isn't it?

ED. Eight, anyway.

ELLEN. Look, you two, will you break it up and say hello to people?

ED. All right, Ellen, but it sure is fine to see The Whirler again. How do you do, Doctor Damon? Not drinking straight Scotch, I hope?

DAMON. If I did that, my stomach—and Mrs. Damon—would punish me severely.

ELLEN. Won't you have a cocktail, Ed? (*Brings drink to* ED.)

ED. Thanks.

JOE. Say, this is Ellen's birthday. How about a little toast?

TOMMY. Well, fill 'em up. (*Pours drinks, one for himself.*)

ED. Well, happy birthday, Ellen! (ED *starts "Happy Birthday To You," and they* ALL *sing. It is obvious* TOMMY *is bored; he sits down, sips his drink, then noticing everybody standing, he rises, sings the last line very off key.* CLEOTA *enters, comes up behind* DAMON *with plate of canapés.*)

CLEOTA (*after song dies*). Hor doves?

DAMON (*startled*). I beg your pardon —oh! Thank you.

JOE (*as* TOMMY *pours another round*). Let's drink one toast to The Big Red Team. What do you say! (TOMMY *starts humming "The Big Bad Wolf."*)

ED. The Big Red Team.

TOMMY (*singing softly to himself*). "The Big Red Team—
Big Red Team.
Who's afraid of The Big Red Team—"

ED. What's that?

TOMMY. Huh? (ED *glares at him. To* ELLEN.) What did I do?

ELLEN. Tommy! You'd better eat something. Those cocktails are strong.

TOMMY I'm doing all right, honey. How's everything in Detroit, Joe?

JOE. I don't know. All right, I guess. (ED *and* JOE *seat themselves on settee away from the women.*)

ELLEN. Tommy means Pittsburgh. The Bryson Steel Company is in Pittsburgh, Tommy. (CLEOTA *gives* ELLEN *tray and goes out.*)

TOMMY. Oh, yes, sure. Well, how's everything in Pittsburgh?

JOE. Well, it might be worse.

ED. Couldn't be much worse out here.

TOMMY. Have a drink.

ELLEN (*takes canapés to* MYRTLE). How are the kids, Myrtle?

MYRTLE. They're all right. The baby has some kind of rash on her little hips, but it's nothing, really. Makes her cross, though.

ED. Time sure does fly. Now Buster wants to go to Princeton. No matter how you watch 'em, they get in with the wrong kids. (*The* WOMEN's *voices predominate.*)

BLANCHE. How's your sister?

MYRTLE. They took a stone out of her as big as a walnut. She can't weigh more than ninety pounds.

JOE. I remember when I actually got along with only one car, and thought it was plenty. Now I've got three, and the bills are terrific. Do you know what my gas bill was last month? (DAMON *rises, bored, picks out book and glances through it.*)

BLANCHE. They cut old Mrs. Wilmot open for the same trouble, and didn't find a thing!

MYRTLE. Ed, when was it I had that impacted tooth out?

ED. Seven years ago. Year the banks closed. 'Thirty-three.

TOMMY. Fill 'em up. (*Pours himself another.*)

ELLEN. Tommy! (*She takes shaker away from him.*) Dividend for the women folks. Give me your glass, Myrtle.

MYRTLE. Thanks.

BLANCHE. No more for us. Mercy, we'll be light-headed.

TOMMY (*follows* ELLEN, *takes shaker, pours himself another*). But we're celebrating the homecoming game. Banks closing and everything.

JOE. How's building out here now, Ed?

TOMMY (*sauntering over to the men*). Yeh, how's building?

ED. Lousy. Whatta ya expect with that man in the White House? You know what *I* think? I think he's crazy.

JOE. You know what I heard? (*The* WOMEN *stop their talk to listen, but* JOE *whispers in* ED's *ear.* TOMMY *puts down shaker.*)

ED. I wouldn't be a damn bit surprised. (ED's *voice predominates in the following.*)

ED. Only hope for business I see is

some big new industry. And he'll probably do something to ruin that.

BLANCHE (*sotto voce*). Patricia, may I see the little girl's room?

MYRTLE. Me, too.

PATRICIA. Yes, I'll show you. (*They start toward stairs.*)

MYRTLE (*as they start upstairs*). Is it serious?

BLANCHE. They took a pint of pus out of her! (*Men react to this. The women go off, still chattering.*)

ED. Well, Doctor Damon, we men on the Board of Trustees are certainly glad that this Red scare is over.

DAMON. No doubt you are.

ED. Now maybe the new stadium project will get somewhere.

DAMON (*eagerly moving forward*). And the Endowment Fund?

ED. Yeh, sure—that's important too. I'm working to convince the substantial alumni that we've got all this Parlor Pink business over and done with. Got 'em all weeded out.

JOE. Yeah—all that newspaper stuff was pretty bad.

ED. Sure! Nobody felt like coming through for anything when they read about men like Kennedy and Sykes and Chapman being in the faculty. That Chapman was nothing but a damn Red. (DAMON *covers his disgust and turns to* ELLEN.)

TOMMY. No, he wasn't, Mr. Keller. Don Chapman was a humanist.

ELLEN (*laying a quieting hand on* TOMMY's *arm*). We knew him very well.

JOE. How do you know he wasn't a Red, Tommy?

ED. He went to Soviet Russia for his vacation once, didn't he?

TOMMY (*rising*). He just went to see the Drama Festival.

ED (*suspiciously*). Well, it's a mighty long way to go to see a show.

CLEOTA (*who has just entered*). Suppah is se'ved. (*Retires to dining room.*)

ELLEN. Shall we go into the dining room? It's only a salad. We're going out to eat afterwards. Come along, Ed, we

don't want to miss that rally. (*She links her arm through* ED's *and they go out to dining room.*)

ED. Say, that's right. I haven't missed a Michigan rally in seventeen years.

ELLEN (*reenters; goes to stairs; calls*). Supper's ready! (PATRICIA, BLANCHE, *and* MYRTLE *come downstairs.*)

BLANCHE. Thank you. Come, Frederick. (DAMON *and* BLANCHE *go into dining room.*)

ELLEN. Patricia, you get a plate for Mr. Ferguson. He's the guest of honor you know.

JOE. And I'll get a plate for you, Ellen. Come on. (JOE *and* PATRICIA *follow the* DAMONS.)

MYRTLE (*as she goes into dining room*). Oh, what a lovely table, Ellen! (*During the following scene until* ED's *reentrance, there is the general conversation in the dining room, as* EVERYBODY *is finding his supper and beginning to eat.*)

ELLEN (*crossing to* TOMMY). Tommy, don't say any more about Don Chapman tonight, please.

TOMMY. All right, I won't. Let's get something to eat. (ELLEN *takes his arm. They start for dining room.*) Joe looks better, doesn't he?

ELLEN. Better?

TOMMY. Well, bigger anyway. (*They exit.* CLEOTA *has entered with cleanup tray. She clears away drinks and canapés, singing "I Can't Give You Anything but Love" softly. She finds one glass with some liquor in it. After a long scrutiny she raises it to her lips.*)

ED (*off*). Come on, Myrtle! Hurry up! Joe's got to speak at this rally. (CLEOTA *drinks and quickly puts glass on tray and resumes song as* ED *enters with plate of food. He plants himself in the center of a settee, and also takes possession of a coffe table.* BLANCHE *and* MYRTLE *enter, with* DAMON *following them and carrying two plates.*)

BLANCHE. Come, Myrtle, sit over here with me. Frederick, put it down over there on that table.

MYRTLE (*as they cross the room*).

What makes you think there was something suspicious about it? (*The women settle themselves on settee.*)

BLANCHE. Well, his family won't allow a post mortem. Thank you, Frederick, that's fine. (ELLEN *and* JOE *come in.*)

ELLEN. I hope you can all find a place to sit.

JOE (*crossing to long sofa*). What's the matter with this? Come on Ellen, give me a break.

ELLEN (*smiles and sits beside him, speaking to* PATRICIA, *who appears in dining room door*). Pat, is Tommy getting some food?

PATRICIA. Yeh, he's all right. (*She joins the women and* DAMON, *who is eating standing up at the mantel.*)

TOMMY (*entering*). Sure, I'm fine. (*He looks around for a place to settle.*)

ELLEN. Bring in the coffee, please, Cleota. (CLEOTA *nods and goes out.*)

ED. There's room here for somebody.

TOMMY. No, thanks, I'll sit— (*Looks around for any place away from* ED— *the only vacant space is a chair beside* ED's *settee.*) here.

MYRTLE. Eat your vegetables, Ed.

ED. Aw, this is a party.

BLANCHE. Where's Michael Barnes this evening, Patricia? Frederick tells me he's written a remarkable editorial. (DAMON *drops his fork.*) Be careful, Frederick!

ED. Barnes—Barnes—? I haven't read a decent editorial since Brisbane died.[3]

PATRICIA. Michael couldn't come. He doesn't like Mr.—er—

MYRTLE. Doesn't like what?

PATRICIA. Doesn't like parties.

BLANCHE. I'm always so interested in *The Literary Magazine.* What was the editorial, Patricia?

DAMON. Eat your dinner, my dear. Remember, Mr. Keller—wants to get to the rally.

ED. Huh?

BLANCHE (*staring at him*). What's the matter with you? (*He shushes her. To*

PATRICIA.) I hope I haven't said anything, dear. (PATRICIA *shakes her head.* CLEOTA *enters with coffee and serves the guests.*)

ED. What's going on over there? Who is this Barnes?

TOMMY. One of Patricia's beaux.

ED. Some writer?

TOMMY. He's a student. Editor on *The Literary Magazine.*

ED. Oh, yeah, I've heard of him. What's he done now?

ELLEN. Oh, it's nothing really.

TOMMY. Well, since it's come up, Ellen, we might as well tell Mr. Keller. He'll read about it tomorrow— (ELLEN *rises.*) I told Michael I was going to read something to one of my English classes and he got a mistaken idea about it and wrote a sort of—

ELLEN (*breaking in quickly*). Just a silly little editorial—that's all.

ED. I see.

PATRICIA. Because Tommy isn't really going to read it at all. (MYRTLE *murmurs to* BLANCHE, *rises and goes to dining room.*)

ED. What was it this kid said, you were going to read? Anything important?

TOMMY (*after a moment*). It's a short, but beautifully written piece of English by Bartolomeo Vanzetti.

ED. Never heard of him. (*Then, as the name registers.*) Hey, you don't mean Vanzetti of Sacco and Vanzetti!

TOMMY. Yes, the same man.

ED. You mean you're going to read something *he* wrote?

TOMMY. Yes, I was going to.

ELLEN (*quickly*). But now he's not— Michael didn't understand.

ED. Why would you ever think of such a dumb thing in the first place? (TOMMY *has lost any appetite he may have had. He rises and puts his plate and cup on the table.*)

TOMMY. It's part of a series. I read many such letters to my class.

ED. You mean letters by anarchists?

[3] Arthur Brisbane (1864–1936), influential newspaper editor and columnist on the New York *Journal* and the Chicago *Herald and Examiner.*

TOMMY (*restrains himself*). No, letters by men who were not professional writers—like Lincoln, General Sherman—

ED. Well, it's a damn good thing you changed your mind. Putting Lincoln and General Sherman in a class with Vanzetti! Wouldn't look very good.

JOE. What's this?

ED. Wait a minute. (*To* TOMMY.) Is this thing going to be printed? This editorial?

DAMON. We discovered it too late to stop it.

ED. And this kid didn't submit it to the Publications Committee?

DAMON. Unfortunately, he did not. Ellen dear, Mrs. Damon and I must be running along.

ELLEN. Oh, I'm sorry.

DAMON. I have a committee meeting.

BLANCHE (*astonished*). What committee?

DAMON. Come, Blanche.

BLANCHE (*rising*). Oh, yes, that little committee.

ED. Well, I hope this thing's not too bad. You better deny it quick, Turner. I tell you. I'll call the papers in the morning.

TOMMY. No, I'll take care of it. (MYRTLE *enters from dining room with two dishes of sherbet.*)

JOE. What's going on here? (*Rises.*)

MYRTLE. Here's some sherbet, Ed.

ED. Put it down there. (*To* JOE.) I'm just telling Turner here we've had enough of this Red business among the students and the faculty. Don't want any more.

TOMMY (*returning to his chair*). This isn't Red, Mr. Keller.

ED. Maybe not, but it looks bad. We don't want anything Red—or even Pink—taught here.

TOMMY. But who's to decide what is Red or what is Pink?

ED. We are! Somebody's got to decide what's fit to teach. If we don't, who would?

DAMON. I thought that perhaps the faculty had—

ED. No sir. You fellows are too wishy-washy. We saw that in the Chapman case. Americanism is what we want taught here.

JOE. Americanism is a fine thing.

TOMMY. Fine! But how would you define Americanism?

ED. Why—er—everybody knows what Americanism is! What do you believe in?

TOMMY. I believe that a college should be concerned with ideas. Not just your ideas or my ideas, but all ideas.

ED. No, sir! That's the *trouble*—too damn many ideas floating around— You put ideas of any kind into young people's heads, and the first thing you know, they start believing them.

DAMON. On the contrary. I have been putting ideas into young people's heads for forty-two years with no—visible—results whatever. (*There is a dubious laugh from* ED.)

BLANCHE. Come, Frederick. Good night, Ellen! Lovely party! (*She bustles* DAMON *out.*)

ED (*rises*). Turner, you better think twice before you read anything. I can promise you the trustees will clamp down on any professor who tries anything funny. I'm telling you that for your own good.

JOE. Say, I thought we were going to have some fun. Let's break this up. How about some music? (*He goes over to* Victrola *and puts on a record.*)

ED. That's right. We're celebrating tonight. Just wanted to get that out of my system. (*He picks up the dish of ice.*) Oh, I didn't want this—I wanted some of that ice cream. (*He starts for the dining room.*)

MYRTLE. He means he wants both. Here, I'll show you. (*She follows him out.* PATRICIA *starts to go, too;* ELLEN, *worried about* TOMMY, *stops her, whispering to her.* PAT *nods and turns to* JOE, *who is looking through the records.*)

PATRICIA. I'll bet you'd like some ice cream, too, Mr. Ferguson.

JOE. No. I . . . (PATRICIA *winks at him; he glances at* TOMMY.) Oh, sure! Sure, I would.

PATRICIA (*linking an arm through his*). Can you still skip?

JOE. No—not at my age. (*They go into the dining room,* PAT *closing the door softly.* TOMMY *pours himself a drink.*)

ELLEN. Tommy, have you had too much to drink?

TOMMY. No. Not enough.

ELLEN. Your eyes have that funny look.

TOMMY. Did you hear what Mr. Keller said to me? I don't like to be talked to like that.

ELLEN. Just because he was nasty and you've had a few drinks. Tommy, you're not going to go ahead and read that letter.

TOMMY. Yes, Ellen, I think I have to.

ELLEN. Tommy, try to be practical for once. At least wait until you're not so mad. Try to think of this the way any other man would think of it.

TOMMY. I'm not any other man.

ELLEN. Well, try to be. Do you think Joe would do something that would get him into trouble just because somebody irritated him?

TOMMY. *Joe!* I don't see why you don't try to understand how *I* feel about this.

ELLEN. I'm simply trying to keep you out of a lot of trouble. I don't see why—

TOMMY. But you see how Joe would feel. That's very plain to you, isn't it?

ELLEN. Yes, it is. Joe wouldn't get all mixed up.

TOMMY. I'm not mixed up. I'm trying to understand what goes on in your mind. It *can't* be like Joe Ferguson's mind!

ELLEN. Oh, you and your mind! (*Turns away exasperated.*) I have to go through such a lot with your mind!

TOMMY. Maybe you wouldn't if you understood it better.

ELLEN. Oh, I know, I know! I'm too dumb for you!

TOMMY. Now, Ellen, I didn't say that.

ELLEN. You said Joe and I were stupid.

TOMMY. I said he was.

ELLEN. But he isn't. He's a big man. In some ways he's smarter than you.

TOMMY. Well, you ought to know. (*He turns away from her.*)

ELLEN (*catching his arm*). Oh, look, Tommy—what are we fighting about?

TOMMY (*turns*). You said I was dumb.

ELLEN. Tommy, you've had too many drinks or you wouldn't say that.

TOMMY. No, I haven't, but I don't feel very well. I feel very unhappy and slightly sick.

ELLEN. I'll get you some bicarbonate of soda.

TOMMY. No, you won't. I'll go upstairs and lie down for a few minutes myself. I can do that much. Let's not bring this down to the level of bicarbonate of soda. (*He starts slowly, then suddenly feels squeamish and makes a mad dash for it.*)

ELLEN (*hesitates for a minute at the foot of the stairs—calls after him*). Tommy! Tommy, I didn't— (JOE *comes from the dining room with a dish of ice cream.*)

JOE. Anything the matter?

ELLEN. Oh—no. Tommy's not feeling well. He got sick once before at a party. He's not used to drinking, and he's very sensitive about it. Cleota! (JOE *nods and goes to turn off the Victrola.* CLEOTA *comes in, starts clearing away supper plates.* ELLEN *goes to her, speaks in a low voice.*) Cleota, will you get Mr. Turner some bicarbonate of soda from the kitchen? (CLEOTA *nods, retires to the dining room.*) Cleota will get him some bicarbonate of soda from the kitchen. He'd never find it upstairs.

JOE (*takes off the record and hunts for another one to his liking*). Why wouldn't he? Where do you keep it?

ELLEN. In the medicine chest.

JOE. What was that stuff between him and Ed?

ELLEN. Oh, it's nothing, really. I'll tell you about it tomorrow. (*Her mind is on* TOMMY *upstairs.*)

JOE. Fine— Say, look what I found! "Who?" Remember that, Ellen? (*He puts the record on, starts it.* ELLEN *moves closer to the Victrola and listens as it plays:*

"Who-o-o stole my heart away?
Who-o-o makes me dream all day?
Dreams I know can never come true.
Seems as though I'd ever be blue
Who-o-o means my happiness—"
(*As naturally as if they were always danc-ing to this song, they* BOTH *begin to dance.*) Gee, this takes me back—The May Dance. Remember?

ELLEN. Um-huh—it rained.

JOE. You said you didn't know it was raining. I know I didn't. (*Holds her closer.*)

ELLEN (*breaks away*). I'm a little rusty, Joe. I haven't danced in—oh, I don't remember when. Makes me feel young.

JOE. Then what are we stopping for? Come on.

ELLEN. Well—all right. (*They go back into the dance. Dreaming.* ELLEN *glances up at* JOE. *They slow down to a stop and stand looking at each other, he ardently, she caught up in the music.*)

JOE. I can answer all those questions— (*As the music goes into the instrumental reprise,* JOE *kisses her, and she kisses back for a long moment, then tries to pull away.*) No one but you—

ELLEN (*as he tries to kiss her again*). Oh, no, Joe, please, I— Say, how many cocktails did *I* have? (*They stand for an instant, looking at each other. Offstage we hear:*)

MYRTLE. Ed, get away from that ice cream. You've had enough. (JOE *and* ELLEN *quietly start dancing again smil-ing.*)

ED. Oh—all right. (TOMMY, *a little pale and disheveled, comes down the stairs and sees them dancing there; he stops;* MYRTLE *and* ED *enter.*)

MYRTLE (*nudging* ED). Look, Ed! Just like the old days, isn't it? Seeing them dancing together?

ED. I'll say. (*Then, loudly.*) They make a darn handsome couple, don't they? (TOMMY, *although he has not seen the kiss, has sensed the whole intimacy of the scene and the meaning of* ED's *remark; he nods soberly.*)

JOE. She dances like a dream.

ED (*chuckling*). Like a "dream can never come true," eh, Joe? You look mighty sweet in there, boy. (ELLEN *sees* TOMMY. *Following her glance,* ED *and* MYRTLE *and* JOE *turn and look at* TOMMY.)

ELLEN (*breaking away*). Oh—Tommy —are you all right?

TOMMY (*coming down*). Yes, thanks.— Don't—let me spoil the party.

ED. Party's breaking up anyway, Tom-my. (JOE *turns off Victrola.*)

TOMMY. I just thought I'd get some more air— (*Crosses to door which leads out to the garden.*)

ED. I don't want to miss any of that rally. (*A band is heard in the distance, approaching. Holds out* MYRTLE's *coat.*) Myrtle! (MYRTLE *crosses to him.*)

PATRICIA (*enters from dining room with bicarbonate of soda in glass*). Who's this for, Ellen?

ELLEN. Tommy! (*To* TOMMY, *as he stands with his back turned, breathing the fresh air.*) Tommy, will you take this bicarbonate?

TOMMY. Just—put it by for a moment. You go to the rally, Ellen— I'm going to walk around out here—until I feel better. Good night, everybody— You're coming to lunch tomorrow, aren't you, Joe?

JOE. Yes, sir!

TOMMY. That's what I thought. (*He goes out, closing the screen door.* PATRI-CIA *looks out the window; the band is heard louder.*)

PATRICIA. Ellen! It's the team and the band and a lot of the kids! They must be going in the Neil Avenue gate!

ED. Come on, let's step on it!

JOE. Yeh. (*Listens to music.*) Boy, that sounds good! God, doesn't that take you back?

MYRTLE. Where'll we go after the rally?

JOE. I'll take you all to the Dixie Club! Whatta ya say, Ellen?

ELLEN. Oh, I haven't been there in years! It would be fun— But, no, I'm not going. (*Calls.*) I'm going to stay here with you, Tommy.

TOMMY'S VOICE (*offstage*). No, I'd rather you didn't—really.

PATRICIA (*as music gets much louder*).

Hey! They're stopping in front of the house!

WALLY (*runs in as the music stops*). Ready, Pat?

PATRICIA. Sure!

WALLY (*breathless and excited goes to* JOE). Look, Mr. Ferguson, we brought the band over to escort you to the chapel. You're going to ride in the Axline Buggy! We hauled it out of the trophy rooms!

ED. The Axline Buggy! Wow!

WALLY. Yes! We got two horses—not the old black ones, but we got two horses! Whatta ya say?

ED. Fine! Fine!

NUTSY (*runs in, dressed in bandleader's uniform and carrying his glistening stick*). Hey, come on! Let's get going! The carriage waits, Mr. Ferguson! (*Does drum major's salute and clicks heels.*)

WALLY. This is Nutsy Miller, the leader of the band.

JOE (*shaking hands*). Hiya, Nutsy?

NUTSY. Hiya, Joe?

JOE. Okay, fellas! Whatta ya say, Ellen —you ride with me.—Some fun, huh?

ELLEN (*in the spirit of it*). Oh—all right. Hurray!

JOE. Hit her, Ed!

ED, JOE, WALLY, ELLEN, PATRICIA, NUTSY (*sing*).

"And if we win the game,
We'll buy a keg of booze,
And we'll drink to old Midwestern
Till we wobble in our shoes."

(*They all go out,* JOE *and* ELLEN *the center of the gay, excited group, arm in arm. A shout goes up as* JOE *appears outside. You hear a triple "rah-team" for* JOE.)

VOICES (*outside*). Rah-rah-rah! Rah-rah-rah! Rah-rah-rah! Ferguson! Ferguson! *Ferguson!* (*The band starts another march.* TOMMY *has reappeared in the lower door a moment after the general exit. He crosses slowly and closes upper door. The cheers for* FERGUSON *and the band music slowly die away as* TOMMY *turns and sees the glass of soda. He picks it up, looks at it in distaste—distaste for himself.*)

TOMMY. Rah-rah-rah! (*He throws down the spoon, crosses to the Victrola and starts the record.*)

VICTROLA. ". . . Dreams I know can never come true. . . ." (TOMMY *listens for a moment, then makes awkwardly, solemnly, a couple of dance steps, frowns, shakes his head, and drops into settee, giving it up. He drinks the bitter cup of soda as the music ends and*)

THE CURTAIN FALLS.

ACT TWO

SCENE 1: *Same as Act One. About 1 P. M., the following day.*

AT RISE: JOE, *with coat off, is arranging plates, knives, saucers and forks, on the floor in the form of a football formation. The end table has evidently been used for serving luncheon as there are still a plate and cup.* ELLEN *is seated center, finishing her coffee and watching* JOE. PATRICIA *is down on her knees on the floor, studying the array of dishes, napkins, salt cellars and glasses which are ankle-deep around* JOE. CLEOTA *enters from the dining room, carrying an empty tray. She crosses to the end table, and begins clearing away the dishes, keeping a suspicious eye on* JOE *and the black magic he is up to.*)

JOE. Now here—it's a balanced line. Move those two men out a little more. (PATRICIA *moves men out.*) This is a wonderful play. The coach gave it to me in strictest confidence.

ELLEN. Cleota, did you phone Mr. Turner's office again?

CLEOTA (*at end table clearing away dishes*). Yessum. Dey ain' no answeh.

PATRICIA. I saw Tommy, Ellen—about an hour ago.

ELLEN. Where?

PATRICIA. He was walking out on the little road back of the Ag buildings. Just moping along. I yelled at him, but he didn't hear me.

ELLEN. I'm getting worried.

JOE (*intent on his own activity*).

Everything's going to be okay. Nothing to worry about— Now, study this play, girls, or you won't know it when you see it this afternoon. This is Michigan. And this is Midwestern.—Now! From the balanced line, we shift. Hup! (*He executes a Notre Dame shift. Grimaces a little as his right knee resents this activity.*) Wally takes the left end's place, but he plays out a little.

PATRICIA (*exchanges cup and cream pitcher*). Isn't Wally going to carry the ball?

JOE. Shh! Michigan spreads out. They're watching that wide end, but it's too obvious. They're watching the other side of the line, too.

CLEOTA (*moving down, wide-eyed*). What's goin' on heah?

ELLEN. Football game.

JOE (*ignoring her*). The ball is snapped back. Now look, here we go! Both of us. (*Carrying a plate and a napkin.*) Close together. Fading back but threatening a left end run as well as a pass.

PATRICIA. But who are you?

JOE. I'm both of them—Lindstrom and Wierasocka.—(*Comes forward.*) Skolsky cuts down the left side line deep and takes out Wupperman—that's the jam pot. (*Picks up "Wally."*) Wally is running wide around right end, (*Runs around end.*) faking as though he had the ball but hasn't really got it—apparently! Now, then, just as Michigan is charging in on Lindstrom and Wierasocka, trying to decide which one has the ball, Wally lets himself out! *He's really got it!*

PATRICIA. Hooray!

JOE. It's a fake fake. It's an old play, so corny only a football genius like Coach Sprague would use it. With no interference at all, Wally cuts over and goes straight down the right side of the field! He stiff-arms the safety man— (*Running with the cream pitcher.*) Touchdown!

PATRICIA. Whoopee! (*She knocks over the jam pot.*) Oh, Lord, there goes Wupperman! (*During* JOE'S *"touchdown,"* TOMMY *has appeared quietly in door to the back yard. He watches* JOE

with distaste. No one notices him in the confusion.)

CLEOTA. Um-hm. You through playin' now? (PAT *and* JOE *help her pick up dishes.*)

PATRICIA. I'm sorry, Ellen.

ELLEN. It's all right. You can take the teams to the showers now, Cleota. Can't she, Joe?

JOE. Sure! How do you like it?

ELLEN. I think it's nice.

JOE. Nice?! It's marvelous! That play is going to put us in the Rose Bowl. (*To* PATRICIA.) Did I ever tell you about how we used the Statue of Liberty play? (*He uses a cream pitcher for a football.*) I would go back for a pass, and Jonesy would take it out of my hand and cut around to the left. (*He loses himself in the play, then suddenly realizes that not the imaginary ball but the cream pitcher has been taken out of his hand and that there is no Jonesy. He looks around slowly, puzzled, too late to have seen* TOMMY *quietly returning to the outdoors with the pitcher which he has snatched from* JOE'S *hand. Doorbell rings.*)

ELLEN. I'll answer it. (*She goes to the front door.* JOE *looks to see where he might have dropped the pitcher, he is vastly puzzled.*)

PATRICIA. It's a wonderful play, Mr. Ferguson. If it works. (*She runs upstairs.*)

JOE. The coach gave it to me in strictest confidence. (*He gives another look for the pitcher with the expression of a prize bloodhound who has lost a scent.* ELLEN *admits* DEAN DAMON.)

ELLEN. Can you come in and wait, Doctor Damon? Tommy is out somewhere, but I'm expecting him back. (CLEOTA *goes out with tray and dishes, leaving coffee things on table.*)

DAMON. I can't wait very long. (*Indicates magazine in pocket.*)

ELLEN. Is that *The Literary Magazine?*

DAMON. It's a powder magazine. Bombs are bursting all around. (*Sees* JOE, *who has been putting on coat and looking in the door drapes for pitcher.*) Oh—good afternoon.

JOE. How are you, Doctor Damon? (*Phone rings.*)

ELLEN. Excuse me, I'll— (*She goes to phone.*) Hello— Yes, thank you. (*Hangs up.*) That was Ed Keller's office, Joe. He's on his way over here.

JOE. Oh, yeah. He called me this morning. He's fit to be tied about this *Literary Magazine* thing. Have you seen it?

DAMON. Yes. This is it.

JOE. May I take a look at it? Gosh, I didn't realize what this thing was— (*He takes magazine and scans editorial.*) Calls the trustees Fascists! This kid's dangerous—un-American.

DAMON. Oh, no!

ELLEN. Oh, no, not really. He's from an old Chillicothe family.

JOE. This is bad stuff for the university. I'm afraid all hell's going to break loose. Of course, it's none of my business, but—

DAMON (*taking the magazine out of JOE's hand*). You take the words right out of my mouth. It's been a very trying morning. I haven't had such a day since poor Doctor Prendergast shot his secretary.

JOE. Well, I'm not a trustee, but I know how they feel.

ELLEN (*anxiously*). I know.

JOE. Tommy'd better deny this, pretty fast, and get himself out in the clear. I'm telling you. I'm sorry about this, Ellen— Where is Tommy?

ELLEN. I don't know.

JOE. You don't think— (*Lowers voice.*) You don't think he may be a little sore about your going out with me last night?

ELLEN. I don't know. Oh, Joe, I'm all upset. (*Doorbell rings.*)

JOE. Shall I open it? (*He does.*) Hi, Ed.

ED (*offstage*). Turner here?

ELLEN. No, he isn't.

ED (*sternly*). Well, I want to see him before the game. Tell him to call my office. Coming, Joe?

ELLEN (*quickly*). I don't know just when he'll—Won't you come in? Dean Damon is here.

ED. Oh! (*He comes into the room a few steps.* JOE *closes the door.*) Well, I'm glad somebody's here. How do you do, sir. Do you know where I could find President Cartwright?

DAMON. His secretary informed me that he is at the barber shop, having his beard trimmed.

ED (*his anger going up fast*). That'll be a big help! I thought Turner was going to deny this story. Papers keep calling *me*—they say he hasn't. Here I am, bearing the brunt of this damn disgraceful attack. "Fascists!" You oughtta heard Si McMillan! And do you know Kressinger's in town from Detroit?

ELLEN. Is he a trustee, too?

DAMON. Oh, yes, young Michael has exploded his dynamite at a moment when the concentration of trustees is at its thickest.

ED. Yeh. There goes the new stadium. There goes your Endowment Fund! Unless something is done, and done quick! (*He turns on* ELLEN *with a roar.*) Ellen, you tell your husband what I said!

JOE (*moving in*). Look, Ed, it isn't Ellen's fault.

ED (*between fury and tears*). It isn't my fault, either. Here, I kept this whole week end free. I've got my office full of eighteen-year-old Bourbon so we fellows could cut loose a little. And look what happens! All we need now is for Wierasocka to fumble a punt! (*He stomps out of the house.*)

JOE. I'll—see you later. (*He goes out after* ED.)

DAMON. I didn't like the way Mr. Keller said "There goes your Endowment Fund." (*Phone rings.*) If that's the newspapers I'm not here.

ELLEN. Oh, I don't want to talk to them either. Cleota— (*As the phone rings again,* PATRICIA *runs down the stairs.*)

PATRICIA (*angrily*). I'm going out to talk to Michael. I got him on the phone but he hung up on me! Good afternoon, Doctor Damon. I'll knock his ears off. (*She slams out the door. The phone rings on.*)

DAMON. Good afternoon, Patricia. (CLEOTA *enters from the dining room.*)

ELLEN. Answer the phone, Cleota.

CLEOTA (*picking up the receiver cautiously*). Hello—Says what?—Says he is? —Ah didn't say you said he was, I say what is it?—No, he ain't heah— No, dis ain' Miz Turner. (*She is getting a little surly.*)

ELLEN. *Who is calling, please.*

CLEOTA. Who's dis?—Wait a minute— (*Puts hand over mouthpiece—to* ELLEN.) It's de *Daily* sump'n.

ELLEN. Hang up, Cleota.

CLEOTA (*brightly*). G'bye. (*Hangs up and exits.*)

ELLEN. Oh, Lord, see what's happened already! Doctor Damon, suppose Tommy *didn't* read this letter?

DAMON. Let us not take refuge in conditional clauses, my dear.

ELLEN. Would you read it if you were Tommy?

DAMON. Now we go into the subjunctive. My dear, for forty-two years I have read nothing to *my* classes which was written later than the first half of the seventeenth century.

ELLEN. There must be some way— some compromise—that wouldn't be too humiliating.

DAMON. The policy of appeasement? Yes, it has its merits. (*Rises.*) I can't wait any longer for Thomas. Tell him that if he decides not to read the letter, I shall feel easier in my mind. Much easier. (*Picks up hat.*) And—slightly disappointed— Good afternoon, my dear— (*He opens the door, and in flies* PATRICIA. *They collide.*) Wup, wup, *wup!*

PATRICIA. Don't let Michael in! I don't want to talk to him any more!

DAMON. Did you—uh—knock his ears off?

PATRICIA (*loudly*). I got him told. But he wants to tell me *his* side of it. He thinks *he* has a side.

DAMON (*quietly*). A common failing, my dear— Good afternoon. (*He goes out and* PATRICIA *bolts the door after him, hotly.*)

PATRICIA. There, I've bolted that young genius out! Oh, Ellen! Give me a football player any time. (*She crosses to her sister for comfort.*) Give me a guy without so much intellect or whatever it is. Somebody that doesn't want to be bawling the world out all the time—always doing something brave or fine or something. (*MICHAEL, greatly upset, steps into the room from the back yard.*) Go away!

ELLEN. Quiet down, Patricia— Come in, Michael.

MICHAEL (*to* PATRICIA). You're being very silly.

ELLEN (*noticing* MICHAEL's *distraught look*). Can I give you a glass of milk?

MICHAEL. No, thank you. She won't listen to me, Mrs. Turner. I'm not trying to ruin your husband's life or my life or anybody's life. It's the principle of the thing she won't see.

PATRICIA. Oh, the principle! (*She stomps over to him.*) I'll bet nobody else would make a fool of himself and his friends and—my brother-in-law—over a principle. (*ELLEN, taking the dishes with her, quietly slips out toward the kitchen, unnoticed by* MICHAEL.)

MICHAEL (*with the enormous gravity of the young man in love*). All right, Pat. I'm very glad to know the qualities you admire in a man. They are certainly the noble virtues, and I'm sure Wally is lousy with them.

PATRICIA. Oh, make up your mind who you're imitating, Ralph Waldo Emerson or Hemingway! You—you *writer!*

MICHAEL. *Now* who's imitating Hemingway?

PATRICIA. I wish you'd go away!

MICHAEL (*rushing to the front door*). I'm going! I'm going for good! I'm going out of your life! (*On the last word he jerks at door to make a dramatic exit, but it won't open, since* PAT *bolted it. Doorknob comes off in his hand.*)

PATRICIA (*going out the lower door to the porch*). It's bolted, you dope! (MICHAEL *gets the door open finally and in walks an extremely puzzled* TOMMY *with the other doorknob in his hand. The two stand and look at each other.*)

MICHAEL (*a little guiltily*). Sorry, Mr. Turner!

TOMMY. What's going on here? (MI-CHAEL *puts the knob in.* TOMMY *screws the other knob on.*)

MICHAEL. I was just going.

TOMMY. That's all right. Come in if you want to.

MICHAEL (*noticing* TOMMY's *haggard look*). Say, you look terrible.

TOMMY. Me? Why, what's the matter?

MICHAEL (*his mind on his own woes*). I've got to get out of here.

TOMMY. Why? Did somebody do something to you?

MICHAEL. Patricia. She did plenty. I suppose it's just as well. I've found out what she wants in life: a handsome, half-witted half-back.

TOMMY. Yes, I know how that feels.

MICHAEL. Yes, sir. Well, you can't get anywhere with a woman who doesn't understand what you have to do.

TOMMY. No. No, you can't, Michael. You'd like to, but you can't— Well— Good-bye, Michael. (*He shakes hands with* MICHAEL, *grimly.*) Come back in about an hour, will you? I want to give you a piece of my mind.

MICHAEL (*puzzled*). Yes, sir. (*He goes slowly out the front door, as* TOMMY *takes the pitcher he snatched from* JOE *out of his overcoat pocket.* TOMMY *sits sadly, and sighs as* ELLEN *enters.*)

ELLEN. Oh, hello, darling!

TOMMY. Hello!

ELLEN (*uneasily*). Well, I'm glad you remembered where you live. I was beginning to be worried. We phoned your office three times, but nobody knew where you were.

TOMMY (*looking up slowly*). Huh?

ELLEN. I say nobody knew where you were—since early this morning.

TOMMY. I was walking.

ELLEN. Without any breakfast? All this time?

TOMMY. Well, I—came around to the back door a while ago, but Joe was doing the Statue of Liberty or something again, so I went away.

ELLEN. You were right here and you went away?

TOMMY. Yes, I couldn't face that right now. Not the Statue of Liberty.

ELLEN. Oh! Well, Doctor Damon's been here—and Ed Keller, and the newspapers have been calling up. There's going to be a lot of trouble if you don't hurry up and deny that story of Michael's—or have you done it?

TOMMY. No—I haven't denied it.

ELLEN (*troubled*). You mean you've made up your mind to read it? Is that what you've been—walking around for? Tommy, I don't know what to say to you.

TOMMY. I think maybe you've said enough already.

ELLEN. That isn't very kind.

TOMMY. None of this is going to sound very kind but I've figured out exactly what I want to say, and I have to get it out before I get all mixed up.

ELLEN. I don't see why you are being so mean.

TOMMY. It's just that last night I began to see you, and myself, clearly for the first time.

ELLEN. If this is a story you're writing, and you're trying it out on me, it isn't very good.

TOMMY. Oh, I saw you and Joe clearly, too.

ELLEN (*relieved. Crossing to* TOMMY). Oh, you saw him kiss me— I thought that was it—

TOMMY. No—No, I didn't—Did he kiss you? Well, that's fine—I've been meaning to ask you, what became of Housman's "Last Poems"? (*Turns to book shelves.*)

ELLEN. Tommy, (*Puts her hand on his shoulder.*) listen to me—I wanted to have a good time last night, and you spoiled it—

TOMMY. Didn't you enjoy it at all?

ELLEN (*piqued*). Yes, I did. I'm not a hundred years old—yet. I just decided to quit worrying about you, and have a little fun. For about an hour I felt like a girl again—wearing flowers at a Spring Dance—when I was young and silly—

TOMMY. Young and happy.

ELLEN. All right, he—kissed me. I

kissed him, too. We didn't go out in the dark to do it.

TOMMY (*piling books he is taking from book shelves on settee*). I hope you didn't lend that book to anybody; it was a first edition.

ELLEN. Did you *hear* what I *said*?

TOMMY. Sure, I heard you. I'm listening— You said you went out in the dark and kissed Joe.

ELLEN. I said no such thing, and you know it.

TOMMY. I wish we had had separate book-plates.

ELLEN. (*beginning to flame*). So that when you really make me mad and I get out of here, I can find my own books quickly?

TOMMY. I hate sentimental pawing over things by a couple breaking up. We're not living in the days of Henry James and Meredith. Look at Joe and his wife.

ELLEN. Tommy, (*She goes to him again.*) I want you to stop this. If you're going to be jealous *be* jealous, rave or throw things, but don't act like the lead in a Senior Class play! (*This thrust gets home.*)

TOMMY (*angrily*). I'm trying to tell you that I don't care what you and Joe do. I'm trying to tell you that it's fine. It's very lucky that he came back just now.

ELLEN. What do you mean?

TOMMY. I mean on the money *I* make, I can go on fine alone, reading whatever I want to to my classes. That's what I want. And that's what I'm going to do.

ELLEN. Oh, that's what you want! Suddenly that's what you want. More than me?

TOMMY. It isn't so sudden. Not any more sudden than your feeling for Joe. It's logical. We get in each other's way. You wear yourself out picking up after me. Taking matches out of my pockets. Disarranging my whole way of life. (*She follows him as he moves away from her.*)

ELLEN. Why haven't you said all this before?

TOMMY. I couldn't very well.

ELLEN. Why couldn't you? If you felt this way?

TOMMY. Well, we hadn't split up on this letter issue, for one thing—and then there was no place for you to go. (*He sits on a sofa.*) I didn't want you to have to go back to Cleveland, or to work in some tea shoppe.

ELLEN. Oh, I see. Some tea shoppe! That's what you think I'd have to do! Well, you needn't have spared my feelings. I can make as much money as you.

TOMMY. You don't have to, now.

ELLEN (*whirling*). Oh, you mean you waited to tell me this till Joe came along! I thought you were jealous of Joe. I could understand that. You aren't the least bit aroused at the idea of his kissing me—*out in the dark—for hours!*

TOMMY. No, I'm not.

ELLEN (*full of exclamation points*). So that's why you've been wandering around! That's what you've been figuring out! How nice it would be if he would take me off your hands, so you could be left alone with your books and match-boxes and *litter!* I suppose any man would do as well as Joe. (*She rushes up to him.*)

TOMMY (*rising to face her*). He's not just any man, and you know that. He's always been in love with you, and you've always been in love with him! (*He is angry and jealous now and brings up his own exclamation points.*)

ELLEN. That's ridiculous!

TOMMY (*moving toward her*). I felt it when I saw you dancing together. It was unmistakable. You've just admitted it.

ELLEN. Oh, you can't do that *now!* You can't be jealous *now* just because you think I want you to be!

TOMMY (*rising to his big denunciation*). I saw you dancing together—like angels! I saw you go out in that goddamn carriage together! I saw you together years ago, when I was young enough and dumb enough to believe that I really took you away from him. There's something that happens when you two dance together that doesn't happen when *we* dance together!

ELLEN (*worried, angry, and tired*). All right—have it your way. If you want to be free, then I want to be free—and I've gone around for ten years mooning about Joe— Well, maybe I have—maybe I have, because I'm certainly sick of you right now! (*Whirls away from him.*)

TOMMY (*deathly afraid of her being sick of him*). Ellen—Ellen, listen—

ELLEN. Never mind—all right—*all right* —ALL RIGHT! (*She is shouting as* JOE *enters brightly.*)

JOE. Oh, I'm sorry—if I— (*He stops in embarrassment. There is a pause. He has caught only the tone; but he sees and feels the tension. He is carrying a wrapped bottle and a newspaper.*)

TOMMY. Hello, Joe!

JOE. Hello. I brought the rum. (*He crosses to the coffee table, puts the bottle on the table; holds up the newspaper.*) Big picture of Wally all over the front page. (*ELLEN stares out the window.* TOMMY *stares at* JOE.) Good picture, isn't it?

TOMMY. You and Ellen have some rum.

JOE. The rum's for the punch—later.

ELLEN. Could I have some—now? (*TOMMY goes out to the dining room.*)

JOE (*surprised*). Right now?—Sure.

TOMMY (*yelling from dining room*). I'll get you some glasses. (*Reappears with two glasses.*)

JOE (*unscrewing the top of the rum bottle*). Tommy, old man, I just left Ed Keller and Si McMillan. This thing your young friend wrote in the magazine. (*Pours drink.*) I read the piece over again. He's got you on a spot, Tommy. (*He gives* ELLEN *her drink.*)

ELLEN. Want to drink a toast, Joe?— To Tommy's happiness?

JOE (*looks at both of them—puzzled*). Sure— (*Pours himself drink.*) Your happiness, Tommy. (*They drink amid a long silence,* JOE *nervously finishing his;* ELLEN *taking a long drink, grimacing as the drink burns her throat.* JOE *decides to dive in.*) What's the matter? What's it about? Maybe I could talk to Ed—

TOMMY. No. I don't want that. I'll run my own life my own way.

ELLEN. That's what it's about. Tommy wants to—live alone.

JOE. What?

ELLEN. He wants to be left alone—

JOE. I beg your pardon?

ELLEN (*almost shouting*). Us! Tommy and me! We're breaking up!

JOE (*awed*). *Just before the game—?* You're both crazy! Maybe I better go.

TOMMY. Not at all! You're not exactly a stranger around here. You knew Ellen as long ago as I did.

JOE. I knew her a long time before you did—and this is a fine way to be treating her.

TOMMY (*baiting a hook*). Yes, I know. I was just saying I barged in and took her away from you. (*ELLEN stares at* TOMMY.)

JOE (*taking the bait*). Oh, no, you didn't. You had nothing to do with it. She got sore at me on account of another girl.

TOMMY (*triumphantly*). Oh, *that's* where I came in?

JOE. Sure! If you think you took her away from me, you're crazy. Here, you better have some rum.

ELLEN (*the wife*). He can't drink this early.

TOMMY. *I* don't *need* any rum. Go on, Joe.

JOE (*sitting near* TOMMY). Well, Ellen and I had a fight. You weren't in on it. You came in later—

ELLEN (*wearily, also warily*). Joe, do we have to—

TOMMY. It's all right. It's his turn.

JOE. She said she hated me and never wanted to see me again. She threw something at me. She thought I slept with this girl—I mean—

TOMMY (*cooly*).—I know what you mean—

ELLEN (*indignantly*). I never said you sl—. I never said that.

JOE (*turning from* TOMMY *to* ELLEN). Oh, yes, you did—you intimated it.

ELLEN. No, that was *your* idea. I thought you were bragging about it.

JOE (*turning farther away from* TOM-

MY). Well, you got awfully mad. I thought you never did want to see me again. I guess I was dumb. Brenda says it shows you liked me. (*From* ELLEN's *expression,* JOE *is reminded of* TOMMY's *presence; he turns to* TOMMY, *a little sheepishly.*) Oh— sorry.

TOMMY (*the tolerant man of the world*). Oh, don't mind me. Who's Brenda? Another girl?

JOE. My wife.

TOMMY. Oh, sorry!

JOE. Ellen knows her. She's from Cleveland. Brenda's always been jealous of Ellen. She found a picture of you.

TOMMY (*not so tolerant*). What picture?

ELLEN. I gave him a picture. He wouldn't give it back.

JOE. It's a swell picture. You were wearing that floppy hat. Red.

ELLEN. Blue.

JOE. It had ribbons. Made you look like you were sixteen.

TOMMY. *I've* never seen it.

ELLEN. It was a silly hat. This was ages ago.

TOMMY. I mean, I've never seen the picture.

ELLEN (*angrily*). I threw them all away.

JOE (*looking back over the years*). It kind of went down over one eye.

TOMMY (*remembering an old lovely hat*). She looks nice in hats like that. (ELLEN *suddenly begins to cry; collapses on sofa.*)

JOE (*rising*). Now look what you've done!

TOMMY (*rising*). Look what *you've* done! Bringing up old floppy blue hats! (JOE *moves to* ELLEN.) Don't touch her! She doesn't like to be touched when she's crying.

JOE. I've seen her cry. I know what to do.

TOMMY. Oh, you do?

JOE. She cried when we had that fight about the girl. She was lying on the floor and kicking and crying—on her stomach.

ELLEN. I was not!

TOMMY. Be careful what you say!

JOE. Well, I mean I knew what to do. (*Crosses to other end of sofa.*) I picked her up then.

TOMMY (*following him*). Well, you're not going to pick her up now.

ELLEN. Will you both please let me alone?! Will you please go away!

JOE (*getting sore*). She wants you to go away. And I don't blame her, if this is the way you treat her. I wouldn't have stood for it ten years ago, and I'm not going to stand for it now.

TOMMY. But what are you going to do?

JOE. I'm going to get her away from all this! It isn't *nice*!

TOMMY. It isn't exactly to my taste, either. I didn't want it to turn out this way, but it did: me feeling like a cad, Ellen crying, and you acting like a fool.

JOE. *Me* acting like a fool?

ELLEN (*sitting up*). Everybody's acting like a fool.

JOE. You've certainly messed things up, brother.

TOMMY. Don't call me brother! I can't stand that, now!

JOE. If Ellen weren't here, I'd call you worse than brother.

ELLEN. Well, I'm not going to be here! Please, please, stop—both of you! Nobody has said a word about what *I* want to do. You're going to settle that between yourselves. Bandying me back and forth!

TOMMY. Nobody's bandying you, Ellen.

ELLEN (*mad*). I know when I'm being bandied! (*On her feet.*) I don't want either of you! You can both go to hell! (*Runs upstairs, crying. Both men follow and look after her.*)

TOMMY. She means me.

JOE. She said both of us.

TOMMY. She was looking at me.

JOE. How did we get into this anyway?

TOMMY. You two-stepped into it. You kissed your way into it.

JOE. I'm sorry about that. Sorry it happened.

TOMMY. You're not sorry it happened. You're sorry I found it out. Do you know anything about women? Didn't you know what she was thinking about when she was dancing with you?

JOE. No. I don't think when I'm dancing.

TOMMY. I know. You think in your office. Well, you'll have to think in your home after this. She likes to be thought about.

JOE. I thought about her. I remembered her birthday. I brought her flowers.

TOMMY. Well, you'll have to keep on bringing her things whether it's her birthday or not—fur coats and things —She's still young and pretty.

JOE (*narrowing his eyes*). I don't get you.

TOMMY. I'm being broadminded. I'm taking things in my stride. It's the modern way of doing things. You ought to know that.

JOE (*shrewdly*). Um, hm. But what makes me think you're still crazy about her and are up to some goddamn something or other?

TOMMY (*a little taken aback*). Don't be acute. I couldn't stand you being acute.

JOE. I'm not dumb.

TOMMY. Yes, you are. It isn't what I feel that counts. It's what she feels. I think she's always been in love with you. Why, I don't know. It's supposed to be beyond reason. I guess it is.

JOE. You just think that because of last night?

TOMMY. No. Because of what lay behind last night. That wasn't just a kiss. That's nothing. This thing is too deep for jealousy or for anything but honesty. A woman must not go on living with a man when she dances better with another man.

JOE. That's silly. *That's the silliest—* Dancing doesn't mean everything.

TOMMY. The way *you* do it does. The things that happen to you. The *light* you give off.

JOE. *Light?!*

TOMMY. Oh, these things are too subtle for you, Joe. I've made some study of them. (*Turns away.*)

JOE. Maybe all this studying's bad for you.

TOMMY (*pinning him down*). All I want to know is whether you felt the same thing she felt last night.

JOE. I felt fine. This is goddamn embarrassing! A man makes love to a woman. He doesn't talk it over with her husband!

TOMMY. I'm just trying to be honest.

JOE. You're a funny guy. Conscientious. What does it get you? Like this letter you're going to read— Say, is that what started the trouble?

TOMMY. Yes, it's an integral part of the trouble—things like that.

JOE. Well, what are we going to do? I mean now? I mean from now on?

TOMMY. From now on will work itself out. Right now you'd better go upstairs and comfort her. She'll be expecting you.

JOE. Oh, no. Not me! You ought to know more what to do right now. It's your house. She's still your wife.

TOMMY. She doesn't want to talk to me. She's just done that. But she oughtn't to be left alone right now.

JOE (*rises*). Well— (*He takes a few steps.*) What'll I say?

TOMMY. What did you say last night, when you were dancing?

JOE (*going to the foot of the stairs*). It doesn't seem right somehow for me to go upstairs.

TOMMY. This is not a moment for cheap moralizing!

JOE. Well—good God Almighty! (*Goes upstairs. MICHAEL has come in the front door in time to hear JOE's last expletive.*)

MICHAEL (*as TOMMY looks after JOE*). What's the matter?

TOMMY. Never mind— (*He paces, glares upstairs, still has his glare when he turns back to MICHAEL.*)

MICHAEL. Well, I came back like you said. Before you start in on me, Mr. Turner, please remember that I've been through a lot today. I can't stand much more. (*TOMMY pats him on shoulder.*) They'll probably do something to you— especially if we lose to Michigan. You know what Keller did the last time they beat us in a Homecoming Game? He ran the flag on his office building down to half-mast.

TOMMY (*looking upstairs—distracted*). Don't worry about me.

MICHAEL. Well, I'm feeling better. I've put her out of my mind. It's ended as simply as that. (*Drops into chair.*) There's a girl who could sit with you and talk about Shelley. Well, I'm glad I found out about women. (*Crash upstairs.*) What was that?

TOMMY. I'm sure I don't know. What were you saying?

MICHAEL. I say Patricia knew things. She knew odd things like, "A Sonnet on Political Greatness"; she quoted that one night. Wouldn't you think a girl like that had some social consciousness?

TOMMY. That's the sonnet that ends:
"Quelling the anarchy of hopes
    and fears,
Being himself alone."

MICHAEL. Yes, but when an issue comes up and a man has to be himself alone, she reveals the true stature of her character and goes off to Hennick's with that football player. I saw them—right in the front window—drinking Seven-Up—he uses a straw.

TOMMY. Yes, but he's handsome. What is more, he whirls. He's a hunter. He comes home at night with meat slung over his shoulders, and you sit there drawing pictures on the wall of your cave.

MICHAEL. I see. Maybe I ought to sock him with a ball bat.

TOMMY. No. You are a civilized man, Michael. If the male animal in you doesn't like the full implications of that, he must nevertheless be swayed by Reason. You are not living in the days of King Arthur when you fought for your woman. Nowadays, the man and his wife and the other man talk it over. Quietly and calmly. They all go out to dinner together. (*He sits on the sofa across the stage from* MICHAEL.)

MICHAEL. Intellectually, Patricia is sleeping with that guy. I feel like going out tonight with the Hot Garters.

TOMMY. With the what?

MICHAEL. It's a girl. They call her that. What if she was kicked out of the Pi Phi House? She's honest! She does what she believes in! And—well, Hot Garters doesn't argue all the time anyway.

TOMMY (*removing his glasses*). Look, Michael, hasn't she got a name? You don't call her *that*, do you?

MICHAEL. Marcia Gardner. They just call her—

TOMMY. Yes, you told me what they call her. (*Slight pause.*)

MICHAEL. Patricia's not coming to class when you read that letter. She's gone over to the Philistines— Oh, Mr. Turner, I wish I were like you! Middle-aged, settled down, happily married—and through with all this hell you feel when you're young and in love.

TOMMY (*nettled*). Middle-aged?

MICHAEL. Yes, you know what Rupert Brooke says:
"That time when all is over,
(TOMMY *writhes, turns his back.*)
And love has turned to kindliness."
Is kindliness peaceful?

TOMMY. Don't ask *me*. (*Two quick crashes from upstairs bring* TOMMY *to his feet as* JOE *hurries down the stairs, looking worn and worried, his hair slightly disarranged. Sharply.*) You look ruffled!

JOE (*just as sharply, but a bit absently*). What? (*The two men look each other over.*)

TOMMY. I say—what ruffled you?

JOE. Do we have to discuss these things in front of this boy?

MICHAEL (*rising*). I am not a boy.

TOMMY. This is Michael Barnes.

JOE. Oh, so you're the little boy that started all this! I want to tell you that you write too much, you have too much to say, you get too many people into too much trouble. You've not only got Tommy and Ellen involved, but me.

MICHAEL. I don't see how this concerns you, do you, Mr. Turner?

TOMMY. Yes.

MICHAEL. Oh, well, I'll go out and climb a tree, Mr. Turner. I'll come back when this blows over. (*Goes out into the garden.*)

JOE. Oh, God, I wish I was in Pittsburgh! (*He sits heavily in chair vacated by* MICHAEL.)

TOMMY (*eagerly*). What happened?

JOE. Well, old man, I guess you're right. She was pretty bitter—about you. She picked up something you'd given her and threw it against the wall and broke it into a thousand pieces.

TOMMY. What was it?

JOE. I didn't see it till after she threw it.

TOMMY. Oh!

JOE. Every time she mentioned your name, she threw something. Kept me ducking.

TOMMY (*sadly*). I see. (*He, too, sits heavily on the large sofa.*) You want to marry Ellen, don't you?

JOE. Well, I always liked her, but I don't like to go through so much. (*Pause.*) Are you sure you understand women?

TOMMY. Yes.

JOE. Well, when Ellen and I had that fight about the girl, she threw things on account of me, and Brenda thinks that meant she was in love with me. Now she throws things on account of *you.*

TOMMY (*after an instant of hope*). In both instances, she threw them at *you,* didn't she?

JOE (*glumly*). Yeh, I guess so.

TOMMY. Well, there you are. What did she say when you left? What was she doing?

JOE. She was in a terrible state. I don't think she'll be able to go to the game. She may have a sick headache for days. What do you do then?

TOMMY (*rises and goes to dining room with sudden efficiency*). Get her a hot-water bottle. Cleota!—Cleota!

CLEOTA (*off*). Yes, suh?

TOMMY (*off-stage*). There's a hot-water bottle out there in the—somewhere. Fill it and bring it in, please.

CLEOTA (*off*). Yes, suh. (TOMMY *returns.* JOE *glances at his wrist watch, rises, and paces across stage.*)

JOE. I don't want to miss this game. I sort of wish Stalenkiwiecz wasn't laid up, don't you?

TOMMY (*sits on sofa again*). I haven't

given it much thought one way or another.

JOE. Of course, Wierasocka's all right, but Stalenkiwiecz is a better pass-receiver.

TOMMY. Is he? Why?

JOE. I don't know why. He just is. "Why!" (*His pacing has carried him to the door, leading to the garden. He remembers the vanishing pitcher and takes one more look, then resumes his prowl.*) 'Course they may not give Brenda a divorce.

TOMMY. I think they will.

JOE. I don't know.

CLEOTA (*comes in with hot-water bottle and towel. She hands them to* TOMMY *on sofa*). Is you gotta pain?

TOMMY. No.—Oh, thank you. (CLEOTA *retires.*)

JOE. I don't suppose we ought to go and leave her.

TOMMY (*going to him with bottle*). Oh, I'm not going. Here. (*Hands him bottle and towel.*)

JOE (*taking it, as if it were a baby*). Ow!

TOMMY. Hold it by the end.

JOE. Won't this thing burn her?

TOMMY (*impatiently, showing him*). You wrap the towel around it.

JOE. You shouldn't stay here in the house alone with her, things being the way they are, should you?

TOMMY (*turning away*). Please don't worry about that!

JOE (*looking at the bottle*). I thought these things were different now than they used to be.

TOMMY. What do you mean, different?

JOE. I mean better looking—somehow. (*There is a pause during which* JOE *tries to wrap the towel around the hot-water bottle but various parts of it insist on remaining exposed. Finally* TOMMY *crosses down to* JOE *angrily.*)

TOMMY. Well, why don't you take it up to her?

ELLEN (*coming down the stairs*). It's time to get started, isn't it? (*The two men turn and stare at her,* JOE *still holding the hot-water bottle.* ELLEN *is utterly serene, with no sign of tears or hysterics. Washed and powdered, with her hat on, she stands at the foot of the stairs, ready for the game.*) Do you realize what time it is? The Kellers will be waiting for us at Esther Baker's. We'll leave the car there and walk to the stadium. It's only a block. (*The men are still staring.*) What are you doing with that thing, Joe?

TOMMY. He was going to lie down with it for a while.

JOE. I was not! Here! (*Tries to hand it to* TOMMY.)

TOMMY. I don't want it.

ELLEN. We've got to hurry, Joe. (*Takes the bottle from* JOE *and puts it on sofa.*) Have you got the tickets?

JOE. Yeh, I've got them. (*Goes to radio.*) Say, what number is the game on?

ELLEN. It's around 1210 on the dial. (*As* JOE *turns on radio and fiddles with dial—to* TOMMY.) Sure you won't go to the game?

TOMMY. Oh, no— (*With shy politeness.*) How are you?

ELLEN (*as if surprised at the question*). Me? I'm fine. (*As* JOE *keeps fiddling with dials, dance music comes on, then band music.*)

TOMMY. That's good.

JOE. Well, it hasn't started yet—just music. Let's go. (*Get's* ELLEN's *coat from hook.*) This yours?

ELLEN. Yes.

JOE. Well, is it warm enough?

ELLEN. Yes. Oh, it's very warm.

TOMMY (*angrily*). No, it isn't.

CLEOTA (*enters with Thermos. Gives it to* TOMMY). Here's your Thermos bottle, Mr. Turner.

TOMMY. Thank you. (*Takes it.*) (CLEOTA *goes out.*)

ELLEN. It's a very warm day, anyway, and we'll have the laprobe from the car.

TOMMY. Ellen. (*She goes to him eagerly.*) You forgot your Thermos bottle— (*His tone is jocular, and he pretends to screw the cap on tighter to cover his hurt.*) You'd better make a note of this, Joe. It gets cold in stadiums late in the afternoon. Ellen gets chilly sometimes, so she likes hot coffee— Well, here. (*He hands Thermos to* ELLEN. JOE *nods, goes to the front door, and*

opens it. ELLEN, *who has been staring at* TOMMY, *suddenly throws the Thermos bottle on the floor, then rushes out, passing* JOE. JOE *looks after her, then comes back to face* TOMMY *threateningly.*)

JOE. Did you slap her?

TOMMY. No, I kicked her.

JOE. Well, you did something! (*An* ANNOUNCER's *voice breaks into the band music.*)

ANNOUNCER'S VOICE. Well, here we are on Midwestern field on a mighty fine afternoon for a football game. It looks like the Big Day of the year, folks. Neither one of these great teams has lost a game. The Michigan squad is out on the field, warming up. They look even bigger than last year.—

JOE (*torn between interest in the announcement and his aroused chivalry*). Here I get her all calmed down and you make her cry again. I see now what kind of a life she has here. I'm going to take her away from this and keep her away!

TOMMY (*shouting*). All right! Why don't you get started?

JOE (*topping him*). Because I've got a few more things to say to you. First! (*As he takes a breath, the* ANNOUNCER's VOICE *comes through clearly.*)

ANNOUNCER'S VOICE. Here comes the Scarlet Stampede now! (*There is a roar of cheering.*)

JOE. My God, they're coming out on the field! We'll miss the kick-off! *God damn it!* (*Turns and dashes out the front door.* TOMMY *stands looking after them as the band blares and*)

THE CURTAIN FALLS.

SCENE 2: *The Turner living room, two hours later. It is growing dark outside.*

TOMMY *and* MICHAEL *are sitting in chairs, wide apart, facing the audience, so that they have to turn their heads to see each other. Each has a glass in his hand, and they are sprawled in their chairs silent, brooding. The room shows indications of quite a bout: a bottle here, a few magazines flung there, a cushion on the floor.* TOMMY *gets the Scotch bottle, pours a little into* MICHAEL's *glass, emptying the bottle. He starts to* **pour** *some into his own glass, finds the bottle empty so pours some from* MICHAEL'S *glass into his own. Throws the bottle into waste-basket. There is a pause.*

MICHAEL. He is probably still running with that ball—

TOMMY (*pause*). Quiet—quiet!— What time is it?

MICHAEL (*looks at wrist-watch, has trouble seeing it*). It's getting dark.

TOMMY (*pause*). Do you know the first law of human nature?

MICHAEL. Yes. Self-propagation.

TOMMY. Not any more. That's gone with last year's nightingale.

MICHAEL. Gone with last year's rose.

TOMMY (*slight pause*). Yes— Defense of the home—against prowlers and predatory—prowlers— Do you know what the tiger does when the sanctity of his home is jeopardized?

MICHAEL. I know. You told me. He talks it over with the other man, quietly and calmly.

TOMMY. He does not. I'm ashamed of you.

MICHAEL. I think we must have another drink—possibly.

TOMMY. All right. Hey! *Hey!* (*He is pleased with this shouting.*) That's the way to talk to 'em. (*He puts back his head and yells.*) HEYYY!! (CLEOTA *enters and turns on the lights.*)

CLEOTA. Mistah Turner, what is it?

TOMMY. What do you want?—Oh, we should like to have something more to drink.

CLEOTA. Dey ain' no more to drink. I'll make you all some black coffee. (*She goes out.*)

TOMMY (*pause*). What'd she say?

MICHAEL. Nothing.

TOMMY. Where was I?

MICHAEL. Let's see—you were talking about tigers.

TOMMY. Oh, yes. But let us take the wolf. What does he do? I mean, when they come for his mate. He tears 'em to pieces.

MICHAEL. But we are civilized men. Aren't we?

TOMMY. And so does the leopard, and the lion, and the hawk. They tear 'em to pieces. Without a word.

MICHAEL. You had it figured out the other way around a while ago. You said we should give up our women. (TOMMY *stands, falters.*) It's better sitting down. (TOMMY *sits.*)

TOMMY. Let us say that the tiger wakes up one morning and finds that the wolf has come down on the fold. What does he—? Before I tell you what he does, I will tell you what he does not do.

MICHAEL. Yes, sir.

TOMMY. He does not expose everyone to a humiliating intellectual analysis. He comes out of his corner like this— (*Rises, assumes awkward fighting pose, fists up —then sits quickly again.*) The bull elephant in him is aroused.

MICHAEL (*plaintively*). Can't you stick to one animal?

TOMMY. No, that's my point. All animals are the same, including the human being. We are male animals, too.

MICHAEL (*stares at him, bewildered*). You said—

TOMMY. Even the penguin. (*His voice shows emotion as he thinks of the penguin.*) He stands for no monkey business where his mate is concerned. Swans have been known to drown Scotties who threatened their nests.

MICHAEL. I don't think so.

TOMMY. There it is, in us always, though it may be asleep. The male animal. The mate. When you are married long enough, you become a mate— Think of the sea lion for a minute.

MICHAEL. All right.

TOMMY. His mate is lying there in a corner of the cave on a bed of tender boughs or something. (*Turns to* MICHAEL *for confirmation.*) Is that all right, "tender boughs"?

MICHAEL. Yeah!

TOMMY (*illustrating by gesture, a great seal, or eel*). Now, who comes swimming quietly in through the early morning mist, sleek and powerful, dancing and whirling and throwing kisses?

MICHAEL. Joe Ferguson.

TOMMY. And what do I do?

MICHAEL. You say, "Hello."

TOMMY (*in self-disgust*). The sea lion knows better. He snarls. He gores. He roars with his antlers. He knows that love is a thing you do something about. He knows it is a thing that words can kill. You do something. You don't just sit there. (MICHAEL *rises*.) I don't mean you. (MICHAEL *sits*.) A woman likes a man who does something. All the male animals fight for the female, from the land crab to the bird of paradise. They don't just sit and talk. They act. (*He removes glasses and blinks owlishly around.*) I hope I have made all this clear to you. Are there any questions?

MICHAEL. No, sir. (ELLEN *and* JOE *enter*. ELLEN *takes in the disordered room, bottles on the floor*, TOMMY's *and* MICHAEL's *condition*. MICHAEL *and* TOMMY *rise*.)

ELLEN. Tommy! What in the world have you been doing?

TOMMY. Drinking.

ELLEN. What for?

TOMMY. I was celebrating. Ellen, I have found myself. (*Glances at* JOE.) I know now what I have to do.

ELLEN. Yes, I know. We've been through all that.

TOMMY. I think perhaps you had better go away for a little while. (*Waves toward upstairs.*)

ELLEN. I'm going. I'll be down in a minute, Joe. (*She slams upstairs.*)

JOE. Boy, wasn't that some football game? I'm running Wally Myers for President.

TOMMY (*beckoning to* MICHAEL). Come on. (*With drunken carefulness he and* MICHAEL *begin moving furniture to the sides of the room.*)

JOE (*watches, slightly puzzled, making talk*). Yes, sir, some game, wasn't it? What did you think of Michigan going into the lead like that? If Wally hadn't snared that pass—

MICHAEL. We didn't listen to the game.

JOE. You didn't listen to the game?

MICHAEL. No, we turned it off. (*He flips an imaginary dial.*)

TOMMY. The game didn't last all this time. Where have you been?

JOE. Well, we stopped in at President Cartwright's house.

TOMMY. What for?

JOE. 'Cause Ellen and I were making one last effort to get you out of this mess.

TOMMY. Ellen and you. You would know exactly what to do, wou'nt you?

JOE. You guys are pie-eyed!

TOMMY (*to* MICHAEL). Did you hear that?

MICHAEL. Yes.

JOE. What's the idea of moving all the furniture around like this?

TOMMY. I don't want you to break anything when you fall.

JOE. I'm not going to fall.

TOMMY. Yes, you are. I am going to knock you cold. (*The furniture safe*, TOMMY *rolls up his sleeves, and* MICHAEL *sits on the arm of a settee, watching.*)

JOE (*kindly*). Let's sit down and talk this over.

TOMMY (*turning to* MICHAEL). "Talk," he says, to a man of action. "Sit down," he says, to a tigress and her cubs!

JOE. How in hell did you guys get so cock-eyed? I wish Ellen'd hurry up. (*Goes to dining room door.*) Cleota!

TOMMY. Don't call for help. I could take Cleota and you in the same ring!

JOE. Well, what's this all about?

TOMMY. You crept into this house to take Ellen away, didn't you? You thought it was the house of a professor who would talk and *talk* and TALK—

JOE. And by God you have! I came here to see a football game—

MICHAEL. That's a lie.

JOE. Why don't you go home?

MICHAEL. 'Cause I want to watch.

JOE. Well, there isn't going to be anything to watch.

TOMMY (*assuming fighter's pose*). Come on, put up your fists.

JOE. Get away from me, Tommy. (*Pushes* TOMMY's *arm which pivots* TOMMY *around so he faces* MICHAEL.) I'd break you in two, and I don't want to do that.

TOMMY (*at first to* MICHAEL, *then realizing he is facing the wrong way he turns to* JOE). Why don't you want to do that?

JOE. 'Cause how would it look if I came here and took Ellen and knocked you down on the way out?

MICHAEL. Maybe he's right. That's a point of honor, Mr. Turner.

TOMMY. Is it?

MICHAEL. But we could fight him about something else.

TOMMY. About what?

MICHAEL. He doesn't want you to read that letter.

TOMMY. That's right. (MICHAEL *rises and slowly moves to a spot behind* JOE.) Going to President Cartwright's house. Trying to make me lose my job.

JOE. Why the hell should I?

TOMMY. So you could get Ellen.

JOE. Now, listen—

TOMMY. Yes! Now I'm going to have to knock you further than I had previously decided upon. Come out in the back yard. (*He tugs at* JOE, *but doesn't move him.* MICHAEL *helpfully gives* JOE *a good push.*)

JOE (*turns and strides back to* MICHAEL). Don't push me!

TOMMY. *HEY!!* (*He lunges at* JOE *with a badly aimed "haymaker."*)

JOE (*ducks and catches* TOMMY *to keep him from falling*). Now look, if you do ever get in a fight, Tommy, don't lead with your right. It leaves you wide open.

TOMMY. Oh, does it?

ELLEN (*comes down stairs with suitcase, which she drops when she sees odd positions of belligerents*). Tommy! What's happened? What are you doing now?

TOMMY. Fighting. (*The music of the band is heard in the distance. Through the following scene it grows louder to* ELLEN'S *exit, then dies away as the band goes around the corner and comes up again for the end of the scene.*)

ELLEN (*hopefully*). Fighting! What about?

MICHAEL. Penguins.

ELLEN. What!

JOE (*trying to explain*). Oh, it was all mixed up—about a lot of tigers and a cub. Tommy doesn't care what you and I are trying to do! He wants us to stay out of it!

ELLEN (*disappointed bitterly*). Oh, I see. That's what you were fighting about.

TOMMY. It wasn't about you.—Point of honor.

ELLEN. Oh yes, I see. You don't want me mixed up with anything. All right. You can pull the house down on top of you with your damn birds and letters and whisky. Just let me get out of—what is all that racket?

JOE (*opens the door a crack—then closes it*). Oh, they're having a victory parade and they want me to ride in that damn carriage with Wally Myers and the band.

TOMMY. You attract bands like flies, don't you!

ELLEN (*as she starts for the door*). Goodbye, Tommy! I'll be out in the car, Joe. Bring my bag, please! (*She slams out. The men look after her then* JOE *gets* ELLEN'S *bag and faces* TOMMY.)

JOE. You're getting me in deeper and deeper. I should'a taken a poke at you when I had the chance!

TOMMY. Fine! Come out in the back yard! (*Walks to garden door and holds it open.*)

JOE. I'm not coming out in the back yard! (MICHAEL *pushes him and* TOMMY, *catching him, turns him around to the lower door.*) Don't push me! I said, I don't like to be pushed!

TOMMY. No— You said, "Don't lead with your right." (*He hits* JOE *on the nose with his left fist.*)

JOE (*pinching bridge of nose*). Ow-w-w! Now you've started my sinus trouble! (*He flings down suitcase and spreads his hand easily across* TOMMY'S *face.*) By God, if you want a fight, you've got a fight! (*He pushes* TOMMY *outside, his arms flailing the air.*)

MICHAEL (*plants a chair in front of the door and sits watching the fight offstage. He applauds its progress*). Hit him! Hit him! (*Quotes softly.*)

"And all the summer afternoon
They hunted us and slew!
But tomorrow—by the living God!
We'll try the game again!"

Don't forget to lead with your right, Mr. Turner! That's right! Right in the eye! (CLEOTA *is attracted from the dining room by the noise.* WALLY *and* PATRICIA *come in the front door, rush over* to MICHAEL *who bars the door with out-stretched arms.*)

PATRICIA. Michael!!

WALLY. What's going on here?

CLEOTA (*peering at fight off scene*). Godamighty!

PATRICIA. Oh—Michael, stop them! Wally, stop them!

MICHAEL. No, don't stop them! Let Mr. Turner alone and he'll tear him to pieces! (*Crash outside.*)

WALLY. Get away from that door! (*He hurls MICHAEL aside.*)

PATRICIA (*runs and kneels beside MICHAEL*). Michael! Michael!

ELLEN (*reenters the front door, calling*). Joe, are you coming? (*She sees MICHAEL and PATRICIA, and looks around the room for TOMMY and JOE.*)

MICHAEL (*continues to quote poetry dramatically. With rapid fervor*).

"And many a broken heart is here,"

ELLEN. What is it?

MICHAEL.

"And many a broken head,
But tomorrow—by the living God!—
We'll try the game again!"

(*He tries to rise. PATRICIA drops him in disgust.*)

PATRICIA. Oh, Michael! (*JOE and WALLY carry in the unconscious TOMMY, and deposit him on the sofa.*)

ELLEN (*screaming*). Tommy!! (*The phone rings insistently.*)

CLEOTA (*shouts imperturbably into phone*). Professah Turner's res-i-dence!

THE CURTAIN FALLS SWIFTLY.

ACT THREE

SCENE: *The Turner living room. Same as Acts One and Two. About noon, Monday. The room is neat and orderly, but the flowers and other signs of festivity have been removed.*

The stage is empty, but the phone bell is ringing. A moment later, the doorbell also begins to sound insistently. CLEOTA *enters from the dining room, wiping her hands on her apron, scuttles for an instant between the bells, picks up phone.*

CLEOTA (*into phone*). Stop ringin' dis thing both at once—Who?—Ah cain' heah you foh de ringin'. Hol' on— (*Putting down the receiver, she hurries to the front door and opens it cautiously, bracing herself to prevent a forced entrance. She speaks through the crack of the door to the man standing there.*) Ah tol' you stop ringin' eve'ything. Ah'm heah, ain' I?

REPORTER'S VOICE. I'd like to see Mr. Turner.

CLEOTA. Is you a newspapah?

REPORTER'S VOICE. Yeh, I'm from the *Daily Journal.*

CLEOTA. He cain' see nobody—he's sick.

REPORTER. I know—but will he be up today? Is he going to his class?

CLEOTA. He ain' goin' nowheah. His haid huts him. He's sick. Go 'way. (*She forces the door shut, bolts it, returns to the telephone.*) Professah Turner's res-i-dence— *Daily* what?—You jus' *was* heah — No, Professah Turner ain' talkin' to nobody. He's sick in bed with his haid— No, he ain' goin' an' you ain' comin'. He ain't not talkin' 'cause he don' wanta talk. He jus' ain' talkin' cause he cain' talk. Goodbye. (*The bolted door is rattled from outside, then the doorbell begins to ring insistently.* CLEOTA *looks at the door angrily and starts for it. Looks back at the phone and mutters.*) What's goin' on heah? —I told you to go 'way. (*She opens the door and* PATRICIA *enters.*)

PATRICIA. What's the matter?

CLEOTA (*giggling in embarrassment*). Oh, it's you. I thought it was that newspapah again. He just went.

PATRICIA. He didn't go—he's outside picketing. Where's my sister, Cleota?

CLEOTA. Upstaihs. Miss Patricia, Ah wish Ah knew bettah what's goin' on heah.

PATRICIA. Never mind.

CLEOTA. Mr. Michael jus' left.

PATRICIA. Oh. Well, if Mr. Michael

Barnes comes here again, *don't let him in!*

CLEOTA. No, ma'am. (CLEOTA *goes into the dining room just as* ELLEN, *looking very depressed, comes from upstairs.*)

PATRICIA. Hello, Ellen! How's Tommy? Is he still asleep?

ELLEN. Yes, but he tosses around and mutters. The doctor says he can get up this afternoon.

PATRICIA. No concussion, then?

ELLEN. Yes, a little.

PATRICIA (*seating herself on settee*). I guess when anybody's as crazy as Tommy or Michael, a little concussion doesn't make any difference.

ELLEN. Did you get the butter?

PATRICIA. Oh, Lord, no—I'll go back.

ELLEN. Never mind. I need a little air.

PATRICIA. How's *your* head?

ELLEN. Oh, all right.

PATRICIA. Is it? Say, what is this second springtime you're all going through, anyway?

ELLEN. Tommy won't let me in on what he's really thinking about. He thinks I'm not smart enough to understand it—that's what it comes down to.

PATRICIA. Oh, a mental problem! I haven't been exactly listening at keyholes, but isn't there a Joe Something-or-other mixed up in this?

ELLEN. Oh, there's more to it than a fight about Joe.

PATRICIA. Pretty good one round here Saturday about Joe. (*Then, directly.*) You know Tommy was fighting for you in his mid-Victorian way, don't you?

ELLEN. Oh, but he was drunk. When he's sober he despises me. He thinks I'm a dimwit.

PATRICIA. But he wouldn't want you any other way than you are.

ELLEN. Thanks.

PATRICIA. I mean you're smart enough for Tommy and you know it, and he knows it.

ELLEN (*unhappily*). I'm all mixed up. I want to go away some place where I can think.

PATRICIA. Look, this is a new century. You're not Diana of the Crossways or somebody.

ELLEN. Well, what do you want me to do—stay here when he doesn't want me?

PATRICIA (*vigorously*). No, but if you're going away, go away with Joe. Tommy's certainly been throwing you at him. Why don't you take him up on it? See what happens.

ELLEN. Is this advice to the lovelorn? Do you think he would come running after me?

PATRICIA. Well, you've got to quit moping around and do something. I thought we Stanley women were supposed to have some resources. (*Rises and faces* ELLEN.) Look, your great-grandmother chased her man all the way to Nebraska in a covered wagon.

ELLEN. Well, I'm not going to chase anybody anywhere! I'm going to talk this over with Tommy, fairly and squarely, face to face. (*Starts to front door.*)

PATRICIA. "Fairly and squarely!" How did your generation ever get through the 1920s?

ELLEN (*sadly*). We didn't. (*She goes out.* PATRICIA *sighs in despair.*)

TOMMY (*comes slowly down stairs. He wears terrycloth bathrobe, and has a wet turkish towel twisted about his head*). Hello, Pat!

PATRICIA. Tommy—you shouldn't be up!

TOMMY. I'm all right. What day is this?

PATRICIA. Monday.

TOMMY. Cleota—Cleota! (*To* PATRICIA.) Can I take this thing off?

PATRICIA. You're not supposed to. You ought to lie down. (TOMMY *sinks in chair.*)

TOMMY. I'll just lean back. (*Winces as he tries it.*) No—I guess I won't.

CLEOTA (*appears in dining room door*). Mistah Turner—is you up?

TOMMY. Yes, I'm up. Cleota, don't let anyone in this house except Mr. Michael Barnes. (PATRICIA *shakes her head "No" to* CLEOTA.)

CLEOTA (*nodding to both*). Yessuh— Ah do de best Ah can. (*Backs out of room.*)

TOMMY. Where's Ellen?

PATRICIA. She went out to get the transfer man—for her trunk.

TOMMY. She's going away?

PATRICIA. Oh, no. She just likes to call on transfer men. Didn't you know that?

TOMMY. I can't stand irony so early in the day, Patricia.

PATRICIA. You're all right now, you see. She wouldn't go before. I don't know why.

TOMMY. You ought to know why. Your sister wouldn't walk out on anybody when he's down—even when he's down with delirium tremens.

PATRICIA. You didn't have D.T.'s. You had concussion.

TOMMY. Seemed more like D.T.'s.

PATRICIA. You don't know very much about my little sister, do you?

TOMMY. I know a lot more than I did last Friday. (*Goes to sofa.*) I think I will lie down.

PATRICIA. Why do you have to make everything as hard as you can? (TOMMY *groans a little with pain.*) Do you want another cold towel?

TOMMY. No, thanks. (*Phone rings.*)

PATRICIA (*answering phone*). Yes?— Who? No, Michael Barnes isn't here.

TOMMY (*lying down carefully*). He was here and he's coming back.

PATRICIA. This is Patricia Stanley— Yes— Yes— I'll be very glad to tell him to call you—if I see him. Good-bye! (*Slams receiver down.*) That was Hot Garters Gardner.

TOMMY. Oh-oh! Why did she call here?

PATRICIA. She said they told her Michael was on his way here, but obviously she just called for my benefit— So that's where he went Saturday night! You had that Hot—that Miss Gardner in some of your classes; do you remember her?

TOMMY (*reflectively*). I don't know. What does she look like?

PATRICIA. Well, she—doesn't wear any— (*Gestures a brassière.*)

TOMMY. I only had her in Wordsworth.

PATRICIA. Calling up here! (*There is a knock at the door;* PATRICIA *smiles grimly. She goes to the door and opens*

it. MICHAEL *steps in; he is taken aback at seeing* PATRICIA.) Good-morning, Michael! Come in.

TOMMY (*in warning, sepulchral tones*). Yes, come in, Michael. (PATRICIA'S *back is turned so* TOMMY *pantomimes "telephone" for* MICHAEL'S *benefit.* MICHAEL *peers at him nervously.*)

MICHAEL. I got the car for you— Feel better now that you're up? (*Doesn't get the pantomime.*)

TOMMY. Yes, much better. How do you feel?

MICHAEL. I feel all right.

TOMMY. That's good. (*Mimics* PATRICIA'S *brassière gesture.*)

PATRICIA (*turning*). If you'll excuse me—

MICHAEL. Oh, Pat, wait!—I—could I talk to you for a minute? Couldn't we go outside there and—

PATRICIA. No, we couldn't go outside there. Is it anything you're ashamed to say in front of Tommy?

MICHAEL (*stiffening*). No. No, I'm not. Only— Well, I don't want to get off on the wrong foot again. I'm sorry I got so mad Saturday. I said things and did things that—

PATRICIA. You certainly did.

MICHAEL. Well, I'm sorry, and— Oh, Pat, you ought to be able to see this my way. We just lost our tempers and— well—Mr. Turner and I are in a jam. I think you ought to—well—make an effort to understand what we're trying to do and stand by us—that is, if you care anything about me at all.

PATRICIA (*so sweetly*). Oh, I certainly do. I've been standing by—taking messages for you—phone calls. I'm so glad we had this nice talk. (*Shakes his hand.*) And before you go, be sure to call Maple 4307. (*She hurls the last at him furiously, then sweeps out the front door.*)

MICHAEL (*looking after her*). Maple 430— (*Horrified, as he realizes whom the number belongs to.*) Did The Garters call here?

TOMMY. That's what I was trying to tell you. Patricia answered the phone. The—elastics—snapped right in her face.

MICHAEL. And I didn't even *do* anything. (*Sits beside* TOMMY *on sofa.*) I hope.

TOMMY. Michael, you're making me nervous. (*A pause.*)

MICHAEL. Will you be able to go to the faculty meeting tonight?

TOMMY. I'll be there.

MICHAEL. They'll be out to get you— I know this is all my fault, Mr. Turner.

TOMMY. Yes, you're certainly the man that lighted the match.

MICHAEL. I just came from the President's office; he flayed me alive.

TOMMY. Are you kicked out?

MICHAEL. Suspended.

TOMMY. Michael, tell me— Are you really a Communist?

MICHAEL. Me?—No—I only know one guy who is. I'm—well, I guess I'm an unconfused liberal. I think I'll go to Stringfellow Barr's school in Annapolis and read the classics.

TOMMY. I wonder where I'll go? (ELLEN *enters front door with parcel.*)

ELLEN. Good morning, Michael.

MICHAEL (*rises*). Hello, Mrs. Turner!

ELLEN (*sees* TOMMY). Good morning, Tommy— (*Goes to dining room door and calls.*) Cleota—

TOMMY. Good morning. (CLEOTA *enters.*)

ELLEN. Here's the butter, Cleota. Will you make Mr. Turner a cup of tea? (*Turns back to him.*) Would you like a hard-boiled egg?

TOMMY. No, thanks. Nothing hard. My teeth hurt. (CLEOTA *retires.*)

ELLEN. Are you waiting for Patricia, Michael?

MICHAEL. I saw her. I'm leaving town, Mrs. Turner.

ELLEN. I'm awfully sorry, Michael.

WALLY's VOICE (*offstage*). Pat! Oh, Pat!

ELLEN. Come in, Wally. (WALLY *comes in from the garden.*) Patricia's gone out somewhere.

WALLY. Oh, I see. (*To* MICHAEL.) You waiting for her?

MICHAEL. That's none of your business. Why? (*He strides over to* WALLY.)

WALLY (*lowers his voice*). I know

what you did Saturday night, that's why. Well, thanks, Mrs. Turner. I just cut across the back way. I'll walk on down to the house. (*Starts out.*)

MICHAEL (*stops him*). I think I'll walk along. I want to talk to you.

WALLY. You don't have to.

MICHAEL. If I didn't have to, I wouldn't do it. I'm no masochist. (*Starts out.*)

WALLY (*stares after him blankly, then follows*). You don't have to use words like that in front of ladies.

MICHAEL. I'll be back in time to drive you to class, Mr. Turner. (*Both boys go out.*)

TOMMY. Thanks. (CLEOTA *enters, and* ELLEN *takes the tray from her.*)

ELLEN. Here's your tea. (CLEOTA *goes out.*)

TOMMY. Thanks.

ELLEN (*with some constraint*). How do you feel?

TOMMY. Very strange.

ELLEN. Is everything clear to you now?

TOMMY. Clear in the center. It's kind of fuzzy around the edges.

ELLEN. (ELLEN *has made up her mind what she wants to say; she seats herself and begins.*) I hope it's clear enough to give me a chance to say something without your going off on one of your literary tangents.

TOMMY. I don't do that.

ELLEN. I know you think I'm not very bright or something, (TOMMY *tries to demur, but she continues.*) but you must realize that you got me all mixed up Friday and that you were even less helpful Saturday.

TOMMY. That wasn't me, Saturday. That was a drunken sea lion.

ELLEN. I rather liked you as a sea lion.

TOMMY. Yes, I must have been very funny. Did you ever read Hodgson's poem, "The Bull"?

ELLEN. Oh, Tommy!

TOMMY. It's the story of the defeated male. There is no defeat that can be quite so complete.

ELLEN. You wouldn't admit that this defeat was on account of— No, it has to be something out of a book.

TOMMY. "When the bull's head is in the dust, life goes on and leaves him there"; it's a psychological fact. The poets understand these things.

ELLEN. And all the cows react the same way? As if they were reading instructions from a blackboard? Oh, Tommy, listen to me— (*Doorbell rings.*)

TOMMY. The point is, I don't want any pity.

CLEOTA (*hurrying from dining room*). It's dat prize fightah. I seen him from de windah. (ELLEN *admits* JOE, *who comes in without his old bounce; he is worried and restless.*)

ELLEN. Hello, Joe!

JOE. Hello. (*Awkwardly to* TOMMY.) Hello.

TOMMY. Hello!

JOE. I'm sorry, Tommy. I didn't hit you hard. You slipped and hit your head on a bench.

TOMMY. Yeh, I know. What's the matter with your hand?

JOE. You kinda bit me. Ed's out in the car. We just chased a reporter away hanging around out there.

ELLEN. Well, don't let any reporters in, Cleota.

TOMMY. And don't let Keller in. (CLEOTA *nods and exits to kitchen.*)

JOE (*indicating wet towel*). Do you have to keep that thing on?

TOMMY. No, I just do it because I like it. (*Throws down towel.*)

JOE. Could I have a little slug of something? I—

ELLEN. Certainly! Scotch?

JOE. Yeh, fine. (ELLEN *goes to dining room.* JOE *paces.*) I got the galloping jumps. I can use a little drink. Haven't slept for two nights.

TOMMY. Worrying about something?

JOE. Yeh, worrying about something— And my cold's worse.

TOMMY. Want some Kleenex?

JOE (*irritated*). No, I don't want some Kleenex. Darn reporters been bothering me, too.

TOMMY. What do they want with you?

JOE. Oh, they wanted me to pick an all-American team.

TOMMY (*incredulously—almost*). Did you?

JOE. Yeh. Kinda took my mind off things.

TOMMY (*sarcastically*). Who'd you pick for right guard?

JOE. Shulig—Kansas State Teachers'. (*Faces* TOMMY.) Look, Tommy, where the hell do we all stand now? (TOMMY *picks up towel, presses it to his head again.*) Does that kinda throb?

TOMMY. No.

JOE. Well, I wanta know where we all stand.

TOMMY. Oh, let it alone, Joe. It'll work out. You and I can handle this. I don't want Ellen worried about details now. She's got enough trouble with me —sitting around the house looking like a hot-oil shampoo—

ELLEN (*enters with bowl of ice. She fixes a drink*). There's been more drinking in this house in the last two days than we've done in ten years. (JOE *sits on settee at far side of room.*)

TOMMY (*after a pause*). Ellen, Joe picked Shulig of Kansas State Teachers' for right guard, on his all-American. Isn't that nice? (ELLEN *looks annoyed.*)

JOE (*reminiscently*). It was kinda hard choosing between him and Feldkamp of Western Reserve. Both big and fast.

ELLEN (*crossing with drink*). Here you are, dear— (*She is coolly oblivious of* TOMMY's *hand which he puts out for drink; goes on to* JOE, *who doesn't realize she means him.*) Dear. (*He looks up at her with a start—glances at* TOMMY, *then takes drink.*)

TOMMY (*sulkily*). I don't want any.

JOE. Say, have you got a Pennsylvania timetable around?

ELLEN. Where are you going, Joe?

JOE. Well, I've got to be in Washington tomorrow.

ELLEN. That's going to rush me.

JOE. What do you mean?

ELLEN. Well, Joe, I thought you and I might start out late this afternoon and go as far as that little Inn at Granville tonight. Just for a few days. (*She sits close to* JOE *on settee.*)

TOMMY (*rises*). What did you say?

ELLEN (*to* JOE). I think it's the nicest place around here. Don't you?

JOE (*flopping on the hook*). I—I—eh—Could I have a little more Scotch? (*He hurries across the room, pours himself another drink.*)

ELLEN (*gaily*). I don't want you to get drunk, Joe.

JOE. I'll be all right—I'll be all right. What time is it?

TOMMY. Never mind what time it is. (*To* ELLEN.) Would you mind explaining this a little better?

ELLEN. I'll try to make it as clear as I can for both of you. I simply have to make a fresh start now, Tommy. You understand women; you must see that. I can't stay here now. You've made your plans, and now I have to make mine.

TOMMY. Yes—but not like this—not running off to Granville!

ELLEN. All right, if you're afraid of a scandal, we'll go farther away. Put Granville out of your mind, then. We'll go directly to Pittsburgh.

JOE. Huh?

ELLEN. It's a very big town. Nobody need know anything about it.

JOE. About what?

ELLEN. About us. About our living together. (*Both men stop cold.*)

TOMMY. Ellen!

JOE (*desperately*). But you see—I don't live in Pittsburgh. (*He makes a large circular gesture with both hands.*) I live in Sewickly. (*The gesture is small and loving now.*) And my boss lives there too. And my mother. My mother's not very well. My mother—

TOMMY. Oh, you and your mother!

JOE. Besides, it's a Presbyterian town.

ELLEN. You're not being very gallant, Joe.

TOMMY. No. Are you trying to get out of this?

JOE. No, but I come from a long line of married people! And besides, I'm not going to Pittsburgh directly. I've got to go to Washington, and that's one place I couldn't take you, Ellen!

TOMMY. You'll take her any place she wants to go, but she's not going any place!

ELLEN. Oh, yes, I am! (*There is a loud knock, and* ED KELLER *enters.*)

ED. I can't sit out in that car all day, you know.

JOE. Oh, I'm sorry, Ed, but—jees, I forgot all about you. (*Turns to* TOMMY.) I persuaded Ed to come over and talk to you before this thing gets too bad. (*Leads* ED *to* TOMMY.)

TOMMY. It couldn't get any worse!

JOE. I mean about the trustees.

TOMMY. Let the trustees take care of themselves. We have troubles of our own.

ED. You'll find out this is your trouble. Is he able to talk?

JOE. God, yes!

ED (*to* TOMMY). Well, then, listen. We just had a trustees' meeting in the President's office. Michael Barnes is out, and you're on your way out. You'll be asked to resign tonight.

ELLEN (*rising*). Oh, Tommy!

JOE. Ed's trying to help him while there's still time. After tonight, it will be too late.

TOMMY. What do you care what happens tonight? You won't be here. You'll be in Granville or somewhere.

ED. What're you going to be doing in Granville?

TOMMY. Please don't ask personal questions.

ELLEN. Do you mind if I stay a little while, Tommy?

TOMMY (*angrily*). Why shouldn't you stay? It's your house.

ED. Sit down, Ellen. (*She sits. To* TOMMY.) There's just one thing you can do: come out with a statement to the papers quick. Say you were sick. Say you didn't know anything about Barnes' editorial. You think it's an outrage. You're not going to read this Vanzetti thing, and you think Barnes is getting what he deserves. That's the only thing that'll save your neck.

ELLEN. Tommy wouldn't say that about Michael, Ed, and you shouldn't ask him to.

TOMMY. Thank you.

ED. All right, then! That's all I had to say. Goodbye! This is on your own head.

ELLEN. Ed! Just a minute, please. (*Faces* TOMMY.) I know that reading this letter must mean something to you, Tommy. Something none of us can quite understand. I wish I could. It might help me to understand a lot of other things, when I can get away where I can think.

TOMMY. Such as what?

ELLEN. Such as what is important to you. What you've been fighting for. Whether it's something you really believe in and love, or just your own selfish pride. I think you got into this just because you were mad at me. And that's ridiculous, because now you don't care what I do or say about it. You're out of that.

ED (*to* JOE). I don't see what she's talking about. (JOE *motions him to be quiet.*)

TOMMY. All right, I'll try to explain what it means to me. Perhaps originally pride had something to do with this. And jealousy.

ELLEN. And stubbornness—

TOMMY. And—please. I am trying to say that—now—I am not fighting about you and me at all. This is bigger than you and me or any of us.

ELLEN. Is it?

ED (*ironically*). It must be a masterpiece. That letter must be quite a nice piece of propaganda.

TOMMY. Why don't you read it and find out?

ED. I don't read things like that.

TOMMY. My God, you don't even know what you're objecting to.

JOE. Well, Tommy, why don't you read the letter to us, and let us see what it is?

TOMMY. I'll be glad to read it to you, but I'll read it to my class too. (*He goes to bookcase and hunts for the book; not finding it, he remembers it is upstairs and goes up.*)

ED. You don't have to read it to me. I know what kind of stuff it is. (*The front door bursts open, and* PATRICIA *backs in, followed by* WALLY, *leaving the door open.*)

PATRICIA. But I can't go with you now! I told you I've got to wait here and see what Tommy's going to do.

WALLY. But you're not going to the class! You said you're not going!

PATRICIA. I'm not! I just want to know!

WALLY. I'll bet you *are* going! You're waiting here for Michael to go with you!

PATRICIA. Oh, go away! (*Turning, she sees others, who are listening.*) Oh—I'm sorry. (*She rushes across to the door leading to the garden.*)

ED. What's this now?

JOE (*grinning*). Hey, Pat, you better think twice before you scrap with Wally here. He's coming in with me at Pittsburgh next year.

WALLY. A lot she cares about Pittsburgh! I run sixty-two yards through Michigan and all she wants is to listen to Mike Barnes talk about free love. (*He stalks over to* PATRICIA.)

ED. She does?

ELLEN (*trying to stop* WALLY). Wally, how's Stalenkiwiecz?

WALLY (*brushing past her*). He's much better. (*To* PATRICIA.) If you knew what I know about that guy Barnes—

PATRICIA. I know what you're hinting at! And what if he did? It only shows what an intense person Michael is. I know that no matter what he did, he was thinking of me.

WALLY. That's disgusting!

PATRICIA. And aren't you a little bit disgusting to mention it? I thought *men* had some loyalty! (*She goes out.*)

WALLY (*following her out*). Now, listen here— Do you know what he did? —I'll tell you what he did.

ED (*sitting on sofa*). What kind of a house is this? (*As* TOMMY *comes downstairs with an open book in his hand,* DAMON, *carrying his ever-present umbrella, walks quietly in the open front door and looks around.*)

TOMMY. All right, here it is. Now sit down—or stand up—but listen!— Oh, hello, Doctor Damon. You're just in time.

DAMON. In time for what? (*Sees* ED, *moves toward him.*) Has the Inquisition moved its headquarters?

TOMMY. I'm just going to read the Inquisition a letter from one of its victims.

ED. That's about enough of that.

DAMON. Gentlemen, gentlemen—This may not be wise, Thomas.

TOMMY. It may not be wise, but it's necessary. I think you'll have to take a stand, too, Doctor Damon.

DAMON. I hope not. (*Sits on settee;* JOE *seats himself on the fireplace bench:* ELLEN *sits opposite side of the room.*)

TOMMY. So did I hope not. I didn't start out to lead a crusade. I simply mentioned one day that I meant to read to my class three letters by men whose profession was not literature, but who had something sincere to say. Once I had declared that very harmless intention, the world began to shake, great institutions trembled, and football players descended upon me and my wife. I realized then that I was doing something important.

ED (*sarcastically*). You make it sound mighty innocent. Reading Lincoln and General Sherman—and Vanzetti. What was the reason you gave for picking out Vanzetti?

TOMMY (*to* ED). *Originally* I chose him to show that broken English can sometimes be very moving and eloquent, but now—

ED. We wouldn't object if this was just a case of broken English—it's more than that.

TOMMY. Yes, you've made it more than that.

ED. Vanzetti was an anarchist! He was executed for murder.

TOMMY. He was accused of murder, but thousands of people believe he was executed simply because of the ideas he believed in.

ED. That's a dangerous thing to bring up.

TOMMY (*getting really mad*). No, it's a dangerous thing to keep down. I'm fighting for a teacher's rights. But if you want to make it political, all right! You can't suppress ideas because you don't like them—not in this country—not yet. (*To* DAMON.) This is a university! It's our business to bring what light we can into this muddled world—to try to follow truth!

DAMON. You are quite right, Thomas, but I wish you would make an effort not to—uh—uh—intone.

TOMMY. I'm not intoning—I'm yelling! And for God's sake, sir, put away that umbrella! (DAMON *covers his umbrella with his hat.*) Don't you see this isn't about Vanzetti. This is about us! If I can't read this letter today, tomorrow none of us will be able to teach anything except what Mr. Keller here and the Legislature permit us to teach. Can't you see what that leads to—what it has led to in other places? We're holding the last fortress of free thought, and if we surrender to prejudice and dictation, we're cowards. (*He strides across the room.*)

ELLEN. Tommy, no matter how deeply you feel about this, what can you *do?* What can any one man do? Except to lose everything—

TOMMY. I have very little more to lose. And I can't tell you what I hope to gain. I can't answer that. I only know that I have to do it. (PATRICIA *appears in doorway, stops and listens.*)

DAMON. May we hear the letter—in a slightly calmer mood, perhaps?

TOMMY. Yes, sir— This may disappoint you a little, Mr. Keller. It isn't inflammatory, so it may make you feel a little silly. At least, I hope so— (*He holds up the book, pauses.* ED *and* JOE *get set in their chairs.*) Vanzetti wrote this in April, 1927, after he was sentenced to die. It has been printed in many newspapers. It appears in this book. You could destroy every printed copy of it, but it would not die out of the language, because a great many people know it by heart. (*He reads, hardly referring to the book, watching them.*) "If it had not been for these thing, I might have live out my life talking at street corners to scorning men. I might have die, unmarked, unknown, a failure. Now we are not a failure. Never in our full life could we hope to do so much work for tolerance, for Justice, for man's understanding of man, as now we do by accident. Our words—our lives—our pain—nothing! The taking of our lives—the lives of a good shoemaker and a poor fish-peddler—all! That last moment belongs to us—that agony is our triumph!" Well, that's it— (*He closes the book and drops it on the table. There is silence for a moment; KELLER is puzzled; ELLEN, who has been moved by the letter, looks up in surprise, meets TOMMY's eyes, then drops hers.*)

JOE (*uncomfortably*). Well, that isn't so bad! That isn't a bad letter.

ED. Is that all of it?

TOMMY. Yes, that's all.

JOE (*rises*). Maybe Tommy's right. I don't see that it would do so much harm.

ED (*slowly*). Yes, it will. If he reads this letter to his class he'll get a lot of those kids worried about that man. Make socialists out of 'em.

JOE. It's got me worried already.

ED (*rises, facing* TOMMY). No— I won't have it— You fellows are trying to defy the authority of the trustees. You say you're going to take a stand. Well, we've *taken* a stand. I wouldn't care if that letter were by Alexander Hamilton.

TOMMY (*measuring him*). Neither would I. The principle is exactly the same.

JOE (*speaking hopefully*). Well, then, read something else. Why can't you read Hoover?

ED. Yeah.

JOE. He writes a lot of stuff—a lot of good stuff in his book.

TOMMY (*his artistic ire is aroused*). Hoover can't *write* as well as Vanzetti.

ED (*winces*). That's a terrible thing to say. You'll get in trouble saying things like that.

TOMMY. Very likely. (*He strides to the garden door.*)

JOE. Ed, look—can't we compromise somehow? Seems a shame that a little thing like this should—

ELLEN (*rises*). It isn't little! Joe, you have some influence around here.

TOMMY. I can fight my own battles, Ellen.

ELLEN. Can't I say anything any more —even on your side?

ED. Turner, I've heard the letter and—

TOMMY (*answering* ELLEN). Not out

of a sense of self-sacrifice or something.

ED. What?

ELLEN. Oh, yes, you always know—

ED (*to* JOE). Do we always have to have women butting into this?

JOE. Ellen isn't women. She's Tommy's wife.

ELLEN (*furiously*). No, I'm not—

ED. No, Turner, it comes to this— (*Turns to* ELLEN.) You're not what? Do you mean to stand there and tell me you two are not—

TOMMY (*raging*). Will you please not ask personal questions?

ED (*to* TOMMY). No. *We can't have that in this school!*

ELLEN (*with a glance at* JOE). It's Joe and I who are going to live together.

ED. Yeh, will you let me— (*Turns to* ELLEN.) You and Joe are going to what! (*Turns on* JOE.) What the hell is going on here anyway?

JOE. Now don't look at me!

ED. You can't go away with Ellen!

JOE. I didn't say—

ELLEN (*twisting the knife in both men's backs*). We might as well tell him now. I'm going to Pittsburgh with Joe. (*Plants herself on settee.*)

ED (*turning back to* ELLEN). Why, you can't do that! Why, the newspapers would make Midwestern University look like some kind of a honky-tonk or something. This is worse than that goddamn letter!

TOMMY. Aren't you getting off the subject?

ED. No! What kind of a woman are you?

TOMMY (*advancing on* ED). Why don't you come out in the back yard!

JOE. Better be careful, Ed!

ELLEN. No more fights please!

DAMON (*rises*). I think I shall get a breath of fresh air. (*Goes to front door and opens it.*)

ELLEN. Well, I can't stay *here* now.

JOE. Look, Ed, you don't understand. You get things all mixed up.

ED. Well, I've got this much straight —if we can keep sex out of this for a minute. I came here to say to you that if you read this letter today you're out of this university tomorrow! You take this stand and you stand alone!

DAMON (*turning, walks deliberately over to* ED). Mr. Keller, for forty-two years I have followed a policy of appeasement. I might say I have been kicked around in this institution by one Edward K. Keller after another—

ED. There is only one Edward K. Keller.

DAMON. There has always been at least one. But there is an increasing element in the faculty which resents your attitude toward any teacher who raises his voice or so much as clears his throat. I warn you that if you persist in persecuting Thomas Turner, you will have a fight on your hands, my friend.

ED. Do you think that Bryson and Kressinger and I are afraid of a few dissatisfied bookworms who work for twenty-five hundred a year?

DAMON (*with strong indignation*). These men are not malcontents! Some of them are distinguished scholars who have made this University what it is!

ED (*aghast*). They've made it what it is! What about me? Who's getting this new stadium? Who brought Coach Sprague here from Southern Methodist?

JOE. He means that this thing is bigger than stadiums and coaches.

ED. Nothing's bigger than the new stadium.

JOE. We've all had a bad week end around here, Ed, and you're not helping any.

ED. Do you think I've had a good week end! (MICHAEL *and* NUTSY *come in the front door.*)

MICHAEL. Come in, Nutsy.

ED. Now what!

MICHAEL. We're circulating petitions for Mr. Turner. Show 'em, Nutsy.

NUTSY (*whipping out some sheets full of signatures*). This one's just from 14th Avenue and the Athletic house. We've got three hundred and fifty-seven names.

DAMON. We want no student insurrections!

JOE. Let me see that thing. (*Takes petition from* NUTSY; *scans it hurriedly.*)

ED. You're wasting your time with that handful of names. Turner will be out tomorrow and Barnes is on his way home now.

MICHAEL. I'm not on my way home yet, sir.

ED. *Ohhh!* So you're Barnes! So you're the little puppy that called me a Fascist!

PATRICIA. (*comes between* ED *and* MICHAEL. *To* ED). Well, the way you're treating everybody, I think you *are* a Fascist!

ELLEN. Patricia!

TOMMY. Let her alone.

ELLEN. Oh, she can stand up for Michael, but I can't stand up for you! Is that it?

ED. Do I have to stand here and be insulted by every sixteen-year-old child that comes into this room?

PATRICIA. I'm not sixteen, I'm nineteen!

MICHAEL. She'll soon be twenty.

ED. Why don't *you* get packing?

MICHAEL. You don't need to worry about me. I'll be far away from here by tomorrow. Come on, Nutsy! (NUTSY *starts out;* MICHAEL *following.*)

PATRICIA (*starts after him*). If you throw him out, I'm going with him! Wait, Michael!

ED. Are you married to this little radical?

PATRICIA. You don't have to be married to somebody to go away with him —*do you, Ellen?* (*She and* MICHAEL *go out.*)

DAMON (*who can't cope with any more*). I think I shall go home, have my Ovaltine and lie down. (*He goes out the front door.*)

ED. He'll need his Ovaltine.

JOE (*suddenly, awesomely*). Say, Ed, look! This thing has been signed by Stalenkiwiecz and Wierasocka.

ED. What! I don't believe it. (*Snatches petition, scans it, in all its terrible significance.*)

JOE. Ed, you ought to have some respect for men like Dean Damon and Stalenkiwiecz and Wierasocka.

ED (*stricken*). They can't do this to me! Two of the biggest men in the university signing the Red petition! You, the greatest half-back we ever had, running away with a woman! Why—*they'll never ask us to the Rose Bowl now!*

TOMMY. What is the Rose Bowl?

ED (*almost screams*). I'm getting out of this house! Coming Joe?

JOE. No.

ED. By God, you can't depend on anybody! I've a damn good notion to resign from the board of trustees. (*Stiffening.*) But I'll kick you out if it's the last thing I do.

TOMMY (*grimly*). Just to make things even—I'll kick you out. Here's your hat. (*Gives him* JOE's *derby.*)

ED. Very well! (*Puts on hat and leaves angrily.*)

JOE. Hey, that's *my* hat!

TOMMY. Well, get another one. (*He closes door.*) Well, that's that. (*They look at each other. Here they are again, the triangle.*)

JOE. Yeh, that's that. (*Pause. He eyes the others doubtfully.*) Well, I s'pose Ed will never speak to me again.

TOMMY. I have to go to class. I'll be late. (*Starts for stairs.*)

ELLEN (*appealingly to* TOMMY). Tommy—I—

TOMMY. I know. I know.

ELLEN. You know what?

TOMMY. I know what you're going to say—but I don't want substitutes. I don't want *loyalty.* (ELLEN *turns away.*)

JOE. What's the matter with that?

TOMMY. I just don't want Ellen standing by like a Red Cross nurse because she knows I'm in trouble.

JOE. I don't know whether you need a nurse or a psychoanalyst!

ELLEN. I think he's analyzed it very well himself. It isn't because you think I don't care, it's because you don't.

TOMMY (*almost bursting*). I thought we could settle this *quietly* and *calmly.*

ELLEN. Quietly and calmly! Oh, God! (*Picks up large ashtray from a table and smashes it on the floor.*)

TOMMY. Now, don't do that! I can throw things, too! (*Picks up his teacup.*)

ELLEN. No, you can't—you haven't got enough blood in you! (TOMMY *glares at her, puts cup down coldly—suddenly*

snatches it and hurls it into fireplace—reaches for saucer.*)

JOE (*leaps for* TOMMY—*grabs saucer from him*). Now wait—let me handle this. *I don't throw things—* I just want to say that I came to this city *to see a football game.*

ELLEN (*right into* JOE's *face*). Oh, no, you didn't! You came for me. You haven't been here for a ball-game in ten years. You wait till Brenda and you are separated, then you come for me!

JOE. Oh, hell! (*Throws saucer in fireplace then wilts as he realizes this household has affected him, too.*)

TOMMY (*desperately insisting upon his own doom*). That's very smart, Ellen. That's very penetrating. That's all I wanted to know. (*To* JOE.) Subconsciously, you came here for Ellen, so don't try to deny it.

JOE. I don't do things subconsciously! You're full of childish explanations of everything that comes up!

TOMMY. And you're full of psychological evasions!

ELLEN (*screaming. It's a madhouse now*). Oh, shut up! Both of you! I am not going to listen to any more of this! (*She runs upstairs.* TOMMY *sits limply on sofa and covers his face with his hands. There is a long pause.*)

JOE (*slowly and with determination*). Well I'll tell you one thing! I'm not going upstairs this time! If you'd explained what you were standing for on Saturday, things would have cleared up around here and I'd be in Washington now, talking to Ickes.

TOMMY (*in a low grim tone*). Are you still in love with Norma?

JOE. Norma who?

TOMMY. Your wife.

JOE. My wife's name is Brenda. And you're not going to talk her over with me. I can't be alone with you two minutes and have any private life left!

ELLEN'S VOICE (*from upstairs*). Tommy! *What did you do with my nail file???!*

JOE. Oh, Lord—she sounds worse than last Saturday.

TOMMY. I haven't got it. (*He absently goes through a pocket, finds it, brings it out.*) Oh! Yeh, I've got it.

JOE. I've gone through more hell here in three days than I've had with Phyllis in three years.

TOMMY. Yeh! (*grimly; rising.*) Phyllis? Who is Phyllis? Are you carrying on with some other woman in Pittsburgh? You can't do this.

JOE (*springing to his feet*). I'm not carrying on with anybody. Phyllis is my secretary and there's nothing between us!

TOMMY. *Then why did you say you've been going through hell for three years?*

JOE (*yelling*). 'Cause you get me all balled up. (ELLEN *stomps downstairs with a suitcase and sets it down.*)

TOMMY. Here—here's your nail file. (*Hands it to her.*) You didn't pack anything!

ELLEN. I've been packed for three days.

TOMMY (*his voice threatens to break, but he holds out*). Well, you can't go with just one suitcase— There isn't much here, but—there're the books. They're yours. Most of them I gave to you. (*Turns away.*)

ELLEN. Can I have "The Shropshire Lad"? Isn't that the one that has:

"And now the fancy passes by—"

TOMMY. "And nothing will remain—" (*He brings her the book from the bookcase. Everyone is miserable.*)

MICHAEL (*sticks his head in door*). You've just five minutes to get to your class, Mr. Turner. We'll wait for you in the car. (*He goes out.*)

TOMMY (*bravely*). Well, so long, Joe. I know you'll get her a place of her own for a while anyway. You can take that four-poster money with you, Ellen. I'll have one more check coming, too. (*He starts slowly upstairs.*)

JOE. What's "four-poster money"?

ELLEN (*her voice trembling pathetically*). We were saving up to buy a new bed. (*She cries and collapses on settee.*)

JOE. Oh, God, here we go again!

TOMMY (*comes back again, desperately*). Why did you have to ask what four-poster money is? (*To* ELLEN.) Ellen, please.

ELLEN (*hysterically*). Oh, go on! Go on! Put on your coat! If you're going to be kicked out of school, you can't go over there looking like a tramp.

TOMMY (*balefully*). All right. (*He clumps upstairs like King Lear.*)

JOE. Look, Ellen, everything's gonna be all right.

ELLEN. Is it?

JOE (*looking after* TOMMY). I wouldn't worry about that guy.

ELLEN. I don't.

JOE. I mean he's sure to get another job. He's had more publicity than Wally Myers.

ELLEN. I don't care what becomes of him. (JOE *studies her drooping figure narrowly.*)

JOE. Come here. (*He pulls her to her feet, facing him.*) You're still crazy about that guy, aren't you?

ELLEN. I'm kind of scared of him. He used to be just—nice, but now he's wonderful! (TOMMY *appears on stairs in time to catch the end of this. Very slowly a light begins to dawn upon him.* JOE *sees him but* ELLEN *doesn't.*)

JOE. I don't think he's so wonderful!

ELLEN. Yes, he is! That letter's wonderful. What he's trying to do is wonderful. He wouldn't let me or you or anyone stop him. Even Ed.

JOE. He's a scrapper all right, but he can't dance. (*He crosses to the Victrola, pulling her along. He has an idea and does everything for* TOMMY's *benefit.* TOMMY *comes down slowly.* JOE *turns on Victrola which plays "Who."*)

ELLEN. Oh, who wants to dance now? (JOE *makes her dance, keeping her back to* TOMMY.)

JOE. This is important. It's all in the light you give off.

ELLEN. Light? What are you talking about?

JOE (*with intensity*). The important thing about dancing is that the man has got to lead. (*He beckons to* TOMMY;

with one stride, Tommy *turns her away from* Joe.)

Tommy. May I cut in?

Ellen. Tommy! Let me go!

Tommy (*shouting*). No, I think you're wonderful too!

Ellen. You think I'm dumb! Were you listening?

Tommy. No, I wasn't.

Joe (*up near door*). Hey—don't start that again!

Tommy (*puts on his hat, still dancing feverishly*). Joe—why don't you go back to your wife? We can send her a wire.

Joe. Don't worry about me, Brother. I sent her a wire this morning. (*He goes out into the fresh air, a happy man.* Tommy *still dances with* Ellen—*they are almost in tears.*)

Tommy. Quit leading!

Ellen. I'm not leading. You *were* listening!

Tommy. You were yelling. Well, turn!

Ellen. Make me turn. (*He does.*) Don't be so rough—and put your hat on straight. You look terrible. (*Half crying, she throws her arms around* Tommy. *They are kissing each other very, very hard as*)

THE CURTAIN FALLS.

SUGGESTED TOPICS FOR FURTHER INVESTIGATION AND REPORT

1. Aristophanic comedy was satire in a unique and highly distinguished form. Plays like *Peace, Lysistrata, The Clouds, The Thesmophoriazusae, The Frogs*—in fact, nearly all the plays are strongly satiric. Make a study of some of them, and indicate how much of their form and style has failed to transfer to modern drama. What amount of satire, if any, is still apparent?

2. If possible, locate and read some complete Revolutionary satires. Those known to have been published are included in the Readex Microcard reprints, and your library may have other copies. Study their style as compared with modern comedies with a purpose.

3. Read all of Fitch's *The Climbers.* Show how it fails to sustain the satire, or discover, if you can, further elements beyond the famous opening scene. Read Harry James Smith's *Mrs. Bumpstead-Leigh,* available in the Burns Mantle annual for 1909–1919. Compare the two plays.

4. A true appreciation of James Thurber can be gained only from his stories and articles. Read several from any of his many collections. How many of them are pure fun, and how many contain the barb of satire or the pointed jab of caricature? Compare their style and message with *The Male Animal.*

5. Read all of Clare Boothe's *The Women* or O'Neill's *Marco Millions.* Evaluate the satire. Determine whether the play you read goes beyond its purpose and loses strength in its attack.

6. Read one of Sinclair Lewis' novels: "Babbitt," "Arrowsmith," or "Main Street." Compare the similarity of O'Neill's attack on materialism found in *Marco Millions.*

7. Two excellent comedies with a purpose which are not as heavily satiric as others we have discussed are Lindsay and Crouse's *State of the Union,* 1945, and Garson Kanin's *Born Yesterday,* of 1945. They are both comedies, but in different veins. Compare their treatment of big business and politics. Which is the more successful, or can they be compared on equal terms?

8. The endless bumbling and complications of military red tape have brought all kinds of official and unofficial attack. We have already mentioned *Johnny Johnson,* by Paul Green, an expressionistic antiwar play of the 1930s. Study it now as a piece of satire. From what does it derive its laughter? Would it still have an appeal today? Probably the best play after World War II which spoofs military pomposity and nearsightedness is John Patrick's *The Teahouse of the August Moon,* 1953. Discuss it as satire, burlesque, or whatever you determine its main approach to be. If you read both plays, make a comparative study of their attitudes.

9. A number of popular farces since the 1920s have made fun of modern habits and ideas. Though many of them can still be played, a number of them show their age. Read two or three, like Kaufman and Connelly's *Merton of the Movies,* 1922, Bella and Samuel Spewack's *Boy Meets Girl,* 1935, Kaufman and Hart's *The Man who Came to Dinner* and *You Can't Take It with You.* Wherein do these plays seem dated and the fun no longer applicable? (Notice the timely "wisecrack" and its vulnerability to old age.)

The Comic and the Sentimental

The eighteenth-century sentimental drama all but destroyed true comedy. The new comedies of sentiment asked for the one audience reaction which kills the comic spirit more quickly than anything else—intense emotional response. They sought applause at the already well-known *virtues* of life, protested Oliver Goldsmith in the 1770s, instead of laughter at the exposed *vices*, while they emphasized the *distresses* of mankind, rather than the *faults*. Henri Bergson, in his essay, "Laughter," shows why the sentimental appeal is not comic when he says that we may laugh at a person who inspires affection or pity, but that while we do so we must put affection aside and silence our pity. The comic, he explains, demands indifference, and the heart must undergo a "momentary anesthesia."

The dictionary[1] defines *sensibility* as "refined sensitiveness in emotion and taste with especial responsiveness to the pathetic." Although this could suggest the dangers of sentimentality, it is possible to create a comedy of sensibility if the appeal to refined sensitiveness and the pathetic remains as an undercurrent, without being dwelt on for its own sake. The audience may then laugh heartily at the behavior of the comic characters while momentarily dismissing its affection and pity; simultaneously, the quiet flow of emotional sensitivity can remain.

The comedy of sensibility is a product of modern realism. It depends upon characters who are beyond the artistic "laws" of Bronson Howard's romanticism and safely removed from overwrought sentimentality. Their experiences must appeal directly to audience sensibilities without producing a feeling of contrivance for an emotional effect. Plot development is minimal; the strength of the play depends upon those incidents which illuminate character behavior and attitude. The comedy of sensibility avoids the low broad strokes of farce as well as the polished wit of sophistication. It is a comedy of reality, which includes, if need be, the unpleasantness of suffering or death. It may draw tears, but they will be genuine tears of compassion. There can be no lingering tearfulness. The comedy of sensibility must hold to its purpose of showing the fundamental charm of average, plodding human beings, who are good, ordinary, and consistently comic.

Comparison of Two Eras

Two of the most popular plays in the history of the American theatre provide interesting comparisons in the development of comic sensibility. The first, *The Old Homestead*, by Denman Thompson, a standard production on

[1] By permission from *Webster's New International Dictionary*, 2d ed., copyright 1934, 1939, 1945, 1950, 1954, 1957, G. & C. Merriam Company, Springfield, Mass.

many a stock-company stage fifty years ago, appeared in New York in 1877. The second, *Lightnin'*, by Winchell Smith and Frank Bacon, which had one of the longest runs in the history of the Broadway theatre, opened in 1918. Both revolve their insubstantial plots around a kind and lovable man whose honest innocence heads everybody away from possible disaster toward a happy solution of all problems, while he himself remains the good-to-the-core, down-to-earth creature he first appeared. Both plays set out to gain our wholehearted sentimental involvement, but the difference between the nineteenth-century hearts-and-flowers atmosphere and the beginnings of twentieth-century comic realism shows how much audience tastes were changing.

With no pretension to subtlety, *The Old Homestead* capitalizes outrageously on the slushy emotions of the cozy old house down on the farm, inhabited by Ma and Pa amidst a passel of friends and relatives, where the best things of life must triumph. The "plot" concerns the search by Joshua Whitcomb for his son, who has fled the New England farm for New York after being acquitted of bank robbery, and the prodigal's eventual return. In an early scene a tramp called Happy Jack encounters Joshua, who promptly tries to convert him to the ways of righteousness by telling him what he owes to his dear old mother:

> JACK (*sits, penitently, with lowered head*). Say, old gentleman, you've set me thinking.
> JOSH. I'm glad of it if I have. Now look here, will you go home if I give you money enough to pay your fare?
> JACK. Yes.
> JOSH. And stop drinking?
> JACK. Whew! Say, old gentleman, that's a corker, but I'll try it.

*   *   *

> JOSHUA. All right, sir—there's a ten-dollar bill. . . .
> JACK. . . . Say, old gentleman— (*offering money to* JOSH.)—you had better take this money back. I don't honestly believe I can do as I have agreed.
> JOSH (*rising*). Well, you can try, can't you?
> JACK. Yes, I can try.
> JOSH (*putting hand on* JACK'S *shoulder*). That's right! Go home and try to be somebody, it ain't too late.
> JACK (*with determination*). Well, I will! And if I don't win, I'll give old John Barleycorn the toughest scuffle he ever had for the underhold. Good-by, old friend, good-by!

Lightnin' Bill Jones is a significant and encouraging improvement upon Joshua Whitcomb. *Lightnin'* possesses a plot only a little better than *The Old Homestead*, but the genial, inoffensive sot, given to tall tales about himself, is closer to valid character creation. Bill and his wife operate a Lake Tahoe resort hotel, half in Nevada and half in California. They make good money catering to women who live in the Nevada half for six months prior to divorce. Conspiring railroad interests try to get the property, but young John Marvin, who eventually marries the couple's foster daughter, Millie, convinces Lightnin' that there is skulduggery afoot. Bill refuses to sign, and Mrs. Jones is furious. The first act ends with the following scene. Bill has offered everybody a drink for "sociability," protesting that "I don't drink." (When Mrs. Jones enters she wears an elaborate and revealing gown given her by an actress guest.)

SHERIFF. Don't tell me that. You're a booze fighter. (*Sits.*)

BILL. No, I ain't—I'm a Indian fighter.

SHERIFF. Is that so?

BILL. Yes, that's so. Did you ever know Buffalo Bill?

SHERIFF. Yes, I knew him well. (BILL *turns, takes a good look at him.*)

BILL. I learned him all he knew about killing Indians. (*Sits.*) Did he ever tell you about the duel I fought with Settin' Bull?

SHERIFF. Settin' Bull?

BILL. He was standin' when I shot him. I never took advantage of nobody, not even a Indian.

SHERIFF. Say, you got a bee in your bonnet, ain't you?

BILL. What do you know about bees?

SHERIFF. Not much, do you?

BILL. Yes, I do—I know all about 'em. I used to be in the bee business. Why, I drove a swarm of bees across the plains in the dead of winter. And never lost a bee. Got stung twice.

* * *

HAMMOND. Now look here, Mr. Jones—

BILL. Won't do no good. I promised John not to sign nothing, and I ain't going to sign nothing—understand that.

HAMMOND. Well, if you don't you'll find yourself without a home. (*Enter* MRS. JONES. . . .*) You understand that—if you're not too drunk.

BILL. Do you think I'm drunk? (*Turns, sees* MRS. JONES *crossing to left; thinks she is one of the guests. Rises. Crosses to* MRS. JONES.) Do you want your key? (MRS. JONES *turns with key in one hand and pen in the other.* BILL *recognizes her.*) Mother, it ain't you?

MRS. JONES (*angrily*). Yes, it's me.

BILL (*to* HAMMOND). You're right. I'm drunk.

Bill eventually vindicates himself in court and the rascals who would bilk him are properly exposed.

Sidney Howard's Pulitzer Prize play of the 1924–1925 season, *They Knew What They Wanted*, is probably the first that can be considered a legitimate "comedy of sensibility." Its vigorous story is simple and direct, and its characters come to life in full-drawn strokes. The dramatic complications are serious and potentially dangerous. Important problems with no comic intent involve the audience emotionally with practically every individual. But still the play remains at heart comic, through its appeal to audience sensitiveness and awareness of the pathetic. We can laugh heartily and smile understandingly as we see these confused people make the best of a bad situation.

The story concerns the marriage of a portly, middle-aged Italian wine grower, Tony, to an attractive young waitress, Amy, whom he has wooed by mail. The comic and the pathetic merge in many situations, such as Tony's substitution of the photograph of his good-looking hired hand, Joe, for his own; his fracture of both legs in his rush to meet his bride; and Amy's bewilderment and rage at learning the truth. In her distress and loneliness Amy finds momentary understanding in Joe, and a wedding-night indiscretion results in her conceiving Joe's child.

The final scene would have been impossible fifty years earlier, and rashly daring only twenty years before. The lack of protest against it proved how much the moral atmosphere had changed. The wise ending reflects the tone of the entire play: that is, a comedy of sensitive refinement in emotion, charming and pathetic, full of legitimate sentiment but totally lacking in destructive sentimentality. In the following scene, Amy is preparing to leave with Joe, and Tony hysterically tries to stop her:

> Tony (*a last frantic appeal*). No! No! NO! (*Leaning back in his chair and looking around the room.*) W'at's good for me havin' dees fine house? W'at's good for me havin' all dis money w'at I got? I got nobody for give my house an' my money w'en I die. Ees for dat I want dis baby, Amy. Joe don't want him. Ees Tony want him. Amy, . . . Amy, . . . for God's sake don't go away an' leave Tony!
>
> Amy. But, Tony! Think of what I done!
>
> Tony. What you done was mistake in da head, not in da heart. . . . Mistake in da head is no matter.
>
> Amy. You—you ain't kiddin' me, are you? . . . You're serious, ain't you—Tony? You'll stick to this afterwards, won't you, Tony? (*She walks slowly over to him. She throws her arms around his neck and presses his head against her breast. A prolonged pause.*) Well, Joe, I guess you better be going.
>
> Joe. You mean?
>
> Amy. I guess you'd better be going. (*Joe straightens in great relief.*)
>
> Joe. All right. (*He picks up his knapsack which he dropped when he came in.*) I guess you're right. (*He pulls on his cap and stands a moment in the doorway, a broad grin spreading over his face.*) I guess there ain't none of us got any kick comin', at that. No real kick. (*He goes out slowly.*)
>
> Amy (*lifting her face*). No. (*Tony clutches her even closer as the curtain falls.*)

The Member of the Wedding

The protagonist of *The Member of the Wedding* is a gawky, uncouth, loud voiced pre-teen girl. The antagonist, says the author, Carson McCullers, is not a person but a "human condition." The plot is nonexistent. An unlikely heroine, an abstract source of conflict, and no story to speak of combine to form an exceptionally touching play and a superlative example of the *comedy of sensibility*.

A favorite literary topic has always been the essential loneliness of the individual. Strong cases have been made for the "no-man-is-an-island" contention, but there can never be a complete denial of the manifest isolation of one human being from another. When the realization of this circumstance begins to register in the mind of a child, it can be terrifying. The gradual awareness that heavy reliance on others for security, pleasure, and happiness may not always be possible, and that most people in the world are far less concerned with others than with themselves, can alter the perspective of many things.

Carson McCullers has consistently stressed the individual's loneliness in her stories and novels, and this, her first attempt at playwriting (an adaptation of her own 1946 novel) is her best handling of the subject. She has drawn in the ungainly, impetuous Frankie Addams a character at once hilariously amusing and tearfully pathetic, but never does she permit her scrawny heroine to move either too far from reality or toward undue sentimentality. When Frankie begins to draw upon our sympathies and we would weep at her pathetic search for social identification, she bursts forth with a violent "son-of-a-bitches" hurled defiantly at her girlish enemies, or comes traipsing onstage in her frightful wedding costume. The only possible audience expression is laughter, temporarily setting aside subjective emotions and pity, as the grotesque world of a twelve-year-old is abruptly tossed into view with the sudden violence of changing adolescent emotions.

Forced into self-reliance at an early age, Frankie suddenly feels the need for companionship and mutual sharing heretofore denied her. Ironically, she discovers the need at a time in her own age and in her family situation when she must remain even more alone than she has been in the past. Her realization that she cannot join the wedding party is a profound shock that forms a lesson all the better taught by her forced ejection from the honeymoon car. Nobody could tell her. And nobody else could realize the sickening pain when she finally recognizes what is taking place.

Mrs. McCullers provides Frankie with two companions of equal loneliness, but on different planes. One is a seven-year-old cousin, who seems to have no other companions with whom he may play, and whose interests are attracted more by the pictures on the playing cards than by the game, more by the mysteries of Berenice's glass eye than by Frankie's problems. The other is a mature Negro servant, much married, wise in the manners of social segregation.

resigned to a loneliness that Frankie will never experience because she is white. The trio are about as unlikely a lot to share their lives as one could expect, yet all are a part of the author's emphasis upon the "human condition" about which she writes. The adolescent girl, the doomed little boy, and the philosophical Negress join in creating the drama's universality.

The play is admittedly fragmentary. There is no place for logical story telling or neatly dovetailed plot lines. Frankie comes to face the truth about herself through the haphazard encounters of ordinary life. Her decision to become a member of the wedding precipitates no immediate action and brings only an uncomprehending "What?" from John Henry when she reveals it to him. Her plans and their attempted execution provide impetus for the entire play without need for a fabricated story. The world as a "sudden place" is expertly defined without it.

There are some pertinent questions concerning a few other matters which Mrs. McCullers treats in *The Member of the Wedding*. To what purpose is the injection of Mr. Addams' brief but sharp clash with T. T. and Honey? What is the point of Honey's stereotyped razor-secured "freedom" and subsequent suicide? Why is his death so casually related? Is John Henry's death justified? He has been a major character, amusing, delightful, pathetic, an important part of Frankie's life. Suddenly, after a few obscure references to being "sick," he is dead from a terribly painful disease. Why are his suffering and passing all but ignored?

One thing to be said in favor of this casual treatment is that it helps keep the play within the bounds of comedy. On no occasion does the author permit the sentimentalities or emotional responses to gain control of the play's spirit. In fact, it is a very unsentimental play. Frankie is the adolescence of all of us, and she must learn most of her lessons in the same hard way the rest of us do, but she is not a nostalgic re-creation of happy childhood. She represents what few writers have honestly attempted to show: that childhood is, more frequently than we realize, a confused, painful, and often very lonely time. It is free and without responsibility, and an age of great discovery, while simultaneously it mystifies and hurts without satisfactory explanation. Even then, Frankie does not ask for our pity. She is pathetic in many ways, but the pathos brings genuine laughter. The wedding dress is not a pitiful thing; it is so outlandish a getup that it cannot be taken seriously. When the showdown arrives, we are mercifully spared watching the agony. Instead, most of it is described through John Henry's innocent eyes and neatly summarized in Frankie's expression of the whole affair: "It was a frame-up all around." Although she grabs the gun and runs off to "kill" herself (none of which is seen), we feel hardly more concern for her fate than we have for any other of her wild ideas. They are mainly "child plans that won't work," as she herself realizes when she returns.

The Member of the Wedding is a thoroughly pleasant play. Sadness and death notwithstanding, it ends pleasantly. Frankie finds a more realistic "we" in her sudden friendship with Mary Littlejohn. The warm comic quality of Frankie, John Henry, and Berenice arouses our sensitivities by its refinement of taste and by gentle play on our emotions, while asking us to laugh in sympathy and understanding. *The Member of the Wedding* is in all ways a superior creation of the comedy of sensibility.

Carson McCullers

Carson (Smith) McCullers was born in Columbus, Georgia, in February, 1917. She finished high school at an early age and reports that she "loafed" around for a year or two before beginning to write at the age of sixteen. Her interests before that time had been mainly musical; she had aspired to be a concert pianist. When she began writing, Eugene O'Neill was her ideal, and she composed early plays "thick with incest, lunacy, and murder" which got rather questioning approval from her family and none anywhere else. At the age of seventeen she ventured to New York, intent on attending Columbia University and/or the Julliard School of Music, but lost her tuition money on the subway the first day and had to go to work at anything she could get. She attended night school, entered and left an assortment of jobs, and at eighteen sold two short stories to the magazine *Story*.

She married Reeves McCullers in 1937 (he died in 1953) and moved to North Carolina where she continued to write. Her first success was "The Heart is a Lonely Hunter" in 1940, a novel about a deaf-mute. It contained one of the most honestly drawn Negro characters in contemporary fiction. A "neurotic" novel about an Army officer in a Southern camp called "Reflections in a Golden Eye" appeared in 1941. After the 1946 success of "The Member of the Wedding" and its subsequent dramatization, she published "The Ballad of the Sad Café" in 1951, a collection of her short stories, three novels, and the novelette which gave the book its name. Another play, *The Square Root of Wonderful*, failed on Broadway in late 1957.

Mrs. McCullers has been a Fellow at the Bread Loaf Writers' Conference in Vermont. She is a Fellow of the American Academy of Arts and Sciences, and has received two Guggenheim awards.

THE MEMBER OF THE WEDDING
by
Carson McCullers

Setting for *The Member of the Wedding*. This portrayal of both interior and exterior acting areas at the same time descends from the medieval simultaneous stage. Its use has been increasingly popular and was outstandingly effective in Williams' *A Streetcar Named Desire* and *The Rose Tattoo* and in Miller's *Death of a Salesman*, to name a few other instances. *(Courtesy Lester Polakov.)*

The Member of the Wedding was first produced in New York on January 5, 1950, at the Empire Theatre. It ran for a total of 501 performances. The play was critically well received, but the highest praise went to Julie Harris in her first starring role and to Brandon de Wilde for his outstanding performance as an exceptionally talented child actor. The following cast appeared in the opening night production:

BERENICE SADIE BROWN	*Ethel Waters*
FRANKIE ADDAMS	*Julie Harris*
JOHN HENRY WEST	*Brandon de Wilde*
JARVIS	*James Holden*
JANICE	*Janet de Gore*
MR. ADDAMS	*William Hansen*
MRS. WEST	*Margaret Barker*
HELEN FLETCHER	*Mitzie Blake*
DORIS	*Joan Shepard*
SIS LAURA	*Phyliss Walker*
T. T. WILLIAMS	*Harry Bolden*
HONEY CAMDEN BROWN	*Henry Scott*
BARNEY MACKEAN	*Jimmy Dutton*

Produced by Robert Whitehead, Oliver Rea, and Stanley Martineau
Directed by Harold Clurman
Sets designed by Lester Polakov

ACT ONE

SCENE: *A part of a Southern back yard and kitchen. At stage left there is a scuppernong arbor. A sheet, used as a stage curtain, hangs raggedly at one side of the arbor. There is an elm tree in the yard. The kitchen has in the center a table with chairs. The walls are drawn with child drawings. There is a stove to the right and a small coal heating stove with coal scuttle in rear center of kitchen. The kitchen opens on the left into the yard. At the interior right a door leads to a small inner room. A door at the left leads into the front hall. The lights go on dimly, with a dreamlike effect, gradually revealing the family in the yard and* BERENICE SADIE BROWN *in the kitchen.* BERENICE, *the cook, is a stout, motherly Negro woman with an air of great capability and devoted protection. She is about forty-five years old. She has a quiet, flat face and one of her eyes is made of blue glass. Sometimes, when her socket bothers her, she dispenses with the false eye and wears a black patch. When we first see her she is wearing the patch and is dressed in a simple print work dress and apron.*

FRANKIE, *a gangling girl of twelve with blonde hair cut like a boy's, is wearing shorts and a sombrero and is standing in the arbor gazing adoringly at her brother* JARVIS *and his fiancée* JANICE. *She is a dreamy, restless girl, and periods of energetic activity alternate with a rapt attention to her inward world of fantasy. She is thin and awkward and very much aware of being too tall.* JARVIS, *a good-looking boy of twenty-one, wearing an army uniform, stands by* JANICE. *He is awkward when he first appears because this is his betrothal visit.* JANICE, *a young, pretty, fresh-looking girl of eighteen or nineteen is charming but rather ordinary, with brown hair done up in a small knot. She is dressed in her best clothes and is anxious to be liked by her new family.* MR. ADDAMS, FRANKIE's *father, is a deliberate and absent-minded man of about forty-five. A widower of many years, he has become set in his habits. He is dressed conservatively, and there is about him an old-fashioned look and manner.* JOHN HENRY, FRANKIE's *small cousin, aged seven, picks and eats any scuppernongs he can reach. He is a delicate, active boy and wears gold-rimmed spectacles which give him an oddly judicious look. He is blond and sunburned and when we first see him he is wearing a sun-suit and is barefooted.* BERENICE SADIE BROWN *is busy in the kitchen.*

JARVIS. Seems to me like this old arbor has shrunk. I remember when I was a child it used to seem absolutely enormous. When I was Frankie's age, I had a vine swing here. Remember, Papa?

FRANKIE. It don't seem so absolutely enormous to me, because I am so tall.

JARVIS. I never saw a human grow so fast in all my life. I think maybe we ought to tie a brick to your head.

FRANKIE (*hunching down in obvious distress*). Oh, Jarvis! Don't.

JANICE. Don't tease your little sister. I don't think Frankie is too tall. She probably won't grow much more. I had the biggest portion of my growth by the time I was thirteen.

FRANKIE. But I'm just twelve. When I think of all the growing years ahead of me, I get scared. (JANICE *goes to* FRANKIE *and puts her arms around her comfortingly.* FRANKIE *stands rigid, embarrassed and blissful.*)

JANICE. I wouldn't worry. (BERENICE *comes from the kitchen with a tray of drinks.* FRANKIE *rushes eagerly to help her serve them.*)

FRANKIE. Let me help.

BERENICE. Them two drinks is lemonade for you and John Henry. The others got liquor in them.

FRANKIE. Janice, come sit on the arbor seat. Jarvis, you sit down too. (JARVIS *and* JANICE *sit close together on the wicker bench in the arbor.* FRANKIE *hands the drinks around, then perches on the ground before* JANICE *and* JARVIS *and stares adoringly at them.*)

FRANKIE. It was such a surprise when Jarvis wrote home you are going to be married.

JANICE. I hope it wasn't a bad surprise.

FRANKIE. Oh, Heavens no! (*With great feeling.*) As a matter of fact . . . (*She strokes* JANICE's *shoes tenderly and* JARVIS' *army boot.*) If only you knew how I feel.

MR. ADDAMS. Frankie's been bending my ears ever since your letter came, Jarvis. Going on about weddings, brides, grooms, etc.

JANICE. It's lovely that we can be married at Jarvis' home.

MR. ADDAMS. That's the way to feel, Janice. Marriage is a sacred institution.

FRANKIE. Oh, it will be beautiful.

JARVIS. Pretty soon we'd better be shoving off for Winter Hill. I have to be back in barracks tonight.

FRANKIE. Winter Hill is such a lovely, cold name. It reminds me of ice and snow.

JANICE. You know it's just a hundred miles away, darling.

JARVIS. Ice and snow indeed! Yesterday the temperature on the parade ground reached 102. (FRANKIE *takes a palmetto fan from the table and fans first* JANICE, *then* JARVIS.)

JANICE. That feels so good, darling. Thanks.

FRANKIE. I wrote you so many letters, Jarvis, and you never, never would answer me. When you were stationed in Alaska, I wanted so much to hear about Alaska. I sent you so many boxes of homemade candy, but you never answered me.

JARVIS. Oh, Frankie. You know how it is . . .

FRANKIE (*sipping her drink*). You know this lemonade tastes funny. Kind of sharp and hot. I believe I got the drinks mixed up.

JARVIS. I was thinking my drink tasted mighty sissy. Just plain lemonade—no liquor at all. (FRANKIE *and* JARVIS *exchange their drinks.* JARVIS *sips his.*) This is better.

FRANKIE. I drank a lot. I wonder if I'm drunk. It makes me feel like I had four legs instead of two. I think I'm drunk. (*She gets up and begins to stagger around in imitation of drunkenness.*) See! I'm drunk! Look, Papa, how drunk I am! (*Suddenly she turns a handspring; then there is a blare of music from the club-house gramophone off to the right.*)

JANICE. Where does the music come from? It sounds so close.

FRANKIE. It is. Right over there. They have club meetings and parties with boys on Friday nights. I watch them here from the yard.

JANICE. It must be nice having your club house so near.

FRANKIE. I'm not a member now. But they are holding an election this afternoon, and maybe I'll be elected.

JOHN HENRY. Here comes Mama. (MRS. WEST, JOHN HENRY's *mother, crosses the yard from the right. She is a vivacious, blonde woman of about thirty-three. She is dressed in sleazy, rather dowdy summer clothes.*)

MR. ADDAMS. Hello, Pet. Just in time to meet our new family member.

MRS. WEST. I saw you out here from the window.

JARVIS (*rising, with* JANICE). Hi, Aunt Pet. How is Uncle Eustace?

MRS. WEST. He's at the office.

JANICE (*offering her hand with the engagement ring on it*). Look, Aunt Pet. May I call you Aunt Pet?

MRS. WEST (*hugging her*). Of course, Janice. What a gorgeous ring!

JANICE. Jarvis just gave it to me this morning. He wanted to consult his father and get it from his store, naturally.

MRS. WEST. How lovely.

MR. ADDAMS. A quarter carat—not too flashy but a good stone.

MRS. WEST (*to* BERENICE, *who is gathering up the empty glasses*). Berenice, what have you and Frankie been doing to my John Henry? He sticks over here in your kitchen morning, noon and night.

BERENICE. We enjoys him and Candy seems to like it over here.

MRS. WEST. What on earth do you do to him?

BERENICE. We just talks and passes the time of day. Occasionally plays cards.

MRS. WEST. Well, if he gets in your way just shoo him home.

BERENICE. Candy don't bother nobody.

JOHN HENRY (*walking around barefooted in the arbor*). These grapes are so squelchy when I step on them.

MRS. WEST. Run home, darling, and wash your feet and put on your sandals.

JOHN HENRY. I like to squelch on the grapes. (BERENICE *goes back to the kitchen.*)

JANICE. That looks like a stage curtain. Jarvis told me how you used to write plays and act in them out here in the arbor. What kind of shows do you have?

FRANKIE. Oh, crook shows and cowboy shows. This summer I've had some cold shows—about Esquimos and explorers—on account of the hot weather.

JANICE. Do you ever have romances?

FRANKIE. Naw . . . (*with bravado.*) I had crook shows for the most part. You see I never believed in love until now. (*Her look lingers on* JANICE *and* JARVIS. *She hugs* JANICE *and* JARVIS, *bending over them from the back of the bench.*)

MRS. WEST. Frankie and this little friend of hers gave a performance of "The Vagabond King" out here last spring. (JOHN HENRY *spreads out his arms and imitates the heroine of the play from memory, singing in his high childish voice.*)

JOHN HENRY. Never hope to bind me. Never hope to know. (*Speaking.*) Frankie was the king-boy. I sold the tickets.

MRS. WEST. Yes, I have always said that Frankie has talent.

FRANKIE. Aw, I'm afraid I don't have much talent.

JOHN HENRY. Frankie can laugh and kill people good. She can die, too.

FRANKIE (*with some pride*). Yeah, I guess I die all right.

MR. ADDAMS. Frankie rounds up John Henry and those smaller children, but by the time she dresses them in the costumes, they're worn out and won't act in the show.

JARVIS (*looking at his watch*). Well, it's time we shove off for Winter Hill—Frankie's land of icebergs and snow—where the temperature goes up to 102. (JARVIS *takes* JANICE's *hand. He gets up and gazes fondly around the yard and the arbor. He pulls her up and stands with his arm around her, gazing around him at the arbor and yard.*) It carries me back—this smell of mashed grapes and dust. I remember all the endless summer afternoons of my childhood. It does carry me back.

FRANKIE. Me too. It carries me back, too.

MR. ADDAMS (*putting one arm around* JANICE *and shaking* JARVIS' *hand*). Merciful Heavens! It seems I have two Methuselahs in my family! Does it carry you back to your childhood too, John Henry?

JOHN HENRY. Yes, Uncle Royal.

MR. ADDAMS. Son, this visit was a real pleasure. Janice, I'm mighty pleased to see my boy has such lucky judgment in choosing a wife.

FRANKIE. I hate to think you have to go. I'm just now realizing you're here.

JARVIS. We'll be back in two days. The wedding is Sunday. (*The family move around the house toward the street.* JOHN HENRY *enters the kitchen through the back door. There are the sounds of "good-byes" from the front yard.*)

JOHN HENRY. Frankie was drunk. She drank a liquor drink.

BERENICE. She just made out like she was drunk—pretended.

JOHN HENRY. She said, "Look, Papa, how drunk I am," and she couldn't walk.

FRANKIE's VOICE. Good-bye, Jarvis. Good-bye, Janice.

JARVIS' VOICE. See you Sunday.

MR. ADDAMS' VOICE. Drive carefully, son. Good-bye, Janice.

JANICE's VOICE. Good-bye and thanks, Mr. Addams. Good-bye, Frankie darling.

ALL THE VOICES. Good-bye! Good-bye!

JOHN HENRY. They are going now to Winter Hill. (*There is the sound of the front door opening, then of steps in the hall.* FRANKIE *enters through the hall.*)

FRANKIE. Oh, I can't understand it! The way it all just suddenly happened.

BERENICE. Happened? Happened?

FRANKIE. I have never been so puzzled.

BERENICE. Puzzled about what?

FRANKIE. The whole thing. They are so beautiful.

BERENICE (*after a pause*). I believe the sun done fried your brains.

JOHN HENRY (*whispering*). Me too.

BERENICE. Look here at me. You jealous.

FRANKIE. Jealous?

BERENICE. Jealous because your brother's going to be married.

FRANKIE (*slowly*). No. I just never saw any two people like them. When they walked in the house today it was so queer.

BERENICE. You jealous. Go and behold yourself in the mirror. I can see from the color of your eyes. (FRANKIE *goes to the mirror and stares. She draws up her left shoulder, shakes her head, and turns away.*)

FRANKIE (*with feeling*). Oh! They were the two prettiest people I ever saw. I just can't understand how it happened.

BERENICE. Whatever ails you?—actin' so queer.

FRANKIE. I don't know. I bet they have a good time every minute of the day.

JOHN HENRY. Less us have a good time.

FRANKIE. Us have a good time? Us? (*She rises and walks around the table.*)

BERENICE. Come on. Less have a game of three-handed bridge. (*They sit down to the table, shuffle the cards, deal, and play a game.*)

FRANKIE. Oregon, Alaska, Winter Hill, the wedding. It's all so queer.

BERENICE. I can't bid, never have a hand these days.

FRANKIE. A spade.

JOHN HENRY. I want to bid spades. That's what I was going to bid.

FRANKIE. Well, that's your tough luck. I bid them first.

JOHN HENRY. Oh, you fool jackass! It's not fair!

BERENICE. Hush quarreling, you two. (*She looks at both their hands.*) To tell the truth, I don't think either of you got such a grand hand to fight over the bid about. Where is the cards? I haven't had no kind of a hand all week.

FRANKIE. I don't give a durn about it. It is immaterial with me. (*There is a long pause. She sits with her head propped on her hand, her legs wound around each other.*) Let's talk about them—and the wedding.

BERENICE. What you want to talk about?

FRANKIE. My heart feels them going away—going farther and farther away—while I am stuck here by myself.

BERENICE. You ain't here by yourself. By the way, where's your Pa?

FRANKIE. He went to the store. I think about them, but I remembered them more as a feeling than as a picture.

BERENICE. A feeling?

FRANKIE. They were the two prettiest people I ever saw. Yet it was like I couldn't see all of them I wanted to see. My brains couldn't gather together quick enough to take it all in. And then they were gone.

BERENICE. Well, stop commenting about it. You don't have your mind on the game.

FRANKIE (*playing her cards, followed by* JOHN HENRY). Spades are trumps and you got a spade. I have some of my mind on the game. (JOHN HENRY *puts his donkey necklace in his mouth and looks away.*)

FRANKIE. Go on, cheater.

BERENICE. Make haste.

JOHN HENRY. I can't. It's a king. The only spade I got is a king, and I don't want to play my king under Frankie's ace. And I'm not going to do it either.

FRANKIE (*throwing her cards down on the table*). See, Berenice, he cheats!

BERENICE. Play your king, John Henry. You have to follow the rules of the game.

JOHN HENRY. My king. It isn't fair.

FRANKIE. Even with this trick, I can't win.

BERENICE. Where is the cards? For three days I haven't had a decent hand. I'm beginning to suspicion something. Come on less us count these old cards.

FRANKIE. We've worn these old cards out. If you would eat these old cards, they would taste like a combination of all the dinners of this summer together with a sweaty-handed, nasty taste. Why, the jacks and the queens are missing.

BERENICE. John Henry, how come you do a thing like that? So that's why you asked for the scissors and stole off quiet behind the arbor. Now Candy, how come you took our playing cards and cut out the pictures?

JOHN HENRY. Because I wanted them. They're cute.

FRANKIE. See? He's nothing but a child. It's hopeless. Hopeless!

BERENICE. Maybe so.

FRANKIE. We'll just have to put him out of the game. He's entirely too young. (JOHN HENRY *whimpers.*)

BERENICE. Well, we can't put Candy out of the game. We gotta have a third to play. Besides, by the last count he owes me close to three million dollars.

FRANKIE. Oh, I am sick unto death. (*She sweeps the cards from the table, then gets up and begins walking around the kitchen.* JOHN HENRY *leaves the table and picks up a large blonde doll on the chair in the corner.*) I wish they'd taken me with them to Winter Hill this afternoon. I wish tomorrow was Sunday instead of Saturday.

BERENICE. Sunday will come.

FRANKIE. I doubt it. I wish I was going somewhere for good. I wish I had a hundred dollars and could just light out and never see this town again.

BERENICE. It seems like you wish for a lot of things.

FRANKIE. I wish I was somebody else except me.

JOHN HENRY (*holding the doll*). You serious when you gave me the doll a while ago?

FRANKIE. It gives me a pain just to think about them.

BERENICE. It is a known truth that

gray-eyed peoples are jealous. (*There are sounds of children playing in the neighboring yard.*)

JOHN HENRY. Let's go out and play with the children.

FRANKIE. I don't want to.

JOHN HENRY. There's a big crowd, and they sound like they having a mighty good time. Less go.

FRANKIE. You got ears. You heard me.

JOHN HENRY. I think maybe I better go home.

FRANKIE. Why, you said you were going to spend the night. You just can't eat dinner and then go off in the afternoon like that.

JOHN HENRY. I know it.

BERENICE. Candy, Lamb, you can go home if you want to.

JOHN HENRY. But less go out, Frankie. They sound like they having a lot of fun.

FRANKIE. No, they're not. Just a crowd of ugly, silly children. Running and hollering and running and hollering. Nothing to it.

JOHN HENRY. Less go!

FRANKIE. Well, then I'll entertain you. What do you want to do? Would you like for me to read to you out of The Book of Knowledge, or would you rather do something else?

JOHN HENRY. I rather do something else. (*He goes to the back door, and looks into the yard. Several young girls of thirteen or fourteen, dressed in clean print frocks, file slowly across the back yard.*) Look. Those big girls.

FRANKIE (*running out into the yard*). Hey, there. I'm mighty glad to see you. Come on in.

HELEN. We can't. We were just passing through to notify our new member.

FRANKIE (*overjoyed*). Am I the new member?

DORIS. No, you're not the one the club elected.

FRANKIE. Not elected?

HELEN. Every ballot was unanimous for Mary Littlejohn.

FRANKIE. Mary Littlejohn! You mean that girl who just moved in next door? That pasty fat girl with those tacky pigtails? The one who plays the piano all day long?

DORIS. Yes. The club unanimously elected Mary.

FRANKIE. Why, she's not even cute.

HELEN. She is too; and, furthermore, she's talented.

FRANKIE. I think it's sissy to sit around the house all day playing classical music.

DORIS. Why, Mary is training for a concert career.

FRANKIE. Well, I wish to Jesus she would train somewhere else.

DORIS. You don't have enough sense to appreciate a talented girl like Mary.

FRANKIE. What are you doing in my yard? You're never to set foot on my Papa's property again. (FRANKIE *shakes* HELEN.) Son-of-a-bitches. I could shoot you with my Papa's pistol.

JOHN HENRY (*shaking his fists*). Son-of-a-bitches.

FRANKIE. Why didn't you elect me? (*She goes back into the house.*) Why can't I be a member?

JOHN HENRY. Maybe they'll change their mind and invite you.

BERENICE. I wouldn't pay them no mind. All my life I've been wantin' things that I ain't been gettin'. Anyhow those club girls is fully two years older than you.

FRANKIE. I think they have been spreading it all over town that I smell bad. When I had those boils and had to use that black bitter-smelling ointment, old Helen Fletcher asked me what was that funny smell I had. Oh, I could shoot every one of them with a pistol. (FRANKIE *sits with her head on the table.* JOHN HENRY *approaches and pats the back of* FRANKIE's *neck.*)

JOHN HENRY. I don't think you smell so bad. You smell sweet, like a hundred flowers.

FRANKIE. The son-of-a-bitches. And there was something else. They were telling nasty lies about married people. When I think of Aunt Pet and Uncle Eustace! And my own father! The nasty lies! I don't know what kind of fool they take me for.

BERENICE. That's what I tell you. They too old for you. (JOHN HENRY *raises his head, expands his nostrils and sniffs at himself. Then* FRANKIE *goes into the in-*

terior bedroom and returns with a bottle of perfume.)

FRANKIE. Boy! I bet I use more perfume than anybody else in town. Want some on you, John Henry? You want some, Berenice? (*She sprinkles perfume.*)

JOHN HENRY. Like a thousand flowers.

BERENICE. Frankie, the whole idea of a club is that there are members who are included and the nonmembers who are not included. Now what you ought to do is to round you up a club of your own. And you could be the president yourself. (*There is a pause.*)

FRANKIE. Who would I get?

BERENICE. Why, those little children you hear playing in the neighborhood.

FRANKIE. I don't want to be the president of all those little young left-over people.

BERENICE. Well, then enjoy your misery. That perfume smells so strong it kind of makes me sick. (JOHN HENRY *plays with the doll at the kitchen table and* FRANKIE *watches.*)

FRANKIE. Look here at me, John Henry. Take off those glasses. (JOHN HENRY *takes off his glasses.*) I bet you don't need those glasses. (*She points to the coal scuttle.*) What is this?

JOHN HENRY. The coal scuttle.

FRANKIE (*taking a shell from the kitchen shelf*). And this?

JOHN HENRY. The shell we got at Saint Peter's Bay last summer.

FRANKIE. What is that little thing crawling around on the floor?

JOHN HENRY. Where?

FRANKIE. That little thing crawling around near your feet.

JOHN HENRY. Oh. (*He squats down.*) Why, it's an ant. How did that get in here?

FRANKIE. If I were you I'd just throw those glasses away. You can see good as anybody.

BERENICE. Now quit picking with John Henry.

FRANKIE. They don't look becoming. (JOHN HENRY *wipes his glasses and puts them back on.*) He can suit himself. I was only telling him for his own good. (*She walks restlessly around the kitch-*

en.) I bet Janice and Jarvis are members of a lot of clubs. In fact, the army is kind of like a club. (JOHN HENRY *searches through* BERENICE'S *pocketbook.*)

BERENICE. Don't root through my pocketbook like that, Candy. Ain't a wise policy to search folks' pocketbooks. They might think you trying to steal their money.

JOHN HENRY. I'm looking for your new glass eye. Here it is. (*He hands* BERENICE *the glass eye.*) You got two nickels and a dime. (BERENICE *takes off her patch, turns away and inserts the glass eye.*)

BERENICE. I ain't used to it yet. The socket bothers me. Maybe it don't fit properly.

JOHN HENRY. The blue glass eye looks very cute.

FRANKIE. I don't see why you had to get that eye. It has a wrong expression— let alone being blue.

BERENICE. Ain't anybody ask your judgment, wise-mouth.

JOHN HENRY. Which one of your eyes do you see out of the best?

BERENICE. The left eye, of course. The glass eye don't do me no seeing good at all.

JOHN HENRY. I like the glass eye better. It is so bright and shiny—a real pretty eye. Frankie, you serious when you gave me this doll a while ago?

FRANKIE. Janice and Jarvis. It gives me this pain just to think about them.

BERENICE. It is a known truth that gray-eyed people are jealous.

FRANKIE. I told you I wasn't jealous. I couldn't be jealous of one of them without being jealous of them both. I 'sociate the two of them together. Somehow they're just so different from us.

BERENICE. Well, I were jealous when my foster-brother, Honey, married Clorina. I sent a warning I could tear the ears off her head. But you see I didn't. Clorina's got ears just like anybody else. And now I love her.

FRANKIE (*stopping her walking suddenly*). J.A.—Janice and Jarvis. Isn't that the strangest thing?

BERENICE. What?

FRANKIE. J.A.—Both their names begin with "J.A."

BERENICE. And? What about it?

FRANKIE (*walking around the kitchen table*). If only my name was Jane. Jane or Jasmine.

BERENICE. I don't follow your frame of mind.

FRANKIE. Jarvis and Janice and Jasmine. See?

BERENICE. No. I don't see.

FRANKIE. I wonder if it's against the law to change your name. Or add to it.

BERENICE. Naturally. It's against the law.

FRANKIE (*impetuously*). Well, I don't care. F. Jasmine Addams.

JOHN HENRY (*approaching with the doll*). You serious when you give me this? (*He pulls up the doll's dress and pats her.*) I will name her Belle.

FRANKIE. I don't know what went on in Jarvis' mind when he brought me that doll. Imagine bringing me a doll! I had counted on Jarvis bringing me something from Alaska.

BERENICE. Your face when you unwrapped that package was a study.

FRANKIE. John Henry, quit pickin' at the doll's eyes. It makes me so nervous. You hear me! (*He sits the doll up.*) In fact, take the doll somewhere out of my sight.

JOHN HENRY. Her name is Lily Belle. (JOHN HENRY *goes out and props the doll up on the back steps. There is the sound of an unseen Negro singing from the neighboring yard.*)

FRANKIE (*going to the mirror*). The big mistake I made was to get this close crew cut. For the wedding, I ought to have long brunette hair. Don't you think so?

BERENICE. I don't see how come brunette hair is necessary. But I warned you about getting your head shaved off like that before you did it. But nothing would do but you shave it like that.

FRANKIE (*stepping back from the mirror and slumping her shoulders*). Oh, I am so worried about being so tall. I'm twelve and five-sixths years old and already five feet five and three-fourths inches tall. If I keep on growing like this until I'm twenty-one, I figure I will be nearly ten feet tall.

JOHN HENRY (*reentering the kitchen*). Lily Belle is taking a nap on the back steps. Don't talk so loud, Frankie.

FRANKIE (*after a pause*). I doubt if they ever get married or go to a wedding. Those freaks.

BERENICE. Freaks. What freaks you talking about?

FRANKIE. At the fair. The ones we saw there last October.

JOHN HENRY. Oh, the freaks at the fair! (*He holds out an imaginary skirt and begins to skip around the room with one finger resting on the top of his head.*) Oh, she was the cutest little girl I ever saw. I never saw anything so cute in my whole life. Did you, Frankie?

FRANKIE. No. I don't think she was cute.

BERENICE. Who is that he's talking about?

FRANKIE. That little old pin-head at the fair. A head no bigger than an orange. With the hair shaved off and a big pink bow at the top. Bow was bigger than the head.

JOHN HENRY. Shoo! She was too cute.

BERENICE. That little old squeezed-looking midget in them little trick evening clothes. And that giant with the hang-jaw face and them huge loose hands. And that morphidite! Half man —half woman. With that tiger skin on one side and that spangled skirt on the other.

JOHN HENRY. But that little-headed girl was cute.

FRANKIE. And that wild colored man they said came from a savage island and ate those real live rats. Do you think they make a very big salary?

BERENICE. How would I know? In fact, all them freak folks down at the fair every October just gives me the creeps.

FRANKIE (*after a pause, and slowly*). Do I give you the creeps?

BERENICE. You?

FRANKIE. Do you think I will grow into a freak?

BERENICE. You? Why certainly not, I trust Jesus!

FRANKIE (*going over to the mirror, and looking at herself*). Well, do you think I will be pretty?

BERENICE. Maybe. If you file down them horns a inch or two.

FRANKIE (*turning to face* BERENICE, *and shuffling one bare foot on the floor*). Seriously.

BERENICE. Seriously, I think when you fill out you will do very well. If you behave.

FRANKIE. But by Sunday, I want to do something to improve myself before the wedding.

BERENICE. Get clean for a change. Scrub your elbows and fix yourself nice. You will do very well.

JOHN HENRY. You will be all right if you file down them horns.

FRANKIE (*raising her right shoulder and turning from the mirror*). I don't know what to do. I just wish I would die.

BERENICE. Well, die then!

JOHN HENRY. Die.

FRANKIE (*suddenly exasperated*). Go home! (*There is a pause.*) You heard me! (*She makes a face at him and threatens him with the fly swatter. They run twice around the table.*) Go home! I'm sick and tired of you, you little midget. (JOHN HENRY *goes out, taking the doll with him.*)

BERENICE. Now what makes you act like that? You are too mean to live.

FRANKIE. I know it. (*She takes a carving knife from the table drawer.*) Something about John Henry just gets on my nerves these days. (*She puts her left ankle over her right knee and begins to pick with the knife at a splinter in her foot.*) I've got a splinter in my foot.

BERENICE. That knife ain't the proper thing for a splinter.

FRANKIE. It seems to me that before this summer I used always to have such a good time. Remember this spring when Evelyn Owen and me used to dress up in costumes and go down town and shop at the five-and-dime? And how every Friday night we'd spend the night with each other either at her house or here? And then Evelyn Owen had to go and move away to Florida. And now she won't even write to me.

BERENICE. Honey, you are not crying, is you? Don't that hurt you none?

FRANKIE. It would hurt anybody else except me. And how the wisteria in town was so blue and pretty in April but somehow it was so pretty it made me sad. And how Evelyn and me put on that show the Glee Club did at the High School Auditorium? (*She raises her head and beats time with the knife and her fist on the table, singing loudly with sudden energy.*) Sons of toil and danger! Will you serve a stranger! And bow down to Burgundy! (BERENICE *joins in on "Burgundy."* FRANKIE *pauses, then begins to pick her foot again, humming the tune sadly.*)

BERENICE. That was a nice show you children copied in the arbor. You will meet another girl friend you like as well as Evelyn Owen. Or maybe Mr. Owen will move back into town. (*There is a pause.*) Frankie, what you need is a needle.

FRANKIE. I don't care anything about my old feet. (*She stomps her foot on the floor and lays down the knife on the table.*) It was just so queer the way it happened this afternoon. The minute I laid eyes on the pair of them I had this funny feeling. (*She goes over and picks up a saucer of milk near the cat-hole in back of the door and pours the milk in the sink.*) How old were you, Berenice, when you married your first husband?

BERENICE. I were thirteen years old.

FRANKIE. What made you get married so young for?

BERENICE. Because I wanted to.

FRANKIE. You never loved any of your four husbands but Ludie.

BERENICE. Ludie Maxwell Freeman was my only true husband. The other ones were just scraps.

FRANKIE. Did you marry with a veil every time?

BERENICE. Three times with a veil.

FRANKIE (*pouring milk into the saucer and returning the saucer to the cat-hole*). If only I just knew where he is gone. Ps, ps, ps . . . Charles, Charles.

BERENICE. Quit worrying yourself about that old alley cat. He's gone off to hunt a friend.

FRANKIE. To hunt a friend?

BERENICE. Why certainly. He roamed off to find himself a lady friend.

FRANKIE. Well, why don't he bring his friend home with him? He ought to know I would be only too glad to have a whole family of cats.

BERENICE. You done seen the last of that old alley cat.

FRANKIE (crossing the room). I ought to notify the police force. They will find Charles.

BERENICE. I wouldn't do that.

FRANKIE (at the telephone). I want the police force, please . . . Police force? . . . I am notifying you about my cat . . . Cat! He's lost. He is almost pure Persian.

BERENICE. As Persian as I is.

FRANKIE. But with short hair. A lovely color of gray with a little white spot on his throat. He answers to the name of Charles, but if he don't answer to that, he might come if you call "Charlina." . . . My name is Miss F. Jasmine Addams and the address is 124 Grove Street.

BERENICE (giggling as FRANKIE reenters). Gal, they going to send around here and tie you up and drag you off to Milledgeville. Just picture them fat blue police chasing tomcats around alleys and hollering, "Oh Charles! Oh come here, Charlina!" Merciful Heavens.

FRANKIE. Aw, shut up! (Outside a voice is heard calling in a drawn-out chant, the words almost indistinguishable: "Lot of okra, peas, fresh butter beans . . .")

BERENICE. The trouble with you is that you don't have no sense of humor no more.

FRANKIE (disconsolately). Maybe I'd be better off in jail. (The chanting voice continues and an ancient Negro woman, dressed in a clean print dress with several petticoats, the ruffle of one of which shows, crosses the yard. She stops and leans on a gnarled stick.)

FRANKIE. Here comes the old vegetable lady.

BERENICE. Sis Laura is getting mighty feeble to peddle this hot weather.

FRANKIE. She is about ninety. Other old folks lose their faculties, but she found some faculty. She reads futures, too.

BERENICE. Hi, Sis Laura. How is your folks getting on?

SIS LAURA. We ain't much, and I feels my age these days. Want any peas today? (She shuffles across the yard.)

BERENICE. I'm sorry, I still have some left over from yesterday. Good-bye, Sis Laura.

SIS LAURA. Good-bye. (She goes off behind the house to the right, continuing her chant. When the old woman is gone FRANKIE begins walking around the kitchen.)

FRANKIE. I expect Janice and Jarvis are almost to Winter Hill by now.

BERENICE. Sit down. You make me nervous.

FRANKIE. Jarvis talked about Granny. He remembers her very good. But when I try to remember Granny, it is like her face is changing—like a face seen under water. Jarvis remembers Mother too, and I don't remember her at all.

BERENICE. Naturally! Your mother died the day that you were born.

FRANKIE (standing with one foot on the seat of the chair, leaning over the chair back and laughing). Did you hear what Jarvis said?

BERENICE. What?

FRANKIE (after laughing more). They were talking about whether to vote for C. P. MacDonald. And Jarvis said, "Why I wouldn't vote for that scoundrel if he was running to be dogcatcher." I never heard anything so witty in my life. (There is a silence during which BERENICE watches FRANKIE, but does not smile.) And you know what Janice remarked. When Jarvis mentioned about how much I've grown, she said she didn't think I looked so terribly big. She said she got the major portion of her growth before she was thirteen. She said I was the right height and had acting talent and ought to go to Hollywood. She did, Berenice.

BERENICE. O.K. All right! She did!

FRANKIE. She said she thought I was a lovely size and would probably not grow any taller. She said all fashion models and movie stars . . .

BERENICE. She did not. I heard her from the window. She only remarked that you probably had already got your growth. But she didn't go on and on like that or mention Hollywood.

FRANKIE. She said to me . . .

BERENICE. She said to you! This is a serious fault with you, Frankie. Somebody just makes a loose remark and then you cozen it in your mind until nobody would recognize it. Your Aunt Pet happened to mention to Clorina that you had sweet manners and Clorina passed it on to you. For what it was worth. Then next thing I know you are going all around and bragging how Mrs. West thought you had the finest manners in town and ought to go to Hollywood, and I don't know what-all you didn't say. And that is a serious fault.

FRANKIE. Aw, quit preaching at me.

BERENICE. I ain't preaching. It's the solemn truth and you know it.

FRANKIE. I admit it a little. (*She sits down at the table and puts her forehead on the palms of her hands. There is a pause, and then she speaks softly.*) What I need to know is this. Do you think I made a good impression?

BERENICE. Impression?

FRANKIE. Yes.

BERENICE. Well, how would I know?

FRANKIE. I mean, how did I act? What did I do?

BERENICE. Why, you didn't do anything to speak of.

FRANKIE. Nothing?

BERENICE. No. You just watched the pair of them like they was ghosts. Then, when they talked about the wedding, them ears of yours stiffened out the size of cabbage leaves . . .

FRANKIE (*raising her hand to her ear*). They didn't!

BERENICE. They did.

FRANKIE. Some day you going to look down and find that big fat tongue of yours pulled out by the roots and laying there before you on the table.

BERENICE. Quit talking so rude.

FRANKIE (*after a pause*). I'm so scared I didn't make a good impression.

BERENICE. What of it? I got a date with T. T. and he's supposed to pick me up here. I wish him and Honey would come on. You make me nervous. (*FRANKIE sits miserably, her shoulders hunched. Then with a sudden gesture she bangs her forehead on the table. Her fists are clenched and she is sobbing.*)

BERENICE. Come on. Don't act like that.

FRANKIE (*her voice muffled*). They were so pretty. They must have such a good time. And they went away and left me.

BERENICE. Sit up. Behave yourself.

FRANKIE. They came and went away, and left me with this feeling.

BERENICE. Hosee! I bet I know something. (*She begins tapping with her heel: one, two, three—bang! After a pause, in which the rhythm is established, she begins singing.*) Frankie's got a crush! Frankie's got a crush! Frankie's got a crush on the *wedding!*

FRANKIE. Quit!

BERENICE. Frankie's got a crush! Frankie's got a crush!

FRANKIE. You better quit! (*She rises suddenly and snatches up the carving knife.*)

BERENICE. You lay down that knife.

FRANKIE. Make me. (*She bends the blade slowly.*)

BERENICE. Lay it down, *Devil.* (*There is a silence.*) Just throw it! You just! (*After a pause FRANKIE aims the knife carefully at the closed door leading to the bedroom and throws it. The knife does not stick in the wall.*)

FRANKIE. I used to be the best knife thrower in this town.

BERENICE. Frances Addams, you goin' to try that stunt once too often.

FRANKIE. I warned you to quit pickin' with me.

BERENICE. You are not fit to live in a house.

FRANKIE. I won't be living in this one

much longer; I'm going to run away from home.

BERENICE. And a good riddance to a big old bag of rubbage.

FRANKIE. You wait and see. I'm leaving town.

BERENICE. And where do you think you are going?

FRANKIE (*gazing around the walls*). I don't know.

BERENICE. You're going crazy. That's where you going.

FRANKIE. No. (*Solemnly.*) This coming Sunday after the wedding, I'm leaving town. And I swear to Jesus by my two eyes I'm never coming back here any more.

BERENICE (*going to* FRANKIE *and pushing her damp bangs back from her forehead*). Sugar? You serious?

FRANKIE (*exasperated*). Of course! Do you think I would stand here and say that swear and tell a story? Sometimes, Berenice, I think it takes you longer to realize a fact than it does anybody who ever lived.

BERENICE. But you say you don't know where you going. You going, but you don't know where. That don't make no sense to me.

FRANKIE (*after a long pause in which she again gazes around the walls of the room*). I feel just exactly like somebody has peeled all the skin off me. I wish I had some good cold peach ice cream. (BERENICE *takes her by the shoulders. During the last speech,* T. T. WILLIAMS *and* HONEY CAMDEN BROWN *have been approaching through the back yard.* T. T. *is a large and pompous-looking Negro man of about fifty. He is dressed like a church deacon, in a black suit with a red emblem in the lapel. His manner is timid and overpolite.* HONEY *is a slender, limber Negro boy of about twenty. He is quite light in color and he wears loud-colored, snappy clothes. He is brusque and there is about him an odd mixture of hostility and playfulness. He is very high-strung and volatile. They are trailed by* JOHN HENRY. JOHN HENRY *is dressed for afternoon in a clean white linen suit, white shoes and socks.* HONEY *carries a horn. They cross the back yard and knock at the back door.* HONEY *holds his hand to his head.*)

FRANKIE. But every word I told you was the solemn truth. I'm leaving here after the wedding.

BERENICE (*taking her hands from* FRANKIE'S *shoulders and answering the door*). Hello, Honey and T. T. I didn't hear you coming.

T. T. You and Frankie too busy discussing something. Well, your foster-brother, Honey, got into a ruckus standing on the sidewalk in front of the Blue Moon Café. Police cracked him on the haid.

BERENICE (*turning on the kitchen light*). What! (*She examines* HONEY'S *head.*) Why, it's a welt the size of a small egg.

HONEY. Times like this I feel like I got to bust loose or die.

BERENICE. What were you doing?

HONEY. Nothing. I was just passing along the street minding my own business when this drunk soldier came out of the Blue Moon Café and ran into me. I looked at him and he gave me a push. I pushed him back and he raised a ruckus. This white M.P. came up and slammed me with his stick.

T. T. It was one of those accidents can happen to any colored person.

JOHN HENRY (*reaching for the horn*). Toot some on your horn, Honey.

FRANKIE. Please blow.

HONEY (*to* JOHN HENRY, *who has taken the horn*). Now, don't bother my horn, Butch.

JOHN HENRY. I want to toot it some. (JOHN HENRY *takes the horn, tries to blow it, but only succeeds in slobbering in it. He holds the horn away from his mouth and sings: "Too-ty-toot, too-ty-toot."* HONEY *snatches the horn away from him and puts it on the sewing table.*)

HONEY. I told you not to touch my horn. You got it full of slobber inside and out. It's ruined! (*He loses his temper, grabs* JOHN HENRY *by the shoulders and shakes him hard.*)

BERENICE (*slapping* HONEY). Satan!

Don't you dare touch that little boy! I'm going to stomp out your brains!

HONEY. You ain't mad because John Henry is a little boy. It's because he's a white boy. John Henry knows he needs a good shake. Don't you, Butch?

BERENICE. Ornery—no good! (HONEY *lifts* JOHN HENRY *and swings him, then reaches in his pocket and brings out some coins.*)

HONEY. John Henry, which would you rather have—the nigger money or the white money?

JOHN HENRY. I rather have the dime. (*He takes it.*) Much obliged. (*He goes out and crosses the yard to his house.*)

BERENICE. You troubled and beat down and try to take it out on a little boy. You and Frankie just alike. The club girls don't elect her and she turns on John Henry too. When folks are lonesome and left out, they turn so mean. T. T. do you wish a small little quickie before we start?

T. T. (*looking at* FRANKIE *and pointing toward her*). Frankie ain't no tattletale. Is you? (BERENICE *pours a drink for* T. T.)

FRANKIE (*disdaining his question*). That sure is a cute suit you got on, Honey. Today I heard somebody speak of you as Lightfoot Brown. I think that's such a grand nickname. It's on account of your travelling—to Harlem, and all the different places where you have run away, and your dancing. Lightfoot! I wish somebody would call me Lightfoot Addams.

BERENICE. It would suit me better if Honey Camden had brick feets. As it is, he keeps me so anxious-worried. C'mon, Honey and T. T. Let's go! (HONEY *and* T. T. *go out.*)

FRANKIE. I'll go out into the yard. (FRANKIE, *feeling excluded, goes out into the yard. Throughout the act the light in the yard has been darkening steadily. Now the light in the kitchen is throwing a yellow rectangle in the yard.*)

BERENICE. Now Frankie, you forget all that foolishness we were discussing. And if Mr. Addams don't come home

by good dark, you go over to the Wests'. Go play with John Henry.

HONEY AND T. T. (*from outside*). So long!

FRANKIE. So long, you all. Since when have I been scared of the dark? I'll invite John Henry to spend the night with me.

BERENICE. I thought you were sick and tired of him.

FRANKIE. I am.

BERENICE (*kissing* FRANKIE). Good night, Sugar!

FRANKIE. Seems like everybody goes off and leaves me. (*She walks towards the* WESTS' *yard, calling, with cupped hands.*) John Henry. John Henry.

JOHN HENRY'S VOICE. What do you want, Frankie?

FRANKIE. Come over and spend the night with me.

JOHN HENRY'S VOICE. I can't.

FRANKIE. Why?

JOHN HENRY. Just because.

FRANKIE. Because why? (JOHN HENRY *does not answer.*) I thought maybe me and you could put up my Indian tepee and sleep out here in the yard. And have a good time. (*There is still no answer.*) Sure enough. Why don't you stay and spend the night?

JOHN HENRY (*quite loudly*). Because, Frankie. I don't want to.

FRANKIE (*angrily*). Fool Jackass! Suit yourself! I only asked you because you looked so ugly and so lonesome.

JOHN HENRY (*skipping toward the arbor*). Why, I'm not a bit lonesome.

FRANKIE (*looking at the house*). I wonder when that Papa of mine is coming home. He always comes home by dark. I don't want to go into that empty, ugly house all by myself.

JOHN HENRY. Me neither.

FRANKIE (*standing with outstretched arms, and looking around her*). I think something is wrong. It is too quiet. I have a peculiar warning in my bones. I bet you a hundred dollars it's going to storm.

JOHN HENRY. I don't want to spend the night with you.

FRANKIE. A terrible, terrible dog-day storm. Or maybe even a cyclone.

JOHN HENRY. Huh.

FRANKIE. I bet Jarvis and Janice are now at Winter Hill. I see them just plain as I see you. Plainer. Something is wrong. It is too quiet. (*A clear horn begins to play a blues tune in the distance.*)

JOHN HENRY. Frankie?

FRANKIE. Hush! It sounds like Honey. (*The horn music becomes jazzy and spangling, then the first blues tune is repeated. Suddenly, while still unfinished, the music stops. FRANKIE waits tensely.*) He has stopped to bang the spit out of his horn. In a second he will finish. (*After a wait.*) Please, Honey, go on finish!

JOHN HENRY (*softly*). He done quit now.

FRANKIE (*moving restlessly*). I told Berenice that I was leavin' town for good and she did not believe me. Sometimes I honestly think she is the biggest fool that ever drew breath. You try to impress something on a big fool like that, and it's just like talking to a block of cement. I kept on telling and telling and telling her. I told her I had to leave this town for good because it is inevitable. Inevitable. (*MR. ADDAMS enters the kitchen from the house, calling: "Frankie, Frankie."*)

MR. ADDAMS (*calling from the kitchen door*). Frankie, Frankie.

FRANKIE. Yes, Papa.

MR. ADDAMS (*opening the back door*). You had supper?

FRANKIE. I'm not hungry.

MR. ADDAMS. Was a little later than I intended, fixing a timepiece for a railroad man. (*He goes back through the kitchen and into the hall, calling: "Don't leave the yard!"*)

JOHN HENRY. You want me to get the weekend bag?

FRANKIE. Don't bother me, John Henry. I'm thinking.

JOHN HENRY. What you thinking about?

FRANKIE. About the wedding. About my brother and the bride. Everything's been so sudden today. I never believed before about the fact that the earth turns at the rate of about a thousand miles a day. I didn't understand why it was that if you jumped up in the air you wouldn't land in Selma or Fairview or somewhere else instead of the same back yard. But now it seems to me I feel the world going around very fast. (*FRANKIE begins turning around in circles with arms outstretched. JOHN HENRY copies her. They both turn.*) I feel it turning and it makes me dizzy.

JOHN HENRY. I'll stay and spend the night with you.

FRANKIE (*suddenly stopping her turning*). No. I just now thought of something.

JOHN HENRY. You just a little while ago was begging me.

FRANKIE. I know where I'm going. (*There are sounds of children playing in the distance.*)

JOHN HENRY. Let's go play with the children, Frankie.

FRANKIE. I tell you I know where I'm going. It's like I've known it all my life. Tomorrow I will tell everybody.

JOHN HENRY. Where?

FRANKIE (*dreamily*). After the wedding I'm going with them to Winter Hill. I'm going off with them after the wedding.

JOHN HENRY. You serious?

FRANKIE. Shush, just now I realized something. The trouble with me is that for a long time I have been just an "I" person. All other people can say "we." When Berenice says "we" she means her lodge and church and colored people. Soldiers can say "we" and mean the army. All people belong to a "we" except me.

JOHN HENRY. What are we going to do?

FRANKIE. Not to belong to a "we" makes you too lonesome. Until this afternoon I didn't have a "we," but now after seeing Janice and Jarvis I suddenly realize something.

JOHN HENRY. What?

FRANKIE. I know that the bride and my brother are the "we" of me. So I'm going with them, and joining with the wedding. This coming Sunday when my brother and the bride leave this town, I'm going with the two of them to Winter Hill. And after that to whatever place that they will ever go. (*There is a pause.*) I love the two of them so much and we belong to be together. I love the two of them so much because they are the *we* of me.

THE CURTAIN FALLS.

ACT TWO

The scene is the same: the kitchen of the ADDAMS *home.* BERENICE *is cooking.* JOHN HENRY *sits on the stool, blowing soap bubbles with a spool. It is the afternoon of the next day. The front door slams and* FRANKIE *enters from the hall.*

BERENICE. I been phoning all over town trying to locate you. Where on earth have you been?

FRANKIE. Everywhere. All over town.

BERENICE. I been so worried I got a good mind to be seriously mad with you. Your Papa came home to dinner today. He was mad when you didn't show up. He's taking a nap now in his room.

FRANKIE. I walked up and down Main Street and stopped in almost every store. Bought my wedding dress and silver shoes. Went around by the mills. Went all over the complete town and talked to nearly everybody in it.

BERENICE. What for, pray tell me?

FRANKIE. I was telling everybody about the wedding and my plans. (*She takes off her dress and remains barefooted in her slip.*)

BERENICE. You mean just people on the street? (*She is creaming butter and sugar for cookies.*)

FRANKIE. Everybody. Storekeepers. The monkey and monkey man. A soldier. Everybody. And you know the soldier wanted to join with me and asked me for a date this evening. I wonder what you do on dates.

BERENICE. Frankie, I honestly believe you have turned crazy on us. Walking all over town and telling total strangers this big tale. You know in your soul this mania of yours is pure foolishness.

FRANKIE. Please call me F. Jasmine. I don't wish to have to remind you any more. Everything good of mine has got to be washed and ironed so I can pack them in the suitcase. (*She brings in a suitcase and opens it.*) Everybody in town believes that I'm going. All except Papa. He's stubborn as an old mule. No use arguing with people like that.

BERENICE. Me and Mr. Addams has some sense.

FRANKIE. Papa was bent over working on a watch when I went by the store. I asked him could I buy the wedding clothes and he said charge them at Mac-Dougal's. But he wouldn't listen to any of my plans. Just sat there with his nose to the grindstone and answered with— kind of grunts. He never listens to what I say. (*There is a pause.*) Sometimes I wonder if Papa loves me or not.

BERENICE. Course he loves you. He is just a busy widowman—set in his ways.

FRANKIE. Now I wonder if I can find some tissue paper to line this suitcase.

BERENICE. Truly, Frankie, what makes you think they want you taggin' along with them? Two is company and three is a crowd. And that's the main thing about a wedding. Two is company and three is a crowd.

FRANKIE. You wait and see.

BERENICE. Remember back to the time of the flood. Remember Noah and the Ark.

FRANKIE. And what has that got to do with it?

BERENICE. Remember the way he admitted them creatures.

FRANKIE. Oh, shut up your big old mouth!

BERENICE. Two by two. He admitted them creatures two by two.

FRANKIE (*after a pause*). That's all right. But you wait and see. They will take me.

BERENICE. And if they don't?

FRANKIE (*turning suddenly from washing her hands at the sink*). If they don't, I will kill myself.

BERENICE. Kill yourself, how?

FRANKIE. I will shoot myself in the side of the head with the pistol that Papa keeps under his handkerchiefs with Mother's picture in the bureau drawer.

BERENICE. You heard what Mr. Addams said about playing with that pistol. I'll just put this cookie dough in the icebox. Set the table and your dinner is ready. Set John Henry a plate and one for me. (BERENICE *puts the dough in the icebox.* FRANKIE *hurriedly sets the table.* BERENICE *takes dishes from the stove and ties a napkin around* JOHN HENRY'S *neck.*) I have heard of many a peculiar thing. I have knew men to fall in love with girls so ugly that you wonder if their eyes is straight.

JOHN HENRY. Who?

BERENICE. I have knew women to love veritable satans and thank Jesus when they put their split hooves over the threshold. I have knew boys to take it into their heads to fall in love with other boys. You know Lily Mae Jenkins?

FRANKIE. I'm not sure. I know a lot of people.

BERENICE. Well, you either know him or you don't know him. He prisses around in a girl's blouse with one arm akimbo. Now this Lily Mae Jenkins fell in love with a man name Juney Jones. A man, mind you. And Lily Mae turned into a girl. He changed his nature and his sex and turned into a girl.

FRANKIE. What?

BERENICE. He did. To all intents and purposes. (BERENICE *is sitting in the center chair at the table. She says grace.*) Lord, make us thankful for what we are about to receive to nourish our bodies. Amen.

FRANKIE. It's funny I can't think who you are talking about. I used to think I knew so many people.

BERENICE. Well, you don't need to know Lily Mae Jenkins. You can live without knowing him.

FRANKIE. Anyway, I don't believe you.

BERENICE. I ain't arguing with you. What was we speaking about?

FRANKIE. About peculiar things.

BERENICE. Oh, yes. As I was just now telling you I have seen many a peculiar thing in my day. But one thing I never knew and never heard tell about. No, siree. I never in all my days heard of anybody falling in love with a wedding. (*There is a pause.*) And thinking it all over I have come to a conclusion.

JOHN HENRY. How? How did that boy change into a girl? Did he kiss his elbow? (*He tries to kiss his elbow.*)

BERENICE. It was just one of them things, Candy Lamb. Yep, I have come to the conclusion that what you ought to be thinking about is a beau. A nice little white boy beau.

FRANKIE. I don't want any beau. What would I do with one? Do you mean something like a soldier who would maybe take me to the Idle Hour?

BERENICE. Who's talking about soldiers? I'm talking about a nice little white boy beau your own age. How 'bout that little old Barney next door?

FRANKIE. Barney MacKean! That nasty Barney!

BERENICE. Certainly! You could make out with him until somebody better comes along. He would do.

FRANKIE. You are the biggest crazy in this town.

BERENICE. The crazy calls the sane the crazy. (BARNEY MACKEAN, *a boy of twelve, shirtless and wearing shorts, and* HELEN FLETCHER, *a girl of twelve or fourteen, cross the yard from the left, go through the arbor and out on the right.* FRANKIE *and* JOHN HENRY *watch them from the window.*)

FRANKIE. Yonder's Barney now with Helen Fletcher. They are going to the alley behind the Wests' garage. They do something bad back there. I don't know what it is.

BERENICE. If you don't know what it is, how come you know it is bad?

FRANKIE. I just know it. I think maybe they look at each other and peepee or something. They don't let anybody watch them.

JOHN HENRY. I watched them once.

FRANKIE. What do they do?

JOHN HENRY. I saw. They don't peepee.

FRANKIE. Then what do they do?

JOHN HENRY. I don't know what it was. But I watched them. How many of them did you catch, Berenice? Them beaus?

BERENICE. How many? Candy Lamb, how many hairs is in this plait? You're talking to Miss Berenice Sadie Brown.

FRANKIE. I think you ought to quit worrying about beaus and be content with T. T. I bet you are forty years old.

BERENICE. Wise-mouth. How do you know so much? I got as much right as anybody else to continue to have a good time as long as I can. And as far as that goes, I'm not so old as some peoples would try and make out. I ain't changed life yet.

JOHN HENRY. Did they all treat you to the picture show, them beaus?

BERENICE. To the show, or one thing or another. Wipe off your mouth. (*There is the sound of piano tuning.*)

JOHN HENRY. The piano tuning man.

BERENICE. Ye Gods, I seriously believe this will be the last straw.

JOHN HENRY. Me too.

FRANKIE. It makes me sad. And jittery too. (*She walks around the room.*) They tell me that when they want to punish the crazy people in Milledgeville, they tie them up and make them listen to piano tuning. (*She puts the empty coal scuttle on her head and walks around the table.*)

BERENICE. We could turn on the radio and drown him out.

FRANKIE. I don't want the radio on. (*She goes into the interior room and takes off her dress, speaking from inside.*) But I advise you to keep the radio on after I leave. Some day you will very likely hear us speak over the radio.

BERENICE. Speak about what, pray tell me?

FRANKIE. I don't know exactly what about. But probably some eye witness account about something. We will be asked to speak.

BERENICE. I don't follow you. What are we going to eye witness? And who will ask us to speak?

JOHN HENRY (*excitedly*). What, Frankie? Who is speaking on the radio?

FRANKIE. When I said *we*, you thought I meant you and me and John Henry West. To speak over the world radio. I have never heard of anything so funny since I was born.

JOHN HENRY (*climbing up to kneel on the seat of the chair*). Who? What?

FRANKIE. Ha! Ha! Ho! Ho! Ho! Ho! (*FRANKIE goes around punching things with her fist, and shadow boxing. BERENICE raises her right hand for peace. Then suddenly they all stop. FRANKIE goes to the windows, and JOHN HENRY hurries there also and stands on tiptoe with his hands on the sill. BERENICE turns her head to see what has happened. The piano is still. Three young girls in clean dresses are passing before the arbor. FRANKIE watches them silently at the window.*)

JOHN HENRY (*softly*). The club of girls.

FRANKIE. What do you son-of-a-bitches mean crossing my yard? How many times must I tell you not to set foot on my Papa's property?

BERENICE. Just ignore them and make like you don't see them pass.

FRANKIE. Don't mention those crooks to me. (T. T. *and* HONEY *approach by way of the back yard.* HONEY *is whistling a blues tune.*)

BERENICE. Why don't you show me the new dress? I'm anxious to see what you selected. (FRANKIE *goes into the interior room.* T. T. *knocks on the door. He and* HONEY *enter.*) Why T. T. what you doing around here this time of day?

T. T. Good afternoon, Miss Berenice. I'm here on a sad mission.

BERENICE (*startled*). What's wrong?

T. T. It's about Sis Laura Thompson. She suddenly had a stroke and died.

BERENICE. What! Why she was by here just yesterday. We just ate her peas. They in my stomach right now, and her lyin' dead on the cooling board this minute. The Lord works in strange ways.

T. T. Passed away at dawn this morning.

FRANKIE (*putting her head in the doorway*). Who is it that's dead?

BERENICE. Sis Laura, Sugar. That old vegetable lady.

FRANKIE (*unseen, from the interior room*). Just to think—she passed by yesterday.

T. T. Miss Berenice, I'm going around to take up a donation for the funeral. The policy people say Sis Laura's claim has lapsed.

BERENICE. Well, here's fifty cents. The poor old soul.

T. T. She was brisk as a chipmunk to the last. The Lord had appointed the time for her. I hope I go that way.

FRANKIE (*from the interior room*). I've got something to show you all. Shut your eyes and don't open them until I tell you. (*She enters the room dressed in an orange satin evening dress with silver shoes and stockings.*) These are the wedding clothes. (BERENICE, T. T. *and* JOHN HENRY *stare.*)

JOHN HENRY. Oh, how pretty!

FRANKIE. Now tell me your honest opinion. (*There is a pause.*) What's the matter? Don't you like it, Berenice?

BERENICE. No. It don't do.

FRANKIE. What do you mean? It don't do.

BERENICE. Exactly that. It just don't do. (*She shakes her head while* FRANKIE *looks at the dress.*)

FRANKIE. But I don't see what you mean. What is wrong?

BERENICE. Well, if you don't see it I can't explain it to you. Look there at your head, to begin with. (FRANKIE *goes to the mirror.*) You had all your hair shaved off like a convict and now you tie this ribbon around this head without any hair. Just looks peculiar.

FRANKIE. But I'm going to wash and try to stretch my hair tonight.

BERENICE. Stretch your hair! How you going to stretch your hair? And look at them elbows. Here you got on a grown woman's evening dress. And that brown crust on your elbows. The two things just don't mix. (FRANKIE, *embarrassed, covers her elbows with her hands.* BERENICE *is still shaking her head.*) Take it back down to the store.

T. T. The dress is too growny looking.

FRANKIE. But I can't take it back. It's bargain basement.

BERENICE. Very well then. Come here. Let me see what I can do.

FRANKIE (*going to* BERENICE, *who works with the dress*). I think you're just not accustomed to seeing anybody dressed up.

BERENICE. I'm not accustomed to seein' a human Christmas tree in August.

JOHN HENRY. Frankie's dress looks like a Christmas tree.

FRANKIE. Two-faced Judas! You just now said it was pretty. Old double-faced Judas! (*The sounds of piano tuning are heard again.*) Oh, that piano tuner!

BERENICE. Step back a little now.

FRANKIE (*looking in the mirror*). Don't you honestly think it's pretty? Give me your candy opinion.

BERENICE. I never knew anybody so unreasonable! You ask me my candy opinion, I give you my candy opinion. You ask me again, and I give it to you again. But what you want is not my honest opinion, but my good opinion of something I know is wrong.

FRANKIE. I only want to look pretty.

BERENICE. Pretty is as pretty does. Ain't that right, T. T.? You will look well enough for anybody's wedding. Excepting your own. (MR. ADDAMS *enters through the hall door.*)

MR. ADDAMS. Hello, everybody. (*To* FRANKIE.) I don't want you roaming around the streets all morning and not coming home at dinner time. Looks like I'll have to tie you up in the back yard.

FRANKIE. I had business to tend to. Papa, look!

MR. ADDAMS. What is it, Miss Picklepriss?

FRANKIE. Sometimes I think you have turned stone blind. You never even noticed my new dress.

MR. ADDAMS. I thought it was a show costume.

FRANKIE. Show costume! Papa, why is it you don't ever notice what I have on or pay any serious mind to me? You just walk around like a mule with blinders on, not seeing or caring.

MR. ADDAMS. Never mind that now. (*To* T. T. *and* HONEY.) I need some help down at my store. My porter failed me again. I wonder if you or Honey could help me next week.

T. T. I will if I can, sir, Mr. Addams. What days would be convenient for you, sir?

MR. ADDAMS. Say Wednesday afternoon.

T. T. Now, Mr. Addams, that's one afternoon I promised to work for Mr. Finny, sir. I can't promise anything, Mr. Addams. But if Mr. Finny change his mind about needing me, I'll work for you, sir.

MR. ADDAMS. How about you, Honey?

HONEY (*shortly*). I ain't got the time.

MR. ADDAMS. I'll be so glad when the war is over and you biggety, worthless niggers get back to work. And, furthermore, you *sir* me! Hear me?

HONEY (*reluctantly*). Yes,—sir.

MR. ADDAMS. I better go back to the store now and get my nose down to the grindstone. You stay home, Frankie. (*He goes out through the hall door.*)

JOHN HENRY. Uncle Royal called Honey a nigger. Is Honey a nigger?

BERENICE. Be quiet now, John Henry. (*To* HONEY.) Honey, I got a good mind to shake you till you spit. Not saying *sir* to Mr. Addams, and acting so impudent.

HONEY. T. T. said sir enough for a whole crowd of niggers. But for folks that calls me nigger, I got a real good nigger razor. (*He takes a razor from his pocket.* FRANKIE *and* JOHN HENRY *crowd close to look. When* JOHN HENRY *touches the razor* HONEY *says:*) Don't touch it, Butch, it's sharp. Liable to hurt yourself.

BERENICE. Put up that razor, Satan! I worry myself sick over you. You going to die before your appointed span.

JOHN HENRY. Why is Honey a nigger?

BERENICE. Jesus knows.

HONEY. I'm so tensed up. My nerves been scraped with a razor. Berenice, loan me a dollar.

BERENICE. I ain't handing you no dollar, worthless, to get high on them reefer cigarettes.

HONEY. Gimme, Berenice, I'm so tensed up and miserable. The nigger hole. I'm sick of smothering in the nigger hole. I can't stand it no more. (*Relenting,* BERENICE *gets her pocketbook from the shelf, opens it, and takes out some change.*)

BERENICE. Here's thirty cents. You can buy two beers.

HONEY. Well, thankful for tiny, infinitesimal favors. I better be dancing off now.

T. T. Same here. I still have to make a good deal of donation visits this afternoon. (HONEY *and* T. T. *go to the door.*)

BERENICE. So long, T. T. I'm counting on you for tomorrow and you too, Honey.

FRANKIE *and* JOHN HENRY. So long.

T. T. Good-bye, you all. Good-bye. (*He goes out, crossing the yard.*)

BERENICE. Poor ole Sis Laura. I certainly hope that when my time comes I will have kept up my policy. I dread to think the church would ever have to bury me. When I die.

JOHN HENRY. Are you going to die, Berenice?

BERENICE. Why, Candy, everybody has to die.

JOHN HENRY. Everybody? Are you going to die, Frankie?

FRANKIE. I doubt it. I honestly don't think I'll ever die.

JOHN HENRY. What is "die"?

FRANKIE. It must be terrible to be nothing but black, black, black.

BERENICE. Yes, baby.

FRANKIE. How many dead people do you know? I know six dead people in all. I'm not counting my mother. There's William Boyd who was killed in Italy. I knew him by sight and name. An' that man who climbed poles for the telephone company. An' Lou Baker. The porter at Finny's place who was murdered in the alley back of Papa's store. Somebody drew a razor on him and the alley people said that his cut throat shivered like a mouth and spoke ghost words to the sun.

JOHN HENRY. Ludie Maxwell Freeman is dead.

FRANKIE. I didn't count Ludie; it wouldn't be fair. Because he died just before I was born. (*To* BERENICE.) Do you think very frequently about Ludie?

BERENICE. You know I do. I think about the five years when me and Ludie was together, and about all the bad times I seen since. Sometimes I almost wish I had never knew Ludie at all. It leaves you too lonesome afterward. When you walk home in the evening on the way from work, it makes a little lonesome quinch come in you. And you take up with too many sorry men to try to get over the feeling.

FRANKIE. But T. T. is not sorry.

BERENICE. I wasn't referring to T. T. He is a fine upstanding colored gentleman, who has walked in a state of grace all his life.

FRANKIE. When are you going to marry with him?

BERENICE. I ain't going to marry with him.

FRANKIE. But you were just now saying . . .

BERENICE. I was saying how sincerely I respect T. T. and sincerely regard T. T. (*There is a pause.*) But he don't make me shiver none.

FRANKIE. Listen, Berenice, I have something queer to tell you. It's something that happened when I was walking around town today. Now I don't exactly know how to explain what I mean.

BERENICE. What is it?

FRANKIE (*now and then pulling her bangs or lower lip*). I was walking along and I passed two stores with a alley in between. The sun was frying hot. And just as I passed this alley, I caught a *glimpse* of something in the corner of my left eye. A dark double shape. And this glimpse brought to my mind—so sudden and clear—my brother and the bride that I just stood there and couldn't hardly bear to look and see what it was.

It was like they were there in that alley, although I knew that they are in Winter Hill almost a hundred miles away. (*There is a pause.*) Then I turn slowly and look. And you know what was there? (*There is a pause.*) It was just two colored boys. That was all. But it gave me such a queer feeling. (BERENICE *has been listening attentively. She stares at* FRANKIE, *then draws a package of cigarettes from her bosom and lights one.*)

BERENICE. Listen at me! Can you see through these bones in my forehead? (*She points to her forehead.*) Have you, Frankie Addams, been reading my mind? (*There is a pause.*) That's the most remarkable thing I ever heard of.

FRANKIE. What I mean is that . . .

BERENICE. I know what you mean. You mean right here in the corner of your eye. (*She points to her eye.*) You suddenly catch something there. And this cold shiver run all the way down you. And you whirl around. And you stand there facing Jesus knows what. But not Ludie, not who you want. And for a minute you feel like you been dropped down a well.

FRANKIE. Yes. That is it. (FRANKIE *reaches for a cigarette and lights it, coughing a bit.*)

BERENICE. Well, that is mighty remarkable. This is a thing been happening to me all my life. Yet just now is the first time I ever heard it put into words. (*There is a pause.*) Yes, that is the way it is when you are in love. A thing known and not spoken.

FRANKIE (*patting her foot*). Yet I always maintained I never believed in love. I didn't admit it and never put any of it in my shows.

JOHN HENRY. I never believed in love.

BERENICE. Now I will tell you something. And it is to be a warning to you. You hear me, John Henry. You hear me, Frankie.

JOHN HENRY. Yes. (*He points his forefinger.*) Frankie is smoking.

BERENICE (*squaring her shoulders*). Now I am here to tell you I was happy. There was no human woman in all the world more happy than I was in them days. And that includes everybody. You listening to me, John Henry? It includes all queens and millionaires and first ladies of the land. And I mean it includes people of all color. You hear me, Frankie? No human woman in all the world was happier than Berenice Sadie Brown.

FRANKIE. The five years you were married to Ludie.

BERENICE. From that autumn morning when I first met him on the road in front of Campbell's Filling Station until the very night he died, November, the year 1933.

FRANKIE. The very year and the very month I was born.

BERENICE. The coldest November I ever seen. Every morning there was frost and puddles were crusted with ice. The sunshine was pale yellow like it is in winter time. Sounds carried far away, and I remember a hound dog that used to howl toward sundown. And everything I seen come to me as a kind of sign.

FRANKIE. I think it is a kind of sign I was born the same year and the same month he died.

BERENICE. And it was a Thursday towards six o'clock. About this time of day. Only November. I remember I went to the passage and opened the front door. Dark was coming on; the old hound was howling far away. And I go back in the room and lay down on Ludie's bed. I lay myself down over Ludie with my arms spread out and my face on his face. And I pray that the Lord would contage my strength to him. And I ask the Lord let it be anybody, but not let it be Ludie. And I lay there and pray for a long time. Until night.

JOHN HENRY. How? (*In a higher, wailing voice.*) How, Berenice?

BERENICE. That night he died. I tell you he died. Ludie! Ludie Freeman! Ludie Maxwell Freeman died! (*She hums.*)

FRANKIE (*after a pause*). It seems to me I feel sadder about Ludie than any other dead person. Although I never knew him. I know I ought to cry sometimes about my mother, or anyhow Granny. But it looks like I can't. But Ludie—maybe it was because I was born so soon after Ludie died. But you were starting out to tell some kind of a warning.

BERENICE (*looking puzzled for a moment*). Warning? Oh, yes! I was going to tell you how this thing we was talking about applies to me. (*As BERENICE begins to talk FRANKIE goes to a shelf above the refrigerator and brings back a fig bar to the table.*) It was the April of the following year that I went one Sunday to the church where the congregation was strange to me. I had my forehead down on the top of the pew in front of me, and my eyes were open—not peeping around in secret, mind you, but just open. When suddenly this shiver ran all the way through me. I had caught sight of something from the corner of my eye. And I looked slowly to the left. There on the pew, just six inches from my eyes, was this *thumb*.

FRANKIE. What thumb?

BERENICE. Now I have to tell you. There was only one small portion of Ludie Freeman which was not pretty. Every other part about him was handsome and pretty as anyone would wish. All except this right thumb. This one thumb had a mashed, chewed appearance that was not pretty. You understand?

FRANKIE. You mean you suddenly saw Ludie's thumb when you were praying?

BERENICE. I mean I seen *this* thumb. And as I knelt there just staring at this thumb, I began to pray in earnest. I prayed out loud! Lord, manifest! Lord, manifest!

FRANKIE. And did He—manifest?

BERENICE. Manifest, my foot! (*Spitting.*) You know who that thumb belonged to?

FRANKIE. Who?

BERENICE. Why, Jamie Beale. That big old no-good Jamie Beale. It was the first time I ever laid eyes on him.

FRANKIE. Is that why you married him? Because he had a mashed thumb like Ludie's?

BERENICE. Lord only knows. I don't. I guess I felt drawn to him on account of that thumb. And then one thing led to another. First thing I know I had married him.

FRANKIE. Well, I think that was silly. To marry him just because of that thumb.

BERENICE. I'm not trying to dispute with you. I'm just telling you what actually happened. And the very same thing occurred in the case of Henry Johnson.

FRANKIE. You mean to sit there and tell me Henry Johnson had one of those mashed thumbs too?

BERENICE. No. It was not the thumb this time. It was the coat. (FRANKIE and JOHN HENRY look at each other in amazement. After a pause BERENICE continues.) Now when Ludie died, them policy people cheated me out of fifty dollars so I pawned everything I could lay hands on, and I sold my coat and Ludie's coat. Because I couldn't let Ludie be put away cheap.

FRANKIE. Oh! Then you mean Henry Johnson bought Ludie's coat and you married him because of it?

BERENICE. Not exactly. I was walking down the street one evening when I suddenly seen this shape appear before me. Now the shape of this boy ahead of me was so similar to Ludie through the shoulders and the back of the head that I almost dropped dead there on the sidewalk. I followed and run behind him. It was Henry Johnson. Since he lived in the country and didn't come into town, he had chanced to buy Ludie's coat and from the back view it looked like he was Ludie's ghost or Ludie's twin. But how I married him I don't exactly know, for, to begin with, it was clear that he did not have his share of sense. But you let a boy hang around and you get fond of him. Anyway, that's how I married Henry Johnson.

FRANKIE. He was the one went crazy

on you. Had eatin' dreams and swallowed the corner of the sheet. (There is a pause.) But I don't understand the point of what you was telling. I don't see how that about Jamie Beale and Henry Johnson applies to me.

BERENICE. Why, it applies to everybody and it is a warning.

FRANKIE. But how?

BERENICE. Why, Frankie, don't you see what I was doing? I loved Ludie and he was the first man I loved. Therefore I had to go and copy myself forever afterward. What I did was to marry off little pieces of Ludie whenever I come across them. It was just my misfortune they all turned out to be the wrong pieces. My intention was to repeat me and Ludie. Now don't you see?

FRANKIE. I see what you're driving at. But I don't see how it is a warning applied to me.

BERENICE. You don't! Then I'll tell you. (FRANKIE does not nod or answer. The piano tuner plays an arpeggio.) You and that wedding tomorrow. That is what I am warning about. I can see right through them two gray eyes of yours like they was glass. And what I see is the saddest piece of foolishness I ever knew.

JOHN HENRY (in a low voice). Gray eyes is glass. (FRANKIE tenses her brows and looks steadily at BERENICE.)

BERENICE. I see what you have in mind. Don't think I don't. You see something unheard of tomorrow, and you right in the center. You think you going to march to the preacher right in between your brother and the bride. You think you going to break into that wedding, and then Jesus knows what else.

FRANKIE. No. I don't see myself walking to the preacher with them.

BERENICE. I see through them eyes. Don't argue with me.

JOHN HENRY (repeating softly). Gray eyes is glass.

BERENICE. But what I'm warning is this. If you start out falling in love with some unheard-of thing like that, what is going to happen to you? If you take a mania like this, it won't be the last time and of that you can be sure. So what will become of you? Will you be trying to break into weddings the rest of your days?

FRANKIE. It makes me sick to listen to people who don't have any sense. (*She sticks her fingers in her ears and hums.*)

BERENICE. You just settin' yourself this fancy trap to catch yourself in trouble. And you know it.

FRANKIE. They will take me. You wait and see.

BERENICE. Well, I been trying to reason seriously. But I see it is no use.

FRANKIE. You are just jealous. You are just trying to deprive me of all the pleasure of leaving town.

BERENICE. I am just trying to head this off. But I still see it is no use.

JOHN HENRY. Gray eyes is glass. (*The piano is played to the seventh note of the scale and this is repeated.*)

FRANKIE (*singing*). Do, ray, mee, fa, sol, la, tee, do. Tee. Tee. It could drive you wild. (*She crosses to the screen door and slams it.*) You didn't say anything about Willis Rhodes. Did he have a mashed thumb or a coat or something? (*She returns to the table and sits down.*)

BERENICE. Lord, now that really was something.

FRANKIE. I only know he stole your furniture and was so terrible you had to call the Law on him.

BERENICE. Well, imagine this! Imagine a cold bitter January night. And me laying all by myself in the big parlor bed. Alone in the house because everybody else had gone for the Saturday night. Me, mind you, who hates to sleep in a big empty bed all by myself at any time. Past twelve o'clock on this cold, bitter January night. Can you remember winter time, John Henry? (JOHN HENRY *nods.*) Imagine! Suddenly there comes a sloughing sound and a tap, tap, tap. So Miss Me . . . (*She laughs uproariously and stops suddenly, putting her hand over her mouth.*)

FRANKIE. What? (*Leaning closer across the table and looking intently at* BERENICE.) What happened? (BERENICE *looks* from one to the other, shaking her head slowly. Then she speaks in a changed voice.*)

BERENICE. Why, I wish you would look yonder. I wish you would look. (FRANKIE *glances quickly behind her, then turns back to* BERENICE.)

FRANKIE. What? What happened?

BERENICE. Look at them two little pitchers and them four big ears. (BERENICE *gets up suddenly from the table.*) Come on, chillin, less us roll out the dough for the cookies tomorrow. (BERENICE *clears the table and begins washing dishes at the sink.*)

FRANKIE. If it's anything I mortally despise, it's a person who starts out to tell something and works up people's interest, and then stops.

BERENICE (*still laughing*). I admit it. And I am sorry. But it was just one of them things I suddenly realized I couldn't tell you and John Henry. (JOHN HENRY *skips up to the sink.*)

JOHN HENRY (*singing*). Cookies! Cookies! Cookies!

FRANKIE. You could have sent him out of the room and told me. But don't think I care a particle about what happened. I just wish Willis Rhodes had come in about that time and slit your throat. (*She goes out into the hall.*)

BERENICE (*still chuckling*). That is a ugly way to talk. You ought to be ashamed. Here, John Henry, I'll give you a scrap of dough to make a cookie man. (BERENICE *gives* JOHN HENRY *some dough. He climbs up on a chair and begins to work with it.* FRANKIE *enters with the evening newspaper. She stands in the doorway, then puts the newspaper on the table.*)

FRANKIE. I see in the paper where we dropped a new bomb—the biggest one dropped yet. They call it a atom bomb. I intend to take two baths tonight. One long soaking bath and scrub with a brush. I'm going to try to scrape this crust off my elbows. Then let out the dirty water and take a second bath.

BERENICE. Hooray, that's a good idea. I will be glad to see you clean.

JOHN HENRY. I will take two baths.

(BERENICE *has picked up the paper and is sitting in a chair against the pale white light of the window. She holds the newspaper open before her and her head is twisted down to one side as she strains to see what is printed there.*)

FRANKIE. Why is it against the law to change your name?

BERENICE. What is that on your neck? I thought it was a head you carried on that neck. Just think. Suppose I would suddenly up and call myself Mrs. Eleanor Roosevelt. And you would begin naming yourself Joe Louis. And John Henry here tried to pawn himself off as Henry Ford.

FRANKIE. Don't talk childish; that is not the kind of changing I mean. I mean from a name that doesn't suit you to a name you prefer. Like I changed from Frankie to F. Jasmine.

BERENICE. But it would be a confusion. Suppose we all suddenly change to entirely different names. Nobody would ever know who anybody was talking about. The whole world would go crazy.

FRANKIE. I don't see what that has to do with it.

BERENICE. Because things accumulate around your name. You have a name and one thing after another happens to you and things have accumulated around the name.

FRANKIE. But what has accumulated around my old name? (BERENICE *does not reply.*) Nothing! See! My name just didn't mean anything. Nothing ever happened to me.

BERENICE. But it will. Things will happen.

FRANKIE. What?

BERENICE. You pin me down like that and I can't tell you truthfully. If I could, I wouldn't be sitting here in this kitchen right now, but making a fine living on Wall Street as a wizard. All I can say is that things will happen. Just what, I don't know.

FRANKIE. Until yesterday, nothing ever happened to me. (JOHN HENRY *crosses to the door and puts on* BERENICE'S *hat and shoes, takes her pocketbook and walks around the table twice.*)

BERENICE. John Henry, take off my hat and my shoes and put up my pocketbook. Thank you very much. (JOHN HENRY *does so.*)

FRANKIE. Listen, Berenice. Doesn't it strike you as strange that I am I and you are you? Like when you are walking down a street and you meet somebody. And you are you. And he is him. Yet when you look at each other, the eyes make a connection. Then you go off one way. And he goes off another way. You go off into different parts of town, and maybe you never see each other again. Not in your whole life. Do you see what I mean?

BERENICE. Not exactly.

FRANKIE. That's not what I meant to say anyway. There are all these people here in town I don't even know by sight or name. And we pass alongside each other and don't have any connection. And they don't know me and I don't know them. And now I'm leaving town and there are all these people I will never know.

BERENICE. But who do you want to know?

FRANKIE. Everybody. Everybody in the world.

BERENICE. Why, I wish you would listen to that. How about people like Willis Rhodes? How about them Germans? How about them Japanese? (FRANKIE *knocks her head against the door jamb and looks up at the ceiling.*)

FRANKIE. That's not what I mean. That's not what I'm talking about.

BERENICE. Well, what *is* you talking about? (*A child's voice is heard outside, calling: "Batter up! Batter up!"*)

JOHN HENRY (*in a low voice*). Less play out, Frankie.

FRANKIE. No. You go. (*After a pause.*) This is what I mean. (BERENICE *waits, and when* FRANKIE *does not speak again, says:*)

BERENICE. What on earth is wrong with you?

FRANKIE (*after a long pause, then suddenly, with hysteria*). Boyoman! Manoboy! When we leave Winter Hill we're going to more places than you ever thought about or even knew existed. Just where we will go first I don't know, and it don't matter. Because after we go to that place we're going on to another. Alaska, China, Iceland, South America. Travelling on trains. Letting her rip on motorcycles. Flying around all over the world in airplanes. Here today and gone tomorrow. All over the world. It's the damn truth. Boyoman! (*She runs around the table.*)

BERENICE. Frankie!

FRANKIE. And talking of things happening. Things will happen so fast we won't hardly have time to realize them. Captain Jarvis Addams wins highest medals and is decorated by the President. Miss F. Jasmine Addams breaks all records. Mrs. Janice Addams elected Miss United Nations in beauty contest. One thing after another happening so fast we don't hardly notice them.

BERENICE. Hold still, fool.

FRANKIE (*her excitement growing more and more intense*). And we will meet them. Everybody. We will just walk up to people and know them right away. We will be walking down a dark road and see a lighted house and knock on the door and strangers will rush to meet us and say: "Come in! Come in!" We will know decorated aviators and New York people and movie stars. We will have thousands and thousands of friends. And we will belong to so many clubs that we can't even keep track of all of them. We will be members of the whole world. Boyoman! Manoboy! (*FRANKIE has been running round and round the table in wild excitement and when she passes the next time BERENICE catches her slip so quickly that she is caught up with a jerk.*)

BERENICE. Is you gone raving wild? (*She pulls FRANKIE closer and puts her arm around her waist.*) Sit here in my lap and rest a minute. (*FRANKIE sits in BERENICE's lap. JOHN HENRY comes close and jealously pinches FRANKIE.*) Leave Frankie alone. She ain't bothered you.

JOHN HENRY. I'm sick.

BERENICE. Now no, you ain't. Be quiet and don't grudge your cousin a little bit love.

JOHN HENRY (*hitting FRANKIE*). Old mean bossy Frankie.

BERENICE. What she doing so mean right now? She just laying here wore out. (*They continue sitting. FRANKIE is relaxed now.*)

FRANKIE. Today I went to the Blue Moon—this place that all the soldiers are so fond of and I met a soldier—a red-headed boy.

BERENICE. What is all this talk about the Blue Moon and soldiers?

FRANKIE. Berenice, you treat me like a child. When I see all these soldiers milling around town I always wonder where they came from and where they are going.

BERENICE. They were born and they going to die.

FRANKIE. There are so many things about the world I do not understand.

BERENICE. If you did understand you would be God. Didn't you know that?

FRANKIE. Maybe so. (*She stares and stretches herself on BERENICE's lap, her long legs sprawled out beneath the kitchen table.*) Anyway, after the wedding I won't have to worry about things any more.

BERENICE. You don't have to now. Nobody requires you to solve the riddles of the world.

FRANKIE (*looking at newspaper*). The paper says this new atom bomb is worth twenty thousand tons of TNT.

BERENICE. Twenty thousand tons? And there ain't but two tons of coal in the coal house—all that coal.

FRANKIE. The paper says the bomb is a very important science discovery.

BERENICE. The figures these days have got too high for me. Read in the paper about ten million peoples killed. I can't crowd that many peoples in my mind's eye.

JOHN HENRY. Berenice, is the glass eye your mind's eye? (*JOHN HENRY has climbed up on the back rungs of BERENICE's chair and has been hugging her head. He is now holding her ears.*)

BERENICE. Don't yank my head back like that, Candy. Me and Frankie ain't going to float up through the ceiling and leave you.

FRANKIE. I wonder if you have ever thought about this? Here we are—right now. This very minute. Now. But while we're talking right now, this minute is passing. And it will never come again. Never in all the world. When it is gone, it is gone. No power on earth could bring it back again.

JOHN HENRY (*beginning to sing*).
I sing because I'm happy,
I sing because I'm free,
For His eye is on the sparrow,
And I know He watches me.

BERENICE (*singing*).
Why should I feel discouraged?
Why should the shadows come?
Why should my heart be lonely,

Away from heaven and home?
For Jesus is my portion,
My constant friend is He,
For His eye is on the sparrow,
And I know He watches me.
So, I sing because I'm happy.

(JOHN HENRY *and* FRANKIE *join on the last three lines.*)
I sing because I'm happy,
I sing because I'm free,
For His eye is on the sparrow,
And I know He watches . . .

BERENICE. Frankie, you got the sharpest set of human bones I ever felt.

THE CURTAIN FALLS

ACT THREE

SCENE 1: *The scene is the same: the kitchen. It is the day of the wedding. When the curtain rises* BERENICE, *in her apron, and* T. T. WILLIAMS, *in a white coat, have just finished preparations for the wedding refreshments.* BERENICE *has been watching the ceremony through the half-open door leading into the hall. There are sounds of congratulations off-stage, the wedding ceremony having just finished.*

BERENICE (*to* T. T. WILLIAMS). Can't see much from this door. But I can see Frankie. And her face is a study. And John Henry's chewing away at the bubble gum that Jarvis bought him. Well, sounds like it's all over. They crowding in now to kiss the bride. We better take this cloth off the sandwiches. Frankie said she would help you serve.

T. T. From the way she's been acting, I don't think we can count much on her.

BERENICE. I wish Honey was here. I'm so worried about him since what you told me. It's going to storm. It's a mercy they didn't decide to have the wedding in the back yard like they first planned.

T. T. I thought I'd better not minch the matter. Honey was in a bad way when I saw him this morning.

BERENICE. Honey Camden don't have too large a share of judgment as it is, but when he gets high on them reefers,

he's got no more judgment than a four-year-old child. Remember that time he swung at the police and nearly got his eyes beat out?

T. T. Not to mention six months on the road.

BERENICE. I haven't been so anxious in all my life. I've got two people scouring Sugarville to find him. (*In a fervent voice.*) God, you took Ludie but please watch over my Honey Camden. He's all the family I got.

T. T. And Frankie behaving this way about the wedding. Poor little critter.

BERENICE. And the sorry part is that she's perfectly serious about all this foolishness. (FRANKIE *enters the kitchen through the hall door.*) Is it all over? (T. T. *crosses to the icebox with sandwiches.*)

FRANKIE. Yes. And it was such a pretty wedding I wanted to cry.

BERENICE. You told them yet?

FRANKIE. About my plans—no, I haven't yet told them. (JOHN HENRY *comes in and goes out.*)

BERENICE. Well, you better hurry up and do it, for they going to leave the house right after the refreshments.

FRANKIE. Oh, I know it. But something just seems to happen to my throat; every time I tried to tell them, different words came out.

BERENICE. What words?

FRANKIE. I asked Janice how come she didn't marry with a veil. (*With feeling.*) Oh, I'm so embarrassed. Here I am all dressed up in this tacky evening dress. Oh, why didn't I listen to you! I'm so ashamed. (T. T. *goes out with a platter of sandwiches.*)

BERENICE. Don't take everything so strenuous like.

FRANKIE. I'm going in there and tell them now! (*She goes.*)

JOHN HENRY (*coming out of the interior bedroom, carrying several costumes*). Frankie sure gave me a lot of presents when she was packing the suitcase. Berenice, she gave me all the beautiful show costumes.

BERENICE. Don't set so much store by all those presents. Come tomorrow morning and she'll be demanding them back again.

JOHN HENRY. And she even gave me the shell from the Bay. (*He puts the shell to his ear and listens.*)

BERENICE. I wonder what's going on up there. (*She goes to the door and opens it and looks through.*)

T. T. (*returning to the kitchen*). They all complimenting the wedding cake. And drinking the wine punch.

BERENICE. What's Frankie doing? When she left the kitchen a minute ago she was going to tell them. I wonder how they'll take this total surprise. I have a feeling like you get just before a big thunder storm. (FRANKIE *enters, holding a punch cup.*)

BERENICE. You told them yet?

FRANKIE. There are all the family around and I can't seem to tell them. I wish I had written it down on the typewriter beforehand. I try to tell them and the words just—die.

BERENICE. The words just die because the very idea is so silly.

FRANKIE. I love the two of them so much. Janice put her arms around me and said she had always wanted a little sister. And she kissed me. She asked me again what grade I was in in school. That's the third time she's asked me. In fact, that's the main question I've been asked at the wedding. (JOHN HENRY *comes in, wearing a fairy costume, and*

goes out. BERENICE *notices* FRANKIE's *punch and takes it from her.*)

FRANKIE. And Jarvis was out in the street seeing about this car he borrowed for the wedding. And I followed him out and tried to tell him. But while I was trying to reach the point, he suddenly grabbed me by the elbows and lifted me up and sort of swung me. He said: "Frankie, the lankie, the alaga fankie, the tee-legged, toe-legged, bow-legged Frankie." And he gave me a dollar bill.

BERENICE. That's nice.

FRANKIE. I just don't know what to do. I have to tell them and yet I don't know how to.

BERENICE. Maybe when they're settled, they will invite you to come and visit with them.

FRANKIE. Oh no! I'm going *with* them. (FRANKIE *goes back into the house. There are louder sounds of voices from the interior.* JOHN HENRY *comes in again.*)

JOHN HENRY. The bride and the groom are leaving. Uncle Royal is taking their suitcases out to the car. (FRANKIE *runs to the interior room and returns with her suitcase. She kisses* BERENICE.)

FRANKIE. Good-bye, Berenice. Good-bye, John Henry. (*She stands a moment and looks around the kitchen.*) Farewell, old ugly kitchen. (*She runs out. There are sounds of good-byes as the wedding party and the family guests move out of the house to the sidewalk. The voices get fainter in the distance. Then, from the front sidewalk there is the sound of disturbance.* FRANKIE's *voice is heard, diminished by distance, although she is speaking loudly.*)

FRANKIE'S VOICE. That's what I am telling you. (*Indistinct protesting voices are heard.*)

MR. ADDAMS' VOICE (*indistinctly*). Now be reasonable, Frankie.

FRANKIE'S VOICE (*screaming*). I have to go. Take me! Take me!

JOHN HENRY (*entering excitedly*). Frankie is in the wedding car and they can't get her out. (*He runs out but soon returns.*) Uncle Royal and my Daddy are having to haul and drag old Frankie. She's holding onto the steering wheel.

MR. ADDAMS' VOICE. You march right

along here. What in the world has come into you? (*He comes into the kitchen with* FRANKIE *who is sobbing.*) I never heard of such an exhibition in my life. Berenice, you take charge of her. (FRANKIE *flings herself on the kitchen chair and sobs with her head in her arms on the kitchen table.*)

JOHN HENRY. They put old Frankie out of the wedding. They hauled her out of the wedding car.

MR. ADDAMS (*clearing his throat*). That's sufficient, John Henry. Leave Frankie alone. (*He puts a caressing hand on* FRANKIE'S *head.*) What makes you want to leave your old papa like this? You've got Janice and Jarvis all upset on their wedding day.

FRANKIE. I love them so!

BERENICE (*looking down the hall*). Here they come. Now please be reasonable, Sugar. (*The bride and groom come in.* FRANKIE *keeps her face buried in her arms and does not look up. The bride wears a blue suit with a white flower corsage pinned at the shoulder.*)

JARVIS. Frankie, we came to tell you good-bye. I'm sorry you're taking it like this.

JANICE. Darling, when we are settled we want you to come for a nice visit with us. But we don't yet have any place to live. (*She goes to* FRANKIE *and caresses her head.* FRANKIE *jerks.*) Won't you tell us good-bye now?

FRANKIE (*with passion*). We! When you say *we*, you only mean you and Jarvis. And I am not included. (*She buries her head in her arms again and sobs.*)

JANICE. Please, darling, don't make us unhappy on our wedding day. You know we love you.

FRANKIE. See! *We*—when you say we, I am not included. It's not fair.

JANICE. When you come visit us you must write beautiful plays, and we'll all act in them. Come, Frankie, don't hide your sweet face from us. Sit up. (FRANKIE *raises her head slowly and stares with a look of wonder and misery.*) Good-bye, Frankie, darling.

JARVIS. So long, now, kiddo. (*They go out and* FRANKIE *still stares at them as*

they go down the hall. She rises, crosses towards the door and falls on her knees.)

FRANKIE. Take me! Take me! (BERENICE *puts* FRANKIE *back on her chair.*)

JOHN HENRY. They put Frankie out of the wedding. They hauled her out of the wedding car.

BERENICE. Don't tease your cousin, John Henry.

FRANKIE. It was a frame-up all around.

BERENICE. Well, don't bother no more about it. It's over now. Now cheer up.

FRANKIE. I wish the whole world would die.

BERENICE. School will begin now in only three more weeks and you'll find another bosom friend like Evelyn Owen you so wild about.

JOHN HENRY (*seated below the sewing machine*). I'm sick, Berenice. My head hurts.

BERENICE. No you're not. Be quiet, I don't have the patience to fool with you.

FRANKIE (*hugging her hunched shoulders*). Oh, my heart feels so cheap!

BERENICE. Soon as you get started in school and have a chance to make these here friends, I think it would be a good idea to have a party.

FRANKIE. Those baby promises rasp on my nerves.

BERENICE. You could call up the society editor of the *Evening Journal* and have the party written up in the paper. And that would make the fourth time your name has been published in the paper.

FRANKIE (*with a trace of interest*). When my bike ran into that automobile, the paper called me Fankie Addams, F-A-N-K-I-E. (*She puts her head down again.*)

JOHN HENRY. Frankie, don't cry. This evening we can put up the teepee and have a good time.

FRANKIE. Oh, hush up your mouth.

BERENICE. Listen to me. Tell me what you would like and I will try to do it if it is in my power.

FRANKIE. All I wish in the world, is for no human being ever to speak to me as long as I live.

BERENICE. Bawl, then, misery. (MR. ADDAMS *enters the kitchen, carrying*

FRANKIE'S *suitcase, which he sets in the middle of the kitchen floor. He cracks his finger joints.* FRANKIE *stares at him resentfully, then fastens her gaze on the suitcase.*)

MR. ADDAMS. Well, it looks like the show is over and the monkey's dead.

FRANKIE. You think it's over, but it's not.

MR. ADDAMS. You want to come down and help me at the store tomorrow? Or polish some silver with the shammy rag? You can even play with those old watch springs.

FRANKIE (*still looking at her suitcase*). That's my suitcase I packed. If you think it's all over, that only shows how little you know. (T. T. *comes in.*) If I can't go with the bride and my brother as I was meant to leave this town, I'm going anyway. Somehow, anyhow, I'm leaving town. (FRANKIE *raises up in her chair.*) I can't stand this existence—this kitchen—this town—any longer! I will hop a train and go to New York. Or hitch rides to Hollywood, and get a job there. If worse comes to worse, I can act in comedies. (*She rises.*) Or I could dress up like a boy and join the Merchant Marines and run away to sea. Somehow, anyhow, I'm running away.

BERENICE. Now quiet down—

FRANKIE (*grabbing the suitcase and running into the hall*). Please, Papa, don't try to capture me. (*Outside the wind starts to blow.*)

JOHN HENRY (*from the doorway*). Uncle Royal, Frankie's got your pistol in her suitcase. (*There is the sound of running footsteps and of the screen door slamming.*)

BERENICE. Run catch her. (T. T. *and* MR. ADDAMS *rush into the hall, followed by* JOHN HENRY.)

MR. ADDAMS' VOICE. Frankie! Frankie! Frankie! (BERENICE *is left alone in the kitchen. Outside the wind is higher and the hall door is blown shut. There is a rumble of thunder, then a loud clap. Thunder and flashes of lightning continue.* BERENICE *is seated in her chair, when* JOHN HENRY *comes in.*)

JOHN HENRY. Uncle Royal is going with my Daddy, and they are chasing her in our car. (*There is a thunder clap.*) The thunder scares me, Berenice.

BERENICE (*taking him in her lap*). Ain't nothing going to hurt you.

JOHN HENRY. You think they're going to catch her?

BERENICE (*putting her hand to her head*). Certainly. They'll be bringing her home directly. I've got such a headache. Maybe my eye socket and all these troubles.

JOHN HENRY (*with his arms around* BERENICE). I've got a headache, too. I'm sick, Berenice.

BERENICE. No you ain't. Run along, Candy. I ain't got the patience to fool with you now. (*Suddenly the lights go out in the kitchen, plunging it in gloom. The sound of wind and storm continues and the yard is a dark storm-green.*)

JOHN HENRY. Berenice!

BERENICE. Ain't nothing. Just the lights went out.

JOHN HENRY. I'm scared.

BERENICE. Stand still, I'll just light a candle. (*Muttering.*) I always keep one around, for such like emergencies. (*She opens a drawer.*)

JOHN HENRY. What makes the lights go out so scarey like this?

BERENICE. Just one of them things, Candy.

JOHN HENRY. I'm scared. Where's Honey?

BERENICE. Jesus knows. I'm scared, too. With Honey snow-crazy and loose like this—and Frankie run off with a suitcase and her Papa's pistol. I feel like every nerve been picked out of me.

JOHN HENRY (*holding out his seashell and stroking* BERENICE). You want to listen to the ocean?

THE CURTAIN FALLS.

SCENE 2: *The scene is the same. There are still signs in the kitchen of the wedding: punch glasses and the punch bowl on the drainboard. It is four o'clock in the morning. As the curtain rises,* BERENICE *and* MR. ADDAMS *are alone in the kitchen. There is a crepuscular glow in the yard.*

MR. ADDAMS. I never was a believer in

corporal punishment. Never spanked Frankie in my life, but when I lay my hands on her . . .

BERENICE. She'll show up soon—but I know how you feel. What with worrying about Honey Camden, John Henry's sickness and Frankie, I've never lived through such a anxious night. (*She looks through the window. It is dawning now.*)

MR. ADDAMS. I'd better go and find out the last news of John Henry, poor baby. (*He goes through the hall door. FRANKIE comes into the yard and crosses to the arbor. She looks exhausted and almost beaten. BERENICE has seen her from the window, rushes into the yard and grabs her by the shoulders and shakes her.*)

BERENICE. Frankie Addams, you ought to be skinned alive. I been so worried.

FRANKIE. I've been so worried too.

BERENICE. Where have you been this night? Tell me everything.

FRANKIE. I will, but quit shaking me.

BERENICE. Now tell me the A and the Z of this.

FRANKIE. When I was running around the dark scarey streets, I begun to realize that my plans for Hollywood and the Merchant Marines were child plans that would not work. I hid in the alley behind Papa's store, and it was dark and I was scared. I opened the suitcase and took out Papa's pistol. (*She sits down on her suitcase.*) I vowed I was going to shoot myself. I said I was going to count three and on three pull the trigger. I counted one—two—but I didn't count three—because at the last minute, I changed my mind.

BERENICE. You march right along with me. You going to bed.

FRANKIE. Oh, Honey Camden! (*HONEY CAMDEN BROWN, who has been hiding behind the arbor, has suddenly appeared.*)

BERENICE. Oh, Honey, Honey. (*They embrace.*)

HONEY. Shush, don't make any noise; the law is after me.

BERENICE (*in a whisper*). Tell me.

HONEY. Mr. Wilson wouldn't serve me so I drew a razor on him.

BERENICE. You kill him?

HONEY. Didn't have no time to find out. I been runnin' all night.

FRANKIE. Lightfoot, if you drew a razor on a white man, you'd better not let them catch you.

BERENICE. Here's six dolla's. If you can get to Fork Falls and then to Atlanta. But be careful slippin' through the white folks' section. They'll be combing the county looking for you.

HONEY (*with passion*). Don't cry, Berenice.

BERENICE. Already I feel that rope.

HONEY. Don't you dare cry. I know now all my days have been leading up to this minute. No more "boy this—boy that"—no bowing, no scraping. For the first time, I'm free and it makes me happy. (*He begins to laugh hysterically.*)

BERENICE. When they catch you, they'll string you up.

HONEY (*beside himself, brutally*). Let them hang me—I don't care. I tell you I'm glad. I tell you I'm happy. (*He goes out behind the arbor.*)

FRANKIE (*calling after him*). Honey, remember you are Lightfoot. Nothing can stop you if you want to run away. (*MRS. WEST, JOHN HENRY's mother, comes into the yard.*)

MRS. WEST. What was all that racket? John Henry is critically ill. He's got to have perfect quiet.

FRANKIE. John Henry's sick, Aunt Pet?

MRS. WEST. The doctors say he has meningitis. He must have perfect quiet.

BERENICE. I haven't had time to tell you yet. John Henry took sick sudden last night. Yesterday afternoon when I complained of my head, he said he had a headache too and thinking he copies me I said, "Run along, I don't have the patience to fool with you." Looks like a judgment on me. There won't be no more noise, Mrs. West.

MRS. WEST. Make sure of that. (*She goes away.*)

FRANKIE (*putting her arm around BERENICE*). Oh, Berenice, what can we do?

BERENICE (*stroking FRANKIE's head*). Ain't nothing we can do but wait.

FRANKIE. The wedding—Honey—John Henry—so much has happened that my brain can't hardly gather it in. Now for the first time I realize that the world is certainly—a sudden place.

BERENICE. Sometimes sudden, but when you are waiting, like this, it seems so slow.

THE CURTAIN FALLS.

SCENE 3: *The scene is the same: the kitchen and arbor. It is months later, a November day, about sunset. The arbor is brittle and withered. The elm tree is bare except for a few ragged leaves. The yard is tidy and the lemonade stand and sheet stage curtain are now missing. The kitchen is neat and bare and the furniture has been removed.* BERENICE, *wearing a fox fur, is sitting in a chair with an old suitcase and doll at her feet.* FRANKIE *enters.*

FRANKIE. Oh, I am just mad about these Old Masters.

BERENICE. Humph!

FRANKIE. The house seems so hollow. Now that the furniture is packed. It gives me a creepy feeling in the front. That's why I came back here.

BERENICE. Is that the only reason why you came back here?

FRANKIE. Oh, Berenice, you know. I wish you hadn't given quit notice just because Papa and I are moving into a new house with Uncle Eustace and Aunt Pet out in Limewood.

BERENICE. I respect and admire Mrs. West but I'd never get used to working for her.

FRANKIE. Mary is just beginning this Rachmaninoff Concerto. She may play it for her debut when she is eighteen years old. Mary playing the piano and the whole orchestra playing at one and the same time, mind you. Awfully hard.

BERENICE. Ma-ry Littlejohn.

FRANKIE. I don't know why you always have to speak her name in a tinged voice like that.

BERENICE. Have I ever said anything against her? All I said was that she is too lumpy and marshmallow white and it makes me nervous to see her just setting there sucking them pigtails.

FRANKIE. Braids. Furthermore, it is no use our discussing a certain party. You could never possibly understand it. It's just not in you. (BERENICE *looks at her sadly, with faded stillness, then pats and strokes the fox fur.*)

BERENICE. Be that as it may. Less us not fuss and quarrel this last afternoon.

FRANKIE. I don't want to fuss either. Anyway, this is not our last afternoon. I will come and see you often.

BERENICE. No, you won't, baby. You'll have other things to do. Your road is already strange to me. (FRANKIE *goes to* BERENICE, *pats her on the shoulder, then takes her fox fur and examines it.*)

FRANKIE. You still have the fox fur that Ludie gave you. Somehow this little fur looks so sad—so thin and with a sad little fox-wise face.

BERENICE (*taking the fur back and continuing to stroke it*). Got every reason to be sad. With what has happened in these two last months. I just don't know what I have done to deserve it. (*She sits, the fur in her lap, bent over with her forearms on her knees and her hands limply dangling.*) Honey gone and John Henry, my little boy gone.

FRANKIE. You did all you could. You got poor Honey's body and gave him a Christian funeral and nursed John Henry.

BERENICE. It's the way Honey died and the fact that John Henry had to suffer so. Little soul!

FRANKIE. It's peculiar—the way it all happened so fast. First Honey caught and hanging himself in the jail. Then later in that same week, John Henry died and then I met Mary. As the irony of fate would have it, we first got to know each other in front of the lipstick and cosmetics counter at Woolworth's. And it was the week of the fair.

BERENICE. The most beautiful September I ever seen. Countless white and yellow butterflies flying around them autumn flowers—Honey dead and John Henry suffering like he did and daisies, golden weather, butterflies—such strange death weather.

FRANKIE. I never believed John Henry

would die. (*There is a long pause. She looks out the window.*) Don't it seem quiet to you in here? (*There is another, longer pause.*) When I was a little child I believed that out under the arbor at night there would come three ghosts and one of the ghosts wore a silver ring. (*Whispering.*) Occasionally when it gets so quiet like this I have a strange feeling. It's like John Henry is hovering somewhere in this kitchen—solemn looking and ghost-grey.

A Boy's Voice (*from the neighboring yard*). Frankie, Frankie.

FRANKIE (*calling to the boy*). Yes, Barney. (*To* BERENICE.) Clock stopped. (*She shakes the clock.*)

THE BOY'S VOICE. Is Mary there?

FRANKIE (*to* BERENICE). It's Barney MacKean. (*To the boy, in a sweet voice.*) Not yet. I'm meeting her at five. Come on in, Barney, won't you?

BARNEY. Just a minute.

FRANKIE (*to* BERENICE). Barney puts me in mind of a Greek god.

BERENICE. What? Barney puts you in mind of a what?

FRANKIE. Of a Greek god. Mary remarked that Barney reminded her of a Greek god.

BERENICE. It looks like I can't understand a thing you say no more.

FRANKIE. You know, those old-timey Greeks worship those Greek gods.

BERENICE. But what has that got to do with Barney MacKean?

FRANKIE. On account of the figure. (BARNEY MACKEAN, *a boy of thirteen, wearing a football suit, bright sweater and cleated shoes, runs up the back steps into the kitchen.*)

BERENICE. Hi, Greek god Barney. This afternoon I saw your initials chalked down on the front sidewalk. M. L. loves B. M.

BARNEY. If I could find out who wrote it, I would rub it out with their faces. Did you do it, Frankie?

FRANKIE (*drawing herself up with sudden dignity*). I wouldn't do a kid thing like that. I even resent you asking me. (*She repeats the phrase to herself in a pleased undertone.*) Resent you asking me.

BARNEY. Mary can't stand me anyhow.

FRANKIE. Yes she can stand you. I am her most intimate friend. I ought to know. As a matter of fact she's told me several lovely compliments about you. Mary and I are riding on the moving van to our new house. Would you like to go?

BARNEY. Sure.

FRANKIE. O.K. You will have to ride back with the furniture 'cause Mary and I are riding on the front seat with the driver. We had a letter from Jarvis and Janice this afternoon. Jarvis is with the Occupation Forces in Germany and they took a vacation trip to Luxembourg. (*She repeats in a pleased voice:*) Luxembourg. Berenice, don't you think that's a lovely name?

BERENICE. It's kind of a pretty name, but it reminds me of soapy water.

FRANKIE. Mary and I will most likely pass through Luxembourg when we—are going around the world together. (FRANKIE *goes out followed by* BARNEY *and* BERENICE *sits in the kitchen alone and motionless. She picks up the doll, looks at it and hums the first two lines of "I Sing Because I'm Happy." In the next house the piano is heard again, as*)

THE CURTAIN FALLS.

SUGGESTED TOPICS FOR FURTHER STUDY AND DISCUSSION

1. Read a good example of the Restoration comedy of manners, something like Etherege's *The Man of Mode*, Vanbrugh's *The Relapse*, or Congreve's *The Way of the World*. Read one of the "better" sentimental comedies of the eighteenth century, like Cibber's *The Careless Husband*, or Steele's *The Conscious Lovers*. Then study a "laughing" comedy, such as Goldsmith's *She Stoops to Conquer* or Sheridan's *The Rivals*. Trace the elements of genuine comedy in each, and show how the sentimental comedy failed as good drama.

2. The "melodrama of tears" has much in common with the sentimental comedies of the nineteenth and early twentieth centuries. Read *East Lynne*, *Way Down East*, *The Two Orphans*, *The Old Homestead*, or others. Which are "melodrama" and which are "comedy"? Does Herne's *Shore Acres* belong in this category? Why, or why not?

3. Read all of *Lightnin'*. Evaluate it by today's standards of comedy in plot, character, and dialogue. Try to determine why it had one of the longest runs in history.

4. Read *They Knew What They Wanted*. If you do not consider it a comedy, defend your judgment of whatever classification you use. You might find it interesting to read Robert E. Sherwood's *The Petrified Forest*, which is also inhabited by some rather pathetic characters who appeal to our sensibilities. It is often called a melodrama. Is it? Does it have some of the qualities of the comedy of sensibility?

5. Sentimentality was one of the trademarks of the British writer, James M. Barrie, who wrote many of his plays for the beautiful Maude Adams, an American star. She often appeared in his plays in New York before they were given in London. In revival today, Barrie appears too obviously "cute" in many respects. Read and evaluate two or three: *What Every Woman Knows*, *The Little Minister*, *The Old Lady Shows Her Medals* (one-act), *Quality Street*, *Alice Sit-by-the-Fire*. Do not include his fantasies like *Peter Pan*, *Mary Rose*, or *Dear Brutus*.

6. "Domestic" comedies of recent decades have often been popular. In fact, one of them, Lindsay and Crouse's *Life with Father*, established the all-time record run for a Broadway play—more than seven years. Study it in conjunction with Eugene O'Neill's *Ah, Wilderness!* John Van Druten's *I Remember Mamma*, Rose Franken's *Claudia*, and even Thornton Wilder's *Our Town*. Is *Life with Father* a domestic comedy, or a comedy of sensibility, or is it a comedy at all? How much of the value of these plays rests upon genuine drama? Upon legitimate comedy? Upon overt sentimentality?

7. Study plays by William Saroyan: *The Beautiful People*, *My Heart's in the Highlands*, *The Time of Your Life*. Discuss them in terms of the comedy of sensibility. Also read some of his stories. What is Saroyan's attitude toward mankind in general? Can you compare him with Barrie or another modern playwright?

8. William Inge has written both seriously and comically about the pathos of ordinary life. Read his *Picnic*, *Bus Stop*, and *The Dark at the Top of the Stairs*. Could you classify them as comedies of sensibility? What theme runs through all of Inge's plays? Can you discover why his first four plays (beginning with *Come Back, Little Sheba*) were four consecutive major successes on Broadway?

9. Tennessee Williams is not normally associated with comedy of any sort. *The Rose Tattoo* is his closest approach. Judge it as a comedy. If you cannot accept it as comedy, what is it?

Fantasy suggests pleasant associations attendant upon the play of imagination, involving caprice and whimsy, without exaggeration or distortion. *Fantastic* has the connotation of strangeness, weird appearance and extravagance, lack of imaginative restraint, and a tendency toward the grotesque. Both may touch the *supernatural*, based upon miraculous forces and, frequently, objects of fear. *Whimsy* and *caprice* each suggest impulsive and often freakish departure from what is expected. Whimsy is quaint and fanciful, with a warm and attractive charm. Caprice, less motivated, can be arbitrary and even unpleasant. Comedy survives best under the gentler hand of fantasy emphasizing the quiet subtleties of whimsy.

The fantastic as a dramatic form is more closely allied with expressionism, which distorts and exaggerates by fantastic images. The expressionist, however, is interpreting reality in a world that *does* exist; the writer of fantasy creates a world that *might* exist. Dramatic expressionism and dramatic fantasy use the same theatrical tools, but each is sold on different terms.

Historically, fantasy has been an important dramatic ingredient. Ever since the fifth century B.C., when in *The Frogs*, Aristophanes dispatched Dionysus into Hades to conduct a poetry contest between Aeschylus and Euripides, stage comedy has often been at its best in the imaginative flights of its author's fancy. The display of flaming Hellmouth and the fork-tailed demons of medieval religious drama was a familiar interpretation of a place that very much concerned the lives of those who watched. To the Elizabethan citizen ghostly spirits, fairies, and elves interfered directly in human affairs. Shakespeare in *A Midsummer Night's Dream* and *The Tempest* relied upon the imaginative enjoyment of fantasy and the fantastic. The ultrasophistication of the Restoration and the sentimentalities of the eighteenth century were poor ground for pleasant fantasy, and its best revival in the late eighteenth and early nineteenth centuries came from Germany, where it achieved great heights in Goethe's *Faust*. Most fantasies, however, were wild melodramas in the style of Kotzebue's Gothic horrors, so popular in the early American theatre.

Throughout Europe good drama of fantasy, as distinct from the elaborately fantastic, began to appear in the 1890s and the early twentieth century. Maeterlinck's *Pelléas et Mélisande* (1892) and *The Bluebird* (1908), Barrie's *Peter Pan* (1905), perhaps the most famous of all, and Molnar's *Liliom* in 1909 dwelt in lands beyond normal existence. In 1922 Pirandello's search for the "real" in reality supplied the fantasy drama of *Six Characters in Search of an Author*.

Twentieth-century Fantasy

Augustus Thomas' *The Witching Hour* (1907) and William Vaughn Moody's *The Faith Healer* (1909) were early twentieth-century American plays which made considerable use of the fantastic and the supernatural but Percy MacKaye's *The Scarecrow* (1908) was the first to strike at the heart of true fantasy in its make-believe, fairy-tale basis.

MacKaye's play was not produced until 1910. It is an adaptation of Nathaniel Hawthorne's tale, "Feathertop," about a New England witch who creates a fine-looking seventeenth-century gentleman from a broomstick and a pumpkin. Hawthorne's story is a satire upon the foppish foolishness of artificial society, which will accept an individual without question so long as his dress is elegant and his pedigree impressive. MacKaye goes beyond Hawthorne's basic idea and calls his play *A Tragedy of the Ludicrous*, explaining that he conceived his scarecrow, Ravensbane, as "an emblem of human bathos" rather than the superficial fop of Hawthorne's Feathertop. Although changed in many respects, MacKaye's adaptation retains the essence of Hawthorne's fantasy in the creation of his hero and in the amusing byplay of Goody Rickby, the witch, and Dickon, the devil. As the following scene demonstrates, he also hands his producer some tricky stage problems.

MacKaye's Mother Rickby designs her scarecrow to avenge herself upon the local Justice Merton for having fathered a child upon her and for having deserted them both. She sends her fantastic handiwork to woo and win the Judge's daughter, Rachel. The Judge believes the creature is his illegitimate son, but Rachel's betrothed, Richard, begins to suspect witchcraft, especially since the otherwise dignified Lord Ravensbane smokes his pipe unceasingly. At a family gathering, Richard decides to force the issue with a "Mirror of Truth" which Rachel has purchased from Goody Rickby. Just as Ravensbane is pinning a tassel from his uniform on Rachel's breast, Richard pulls back the curtain and uncovers the mirror. Rachel screams, "Do not look!"

> (*In the glass are reflected the figures of* RACHEL *and* RAVENSBANE—RACHEL *just as she herself appears, but* RAVENSBANE *in his essential form of a scarecrow, in every movement reflecting* RAVENSBANE's *motions. The thing in the glass is about to pin a wisp of corn silk on the mirrored breast of the maiden.*)
>
> RAVENSBANE. What is there?
>
> RACHEL (*looking again, starts away from* RAVENSBANE). Leave me! Leave me!—Richard!
>
> RAVENSBANE (*gazing at the glass, clings to* RACHEL *as though to protect her*). Help her! See! It is seizing her.
>
> RACHEL. Richard! (*She faints in* RICHARD's *arms.*)
>
> RAVENSBANE. Fear not, mistress, I will kill the thing. (*Drawing his sword, he rushes at the glass. Within, the scarecrow, with a drawn wheel spoke, approaches him at equal speed. They come face to face and recoil.*) Ah! ah! fear'st thou me? What art thou? Why, 'tis a glass. Thou mockest me? Look, look, mistress, it mocks me! O God, no! no! Take it away. Dear God, do not look!—It is I!
>
> ALL (*rushing to the doors*). Witchcraft! Witchcraft! (*As* RAVENSBANE *stands frantically confronting his abject reflection, struck in a like posture of despair, the curtain falls.*)

Later, Ravensbane attempts to solve his problem and converses with Dickon:

RAVENSBANE. This pipe, this ludicrous pipe that I forever set to my lips and puff! Why must I, Dickon? Why?

DICKON. To avoid extinction—merely. You see, 'tis just as your fellow in there (*Pointing to the glass.*) explained. You yourself are the subtlest of mirrors, polished out of pumpkin and pipesmoke. Into this mirror the fair Mistress Rachel has projected her lovely image, and thus provided you with what men call a soul.

RAVENSBANE. Ah! then, I have a soul—the truth of me? Mistress Rachel has indeed made me a man?

DICKON. Don't flatter thyself, cobby. Break thy pipe, and whiff—soul, Mistress Rachel, man, truth, and this pretty world itself, go up in the last smoke.

RAVENSBANE. No, no! not Mistress Rachel—for she is beautiful; and the images of beauty are immutable. She told me so.

At the end of the play, Ravensbane dares to defy the powers of Dickon and Goody Ricky, breaks the pipe, and dies no longer a scarecrow but a man. His love for Rachel has brought him his soul. The denouement is not Hawthorne, but it is good theatre.

A poetic fantasy by Josephine Preston Peabody called *The Piper* won first prize in a contest for the best original play with which to open England's new Stratford-on-Avon Theatre in 1910. Based mainly on Browning's version of the Pied Piper, it uses fantasy to expose human faults of narrow selfishness without the harsh tone of the satirist. Mrs. Peabody also adds a happy ending to the tragedy of Hamelin by returning the children to their homes. The play is of minor importance today but remains unique as one of the few successful poetic dramas at the beginning of the twentieth century.

Postwar Adventures in Time Travel

The sophisticated 1920s had little patience for the quiet charms of fantasy. This was an era of gay sexual freedom, social emancipation, prosperity and "normalcy." On the stage experimentation with Continental expressionism vied with high-comedy chitchat. It is therefore somewhat surprising to see a "gentle" play like John Balderston's *Berkeley Square* become one of the more popular dramas of 1929. It raises a favorite question: is it possible to travel in time?

Berkeley Square (the British pronounce it "Barkly") is based on Henry James' unfinished novel, "A Sense of the Past." Peter Standish, a descendant of an eighteenth-century English family, lives in his ancestral mansion on Berkeley Square, London. He has become convinced that it is possible to exist simultaneously in two different periods of time. Physically ill with the obsession of his idea, he attempts to explain it to his friend, the Ambassador:

PETER. . . . Now look here. Here's an idea. Suppose you are in a boat, sailing down a winding stream. You watch the banks as they pass you. You went by a grove of maple trees, upstream. But you can't see them now, so you saw them in the *past*, didn't you? You're watching a field of clover now;

it's before your eyes at this moment, in the *present*. But you don't know
yet what's around the bend in the stream there ahead of you. There may
be wonderful things, but you can't see them until you get around the bend
in the *future*, can you? (AMBASSADOR *nods; he listens politely.*) Now remember, *you're* in the boat. But *I'm* up in the sky above you, in a plane.
I'm looking down on it all. I can see *all at once!* So the past, present, and
future to the man in the boat are all *one* to the man in the plane. Doesn't
that show how all Time must really be one? Real Time—real Time is nothing but an idea in the mind of God!

The scene closes as Peter finds that his theories have gone beyond speculation
and that he is able to thrust himself into the English world of 1784. He discovers, of course, that the beautiful pure life he was sure he would find is an
ugly, uncouth existence. His weird behavior is taken for witchcraft, and the
local churchman, Throstle, attempts to exorcise the devil in him. Only Helen
Pettigrew, with whom he has fallen in love and whom he cannot marry
because of the facts of history, finally realizes what he is. When he is at last
crowded to the wall and accused of being a demon out of hell, he turns on his
tormentors:

PETER. . . . Insolence, ignorance and dirt! . . . God! What a Period! Dirt,
disease, cruelty, smells! A new fire of London, that's what's needed here;
yes, and a new plague, too! God, how the Eighteenth Century stinks! . . .
What do I care about you? You're all over and done with! (*Sidles along
rear wall, afraid, grasping curtain of window for support.*) You're all dead
—you've all rotted in your graves—you're all ghosts, that's what you are—
ghosts!

Peter is finally forced back into the present age by his recognition that he
can never be a part of two worlds. At the final curtain he is still grieving for
the girl he had to leave behind nearly a century and a half before.

High-quality fantasy is a rare thing on the modern stage. There have been
some excellent plays of remarkable imaginative quality, but they have been
infrequent. The poet, Edna St. Vincent Millay, made life a harlequinade on
a make-believe stage in her beautiful and poetic one-act *Aria da Capo* in
1920. Philip Barry's *Hotel Universe* turned grownups into children in 1930,
and Elmer Rice's *Dream Girl* of 1945 underscored many human wishes. In
1950 the British John Van Druten delighted audiences with his gentle witches
in *Bell, Book, and Candle,* and Gore Vidal brought a suave and appealing
gentleman from outer space into the maze of Washington's red tape in 1957
with *Visit to a Small Planet.*

Fantasy has its important place in modern drama. There is absolutely nothing
wrong in seeking theatrical entertainment in a full evening of unbridled make-
believe. After all, it is the province of the theatre to be a place where man's
ideas, fears, and joys receive their graphic interpretation without artistic
restriction. Perhaps we need more of good fantasy to counter the heavy dosage
of "grim reality" that threatens to overwhelm the midcentury stage.

Harvey

Harvey was one of those sensational New York successes which, by all conventional standards of good theatre, should not have lasted a week. In style it is at once realism and whimsical fantasy; satire alternates with broad, almost slapstick, farce. The play is constructed with a lopsided first act, overweighted with wild improbabilities; afterward, it slows down to an unhurried walk. It has an uninteresting love affair that soon atrophies for lack of nourishment. Though some of the important characters are wonderfully rounded, others enter and exit with little more than sketchy outline of their personalities. The play endures without plot and works a single situation—a question—for its entire length: does or does not a 6-foot-1½-inch white rabbit exist? Fortunately, *Harvey* has something to offer beyond these "violations" of form, and its phenomenal appeal as one of America's longest-running plays can readily be explained.

First of all, the gentle Elwood Dowd and his unseen friend have won sympathetic understanding in nations around the world and in almost every language because of their plea for tolerance of human individuality, however eccentric. There is universal meaning in the play's message about deadening conformity, with its spoof of scientific effort to eliminate social deviation. The appeal that has carried *Harvey* into every type of civilized community probably remains where it did the first night it opened to a sophisticated New York audience which would be least expected to approve a whimsical fairy tale about talking bunnies. If it is nothing else, *Harvey* is a superb example of modern theatrical escapism.

While it is a play of whimsy, *Harvey* never turns to the unnecessary pursuit of whimsicality for its own sake. Its witty dialogue and its madhouse antics give it a quality best described in words like wacky, cockeyed, or zany, all fittingly descriptive of fine comic escapism. The miracle, so termed by one critic, is in the common sense that comes through it. For all its departure into the delights of pure nonsense, it reveals the fundamental wisdom to be gained from those whose grip on reality is not as deathlike as the rest of us maintain it should be. As Joseph Wood Krutch remarked in his review, *Harvey* makes a good lesson out of the statement "It's great to be crazy," teaching the lesson in sheer, unhackneyed fun.

The minute the play begins we are in complete sympathy with Elwood. The horrors of a musical afternoon at the Wednesday Forum, full of hypocrisies, fake intellectualism, and childish desires to be properly listed in the society column, are contrasted with Elwood's forthright geniality and innocent sincerity. Everyone can experience a vicarious joy in his intrusion upon the sham of Veta's circle. There are occasions when many of us would be delighted to introduce both our own Harveys and Miss Greenawalt's quart of gin into the midst of these gossiping dowagers. Before we know it, we have accepted Harvey and we are quite willing to sit down with him and listen to Elwood's meticulous reading of Jane Austen.

Mrs. Chase exhibits her finest sense of the comically ludicrous when she gives the confused Veta the duty of explaining Harvey to the young psychiatrist. It is unfortunate that most of the scenes which follow fail to top this wholly preposterous sequence, for it is farce at its very best. By the time Elwood has left the office with his companion and the doctor has discovered the punctured hat, most of the play's highest comic levels have passed. Mrs. Chase has, however, now firmly convinced the most skeptical that Harvey exists. She leaves no doubt at all as Wilson reads the cheerfully mocking greeting in the encyclopedia. By the end of the first act, the audience knows that everybody onstage, except Elwood, is quite, quite mad.

Throughout the rest of the play, Mrs. Chase carries us through a clever satire upon the idea of "normal" life. Elwood remains calmly unperturbed, displays more common sense than all the others, and ends up giving more sound psychiatric advice to the medical profession than it can give to him. The climax occurs in the ingenious twist of forcing the weary doctor, tired of hearing the frustrations of others, to pour out his own dreams of Ohio and idyllic days with lovely maidens to the sympathetic and comprehending Elwood. After all, Elwood has long been able to do what Dr. Chumley dreams of, and he has overcome reality in order to make his own life a thoroughly bearable existence. Chumley, however, is not sure whether to fear or to welcome Harvey, but finally, in desperation, is resolved to capture him by very proper and very underhanded scientific means, even if his method involves the destruction of a happy man. Fortunately, Elwood's loving sister realizes the meaning of his "abnormality" in time to end the threat.

The satire of Harvey remains secondary; the signal value comes from the portrayal of Elwood and his friend in a matter-of-fact style that makes the fantasy so enjoyable. After seeing the tryout performances, Mrs. Chase realized that her first strong insistence on using an actor onstage in a monstrous rabbit costume was entirely out of place. There must always be the question of Harvey's existence, regardless of each spectator's private conviction that he is present. The hat, the opening of locked doors, and the accurate predictions of the future of which Elwood is capable are fair proofs,—except that we are never going to admit publicly that Harvey is there. After all, the power of suggestion is strong. Perhaps we are suffering like Dr. Chumley. Or perhaps Dr. Chumley is not suffering anything but only realizing at last that there are facts of life which his training simply cannot tell him. All the professionalism of Dr. Sanderson's attempt to discredit Harvey is lost in Elwood's rational explanations. Harvey cannot be explained away in medical jargon as an alcoholic carry-over from delirium tremens. True, Dr. Sanderson's formula can restore Elwood to "normal" living, and Harvey will disappear, but one feels that no scientific process would have exorcised Harvey. Harvey would have departed in disgust, wishing to be no part of the uninteresting but acceptable life of a thoroughly "respectable" person.

As for the "pooka," he is Celtic in origin. Most pookas take the form of horses, but they can be any animal they wish. Normally they are not so congenial as Harvey, and prefer to create disturbances rather than to ingratiate themselves with their human friends. They seldom appear to very many people at once. Some say they cannot be felt to the touch. The nearest equivalent in English lore would be Puck, the mischievous elf who can do good if properly treated, but who prefers to confuse and confound human beings just for the deviltry of it.

Mary Chase

Mary (Coyle) Chase was born on February 25, 1907 in Denver, Colorado. Her taste for pookas and banshees comes from the Celtic origin of her parents, who came to this country from Ireland. She attended the University of Denver for 2½ years and the University of Colorado for one more, but graduated from neither. She became a reporter for the *Rocky Mountain News* after her college work, and married Robert L. Chase in June, 1928.

After her marriage she quit newspaper work, but continued to write short stories and plays and wrote a radio program for the Teamsters' Union. She was also a free-lance writer for the International News Service and the United Press. In 1937 she wrote a play called *Me Three*, produced by the Federal Theatre Project in New York by Brock Pemberton under the title *Now I've Done It*, but it was a failure. Other plays, including *Banshee*, got nowhere. From 1941 to 1944 she became publicity director for the National Youth Administration in Denver.

Brock Pemberton was confident of Mrs. Chase's ability and undertook to produce *Harvey*, its title changed from *The White Rabbit* of its original copyright. Its November, 1944 opening became history. The play was an immediate hit and was awarded the Pulitzer Prize for 1944–1945. Mrs. Chase did not follow up her initial success until 1952, when Helen Hayes starred in her *Mrs. McThing*, another bit of whimsical fantasy involving witchcraft. *Bernadine*, concerning teen-age boys' dreams of their ideal woman, was a success of 1953.

Mrs. Chase is a member of the Dramatists Guild and was given the William MacLeod Raine Award from the Colorado Authors League in 1944. In 1947 the University of Denver honored her with the degree of doctor of letters.

HARVEY

by

Mary Chase

Frank Fay, well known to an earlier generation, but long absent from the Broadway stage, made a widely acclaimed comeback as Elwood P. Dowd in *Harvey*. In this closing portion of the first scene, Elwood settles down to read aloud from Jane Austen, while Harvey listens attentively. (*Life Magazine. Photo by Graphic House.*)

Harvey was first produced at the Forty-eighth Street Theatre in New York on November 1, 1944. It became one of the extraordinary successes of the modern theatre, running for 1775 performances before closing on January 15, 1949. The play provided a successful comeback for veteran actor Frank Fay, and gave actress Josephine Hull one of her best comedy roles. The following cast appeared in the opening performance:

Myrtle Mae Simmons	*Jane Van Duser*
Veta Louise Simmons	*Josephine Hull*
Elwood P. Dowd	*Frank Fay*
Miss Johnson	*Eloise Sheldon*
Mrs. Ethel Chauvenet	*Frederica Going*
Ruth Kelly, R.N.	*Janet Tyler*
Duane Wilson	*Jesse White*
Lyman Sanderson, M.D.	*Tom Seidel*
William R. Chumley, M.D.	*Fred Irving Lewis*
Betty Chumley	*Dora Clement*
Judge Omar Gaffney	*John Kirk*
E. J. Lofgren	*Robert Gist*

Produced by Brock Pemberton
Directed by Antoinette Perry
Settings by John Root

ACT ONE

SCENE 1: *The time is midafternoon of a spring day. The scene is the library of the old Dowd family mansion—a room lined with books and set with heavy, old-fashioned furniture of a faded grandeur. The most conspicuous item in the room is an oil painting over a black marble Victorian mantelpiece. This is the portrait of a lantern-jawed older woman. There are double doors at the right. These doors, now pulled apart, lead to the hallway and across to the parlor, which is not seen. Telephone is on small table at left. This afternoon there is a festive look to the room—silver bowls with spring flowers set about.*

From the parlor to the right comes the sound of a bad female voice singing, "I'm Called Little Buttercup."

AT RISE: MYRTLE MAE *is discovered coming through door from parlor, and as telephone rings, she goes to it.*

MYRTLE. Mrs. Simmons? Mrs. Simmons is my mother, but she has guests this afternoon. Who wants her? (*Respectful change in tone after she hears who it is.*) Oh—wait just a minute. Hang on just a minute. (*Goes to doorway and calls.*) Psst— Mother! (*Cranes her neck more.*) Psst— Mother! (*Crooks her finger insistently several times. Singing continues.*)

VETA (*enters, humming "Buttercup"*). Yes, dear?

MYRTLE. Telephone.

VETA (*turning to go out again*). Oh, no, dear. Not with all of them in there. Say I'm busy.

MYRTLE. But, Mother. It's the Society Editor of the Evening News Bee—

VETA (*turning*). Oh—the Society Editor. She's very important. (*She fixes her hair and goes to phone. Her voice is very sweet. She throws out chest and assumes dignified pose.*) Good afternoon, Miss Ellerbe. This is Veta Simmons. Yes —a tea and reception for the members of the Wednesday Forum. You might say— program tea. My mother, you know— (*Waves hand toward portrait.*) the late Marcella Pinney Dowd, pioneer cultural leader she came here by ox team as a child and she founded the Wednesday Forum. (MYRTLE *is watching out door.*) Myrtle—how many would you say?

MYRTLE. Seventy-five, at least. Say a hundred.

VETA (*on phone*). Seventy-five. Miss Tewksbury is the soloist, accompanied by Wilda McCurdy, accompanist.

MYRTLE. Come on! Miss Tewksbury is almost finished with her number.

VETA. She'll do an encore.

MYRTLE. What if they don't give her a lot of applause?

VETA. I've known her for years. She'll do an encore. (MYRTLE *again starts to leave.*) You might say that I am entertaining, assisted by my daughter, Miss Myrtle Mae Simmons. (*To* MYRTLE—*indicates her dress.*) What color would you call that?

MYRTLE. Rancho Rose, they told me.

VETA (*into phone*). Miss Myrtle Mae Simmons looked charming in a modish Rancho Rose-toned crepe, picked up at the girdle with a touch of magenta on emerald. I wish you could see her, Miss Ellerbe.

MYRTLE (*looks through door*). Mother —please—she's almost finished and where's the cateress?

VETA (*to* MYRTLE). Everything's ready. The minute she's finished singing we open the dining-room doors and we begin pouring. (*Into phone.*) The parlors and halls are festooned with smilax. Yes, festooned. (*Makes motion in air with finger.*) That's right. Yes, Miss Ellerbe, this is the first party we've had in years. There's a reason but I don't want it in the papers. We all have our troubles, Miss Ellerbe. The guest list? Oh, yes—

MYRTLE. Mother—come.

VETA. If you'll excuse me now, Miss Ellerbe. I'll call you later. (*Hangs up.*)

MYRTLE. Mother—Mrs. Chauvenet just came in!

VETA (*arranging flowers on phone table*). Mrs. Eugene Chauvenet Senior! Her father was a scout with Buffalo Bill.

MYRTLE. So that's where she got that hat!

VETA (*as she and* MYRTLE *start to exit*). Myrtle, you must be nice to Mrs. Chauvenet. She has a grandson about your age.

MYRTLE. But what difference will it make, with Uncle Elwood?

VETA. Myrtle—remember! We agreed not to talk about that this afternoon. The point of this whole party is to get you started. We work through those older women to the younger group.

MYRTLE. We can't have anyone here in the evenings, and that's when men come to see you—in the evenings. The only reason we can even have a party this afternoon is because Uncle Elwood is playing pinochle at the Fourth Avenue Firehouse. Thank God for the firehouse!

VETA. I know—but they'll just have to invite you out and it won't hurt them one bit. Oh, Myrtle—you've got so much to offer. I don't care what anyone says, there's something sweet about every young girl. And a man takes that sweetness, and look what he does with it! (*Crosses to mantel with flowers.*) But you've got to meet somebody, Myrtle. That's all there is to it.

MYRTLE. If I do they say, That's Myrtle Mae Simmons! Her uncle is Elwood P. Dowd—the biggest screwball in town. Elwood P. Dowd and his pal—

VETA (*puts hand on her mouth*). You promised.

MYRTLE (*crossing above table, sighs*). All right—let's get them into the dining room.

VETA. Now when the members come in here and you make your little welcome speech on behalf of your grandmother—be sure to do this. (*Gestures toward portrait on mantel.*)

MYRTLE (*in fine disgust—business with flowers*). And then after that, I mention my Uncle Elwood and say a few words about his pal Harvey. Damn Harvey! (*In front of table, as she squats.*)

VETA (*the effect on her is electric. She runs over and closes doors*). Myrtle Mae —that's right! Let everybody in the Wednesday Forum hear you. You said that name. You promised you wouldn't say that name and you said it.

MYRTLE (*rising*). I'm sorry, Mother. But how do you know Uncle Elwood won't come in and introduce Harvey to everybody? (*Places flowers on mantel.*)

VETA. This is unkind of you, Myrtle Mae. Elwood is the biggest heartache I have. Even if people do call him peculiar he's still my brother, and he won't be home this afternoon.

MYRTLE. Are you sure?

VETA. Of course I'm sure.

MYRTLE. But Mother, why can't we live like other people?

VETA. Must I remind you again? Elwood is not living with us—we are living with him.

MYRTLE. Living with him and Harvey! Did Grandmother know about Harvey?

VETA. I've wondered and wondered about that. She never wrote me if she did.

MYRTLE. Why did she have to leave all her property to Uncle Elwood?

VETA. Well, I suppose it was because she died in his arms. People are sentimental about things like that.

MYRTLE. You always say that and it doesn't make sense. She couldn't make out her will after she died, could she?

VETA. Don't be didactic, Myrtle Mae. It's not becoming in a young girl, and

men loathe it. Now don't forget to wave your hand.

MYRTLE. I'll do my best. (*Opens door.*)

VETA. Oh, dear—Miss Tewksbury's voice is certainly fading!

MYRTLE. But not fast enough. (*She exits.*)

VETA (*exits through door, clapping hands, pulling down girdle*). Lovely, Miss Tewksbury—perfectly lovely. I loved it. (*Through door at left enters* ELWOOD P. DOWD. *He is a man about forty-seven years old with a dignified bearing, and yet a dreamy expression in his eyes. His expression is benign, yet serious to the point of gravity. He wears an overcoat and a battered old hat. This hat, reminiscent of the Joe College era, sits on the top of his head. Over his arm he carries another hat and coat. As he enters, although he is alone, he seems to be ushering and bowing someone else in with him. He bows the invisible person over to a chair. His step is light, his movements quiet and his voice low-pitched.*)

ELWOOD (*to invisible person*). Excuse me a moment. I have to answer the phone. Make yourself comfortable, Harvey. (*Phone rings.*) Hello. Oh, you've got the wrong number. But how are you, anyway? This is Elwood P. Dowd speaking. I'll do? Well, thank you. And what is your name, my dear? Miss Elsie Greenawalt? (*To chair.*) Harvey, it's a Miss Elsie Greenawalt. How are you today, Miss Greenawalt? That's fine. Yes, my dear. I would be happy to join your club. I belong to several clubs now —the University Club, the Country Club and the Pinochle Club at the Fourth Avenue Firehouse. I spend a good deal of my time there, or at Charlie's Place, or over at Eddie's Bar. And what is your club, Miss Greenawalt? (*He listens— then turns to empty chair.*) Harvey, I get the Ladies Home Journal, Good Housekeeping and the Open Road for Boys for two years for six twenty-five. (*Back to phone.*) It sounds fine to me. I'll join it. (*To chair.*) How does it sound to you, Harvey? (*Back to phone.*) Harvey says it sounds fine to him also, Miss Greenawalt. He says he will join, too. Yes—two subscriptions. Mail everything to this address. . . . I hope I will have the pleasure of meeting you some time, my dear. Harvey, she says she would like to meet me. When? When would you like to meet me, Miss Greenawalt? Why not right now? My sister seems to be having a few friends in and we would consider it an honor if you would come and join us. My sister will be delighted. 343 Temple Drive—I hope to see you in a very few minutes. Goodbye, my dear. (*Hangs up.*) She's coming right over. (*Moves to* HARVEY.) Harvey, don't you think we'd better freshen up? Yes, so do I. (*He takes up hats and coats and exits.*)

VETA (*enters, followed by* MAID). I can't seem to remember where I put that guest list. I must read it to Miss Ellerbe . . . Have you seen it, Miss Johnson?

MAID. No, I haven't, Mrs. Simmons.

VETA. Look on my dresser. (*MAID exits.*)

MYRTLE (*enters*). Mother—Mrs. Chauvenet—she's asking for you. (*Turning—speaking in oh-so-sweet tone to someone in hall.*) Here's Mother, Mrs. Chauvenet. Here she is. (*Enter* MRS. CHAUVENET. *She is a woman of about sixty-five—heavy, dressed with the casual sumptuousness of a wealthy Western society woman—in silvery gold and plush, and mink scarf even though it is a spring day. She rushes over to* VETA.)

MRS. CHAUVENET. Veta Louise Simmons! I thought you were dead. (*Gets to her and takes hold of her.*)

VETA (*rushing to her, they kiss*). Aunt Ethel! (*Motioning to* MYRTLE *to come forward and meet the great lady.*) Oh, no—I'm very much alive—thank you—

MRS. CHAUVENET (*turning to* MYRTLE). And this full-grown girl is your daughter —I've known you since you were a baby.

MYRTLE. I know.

MRS. CHAUVENET. What's your name, dear?

VETA (*proudly*). This is Myrtle—Aunt

Ethel. Myrtle Mae—for the two sisters of her father. He's dead. That's what confused you.

MRS. CHAUVENET. Where's Elwood?

VETA (*with a nervous glance at* MYRTLE MAE). He couldn't be here, Aunt Ethel—now let me get you some tea.

MRS. CHAUVENET. Elwood isn't here?

VETA. No—

MRS. CHAUVENET. Oh, shame on him. That was the main reason I came. (*Takes off scarf—puts it on chair.*) I want to see Elwood.

VETA. Come—there are loads of people anxious to speak to you.

MRS. CHAUVENET. Do you realize, Veta, it's been years since I've seen Elwood?

VETA. No—where does the time go?

MRS. CHAUVENET. But I don't understand it. I was saying to Mr. Chauvenet only the other night—what on earth do you suppose has happened to Elwood Dowd? He never comes to the club dances any more. I haven't seen him at a horse show in years. Does Elwood see anybody these days?

VETA (*and* MYRTLE, *with a glance at each other*). Oh, yes—Aunt Ethel. Elwood sees somebody.

MYRTLE. Oh, yes.

MRS. CHAUVENET (*to* MYRTLE). Your Uncle Elwood, child, is one of my favorite people. (*VETA rises.*) Always has been.

VETA. Yes, I remember.

MRS. CHAUVENET. Is Elwood happy, Veta?

VETA. Elwood's very happy, Aunt Ethel. You don't need to worry about Elwood— (*Looks through doorway. She is anxious to get the subject on something else.*) Why, there's Mrs. Frank Cummings—just came in. Don't you want to speak to her?

MRS. CHAUVENET (*peers out*). My—but she looks ghastly! Hasn't she failed though?

VETA. If you think she looks badly—you should see him!

MRS. CHAUVENET. Is that so? I must

have them over. (*Looks again.*) She looks frightful. I thought she was dead.

VETA. Oh, no.

MRS. CHAUVENET. Now—what about tea, Veta?

VETA. Certainly— (*Starts forward to lead the way.*) If you will forgive me, I will precede you— (ELWOOD *enters,* MRS. CHAUVENET *turns back to pick up her scarf from chair, and sees him.*)

MRS. CHAUVENET (*rushing forward*). Elwood! Elwood Dowd! Bless your heart.

ELWOOD (*coming forward and bowing as he takes her hand*). Aunt Ethel! What a pleasure to come in and find a beautiful woman waiting for me!

MRS. CHAUVENET (*looking at him fondly*). Elwood—you haven't changed.

VETA (*moves forward quickly, takes hold of her*). Come along, Aunt Ethel—you mustn't miss the party.

MYRTLE. There's punch if you don't like tea.

MRS. CHAUVENET. But I do like tea. Stop pulling at me, you two. Elwood, what night next week can you come to dinner?

ELWOOD. Any night. Any night at all, Aunt Ethel—I would be delighted.

VETA. Elwood, there's some mail for you today. I took it up to your room.

ELWOOD. Did you, Veta? That was nice of you. Aunt Ethel—I want you to meet Harvey. As you can see he's a Pooka. (*Turns toward air beside him.*) Harvey, you've heard me speak of Mrs. Chauvenet? We always called her Aunt Ethel. She is one of my oldest and dearest friends. (*Inclines head toward space and goes "Hmm!" and then listens as though not hearing first time. Nods as though having heard someone next to him speak.*) Yes—yes—that's right. She's the one. This is the one. (*To* MRS. CHAUVENET.) He says he would have known you anywhere. (*Then as a confused, bewildered look comes over* MRS. CHAUVENET's *face and as she looks to left and right of* ELWOOD *and cranes her neck to see behind him—*ELWOOD *not seeing her expression, crosses towards*

VETA *and* MYRTLE MAE.) You both look lovely. (*Turns to the air next to him.*) Come on in with me, Harvey— We must say hello to all of our friends—(*Bows to* MRS. CHAUVENET.) I beg your pardon, Aunt Ethel. If you'll excuse me for one moment— (*Puts his hand gently on her arm, trying to turn her.*)

MRS. CHAUVENET. What?

ELWOOD. You are standing in his way— (*She gives a little—her eyes wide on him.*) Come along, Harvey. (*He watches the invisible Harvey cross to door, then stops him.*) Uh-uh! (ELWOOD *goes over to door. He turns and pantomimes as he arranges the tie and brushes off the head of the invisible Harvey. Then he does the same thing to his own tie. They are all watching him,* MRS. CHAUVENET *in horrified fascination, the heads of* VETA *and* MYRTLE *bowed in agony.*) Go right on in, Harvey. I'll join you in a minute. (*He pantomimes as though slapping him on the back, and ushers him out. Then turns and comes back to* MRS. CHAUVENET.) Aunt Ethel, I can see you are disturbed about Harvey. Please don't be. He stares like that at everybody. It's his way. But he liked you. I could tell. He liked you very much. (*Pats her arm reassuringly, smiles at her, then calmly and confidently goes on out. After his exit* MRS. CHAUVENET, MYRTLE *and* VETA *are silent. Finally* VETA—*with a resigned tone—clears her throat.*)

VETA (*looking at* MRS. CHAUVENET). Some tea—perhaps—?

MRS. CHAUVENET. Why, I—not right now—I—well—I think I'll be running along.

MYRTLE. But—

VETA (*putting a hand over hers to quiet her*). I'm so sorry—

MRS. CHAUVENET. I'll—I'll be talking to you soon. Goodbye—goodbye— (*She exits quickly.* VETA *stands stiffly—her anger paralyzing her.* MYRTLE *finally tiptoes over and closes one side of door—peeking over, but keeping herself out of sight.*)

MYRTLE. Oh, God— (*Starts to run for doorway.*) Oh, my God!

VETA. Myrtle—where are you going?

MYRTLE. Up to my room. He's introducing Harvey to everybody. I can't face those people now. I wish I were dead.

VETA. Come back here. Stay with me. We'll get him out of there and upstairs to his room.

MYRTLE. I won't do it. I can't. I can't.

VETA. Myrtle Mae! (MYRTLE *stops.* VETA *goes over to her and pulls her to where they are directly in line with doorway.*) Now—pretend I'm fixing your corsage.

MYRTLE (*covering her face with her hands in shame*). Oh, Mother!

VETA. We've got to. Pretend we're having a gay little chat. Keep looking. When you catch his eye, tell me. He always comes when I call him. Now, then—do you see him yet?

MYRTLE. No—not yet. How do you do, Mrs. Cummings.

VETA. Smile, can't you? Have you no pride? I'm smiling— (*Waves and laughs.*) and he's my own brother!

MYRTLE. Oh, Mother—people get run over by trucks every day. Why can't something like that happen to Uncle Elwood?

VETA. Myrtle Mae Simmons, I'm ashamed of you. This thing is not your uncle's fault. (*Phone rings.*)

MYRTLE. Ouch! You're sticking me with that pin!

VETA. That's Miss Ellerbe. Keep looking. Keep smiling. (*She goes to phone.*)

MYRTLE. Mrs. Cummings is leaving. Uncle Elwood must have told her what Harvey is. Oh, God!

VETA (*on phone*). Hello—this is Mrs. Simmons. Should you come in the clothes you have on— What have you on? Who is this? But I don't know any Miss Greenawalt. Should you what?— May I ask who invited you? Mr. Dowd! Thank you just the same, but I believe there has been a mistake.—Well, I never!

MYRTLE. Never what?

VETA. One of your Uncle Elwood's friends. She asked me if she should bring a quart of gin to the Wednesday Forum!

MYRTLE. There he is—he's talking to Mrs. Halsey.

VETA. Is Harvey with him?

MYRTLE. What a thing to ask! How can I tell? How can anybody tell but Uncle Elwood?

VETA (*calls*). Oh, Elwood, could I see you a moment, dear? (*To* MYRTLE.) I promise you your Uncle Elwood has disgraced us for the last time in this house. I'm going to do something I've never done before.

MYRTLE. What did you mean just now when you said this was not Uncle Elwood's fault? If it's not his fault, whose fault is it?

VETA. Never you mind. I know whose fault it is. Now lift up your head and smile and go back in as though nothing had happened.

MYRTLE. You're no match for Uncle Elwood.

VETA. You'll see. (ELWOOD *is coming.*)

MYRTLE (*as they pass at door*). Mother's waiting for you. (*She exits.*)

VETA. Elwood! Could I see you for a moment, dear?

ELWOOD. Yes, sister. Excuse me, Harvey. (VETA *steps quickly over and pulls double doors together.*)

VETA. Elwood, would you mind sitting down in here and waiting for me until the party is over? I want to talk to you. It's very important.

ELWOOD. Of course, sister. I happen to have a little free time right now and you're welcome to all of it, Veta. Do you want Harvey to wait too?

VETA (*quite seriously—not in a pampering, humoring tone at all*). Yes, Elwood. I certainly do. (*She steals out—watching him as she crosses through door. After she has gone out we see doors being pulled together from the outside and hear the click of a lock.* ELWOOD *goes calmly over to bookcase, peruses it carefully, and then when he has found the book he wants, takes it out and from behind it pulls a half-filled pint bottle of liquor.*)

ELWOOD (*looking at book he holds in one hand*). Ah—Jane Austen. (*He gets one chair, pulls it down, facing front.*

Gets chair and pulls it right alongside. Sits down, sets bottle on floor between chairs.) Sit down, Harvey. Veta wants to talk to us. She said it was important. I think she wants to congratulate us on the impression we made at her party. (*Reads. Turns to Harvey. Inclines head and listens, then looks at back of book and answers as though Harvey had asked what edition it is, who published it and what are those names on the fly leaf; turning head toward empty chair each time and twice saying "Hmm?"*) Jane Austen—De Luxe Edition—Limited—Grosset and Dunlap—The usual acknowledgements. Chapter One—

AND THE CURTAIN FALLS.

SCENE 2: *The office in the main building of Chumley's Rest—a sanitarium for mental patients. The wall at back is half plaster and half glass. There is a door up center, through which we can see the corridor of the sanitarium itself. In the right wall is a door which is lettered "Dr. Chumley." On right wall is a bookcase, a small filing-case on top of it. Across the room is another door lettered "Dr. Sanderson." Down left is the door leading from the outside. There is a big desk at right angles with footlights, with chair either side of desk. At right is a table with chairs on either side.*

The time is an hour after the close of Scene 1.

AT RISE: MISS RUTH KELLY, *head nurse at Chumley's Rest, is seated left of desk, taking notes as she talks to* VETA SIMMONS, *who stands. Miss* KELLY *is a very pretty young woman of about twenty-four. She is wearing a starched white uniform and cap. As she talks to* VETA *she writes on a slip of paper with a pencil.*

KELLY (*writing*). Mrs. O. R. Simmons, 343 Temple Drive, is that right?

VETA (*nodding, taking handkerchief from handbag*). We were born and raised there. It's old but we love it. It's our home. (*Crosses to table, puts down handbag.*)

KELLY. And you wish to enter your brother here at the sanitarium for treatment. Your brother's name?

VETA (*coming back to desk—raising handkerchief to eyes and dabbing*). It's—oh—

KELLY. Mrs. Simmons, what is your brother's name?

VETA. I'm sorry. Life is not easy for any of us. I'll have to hold my head up and go on just the same. That's what I keep telling Myrtle and that's what Myrtle Mae keeps telling me. She's heartbroken about her Uncle Elwood—Elwood P. Dowd. That's it. (*Sits on chair beside desk.*)

KELLY (*writing*). Elwood P. Dowd. His age?

VETA. Forty-seven the twenty-fourth of last April. He's Taurus—Taurus—the bull. I'm Leo, and Myrtle is on a cusp.

KELLY. Forty-seven. Is he married?

VETA. No, Elwood has never married. He stayed with mother. He was always a great home boy. He loved his home.

KELLY. You have him with you now?

VETA. He's in a taxicab down in the driveway. (KELLY *rings buzzer.*) I gave the driver a dollar to watch him, but I didn't tell the man why. You can't tell these things to perfect strangers. (*Enter* WILSON. *He is the sanitarium strongarm. He is a big burly attendant, black-browed, about twenty-eight.* KELLY *crosses in front of desk toward bookcase.*)

KELLY. Mr. Wilson, would you step down to a taxi in the driveway and ask a Mr. Dowd if he would be good enough to step up to Room number 24—South Wing G?

WILSON (*glaring*). Ask him?

KELLY (*with a warning glance toward* VETA). This is his sister, Mrs. Simmons. (KELLY *crosses to cabinet for card.*)

WILSON (*with a feeble grin*). How do—why, certainly—be glad to escort him. (*Exits.*)

VETA. Thank you.

KELLY (*handing* VETA *her printed slip*). The rates here, Mrs. Simmons—you'll find them printed on this card.

VETA (*waving it away*). That will all be taken care of by my mother's estate.

The late Marcella Pinney Dowd. Judge Gaffney is our attorney.

KELLY. Now I'll see if Dr. Sanderson can see you.

VETA. Dr. Sanderson? I want to see Dr. Chumley himself.

KELLY. Oh, Mrs. Simmons, Dr. Sanderson is the one who sees everybody. Dr. Chumley sees no one.

VETA. He's still head of this institution, isn't he? He's still a psychiatrist, isn't he?

KELLY (*shocked at such heresy*). Still a psychiatrist! Dr. Chumley is more than that. He is a psychiatrist with a national reputation. Whenever people have mental breakdowns they at once think of Dr. Chumley.

VETA (*pointing*). That's his office, isn't it? Well, you march right in and tell him I want to see him. If he knows who's in here he'll come out here.

KELLY. I wouldn't dare disturb him, Mrs. Simmons. I would be discharged if I did.

VETA. Well, I don't like to be pushed off onto any second fiddle.

KELLY. Dr. Sanderson is nobody's second fiddle. (*Her eyes aglow.*) He's young, of course, and he hasn't been out of medical school very long, but Dr. Chumley tried out twelve and kept Dr. Sanderson. He's really wonderful— (*Catches herself.*) to the patients.

VETA. Very well. Tell him I'm here.

KELLY (*straightens her cap. As she exits into door, primps*). Right away. (VETA *rises, takes off coat—puts it on back of chair, sighs.*) Oh dear—oh dear. (WILSON *and* ELWOOD *appear in corridor.* ELWOOD *pulls over a little from* WILSON *and sees* VETA.)

ELWOOD. Veta—isn't this wonderful—! (WILSON *takes him forcefully off upstairs.* VETA *is still jumpy and nervous from the surprise. Enter* DR. SANDERSON. LYMAN SANDERSON *is a good-looking young man of twenty-seven or twenty-eight. He is wearing a starched white coat over dark trousers. His eyes follow* MISS KELLY, *who has walked out before him and gone out, closing doors. Then he sees* VETA, *pulls down his jacket and*

gets a professional bearing. VETA *has not heard him come in. She is still busy with the compact.*)

SANDERSON (*looking at slip in his hand*). Mrs. Simmons?

VETA (*startled—she jumps*). Oh—oh dear—I didn't hear you come in. You startled me. You're Dr. Sanderson?

SANDERSON (*he nods*). Yes. Will you be seated, please?

VETA (*sits*). Thank you. I hope you don't think I'm jumpy like that all the time, but I—

SANDERSON. Of course not. Miss Kelly tells me you are concerned about your brother. Dowd, is it? Elwood P. Dowd?

VETA. Yes, Doctor—he's—this isn't easy for me, Doctor.

SANDERSON (*kindly*). Naturally these things aren't easy for the families of patients. I understand.

VETA (*twisting her handkerchief nervously*). It's what Elwood's doing to himself, Doctor—that's the thing. Myrtle Mae has a right to nice friends. She's young and her whole life is before her. That's my daughter.

SANDERSON. Your daughter. How long has it been since you began to notice any peculiarity in your brother's actions?

VETA. I noticed it right away when Mother died, and Myrtle Mae and I came back home from Des Moines to live with Elwood. I could see that he—that he— (*Twists handkerchief—looks pleadingly at* SANDERSON.)

SANDERSON. That he—what? Take your time, Mrs. Simmons. Don't strain. Let it come. I'll wait for it.

VETA. Doctor—everything I say to you is confidential? Isn't it?

SANDERSON. That's understood.

VETA. Because it's a slap in the face to everything we've stood for in this community the way Elwood is acting now.

SANDERSON. I am not a gossip, Mrs. Simmons. I am a psychiatrist.

VETA. Well—for one thing—he drinks.

SANDERSON. To excess?

VETA. To excess? Well—don't you call it excess when a man never lets a day go by without stepping into one of those cheap taverns, sitting around with riffraff and people you never heard of? Inviting them to the house—playing cards with them—giving them food and money. And here I am trying to get Myrtle Mae started with a nice group of young people. If that isn't excess I'm sure I don't know what excess is.

SANDERSON. I didn't doubt your statement, Mrs. Simmons. I merely asked if your brother drinks.

VETA. Well, yes, I say definitely Elwood drinks and I want him committed out here permanently, because I cannot stand another day of that Harvey. Myrtle and I have to set a place at the table for Harvey. We have to move over on the sofa and make room for Harvey. We have to answer the telephone when Elwood calls and asks to speak to Harvey. Then at the party this afternoon with Mrs. Chauvenet there— We didn't even know anything about Harvey until we came back here. Doctor, don't you think it would have been a little bit kinder of Mother to have written and told me about Harvey? Be honest, now —don't you?

SANDERSON. I really couldn't answer that question, because I—

VETA. I can. Yes—it certainly would have.

SANDERSON. This person you call Harvey—who is he?

VETA. He's a rabbit.

SANDERSON. Perhaps—but just who is he? Some companion—someone your brother has picked up in these bars, of whom you disapprove?

VETA (patiently). Doctor—I've been telling you. Harvey is a rabbit—a big white rabbit—six feet high—or is it six feet and a half? Heaven knows I ought to know. He's been around the house long enough.

SANDERSON (regarding her narrowly). Now, Mrs. Simmons, let me understand this—you say—

VETA (impatient). Doctor—do I have to keep repeating myself? My brother insists that his closest friend is this big

white rabbit. This rabbit is named Harvey. Harvey lives at our house. Don't you understand? He and Elwood go every place together. Elwood buys railroad tickets, theater tickets, for both of them. As I told Myrtle Mae—if your uncle was so lonesome he had to bring something home—why couldn't he bring home something human? He has me, doesn't he? He has Myrtle Mae, doesn't he? (She leans forward.) Doctor— (She rises to him. He inclines toward her.) I'm going to tell you something I've never told anybody in the world before. (Puts her hand on his shoulder.) Every once in a while I see that big white rabbit myself. Now isn't that terrible? I've never even told that to Myrtle Mae.

SANDERSON (now convinced. Starts to rise). Mrs. Simmons—

VETA (straightening). And what's more—he's every bit as big as Elwood says he is. Now don't ever tell that to anybody, Doctor. I'm ashamed of it.

SANDERSON. I can see that you have been under a great nervous strain recently.

VETA. Well—I certainly have.

SANDERSON. Grief over your mother's death depressed you considerably?

VETA. Nobody knows how much.

SANDERSON. Been losing sleep?

VETA. How could anybody sleep with that going on?

SANDERSON. Short-tempered over trifles?

VETA. You just try living with those two and see how your temper holds up.

SANDERSON (presses buzzer). Loss of appetite?

VETA. No one could eat at a table with my brother and a big white rabbit. Well, I'm finished with it. I'll sell the house—be appointed conservator of Elwood's estate, and Myrtle Mae and I will be able to entertain our friends in peace. It's too much, Doctor. I just can't stand it.

SANDERSON (has been repeatedly pressing a buzzer on his desk. He looks with annoyance toward hall door. His answer now to VETA is gentle). Of course, Mrs Simmons. Of course it is. You're tired.

VETA (*she nods*). Oh, yes I am.

SANDERSON. You've been worrying a great deal.

VETA (*nods*). Yes, I have. I can't help it.

SANDERSON. And now I'm going to help you.

VETA. Oh, Doctor . . .

SANDERSON (*goes cautiously to door—watching her*). Just sit there quietly, Mrs. Simmons. I'll be right back. (*He exits.*)

VETA (*sighing with relief, rises and calls out as she takes coat*). I'll just go down to the cab and get Elwood's things. (*She exits out. SANDERSON, KELLY and WILSON come in.*)

SANDERSON. Why didn't someone answer the buzzer?

KELLY. I didn't hear you, Doctor—

SANDERSON. I rang and rang. (*Looks into his office. It is empty.*) Mrs. Simmons— (*Looks out door, shuts it, comes back.*) Sound the gong, Wilson. That poor woman must not leave the grounds.

WILSON. She's made with a getaway, huh, doc? (*WILSON presses a button on the wall and we hear a loud gong sounding.*)

SANDERSON. Her condition is serious. Go after her. (*WILSON exits.*)

KELLY. I can't believe it. (*SANDERSON picks up phone.*)

SANDERSON. Main gate. Henry, Dr. Sanderson. Allow no one out of the main gate. We're looking for a patient. (*Hangs up.*) I shouldn't have left her alone, but no one answered the buzzer.

KELLY. Wilson was in South, Doctor.

SANDERSON (*making out papers*). What have we available, Miss Kelly?

KELLY. Number 13, upper West R., is ready, Doctor.

SANDERSON. Have her taken there immediately, and I will prescribe preliminary treatment. I must contact her brother. Dowd is the name, Elwood P. Dowd. Get him on the telephone for me, will you please, Miss Kelly?

KELLY. But Doctor—I didn't know it was the woman who needed the treatment. She said it was for her brother.

SANDERSON. Of course she did. It's the oldest dodge in the world—always used by a cunning type of psychopath. She apparently knew her brother was about to commit her, so she came out to discredit him. Get him on the telephone, please.

KELLY. But, Doctor—I thought the woman was all right, so I had Wilson take the brother up to No. 24 South Wing G. He's there now.

SANDERSON (*staring at her with horror*). You had Wilson take the brother in? No gags, please Kelly. You're not serious, are you?

KELLY. Oh, I did, Doctor. I did. Oh, Doctor, I'm terribly sorry.

SANDERSON. Oh, well then, if you're sorry, that fixes everything. (*He starts to pick up house phone and finishes the curse under his breath.*) Oh—no! (*Buries his head in his hands.*)

KELLY. I'll do it, Doctor. I'll do it. (*She takes phone.*) Miss Dumphy—will you please unlock the door to Number 24—and give Mr. Dowd his clothes and—? (*Looks at SANDERSON for direction.*)

SANDERSON. Ask him to step down to the office right away.

KELLY (*into phone*). Ask him to step down to the office right away. There's been a terrible mistake and Dr. Sanderson wants to explain—

SANDERSON. Explain? Apologize!

KELLY. Thank heaven they hadn't put him in a hydro tub yet. She'll let him out.

SANDERSON (*staring at her*). Beautiful —and dumb, too. It's almost too good to be true.

KELLY. Doctor—I feel terrible. I didn't know. Judge Gaffney called and said Mrs. Simmons and her brother would be out here, and when she came in here— you don't have to be sarcastic.

SANDERSON. Oh, don't I? Stop worrying. We'll squirm out of it some way. (*Thinking—starts toward right door.*)

KELLY. Where are you going?

SANDERSON. I've got to tell the chief about it, Kelly. He may want to handle this himself.

KELLY. He'll be furious. I know he will.

He'll die. And then he'll terminate me.

SANDERSON (*catches her shoulders*). The responsibility is all mine, Kelly.

KELLY. Oh, no—tell him it was all my fault, Doctor.

SANDERSON. I never mention your name. Except in my sleep.

KELLY. But this man Dowd—

SANDERSON. Don't let him get away. I'll be right back.

KELLY. But what shall I say to him? What shall I do? He'll be furious.

SANDERSON. Look, Kelly—he'll probably be fit to be tied—but he's a man, isn't he?

KELLY. I guess so—his name is Mister.

SANDERSON. Go into your old routine —you know—the eyes—the swish—the works. I'm immune—but I've seen it work with some people—some of the patients out here. Keep him here, Kelly—if you have to do a strip tease. (*He exits.*)

KELLY (*very angry. Speaks to closed door*). Well, of all the—oh—you're wonderful, Dr. Sanderson! You're just about the most wonderful person I ever met in my life. (*Kicks chair.*)

WILSON (*has entered in time to hear last sentence*). Yeah—but how about giving me a lift here just the same?

KELLY. What?

WILSON. That Simmons dame.

KELLY. Did you catch her?

WILSON. Slick as a whistle. She was comin' along the path hummin' a little tune. I jumped out at her from behind a tree. I says "Sister—there's a man wants to see you." Shoulda heard her yell! She's whacky, all right.

KELLY. Take her to No. 13 upper West R.

WILSON. She's there now. Brought her in through the diet kitchen. She's screamin' and kickin' like hell. I'll hold her if you'll come and undress her.

KELLY. Just a second, Wilson. Dr. Sanderson told me to stay here till her brother comes down.

WILSON. Make it snappy— (*Goes out. ELWOOD enters. KELLY rises.*)

KELLY. You're Mr. Dowd?

ELWOOD (*carrying other hat and coat over his arm. He bows*). Elwood P.

KELLY. I'm Miss Kelly.

ELWOOD. Let me give you one of my cards. (*Fishes in vest pocket—pulls out card.*) If you should want to call me— call me at this number. Don't call me at that one. That's the old one.

KELLY. Thank you.

ELWOOD. Perfectly all right, and if you lose it—don't worry, my dear. I have plenty more.

KELLY. Won't you have a chair, please, Mr. Dowd?

ELWOOD. Thank you. I'll have two. Allow me. (*He brings another chair. Puts extra hat and coat on table. Motions Harvey to sit in chair. He stands waiting.*)

KELLY. Dr. Sanderson is very anxious to talk to you. He'll be here in a minute. Please be seated.

ELWOOD (*waving her toward chair right of desk*). After you, my dear.

KELLY. Oh, I really can't, thank you. I'm in and out all the time. But you mustn't mind me. Please sit down.

ELWOOD (*bowing*). After you.

KELLY (*sits. ELWOOD sits on chair he has just put in place*). Could I get you a magazine to look at?

ELWOOD. I would much rather look at you, Miss Kelly, if you don't mind. You really are very lovely.

KELLY. Oh—well. Thank you. Some people don't seem to think so.

ELWOOD. Some people are blind. That is often brought to my attention. And now, Miss Kelly—I would like to have you meet—(*Enter SANDERSON. MISS KELLY rises and backs up to below desk. ELWOOD rises when she does, and he makes a motion to the invisible Harvey to rise, too.*)

SANDERSON (*going to him, extending hand*). Mr. Dowd?

ELWOOD. Elwood P. Let me give you one of my cards. If you should want—

SANDERSON. Mr. Dowd—I am Dr. Lyman Sanderson, Dr. Chumley's assistant out here.

ELWOOD. Well, good for you! I'm happy to know you. How are you, Doctor?

SANDERSON. That's going to depend on

you, I'm afraid. Please sit down. You've met Miss Kelly, Mr. Dowd?

ELWOOD. I have had that pleasure, and I want both of you to meet a very dear friend of mine—

SANDERSON. Later on—be glad to. Won't you be seated, because first I want to say—

ELWOOD. After Miss Kelly—

SANDERSON. Sit down, Kelly—(*She sits, as does* ELWOOD—*who indicates to Harvey to sit also.*) Is that chair quite comfortable, Mr. Dowd?

ELWOOD. Yes, thank you. Would you care to try it? (*He takes out a cigarette.*)

SANDERSON. No, thank you. How about an ash tray there? Could we give Mr. Dowd an ash tray? (KELLY *gets it.* EL-WOOD *and Harvey rise also.* ELWOOD *beams as he turns and watches her.* KELLY *puts ash tray by* DOWD, *who moves it to share with Harvey.*) Is it too warm in here for you, Mr. Dowd? Would you like me to open a window? (ELWOOD *hasn't heard. He is watching* MISS KELLY.)

KELLY (*turning, smiling at him*). Mr. Dowd—Dr. Sanderson wants to know if he should open a window?

ELWOOD. That's entirely up to him. I wouldn't presume to live his life for him. (*During this dialogue* SANDERSON *is near window.* KELLY *has her eyes on his face.* ELWOOD *smiles at Harvey fondly.*)

SANDERSON. Now then, Mr. Dowd, I can see that you're not the type of person to be taken in by any high-flown phrases or beating about the bush.

ELWOOD (*politely*). Is that so, Doctor?

SANDERSON. You have us at a disadvantage here. You know it. We know it. Let's lay the cards on the table.

ELWOOD. That certainly appeals to me, Doctor.

SANDERSON. Best way in the long run. People are people, no matter where you go.

ELWOOD. That is very often the case.

SANDERSON. And being human are therefore liable to mistakes. Miss Kelly and I have made a mistake here this afternoon, Mr. Dowd, and we'd like to explain it to you.

KELLY. It wasn't Doctor Sanderson's fault, Mr. Dowd. It was mine.

SANDERSON. A human failing—as I said.

ELWOOD. I find it very interesting, nevertheless. You and Miss Kelly here? (*They nod.*) This afternoon—you say? (*They nod.* ELWOOD *gives Harvey a knowing look.*)

KELLY. We do hope you'll understand, Mr. Dowd.

ELWOOD. Oh, yes. Yes. These things are often the basis of a long and warm friendship.

SANDERSON. And the responsibility is, of course, not hers—but mine.

ELWOOD. Your attitude may be old-fashioned, Doctor—but I like it.

SANDERSON. Now, if I had seen your sister first—that would have been an entirely different story.

ELWOOD. Now there you surprise me. I think the world and all of Veta—but I had supposed she had seen her day.

SANDERSON. You must not attach any blame to her. She is a very sick woman. Came in here insisting you were in need of treatment. That's perfectly ridiculous.

ELWOOD. Veta shouldn't be upset about me. I get along fine.

SANDERSON. Exactly—but your sister had already talked to Miss Kelly, and there had been a call from your family lawyer, Judge Gaffney—

ELWOOD. Oh, yes. I know him. Know his wife, too. Nice people. (*He turns to* Harvey—*cigarette business: he needs a match.*)

SANDERSON. Is there something I can get for you, Mr. Dowd?

ELWOOD. What did you have in mind?

SANDERSON. A light—here—let me give you a light. (*Crosses to* DOWD, *lights his cigarette.* ELWOOD *brushes smoke away from the rabbit.*) Your sister was extremely nervous and plunged right away into a heated tirade on your drinking.

ELWOOD. That was Veta.

SANDERSON. She became hysterical.

ELWOOD. I tell Veta not to worry about that. I'll take care of that.

SANDERSON. Exactly. Oh, I suppose you take a drink now and then—the same as the rest of us?

ELWOOD. Yes, I do. As a matter of fact, I would like one right now.

SANDERSON. Matter of fact, so would I, but your sister's reaction to the whole matter of drinking was entirely too intense. Does your sister drink, Mr. Dowd?

ELWOOD. Oh, no, Doctor. No. I don't believe Veta has ever taken a drink.

SANDERSON. Well, I'm going to surprise you. I think she has and does—constantly.

ELWOOD. I am certainly surprised.

SANDERSON. But it's not her alcoholism that's going to be the basis for my diagnosis of her case. It's much more serious than that. It was when she began talking so emotionally about this big white rabbit—Harvey—yes, I believe she called him Harvey—

ELWOOD (nodding). Harvey is his name.

SANDERSON. She claimed you were persecuting her with this Harvey.

ELWOOD. I haven't been persecuting her with Harvey. Veta shouldn't feel that way. And now, Doctor, before we go any further I must insist you let me introduce—(He starts to rise.)

SANDERSON. Let me make my point first, Mr. Dowd. This trouble of your sister's didn't spring up overnight. Her condition stems from trauma.

ELWOOD (sits down again). From what?

SANDERSON. From trauma.—Spelled T-R-A-U-M-A. It means shock. Nothing unusual about it. There is the birth trauma. The shock to the act of being born.

ELWOOD (nodding). That's the one we never get over—

SANDERSON. You have a nice sense of humor, Dowd—hasn't he, Miss Kelly?

KELLY. Oh, yes, Doctor.

ELWOOD. May I say the same about both of you?

SANDERSON. To sum it all up—your sister's condition is serious, but I can help her. She must however remain out here temporarily.

ELWOOD. I've always wanted Veta to have everything she needs.

SANDERSON. Exactly.

ELWOOD. But I wouldn't want Veta to stay out here unless she liked it out here and wanted to stay here.

SANDERSON. Of course. (To KELLY.) Did Wilson get what he went after? (KELLY nods.)

KELLY. Yes, Doctor. (She rises.)

SANDERSON. What was Mrs. Simmons' attitude, Miss Kelly?

KELLY. Not unusual, Doctor.

SANDERSON (rising). Mr. Dowd, if this were an ordinary delusion—something reflected on the memory picture—in other words, if she were seeing something she had seen once—that would be one thing. But this is more serious. It stands to reason nobody has ever seen a white rabbit six feet high.

ELWOOD (smiles at Harvey). Not very often, Doctor.

SANDERSON. I like you, Dowd.

ELWOOD. I like you, too, Doctor. And Miss Kelly here. (Looks for MISS KELLY, who is just crossing in front of window seat. ELWOOD springs to his feet. KELLY sits quickly. ELWOOD motions Harvey down and sits, himself.) I like her, too.

SANDERSON. So she must be committed here temporarily. Under these circumstances I would commit my own grandmother. (Goes to desk.)

ELWOOD. Does your grandmother drink, too?

SANDERSON. It's just an expression. Now will you sign these temporary commitment papers as next-of-kin—just a formality?

ELWOOD. You'd better have Veta do that, Doctor. She always does all the signing and managing for the family. She's good at it.

SANDERSON. We can't disturb her now.

ELWOOD. Perhaps I'd better talk it over with Judge Gaffney?

SANDERSON. You can explain it all to him later. Tell him I advised it. And it isn't as if you couldn't drop in here any time and make inquiries. Glad to have you. I'll make out a full visitor's pass for you. When would you like to come back? Wednesday, say? Friday, say?

ELWOOD. You and Miss Kelly have been so pleasant I can come back right after dinner. About an hour.

SANDERSON (*taken aback*). Well—we're pretty busy around here, but I guess that's all right.

ELWOOD. I don't really have to go now. I'm not very hungry.

SANDERSON. Delighted to have you stay —but Miss Kelly and I have to get on upstairs now. Plenty of work to do. But I tell you what you might like to do.

ELWOOD. What might I like to do?

SANDERSON. We don't usually do this —but just to make sure in your mind that your sister is in good hands—why don't you look around here? If you go through that door—(*Rises—points beyond stairway.*) and turn right just beyond the stairway you'll find the occupational therapy room down the hall, and beyond that the conservatory, the library, and the diet kitchen.

ELWOOD. For Veta's sake I believe I'd better do that, Doctor.

SANDERSON. Very well, then. (*He is now anxious to terminate the interview. Rises, shakes hands.*) It's been a great pleasure to have this little talk with you, Mr. Dowd. (*Gives him pass.*)

ELWOOD (*walking toward him*). I've enjoyed it too, Doctor—meeting you and Miss Kelly.

SANDERSON. And I will say that for a layman you show an unusually acute perception into psychiatric problems.

ELWOOD. Is that a fact? I never thought I knew anything about it. Nobody does, do you think?

SANDERSON. Well—the good psychiatrist is not found under every bush.

ELWOOD. You have to pick the right bush. Since we all seem to have enjoyed this so much, let us keep right on. I would like to invite you to come with me now down to Charlie's Place and have a drink. When I enjoy people I like to stay right with them.

SANDERSON. Sorry—we're on duty now. Give us a rain-check. Some other time be glad to.

ELWOOD. When?

SANDERSON. Oh—can't say right now. Miss Kelly and I don't go off duty till ten o'clock at night.

ELWOOD. Let us go to Charlie's at ten o'clock tonight.

SANDERSON. Well—

ELWOOD. And you, Miss Kelly?

KELLY. I—(*Looks at* SANDERSON.)

SANDERSON. Dr. Chumley doesn't approve of members of the staff fraternizing, but since you've been so understanding perhaps we could manage it.

ELWOOD. I'll pick you up out here in a cab at ten o'clock tonight and the four of us will spend a happy evening. I want you both to become friends with a very dear friend of mine. You said later on— so later on it will be. Goodbye, now. (*Motions goodbye to Harvey. Tips hat, exits.*)

KELLY. Whew—now I can breathe again!

SANDERSON. Boy, that was a close shave all right, but he seemed to be a pretty reasonable sort of fellow. That man is proud—what he has to be proud of I don't know. I played up to that pride. You can get to almost anybody if you want to. Now I must look in on that Simmons woman.

KELLY. Dr. Sanderson—! (SANDERSON turns.) You say you can get to anybody if you want to. How can you do that?

SANDERSON. Takes study, Kelly. Years of specialized training. There's only one thing I don't like about this Dowd business.

KELLY. What's that?

SANDERSON. Having to make that date with him. Of course the man has left here as a good friend and booster of this sanitarium—so I guess I'll have to go with him tonight—but you don't have to go.

KELLY. Oh!

SANDERSON. No point in it. I'll have a drink with him, pat him on the back and leave. I've got a date tonight, anyway.

KELLY (*freezing*). Oh, yes—by all means. I didn't intend to go, anyway. The idea bored me stiff. I wouldn't go if I never went anywhere again. I wouldn't go if my life depended on it.

SANDERSON (*stepping back to her*). What's the matter with you, Kelly?

What are you getting so emotional about?

KELLY. He may be a peculiar man with funny clothes, but he knows how to act. His manners were perfect.

SANDERSON. I saw you giving him the doll-puss stare. I didn't miss that.

KELLY. He wouldn't sit down till I sat down. He told me I was lovely and he called me dear. I'd go to have a drink with him if you weren't going.

SANDERSON. Sure you would. And look at him! All he does is hang around bars. He doesn't work. All that corny bowing and getting up out of his chair every time a woman makes a move. Why, he's as outdated as a cast-iron deer. But you'd sit with him in a bar and let him flatter you.—You're a wonderful girl, Kelly.

KELLY. Now let me tell you something—you— (*Enter the great* DR. WILLIAM CHUMLEY. DR. CHUMLEY *is a large, handsome man of about fifty-seven. He has gray hair and wears rimless glasses which he removes now and then to tap on his hand for emphasis. He is smartly dressed. His manner is confident, pompous, and lordly. He is good and he knows it.*)

CHUMLEY. Dr. Sanderson! Miss Kelly! (*They break apart and jump to attention like two buck privates before a* C.O.)

KELLY AND SANDERSON. Yes, Doctor?

CHUMLEY. Tell the gardener to prune more carefully around my prize dahlias along the fence by the main road. They'll be ready for cutting next week. The difficulty of the woman who has the big white rabbit—has it been smoothed over?

SANDERSON. Yes, Doctor. I spoke to her brother and he was quite reasonable.

CHUMLEY. While I have had many patients out here who saw animals, I have never before had a patient with an animal that large. (*Puts book in bookcase.*)

SANDERSON. Yes, Doctor. She called him Harvey.

CHUMLEY. Harvey. Unusual name for an animal of any kind. Harvey is a man's name. I have known several men in my day named Harvey, but I have never heard of any type of animal whatsoever with that name. The case has an interesting phase, Doctor. (*Finishes straightening books.*)

SANDERSON. Yes, Doctor.

CHUMLEY. I will now go upstairs with you and look in on this woman. It may be that we can use my formula 977 on her. I will give you my advice in prescribing the treatment, Doctor.

SANDERSON. Thank you, Doctor.

CHUMLEY (*starts to move across stage and stops, draws himself up sternly*). And now—may I ask—what is that hat and coat doing on that table? Whose is it?

SANDERSON. I don't know. Do you know, Miss Kelly? Was it Dowd's?

KELLY (*above table, picking up hat and coat*). He had his hat on, Doctor. Perhaps it belongs to a relative of one of the patients.

CHUMLEY. *Hand me the hat.* (KELLY *hands it. Looking inside.*) There may be some kind of identification— Here—what's this—what's this? (*Pushes two fingers up through the holes.*) Two holes cut in the crown of his hat. See!

KELLY. That's strange!

CHUMLEY. Some new fad—put them away. Hang them up—get them out of here. (KELLY *takes them into office and comes out again.* WILSON *comes in.*)

WILSON (*very impressed with* DR. CHUMLEY *and very fond of him*). Hello, Dr. Chumley.

CHUMLEY. Oh, there you are.

WILSON. How is every little old thing? (DR. CHUMLEY *picks up pad of notes from desk.*)

CHUMLEY. Fair, thank you, Wilson, fair.

WILSON. Look—somebody's gonna have to give me a hand with this Simmons dame—order a restraining jacket or something. She's terrible. (*To* KELLY.) *Forgot me*, didn't you? Well, I got her corset off all by myself.

CHUMLEY. We're going up to see this patient right now, Wilson.

WILSON. She's in a hydro-tub now— my God—I left the water *running on her!* (*Runs off upstairs, followed by* KELLY. BETTY CHUMLEY, *the Doctor's wife, enters. She is a good-natured, gay, bustling woman of about fifty-five.*)

BETTY. Willie—remember your promise—. Hello, Dr. Sanderson. Willie, you haven't forgotten Dr. McClure's cocktail party? We promised them faithfully.

CHUMLEY. That's right. I have to go upstairs now and look in on a patient. Be down shortly— (*Exits upstairs.*)

BETTY (*calling after him*). Give a little quick diagnosis, Willie—we don't want to be late to the party. I'm dying to see the inside of that house. (*Enter* ELWOOD. *He doesn't see* BETTY *at first. He looks around the room carefully.*) Good evening.

ELWOOD (*removing his hat and bowing*). Good evening. (*Puts hat on desk. Walks over to her.*)

BETTY. I am Mrs. Chumley. Doctor Chumley's wife.

ELWOOD. I'm happy to know that. Dowd is my name. Elwood P. Let me give you one of my cards. (*Gives her one.*) If you should want to call me—call me at this one. Don't call me at that one, because that's—(*Points at card.*) the old one. (*Starts one step. Looking.*)

BETTY. Thank you. Is there something I can do for you?

ELWOOD (*turns to her*). What did you have in mind?

BETTY. You seem to be looking for someone.

ELWOOD (*walking*). Yes, I am. I'm looking for Harvey. I went off without him.

BETTY. Harvey? Is he a patient here?

ELWOOD (*turns*). Oh, no. Nothing like that.

BETTY. Does he work here?

ELWOOD (*looking out door*). Oh no. He is what you might call my best friend. He is also a pooka. He came out here with me and Veta this afternoon.

BETTY. Where was he when you last saw him?

ELWOOD. In that chair there—with his hat and coat on the table.

BETTY. There doesn't seem to be any hat and coat around here now. Perhaps he left?

ELWOOD. Apparently. I don't see him anywhere. (*Looks in* SANDERSON'S *office.*)

BETTY. What was that word you just said—pooka?

ELWOOD (*looking in hallway*). Yes—that's it.

BETTY. Is that something new? (*Looks in hallway.*)

ELWOOD. Oh, no. As I understand it. That's something very old.

BETTY. Oh, really? I had never happened to hear it before.

ELWOOD. I'm not too surprised at that. I hadn't myself, until I met him. I do hope you get an opportunity to meet him. I'm sure he would be quite taken with you.

BETTY. Oh, really? Well, that's very nice of you to say so, I'm sure.

ELWOOD. Not at all. If Harvey happens to take a liking to people he expresses himself quite definitely. If he's not particularly interested, he sits there like an empty chair or an empty space on the floor. Harvey takes his time making his mind up about people. Choosey, you see.

BETTY. That's not such a bad way to be in this day and age.

ELWOOD. Harvey is fond of my sister, Veta. That's because he is fond of me, and Veta and I come from the same family. Now you'd think that feeling would be mutual, wouldn't you? But Veta doesn't seem to care for Harvey. Don't you think that's rather too bad, Mrs. Chumley?

BETTY. Oh, I don't know, Mr. Dowd. I gave up a long time ago expecting my family to like my friends. It's useless.

ELWOOD. But we must keep on trying. (*Sits.*)

BETTY. Well, there's no harm in trying, I suppose.

ELWOOD. Because if Harvey has said to me once he has said a million times— "Mr. Dowd, I would do anything for you." Mrs. Chumley—

BETTY. Yes—

ELWOOD. Did you know that Mrs.

McElhinney's Aunt Rose is going to drop in on her unexpectedly tonight from Cleveland?

BETTY. Why, no I didn't—

ELWOOD. Neither does she. That puts you both in the same boat, doesn't it?

BETTY. Well, I don't know anybody named—Mrs.—

ELWOOD. Mrs. McElhinney? Lives next door to us. She is a wonderful woman. Harvey told me about her Aunt Rose. That's an interesting little news item, and you are perfectly free to pass it around.

BETTY. Well, I—

ELWOOD. Would you care to come downtown with me now, my dear? I would be glad to buy you a drink.

BETTY. Thank you very much, but I am waiting for Dr. Chumley and if he came down and found me gone he would be liable to raise—he would be irritated!

ELWOOD. We wouldn't want that, would we? Some other time, maybe? (He rises.)

BETTY. I'll tell you what I'll do, however.

ELWOOD. What will you do, however? I'm interested.

BETTY. If your friend comes in while I'm here I'd be glad to give him a message for you.

ELWOOD (gratefully). Would you do that? I'd certainly appreciate that. (Goes to desk for his hat.)

BETTY. No trouble at all. I'll write it down on the back of this. (Holds up card. Takes pencil from purse.) What would you like me to tell him if he comes in while I'm still here?

ELWOOD. Ask him to meet me downtown—if he has no other plans.

BETTY (writing). Meet Mr. Dowd downtown. Any particular place downtown?

ELWOOD. He knows where. Harvey knows this town like a book.

BETTY (writing). Harvey—you know where. Harvey what?

ELWOOD. Just Harvey.

BETTY. I'll tell you what.

ELWOOD. What?

BETTY. Doctor and I are going right downtown—to Twelfth and Montview. Dr. McClure is having a cocktail party.

ELWOOD (he writes that down on pad on desk). A cocktail party at Twelfth and Montview.

BETTY. We're driving there in a few minutes. We could give your friend a lift into town.

ELWOOD. I hate to impose on you—but I would certainly appreciate that.

BETTY. No trouble at all. Dr. McClure is having this party for his sister from Wichita.

ELWOOD. I didn't know Dr. McClure had a sister in Wichita.

BETTY. Oh—you know Dr. McClure?

ELWOOD. No.

BETTY (puts ELWOOD's card down on desk). But—(Sits.)

ELWOOD. You're quite sure you haven't time to come into town with me and have a drink?

BETTY. I really couldn't—but thank you just the same.

ELWOOD. Some other time, perhaps?

BETTY. Thank you.

ELWOOD. It's been very pleasant to meet you, and I hope to see you again.

BETTY. Yes, so do I.

ELWOOD. Goodnight, my dear. (Tips hat—bows—goes to door, turns.) You can't miss Harvey. He's very tall—(Shows with hands.) Like that—(Exits. CHUMLEY enters, followed by SANDERSON and KELLY. CHUMLEY goes to desk. KELLY crosses to office for CHUMLEY's hat and coat.)

CHUMLEY (working with pen on desk-pad). That Simmons woman is uncooperative, Doctor. She refused to admit to me that she has this big rabbit. Insists it's her brother. Give her two of these at nine—another at ten—if she continues to be so restless. Another trip to the hydro-room at eight, and one in the morning at seven. Then we'll see if she won't cooperate tomorrow, won't we, Doctor?

SANDERSON. Yes, Doctor.

CHUMLEY. You know where to call me if you need me. Ready, pet?

BETTY. Yes, Willie—and oh, Willie—

CHUMLEY. Yes—

BETTY. There was a man in here—a man named—let me see—(*Picks up card from desk.*) Oh, here is his card— Dowd —Elwood P. Dowd. (KELLY *enters. She has* DR. CHUMLEY'S *hat.*)

SANDERSON. That's Mrs. Simmons' brother, Doctor. I told him he could look around, and I gave him full visiting privileges.

CHUMLEY. She mustn't see anyone tonight. Not anyone at all. Tell him that.

SANDERSON. Yes, Doctor.

BETTY. He didn't ask to see her? He was looking for someone—some friend of his.

CHUMLEY. Who could that be, Dr. Sanderson?

SANDERSON. I don't know, Doctor.

BETTY. He said it was someone he came out here with this afternoon.

SANDERSON. Was there anyone with Dowd when you saw him, Miss Kelly?

KELLY. No, Doctor—not when I saw him.

BETTY. Well, he said there was. He said he last saw his friend sitting right in that chair there with his hat and coat. He seemed quite disappointed.

KELLY (*a funny look is crossing her face*). Dr. Sanderson—

BETTY. I told him if we located his friend we'd give him a lift into town. He could ride in the back seat. Was that all right, Willie?

CHUMLEY. Of course—of course—

BETTY. Oh here it is. I wrote it down on the back of this card. His friend's name was Harvey.

KELLY. Harvey!

BETTY. He didn't give me his last name. He mentioned something else about him —pooka—but I didn't quite get what that was.

SANDERSON *and* CHUMLEY. Harvey!

BETTY (*rises*). He said his friend was very tall—. Well, why are you looking like that, Willie? This man was a very nice, polite man, and he merely asked that we give his friend a lift into town, and if we can't do a favor for someone, why are we living?

SANDERSON (*gasping*). Where—where did he go, Mrs. Chumley? How long ago was he in here?

CHUMLEY (*thundering*). Get me that hat! By George, we'll find out about this! (KELLY *goes out to get it.*)

BETTY. I don't know where he went. Just a second ago. (SANDERSON, *his face drawn, sits at desk and picks up house phone.* CHUMLEY, *with a terrible look on his face, has started to thumb through phone book.*)

SANDERSON (*on house phone*). Main gate—Henry—Dr. Sanderson—

CHUMLEY (*thumbing through book*). Gaffney—Judge Gaffney—

SANDERSON. Henry—did a man in a brown suit go out through the gate a minute ago? He did? He's gone? (*Hangs up and looks stricken.* KELLY *enters with hat.*)

CHUMLEY (*has been dialing*). Judge Gaffney—this is Dr. William Chumley— the psychiatrist. I'm making a routine checkup on the spelling of a name before entering it into our records. Judge —you telephoned out here this afternoon about having a client of yours committed? How is that name spelled? With a W, not a U—Mr. Elwood P. Dowd. Thank you, Judge—(*Hangs up—rises— pushes chair in to desk—takes hat from* KELLY. *Stands silently for a moment, contemplating* SANDERSON.) Dr. Sanderson—I believe your name is Sanderson?

SANDERSON. Yes, Doctor.

CHUMLEY. You know that much, do you? You went to medical school—you specialized in the study of psychiatry? You graduated—you went forth. (*Holds up hat and runs two fingers up through holes in it.*) Perhaps they neglected to tell you that a rabbit has large pointed ears! That a hat for a rabbit would have to be perforated to make room for those ears?

SANDERSON. Dowd seemed reasonable enough this afternoon, Doctor.

CHUMLEY. Doctor—the function of a psychiatrist is to tell the difference between those who are reasonable, and those who merely talk and act reasonably. (*Presses buzzer. Flings hat on desk.*) Do you realize what you have done to me? You don't answer. I'll tell you. You have permitted a psychopathic case to walk off these grounds and roam around with an overgrown white rabbit. You have subjected me—a psychiatrist—to the humiliation of having to call—of all things —a lawyer to find out who came out here to be committed—and who came out here to commit! (WILSON *enters.*)

SANDERSON. Dr. Chumley—I—

CHUMLEY. Just a minute, Wilson—I want you. (*Back to* SANDERSON.) I will now have to do something I haven't done in fifteen years. I will have to go out after this patient, Elwood P. Dowd, and I will have to bring him back, and when I do bring him back your connection with this institution is ended—as of that moment! (*Turns to* WILSON—*others are standing frightened.*) Wilson, get the car. (*To* BETTY.) Pet, call the McClures and say we can't make it. Miss Kelly—come upstairs with me and we'll get that woman out of the tub—(*Starts upstairs on the run.*)

KELLY (*follows him upstairs*). Yes—Doctor—(SANDERSON *turns on his heel, goes into his office.* WILSON *is getting into a coat in hall.*)

BETTY. I'll have to tell the cook we'll be home for dinner. She'll be furious. (*She turns.*) Wilson—

WILSON. Yes, ma'am.

BETTY. What is a pooka?

WILSON. A what?

BETTY. A pooka.

WILSON. You can search me, Mrs. Chumley.

BETTY. I wonder if it would be in the Encyclopedia here? (*Goes to bookcase and takes out book.*) They have everything here. I wonder if it is a lodge, or what it is! (*Starts to look in it, then puts it on table open.*) Oh, I don't dare to stop to do this now. Dr. Chumley won't want to find me still here when he comes down. (*Starts to door very fast.*) He'll raise—I mean—oh, dear! (*She exits.*)

WILSON (*picks up book, looks in it. Runs forefinger under words*). P-o-o-k-a. "Pooka. From old Celtic mythology. A fairy spirit in animal form. Always very large. The pooka appears here and there, now and then, to this one and that one at his own caprice. A wise but mischievous creature. Very fond of rum-pots, crack-pots," and how are you, Mr. Wilson. (*Looks at book startled—looks at doorway fearfully—then back to book.*) How are you, Mr. Wilson? (*Shakes book, looks at it in surprise.*) Who in the encyclopedia wants to know? (*Looks at book again, drops it on table.*) Oh—to hell with it! (*He exits quickly.*)

CURTAIN

ACT TWO

SCENE 1: *The Dowd library again, about an hour later.*

AT RISE: *Doorbell is ringing and* MYRTLE *enters. She calls behind her.*

MYRTLE. That's right. The stairs at the end of the hall. It goes to the third floor. Go right up. I'll be with you in a minute. (JUDGE OMAR GAFFNEY *enters, an elderly white-haired man. He looks displeased.*)

JUDGE (*looking around*). Well, where is she?

MYRTLE. Where is who? Whom do you mean, Judge Gaffney? Sit down, won't you?

JUDGE. I mean your mother. Where's Veta Louise?

MYRTLE. Why Judge Gaffney! You know where she is. She took Uncle Elwood out to the sanitarium.

JUDGE. I know that. But why was I called at the club with a lot of hysteria? Couldn't even get what she was talking about. Carrying on something fierce.

MYRTLE. Mother carrying on! What about?

JUDGE. I don't know. She was hysterical.

MYRTLE. That's strange! She took Uncle Elwood out to the sanitarium. All she had to do was put him in. (*Goes back, opens door, and looks through, calling.*) Did you find it? I'll be right up. (*Waits. Turns to him.*) They found it.

JUDGE. Who? Found what? What are you talking about?

MYRTLE. When Mother left the house with Uncle Elwood I went over to the real-estate office to put the house on the market. And what do you think I found there? (*She sits.*)

JUDGE. I'm not a quiz kid.

MYRTLE. Well, I found a man there who was looking for an old house just like this to cut up into buffet apartments. He's going through it now.

JUDGE. Now see here, Myrtle Mae. This house doesn't belong to you. It belongs to your Uncle Elwood.

MYRTLE. But now that Elwood is locked up, Mother controls the property, doesn't she?

JUDGE. Where is your mother? Where is Veta Louise?

MYRTLE. Judge, she went out to Chumley's Rest to tell them about Harvey and put Uncle Elwood in.

JUDGE. Why did she call me at the club when I was in the middle of a game, and scream at me to meet her here about something important?

MYRTLE. I don't know. I simply don't know. Have you got the deed to this house?

JUDGE. Certainly, it's in my safe. Myrtle, I feel pretty bad about this thing of locking Elwood up.

MYRTLE. Mother and I will be able to take a long trip now—out to Pasadena.

JUDGE. I always liked that boy. He could have done anything—been anything—made a place for himself in this community.

MYRTLE. And all he did was get a big rabbit.

JUDGE. He had everything. Brains, personality, friends. Men liked him. Women liked him. I liked him.

MYRTLE. Are you telling me that once Uncle Elwood was like other men—that women actually liked him—I mean in that way?

JUDGE. Oh, not since he started running around with this big rabbit. But they did once. Once that mail-box of your grandmother's was full of those little blue-scented envelopes for Elwood.

MYRTLE. I can't believe it.

JUDGE. Of course there was always something different about Elwood.

MYRTLE. I don't doubt that.

JUDGE. Yes—he was always so calm about any sudden change in plans. I used to admire it. I should have been suspicious. Take your average man looking up and seeing a big white rabbit. He'd do something about it. But not Elwood. He took that calmly, too. And look where it got him!

MYRTLE. You don't dream how far overboard he's gone on this rabbit.

JUDGE. Oh, yes I do. He's had that rabbit in my office many's the time. I'm old but I don't miss much. (*Noise from upstairs.*) What's that noise?

MYRTLE. The prospective buyer on the third floor. (*Looks up. VETA is standing in doorway, looking like something the cat dragged in. Shakes her head sadly; looks into the room and sighs; her hat is crooked. MYRTLE jumps up.*) Mother! Look, Judge—

JUDGE (*rising*). Veta Louise—what's wrong, girl?

VETA (*shaking her head*). I never thought I'd see either of you again. (*MYRTLE and JUDGE take VETA to chair.*)

MYRTLE. Take hold of her, Judge. She looks like she's going to faint. (*JUDGE gets hold of her on one side and MYRTLE on the other. They start to bring her into the room.*) Now, Mother—you're all right. You're going to be perfectly all right.

JUDGE. Steady—steady, girl, steady.

VETA. Please—not so fast.

JUDGE. Don't rush her, Myrtle— Ease her in.

VETA. Let me sit down. Only get me some place where I can sit down.

JUDGE (*guiding her to a big chair*). Here you are, girl. Easy, Myrtle—easy. (*VETA is about to lower herself into chair. She sighs. But before she can complete the lowering, MYRTLE MAE lets out a yelp and VETA straightens up quickly.*)

MYRTLE. Oh—(*She picks up envelope off chair. Holds it up.*) The gas bill.

VETA (*hand at head*). Oh—oh, my—(*Sits.*)

JUDGE. Get her some tea, Myrtle. Do you want some tea, Veta?

MYRTLE. I'll get you some tea, Mother. Get her coat off, Judge.

JUDGE. Let Myrtle get your coat off, Veta. Get her coat off, Myrtle.

VETA. Leave me alone. Let me sit here. Let me get my breath.

MYRTLE. Let her get her breath, Judge.

VETA. Let me sit here a minute and then let me get upstairs to my own bed where I can let go.

MYRTLE. What happened to you, Mother?

VETA. Omar, I want you to sue them. They put me in and let Elwood out.

JUDGE. What's this?

MYRTLE. Mother!

VETA (taking off hat). Just look at my hair.

MYRTLE. But why? What did you say? What did you do? (Kneels at VETA's feet.) You must have done something.

VETA. I didn't do one thing. I simply told them about Elwood and Harvey.

JUDGE. Then how could it happen to you? I don't understand it.

VETA. I told them about Elwood, and then I went down to the cab to get his things. As I was walking along the path —this awful man stepped out. He was a white slaver. I know he was. He had on one of those white suits. That's how they advertise.

MYRTLE. A man—what did he do, Mother?

VETA. What did he do? He took hold of me and took me in there and then he— (Bows her head. MYRTLE and JUDGE exchange a look.)

JUDGE (softly). Go on, Veta Louise. Go on, girl.

MYRTLE (goes over, takes her hand). Poor Mother— Was he a young man?

JUDGE. Myrtle Mae—perhaps you'd better leave the room.

MYRTLE. Now? I should say not! Go on, Mother.

JUDGE (edging closer). What did he do, Veta?

VETA. He took me upstairs and tore my clothes off.

MYRTLE (shrieking). Oh—did you hear

that, Judge! Go on, Mother. (She is all ears.)

JUDGE. By God—I'll sue them for this!

VETA. And then he set me down in a tub of water.

MYRTLE (disappointed). Oh! For heaven's sake! (Rises.)

VETA. I always thought that what you were showed on your face. Don't you believe it, Judge! Don't you believe it, Myrtle. This man took hold of me like I was a woman of the streets—but I fought. I always said if a man jumped at me—I'd fight. Haven't I always said that, Myrtle?

MYRTLE. She's always said that, Judge. That's what Mother always told me to do.

VETA. And then he hustled me into that sanitarium and set me down in that tub of water and began treating me like I was a—

MYRTLE. A what—?

VETA. A crazy woman—but he did that just for spite.

JUDGE. Well, I'll be damned!

VETA. And those doctors came upstairs and asked me a lot of questions—all about sex-urges—and all that filthy stuff. That place ought to be cleaned up, Omar. You better get the authorities to clean it up. Myrtle, don't you ever go out there. You hear me?

JUDGE. This stinks to high heaven, Veta. By God, it stinks!

VETA. You've got to do something about it, Judge. You've got to sue them.

JUDGE. I will, girl. By God, I will! If Chumley thinks he can run an unsavory place like this on the outskirts of town he'll be publicly chastised. By God, I'll run him out of the State!

VETA. Tell me, Judge. Is that all those doctors do at places like that—think about sex?

JUDGE. I don't know.

VETA. Because if it is they ought to be ashamed—of themselves. It's all in their head anyway. Why don't they get out and go for long walks in the fresh air? (To MYRTLE.) Judge Gaffney walked everywhere for years—didn't you, Judge?

JUDGE. Now let me take some notes on

this. You said—these doctors came up to talk to you—Dr. Chumley and— What was the other doctor's name?

VETA. Sanderson— (*Sits up straight—glances covertly at them and becomes very alert.*) But, Judge, don't you pay any attention to anything he tells you. He's a liar. Close-set eyes. They're always liars. Besides—I told him something in strictest confidence and he blabbed it.

MYRTLE. What did you tell him, Mother?

VETA. Oh, what difference does it make? Let's forget it. I don't even want to talk about it. You can't trust anybody.

JUDGE. Anything you told this Dr. Sanderson you can tell us, Veta Louise. This is your daughter and I am your lawyer.

VETA. I know which is which. I don't want to talk about it. I want to sue them and I want to get in my own bed. (JUDGE *rises.*)

MYRTLE. But, Mother—this is the important thing, anyway. Where is Uncle Elwood?

VETA (*to herself*). I should have known better than to try to do anything about him. Something protects him—that awful Pooka—

MYRTLE. Where is Uncle Elwood? Answer me.

VETA (*trying to be casual*). How should I know? They let him go. They're not interested in men at places like that. Don't act so naïve, Myrtle Mae. (*Noise from upstairs.*) What's that noise?

MYRTLE. I've found a buyer for the house.

VETA. What?

MYRTLE. Listen, Mother, we've got to find Uncle Elwood—no matter who jumped at you we've still got to lock up Uncle Elwood.

VETA. I don't know where he is. The next time *you* take him, Judge. Wait until Elwood hears what they did to me. He won't stand for it. Don't forget to sue them, Judge— Myrtle Mae, all I hope is that never, never as long as you live a man pulls the clothes off you and dumps you down into a tub of water. (*She exits.*)

MYRTLE (*turning to* JUDGE). Now, see —Mother muffed everything. No matter what happened out there—Uncle Elwood's still wandering around with Harvey.

JUDGE (*pondering*). The thing for me to do is take some more notes.

MYRTLE. It's all Uncle Elwood's fault. He found out what she was up to—and he had her put in. Then he ran.

JUDGE. Oh, no—don't talk like that. Your uncle thinks the world and all of your mother. Ever since he was a little boy he always wanted to share everything he had with her.

MYRTLE. I'm not giving up. We'll get detectives. We'll find him. And, besides —you'd better save some of that sympathy for me and Mother—you don't realize what we have to put up with. Wait till I show you something he brought home about six months ago, and we hid it out in the garage. You just wait—

JUDGE. I'm going up to talk to Veta. There's more in this than she's telling. I sense that.

MYRTLE (*as she exits*). Wait till I show you, Judge.

JUDGE. All right. I'll wait. (WILSON *enters.*)

WILSON. Okay—is he here?

JUDGE. What? What's this?

WILSON. That crackpot with the rabbit. Is he here?

JUDGE. No—and who, may I ask, are you?

WILSON (*stepping into hallway, calling*). Not here, Doctor—okay—(*To* JUDGE.) Doctor Chumley's comin' in, anyway. What's your name?

JUDGE. Chumley—well, well, well—I've got something to say to him! (*Sits.*)

WILSON. What's your name? Let's have it.

JUDGE. I am Judge Gaffney—where is Chumley?

WILSON. The reason I asked your name is the Doctor always likes to know who he's talkin' to. (*Enter* CHUMLEY.) This guy says his name is Judge Gaffney, Doctor.

JUDGE. Well, well, Chumley—

CHUMLEY. Good evening, Judge. Let's not waste time. Has he been here?

JUDGE. Who? Elwood—no—but see here, Doctor—

WILSON. Sure he ain't been here? He's wise now. He's hidin'. It'll be an awful job to smoke him out.

CHUMLEY. It will be more difficult, but I'll do it. They're sly. They're cunning. But I get them. I always get them. Have you got the list of the places we've been, Wilson?

WILSON (pulling paper out of his pocket). Right here, Doctor.

CHUMLEY (sits). Read it.

WILSON. We've been to seventeen bars, Eddie's Place, Charlie's Place, Bessie's Barn-dance, the Fourth Avenue Firehouse, the Tenth and Twelfth and Ninth Avenue firehouses, just to make sure. The Union Station, the grain elevator—say, why does this guy go down to a grain elevator?

JUDGE. The foreman is a friend of his. He has many friends—many places.

CHUMLEY. I have stopped by here to ask Mrs. Simmons if she has any other suggestions as to where we might look for him.

JUDGE. Doctor Chumley, I have to inform you that Mrs. Simmons has retained me to file suit against you—

DR. CHUMLEY. What?

JUDGE. For what happened to her at the sanitarium this afternoon . . .

CHUMLEY. A suit!

JUDGE. And while we're on that subject—

WILSON. That's pretty, ain't it, Doctor? After us draggin' your tail all over town trying to find that guy.

CHUMLEY. What happened this afternoon was an unfortunate mistake. I've discharged my assistant who made it. And I am prepared to take charge of this man's case personally. It interests me. And my interest in a case is something no amount of money can buy. You can ask any of them.

JUDGE. But this business this afternoon, Doctor—

CHUMLEY. Water under the dam. This is how I see this thing. I see it this way— (MYRTLE has come into the room. She is carrying a big flat parcel, wrapped in brown paper. Stands it up against wall and listens.) The important item now is to get this man and take him out to the sanitarium where he belongs.

MYRTLE (coming forward). That's right, Judge—that's just what I think—

JUDGE. Let me introduce Miss Myrtle Mae Simmons, Mr. Dowd's niece, Mrs. Simmons's daughter. (CHUMLEY rises.)

MYRTLE. How do you do, Dr. Chumley.

CHUMLEY (giving her the careful scrutiny he gives all women). How do you do, Miss Simmons.

WILSON. Hello, Myrtle—

MYRTLE (now seeing him and looking at him with a mixture of horror and intense curiosity). What? Oh—

CHUMLEY. Now, then—let me talk to Mrs. Simmons.

MYRTLE. Mother won't come down, Doctor. I know she won't. (To JUDGE.) You try to get Mother to talk to him, Judge. (Puts package down.)

JUDGE. But, see here; your mother was manhandled. She was—God knows what she was—the man's approach to her was not professional, it was personal. (Looks at WILSON.)

CHUMLEY. Wilson—this is a serious charge.

WILSON. Dr. Chumley, I've been with you for ten years. Are you gonna believe—what's your name again?

JUDGE. Gaffney. Judge Omar Gaffney.

WILSON. Thanks. You take the word of this old blister Gaffney—

CHUMLEY. Wilson!

WILSON. Me! Me and a dame who sees a rabbit!

JUDGE. It's not Mrs. Simmons who sees a rabbit. It's her brother.

MYRTLE. Yes, it's Uncle Elwood.

JUDGE. If you'll come with me, Doctor—

CHUMLEY. Very well, Judge. Wilson, I have a situation here. Wait for me. (He and JUDGE exit.)

WILSON. O.K. Doctor. (MYRTLE MAE *is fascinated by* WILSON. *She lingers and looks at him. He comes over to her, grinning.*)

WILSON. So your name's Myrtle Mae?

MYRTLE. What? Oh—yes— (*She backs up. He follows.*)

WILSON. If we grab your uncle you're liable to be comin' out to the sanitarium on visiting days?

MYRTLE. Oh, I don't really know—I—

WILSON. Well, if you do, I'll be there.

MYRTLE. You will? Oh—

WILSON. And if you don't see me right away—don't give up. Stick around. I'll show up.

MYRTLE. You will—? Oh—

WILSON. Sure. (*He is still following her.*) You heard Dr. Chumley tell me to wait?

MYRTLE. Yeah—

WILSON. Tell you what—while I'm waiting I sure could use a sandwich and a cup of coffee.

MYRTLE. Certainly. If you'll forgive me I'll precede you into the kitchen. (*She tries to go. He traps her.*)

WILSON. Yessir—you're all right, Myrtle.

MYRTLE. What?

WILSON. Doctor Chumley noticed it right away. He don't miss a trick. (*Crowds closer; raises finger and pokes her arm for emphasis.*) Tell you somethin' else, Myrtle—

MYRTLE. What?

WILSON. You not only got a nice build —but, kid, you got something else, too.

MYRTLE. What?

WILSON. You got the screwiest uncle that ever stuck his puss inside our nuthouse. (MYRTLE *starts to exit in a huff, and* WILSON *raises hand to give her a spank, but she turns and so he puts up raised hand to his hair. They exit. The stage is empty for a half second and then* ELWOOD *comes in, goes to phone, dials a number.*)

ELWOOD. Hello, Chumley's Rest? Is Doctor Chumley there? Oh—it's Mrs. Chumley! This is Elwood P. Dowd speaking. How are you tonight? Tell me, Mrs. Chumley, were you able to locate Harvey?—Don't worry about it. I'll find him. I'm sorry I missed you at the McClure cocktail party. The people were all charming and I was able to leave quite a few of my cards. I waited until you phoned and said you couldn't come because a patient had escaped. Where am I? I'm here. But I'm leaving right away. I must find Harvey. Well, goodbye, Mrs. Chumley. My regards to you and anybody else you happen to run into. Goodbye. (*Hangs up, then he sees the big flat parcel against wall. He gets an "Ah, there it is!" expression on his face, goes over and takes off paper. We see revealed a very strange thing. It is an oil painting of* ELWOOD *seated on a chair while behind him stands a large white rabbit, in a blue polka-dot collar and red necktie.* ELWOOD *holds it away from him and surveys it proudly, then looks around for a place to put it. Takes it over and sets it on mantel. It obscures the picture of Marcella Pinney Dowd completely. He gathers up wrapping-paper, admires the rabbit again, tips his hat to it and exits. Phone rings and* VETA *enters, followed by* DR. CHUMLEY.*)

VETA. Doctor, you might as well go home and wait. I'm suing you for fifty thousand dollars and that's final. (*Crosses to phone—her back is to mantel; she hasn't looked up.*)

CHUMLEY (*follows her*). Mrs. Simmons—

VETA (*into phone*). Yes— Well, all right.

CHUMLEY. This picture over your mantel.

VETA. That portrait happens to be the pride of this house.

CHUMLEY (*looking at her*). Who painted it?

VETA. Oh, some man. I forget his name. He was around here for the sittings, and then we paid him and he went away. Hello—yes— No. This is Dexter 1567. (*Hangs up.*)

CHUMLEY. I suppose if you have the money to pay people, you can persuade them to do anything.

VETA. Well, Dr. Chumley— (*Walks over and faces him.*) When you helped me out of that tub at your place, what did I say to you?

CHUMLEY. You expressed yourself. I don't remember the words.

VETA. I said, "Dr. Chumley, this is a belated civility." Isn't that what I said?

CHUMLEY. You said something of the sort—

VETA. You brought this up; you may as well learn something quick. I took a course in art this last winter. The difference between a fine oil painting and a mechanical thing like a photograph is simply this: a photograph shows only the reality; a painting shows not only the reality but the dream behind it—. It's our dreams that keep us going. That separate us from the beasts. I wouldn't even want to live if I thought it was all just eating and sleeping and taking off my clothes. Well—putting them on again— (*Turns—sees picture—screams—totters—falls back.*) Oh—Doctor—oh—hold me—oh—

CHUMLEY (*taking hold of her*). Steady now—steady—don't get excited. Everything's all right. (*Seats her in chair.*) Now—what's the matter?

VETA (*pointing*). Doctor—that is *not* my mother!

CHUMLEY. I'm glad to hear that.

VETA. Oh, Doctor. Elwood's been here. He's been here.

CHUMLEY. Better be quiet. (*Phone rings.*) I'll take it. (*He answers it.*) Hello. Yes, yes—who's calling? (*Drops his hand over mouthpiece quickly.*) Here he is. Mrs. Simmons, it's your brother!

VETA (*getting up. Weak no longer*). Oh—let me talk to him!

CHUMLEY. Don't tell him I'm here. Be casual.

VETA. Hello, Elwood—(*Laughs.*) Where are you? What? Oh—just a minute. (*Covers phone.*) He won't say where he is. He wants to know if Harvey is here.

CHUMLEY. Tell him Harvey *is* here.

VETA. But he isn't.

CHUMLEY. Tell him. That will bring him here, perhaps. Humor him. We have to humor them.

VETA. Yes—Elwood. Yes, dear. Harvey is here. Why don't you come home? Oh, oh, oh—well—all right. (*Looks around uncomfortably. Covers phone again.*) It won't work. He says for me to call Harvey to the telephone.

CHUMLEY. Say Harvey is here, but can't come to the telephone. Say—he—say—he's in the bathtub.

VETA. Bathtub?

CHUMLEY. Say he's in the bathtub, and you'll send him over there. That way we'll find out where he is.

VETA. Oh, Doctor!

CHUMLEY. Now, you've got to do it, Mrs. Simmons.

VETA. Hello, Elwood. Yes, dear. Harvey is here but he can't come to the telephone, he's in the bathtub. I'll send him over as soon as he's dry. Where are you? Where, Elwood? (*Bangs phone.*)

CHUMLEY. Did he hang up?

VETA. Harvey just walked in the door! He told me to look in the bathtub—it must be a stranger. But I know where he is. He's at Charlie's Place. That's a bar over at Twelfth and Main.

CHUMLEY (*picking up his hat from table*). Twelfth and Main. That's two blocks down and one over, isn't it?

VETA. Doctor—where are you going?

CHUMLEY. I'm going over there to get your brother and take him out to the sanitarium, where he belongs.

VETA. Oh, Dr. Chumley—don't do that. Send one of your attendants. I'm warning you.

CHUMLEY. But, Mrs. Simmons, if I am to help your brother—

VETA. He can't be helped. (*Looks at picture.*) There is no help for him. He must be picked up and locked up and left.

CHUMLEY. You consider your brother a dangerous man?

VETA. Dangerous!

CHUMLEY. Why?

VETA. I won't tell you why, but if I didn't, why would I be asking for a permanent commitment for him?

CHUMLEY. Then I must observe this man. I must watch the expression on his face as he talks to this rabbit. He does talk to the rabbit, you say?

VETA. They tell each other everything.

CHUMLEY. What's that?

VETA. I said, of course he talks to him. But don't go after him, Doctor. You'll regret it if you do.

CHUMLEY. Nonsense. You underestimate me, Mrs. Simmons.

VETA. Oh, no, Doctor. You underestimate my brother.

CHUMLEY. Not at all. Don't worry now. I can handle him! (*He exits.*)

VETA (*after he has gone*). You can handle him? That's what you think! (*Calls.*) Myrtle Mae! See who's in the bathtub. OH!

CURTAIN

SCENE 2: *The main office at Chumley's Rest again, four hours later.*

AT RISE: KELLY *is on the phone.* WILSON *is helping* SANDERSON *carry boxes of books out of his office and onto table.*

KELLY. Thank you. I may call later. (*Hangs up.*)

WILSON. How about the stuff in your room, Doctor—upstairs?

SANDERSON. All packed—thanks—Wilson.

WILSON. Tough your gettin' bounced. I had you pegged for the one who'd make the grade.

SANDERSON. Those are the breaks.

WILSON. When you takin' off?

SANDERSON. As soon as Dr. Chumley gets back.

WILSON (*to* KELLY). Did you get a report back yet from the desk sergeant in the police accident bureau?

KELLY. Not yet. I just talked to the downtown dispensary. They haven't seen him.

WILSON. It's beginning to smell awful funny to me. Four hours he's been gone and not a word from him. (*Goes to* SANDERSON—*extends hand.*) I may not see you again, Doctor, so I want to say I wish you a lot of luck and I'm mighty sorry you got a kick in the atpray.

SANDERSON. Thanks, Wilson—good luck to you, too—

WILSON (*starts to exit, but stops at door, turns toward* KELLY). Look, Kelly, let me know when you hear from the desk sergeant again. If there's no sign of the doctor, I'm goin' into town and look for him. He should know better'n to go after a psycho without me.

SANDERSON. I'd like to help look for the doctor, too, Wilson.

WILSON. That's swell of you, Doctor, right after he give you the brush.

SANDERSON. I've no resentment against Dr. Chumley. He was right. I was wrong. (*He rises.*) Chumley is the biggest man in his field. It's my loss not to be able to work with him.

WILSON. You're not so small yourself, Doctor—

SANDERSON. Thanks, Wilson.

WILSON. Don't mention it. (*Exits.*)

KELLY (*taking deep breath*). Dr. Sanderson—

SANDERSON (*without looking up*). Yes—

KELLY (*plunging in*). Well, Doctor— (*Takes another deep breath.*) I'd like to say that *I* wish you a lot of luck, too, and I'm sorry to see you leave.

SANDERSON (*going on with his work*). Are you sure you can spare these good wishes, Miss Kelly?

KELLY (*she flushes*). On second thought—I guess I can't. Forget it.

SANDERSON (*now looking up*). Miss Kelly— This is for nothing—just a little advice. I'd be a little careful if I were you about the kind of company I kept.

KELLY. I beg your pardon, Doctor?

SANDERSON. You don't have to. I told you it was free. I saw you Saturday night—dancing with that drip in the Rose Room down at the Frontier Hotel.

KELLY (*putting books on desk*). Oh, did you? I didn't notice you.

SANDERSON. I'd be a little careful of him, Kelly. He looked to me like a schizophrenic all the way across the floor.

KELLY. You really shouldn't have given him a thought, Doctor. He was my date—not yours. (*Hands book to* SANDERSON.)

SANDERSON. That was his mentality. The rest of him—well—

KELLY. But she was beautiful, though—

SANDERSON. Who?

KELLY. That girl you were with—

SANDERSON. I thought you didn't notice?

KELLY. You bumped into us twice. How could I help it?

SANDERSON. Not that it makes any difference to you, but that girl is a charming little lady. *She* has a sweet kind disposition and *she* knows how to conduct herself.

KELLY. Funny she couldn't rate a better date on a Saturday night!

SANDERSON. And she has an excellent mind.

KELLY. Why doesn't she use it?

SANDERSON. Oh, I don't suppose you're to be censured for the flippant hard shell you have. You're probably compensating for something.

KELLY. I am not, and don't you use any of your psychiatry on me.

SANDERSON. Oh—if I could try something else on you—just once! Just to see if you'd melt under any circumstances. I doubt it.

KELLY. You'll never know, Doctor.

SANDERSON. Because you interest me as a case history—that's all. I'd like to know where you get that inflated ego—

KELLY (*now close to tears*). If you aren't the meanest person—inflated ego—case history! (*Turns and starts out.*)

SANDERSON. Don't run away. Let's finish it. (*Phone rings.*)

KELLY. Oh, leave me alone. (*Goes to answer it.*)

SANDERSON. Gladly. (*Exits.*)

KELLY (*in angry, loud voice*). Chumley's Rest. Yes—Sergeant. No accident report on him either in town or the suburbs. Look, Sergeant—maybe we better—(*Looks up as door opens and* ELWOOD *enters. He is carrying a bouquet of dahlias.*) Oh, never mind, Sergeant. They're here now. (*Hangs up. Goes toward* ELWOOD.) Mr. Dowd—!

ELWOOD (*handing her flowers*). Good evening, my dear. These are for you.

KELLY. For me—oh, thank you!

ELWOOD. They're quite fresh, too. I just picked them outside.

KELLY. I hope Dr. Chumley didn't see you. They're his prize dahlias. Did he go upstairs?

ELWOOD. Not knowing, I cannot state. Those colors are lovely against your hair.

KELLY. I've never worn burnt orange. It's such a trying color.

ELWOOD. You would improve any color, my dear.

KELLY. Thank you. Did Dr. Chumley go over to his house?

ELWOOD. I don't know. Where is Dr. Sanderson?

KELLY. In his office there—I think.

ELWOOD (*going over to door and knocking*). Thank you.

SANDERSON (*enters*). Dowd! There you are!

ELWOOD. I have a cab outside, if it's possible for you and Miss Kelly to get away now.

SANDERSON. Where is Dr. Chumley?

ELWOOD. Is he coming with us? That's nice.

KELLY (*answering question on* SANDERSON's *face*). I don't know, Doctor.

ELWOOD. I must apologize for being a few seconds late. I thought Miss Kelly should have some flowers. After what happened out here this afternoon the flowers really should be from you, Doctor. As you grow older and pretty women pass you by, you will think with deep gratitude of these generous girls of your youth. Shall we go now? (KELLY *exits.*)

SANDERSON (*pressing buzzer*). Just a moment, Dowd— The situation has changed since we met this afternoon. But I urge you to have no resentments. Dr. Chumley is your friend. He only wants to help you.

ELWOOD. That's very nice of him. I would like to help him, too.

SANDERSON. If you'll begin by taking a cooperative attitude—that's half the battle. We all have to face reality, Dowd —sooner or later.

ELWOOD. Doctor, I wrestled with reality for forty years, and I am happy to state that I finally won out over it. (KELLY *enters.*) Won't you and Miss

Kelly join me—down at Charlie's? (*Enter* WILSON.)

WILSON. Here you are! (*Goes over to* ELWOOD.) Upstairs, buddy—we're going upstairs. Is the doctor O.K.? (*He asks* SANDERSON *this.*)

ELWOOD. There must be some mistake. Miss Kelly and Dr. Sanderson and I are going downtown for a drink. I'd be glad to have you come with us, Mr.—

WILSON. Wilson.

ELWOOD. —Wilson. They have a wonderful floor show.

WILSON. Yeah? Well—wait'll you see the floor show we've got— Upstairs, buddy!

SANDERSON. Just a minute, Wilson. Where did you say Dr. Chumley went, Dowd?

ELWOOD. As I said, he did not confide his plans in me.

WILSON. You mean the doctor ain't showed up yet?

KELLY. Not yet.

WILSON. Where is he?

SANDERSON. That's what we're trying to find out.

KELLY. Mr. Dowd walked in here by himself.

WILSON. Oh, he did, eh? Listen, you —talk fast or I'm workin' you over!

ELWOOD. I'd rather you didn't do that, and I'd rather you didn't even mention such a thing in the presence of a lovely young lady like Miss Kelly—

SANDERSON. Mr. Dowd, Dr. Chumley went into town to pick you up. That was four hours ago.

ELWOOD. Where has the evening gone to?

WILSON. Listen to that! Smart, eh?

SANDERSON. Just a minute, Wilson. Did you see Dr. Chumley tonight, Dowd?

ELWOOD. Yes, I did. He came into Charlie's Place at dinner-time. It is a cozy spot. Let's all go there and talk it over with a tall one.

WILSON. We're going no place— Now I'm askin' you a question, and if you don't button up your lip and give me some straight answers I'm gonna beat it out of you!

ELWOOD. What you suggest is impossible.

WILSON. What's that?

ELWOOD. You suggest that I button up my lip and give you some straight answers. It can't be done.

SANDERSON. Let me handle this, Wilson.

WILSON. Well, handle it, then. But find out where the Doctor is.

SANDERSON. Dr. Chumley *did* come into Charlie's Place, you say?

ELWOOD. He did, and I was very glad to see him.

WILSON. Go on—

ELWOOD. He had asked for me, and naturally the proprietor brought him over and left him. We exchanged the conventional greetings. I said, "How do you do, Dr. Chumley," and he said, "How do you do, Mr. Dowd." I believe we said that at least once.

WILSON. Okay—okay—

ELWOOD. I am trying to be factual. I then introduced him to Harvey.

WILSON. To who?

KELLY. A white rabbit. Six feet tall.

WILSON. Six feet!

ELWOOD. Six feet one and a half!

WILSON. Okay—fool around with him, and the Doctor is probably some place bleedin' to death in a ditch.

ELWOOD. If those were his plans for the evening he did not tell me.

SANDERSON. Go on, Dowd.

ELWOOD. Dr. Chumley sat down in the booth with us. I was sitting on the outside like this. (*Shows.*) Harvey was on the inside near the wall, and Dr. Chumley was seated directly across from Harvey where he could look at him.

WILSON. That's right. Spend all night on the seatin' arrangements!

ELWOOD. Harvey then suggested that I buy him a drink. Knowing that he does not like to drink alone, I suggested to Dr. Chumley that we join him.

WILSON. And so?

ELWOOD. We joined him.

WILSON. Go on—go on.

ELWOOD. We joined him again.

WILSON. Then what?

ELWOOD. We kept right on joining him.

WILSON. Oh, skip all the joining!

ELWOOD. You are asking me to skip a large portion of the evening—

WILSON. Tell us what happened—come on—please—

ELWOOD. Dr. Chumley and Harvey got into a conversation—quietly at first. Later it became rather heated and Dr. Chumley raised his voice.

WILSON. Yeah—why?

ELWOOD. Harvey seemed to feel that Dr. Chumley should assume part of the financial responsibility of the joining, but Dr. Chumley didn't seem to want to do that.

KELLY (it breaks out from her). I can believe that part of it!

WILSON. Let him talk. See how far he'll go. This guy's got guts.

ELWOOD. I agreed to take the whole thing because I did not want any trouble. We go down to Charlie's quite often—Harvey and I—and the proprietor is a fine man with an interesting approach to life. Then the other matter came up.

WILSON. Cut the damned double talk and get on with it!

ELWOOD. Mr. Wilson, you are a sincere type of person, but I must ask you not to use that language in the presence of Miss Kelly. (He makes a short bow to her.)

SANDERSON. You're right, Dowd, and we're sorry. You say—the other matter came up?

ELWOOD. There was a beautiful blonde woman—a Mrs. Smethills—and her escort seated in the booth across from us. Dr. Chumley went over to sit next to her, explaining to her that they had once met. In Chicago. Her escort escorted Dr. Chumley back to me and Harvey and tried to point out that it would be better for Dr. Chumley to mind his own affairs. Does he have any?

WILSON. Does he have any what?

ELWOOD. Does he have any affairs?

WILSON. How would I know?

KELLY. Please hurry, Mr. Dowd—we're all so worried.

ELWOOD. Dr. Chumley then urged Harvey to go with him over to Blondie's Chicken Inn. Harvey wanted to go to Eddie's instead. While they were arguing about it I went to the bar to order another drink, and when I came back they were gone.

WILSON. Where did they go? I mean where did the Doctor go?

ELWOOD. I don't know—I had a date out here with Dr. Sanderson and Miss Kelly, and I came out to pick them up—hoping that later on we might run into Harvey and the Doctor and make a party of it.

WILSON. So—you satisfied? You got his story—(Goes over to ELWOOD, fists clenched.) O.K. You're lyin' and we know it!

ELWOOD. I never lie, Mr. Wilson.

WILSON. You've done somethin' with the Doctor and I'm findin' out what it is—

SANDERSON (moving after him). Don't touch him, Wilson—

KELLY. Maybe he isn't lying, Wilson—

WILSON (turning on them. Furiously). That's all this guy is, is a bunch of lies! You two don't believe this story he tells about the Doctor sittin' there talkin' to a big white rabbit, do you?

KELLY. Maybe Dr. Chumley did go to Charlie's Place.

WILSON. And saw a big rabbit, I suppose.

ELWOOD. And why not? Harvey was there. At first the Doctor seemed a little frightened of Harvey but that gave way to admiration as the evening wore on—. The evening wore on! That's a nice expression. With your permission I'll say it again. The evening wore on.

WILSON (lunging at him). With your permission I'm gonna knock your teeth down your throat!

ELWOOD (not moving an inch). Mr. Wilson—haven't you some old friends you can go play with? (SANDERSON has grabbed WILSON and is struggling with him.)

WILSON (he is being held. Glares fiercely at ELWOOD. KELLY dials phone).

The nerve of this guy! He couldn't come out here with an ordinary case of d.t.'s. No. He has to come out with a six-foot rabbit.

ELWOOD. Stimulating as all this is, I really must be getting downtown.

KELLY (*on phone*). Charlie's Place? Is Dr. Chumley anywhere around there? He was there with Mr. Dowd earlier in the evening. What? Well, don't bite my head off! (*Hangs up.*) My, that man was mad. He said Mr. Dowd was welcome any time, but his friend was not.

ELWOOD. That's Mr. McNulty the bartender. He thinks a lot of me. Now let's all go down and have a drink.

WILSON. Wait a minute—

KELLY. Mr. Dowd—(*Goes over to him.*)

ELWOOD. Yes, my dear—may I hold your hand?

KELLY. Yes—if you want to. (ELWOOD *does.*) Poor Mrs. Chumley is so worried. Something must have happened to the Doctor. Won't you please try and remember something—something else that might help her? Please—

ELWOOD. For you I would do anything. I would almost be willing to live my life over again. Almost. But I've told it all.

KELLY. You're sure?

ELWOOD. Quite sure—but ask me again, anyway, won't you? I liked that warm tone you had in your voice just then.

SANDERSON (*without realizing he is saying it*). So did I. (*Looks at* KELLY.)

WILSON. Oh, nuts!

ELWOOD. What?

WILSON. Nuts!

ELWOOD. Oh! I must be going. I have things to do.

KELLY. Mr. Dowd, what is it you do?

ELWOOD (*sits, as* KELLY *sits at desk*). Harvey and I sit in the bars and we have a drink or two and play the juke box. Soon the faces of the other people turn toward mine and smile. They are saying: "We don't know your name, Mister, but you're a lovely fellow." Harvey and I warm ourselves in all these golden moments. We have entered as strangers—soon we have friends. They come over. They sit with us. They drink with us. They talk to us. They tell about the big terrible things they have done. The big wonderful things they *will* do. Their hopes, their regrets, their loves, their hates. All very large because nobody ever brings anything small into a bar. Then I introduce them to Harvey. And he is bigger and grander than anything they offer me. When they leave, they leave impressed. The same people seldom come back—but that's envy, my dear. There's a little bit of envy in the best of us—too bad, isn't it?

SANDERSON (*leaning forward*). How did you happen to call him Harvey?

ELWOOD. Harvey is his name.

SANDERSON. How do you know that?

ELWOOD. That was rather an interesting coincidence, Doctor. One night several years ago I was walking early in the evening along Fairfax Street—between Eighteenth and Nineteenth. You know that block?

SANDERSON. Yes, yes.

ELWOOD. I had just helped Ed Hickey into a taxi. Ed had been mixing his rye with his gin, and I felt he needed conveying. I started to walk down the street when I heard a voice saying: "Good evening, Mr. Dowd." I turned and there was this great white rabbit leaning against a lamp post. Well, I thought nothing of that, because when you have lived in a town as long as I have lived in this one, you get used to the fact that everybody knows your name. Naturally, I went over to chat with him. He said to me: "Ed Hickey is a little spiffed this evening, or could I be mistaken?" Well, of course he was not mistaken. I think the world and all of Ed but he was spiffed. Well, anyway, we stood there and talked, and finally I said—"You have the advantage of me. You know my name and I don't know yours." Right back at me he said: "What name do you like?" Well, I didn't even have to think a minute: Harvey has always been my favorite name. So I said, "Harvey," and this is the interesting part of the whole thing. He said—"What a coincidence! My name happens to be Harvey."

SANDERSON. What was your father's name, Dowd?

ELWOOD. John. John Frederick.

SANDERSON. Dowd, when you were a child you had a playmate, didn't you? Someone you were very fond of—with whom you spent many happy, carefree hours?

ELWOOD. Oh, yes, Doctor. Didn't you?

SANDERSON. What was his name?

ELWOOD. Verne. Verne McElhinney. Did you ever know the McElhinneys, Doctor?

SANDERSON. No.

ELWOOD. Too bad. There were a lot of them, and they circulated. Wonderful people.

SANDERSON. Think carefully, Dowd. Wasn't there someone, somewhere, some time, whom you knew—by the name of Harvey? Didn't you ever know anybody by that name?

ELWOOD. No, Doctor. No one. Maybe that's why I always had such hopes for it.

SANDERSON. Come on, Wilson, we'll take Mr. Dowd upstairs now.

WILSON. I'm taking him nowhere. You've made this your show—now run it. Lettin' him sit here—forgettin' all about Dr. Chumley! O.K. It's your show —you run it.

SANDERSON. Come on, Dowd— (*Pause. Putting out his hand.*) Come on, Elwood—

ELWOOD (*rises*). Very well, Lyman. (SANDERSON *and* KELLY *take him to door.*) But I'm afraid I won't be able to visit with you for long. I have promised Harvey I will take him to the floor show. (*They exit.* WILSON *is alone. Sits at desk, looks at his watch.*)

WILSON. Oh, boy! (*Puts head in arms on desk.* DR. CHUMLEY *enters.* WILSON *does not see him until he gets almost to the center of the room.*)

WILSON (*jumping up, going to him*). Dr. Chumley—Are you all right?

CHUMLEY. All right? Of course I'm all right. I'm being followed. Lock that door.

WILSON (*goes to door, locks it*). Who's following you?

CHUMLEY. None of your business. (*Exits into office and locks door behind him.* WILSON *stands a moment perplexed, then shrugs shoulders, turns off lights and exits. The stage is dimly lit. Then from door left comes the rattle of the doorknob. Door opens and shuts, and we hear locks opening and closing, and see light from the hall. The invisible Harvey has come in. There is a count of eight while he crosses the stage, then door of* CHUMLEY'S *office opens and closes, with sound of locks clicking. Harvey has gone in—and then—*)

CURTAIN

ACT THREE

SCENE: *The sanitarium office at Chumley's Rest, a few minutes later.*

AT RISE: *Lights are still dim as at preceding curtain. There is a loud knocking and the sound of* CHUMLEY'S *voice calling,* "Wilson! Wilson!"

WILSON (*enters, opens outside door.* CHUMLEY *enters, white-faced*). How didja get out here, Doctor? I just saw you go in there.

CHUMLEY. I went out through my window. Wilson—don't leave me!

WILSON. No, Doctor.

CHUMLEY. Get that man Dowd out of here.

WILSON. Yes, Doctor. (*Starts to exit.*)

CHUMLEY. No—don't leave me!

WILSON (*turning back—confused*). But you said—

CHUMLEY. Dumphy—on the telephone.

WILSON. Yes, Doctor. (*Crosses to phone.*) Dumphy—give that guy Dowd his clothes and get him down here right away. (*A knock on the door.*)

CHUMLEY. Don't leave me!

WILSON. Just a minute, Doctor.

(*Turns on lights. Opens door.*) Judge Gaffney.

JUDGE. I want to see Dr. Chumley. (*Enter* JUDGE *and* MYRTLE MAE.)

WILSON. Hiya, Myrtle.

MYRTLE. Hello.

JUDGE. Chumley, we've got to talk to you. This thing is serious.

MYRTLE. It certainly is.

GAFFNEY. More serious than you suspect. Where can we go to talk? (*Moves toward* CHUMLEY's *office.*)

CHUMLEY (*blocking door*). Not in there.

WILSON. The Doctor doesn't want you in his office.

CHUMLEY. No, sir.

JUDGE. Then sit down, Dr. Chumley. Sit down, Myrtle Mae.

CHUMLEY (*dazed*). Sit down, Dr. Chumley. Sit down, Myrtle Mae. Don't go, Wilson. Don't leave me.

JUDGE. Now, Chumley, here are my notes—the facts. Can anybody hear me?

WILSON. Yeah, we can all hear you. Is that good?

JUDGE (*gives* WILSON *a look of reproof*). Now, Chumley, has it ever occurred to you that possibly there might *be* something like this rabbit Harvey?

MYRTLE. Of course there isn't. And anybody who thinks so is crazy. (CHUMLEY *stares at her.*) Well, don't look at me like that. There's nothing funny about me. I'm like my father's family—they're all dead.

JUDGE. Now, then, my client, the plaintiff, Mrs. Veta Louise Simmons, under oath, swears that on the morning of November second while standing in the kitchen of her home, hearing her name called, she turned and saw this great white rabbit, Harvey. He was staring at her. Resenting the intrusion, the plaintiff made certain remarks and drove the creature from the room. He went.

CHUMLEY. What did she say to him?

JUDGE. She was emphatic. The remarks are not important.

CHUMLEY. I want to know how she got this creature out of her sanitarium —I mean—her home.

MYRTLE. I hate to have you tell him, Judge. It isn't a bit like Mother.

WILSON. Quit stalling. Let's have it.

GAFFNEY. She looked him right in the eye and exclaimed in the heat of anger— "To hell with you!"

CHUMLEY (*looking at door*). "To hell with you!" He left?

JUDGE. Yes, he left. But that's beside the point. The point is—is it perjury or is it something we can cope with? I ask for your opinion. (KELLY *enters from stairs;* SANDERSON *comes from diet kitchen.*)

SANDERSON. Ruthie! I've been looking all over for you.

CHUMLEY. Dr. Sanderson, disregard what I said this afternoon. I want you on my staff. You are a very astute young man.

KELLY. Oh, Lyman! Did you hear?

SANDERSON. Oh, baby!

KELLY. See you later. (*Exits, blowing him a kiss.* SANDERSON *exits into his office.*)

MYRTLE. You've just got to keep Uncle Elwood out here, Doctor.

CHUMLEY. No. I want this sanitarium the way it was before that man came out here this afternoon.

MYRTLE. I know what you mean.

CHUMLEY. You do?

MYRTLE. Well, it certainly gets on anyone's nerves the way Uncle Elwood knows what's going to happen before it happens. This morning, for instance, he told us that Harvey told him Mrs. McElhinney's Aunt Rose would drop in on her unexpectedly tonight from Cleveland.

CHUMLEY. And did she?

MYRTLE. Did she what?

CHUMLEY. Aunt Rose—did she come just as Harvey said she would?

MYRTLE. Oh, yes. Those things always turn out the way Uncle Elwood says they will—but what of it? What do we care about the McElhinneys?

CHUMLEY. You say this sort of thing happens often?

MYRTLE. Yes, and isn't it silly? Uncle Elwood says Harvey tells him everything. Harvey knows everything. How could he when there is no such thing as Harvey?

CHUMLEY (*goes over, tries lock at door*). Fly-specks. I've been spending my life among fly-specks while miracles have been leaning on lamp-posts on Eighteenth and Fairfax.

VETA (*enters. Looks around cautiously. Sighs with relief*). Good. Nobody here but people.

MYRTLE. Oh, Mother! You promised you wouldn't come out here.

VETA. Well, good evening. Now, Myrtle Mae, I brought Elwood's bathrobe. Well, why are you all just sitting here? I thought you'd be committing him.

JUDGE. Sit down there, girl. (*Motioning to chair near* WILSON.)

VETA. I will not sit down there.

WILSON. How about you and me stepping out Saturday night, Myrtle Mae?

VETA. Certainly not. Myrtle Mae, come here.

MYRTLE. I'm sorry.

VETA. Is everything settled?

CHUMLEY. It will be. (SANDERSON *enters from his office.*)

SANDERSON. Doctor, may I give an opinion?

CHUMLEY. Yes, do. By all means.

VETA (*sniffing*). His opinion! Omar—he's the doctor I told you about. The eyes!

SANDERSON. It's my opinion that Elwood P. Dowd is suffering from a third-degree hallucination and the—(*Pointing at* VETA'*s back.*) other party concerned is the victim of auto-suggestion. I recommend shock formula number 977 for him and bed rest at home for—(*Points again.*)

CHUMLEY. You do?

SANDERSON. That's my diagnosis, Doctor. (*To* VETA.) Mr. Dowd will not see this rabbit any more after this injection. We've used it in hundreds of psychopathic cases.

VETA. Don't you call my brother a psychopathic case! There's never been anything like that in our family.

MYRTLE. If you didn't think Uncle Elwood was psychopathic, why did you bring him out here?

VETA. Where else could I take him, I couldn't take him to jail, could I? Besides, this is not your uncle's fault. Why did Harvey have to speak to him in the first place? With the town full of people, why did he have to bother Elwood?

JUDGE. Stop putting your oar in. Keep your oar out. If this shock formula brings people back to reality, give it to him. That's where we want Elwood.

CHUMLEY. I'm not sure that it would work in a case of this kind, Doctor.

SANDERSON. It always has.

VETA. Harvey always follows Elwood home.

CHUMLEY. He does?

VETA. Yes. But if you give him the formula and Elwood doesn't see Harvey, he won't let him in. Then when he comes to the door, I'll deal with him.

MYRTLE. Mother, won't you stop talking about Harvey as if there was such a thing?

VETA. Myrtle Mae, you've got a lot to learn and I hope you never learn it. (*She starts up toward* WILSON. ELWOOD *is heard off stage humming.*)

JUDGE. Sh! Here he is. (ELWOOD *enters.*)

ELWOOD. Good evening, everybody.

VETA. Good evening, Elwood. I've brought you your bathrobe.

ELWOOD. Thank you, Veta.

JUDGE. Well, Chumley, what do we do? We've got to do something.

VETA. Oh, yes, we must.

MYRTLE. I should say so.

CHUMLEY (*looking at door*). Yes, it's imperative.

ELWOOD. Well, while you're making up your minds, why don't we all go down to Charlie's and have a drink?

VETA. You're not going anywhere, Elwood. You're staying here.

MYRTLE. Yes, Uncle Elwood.

JUDGE. Stay here, son.

ELWOOD. I plan to leave. You want me to stay. An element of conflict in any discussion is a good thing. It means everybody is taking part and nobody is left out. I like that. Oh—how did you get along with Harvey, Doctor?

CHUMLEY. Sh-h!

JUDGE. We're waiting for your answer, Doctor.

CHUMLEY. What?

JUDGE. What is your decision?

CHUMLEY. I must be alone with this man. Will you all step into the other room? (MYRTLE *exits*.) I'll have my diagnosis in a moment.

VETA. Do hurry, Doctor.

CHUMLEY. I will.

VETA. You stay here, Elwood. (*She and* JUDGE GAFFNEY *exit*.)

CHUMLEY. Here, Mr. Dowd. Let me give you this chair. (*Indicates chair*.) Let me give you a cigar. (*Does so*.) Is there anything else I can get you?

ELWOOD (*seated in chair*). What did you have in mind?

CHUMLEY. Mr. Dowd—(*Lowers voice, looks toward office*.) What kind of a man are you? Where do you come from?

ELWOOD (*getting out card*). Didn't I give you one of my cards?

CHUMLEY. And where on the face of this tired old earth did you find a thing like him?

ELWOOD. Harvey the Pooka?

CHUMLEY (*sits*). Is it true that he has a function—that he—?

ELWOOD. Gets advance notice? I'm happy to say it is. Harvey is versatile. Harvey can stop clocks.

CHUMLEY. What?

ELWOOD. You've heard that expression, "His face would stop a clock"?

CHUMLEY. Yes. But why? To what purpose?

ELWOOD. Harvey says that he can look at your clock and stop it and you can go away as long as you like with whomever you like and go as far as you like. And when you come back not one minute will have ticked by.

CHUMLEY. You mean that he actually—? (*Looks toward office*.)

ELWOOD. Einstein has overcome time and space. Harvey has overcome not

only time and space—but any objections.

CHUMLEY. And does he do this for you?

ELWOOD. He is willing to at any time, but so far I've never been able to think of any place I'd rather be. I always have a wonderful time just where I am, whomever I'm with. I'm having a fine time right now with you, Doctor. (*Holds up cigar*.) Corona-Corona.

CHUMLEY. I know where I'd go.

ELWOOD. Where?

CHUMLEY. I'd go to Akron.

ELWOOD. Akron?

CHUMLEY. There's a cottage camp outside Akron in a grove of maple trees, cool, green, beautiful.

ELWOOD. My favorite tree.

CHUMLEY. I would go there with a pretty young woman, a strange woman, a quiet woman.

ELWOOD. Under a tree?

CHUMLEY. I wouldn't even want to know her name. I would be—just Mr. Brown.

ELWOOD. Why wouldn't you want to know her name? You might be acquainted with the same people.

CHUMLEY. I would send out for cold beer. I would talk to her. I would tell her things I have never told anyone— things that are locked in here. (*Beats his breast*. ELWOOD *looks over at his chest with interest*.) And then I would send out for more cold beer.

ELWOOD. No whisky?

CHUMLEY. Beer is better.

ELWOOD. Maybe under a tree. But she might like a highball.

CHUMLEY. I wouldn't let her talk to me, but as I talked I would want her to reach out a soft white hand and stroke my head and say, "Poor thing! Oh, you poor, poor thing!"

ELWOOD. How long would you like that to go on?

CHUMLEY. Two weeks.

ELWOOD. Wouldn't that get monotonous? Just Akron, beer, and "poor, poor thing" for two weeks?

CHUMLEY. No. No, it would not. It would be wonderful.

ELWOOD. I can't help but feel you're making a mistake in not allowing that woman to talk. If she gets around at all, she may have picked up some very interesting little news items. And I'm sure you're making a mistake with all that beer and no whisky. But it's your two weeks.

CHUMLEY (*dreamily*). Cold beer at Akron and one last fling! God, man!

ELWOOD. Do you think you'd like to lie down for awhile?

CHUMLEY. No. No. Tell me Mr. Dowd, could he—would he do this for me?

ELWOOD. He could and he might. I have never heard Harvey say a word against Akron. By the way, Doctor, where is Harvey?

CHUMLEY (*rising. Very cautiously*). Why, don't you know?

ELWOOD. The last time I saw him he was with you.

CHUMLEY. Ah!

ELWOOD. Oh! He's probably waiting for me down at Charlie's.

CHUMLEY (*with a look of cunning toward his office*). That's it! He's down at Charlie's.

ELWOOD. Excuse me, Doctor. (*Rises.*)

CHUMLEY. No, no, Mr. Dowd. Not in there.

ELWOOD. I couldn't leave without saying good-night to my friend, Dr. Sanderson.

CHUMLEY. Mr. Dowd, Dr. Sanderson is not your friend. None of those people are your friends. *I* am your friend.

ELWOOD. Thank you, Doctor. And I'm yours.

CHUMLEY. And this sister of yours—she is at the bottom of this conspiracy against you. She's trying to persuade me to lock you up. Today she had commitment papers drawn up. She's got your power of attorney and the key to your safety box. She brought you out here—

ELWOOD. My sister did all that in one afternoon? Veta is certainly a whirlwind.

CHUMLEY. God, man, haven't you any righteous indignation?

ELWOOD. Dr. Chumley, my mother used to say to me, "In this world, Elwood"—she always called me Elwood—she'd say, "In this world, Elwood, you must be oh, so smart or oh, so pleasant." For years I was smart. I recommend pleasant. You may quote me.

CHUMLEY. Just the same, I will protect you if I have to commit her. Would you like me to do that?

ELWOOD. No, Doctor, not unless Veta wanted it that way. Oh, not that you don't have a nice place out here, but I think Veta would be happier at home with me and Harvey and Myrtle Mae. (KELLY *enters with flower in hair, goes to put magazines on table.* ELWOOD *turns to her.*) Miss Kelly! "Diviner grace has never brightened this enchanting face!" (*To* CHUMLEY.) Ovid's Fifth Elegy. (*To* MISS KELLY.) My dear, you will never look lovelier!

KELLY. I'll never feel happier, Mr. Dowd. I know it. (*Kisses him.*)

CHUMLEY. Well!

KELLY. Yes, Doctor. (*Exits.* WILSON *enters hall in time to see the kiss.*)

ELWOOD. I wonder if I would be able to remember any more of that poem?

WILSON. Say, maybe this rabbit gag is a good one. Kelly never kissed me.

ELWOOD (*looking at* WILSON). Ovid has always been my favorite poet.

WILSON. O.K., pal— You're discharged. This way out—(*Takes him by arm downstage.*)

CHUMLEY. Wilson! Take your hands off that man!

WILSON. What?

CHUMLEY. Apologize to Mr. Dowd.

WILSON. Apologize to him—this guy with the rabbit?

CHUMLEY (*looking toward his office*). Apologize! Apologize—

WILSON. I apologize. This is the door.

ELWOOD. If I leave, I'll remember. (WILSON *exits.*)

CHUMLEY. Wait a minute, Dowd. Do women often come up to you and kiss you like Miss Kelly did just now?

ELWOOD. Every once in a while.

CHUMLEY. Yes?

ELWOOD. I encourage it, too.

CHUMLEY (*to himself*). To hell with decency! I've got to have that rabbit! Go ahead and knock. (ELWOOD *starts for* SANDERSON's *door just as* SANDERSON *comes out.*)

ELWOOD. Dr. Sanderson, I couldn't leave without—

SANDERSON. Just a minute, Dowd—(*To* CHUMLEY.) Doctor, do you agree with my diagnosis?

CHUMLEY. Yes, yes! Call them all in.

SANDERSON. Thank you, Doctor. Mrs. Simmons—Judge Gaffney—will you step in here for a minute, please? (VETA *enters.*)

VETA. Is it settled? (MYRTLE *and* JUDGE *enter.*)

CHUMLEY. I find I concur with Dr. Sanderson!

SANDERSON. Thank you, Doctor.

MYRTLE. Oh, that's wonderful! What a relief!

JUDGE. Good boy!

ELWOOD. Well, let's celebrate—(*Takes little book out of his pocket.*) I've got some new bars listed in the back of this book.

CHUMLEY (*speaking to others in low tone*). This injection carries a violent reaction. We can't give it to him without his consent. Will he give it?

VETA. Of course he will, if I ask him.

CHUMLEY. To give up this rabbit—I doubt it.

MYRTLE. Don't ask him. Just give it to him.

ELWOOD. "Bessie's Barn Dance. Blondie's Chicken Inn. Better Late Than Never—Bennie's Drive In"—

VETA. Elwood!

ELWOOD. We'll go to Bennie's Drive In. We should telephone for a table. How many of us will there be, Veta?

VETA (*starting to count, then catching herself*). Oh—Elwood!

CHUMLEY. Mr. Dowd, I have a formula —977—that will be good for you. Will you take it?

JUDGE. Elwood, you won't see this rabbit any more.

SANDERSON. But you will see your responsibilities, your duties—

ELWOOD. I'm sure if you thought of it, Doctor, it must be a very fine thing. And if I happen to run into anyone who needs it, I'll be glad to recommend it. For myself, I wouldn't care for it.

VETA. Hear that, Judge! Hear that, Doctor! That's what we have to put up with.

ELWOOD (*turning to look at her*). Veta, do you want me to take this?

VETA. Elwood, I'm only thinking of you. You're my brother and I've known you for years. I'd do anything for you. That Harvey wouldn't do anything for you. He's making a fool out of you, Elwood. Don't be a fool.

ELWOOD. Oh, I won't.

VETA. Why, you could amount to something. You could be sitting on the Western Slope Water Board right now if you'd only go over and ask them.

ELWOOD. All right, Veta. If that's what you want, Harvey and I will go over and ask them tomorrow.

VETA. Tomorrow! I never want to see another tomorrow. Not if Myrtle Mae and I have to live in the house with that rabbit. Our friends never come to see us —we have no social life; we have no life at all. We're both miserable. I wish I were dead—but maybe you don't care!

ELWOOD (*slowly*). I've always felt that Veta should have everything she wants. Veta, are you sure? (VETA *nods.*) I'll take it. Where do I go, Doctor?

CHUMLEY. In Dr. Sanderson's office, Dowd.

ELWOOD. Say goodbye to the old fellow for me, won't you? (*Exits.* CHUMLEY *exits.*)

JUDGE. How long will this take, Doctor?

SANDERSON. Only a few minutes. Why don't you wait? (*Exits.*)

JUDGE. We'll wait. (*Sits.*)

VETA (*sighs*). Dr. Sanderson said it wouldn't take long.

MYRTLE. Now, Mother, don't fidget.

VETA. Oh, how can I help it?

MYRTLE (*picks up edge of draperies*). How stunning! Mother, could you see me in a housecoat of this material?

VETA (*to* MYRTLE—*first looking at draperies. Sighs again*). Yes, dear, but let me get a good night's sleep first. (*Loud knocking at door.*)

JUDGE. Come in. (*Enter* CAB DRIVER.) What do you want?

CAB DRIVER. I'm lookin' for a little, short— (*Seeing* VETA.) Oh, there you are! Lady, you jumped outta the cab without payin' me.

VETA. Oh, yes. I forgot. How much is it?

CAB DRIVER. All the way out here from town? $2.75.

VETA (*looking in purse*). Two seventy-five! I could have sworn I brought my coin purse—where is it? (*Gets up, goes to table, turns pocketbook upside down, in full view of audience. Nothing comes out of it but a compact and a handkerchief.*) Myrtle, do you have any money?

MYRTLE. I spent that money Uncle Elwood gave me for my new hairdo for the party.

VETA. Judge, do you have $2.75 I could give this man?

JUDGE. Sorry. Nothing but a check

CAB DRIVER. We don't take checks.

JUDGE. I know.

VETA. Dr. Chumley, do you happen to have $2.75 I could borrow to pay this cab driver?

CHUMLEY (*he has just entered, now wearing white starched jacket*). Haven't got my wallet. No time to get it now. Have to get on with this injection. Sorry. (*Exits.*)

VETA. Well, I'll get it for you from my brother, but I can't get it right now. He's in there to get an injection. It won't be long. You'll have to wait.

CAB DRIVER. You're gonna get my money from your brother and he's in there to get some of that stuff they shoot out here?

VETA. Yes, it won't be but a few minutes.

CAB DRIVER. Lady, I want my money now.

VETA. But I told you it would only be a few minutes. I want you to drive us back to town, anyway.

CAB DRIVER. And I told you I want my money now or I'm nosin' the cab back to town, and you can wait for the bus—at six in the morning.

VETA. Well, of all the pig-headed, stubborn things—!

MYRTLE. I should say so.

JUDGE. What's the matter with you?

CAB DRIVER. Nothin' that $2.75 won't fix. You heard me. Take it or leave it.

VETA (*getting up*). I never heard of anything so unreasonable in my life. (*Knocks.*) Dr. Chumley, will you let Elwood step out here a minute. This cab driver won't wait.

CHUMLEY (*off*). Don't be too long. (*Enter* ELWOOD. CHUMLEY *follows.*)

VETA. Elwood, I came off without my coin purse. Will you give this man $2.75? But don't give him any more. He's been very rude.

ELWOOD (*extending his hand*). How do you do? Dowd is my name. Elwood P.

CAB DRIVER. Lofgren's mine. E. J.

ELWOOD. I'm glad to meet you, Mr. Lofgren. This is my sister, Mrs. Simmons. My charming little niece, Myrtle Mae Simmons. Judge Gaffney and Dr. Chumley. (*All bow coldly.*)

CAB DRIVER. Hi—

ELWOOD. Have you lived around here long, Mr. Lofgren?

CAB DRIVER. Yeah, I've lived around here all my life.

ELWOOD. Do you enjoy your work?

CAB DRIVER. It's O.K. I been with the Apex Cabs fifteen years and my brother Joe's been drivin' for Brown Cabs pretty near twelve.

ELWOOD. You drive for Apex and your brother Joe for Brown's? That's interesting, isn't it, Veta? (VETA *reacts with a sniff.*) Mr. Lofgren—let me give you one of my cards. (*Gives him one.*)

CHUMLEY. Better get on with this, Mr. Dowd.

ELWOOD. Certainly. One minute. My sister and my charming little niece live here with me at this address. Won't you and your brother come and have dinner with us some time?

CAB DRIVER. Sure—be glad to.

ELWOOD. When—when would you be glad to?

CAB DRIVER. I couldn't come any night but Tuesday. I'm on duty all the rest of the week.

ELWOOD. You must come on Tuesday, then. We'll expect you and be delighted to see you, won't we, Veta?

VETA. Oh, Elwood, I'm sure this man has friends of his own.

ELWOOD. Veta, one can't have too many friends.

VETA. Elwood, don't keep Dr. Chumley waiting—that's rude.

ELWOOD. Of course. (*Gives him bill.*) Here you are—keep the change. I'm glad to have met you and I'll expect you Tuesday with your brother. Will you excuse me now?

CAB DRIVER. Sure. (ELWOOD *exits.* CHUMLEY *follows.*) A sweet guy.

VETA. Certainly. You could just as well have waited.

CAB DRIVER. Oh, no. Listen, lady. I've been drivin' this route fifteen years. I've brought 'em out here to get that stuff and drove 'em back after they had it. It changes 'em.

VETA. Well, I certainly hope so.

CAB DRIVER. And you ain't kiddin'. On the way out here they sit back and enjoy the ride. They talk to me. Sometimes we stop and watch the sunsets and look at the birds flyin'. Sometimes we stop and watch the birds when there ain't no birds and look at the sunsets when it's rainin'. We have a swell time and I always get a big tip. But afterward —oh—oh—(*Starts to exit again.*)

VETA. Afterwards—oh—oh! What do you mean afterwards—oh—oh?

CAB DRIVER. They crab, crab, crab. They yell at me to watch the lights, watch the brakes, watch the intersections. They scream at me to hurry. They got no faith—in me or my buggy—yet it's the same cab—the same driver—and we're goin' back over the very same road. It's no fun—and no tips—(*Turns to door.*)

VETA. But my brother would have tipped you, anyway. He's very generous. Always has been.

CAB DRIVER. Not after this he won't be. Lady, after this, he'll be a perfectly normal human being and you know what bastards they are! Glad I met you. I'll wait. (*Exits.*)

VETA (*starts to run for door*). Oh, Judge Gaffney—Myrtle Mae! Stop it—stop it—don't give it to him! Elwood, come out of there.

JUDGE. You can't do that. Dr. Chumley is giving the injection.

MYRTLE. Mother—stop this—

VETA (*pounding on door*). I don't want Elwood to have it! I don't want Elwood that way. I don't like people like that.

MYRTLE. Do something with her, Judge —Mother, stop it—

VETA (*turning to her*). You shut up! I've lived longer than you have. I remember my father. I remember your father. I remember—

CHUMLEY (*opens door*). What's this? What's all this commotion?

WILSON (*enters*). What's the trouble, Doctor? She soundin' off again?

JUDGE. She wants to stop the injection.

VETA. You haven't—you haven't already given it to him, have you?

CHUMLEY. No, but we're ready. Take Mrs. Simmons away, Wilson.

VETA. Leave me alone. Take your hands off me, you white slaver!

JUDGE. You don't know what you want. You didn't want that rabbit, either.

VETA. And what's wrong with Harvey? If Elwood and Myrtle Mae and I want to live with Harvey it's nothing to you! You don't even have to come around. It's our business. Elwood—Elwood! (ELWOOD *enters. She throws herself weepingly into his arms. He pats her shoulder.*)

ELWOOD. There, there, Veta. (*To others.*) Veta is all tired out. She's done a lot today.

JUDGE. Have it your own way. I'm not giving up my game at the club again, no matter how big the animal is. (*He exits.*)

VETA. Come on, Elwood—let's get out of here. I hate this place. I wish I'd never seen it!

CHUMLEY. But—see—here—

ELWOOD. It's whatever Veta says, Doctor.

VETA. Why, look at this! That's funny. (*It's her coin purse.*) It must have been there all the time. I could have paid that cab driver myself. Harvey! Come on, Myrtle Mae. Come on, Elwood. Hurry up. (*She exits.* MYRTLE *follows.*)

ELWOOD. Good night, Doctor Chumley. Good night, Mr. Wilson.

VETA (*offstage*). Come along, Elwood.

ELWOOD. Doctor, for years I've known what my family thinks of Harvey. But I've often wondered what Harvey's family thinks of me. (*He looks beyond* CHUMLEY *to the door of his office.*) Oh —there you are! Doctor—do you mind? (*Gestures for him to step back.*) You're standing in his way. (*There is the sound of a lock clicking open and the door of* CHUMLEY'S *office opens wide. The invisible Harvey crosses to him and as they exit together.*) Where've you been? I've been looking all over for you—

CURTAIN

SUGGESTED TOPICS FOR FURTHER INVESTIGATION AND REPORT

1. Make a study of the progress of dramatic fantasy during the Elizabethan period. Read Lyly's *Endymion*, Greene's *Friar Bacon and Friar Bungay*, Marlowe's *Doctor Faustus*, Shakespeare's *A Midsummer Night's Dream* and *The Tempest*, and Dekker's *Old Fortunatus*. What similarities can you find? What are the main differences? Compare Elizabethan ideas of fantasy with those of today.

2. The legend of Faust, the man who sold his soul to the devil for renewed youth, is a popular theme. Compare Marlowe's approach with Goethe's. Try to get a libretto of the Gounod opera. Show the similarities and differences among all three.

3. Two important European writers of realism also wrote plays of fantasy. Ibsen wrote *Peer Gynt* in 1867, early in his career. Strindberg wrote *The Ghost* (or *Spook*) *Sonata* in 1907, quite late in his. Are these plays of fantasy, or are they more accurately "expressionism"? Ibsen combines his serious thoughts with some good fun as well. Do you find this combination in Strindberg?

4. One of the dangers of fantasy is that it may become "precious," that is, over-refined and affected. This charge is frequently leveled against J. M. Barrie. Read his *Dear Brutus*, *Mary Rose*, and *Peter Pan*. Attack or defend the charge. Compare Barrie with the Belgian Maeterlinck in a play like *The Blue Bird*.

5. Time travel is always a favorite subject. You might want to read such famous stories as H. G. Wells' "The Time Machine" or Mark Twain's "A Connecticut Yankee at King Arthur's Court." How effectively is the adventure in time used in plays such as *Berkeley Square*, Maxwell Anderson's comic fantasy, *The Star Wagon*, and Philip Barry's more serious *Hotel Universe?* J. B. Priestley's *Dangerous Corner* is a well-known English play of this type.

6. Death or some similar representative of the hereafter appears frequently in fantasy. Paul Osborn treats the subject in *On Borrowed Time*. In *Death Takes a Holiday* the Italian Alberto Casella placed Death onstage with considerable success. Priestley's *An Inspector Calls* introduces a mysterious individual not of this world. Compare the characterizations in these or other plays of similar nature.

7. Henry James' exciting novel, "The Turn of the Screw," was made into a very successful play, *The Innocents*, by William Archibald. The story involves ghosts, actual or imagined. Read both the novel (it is quite short) and the play. Where does the adaptation succeed or fail? Are the ghosts real, or the product of a psychosis?

8. The treatment of life after death appears in many types of plays. Molnar's *Liliom* (made into the successful Rodgers and Hammerstein *Carousel*), Sutton Vane's *Outward Bound*, Thornton Wilder's *Our Town* are three separate approaches. Evaluate them, or other treatments, for their dramatic effectiveness.

9. Read one or two of the early-century American fantasies, particularly those mentioned here, like *The Piper* and *The Scarecrow*, along with *The Witching Hour* and *The Faith Healer*. In what manner do they fall short of present-day standards? Or how do they show strengths which might make them play effectively today?

10. Read other comedies or comedy-dramas, like Anderson's *High Tor*, Noel Coward's *Blithe Spirit*, Elmer Rice's *Dream Girl*. Or read one of the successful musical-comedy books like *Finian's Rainbow*, *Brigadoon*, or *Lady in the Dark*, which make heavy use of fairy tale and fantasy. Compare or contrast these with *Harvey*, or with one another, as far as the success of their fantasy is concerned.

TRAGEDY: MOST ANCIENT AND
MOST NEGLECTED

The Form of Tragedy

Tragedy, the most ancient of dramatic forms, for centuries the only name for serious drama, is today's most neglected dramatic art. We have problem plays and thesis plays, satires and social documents, realistic dramas and naturalistic case histories, but we have very few tragedies. Tragedy does not mean simply a "sad" play, nor a play with an "unhappy" ending. It is not involved with the pathetic nor the unexpectedly disastrous in the journalistic meaning of the term; it has no connection with sentimentality. Although it must show the destruction of a human being, it demands not tearful sorrow but awe and admiration. Tragedy strives for majesty, not pathos. Its catastrophe, although irrevocably final, exalts and elevates; it cannot under any circumstances depress. Tragedy is positive and optimistic. The playwright who finds man a hopeless product of his environment, incapable of greatness, or who moralizes upon his hero's fall, is not entertaining the tragic view.

The Chorus in Jean Anouilh's modern-dress version of Sophocles' *Antigone* gives an unusually effective summary of the meaning of tragedy:

> Tragedy is clean, it is firm, it is flawless. It has nothing to do with melodrama—with wicked villains, persecuted maidens, avengers, sudden revelations and eleventh-hour repentances. Death, in a melodrama, is really horrible because it is never inevitable. The dear old father might so easily have been saved; the honest young man might so easily have brought in the police five minutes earlier.
>
> In a tragedy, nothing is in doubt and everyone's destiny is known. That makes for tranquillity. There is a sort of fellow feeling among characters in a tragedy: he who kills is as innocent as he who gets killed: it's all a matter of what part you are playing. Tragedy is restful; and the reason is that hope, that foul, deceitful thing, has no part in it. There isn't any hope. You're trapped. The whole sky has fallen on you, and all you can do about it is to shout.
>
> Don't mistake me: I said "shout": I did not say groan, whimper, complain. That, you cannot do. But you can shout aloud; you can get all those things said that you never thought you'd be able to say—or never even knew you had it in you to say. And you don't say these things because it will do any good to say them: you know better than that. You say them for their own sake; you say them because you learn a lot from them.

When it is all over, the tragic hero is destroyed, but he has added that much more glory to mankind. The events, including his physical or symbolic death, are in themselves unimportant. It is what he does to counter his fate and how he acts when death finally overcomes him that become important. Moreover, he has also taken with him the evil that destroyed him. There is no question of anything coming afterwards. Tragedy is *finality*.

The tragic death cannot be regarded as pitiful, pathetic, or sentimental. Realistic drama, like *The Little Foxes*, shows man *as he is;* tragedy exhibits man as *greater than he is*. Most serious plays of the past three-quarters of a century have not been tragic because of their failure to demonstrate this greatness. The late nineteenth-century departure from romanticism and the break with the formulas of the well-made play impelled writers to compose heavy, sordid pieces, loosely called "tragedies," full of the inherited diseases, corruption, and marital combats of Ibsen or Strindberg. Central characters became suicidal Hedda Gablers or persecuted husbands beset by vicious and unscrupulous wives.

Today the question remains whether or not tragedy can exist in the world of the "common man." Are his ordinary deeds in his ordinary life fair subject for tragedy? Is there tragedy in the city slums, on rocky New England farms, or in the jungle of the business world? Can a man today speak with the lyricism demanded of fine tragic dialogue and force the awed admiration of the world upon him? The contemporary writer may courageously say "Yes," but he cannot say it without defining tragedy in modern terms. Even then, tragedy must maintain the optimistic view of man's greatness, a difficult artistic philosophy in the face of threatened annihilation and human insignificance unimagined as recently as 150 years ago.

Tragedy of the Early Republic

The first play to be written by a native American and to be staged by a professional company was Thomas Godfrey's *The Prince of Parthia*, produced in 1767. It is typical of its period; its limited originality shows the deterioration which had begun to infect English-language tragedy. During the late seventeenth century, tragedy had turned into a parroting of Continental neoclassic forms, complete with rigid unities of time, place, and action. The standard subjects were Caesar, Brutus, Cato, and other ancient or exotic nobility. Shakespeare was driven off the stage by more "proper" forms, or he became so altered by the mutilations of contemporary authors that the plays sometimes became unrecognizable. During the eighteenth century the tragedies of Addison and Otway—stilted, stuffy and tedious—brought uniform praise.

Godfrey moves his characters on and off the stage in French-style scenes. The clean plot lines of good tragedy are obscured in the intrigues and complexities of love and hate that turn the play more toward melodrama than tragedy. Murderers, cursing ghosts, and star-crossed lovers enter and exit in quick sequence, reminiscent of late Jacobean tragedies by Webster and Tourneur. Characters speak a blank verse of dubious distinction.

Prince Arsaces, son of King Artabanus of Parthia, loves Evanthe, who is also loved by Vardanes, his brother. After a final battle for power, when Vardanes and Arsaces come face to face on the battlefield, Evanthe is told that Arsaces is dead, and she promptly takes poison. The news is false, however, and Arsaces, very much alive and victorious, enters for this final scene:

ARSACES.   Save her, ye Gods!—oh! save her!
    And I will bribe ye with clouds of incense;
    Such num'rous sacrifices, that your altars
    Shall even sink beneath the mighty load.
EVANTHE. When I am dead, dissolv'd to native dust,
    Yet let me live in thy dear mem'ry—
    One tear will not be much to give *Evanthe*.
ARSACES. My eyes shall e'er two running fountains be,
    And wet thy urn with everflowing tears,
    Joy ne'er again within my breast shall find
    A residence— Oh! speak, once more—
EVANTHE.   Life's just out—
    My Father— Oh! protect his honour'd age,
    And give him shelter from the storms of fate,
    He's long been fortune's sport— Support me— Ah!—
    I can no more—my glass is spent—farewell—
    Forever—*Arsaces!* —Oh!   (*Dies.*)
ARSACES.   Stay, oh! stay,
    Or take me with thee—dead! she's cold and dead!
    Her eyes are clos'd, and all my joys are flown—
    Now burst ye elements, from your restraint,
    Let order cease, and chaos be again.
    Break! break tough heart!—oh! torture—life dissolve—
    Why stand ye idle? Have I not one friend
    To kindly free me from this pain? One blow,
    One friendly blow would give me ease. . . .
    Ha!—this, shall make a passage for my soul—
      (*Snatches* BARZAPHERNES' *sword.*)
    Out, out vile cares, from your distress'd abode—(*Stabs himself.*)

James Nelson Barker's *Superstition* of 1824 was one of the first plays to be based on colonial American history, and it makes interesting comparison with Arthur Miller's later treatment of witchcraft in *The Crucible*. Its best effects rely on the Gothic quality of its melodrama. Although the native theme is encouraging, the play has small indication of progress toward good tragedy.

On the edge of an unnamed New England village live the beautiful but mysterious Isabella and her profligate son, Charles. Beyond the town in a cave resides the "Unknown," who clothes himself in skins of animals. Within the village lives a hell-fire-and-damnation Puritan preacher, Ravensworth, whose daughter Mary is forcibly kept from Charles, her lover. After a series of melodramatic complications in which Charles' rescue of Mary from assault is wholly misinterpreted, Ravensworth brings charges against both Isabella and Charles. He accuses her of witchcraft and Charles of possible sorcery and attempted rape and murder. "What evidence have you against this woman?" asks the judge. Ravensworth offers the "red comet" everybody has seen, the current drought and famine, and the Indian attacks to support his accusations.

Barker gives his Judge more leniency than might be expected in these matters; he is unimpressed by Ravensworth's charges. When his attack fails, Ravensworth turns to Charles and produces the sword and bloody handkerchief involved in Charles' rescue of Mary. Ravensworth charges sorcery:

> JUDGE. Bid him stand forth. We wait your answer, youth.
> CHARLES. You wait in vain—I shall not plead.
> JUDGE.   Not plead!
> RAVENSWORTH (aside). This is beyond my hopes.
> ISABELLA.   O Charles, my son!
> JUDGE. What do you mean?
> CHARLES.   Simply, sir, that I will not
>   Place myself on my trial here.
> JUDGE.   Your reason?
>   Do you question then the justice of the court?
> RAVENSWORTH. He does, no doubt he does.
> CHARLES.   However strong
>   Might be the ground for question—'tis not that
>   Determines me to silence.
> JUDGE.   If you hope
>   To purchase safety by this contumacy;
>   'Tis fit you be aware that clinging there,
>   You may pull ruin on your head.
> CHARLES.   I know
>   The danger I incur, but dare to meet it.

As a terrible storm rages, Charles is convicted on his refusal to stand trial and is removed for execution just as Mary revives from a faint to scream that he is her betrothed husband. The "Unknown" rushes in to reveal that Charles is actually a son of Charles II of England, but all is too late. The victim is brought in dead, and as the storm continues to howl Mary goes insane with grief and dies while the curtain descends.

The list of tragedies up to about the middle of the nineteenth century includes Robert Montgomery Bird's *The Broker of Bogota*, George Henry Boker's *Francesca da Rimini*, certain of John Howard Payne's romantic dramas, William Dunlap's *André*, and others, but they are all of the same cloth. The tragic themes are exotic, highly imaginative, presented in blank verse at times effective but generally uninspired.

Seven Decades Later

To search for the tragic approach in the works of any important American playwright between 1850 and 1920 is unrewarding. As the popularity of the Boker-Bird-Payne romantic tragedy ebbed, nothing replaced it. Serious plays existed, but none achieved the grandeur of theme that tragedy demands. The nearest date we can choose for modern tragedy is 1920, the year of *Beyond the Horizon*, Eugene O'Neill's first full-length Broadway play. Here is a conscious, if faulty, attempt to re-create tragedy as a modern dramatic art. It won the Pulitzer Prize along with the wide critical acclaim of New York reviewers.

Beyond the Horizon avoids the melodramatic decorations of earlier "tragedies" and reduces plot complications to the absolute minimum. Dramatic strength is drawn from the decline and death of a helplessly romantic soul in the midst of a world he despises and cannot control. The relentless push toward his extermination in scene after scene of increasing spiritual decay and physical violence was new to the modern commercial theatre. Robert Mayo, the protagonist, has long dreamed of the romantic life beyond the narrow horizon of his father's New England farm, but at the last minute he gives up a chance to take a sea voyage with his uncle in order to stay home and marry Ruth, the girl next door. Andrew, his brother, who had assumed that he himself would marry Ruth and settle down on the farm, decides to take Robert's place aboard the uncle's ship. After five years of struggle it is dismally evident that Robert has failed as a farmer and that he and Ruth no longer share the romance of their betrothal night. When Andrew returns again to a poverty-stricken farm and a dying Robert in the last phases of tuberculosis, Robert begins to realize what the tragedy of his life means. He speaks to Andrew, who has wasted his own years in get-rich-quick schemes:

ROBERT (*thoughtfully*). I've been wondering what the great change was in you. (*After a pause.*) You—a farmer—to gamble in a wheat pit with scraps of paper. There's a spiritual significance in that picture, Andy. (*He smiles bitterly.*) I'm a failure, and Ruth's another—but we can both justly lay some of the blame for our stumbling on God. But you're the deepest-dyed failure of the three, Andy. You've spent eight years running away from yourself. Do you see what I mean? You used to be a creator when you loved the farm. You and life were in harmonious partnership. And now— (*He stops as if vainly seeking for words.*) My brain is muddled. But part of what I mean is that your gambling with the thing you used to love to create proves how far astray— So you'll be punished. You'll have to suffer to win back— (*His voice grows weaker and he sighs wearily.*) It's no use. I can't say it. (*He lies back and closes his eyes, breathing pantingly.*)

ANDREW (*slowly*). I think I know what you're driving at, Rob—and it's true, I guess. (ROBERT *smiles gratefully and stretches out his hand, which* ANDREW *takes in his.*)

ROBERT. Remember, Andy, Ruth has suffered double her share. (*His voice faltering with weakness.*) Only through contact with suffering, Andy, will you—awaken. . . .

As Robert dies on the roadside, looking out to the horizon he never crossed, he tries to tell the horrified Andrew and Ruth that he is now free and happy. "It isn't the end," he says. "It's a free beginning—the start of my voyage! I've won my trip—the right of release—beyond the horizon! Oh, you ought to be glad—glad—for my sake!"

Venture into Verse

Before the appearance of Tennessee Williams and Arthur Miller after the Second World War, the only other American playwright who shared O'Neill's tragic view was Maxwell Anderson. There are wide differences between the styles of the two writers, but they both felt that there was more of the genuinely tragic to be found in contemporary life than others recognized. *Winterset*, 1935, was Anderson's demonstration of the possibilities of lyricism and tragedy in a modern story of crime and detection set in the New York slums.

The background of *Winterset* is the Sacco-Vanzetti case. Using fictitious names, Anderson tells the story of Mio, the teen-age son of one of the victims, who is searching the country for the gang who actually committed the murder and let his father die, an innocent man. He has tracked the leading suspect to a tenement beneath the Brooklyn Bridge. His passionate desire to avenge the wrong is temporarily disrupted by his Romeo-and-Juliet-style love affair with Miriamne, the fifteen-year-old sister of the one living witness who could clear his family name. Anderson succumbs to melodrama as he gathers together in a slum apartment the leading figures of the case, from the gunman who did the shooting to the judge who presided at the trial, all facing one another as a wild storm rages outside. Mio seems on the edge of triumph, but his foreordained fate turns the tables in a series of quick misfortunes, and the murderer escapes to take his inevitable revenge.

Happily, Anderson does not permit this overcontrived climax to ruin his play. Mere incident becomes unimportant when compared with the unfolding of the tragic view of modern life that is expressed in Mio's fate and the love and devotion of the pathetic Miriamne. Anderson's power is strongest in the long closing scene. Mio's attempt to evade the gunmen has failed, and he crawls back to Miriamne, mortally wounded. To prove that she has had no part in his ambush, Miriamne calls out as she walks toward the killers, "I can die, too, see! You! There! You in the shadows!—You killed him to silence him!" She, too, collapses in a burst of machine-gun fire and dies with Mio. Esdras, her father, and Garth, the brother who could have saved both, stand helplessly over them. Esdras speaks:

ESDRAS. Well, they were wiser than you and I. To die
    when you are young and untouched, that's beggary
    to a miser of years, but the devils locked in synod
    shake and are daunted when men set their lives
    at hazard for the heart's love, and lose. And these,
    who were yet children, will weigh more than all
    a city's elders when the experiment
    is reckoned up in the end. Oh, Miriamne,
    and Mio—Mio, my son—know this where you lie,
    this is the glory of earth-born men and women,
    not to cringe, never to yield, but standing,
    take defeat implacable and defiant,
    die unsubmitting. I wish that I'd died so. . . .

Desire Under the Elms

Desire Under the Elms was welcomed as O'Neill's first tragedy in the classic Greek manner. Simultaneously it was condemned as a dismal failure, written about ugly people and repulsive deeds. In 1926 a Los Angeles police officer arrested the entire cast for presenting an immoral play. The Lord Chamberlain forbade its appearance in England until 1940. Praise for its "classic" nature and "overwhelming elemental power" greeted a brief revival in 1952, but an interesting and somewhat altered motion picture version in 1957 encountered mixed reactions. Whether or not the play is judged as tragedy, morbid melodrama, or the case history of a decaying New England family, the play has survived as one of the most respected works in the entire O'Neill canon.

Desire Under the Elms cannot be considered tragedy if the criterion is "high prosperity" or "nobility" in Aristotle's terms. The unattractive, superstitious characters who endure their suffering on a bleak and primitive New England farm are only a few steps above poverty. The goals toward which they strive and the motivations behind their violent displays of lust and anger are not admirable. An acceptable way to see the tragedy is in terms of naturalistic determinism. The human, realistically conceived characters in the drama act in the midst of a natural environment from which they have no chance of escape and over which they have minimal control. As direct products of their surroundings, given virtually no opportunity for self-betterment, they operate on a fundamental level of animal lust, elemental passion, and appalling ignorance. Theirs is the tragedy of a life forced upon them by a callous and indifferent nature, which they cannot possibly understand but can aspire to combat even though the struggle means their ultimate destruction.

If the characters are to be admired as tragic, the tragedy must come from what they are as human beings facing the catastrophe brought upon them by their situation. Old Cabot, immovable in his rigid way and often bestial (the association with the understanding cows in the stable is not without significance) is least likely to receive sympathy. But because he is drawn so much larger than life, and because he is so devoted to the furtherance of what he maintains to be right and good, he becomes a character we must finally, if reluctantly, admire. He is not an evil person; what he does is with the full conviction that he stands justified in the eyes of God. When given the opportunity to prosper easily in a land which produced fruitfully without hard labor, he obeyed the call of his primitive, rock-hard, patriarchal God and went back to the stony hills of New England where a grueling life offered him purpose in existence. Cabot falls short of tragic proportions mainly because the suffering he endures at the hands of his children and as a result of his own limited views on what is "right" leaves him unchanged, adamant as ever. At the close of the play he rounds up the cattle to start life anew, the same man that he has always been. What he has endured is part of God's hard way. He survives as hale and hardy in his ancient body and his mind as when he first walked on stage. If not fully tragic, he still remains as an extraordinary figure, one of the most powerful characters in contemporary American drama.

Eben and Abbie develop more nearly along the directions expected of tragic characters. They do not understand the forces which move them, and they are unable to question them intelligently. They fiercely seek their rights of material possession and economic security, and just as fiercely pursue their violent physical attraction toward each other. The most basic of natural urges, which grips them and leaves them powerless, now compounds their danger, but in the end it joins them together in a tragic realization of their doom. At first they react in the only way they know, with more violence. Abbie has but one way to demonstrate the truth of her love. Her rash murder of the child seals the doom of all, for it is no more the way out of a frightful situation than was the illicit love affair a solution to loneliness and fear in the first place. Eben's abhorrence inspires his own impetuous move when he runs for the law, but it solves no more than Abbie's murder. Together, then, Eben and Abbie realize what has grasped them and understand that neither one nor the other can suffer alone for the horror of their crimes. Their agony has brought them the genuine unchanging love they at one time so fervently sought but could not hope to find in the world as it was. Eben and Abbie have, in their way, redeemed themselves for what they have done. As they are led away, tranquility is restored. The evil thing which has destroyed, the thing of lust, revenge, and greed, is dead.

O'Neill's sense of good theatre has served him well in *Desire Under the Elms*. It is more successful here than in many of his other plays because it does not rely on the mechanical effects of the masks and soliloquies which became the O'Neill trademark. Neither does O'Neill's theatricalism rely on the melodramatic in the way Anderson employed it in *Winterset*. Compare the climactic sequence in *Winterset* with the bedroom scene in *Desire*, one of the best scenes which O'Neill ever wrote. It carries the highest qualities of theatrical suspense and anticipation without violence or artificial flourish. When the bored, somewhat terrified young wife stares at the center wall, and her companion in tragedy moves toward her from the opposite side as if her gaze penetrated the opaque plaster, there is more genuine drama and vivid theatre than will be found in several pages of dialogue and elaborate stage directions.

You will not find that O'Neill writes in a style easily compared with other modern writers. His characters often move with heavy, ponderous steps. They repeat incessantly, and their speech is sterile and artificial. There is not a memorable line, aside from "purty," in the entire play. O'Neill is not a facile writer like Anderson. He does not give the feel of natural talk like Miller, nor of the poetry with which Williams can infuse some of his characters. But by the time you have finished the play, you will realize that O'Neill's intensity and devotion to his purpose is not often equaled by other playwrights. *Desire Under the Elms* has flaws which could possibly be fatal in another writer. In this play they do not destroy, and it becomes an outstanding example of a serious try at genuine native American tragedy.

Eugene O'Neill

Eugene O'Neill was born on October 16, 1888, in New York City. His parents were James O'Neill, the actor, who had come to this country from Ireland as a boy, and Ellen Quinlan O'Neill, a quiet, convent-bred girl born in New Haven, Connecticut. The elder O'Neill was nationally famous for his role of Edmund Dantes in *The Count of Monte Cristo*, which he played up and down the nation for decades.

Young O'Neill was educated at private and public schools in New York and New England and traveled with his parents on road tours of *Monte Cristo*. He entered Princeton with the class of 1910 but left in 1907 without completing the freshman year. The O'Neill family life has only recently become revealed through the long biographical *Long Day's Journey into Night*, produced in 1956, and through a series of books published by individuals in one way or another close to the playwright. We know that his father, a heavy drinker, was a parsimonious penny pincher, who never supplied the family with the comforts and the full life which his fortune could have brought them. His mother was addicted to morphine, and his brother, James, ten years his elder, was a hopeless alcoholic. The entire story is yet to be told.

In 1909 Eugene O'Neill married Kathleen Jenkins, with whom he lived only briefly before departing for a gold-prospecting tour in Honduras, which resulted in malarial fever and no gold. His son, Eugene, Jr., whom he did not see for nearly twelve years, was born in 1910, and this first marriage was soon ended. From 1910 to 1912 O'Neill shipped on an assortment of tramp steamers, mainly to South America, and lived in destitution in a New York water-front dive. After a futile attempt at suicide, he shipped out as a sailor again and then returned to New London, Connecticut, where he worked on the local paper. His health broke, and in December, 1912, he entered a sanatorium at Wallingford, Connecticut, where he remained six months. While there he began his intense reading of modern writers, particularly of the dramatist Strindberg.

In the winter of 1913–1914 O'Neill wrote several one-act plays, some of which his father financed for publication as *Thirst, and Other One-act Plays* in 1914. The book was a failure but is now a collector's item. In the fall of 1914 he enrolled in George Pierce Baker's English 47 class at Harvard, where he briefly studied playwriting. By 1916 he was living in Provincetown, still without income to speak of. Here he met the Provincetown Players, who produced *Bound East for Cardiff* in the summer of 1916, and started him on his way. In 1918 he married Agnes Boulton, a short-story writer and journalist.

With the staging on Broadway of *Beyond the Horizon* in February, 1920, he was an established playwright. Thereupon followed play after play, four or five bunched together in one season, playing both uptown on Broadway stages, or downtown in the smaller Off Broadway houses of that day. Many of the plays were terrible failures; three of them won Pulitzer Prizes.

O'Neill was ever a restless soul. After his marriage to Miss Boulton, he lived with his family (daughter Oona, now married to Charlie Chaplin, and son Shane) in a made-over Cape Cod Coast Guard rescue shack that had been abandoned, and in a large manor house in Bermuda. During this period he successfully overcame his alcoholism and remained a teetotaler for the rest of his life. In 1929 he divorced Agnes Boulton and immediately married actress Carlotta Monterey. They resided in a French château for a few years, and then in a mansion on Sea Island, Georgia, in 1932. In 1936 O'Neill and his wife moved to an isolated valley in California where they lived until 1946, when they returned to the East to live in New York and in Marblehead, Massachusetts.

During the time in California, O'Neill's health had deteriorated. The uncontrolled trembling of a rare nerve disease prevented his completing any work. He had started a great play cycle which was to include as many as eleven plays, but only *A Touch of the Poet*, produced in New York in 1958, has survived. O'Neill died of bronchial pneumonia in Boston on November 27, 1953.

This sketch cannot do justice to the man or his work. O'Neill's life was continually full, continually restless, and often tragic. (His brilliant son, Eugene, Jr., a classical scholar of considerable fame, committed suicide in 1950, and he disinherited his daughter when she married Chaplin.) He wrote nothing but plays and refused all requests to appear in public on any occasion whatsoever. He had one burning desire—to write tragedy based on the American scene. His many awards, including the Nobel Prize, attest his international fame, but as a man he remained until his death a fascinating enigma.

A LIST OF THE MOST IMPORTANT PLAYS OF EUGENE O'NEILL

Ah, Wilderness!, 1933.
All God's Chillun Got Wings, 1924.
Anna Christie, 1921. Pulitzer Prize.
Beyond the Horizon, 1920. Pulitzer Prize.
Bound East for Cardiff, 1916. One act; his first produced play.
Days Without End, 1934.
Desire Under the Elms, 1924.
Dynamo, 1929.
The Emperor Jones, 1920.
The Great God Brown, 1926.
The Hairy Ape, 1922.
The Iceman Cometh, 1946. Copyrighted, but unpublished, 1940.

In the Zone, 1917. One act.

Lazarus Laughed, 1928. Produced only by Pasadena Playhouse in original version. Never professionally produced.

Long Day's Journey into Night, 1956. First produced earlier the same year in Stockholm, Sweden. The play was completed in 1941 and given to his wife as an anniversary present. He specified that it not be produced until twenty-five years after his death, but Mrs. O'Neill decided that it should be seen. It won O'Neill's fourth Pulitzer Prize.

The Long Voyage Home, 1917. One act.

Marco Millions, 1928.

A Moon for the Misbegotten, 1947. First produced at Columbus, Ohio, this play ran afoul of censors and did not enter New York. It was revived for a moderate Broadway run in 1957.

The Moon of the Caribbees, 1918. One act.

Mourning Becomes Electra, 1931.

Strange Interlude, 1928. Pulitzer Prize.

A Touch of the Poet, 1958. Completed about 1940, as a part of his multiplay cycle entitled *A Tale of Possessors Self-dispossessed*, at one time supposed to have reached eleven plays. This is the only play surviving in condition to be acted. *More Stately Mansions* exists but is reported to be so garbled that production is impractical.

One other play, *Hughie*, a long one-act play, was produced in Stockholm in the 1957–1958 season. It involves only two characters and becomes almost a monologue. As of this time, it has not yet appeared in New York, but its production is undoubtedly not far away.

DESIRE UNDER THE ELMS
by
Eugene O'Neill

Right. O'Neill's original sketches for the setting of *Desire Under the Elms* included a form of simultaneous staging. Compare these to his explicit stage directions as printed in the play. (*The Provincetown Playbill. Courtesy Kenneth Macgowan*.)

Below. Robert Edmond Jones directed the original Provincetown production of *Desire,* and his scene design is based directly on O'Neill's sketches. (*Courtesy Museum of the City of New York*.)

Desire Under the Elms was first produced at the Greenwich Village Theatre, New York, on November 11, 1924. It moved uptown to the Earl Carroll Theatre in January, 1925, and thence to the George M. Cohan and Daly's Sixty-third Street Theatres. Its performances totalled 208, the longest run of any O'Neill play up to that time. The following cast appeared in the original production:

SIMEON CABOT	*Allen Nagle*
PETER CABOT	*Perry Ivins*
EBEN CABOT	*Charles Ellis*
EPHRAIM CABOT	*Walter Huston*
ABBIE PUTNAM	*Mary Morris*

Produced by the Provincetown Players downtown
Produced by A. L. Jones and Morris Green uptown
Setting designed by Robert Edmond Jones

The action of the entire play takes place in, and immediately outside of, the Cabot farmhouse in New England, in the year 1850. The south end of the house faces front to a stone wall with a wooden gate at center opening on a country road. The house is in good condition but in need of paint. Its walls are a sickly grayish, the green of the shutters faded. Two enormous elms are on each side of the house. They bend their trailing branches down over the roof. They appear to protect and at the same time subdue. There is a sinister maternity in their aspect, a crushing, jealous absorption. They have developed from their intimate contact with the life of man in the house an appalling humaneness. They brood oppressively over the house. They are like exhausted women resting their sagging breasts and hands and hair on its roof, and when it rains their tears trickle down monotonously and rot on the shingles.

There is a path running from the gate around the right corner of the house to the front door. A narrow porch is on this side. The end wall facing us has two windows in its upper story, two larger ones on the floor below. The two upper are those of the father's bedroom and that of the brothers. On the left, ground floor, is the kitchen—on the right, the parlor, the shades of which are always drawn down.

PART ONE

SCENE 1: *Exterior of the farmhouse. It is sunset of a day at the beginning of summer in the year 1850. There is no wind and everything is still. The sky above the roof is suffused with deep colors, the green of the elms glows, but the house is in shadow, seeming pale and washed out by contrast.*

A door opens and EBEN CABOT *comes to the end of the porch and stands looking down the road to the right. He has a large bell in his hand and this he swings* mechanically, awakening a deafening clangor. Then he puts his hands on his hips and stares up at the sky. He sighs with a puzzled awe and blurts out with halting appreciation.

EBEN. God! Purty! (*His eyes fall and he stares about him frowningly. He is twenty-five, tall and sinewy. His face is well-formed, good-looking, but its expression is resentful and defensive. His defiant, dark eyes remind one of a wild animal's in captivity. Each day is a cage in which he finds himself trapped but inwardly unsubdued. There is a fierçe repressed vitality about him. He has black hair, mustache, a thin curly trace of beard. He is dressed in rough farm clothes.*

He spits on the ground with intense disgust, turns and goes back into the house.

SIMEON *and* PETER *come in from their work in the fields. They are tall men, much older than their half-brother* [SIMEON *is thirty-nine and* PETER *thirty-seven*], *built on a squarer, simpler model, fleshier in body, more bovine and homelier in face, shrewder and more practical. Their shoulders stoop a bit from years of farm work. They clump heavily along in their clumsy thick-soled boots caked with earth. Their clothes, their faces, hands, bare arms and throats are earth-stained. They smell of earth. They stand together for a moment in front of the house and, as if with the one impulse, stare dumbly up at the sky, leaning on their hoes. Their faces have a compressed, unresigned expression. As they look upward, this softens.)*

SIMEON (*grudgingly*). Purty.

PETER. Ay-eh.

SIMEON (*suddenly*). Eighteen year ago.

PETER. What?

SIMEON. Jenn. My woman. She died.

PETER. I'd fergot.

SIMEON. I rec'lect—now an' agin. Makes it lonesome. She'd hair long's a hoss' tail—an' yaller like gold!

PETER. Waal—she's gone. (*This with indifferent finality—then after a pause.*) They's gold in the West, Sim.

SIMEON (*still under the influence of sunset—vaguely*). In the sky?

PETER. Waal—in a manner o' speakin' —thar's the promise. (*Growing excited.*) Gold in the sky—in the West—Golden Gate—Californi-a!—Golden West!—fields o' gold!

SIMEON (*excited in his turn*). Fortunes layin' just atop o' the ground waitin' t' be picked! Solomon's mines, they says! (*For a moment they continue looking up at the sky—then their eyes drop.*)

PETER (*with sardonic bitterness*). Here —it's stones atop o' the ground—stones atop o' stones—makin' stone walls—year atop o' year—him 'n' yew 'n' me 'n' then Eben—makin' stone walls fur him to fence us in!

SIMEON. We've wuked. Give our strength. Give our years. Plowed 'em under in the ground,—(*He stamps rebelliously.*)—rottin'—makin' soil for his crops! (*A pause.*) Waal—the farm pays good for hereabouts.

PETER. If we plowed in Californi-a, they'd be lumps o' gold in the furrow!

SIMEON. Californi-a's t'other side o' earth, a'most. We got t' calc'late—

PETER (*after a pause*). 'Twould be hard fur me, too, to give up what we've 'arned here by our sweat. (*A pause.* EBEN *sticks his head out of the dining-room window, listening.*)

SIMEON. Ay-eh. (*A pause.*) Mebbe— he'll die soon.

PETER (*doubtfully*). Mebbe.

SIMEON. Mebbe—fur all we knows— he's dead now.

PETER. Ye'd need proof.

SIMEON. He's been gone two months— with no word.

PETER. Left us in the fields an evenin' like this. Hitched up an' druv off into the West. That's plum onnateral. He hain't never been off this farm 'ceptin' t' the village in thirty year or more, not since he married Eben's maw. (*A pause. Shrewdly.*) I calc'late we might git him declared crazy by the court.

SIMEON. He skinned 'em too slick. He got the best o' all on 'em. They'd never b'lieve him crazy. (*A pause.*) We got t' wait—till he's under ground.

EBEN (*with a sardonic chuckle*). Honor thy father! (*They turn, startled, and stare at him. He grins, then scowls.*) I pray he's died. (*They stare at him. He continues matter-of-factly.*) Supper's ready.

SIMEON *and* PETER (*together*). Ay-eh.

EBEN (*gazing up at the sky*). Sun's downin' purty.

SIMEON *and* PETER (*together*). Ay-eh. They's gold in the West.

EBEN. Ay-eh. (*Pointing.*) Yonder atop o' the hill pasture, ye mean?

SIMEON *and* PETER (*together*). In Californi-a!

EBEN. Hunh? (*Stares at them indifferently for a second, then drawls.*) Waal—supper's gittin' cold. (*He turns back into kitchen.*)

SIMEON (*startled—smacks his lips*). I air hungry!

PETER (*sniffing*). I smells bacon!

SIMEON (*with hungry appreciation*). Bacon's good!

PETER (*in same tone*). Bacon's bacon! (*They turn, shouldering each other, their bodies bumping and rubbing together as they hurry clumsily to their food, like two friendly oxen toward their evening meal. They disappear around the right corner of house and can be heard entering the door.*)

CURTAIN

SCENE 2: *The color fades from the sky. Twilight begins. The interior of the kitchen is now visible. A pine table is at center, a cookstove in the right rear corner, four rough wooden chairs, a tallow candle on the table. In the middle of the rear wall is fastened a big advertising poster with a ship in full sail and the word "California" in big letters. Kitchen utensils hang from nails. Everything is neat and in order but the atmosphere is of a men's camp kitchen rather than that of a home.*

Places for three are laid. EBEN takes boiled potatoes and bacon from the stove and puts them on the table, also a loaf of bread and a crock of water. SIMEON and PETER shoulder in, slump down in their chairs without a word. EBEN joins them. The three eat in silence for a moment, the two elder as naturally unrestrained as beasts of the field, EBEN picking at his food without appetite, glancing at them with a tolerant dislike.

SIMEON (*suddenly turns to EBEN*). Looky here! Ye'd oughtn't t' said that, Eben.

PETER. 'Twa'n't righteous.

EBEN. What?

SIMEON. Ye prayed he'd died.

EBEN. Waal—don't yew pray it? (*A pause.*)

PETER. He's our Paw.

EBEN (*violently*). Not mine!

SIMEON (*dryly*). Ye'd not let no one else say that about yer Maw! Ha! (*He gives one abrupt sardonic guffaw. PETER grins.*)

EBEN (*very pale*). I meant—I hain't his'n—I hain't like him—he hain't me!

PETER (*dryly*). Wait till ye've growed his age!

EBEN (*intensely*). I'm Maw—every drop o' blood! (*A pause. They stare at him with indifferent curiosity.*)

PETER (*reminiscently*). She was good t' Sim 'n' me. A good stepmaw's scurse.

SIMEON. She was good t' everyone.

EBEN (*greatly moved, gets to his feet and makes an awkward bow to each of them—stammering*). I be thankful t' ye. I'm her—her heir. (*He sits down in confusion.*)

PETER (*after a pause—judicially*). She was good even t' him.

EBEN (*fiercely*). An' fur thanks he killed her!

SIMEON (*after a pause*). No one never kills nobody. It's allus somethin'. That's the murderer.

EBEN. Didn't he slave Maw t' death?

PETER. He's slaved himself t' death. He's slaved Sim 'n' me 'n' yew t' death—on'y none o' us hain't died—yit.

SIMEON. It's somethin'—drivin' him—t' drive us!

EBEN (*vengefully*). Waal—I hold him t' jedgment! (*Then scornfully.*) Somethin'! What's somethin'?

SIMEON. Dunno.

EBEN (*sardonically*). What's drivin' yew to Californi-a, mebbe? (*They look at him in surprise.*) Oh, I've heerd ye! (*Then, after a pause.*) But ye'll never go t' the gold fields!

PETER (*assertively*). Mebbe!

EBEN. Whar'll ye git the money?

PETER. We kin walk. It's an a'mighty ways—Californi-a—but if yew was t' put all the steps we've walked on this farm end t' end we'd be in the moon!

EBEN. The Injuns'll skulp ye on the plains.

SIMEON (*with grim humor*). We'll mebbe make 'em pay a hair fur a hair!

EBEN (*decisively*). But t'aint that. Ye

won't never go because ye'll wait here fur yer share o' the farm, thinkin' allus he'll die soon.

SIMEON (*after a pause*). We've a right.

PETER. Two-thirds belongs t' us.

EBEN (*jumping to his feet*). Ye've no right! She wa'n't yewr Maw! It was her farm! Didn't he steal it from her? She's dead. It's my farm.

SIMEON (*sardonically*). Tell that t' Paw—when he comes! I'll bet ye a dollar he'll laugh—fur once in his life. Ha! (*He laughs himself in one single mirthless bark.*)

PETER (*amused in turn, echoes his brother*). Ha!

SIMEON (*after a pause*). What've ye got held agin us, Eben? Year arter year it's skulked in yer eye—somethin'.

PETER. Ay-eh.

EBEN. Ay-eh. They's somethin'. (*Suddenly exploding.*) Why didn't ye never stand between him 'n' my Maw when he was slavin' her to her grave—t' pay her back fur the kindness she done t' yew? (*There is a long pause. They stare at him in surprise.*)

SIMEON. Waal—the stock'd got t' be watered.

PETER. 'R they was woodin' t' do.

SIMEON. 'R plowin'.

PETER. 'R hayin'.

SIMEON. 'R spreadin' manure.

PETER. 'R weedin'.

SIMEON. 'R prunin'.

PETER. 'R milkin'.

EBEN (*breaking in harshly*). An' makin' walls—stone atop o' stone—makin' walls till yer heart's a stone ye heft up out o' the way o' growth onto a stone wall t' wall in yer heart!

SIMEON (*matter-of-factly*). We never had no time t' meddle.

PETER (*to EBEN*). Yew was fifteen afore yer Maw died—an' big fur yer age. Why didn't ye never do nothin'?

EBEN (*harshly*). They was chores t' do, wa'n't they? (*A pause—then slowly.*) It was on'y arter she died I come to think o' it. Me cookin'—doin' her work —that made me know her, suffer her sufferin'—she'd come back t' help—come back t' bile potatoes—come back t' fry bacon—come back t' bake biscuits—come

back all cramped up t' shake the fire, an' carry ashes, her eyes weepin' an' bloody with smoke an' cinders same's they used t' be. She still comes back—stands by the stove thar in the evenin'—she can't find it nateral sleepin' an' restin' in peace. She can't git used t' bein' free—even in her grave.

SIMEON. She never complained none.

EBEN. She'd got too tired. She'd got too used t' bein' too tired. That was what he done. (*With vengeful passion.*) An' sooner'r later, I'll meddle. I'll say the thin's I didn't say then t' him! I'll yell 'em at the top o' my lungs. I'll see t' it my Maw gits some rest an' sleep in her grave! (*He sits down again, relapsing into a brooding silence. They look at him with a queer indifferent curiosity.*)

PETER (*after a pause*). Whar in tarnation d'ye s'pose he went, Sim?

SIMEON. Dunno. He druv off in the buggy, all spick an' span, with the mare all breshed an' shiny, druv off clackin' his tongue an' wavin' his whip. I remember it right well. I was finishin' plowin', it was spring an' May an' sunset, an' gold in the West, an' he druv off into it. I yells "Whar ye goin', Paw?" an' he hauls up by the stone wall a jiffy. His old snake's eyes was glitterin' in the sun like he'd been drinkin' a jugful an' he says with a mule's grin: "Don't ye run away till I come back!"

PETER. Wonder if he knowed we was wantin' fur Californi-a?

SIMEON. Mebbe. I didn't say nothin' an' he says, lookin' kinder queer an' sick: "I been hearin' the hens cluckin' an' the roosters crowin' all the durn day. I been listenin' t' the cows lowin' an' everythin' else kickin' up till I can't stand it no more. It's spring an' I'm feelin' damned," he says. "Damned like an old bare hickory tree fit on'y fur burnin'," he says. An' then I calc'late I must've looked a mite hopeful, fur he adds real spry and vicious: "But don't git no fool idee I'm dead. I've sworn t' live a hundred an' I'll do it, if on'y t' spite yer sinful greed! An' now I'm ridin' out t' learn God's message t' me in the spring, like the prophets done. An' yew git back t' yer plowin'," he says. An' he druv off singin' a hymn. I thought he was drunk—'r I'd stopped him goin'.

EBEN (*scornfully*). No, ye wouldn't! Ye're scared o' him. He's stronger—inside —than both o' ye put together!

PETER (*sardonically*). An' yew—be yew Samson?

EBEN. I'm gittin' stronger. I kin feel it growin' in me—growin' an' growin'—till it'll bust out—! (*He gets up and puts on his coat and a hat. They watch him, gradually breaking into grins. EBEN avoids their eyes sheepishly.*) I'm goin' out fur a spell—up the road.

PETER. T' the village?

SIMEON. T' see Minnie?

EBEN (*defiantly*). Ay-eh!

PETER (*jeeringly*). The Scarlet Woman!

SIMEON. Lust—that's what's growin' in ye!

EBEN. Waal—she's purty!

PETER. She's been purty fur twenty year!

SIMEON. A new coat o' paint'll make a heifer out of forty.

EBEN. She hain't forty!

PETER. If she hain't, she's teeterin' on the edge.

EBEN (*desperately*). What d'yew know—

PETER. All they is . . . Sim knew her —an' then me arter—

SIMEON. An' Paw kin tell yew somethin' too! He was fust!

EBEN. D'ye mean t' say he . . . ?

SIMEON (*with a grin*). Ay-eh! We air his heirs in everythin'!

EBEN (*intensely*). That's more to it! That grows on it! It'll bust soon! (*Then violently.*) I'll go smash my fist in her face! (*He pulls open the door in rear violently.*)

SIMEON (*with a wink at PETER—drawlingly*). Mebbe—but the night's wa'm—purty—by the time ye git thar mebbe ye'll kiss her instead!

PETER. Sart'n he will! (*They both roar with coarse laughter. EBEN rushes out and slams the door—then the outside front door—comes around the corner of the house and stands still by the gate, staring up at the sky.*)

SIMEON (*looking after him*). Like his Paw.

PETER. Dead spit an' image!

SIMEON. Dog'll eat dog!

PETER. Ay-eh. (*Pause. With yearning.*) Mebbe a year from now we'll be in Californi-a.

SIMEON. Ay-eh. (*A pause. Both yawn.*) Let's git t'bed. (*He blows out the candle. They go out door in rear. EBEN stretches his arms up to the sky—rebelliously.*)

EBEN. Waal—thar's a star, an' somewhar's they's him, an' here's me, an' thar's Min up the road—in the same night. What if I does kiss her? She's like t'night, she's soft 'n' wa'm, her eyes kin wink like a star, her mouth's wa'm, her arms're wa'm, she smells like a wa'm plowed field, she's purty . . . Ay-eh! By God Almighty she's purty, an' I don't give a damn how many sins she's sinned afore mine or who she's sinned 'em with, my sin's as purty as any one of 'em! (*He strides off down the road to the left.*)

SCENE 3: *It is the pitch darkness just before dawn.* EBEN *comes in from the left and goes around to the porch, feeling his way, chuckling bitterly and cursing half-aloud to himself.*

EBEN. The cussed old miser! (*He can be heard going in the front door. There is a pause as he goes upstairs, then a loud knock on the bedroom door of the brothers.*) Wake up!

SIMEON (*startledly*). Who's thar?

EBEN (*pushing open the door and coming in, a lighted candle in his hand. The bedroom of the brothers is revealed. Its ceiling is the sloping roof. They can stand upright only close to the center dividing wall of the upstairs.* SIMEON *and* PETER *are in a double bed, front.* EBEN's *cot is to the rear.* EBEN *has a mixture of silly grin and vicious scowl on his face*). I be!

PETER (*angrily*). What in hell's-fire . . . ?

EBEN. I got news fur ye! Ha! (*He gives one abrupt sardonic guffaw.*)

SIMEON (*angrily*). Couldn't ye hold it 'til we'd got our sleep?

EBEN. It's nigh sunup. (*Then explosively.*) He's gone an' married agen!

SIMEON and PETER (*explosively*). Paw?

EBEN. Got himself hitched to a female 'bout thirty-five—an' purty, they says . . .

SIMEON (*aghast*). It's a durn lie!

PETER. Who says?

SIMEON. They been stringin' ye!

EBEN. Think I'm a dunce, do ye? The hull village says. The preacher from New Dover, he brung the news—told it t' our preacher—New Dover, that's whar the old loon got himself hitched—that's whar the woman lived—

PETER (*no longer doubting—stunned*). Waal . . . !

SIMEON (*the same*). Waal . . . !

EBEN (*sitting down on a bed—with vicious hatred*). Ain't he a devil out o' hell? It's jest t' spite us—the damned old mule!

PETER (*after a pause*). Everythin'll go t' her now.

SIMEON. Ay-eh. (*A pause—dully.*) Waal—if it's done—

PETER. It's done us. (*Pause—then persuasively.*) They's gold in the fields o' Californi-a, Sim. No good a-stayin' here now.

SIMEON. Jest what I was a-thinkin'. (*Then with decision.*) S'well fust's last! Let's light out and git this mornin'.

PETER. Suits me.

EBEN. Ye must like walkin'.

SIMEON (*sardonically*). If ye'd grow wings on us we'd fly thar!

EBEN. Ye'd like ridin' better—on a boat, wouldn't ye? (*Fumbles in his pocket and takes out a crumpled sheet of foolscap.*) Waal, if ye sign this ye kin ride on a boat. I've had it writ out an' ready in case ye'd ever go. It says fur three hundred dollars t' each ye agree yewr shares o' the farm is sold t' me. (*They look suspiciously at the paper. A pause.*)

SIMEON (*wonderingly*). But if he's hitched agen—

PETER. An' whar'd yew git that sum o' money, anyways?

EBEN (*cunningly*). I know whar it's hid. I been waitin'—Maw told me. She knew whar it lay fur years, but she was waitin' . . . It's her'n—the money he hoarded from her farm an' hid from Maw. It's my money by rights now.

PETER. Whar's it hid?

EBEN (*cunningly*). Whar yew won't never find it without me. Maw spied on him—'r she'd never knowed. (*A pause. They look at him suspiciously, and he at them.*) Waal, is it fa'r trade?

SIMEON. Dunno.

PETER. Dunno.

SIMEON (*looking at window*). Sky's grayin'.

PETER. Ye better start the fire, Eben.

SIMEON. An' fix some vittles.

EBEN. Ay-eh. (*Then with a forced jocular heartiness.*) I'll git ye a good one. If ye're startin' t' hoof it t' Californi-a ye'll need somethin' that'll stick t' yer ribs. (*He turns to the door, adding meaningly.*) But ye kin ride on a boat if ye'll swap. (*He stops at the door and pauses. They stare at him.*)

SIMEON (*suspiciously*). Whar was ye all night?

EBEN (*defiantly*). Up t' Min's. (*Then slowly.*) Walkin' thar, fust I felt 's if I'd kiss her; then I got a-thinkin' o' what ye'd said o' him an' her an' I says, I'll bust her nose fur that! Then I got t' the village an' heerd the news an' I got madder'n hell an' run all the way t' Min's not knowin' what I'd do— (*He pauses—then sheepishly but more defiantly.*) Waal—when I seen her, I didn't hit her—nor I didn't kiss her nuther—I begun t' beller like a calf an' cuss at the same time, I was so durn mad—an' she got scared—an' I jest grabbed holt an' tuk her! (*Proudly.*) Yes, sirree! I tuk her. She may've been his'n—an' your'n, too—but she's mine now!

SIMEON (*dryly*). In love, air yew?

EBEN (*with lofty scorn*). Love! I don't take no stock in sech slop!

PETER (*winking at* SIMEON). Mebbe Eben's aimin' t' marry, too.

SIMEON. Min'd make a true faithful he'pmeet! (*They snicker.*)

EBEN. What do I care fur her—'ceptin' she's round an' wa'm? The p'int is she was his'n—an' now she b'longs t' me! (*He goes to the door—then turns—rebelliously.*) An' Min hain't sech a bad un. They's worse'n Min in the world, I'll bet ye! Wait'll we see this cow the Old Man's hitched t'! She'll beat Min, I got a notion! (*He starts to go out.*)

SIMEON (*suddenly*). Mebbe ye'll try t' make her your'n, too?

PETER. Ha! (*He gives a sardonic laugh of relish at this idea.*)

EBEN (*spitting with disgust*). Her—here—sleepin' with him—stealin' my Maw's farm! I'd as soon pet a skunk 'r kiss a snake! (*He goes out. The two stare after him suspiciously. A pause. They listen to his steps receding.*)

PETER. He's startin' the fire.

SIMEON. I'd like t' ride t' Californi-a—but—

PETER. Min might o' put some scheme in his head.

SIMEON. Mebbe it's all a lie 'bout Paw marryin'. We'd best wait an' see the bride.

PETER. An' don't sign nothin' till we does!

SIMEON. Nor till we've tested it's good money! (*Then with a grin.*) But if Paw's hitched we'd be sellin' Eben somethin' we'd never git nohow!

PETER. We'll wait an' see. (*Then with sudden vindictive anger.*) An' till he comes, let's yew 'n' me not wuk a lick, let Eben tend to thin's if he's a mind t', let's us jest sleep an' eat an' drink likker, an' let the hull damned farm go t' blazes!

SIMEON (*excitedly*). By God, we've 'arned a rest! We'll play rich fur a change. I hain't a'goin' to stir outa bed till breakfast's ready.

PETER. An' on the table!

SIMEON (*after a pause—thoughtfully*). What d'ye calc'late she'll be like—our new Maw? Like Eben thinks?

PETER. More'n' likely.

SIMEON (*vindictively*). Waal—I hope she's a she-devil that'll make him wish he was dead an' livin' in the pit o' hell fur comfort!

PETER (*fervently*). Amen!

SIMEON (*imitating his father's voice*). "I'm ridin' out t' learn God's message t' me in the spring like the prophets done," he says. I'll bet right then an' thar he knew plumb well he was goin' whorin', the stinkin' old hypocrite!

SCENE 4: *Same as Scene 2—shows the interior of the kitchen with a lighted candle on table. It is gray dawn outside.* SIMEON *and* PETER *are just finishing their breakfast.* EBEN *sits before his plate of untouched food, brooding frowningly.*

PETER (*glancing at him rather irritably*). Lookin' glum don't help none.

SIMEON (*sarcastically*). Sorrowin' over his lust o' the flesh!

PETER (*with a grin*). Was she yer fust?

EBEN (*angrily*). None o' yer business. (*A pause.*) I was thinkin' o' him. I got a notion he's gittin' near—I kin feel him comin' on like yew kin feel malaria chill afore it takes ye.

PETER. It's too early yet.

SIMEON. Dunno. He'd like t' catch us nappin'—jest t' have somethin' t' hoss us 'round over.

PETER (*mechanically gets to his feet.* SIMEON *does the same*). Waal—let's git t' wuk. (*They both plod mechanically toward the door before they realize. Then they stop short.*)

SIMEON (*grinning*). Ye're a cussed fool, Pete—an' I be wuss! Let him see we hain't wukin'! We don't give a durn!

PETER (*as they go back to the table*). Not a damned durn! It'll serve t' show him we're done with him. (*They sit down again.* EBEN *stares from one to the other with surprise.*)

SIMEON (*grins at him*). We're aimin' t' start bein' lilies o' the field.

PETER. Nary a toil 'r spin 'r lick o' wuk do we put in!

SIMEON. Ye're sole owner—till he comes—that's what ye wanted. Waal, ye got t' be sole hand, too.

PETER. The cows air bellerin'. Ye better hustle at the milkin'.

EBEN (*with excited joy*). Ye mean ye'll sign the paper?

SIMEON (*dryly*). Mebbe.

PETER. Mebbe.

SIMEON. We're considerin'. (*Peremptorily.*) Ye better git t' wuk.

EBEN (*with queer excitement*). It's Maw's farm agen! It's my farm! Them's my cows! I'll milk my durn fingers off fur cows o' mine! (*He goes out door in rear, they stare after him indifferently.*)

SIMEON. Like his Paw.

PETER. Dead spit 'n' image!

SIMEON. Waal—let dog eat dog! (EBEN *comes out of front door and around the corner of the house. The sky is beginning to grow flushed with sunrise. EBEN stops by the gate and stares around him with glowing, possessive eyes. He takes in the whole farm with his embracing glance of desire.*)

EBEN. It's purty! It's damned purty! It's mine! (*He suddenly throws his head back boldly and glares with hard, defiant eyes at the sky.*) Mine, d'ye hear? Mine! (*He turns and walks quickly off left, rear, toward the barn. The two brothers light their pipes.*)

SIMEON (*putting his muddy boots up on the table, tilting back his chair, and puffing defiantly*). Waal—this air solid comfort—fur once.

PETER. Ay-eh. (*He follows suit. A pause. Unconsciously they both sigh.*)

SIMEON (*suddenly*). He never was much o' a hand at milkin', Eben wa'n't.

PETER (*with a snort*). His hands air like hoofs! (*A pause.*)

SIMEON. Reach down the jug thar! Let's take a swaller. I'm feelin'. kind o' low.

PETER. Good idee! (*He does so—gets two glasses—they pour out drinks of whisky.*) Here's t' the gold in Californi-a!

SIMEON. An' luck t' find it! (*They drink—puff resolutely—sigh—take their feet down from the table.*)

PETER. Likker don't pear t' sot right.

SIMEON. We hain't used t' it this early. (*A pause. They become very restless.*)

PETER. Gittin' close in this kitchen.

SIMEON (*with immense relief*). Let's git a breath o' air. (*They arise briskly and go out rear—appear around house and stop by the gate. They stare up at the sky with a numbed appreciation.*)

PETER. Purty!

SIMEON. Ay-eh. Gold's t' the East now.

PETER. Sun's startin' with us fur the Golden West.

SIMEON (*staring around the farm, his compressed face tightened, unable to conceal his emotion*). Waal—it's our last mornin'—mebbe.

PETER (*the same*). Ay-eh.

SIMEON (*stamps his foot on the earth and addresses it desperately*). Waal—ye've thirty year o' me buried in ye—spread out over ye—blood an' bone an' sweat—rotted away—fertilizin' ye—richin' yer soul—prime manure, by God, that's what I been t' ye!

PETER. Ay-eh! An' me!

SIMEON. An' yew, Peter. (*He sighs—then spits.*) Waal—no use'n cryin' over spilt milk.

PETER. They's gold in the West—an' freedom, mebbe. We been slaves t' stone walls here.

SIMEON (*defiantly*). We hain't nobody's slaves from this out—nor no thin's slaves nuther. (*A pause—restlessly.*) Speakin' o' milk, wonder how Eben's managin'?

PETER. I s'pose he's managin'.

SIMEON. Mebbe we'd ought t' help—this once.

PETER. Mebbe. The cows knows us.

SIMEON. An' likes us. They don't know him much.

PETER. An' the hosses, an' pigs, an' chickens. They don't know him much.

SIMEON. They knows us like brothers—an' likes us! (*Proudly.*) Hain't we raised 'em t' be fust-rate, number one prize stock?

PETER. We hain't—not no more.

SIMEON (*dully*). I was fergittin'. (*Then resignedly.*) Waal, let's go help Eben a spell an' git waked up.

PETER. Suits me. (*They are starting off down left, rear, for the barn when* EBEN *appears from there hurrying toward them, his face excited.*)

EBEN (*breathlessly*). Waal—har they be! The old mule an' the bride! I seen 'em from the barn down below at the turnin'.

PETER. How could ye tell that far?

EBEN. Hain't I as far-sight as he's near-sight? Don't I know the mare 'n' buggy, an' two people settin' in it? Who else . . . ? An' I tell ye I kin feel 'em a-comin', too! (*He squirms as if he had the itch.*)

PETER (*beginning to be angry*). Waal—let him do his own unhitchin'!

SIMEON (*angry in his turn*). Let's hustle in an' git our bundles an' be a-goin' as he's a-comin'. I don't want never t' step inside the door agen arter he's back. (*They both start back around the corner of the house.* EBEN *follows them.*)

EBEN (*anxiously*). Will ye sign it afore ye go?

PETER. Let's see the color o' the old skinflint's money an' we'll sign. (*They disappear left. The two brothers clump upstairs to get their bundles.* EBEN *appears in the kitchen, runs to window, peers out, comes back and pulls up a strip of flooring in under stove, takes out a canvas bag and puts it on table, then sets the floorboard back in place. The two brothers appear a moment after. They carry old carpet bags.*)

EBEN (*puts his hand on bag guardingly*). Have ye signed?

SIMEON (*shows paper in his hand*). Ay-eh. (*Greedily.*) Be that the money?

EBEN (*opens bag and pours out pile of twenty-dollar gold pieces*). Twenty-dollar pieces—thirty on 'em. Count 'em. (PETER *does so, arranging them in stacks of five, biting one or two to test them.*)

PETER. Six hundred. (*He puts them in bag and puts it inside his shirt carefully.*)

SIMEON (*handing paper to* EBEN). Har ye be.

EBEN (*after a glance, folds it carefully and hides it under his shirt—gratefully*). Thank yew.

PETER. Thank yew fur the ride.

SIMEON. We'll send ye a lump o' gold fur Christmas. (*A pause.* EBEN *stares at them and they at him.*)

PETER (*awkwardly*). Waal—we're a-goin'.

SIMEON. Comin' out t' the yard?

EBEN. No. I'm waitin' in here a spell. (*Another silence. The brothers edge awkwardly to door in rear—then turn and stand.*)

SIMEON. Waal—good-by.

PETER. Good-by.

EBEN. Good-by. (*They go out. He sits down at the table, faces the stove and pulls out the paper. He looks from it to the stove. His face, lighted up by the shaft of sunlight from the window, has an expression of trance. His lips move. The two brothers come out to the gate.*)

PETER (*looking off toward barn*). Thar he be—unhitchin'.

SIMEON (*with a chuckle*). I'll bet ye he's riled!

PETER. An' thar she be.

SIMEON. Let's wait 'n' see what our new Maw looks like.

PETER (*with a grin*). An' give him our partin' cuss!

SIMEON (*grinning*). I feel like raisin' fun. I feel light in my head an' feet.

PETER. Me, too. I feel like laffin' till I'd split up the middle.

SIMEON. Reckon it's the likker?

PETER. No. My feet feel itchin' t' walk an' walk—an' jump high over thin's—an' . . .

SIMEON. Dance? (*A pause.*)

PETER (*puzzled*). It's plumb onnateral.

SIMEON (*a light coming over his face*). I calc'late it's 'cause school's out. It's holiday. Fur once we're free!

PETER (*dazedly*). Free?

SIMEON. The halter's broke—the harness is busted—the fence bars is down—the stone walls air crumblin' an' tumblin'! We'll be kickin' up an' tearin' away down the road!

PETER (*drawing a deep breath—oratorically*). Anybody that wants this stinkin' old rock-pile of a farm kin hev it. T'ain't our'n, no sirree!

SIMEON (*takes the gate off its hinges and puts it under his arm*). We harby 'bolishes shet gates, an' open gates, an' all gates, by thunder!

PETER. We'll take it with us fur luck an' let 'er sail free down some river.

SIMEON (*as a sound of voices comes from left, rear*). Har they comes! (*The two brothers congeal into two stiff, grim-visaged statues.* EPHRAIM CABOT *and* ABBIE PUTNAM *come in.* CABOT *is seventy-five, tall and gaunt, with great, wiry, concentrated power, but stoop-shouldered from toil. His face is as hard as if it were hewn out of a boulder, yet there is a weakness in it, a petty pride in its own narrow strength. His eyes are small, close together, and extremely nearsighted, blinking continually in the effort to focus on objects, their stare having a straining, ingrowing quality.*

He is dressed in his dismal black Sunday suit. ABBIE *is thirty-five, buxom, full of vitality. Her round face is pretty but marred by its rather gross sensuality. There is strength and obstinacy in her jaw, a hard determination in her eyes, and about her whole personality the same unsettled, untamed, desperate quality which is so apparent in* EBEN.)

CABOT (*as they enter—a queer strangled emotion in his dry cracking voice*). Har we be t' hum, Abbie.

ABBIE (*with lust for the word*). Hum! (*Her eyes gloating on the house without seeming to see the two stiff figures at the gate.*) It's purty—purty! I can't b'lieve it's r'ally mine.

CABOT (*sharply*). Yewr'n? Mine! (*He stares at her penetratingly. She stares back. He adds relentingly.*) Our'n—mebbe! It was lonesome too long. I was growin' old in the spring. A hum's got t' hev a woman.

ABBIE (*her voice taking possession*). A woman's got t' hev a hum!

CABOT (*nodding uncertainly*). Ay-eh. (*Then irritably.*) Whar be they? Ain't thar nobody about—'r wukin'—'r nothin'?

ABBIE (*sees the brothers. She returns their stare of cold appraising contempt with interest—slowly*). Thar's two men loafin' at the gate an' starin' at me like a couple o' strayed hogs.

CABOT (*straining his eyes*). I kin see 'em—but I can't make out. . . .

SIMEON. It's Simeon.

PETER. It's Peter.

CABOT (*exploding*). Why hain't ye wukin'?

SIMEON (*dryly*). We're waitin' t' welcome ye hum—yew an' the bride!

CABOT (*confusedly*). Huh? Waal—this be yer new Maw, boys. (*She stares at them and they at her.*)

SIMEON (*turns away and spits contemptuously*). I see her!

PETER (*spits also*). An' I see her!

ABBIE (*with the conqueror's conscious superiority*). I'll go in an' look at *my* house. (*She goes slowly around to porch.*)

SIMEON (*with a snort*). Her house!

PETER (*calls after her*). Ye'll find Eben inside. Ye better not tell him it's *yewr* house.

ABBIE (*mouthing the name*). Eben. (*Then quietly.*) I'll tell Eben.

CABOT (*with a contemptuous sneer*). Ye needn't heed Eben. Eben's a dumb fool—like his Maw—soft an' simple!

SIMEON (*with his sardonic burst of laughter*). Ha! Eben's a chip o' yew—spit 'n' image—hard 'n' bitter's a hickory tree! Dog'll eat dog. He'll eat ye yet, old man!

CABOT (*commandingly*). Ye git t' wuk!

SIMEON (*as* ABBIE *disappears in house—winks at* PETER *and says tauntingly*). So that thar's our new Maw, be it? Whar in hell did ye dig her up? (*He and* PETER *laugh.*)

PETER. Ha! Ye'd better turn her in the pen with the other sows. (*They laugh uproariously, slapping their thighs.*)

CABOT (*so amazed at their effrontery that he stutters in confusion*). Simeon! Peter! What's come over ye? Air ye drunk?

SIMEON. We're free, old man—free o' yew an' the hull damned farm! (*They grow more and more hilarious and excited.*)

PETER. An' we're startin' out fur the gold fields o' Californi-a!

SIMEON. Ye kin take this place an' burn it!

PETER. An' bury it—fur all we cares!

SIMEON. We're free, old man! (*He cuts a caper.*)

PETER. Free! (*He gives a kick in the air.*)

SIMEON (*in a frenzy*). Whoop!

PETER. Whoop! (*They do an absurd Indian war dance about the old man who is petrified between rage and the fear that they are insane.*)

SIMEON. We're free as Injuns! Lucky we don't skulp ye!

PETER. An' burn yer barn an' kill the stock!

SIMEON. An' rape yer new woman! Whoop! (*He and* PETER *stop their dance, holding their sides, rocking with wild laughter.*)

CABOT (*edging away*). Lust fur gold—fur the sinful, easy gold o' Californi-a! It's made ye mad!

SIMEON (*tauntingly*). Wouldn't ye like us to send ye back some sinful gold, ye old sinner?

PETER. They's gold besides what's in Californi-a! (*He retreats back beyond the vision of the old man and takes the bag of money and flaunts it in the air above his head, laughing.*)

SIMEON. And sinfuller, too!

PETER. We'll be voyagin' on the sea! Whoop! (*He leaps up and down.*)

SIMEON. Livin' free! Whoop! (*He leaps in turn.*)

CABOT (*suddenly roaring with rage*). My cuss on ye!

SIMEON. Take our'n in trade fur it! Whoop!

CABOT. I'll hev ye both chained up in the asylum!

PETER. Ye old skinflint! Good-by!

SIMEON. Ye old bloodsucker! Good-by!

CABOT. Go afore I . . . !

PETER. Whoop! (*He picks a stone from the road. SIMEON does the same.*)

SIMEON. Maw'll be in the parlor.

PETER. Ay-eh! One! Two!

CABOT (*frightened*). What air ye . . . ?

PETER. Three! (*They both throw, the stones hitting the parlor window with a crash of glass, tearing the shade.*)

SIMEON. Whoop!

PETER. Whoop!

CABOT (*in a fury now, rushing toward them*). If I kin lay hands on ye—I'll break yer bones fur ye! (*But they beat a capering retreat before him, SIMEON with the gate still under his arm. CABOT comes back, panting with impotent rage. Their voices as they go off take up the song of the gold-seekers to the old tune of "Oh, Susannah!"*)

"I jumped aboard the Liza ship,
  And traveled on the sea,
  And every time I thought of home
  I wished it wasn't me!
  Oh! Californi-a,
  That's the land fur me!
  I'm off to Californi-a!
  With my wash bowl on my knee."

In the meantime, the window of the upper bedroom on right is raised and AB-BIE sticks her head out. She looks down at CABOT—with a sigh of relief.)

ABBIE. Waal—that's the last o' them two, hain't it? (*He doesn't answer. Then in possessive tones.*) This here's a nice bedroom, Ephraim. It's a r'al nice bed. Is it my room, Ephraim?

CABOT (*grimly—without looking up*). Our'n! (*She cannot control a grimace of aversion and pulls back her head slowly and shuts the window. A sudden horrible thought seems to enter CABOT's head.*) They been up to somethin'! Mebbe—mebbe they've pizened the stock—'r somethin'! (*He almost runs off down toward the barn. A moment later the kitchen door is slowly pushed open and ABBIE enters. For a moment she stands looking at EBEN. He does not notice her at first. Her eyes take him in penetratingly with a calculating appraisal of his strength as against hers. But under this her desire is dimly awakened by his youth and good looks. Suddenly he becomes conscious of her presence and looks up. Their eyes meet. He leaps to his feet, glowering at her speechlessly.*)

ABBIE (*in her most seductive tones which she uses all through this scene*). Be you—Eben? I'm Abbie— (*She laughs.*) I mean, I'm yer new Maw.

EBEN (*viciously*). No, damn ye!

ABBIE (*as if she hadn't heard—with a queer smile*). Yer Paw's spoke a lot o' yew. . . .

EBEN. Ha!

ABBIE. Ye mustn't mind him. He's an old man. (*A long pause. They stare at each other.*) I don't want t' pretend playin' Maw t' ye, Eben. (*Admiringly.*) Ye're too big an' too strong fur that. I want t' be frens with ye. Mebbe with me fur a fren ye'd find ye'd like livin' here better. I kin make it easy fur ye with him, mebbe. (*With a scornful sense of power.*) I calc'late I kin git him t' do most anythin' fur me.

EBEN (*with bitter scorn*). Ha! (*They stare again, EBEN obscurely moved, physically attracted to her—in forced stilted tones.*) Yew kin go t' the devil!

ABBIE (*calmly*). If cussin' me does ye good, cuss all ye've a mind t'. I'm all prepared t' have ye agin me—at fust. I don't blame ye nuther. I'd feel the same at any stranger comin' t' take my Maw's place. (*He shudders. She is watching him carefully.*) Yew must've cared a lot fur yewr Maw, didn't ye? My Maw died afore I'd growed. I don't remember her none. (*A pause.*) But yew won't hate me long, Eben. I'm not the wust in the world—an' yew an' me've got a lot in common. I kin tell that by lookin' at ye. Waal—I've had a hard life, too— oceans o' trouble an' nuthin' but wuk fur reward. I was a orphan early an' had t' wuk fur others in other folks' hums. Then I married an' he turned out a drunken spreer an' so he had to wuk fur others an' me too agen in other folks' hums, an' the baby died, an' my husband got sick an' died too, an' I was glad sayin' now I'm free fur once, on'y I diskivered right away all I was free fur was t' wuk agen in other folks' hums, doin' other folks' wuk till I'd most give up hope o' ever doin' my own wuk in my own hum, an' then your Paw come. . . . (*Cabot appears returning from the barn. He comes to the gate and looks down the road the brothers have gone. A faint strain of their retreating voices is heard: "Oh, Californi-a! That's the place for me." He stands glowering, his fist clenched, his face grim with rage.*)

Eben (*fighting against his growing attraction and sympathy—harshly*). An' bought yew—like a harlot! (*She is stung and flushes angrily. She has been sincerely moved by the recital of her troubles. He adds furiously.*) An' the price he's payin' ye—this farm—was my Maw's, damn ye!—an' mine now!

Abbie (*with a cool laugh of confidence*). Yewr'n? We'll see 'bout that! (*Then strongly.*) Waal—what if I did need a hum? What else'd I marry an old man like him fur?

Eben (*maliciously*). I'll tell him ye said that!

Abbie (*smiling*). I'll say ye're lyin' a-purpose—an' he'll drive ye off the place!

Eben. Ye devil!

Abbie (*defying him*). This be my farm—this be my hum—this be my kitch-en—!

Eben (*furiously, as if he were going to attack her*). Shut up, damn ye!

Abbie (*walks up to him—a queer coarse expression of desire in her face and body—slowly*). An' upstairs—that be my bedroom—an' my bed! (*He stares into her eyes, terribly confused and torn. She adds softly.*) I hain't bad nor mean —'ceptin' fur an enemy—but I got t' fight fur what's due me out o' life, if I ever 'spect t' git it. (*Then putting her hand on his arm—seductively.*) Let's yew 'n' me be frens, Eben.

Eben (*stupidly—as if hypnotized*). Ay-eh. (*Then furiously flinging off her arm.*) No, ye durned old witch! I hate ye! (*He rushes out the door.*)

Abbie (*looks after him smiling satisfiedly—then half to herself, mouthing the word*). Eben's nice. (*She looks at the table, proudly.*) I'll wash up *my* dishes now. (*Eben appears outside, slamming the door behind him. He comes around corner, stops on seeing his father, and stands staring at him with hate.*)

Cabot (*raising his arms to heaven in the fury he can no longer control*). Lord God o' Hosts, smite the undutiful sons with Thy wust cuss!

Eben (*breaking in violently*). Yew 'n' yewr God! Allus cussin' folks—allus naggin' 'em!

Cabot (*oblivious to him—summoningly*). God o' the old! God o' the lonesome!

Eben (*mockingly*). Naggin' His sheep t' sin! T' hell with yewr God! (*Cabot turns. He and Eben glower at each other.*)

Cabot (*harshly*). So it's yew. I might've knowed it. (*Shaking his finger threateningly at him.*) Blasphemin' fool! (*Then quickly.*) Why hain't ye t' wuk?

Eben. Why hain't yew? They've went. I can't wuk it all alone.

Cabot (*contemptuously*). Nor noways! I'm wuth ten o' ye yit, old's I be! Ye'll never be more'n half a man! (*Then, matter-of-factly.*) Waal—let's git t' the barn. (*They go. A last faint note of the "Californi-a" song is heard from the distance. Abbie is washing her dishes.*)

CURTAIN

PART TWO

SCENE 1: *The exterior of the farm-house, as in Part One—a hot Sunday afternoon two months later.* ABBIE, *dressed in her best, is discovered sitting in a rocker at the end of the porch. She rocks listlessly, enervated by the heat, staring in front of her with bored, half-closed eyes.*

EBEN *sticks his head out of his bed-room window. He looks around fur-tively and tries to see—or hear—if anyone is on the porch, but although he has been careful to make no noise,* ABBIE *has sensed his movement. She stops rock-ing, her face grows animated and eager, she waits attentively.* EBEN *seems to feel her presence, he scowls back his thoughts of her and spits with exaggerated disdain —then withdraws back into the room.* ABBIE *waits, holding her breath as she listens with passionate eagerness for ev-ery sound within the house.*

EBEN *comes out. Their eyes meet. His falter, he is confused, he turns away and slams the door resentfully. At this ges-ture,* ABBIE *laughs tantalizingly, amused but at the same time piqued and irritated. He scowls, strides off the porch to the path and starts to walk past her to the road with a grand swagger of ignoring her existence. He is dressed in his store suit, spruced up, his face shines from soap and water.* ABBIE *leans forward on her chair, her eyes hard and angry now, and, as he passes her, gives a sneering, taunting chuckle.*

EBEN (*stung—turns on her furiously*). What air yew cacklin' 'bout?

ABBIE (*triumphant*). Yew!

EBEN. What about me?

ABBIE. Ye look all slicked up like a prize bull.

EBEN (*with a sneer*). Waal—ye hain't so durned purty yerself, be ye? (*They stare into each other's eyes, his held by hers in spite of himself, hers glowingly possessive. Their physical attraction be-comes a palpable force quivering in the hot air.*)

ABBIE (*softly*). Ye don't mean that, Eben. Ye may think ye mean it, mebbe, but ye don't. Ye can't. It's agin nature,

Eben. Ye been fightin' yer nature ever since the day I come—tryin' t' tell yer-self I hain't purty t'ye. (*She laughs a low humid laugh without taking her eyes from his. A pause—her body squirms desirously—she murmurs lan-guorously.*) Hain't the sun strong an' hot? Ye kin feel it burnin' into the earth— Nature—makin' thin's grow—bigger 'n' bigger—burnin' inside ye—makin' ye want t' grow—into somethin' else—till ye're jined with it—an' it's your'n—but it owns ye, too—an' makes ye grow bigger—like a tree—like them elums— (*She laughs again softly, holding his eyes. He takes a step toward her, compelled against his will.*) Nature'll beat ye, Eben. Ye might's well own up t' it fust 's last.

EBEN (*trying to break from her spell— confusedly*). If Paw'd hear ye goin' on. . . . (*Resentfully.*) But ye've made such a damned idjit out o' the old devil . . . ! (*ABBIE laughs.*)

ABBIE. Waal—hain't it easier fur yew with him changed softer?

EBEN (*defiantly*). No. I'm fightin' him —fightin' yew—fightin' fur Maw's rights t' her hum! (*This breaks her spell for him. He glowers at her.*) An' I'm onto ye. Ye hain't foolin' me a mite. Ye're aimin' t' swaller up everythin' an' make it your'n. Waal, you'll find I'm a heap sight bigger hunk nor yew kin chew! (*He turns from her with a sneer.*)

ABBIE (*trying to regain her ascendancy —seductively*). Eben!

EBEN. Leave me be! (*He starts to walk away.*)

ABBIE (*more commandingly*). Eben!

EBEN (*stops—resentfully*). What d'ye want?

ABBIE (*trying to conceal a growing excitement*). Whar air ye goin'?

EBEN (*with malicious nonchalance*). Oh—up the road a spell.

ABBIE. T' the village?

EBEN (*airily*). Mebbe.

ABBIE (*excitedly*). T' see that Min, I s'pose?

EBEN. Mebbe.

ABBIE (*weakly*). What d'ye want t' waste time on her fur?

EBEN (*revenging himself now—grinning at her*). Ye can't beat Nature, didn't ye say? (*He laughs and again starts to walk away.*)

ABBIE (*bursting out*). An ugly old hake!

EBEN (*with a tantalizing sneer*). She's purtier'n yew be!

ABBIE. That every wuthless drunk in the country has. . . .

EBEN (*tauntingly*). Mebbe—but she's better'n yew be. She owns up fa'r 'n' squar' t' her doin's.

ABBIE (*furiously*). Don't ye dare compare. . . .

EBEN. She don't go sneakin' an' stealin' —what's mine.

ABBIE (*savagely seizing on his weak point*). Your'n? Yew mean—my farm?

EBEN. I mean the farm yew sold yerself fur like any other old whore—my farm!

ABBIE (*stung—fiercely*). Ye'll never live t' see the day when even a stinkin' weed on it 'll belong t' ye! (*Then in a scream.*) Git out o' my sight! Go on t' yer slut—disgracin' yer Paw 'n' me! I'll git yer Paw t' horsewhip ye off the place if I want t'! Ye're only livin' here 'cause I tolerate ye! Git along! I hate the sight o' ye! (*She stops, panting and glaring at him.*)

EBEN (*returning her glance in kind*). An' I hate the sight o' yew! (*He turns and strides off up the road. She follows his retreating figure with concentrated hate. Old* CABOT *appears coming up from the barn. The hard, grim expression of his face has changed. He seems in some queer way softened, mellowed. His eyes have taken on a strange, incongruous dreamy quality. Yet there is no hint of physical weakness about him—rather he looks more robust and younger.* ABBIE *sees him and turns away quickly with unconcealed aversion. He comes slowly up to her.*)

CABOT (*mildly*). War yew an' Eben quarrelin' agen?

ABBIE (*shortly*). No.

CABOT. Ye was talkin' a'mighty loud. (*He sits down on the edge of porch.*)

ABBIE (*snappishly*). If ye heerd us they hain't no need askin' questions.

CABOT. I didn't hear what ye said.

ABBIE (*relieved*). Waal—it wa'n't nothin' t' speak on.

CABOT (*after a pause*). Eben's queer.

ABBIE (*bitterly*). He's the dead spit 'n' image o' yew!

CABOT (*queerly interested*). D'ye think so, Abbie? (*After a pause, ruminatingly.*) Me 'n' Eben's allus fit 'n' fit. I never could b'ar him noways. He's so thunderin' soft—like his Maw.

ABBIE (*scornfully*). Ay-eh! 'Bout as soft as yew be!

CABOT (*as if he hadn't heard*). Mebbe I been too hard on him.

ABBIE (*jeeringly*). Waal—ye're gittin' soft now—soft as slop! That's what Eben was sayin'.

CABOT (*his face instantly grim and ominous*). Eben was sayin'? Waal, he'd best not do nothin' t' try me 'r he'll soon diskiver . . . (*A pause. She keeps her face turned away. His gradually softens. He stares up at the sky.*) Purty, hain't it?

ABBIE (*crossly*). I don't see nothin' purty.

CABOT. The sky. Feels like a wa'm field up thar.

ABBIE (*sarcastically*). Air yew aimin' t' buy up over the farm too? (*She snickers contemptuously.*)

CABOT (*strangely*). I'd like t' own my place up thar. (*A pause.*) I'm gittin' old, Abbie. I'm gittin' ripe on the bough. (*A pause. She stares at him mystified. He goes on.*) It's allus lonesome cold in the house—even when it's bilin' hot outside. Hain't yew noticed?

ABBIE. No.

CABOT. It's wa'm down t' the barn— nice smellin' an' wa'm—with the cows. (*A pause.*) Cows is queer.

ABBIE. Like yew?

CABOT. Like Eben. (*A pause.*) I'm gittin' t' feel resigned t' Eben—jest as I got t' feel 'bout his Maw. I'm gittin' t' learn to b'ar his softness—jest like her'n. I calc'late I c'd a'most take t' him—if he wa'n't sech a dumb fool! (*A pause.*) I s'pose it's old age a-creepin' in my bones.

ABBIE (*indifferently*). Waal—ye hain't dead yet.

CABOT (*roused*). No, I hain't, yew bet

—not by a hell of a sight—I'm sound 'n' tough as hickory! (*Then moodily.*) But arter three score and ten the Lord warns ye t' prepare. (*A pause.*) That's why Eben's come in my head. Now that his cussed sinful brothers is gone their path t' hell, they's no one left but Eben.

ABBIE (*resentfully*). They's me, hain't they? (*Agitatedly.*) What's all this sudden likin' ye've tuk to Eben? Why don't ye say nothin' 'bout me? Hain't I yer lawful wife?

CABOT (*simply*). Ay-eh. Ye be. (*A pause—he stares at her desirously—his eyes grow avid—then with a sudden movement he seizes her hands and squeezes them, declaiming in a queer camp meeting preacher's tempo.*) Yew air my Rose o' Sharon! Behold, yew air fair; yer eyes air doves; yer lips air like scarlet; yer two breasts air like two fawns; yer navel be like a round goblet; yer belly be like a heap o' wheat. . . . (*He covers her hand with kisses. She does not seem to notice. She stares before her with hard angry eyes.*)

ABBIE (*jerking her hands away—harshly*). So ye're plannin' t' leave the farm t' Eben, air ye?

CABOT (*dazedly*). Leave . . . ? (*Then with resentful obstinacy.*) I hain't a-givin' it t' no one!

ABBIE (*remorselessly*). Ye can't take it with ye.

CABOT (*thinks a moment—then reluctantly*). No, I calc'late not. (*After a pause —with a strange passion.*) But if I could, I would, by the Etarnal! 'R if I could, in my dyin' hour, I'd set it afire an' watch it burn—this house an' every ear o' corn an' every tree down t' the last blade o' hay! I'd sit an' know it was all a-dying with me an' no one else'd ever own what was mine, what I'd made out o' nothin' with my own sweat 'n' blood! (*A pause—then he adds with a queer affection.*) 'Ceptin' the cows. Them I'd turn free.

ABBIE (*harshly*). An' me?

CABOT (*with a queer smile*). Ye'd be turned free, too.

ABBIE (*furiously*). So that's the thanks I git fur marryin' ye—t' have ye change kind to Eben who hates ye, an' talk o' turnin' me out in the road.

CABOT (*hastily*). Abbie! Ye know I wa'n't. . . .

ABBIE (*vengefully*). Just let me tell ye a thing or two 'bout Eben! Whar's he gone? T' see that harlot, Min! I tried fur t' stop him. Disgracin' yew an' me—on the Sabbath, too!

CABOT (*rather guiltily*). He's a sinner —nateral-born. It's lust eatin' his heart.

ABBIE (*enraged beyond endurance— wildly vindictive*). An' his lust fur me! Kin ye find excuses fur that?

CABOT (*stares at her—after a dead pause*). Lust—fur yew?

ABBIE (*defiantly*). He was tryin' t' make love t' me—when ye heerd us quarrelin'.

CABOT (*stares at her—then a terrible expression of rage comes over his face— he springs to his feet shaking all over*). By the A'mighty God—I'll end him!

ABBIE (*frightened now for* EBEN). No! Don't ye!

CABOT (*violently*). I'll git the shotgun an' blow his soft brains t' the top o' them elums!

ABBIE (*throwing her arms around him*). No, Ephraim!

CABOT (*pushing her away violently*). I will, by God!

ABBIE (*in a quieting tone*). Listen, Ephraim. 'Twa'n't nothin' bad—on'y a boy's foolin'—'twa'n't meant serious—jest jokin' an' teasin'. . . .

CABOT. Then why did ye say—lust?

ABBIE. It must hev sounded wusser'n I meant. An' I was mad at thinkin'—ye'd leave him the farm.

CABOT (*quieter but still grim and cruel*). Waal then, I'll horsewhip him off the place if that much'll content ye.

ABBIE (*reaching out and taking his hand*). No. Don't think o' me! Ye mustn't drive him off. 'Tain't sensible. Who'll ye get to help ye on the farm? They's no one hereabouts.

CABOT (*considers this—then nodding his appreciation*). Ye got a head on ye. (*Then irritably.*) Waal, let him stay. (*He sits down on the edge of the porch. She sits beside him. He murmurs con-*

temptuously.) I oughtn't t' git riled so—at that 'ere fool calf. (*A pause.*) But har's the p'int. What son o' mine'll keep on here t' the farm—when the Lord does call me? Simeon an' Peter air gone t' hell—an' Eben's follerin' 'em.

ABBIE. They's me.

CABOT. Ye're on'y a woman.

ABBIE. I'm yewr wife.

CABOT. That hain't me. A son is me—my blood—mine. Mine ought t' git mine. An' then it's still mine—even though I be six foot under. D'ye see?

ABBIE (*giving him a look of hatred*). Ay-eh. I see. (*She becomes very thoughtful, her face growing shrewd, her eyes studying* CABOT *craftily.*)

CABOT. I'm gittin' old—ripe on the bough. (*Then with a sudden forced reassurance.*) Not but what I hain't a hard nut t' crack even yet—an' fur many a year t' come! By the Etarnal, I kin break most o' the young fellers' backs at any kind o' work any day o' the year!

ABBIE (*suddenly*). Mebbe the Lord'll give *us* a son.

CABOT (*turns and stares at her eagerly*). Ye mean—a son—t' me 'n' yew?

ABBIE (*with a cajoling smile*). Ye're a strong man yet, hain't ye? 'Tain't noways impossible, be it? We know that. Why d'ye stare so? Hain't ye never thought o' that afore? I been thinkin' o' it all along. Ay-eh—an' I been prayin' it'd happen, too.

CABOT (*his face growing full of joyous pride and a sort of religious ecstasy*). Ye been prayin', Abbie?—fur a son?—t' us?

ABBIE. Ay-eh. (*With a grim resolution.*) I want a son now.

CABOT (*excitedly clutching both of her hands in his*). It'd be the blessin' o' God, Abbie—the blessin' o' God A'mighty on me—in my old age—in my lonesomeness! They hain't nothin' I wouldn't do fur ye then, Abbie. Ye'd hev on'y t' ask it—anythin' ye'd a mind t'!

ABBIE (*interrupting*). Would ye will the farm t' me then—t' me an' it . . . ?

CABOT (*vehemently*). I'd do anythin' ye axed, I tell ye! I swar it! May I be everlastin' damned t' hell if I wouldn't! (*He sinks to his knees pulling her down*

with him. He trembles all over with the fervor of his hopes.*) Pray t' the Lord agen, Abbie. It's the Sabbath! I'll jine ye! Two prayers air better nor one. "An' God hearkened unto Rachel"! An' God hearkened unto Abbie! Pray, Abbie! Pray fur him to hearken! (*He bows his head, mumbling. She pretends to do likewise but gives him a side glance of scorn and triumph.*)

SCENE 2: *About eight in the evening. The interior of the two bedrooms on the top floor is shown.* EBEN *is sitting on the side of his bed in the room on the left. On account of the heat he has taken off everything but his undershirt and pants. His feet are bare. He faces front, brooding moodily, his chin propped on his hands, a desperate expression on his face.*

In the other room CABOT *and* ABBIE *are sitting side by side on the edge of their bed, an old four-poster with feather mattress. He is in his night shirt, she in her nightdress. He is still in the queer, excited mood into which the notion of a son has thrown him. Both rooms are lighted dimly and flickeringly by tallow candles.*

CABOT. The farm needs a son.

ABBIE. I need a son.

CABOT. Ay-eh. Sometimes ye air the farm an' sometimes the farm be yew. That's why I clove t' ye in my lonesomeness. (*A pause. He pounds his knee with his fist.*) Me an' the farm has got t' beget a son!

ABBIE. Ye'd best go t' sleep. Ye're gittin' thin's all mixed.

CABOT (*with an impatient gesture*). No, I hain't. My mind's clear's a well. Ye don't know me, that's it. (*He stares hopelessly at the floor.*)

ABBIE (*indifferently*). Mebbe. (*In the next room* EBEN *gets up and paces up and down distractedly.* ABBIE *hears him. Her eyes fasten on the intervening wall with concentrated attention.* EBEN *stops and stares. Their hot glances seem to meet through the wall. Unconsciously he stretches out his arms for her and she half rises. Then aware, he mutters a curse at himself and flings himself face down-*

ward on the bed, his clenched fists above his head, his face buried in the pillow. ABBIE *relaxes with a faint sigh but her eyes remain fixed on the wall; she listens with all her attention for some movement from* EBEN.)

CABOT (*suddenly raises his head and looks at her—scornfully*). Will ye ever know me—'r will any man 'r woman? (*Shaking his head.*) No. I calc'late 't wa'n't t' be. (*He turns away.* ABBIE *looks at the wall. Then, evidently unable to keep silent about his thoughts, without looking at his wife, he puts out his hand and clutches her knee. She starts violently, looks at him, sees he is not watching her, concentrates again on the wall and pays no attention to what he says.*) Listen, Abbie. When I come here fifty odd year ago—I was jest twenty an' the strongest an' hardest ye ever seen—ten times as strong an' fifty times as hard as Eben. Waal—this place was nothin' but fields o' stones. Folks laughed when I tuk it. They couldn't know what I knowed. When ye kin make corn sprout out o' stones, God's livin' in yew! They wa'n't strong enuf fur that! They reckoned God was easy. They laughed. They don't laugh no more. Some died hereabouts. Some went West an' died. They're all under ground—fur follerin' arter an easy God. God hain't easy. (*He shakes his head slowly.*) An' I growed hard. Folks kept allus sayin' he's a hard man like 'twas sinful t' be hard, so's at last I said back at 'em: Waal then, by thunder, ye'll git me hard an' see how ye like it! (*Then suddenly.*) But I give in t' weakness once. 'Twas arter I'd been here two year. I got weak—despairful—they was so many stones. They was a party leavin', givin' up, goin' West. I jined 'em. We tracked on 'n' on. We come t' broad medders, plains, whar the soil was black an' rich as gold. Nary a stone. Easy. Ye'd on'y to plow an' sow an' then set an' smoke yer pipe an' watch thin's grow. I could o' been a rich man—but somethin' in me fit me an' fit me—the voice o' God sayin': "This hain't wuth nothin' t' Me. Git ye back t' hum!" I got afeerd o' that voice an' I lit out back t' hum here, leavin' my claim an' crops t' whoever'd

a mind t' take 'em. Ay-eh. I actoolly give up what was rightful mine! God's hard, not easy! God's in the stones! Build my church on a rock—out o' stones an' I'll be in them! That's what He meant t' Peter! (*He sighs heavily—a pause.*) Stones. I picked 'em up an' piled 'em into walls. Ye kin read the years o' my life in them walls, every day a hefted stone, climbin' over the hills up and down, fencin' in the fields that was mine, whar I'd made thin's grow out o' nothin' —like the will o' God, like the servant o' His hand. It wa'n't easy. It was hard an' He made me hard fur it. (*He pauses.*) All the time I kept gittin' lonesomer. I tuk a wife. She bore Simeon an' Peter. She was a good woman. She wuked hard. We was married twenty year. She never knowed me. She helped but she never knowed what she was helpin'. I was allus lonesome. She died. After that it wa'n't so lonesome fur a spell. (*A pause.*) I lost count o' the years. I had no time t' fool away countin' 'em. Sim an' Peter helped. The farm growed. It was all mine! When I thought o' that I didn't feel lonesome. (*A pause.*) But ye can't hitch yer mind t' one thin' day an' night. I tuk another wife—Eben's Maw. Her folks was contestin' me at law over my deeds t' the farm—my farm! That's why Eben keeps a-talkin' his fool talk o' this bein' his Maw's farm. She bore Eben. She was purty—but soft. She tried t' be hard. She couldn't. She never knowed me nor nothin'. It was lonesomer 'n hell with her. After a matter o' sixteen odd years, she died. (*A pause.*) I lived with the boys. They hated me 'cause I was hard. I hated them 'cause they was soft. They coveted the farm without knowin' what it meant. It made me bitter 'n wormwood. It aged me—them coveting what I'd made fur mine. Then this spring the call come—the voice o' God cryin' in my wilderness, in my lonesomeness—t' go out an' seek an' find! (*Turning to her with strange passion.*) I sought ye an' I found ye! Yew air my Rose o' Sharon! Yer eyes air like . . . (*She has turned a blank face, resentful eyes to his. He stares at her for a moment—then harshly.*) Air ye any the wiser fur all I've told ye?

ABBIE (*confusedly*). Mebbe.

CABOT (*pushing her away from him—angrily*). Ye don't know nothin'—nor never will. If ye don't hev a son t' redeem ye . . . (*This in a tone of cold threat.*)

ABBIE (*resentfully*). I've prayed, hain't I?

CABOT (*bitterly*). Pray agen—fur understandin'!

ABBIE (*a veiled threat in her tone*). Ye'll have a son out o' me, I promise ye.

CABOT. How kin ye promise?

ABBIE. I got second sight mebbe. I kin foretell. (*She gives a queer smile.*)

CABOT. I believe ye have. Ye give me the chills sometimes. (*He shivers.*) It's cold in this house. It's oneasy. They's thin's pokin' about in the dark—in the corners. (*He pulls on his trousers, tucking in his night shirt, and pulls on his boots.*)

ABBIE (*surprised*). Whar air ye goin'?

CABOT (*queerly*). Down whar it's restful—whar it's warm—down t' the barn. (*Bitterly.*) I kin talk t' the cows. They know. They know the farm an' me. They'll give me peace. (*He turns to go out the door.*)

ABBIE (*a bit frightenedly*). Air ye ailin' tonight, Ephraim?

CABOT. Growin'. Growin' ripe on the bough. (*He turns and goes, his boots clumping down the stairs. EBEN sits up with a start, listening. ABBIE is conscious of his movement and stares at the wall. CABOT comes out of the house around the corner and stands by the gate, blinking at the sky. He stretches up his hands in a tortured gesture.*) God A'mighty, call from the dark! (*He listens as if expecting an answer. Then his arms drop, he shakes his head and plods off toward the barn. EBEN and ABBIE stare at each other through the wall. EBEN sighs heavily and ABBIE echoes it. Both become terribly nervous, uneasy. Finally ABBIE gets up and listens, her ear to the wall. He acts as if he saw every move she was making, he becomes resolutely still. She seems driven into a decision—goes out the door in rear determinedly. His eyes follow her. Then as the door of his*

room *is opened softly, he turns away, waits in an attitude of strained fixity.* ABBIE *stands for a second staring at him, her eyes burning with desire. Then with a little cry she runs over and throws her arms about his neck, she pulls his head back and covers his mouth with kisses. At first, he submits dumbly; then he puts his arms about her neck and returns her kisses, but finally, suddenly aware of his hatred, he hurls her away from him, springing to his feet. They stand speechless and breathless, panting like two animals.*)

ABBIE (*at last—painfully*). Ye shouldn't, Eben—ye shouldn't—I'd make ye happy!

EBEN (*harshly*). I don't want t' be happy—from yew!

ABBIE (*helplessly*). Ye do, Eben! Ye do! Why d'ye lie?

EBEN (*viciously*). I don't take t'ye, I tell ye! I hate the sight o' ye!

ABBIE (*with an uncertain troubled laugh*). Waal, I kissed ye anyways—an' ye kissed back—yer lips was burnin'—ye can't lie 'bout that! (*Intensely.*) If ye don't care, why did ye kiss me back—why was yer lips burnin'?

EBEN (*wiping his mouth*). It was like pizen on 'em. (*Then tauntingly.*) When I kissed ye back, mebbe I thought 'twas someone else.

ABBIE (*wildly*). Min?

EBEN. Mebbe.

ABBIE (*torturedly*). Did ye go t' see her? Did ye r'ally go? I thought ye mightn't. Is that why ye throwed me off jest now?

EBEN (*sneeringly*). What if it be?

ABBIE (*raging*). Then ye're a dog, Eben Cabot!

EBEN (*threateningly*). Ye can't talk that way t' me!

ABBIE (*with a shrill laugh*). Can't I? Did ye think I was in love with ye—a weak thin' like yew? Not much! I on'y wanted ye fur a purpose o' my own—an' I'll hev ye fur it yet 'cause I'm stronger'n yew be!

EBEN (*resentfully*). I knowed well it was on'y part o' yer plan t' swaller everythin'!

ABBIE (*tauntingly*). Mebbe!

EBEN (*furious*). Git out o' my room!

ABBIE. This air my room an' ye're on'y hired help!

EBEN (*threateningly*). Git out afore I murder ye!

ABBIE (*quite confident now*). I hain't a mite afeerd. Ye want me, don't ye? Yes, ye do! An' yer Paw's son'll never kill what he wants! Look at yer eyes! They's lust fur me in 'em, burnin' 'em up! Look at yer lips now! They're tremblin' an' longin' t' kiss me, an' yer teeth t' bite! (*He is watching her now with a horrible fascination. She laughs a crazy triumphant laugh.*) I'm a-goin' t' make all o' this hum my hum! They's one room hain't mine yet, but it's a-goin t' be tonight. I'm a-goin' down now an' light up! (*She makes him a mocking bow.*) Won't ye come courtin' me in the best parlor, Mister Cabot?

EBEN (*staring at her—horribly confused—dully*). Don't ye dare! It hain't been opened since Maw died an' was laid out thar! Don't ye . . . ! (*But her eyes are fixed on his so burningly that his will seems to wither before hers. He stands swaying toward her helplessly.*)

ABBIE (*holding his eyes and putting all her will into her words as she backs out the door*). I'll expect ye afore long, Eben.

EBEN (*stares after her for a while, walking toward the door. A light appears in the parlor window. He murmurs*). In the parlor? (*This seems to arouse connotations for he comes back and puts on his white shirt, collar, half ties the tie mechanically, puts on coat, takes his hat, stands barefooted looking about him in bewilderment, mutters wonderingly.*) Maw! Whar air yew? (*Then goes slowly toward the door in rear.*)

SCENE 3: *A few minutes later. The interior of the parlor is shown. A grim, repressed room like a tomb in which the family has been interred alive.* ABBIE *sits on the edge of the horsehair sofa. She has lighted all the candles and the room is revealed in all its preserved ugliness. A change has come over the woman. She looks awed and frightened now, ready to run away.*

The door is opened and EBEN *appears.*

His face wears an expression of obsessed confusion. He stands staring at her, his arms hanging disjointedly from his shoulders, his feet bare, his hat in his hand.

ABBIE (*after a pause—with a nervous, formal politeness*). Won't ye set?

EBEN (*dully*). Ay-eh. (*Mechanically he places his hat carefully on the floor near the door and sits stiffly beside her on the edge of the sofa. A pause. They both remain rigid, looking straight ahead with eyes full of fear.*)

ABBIE. When I fust come in—in the dark—they seemed somethin' here.

EBEN (*simply*). Maw.

ABBIE. I kin still feel—somethin'. . . .

EBEN. It's Maw.

ABBIE. At first I was feered o' it. I wanted t' yell an' run. Now—since yew come—seems like it's growin' soft an' kind t' me. (*Addressing the air—queerly.*) Thank yew.

EBEN. Maw allus loved me.

ABBIE. Mebbe it knows I love yew, too. Mebbe that makes it kind to me.

EBEN (*dully*). I dunno. I should think she'd hate ye.

ABBIE (*with certainty*). No. I kin feel it don't—not no more.

EBEN. Hate ye fur stealin' her place—here in her hum—settin' in her parlor whar she was laid— (*He suddenly stops, staring stupidly before him.*)

ABBIE. What is it, Eben?

EBEN (*in a whisper*). Seems like Maw didn't want me t' remind ye.

ABBIE (*excitedly*). I knowed, Eben! It's kind t' me! It don't b'ar me no grudges fur what I never knowed an' couldn't help!

EBEN. Maw b'ars him a grudge.

ABBIE. Waal, so does all o' us.

EBEN. Ay-eh. (*With passion.*) I does, by God!

ABBIE (*taking one of his hands in hers and patting it*). Thar! Don't git riled thinkin' o' him. Think o' yer Maw who's kind t' us. Tell me about yer Maw, Eben.

EBEN. They hain't nothin' much. She was kind. She was good.

ABBIE (*putting one arm over his shoulder. He does not seem to notice—passionately*). I'll be kind an' good t' ye!

EBEN. Sometimes she used t' sing fur me.

ABBIE. I'll sing fur ye!

EBEN. This was her hum. This was her farm.

ABBIE. This is my hum! This is my farm!

EBEN. He married her t' steal 'em. She was soft an' easy. He couldn't 'preciate her.

ABBIE. He can't 'preciate me!

EBEN. He murdered her with his hardness.

ABBIE. He's murderin' me!

EBEN. She died. (*A pause.*) Sometimes she used to sing fur me. (*He bursts into a fit of sobbing.*)

ABBIE (*both her arms around him—with wild passion*). I'll sing fur ye! I'll die fur ye! (*In spite of her overwhelming desire for him, there is a sincere maternal love in her manner and voice—a horribly frank mixture of lust and mother love.*) Don't cry, Eben! I'll take yer Maw's place! I'll be everythin' she was t' ye! Let me kiss ye, Eben! (*She pulls his head around. He makes a bewildered pretense of resistance. She is tender.*) Don't be afeered! I'll kiss ye pure, Eben—same 's if I was a Maw t' ye —an' ye kin kiss me back 's if yew was my son—my boy—sayin' good-night t' me! Kiss me, Eben. (*They kiss in restrained fashion. Then suddenly wild passion overcomes her. She kisses him lustfully again and again and he flings his arms about her and returns her kisses. Suddenly, as in the bedroom, he frees himself from her violently and springs to his feet. He is trembling all over, in a strange state of terror. ABBIE strains her arms toward him with fierce pleading.*) Don't ye leave me, Eben! Can't ye see it hain't enuf—lovin' ye like a Maw— can't ye see it's got t' be that an' more— much more—a hundred times more—fur me t' be happy—fur yew t' be happy?

EBEN (*to the presence he feels in the room*). Maw! Maw! What d'ye want? What air ye tellin' me?

ABBIE. She's tellin' ye t' love me. She knows I love ye an' I'll be good t' ye. Can't ye feel it? Don't ye know? She's tellin' ye t' love me, Eben!

EBEN. Ay-eh. I feel—mebbe she—but— I can't figger out—why—when ye've stole her place—here in her hum—in the parlor whar she was—

ABBIE (*fiercely*). She knows I love ye!

EBEN (*his face suddenly lighting up with a fierce, triumphant grin*). I see it! I sees why. It's her vengeance on him— so's she kin rest quiet in her grave!

ABBIE (*wildly*). Vengeance o' God on the hull o' us! What d'we give a durn? I love ye, Eben! God knows I love ye! (*She stretches out her arms for him.*)

EBEN (*throws himself on his knees beside the sofa and grabs her in his arms —releasing all his pent-up passion*). An' I love yew, Abbie!—now I kin say it! I been dyin' fur want o' ye—every hour since ye come! I love ye! (*Their lips meet in a fierce, bruising kiss.*)

SCENE 4: *Exterior of the farmhouse. It is just dawn. The front door at right is opened and EBEN comes out and walks around to the gate. He is dressed in his working clothes. He seems changed. His face wears a bold and confident expression, he is grinning to himself with evident satisfaction. As he gets near the gate, the window of the parlor is heard opening and the shutters are flung back and ABBIE sticks her head out. Her hair tumbles over her shoulders in disarray, her face is flushed, she looks at EBEN with tender, languorous eyes and calls softly.*

ABBIE. Eben. (*As he turns—playfully.*) Jest one more kiss afore ye go. I'm goin' to miss ye fearful all day.

EBEN. An' me yew, ye kin bet! (*He goes to her. They kiss several times. He draws away, laughingly.*) Thar. That's enuf, hain't it? Ye won't hev none left fur next time.

ABBIE. I got a million o' 'em left fur yew! (*Then a bit anxiously.*) D'ye r'ally love me, Eben?

EBEN (*emphatically*). I like ye better'n any gal I ever knowed! That's gospel!

ABBIE. Likin' hain't lovin'.

EBEN. Waal then—I love ye. Now air yew satisfied?

ABBIE. Ay-eh, I be. (*She smiles at him adoringly.*)

EBEN. I better git t' the barn. The old critter's liable t' suspicion an' come sneakin' up.

ABBIE (*with a confident laugh*). Let him! I kin allus pull the wool over his eyes. I'm goin' t' leave the shutters open and let in the sun 'n' air. This room's been dead long enuf. Now it's goin' t' be my room!

EBEN (*frowning*). Ay-eh.

ABBIE (*hastily*). I meant—our room.

EBEN. Ay-eh.

ABBIE. We made it our'n last night, didn't we? We give it life—our lovin' did. (*A pause.*)

EBEN (*with a strange look*). Maw's gone back t' her grave. She kin sleep now.

ABBIE. May she rest in peace! (*Then tenderly rebuking.*) Ye oughtn't t' talk o' sad thin's—this mornin'.

EBEN. It jest come up in my mind o' itself.

ABBIE. Don't let it. (*He doesn't answer. She yawns.*) Waal, I'm a-goin' t' steal a wink o' sleep. I'll tell the Old Man I hain't feelin' pert. Let him git his own vittles.

EBEN. I see him comin' from the barn. Ye better look smart an' git upstairs.

ABBIE. Ay-eh. Good-by. Don't ferget me. (*She throws him a kiss. He grins—then squares his shoulders and awaits his father confidently. CABOT walks slowly up from the left, staring up at the sky with a vague face.*)

EBEN (*jovially*). Mornin', Paw. Stargazin' in daylight?

CABOT. Purty, hain't it?

EBEN (*looking around him possessively*). It's a durned purty farm.

CABOT. I mean the sky.

EBEN (*grinning*). How d'ye know? Them eyes o' your'n can't see that fur. (*This tickles his humor and he slaps his thigh and laughs.*) Ho-ho! That's a good un!

CABOT (*grimly sarcastic*). Ye're feelin' right chipper, hain't ye? Whar'd ye steal the likker?

EBEN (*good-naturedly*). 'Tain't likker. Jest life. (*Suddenly holding out his hand—soberly.*) Yew 'n' me is quits. Let's shake hands.

CABOT (*suspiciously*). What's come over ye?

EBEN. Then don't. Mebbe it's jest as well. (*A moment's pause.*) What's come over me? (*Queerly.*) Didn't ye feel her passin'—goin' back t' her grave?

CABOT (*dully*). Who?

EBEN. Maw. She kin rest now an' sleep content. She's quits with ye.

CABOT (*confusedly*). I rested. I slept good—down with the cows. They know how t' sleep. They're teachin' me.

EBEN (*suddenly jovial again*). Good fur the cows! Waal—ye better git t' work.

CABOT (*grimly amused*). Air yew bossin' me, ye calf?

EBEN (*beginning to laugh*). Ay-eh! I'm bossin' yew! Ha-ha-ha! See how ye like it! Ha-ha-ha! I'm the prize rooster o' this roost. Ha-ha-ha! (*He goes off toward the barn laughing.*)

CABOT (*looks after him with scornful pity*). Soft-headed. Like his Maw. Dead spit 'n' image. No hope in him! (*He spits with contemptuous disgust.*) A born fool! (*Then matter-of-factly.*) Waal—I'm gittin' peckish. (*He goes toward door.*)

CURTAIN

PART THREE

SCENE 1: *A night in late spring the following year. The kitchen and the two bedrooms upstairs are shown. The two bedrooms are dimly lighted by a tallow candle in each. EBEN is sitting on the side of the bed in his room, his chin propped on his fists, his face a study of the struggle he is making to understand his con-* flicting emotions. *The noisy laughter and music from below where a kitchen dance is in progress annoy and distract him. He scowls at the floor.*

In the next room a cradle stands beside the double bed.

In the kitchen all is festivity. The stove has been taken down to give more room to the dancers. The chairs, with wooden benches added, have been pushed back against the walls. On these are seated, squeezed in tight against one another, farmers and their wives and their young folks of both sexes from the neighboring farms. They are all chattering and laughing loudly. They evidently have some secret joke in common. There is no end of winking, of nudging, of meaning nods of the head toward CABOT *who, in a state of extreme hilarious excitement increased by the amount he has drunk, is standing near the rear door where there is a small keg of whisky and serving drinks to all the men. In the left corner, front, dividing the attention with her husband,* ABBIE *is sitting in a rocking chair, a shawl wrapped about her shoulders. She is very pale, her face is thin and drawn, her eyes are fixed anxiously on the open door in rear as if waiting for someone.*

The musician is tuning up his fiddle, seated in the far right corner. He is a lanky young fellow with a long, weak face. His pale eyes blink incessantly and he grins about him slyly with a greedy malice.

ABBIE (*suddenly turning to a young girl on her right*). Whar's Eben?

YOUNG GIRL (*eying her scornfully*). I dunno, Mrs. Cabot. I hain't seen Eben in ages. (*Meaningly.*) Seems like he's spent most o' his time t' hum since yew come.

ABBIE (*vaguely*). I tuk his Maw's place.

YOUNG GIRL. Ay-eh. So I've heerd. (*She turns away to retail this bit of gossip to her mother sitting next to her.* ABBIE *turns to her left to a big stoutish middle-aged man whose flushed face and starting eyes show the amount of "likker" he has consumed.*)

ABBIE. Ye hain't seen Eben, hev ye?

MAN. No, I hain't. (*Then he adds with a wink.*) If yew hain't, who would?

ABBIE. He's the best dancer in the county. He'd ought t' come an' dance.

MAN (*with a wink*). Mebbe he's doin' the dutiful an' walkin' the kid t' sleep. It's a boy, hain't it?

ABBIE (*nodding vaguely*). Ay-eh—born two weeks back—purty's a picter.

MAN. They all is—t' their Maws. (*Then in a whisper, with a nudge and a leer.*) Listen, Abbie—if ye ever git tired o' Eben, remember me! Don't fergit now! (*He looks at her uncomprehending face for a second—then grunts disgustedly.*) Waal—guess I'll likker agin. (*He goes over and joins* CABOT *who is arguing noisily with an old farmer over cows. They all drink.*)

ABBIE (*this time appealing to nobody in particular*). Wonder what Eben's a-doin'? (*Her remark is repeated down the line with many a guffaw and titter until it reaches the fiddler. He fastens his blinking eyes on* ABBIE.)

FIDDLER (*raising his voice*). Bet I kin tell ye, Abbie, what Eben's doin'! He's down t' the church offerin' up prayers o' thanksgivin'. (*They all titter expectantly.*)

MAN. What fur? (*Another titter.*)

FIDDLER. 'Cause unto him a—(*He hesitates just long enough.*) brother is born! (*A roar of laughter. They all look from* ABBIE *to* CABOT. *She is oblivious, staring at the door.* CABOT, *although he hasn't heard the words, is irritated by the laughter and steps forward, glaring about him. There is an immediate silence.*)

CABOT. What're ye all bleatin' about—like a flock o' goats? Why don't ye dance, damn ye? I axed ye here t' dance—t' eat, drink an' be merry—an' thar ye set cacklin' like a lot o' wet hens with the pip! Ye've swilled my likker an' guzzled my vittles like hogs, hain't ye? Then dance fur me, can't ye? That's fa'r an' squar', hain't it? (*A grumble of resentment goes around but they are all evidently in too much awe of him to express it openly.*)

FIDDLER (*slyly*). We're waitin' fur Eben. (*A suppressed laugh.*)

CABOT (*with a fierce exultation*). T'hell with Eben! Eben's done fur now! I got a new son! (*His mood switching with drunken suddenness.*) But ye needn't t' laugh at Eben, none o' ye! He's my blood, if he be a dumb fool. He's better nor any o' yew! He kin do a day's work a'most up t' what I kin—an' that'd put any o' yew pore critters t' shame!

FIDDLER. An' he kin do a good night's work, too! (*A roar of laughter.*)

CABOT. Laugh, ye damn fools! Ye're right jist the same, Fiddler. He kin work day an' night too, like I kin, if need be!

OLD FARMER (*from behind the keg where he is weaving drunkenly back and forth—with great simplicity*). They hain't many t' touch ye, Ephraim—a son at seventy-six. That's a hard man fur ye! I be on'y sixty-eight an' I couldn't do it. (*A roar of laughter in which CABOT joins uproariously.*)

CABOT (*slapping him on the back*). I'm sorry fur ye, Hi. I'd never suspicion sech weakness from a boy like yew!

OLD FARMER. An' I never reckoned yew had it in ye nuther, Ephraim. (*There is another laugh.*)

CABOT (*suddenly grim*). I got a lot in me—a hell of a lot—folks don't know on. (*Turning to the fiddler.*) Fiddle 'er up, darn ye! Give 'em somethin' t' dance t'! What air ye, an ornament? Hain't this a celebration? Then grease yer elbow an' go it!

FIDDLER (*seizes a drink which the OLD FARMER holds out to him and downs it*). Here goes! (*He starts to fiddle "Lady of the Lake." Four young fellows and four girls form in two lines and dance a square dance. The FIDDLER shouts directions for the different movements, keeping his words in the rhythm of the music and interspersing them with jocular personal remarks to the dancers themselves. The people seated along the walls stamp their feet and clap their hands in unison. CABOT is especially active in this respect. Only ABBIE remains apathetic, staring at the door as if she were alone in a silent room.*)

FIDDLER. Swing your partner t' the right! That's it, Jim! Give her a b'ar hug! Her Maw hain't lookin'. (*Laughter.*) Change partners! That suits ye, don't it, Essie, now ye got Reub afore ye? Look at her redden up, will ye? Waal, life is short an' so's love, as the feller says. (*Laughter.*)

CABOT (*excitedly, stamping his foot*). Go it, boys! Go it, gals!

FIDDLER (*with a wink at the others*). Ye're the spryest seventy-six ever I sees, Ephraim! Now if ye'd on'y good eyesight . . . ! (*Suppressed laughter. He gives CABOT no chance to retort but roars.*) Promenade! Ye're walkin' like a bride down the aisle, Sarah! Waal while they's life they's allus hope, I've heerd tell. Swing your partner to the left! Gosh A'mighty, look at Johnny Cook high-steppin'! They hain't goin' t'be much strength left fur howin' in the corn lot t'morrow. (*Laughter.*)

CABOT. Go it! Go it! (*Then suddenly, unable to restrain himself any longer, he prances into the midst of the dancers, scattering them, waving his arms about wildly.*) Ye're all hoofs! Git out o' my road! Give me room! I'll show ye dancin'. Ye're all too soft! (*He pushes them roughly away. They crowd back toward the walls, muttering, looking at him resentfully.*)

FIDDLER (*jeeringly*). Go it, Ephraim! Go it! (*He starts "Pop Goes the Weasel," increasing the tempo with every verse until at the end he is fiddling crazily as fast as he can go.*)

CABOT (*starts to dance, which he does very well and with tremendous vigor. Then he begins to improvise, cuts incredibly grotesque capers, leaping up and cracking his heels together, prancing around in a circle with body bent in an Indian war dance, then suddenly straightening up and kicking as high as he can with both legs. He is like a monkey on a string. And all the while he intersperses his antics with shouts and derisive comments*). Whoop! Here's dancin' fur ye! Whoop! See that! Seventy-six, if I'm a day! Hard as iron yet! Beatin' the young 'uns like I allus done! Look at me! I'd invite ye t' dance on my hundredth birthday on'y ye'll all be dead by then. Ye're a sickly generation! Yer hearts air pink, not red! Yer veins is full o' mud an' water! I be the on'y man in the county! Whoop! See that! I'm a Injun! I've killed Injuns in the West afore ye was born—an' skulped 'em too! They's a arrer wound on my backside I c'd show ye! The hull tribe chased me. I outrun 'em all—with the arrer stuck in me! An' I tuk vengeance on 'em. Ten eyes fur an eye, that was my motter! Whoop! Look at me! I kin kick the ceilin' off the room! Whoop!

FIDDLER (*stops playing—exhaustedly*). God A'mighty, I got enuf. Ye got the devil's strength in ye.

CABOT (*delightedly*). Did I beat yew, too? Waal, ye played smart. Hev a swig. (*He pours whisky for himself and* FIDDLER. *They drink. The others watch* CABOT *silently with cold, hostile eyes. There is a dead pause. The* FIDDLER *rests.* CABOT *leans against the keg, panting, glaring around him confusedly. In the room above,* EBEN *gets to his feet and tiptoes out the door in rear, appearing a moment later in the other bedroom. He moves silently, even frightenedly, toward the cradle and stands there looking down at the baby. His face is as vague as his reactions are confused, but there is a trace of tenderness, of interested discovery. At the same moment that he reaches the cradle,* ABBIE *seems to sense something. She gets up weakly and goes to* CABOT.)

ABBIE. I'm goin' up t' the baby.

CABOT (*with real solicitation*). Air ye able fur the stairs? D'ye want me t'help ye, Abbie?

ABBIE. No. I'm able. I'll be down agen soon.

CABOT. Don't ye git wore out! He needs ye, remember—our son does! (*He grins affectionately, patting her on the back. She shrinks from his touch.*)

ABBIE (*dully*). Don't—tech me. I'm goin'—up. (*She goes.* CABOT *looks after her. A whisper goes around the room.* CABOT *turns. It ceases. He wipes his forehead streaming with sweat. He is breathing pantingly.*)

CABOT. I'm a-goin' out t' git fresh air. I'm feelin' a mite dizzy. Fiddle up thar! Dance, all o' ye! Here's likker fur them as wants it. Enjoy yerselves. I'll be back. (*He goes, closing the door behind him.*)

FIDDLER (*sarcastically*). Don't hurry none on our account! (*A suppressed laugh. He imitates* ABBIE.) Whar's Eben? (*More laughter.*)

A WOMAN (*loudly*). What's happened in this house is plain as the nose on yer face! (ABBIE *appears in the doorway upstairs and stands looking in surprise and adoration at* EBEN *who does not see her.*)

A MAN. Ssshh! He's li'ble t' be listenin' at the door. That'd be like him. (*Their voices die to an intensive whispering. Their faces are concentrated on this gossip. A noise as of dead leaves in the wind comes from the room.* CABOT *has come out from the porch and stands by the gate, leaning on it, staring at the sky blinkingly.* ABBIE *comes across the room silently.* EBEN *does not notice her until quite near.*)

EBEN (*starting*). Abbie!

ABBIE. Ssshh! (*She throws her arms around him. They kiss—then bend over the cradle together.*) Ain't he purty?—dead spit 'n' image o' yew!

EBEN (*pleased*). Air he? I can't tell none.

ABBIE. E-zactly like!

EBEN (*frowningly*). I don't like this. I don't like lettin' on what's mine's his'n. I been doin' that all my life. I'm gittin' t' the end o' b'arin' it!

ABBIE (*putting her finger on his lips*). We're doin' the best we kin. We got t' wait. Somethin's bound t' happen. (*She puts her arms around him.*) I got t' go back.

EBEN. I'm goin' out. I can't b'ar it with the fiddle playin' an' the laughin'.

ABBIE. Don't git feelin' low. I love ye, Eben. Kiss me. (*He kisses her. They remain in each other's arms.*)

CABOT (*at the gate, confusedly*). Even the music can't drive it out—somethin'. Ye kin feel it droppin' off the elums, climbin' up the roof, sneakin' down the chimney, pokin' in the corners! They's no peace in houses, they's no rest livin' with folks. Somethin's always livin' with ye. (*With a deep sigh.*) I'll go t' the barn an' rest a spell. (*He goes wearily toward the barn.*)

FIDDLER (*tuning up*). Let's celebrate the old skunk gittin' fooled! We kin have some fun now he's went. (*He starts to fiddle "Turkey in the Straw." There is real merriment now. The young folks get up to dance.*)

SCENE 2: *A half hour later—Exterior—* EBEN *is standing by the gate looking up at the sky, an expression of dumb pain bewildered by itself on his face.* CABOT *appears, returning from the barn, walking wearily, his eyes on the ground. He sees* EBEN *and his whole mood immediately changes. He becomes excited, a cruel, triumphant grin comes to his lips, he strides up and slaps* EBEN *on the back. From within comes the whining of the fiddle and the noise of stamping feet and laughing voices.*

CABOT. So har ye be!

EBEN (*startled, stares at him with hatred for a moment—then dully*). Ay-eh.

CABOT (*surveying him jeeringly*). Why hain't ye been in t' dance? They was all axin' fur ye.

EBEN. Let 'em ax!

CABOT. They's a hull passel o' purty gals.

EBEN. T' hell with 'em!

CABOT. Ye'd ought t' be marryin' one o' 'em soon.

EBEN. I hain't marryin' no one.

CABOT. Ye might 'arn a share o' a farm that way.

EBEN (*with a sneer*). Like yew did, ye mean? I hain't that kind.

CABOT (*stung*). Ye lie! 'Twas yer Maw's folks aimed t' steal my farm from me.

EBEN. Other folks don't say so. (*After a pause—defiantly.*) An' I got a farm, anyways!

CABOT (*derisively*). Whar?

EBEN (*stamps a foot on the ground*). Har!

CABOT (*throws his head back and laughs coarsely*). Ho-ho! Ye hev, hev ye? Waal, that's a good un!

EBEN (*controlling himself—grimly*). Ye'll see!

CABOT (*stares at him suspiciously, trying to make him out—a pause—then with scornful confidence*). Ay-eh. I'll see. So'll ye. It's ye that's blind—blind as a mole underground. (*EBEN suddenly laughs, one short sardonic bark: "Ha." A pause. CABOT peers at him with renewed suspicion.*) Whar air ye hawin' 'bout? (*EBEN turns away without answering. CABOT grows angry.*) God A'mighty, yew air a dumb dunce! They's nothin' in that thick skull o' your'n but noise—like a empty keg it be! (*EBEN doesn't seem to hear. CABOT's rage grows.*) Yewr farm! God A'mighty! If ye wa'n't a born donkey ye'd know ye'll never own stick nor stone on it, specially now arter him bein' born—it's his'n, I tell ye—his'n arter I die—but I'll live a hundred jest t' fool ye all—an' he'll be growed then—yewr age a'most! (*EBEN laughs again his sardonic "Ha." This drives CABOT into a fury.*) Ha? Ye think ye kin git 'round that someways, do ye? Waal, it'll be her'n, too—Abbie's—ye won't git 'round her—she knows yer tricks—she'll be too much fur ye—she wants the farm her'n—she was afeerd o' ye—she told me ye was sneakin' 'round tryin' t' make love t' her t' git her on yer side . . . ye . . . ye mad fool, ye! (*He raises his clenched fists threateningly.*)

EBEN (*is confronting him choking with rage*). Ye lie, ye old skunk! Abbie never said no sech thing!

CABOT (*suddenly triumphant when he sees how shaken* EBEN *is*). She did. An' I says, I'll blow his brains t' the top o' them elums—an' she says no, that hain't sense, who'll ye git t'help ye on the farm in his place—an' then she says yew'n me ought t' have a son—I know we kin, she says—an' I says, if we do, ye kin have anythin' I've got ye've a mind t'. An' she says, I wants Eben cut off so's this farm'll be mine when ye die! (*With terrible gloating.*) An' that's what's happened, hain't it? An' the farm's her'n! An' the dust o' the road—that's your'n! Ha! Now who's hawin'?

EBEN (*has been listening, petrified with grief and rage—suddenly laughs wildly and brokenly*). Ha-ha-ha! So that's her sneakin' game—all along!—like I suspicioned at fust—t' swaller it all—an' me, too . . . ! (*Madly.*) I'll murder her! (*He springs toward the porch but* CABOT *is quicker and gets in between.*)

CABOT. No, ye don't!

EBEN. Git out o' my road! (*He tries to throw* CABOT *aside. They grapple in what becomes immediately a murderous struggle. The old man's concentrated strength is too much for* EBEN. CABOT *gets one hand on his throat and presses him back across the stone wall. At the same moment,* ABBIE *comes out on the porch. With a stifled cry she runs toward them.*)

ABBIE. Eben! Ephraim! (*She tugs at the hand on* EBEN's *throat.*) Let go, Ephraim! Ye're chokin' him!

CABOT (*removes his hand and flings* EBEN *sideways full length on the grass, gasping and choking. With a cry,* ABBIE *kneels beside him, trying to take his head on her lap, but he pushes her away.* CABOT *stands looking down with fierce triumph*). Ye needn't t've fret, Abbie, I wa'n't aimin' t' kill him. He hain't wuth hangin' fur—not by a hell of a sight! (*More and more triumphant.*) Seventy-six an' him not thirty yit—an' look whar he be fur thinkin' his Paw was easy! No, by God, I hain't easy! An' him upstairs, I'll raise him t' be like me! (*He turns to leave them.*) I'm goin' in an' dance!—sing an' celebrate! (*He walks to the porch—then turns with a great grin.*) I don't calc'late it's left in him, but if he gits pesky, Abbie, ye jest sing out. I'll come a-runnin' an' by the Eternal, I'll put him across my knee an' birch him! Ha-ha-ha! (*He goes into the house laughing. A moment later his loud "whoop" is heard.*)

ABBIE (*tenderly*). Eben. Air ye hurt? (*She tries to kiss him but he pushes her violently away and struggles to a sitting position.*)

EBEN (*gaspingly*). T'hell—with ye!

ABBIE (*not believing her ears*). It's me, Eben—Abbie—don't ye know me?

EBEN (*glowering at her with hatred*). Ay-eh—I know ye—now! (*He suddenly breaks down, sobbing weakly.*)

ABBIE (*fearfully*). Eben—what's happened t' ye—why did ye look at me 's if ye hated me?

EBEN (*violently, between sobs and gasps*). I do hate ye! Ye're a whore—a damn trickin' whore!

ABBIE (*shrinking back horrified*). Eben! Ye don't know what ye're sayin'!

EBEN (*scrambling to his feet and following her—accusingly*). Ye're nothin' but a stinkin' passel o' lies! Ye've been lyin' t' me every word ye spoke, day an' night, since we fust—done it. Ye've kept sayin' ye loved me . . .

ABBIE (*frantically*). I do love ye! (*She takes his hand but he flings her away.*)

EBEN (*unheeding*). Ye've made a fool o' me—a sick, dumb fool—a-purpose! Ye've been on'y playin' yer sneakin' stealin' game all along—gittin' me t' lie with ye so's ye'd hev a son he'd think was his'n, an' makin' him promise he'd give ye the farm and let me eat dust, if ye did git him a son! (*Staring at her with anguished, bewildered eyes.*) They must be a devil livin' in ye! 'Tain't human t' be as bad as that be!

ABBIE (*stunned—dully*). He told yew . . ?

EBEN. Hain't it true? It hain't no good in yew lyin'.

ABBIE (*pleadingly*). Eben, listen—ye must listen—it was long ago—afore we done nothin'—yew was scornin' me—goin' t' see Min—when I was lovin' ye—an' I said it t' him t' git vengeance on ye!

EBEN (*unheedingly. With tortured passion*). I wish ye was dead! I wish I was dead along with ye afore this come! (*Ragingly.*) But I'll git my vengeance too! I'll pray Maw t' come back t' help me—t' put her cuss on yew an' him!

ABBIE (*brokenly*). Don't ye, Eben! Don't ye! (*She throws herself on her knees before him, weeping.*) I didn't mean t' do bad t'ye! Fergive me, won't ye?

EBEN (*not seeming to hear her—fiercely*). I'll git squar' with the old skunk—an' yew! I'll tell him the truth 'bout the son he's so proud o'! Then I'll leave ye here t' pizen each other—with Maw comin' out o' her grave at nights—

an' I'll go t' the gold fields o' Californi-a whar Sim an' Peter be!

ABBIE (*terrified*). Ye won't—leave me? Ye can't!

EBEN (*with fierce determination*). I'm a-goin', I tell ye! I'll git rich thar an' come back an' fight him fur the farm he stole—an' I'll kick ye both out in the road—t' beg an' sleep in the woods—an' yer son along with ye—t' starve an' die! (*He is hysterical at the end.*)

ABBIE (*with a shudder—humbly*). He's yewr son, too, Eben.

EBEN (*torturedly*). I wish he never was born! I wish he'd die this minit! I wish I'd never sot eyes on him! It's him —yew havin' him—a-purpose t' steal!— that's changed everythin'!

ABBIE (*gently*). Did ye believe I loved ye—afore he come?

EBEN. Ay-eh—like a dumb ox!

ABBIE. An' ye don't believe no more?

EBEN. B'lieve a lyin' thief! Ha!

ABBIE (*shudders—then humbly*). An' did ye r'ally love me afore?

EBEN (*brokenly*). Ay-eh—an' ye was trickin' me!

ABBIE. An' ye don't love me now!

EBEN (*violently*). I hate ye, I tell ye!

ABBIE. An' ye're truly goin' West— goin' t' leave me—all account o' him be-in' born?

EBEN. I'm a-goin' in the mornin'—or may God strike me t' hell!

ABBIE (*after a pause—with a dreadful cold intensity—slowly*). If that's what his comin's done t' me—killin' yewr love —takin' yew away—my on'y joy—the on'y joy I ever knowed—like heaven t' me— purtier'n heaven—then I hate him, too, even if I be his Maw!

EBEN (*bitterly*). Lies! Ye love him! He'll steal the farm fur ye! (*Brokenly.*) But t'ain't the farm so much—not no more—it's yew foolin' me—gittin' me t' love ye—lyin' yew loved me—jest t' git a son t' steal!

ABBIE (*distractedly*). He won't steal! I'd kill him fust! I do love ye! I'll prove t' ye . . . !

EBEN (*harshly*). 'Tain't no use lyin' no more. I'm deaf t' ye! (*He turns away.*) I hain't seein' ye agen. Good-by!

ABBIE (*pale with anguish*). Hain't ye even goin' t' kiss me—not once—arter all we loved?

EBEN (*in a hard voice*). I hain't want-in' t' kiss ye never agen! I'm wantin' t' forgit I ever sot eyes on ye!

ABBIE. Eben!—ye mustn't—wait a spell —I want t' tell ye . . .

EBEN. I'm a'goin' in t' git drunk. I'm a-goin' t' dance.

ABBIE (*clinging to his arm—with passionate earnestness*). If I could make it —'s if he'd never come up between us— if I could prove t' ye I wa'n't schemin' t' steal from ye—so's everythin' could be jest the same with us, lovin' each other jest the same, kissin' an' happy the same's we've been happy afore he come —if I could do it—ye'd love me agen, wouldn't ye? Ye'd kiss me agen? Ye wouldn't never leave me, would ye?

EBEN (*moved*). Calc'late not. (*Then shaking her hand off his arm—with a bitter smile.*) But ye hain't God, be ye?

ABBIE (*exultantly*). Remember ye've promised! (*Then with strange intensity.*) Mebbe I kin take back one thin' God does!

EBEN (*peering at her*). Ye're gittin' cracked, hain't ye? (*Then going towards door.*) I'm a-goin' t' dance.

ABBIE (*calls after him intensely*). I'll prove t' ye! I'll prove I love ye better'n . . . (*He goes in the door, not seeming to hear. She remains standing where she is, looking after him—then she finishes desperately.*) Better'n everythin' else in the world!

SCENE 3: *Just before dawn in the morning—shows the kitchen and CAB-OT's bedroom. In the kitchen, by the light of a tallow candle on the table EBEN is sitting, his chin propped on his hands, his drawn face blank and expressionless. His carpetbag is on the floor beside him. In the bedroom, dimly lighted by a small whale-oil lamp, CAB-OT lies asleep. ABBIE is bending over the cradle, listening, her face full of terror yet with an undercurrent of desperate triumph. Suddenly, she breaks down and sobs, appears about to throw herself on her knees beside the cradle; but the old man turns restlessly, groaning in his sleep, and she controls herself, and, shrinking away from the cradle with a gesture of horror, backs swiftly toward the door in rear and goes out. A moment later she comes into the kitchen and, running to* EBEN, *flings her arms about his neck and kisses him wildly. He hardens himself, he remains unmoved and cold, he keeps his eyes straight ahead.*

ABBIE (*hysterically*). I done it, Eben! I told ye I'd do it! I've proved I love ye —better'n everythin'—so's ye cain't never doubt me no more!

EBEN (*dully*). Whatever ye done, it hain't no good now.

ABBIE (*wildly*). Don't ye say that! Kiss me, Eben, won't ye? I need ye t' kiss me arter what I done! I need ye t' say ye loved me!

EBEN (*kisses her without emotion—dully*). That's fur good-by. I'm a-goin' soon.

ABBIE. No! No! Ye won't go—not now!

EBEN (*going on with his own thoughts*). I been a-thinkin'—an' I hain't goin' t' tell Paw nothin'. I'll leave Maw t' take vengeance on ye. If I told him, the old skunk'd jest be stinkin' mean enuf to take it out on that baby. (*His voice showing emotion in spite of him.*) An' I don't want nothin' bad t' happen t' him. He hain't t' blame fur yew. (*He adds with a certain queer pride.*) An' he looks like me! An' by God, he's mine! An' some day I'll be a-comin' back an' . . . !

ABBIE (*too absorbed in her own thoughts to listen to him—pleadingly*). They's no cause fur ye t' go now—they's no sense—it's all the same's it was—they's nothin' come b'tween us now—arter what I done!

EBEN (*something in her voice arouses him. He stares at her a bit frightenedly*). Ye look mad, Abbie. What did ye do?

ABBIE. I—I killed him, Eben.

EBEN (*amazed*). Ye killed him?

ABBIE (*dully*). Ay-eh.

EBEN (*recovering from his astonishment—savagely*). An' serves him right!

But we got t' do somethin' quick t' make it look s'if the old skunk'd killed himself when he was drunk. We kin prove by 'em all how drunk he got.

ABBIE (*wildly*). No! No! Not him! (*Laughing distractedly.*) But that's what I ought t' done, hain't it? I oughter killed him instead! Why didn't ye tell me?

EBEN (*appalled*). Instead? What d'ye mean?

ABBIE. Not him.

EBEN (*his face grown ghastly*). Not—not that baby!

ABBIE (*dully*). Ay-eh!

EBEN (*falls to his knees as if he'd been struck—his voice trembling with horror*). Oh, God A'mighty! A'mighty God! Maw, whar was ye, why didn't ye stop her?

ABBIE (*simply*). She went back t' her grave that night we fust done it, remember? I hain't felt her about since. (*A pause.* EBEN *hides his head in his hands, trembling all over as if he had the ague. She goes on dully.*) I left the piller over his little face. Then he killed himself. He stopped breathin'. (*She begins to weep softly.*)

EBEN (*rage beginning to mingle with grief*). He looked like me. He was mine, damn ye!

ABBIE (*slowly and brokenly*). I didn't want t' do it. I hated myself fur doin' it. I loved him. He was so purty—dead spit 'n' image o' yew. But I loved yew more—an' yew was goin' away—far off whar I'd never see ye agen, never kiss ye, never feel ye pressed agin me agen—an' ye said ye hated me fur havin' him—ye said ye hated him an' wished he was dead—ye said if it hadn't been fur him comin' it'd be the same's afore between us.

EBEN (*unable to endure this, springs to his feet in a fury, threatening her, his twitching fingers seeming to reach out for her throat*). Ye lie! I never said— I never dreamed ye'd— I'd cut off my head afore I'd hurt his finger!

ABBIE (*piteously, sinking on her knees*). Eben, don't ye look at me like that—hatin' me—not after what I done fur ye—fur us—so's we could be happy agen—

EBEN (*furiously now*). Shut up, or I'll kill ye! I see yer game now—the same old sneakin' trick—ye're aimin' t' blame me fur the murder ye done!

ABBIE (*moaning—putting her hands over her ears*). Don't ye, Eben! Don't ye! (*She grasps his legs.*)

EBEN (*his mood suddenly changing to horror, shrinks away from her*). Don't ye tech me! Ye're pizen! How could ye —t' murder a pore little critter— Ye must've swapped yer soul t' hell! (*Suddenly raging.*) Ha! I kin see why ye done it! Not the lies ye jest told—but 'cause ye wanted t' steal agen—steal the last thin' ye'd left me—my part o' him— no, the hull o' him—ye saw he looked like me—ye knowed he was all mine— an' ye couldn't b'ar it—I know ye! Ye killed him fur bein' mine! (*All this has driven him almost insane. He makes a rush past her for the door—then turns— shaking both fists at her, violently.*) But I'll take vengeance now! I'll git the Sheriff! I'll tell him everythin'! Then I'll sing "I'm off to Californi-a!" an' go —gold—Golden Gate—gold sun—fields o' gold in the West! (*This last he half shouts, half croons incoherently, suddenly breaking off passionately.*) I'm a- goin' fur the Sheriff t' come an' git ye! I want ye tuk away, locked up from me! I can't stand t' luk at ye! Murderer an' thief 'r not, ye still tempt me! I'll give ye up t' the Sheriff! (*He turns and runs out, around the corner of house, panting and sobbing, and breaks into a swerving sprint down the road.*)

ABBIE (*struggling to her feet, runs to the door, calling after him*). I love ye, Eben! I love ye! (*She stops at the door weakly, swaying, about to fall.*) I don't care what ye do—if ye'll on'y love me agen— (*She falls limply to the floor in a faint.*)

SCENE 4: *About an hour later. Same as Scene 3. Shows the kitchen and* CABOT's *bedroom. It is after dawn. The sky is brilliant with the sunrise. In the kitchen,* ABBIE *sits at the table, her body limp and*

exhausted, her head bowed down over her arms, her face hidden. Upstairs, CAB- OT *is still asleep but awakens with a start. He looks toward the window and gives a snort of surprise and irritation— throws back the covers and begins hur- riedly pulling on his clothes. Without looking behind him, he begins talking to* ABBIE *whom he supposes beside him.*

CABOT. Thunder 'n' lightnin', Abbie! I hain't slept this late in fifty year! Looks 's if the sun was full riz a'most. Must've been the dancin' an' likker. Must be git- tin' old. I hope Eben's t' wuk. Ye might've tuk the trouble t' rouse me, Abbie. (*He turns—sees no one there— surprised.*) Waal—whar air she? Gittin' vittles, I calc'late. (*He tiptoes to the cradle and peers down—proudly.*) Morn- in', sonny. Purty's a picter! Sleepin' sound. He don't beller all night like most o' 'em. (*He goes quietly out the door in rear—a few moments later enters kitchen—sees* ABBIE—*with satisfaction.*) So thar ye be. Ye got any vittles cooked?

ABBIE (*without moving*). No.

CABOT (*coming to her, almost sympa- thetically*). Ye feelin' sick?

ABBIE. No.

CABOT (*pats her on shoulder. She shudders*). Ye'd best lie down a spell. (*Half jocularly.*) Yer son'll be needin' ye soon. He'd ought t' wake up with a gnashin' appetite, the sound way he's sleepin'.

ABBIE (*shudders—then in a dead voice*). He hain't never goin' t' wake up.

CABOT (*jokingly*). Takes after me this mornin'. I hain't slept so late in . . .

ABBIE. He's dead.

CABOT (*stares at her—bewilderedly*). What. . . .

ABBIE. I killed him.

CABOT (*stepping back from her— aghast*). Air ye drunk—'r crazy—'r . . . !

ABBIE (*suddenly lifts her head and turns on him—wildly*). I killed him, I tell ye! I smothered him. Go up an' see if ye don't b'lieve me! (*CABOT stares at her a second, then bolts out the rear door, can be heard bounding up the stairs, and rushes into the bedroom and over to the cradle.* ABBIE *has sunk back lifelessly into her former position.* CABOT *puts his hand down on the body in the crib. An expression of fear and horror comes over his face.*)

CABOT (*shrinking away—tremblingly*). God A'mighty! God A'mighty. (*He stumbles out the door—in a short while returns to the kitchen—comes to* ABBIE, *the stunned expression still on his face —hoarsely.*) Why did ye do it? Why? (*As she doesn't answer, he grabs her violently by the shoulder and shakes her.*) I ax ye why ye done it! Ye'd better tell me 'r . . . !

ABBIE (*gives him a furious push which sends him staggering back and springs to her feet—with wild rage and hatred*). Don't ye dare tech me! What right hev ye t' question me 'bout him? He wa'n't yewr son! Think I'd have a son by yew? I'd die fust! I hate the sight o' ye an' allus did! It's yew I should've murdered, if I'd had good sense! I hate ye! I love Eben. I did from the fust. An' he was Eben's son—mine an' Eben's—not your'n!

CABOT (*stands looking at her dazedly— a pause—finding his words with an effort—dully*). That was it—what I felt— pokin' round the corners—while ye lied —holdin' yerself from me—sayin' ye'd a'ready conceived— (*He lapses into crushed silence—then with a strange emotion.*) He's dead, sart'n. I felt his heart. Pore little critter! (*He blinks back one tear, wiping his sleeve across his nose.*)

ABBIE (*hysterically*). Don't ye! Don't ye! (*She sobs unrestrainedly.*)

CABOT (*with a concentrated effort that stiffens his body into a rigid line and hardens his face into a stony mask— through his teeth to himself*). I got t' be —like a stone—a rock o' jedgment! (*A pause. He gets complete control over himself—harshly.*) If he was Eben's, I be glad he air gone! An' mebbe I suspicioned it all along. I felt they was somethin' onnateral—somewhars—the house got so lonesome—an' cold—drivin' me down t' the barn—t' the beasts o' the field. . . . Ay-eh. I must've suspicioned —somethin'. Ye didn't fool me—not altogether, leastways—I'm too old a bird

—growin' ripe on the bough. . . . (*He becomes aware he is wandering, straightens again, looks at* ABBIE *with a cruel grin.*) So ye'd liked t' hev murdered me 'stead o' him, would ye? Waal, I'll live to a hundred! I'll live t' see ye hung! I'll deliver ye up t' the jedgment o' God an' the law! I'll git the Sheriff now. (*Starts for the door.*)

ABBIE (*dully*). Ye needn't. Eben's gone fur him.

CABOT (*amazed*). Eben—gone fur the Sheriff?

ABBIE. Ay-eh.

CABOT. T' inform agen ye?

ABBIE. Ay-eh.

CABOT (*considers this—a pause—then in a hard voice*). Waal, I'm thankful fur him savin' me the trouble. I'll git t' wuk. (*He goes to the door—then turns—in a voice full of strange emotion.*) He'd ought t' been my son, Abbie. Ye'd ought t' loved me. I'm a man. If ye'd loved me, I'd never told no Sheriff on ye no matter what ye did, if they was t' brile me alive!

ABBIE (*defensively*). They's more to it nor yew know, makes him tell.

CABOT (*dryly*). Fur yewr sake, I hope they be. (*He goes out—comes around to the gate—stares up at the sky. His control relaxes. For a moment he is old and weary. He murmurs despairingly.*) God A'mighty, I be lonesomer'n ever! (*He hears running footsteps from the left, immediately is himself again.* EBEN *runs in, panting exhaustedly, wild-eyed and mad looking. He lurches through the gate.* CABOT *grabs him by the shoulder.* EBEN *stares at him dumbly.*) Did ye tell the Sheriff?

EBEN (*nodding stupidly*). Ay-eh.

CABOT (*gives him a push away that sends him sprawling—laughing with withering contempt*). Good fur ye! A prime chip o' yer Maw ye be! (*He goes toward the barn, laughing harshly.* EBEN *scrambles to his feet. Suddenly* CABOT *turns—grimly threatening.*) Git off this farm when the Sheriff takes her—or, by God, he'll have t' come back an' git me fur murder, too! (*He stalks off.* EBEN *does not appear to have heard him. He runs to the door and comes into the kitchen.* ABBIE *looks up with a cry of anguished joy.* EBEN *stumbles over and throws himself on his knees beside her—sobbing brokenly.*)

EBEN. Fergive me!

ABBIE (*happily*). Eben! (*She kisses him and pulls his head over against her breast.*)

EBEN. I love ye! Fergive me!

ABBIE (*ecstatically*). I'd fergive ye all the sins in hell fur sayin' that! (*She kisses his head, pressing it to her with a fierce passion of possession.*)

EBEN (*brokenly*). But I told the Sheriff. He's comin' fur ye!

ABBIE. I kin b'ar what happens t' me —now!

EBEN. I woke him up. I told him. He says, wait 'til I git dressed. I was waitin'. I got to thinkin' o' yew. I got to thinkin' how I'd loved ye. It hurt like somethin' was bustin' in my chest an' head. I got t' cryin'. I knowed sudden I loved ye yet, an' allus would love ye!

ABBIE (*caressing his hair—tenderly*). My boy, hain't ye?

EBEN. I begun t' run back. I cut across the fields an' through the woods. I thought ye might have time t' run away —with me—an' . . .

ABBIE (*shaking her head*). I got t' take my punishment—t' pay fur my sin.

EBEN. Then I want t' share it with ye.

ABBIE. Ye didn't do nothin'.

EBEN. I put it in yer head. I wisht he was dead! I as much as urged ye t' do it!

ABBIE. No. It was me alone!

EBEN. I'm as guilty as yew be! He was the child o' our sin.

ABBIE (*lifting her head as if defying God*). I don't repent that sin! I hain't askin' God t' fergive that!

EBEN. Nor me—but it led up t' the other—an' the murder ye did, ye did 'count o' me—an' it's my murder, too, I'll tell the Sheriff—an' if ye deny it, I'll say we planned it t'gether—an' they'll all b'lieve me, fur they suspicion everythin' we've done, an' it'll seem likely an' true to 'em. An' it is true—way down. I did help ye—somehow.

ABBIE (*laying her head on his—sobbing*). No! I don't want yew t' suffer!

EBEN. I got t' pay fur my part o' the sin! An' I'd suffer wuss leavin' ye, goin' West, thinkin' o' ye day an' night, bein' out when yew was in— (*Lowering his voice.*) 'r bein' alive when yew was dead. (*A pause.*) I want t' share with ye, Abbie—prison 'r death 'r hell 'r anythin'! (*He looks into her eyes and forces a trembling smile.*) If I'm sharin' with ye, I won't feel lonesome, leastways.

ABBIE (*weakly*). Eben! I won't let ye! I can't let ye!

EBEN (*kissing her—tenderly*). Ye can't he'p yerself. I got ye beat fur once!

ABBIE (*forcing a smile—adoringly*). I hain't beat—s'long's I got ye!

EBEN (*hears the sound of feet outside*). Ssshh! Listen! They've come t' take us!

ABBIE. No, it's him. Don't give him no chance to fight ye, Eben. Don't say nothin'—no matter what he says. An' I won't neither. (*It is* CABOT. *He comes up from the barn in a great state of excitement and strides into the house and then into the kitchen.* EBEN *is kneeling beside* ABBIE, *his arm around her, hers around him. They stare straight ahead.*)

CABOT (*stares at them, his face hard. A long pause—vindictively*). Ye make a slick pair o' murderin' turtle doves! Ye'd ought t' be both hung on the same limb an' left thar t' swing in the breeze an' rot—a warnin' t' old fools like me t' b'ar their lonesomeness alone—an' fur young fools like ye t' hobble their lust. (*A pause. The excitement returns to his face, his eyes snap, he looks a bit crazy.*) I couldn't work today. I couldn't take no interest. T' hell with the farm! I'm leavin' it! I've turned the cows an' other stock loose! I've druv 'em into the woods whar they kin be free! By freein' 'em, I'm freein' myself! I'm quittin' here today! I'll set fire t' house an' barn an' watch 'em burn, an' I'll leave yer Maw t' haunt the ashes, an' I'll will the fields back t' God, so that nothin' human kin never touch 'em! I'll be a-goin' to California-t' jine Simeon an' Peter—true sons o' mine if they be dumb fools—an' the Cabots'll find Solomon's Mines t'gether! (*He suddenly cuts a mad caper.*) Whoop! What was the song they sung? "Oh, Californi-a! That's the land fur me." (*He sings this—then gets on his knees by the floor-board under which the money was hid.*) An' I'll sail thar on one o' the finest clippers I kin find! I've got the money! Pity ye didn't know whar this was hidden so's ye could steal . . . (*He has pulled up the board. He stares—feels—stares again. A pause of dead silence. He slowly turns, slumping into a sitting position on the floor, his eyes like those of a dead fish, his face the sickly green of an attack of nausea. He swallows painfully several times—forces a weak smile at last.*) So—ye did steal it!

EBEN (*emotionlessly*). I swapped it t' Sim an' Peter fur their share o' the farm —t' pay their passage t' Californi-a.

CABOT (*with one sardonic*). Ha! (*He begins to recover. Gets slowly to his feet —strangely.*) I calc'late God give it to 'em—not yew! God's hard, not easy! Mebbe they's easy gold in the West but it hain't God's gold. It hain't fur me. I kin hear His voice warnin' me agen t' be hard an' stay on my farm. I kin see his hand usin' Eben t' steal t' keep me from weakness. I kin feel I be in the palm o' His hand, His fingers guidin' me. (*A pause—then he mutters sadly.*) It's a-goin' t' be lonesomer now than ever it war afore—an' I'm gittin' old, Lord—ripe on the bough. . . . (*Then stiffening.*) Waal—what d'ye want? God's lonesome, hain't He? God's hard an' lonesome! (*A pause. The* SHERIFF *with two men comes up the road from the left. They move cautiously to the door. The* SHERIFF *knocks on it with the butt of his pistol.*)

SHERIFF. Open in the name o' the law! (*They start.*)

CABOT. They've come fur ye. (*He goes to the rear door.*) Come in, Jim! (*The three men enter.* CABOT *meets them in doorway.*) Jest a minit, Jim. I got 'em safe here. (*The* SHERIFF *nods. He and his companions remain in the doorway.*)

EBEN (*suddenly calls*). I lied this mornin', Jim. I helped her to do it. Ye kin take me, too.

ABBIE (*brokenly*). No!

CABOT. Take 'em both. (*He comes forward—stares at* EBEN *with a trace of grudging admiration.*) Purty good—fur yew! Waal, I got t' round up the stock. Good-by.

EBEN. Good-by.

ABBIE. Good-by. (*CABOT turns and strides past the men—comes out and around the corner of the house, his shoulders squared, his face stony, and stalks grimly toward the barn. In the meantime the* SHERIFF *and men have come into the room.*)

SHERIFF (*embarrassedly*). Waal—we'd best start.

ABBIE. Wait. (*Turns to* EBEN.) I love ye, Eben.

EBEN. I love ye, Abbie. (*They kiss. The three men grin and shuffle embarrassedly.* EBEN *takes* ABBIE's *hand. They go out the door in rear, the men following, and come from the house, walking hand in hand to the gate.* EBEN *stops there and points to the sunrise sky.*) Sun's a-rizin'. Purty, hain't it?

ABBIE. Ay-eh. (*They both stand for a moment looking up raptly in attitudes strangely aloof and devout.*)

SHERIFF (*looking around at the farm enviously—to his companion*). It's a jim-dandy farm, no denyin'. Wished I owned it!

CURTAIN

The Crucible

Tragedy is not often associated with American history. With no tradition of battling royal houses or courtly intrigues of Europe, the American national background has most often been personified in the hero of the Revolution, the dauntless pioneer, and the "rugged" individualist whose empires were of steel and oil. Courage, endurance, sacrifice, along with ruthless exploitation and cruel indifference to others' well-being, have been a part of this country's growth, but very seldom have any of the important events been associated with tragedy. The hallmark of American enterprise, either on the prairie or in the factory, has been the "success story," instead of the tragic sacrifice of the individual for the benefit of others. Martyrs there have been—Nathan Hale, Abraham Lincoln, Woodrow Wilson—who died for a cause and became revered names in history. Heroes of brawn and bravado from Daniel Boone and Davy Crockett to Sergeant York and Colin Kelly have been plentiful. The tragic victim, however, has appeared infrequently.

Eugene O'Neill and Maxwell Anderson saw tragedy as an individual matter, giving it a modern "domestic" flavor. Tennessee Williams and Arthur Miller also have investigated tragedy in the "common man." Few writers have found the facts of American history a source for the tragic outlook. *The Crucible* is a notable exception.

The scope of the Salem witch trials was limited, without implication beyond the boundaries of the Massachusetts Bay colony. At the time there was no American nation, and the attempt to weed out the Devil in a tiny village buried in the wilderness could have no international repercussions. Witch hunting was not, for all its dreadful consequences to those involved, an unknown thing in the seventeenth-century world. The existence of super-natural powers of darkness as an everyday threat to good people was assumed without question. The savagery and the hysteria of the Salem terror made as little impression beyond the Colony as the family problems of the Cabots would have made in the rural New England of the midnineteenth century.

In their historical perspective, however, the trials have become a livid and shameful mark which has never been completely effaced from our national record. Furthermore, the trials and the executions carried with them the essence of tragedy as they put certain individuals to the farthest test of their human capacities. Arthur Miller has endowed the documented facts of history with the universality of tragedy.

The relentless power that destroys John Proctor is a human power, fueled by superstition, fanaticism, and a great deal of ignorance. To see this ugly force at work in the minds of supposedly intelligent beings becomes in many ways a more terrifying experience than to watch the crushing of the protagonists in *Desire Under the Elms* by the weight of a natural force beyond their ken. Hathorne, Danforth, and the entire court, including Parris, are supposedly rational men. The frightfulness of the situation is amplified many times over as they are bewitched exactly as much by the delirious girls as the girls themselves are transfixed by their own self-hypnosis, while Abigail's total insensibility to the devastation she is wreaking keeps supplying the impetus. For the honest victim there is no way out. Miller forms his destructive fate with conviction and skill, drawing it from the minds and actions of a "civilized" humanity which can recognize the deadly fraud, but which finds itself unable to halt its progress.

The deaths of the innocent victims and the curse on the entire settlement are horrifying and pathetic, but are not tragic until the accusation falls upon the Proctor household. Words and deeds hitherto innocent explode into damning evidence against the good Elizabeth. As Proctor reacts in justified rage at the preposterous charges against his wife and she is led away in chains, the couple begins to acquire some of the necessary tragic stature. Full achievement follows quickly.

The white-hot fire which will cleanse and purify the contaminated village in the merciless crucible of the court radiates its heat with greatest intensity in the paralyzing terror of the inquisition of Act III. Indications of the possibilities have been suggested in the Reverend Hale's carefully probing questions just before Elizabeth Proctor's arrest. The full force of the blasting flame is now released. In the midst stands the satanic Danforth, surrounded by the crowd of "bewitched" girls and the frantic men and women on both sides who seek the court's "justice." Miller injects some excellent tragic irony as the climax approaches and the Proctors' doom becomes inevitable. John and Elizabeth, confronted by the raging Parris and the demoniac Danforth, must draw from their souls' depths the statements that they believe will save both themselves and Salem. Proctor has gone far beyond merely attempting to save his wife, and he pursues his advantage in a desperate effort to destroy the court by proving Abigail's true character. But the tragedy is relentless, and the two people most able to end the unmerciful torture are trapped by their noblest efforts. Proctor's admission of lechery and Elizabeth's first lie in her life combine with the frenzy of Mary's last-ditch effort to extricate herself in a tragic climax as well designed as anyone can find in modern dramatic literature.

The final act reveals that Proctor's tragic dimensions are not a delusion. Both he and the wife who unwittingly condemns him have suffered, and both have reached the understanding of themselves which tragic suffering must bring. It is clear that Proctor cannot survive, for the living lie and walking shame that his freedom offers would be infinitely worse than the relief his death will bring. He has his goodness now, says Elizabeth, deaf to Hale's hysterical pleas. With Proctor's death there is peace in Elizabeth's heart, and there will soon be peace in Salem. As he dies, John Proctor raises human nobility to the level expected of the tragic hero. He was no "great" man, and his worldly position was of little consequence. But faced with the decision to keep his life and lose all human respect for himself, or to die in defiance of those who would declare themselves his betters and thus redeem all the pain and sorrow he had caused within his limited world, he made the choice that broke the back of the power that executed him. And that is tragedy.

The Crucible is more than the tragedy of John or Elizabeth Proctor. It is the tragedy of man's own stupidity as well. Proctor's death becomes a symbol of the waste of human lives which, somehow, mankind has always been able to permit under the guise of law and order, be it theological, political, or otherwise. *The Crucible* is a tragedy of Salem and a tragedy of all the Salems that have existed. Miller admits that he meant the play to reflect directly upon the time in which he wrote it, as a warning of the consequences of modern governmental "witchhunts." Fortunately, *The Crucible* does more than draw parallels, for it is a play which can stand on its own, independent of current political trends. The acceptance of the play outside America and the success of the New York revival in 1958 support this opinion. It is not just a polemic, nor is it an overmelodramatic Sunday sermon. It survives as an outstanding drama in the tragic tradition, in which the perpetual truths of man's brutality and the nobility that can arise from it are impressively expounded.

Arthur Miller

Arthur Miller was born on October 17, 1915, in the Harlem section of New York, son of a manufacturer who had come to this country as a small boy from Austria. Miller's secondary education in the New York public schools was without distinction, and he displayed very little interest in books outside of the Tom Swift or Rover Boy category. After his formal schooling he went to work in a Tenth Avenue warehouse during the Depression, to help with the now depleted family fortunes. His experiences in this position are reflected in his short play, *A Memory of Two Mondays*.

While riding the subway to work he started to read "The Brothers Karamazov" and decided that he was meant to be a writer. When he applied to the University of Michigan, he was refused because of his poor high school record, but his pleas to be accepted because of his desire to write finally admitted him as a student of journalism. During his first spring vacation he wrote a play which won some scholastic prizes, and he continued, as he studied under Prof. Kenneth Rowe, to produce plays of modest distinction.

From Michigan he returned to New York and wrote radio scripts and a novel called "Focus" in 1945. A story of Army camps in 1944 entitled "Situation Normal," had received some praise, but his first try at a New York play, *The Man Who Had All the Luck*, the same year was a total failure. Success was forthcoming in 1947 with *All My Sons*, followed in 1948 by the Pulitzer Prize play, *Death of a Salesman*, which is said to have been composed in six weeks. *The Crucible*, 1953, was not commercially successful, but its

Off Broadway revival in the 1958–1959 season brought high praise and a long run. In 1955 his bill of two short plays, *A View from the Bridge* and *A Memory of Two Mondays* appeared in New York, and he published a collection of his major plays in 1957, including a full-length version of *A View from the Bridge*. His first venture into screen writing, *The Misfits*, appeared in 1961.

THE CRUCIBLE

by

Arthur Miller

The highly dramatic third-act climax of *The Crucible*, from the original Broadway production. With the two antagonists, Abigail Williams and John Proctor, placed back to back downstage, and the judges interrogating Elizabeth Proctor in the background, the director has brilliantly emphasized the terrible forces that are moving the tragedy with violent swiftness toward its highest point. (*Life Magazine. Courtesy Gjon Mili.*)

The Crucible opened at the Martin Beck Theatre in New York on January 22, 1953. It ran for a total of 197 performances. The following cast appeared in the original production:

BETTY PARRIS	*Janet Alexander*
TITUBA	*Jacqueline Andre*
REV. SAMUEL PARRIS	*Fred Stewart*
ABIGAIL WILLIAMS	*Madeleine Sherwood*
SUSANNA WALCOTT	*Barbara Stanton*
MRS. ANN PUTNAM	*Jane Hoffman*
THOMAS PUTNAM	*Raymond Bramley*
MERCY LEWIS	*Dorothy Jolliffe*
MARY WARREN	*Jenny Egan*
JOHN PROCTOR	*Arthur Kennedy*
REBECCA NURSE	*Jean Adair*
GILES COREY	*Joseph Sweeney*
REV. JOHN HALE	*E. G. Marshall*
ELIZABETH PROCTOR	*Beatrice Straight*
FRANCIS NURSE	*Graham Velsey*
EZEKIEL CHEEVER	*Don McHenry*
JOHN WILLARD	*George Mitchell*
JUDGE HATHORNE	*Philip Coolidge*
DEPUTY GOVERNOR DANFORTH	*Walter Hampden*
SARAH GOOD	*Adele Fortin*
HOPKINS	*Donald Marye*

Produced by Kermit Bloomgarden
Directed by Jed Harris
Scenery designed by Boris Aronson
Costumes designed by Edith Lutyens

A Note on the Historical Accuracy
of This Play

This play is not history in the sense in which the word is used by the academic historian. Dramatic purposes have sometimes required many characters to be fused into one; the number of girls involved in the "crying-out" has been reduced; Abigail's age has been raised; while there were several judges of almost equal authority, I have symbolized them all in Hathorne and Danforth. However, I believe that the reader will discover here the essential nature of one of the strangest and most awful chapters in human history. The fate of each character is exactly that of his historical model, and there is no one in the drama who did not play a similar—and in some cases exactly the same—role in history.

As for the characters of the persons, little is known about most of them excepting what may be surmised from a few letters, the trial record, certain broadsides written at the time, and references to their conduct in sources of varying reliability. They may therefore be taken as creations of my own, drawn to the best of my ability in conformity with their known behavior, except as indicated in the commentary I have written for this text.

ACT ONE: AN OVERTURE

A small upper bedroom in the home of REVEREND SAMUEL PARRIS, *Salem, Massachusetts, in the spring of the year 1692. There is a narrow window at the left. Through its leaded panes the morning sunlight streams. A candle still burns near the bed, which is at the right. A chest, a chair, and a small table are the other furnishings. At the back a door opens on the landing of the stairway to the ground floor. The room gives off an air of clean spareness. The roof rafters are exposed, and the wood colors are raw and unmellowed.*

As the curtain rises, REVEREND PARRIS *is discovered kneeling beside the bed, evidently in prayer. His daughter,* BETTY PARRIS, *aged ten, is lying on the bed, inert.*

At the time of these events Parris was in his middle forties. In history he cut a villainous path, and there is very little good to be said for him. He believed he was being persecuted wherever he went, despite his best efforts to win people and God to his side. In meeting, he felt insulted if someone rose to shut the door without first asking his permission. He was a widower with no interest in children, or talent with them. He regarded them as young adults, and until this strange crisis he, like the rest of Salem, never conceived that the children were anything but thankful for being permitted to walk straight, eyes slightly lowered, arms at the sides, and mouths shut until bidden to speak.

His house stood in the "town"—but we today would hardly call it a village. The meeting house was nearby, and from this point outward—toward the bay or inland—there were a few small-windowed, dark houses snuggling against the raw Massachusetts winter. Salem had been established hardly forty years before. To the European world the whole province was a barbaric frontier inhabited by a sect of fanatics who, nevertheless, were shipping out products of slowly increasing quantity and value.

No one can really know what their lives were like. They had no novelists—and would not have permitted anyone to read a novel if one were handy. Their creed forbade anything resembling a theater or "vain enjoyment." They did not celebrate Christmas, and a holiday from work meant only that they must concentrate even more upon prayer.

Which is not to say that nothing broke into this strict and somber way of life. When a new farmhouse was built, friends assembled to "raise the roof," and there would be special foods cooked and probably some potent cider passed around. There was a good supply of ne'er-do-wells in Salem, who dallied at the shovelboard in Bridget Bishop's tavern. Probably more than the creed, hard work kept the morals of the place from spoiling, for the people were forced to fight the land like heroes for every grain of corn, and no man had very much time for fooling around.

That there were some jokers, however, is indicated by the practice of appointing a two-man patrol whose duty was to "walk forth in the time of God's worship to take notice of such as either lye about the meeting house, without attending to the word and ordinances, or that lye at home or in the fields without giving good account thereof, and to take the names of such persons, and to present them to the magistrates, whereby they may be accordingly proceeded against." This predilection for minding other people's business was time-honored among the people of Salem, and it undoubtedly created many of the suspicions which were to feed the coming madness. It was also, in my opinion, one of the things that a John Proctor would rebel against, for the time of the armed camp had almost passed, and since the country was reasonably—although not wholly—safe, the old disciplines were beginning to rankle. But, as in all such matters, the issue was not clear-cut, for danger was still a possibility, and in unity still lay the best promise of safety.

The edge of the wilderness was close by. The American continent stretched endlessly west, and it was full of mystery for them. It stood, dark and threatening, over their shoulders night and day, for out of it Indian tribes marauded from time to time, and Reverend Parris had parishioners who had lost relatives to these heathen.

The parochial snobbery of these people was partly responsible for their failure to convert the Indians. Probably they also preferred to take land from heathens rather than from fellow Christians. At any rate, very few Indians were converted, and the Salem folk believed that the virgin forest was the Devil's last preserve, his home base and the citadel of his final stand. To the best of their knowledge the American forest was the last place on earth that was not paying homage to God.

For these reasons, among others, they carried about an air of innate resistance, even of persecution. Their fathers had, of course, been persecuted in England. So now they and their church found it necessary to deny any other sect its freedom, lest their New Jerusalem be defiled and corrupted by wrong ways and deceitful ideas.

They believed, in short, that they held in their steady hands the candle that would light the world. We have inherited this belief, and it has helped and hurt us. It helped them with the discipline it gave them. They were a dedicated folk, by and large, and they had to be to survive the life they had chosen or been born into in this country.

The proof of their belief's value to them may be taken from the opposite character of the first Jamestown settlement, farther south, in Virginia. The Englishmen who landed there were motivated mainly by a hunt for profit. They had thought to pick off the wealth of the new country and then return rich to England. They were a band of individualists, and a much more ingratiating group than the Massachusetts men. But Virginia destroyed them. Massachusetts tried to kill off the Puritans, but they combined; they set up a communal society which, in the beginning, was little more than an armed camp with an autocratic and very devoted leadership. It was, however, an autocracy by consent, for they were united from top to bottom by a commonly held ideology whose perpetuation was the reason and justification for all their sufferings. So their self-denial, their purposefulness, their suspicion of all vain pursuits, their hard-handed justice, were altogether perfect instruments for the conquest of this space so antagonistic to man.

But the people of Salem in 1692 were not quite the dedicated folk that arrived on the *Mayflower*. A vast differentiation had taken place, and in their own time a revolution had unseated the royal government and substituted a junta which was at this moment in power. The times, to their eyes, must have been out of joint, and to the common folk must have seemed as insoluble and complicated as do ours today. It is not hard to see how easily many could have been led to believe that the time of confusion had been brought upon them by deep and darkling forces. No hint of such speculation appears on the court record, but social disorder in any age breeds such mystical suspicions, and when, as in Salem, wonders are brought forth from below the social surface, it is too much to expect people to hold back very long from laying on the victims with all the force of their frustrations.

The Salem tragedy, which is about to begin in these pages, developed from a paradox. It is a paradox in whose grip we still live, and there is no prospect yet that we will discover its resolution. Simply, it was this: for good purposes, even high purposes, the people of Salem developed a theocracy, a combine of state and religious power whose function was to keep the community together, and to prevent any kind of disunity that might open it to destruction by material or ideological enemies. It was forged for a necessary purpose and accomplished that purpose. But all organization is and must be grounded on the idea of exclusion and prohibition, just as two objects cannot occupy the same place. Evidently the time came in New England when the repressions of order were heavier than seemed warranted by the dangers against which the order was organized. The witch-hunt was a perverse manifestation of the panic which set in among all classes when the balance began to turn toward greater individual freedom.

When one rises above the individual villainy displayed, one can only pity them all, just as we shall be pitied someday. It is still impossible for man to organize his social life without repressions, and the balance has yet to be struck between order and freedom.

The witch-hunt was not, however, a mere repression. It was also, and as importantly, a long overdue opportunity for everyone so inclined to express publicly his guilt and sins, under the cover of accusations against the victims. It suddenly became possible—and patriotic and holy—for a man to say that Martha Corey had come into his bedroom at night, and that, while his wife was sleeping at his side, Martha laid herself down on his chest and "nearly suffocated him." Of course it was her spirit only, but his satisfaction at confessing himself was no lighter than if it had been Martha herself. One could not ordinarily speak such things in public.

Long-held hatreds of neighbors could now be openly expressed, and vengeance taken, despite the Bible's charitable injunctions. Land-lust which had been expressed before by constant bickering over boundaries and deeds, could now be elevated to the arena of morality; one could cry witch against one's neighbor and feel perfectly justified in the bargain. Old scores could be settled on a plane of heavenly combat between Lucifer and the Lord; suspicions and the envy of the miserable toward the happy could and did burst out in the general revenge.

REVEREND PARRIS *is praying now, and, though we cannot hear his words, a sense of his confusion hangs about him. He mumbles, then seems about to weep; then he weeps, then prays again; but his daughter does not stir on the bed.*

The door opens, and his Negro slave enters. TITUBA *is in her forties.* PARRIS *brought her with him from Barbados, where he spent some years as a merchant before entering the ministry. She enters as one does who can no longer bear to be barred from the sight of her beloved, but she is also very frightened because her slave sense has warned her that, as always, trouble in this house eventually lands on her back.*

TITUBA (*already taking a step backward*). My Betty be hearty soon?

PARRIS. Out of here!

TITUBA (*backing to the door*). My Betty not goin' die . . .

PARRIS (*scrambling to his feet in a fury*). Out of my sight. (*She is gone.*) Out of my— (*He is overcome with sobs. He clamps his teeth against them and closes the door and leans against it, exhausted.*) Oh, my God! God help me! (*Quaking with fear, mumbling to himself through his sobs, he goes to the bed and gently takes Betty's hand.*) Betty. Child. Dear child. Will you wake, will you open up your eyes! Betty, little one . . . (*He is bending to kneel again when his niece,* ABIGAIL WILLIAMS, *seventeen, enters—a strikingly beautiful girl, an orphan, with an endless capacity for dissembling. Now she is all worry and apprehension and propriety.*)

ABIGAIL. Uncle? (*He looks to her.*) Susanna Walcott's here from Doctor Griggs.

PARRIS. Oh? Let her come, let her come.

ABIGAIL (*leaning out the door to call to* SUSANNA, *who is down the hall a few steps*). Come in, Susanna. (SUSANNA WALCOTT, *a little younger than* ABIGAIL, *a nervous, hurried girl, enters.*)

PARRIS (*eagerly*). What does the doctor say, child?

SUSANNA (*craning around* PARRIS *to get a look at* BETTY). He bid me come and tell you, reverend sir, that he cannot discover no medicine for it in his books.

PARRIS. Then he must search on.

SUSANNA. Aye, sir, he have been searchin' his books since he left you, sir. But he bid me tell you, that you might look to unnatural things for the cause of it.

PARRIS (*his eyes going wide*). No—no. There be no unnatural cause here. Tell him I have sent for Reverend Hale of Beverly, and Mr. Hale will surely confirm that. Let him look to medicine and put out all thought of unnatural causes here. There be none.

SUSANNA. Aye, sir. He bid me tell you. (*She turns to go.*)

ABIGAIL. Speak nothin' of it in the village, Susanna.

PARRIS. Go directly home and speak nothing of unnatural causes.

SUSANNA. Aye, sir. I pray for her. (*She goes out.*)

ABIGAIL. Uncle, the rumor of witchcraft is all about; I think you'd best go down and deny it yourself. The parlor's packed with people, sir. I'll sit with her.

PARRIS (*pressed, turns on her*). And what shall I say to them? That my daughter and my niece I discovered dancing like heathen in the forest?

ABIGAIL. Uncle, we did dance; let you tell them I confessed it—and I'll be whipped if I must be. But they're speakin' of witchcraft. Betty's not witched.

PARRIS. Abigail, I cannot go before the congregation when I know you have not opened with me. What did you do with her in the forest?

ABIGAIL. We did dance, uncle, and when you leaped out of the bush so suddenly, Betty was frightened and then she fainted. And there's the whole of it.

PARRIS. Child. Sit you down.

ABIGAIL (*quavering, as she sits*). I would never hurt Betty. I love her dearly.

PARRIS. Now look you, child, your punishment will come in its time. But if you trafficked with spirits in the forest I must know it now, for surely my enemies will, and they will ruin me with it.

ABIGAIL. But we never conjured spirits.

PARRIS. Then why can she not move herself since midnight? This child is desperate! (ABIGAIL *lowers her eyes.*) It must come out—my enemies will bring it out. Let me know what you done there. Abigail, do you understand that I have many enemies?

ABIGAIL. I have heard of it, uncle.

PARRIS. There is a faction that is sworn to drive me from my pulpit. Do you understand that?

ABIGAIL. I think so, sir.

PARRIS. Now then, in the midst of such disruption, my own household is discovered to be the very center of some obscene practice. Abominations are done in the forest—

ABIGAIL. It were sport, uncle!

PARRIS (*pointing at* BETTY). You call this sport? (*She lowers her eyes. He pleads.*) Abigail, if you know something that may help the doctor, for God's sake tell it to me. (*She is silent.*) I saw Tituba waving her arms over the fire when I came on you. Why was she doing that? And I heard a screeching and gibberish coming from her mouth. She were swaying like a dumb beast over that fire!

ABIGAIL. She always sings her Barbados songs, and we dance.

PARRIS. I cannot blink what I saw, Abigail, for my enemies will not blink it. I saw a dress lying on the grass.

ABIGAIL (*innocently*). A dress?

PARRIS (*it is very hard to say*). Aye, a dress. And I thought I saw—someone naked running through the trees!

ABIGAIL (*in terror*). No one was naked! You mistake yourself, uncle!

PARRIS (*with anger*). I saw it! (*He moves from her. Then, resolved.*) Now tell me true, Abigail. And I pray you feel the weight of truth upon you, for now my ministry's at stake, my ministry and perhaps your cousin's life. Whatever abomination you have done, give me all of it now, for I dare not be taken unaware when I go before them down there.

ABIGAIL. There is nothin' more. I swear it, uncle.

PARRIS (*studies her, then nods, half convinced*). Abigail, I have fought here three long years to bend these stiff-necked people to me, and now, just now when some good respect is rising for me in the parish, you compromise my very character. I have given you a home, child. I have put clothes upon your back —now give me upright answer. Your name in the town—it is entirely white, is it not?

ABIGAIL (*with an edge of resentment*). Why, I am sure it is, sir. There be no blush about my name.

PARRIS (*to the point*). Abigail, is there any other cause than you have told me, for your being discharged from Goody Proctor's service? I have heard it said, and I tell you as I heard it, that she comes so rarely to the church this year for she will not sit so close to something soiled. What signified that remark?

ABIGAIL. She hates me, uncle, she must, for I would not be her slave. It's a bitter woman, a lying, cold, sniveling woman, and I will not work for such a woman!

PARRIS. She may be. And yet it has troubled me that you are now seven month out of their house, and in all this time no other family has ever called for your service.

ABIGAIL. They want slaves, not such as I. Let them send to Barbados for that. I will not black my face for any of them! (*With ill-concealed resentment at him.*) Do you begrudge my bed, uncle?

PARRIS. No—no.

ABIGAIL (*in a temper*). My name is good in the village! I will not have it said my name is soiled! Goody Proctor is a gossiping liar! (*Enter* MRS. ANN PUTNAM. *She is a twisted soul of forty-five, a death-ridden woman, haunted by dreams.*)

PARRIS (*as soon as the door begins to open*). No—no, I cannot have anyone. (*He sees her, and a certain deference springs into him, although his worry remains.*) Why, Goody Putnam, come in.

MRS. PUTNAM (*full of breath, shiny-eyed*). It is a marvel. It is surely a stroke of hell upon you.

PARRIS. No, Goody Putnam, it is—

MRS. PUTNAM (*glancing at* BETTY). How high did she fly, how high?

PARRIS. No, no, she never flew—

MRS. PUTNAM (*very pleased with it*). Why, it's sure she did. Mr. Collins saw her goin' over Ingersoll's barn, and come down light as bird, he says!

PARRIS. Now, look you, Goody Putnam, she never— (*Enter* THOMAS PUTNAM, *a well-to-do, hard-handed landowner, near fifty.*) Oh, good morning, Mr. Putnam.

PUTNAM. It is a providence the thing is out now! It is a providence. (*He goes directly to the bed.*)

PARRIS. What's out, sir, what's—? (*MRS. PUTNAM goes to the bed.*)

PUTNAM (*looking down at* BETTY). Why, her eyes is closed! Look you, Ann.

MRS. PUTNAM. Why, that's strange. (*To* PARRIS.) Ours is open.

PARRIS (*shocked*). Your Ruth is sick?

MRS. PUTNAM (*with vicious certainty*). I'd not call it sick; the Devil's touch is heavier than sick. It's death, y'know, it's death drivin' into them, forked and hoofed.

PARRIS. Oh, pray not! Why, how does Ruth ail?

MRS. PUTNAM. She ails as she must— she never waked this morning, but her eyes open and she walks, and hears naught, sees naught, and cannot eat. Her soul is taken, surely. (PARRIS *is struck.*)

PUTNAM (*as though for further details*). They say you've sent for Reverend Hale of Beverly?

PARRIS (*with dwindling conviction now*). A precaution only. He has much experience in all demonic arts, and I—

MRS. PUTNAM. He has indeed; and found a witch in Beverly last year, and let you remember that.

PARRIS. Now, Goody Ann, they only thought that were a witch, and I am certain there be no element of witchcraft here.

PUTNAM. No witchcraft! Now look you, Mr. Parris—

PARRIS. Thomas, Thomas, I pray you, leap not to witchcraft. I know that you— you least of all, Thomas, would ever wish so disastrous a charge laid upon me. We cannot leap to witchcraft. They will howl me out of Salem for such corruption in my house.

A word about Thomas Putnam. He was a man with many grievances, at least one of which appears justified. Some time before, his wife's brother-in-law, James Bayley, had been turned down as minister of Salem. Bayley had all the qualifications, and a two-thirds vote into the bargain, but a faction stopped his acceptance, for reasons that are not clear.

Thomas Putnam was the eldest son of the richest man in the village. He had fought the Indians at Narragansett, and was deeply interested in parish affairs. He undoubtedly felt it poor payment that the village should so blatantly disregard his candidate for one of its more important offices, especially since he regarded himself as the intellectual superior of most of the people around him.

His vindictive nature was demonstrated long before the witchcraft began. An-

other former Salem minister, George Burroughs, had had to borrow money to pay for his wife's funeral, and, since the parish was remiss in his salary, he was soon bankrupt. Thomas and his brother John had Burroughs jailed for debts the man did not owe. The incident is important only in that Burroughs succeeded in becoming minister where Bayley, Thomas Putnam's brother-in-law, had been rejected; the motif of resentment is clear here. Thomas Putnam felt that his own name and the honor of his family had been smirched by the village, and he meant to right matters however he could.

Another reason to believe him a deeply embittered man was his attempt to break his father's will, which left a disproportionate amount to a stepbrother. As with every other public cause in which he tried to force his way, he failed in this.

So it is not surprising to find that so many accusations against people are in the handwriting of Thomas Putnam, or that his name is so often found as a witness corroborating the supernatural testimony, or that his daughter led the crying-out at the most opportune junctures of the trials, especially when— But we'll speak of that when we come to it.

PUTNAM (*at the moment he is intent upon getting* PARRIS, *for whom he has only contempt, to move toward the abyss*). Mr. Parris, I have taken your part in all contention here, and I would continue; but I cannot if you hold back in this. There are hurtful, vengeful spirits layin' hands on these children.

PARRIS. But, Thomas, you cannot—

PUTNAM. Ann! Tell Mr. Parris what you have done.

MRS. PUTNAM. Reverend Parris, I have laid seven babies unbaptized in the earth. Believe me, sir, you never saw more hearty babies born. And yet, each would wither in my arms the very night of their birth. I have spoke nothin', but my heart has clamored intimations. And now, this year, my Ruth, my only— I see her turning strange. A secret child she has become this year, and shrivels like a sucking mouth were pullin' on her life too. And so I thought to send her to your Tituba—

PARRIS. To Tituba! What may Tituba—?

MRS. PUTNAM. Tituba knows how to speak to the dead, Mr. Parris.

PARRIS. Goody Ann, it is a formidable sin to conjure up the dead!

MRS. PUTNAM. I take it on my soul, but who else may surely tell us what person murdered my babies?

PARRIS (horrified). Woman!

MRS. PUTNAM. They were murdered, Mr. Parris! And mark this proof! Mark it! Last night my Ruth were ever so close to their little spirits; I know it, sir. For how else is she struck dumb now except some power of darkness would stop her mouth? It is a marvelous sign, Mr. Parris!

PUTNAM. Don't you understand it, sir? There is a murdering witch among us, bound to keep herself in the dark. (PARRIS turns to BETTY, a frantic terror rising in him.) Let your enemies make of it what they will, you cannot blink it more.

PARRIS (to ABIGAIL). Then you were conjuring spirits last night.

ABIGAIL (whispering). Not I, sir—Tituba and Ruth.

PARRIS (turns now, with new fear, and goes to BETTY, looks down at her, and then, gazing off). Oh, Abigail, what proper payment for my charity! Now I am undone.

PUTNAM. You are not undone! Let you take hold here. Wait for no one to charge you—declare it yourself. You have discovered witchcraft—

PARRIS. In my house? In my house, Thomas? They will topple me with this! They will make of it a— (Enter MERCY LEWIS, the PUTNAMS' servant, a fat, sly, merciless girl of eighteen.)

MERCY. Your pardons. I only thought to see how Betty is.

PUTNAM. Why aren't you home? Who's with Ruth?

MERCY. Her grandma come. She's improved a little, I think—she give a powerful sneeze before.

MRS. PUTNAM. Ah, there's a sign of life!

MERCY. I'd fear no more, Goody Putnam. It were a grand sneeze; another like it will shake her wits together, I'm sure. (She goes to the bed to look.)

PARRIS. Will you leave me now, Thomas? I would pray a while alone.

ABIGAIL. Uncle, you've prayed since midnight. Why do you not go down and—

PARRIS. No—no. (To PUTNAM.) I have no answer for that crowd. I'll wait till Mr. Hale arrives. (To get MRS. PUTNAM to leave.) If you will, Goody Ann . . .

PUTNAM. Now look you, sir. Let you strike out against the Devil, and the village will bless you for it! Come down, speak to them—pray with them. They're thirsting for your word, Mister! Surely you'll pray with them.

PARRIS (swayed). I'll lead them in a psalm, but let you say nothing of witchcraft yet. I will not discuss it. The cause is yet unknown. I have had enough contention since I came; I want no more.

MRS. PUTNAM. Mercy, you go home to Ruth, d'y'hear?

MERCY. Aye, mum. (MRS. PUTNAM goes out.)

PARRIS (to ABIGAIL). If she starts for the window, cry for me at once.

ABIGAIL. I will, uncle.

PARRIS (to PUTNAM). There is a terrible power in her arms today. (He goes out with PUTNAM.)

ABIGAIL (with hushed trepidation). How is Ruth sick?

MERCY. It's weirdish, I know not—she seems to walk like a dead one since last night.

ABIGAIL (turns at once and goes to BETTY, and now, with fear in her voice). Betty? (BETTY doesn't move. She shakes her.) Now stop this! Betty! Sit up now! (BETTY doesn't stir. MERCY comes over.)

MERCY. Have you tried beatin' her? I gave Ruth a good one and it waked her for a minute. Here, let me have her.

ABIGAIL (holding MERCY back). No, he'll be comin' up. Listen, now; if they be questioning us, tell them we danced —I told him as much already.

MERCY. Aye. And what more?

ABIGAIL. He knows Tituba conjured Ruth's sisters to come out of the grave.

MERCY. And what more?

ABIGAIL. He saw you naked.

MERCY (*clapping her hands together with a frightened laugh*). Oh, Jesus! (*Enter* MARY WARREN, *breathless. She is seventeen, a subservient, naive, lonely girl.*)

MARY WARREN. What'll we do? The village is out! I just come from the farm; the whole country's talkin' witchcraft! They'll be callin' us witches, Abby!

MERCY (*pointing and looking at* MARY WARREN). She means to tell, I know it.

MARY WARREN. Abby, we've got to tell. Witchery's a hangin' error, a hangin' like they done in Boston two year ago! We must tell the truth, Abby! You'll only be whipped for dancin', and the other things!

ABIGAIL. Oh, *we'll* be whipped!

MARY WARREN. I never done none of it, Abby. I only looked!

MERCY (*moving menacingly toward* MARY). Oh, you're a great one for lookin', aren't you, Mary Warren? What a grand peeping courage you have! (BETTY, *on the bed, whimpers.* ABIGAIL *turns to her at once.*)

ABIGAIL. Betty? (*She goes to* BETTY.) Now, Betty, dear, wake up now. It's Abigail. (*She sits* BETTY *up and furiously shakes her.*) I'll beat you, Betty! (BETTY *whimpers.*) My, you seem improving. I talked to your papa and I told him everything. So there's nothing to—

BETTY (*darts off the bed, frightened of* ABIGAIL, *and flattens herself against the wall*). I want my mama!

ABIGAIL (*with alarm, as she cautiously approaches* BETTY). What ails you, Betty? Your mama's dead and buried.

BETTY: I'll fly to Mama. Let me fly! (*She raises her arms as though to fly, and streaks for the window, gets one leg out.*)

ABIGAIL (*pulling her away from the window*). I told him everything; he knows now, he knows everything we—

BETTY. You drank blood, Abby! You didn't tell him that!

ABIGAIL. Betty, you never say that again! You will never—

BETTY. You did, you did! You drank a charm to kill John Proctor's wife! You drank a charm to kill Goody Proctor!

ABIGAIL (*smashes her across the face*). Shut it! Now shut it!

BETTY (*collapsing on the bed*). Mama, Mama! (*She dissolves into sobs.*)

ABIGAIL. Now look you. All of you. We danced. And Tituba conjured Ruth Putnam's dead sisters. And that is all. And mark this. Let either of you breathe a word, or the edge of a word, about the other things, and I will come to you in the black of some terrible night and I will bring a pointy reckoning that will shudder you. And you know I can do it; I saw Indians smash my dear parents' heads on the pillow next to mine, and I have seen some reddish work done at night, and I can make you wish you had never seen the sun go down! (*She goes to* BETTY *and roughly sits her up.*) Now, you—sit up and stop this! (*But* BETTY *collapses in her hands and lies inert on the bed.*)

MARY WARREN (*with hysterical fright*). What's got her? (ABIGAIL *stares in fright at* BETTY.) Abby, she's going to die! It's a sin to conjure, and we—

ABIGAIL (*starting for* MARY). I say shut it, Mary Warren! (*Enter* JOHN PROCTOR. *On seeing him,* MARY WARREN *leaps in fright.*)

Proctor was a farmer in his middle thirties. He need not have been a partisan of any faction in the town, but there is evidence to suggest that he had a sharp and biting way with hypocrites. He was the kind of man—powerful of body, even-tempered, and not easily led—who cannot refuse support to partisans without drawing their deepest resentment. In Proctor's presence a fool felt his foolishness instantly—and a Proctor is always marked for calumny therefore.

But as we shall see, the steady manner he displays does not spring from an untroubled soul. He is a sinner, a sinner not only against the moral fashion of the time, but against his own vision of decent conduct. These people had no ritual for the washing away of sins. It is another trait we inherited from them, and it has helped to discipline us as well as to breed hypocrisy among us. Proctor, respected and even feared in Salem, has come to regard himself as a kind of fraud. But no hint of this has yet appeared on the surface, and as he enters from the crowded parlor below it is a man in his prime we see, with a quiet confidence and an unexpressed, hidden force. Mary Warren, his servant, can barely speak for embarrassment and fear.

MARY WARREN. Oh! I'm just going home, Mr. Proctor.

PROCTOR. Be you foolish, Mary Warren? Be you deaf? I forbid you leave the house, did I not? Why shall I pay you? I am looking for you more often than my cows!

MARY WARREN. I only come to see the great doings in the world.

PROCTOR. I'll show you a great doin' on your arse one of these days. Now get you home; my wife is waitin' with your work! (*Trying to retain a shred of dignity, she goes slowly out.*)

MERCY LEWIS (*both afraid of him and strangely titillated*). I'd best be off. I have my Ruth to watch. Good morning, Mr. Proctor. (MERCY *sidles out. Since* PROCTOR's *entrance,* ABIGAIL *has stood as though on tiptoe, absorbing his presence, wide-eyed. He glances at her, then goes to* BETTY *on the bed.*)

ABIGAIL. Gah! I'd almost forgot how strong you are, John Proctor!

PROCTOR (*looking at* ABIGAIL *now, the faintest suggestion of a knowing smile on his face*). What's this mischief here?

ABIGAIL (*with a nervous laugh*). Oh, she's only gone silly somehow.

PROCTOR. The road past my house is a pilgrimage to Salem all morning. The town's mumbling witchcraft.

ABIGAIL. Oh, posh! (*Winningly she comes a little closer, with a confidential, wicked air.*) We were dancin' in the woods last night, and my uncle leaped in on us. She took fright, is all.

PROCTOR (*his smile widening*). Ah, you're wicked yet, aren't y'! (*A trill of expectant laughter escapes her, and she dares come closer, feverishly looking into his eyes.*) You'll be clapped in the stocks before you're twenty. (*He takes a step to go, and she springs into his path.*)

ABIGAIL. Give me a word, John. A soft word. (*Her concentrated desire destroys his smile.*)

PROCTOR. No, no, Abby. That's done with.

ABIGAIL (*tauntingly*). You come five mile to see a silly girl fly? I know you better.

PROCTOR (*setting her firmly out of his path*). I come to see what mischief your uncle's brewin' now. (*With final emphasis.*) Put it out of mind, Abby.

ABIGAIL (*grasping his hand before he can release her*). John—I am waitin' for you every night.

PROCTOR. Abby, I never give you hope to wait for me.

ABIGAIL (*now beginning to anger—she can't believe it*). I have something better than hope, I think!

PROCTOR. Abby, you'll put it out of mind. I'll not be comin' for you more.

ABIGAIL. You're surely sportin' with me.

PROCTOR. You know me better.

ABIGAIL. I know how you clutched my back behind your house and sweated like a stallion whenever I come near! Or did I dream that? It's she put me out, you cannot pretend it were you. I saw your face when she put me out, and you loved me then and you do now!

PROCTOR. Abby, that's a wild thing to say—

ABIGAIL. A wild thing may say wild things. But not so wild, I think. I have seen you since she put me out; I have seen you nights.

PROCTOR. I have hardly stepped off my farm this sevenmonth.

ABIGAIL. I have a sense for heat, John, and yours has drawn me to my window, and I have seen you looking up, burning in your loneliness. Do you tell me you've never looked up at my window?

PROCTOR. I may have looked up.

ABIGAIL (*now softening*). And you must. You are no wintry man. I know you, John. I *know* you. (*She is weeping.*) I cannot sleep for dreamin'; I cannot dream but I wake and walk about the house as though I'd find you comin' through some door. (*She clutches him desperately.*)

PROCTOR (*gently pressing her from him, with great sympathy but firmly*). Child—

ABIGAIL (*with a flash of anger*). How do you call me child!

PROCTOR. Abby, I may think of you softly from time to time. But I will cut off my hand before I'll ever reach for you again. Wipe it out of mind. We never touched, Abby.

ABIGAIL. Aye, but we did.

PROCTOR. Aye, but we did not.

ABIGAIL (*with a bitter anger*). Oh, I marvel how such a strong man may let such a sickly wife be—

PROCTOR (*angered—at himself as well*). You'll speak nothin' of Elizabeth!

ABIGAIL. She is blackening my name in the village! She is telling lies about me! She is a cold, sniveling woman, and you bend to her! Let her turn you like a—

PROCTOR (*shaking her*). Do you look for whippin'? (*A psalm is heard being sung below.*)

ABIGAIL (*in tears*). I look for John Proctor that took me from my sleep and put knowledge in my heart! I never knew what pretense Salem was, I never knew the lying lessons I was taught by all these Christian women and their covenanted men! And now you bid me tear the light out of my eyes? I will not, I cannot! You loved me, John Proctor, and whatever sin it is, you love me yet! (*He turns abruptly to go out. She rushes to him.*) John, pity me, pity me! (*The words "going up to Jesus" are heard in the psalm, and BETTY claps her ears suddenly and whines loudly.*)

ABIGAIL. Betty? (*She hurries to BETTY, who is now sitting up and screaming.*

PROCTOR *goes to* BETTY *as* ABIGAIL *is trying to pull her hands down, calling* "Betty!")

PROCTOR (*growing unnerved*). What's she doing? Girl, what ails you? Stop that wailing! (*The singing has stopped in the midst of this, and now* PARRIS *rushes in.*)

PARRIS. What happened? What are you doing to her? Betty! (*He rushes to the bed, crying, "Betty, Betty!"* MRS. PUTNAM *enters, feverish with curiosity, and with her* THOMAS PUTNAM *and* MERCY LEWIS. PARRIS, *at the bed, keeps lightly slapping* BETTY's *face, while she moans and tries to get up.*)

ABIGAIL. She heard you singin' and suddenly she's up and screamin'.

MRS. PUTNAM. The psalm! The psalm! She cannot bear to hear the Lord's name!

PARRIS. No, God forbid. Mercy, run to the doctor! Tell him what's happened here! (MERCY LEWIS *rushes out.*)

MRS. PUTNAM. Mark it for a sign, mark it! (REBECCA NURSE, *seventy-two, enters. She is white-haired, leaning upon her walking-stick.*)

PUTNAM (*pointing at the whimpering* BETTY). That is a notorious sign of witchcraft afoot, Goody Nurse, a prodigious sign!

MRS. PUTNAM. My mother told me that! When they cannot bear to hear the name of—

PARRIS (*trembling*). Rebecca, Rebecca, go to her, we're lost. She suddenly cannot bear to hear the Lord's— (GILES COREY, *eighty-three, enters. He is knotted with muscle, canny, inquisitive, and still powerful.*)

REBECCA. There is hard sickness here, Giles Corey, so please to keep the quiet.

GILES. I've not said a word. No one here can testify I've said a word. Is she going to fly again? I hear she flies.

PUTNAM. Man, be quiet now! (*Everything is quiet.* REBECCA *walks across the room to the bed. Gentleness exudes from her.* BETTY *is quietly whimpering, eyes shut.* REBECCA *simply stands over the child, who gradually quiets.*)

And while they are so absorbed, we may put a word in for Rebecca. Rebecca was the wife of Francis Nurse, who, from all accounts, was one of those men for whom both sides of the argument had to have respect. He was called upon to arbitrate disputes as though he were an unofficial judge, and Rebecca also enjoyed the high opinion most people had for him. By the time of the delusion, they had three hundred acres, and their children were settled in separate homesteads within the same estate. However, Francis had originally rented the land, and one theory has it that, as he gradually paid for it and raised his social status, there were those who resented his rise.

Another suggestion to explain the systematic campaign against Rebecca, and inferentially against Francis, is the land war he fought with his neighbors, one of whom was a Putnam. This squabble grew to the proportions of a battle in the woods between partisans of both sides, and it is said to have lasted for two days. As for Rebecca herself, the general opinion of her character was so high that to explain how anyone dared cry her out for a witch—and more, how adults could bring themselves to lay hands on her—we must look to the fields and boundaries of that time.

As we have seen, Thomas Putnam's man for the Salem ministry was Bayley. The Nurse clan had been in the faction that prevented Bayley's taking office. In addition, certain families allied to the Nurses by blood or friendship, and whose farms were contiguous with the Nurse farm or close to it, combined to break away from the Salem town authority and set up Topsfield, a new and independent entity whose existence was resented by old Salemites.

That the guiding hand behind the outcry was Putnam's is indicated by the fact that, as soon as it began, this Topsfield-Nurse faction absented themselves from church in protest and disbelief. It was Edward and Jonathan Putnam who signed the first complaint against Rebecca; and Thomas Putnam's little daughter was the one who fell into a fit at the hearing and pointed to Rebecca as her attacker. To top it all, Mrs. Putnam—who is now staring at the bewitched child on the bed—soon accused Rebecca's spirit of "tempting her to iniquity," a charge that had more truth in it than Mrs. Putnam could know.

MRS. PUTNAM (*astonished*). What have you done? (REBECCA, *in thought, now leaves the bedside and sits.*)

PARRIS (*wondrous and relieved*). What do you make of it, Rebecca?

PUTNAM (*eagerly*). Goody Nurse, will you go to my Ruth and see if you can wake her?

REBECCA (*sitting*). I think she'll wake in time. Pray calm yourselves. I have eleven children, and I am twenty-six times a grandma, and I have seen them all through their silly seasons, and when it come on them they will run the Devil bowlegged keeping up with their mischief. I think she'll wake when she tires of it. A child's spirit is like a child, you can never catch it by running after it; you must stand still, and, for love, it will soon itself come back.

PROCTOR. Aye, that's the truth of it, Rebecca.

MRS. PUTNAM. This is no silly season, Rebecca. My Ruth is bewildered, Rebecca; she cannot eat.

REBECCA. Perhaps she is not hungered yet. (*To* PARRIS.) I hope you are not decided to go in search of loose spirits, Mr. Parris. I've heard promise of that outside.

PARRIS. A wide opinion's running in the parish that the Devil may be among us, and I would satisfy them that they are wrong.

PROCTOR. Then let you come out and call them wrong. Did you consult the wardens before you called this minister to look for devils?

PARRIS. He is not coming to look for devils!

PROCTOR. Then what's he coming for?

PUTNAM. There be children dyin' in the village, Mister!

PROCTOR. I seen none dyin'. This society will not be a bag to swing around your head, Mr. Putnam. (*To* PARRIS.) Did you call a meeting before you—?

PUTNAM. I am sick of meetings; cannot the man turn his head without he have a meeting?

PROCTOR. He may turn his head, but not to Hell!

REBECCA. Pray, John, be calm. (*Pause. He defers to her.*) Mr. Parris, I think you'd best send Reverend Hale back as soon as he come. This will set us all to arguin' again in the society, and we thought to have peace this year. I think we ought rely on the doctor now, and good prayer.

MRS. PUTNAM. Rebecca, the doctor's baffled!

REBECCA. If so he is, then let us go to God for the cause of it. There is prodigious danger in the seeking of loose spirits. I fear it, I fear it. Let us rather blame ourselves and—

PUTNAM. How may we blame ourselves? I am one of nine sons; the Putnam seed have peopled this province. And yet I have but one child left of eight—and now she shrivels!

REBECCA. I cannot fathom that.

MRS. PUTNAM (*with a growing edge of sarcasm*). But I must! You think it God's work you should never lose a child, nor grandchild either, and I bury all but one? There are wheels within wheels in this village, and fires within fires!

PUTNAM (*to* PARRIS). When Reverend Hale comes, you will proceed to look for signs of witchcraft here.

PROCTOR (*to* PUTNAM). You cannot command Mr. Parris. We vote by name in this society, not by acreage.

PUTNAM. I never heard you worried so on this society, Mr. Proctor. I do not think I saw you at Sabbath meeting since snow flew.

PROCTOR. I have trouble enough without I come five mile to hear him preach only hellfire and bloody damnation. Take it to heart, Mr. Parris. There are many others who stay away from church these days because you hardly ever mention God any more.

PARRIS (*now aroused*). Why, that's a drastic charge!

REBECCA. It's somewhat true; there are many that quail to bring their children—

PARRIS. I do not preach for children, Rebecca. It is not the children who are unmindful of their obligations toward this ministry.

REBECCA. Are there really those unmindful?

PARRIS. I should say the better half of Salem village—

PUTNAM. And more than that!

PARRIS. Where is my wood? My contract provides I be supplied with all my firewood. I am waiting since November for a stick, and even in November I had to show my frostbitten hands like some London beggar!

GILES. You are allowed six pound a year to buy your wood, Mr. Parris.

PARRIS. I regard that six pound as part of my salary. I am paid little enough without I spend six pound on firewood.

PROCTOR. Sixty, plus six for firewood—

PARRIS. The salary is sixty-six pound, Mr. Proctor! I am not some preaching farmer with a book under my arm; I am a graduate of Harvard College.

GILES. Aye, and well instructed in arithmetic!

PARRIS. Mr. Corey, you will look far for a man of my kind at sixty pound a year! I am not used to this poverty; I left a thrifty business in the Barbados to serve the Lord. I do not fathom it, why am I persecuted here? I cannot offer one proposition but there be a howling riot of argument. I have often wondered if the Devil be in it somewhere; I cannot understand you people otherwise.

PROCTOR. Mr. Parris, you are the first minister ever did demand the deed to this house—

PARRIS. Man! Don't a minister deserve a house to live in?

PROCTOR. To live in, yes. But to ask ownership is like you shall own the meeting house itself; the last meeting I were at you spoke so long on deeds and mortgages I thought it were an auction.

PARRIS. I want a mark of confidence, is all! I am your third preacher in seven years. I do not wish to be put out like the cat whenever some majority feels the whim. You people seem not to comprehend that a minister is the Lord's man in the parish; a minister is not to be so lightly crossed and contradicted—

PUTNAM. Aye!

PARRIS. There is either obedience or the church will burn like Hell is burning!

PROCTOR. Can you speak one minute without we land in Hell again? I am sick of Hell!

PARRIS. It is not for you to say what is good for you to hear!

PROCTOR. I may speak my heart, I think!

PARRIS (in a fury). What, are we Quakers? We are not Quakers here yet, Mr. Proctor. And you may tell that to your followers!

PROCTOR. My followers!

PARRIS (now he's out with it). There is a party in this church. I am not blind; there is a faction and a party.

PROCTOR. Against you?

PUTNAM. Against him and all authority!

PROCTOR. Why, then I must find it and join it. (There is shock among the others.)

REBECCA. He does not mean that.

PUTNAM. He confessed it now!

PROCTOR. I mean it solemnly, Rebecca; I like not the smell of this "authority."

REBECCA. No, you cannot break charity with your minister. You are another kind, John. Clasp his hand, make your peace.

PROCTOR. I have a crop to sow and lumber to drag home. (He goes angrily to the door and turns to COREY with a smile.) What say you, Giles, let's find the party. He says there's a party.

GILES. I've changed my opinion of this man, John. Mr. Parris, I beg your pardon. I never thought you had so much iron in you.

PARRIS (surprised). Why, thank you, Giles!

GILES. It suggests to the mind what the trouble be among us all these years. (To all.) Think on it. Wherefore is everybody suing everybody else? Think on it now, it's a deep thing, and dark as a pit. I have been six time in court this year—

PROCTOR (familiarly, with warmth, although he knows he is approaching the edge of GILES' tolerance with this). Is it the Devil's fault that a man cannot say you good morning without you clap him for defamation? You're old, Giles, and you're not hearin' so well as you did.

GILES (he cannot be crossed). John Proctor, I have only last month collected four pound damages for you publicly sayin' I burned the roof off your house, and I—

PROCTOR (laughing). I never said no such thing, but I've paid you for it, so I hope I can call you deaf without charge. Now come along, Giles, and help me drag my lumber home.

PUTNAM. A moment, Mr. Proctor. What lumber is that you're draggin', if I may ask you?

PROCTOR. My lumber. From out my forest by the riverside.

PUTNAM. Why, we are surely gone wild this year. What anarchy is this? That tract is in my bounds, it's in my bounds, Mr. Proctor.

PROCTOR. In your bounds! (Indicating REBECCA.) I bought that tract from Goody Nurse's husband five months ago.

PUTNAM. He had no right to sell it. It stands clear in my grandfather's will that all the land between the river and—

PROCTOR. Your grandfather had a habit of willing land that never belonged to him, if I may say it plain.

GILES. That's God's truth; he nearly willed away my north pasture but he knew I'd break his fingers before he'd set his name to it. Let's get your lumber home, John. I feel a sudden will to work coming on.

PUTNAM. You load one oak of mine and you'll fight to drag it home!

GILES. Aye, and we'll win too, Putnam—this fool and I. Come on! (He turns to PROCTOR and starts out.)

PUTNAM. I'll have my men on you, Corey! I'll clap a writ on you! (*Enter* REVEREND JOHN HALE *of Beverly.*)

Mr. Hale is nearing forty, a tight-skinned, eager-eyed intellectual. This is a beloved errand for him; on being called here to ascertain witchcraft he felt the pride of the specialist whose unique knowledge has at last been publicly called for. Like almost all men of learning, he spent a good deal of his time pondering the invisible world, especially since he had himself encountered a witch in his parish not long before. That woman, however, turned into a mere pest under his searching scrutiny, and the child she had allegedly been afflicting recovered her normal behavior after Hale had given her his kindness and a few days of rest in his own house. However, that experience never raised a doubt in his mind as to the reality of the underworld or the existence of Lucifer's many-faced lieutenants. And his belief is not to his discredit. Better minds than Hale's were—and still are—convinced that there is a society of spirits beyond our ken. One cannot help noting that one of his lines has never yet raised a laugh in any audience that has seen this play; it is his assurance that "We cannot look to superstition in this. The Devil is precise." Evidently we are not quite certain even now whether diabolism is holy and not to be scoffed at. And it is no accident that we should be so bemused.

Like Reverend Hale and the others on this stage, we conceive the Devil as a necessary part of a respectable view of cosmology. Ours is a divided empire in which certain ideas and emotions and actions are of God, and their opposites are of Lucifer. It is as impossible for most men to conceive of a morality without sin as of an earth without "sky." Since 1692 a great but superficial change has wiped out God's beard and the Devil's horns, but the world is still gripped between two diametrically opposed absolutes. The concept of unity, in which positive and negative are attributes of the same force, in which good and evil are relative, ever-changing, and always joined to the same phenomenon —such a concept is still reserved to the physical sciences and to the few who have grasped the history of ideas. When it is recalled that until the Christian era the underworld was never regarded as a hostile area, that all gods were useful and essentially friendly to man despite occasional lapses; when we see the steady and methodical inculcation into humanity of the idea of man's worthlessness— until redeemed—the necessity of the Devil may become evident as a weapon, a weapon designed and used time and time again in every age to whip men into a surrender to a particular church or church-state.

Our difficulty in believing the—for want of a better word—political inspiration of the Devil is due in great part to the fact that he is called up and damned not only by our social antagonists but by our own side, whatever it may be. The Catholic Church, through its Inquisition, is famous for cultivating Lucifer as the arch-fiend, but the Church's enemies relied no less upon the Old Boy to keep the human mind enthralled. Luther was himself accused of alliance with Hell, and he in turn accused his enemies. To complicate matters further, he believed that he had had contact with the Devil and had argued theology with him. I am not surprised at this, for at my own university a professor of history —a Lutheran, by the way—used to assemble his graduate students, draw the shades, and commune in the classroom with Erasmus. He was never, to my knowledge, officially scoffed at for this, the reason being that the university officials, like most of us, are the children of a history which still sucks at the Devil's teats. At this writing, only England has held back before the temptations of contemporary diabolism. In the countries of the Communist ideology, all resistance of any import is linked to the totally malign capitalist succubi, and in America any man who is not reactionary in his views is open to the charge of alliance with the Red hell. Political opposition, thereby, is given an inhumane overlay which then justifies the abrogation of all normally applied customs of civilized intercourse. A political policy is equated with moral right, and opposition to it with diabolical malevolence. Once such an equation is effectively made, society becomes a congerie of plots and counterplots, and the main role of government changes from that of the arbiter to that of the scourge of God.

The results of this process are no different now from what they ever were, except sometimes in the degree of cruelty inflicted, and not always even in that department. Normally the actions and deeds of a man were all that society felt comfortable in judging. The secret intent of an action was left to the ministers, priests, and rabbis to deal with. When diabolism rises, however, actions are the least important manifests of the true nature of a man. The Devil, as Reverend Hale said, is a wily one, and, until an hour before he fell, even God thought him beautiful in Heaven.

The analogy, however, seems to falter when one considers that, while there were no witches then, there are Communists and capitalists now, and in each camp there is certain proof that spies of each side are at work undermining the other. But this is a snobbish objection and not at all warranted by the facts. I have no doubt that people *were* communing with, and even worshiping, the Devil in Salem, and if the whole truth could be known in this case, as it is in others, we should discover a regular and conventionalized propitiation of the dark spirit. One certain evidence of this is the confession of Tituba, the slave of Reverend Parris, and another is the behavior of the children who were known to have indulged in sorceries with her.

There are accounts of similar *klatches* in Europe, where the daughters of the towns would assemble at night and, sometimes with fetishes, sometimes with a selected young man, give themselves to love, with some bastardly results. The Church, sharp-eyed as it must be when gods long dead are brought to life, condemned these orgies as witchcraft and interpreted them, rightly, as a resurgence of the Dionysiac forces it had crushed long before. Sex, sin, and the Devil were early linked, and so they continued to be in Salem, and are today. From all accounts there are no more puritanical mores in the world than those enforced by the Communists in Russia, where women's fashions, for instance, are as prudent and all-covering as any American Baptist would desire. The divorce laws lay a tremendous responsibility on the father for the care of his children. Even the laxity of divorce regulations in the early years of the revolution was undoubtedly a revulsion from the nineteenth-century Victorian immobility of marriage and the consequent hypocrisy that developed from it. If for no other reasons, a state so powerful, so jealous of the uniformity of its citizens, cannot long tolerate the atomization of the family. And yet, in American eyes at least, there remains the conviction that the Russian attitude toward women is lascivious. It is the Devil working again, just as he is working within the Slav who is shocked at the very idea of a woman's disrobing herself in a burlesque show. Our opposites are always robed in sexual sin, and it is from this unconscious conviction that demonology gains both its attractive sensuality and its capacity to infuriate and frighten.

Coming into Salem now, Reverend Hale conceives of himself much as a young doctor on his first call. His painfully acquired armory of symptoms, catchwords, and diagnostic procedures are now to be put to use at last. The road from Beverly is unusually busy this morning, and he has passed a hundred rumors that make him smile at the ignorance of the yeomanry in this most precise science. He feels himself allied with the best minds of Europe—kings, philosophers, scientists, and ecclesiasts of all churches. His goal is light, goodness and its preservation, and he knows the exaltation of the blessed whose intelligence, sharpened by minute examinations of enormous tracts, is finally called upon to face what may be a bloody fight with the Fiend himself.

(*He appears loaded down with half a dozen heavy books.*)

HALE. Pray you, someone take these!

PARRIS (*delighted*). Mr. Hale! Oh! It's good to see you again! (*Taking some books.*) My, they're heavy!

HALE (*setting down his books*). They must be; they are weighted with authority.

PARRIS (*a little scared*). Well, you do come prepared!

HALE. We shall need hard study if it comes to tracking down the Old Boy. (*Noticing* REBECCA.) You cannot be Rebecca Nurse?

REBECCA. I am, sir. Do you know me?

HALE. It's strange how I knew you, but I suppose you look as such a good soul should. We have all heard of your great charities in Beverly.

PARRIS. Do you know this gentleman? Mr. Thomas Putnam. And his good wife Ann.

HALE. Putnam! I had not expected such distinguished company, sir.

PUTNAM (*pleased*). It does not seem to help us today, Mr. Hale. We look to you to come to our house and save our child.

HALE. Your child ails too?

MRS. PUTNAM. Her soul, her soul seems flown away. She sleeps and yet she walks . . .

PUTNAM. She cannot eat.

HALE. Cannot eat! (*Thinks on it. Then, to* PROCTOR *and* GILES COREY.) Do you men have afflicted children?

PARRIS. No, no, these are farmers. John Proctor—

GILES COREY. He don't believe in witches.

PROCTOR (*to* HALE). I never spoke on witches one way or the other. Will you come, Giles?

GILES. No—no, John, I think not. I have some few queer questions of my own to ask this fellow.

PROCTOR. I've heard you to be a sensible man, Mr. Hale. I hope you'll leave some of it in Salem. (PROCTOR *goes.* HALE *stands embarrassed for an instant.*)

PARRIS (*quickly*). Will you look at my daughter, sir? (*Leads* HALE *to the bed.*) She has tried to leap out the window; we discovered her this morning on the highroad, waving her arms as though she'd fly.

HALE (*narrowing his eyes*). Tries to fly.

PUTNAM. She cannot bear to hear the Lord's name, Mr. Hale; that's a sure sign of witchcraft afloat.

HALE (*holding up his hands*). No, no. Now let me instruct you. We cannot look to superstition in this. The Devil is precise; the marks of his presence are definite as stone, and I must tell you all that I shall not proceed unless you are prepared to believe me if I should find no bruise of hell upon her.

PARRIS. It is agreed, sir—it is agreed—we will abide by your judgment.

HALE. Good then. (*He goes to the bed, looks down at* BETTY. *To* PARRIS.) Now, sir, what were your first warning of this strangeness?

PARRIS. Why, sir—I discovered her— (*indicating* ABIGAIL.) and my niece and ten or twelve of the other girls, dancing in the forest last night.

HALE (*surprised*). You permit dancing?

PARRIS. No, no, it were secret—

MRS. PUTNAM (*unable to wait*). Mr. Parris's slave has knowledge of conjurin', sir.

PARRIS (*to* MRS. PUTNAM). We cannot be sure of that, Goody Ann—

MRS. PUTNAM (*frightened, very softly*). I know it, sir. I sent my child— she should learn from Tituba who murdered her sisters.

REBECCA (*horrified*). Goody Ann! You sent a child to conjure up the dead?

MRS. PUTNAM. Let God blame me, not you, not you, Rebecca! I'll not have you judging me any more! (*To* HALE.) Is it a natural work to lose seven children before they live a day?

PARRIS. Sssh! (REBECCA, *with great*

pain, turns her face away. There is a pause.)

HALE. Seven dead in childbirth.

MRS. PUTNAM (*softly*). Aye. (*Her voice breaks; she looks up at him. Silence.* HALE *is impressed.* PARRIS *looks to him. He goes to his books, opens one, turns pages, then reads. All wait, avidly.*)

PARRIS (*hushed*). What book is that?

MRS. PUTNAM. What's there, sir?

HALE (*with a tasty love of intellectual pursuit*). Here is all the invisible world, caught, defined, and calculated. In these books the Devil stands stripped of all his brute disguises. Here are all your familiar spirits—your incubi and succubi; your witches that go by land, by air, and by sea; your wizards of the night and of the day. Have no fear now—we shall find him out if he has come among us, and I mean to crush him utterly if he has shown his face! (*He starts for the bed.*)

REBECCA. Will it hurt the child, sir?

HALE. I cannot tell. If she is truly in the Devil's grip we may have to rip and tear to get her free.

REBECCA. I think I'll go, then. I am too old for this. (*She rises.*)

PARRIS (*striving for conviction*). Why, Rebecca, we may open up the boil of all our troubles today!

REBECCA. Let us hope for that. I go to God for you, sir.

PARRIS (*with trepidation—and resentment*). I hope you do not mean we go to Satan here! (*Slight pause.*)

REBECCA. I wish I knew. (*She goes out; they feel resentful of her note of moral superiority.*)

PUTNAM (*abruptly*). Come, Mr. Hale, let's get on. Sit you here.

GILES. Mr. Hale, I have always wanted to ask a learned man—what signifies the readin' of strange books?

HALE. What books?

GILES. I cannot tell; she hides them.

HALE. Who does this?

GILES. Martha, my wife. I have waked at night many a time and found her in a corner, readin' of a book. Now what do you make of that?

HALE. Why, that's not necessarily—

GILES. It discomfits me! Last night —mark this—I tried and tried and could not say my prayers. And then she close her book and walks out of the house, and suddenly—mark this—I could pray again!

Old Giles must be spoken for, if only because his fate was to be so remarkable and so different from that of all the others. He was in his early eighties at this time, and was the most comical hero in the history. No man has ever been blamed for so much. If a cow was missed, the first thought was to look for her around Corey's house; a fire blazing up at night brought suspicion of arson to his door. He didn't give a hoot for public opinion, and only in his last years —after he had married Martha—did he bother much with the church. That she stopped his prayer is very probable, but he forgot to say that he'd only recently learned any prayers and it didn't take much to make him stumble over them. He was a crank and a nuisance, but withal a deeply innocent and brave man. In court, once, he was asked if it were true that he had been frightened by the strange behavior of a hog and had then said he knew it to be the Devil in an animal's shape. "What frighted you?" he was asked. He forgot everything but the word "frighted," and instantly replied, "I do not know that I ever spoke that word in my life."

HALE. Ah! The stoppage of prayer— that is strange. I'll speak further on that with you.

GILES. I'm not sayin' she's touched the Devil, now, but I'd admire to know what books she reads and why she hides them. She'll not answer me, y' see.

HALE. Aye, we'll discuss it. (*To all.*) Now mark me, if the Devil is in her you will witness some frightful wonders in this room, so please to keep your wits about you. Mr. Putnam, stand close in case she flies. Now, Betty, dear, will you sit up? (PUTNAM *comes in closer, ready-handed.* HALE *sits* BETTY *up, but she hangs limp in his hands.*) Hmmm. (*He observes her carefully. The others watch breathlessly.*) Can you hear me? I am John Hale, minister of Beverly. I have come to help you, dear. Do you remember my two little girls in Beverly? (*She does not stir in his hands.*)

PARRIS (*in fright*). How can it be the Devil? Why would he choose my house to strike? We have all manner of licentious people in the village!

HALE. What victory would the Devil have to win a soul already bad? It is the best the Devil wants, and who is better than the minister?

GILES. That's deep, Mr. Parris, deep, deep!

PARRIS (*with resolution now*). Betty! Answer Mr. Hale! Betty!

HALE. Does someone afflict you, child? It need not be a woman, mind you, or a man. Perhaps some bird invisible to others comes to you—perhaps a pig, a mouse, or any beast at all. Is there some figure bids you fly? (*The child remains limp in his hands. In silence he lays her back on the pillow. Now, holding out his hands toward her, he intones.*) In nomine Domini Sabaoth sui filiique ite ad infernos. (*She does not stir. He turns to* ABIGAIL, *his eyes narrowing.*) Abigail, what sort of dancing were you doing with her in the forest?

ABIGAIL. Why—common dancing is all.

PARRIS. I think I ought to say that I—I saw a kettle in the grass where they were dancing.

ABIGAIL. That were only soup.

HALE. What sort of soup were in this kettle, Abigail?

ABIGAIL. Why, it were beans—and lentils, I think, and—

HALE. Mr. Parris, you did not notice, did you, any living thing in the kettle? A mouse, perhaps, a spider, a frog—?

PARRIS (*fearfully*). I—do believe there were some movement—in the soup.

ABIGAIL. That jumped in, we never put it in!

HALE (*quickly*). What jumped in?

ABIGAIL. Why, a very little frog jumped—

PARRIS. A frog, Abby!

HALE (*grasping* ABIGAIL). Abigail, it may be your cousin is dying. Did you call the Devil last night?

ABIGAIL. I never called him! Tituba, Tituba . . .

PARRIS (*blanched*). She called the Devil?

HALE. I should like to speak with Tituba.

PARRIS. Goody Ann, will you bring her up? (MRS. PUTNAM *exits.*)

HALE. How did she call him?

ABIGAIL. I know not—she spoke Barbados.

HALE. Did you feel any strangeness when she called him? A sudden cold wind, perhaps? A trembling below the ground?

ABIGAIL. I didn't see no Devil! (*Shaking* BETTY.) Betty, wake up. Betty! Betty!

HALE. You cannot evade me, Abigail. Did your cousin drink any of the brew in that kettle?

ABIGAIL. She never drank it!

HALE. Did you drink it?

ABIGAIL. No, sir!

HALE. Did Tituba ask you to drink it?

ABIGAIL. She tried, but I refused.

HALE. Why are you concealing? Have you sold yourself to Lucifer?

ABIGAIL. I never sold myself! I'm a good girl! I'm a proper girl! (MRS. PUTNAM *enters with* TITUBA, *and instantly* ABIGAIL *points at* TITUBA.)

ABIGAIL. She made me do it! She made Betty do it!

TITUBA (*shocked and angry*). Abby!

ABIGAIL. She makes me drink blood!

PARRIS. Blood!!

MRS. PUTNAM. My baby's blood?

TITUBA. No, no, chicken blood. I give she chicken blood!

HALE. Woman, have you enlisted these children for the Devil?

TITUBA. No, no, sir, I don't truck with no Devil!

HALE. Why can she not wake? Are you silencing this child?

TITUBA. I love me Betty!

HALE. You have sent your spirit out

upon this child, have you not? Are you gathering souls for the Devil?

ABIGAIL. She sends her spirit on me in church; she makes me laugh at prayer!

PARRIS. She have often laughed at prayer!

ABIGAIL. She comes to me every night to go and drink blood!

TITUBA. You beg *me* to conjure! She beg *me* make charm—

ABIGAIL. Don't lie! (*To* HALE.) She comes to me while I sleep; she's always making me dream corruptions!

TITUBA. Why you say that, Abby?

ABIGAIL. Sometimes I wake and find myself standing in the open doorway and not a stitch on my body! I always hear her laughing in my sleep. I hear her singing her Barbados songs and tempting me with—

TITUBA. Mister Reverend, I never—

HALE (*resolved now*). Tituba, I want you to wake this child.

TITUBA. I have no power on this child, sir.

HALE. You most certainly do, and you will free her from it now! When did you compact with the Devil?

TITUBA. I don't compact with no Devil!

PARRIS. You will confess yourself or I will take you out and whip you to your death, Tituba!

PUTNAM. This woman must be hanged! She must be taken and hanged!

TITUBA (*terrified, falls to her knees*). No, no, don't hang Tituba! I tell him I don't desire to work for him, sir.

PARRIS. The Devil?

HALE. Then you saw him! (TITUBA *weeps*.) Now Tituba, I know that when we bind ourselves to Hell it is very hard to break with it. We are going to help you tear yourself free—

TITUBA (*frightened by the coming process*). Mister Reverend, I do believe somebody else be witchin' these children.

HALE. Who?

TITUBA. I don't know, sir, but the Devil got him numerous witches.

HALE. Does he! (*It is a clue.*) Tituba, look into my eyes. Come, look into me.

(*She raises her eyes to his fearfully.*) You would be a good Christian woman, would you not, Tituba?

TITUBA. Aye, sir, a good Christian woman.

HALE. And you love these little children?

TITUBA. Oh, yes, sir, I don't desire to hurt little children.

HALE. And you love God, Tituba?

TITUBA. I love God with all my bein'.

HALE. Now, in God's holy name—

TITUBA. Bless Him. Bless Him. (*She is rocking on her knees, sobbing in terror.*)

HALE. And to His glory—

TITUBA. Eternal glory. Bless Him—bless God . . .

HALE. Open yourself, Tituba—open yourself and let God's holy light shine on you.

TITUBA. Oh, bless the Lord.

HALE. When the Devil comes to you does he ever come—with another person? (*She stares up into his face.*) Perhaps another person in the village? Someone you know.

PARRIS. Who came with him?

PUTNAM. Sarah Good? Did you ever see Sarah Good with him? Or Osburn?

PARRIS. Was it man or woman came with him?

TITUBA. Man or woman. Was—was woman.

PARRIS. What woman? A woman, you said. What woman?

TITUBA. It was black dark, and I—

PARRIS. You could see him, why could you not see her?

TITUBA. Well, they was always talking; they was always runnin' round and carryin' on—

PARRIS. You mean out of Salem? Salem witches?

TITUBA. I believe so, yes, sir. (*Now* HALE *takes her hand. She is surprised.*)

HALE. Tituba. You must have no fear to tell us who they are, do you understand? We will protect you. The Devil can never overcome a minister. You know that, do you not?

TITUBA (*kisses* HALE'*s hand*). Aye, sir, oh, I do.

HALE. You have confessed yourself to witchcraft, and that speaks a wish to come to Heaven's side. And we will bless you, Tituba.

TITUBA (*deeply relieved*). Oh, God bless you, Mr. Hale!

HALE (*with rising exaltation*). You are God's instrument put in our hands to discover the Devil's agents among us. You are selected, Tituba, you are chosen to help us cleanse our village. So speak utterly, Tituba, turn your back on him and face God—face God, Tituba, and God will protect you.

TITUBA (*joining with him*). Oh, God, protect Tituba!

HALE (*kindly*). Who came to you with the Devil? Two? Three? Four? How many? (TITUBA *pants, and begins rocking back and forth again, staring ahead.*)

TITUBA. There was four. There was four.

PARRIS (*pressing in on her*). Who? Who? Their names, their names!

TITUBA (*suddenly bursting out*). Oh, how many times he bid me kill you, Mr. Parris!

PARRIS. Kill me!

TITUBA (*in a fury*). He say Mr. Parris must be kill! Mr. Parris no goodly man, Mr. Parris mean man and no gentle man, and he bid me rise out of my bed and cut your throat! (*They gasp.*) But I tell him "No! I don't hate that man. I don't want kill that man." But he say, "You work for me, Tituba, and I make you free! I give you pretty dress to wear, and put you way high up in the air, and you gone fly back to Barbados!" And I say, "You lie, Devil, you lie!" And then he come one stormy night to me, and he say, "Look! I have *white* people belong to me." And I look—and there was Goody Good.

PARRIS. Sarah Good!

TITUBA (*rocking and weeping*). Aye, sir, and Goody Osburn.

MRS. PUTNAM. I knew it! Goody Osburn were midwife to me three times. I begged you, Thomas, did I not? I begged him not to call Osborn because I feared her. My babies always shriveled in her hands!

HALE. Take courage, you must give us all their names. How can you bear to see this child suffering? Look at her, Tituba. (*He is indicating* BETTY *on the bed.*) Look at her God-given innocence; her soul is so tender; we must protect her, Tituba; the Devil is out and preying on her like a beast upon the flesh of the pure lamb. God will bless you for your help. (ABIGAIL *rises, staring as though inspired, and cries out.*)

ABIGAIL. I want to open myself! (*They turn to her, startled. She is enraptured, as though in a pearly light.*) I want the light of God, I want the sweet love of Jesus! I danced for the Devil; I saw him; I wrote in his book; I go back to Jesus; I kiss His hand. I saw Sarah Good with the Devil! I saw Goody Osburn with the Devil! I saw Bridget Bishop with the Devil! (*As she is speaking,* BETTY *is rising from the bed, a fever in her eyes, and picks up the chant.*)

BETTY (*staring too*). I saw George Jacobs with the Devil! I saw Goody Howe with the Devil!

PARRIS. She speaks! (*He rushes to embrace* BETTY.) She speaks!

HALE. Glory to God! It is broken, they are free!

BETTY (*calling out hysterically and with great relief*). I saw Martha Bellows with the Devil!

ABIGAIL. I saw Goody Sibber with the Devil! (*It is rising to a great glee.*)

PUTNAM. The marshal, I'll call the marshal! (PARRIS *is shouting a prayer of thanksgiving.*)

BETTY. I saw Alice Barrow with the Devil! (*The curtain begins to fall.*)

HALE (*as* PUTNAM *goes out*). Let the marshal bring irons!

ABIGAIL. I saw Goody Hawkins with the Devil!

BETTY. I saw Goody Bibber with the Devil!

ABIGAIL. I saw Goody Booth with the Devil! (*On their ecstatic cries*)

THE CURTAIN FALLS.

ACT TWO

The common room of Proctor's house,
eight days later. At the right is a door
opening on the fields outside. A fireplace
is at the left, and behind it a stairway
leading upstairs. It is the low, dark, and
rather long living room of the time. As
the curtain rises, the room is empty.
From above, ELIZABETH *is heard softly*
singing to the children. Presently the
door opens and JOHN PROCTOR *enters,*
carrying his gun. He glances about the
room as he comes toward the fireplace,
then halts for an instant as he hears her
singing. He continues on to the fireplace,
leans the gun against the wall as he
swings a pot out of the fire and smells
it. Then he lifts out the ladle and tastes.
He is not quite pleased. He reaches to a
cupboard, takes a pinch of salt, and drops
it into the pot. As he is tasting again, her
footsteps are heard on the stair. He
swings the pot into the fireplace and
goes to a basin and washes his hands and
face. ELIZABETH *enters.*

ELIZABETH. What keeps you so late?
It's almost dark.

PROCTOR. I were planting far out to the
forest edge.

ELIZABETH. Oh, you're done then.

PROCTOR. Aye, the farm is seeded. The
boys asleep?

ELIZABETH. They will be soon. (*And*
she goes to the fireplace, proceeds to
ladle up stew in a dish.)

PROCTOR. Pray now for a fair summer.

ELIZABETH. Aye.

PROCTOR. Are you well today?

ELIZABETH. I am. (*She brings the plate*
to the table, and, indicating the food.)
It is a rabbit.

PROCTOR (*going to the table*). Oh, is it!
In Jonathan's trap?

ELIZABETH. No, she walked into the
house this afternoon; I found her sittin'
in the corner like she come to visit.

PROCTOR. Oh, that's a good sign walkin'
in.

ELIZABETH. Pray God. It hurt my heart
to strip her, poor rabbit. (*She sits and*
watches him taste it.)

PROCTOR. It's well seasoned.

ELIZABETH (*blushing with pleasure*). I
took great care. She's tender?

PROCTOR. Aye. (*He eats. She watches*
him.) I think we'll see green fields soon.
It's warm as blood beneath the clods.

ELIZABETH. That's well. (PROCTOR *eats,*
then looks up.)

PROCTOR. If the crop is good I'll buy
George Jacob's heifer. How would that
please you?

ELIZABETH. Aye, it would.

PROCTOR (*with a grin*). I mean to
please you, Elizabeth.

ELIZABETH (*it is hard to say*). I know,
it, John. (*He gets up, goes to her, kisses*
her. She receives it. With a certain dis-
appointment, he returns to the table.)

PROCTOR (*as gently as he can*). Cider?

ELIZABETH (*with a sense of reprimand-*
ing herself for having forgot). Aye!
(*She gets up and goes and pours a glass*
for him. He now arches his back.)

PROCTOR. This farm's a continent when
you go foot by foot droppin' seeds in
it.

ELIZABETH (*coming with the cider*).
It must be.

PROCTOR (*drinks a long draught, then,*
putting the glass down). You ought to
bring some flowers in the house.

ELIZABETH. Oh! I forgot! I will tomorrow.

PROCTOR. It's winter in here yet. On
Sunday let you come with me, and we'll
walk the farm together; I never see such
a load of flowers on the earth. (*With*
good feeling he goes and looks up at the
sky through the open doorway.) Lilacs
have a purple smell. Lilac is the smell
of nightfall, I think. Massachusetts is a
beauty in the spring!

ELIZABETH. Aye, it is. (*There is a*
pause. She is watching him from the
table as he stands there absorbing the
night. It is as though she would speak
but cannot. Instead, now, she takes up
his plate and glass and fork and goes
with them to the basin. Her back is
turned to him. He turns to her and

watches her. A sense of their separation rises.)

PROCTOR. I think you're sad again. Are you?

ELIZABETH (*she doesn't want friction, and yet she must*). You come so late I thought you'd gone to Salem this afternoon.

PROCTOR. Why? I have no business in Salem.

ELIZABETH. You did speak of going, earlier this week.

PROCTOR (*he knows what she means*). I thought better of it since.

ELIZABETH. Mary Warren's there today.

PROCTOR. Why'd you let her? You heard me forbid her go to Salem any more!

ELIZABETH. I couldn't stop her.

PROCTOR (*holding back a full condemnation of her*). It is a fault, it is a fault, Elizabeth—you're the mistress here, not Mary Warren.

ELIZABETH. She frightened all my strength away.

PROCTOR. How may that mouse frighten you, Elizabeth? You—

ELIZABETH. It is a mouse no more. I forbid her go, and she raises up her chin like the daughter of a prince and says to me, "I must go to Salem, Goody Proctor; I am an official of the court!"

PROCTOR. Court! What court?

ELIZABETH. Aye, it is a proper court they have now. They've sent four judges out of Boston, she says, weighty magistrates of the General Court, and at the head sits the Deputy Governor of the Province.

PROCTOR (*astonished*). Why, she's mad.

ELIZABETH. I would to God she were. There be fourteen people in the jail now, she says. (PROCTOR *simply looks at her, unable to grasp it.*) And they'll be tried, and the court have power to hang them too, she says.

PROCTOR (*scoffing, but without conviction*). Ah, they'd never hang—

ELIZABETH. The Deputy Governor promise hangin' if they'll not confess, John. The town's gone wild, I think.

She speak of Abigail, and I thought she were a saint, to hear her. Abigail brings the other girls into the court, and where she walks the crowd will part like the sea for Israel. And folks are brought before them, and if they scream and howl and fall to the floor—the person's clapped in the jail for bewitchin' them.

PROCTOR (*wide-eyed*). Oh, it is a black mischief.

ELIZABETH. I think you must go to Salem, John. (*He turns to her.*) I think so. You must tell them it is a fraud.

PROCTOR (*thinking beyond this*). Aye, it is, it is surely.

ELIZABETH. Let you go to Ezekiel Cheever—he knows you well. And tell him what she said to you last week in her uncle's house. She said it had naught to do with witchcraft, did she not?

PROCTOR (*in thought*). Aye, she did, she did. (*Now, a pause.*)

ELIZABETH (*quietly, fearing to anger him by prodding*). God forbid you keep that from the court, John. I think they must be told.

PROCTOR (*quietly, struggling with his thought*). Aye, they must, they must. It is a wonder they do believe her.

ELIZABETH. I would go to Salem now, John—let you go tonight.

PROCTOR. I'll think on it.

ELIZABETH (*with her courage now*). You cannot keep it, John.

PROCTOR (*angering*). I know I cannot keep it. I say I will think on it!

ELIZABETH (*hurt, and very coldly*). Good, then, let you think on it. (*She stands and starts to walk out of the room.*)

PROCTOR. I am only wondering how I may prove what she told me, Elizabeth. If the girl's a saint now, I think it is not easy to prove she's fraud, and the town gone so silly. She told it to me in a room alone—I have no proof for it.

ELIZABETH. You were alone with her?

PROCTOR (*stubbornly*). For a moment alone, aye.

ELIZABETH. Why, then, it is not as you told me.

PROCTOR (*his anger rising*). For a moment, I say. The others come in soon after.

ELIZABETH (*quietly—she has suddenly lost all faith in him*). Do as you wish, then. (*She starts to turn.*)

PROCTOR. Woman. (*She turns to him.*) I'll not have your suspicion any more.

ELIZABETH (*a little loftily*). I have no—

PROCTOR. I'll not have it!

ELIZABETH. Then let you not earn it.

PROCTOR (*with a violent undertone*). You doubt me yet?

ELIZABETH (*with a smile, to keep her dignity*). John, if it were not Abigail that you must go to hurt, would you falter now? I think not.

PROCTOR. Now look you—

ELIZABETH. I see what I see, John.

PROCTOR (*with solemn warning*). You will not judge me more, Elizabeth. I have good reason to think before I charge fraud on Abigail, and I will think on it. Let you look to your own improvement before you go to judge your husband any more. I have forgot Abigail, and—

ELIZABETH. And I.

PROCTOR. Spare me! You forget nothin' and forgive nothin'. Learn charity, woman. I have gone tiptoe in this house all seven month since she is gone. I have not moved from there to there without I think to please you, and still an everlasting funeral marches round your heart. I cannot speak but I am doubted, every moment judged for lies, as though I come into a court when I come into this house!

ELIZABETH. John, you are not open with me. You saw her with a crowd, you said. Now you—

PROCTOR. I'll plead my honesty no more, Elizabeth.

ELIZABETH (*now she would justify herself*). John, I am only—

PROCTOR. No more! I should have roared you down when first you told me your suspicion. But I wilted, and, like a Christian, I confessed. Confessed! Some dream I had must have mistaken you for God that day. But you're not, you're not, and let you remember it!

Let you look sometimes for the goodness in me, and judge me not.

ELIZABETH. I do not judge you. The magistrate sits in your heart that judges you. I never thought you but a good man, John (*With a smile.*) only somewhat bewildered.

PROCTOR (*laughing bitterly*). Oh, Elizabeth, your justice would freeze beer! (*He turns suddenly toward a sound outside. He starts for the door as MARY WARREN enters. As soon as he sees her, he goes directly to her and grabs her by her cloak, furious.*) How do you go to Salem when I forbid it? Do you mock me? (*Shaking her.*) I'll whip you if you dare leave this house again! (*Strangely, she doesn't resist him, but hangs limply by his grip.*)

MARY WARREN. I am sick, I am sick, Mr. Proctor. Pray, pray, hurt me not. (*Her strangeness throws him off, and her evident pallor and weakness. He frees her.*) My insides are all shuddery; I am in the proceedings all day, sir.

PROCTOR (*with draining anger—his curiosity is draining it*). And what of these proceedings here? When will you proceed to keep this house, as you are paid nine pound a year to do—and my wife not wholly well? (*As though to compensate, MARY WARREN goes to ELIZABETH with a small rag doll.*)

MARY WARREN. I made a gift for you today, Goody Proctor. I had to sit long hours in a chair, and passed the time with sewing.

ELIZABETH (*perplexed, looking at the doll*). Why, thank you, it's a fair poppet.

MARY WARREN (*with a trembling, decayed voice*). We must all love each other now, Goody Proctor.

ELIZABETH (*amazed at her strangeness*). Aye, indeed we must.

MARY WARREN (*glancing at the room*). I'll get up early in the morning and clean the house. I must sleep now. (*She turns and starts off.*)

PROCTOR. Mary. (*She halts.*) Is it true? There be fourteen women arrested?

MARY WARREN. No, sir. There be thirty-nine now— (*She suddenly breaks off and sobs and sits down, exhausted.*)

ELIZABETH. Why, she's weepin'! What ails you, child?

MARY WARREN. Goody Osburn—will hang! (*There is a shocked pause, while she sobs.*)

PROCTOR. Hang! (*He calls into her face.*) Hang, y'say?

MARY WARREN (*through her weeping*). Aye.

PROCTOR. The Deputy Governor will permit it?

MARY WARREN. He sentenced her. He must. (*To ameliorate it.*) But not Sarah Good. For Sarah Good confessed, y'see.

PROCTOR. Confessed! To what?

MARY WARREN. That she—(*In horror at the memory.*) she sometimes made a compact with Lucifer, and wrote her name in his black book—with her blood —and bound herself to torment Christians till God's thrown down—and we all must worship Hell forevermore. (*Pause.*)

PROCTOR. But—surely you know what a jabberer she is. Did you tell them that?

MARY WARREN. Mr. Proctor, in open court she near to choked us all to death.

PROCTOR. How, choked you?

MARY WARREN. She sent her spirit out.

ELIZABETH. Oh, Mary, Mary, surely you—

MARY WARREN (*with an indignant edge*). She tried to kill me many times, Goody Proctor!

ELIZABETH. Why, I never heard you mention that before.

MARY WARREN. I never knew it before. I never knew anything before. When she come into the court I say to myself, I must not accuse this woman, for she sleep in ditches, and so very old and poor. But then—then she sit there, denying and denying, and I feel a misty coldness climbin' up my back, and the skin on my skull begin to creep, and I feel a clamp around my neck and I cannot breathe air; and then (*Entranced.*) I hear a voice, a screamin' voice, and it were my voice—and all at once I remembered everything she done to me!

PROCTOR. Why? What did she do to you?

MARY WARREN (*like one awakened to a marvelous secret insight*). So many time, Mr. Proctor, she come to this very door, beggin' bread and a cup of cider —and mark this: whenever I turned her away empty, she *mumbled*.

ELIZABETH. Mumbled! She may mumble if she's hungry.

MARY WARREN. But *what* does she mumble? You must remember, Goody Proctor. Last month—a Monday, I think —she walked away, and I thought my guts would burst for two days after. Do you remember it?

ELIZABETH. Why—I do, I think, but—

MARY WARREN. And so I told that to Judge Hathorne, and he asks her so. "Goody Osburn," says he, "what curse do you mumble that this girl must fall sick after turning you away?" And then she replies (*Mimicking an old crone.*) "Why, your excellence, no curse at all. I only say my commandments; I hope I may say my commandments," says she!

ELIZABETH. And that's an upright answer.

MARY WARREN. Aye, but then Judge Hathorne say, "Recite for us your commandments!" (*Leaning avidly toward them.*) and of all the ten she could not say a single one. She never knew no commandments, and they had her in a flat lie!

PROCTOR. And so condemned her?

MARY WARREN (*now a little strained, seeing his stubborn doubt*). Why, they must when she condemned herself.

PROCTOR. But the proof, the proof!

MARY WARREN (*with greater impatience with him*). I told you the proof. It's hard proof, hard as rock, the judges said.

PROCTOR (*pauses an instant, then*). You will not go to court again, Mary Warren.

MARY WARREN. I must tell you, sir, I will be gone every day now. I am amazed you do not see what weighty work we do.

PROCTOR. What work you do! It's

strange work for a Christian girl to hang old women!

MARY WARREN. But, Mr. Proctor, they will not hang them if they confess. Sarah Good will only sit in jail some time (*Recalling.*) and here's a wonder for you; think on this. Goody Good is pregnant!

ELIZABETH. Pregnant! Are they mad? The woman's near to sixty!

MARY WARREN. They had Doctor Griggs examine her, and she's full to the brim. And smokin' a pipe all these years, and no husband either! But she's safe, thank God, for they'll not hurt the innocent child. But be that not a marvel? You must see it, sir, it's God's work we do. So I'll be gone every day for some time. I'm—I am an official of the court, they say, and I— (*She has been edging toward offstage.*)

PROCTOR. I'll official you! (*He strides to the mantel, takes down the whip hanging there.*)

MARY WARREN (*terrified, but coming erect, striving for her authority*). I'll not stand whipping any more!

ELIZABETH (*hurriedly, as* PROCTOR *approaches*). Mary, promise now you'll stay at home—

MARY WARREN (*backing from him, but keeping her erect posture, striving, striving for her way*). The Devil's loose in Salem, Mr. Proctor; we must discover where he's hiding!

PROCTOR. I'll whip the Devil out of you! (*With whip raised he reaches out for her, and she streaks away and yells.*)

MARY WARREN (*pointing at* ELIZABETH). I saved her life today! (*Silence. His whip comes down.*)

ELIZABETH (*softly*). I am accused?

MARY WARREN (*quaking*). Somewhat mentioned. But I said I never see no sign you ever sent your spirit out to hurt no one, and seeing I do live so closely with you, they dismissed it.

ELIZABETH. Who accused me?

MARY WARREN. I am bound by law, I cannot tell it. (*To* PROCTOR.) I only hope you'll not be so sarcastical no more. Four judges and the King's deputy sat to dinner with us but an hour ago. I—I would have you speak civilly to me, from this out.

PROCTOR (*in horror, muttering in disgust at her*). Go to bed.

MARY WARREN (*with a stamp of her foot*). I'll not be ordered to bed no more, Mr. Proctor! I am eighteen and a woman, however single!

PROCTOR. Do you wish to sit up? Then sit up.

MARY WARREN. I wish to go to bed!

PROCTOR (*in anger*). Good night, then!

MARY WARREN. Good night. (*Dissatisfied, uncertain of herself, she goes out Wide-eyed, both,* PROCTOR *and* ELIZABETH *stand staring.*)

ELIZABETH (*quietly*). Oh, the noose, the noose is up!

PROCTOR. There'll be no noose.

ELIZABETH. She wants me dead. I knew all week it would come to this!

PROCTOR (*without conviction*). They dismissed it. You heard her say—

ELIZABETH. And what of tomorrow? She will cry me out until they take me!

PROCTOR. Sit you down.

ELIZABETH. She wants me dead, John, you know it!

PROCTOR. I say sit down! (*She sits, trembling. He speaks quietly, trying to keep his wits.*) Now we must be wise, Elizabeth.

ELIZABETH (*with sarcasm, and a sense of being lost*). Oh, indeed, indeed!

PROCTOR. Fear nothing. I'll find Ezekiel Cheever. I'll tell him she said it were all sport.

ELIZABETH. John, with so many in the jail, more than Cheever's help is needed now, I think. Would you favor me with this? Go to Abigail.

PROCTOR (*his soul hardening as he senses . . .*). What have I to say to Abigail?

ELIZABETH (*delicately*). John—grant me this. You have a faulty understanding of young girls. There is a promise made in any bed—

PROCTOR (*striving against his anger*). What promise!

ELIZABETH. Spoke or silent, a promise

is surely made. And she may dote on it now—I am sure she does—and thinks to kill me, then to take my place. (PROCTOR's *anger is rising; he cannot speak.*) It is her dearest hope, John, I know it. There be a thousand names; why does she call mine? There be a certain danger in calling such a name—I am no Goody Good that sleeps in ditches, nor Osburn, drunk and half-witted. She'd dare not call out such a farmer's wife but there be monstrous profit in it. She thinks to take my place, John.

PROCTOR. She cannot think it! (*He knows it is true.*)

ELIZABETH (*reasonably*). John, have you ever shown her somewhat of contempt? She cannot pass you in the church but you will blush—

PROCTOR. I may blush for my sin.

ELIZABETH. I think she sees another meaning in that blush.

PROCTOR. And what see you? What see you, Elizabeth?

ELIZABETH (*conceding*). I think you be somewhat ashamed, for I am there, and she so close.

PROCTOR. When will you know me, woman? Were I stone I would have cracked for shame this seven month!

ELIZABETH. Then go and tell her she's a whore. Whatever promise she may sense—break it, John, break it.

PROCTOR (*between his teeth*). Good, then. I'll go. (*He starts for his rifle.*)

ELIZABETH (*trembling, fearfully*). Oh, how unwillingly!

PROCTOR (*turning on her, rifle in hand*). I will curse her hotter than the oldest cinder in hell. But pray, begrudge me not my anger!

ELIZABETH. Your anger! I only ask you—

PROCTOR. Woman, am I so base? Do you truly think me base?

ELIZABETH. I never called you base.

PROCTOR. Then how do you charge me with such a promise? The promise that a stallion gives a mare I gave that girl!

ELIZABETH. Then why do you anger with me when I bid you break it?

PROCTOR. Because it speaks deceit, and

I am honest! But I'll plead no more! I see now your spirit twists around the single error of my life, and I will never tear it free!

ELIZABETH (*crying out*). You'll tear it free—when you come to know that I will be your only wife, or no wife at all! She has an arrow in you yet, John Proctor, and you know it well! (*Quite suddenly, as though from the air, a figure appears in the doorway. They start slightly. It is* MR. HALE. *He is different now—drawn a little, and there is a quality of deference, even of guilt about his manner now.*)

HALE. Good evening.

PROCTOR (*still in his shock*). Why, Mr. Hale! Good evening to you, sir. Come in, come in.

HALE (*to* ELIZABETH). I hope I do not startle you.

ELIZABETH. No, no, it's only that I heard no horse—

HALE. You are Goodwife Proctor.

PROCTOR. Aye; Elizabeth.

HALE (*nods, then*). I hope you're not off to bed yet.

PROCTOR (*setting down his gun*). No, no. (HALE *comes further into the room. And* PROCTOR, *to explain his nervousness.*) We are not used to visitors after dark, but you're welcome here. Will you sit down, sir?

HALE. I will. (*He sits.*) Let you sit, Goodwife Proctor. (*She does, never letting him out of her sight. There is a pause as* HALE *looks about the room.*)

PROCTOR (*to break the silence*). Will you drink cider, Mr. Hale?

HALE. No, it rebels my stomach; I have some further traveling yet tonight. Sit you down, sir. (PROCTOR *sits.*) I will not keep you long, but I have some business with you.

PROCTOR. Business of the court?

HALE. No—no, ⸺ come of my own, without the court's authority. Hear me. (*He wets his lips.*) I know not if you are aware, but your wife's name is—mentioned in the court.

PROCTOR. We know it, sir. Our Mary Warren told us. We are entirely amazed.

HALE. I am a stranger here, as you know. And in my ignorance I find it hard to draw a clear opinion of them that come accused before the court. And so this afternoon, and now tonight, I go from house to house—I come now from Rebecca Nurse's house and—

ELIZABETH (*shocked*). Rebecca's charged!

HALE. God forbid such a one be charged. She is, however—mentioned somewhat.

ELIZABETH (*with an attempt at a laugh*). You will never believe, I hope, that Rebecca trafficked with the Devil.

HALE. Woman, it is possible.

PROCTOR (*taken aback*). Surely you cannot think so.

HALE. This is a strange time, Mister. No man may longer doubt the powers of the dark are gathered in monstrous attack upon this village. There is too much evidence now to deny it. You will agree, sir?

PROCTOR (*evading*). I—have no knowledge in that line. But it's hard to think so pious a woman be secretly a Devil's bitch after seventy year of such good prayer.

HALE. Aye. But the Devil is a wily one, you cannot deny it. However, she is far from accused, and I know she will not be. (*Pause.*) I thought, sir, to put some questions as to the Christian character of this house, if you'll permit me.

PROCTOR (*coldly, resentful*). Why, we —have no fear of questions, sir.

HALE. Good, then. (*He makes himself more comfortable.*) In the book of record that Mr. Parris keeps, I note that you are rarely in the church on Sabbath Day.

PROCTOR. No, sir, you are mistaken.

HALE. Twenty-six time in seventeen month, sir. I must call that rare. Will you tell me why you are so absent?

PROCTOR. Mr. Hale, I never knew I must account to that man for I come to church or stay at home. My wife were sick this winter.

HALE. So I am told. But you, Mister, why could you not come alone?

PROCTOR. I surely did come when I could, and when I could not I prayed in this house.

HALE. Mr. Proctor, your house is not a church; your theology must tell you that.

PROCTOR. It does, sir, it does; and it tells me that a minister may pray to God without he have golden candlesticks upon the altar.

HALE. What golden candlesticks?

PROCTOR. Since we built the church there were pewter candlesticks upon the altar; Francis Nurse made them, y'know, and a sweeter hand never touched the metal. But Parris came, and for twenty week he preach nothin' but golden candlesticks until he had them. I labor the earth from dawn of day to blink of night, and I tell you true, when I look to heaven and see my money glaring at his elbows—it hurt my prayer, sir, it hurt my prayer. I think, sometimes, the man dreams cathedrals, not clapboard meetin' houses.

HALE (*thinks, then*). And yet, Mister, a Christian on Sabbath Day must be in church. (*Pause.*) Tell me—you have three children?

PROCTOR. Aye. Boys.

HALE. How comes it that only two are baptized?

PROCTOR (*starts to speak, then stops, then, as though unable to restrain this*). I like it not that Mr. Parris should lay his hand upon my baby. I see no light of God in that man. I'll not conceal it.

HALE. I must say it, Mr. Proctor; that is not for you to decide. The man's ordained, therefore the light of God is in him.

PROCTOR (*flushed with resentment but trying to smile*). What's your suspicion, Mr. Hale?

HALE. No, no, I have no—

PROCTOR. I nailed the roof upon the church, I hung the door—

HALE. Oh, did you! That's a good sign, then.

PROCTOR. It may be I have been too quick to bring the man to book, but you cannot think we ever desired the destruction of religion. I think that's in your mind, is it not?

HALE (*not altogether giving way*). I—have—there is a softness in your record, sir, a softness.

ELIZABETH. I think, maybe, we have been too hard with Mr. Parris. I think so. But sure we never loved the Devil here.

HALE (*nods, deliberating this. Then, with the voice of one administering a secret test*). Do you know your Commandments, Elizabeth?

ELIZABETH (*without hesitation, even eagerly*). I surely do. There be no mark of blame upon my life, Mr. Hale. I am a covenanted Christian woman.

HALE. And you, Mister?

PROCTOR (*a trifle unsteadily*). I—am sure I do, sir.

HALE (*glances at her open face, then at* JOHN, *then*). Let you repeat them, if you will.

PROCTOR. The Commandments.

HALE. Aye.

PROCTOR (*looking off, beginning to sweat*). Thou shalt not kill.

HALE. Aye.

PROCTOR (*counting on his fingers*). Thou shalt not steal. Thou shalt not covet thy neighbor's goods, nor make unto thee any graven image. Thou shalt not take the name of the Lord in vain; thou shalt have no other gods before me. (*With some hesitation.*) Thou shalt remember the Sabbath Day and keep it holy. (*Pause. Then.*) Thou shalt honor thy father and mother. Thou shalt not bear false witness. (*He is stuck. He counts back on his fingers, knowing one is missing.*) Thou shalt not make unto thee any graven image.

HALE. You have said that twice, sir.

PROCTOR (*lost*). Aye. (*He is flailing for it.*)

ELIZABETH (*delicately*). Adultery, John.

PROCTOR (*as though a secret arrow had pained his heart*). Aye. (*Trying to grin it away—to* HALE.) You see, sir, between the two of us we do know them all. (HALE *only looks at* PROCTOR, *deep in his attempt to define this man.* PROCTOR *grows more uneasy.*) I think it be a small fault.

HALE. Theology, sir, is a fortress; no crack in a fortress may be accounted small. (*He rises; he seems worried now. He paces a little, in deep thought.*)

PROCTOR. There be no love for Satan in this house, Mister.

HALE. I pray it, I pray it dearly. (*He looks to both of them, an attempt at a smile on his face, but his misgivings are clear.*) Well, then—I'll bid you good night.

ELIZABETH (*unable to restrain herself*). Mr. Hale. (*He turns.*) I do think you are suspecting me somewhat? Are you not?

HALE (*obviously disturbed—and evasive*). Goody Proctor, I do not judge you. My duty is to add what I may to the godly wisdom of the court. I pray you both good health and good fortune. (*To* JOHN.) Good night, sir. (*He starts out.*)

ELIZABETH (*with a note of desperation*). I think you must tell him, John.

HALE. What's that?

ELIZABETH (*restraining a call*). Will you tell him? (*Slight pause.* HALE *looks questioningly at* JOHN.)

PROCTOR (*with difficulty*). I—I have no witness and cannot prove it, except my word be taken. But I know the children's sickness had naught to do with witchcraft.

HALE (*stopped, struck*). Naught to do—?

PROCTOR. Mr. Parris discovered them sportin' in the woods. They were startled and took sick. (*Pause.*)

HALE. Who told you this?

PROCTOR (*hesitates, then*). Abigail Williams.

HALE. Abigail!

PROCTOR. Aye.

HALE (*his eyes wide*). Abigail Williams told you it had naught to do with witchcraft!

PROCTOR. She told me the day you came, sir.

HALE (*suspiciously*). Why—why did you keep this?

PROCTOR. I never knew until tonight that the world is gone daft with this nonsense.

HALE. Nonsense! Mister, I have myself examined Tituba, Sarah Good, and numerous others that have confessed to dealing with the Devil. They have *confessed* it.

PROCTOR. And why not, if they must hang for denyin' it? There are them that will swear to anything before they'll hang; have you never thought of that?

HALE. I have. I—I have indeed. (*It is his own suspicion, but he resists it. He glances at* ELIZABETH, *then at* JOHN.) And you—would you testify to this in court?

PROCTOR. I—had not reckoned with goin' into court. But if I must I will.

HALE. Do you falter here?

PROCTOR. I falter nothing, but I may wonder if my story will be credited in such a court. I do wonder on it, when such a steady-minded minister as you will suspicion such a woman that never lied, and cannot, and the world knows she cannot! I may falter somewhat, Mister; I am no fool.

HALE (*quietly—it has impressed him*). Proctor, let you open with me now, for I have a rumor that troubles me. It's said you hold no belief that there may even be witches in the world. Is that true, sir?

PROCTOR (*he knows this is critical, and is striving against his disgust with* HALE *and with himself for even answering*). I know not what I have said, I may have said it. I have wondered if there be witches in the world—although I cannot believe they come among us now.

HALE. Then you do not believe—

PROCTOR. I have no knowledge of it; the Bible speaks of witches, and I will not deny them.

HALE. And you, woman?

ELIZABETH. I—I cannot believe it.

HALE (*shocked*). You cannot!

PROCTOR. Elizabeth, you bewilder him!

ELIZABETH (*to* HALE). I cannot think the Devil may own a woman's soul, Mr. Hale, when she keeps an upright way, as I have. I am a good woman, I know it; and if you believe I may do only good work in the world, and yet be secretly bound to Satan, then I must tell you, sir, I do not believe it.

HALE. But, woman, you do believe there are witches in—

ELIZABETH. If you think that I am one, then I say there are none.

HALE. You surely do not fly against the Gospel, the Gospel—

PROCTOR. She believe in the Gospel, every word!

ELIZABETH. Question Abigail Williams about the Gospel, not myself! (HALE *stares at her.*)

PROCTOR. She do not mean to doubt the Gospel, sir, you cannot think it. This be a Christian house, sir, a Christian house.

HALE. God keep you both; let the third child be quickly baptized, and go you without fail each Sunday in to Sabbath prayer; and keep a solemn, quiet way among you. I think— (GILES COREY *appears in doorway.*)

GILES. John!

PROCTOR. Giles! What's the matter?

GILES. They take my wife. (FRANCIS NURSE *enters.*) And his Rebecca!

PROCTOR (*to* FRANCIS). Rebecca's in the *jail!*

FRANCIS. Aye, Cheever come and take her in his wagon. We've only now come from the jail, and they'll not even let us in to see them.

ELIZABETH. They've surely gone wild now, Mr. Hale!

FRANCIS (*going to* HALE). Reverend Hale! Can you not speak to the Deputy Governor? I'm sure he mistakes these people—

HALE. Pray calm yourself, Mr. Nurse.

FRANCIS. My wife is the very brick and mortar of the church, Mr. Hale (*Indicating* GILES.) and Martha Corey, there cannot be a woman closer yet to God than Martha.

HALE. How is Rebecca charged, Mr. Nurse?

FRANCIS (*with a mocking, half-hearted laugh*). For murder, she's charged! (*Mockingly quoting the warrant.*) "For the marvelous and supernatural murder of Goody Putnam's babies." What am I to do, Mr. Hale?

HALE (*turns from* FRANCIS, *deeply troubled, then*). Believe me, Mr. Nurse, if Rebecca Nurse be tainted, then nothing's left to stop the whole green world from burning. Let you rest upon the justice of the court; the court will send her home, I know it.

FRANCIS. You cannot mean she will be tried in court!

HALE (*pleading*). Nurse, though our hearts break, we cannot flinch; these are new times, sir. There is a misty plot afoot so subtle we should be criminal to cling to old respects and ancient friendships. I have seen too many frightful proofs in court—the Devil is alive in Salem, and we dare not quail to follow wherever the accusing finger points.

PROCTOR (*angered*). How may such a woman murder children?

HALE (*in great pain*). Man, remember, until an hour before the Devil fell, God thought him beautiful in Heaven.

GILES. I never said my wife were a witch, Mr. Hale; I only said she were reading books!

HALE. Mr. Corey, exactly what complaint were made on your wife?

GILES. That bloody mongrel Walcott charge her. Y'see, he buy a pig of my wife four or five year ago, and the pig died soon after. So he come dancin' in for his money back. So my Martha, she says to him, "Walcott, if you haven't the wit to feed a pig properly, you'll not live to own many," she says. Now he goes to court and claims that from that day to this he cannot keep a pig alive for more than four weeks because my Martha bewitch them with her books! (*Enter EZEKIEL CHEEVER. A shocked silence.*)

CHEEVER. Good evening to you, Proctor.

PROCTOR. Why, Mr. Cheever. Good evening.

CHEEVER. Good evening, all. Good evening, Mr. Hale.

PROCTOR. I hope you come not on business of the court.

CHEEVER. I do, Proctor, aye. I am clerk of the court now, y'know. (*Enter MARSHAL HERRICK, a man in his early thirties, who is somewhat shamefaced at the moment.*)

GILES. It's a pity, Ezekiel, that an honest tailor might have gone to Heaven must burn in Hell. You'll burn for this, do you know it?

CHEEVER. You know yourself I must do as I'm told. You surely know that, Giles. And I'd as lief you'd not be sending me to Hell. I like not the sound of it, I tell you; I like not the sound of it. (*He fears PROCTOR, but starts to reach inside his coat.*) Now believe me, Proctor, how heavy be the law, all its tonnage I do carry on my back tonight. (*He takes out a warrant.*) I have a warrant for your wife.

PROCTOR (*to HALE*). You said she were not charged!

HALE. I know nothin' of it. (*To CHEEVER.*) When were she charged?

CHEEVER. I am given sixteen warrant tonight, sir, and she is one.

PROCTOR. Who charged her?

CHEEVER. Why, Abigail Williams charge her.

PROCTOR. On what proof, what proof?

CHEEVER (*looking about the room*). Mr. Proctor, I have little time. The court bid me search your house, but I like not to search a house. So will you hand me any poppets that your wife may keep here?

PROCTOR. Poppets?

ELIZABETH. I never kept no poppets, not since I were a girl.

CHEEVER (*embarrassed, glancing toward the mantel where sits MARY WARREN's poppet*). I spy a poppet, Goody Proctor.

ELIZABETH. Oh! (*Going for it.*) Why, this is Mary's.

CHEEVER (*shyly*). Would you please to give it to me?

ELIZABETH (*handing it to him, asks HALE*). Has the court discovered a text in poppets now?

CHEEVER (*carefully holding the poppet*). Do you keep any others in this house?

PROCTOR. No, nor this one either till tonight. What signifies a poppet?

CHEEVER. Why, a poppet (*He gingerly turns the poppet over.*) a poppet may signify— Now, woman, will you please to come with me?

PROCTOR. She will not! (*To* ELIZA-BETH.) Fetch Mary here.

CHEEVER (*ineptly reaching toward* ELIZABETH). No, no, I am forbid to leave her from my sight.

PROCTOR (*pushing his arm away*). You'll leave her out of sight and out of mind, Mister. Fetch Mary, Elizabeth. (ELIZABETH *goes upstairs.*)

HALE. What signifies a poppet, Mr. Cheever?

CHEEVER (*turning the poppet over in his hands*). Why, they say it may signify that she— (*He has lifted the poppet's skirt, and his eyes widen in astonished fear.*) Why, this, this—

PROCTOR (*reaching for the poppet*). What's there?

CHEEVER. Why— (*He draws out a long needle from the poppet.*) —it is a needle! Herrick, Herrick, it is a needle! (HERRICK *comes toward him.*)

PROCTOR (*angrily, bewildered*). And what signifies a needle!

CHEEVER (*his hands shaking*). Why, this go hard with her, Proctor, this— I had my doubts, Proctor, I had my doubts, but here's calamity. (*To* HALE, *showing the needle.*) You see it, sir, it is a needle!

HALE. Why? What meanin' has it?

CHEEVER (*wide-eyed, trembling*). The girl, the Williams girl, Abigail Williams, sir. She sat to dinner in Reverend Parris's house tonight, and without word nor warnin' she falls to the floor. Like a struck beast, he says, and screamed a scream that a bull would weep to hear. And he goes to save her, and, stuck two inches in the flesh of her belly, he draw a needle out. And demandin' of her how she come to be so stabbed, she (*To* PROCTOR *now.*) testify it were your wife's familiar spirit pushed it in.

PROCTOR. Why, she done it herself! (*To* HALE.) I hope you're not takin' this for proof, Mister! (HALE, *struck by the proof, is silent.*)

CHEEVER. 'Tis hard proof! (*To* HALE.) I find here a poppet Goody Proctor keeps. I have found it, sir. And in the belly of the poppet a needle's stuck. I tell you true, Proctor, I never warranted to see such proof of Hell, and I bid you obstruct me not, for I— (*Enter* ELIZA-BETH *with* MARY WARREN. PROCTOR, *seeing* MARY WARREN, *draws her by the arm to* HALE.)

PROCTOR. Here now! Mary, how did this poppet come into my house?

MARY WARREN (*frightened for herself, her voice very small*). What poppet's that, sir?

PROCTOR (*impatiently, pointing at the doll in* CHEEVER's *hand*). This poppet, this poppet.

MARY WARREN (*evasively, looking at it*). Why, I—I think it is mine.

PROCTOR. It is your poppet, is it not?

MARY WARREN (*not understanding the direction of this*). It—is, sir.

PROCTOR. And how did it come into this house?

MARY WARREN (*glancing about at the avid faces*). Why—I made it in the court, sir, and—give it to Goody Proctor to-night.

PROCTOR (*to* HALE). Now, sir—do you have it?

HALE. Mary Warren, a needle have been found inside this poppet.

MARY WARREN (*bewildered*). Why, I meant no harm by it, sir.

PROCTOR (*quickly*). You stuck that needle in yourself?

MARY WARREN. I—I believe I did, sir, I—

PROCTOR (*to* HALE). What say you now?

HALE (*watching* MARY WARREN *closely*). Child, you are certain this be your natural memory? May it be, per-haps, that someone conjures you even now to say this?

MARY WARREN. Conjures me? Why, no, sir, I am entirely myself, I think. Let you ask Susanna Walcott—she saw me sewin' it in court. (*Or better still.*) Ask Abby, Abby sat beside me when I made it.

PROCTOR (*to* HALE, *of* CHEEVER). Bid him begone. Your mind is surely settled now. Bid him out, Mr. Hale.

ELIZABETH. What signifies a needle?

HALE. Mary—you charge a cold and cruel murder on Abigail.

MARY WARREN. Murder! I charge no—

HALE. Abigail were stabbed tonight; a

needle were found stuck into her belly—

ELIZABETH. And she charges me?

HALE. Aye.

ELIZABETH (*her breath knocked out*). Why—! The girl is murder! She must be ripped out of the world!

CHEEVER (*pointing at* ELIZABETH). You've heard that, sir! Ripped out of the world! Herrick, you heard it!

PROCTOR (*suddenly snatching the warrant out of* CHEEVER's *hands*). Out with you.

CHEEVER. Proctor, you dare not touch the warrant.

PROCTOR (*ripping the warrant*). Out with you!

CHEEVER. You've ripped the Deputy Governor's warrant, man!

PROCTOR. Damn the Deputy Governor! Out of my house!

HALE. Now, Proctor, Proctor!

PROCTOR. Get y'gone with them! You are a broken minister.

HALE. Proctor, if she is innocent, the court—

PROCTOR. If *she* is innocent! Why do you never wonder if Parris be innocent, or Abigail? Is the accuser always holy now? Were they born this morning as clean as God's fingers? I'll tell you what's walking Salem—vengeance is walking Salem. We are what we always were in Salem, but now the little crazy children are jangling the keys of the kingdom, and common vengeance writes the law! This warrant's vengeance! I'll not give my wife to vengeance!

ELIZABETH. I'll go, John—

PROCTOR. You will not go!

HERRICK. I have nine men outside. You cannot keep her. The law binds me, John, I cannot budge.

PROCTOR (*to* HALE, *ready to break him*). Will you see her taken?

HALE. Proctor, the court is just—

PROCTOR. Pontius Pilate! God will not let you wash your hands of this!

ELIZABETH. John—I think I must go with them. (*He cannot bear to look at her.*) Mary, there is bread enough for the morning; you will bake, in the afternoon. Help Mr. Proctor as you were his daughter—you owe me that, and much more. (*She is fighting her weeping. To* PROCTOR.) When the children wake, speak nothing of witchcraft—it will frighten them. (*She cannot go on.*)

PROCTOR. I will bring you home. I will bring you soon.

ELIZABETH. Oh, John, bring me soon!

PROCTOR. I will fall like an ocean on that court! Fear nothing, Elizabeth.

ELIZABETH (*with great fear*). I will fear nothing. (*She looks about the room, as though to fix it in her mind.*) Tell the children I have gone to visit someone sick. (*She walks out the door,* HERRICK *and* CHEEVER *behind her. For a moment,* PROCTOR *watches from the doorway. The clank of chain is heard.*)

PROCTOR. Herrick! Herrick, don't chain her! (*He rushes out the door. From outside.*) Damn you, man, you will not chain her! Off with them! I'll not have it! I will not have her chained! (*There are other men's voices against his.* HALE, *in a fever of guilt and uncertainty, turns from the door to avoid the sight;* MARY WARREN *bursts into tears and sits weeping.* GILES COREY *calls to* HALE.)

GILES. And yet silent, minister? It is fraud, you know it is fraud! What keeps you, man? (PROCTOR *is half braced, half pushed into the room by two deputies and* HERRICK.)

PROCTOR. I'll pay you, Herrick, I will surely pay you!

HERRICK (*panting*). In God's name, John, I cannot help myself. I must chain them all. Now let you keep inside this house till I am gone! (*He goes out with his deputies.* PROCTOR *stands there, gulping air. Horses and a wagon creaking are heard.*)

HALE (*in great uncertainty*). Mr. Proctor—

PROCTOR. Out of my sight!

HALE. Charity, Proctor, charity. What I have heard in her favor, I will not fear to testify in court. God help me, I cannot judge her guilty or innocent—I know not. Only this consider: the world goes mad, and it profit nothing you should lay the cause to the vengeance of a little girl.

PROCTOR. You are a coward! Though you be ordained in God's own tears, you are a coward now!

HALE. Proctor, I cannot think God be provoked so grandly by such a petty cause. The jails are packed—our greatest judges sit in Salem now—and hangin's promised. Man, we must look to cause proportionate. Were there murder done, perhaps, and never brought to light? Abomination? Some secret blasphemy that stinks to Heaven? Think on cause, man, and let you help me to discover it. For there's your way, believe it, there is your only way, when such confusion strikes upon the world. (*He goes to* GILES *and* FRANCIS.) Let you counsel among yourselves; think on your village and what may have drawn from Heaven such thundering wrath upon you all. I shall pray God open up our eyes. (HALE *goes out.*)

FRANCIS (*struck by* HALE's *mood*). I never heard no murder done in Salem.

PROCTOR (*he has been reached by* HALE's *words*). Leave me, Francis, leave me.

GILES (*shaken*). John—tell me, are we lost?

PROCTOR. Go home now, Giles. We'll speak on it tomorrow.

GILES. Let you think on it. We'll come early, eh?

PROCTOR. Aye. Go now, Giles.

GILES. Good night, then. (GILES COREY *goes out. After a moment.*)

MARY WARREN (*in a fearful squeak of a voice*). Mr. Proctor, very likely they'll let her come home once they're given proper evidence.

PROCTOR. You're coming to the court with me, Mary. You will tell it in the court.

MARY WARREN. I cannot charge murder on Abigail.

PROCTOR (*moving menacingly toward her*). You will tell the court how that poppet come here and who stuck the needle in.

MARY WARREN. She'll kill me for sayin' that! (PROCTOR *continues toward her.*) Abby'll charge lechery on you, Mr. Proctor!

PROCTOR (*halting*). She's told you!

MARY WARREN. I have known it, sir. She'll ruin you with it, I know she will.

PROCTOR (*hesitating, and with deep hatred of himself*). Good. Then her saintliness is done with. (MARY *backs from him.*) We will slide together into our pit; you will tell the court what you know.

MARY WARREN (*in terror*). I cannot, they'll turn on me— (PROCTOR *strides and catches her, and she is repeating, "I cannot, I cannot!"*)

PROCTOR. My wife will never die for me! I will bring your guts into your mouth but that goodness will not die for me!

MARY WARREN (*struggling to escape him*). I cannot do it, I cannot!

PROCTOR (*grasping her by the throat as though he would strangle her*). Make your peace with it! Now Hell and Heaven grapple on our backs, and all our old pretense is ripped away—make your peace! (*He throws her to the floor, where she sobs, "I cannot, I cannot . . ."* And now, half to himself, staring, and turning to the open door.) Peace. It is a providence, and no great change; we are only what we always were, but naked now. (*He walks as though toward a great horror, facing the open sky.*) Aye, naked! And the wind, God's icy wind, will blow! (*And she is over and over again sobbing, "I cannot, I cannot, I cannot," as*)

THE CURTAIN FALLS.

ACT THREE

The vestry room of the Salem meeting house, now serving as the anteroom of the General Court.

As the curtain rises, the room is empty, but for sunlight pouring through two high windows in the back wall. The room is solemn, even forbidding. Heavy beams jut out, boards of random widths make up the walls. At the right are two doors leading into the meeting house proper, where the court is being held. At the left another door leads outside.

*There is a plain bench at the left, and
another at the right. In the center a
rather long meeting table, with stools
and a considerable armchair snugged up
to it.*

*Through the partitioning wall at the
right we hear a prosecutor's voice,*
JUDGE HATHORNE'S, *asking a question;
then a woman's voice,* MARTHA COREY'S,
replying.

HATHORNE'S VOICE. Now, Martha
Corey, there is abundant evidence in our
hands to show that you have given yourself to the reading of fortunes. Do you
deny it?

MARTHA COREY'S VOICE. I am innocent
to a witch. I know not what a witch is.

HATHORNE'S VOICE. How do you
know, then, that you are not a witch?

MARTHA COREY'S VOICE. If I were, I
would know it.

HATHORNE'S VOICE. Why do you hurt
these children?

MARTHA COREY'S VOICE. I do not hurt
them. I scorn it!

GILES' VOICE (*roaring*). I have evidence for the court! (*Voices of towns-
people rise in excitement.*)

DANFORTH'S VOICE. You will keep your
seat!

GILES' VOICE. Thomas Putnam is reaching out for land!

DANFORTH'S VOICE. Remove that man,
Marshal!

GILES' VOICE. You're hearing lies, lies!
(*A roaring goes up from the people.*)

HATHORNE'S VOICE. Arrest him, excellency!

GILES' VOICE. I have evidence. Why
will you not hear my evidence? (*The
door opens and* GILES *is half carried into
the vestry room by* HERRICK.)

GILES. Hands off, damn you, let me
go!

HERRICK. Giles, Giles!

GILES. Out of my way, Herrick! I
bring evidence—

HERRICK. You cannot go in there, Giles;
it's a court! (*Enter* HALE *from the
court.*)

HALE. Pray be calm a moment.

GILES. You, Mr. Hale, go in there and
demand I speak.

HALE. A moment, sir, a moment.

GILES. They'll be hangin' my wife!
(JUDGE HATHORNE *enters. He is in his
sixties, a bitter, remorseless Salem judge.*)

HATHORNE. How do you dare come
roarin' into this court! Are you gone
daft, Corey?

GILES. You're not a Boston judge yet,
Hathorne. You'll not call me daft! (*Enter* DEPUTY GOVERNOR DANFORTH *and,
behind him,* EZEKIEL CHEEVER *and* PARRIS.
On his appearance, silence falls. DAN-
FORTH *is a grave man in his sixties, of
some humor and sophistication that does
not, however, interfere with an exact
loyalty to his position and his cause. He
comes down to* GILES, *who awaits his
wrath.*)

DANFORTH (*looking directly at* GILES).
Who is this man?

PARRIS. Giles Corey, sir, and a more
contentious—

GILES (*to* PARRIS). I am asked the question, and I am old enough to answer it!
(*To* DANFORTH, *who impresses him and
to whom he smiles through his strain.*)
My name is Corey, sir, Giles Corey. I
have six hundred acres, and timber in
addition. It is my wife you are condemning now. (*He indicates the courtroom.*)

DANFORTH. And how do you imagine
to help her cause with such contemptuous riot? Now be gone. Your old age
alone keeps you out of jail for this.

GILES (*beginning to plead*). They be
tellin' lies about my wife, sir, I—

DANFORTH. Do you take it upon yourself to determine what this court shall
believe and what it shall set aside?

GILES. Your Excellency, we mean no
disrespect for—

DANFORTH. Disrespect indeed! It is
disruption, Mister. This is the highest
court of the supreme government of this
province, do you know it?

GILES (*beginning to weep*). Your Excellency, I only said she were readin'
books, sir, and they come and take her
out of my house for—

DANFORTH (*mystified*). Books! What
books?

GILES (*through helpless sobs*). It is
my third wife, sir; I never had no wife

that be so taken with books, and I thought to find the cause of it, d'y'see, but it were no witch I blamed her for. (*He is openly weeping.*) I have broke charity with the woman, I have broke charity with her. (*He covers his face, ashamed.* DANFORTH *is respectfully silent.*)

HALE. Excellency, he claims hard evidence for his wife's defense. I think that in all justice you must—

DANFORTH. Then let him submit his evidence in proper affidavit. You are certainly aware of our procedure here, Mr. Hale. (*To* HERRICK.) Clear this room.

HERRICK. Come now, Giles. (*He gently pushes* COREY *out.*)

FRANCIS. We are desperate, sir; we come here three days now and cannot be heard.

DANFORTH. Who is this man?

FRANCIS. Francis Nurse, Your Excellency.

HALE. His wife's Rebecca that were condemned this morning.

DANFORTH. Indeed! I am amazed to find you in such uproar. I have only good report of your character, Mr. Nurse.

HATHORNE. I think they must both be arrested in contempt, sir.

DANFORTH (*to* FRANCIS). Let you write your plea, and in due time I will—

FRANCIS. Excellency, we have proof for your eyes; God forbid you shut them to it. The girls, sir, the girls are frauds.

DANFORTH. What's that?

FRANCIS. We have proof of it, sir. They are all deceiving you. (DANFORTH *is shocked, but studying* FRANCIS.)

HATHORNE. This is contempt, sir, contempt!

DANFORTH. Peace, Judge Hathorne. Do you know who I am, Mr. Nurse?

FRANCIS. I surely do, sir, and I think you must be a wise judge to be what you are.

DANFORTH. And do you know that near to four hundred are in the jails from Marblehead to Lynn, and upon my signature?

FRANCIS. I—

DANFORTH. And seventy-two condemned to hang by that signature?

FRANCIS. Excellency, I never thought to say it to such a weighty judge, but you are deceived. (*Enter* GILES COREY *from left. All turn to see as he beckons in* MARY WARREN *with* PROCTOR. MARY *is keeping her eyes to the ground;* PROCTOR *has her elbow as though she were near collapse.*)

PARRIS (*on seeing her, in shock*). Mary Warren! (*He goes directly to bend close to her face.*) What are you about here?

PROCTOR (*pressing* PARRIS *away from her with a gentle but firm motion of protectiveness*). She would speak with the Deputy Governor.

DANFORTH (*shocked by this, turns to* HERRICK). Did you not tell me Mary Warren were sick in bed?

HERRICK. She were, Your Honor. When I go to fetch her to the court last week, she said she were sick.

GILES. She has been strivin' with her soul all week, Your Honor; she comes now to tell the truth of this to you.

DANFORTH. Who is this?

PROCTOR. John Proctor, sir. Elizabeth Proctor is my wife.

PARRIS. Beware this man, Your Excellency, this man is mischief.

HALE (*excitedly*). I think you must hear the girl, sir, she—

DANFORTH (*who has become very interested in* MARY WARREN *and only raises a hand toward* HALE). Peace. What would you tell us, Mary Warren? (PROCTOR *looks at her, but she cannot speak.*)

PROCTOR. She never saw no spirits, sir.

DANFORTH (*with great alarm and surprise, to* MARY). Never saw no spirits!

GILES (*eagerly*). Never.

PROCTOR (*reaching into his jacket*). She has signed a deposition, sir—

DANFORTH (*instantly*). No, no, I accept no depositions. (*He is rapidly calculating this; he turns from her to* PROCTOR.) Tell me, Mr. Proctor, have you given out this story in the village?

PROCTOR. We have not.

PARRIS. They've come to overthrow the court, sir! This man is—

DANFORTH. I pray you, Mr. Parris. Do you know, Mr. Proctor, that the entire contention of the state in these trials is that the voice of Heaven is speaking through the children?

PROCTOR. I know that, sir.

DANFORTH (*thinks, staring at* PROCTOR, *then turns to* MARY WARREN). And you, Mary Warren, how came you to cry out people for sending their spirits against you?

MARY WARREN. It were pretense, sir.

DANFORTH. I cannot hear you.

PROCTOR. It were pretense, she says.

DANFORTH. Ah? And the other girls? Susanna Walcott, and—the others? They are also pretending?

MARY WARREN. Aye, sir.

DANFORTH (*wide-eyed*). Indeed. (*Pause. He is baffled by this. He turns to study* PROCTOR's *face.*)

PARRIS (*in a sweat*). Excellency, you surely cannot think to let so vile a lie be spread in open court!

DANFORTH. Indeed not, but it strike hard upon me that she will dare come here with such a tale. Now, Mr. Proctor, before I decide whether I shall hear you or not, it is my duty to tell you this. We burn a hot fire here; it melts down all concealment.

PROCTOR. I know that, sir.

DANFORTH. Let me continue. I understand well, a husband's tenderness may drive him to extravagance in defense of a wife. Are you certain in your conscience, Mister, that your evidence is the truth?

PROCTOR. It is. And you will surely know it.

DANFORTH. And you thought to declare this revelation in the open court before the public?

PROCTOR. I thought I would, aye—with your permission.

DANFORTH (*his eyes narrowing*). Now, sir, what is your purpose in so doing?

PROCTOR. Why, I—I would free my wife, sir.

DANFORTH. There lurks nowhere in your heart, nor hidden in your spirit, any desire to undermine this court?

PROCTOR (*with the faintest faltering*). Why, no, sir.

CHEEVER (*clears his throat, awakening*). I— Your Excellency.

DANFORTH. Mr. Cheever.

CHEEVER. I think it be my duty, sir— (*Kindly, to* PROCTOR.) You'll not deny it, John. (*To* DANFORTH.) When we come to take his wife, he damned the court and ripped your warrant.

PARRIS. Now you have it!

DANFORTH. He did that, Mr. Hale?

HALE (*takes a breath*). Aye, he did.

PROCTOR. It were a temper, sir. I knew not what I did.

DANFORTH (*studying him*). Mr. Proctor.

PROCTOR. Aye, sir.

DANFORTH (*straight into his eyes*). Have you ever seen the Devil?

PROCTOR. No, sir.

DANFORTH. You are in all respects a Gospel Christian?

PROCTOR. I am, sir.

PARRIS. Such a Christian that will not come to church but once in a month!

DANFORTH (*restrained—he is curious*). Not come to church?

PROCTOR. I—I have no love for Mr. Parris. It is no secret. But God I surely love.

CHEEVER. He plow on Sunday, sir.

DANFORTH. Plow on Sunday!

CHEEVER (*apologetically*). I think it be evidence, John. I am an official of the court, I cannot keep it.

PROCTOR. I—I have once or twice plowed on Sunday. I have three children, sir, and until last year my land give little.

GILES. You'll find other Christians that do plow on Sunday if the truth be known.

HALE. Your Honor, I cannot think you may judge the man on such evidence.

DANFORTH. I judge nothing. (*Pause. He keeps watching* PROCTOR, *who tries to meet his gaze.*) I tell you straight, Mister—I have seen marvels in this court. I have seen people choked before my eyes by spirits; I have seen them stuck by pins and slashed by daggers. I have until this moment not the slightest reason to suspect that the children may be deceiving me. Do you understand my meaning?

PROCTOR. Excellency, does it not strike upon you that so many of these women have lived so long with such upright reputation, and—

PARRIS. Do you read the Gospel, Mr. Proctor?

PROCTOR. I read the Gospel.

PARRIS. I think not, or you should surely know that Cain were an upright man, and yet he did kill Abel.

PROCTOR. Aye, God tells us that. (*To* DANFORTH.) But who tells us Rebecca Nurse murdered seven babies by sending out her spirit on them? It is the children only, and this one will swear she lied to you. (DANFORTH *considers, then beckons* HATHORNE *to him.* HATHORNE *leans in, and he speaks in his ear.* HATHORNE *nods.*)

HATHORNE. Aye, she's the one.

DANFORTH. Mr. Proctor, this morning, your wife send me a claim in which she states that she is pregnant now.

PROCTOR. My wife pregnant!

DANFORTH. There be no sign of it—we have examined her body.

PROCTOR. But if she say she is pregnant, then she must be! That woman will never lie, Mr. Danforth.

DANFORTH. She will not?

PROCTOR. Never, sir, never.

DANFORTH. We have thought it too convenient to be credited. However, if I should tell you now that I will let her be kept another month; and if she begin to show her natural signs, you shall have her living yet another year until she is delivered—what say you to that? (JOHN PROCTOR *is struck silent.*) Come now. You say your only purpose is to save your wife. Good, then, she is saved at least this year, and a year is long. What say you, sir? It is done now. (*In conflict,* PROCTOR *glances at* FRANCIS *and* GILES.) Will you drop this charge?

PROCTOR. I—I think I cannot.

DANFORTH (*now an almost imperceptible hardness in his voice*). Then your purpose is somewhat larger.

PARRIS. He's come to overthrow this court, Your Honor!

PROCTOR. These are my friends. Their wives are also accused—

DANFORTH (*with a sudden briskness of manner*). I judge you not, sir. I am ready to hear your evidence.

PROCTOR. I come not to hurt the court; I only—

DANFORTH (*cutting him off*). Marshal, go into the court and bid Judge Stoughton and Judge Sewall declare recess for one hour. And let them go to the tavern, if they will. All witnesses and prisoners are to be kept in the building.

HERRICK. Aye, sir. (*Very deferentially.*) If I may say it, sir, I know this man all my life. It is a good man, sir.

DANFORTH (*it is the reflection on himself he resents*). I am sure of it, Marshal. (HERRICK *nods, then goes out.*) Now, what deposition do you have for us, Mr. Proctor? And I beg you be clear, open as the sky, and honest.

PROCTOR (*as he takes out several papers*). I am no lawyer, so I'll—

DANFORTH. The pure in heart need no lawyers. Proceed as you will.

PROCTOR (*handing* DANFORTH *a paper*). Will you read this first, sir? It's a sort of testament. The people signing it declare their good opinion of Rebecca, and my wife, and Martha Corey. (DANFORTH *looks down at the paper.*)

PARRIS (*to enlist* DANFORTH's *sarcasm*). Their good opinion! (*But* DANFORTH *goes on reading, and* PROCTOR *is heartened.*)

PROCTOR. These are all landholding farmers, members of the church. (*Delicately, trying to point out a paragraph.*) If you'll notice, sir—they've known the women many years and never saw no sign they had dealings with the Devil. (PARRIS *nervously moves over and reads over* DANFORTH's *shoulder.*)

DANFORTH (*glancing down a long list*). How many names are here?

FRANCIS. Ninety-one, Your Excellency.

PARRIS (*sweating*). These people should be summoned. (DANFORTH *looks up at him questioningly.*) For questioning.

FRANCIS (*trembling with anger*). Mr. Danforth, I gave them all my word no harm would come to them for signing this.

PARRIS. This is a clear attack upon the court!

HALE (*to* PARRIS, *trying to contain himself*). Is every defense an attack upon the court? Can no one—?

PARRIS. All innocent and Christian people are happy for the courts in Salem! These people are gloomy for it. (*To* DANFORTH *directly.*) And I think you will want to know, from each and every one of them, what discontents them with you!

HATHORNE. I think they ought to be examined, sir.

DANFORTH. It is not necessarily an attack, I think. Yet—

FRANCIS. These are all covenanted Christians, sir.

DANFORTH. Then I am sure they may have nothing to fear. (*Hands* CHEEVER *the paper.*) Mr. Cheever, have warrants drawn for all of these—arrest for examination. (*To* PROCTOR.) Now, Mister, what other information do you have for us? (FRANCIS *is still standing, horrified.*) You may sit, Mr. Nurse.

FRANCIS. I have brought trouble on these people; I have—

DANFORTH. No, old man, you have not hurt these people if they are of good conscience. But you must understand, sir, that a person is either with this court or he must be counted against it, there be no road between. This is a sharp time, now, a precise time—we live no longer in the dusky afternoon when evil mixed itself with good and befuddled the world. Now, by God's grace, the shining sun is up, and them that fear not light will surely praise it. I hope you will be one of those. (MARY WARREN *suddenly sobs.*) She's not hearty, I see.

PROCTOR. No, she's not, sir. (*To* MARY, *bending to her, holding her hand, quietly.*) Now remember what the angel Raphael said to the boy Tobias. Remember it.

MARY WARREN (*hardly audible*). Aye.

PROCTOR. "Do that which is good, and no harm shall come to thee."

MARY WARREN. Aye.

DANFORTH. Come, man, we wait you. (MARSHAL HERRICK *returns, and takes his post at the door.*)

GILES. John, my deposition, give him mine.

PROCTOR. Aye. (*He hands* DANFORTH *another paper.*) This is Mr. Corey's deposition.

DANFORTH. Oh? (*He looks down at it. Now* HATHORNE *comes behind him and reads with him.*)

HATHORNE (*suspiciously*). What lawyer drew this, Corey?

GILES. You know I never hired a lawyer in my life, Hathorne.

DANFORTH (*finishing the reading*). It is very well phrased. My compliments. Mr. Parris, if Mr. Putnam is in the court, will you bring him in? (HATHORNE *takes the deposition, and walks to the window with it.* PARRIS *goes into the court.*) You have no legal training, Mr. Corey?

GILES (*very pleased*). I have the best, sir—I am thirty-three time in court in my life. And always plaintiff, too.

DANFORTH. Oh, then you're much put-upon.

GILES. I am never put-upon; I know my rights, sir, and I will have them. You know, your father tried a case of mine—might be thirty-five year ago, I think.

DANFORTH. Indeed.

GILES. He never spoke to you of it?

DANFORTH. No, I cannot recall it.

GILES. That's strange, he give me nine pound damages. He were a fair judge, your father. Y'see, I had a white mare that time, and this fellow come to borrow the mare— (*Enter* PARRIS *with* THOMAS PUTNAM. *When he sees* PUTNAM, GILES' *ease goes; he is hard.*) Aye, there he is.

DANFORTH. Mr. Putnam, I have here an accusation by Mr. Corey against you. He states that you coldly prompted your daughter to cry witchery upon George Jacobs that is now in jail.

PUTNAM. It is a lie.

DANFORTH (*turning to* GILES). Mr. Putnam states your charge is a lie. What say you to that?

GILES (*furious, his fists clenched*). A fart on Thomas Putnam, that is what I say to that!

DANFORTH. What proof do you submit for your charge, sir?

GILES. My proof is there! (*Pointing to the paper.*) If Jacobs hangs for a witch he forfeit up his property—that's law! And there is none but Putnam with the coin to buy so great a piece. This man is killing his neighbors for their land!

DANFORTH. But proof, sir, proof.

GILES (*pointing at his deposition*). The proof is there! I have it from an honest man who heard Putnam say it! The day his daughter cried out on Jacobs, he said she'd given him a fair gift of land.

HATHORNE. And the name of this man?

GILES (*taken aback*). What name?

HATHORNE. The man that give you this information.

GILES (*hesitates, then*). Why, I—I cannot give you his name.

HATHORNE. And why not?

GILES (*hesitates, then bursts out*). You know well why not! He'll lay in jail if I give his name!

HATHORNE. This is contempt of the court, Mr. Danforth!

DANFORTH (*to avoid that*). You will surely tell us the name.

GILES. I will not give you no name. I mentioned my wife's name once and I'll burn in hell long enough for that. I stand mute.

DANFORTH. In that case, I have no choice but to arrest you for contempt of this court, do you know that?

GILES. This is a hearing; you cannot clap me for contempt of a hearing.

DANFORTH. Oh, it is a proper lawyer! Do you wish me to declare the court in full session here? Or will you give me good reply?

GILES (*faltering*). I cannot give you no name, sir, I cannot.

DANFORTH. You are a foolish old man. Mr. Cheever, begin the record. The court is now in session. I ask you, Mr. Corey—

PROCTOR (*breaking in*). Your Honor— he has the story in confidence, sir, and he—

PARRIS. The Devil lives on such confidences! (*To* DANFORTH.) Without confidences there could be no conspiracy, Your Honor!

HATHORNE. I think it must be broken, sir.

DANFORTH (*to* GILES). Old man, if your informant tells the truth let him come here openly like a decent man. But if he hide in anonymity I must know why. Now sir, the government and central church demand of you the name of

him who reported Mr. Thomas Putnam a common murderer.

HALE. Excellency—

DANFORTH. Mr. Hale.

HALE. We cannot blink it more. There is a prodigious fear of this court in the country—

DANFORTH. Then there is a prodigious guilt in the country. Are *you* afraid to be questioned here?

HALE. I may only fear the Lord, sir, but there is fear in the country nevertheless.

DANFORTH (*angered now*). Reproach me not with the fear in the country; there is fear in the country because there is a moving plot to topple Christ in the country!

HALE. But it does not follow that everyone accused is part of it.

DANFORTH. No uncorrupted man may fear this court, Mr. Hale! None! (*To* GILES.) You are under arrest in contempt of this court. Now sit down and take counsel with yourself, or you will be set in the jail until you decide to answer all questions. (GILES COREY *makes a rush for* PUTNAM. PROCTOR *lunges and holds him.*)

PROCTOR. No, Giles!

GILES (*over* PROCTOR's *shoulder at* PUTNAM). I'll cut your throat, Putnam, I'll kill you yet!

PROCTOR (*forcing him into a chair*). Peace, Giles, peace. (*Releasing him.*) We'll prove ourselves. Now we will. (*He starts to turn to* DANFORTH.)

GILES. Say nothin' more, John. (*Pointing at* DANFORTH.) He's only playin' you! He means to hang us all! (MARY WARREN *bursts into sobs.*)

DANFORTH. This is a court of law, Mister. I'll have no effrontery here!

PROCTOR. Forgive him, sir, for his old age. Peace, Giles, we'll prove it all now. (*He lifts up* MARY's *chin.*) You cannot weep, Mary. Remember the angel, what he say to the boy. Hold to it, now; there is your rock. (MARY *quiets. He takes out a paper, and turns to* DANFORTH.) This is Mary Warren's deposition. I—I would ask you remember, sir, while you read it, that until two week ago she were no different than the other children are today. (*He is speaking reasonably, re-straining all his fears, his anger, his anxiety.*) You saw her scream, she howled, she swore familiar spirits choked her; she even testified that Satan, in the form of women now in jail, tried to win her soul away, and then when she re-fused—

DANFORTH. We know all this.

PROCTOR. Aye, sir. She swears now that she never saw Satan; nor any spirit, vague or clear, that Satan may have sent to hurt her. And she declares her friends are lying now. (PROCTOR *starts to hand* DANFORTH *the deposition, and* HALE *comes up to* DANFORTH *in a trembling state.*)

HALE. Excellency, a moment. I think this goes to the heart of the matter.

DANFORTH (*with deep misgivings*). It surely does.

HALE. I cannot say he is an honest man; I know him little. But in all justice, sir, a claim so weighty cannot be argued by a farmer. In God's name, sir, stop here; send him home and let him come again with a lawyer—

DANFORTH (*patiently*). Now look you, Mr. Hale—

HALE. Excellency, I have signed sev-enty-two death warrants; I am a minister of the Lord, and I dare not take a life without there be a proof so immaculate no slightest qualm of conscience may doubt it.

DANFORTH. Mr. Hale, you surely do not doubt my justice.

HALE. I have this morning signed away the soul of Rebecca Nurse, Your Honor. I'll not conceal it, my hand shakes yet as with a wound! I pray you, sir, *this* argu-ment let lawyers present to you.

DANFORTH. Mr. Hale, believe me; for a man of such terrible learning you are most bewildered—I hope you will for-give me. I have been thirty-two year at the bar, sir, and I should be confounded were I called upon to defend these peo-ple. Let you consider now—(*To* PROCTOR *and the others.*) And I bid you all do likewise. In an ordinary crime, how does one defend the accused? One calls up witnesses to prove his innocence. But witchcraft is *ipso facto*, on its face and by its nature, an invisible crime, is it not? Therefore, who may possibly be witness to it? The witch and the victim. None other. Now we cannot hope the witch will accuse herself; granted? Therefore, we must rely upon her vic-tims—and they do testify, the children certainly do testify. As for the witches, none will deny that we are most eager for all their confessions. Therefore, what is left for a lawyer to bring out? I think I have made my point. Have I not?

HALE. But this child claims the girls are not truthful, and if they are not—

DANFORTH. That is precisely what I am about to consider, sir. What more may you ask of me? Unless you doubt my probity?

HALE (*defeated*). I surely do not, sir. Let you consider it, then.

DANFORTH. And let you put your heart to rest. Her deposition, Mr. Proctor. (PROCTOR *hands it to him.* HATHORNE *rises, goes beside* DANFORTH, *and starts reading.* PARRIS *comes to his other side.* DANFORTH *looks at* JOHN PROCTOR, *then proceeds to read.* HALE *gets up, finds position near the judge, reads too.* PROC-TOR *glances at* GILES, FRANCIS *prays si-lently, hands pressed together.* CHEEVER *waits placidly, the sublime official, duti-ful.* MARY WARREN *sobs once.* JOHN PROC-TOR *touches her head reassuringly. Presently* DANFORTH *lifts his eyes, stands up, takes out a kerchief and blows his nose. The others stand aside as he moves in thought toward the window.*)

PARRIS (*hardly able to contain his an-ger and fear*). I should like to question—

DANFORTH (*his first real outburst, in which his contempt for* PARRIS *is clear*). Mr. Parris, I bid you be silent! (*He stands in silence, looking out the win-dow. Now, having established that he will set the gait.*) Mr. Cheever, will you go into the court and bring the children here? (CHEEVER *gets up and goes out upstage.* DANFORTH *now turns to* MARY.) Mary Warren, how came you to this turnabout? Has Mr. Proctor threatened you for this deposition?

MARY WARREN. No, sir.

DANFORTH. Has he ever threatened you?

MARY WARREN (*weaker*). No, sir.

DANFORTH (*sensing a weakening*). Has he threatened you?

MARY WARREN. No, sir.

DANFORTH. Then you tell me that you sat in my court, callously lying, when you knew that people would hang by your evidence? (*She does not answer.*) Answer me!

MARY WARREN (*almost inaudibly*). I did, sir.

DANFORTH. How were you instructed in your life? Do you not know that God damns all liars? (*She cannot speak.*) Or is it now that you lie?

MARY WARREN. No, sir—I am with God now.

DANFORTH. You are with God now.

MARY WARREN. Aye, sir.

DANFORTH (*containing himself*). I will tell you this—you are either lying now, or you were lying in the court, and in either case you have committed perjury and you will go to jail for it. You cannot lightly say you lied, Mary. Do you know that?

MARY WARREN. I cannot lie no more. I am with God, I am with God. (*But she breaks into sobs at the thought of it, and the right door opens, and enter* SUSANNA WALCOTT, MERCY LEWIS, BETTY PARRIS, *and finally* ABIGAIL. CHEEVER *comes to* DANFORTH.)

CHEEVER. Ruth Putnam's not in the court, sir, nor the other children.

DANFORTH. These will be sufficient. Sit you down, children. (*Silently they sit.*) Your friend, Mary Warren, has given us a deposition. In which she swears that she never saw familiar spirits, apparitions, nor any manifest of the Devil. She claims as well that none of you have seen these things either. (*Slight pause.*) Now, children, this is a court of law. The law, based upon the Bible, and the Bible, writ by Almighty God, forbid the practice of witchcraft, and describe death as the penalty thereof. But likewise, children, the law and Bible damn all bearers of false witness. (*Slight pause.*) Now then. It does not escape me that this deposition may be devised to blind us; it may well be that Mary Warren has been conquered by Satan, who sends her here to distract our sacred purpose. If so, her neck will break for it. But if she speak true, I bid you now drop your guile and confess your pretense, for a quick confession will go easier with you. (*Pause.*) Abigail Williams, rise. (ABIGAIL *slowly rises.*) Is there any truth in this?

ABIGAIL. No, sir.

DANFORTH (*thinks, glances at* MARY, *then back to* ABIGAIL). Children, a very augur bit will now be turned into your souls until your honesty is proved. Will either of you change your positions now, or do you force me to hard questioning?

ABIGAIL. I have naught to change, sir. She lies.

DANFORTH (*to* MARY). You would still go on with this?

MARY WARREN (*faintly*). Aye, sir.

DANFORTH (*turning to* ABIGAIL). A poppet were discovered in Mr. Proctor's house, stabbed by a needle. Mary Warren claims that you sat beside her in the court when she made it, and that you saw her make it and witnessed how she herself stuck her needle into it for safekeeping. What say you to that?

ABIGAIL (*with a slight note of indignation*). It is a lie, sir.

DANFORTH (*after a slight pause*). While you worked for Mr. Proctor, did you see poppets in that house?

ABIGAIL. Goody Proctor always kept poppets.

PROCTOR. Your Honor, my wife never kept no poppets. Mary Warren confesses it was her poppet.

CHEEVER. Your Excellency.

DANFORTH. Mr. Cheever.

CHEEVER. When I spoke with Goody Proctor in that house, she said she never kept no poppets. But she said she did keep poppets when she were a girl.

PROCTOR. She has not been a girl these fifteen years, Your Honor.

HATHORNE. But a poppet will keep fifteen years, will it not?

PROCTOR. It will keep if it is kept, but Mary Warren swears she never saw no poppets in my house, nor anyone else.

PARRIS. Why could there not have been poppets hid where no one ever saw them?

PROCTOR (*furious*). There might also

be a dragon with five legs in my house, but no one has ever seen it.

PARRIS. We are here, Your Honor, precisely to discover what no one has ever seen.

PROCTOR. Mr. Danforth, what profit this girl to turn herself about? What may Mary Warren gain but hard questioning and worse?

DANFORTH. You are charging Abigail Williams with a marvelous cool plot to murder, do you understand that?

PROCTOR. I do, sir. I believe she means to murder.

DANFORTH (*pointing at* ABIGAIL, *incredulously*). This child would murder your wife?

PROCTOR. It is not a child. Now hear me, sir. In the sight of the congregation she were twice this year put out of this meetin' house for laughter during prayer.

DANFORTH (*shocked, turning to* ABIGAIL). What's this? Laughter during–!

PARRIS. Excellency, she were under Tituba's power at that time, but she is solemn now.

GILES. Aye, now she is solemn and goes to hang people!

DANFORTH. Quiet, man.

HATHORNE. Surely it have no bearing on the question, sir. He charges contemplation of murder.

DANFORTH. Aye. (*He studies* ABIGAIL *for a moment, then.*) Continue, Mr. Proctor.

PROCTOR. Mary. Now tell the Governor how you danced in the woods.

PARRIS (*instantly*). Excellency, since I come to Salem this man is blackening my name. He—

DANFORTH. In a moment, sir. (*To* MARY WARREN, *sternly, and surprised.*) What is this dancing?

MARY WARREN. I– (*She glances at* ABIGAIL, *who is staring down at her remorselessly. Then, appealing to* PROCTOR.) Mr. Proctor—

PROCTOR (*taking it right up*). Abigail leads the girls to the woods, Your Honor, and they have danced there naked—

PARRIS. Your Honor, this—

PROCTOR (*at once*). Mr. Parris discovered them himself in the dead of night! There's the "child" she is!

DANFORTH (*it is growing into a nightmare, and he turns, astonished, to* PARRIS). Mr. Parris—

PARRIS. I can only say, sir, that I never found any of them naked, and this man is—

DANFORTH. But you discovered them dancing in the woods? (*Eyes on* PARRIS, *he points at* ABIGAIL.) Abigail?

HALE. Excellency, when I first arrived from Beverly, Mr. Parris told me that.

DANFORTH. Do you deny it, Mr. Parris?

PARRIS. I do not, sir, but I never saw any of them naked.

DANFORTH. But she have *danced?*

PARRIS (*unwillingly*). Aye, sir. (DANFORTH, *as though with new eyes, looks at* ABIGAIL.)

HATHORNE. Excellency, will you permit me? (*He points at* MARY WARREN.)

DANFORTH (*with great worry*). Pray, proceed.

HATHORNE. You say you never saw no spirits, Mary, were never threatened or afflicted by any manifest of the Devil or the Devil's agents.

MARY WARREN (*very faintly*). No, sir.

HATHORNE (*with a gleam of victory*). And yet, when people accused of witchery confronted you in court, you would faint, saying their spirits came out of their bodies and choked you—

MARY WARREN. That were pretense, sir.

DANFORTH. I cannot hear you.

MARY WARREN. Pretense, sir.

PARRIS. But you did turn cold, did you not? I myself picked you up many times, and your skin were icy. Mr. Danforth, you—

DANFORTH. I saw that many times.

PROCTOR. She only pretended to faint, Your Excellency. They're all marvelous pretenders.

HATHORNE. Then can she pretend to faint now?

PROCTOR. Now?

PARRIS. Why not? Now there are no spirits attacking her, for none in this room is accused of witchcraft. So let her turn herself cold now, let her pretend she is attacked now, let her faint. (*He turns to* MARY WARREN.) Faint!

MARY WARREN. Faint?

PARRIS. Aye, faint. Prove to us how you pretended in the court so many times.

MARY WARREN (*looking to* PROCTOR). I —cannot faint now, sir.

PROCTOR (*alarmed, quietly*). Can you not pretend it?

MARY WARREN. I— (*She looks about as though searching for the passion to faint.*) I—have no *sense* of it now, I—

DANFORTH. Why? What is lacking now?

MARY WARREN. I—cannot tell, sir, I—

DANFORTH. Might it be that here we have no afflicting spirit loose, but in the court there were some?

MARY WARREN. I never saw no spirits.

PARRIS. Then see no spirits now, and prove to us that you can faint by your own will, as you claim.

MARY WARREN (*stares, searching for the emotion of it, and then shakes her head*). I—cannot do it.

PARRIS. Then you will confess, will you not? It were attacking spirits made you faint!

MARY WARREN. No, sir, I—

PARRIS. Your Excellency, this is a trick to blind the court!

MARY WARREN. It's not a trick! (*She stands.*) I—I used to faint because I—I thought I saw spirits.

DANFORTH. *Thought* you saw them!

MARY WARREN. But I did not, Your Honor.

HATHORNE. How could you think you saw them unless you saw them?

MARY WARREN. I—I cannot tell how, but I did. I—I heard the other girls screaming, and you, Your Honor, you seemed to believe them, and I— It were only sport in the beginning, sir, but then the whole world cried spirits, spirits, and I—I promise you, Mr. Danforth, I only thought I saw them but I did not. (DANFORTH *peers at her.*)

PARRIS (*smiling, but nervous because* DANFORTH *seems to be struck by* MARY WARREN'S *story*). Surely Your Excellency is not taken by this simple lie.

DANFORTH (*turning worriedly to* ABIGAIL). Abigail. I bid you now search your heart and tell me this—and beware of it, child, to God every soul is precious and His vengeance is terrible on them that take life without cause. Is it possible, child, that the spirits you have seen are illusion only, some deception that may cross your mind when—

ABIGAIL. Why, this—this—is a base question, sir.

DANFORTH. Child, I would have you consider it—

ABIGAIL. I have been hurt, Mr. Danforth; I have seen my blood runnin' out! I have been near to murdered every day because I done my duty pointing out the Devil's people—and this is my reward? To be mistrusted, denied, questioned like a—

DANFORTH (*weakening*). Child, I do not mistrust you—

ABIGAIL (*in an open threat*). Let *you* beware, Mr. Danforth. Think you to be so mighty that the power of Hell may not turn *your* wits? Beware of it! There is— (*Suddenly, from an accusatory attitude, her face turns, looking into the air above—it is truly frightened.*)

DANFORTH (*apprehensively*). What is it, child?

ABIGAIL (*looking about in the air, clasping her arms about her as though cold*). I—I know not. A wind, a cold wind, has come. (*Her eyes fall on* MARY WARREN.)

MARY WARREN (*terrified, pleading*). Abby!

MERCY LEWIS (*shivering*). Your Honor, I freeze!

PROCTOR. They're pretending!

HATHORNE (*touching* ABIGAIL'S *hand*). She is cold, Your Honor, touch her!

MERCY LEWIS (*through chattering teeth*). Mary, do you send this shadow on me?

MARY WARREN. Lord, save me!

SUSANNA WALCOTT. I freeze, I freeze!

ABIGAIL (*shivering visibly*). It is a wind, a wind!

MARY WARREN. Abby, don't do that!

DANFORTH (*himself engaged and entered by* ABIGAIL). Mary Warren, do you witch her? I say to you, do you send your spirit out? (*With a hysterical*

cry MARY WARREN *starts to run.* PROC-
TOR *catches her.*)

MARY WARREN (*almost collapsing*).
Let me go, Mr. Proctor, I cannot, I cannot—

ABIGAIL (*crying to Heaven*). Oh,
Heavenly Father, take away this shadow!
(*Without warning or hesitation,* PROCTOR
leaps at ABIGAIL *and, grabbing her by
the hair, pulls her to her feet. She
screams in pain.* DANFORTH, *astonished,
cries, "What are you about?" and* HA-
THORNE *and* PARRIS *call, "Take your
hands off her!" and out of it all comes*
PROCTOR's *roaring voice.*)

PROCTOR. How do you call Heaven!
Whore! Whore! (HERRICK *breaks* PROC-
TOR *from her.*)

HERRICK. John!

DANFORTH. Man! Man, what do you—

PROCTOR (*breathless and in agony*). It
is a whore!

DANFORTH (*dumfounded*). You
charge—?

ABIGAIL. Mr. Danforth, he is lying!

PROCTOR. Mark her! Now she'll suck a
scream to stab me with, but—

DANFORTH. You will prove this! This
will not pass!

PROCTOR (*trembling, his life collapsing
about him*). I have known her, sir. I
have known her.

DANFORTH. You—you are a lecher?

FRANCIS (*horrified*). John, you cannot
say such a—

PROCTOR. Oh, Francis, I wish you had
some evil in you that you might know
me! (*To* DANFORTH.) A man will not
cast away his good name. You surely
know that.

DANFORTH (*dumfounded*). In—in what
time? In what place?

PROCTOR (*his voice about to break, and
his shame great*). In the proper place—
where my beasts are bedded. On the last
night of my joy, some eight months past.
She used to serve me in my house, sir.
(*He has to clamp his jaw to keep from
weeping.*) A man may think God sleeps,
but God sees everything, I know it now.
I beg you, sir, I beg you—see her what
she is. My wife, my dear good wife,
took this girl soon after, sir, and put her

out on the highroad. And being what
she is, a lump of vanity, sir— (*He is being overcome.*) Excellency, forgive me,
forgive me. (*Angrily against himself, he
turns away from the Governor for a
moment. Then, as though to cry out is
his only means of speech left.*) She
thinks to dance with me on my wife's
grave! And well she might, for I thought
of her softly. God help me, I lusted, and
there *is* a promise in such sweat. But
it is a whore's vengeance, and you must
see it; I set myself entirely in your hands.
I know you must see it now.

DANFORTH (*blanched, in horror, turning to* ABIGAIL). You deny every scrap
and tittle of this?

ABIGAIL. If I must answer that, I will
leave and I will not come back again.
(DANFORTH *seems unsteady.*)

PROCTOR. I have made a bell of my
honor! I have rung the doom of my
good name—you will believe me, Mr.
Danforth! My wife is innocent, except
she knew a whore when she saw one!

ABIGAIL (*stepping up to* DANFORTH).
What look do you give me? (DAN-
FORTH *cannot speak.*) I'll not have such
looks! (*She turns and starts for the
door.*)

DANFORTH. You will remain where
you are! (HERRICK *steps into her path.
She comes up short, fire in her eyes.*)
Mr. Parris, go into the court and bring
Goodwife Proctor out.

PARRIS (*objecting*). Your Honor, this
is all a—

DANFORTH (*sharply to* PARRIS). Bring
her out! And tell her not one word of
what's been spoken here. And let you
knock before you enter. (PARRIS *goes
out.*) Now we shall touch the bottom of
this swamp. (*To* PROCTOR.) Your wife,
you say, is an honest woman.

PROCTOR. In her life, sir, she have never
lied. There are them that cannot sing,
and them that cannot weep—my wife
cannot lie. I have paid much to learn
it, sir.

DANFORTH. And when she put this girl
out of your house, she put her out for
a harlot?

PROCTOR. Aye, sir.

DANFORTH. And knew her for a harlot?

PROCTOR. Aye, sir, she knew her for a harlot.

DANFORTH. Good then. (*To* ABIGAIL.) And if she tell me, child, it were for harlotry, may God spread His mercy on you. (*There is a knock. He calls to the door.*) Hold! (*To* ABIGAIL.) Turn your back. Turn your back. (*To* PROCTOR.) Do likewise. (*Both turn their backs—* ABIGAIL *with indignant slowness.*) Now let neither of you turn to face Goody Proctor. No one in this room is to speak one word, or raise a gesture aye or nay. (*He turns toward the door, calls.*) Enter! (*The door opens.* ELIZABETH *enters with* PARRIS. PARRIS *leaves her. She stands alone, her eyes looking for* PROCTOR.) Mr. Cheever, report this testimony in all exactness. Are you ready?

CHEEVER. Ready, sir.

DANFORTH. Come here, woman. (ELIZABETH *comes to him, glancing at* PROCTOR's *back.*) Look at me only, not at your husband. In my eyes only.

ELIZABETH (*faintly*). Good, sir.

DANFORTH. We are given to understand that at one time you dismissed your servant, Abigail Williams.

ELIZABETH. That is true, sir.

DANFORTH. For what cause did you dismiss her? (*Slight pause. Then* ELIZABETH *tries to glance at* PROCTOR.) You will look in my eyes only and not at your husband. The answer is in your memory and you need no help to give it to me. Why did you dismiss Abigail Williams?

ELIZABETH (*not knowing what to say, sensing a situation, wetting her lips to stall for time*). She—dissatisfied me. (*Pause.*) And my husband.

DANFORTH. In what way dissatisfied you?

ELIZABETH. She were— (*She glances at* PROCTOR *for a cue.*)

DANFORTH. Woman, look at me! (ELIZABETH *does.*) Were she slovenly? Lazy? What disturbance did she cause?

ELIZABETH. Your Honor, I—in that time I were sick. And I— My husband is a good and righteous man. He is never drunk as some are, nor wastin' his time at the shovelboard, but always at his work. But in my sickness—you see, sir, I were a long time sick after my last baby, and I thought I saw my husband somewhat turning from me. And this girl— (*She turns to* ABIGAIL.)

DANFORTH. Look at me.

ELIZABETH. Aye, sir. Abigail Williams— (*She breaks off.*)

DANFORTH. What of Abigail Williams?

ELIZABETH. I came to think he fancied her. And so one night I lost my wits, I think, and put her out on the highroad.

DANFORTH. Your husband—did he indeed turn from you?

ELIZABETH (*in agony*). My husband—is a goodly man, sir.

DANFORTH. Then he did not turn from you.

ELIZABETH (*starting to glance at* PROCTOR.) He—

DANFORTH (*reaches out and holds her face, then*). Look at me! To your own knowledge, has John Proctor ever committed the crime of lechery? (*In a crisis of indecision she cannot speak.*) Answer my question! Is your husband a lecher!

ELIZABETH (*faintly*). No, sir.

DANFORTH. Remove her, Marshal.

PROCTOR. Elizabeth, tell the truth!

DANFORTH. She has spoken. Remove her!

PROCTOR (*crying out*). Elizabeth, I have confessed it!

ELIZABETH. Oh, God! (*The door closes behind her.*)

PROCTOR. She only thought to save my name!

HALE. Excellency, it is a natural lie to tell; I beg you, stop now before another is condemned! I may shut my conscience to it no more—private vengeance is working through this testimony! From the beginning this man has struck me true. By my oath to Heaven, I believe him now, and I pray you call back his wife before we—

DANFORTH. She spoke nothing of lechery, and this man has lied!

HALE. I believe him! (*Pointing at* ABIGAIL.) This girl has always struck me false! She has— (ABIGAIL, *with a weird, wild, chilling cry, screams up to the ceiling.*)

ABIGAIL. You will not! Begone! Begone, I say!

DANFORTH. What is it, child? (*But* ABIGAIL, *pointing with fear, is now raising up her frightened eyes, her awed face, toward the ceiling—the girls are doing the same—and now* HATHORNE, HALE, PUTNAM, CHEEVER, HERRICK, *and* DANFORTH *do the same.*) What's there? (*He lowers his eyes from the ceiling, and now he is frightened; there is real tension in his voice.*) Child! (*She is transfixed—with all the girls, she is whimpering open-mouthed, agape at the ceiling.*) Girls! Why do you—?

MERCY LEWIS (*pointing*). It's on the beam! Behind the rafter!

DANFORTH (*looking up*). Where!

ABIGAIL. Why—? (*She gulps.*) Why do you come, yellow bird?

PROCTOR. Where's a bird? I see no bird!

ABIGAIL (*to the ceiling*). My face? My face?

PROCTOR. Mr. Hale—

DANFORTH. Be quiet!

PROCTOR (*to* HALE). Do you see a bird?

DANFORTH. Be quiet!!

ABIGAIL (*to the ceiling, in a genuine conversation with the "bird," as though trying to talk it out of attacking her*). But God made my face; you cannot want to tear my face. Envy is a deadly sin, Mary.

MARY WARREN (*on her feet with a spring, and horrified, pleading*). Abby!

ABIGAIL (*unperturbed, continuing to the "bird"*). Oh, Mary, this is a black art to change your shape. No, I cannot, I cannot stop my mouth; it's God's work I do.

MARY WARREN. Abby, I'm *here!*

PROCTOR (*frantically*). They're pretending, Mr. Danforth!

ABIGAIL (*now she takes a backward step, as though in fear the bird will swoop down momentarily*). Oh, please, Mary! Don't come down.

SUSANNA WALCOTT. Her claws, she's stretching her claws!

PROCTOR. Lies, lies.

ABIGAIL (*backing further, eyes still fixed above*). Mary, please don't hurt me!

MARY WARREN (*to* DANFORTH). I'm not hurting her!

DANFORTH (*to* MARY WARREN). Why does she see this vision?

MARY WARREN. She sees nothin'!

ABIGAIL (*now staring full front as though hypnotized, and mimicking the exact tone of* MARY WARREN's *cry*). She sees nothin'!

MARY WARREN (*pleading*). Abby, you mustn't!

ABIGAIL AND ALL THE GIRLS (*all transfixed*). Abby, you mustn't!

MARY WARREN (*to all the girls*). I'm here, I'm here!

GIRLS. I'm here, I'm here!

DANFORTH (*horrified*). Mary Warren! Draw back your spirit out of them!

MARY WARREN. Mr. Danforth!

GIRLS (*cutting her off*). Mr. Danforth!

DANFORTH. Have you compacted with the Devil? Have you?

MARY WARREN. Never! never!

GIRLS. Never, never!

DANFORTH (*growing hysterical*). Why can they only repeat you?

PROCTOR. Give me a whip—I'll stop it!

MARY WARREN. They're sporting. They—!

GIRLS. They're sporting!

MARY WARREN (*turning on them all hysterically and stamping her feet*). Abby, stop it!

GIRLS (*stamping their feet*). Abby, stop it!

MARY WARREN. Stop it!

GIRLS. Stop it!

MARY WARREN (*screaming it out at the top of her lungs, and raising her fists*). Stop it!!

GIRLS (*raising their fists*). Stop it!! (MARY WARREN, *utterly confounded, and becoming overwhelmed by* ABIGAIL's *—and the girls'—utter conviction, starts to whimper, hands half raised, powerless, and all the girls begin whimpering exactly as she does.*)

DANFORTH. A little while ago you were

afflicted. Now it seems you afflict others; where did you find this power?

MARY WARREN (*staring at* ABIGAIL). I—have no power.

GIRLS. I have no power.

PROCTOR. They're gulling you, Mister!

DANFORTH. Why did you turn about this past two weeks? You have seen the Devil, have you not?

HALE (*indicating* ABIGAIL *and the girls*). You cannot believe them!

MARY WARREN. I—

PROCTOR (*sensing her weakening*). Mary, God damns all liars!

DANFORTH (*pounding it into her*). You have seen the Devil, you have made compact with Lucifer, have you not?

PROCTOR. God damns liars, Mary. (MARY *utters something unintelligible, staring at* ABIGAIL, *who keeps watching the "bird" above*.)

DANFORTH. I cannot hear you. What do you say? (MARY *utters again unintelligibly*.) You will confess yourself or you will hang! (*He turns her roughly to face him*.) Do you know who I am? I say you will hang if you do not open with me!

PROCTOR. Mary, remember the angel Raphael—do that which is good and—

ABIGAIL (*pointing upward*). The wings! Her wings are spreading! Mary, please, don't, don't—!

HALE. I see nothing, Your Honor!

DANFORTH. Do you confess this power! (*He is an inch from her face*.) Speak!

ABIGAIL. She's going to come down! She's walking the beam!

DANFORTH. Will you speak!

MARY WARREN (*staring in horror*). I cannot!

GIRLS. I cannot!

PARRIS. Cast the Devil out! Look him in the face! Trample him! We'll save you, Mary, only stand fast against him and—

ABIGAIL (*looking up*). Look out! She's coming down! (*She and all the girls run to one wall, shielding their eyes. And now, as though cornered, they let out a gigantic scream, and* MARY, *as though infected, opens her mouth and screams*

with them. Gradually ABIGAIL *and the girls leave off, until only* MARY *is left there, staring up at the "bird," screaming madly. All watch her, horrified by this evident fit.* PROCTOR *strides to her*.)

PROCTOR. Mary, tell the Governor what they— (*He has hardly got a word out, when, seeing him coming for her, she rushes out of his reach, screaming in horror*.)

MARY WARREN. Don't touch me—don't touch me! (*At which the girls halt at the door*.)

PROCTOR (*astonished*). Mary!

MARY WARREN (*pointing at* PROCTOR). You're the Devil's man! (*He is stopped in his tracks*.)

PARRIS. Praise God!

GIRLS. Praise God!

PROCTOR (*numbed*). Mary, how—?

MARY WARREN. I'll not hang with you! I love God, I love God.

DANFORTH (*to* MARY). He bid you do the Devil's work?

MARY WARREN (*hysterically, indicating* PROCTOR). He come at me by night and every day to sign, to sign, to—

DANFORTH. Sign what?

PARRIS. The Devil's book? He come with a book?

MARY WARREN (*hysterically, pointing at* PROCTOR, *fearful of him*). My name, he want my name. "I'll murder you," he says, "if my wife hangs! We must go and overthrow the court," he says! (DANFORTH's *head jerks toward* PROCTOR, *shock and horror in his face*.)

PROCTOR (*turning, appealing to* HALE). Mr. Hale!

MARY WARREN (*her sobs beginning*). He wake me every night, his eyes were like coals and his fingers claw my neck, and I sign, I sign . . .

HALE. Excellency, this child's gone wild!

PROCTOR (*as* DANFORTH's *wide eyes pour on him*). Mary, Mary!

MARY WARREN (*screaming at him*). No, I love God; I go your way no more. I love God, I bless God. (*Sobbing, she rushes to* ABIGAIL.) Abby, Abby, I'll never hurt you more! (*They all watch, as* ABIGAIL, *out of her infinite charity, reaches out and draws the sobbing* MARY *to her, and then looks up to* DANFORTH.)

DANFORTH (*to* PROCTOR). What are you? (PROCTOR *is beyond speech in his anger.*) You are combined with anti-Christ, are you not? I have seen your power; you will not deny it! What say you, Mister?

HALE. Excellency—

DANFORTH. I will have nothing from you, Mr. Hale! (*To* PROCTOR.) Will you confess yourself befouled with Hell, or do you keep that black allegiance yet? What say you?

PROCTOR (*his mind wild, breathless*). I say—I say—God is dead!

PARRIS. Hear it, hear it!

PROCTOR (*laughs insanely, then*). A fire, a fire is burning! I hear the boot of Lucifer, I see his filthy face! And it is my face, and yours, Danforth! For them that quail to bring men out of ignorance, as I have quailed, and as you quail now when you know in all your black hearts that this be fraud—God damns our kind especially, and we will burn, we will burn together!

DANFORTH. Marshal! Take him and Corey with him to the jail!

HALE (*starting across to the door*). I denounce these proceedings!

PROCTOR. You are pulling Heaven down and raising up a whore!

HALE. I denounce these proceedings, I quit this court! (*He slams the door to the outside behind him.*)

DANFORTH (*calling to him in a fury*). Mr. Hale! Mr. Hale!

THE CURTAIN FALLS.

ACT FOUR

A cell in Salem jail, that fall. At the back is a high barred window; near it, a great, heavy door. Along the walls are two benches. The place is in darkness but for the moonlight seeping through the bars. It appears empty. Presently footsteps are heard coming down a corridor beyond the wall, keys rattle, and the door swings open. MARSHAL HERRICK *enters with a lantern. He is nearly drunk, and heavy-footed. He goes to a bench and nudges a bundle of rags lying on it.*

HERRICK. Sarah, wake up! Sarah Good! (*He then crosses to the other bench.*)

SARAH GOOD (*rising in her rags*). Oh, Majesty! Comin', comin'! Tituba, he's here, His Majesty's come!

HERRICK. Go to the north cell; this place is wanted now. (*He hangs his lantern on the wall.* TITUBA *sits up.*)

TITUBA. That don't look to me like His Majesty; look to me like the marshal.

HERRICK (*taking out a flask*). Get along with you now, clear this place. (*He drinks, and* SARAH GOOD *comes and peers up into his face.*)

SARAH GOOD. Oh, is it you, Marshal! I thought sure you be the devil comin' for us. Could I have a sip of cider for me goin'-away?

HERRICK (*handing her the flask*). And where are you off to, Sarah?

TITUBA (*as* SARAH *drinks*). We goin' to Barbados, soon the Devil gits here with the feathers and the wings.

HERRICK. Oh? A happy voyage to you.

SARAH GOOD. A pair of bluebirds wing-in' southerly, the two of us! Oh, it be a grand transformation, Marshal! (*She raises the flask to drink again.*)

HERRICK (*taking the flask from her lips*). You'd best give me that or you'll never rise off the ground. Come along now.

TITUBA. I'll speak to him for you, if you desires to come along, Marshal.

HERRICK. I'd not refuse it, Tituba; it's the proper morning to fly into Hell.

TITUBA. Oh, it be no Hell in Barbados. Devil, him be pleasureman in Barbados, him be singin' and dancin' in Barbados. It's you folks—you riles him up 'round here; it be too cold 'round here for that Old Boy. He freeze his soul in

Massachusetts, but in Barbados he just as sweet and— (*A bellowing cow is heard, and* TITUBA *leaps up and calls to the window.*) Aye, sir! That's him, Sarah!

SARAH GOOD. I'm here, Majesty! (*They hurriedly pick up their rags as* HOPKINS, *a guard, enters.*)

HOPKINS. The Deputy Governor's arrived.

HERRICK (*grabbing* TITUBA). Come along, come along.

TITUBA (*resisting him*). No, he comin' for me. I goin' home!

HERRICK (*pulling her to the door*). That's not Satan, just a poor old cow with a hatful of milk. Come along now, out with you!

TITUBA (*calling to the window*). Take me home, Devil! Take me home!

SARAH GOOD (*following the shouting* TITUBA *out*). Tell him I'm goin', Tituba! Now you tell him Sarah Good is goin' too! (*In the corridor outside* TITUBA *calls on—"Take me home, Devil; Devil take me home!" and* HOPKINS' *voice orders her to move on.* HERRICK *returns and begins to push old rags and straw into a corner. Hearing footsteps, he turns, and enter* DANFORTH *and* JUDGE HATHORNE. *They are in greatcoats and wear hats against the bitter cold. They are followed in by* CHEEVER, *who carries a dispatch case and a flat wooden box containing his writing materials.*)

HERRICK. Good morning, Excellency.

DANFORTH. Where is Mr. Parris?

HERRICK. I'll fetch him. (*He starts for the door.*)

DANFORTH. Marshal. (HERRICK *stops.*) When did Reverend Hale arrive?

HERRICK. It were toward midnight, I think.

DANFORTH (*suspiciously*). What is he about here?

HERRICK. He goes among them that will hang, sir. And he prays with them. He sits with Goody Nurse now. And Mr. Parris with him.

DANFORTH. Indeed. That man have no authority to enter here, Marshal. Why have you let him in?

HERRICK. Why, Mr. Parris command me, sir. I cannot deny him.

DANFORTH. Are you drunk, Marshal?

HERRICK. No, sir; it is a bitter night, and I have no fire here.

DANFORTH (*containing his anger*). Fetch Mr. Parris.

HERRICK. Aye, sir.

DANFORTH. There is a prodigious stench in this place.

HERRICK. I have only now cleared the people out for you.

DANFORTH. Beware hard drink, Marshal.

HERRICK. Aye, sir. (*He waits an instant for further orders. But* DANFORTH, *in dissatisfaction, turns his back on him, and* HERRICK *goes out. There is a pause.* DANFORTH *stands in thought.*)

HATHORNE. Let you question Hale, Excellency; I should not be surprised he have been preaching in Andover lately.

DANFORTH. We'll come to that; speak nothing of Andover. Parris prays with him. That's strange. (*He blows on his hands, moves toward the window, and looks out.*)

HATHORNE. Excellency, I wonder if it be wise to let Mr. Parris so continuously with the prisoners. (DANFORTH *turns to him, interested.*) I think, sometimes, the man has a mad look these days.

DANFORTH. Mad?

HATHORNE. I met him yesterday coming out of his house, and I bid him good morning—and he wept and went his way. I think it is not well the village sees him so unsteady.

DANFORTH. Perhaps he have some sorrow.

CHEEVER (*stamping his feet against the cold*). I think it be the cows, sir.

DANFORTH. Cows?

CHEEVER. There be so many cows wanderin' the highroads, now their masters are in the jails, and much disagreement who they will belong to now. I know Mr. Parris be arguin' with farmers all yesterday—there is great contention, sir, about the cows. Contention make him weep, sir; it were always a man that weep for contention. (*He turns, as do* HATHORNE *and* DANFORTH, *hearing someone coming up the corridor.* DANFORTH *raises his head as* PARRIS *enters. He is gaunt, frightened, and sweating in his greatcoat.*)

PARRIS (*to* DANFORTH, *instantly*). Oh, good morning, sir, thank you for coming, I beg your pardon wakin' you so early. Good morning, Judge Hathorne.

DANFORTH. Reverend Hale have no right to enter this—

PARRIS. Excellency, a moment. (*He hurries back and shuts the door.*)

HATHORNE. Do you leave him alone with the prisoners?

DANFORTH. What's his business here?

PARRIS (*prayerfully holding up his hands*). Excellency, hear me. It is a providence. Reverend Hale has returned to bring Rebecca Nurse to God.

DANFORTH (*surprised*). He bids her confess?

PARRIS (*sitting*). Hear me. Rebecca have not given me a word this three month since she came. Now she sits with him, and her sister and Martha Corey and two or three others, and he pleads with them, confess their crimes and save their lives.

DANFORTH. Why—this is indeed a providence. And they soften, they soften?

PARRIS. Not yet, not yet. But I thought to summon you, sir, that we might think on whether it be not wise, to— (*He dares not say it.*) I had thought to put a question, sir, and I hope you will not—

DANFORTH. Mr. Parris, be plain, what troubles you?

PARRIS. There is news, sir, that the court—the court must reckon with. My niece, sir, my niece—I believe she has vanished.

DANFORTH. Vanished!

PARRIS. I had thought to advise you of it earlier in the week, but—

DANFORTH. Why? How long is she gone?

PARRIS. This be the third night. You see, sir, she told me she would stay a night with Mercy Lewis. And next day, when she does not return, I send to Mr. Lewis to inquire. Mercy told him she would sleep in *my* house for a night.

DANFORTH. They are both gone?!

PARRIS (*in fear of him*). They are, sir.

DANFORTH (*alarmed*). I will send a party for them. Where may they be?

PARRIS. Excellency, I think they be aboard a ship. (DANFORTH *stands agape.*) My daughter tells me how she heard them speaking of ships last week, and tonight I discover my—my strongbox is broke into. (*He presses his fingers against his eyes to keep back tears.*)

HATHORNE (*astonished*). She have robbed you?

PARRIS. Thirty-one pound is gone. I am penniless. (*He covers his face and sobs.*)

DANFORTH. Mr. Parris, you are a brainless man! (*He walks in thought, deeply worried.*)

PARRIS. Excellency, it profit nothing you should blame me. I cannot think they would run off except they fear to keep in Salem any more. (*He is pleading.*) Mark it, sir, Abigail had close knowledge of the town, and since the news of Andover has broken here—

DANFORTH. Andover is remedied. The court returns there on Friday, and will resume examinations.

PARRIS. I am sure of it, sir. But the rumor here speaks rebellion in Andover, and it—

DANFORTH. There is no rebellion in Andover!

PARRIS. I tell you what is said here, sir. Andover have thrown out the court, they say, and will have no part of witchcraft. There be a faction here, feeding on that news, and I tell you true, sir, I fear there will be riot here.

HATHORNE. Riot! Why at every execution I have seen naught but high satisfaction in the town.

PARRIS. Judge Hathorne—it were another sort that hanged till now. Rebecca Nurse is no Bridget that lived three year with Bishop before she married him. John Proctor is not Isaac Ward that drank his family to ruin. (*To* DANFORTH.) I would to God it were not so,

Excellency, but these people have great weight yet in the town. Let Rebecca stand upon the gibbet and send up some righteous prayer, and I fear she'll wake a vengeance on you.

HATHORNE. Excellency, she is condemned a witch. The court have—

DANFORTH (*in deep concern, raising a hand to* HATHORNE). Pray you. (*To* PARRIS.) How do you propose, then?

PARRIS. Excellency, I would postpone these hangin's for a time.

DANFORTH. There will be no postponement.

PARRIS. Now Mr. Hale's returned, there is hope, I think—for if he bring even one of these to God, that confession surely damns the others in the public eye, and none may doubt more that they are all linked to Hell. This way, unconfessed and claiming innocence, doubts are multiplied, many honest people will weep for them, and our good purpose is lost in their tears.

DANFORTH (*after thinking a moment, then going to* CHEEVER). Give me the list. (CHEEVER *opens the dispatch case, searches.*)

PARRIS. It cannot be forgot, sir, that when I summoned the congregation for John Proctor's excommunication there were hardly thirty people come to hear it. That speak a discontent, I think, and—

DANFORTH (*studying the list*). There will be no postponement.

PARRIS. Excellency—

DANFORTH. Now, sir—which of these in your opinion may be brought to God? I will myself strive with him till dawn. (*He hands the list to* PARRIS, *who merely glances at it.*)

PARRIS. There is not sufficient time till dawn.

DANFORTH. I shall do my utmost. Which of them do you have hope for?

PARRIS (*not even glancing at the list now, and in a quavering voice, quietly*). Excellency—a dagger— (*He chokes up.*)

DANFORTH. What do you say?

PARRIS. Tonight, when I open my door to leave my house—a dagger clattered to the ground. (*Silence.* DANFORTH *absorbs this. Now* PARRIS *cries out.*) You cannot hang this sort. There is danger for me. I dare not step outside at night! (REVEREND HALE *enters. They look at him for an instant in silence. He is steeped in sorrow, exhausted, and more direct than he ever was.*)

DANFORTH. Accept my congratulations, Reverend Hale; we are gladdened to see you returned to your good work.

HALE (*coming to* DANFORTH *now*). You must pardon them. They will not budge. (HERRICK *enters, waits.*)

DANFORTH (*conciliatory*). You misunderstand, sir; I cannot pardon these when twelve are already hanged for the same crime. It is not just.

PARRIS (*with failing heart*). Rebecca will not confess?

HALE. The sun will rise in a few minutes. Excellency, I must have more time.

DANFORTH. Now hear me, and beguile yourselves no more. I will not receive a single plea for pardon or postponement. Them that will not confess will hang. Twelve are already executed; the names of these seven are given out, and the village expects to see them die this morning. Postponement now speaks a floundering on my part; reprieve or pardon must cast doubt upon the guilt of them that died till now. While I speak God's law, I will not crack its voice with whimpering. If retaliation is your fear, know this—I should hang ten thousand that dared to rise against the law, and an ocean of salt tears could not melt the resolution of the statutes. Now draw yourselves up like men and help me, as you are bound by Heaven to do. Have you spoken with them all, Mr. Hale?

HALE. All but Proctor. He is in the dungeon.

DANFORTH (*to* HERRICK). What's Proctor's way now?

HERRICK. He sits like some great bird; you'd not know he lived except he will take food from time to time.

DANFORTH (*after thinking a moment*). His wife—his wife must be well on with child now.

HERRICK. She is, sir.

DANFORTH. What think you, Mr. Parris? You have closer knowledge of this man; might her presence soften him?

PARRIS. It is possible, sir. He have not laid eyes on her these three months. I should summon her.

DANFORTH (to HERRICK). Is he yet adamant? Has he struck at you again?

HERRICK. He cannot, sir, he is chained to the wall now.

DANFORTH (after thinking on it). Fetch Goody Proctor to me. Then let you bring him up.

HERRICK. Aye, sir. (HERRICK goes. There is silence.)

HALE. Excellency, if you postpone a week and publish to the town that you are striving for their confessions, that speak mercy on your part, not faltering.

DANFORTH. Mr. Hale, as God have not empowered me like Joshua to stop this sun from rising, so I cannot withhold from them the perfection of their punishment.

HALE (harder now). If you think God wills you to raise rebellion, Mr. Danforth, you are mistaken!

DANFORTH (instantly). You have heard rebellion spoken in the town?

HALE. Excellency, there are orphans wandering from house to house; abandoned cattle bellow on the highroads, the stink of rotting crops hangs everywhere, and no man knows when the harlots' cry will end his life—and you wonder yet if rebellion's spoke? Better you should marvel how they do not burn your province!

DANFORTH. Mr. Hale, have you preached in Andover this month?

HALE. Thank God they have no need of me in Andover.

DANFORTH. You baffle me, sir. Why have you returned here?

HALE. Why, it is all simple. I come to do the Devil's work. I come to counsel Christians they should belie themselves. (His sarcasm collapses.) There is blood on my head! Can you not see the blood on my head!!

PARRIS. Hush! (For he has heard footsteps. They all face the door. HERRICK enters with ELIZABETH. Her wrists are linked by heavy chain, which HERRICK now removes. Her clothes are dirty; her face is pale and gaunt. HERRICK goes out.)

DANFORTH (very politely). Goody Proctor. (She is silent.) I hope you are hearty?

ELIZABETH (as a warning reminder). I am yet six month before my time.

DANFORTH. Pray be at your ease, we come not for your life. We— (Uncertain how to plead, for he is not accustomed to it.) Mr. Hale, will you speak with the woman?

HALE. Goody Proctor, your husband is marked to hang this morning. (Pause.)

ELIZABETH (quietly). I have heard it.

HALE. You know, do you not, that I have no connection with the court? (She seems to doubt it.) I come of my own, Goody Proctor. I would save your husband's life, for if he is taken I count myself his murderer. Do you understand me?

ELIZABETH. What do you want of me?

HALE. Goody Proctor, I have gone this three month like our Lord into the wilderness. I have sought a Christian way, for damnation's doubled on a minister who counsels men to lie.

HATHORNE. It is no lie, you cannot speak of lies.

HALE. It is a lie! They are innocent.

DANFORTH. I'll hear no more of that!

HALE (continuing to ELIZABETH). Let you not mistake your duty as I mistook my own. I came into this village like a bridegroom to his beloved, bearing gifts of high religion; the very crowns of holy law I brought, and what I touched with my bright confidence, it died; and where I turned the eye of my great faith, blood flowed up. Beware, Goody Proctor—cleave to no faith when faith brings blood. It is mistaken law that leads you to sacrifice. Life, woman, life is God's most precious gift; no principle, however glorious, may justify the taking of it. I beg you, woman, prevail upon your husband to confess. Let him give his lie. Quail not before God's judgment in this, for it may well be God damns a liar less than he that throws his life away for pride. Will you plead with him? I cannot think he will listen to another.

ELIZABETH (*quietly*). I think that be the Devil's argument.

HALE (*with a climactic desperation*). Woman, before the laws of God we are as swine! We cannot read His will!

ELIZABETH. I cannot dispute with you, sir; I lack learning for it.

DANFORTH (*going to her*). Goody Proctor, you are not summoned here for disputation. Be there no wifely tenderness within you? He will die with the sunrise. Your husband. Do you understand it? (*She only looks at him.*) What say you? Will you contend with him? (*She is silent.*) Are you stone? I tell you true, woman, had I no other proof of your unnatural life, your dry eyes now would be sufficient evidence that you delivered up your soul to Hell! A very ape would weep at such calamity! Have the Devil dried up any tear of pity in you? (*She is silent.*) Take her out. It profit nothing she should speak to him!

ELIZABETH (*quietly*). Let me speak with him, Excellency.

PARRIS (*with hope*). You'll strive with him? (*She hesitates.*)

DANFORTH. Will you plead for his confession or will you not?

ELIZABETH. I promise nothing. Let me speak with him. (*A sound—the sibilance of dragging feet on stone. They turn. A pause. HERRICK enters with JOHN PROCTOR. His wrists are chained. He is another man, bearded, filthy, his eyes misty as though webs had overgrown them. He halts inside the doorway, his eye caught by the sight of ELIZABETH. The emotion flowing between them prevents anyone from speaking for an instant. Now HALE, visibly affected, goes to DANFORTH and speaks quietly.*)

HALE. Pray, leave them, Excellency.

DANFORTH (*pressing HALE impatiently aside*). Mr. Proctor, you have been notified, have you not? (*PROCTOR is silent, staring at ELIZABETH.*) I see light in the sky, Mister; let you counsel with your wife, and may God help you turn your back on Hell. (*PROCTOR is silent, staring at ELIZABETH.*)

HALE (*quietly*). Excellency, let— (*DANFORTH brushes past HALE and walks out. HALE follows. CHEEVER stands and follows, HATHORNE behind. HERRICK goes. PARRIS, from a safe distance, offers.*)

PARRIS. If you desire a cup of cider, Mr. Proctor, I am sure I— (*PROCTOR turns an icy stare at him, and he breaks off. PARRIS raises his palms toward PROCTOR.*) God lead you now. (*PARRIS goes out. Alone, PROCTOR walks to her, halts. It is as though they stood in a spinning world. It is beyond sorrow, above it. He reaches out his hand as though toward an embodiment not quite real, and as he touches her, a strange soft sound, half laughter, half amazement, comes from his throat. He pats her hand. She covers his hand with hers. And then, weak, he sits. Then she sits, facing him.*)

PROCTOR. The child?

ELIZABETH. It grows.

PROCTOR. There is no word of the boys?

ELIZABETH. They're well. Rebecca's Samuel keeps them.

PROCTOR. You have not seen them?

ELIZABETH. I have not. (*She catches a weakening in herself and downs it.*)

PROCTOR. You are a—marvel, Elizabeth.

ELIZABETH. You—have been tortured?

PROCTOR. Aye. (*Pause. She will not let herself be drowned in the sea that threatens her.*) They come for my life now.

ELIZABETH. I know it. (*Pause.*)

PROCTOR. None—have yet confessed?

ELIZABETH. There be many confessed.

PROCTOR. Who are they?

ELIZABETH. There be a hundred or more, they say. Goody Ballard is one; Isaiah Goodkind is one. There be many.

PROCTOR. Rebecca?

ELIZABETH. Not Rebecca. She is one foot in Heaven now; naught may hurt her more.

PROCTOR. And Giles?

ELIZABETH. You have not heard of it?

PROCTOR. I hear nothin', where I am kept.

ELIZABETH. Giles is dead. (*He looks at her incredulously.*)

PROCTOR. When were he hanged?

ELIZABETH (*quietly, factually*). He were not hanged. He would not answer aye or nay to his indictment; for if he denied the charge they'd hang him surely, and auction out his property. So he stand mute, and died Christian under the law. And so his sons will have his farm. It is the law, for he could not be condemned a wizard without he answer the indictment, aye or nay.

PROCTOR. Then how does he die?

ELIZABETH (*gently*). They press him, John.

PROCTOR. Press?

ELIZABETH. Great stones they lay upon his chest until he plead aye or nay. (*With a tender smile for the old man.*) They say he give them but two words. "More weight," he says. And died.

PROCTOR (*numbed—a thread to weave into his agony*). "More weight."

ELIZABETH. Aye. It were a fearsome man, Giles Corey. (*Pause.*)

PROCTOR (*with great force of will, but not quite looking at her*). I have been thinking I would confess to them, Elizabeth. (*She shows nothing.*) What say you? If I give them that?

ELIZABETH. I cannot judge you, John. (*Pause.*)

PROCTOR (*simply—a pure question*). What would you have me do?

ELIZABETH. As you will, I would have it. (*Slight pause.*) I want you living, John. That's sure.

PROCTOR (*pauses, then with a flailing of hope*). Giles' wife? Have she confessed?

ELIZABETH. She will not. (*Pause.*)

PROCTOR. It is a pretense, Elizabeth.

ELIZABETH. What is?

PROCTOR. I cannot mount the gibbet like a saint. It is a fraud. I am not that man. (*She is silent.*) My honesty is broke, Elizabeth; I am no good man. Nothing's spoiled by giving them this lie that were not rotten long before.

ELIZABETH. And yet you've not confessed till now. That speak goodness in you.

PROCTOR. Spite only keeps me silent. It is hard to give a lie to dogs. (*Pause, for the first time he turns directly to her.*) I would have your forgiveness, Elizabeth.

ELIZABETH. It is not for me to give, John, I am—

PROCTOR. I'd have you see some honesty in it. Let them that never lied die now to keep their souls. It is pretense for me, a vanity that will not blind God nor keep my children out of the wind. (*Pause.*) What say you?

ELIZABETH (*upon a heaving sob that always threatens*). John, it come to naught that I should forgive you, if you'll not forgive yourself. (*Now he turns away a little, in great agony.*) It is not my soul, John, it is yours. (*He stands, as though in physical pain, slowly rising to his feet with a great immortal longing to find his answer. It is difficult to say, and she is on the verge of tears.*) Only be sure of this, for I know it now: Whatever you will do, it is a good man does it. (*He turns his doubting, searching gaze upon her.*) I have read my heart this three month, John. (*Pause.*) I have sins of my own to count. It needs a cold wife to prompt lechery.

PROCTOR (*in great pain*). Enough, enough—

ELIZABETH (*now pouring out her heart*). Better you should know me!

PROCTOR. I will not hear it! I know you!

ELIZABETH. You take my sins upon you, John—

PROCTOR (*in agony*). No, I take my own, my own!

ELIZABETH. John, I counted myself so plain, so poorly made, no honest love could come to me! Suspicion kissed you when I did; I never knew how I should say my love. It were a cold house I kept! (*In fright, she swerves, as HATHORNE enters.*)

HATHORNE. What say you, Proctor? The sun is soon up. (*PROCTOR, his chest heaving, stares, turns to ELIZABETH. She comes to him as though to plead, her voice quaking.*)

ELIZABETH. Do what you will. But let none be your judge. There be no higher judge under Heaven than Proctor is!

Forgive me, forgive me, John—I never knew such goodness in the world! (*She covers her face, weeping.* PROCTOR *turns from her to* HATHORNE; *he is off the earth, his voice hollow.*)

PROCTOR. I want my life.

HATHORNE (*electrified, surprised*). You'll confess yourself?

PROCTOR. I will have my life.

HATHORNE (*with a mystical tone*). God be praised! It is a providence! (*He rushes out the door, and his voice is heard calling down the corridor.*) He will confess! Proctor will confess!

PROCTOR (*with a cry, as he strides to the door*). Why do you cry it? (*In great pain he turns back to her.*) It is evil, is it not? It is evil.

ELIZABETH (*in terror, weeping*). I cannot judge you, John, I cannot!

PROCTOR. Then who will judge me? (*Suddenly clasping his hands.*) God in Heaven, what is John Proctor, what is John Proctor? (*He moves as an animal, and a fury is riding in him, a tantalized search.*) I think it is honest, I think so; I am no saint. (*As though she had denied this he calls angrily at her.*) Let Rebecca go like a saint; for me it is fraud! (*Voices are heard in the hall, speaking together in suppressed excitement.*)

ELIZABETH. I am not your judge, I cannot be. (*As though giving him release.*) Do as you will, do as you will!

PROCTOR. Would you give them such a lie? Say it. Would you ever give them this? (*She cannot answer.*) You would not; if tongs of fire were singeing you you would not! It is evil. Good, then— it is evil, and I do it! (HATHORNE *enters with* DANFORTH, *and, with them,* CHEEVER, PARRIS, *and* HALE. *It is a businesslike, rapid entrance, as though the ice had been broken.*)

DANFORTH (*with great relief and gratitude*). Praise to God, man, praise to God; you shall be blessed in Heaven for this. (CHEEVER *has hurried to the bench with pen, ink, and paper.* PROCTOR *watches him.*) Now then, let us have it. Are you ready, Mr. Cheever?

PROCTOR (*with a cold, cold horror at their efficiency*). Why must it be written?

DANFORTH. Why, for the good instruction of the village, Mister; this we shall post upon the church door! (*To* PARRIS, *urgently.*) Where is the marshal?

PARRIS (*runs to the door and calls down the corridor*). Marshal! Hurry!

DANFORTH. Now, then, Mister, will you speak slowly, and directly to the point, for Mr. Cheever's sake. (*He is on record now, and is really dictating to* CHEEVER, *who writes.*) Mr. Proctor, have you seen the Devil in your life? (PROCTOR'S *jaws lock.*) Come, man, there is light in the sky; the town waits at the scaffold; I would give out this news. Did you see the Devil?

PROCTOR. I did.

PARRIS. Praise God!

DANFORTH. And when he come to you, what were his demand? (PROCTOR *is silent.* DANFORTH *helps.*) Did he bid you to do his work upon the earth?

PROCTOR. He did.

DANFORTH. And you bound yourself to his service? (DANFORTH *turns, as* REBECCA NURSE *enters, with* HERRICK *helping to support her. She is barely able to walk.*) Come in, come in, woman!

REBECCA (*brightening as she sees* PROCTOR). Ah, John! You are well, then, eh? (PROCTOR *turns his face to the wall.*)

DANFORTH. Courage, man, courage—let her witness your good example that she may come to God herself. Now hear it, Goody Nurse! Say on, Mr. Proctor. Did you bind yourself to the Devil's service?

REBECCA (*astonished*). Why, John!

PROCTOR (*through his teeth, his face turned from* REBECCA). I did.

DANFORTH. Now, woman, you surely see it profit nothin' to keep this conspiracy any further. Will you confess yourself with him?

REBECCA. Oh, John—God send his mercy on you!

DANFORTH. I say, will you confess yourself, Goody Nurse?

REBECCA. Why, it is a lie, it is a lie;

how may I damn myself? I cannot, I cannot.

DANFORTH. Mr. Proctor. When the Devil came to you did you see Rebecca Nurse in his company? (PROCTOR *is silent.*) Come, man, take courage—did you ever see her with the Devil?

PROCTOR (*almost inaudibly*). No. (DANFORTH, *now sensing trouble, glances at* JOHN *and goes to the table, and picks up a sheet—the list of condemned.*)

DANFORTH. Did you ever see her sister, Mary Easty, with the Devil?

PROCTOR. No, I did not.

DANFORTH (*his eyes narrow on* PROCTOR). Did you ever see Martha Corey with the Devil?

PROCTOR. I did not.

DANFORTH (*realizing, slowly putting the sheet down*). Did you ever see anyone with the Devil?

PROCTOR. I did not.

DANFORTH. Proctor, you mistake me. I am not empowered to trade your life for a lie. You have most certainly seen some person with the Devil. (PROCTOR *is silent.*) Mr. Proctor, a score of people have already testified they saw this woman with the Devil.

PROCTOR. Then it is proved. Why must I say it?

DANFORTH. Why "must" you say it! Why, you should rejoice to say it if your soul is truly purged of any love for Hell!

PROCTOR. They think to go like saints. I like not to spoil their names.

DANFORTH (*inquiring, incredulous*). Mr. Proctor, do you think they go like saints?

PROCTOR (*evading*). This woman never thought she done the Devil's work.

DANFORTH. Look you, sir. I think you mistake your duty here. It matters nothing what she thought—she is convicted of the unnatural murder of children, and you for sending your spirit out upon Mary Warren. Your soul alone is the issue here, Mister, and you will prove its whiteness or you cannot live in a Christian country. Will you tell me now what persons conspired with you in the Devil's company? (PROCTOR *is silent.*)

To your knowledge was Rebecca Nurse ever—

PROCTOR. I speak my own sins; I cannot judge another. (*Crying out, with hatred.*) I have no tongue for it.

HALE (*quickly to* DANFORTH). Excellency, it is enough he confess himself. Let him sign it, let him sign it.

PARRIS (*feverishly*). It is a great service, sir. It is a weighty name; it will strike the village that Proctor confess. I beg you, let him sign it. The sun is up, Excellency!

DANFORTH (*considers; then with dissatisfaction*). Come, then, sign your testimony. (*To* CHEEVER.) Give it to him. (CHEEVER *goes to* PROCTOR, *the confession and a pen in hand.* PROCTOR *does not look at it.*) Come, man, sign it.

PROCTOR (*after glancing at the confession*). You have all witnessed it—it is enough.

DANFORTH. You will not sign it?

PROCTOR. You have all witnessed it; what more is needed?

DANFORTH. Do you sport with me? You will sign your name or it is no confession, Mister! (*His breast heaving with agonized breathing,* PROCTOR *now lays the paper down and signs his name.*)

PARRIS. Praise be to the Lord! (PROCTOR *has just finished signing when* DANFORTH *reaches for the paper. But* PROCTOR *snatches it up, and now a wild terror is rising in him, and a boundless anger.*)

DANFORTH (*perplexed, but politely extending his hand*). If you please, sir.

PROCTOR. No.

DANFORTH (*as though* PROCTOR *did not understand*). Mr. Proctor, I must have—

PROCTOR. No, no. I have signed it. You have seen me. It is done! You have no need for this.

PARRIS. Proctor, the village must have proof that—

PROCTOR. Damn the village! I confess to God, and God has seen my name on this! It is enough!

DANFORTH. No, sir, it is—

PROCTOR. You came to save my soul, did you not? Here! I have confessed myself; it is enough!

DANFORTH. You have not con—

PROCTOR. I have confessed myself! Is there no good penitence but it be public? God does not need my name nailed upon the church! God sees my name; God knows how black my sins are! It is enough!

DANFORTH. Mr. Proctor—

PROCTOR. You will not use me! I am no Sarah Good or Tituba, I am John Proctor! You will not use me! It is no part of salvation that you should use me!

DANFORTH. I do not wish to—

PROCTOR. I have three children—how may I teach them to walk like men in the world, and I sold my friends?

DANFORTH. You have not sold your friends.

PROCTOR. Beguile me not! I blacken all of them when this is nailed to the church the very day they hang for silence!

DANFORTH. Mr. Proctor, I must have good and legal proof that you—

PROCTOR. You are the high court, your word is good enough! Tell them I confessed myself; say Proctor broke his knees and wept like a woman; say what you will, but my name cannot—

DANFORTH (with suspicion). It is the same, is it not? If I report it or you sign to it?

PROCTOR (he knows it is insane). No, it is not the same! What others say and what I sign to is not the same!

DANFORTH. Why? Do you mean to deny this confession when you are free?

PROCTOR. I mean to deny nothing!

DANFORTH. Then explain to me, Mr. Proctor, why you will not let—

PROCTOR (with a cry of his whole soul). Because it is my name! Because I cannot have another in my life! Because I lie and sign myself to lies! Because I am not worth the dust on the feet of them that hang! How may I live without my name? I have given you my soul; leave me my name!

DANFORTH (pointing at the confession in PROCTOR's hand). Is that document a lie? If it is a lie I will not accept it! What say you? I will not deal in lies, Mister! (PROCTOR is motionless.) You will give me your honest confession in my hand, or I cannot keep you from the rope. (PROCTOR does not reply.) Which way do you go, Mister? (His breast heaving, his eyes staring, PROCTOR tears the paper and crumples it, and he is weeping in fury, but erect.) Marshal!

PARRIS (hysterically, as though the tearing paper were his life). Proctor, Proctor!

HALE. Man, you will hang! You cannot!

PROCTOR (his eyes full of tears). I can. And there's your first marvel, that I can. You have made your magic now, for now I do think I see some shred of goodness in John Proctor. Not enough to weave a banner with, but white enough to keep it from such dogs. (ELIZABETH, in a burst of terror, rushes to him and weeps against his hand.) Give them no tear! Tears pleasure them! Show honor now, show a stony heart and sink them with it! (He has lifted her, and kisses her now with great passion.)

REBECCA. Let you fear nothing! Another judgment waits us all!

DANFORTH. Hang them high over the town! Who weeps for these, weeps for corruption! (He sweeps out past them. HERRICK starts to lead REBECCA, who almost collapses, but PROCTOR catches her, and she glances up at him apologetically.)

REBECCA. I've had no breakfast.

HERRICK. Come, man. (HERRICK escorts them out, HATHORNE and CHEEVER behind them. ELIZABETH stands staring at the empty doorway.)

PARRIS (in deadly fear, to ELIZABETH). Go to him, Goody Proctor! There is yet time! (From outside a drumroll strikes the air. PARRIS is startled. ELIZABETH jerks about toward the window.)

PARRIS. Go to him! (He rushes out the door, as though to hold back his fate.) Proctor! Proctor! (Again, a short burst of drums.)

HALE. Woman, plead with him! (He starts to rush out the door, and then goes back to her.) Woman! It is pride, it is vanity. (She avoids his eyes, and moves to the window. He drops to his knees.) Be his helper!—What profit him to bleed? Shall the dust praise him? Shall the worms declare his truth? Go to him, take his shame away!

ELIZABETH (*supporting herself against collapse, grips the bars of the window, and with a cry*). He have his goodness now. God forbid I take it from him!

(*The final drumroll crashes, then heightens violently.* HALE *weeps in frantic prayer, and the new sun is pouring in upon her face, and the drums rattle like bones in the morning air.*)

THE CURTAIN FALLS.

Echoes Down the Corridor

Not long after the fever died, Parris was voted from office, walked out on the highroad, and was never heard of again.

The legend has it that Abigail turned up later as a prostitute in Boston.

Twenty years after the last execution, the government awarded compensation to the victims still living, and to the families of the dead. However, it is evident that some people still were unwilling to admit their total guilt, and also that the factionalism was still alive, for some beneficiaries were actually not victims at all, but informers.

Elizabeth Proctor married again, four years after Proctor's death.

In solemn meeting, the congregation rescinded the excommunications—this in March 1712. But they did so upon orders of the government. The jury, however, wrote a statement praying forgiveness of all who had suffered.

Certain farms which had belonged to the victims were left to ruin, and for more than a century no one would buy them or live on them.

To all intents and purposes, the power of theocracy in Massachusetts was broken.

SUGGESTED TOPICS FOR FURTHER INVESTIGATION AND REPORT

1. Read the sections of Aristotle's "Poetics" devoted to tragedy. Remember that he wrote as an observer of tragedy as he knew it, but not necessarily with the object of setting down rules. What aspects do you feel are universally applicable to all tragedy? What points are no longer valid? Compare his ideas with modern views such as are expressed by Maxwell Anderson in "The Essence of Tragedy," or by Arthur Miller in his introduction to his "Collected Plays."

2. Tragedy has changed its format in many ways over its 2000 years of existence. You should make a comparative study of outstanding tragedies if you are thoroughly to understand the form and the modern American attitude. Try to read one play in each of the following groups. Discuss the changes and the consistencies in the tragic attitude which are evident in all of them.

Greek and Roman

    The Oresteia (*Agamemnon, The Libation Bearers, The Eumenides*), by Aeschylus. Available in a fine single-volume edition, edited by Richmond Lattimore, University of Chicago Press, Chicago, 1953, but also readily available in other collections.

    Oedipus the King, or *Antigone,* by Sophocles. These, with *Oedipus at Colonus,* also available in a University of Chicago edition, edited by Grene and Lattimore.

    Electra, by Euripides.

    Thyestes, by Seneca. Read Seneca only after reading at least one Greek play.

Shakespearean

    Hamlet, Lear, Macbeth, Othello, Julius Caesar, Antony and Cleopatra, Romeo and Juliet.

Restoration and Eighteenth Century

    All For Love, by John Dryden. This replaced *Antony and Cleopatra* on the English stage for some time. The comparison between the two is interesting.

    Venice Preserved, by Thomas Otway.

    Cato, by Joseph Addison. One of the most popular and most "correct" of its time.

    Douglas, by John Home.

    The London Merchant, by George Lillo.

French

    The Cid, by Pierre Corneille.

    Phaedra, by Jean Racine.

German

    Maria Stuart, by Friedrich Schiller.

    Faust, by Goethe.

Modern English and Irish

    The Tragedy of Nan, by John Masefield.

    Saint Joan, by Bernard Shaw.

    The Plough and the Stars, by Sean O'Casey.

3. Make a study of early American tragedy. Read all of *The Prince of Parthia, The Broker of Bogota, Superstition, Francesca da Rimini.* (These are available in several different collections. Arthur Hobson Quinn's "Representative American

Plays" has them all.) Report on their success as poetry, effective drama, exciting theatre, and so on.

4. Compare Maxwell Anderson's "Elizabethan"-style tragedies, *Mary of Scotland, Elizabeth the Queen, Anne of the Thousand Days*, with a genuine play of the period. Or compare his Mary with Schiller's in *Maria Stuart*.

5. Discuss O'Neill's attempt at modern Greek style in a comparison of his *Mourning Becomes Electra* with the original Aeschylean trilogy, *The Oresteia*. Note the close similarities and the major changes. (Try to locate a copy of Barrett H. Clark's "European Theories of the Drama," Crown Publishers, Inc., New York, 1947, which contains a number of excerpts from O'Neill's personal diary while he was writing the play.)

6. O'Neill's Nina in *Strange Interlude*, his Lavinia in *Mourning Becomes Electra*, and Tennessee Williams' Blanche in *A Streetcar Named Desire* are three modern tragic heroines of considerable dimension. Discuss which of them most nearly becomes a full-fledged tragic protagonist.

7. Study Arthur Miller's introduction to his "Collected Plays." Read *All My Sons* and *Death of a Salesman*. Do these plays become true tragedies? Does the suffering of the central figures accomplish what is expected? Compare these "tragedies of the common man" with Anderson's attempt in *Winterset*.

8. Perhaps you do not feel that either *Desire Under the Elms* or *The Crucible* is completely successful as tragedy. If this is your feeling, discuss their shortcomings and how the plays might be improved.

9. O'Neill's "personal" tragedy is set forth in his autobiographical *Long Day's Journey into Night*. It was well received for its appeal beyond the revelation it made of O'Neill's life. Is it a tragedy? Does it achieve universality and grandeur?

10. Read Nathaniel Hawthorne's "The Scarlet Letter." Hawthorne was a direct descendant of Judge Hathorne, and his forebear's sins always rested heavily on him. Read Barker's *Superstition*, and then discuss the various approaches to religious superstitions, social customs, and moral behavior as seen in these two works, and in Arthur Miller's play. (You may wish to read other stories by Hawthorne, such as "The Minister's Black Veil," "The Grey Champion," or "Young Goodman Brown.")

A SELECTED BIBLIOGRAPHY FOR FURTHER STUDY OF AMERICAN DRAMATIC LITERATURE

The critical and historical material in periodicals and assorted histories, texts, and anthologies is abundant and easily available in college and university libraries. Therefore, no attempt has been made here to compile any form of "complete" bibliography on the plays and playwrights of Part 2. The following are significant omissions:

1. None of the standard histories of world drama have been included. The average institutional library will have Gassner's "Masters of the Drama," Freedley and Reeves' "History of the Theatre," the important books by Allardyce Nicoll, including "World Drama," or others equally helpful. All of them contain broad facts about the American theatre in noncritical historical accounts.

2. There are no references to periodicals. Many of the comprehensive histories and large anthologies have extensive bibliographies of their own which include periodical references. The student's best friend in this regard is "The Reader's Guide" or a similar index.

3. Because texts and anthologies of all sorts are continually being published, any attempt to list their contents would be tedious and unrewarding. The Ottemiller "Index," listed here, is an important help. Library card catalogues and the Burns Mantle annuals are the best sources for this information.

Significant entries in this bibliography are briefly annotated. An asterisk (*) identifies books also listed in the Bibliography to Part 1.

*Anderson, John: "The American Theatre and the Motion Picture in America," The Dial Press, Inc., New York, 1938.

Anderson, Maxwell: "The Essence of Tragedy," Anderson House, Washington, D.C., 1939.

————: "Off Broadway: Essays about the Theatre," Barnes & Noble, Inc., New York, 1947. *Both of these books discuss Anderson's dramatic theories. "Off Broadway" includes "The Essence of Tragedy" as a separate essay.*

Atkinson, Brooks: "Broadway Scrapbook," Theatre Arts Books, New York, 1947. *Miscellaneous writings by the "dean of New York critics" from his New York Times column.*

Bailey, Mabel: "Maxwell Anderson," Abelard-Schuman, Inc., Publishers, New York, 1957.

Baker, Blanche M.: "The Theatre and Allied Arts: A Guide to Books Dealing with the History, Criticism, and Technic of the Drama and Theatre and Related Arts and Crafts," The H. W. Wilson Company, New York, 1952. *A basic reference volume for any study of the drama or theatre.*

Baker, George Pierce: "Dramatic Technique," Houghton Mifflin Company, Boston, 1919. *The man who taught O'Neill and many others wrote this standard text on the technique of the dramatic writer. A fundamental work for the aspiring playwright.*

Bentley, Eric: "The Dramatic Event: An American Chronicle," Horizon Press, Inc., New York, 1954.

————: "In Search of Theatre," Alfred A. Knopf, Inc., New York, 1953. (Vintage Books, 1954.)

————: "The Playwright as Thinker," Harcourt, Brace and Company, Inc., New York, 1946. (Meridian Books, 1955.)

————: "What Is Theatre?" The Beacon Press, Boston, 1956. *Mr. Bentley is one of today's foremost critics, editors, translators, and teachers of the drama. These are his best-known critical writings on all aspects of theatre, including American drama, for which he has limited enthusiasm. His many anthologies in the "Modern Repertory" and "Modern Theatre" series are valuable collections.*

Blake, Ben: "The Awakening of the American Theatre," Tomorrow Publishers, 1935. *An account of the "left-wing" theatre of the 1930s.*

Block, Anita: "The Changing World in Plays and Theatre," Little, Brown & Company, Boston, 1939. *A review of the attitudes and ideas of the late 1930s. An extended treatment of individual authors.*

Blum, Daniel C.: "Great Stars of the American Stage," Greenberg: Publisher, Inc., New York, 1952.

————: "A Pictorial History of the American Theatre, 1900–1950," Greenberg: Publisher, Inc., New York, 1950. *Both of these folio-sized volumes are packed with illustrations, explained by a minimum of text. The reproduction and arrangement of the pictures are often inferior, but the collections are unavailable in such quantity anywhere else.*

Boulton, Agnes: "Part of a Long Story," Doubleday & Company, Inc., New York, 1958. *The first half of a proposed two-part account of life with Eugene O'Neill as told by his second wife. A revealing, although not always precise, account of some hitherto unknown aspects of the playwright's life and personality.*

Bowen, Croswell, with the assistance of Shane O'Neill: "The Curse of the Misbegotten," McGraw-Hill Book Company, Inc., New York, 1959. *With the help of O'Neill's second son and youngest child, Bowen has written an account of O'Neill's family life. A good supplement to Miss Boulton's volume and to O'Neill's own view in* Long Day's Journey into Night.

Brown, John Mason: "As They Appear," McGraw-Hill Book Company, Inc., New York, 1952.

————: "Broadway in Review," W. W. Norton & Company, Inc., New York, 1940.

————: "Letters from Greenroom Ghosts," The Viking Press, Inc., New York, 1934.

————: "The Modern Theatre in Revolt," W. W. Norton & Company, Inc., New York, 1929.

————: "Seeing Things," McGraw-Hill Book Company, Inc., New York, 1946.

————: "Two on the Aisle," W. W. Norton & Company, Inc., New York, 1938. *Mr. Brown, like Eric Bentley, has written extensively on all phases of the drama. These are but a few of his many titles. Consult your card catalogue for others pertinent to a particular phase.*

*Cheney, Sheldon: "The Art Theatre," Alfred A. Knopf, Inc., New York, 1925.

*————: "The New Movement in the Theatre," Mitchell Kennerley, New York, 1914.

Clark, Barrett H.: "Eugene O'Neill: The Man and His Plays," Dover Publications, New York, 1947. *Beginning in 1926, Barrett Clark, a personal friend of O'Neill, wrote a series of books bearing this title, each a revision of the previous edition. The 1947 edition was the last, published just after the appearance of* The Iceman Cometh. *It is the best single volume of O'Neill criticism, but as biography it has been supplanted by others.*

————: "European Theories of the Drama," Crown Publishers, Inc., New York, 1947. *An unexcelled collection of criticism since Aristotle, with an American supplement, including playwriting notes by O'Neill.*

————: "Maxwell Anderson: The Man and His Plays," Samuel French, Inc., New York, 1933. *An attempt to do with Anderson as he did with O'Neill. No further revisions.*

————: "A Study of the Modern Drama," Appleton-Century-Crofts, Inc., New York, 1938. *Another continuously revised series beginning in 1925. Brief criticisms and historical data.*

Clurman, Harold: "The Fervent Years," Alfred A. Knopf, Inc., New York, 1945. *An account of the thriving Group Theatre of the 1930s, home of Clifford Odets and the best of the "left-wing" drama.*

*Coad, Oral Sumner, and Edwin Mims, Jr.: "The American Stage," Yale University Press, New Haven, Conn., 1929.

Cole, Toby, and Helen K. Chinoy (eds.): "Actors on Acting: The Theories, Techniques and Practices of the Great Actors of All Times As Told in Their Own Words," Crown Publishers, Inc., New York, 1949.

Davis, Hallie Flanagan: "Arena," Duell, Sloan & Pearce, Inc., New York, 1940. *Facts about the Federal Theatre Project.*

————: "Dynamo," Duell, Sloan & Pearce, Inc., New York, 1943. *Report on Mrs. Davis' experimental theatre at Vassar.*

*Deutsch, Helen, and Stella Hanau: "The Provincetown," Farrar, Straus & Cudahy, Inc., New York, 1931.

Dickinson, Thomas H.: "Playwrights of the New American Theatre," The Macmillan Company, New York, 1924. *A discussion of some early-century writers.*

Downer, Alan: "Fifty Years of American Drama, 1900–1950," Henry Regnery Company, Chicago, 1951. *Fifty-year summary by a well-known drama critic.*

Eaton, Walter Prichard: "The Theatre Guild: The First Ten Years," Brentano's, Inc., New York, 1929. *The struggles for survival of America's most important producing company.*

Eliot, T. S.: "Poetry and Drama," Harvard University Press, Cambridge, Mass., 1953. *An important contribution in support of modern poetic drama.*

Engel, Edwin A.: "The Haunted Heroes of Eugene O'Neill," Harvard University Press, Cambridge, Mass., 1953. *A study of the problems of O'Neill's main characters. The plots of most of the plays are reviewed.*

Flexner, Elizabeth: "American Playwrights, 1918–1938," Simon and Schuster, Inc., New York, 1938. *"Left-wing" point of view concerning some leading American writers.*

Gagey, Edmond: "Revolution in the American Drama," Columbia University Press, New York, 1947. *The American theatre's major changes after 1912.*

Gassner, John: "Form and Idea in Modern Theatre," The Dryden Press, Inc., New

York, 1956. *An excellent critical account of modern theatrical styles, emphasizing realism and expressionism.*

————: "The Theatre in Our Time," Crown Publishers, Inc., New York, 1954. *An extensive review of all phases of theatre, particularly in the forties and fifties.*

Geddes, Virgil: "Left Turn for American Drama," "The Melodramadness of Eugene O'Neill," and "The Theatre of Dreadful Nights," Brookfield Players, Brookfield, Conn., 1934. *These three short pamphlets are not easily found in most libraries, but are worth the search for their outspoken opinions, particularly about O'Neill.*

Gilder, Rosamund, and George Freedley: "Theatre Collections in Libraries and Museums," Theatre Arts Books, New York, 1936. *Although now out of date, this provides substantial help in locating outstanding collections of American theatre memorabilia. Valuable for advanced research.*

Goldberg, Isaac: "The Drama of Transition," Stewart Kidd Company, Cincinnati, Ohio, 1922. *One of the first books to discuss the new American realism of O'Neill and others.*

Gorelik, Mordecai: "New Theatres for Old," Samuel French, Inc., New York, 1940. *The standard work treating the new movements in stage techniques of the twentieth century. Written by one of America's greatest scene designers and stage craftsmen. Extensive bibliography on all phases of theatre in all countries. Fundamental reference work for a theatre library.*

Hamilton, Clayton: "The Theory of the Theatre," Henry Holt and Company, Inc., New York, 1939. *Essays by a famous critic, written over a period of years.*

*Hartman, John Geoffrey: "The Development of American Social Comedy, 1787–1936," University of Pennsylvania Press, Philadelphia, 1939.

Heffner, Herbert C., Samuel Selden, and Hunton D. Sellman: "Modern Theatre Practice," Appleton-Century-Crofts, Inc., New York, 1947.

*Hewitt, Barnard: "Theatre U.S.A., 1668–1957," McGraw-Hill Book Company, Inc., New York, 1959.

Houghton, Norris: "Advance from Broadway," Harcourt, Brace and Company, Inc., New York, 1941. *A report on the traveling or "road" companies.*

*Hughes, Glenn: "A History of the American Theatre, 1700–1950," Samuel French, Inc., New York, 1951.

————: "The Penthouse Theatre," University of Washington Press, Seattle, Wash., 1950. *The history of a famous arena theatre.*

*Isaacs, Edith J. R.: "The Negro in the American Theatre," Theatre Arts Books, New York, 1935.

————: "Architecture for the New Theatre," Theatre Arts Books, New York, 1935.

Jones, Margo: "Theatre in the Round," Rinehart & Company, Inc., New York, 1951. *Concerns the successful theatre in Dallas, written by a pioneer in arena staging.*

Jones, Robert Edmond: "The Dramatic Imagination," Duell, Sloan & Pearce, Inc., New York, 1941. *A discussion by one of America's foremost scene designers.*

Kinne, Wisner Payne: "George Pierce Baker and the American Theatre," Harvard University Press, Cambridge, Mass., 1954. *An evaluation of Baker's position in the fast-changing twentieth-century drama.*

Kronenberger, Louis: "The Thread of Laughter: Chapters on English Stage Comedy from Jonson to Somerset Maugham," Alfred A. Knopf, Inc., New York, 1953. *A valuable study of all aspects of comedy by a well-known critic.*

Krutch, Joseph Wood: "The American Drama since 1918," George Braziller, Inc., New York, 1957. *This revision of the 1939 edition is the best available short, informal history of modern American drama.*

————: "Modernism in Modern Drama," Cornell University Press, Ithaca, N.Y., 1953. *Further comments on the content of modern drama.*

Langner, Lawrence: "The Magic Curtain," E. P. Dutton & Co., Inc., New York, 1951. *Personal recollections by a founder of the Theatre Guild. Well illustrated.*

Lawson, John Howard: "Theory and Technique of Playwriting," G. P. Putnam's Sons, New York, 1937. *Artistic viewpoints by one of the "left-wing" writers of the 1930s.*

McCollom, W. G.: "Tragedy," The Macmillan Company, New York, 1957. *Helpful in the study of tragedy in general, although, like Kronenberger's book on laughter, not strictly American.*

Macgowan, Kenneth, and Robert Edmond Jones: "The Theatre of Tomorrow," Liveright Publishing Corporation, New York, 1921. *Stagecraft, theatres, and plays of the "future" as seen in the early 1920s.*

Mantle, Burns: "American Playwrights of Today," Dodd, Mead & Company, Inc., New York, 1938. *A general review of leading writers of the 1930s.*

Miller, Jordan Y.: "A Critical Bibliography of Eugene O'Neill," University Microfilms, University of Michigan, Ann Arbor, Mich., 1957. *An annotated bibliography of all available material on O'Neill. Several sections of factual data concerning his life and plays.*

*Morehouse, Ward: "Matinée Tomorrow," McGraw-Hill Book Company, Inc., New York, 1949.

*Morris, Lloyd: "Curtain Time," Random House, Inc., New York, 1953.

*Moses, Montrose J.: "The American Dramatist," Little, Brown & Company, Boston, 1925.

*———— and John Mason Brown: "The American Theatre as Seen by Its Critics," W. W. Norton & Company, Inc., New York, 1934.

Nathan, George Jean: "Art of the Night," Alfred A. Knopf, Inc., New York, 1928.

————: "The Entertainment of a Nation," Alfred A. Knopf, Inc., New York, 1942.

————: "Passing Judgments," Alfred A. Knopf, Inc., New York, 1935.

————: "The Theatre in the Fifties," Alfred A. Knopf, Inc., New York, 1953.

————: "The World in Falseface," Alfred A. Knopf, Inc., New York, 1923. *As in the case of John Mason Brown, consult the card catalogue for other books by Nathan. This sharp-tongued critic and journalist poured out scores of volumes, some valuable, some questionable, all highly personal and written in a distinctive style. Their subject matter is so varied that individual annotation here is unwarranted.*

"New York Theatre Critics' Reviews," Critics' Theatre Reviews, Inc., New York, 1940 to date. *This weekly series reproduces every opening night review of a Broadway play by the New York newspaper critics. Unfortunately it does not include as many of the important Off Broadway productions as it should, but it is a basic tool in any contemporary critical research.*

Nicoll, Allardyce: "The Theory of Drama," George G. Harrap & Co., Ltd., London, 1931. *Another standard reference for any basic theatre library. Excellent discussion of tragedy and comedy.*

O'Hara, Frank Hurburt: "Today in American Drama," University of Chicago Press, Chicago, 1939. *A short volume on some contemporary dramatic themes.*

Ottemiller, John H.: "Index to Plays in Collections," Scarecrow Press, Washington, D.C., 1951. *Comprehensive indexing of all published anthologies.*

Prideaux, Tom: "World Theatre in Pictures," Greenberg: Publisher, Inc., New York, 1953. *Similar in format to the Blum volumes. Plays from classic to modern are illustrated by photographs of contemporary productions.*

*Quinn, Arthur Hobson: "A History of American Drama from the Civil War to the Present Day," Appleton-Century-Crofts, Inc., New York, 1937.

Sanborn, Ralph, and Barrett H. Clark: "A Bibliography of the Works of Eugene O'Neill," Random House, Inc., New York, 1931. *Limited edition, listing all of the variants in O'Neill texts. Far out-of-date, but valuable for a number of O'Neill poems, written before he started writing plays.*

Sayler, Oliver M.: "Our American Theatre, 1908–1923," Brentano's, Inc., New York, 1923.

Sievers, W. David: "Freud on Broadway," Hermitage House, Inc., New York, 1955. *An analysis of Freudian themes in modern American plays. Revealing, if somewhat overstretched at times.*

Simonson, Lee: "Part of a Lifetime," Duell, Sloan & Pearce, Inc., New York, 1943. *A report on this famous designer's life with the Theatre Guild.*

————: "The Stage is Set," Harcourt, Brace and Company, Inc., New York, 1932. *An excellent discussion of modern theatrical and dramatic techniques seen from the designer's viewpoint.*

Skinner, Richard Dana: "Eugene O'Neill: A Poet's Quest," Longmans, Green & Co., Inc., New York, 1935. *O'Neill's career is seen as similar to a saint's quest for understanding of life. The conclusions are not always convincing.*

Sobel, Bernard: "Theatre Handbook and Digest of Plays," Crown Publishers, Inc., New York, 1940. *A handy theatrical and dramatic reference book.*

Sypher, Wylie (ed.): "Comedy," Doubleday & Company, Inc., New York, 1956. *Includes Bergson's essay on laughter and Meredith's on comedy. Excellent for a study of all types of comedy, on stage and off.*

"Theatre Arts Anthology," Theatre Arts Books, New York, 1950. *A collection of outstanding contributions to* Theatre Arts Magazine.

"Theatre Arts Prints," Theatre Arts Books, New York, various dates. *These are hard to get, have long been out of print, but represent a fine collection of theatre pictures. Larger libraries will probably have a complete set.*

Thompson, Alan Reynolds: "The Anatomy of Drama," University of California Press, Berkeley, Calif., 1946.

Whitman, Willson: "Bread and Circuses: A Study of the Federal Theatre," Oxford University Press, New York, 1937.

Winther, Sophus Keith: "Eugene O'Neill: A Critical Study," Random House, Inc., New York, 1934. *A valuable book written when O'Neill was still a practicing playwright. Its favorable attitude should be compared with Skinner's and Geddes'.*

Young, Stark: "The Flower in Drama," Charles Scribner's Sons, New York, 1955.

————: "Immortal Shadows," Charles Scribner's Sons, New York, 1948. *Collected essays by another of our most respected critics.*

INDEX

The Index covers all of the textual material in Part 1, and all of the introductory essays in Part 2. The Chronology of Significant Events is also covered, but generally in terms of broad subject matter. The few exceptions are important entries not mentioned in the text. Page numbers for the Chronology are indicated in **boldface** type.